THE BOOK OF THE STATES

2015 EDITION
VOLUME 47

ISBN 978-0-87292-796-4

The Council of State Governments
Lexington, Kentucky

Headquarters: (859) 244-8000
Fax: (859) 244-8001
Internet: www.csg.org

Sharing capitol ideas.

Headquarters:
David Adkins, Executive Director/CEO
2760 Research Park Drive, P.O. Box 11910
Lexington, KY 40578-1910
Phone: (859) 244-8000
Internet: www.csg.org

Southern:
Colleen Cousineau, Director
P.O. Box 98129
Atlanta, GA 30359
Phone: (404) 633-1866
Internet: www.slcatlanta.org

Eastern:
Wendell M. Hannaford, Director
22 Cortlandt Street, 22nd Floor
New York, NY 10007
Phone: (212) 482-2320
Internet: www.csgeast.org

Western:
Edgar Ruiz, Director
1107 9th Street, Suite 730
Sacramento, CA 95814
Phone: (916) 553-4423
Internet: www.csgwest.org

Midwestern:
Michael H. McCabe, Director
701 E. 22nd Street, Suite 110
Lombard, IL 60148
Phone: (630) 925-1922
Internet: www.csgmidwest.org

Washington, D.C.:

444 N. Capitol Street, NW, Suite 401
Washington, D.C. 20001
Phone: (202) 624-5460
Internet: www.csgdc.org

Foreword

Dear Friends,

The times we live in present both unprecedented opportunity and challenge. Every day, state leaders throughout America wrestle with complex problems and work to serve their constituents. Collectively, they work to advance the common good. These are difficult times in which to govern and yet, in state after state, leaders are finding ways to reach consensus and craft public policy to help build a brighter future.

At The Council of State Governments, we consider it our obligation to be a relevant resource for state leaders. We were created by the states and we pursue the priorities established by our members, the states. We help empower them to solve problems, create solutions and build better futures.

People from all walks of life run for and are elected to serve in state offices. While many bring to their service specific expertise, they will be called on to decide a broad range of issues. They will spend billions of dollars, they will define the laws by which we live, they will set the course for education and they will approve the construction of roads and bridges. They will arbitrate some of the most contentious and complex issues imaginable.

We know state leaders are interested in using data to guide their decisions. We know that when data is used, decisions are more sound and effective. *The Book of the States* is designed to provide state leaders with a myriad of data points all designed to help inform their decisions and enhance their impact. The Council of State Governments is always focused on helping states achieve results. *The Book of the States* is just one of the many tools we produce to assist states in doing just that.

This edition reflects the good work of the many authors and researchers who have contributed to it. CSG is indebted to the generous contributions of the authors who, by sharing their insights and information, have helped make this tool a valuable resource. CSG also has a number of dedicated staff in our national headquarters that have worked diligently to produce this volume. Audrey Wall leads the team and it is her robust network of friends in the states that helps us compile much of the information contained in these pages. We rely on many people to help us gather the contents of this book and we appreciate every one of them. *The Book of the States* would not be possible without their assistance.

CSG's Policy and Research team is headed by John Mountjoy. John and his team work every day to create opportunities for state leaders to learn from each other and to have access to cutting-edge insights on public policy issues.

Kelley Arnold and her Membership, Marketing and Media team helped edit and print *The Book of the States*. In particular, this edition reflects the hard work of Chris Pryor and Heather Perkins.

I commend the CSG national and regional leaders who tirelessly work to guide CSG and, in concert with their colleagues from all the states and territories, help establish our priorities. They inspire us to achieve excellence in all that we do.

First published in 1935, this year marks the 80th anniversary of *The Book of the States*. CSG's founder, Sen. Henry W. Toll of Colorado, wrote in that first edition, "This volume is nothing but a lick and a promise. It is the meager and unorganized beginning of a periodical publication which may eventually become a very useful reference book." Eight decades hence, *The Book of the States* has become the go-to resource for state leaders, managers, academics, researchers and historians. It truly has earned its unofficial moniker: the encyclopedia of state governments.

To the leaders, readers and researchers who use this book, I hope you will be empowered to take what you find on these pages and put it to work to help create stronger states and a stronger nation.

David Adkins

David Adkins
Executive Director / CEO
The Council of State Governments

The Council of State Governments is our nation's only organization serving all three branches of state government. CSG is a region-based forum that fosters the exchange of insights and ideas to help state officials shape public policy. This offers unparalleled regional, national and international opportunities to network, develop leaders, collaborate and create problem-solving partnerships.

Staff Acknowledgements

The staff wishes to thank the authors who shared their expertise and insights, the hundreds of individuals in the states who responded to surveys conducted by The Council of State Governments, national organizations of state officials, federal agencies and think tank organizations who made their most recent data and information available for this volume.

The Book of the States 2015

Managing Editor .... Audrey S. Wall

Associate Editor .... Heather M. Perkins

Lead Designer............ Chris Pryor

Graphic Designers..... Theresa Carroll
Chad Young

Copy Editor .... Jennifer Ginn

*Other CSG Staff
Contributors*.............. Paige Anderson
Jennifer Horne

Disclaimer

The views and opinions expressed in these articles are those of the authors and may not necessarily reflect the opinions or member-endorsed policies of The Council of State Governments.

Table of Contents

CONTENTS

CONTENTS

Chapter Eight

Chapter Nine

CONTENTS

CONTENTS

Chapter One

STATE CONSTITUTIONS

State Constitutional Developments in 2014

By John Dinan

Although constitutional amendment activity was lower in 2014 than in recent even-numbered years, several of the 72 approved amendments attracted significant attention. These include amendments relaxing legislative term limits in Arkansas, creating a bipartisan redistricting commission in New York, eliminating a judicial merit selection commission in Tennessee, strengthening the right to bear arms in Alabama and Missouri, guaranteeing a right to farm in Missouri, and barring state and local officials from enforcing unconstitutional federal directives in Arizona.

Voters considered and approved fewer state constitutional amendments in 2014 than in any other even-numbered year in the 21st century. In other respects, however, the 105 proposed amendments and 72 adopted amendments demonstrate continuity with recent trends in amendment activity. Voters continue to approve a sizable number of rights-related amendments, sometimes recognizing rights with no counterpart in the U.S. Constitution, such as hunting and fishing rights, and sometimes requiring that certain rights, such as the right to bear arms, be given more protection than at the federal level.

Other amendments reflect ongoing experimentation with ways of selecting governing officials and structuring governing institutions—establishing a bipartisan redistricting commission in New York, relaxing legislative term limits in Arkansas, creating an intermediate appellate court in Nevada and eliminating a judicial merit selection commission in Tennessee. Policy amendments also continue to figure prominently on state ballots, with the adoption of several tax-limitation amendments, various amendments authorizing and, in some cases, limiting gambling, and an unusual Arizona amendment barring state and local officials from enforcing unconstitutional federal directives.

Constitutional Amendment and Revision Methods

Constitutional amendments appeared on the ballot in 36 states in 2014, which is comparable to the number of states considering amendments in recent even-numbered years—35 states in 2012 and 37 states in 2010. The 105 proposed amendments and 72 approved amendments in 2014, however, are substantially below the level of constitutional amendment activity in every even-numbered year in the 21st century. In even-year elections held

between 2002 and 2012, the number of proposed amendments ranged from a high of 175 in 2002 to a low of 135 in 2012. The number of enacted amendments ranged from a high of 125 in 2006 to a low of 87 in 2008.

It is no surprise that Louisiana and Alabama accounted for a quarter of all amendments approved in states in 2014. Louisiana voters considered more amendments, 14, than any other state, and approved six of them. Alabama voters approved more amendments than any other state, ratifying all 12 amendments placed on the ballot in elections in June, July and November. This included six amendments of statewide application as well as six local amendments placed on the ballot only in affected localities, but added to the state constitution upon approval. With the addition of these 12 amendments, Alabama's 1901 Constitution now boasts 892 amendments and comprises more than 388,000 words.

Legislative Proposals and Constitutional Initiatives

As indicated in Table A, all 105 amendments on the ballot in 2014 were formally proposed either by legislatures or via the initiative process. Voters approved 70 of 97 legislature-proposed amendments for a passage rate of 72.2 percent. This is comparable to the approval rate for legislature-proposed amendments in recent years. Voters placed eight amendments on the ballot via the constitutional initiative process, which is available in 18 states. Only two of these citizen-initiated amendments were approved: an equal-rights amendment in Oregon and an amendment dedicating additional money to a land acquisition trust fund in Florida. This passage rate of 25 percent is somewhat below the rate for citizen-initiated amendments in recent years.

Table A: State Constitutional Changes by Method of Initiation: 2010–11, 2012–13 and 2014

Method of initiation	Number of states involved			Total proposals (a)			Total adopted (b)			Percentage adopted (c)		
	2010–2011	2012–2013	2014	2010–2011	2012–2013	2014	2010–2011	2012–2013	2014	2010–2011	2012–2013	2014
All methods...............	40	38	36	191	153(d)	105	136(e)(f)	111	72	70.2	70.6	68.6
Legislative proposal...	37	35	35	170	134	97	124(e)(f)	104	70	71.8	75.4	72.2
Constitutional initiative..................	9	7	6	21	19(d)	8	12	7	2	57.1	36.8	25.0
convention	...	...	...	...	...	...	...	...	...	...	...	...
commission..............	...	...	...	...	...	...	...	...	...	...	...	...

Source: John Dinan and The Council of State Governments.
Key:
(a) Excludes Delaware, where proposals are not submitted to voters.
(b) Includes Delaware.
(c) In calculating the percentages, the amendments adopted in Delaware (where proposals are not submitted to voters) are excluded (one amendment was adopted in 2010, one in 2011 and three in 2013).

(d) Excludes two Arkansas amendments that were placed on the 2012 ballot but whose results were not counted pursuant to a court order.
(e) Excludes one Alabama local amendment approved by voters in November 2010, but not certified pursuant to a court order.
(f) Includes one Oklahoma amendment that was approved by voters in 2010, but whose enforcement was permanently enjoined by a federal district court.

Constitutional Conventions and Commissions

Rhode Island voters rejected, by a 55 to 45 percent margin, an automatically generated proposition on the November 2014 ballot that would have established a convention to consider amendments to the state constitution. Rhode Island is one of 14 states to provide for a periodic convention referendum, which in the case of Rhode Island appears on the ballot every 10 years.[1] In fact, Rhode Island voters approved a periodic convention referendum in 1984, which led in 1986 to the last full-scale convention held in the 50 states.

The 2014 Rhode Island convention referendum attracted a good amount of public attention, much more than recent automatic convention referendums in other states. Convention backers established an organization, Renew RI, and raised funds and published a number of op-ed pieces in support of a yes vote on the referendum. A coalition of convention opponents formed an organization, Citizens for Responsible Government, which raised even more funds and enjoyed the backing of influential public and private-sector unions, along with civil rights and abortion rights groups, and succeeded in defeating the measure.[2]

The Ohio Constitutional Modernization Commission was the only constitutional commission operating in 2014. Established by the state legislature in 2011, this 32-member commission has until 2021 to recommend changes to the state constitution. Recommendations that secure the support of two-thirds of the commissioners are forwarded to the legislature, which can submit them for voter ratification upon a three-fifths vote in both houses. The commission in 2014 focused on considering alternatives to the current method of drawing state legislative and congressional district lines, among other topics.

The Alabama Legislature in 2014 considered several recommendations from a 16-member Alabama Constitutional Revision Commission, but the legislature did not place any of these commission-recommended amendments on the 2014 ballot. The legislature had in 2012 placed on the ballot several amendments recommended by the legislature-established commission, which operated from 2011 to 2013 and was charged with reviewing and suggesting changes to 11 of the 18 articles of the state constitution. As legislators were wrapping up their 2014 session, however, Alabama Supreme Court Chief Justice Roy Moore and Associate Justice Tom Parker issued advisory opinions casting doubt on the legitimacy of this article-by-article approach to constitutional revision. These opinions brought a temporary halt to legislators' consideration of the commission's slate of recommendations. Legislators returned to the task after a brief pause, but the session concluded before both houses could agree on approving any of the commission-recommended amendments for placement on the ballot.

Table B: Substantive Changes in State Constitutions, Proposed and Adopted, 2010–11, 2012–2013 and 2014

Subject matter	Total proposed (a)			Total adopted (b)			Percentage adopted (c)		
	2010–2011	2012–2013	2014	2010–2011	2012–2013	2014	2010–2011	2012–2013	2014
Proposals of statewide applicability	147	132 (a)(d)	99	108 (b)(f)	94 (b)	66	72.1 (c)	68.9 (c)	66.7
Bill of Rights	22	20	14	17	13	12	77.3	65.0	85.7
Suffrage & elections	18	5 (a)	8	15	3 (b)	4	83.3	40.0 (c)	50.0
Legislative branch	6	11	5	5	7	3	83.3	63.6	60.0
Executive branch	6	4	5	5 (b)	4	3	66.7 (c)	100.0	60.0
Judicial branch	7	12 (a)	9	5 (b)(f)	7 (b)	6	57.1 (c)	41.7 (c)	66.7
Local government	7	3	5	4	2	4	57.1	66.7	80.0
Finance & taxation	42	32	25	32	25	19	76.2	78.1	76.0
State & local debt	16	5	5	13	4	4	81.3	80.0	80.0
State functions	9	16	8	3	11	1	33.3	68.8	12.5
Amendment & revision	0	0	0	0	0	0	0.0	0.0	0.0
General revision proposals	0	0	0	0	0	0	0.0	0.0	0.0
Miscellaneous proposals	14	24	15	9	18	10	64.3	75.0	40.0
Local amendments	44	21	16	28 (e)	17	6	63.6	81.0	100.0

Source: John Dinan and The Council of State Governments.
Key:
 (a) Excludes Delaware, where amendments do not require popular approval.
 (b) Includes Delaware.
 (c) In calculating the percentages, the amendments adopted in Delaware (where proposals are not submitted to voters) are excluded (one amendment was adopted in 2010, one in 2011 and three in 2013).

 (d) Excludes two Arkansas amendments placed on the 2012 ballot, but whose results were not counted pursuant to a court order.
 (e) Excludes one Alabama local amendment approved by voters in November 2010 but not certified pursuant to a court order.
 (f) Includes one Oklahoma amendment approved by voters in 2010, but whose enforcement was permanently enjoined by a federal district court.

Constitutional Changes

Finance-related amendments in 2014 far outpaced the number of amendments on any other topic, as is the norm. Excluding miscellaneous amendments, rights-related amendments were the second most common type of amendment approved in 2014, as also has been the norm in recent years. It is notable that judiciary-related amendments were the third-largest category of approved amendments. Table B reports the number of proposed and enacted amendments in these and other categories.

Rights

Rights-related amendments on the 2014 ballot attracted substantial attention, as voters considered several amendments adding or strengthening rights with no counterpart in the text of the U.S. Constitution.[3] Mississippi became the 18th state to recognize a right to hunt and fish in its constitution, with all but one of these states adopting their provisions in the past two decades. Vermont adopted a right to hunt and fish in its inaugural 1777 constitution and remained the only state to recognize such a right until 1996, when Alabama voters approved an amendment adding hunting

and fishing rights to their state constitution. In 2014, Alabama voters approved a "Sportspersons' Bill of Rights" amendment strengthening this original provision, in part by declaring: "The people have a right to hunt, fish, and harvest wildlife, including by the use of traditional methods, subject to reasonable regulations, to promote wildlife conservation and management, and to preserve the future of hunting and fishing." Missouri became the second state to guarantee a right to farm, following passage of a North Dakota measure in 2012. The narrowly approved Missouri amendment states, in part, that: "the right of farmers and ranchers to engage in farming and ranching practices shall be forever guaranteed in this state."

Voters approved several other amendments protecting rights with no counterpart in the text of the U.S. Constitution. The Illinois Constitution is one of more than 30 state constitutions guaranteeing crime victims' rights. In 2014, Illinois voters approved an amendment expanding the original list of rights of crime victims in that state and making it easier for them to assert these rights in court.

Table C: State Constitutional Changes by Legislative and Initiative Proposal: 2014

State	Legislative proposal			Constitutional initiative		
	Number proposed	Number adopted	Percentage adopted	Number proposed	Number adopted	Percentage adopted
Alabama	12	12	100.0			
Arizona	1	1	100.0			
Arkansas	3	3	100.0	1	0	0.0
California	2	2	100.0			
Colorado				2	0	0.0
Connecticut	1	0	0.0			
Florida	1	0	0.0	2	1	50.0
Georgia	2	2	100.0			
Hawaii	5	3	60.0			
Idaho	1	0	0.0			
Illinois	2	2	100.0			
Kansas	1	1	100.0			
Louisiana	14	6	42.9			
Maryland	2	2	100.0			
Mississippi	1	1	100.0			
Missouri	8	5	50.0	1	0	0.0
Montana	1	0	0.0			
Nevada	2	1	50.0			
New Jersey	2	2	100.0			
New Mexico	5	4	80.0			
New York	2	2	100.0			
North Carolina	1	1	100.0			
North Dakota	5	2	40.0	1	0	0.0
Ohio	1	1	100.0			
Oklahoma	3	3	100.0			
Oregon	2	1	50.0	1	1	100.0
Rhode Island	2	1	50.0			
South Carolina	2	2	100.0			
South Dakota	1	1	100.0			
Tennessee	4	4	100.0			
Texas	1	1	100.0			
Utah	3	1	33.3			
Virginia	1	1	100.0			
West Virginia	1	1	100.0			
Wisconsin	1	1	100.0			
Wyoming	1	0	0.0			
Totals	97	70	72.2	8	2	25.0

Source: John Dinan and The Council of State Governments.

Oregon adopted a citizen-initiated equal rights amendment barring state or local governments from denying rights on account of sex. Most states with equal rights provisions of this sort adopted them in the 1970s and 1980s, when a federal equal rights amendment fell just short of being ratified by the requisite number of states.

Several amendments approved in 2014 deal with rights guaranteed in both the U.S. Constitution and state constitutions; their intent is to stipulate that the state constitution affords greater protection than is found in the federal constitution. Following a path taken by several other states in the past few years, Alabama voters approved an amendment declaring the right to bear arms is "fundamental" and "any restriction on this right shall be subject to strict scrutiny." Missouri voters also strengthened their existing right-to-bear-arms provision by declaring that the right "shall be unalienable" and any restriction "shall be subject to strict scrutiny." The Missouri amendment also broadened the right to bear arms to include "ammunition, and accessories typical to the normal function of such arms" and eliminated prior language that qualified this right by saying it did not apply to the carrying of concealed weapons.

Missouri voters also approved an amendment making clear that the state guarantee against unreasonable searches and seizures applies to "electronic communications and data."

Voters approved several amendments adjusting the rights of criminal defendants. Prior to this year, felony defendants in North Carolina could not waive their right to a jury trial. After voters approved a 2014 amendment permitting waiver of a jury trial in noncapital cases, North Carolina joined the other 49 states in permitting jury trial waivers. New Jersey voters approved an amendment adjusting the language in a right-to-bail provision by authorizing judges to deny pretrial release to defendants in certain situations.

State constitutional amendments can, in some instances, expand rights beyond federal guarantees. They also can be a vehicle in other instances for overturning state court decisions that interpret state constitutional rights more expansively than federal guarantees.[4] Voters approved two court-constraining amendments of this sort in 2014. In response to prior Missouri Supreme Court rulings disallowing admission of "propensity" evidence, Missouri voters approved an amendment authorizing prosecutors to introduce such evidence in certain cases. The Missouri amendment declares that notwithstanding other state constitutional provisions, in cases involving sex crimes against minors "relevant evidence of prior criminal acts, whether charged or uncharged, is admissible for the purpose of corroborating the victim's testimony or demonstrating the defendant's propensity to commit the crime with which he or she is presently charged."

Tennessee voters approved an amendment responding to a 2000 Tennessee Supreme Court decision holding that the state constitution provides more protection for abortion rights than is guaranteed by the federal constitution and striking down several abortion restrictions on that ground. The 2014 Tennessee amendment declares, in part: "Nothing in this Constitution secures or protects a right to abortion or requires the funding of an abortion. The people retain this right through their elected state representatives and state senators to enact, amend, or repeal statutes regarding abortion."

Rights-related amendments appearing on the 2014 ballot were approved in nearly all cases; the only two amendments of this sort rejected at the polls were fetal personhood amendments in Colorado and North Dakota seeking in various ways to define life as beginning at conception. Colorado voters rejected personhood amendments on two prior occasions, in 2008 and 2010, as did Mississippi voters in 2011. The 2014 Colorado amendment differed from prior amendments in that it focused narrowly on defining the terms "person" and "child" in the Colorado Criminal Code and Wrongful Death Act to include "unborn human beings." The failed North Dakota amendment in 2014 was similar to the earlier and more broadly applicable personhood amendments in declaring, "The inalienable right to life of every human being at any stage of development must be recognized and protected."

Looking ahead to 2015, Mississippi voters will consider competing education-related amendments. One proposed amendment, which reached the ballot through the initiative process, would amend the current education clause by guaranteeing a "fundamental right to educational opportunity" to be enforced by the state's chancery courts. However, Mississippi's constitutional initiative process is unusual in that the legislature has an opportunity to craft and submit to voters an alternative amendment alongside the citizen-initiated amendment. For the first time since adoption of the initiative process in Mississippi in 1992 the legislature took advantage of this opportunity, by crafting an amendment that makes only modest changes to the current education clause and lacks the fundamental-right or judicial-enforcement language. Voters in 2015 will have a chance to indicate whether they support making any change to the current education clause, and, if so, which amendment they prefer.

Institutions

Voters in 2014 considered a number of amendments altering governing or electoral institutions, with the judicial branch attracting the most attention. Heading the list of judiciary-related amendments is a notable change in the way Tennessee Supreme Court and intermediate appellate court judges are chosen. Although the relevant provision of the Tennessee Constitution had for many years directed that supreme court judges "shall be elected by the qualified voters of the state," this is not how judges actually were selected in recent decades. Rather, Tennessee operated under a merit selection plan. In case of a vacancy, a judicial nominating commission forwarded a list of potential nominees to the governor, who made the appointment. Judges then stood periodically for retention elections. The amendment approved by Tennessee voters in 2014 eliminates the longstanding language providing for elected judges; it also eliminates the nominating commission and provides that the governor, with the consent of the legislature, shall make the initial appointment of appellate judges. Notably, the legislature is understood to have given its consent if it fails to reject a gubernatorial nominee within 60 days. Several other states, including Kansas, continue to debate amendments eliminating their current merit selection commissions and moving toward some version of the federal judicial-selection plan.

One other notable change in judicial selection procedures approved by voters in 2014, aside from a technical change in New Mexico in the filing deadline for incumbent judges, was a Hawaii amendment requiring the merit commission to make public the names of all judicial nominees it forwards to the governor pursuant to the merit selection process in that state. Florida voters rejected an amendment permitting the governor to prospectively fill judicial vacancies. This would have been particularly important when judgeships become vacant on the same day as a gubernatorial inauguration, as will occur in 2019 when three current judges will have to step down by virtue of approaching the judicial retirement age. The failed Florida amendment would have permitted the outgoing, rather than incoming, governor to make judicial appointments in these situations.

Voters considered, and in some cases approved, other judiciary-related amendments. Efforts to raise or eliminate the judicial retirement age invariably have been rejected in recent years, and voters in 2014 defeated two more such amendments. Hawaii voters once again defeated an amendment to raise the retirement age, in this case from 70 to 80. Louisiana voters were unwilling to approve an amendment seeking to eliminate the judicial retirement age altogether. In Nevada, voters finally approved an amendment creating an intermediate appellate court, after defeating similar amendments on four prior occasions dating to the 1970s, most recently in 2010. Alabama voters approved an "American and Alabama Laws for Alabama Courts Amendment" prohibiting courts from applying foreign law when doing so would violate the public policy of the state or rights guaranteed by federal and state constitutions. Although the amendment is motivated by some

of the same concerns that in 2010 led to Oklahoma's adoption of an anti-Sharia amendment—whose enforcement has been permanently enjoined by a federal court—the Alabama amendment does not make explicit mention of Sharia law.

Arkansas voters approved the most important legislature-related amendment in 2014, when they relaxed the current legislative term limits rules by allowing legislators to serve up to 16 years in the house or senate. This amendment also included provisions limiting lobbying, restricting certain campaign contributions and creating an independent commission to set elected officials' salaries; it was seen as securing popular ratification largely on the strength of these other provisions. Prior to adoption of this amendment, legislators could serve a maximum of six years in the house and eight years in the senate. Arkansas becomes the second state to relax its legislative term limits in recent years, following California voters' approval of a similar amendment in 2012.

Meanwhile, Illinois supporters of a measure to institute legislative term limits secured enough signatures to qualify an amendment for the November 2014 ballot via the initiative process. But Cook County Circuit Court Judge Mary Mikva ruled in June 2014 that this amendment could not appear on the ballot because it did not deal with structural or procedural aspects of the legislative branch, as required of initiated amendments in Illinois. Several decades ago, a court held another proposed term limits amendment invalid on the grounds that it dealt with eligibility and qualifications of legislators rather than with structural or procedural aspects of the legislature. Supporters of the proposed 2014 amendment sought to overcome these concerns by packaging the term limits provision with changes in the number of legislators and the percentage of legislators needed to override a gubernatorial veto. But this argument proved unsuccessful in court and the amendment was kept off the 2014 ballot, along with another amendment that would have created an independent redistricting commission. Mikva concluded this other redistricting amendment also extended beyond structural and procedural aspects of the legislature, at least in the form it was drafted.

In other legislature-related amendments, Arkansas voters approved a measure stipulating that rules promulgated by state administrative agencies cannot take effect until they are reviewed and approved by a legislative committee. At the same time, Idaho voters narrowly rejected an amendment empowering the legislature to reject, in whole or in part, rules promulgated by state executive agencies. New York voters approved an amendment permitting legislators to file bills electronically.

Missouri voters approved a complex amendment limiting the governor's budget power. At a time when the Republican-controlled state house and senate were at odds with Democratic Gov. Jay Nixon regarding the budget, the legislature proposed, and voters approved, an amendment barring the governor from reducing appropriations items passed by the legislature without the consent of the legislature, along with various other restrictions on the governor's budget power. Other executive branch-related amendments approved in 2014 included a South Carolina amendment providing that the state adjutant general will now be a gubernatorial appointee rather than a popularly elected official and a Utah amendment clarifying that someone appointed to fill a vacancy in the lieutenant governor position should serve until the next gubernatorial election.

Voters approved several amendments regarding electoral institutions, including a New York amendment establishing a bipartisan commission responsible for drawing state legislative and congressional district lines. Constitutional amendments have been a vehicle on several recent occasions for creating independent citizen redistricting commissions, as in California, or establishing guidelines to restrain the legislature in the line-drawing process, as in Florida. The New York redistricting commission differs from several other redistricting commissions in that the majority and minority leadership of the senate and assembly appoint its members and the legislature can reject and modify any maps drawn up by the commission.

Looking ahead to 2015, Ohio voters will consider a legislature-referred amendment that would alter the current rules for drawing state legislative districts but would not apply to congressional districts. Among other changes, the proposed amendment would increase from five to seven the number of members on the current redistricting commission and ensure that the minority party appoints two members. Commission-drawn maps would have to secure the approval of at least two members of the minority party, or they would only remain in effect for four years, rather than the standard 10 years.

Other elections-related amendments on the 2014 ballot included a pair of defeated amendments in Connecticut and Missouri that sought to authorize an early voting period. Illinois voters approved an amendment barring the denial of the right to vote; the amendment was seen as motivated by opposition to voter identification requirements. Arkansas and North Dakota voters approved amendments changing the procedures for qualifying citizen-initiated measures, generally by making the process more difficult.

Policy

Finance amendments figured prominently on the 2014 ballot and were, in most cases, approved. Voters approved all three tax-limitation amendments on the ballot. Tennessee voters approved an amendment barring any tax on earned individual income and thereby reinforcing the current statutory policy against taxing such income. Dividend and interest income remain the only type of income subject to taxation. Georgia voters approved an amendment prohibiting any increase in the maximum individual tax rate beyond the rate as it stands in January 2015. North Dakota became the latest state to adopt an amendment barring real estate transfer taxes.

Two of the six taxation-related measures defeated in 2014 sought to increase taxes. Missouri voters easily rejected an amendment temporarily increasing the sales tax by three-quarters of one percent and dedicating the revenue to transportation projects. Nevada voters narrowly defeated an amendment eliminating a longstanding 5 percent cap on taxes for mines, mining claims and mineral extraction.

A significant amount of recent finance amendment activity has dealt with creating and regulating budget stabilization funds and trust funds, and 2014 was no exception. Voters in California approved an amendment changing the rules regarding funds that are required to be deposited into an existing budget stabilization (rainy day) fund and the way the fund can be used. This complex amendment also created another rainy day fund dedicated for public schools. Texas voters approved an amendment allowing certain revenue that previously had been deposited in a rainy day fund to be deposited instead into a state highway fund to pay for transportation projects.

Voters in several states approved amendments establishing new funds or in some cases elevating funds that rested on a statutory footing to constitutional status. Voters in Maryland and Wisconsin approved similarly framed amendments elevating existing transportation funds to constitutional status, stipulating that certain transportation-related taxes and fees should be placed in the fund and limiting its use for any other purposes. Louisiana voters approved an amendment creating an Artificial Reef Development Fund. In Florida, voters approved an amendment providing another source of funding—a portion of the proceeds from a document tax—for an existing Land Acquisition Trust Fund. Voters in other states approved amendments providing a dedicated stream of funding for particular programs or projects, as in New Jersey, where a portion of corporate tax revenue will be devoted to preserving open space, farmland and historic sites during the next three decades.

Amendments authorizing or limiting games of chance appeared on a number of state ballots in 2014, as has generally been the case in recent years. In some states—such as Kansas, South Carolina and Tennessee—voters approved amendments allowing certain nonprofit groups to hold raffles, or in some cases lotteries, thereby making exceptions to existing constitutional restrictions on gambling. In Colorado voters rejected an amendment allowing additional forms of limited gaming at certain horse racetracks and depositing the additional tax revenue into a K–12 education fund. Rhode Island voters defeated an amendment that would have allowed additional forms of casino gaming at the Newport Grand facility; in the same election, voters approved an amendment requiring any future changes in the location of this gaming facility to be approved by voters in the state and in the affected locality.

A "Rejection of Unconstitutional Federal Actions" amendment approved by Arizona voters attracted national attention, both in the lead-up to the November election and after the measure's narrow passage. This legislature-referred amendment prohibits state or local governments from "using any personnel or financial resources to enforce, administer or cooperate with" a federal action or program in the event of the passage of a state legislative statute or initiative measure to this effect.

Several other amendments placed on the ballot via the initiative process attracted national attention but were in each case defeated. An amendment allowing use of marijuana for medical purposes attracted the support of 57 percent of Florida voters; but the Florida Constitution has since 2006 required amendments to be approved by at least 60 percent of voters. Missouri voters overwhelmingly rejected an amendment to establish a teacher evaluation system where promotion and salary increases would be determined, in part, by student performance. Arkansas voters rejected by a solid margin an amendment that would have allowed the sale of alcohol in all counties and thereby overturned the local-option system.

Conclusion

One might choose to emphasize the way 2014 amendment activity departed from recent practice by noting that amendment proposals and approvals were lower than in any other even-year election this century. But one might just as easily point to the degree of continuity in that the number of states considering amendments in 2014 was on par with recent even-numbered years. Other examples of continuity with recent amendment activity include passage of rights-related measures guaranteeing more state protection for certain rights than at the federal level; continued tweaking of institutional arrangements regarding judicial selection, legislative term limits and redistricting processes; and the usual slate of policy amendments limiting taxes, creating trust funds, and expanding, and occasionally limiting, gambling.

Notes

[1] John Dinan, "The Political Dynamics of Mandatory State Constitutional Convention Referendums: Lessons from the 2000s Regarding Obstacles and Pathways to their Passage," *Montana Law Review* 71 (Summer 2010): 395–432.

[2] For an analysis, see J.H. Snider, "Post-Mortem: Rhode Island's Nov. 4, 2014 Referendum to Convene a State Constitutional Convention," Nov. 8, 2014, *http://rhodeislandconcon.info/?p=1588*. The website, *http://rhodeislandconcon.info/*, contains an extensive documentary history of the referendum campaign.

[3] John Dinan, "State Constitutional Amendments and Protection of Rights in the Twenty-First Century," *Albany Law Review* 76, 4 (2013): 2105–2140.

[4] John Dinan, "Court-Constraining Amendments and the State Constitutional Tradition," *Rutgers Law Journal* 38 (Summer 2007): 983–1039.

About the Author

John Dinan is professor of politics and international affairs at Wake Forest University in North Carolina. He is the author of *The American State Constitutional Tradition* and various articles on state constitutions.

Table 1.1
GENERAL INFORMATION ON STATE CONSTITUTIONS
(As of January 1, 2015)

State or other jurisdiction	Number of constitutions*	Dates of adoption	Effective date of present constitution	Estimated length (b) (number of words)**	Number of amendments Submitted to voters	Number of amendments Adopted
Alabama	6	1819, 1861, 1865, 1868, 1875, 1901	Nov. 28, 1901	388,882 (a)	1,221	892 (c)
Alaska	1	1956	Jan. 3, 1959	13,479	42	29
Arizona	1	1911	Feb. 14, 1912	47,306	275	152
Arkansas	5	1836, 1861, 1864, 1868, 1874	Oct. 30, 1874	59,120	202	102 (d)
California	2	1849, 1879	July 4, 1879	67,048	896	529
Colorado	1	1876	Aug. 1, 1876	66,140	342	158
Connecticut	2	1818 (f), 1965	Dec. 30, 1965	16,401	32	30
Delaware	4	1776, 1792, 1831, 1897	June 10, 1897	25,445	(e)	145
Florida	6	1839, 1861, 1865, 1868, 1886, 1968	Jan. 7, 1969	56,705	168	122
Georgia	10	1777, 1789, 1798, 1861, 1865, 1868, 1877, 1945, 1976, 1982	July 1, 1983	41,684	98 (g)	75 (g)
Hawaii	1 (h)	1950	Aug. 21, 1959	21,498	138	113
Idaho	1	1889	July 3, 1890	24,626	213	125
Illinois	4	1818, 1848, 1870, 1970	July 1, 1971	16,401	21	14
Indiana	2	1816, 1851	Nov. 1, 1851	11,476	79	47
Iowa	2	1846, 1857	Sept. 3, 1857	11,089	59	54 (i)
Kansas	1	1859	Jan. 29, 1861	14,097	127	97 (i)
Kentucky	4	1792, 1799, 1850, 1891	Sept. 28, 1891	27,234	76	42
Louisiana	11	1812, 1845, 1852, 1861, 1864, 1868, 1879, 1898, 1913, 1921, 1974	Jan. 1, 1975	69,876	262	182
Maine	1	1819	March 15, 1820	16,313	205	172 (j)
Maryland	4	1776, 1851, 1864, 1867	Oct. 5, 1867	43,198	266	230 (k)
Massachusetts	1	1780	Oct. 25, 1780	45,283 (l)	148	120
Michigan	4	1835, 1850, 1908, 1963	Jan. 1, 1964	31,164	73	30
Minnesota	1	1857	May 11, 1858	11,734	217	120
Mississippi	4	1817, 1832, 1869, 1890	Nov. 1, 1890	26,229	162	126
Missouri	4	1820, 1865, 1875, 1945	March 30, 1945	69,394	186	120
Montana	2	1889, 1972	July 1, 1973	12,790	57	31
Nebraska	2	1866, 1875	Oct. 12, 1875	34,934	354 (m)	230 (m)
Nevada	1	1864	Oct. 31, 1864	37,418	235	138
New Hampshire	2	1776, 1784	June 2, 1784	13,060	289 (n)	145
New Jersey	3	1776, 1844, 1947	Jan. 1, 1948	26,360	85	70
New Mexico	1	1911	Jan. 6, 1912	33,198	303 (y)	169 (x)
New York	4	1777, 1822, 1846, 1894	Jan. 1, 1895	44,397	303	227
North Carolina	3	1776, 1868, 1970	July 1, 1971	17,177	39	32
North Dakota	1	1889	Nov. 2, 1889	18,746	277	156 (o)
Ohio	2	1802, 1851	Sept. 1, 1851	53,239	288	173
Oklahoma	1	1907	Nov. 16, 1907	81,666	363 (p)	196 (p)
Oregon	1	1857	Feb. 14, 1859	49,016	498 (q)	255 (q)
Pennsylvania	5	1776, 1790, 1838, 1873, 1968 (r)	1968 (r)	26,078	36 (r)	30 (r)
Rhode Island	2	1842 (f), 1986 (s)	Dec. 4, 1986	11,407	16 (s)	13 (s)
South Carolina	7	1776, 1778, 1790, 1861, 1865, 1868, 1895	Jan. 1, 1896	27,421	689 (t)	500 (t)
South Dakota	1	1889	Nov. 2, 1889	27,774	234	118
Tennessee	3	1796, 1835, 1870	Feb. 23, 1870	13,960	66	43
Texas	5 (u)	1845, 1861, 1866, 1869, 1876	Feb. 15, 1876	86,936	662 (v)	484
Utah	1	1895	Jan. 4, 1896	17,849	172	118
Vermont	3	1777, 1786, 1793	July 9, 1793	8,565	212	54
Virginia	6	1776, 1830, 1851, 1869, 1902, 1970	July 1, 1971	21,899	56	49
Washington	1	1889	Nov. 11, 1889	32,578	180	106
West Virginia	2	1863, 1872	April 9, 1872	33,324	123	72
Wisconsin	1	1848	May 29, 1848	15,102	195	146 (i)
Wyoming	1	1889	July 10, 1890	26,349	129	100
American Samoa	2	1960, 1967	July 1, 1967	6,000	15 (y)	7 (y)
No. Mariana Islands	1	1977	Jan. 9, 1978	13,700	60 (y)	56 (w)(y)
Puerto Rico	1	1952	July 25, 1952	9,400	8 (y)	6 (y)

See footnotes at end of table.

GENERAL INFORMATION ON STATE CONSTITUTIONS — Continued
(As of January 1, 2015)

Source: John Dinan and The Council of State Governments, with research assistance from Wake Forest students Bradley Harper and Alec Papovich.

*The constitutions referred to in this table include those Civil War documents customarily listed by the individual states.

**In calculating word counts, supplemental information regarding dates of adoption and other material not formally a part of the constitution are generally excluded. In some cases, word counts are taken from the total as of January 2011.

Key:

(a) The Alabama constitution includes numerous local amendments that apply to only one county. An estimated 70 percent of all amendments are local. A 1982 amendment provides that after proposal by the legislature to which special procedures apply, only a local vote (with exceptions) is necessary to add them to the constitution.

(b) Computer word count.

(c) The total number of Alabama amendments includes one that is commonly overlooked.

(d) Eight of the approved amendments have been superseded and are not printed in the current edition of the constitution. The total adopted does not include five amendments proposed and adopted since statehood.

(e) Proposed amendments are not submitted to the voters in Delaware.

(f) Colonial charters with some alterations served as the first constitutions in Connecticut (1638, 1662) and in Rhode Island (1663).

(g) The Georgia constitution requires amendments to be of "general and uniform application throughout the state," thus eliminating local amendments that accounted for most of the amendments before 1982.

(h) As a kingdom and republic, Hawaii had five constitutions.

(i) The figure includes amendments approved by the voters and later nullified by the state supreme court in Iowa (three), Kansas (one), Nevada (six) and Wisconsin (two).

(j) The figure does not include one amendment approved by the voters in 1967 that is inoperative until implemented by legislation.

(k) Two sets of identical amendments were on the ballot and adopted in the 1992 Maryland election. The four amendments are counted as two in the table.

(l) The printed constitution includes many provisions that have been annulled.

(m) The 1998 and 2000 Nebraska ballots allowed the voters to vote separately on "parts" of propositions. In 1998, 10 of 18 separate propositions were adopted; in 2000, 6 of 9.

(n) The constitution of 1784 was extensively revised in 1792. Figure shows proposals and adoptions since the constitution was adopted in 1784.

(o) The figures do not include submission and approval of the constitution of 1889 itself and of Article XX; these are constitutional questions included in some counts of constitutional amendments and would add two to the figure in each column.

(p) The figures include six amendments submitted to and approved by the voters which were, by decisions of the Oklahoma or federal courts, rendered inoperative or ruled invalid, unconstitutional, or illegally submitted.

(q) One Oregon amendment on the 2000 ballot was not counted as approved because canvassing was enjoined by the courts.

(r) Certain sections of the constitution were revised by the limited convention of 1967–68. Amendments proposed and adopted are since 1968.

(s) Following approval of the eight amendments and a "rewrite" of the Rhode Island Constitution in 1986, the constitution has been called the 1986 Constitution.

(t) In 1981 approximately two-thirds of the proposed and four-fifths of the adopted amendments were local. Since then the amendments have been statewide propositions.

(u) The Constitution of the Republic of Texas preceded five state constitutions.

(v) The number of proposed amendments to the Texas Constitution excludes three proposed by the legislature but not placed on the ballot.

(w) The total excludes one amendment ruled void by a federal district court.

(x) The total excludes one amendment approved by voters in November 2008 but later declared invalid on single subject grounds by the state supreme court.

(y) These totals for territorial constitutions are in some cases taken from 2011 data.

Table 1.2
CONSTITUTIONAL AMENDMENT PROCEDURE: BY THE LEGISLATURE
Constitutional Provisions

State or other jurisdiction	Legislative vote required for proposal (a)	Consideration by two sessions required	Vote required for ratification	Limitation on the number of amendments submitted at one election
Alabama	3/5	No	Majority vote on amendment	None
Alaska	2/3	No	Majority vote on amendment	None
Arizona	Majority	No	Majority vote on amendment	None
Arkansas	Majority	No	Majority vote on amendment	3
California	2/3	No	Majority vote on amendment	None
Colorado	2/3	No	Majority vote on amendment	None (b)
Connecticut	(c)	(c)	Majority vote on amendment	None
Delaware	2/3	Yes	Not required	No referendum
Florida	3/5	No	3/5 vote on amendment (d)	None
Georgia	2/3	No	Majority vote on amendment	None
Hawaii	(e)	(e)	(f)	None
Idaho	2/3	No	Majority vote on amendment	None
Illinois	3/5	No	(g)	3 articles
Indiana	Majority	Yes	Majority vote on amendment	None
Iowa	Majority	Yes	Majority vote on amendment	None
Kansas	2/3	No	Majority vote on amendment	5
Kentucky	3/5	No	Majority vote on amendment	4
Louisiana	2/3	No	Majority vote on amendment (h)	None
Maine	2/3 (i)	No	Majority vote on amendment	None
Maryland	3/5	No	Majority vote on amendment (h)	None
Massachusetts	Majority (j)	Yes	Majority vote on amendment	None
Michigan	2/3	No	Majority vote on amendment	None
Minnesota	Majority	No	Majority vote in election	None
Mississippi	2/3 (k)	No	Majority vote on amendment	None
Missouri	Majority	No	Majority vote on amendment	None
Montana	2/3 (i)	No	Majority vote on amendment	None
Nebraska	3/5 (w)	No	Majority vote on amendment (f)	None
Nevada	Majority	Yes	Majority vote on amendment	None
New Hampshire	3/5	No	2/3 vote on amendment	None
New Jersey	(l)	(l)	Majority vote on amendment	None (m)
New Mexico	Majority (n)	No	Majority vote on amendment (n)	None
New York	Majority	Yes	Majority vote on amendment	None
North Carolina	3/5	No	Majority vote on amendment	None
North Dakota	Majority	No	Majority vote on amendment	None
Ohio	3/5	No	Majority vote on amendment	None
Oklahoma	Majority (w)	No	Majority vote on amendment	None
Oregon	(o)	No	Majority vote on amendment (x)	None
Pennsylvania	Majority (p)	Yes (p)	Majority vote on amendment	None
Rhode Island	Majority	No	Majority vote on amendment	None
South Carolina	2/3 (q)	Yes (q)	Majority vote on amendment	None
South Dakota	Majority	No	Majority vote on amendment	None
Tennessee	(r)	Yes (r)	Majority vote in election (s)	None
Texas	2/3	No	Majority vote on amendment	None
Utah	2/3	No	Majority vote on amendment	None
Vermont	(t)	Yes	Majority vote on amendment	None
Virginia	Majority	Yes	Majority vote on amendment	None
Washington	2/3	No	Majority vote on amendment	None
West Virginia	2/3	No	Majority vote on amendment	None
Wisconsin	Majority	Yes	Majority vote on amendment	None
Wyoming	2/3	No	Majority vote in election	None
American Samoa	2/3	No	Majority vote on amendment (u)	None
No. Mariana Islands	3/4	No	Majority vote on amendment	None
Puerto Rico	2/3 (v)	No	Majority vote on amendment	3

See footnotes at end of table.

CONSTITUTIONAL AMENDMENT PROCEDURE: BY THE LEGISLATURE — Continued
Constitutional Provisions

Source: John Dinan and The Council of State Governments, Feb. 2015.

Key:

(a) In all states not otherwise noted, the figure shown in the column refers to the proportion of elected members in each house required for approval of proposed constitutional amendments.

(b) Legislature may not propose amendments to more than six articles of the constitution in the same legislative session.

(c) Three-fourths vote in each house at one session, or majority vote in each house in two sessions between which an election has intervened.

(d) Three-fifths vote on amendment, except amendment for "new state tax or fee" not in effect on Nov. 7, 1994 requires two-thirds of voters in the election.

(e) Two-thirds vote in each house at one session, or majority vote in each house in two sessions.

(f) In Hawaii, the majority vote on amendment must be at least 50 percent of the total votes cast at the election; or, at a special election, a majority of the votes tallied which must be at least 30 percent of the total number of registered voters. In Nebraska the majority vote on amendment must be at least 35 percent of the total votes cast at the election.

(g) Majority voting in election or three-fifths voting on amendment.

(h) In Louisiana, if five or fewer political subdivisions of the state are affected, majority in state as a whole and also in each of affected subdivisions is required. In Maryland, if an amendent affects only the City of Baltimore or only one county, majority in state as a whole and also in affected subdivision is required.

(i) Two-thirds of both houses.

(j) Majority of members elected sitting in joint session.

(k) The two-thirds must include not less than a majority elected to each house.

(l) Three-fifths of all members of each house at one session, or majority of all members of each house for two successive sessions.

(m) If a proposed amendment is not approved at the election when submitted, neither the same amendment nor one which would make substantially the same change for the constitution may be again submitted to the people before the third general election thereafter.

(n) Amendments concerning certain elective franchise and education matters require three-fourths vote of members elected and approval by three-fourths of electors voting in state and two-thirds of those voting in each county.

(o) Majority vote to amend constitution, two-thirds to revise ("revise" includes all or a part of the constitution).

(p) Emergency amendments may be passed by two-thirds vote of each house, followed by ratification by majority vote of electors in election held at least one month after legislative approval.

(q) Two-thirds of members of each house, first passage; majority of members of each house after popular ratification.

(r) Majority of members elected to both houses, first passage; two-thirds of members elected to both houses, second passage.

(s) Majority of all citizens voting for governor.

(t) Two-thirds vote senate, majority vote house, first passage; majority both houses, second passage. As of 1974, amendments may be submitted only every four years.

(u) Within 30 days after voter approval, governor must submit amendment(s) to U.S. Secretary of the Interior for approval.

(v) If approved by two-thirds of members of each house, amendment(s) submitted to voters at special referendum; if approved by not less than three-fourths of total members of each house, referendum may be held at next general election.

(w) The legislature may, by a four-fifths vote in Nebraska or a two-thirds vote in Oklahoma, call a special election for voters to consider amendments.

(x) There is an exception for an amendment containing a supermajority voting requirement, which must be ratified by an equal supermajority.

Table 1.3
CONSTITUTIONAL AMENDMENT PROCEDURE: BY INITIATIVE
Constitutional Provisions

State or other jurisdiction	Number of signatures required on initiative petition	Distribution of signatures	Referendum vote
Arizona	15% of total votes cast for all candidates for governor at last election.	None specified.	Majority vote on amendment.
Arkansas	10% of voters for governor at last election.	Must include 5% of voters for governor in each of 15 counties.	Majority vote on amendment.
California	8% of total voters for all candidates for governor at last election.	None specified.	Majority vote on amendment.
Colorado	5% of total legal votes for all candidates for secretary of state at last general election.	None specified.	Majority vote on amendment.
Florida	8% of total votes cast in the state in the last election for presidential electors.	8% of total votes cast in each of 1/2 of the congressional districts.	Three-fifths vote on amendment except amendment for "new state tax or fee" not in effect Nov. 7, 1994 requires 2/3 of voters voting in election.
Illinois (a)	8% of total votes cast for candidates for governor at last election.	None specified.	Majority voting in election or 3/5 voting on amendment.
Massachusetts (b)	3% of total votes cast for governor at preceding biennial state election (not less than 25,000 qualified voters).	No more than 1/4 from any one county.	Majority vote on amendment which must be 30% of total ballots cast at election.
Michigan	10% of total voters for all candidates at last gubernatorial election.	None specified.	Majority vote on amendment.
Mississippi (c)	12% of total votes for all candidates for governor in last election.	No more than 20% from any one congressional district.	Majority vote on amendment and not less than 40% of total vote cast at election.
Missouri	8% of legal voters for all candidates for governor at last election.	The 8% must be in each of 2/3 of the congressional districts in the state.	Majority vote on amendment.
Montana	10% of qualified electors, the number of qualified voters to be determined by number of votes cast for governor in preceding election in each county and in the state.	The 10% to include at least 10% of qualified voters in 1/2 of the counties.	Majority vote on amendment.
Nebraska	10% of registered voters.	The 10% must include 5% in each of 2/5 of the counties.	Majority vote on amendment which must be at least 35% of total vote at the election.
Nevada	10% of voters who voted in entire state in last general election.	None in effect after a U.S. District Court ruling in 2004 invalidated the requirement.	Majority vote on amendment in two consecutive general elections.
North Dakota	4% of population of the state.	None specified.	Majority vote on amendment.
Ohio	10% of total number of electors who voted for governor in last election.	At least 5% of qualified electors in each of 1/2 of counties in the state.	Majority vote on amendment.
Oklahoma	15% of legal voters for state office receiving highest number of voters at last general state election.	None specified.	Majority vote on amendment.
Oregon	8% of total votes for all candidates for governor at last election at which governor was elected for four-year term.	None specified.	Majority vote on amendment except for supermajority equal to supermajority voting requirement contained in proposed amendment.
South Dakota	10% of total votes for governor in last election.	None specified.	Majority vote on amendment.
No. Mariana Islands	50% of qualified voters of commonwealth.	In addition, 25% of qualified voters in each senatorial district.	Majority vote on amendment if legislature approved it by majority vote; if not, at least 2/3 vote in each of two senatorial districts in addition to a majority vote.

Source: John Dinan and The Council of State Governments, Feb. 2015.
Key:
(a) Initiatives can only be used to amend substantive or procedural aspects of Article IV, the Legislature Article, and cannot be used to amend any other articles.
(b) Before being submitted to the electorate for ratification, initiative measures must be approved at two sessions of a successively elected legislature by not less than one-fourth of all members elected, sitting in joint session.
(c) Before being submitted to the electorate, initiated measures are sent to the legislature, which has the option of submitting an amended or alternative measure alongside the original measure.

Table 1.4
PROCEDURES FOR CALLING CONSTITUTIONAL CONVENTIONS
Constitutional Provisions

State or other jurisdiction	Provision for convention	Provision for calling a convention by initiative	Legislative vote for submission of convention question (a)	Popular vote to authorize convention	Periodic submission of convention question required (b)	Popular vote required for ratification of convention proposals
Alabama	Yes	No	Majority	ME	No	Not specified
Alaska	Yes	No	No provision (c)(d)	(c)	10 years; 2012 (c)	Not specified (c)
Arizona	Yes	No	Majority	(e)	No	MP
Arkansas	No	No	No			
California	Yes	No	2/3	MP	No	MP
Colorado	Yes	No	2/3	MP	No	ME
Connecticut	Yes	No	2/3	MP	20 years; 2008 (f)	MP
Delaware	Yes	No	2/3	MP	No	No provision
Florida	Yes	Yes (m)	(g)	MP	No	3/5 voting on proposal
Georgia	Yes	No	(d)	No	No	MP
Hawaii	Yes	No	Not specified	MP	9 years; 2008	MP (h)
Idaho	Yes	No	2/3	MP	No	Not specified
Illinois	Yes	No	3/5	(i)	20 years; 2008	MP
Indiana	No	No	No			
Iowa	Yes	No	Majority	MP	10 years; 2010	MP
Kansas	Yes	No	2/3	MP	No	MP
Kentucky	Yes	No	Majority (j)	MP (k)	No	No provision
Louisiana	Yes	No	(d)	No	No	MP
Maine	Yes	No	(d)	No	No	No provision
Maryland	Yes	No	Majority	ME	20 years; 2010	MP
Massachusetts	No	No		No		
Michigan	Yes	No	Majority	MP	16 years; 2010	MP
Minnesota	Yes	No	2/3	ME	No	3/5 voting on proposal
Mississippi	No	No	No			
Missouri	Yes	No	Majority	MP	20 years; 2002	Not specified (l)
Montana	Yes	Yes (m)	2/3	MP	20 years; 2010	MP
Nebraska	Yes	No	3/5	MP (o)	No	MP
Nevada	Yes	No	2/3	ME	No	No provision
New Hampshire	Yes	No	Majority	MP	10 years; 2012	2/3 voting on proposal
New Jersey	No	No	No			
New Mexico	Yes	No	2/3	MP	No	Not specified
New York	Yes	No	Majority	MP	20 years; 1997	MP
North Carolina	Yes	No	2/3	MP	No	MP
North Dakota	No	Yes (m)	No			
Ohio	Yes	No	2/3	MP	20 years; 2012	MP
Oklahoma	Yes	No	Majority	(e)	20 years; 1970	MP
Oregon	Yes	No	Majority	(e)	No	No provision
Pennsylvania	No	No	No			
Rhode Island	Yes	No	Majority	MP	10 years; 2014	MP
South Carolina	Yes	No	(d)	ME	No	No provision
South Dakota	Yes	Yes (m)	(d)	No	No	(p)
Tennessee	Yes (q)	No	Majority	MP	No	MP
Texas	No	No	No			
Utah	Yes	No	2/3	ME	No	ME
Vermont	No	No	No			
Virginia	Yes	No	(d)	No	No	MP
Washington	Yes	No	2/3	ME	No	Not specified
West Virginia	Yes	No	Majority	MP	No	Not specified
Wisconsin	Yes	No	Majority	MP	No	No provision
Wyoming	Yes	No	2/3	ME	No	Not specified
American Samoa	Yes	No	(r)	No	No	ME (s)
No. Mariana Islands	Yes	Yes (t)	Majority	2/3	10 years	MP and at least 2/3 in each of 2 senatorial districts
Puerto Rico	Yes	No	2/3	MP	No	MP

See footnotes at end of table.

PROCEDURES FOR CALLING CONSTITUTIONAL CONVENTIONS — Continued
Constitutional Provisions

Source: John Dinan and The Council of State Governments, Feb. 2015.
Key:
MP — Majority voting on the proposal.
ME — Majority voting in the election.

(a) In all states not otherwise noted, the entries in this column refer to the proportion of members elected to each house required to submit to the electorate the question of calling a constitutional convention.

(b) The number listed is the interval between required submissions on the question of calling a constitutional convention; where given, the date is that of the most recent submission of the mandatory convention referendum.

(c) Unless provided otherwise by law, convention calls are to conform as nearly as possible to the act calling the 1955 convention, which provided for a legislative vote of a majority of members elected to each house and ratification by a majority vote on the proposals. The legislature may call a constitutional convention at any time.

(d) In these states, the legislature may call a convention without submitting the question to the people. The legislative vote required is two-thirds of the members elected to each house in Georgia, Louisiana, South Carolina and Virginia; two-thirds concurrent vote of both branches in Maine; three-fourths of all members of each house in South Dakota; and not specified in Alaska, but bills require majority vote of membership in each house.

(e) The law calling a convention must be approved by the people.

(f) The legislature shall submit the question 20 years after the last convention, or 20 years after the last vote on the question of calling a convention, whichever date is last.

(g) The power to call a convention is reserved to the people by petition.

(h) The majority must be 50 percent of the total votes cast at a general election or at a special election, a majority of the votes tallied which must be at least 30 percent of the total number of registered voters.

(i) Majority voting in the election, or three-fifths voting on the question.

(j) Must be approved during two legislative sessions.

(k) Majority must equal one-fourth of qualified voters at last general election.

(l) Majority of those voting on the proposal is assumed. Vote must take place at a special election held no less than 60 days and no more than 6 months after convention.

(m) In Montana, North Dakota and South Dakota, conventions can be called by initiative petition in the same manner as provided for initiated amendments (see Table 1.3), and with approval by a majority of voters. In Florida, conventions can be called by filing an initiative petition with signatures equal to 15 percent of the votes cast in the preceding presidential election and also equal to 15 percent of signatures in half of the congressional districts in the state and then obtaining a majority of the voters at the ensuing election.

(n) Two-thirds of all members of the legislature.

(o) Majority must be 35 percent of total votes cast at the election.

(p) Convention proposals are submitted to the electorate at a special election in a manner to be determined by the convention. Ratification by a majority of votes cast.

(q) Conventions may not be held more often than once in six years.

(r) Five years after effective date of constitutions, governor shall call a constitutional convention to consider changes proposed by a constitutional committee appointed by the governor. Delegates to the convention are to be elected by their county councils. A convention was held in 1972.

(s) If proposed amendments are approved by the voters, they must be submitted to the U.S. Secretary of the Interior for approval.

(t) The petition must be signed by 25 percent of the qualified voters or at least 75 percent in a senatorial district.

State Constitutions and Environmental Bills of Rights
By Art English and John J. Carroll

The movement to add environmental bills of rights to state constitutions is important as one manifestation of a wider environmentalism that began to sweep the country in the 1970s, but also because it sheds interesting light on state constitutions and constitutional processes. The states proved to be more hospitable for this type of constitutional reform than the federal because state constitutional traditions diverge substantially from the national model. In particular, the argument is that the openness of state constitutional processes to their political environment facilitated the effort to place environmental rights, as well as a variety of other environmental provisions, in state constitutions.

The provisions to include environmental bills of rights in state constitutions have been crafted in innovative ways. These provisions typify how states amend constitutions, displaying first, uniformities in intent and meaning as new states adopted provisions borrowed from other states and adopted them and, second, increments of innovation as the basic idea was adapted to the needs of a unique state and its environment.

Each state that adopted a provision could claim, like all the others, a unique environmental character. Rhode Island is a coastal state with some of the most unspoiled beaches and best saltwater fishing in the nation and its environmental provisions reflect those characteristics. Pennsylvania is known for its woodlands, deer population and mountains, as well as its many colonial and Civil War historic places. Massachusetts has both freshwater resources and coastline fisheries, while Hawaii is perhaps the most unique American state with eight main islands geographically located almost 2,500 miles from the continental United States. Even the central gateway to the Midwest, Illinois, has thousands of square miles of timberland, lakes and rivers. The state environmental bills of rights reflect each state's unique assets and concerns.

Six Environmental Bills of Rights

Illinois, 1970: Illinois' pioneering environmental rights provision was a product of the constitutional reform that was prevalent in the states during the 1970s. The article was part of a revised state constitution adopted in 1970 and is fairly typical of the kinds of environmental rights that were placed in state constitutions during this active period of environmental constitution making. The environmental bill of rights appears in the Illinois Constitution as a freestanding provision and is not part of the

Table A: Summary of Environmental Rights Provisions in Six States

State	Date	Section	Total words in provision	Mentions state public trust	Mentions future generations	Enforcement mechanism noted
Illinois	1970	Article XI	83	Yes	Yes	Self-Executing
Pennsylvania	1971	Article I Section 27 (in bill of rights)	61	Yes	Yes	Legislative
Montana	1972	Article II, Section 3 (in bill of rights)	60	Yes	Yes	Unclear – Subject to judicial interpretation
Massachusetts	1972	Article 97	191	Yes	No	Legislative
Hawaii	1978	Article XI, Section 9	57	Yes	Yes	Self-Executing
Rhode Island	1987	Article I, Section 17 (in bill of rights)	185	Yes	Yes	Legislative

Source: Art English and John J. Carroll.

document's bill of rights. The key language of the provision is found in Section 2 and states, "Each person has the right to a healthful environment."[1]

Like most of the environmental provisions written into state constitutions during this period, Illinois' provision is short but reflects the unique traditions of state constitution making that drove the selected language. Section 1, for example, offers a uniquely state constitutional twist when it begins by observing that it is "the public policy of the state and the duty of each person to provide and maintain a healthful environment for the benefit of this and future generations." This section bears several of the earmarks of the distinctive state constitution making tradition. The language is a hortatory reminder to the people of Illinois that they bear a direct responsibility for the care of the environment themselves. It is a statement of public policy meant to guide, but not bind, the state legislature to a course of action. The article lays out the public trust doctrine giving the legislature the responsibility for protecting the environment for current and future generations.

Section 2 contains ideas later alluded to in the Montana and Hawaii documents that provide a person may enforce the right to a healthy environment against a governmental or private party, but that the right is subject to reasonable regulation the General Assembly may provide by law. Thus, while Article 1 appears to be completely self-executing, i.e. enforceable by the courts without legislative implementation, nonetheless, Article 2 grants the Illinois General Assembly power to implement the provision.

Pennsylvania, 1971: The Pennsylvania environmental rights provision appears in the constitution's Declaration of Rights and was placed there in 1971 by a referendum that passed by a margin of 4-to-1. The referendum was part of a general awakening in Pennsylvania about matters of environmental concern, and was one of several steps taken during this period to tighten control on coal companies, steel companies and land developers.[2]

In its provision, Pennsylvania enumerates the components of what Illinois had summarily called a "healthful environment." Among the components are values we have since come to expect: clean air, pure water and preservation of natural areas. But the Pennsylvania provision contains some surprises reflecting its historic legacy as one the first 13 colonies. The inclusion of "scenic, historic and aesthetic values" takes the idea of an environmental bill of rights in a new direction and expands its scope. It

also indicates to constitution makers in other states that such a declaration can be sensitive to each state's unique heritage, including, but not limited to, its natural environment.

Like the Illinois document, the Pennsylvania Constitution contains a statement of policy in defining environmental values as a public trust of the state to preserve and articulate on behalf of the people, including "generations yet to come."[3] The Pennsylvania language is unclear as to whether it was meant to follow the self-executing model, or whether it depended on the legislature to provide for its enforcement. This became a matter of contention in the courts.[4]

Montana, 1972: Montana is a particularly interesting case. The Montana provision emanated from a constitutional convention called by the people, which essentially replaced Montana's 1889 statehood constitution. The new constitution was adopted by a razor-thin majority of 116,415 to 113,883 in 1972. At 11,200 words, it was only half the size of the 1889 document. Among its more modern provisions were a right to bring suit against the state for injuries to person and property, a provision that the governor and lieutenant governor run as a team, and an amendatory veto for the governor.[5] Short in length and not excessive in detail, the new Montana Constitution had a decidedly "model" state constitution look.[6] The preamble of the 1972 Montana Constitution demonstrates a forceful commitment to environmental rights, intoning in almost spiritual language the natural wonders of the state:

> We the people of Montana grateful to God for the quiet beauty of our state, the grandeur of our mountains, the vastness of our rolling plains, and desiring to improve the quality of life, equality of opportunity and to secure the blessings of liberty for this and future generations do ordain and establish this constitution.[7]

The language of the preamble demonstrates that environmental protection was a very high value among those who wrote the state's constitution. One of the new constitution's most innovative provisions, however, was Article II, Section 3 of The Declaration of Rights, which enumerates the inalienable rights of a people "born free." In its enumeration of rights, pride of place is given to "the right to a clean and healthful environment," followed in the same sentence by such traditional items as "enjoying and defending lives and liberties," "protecting property," and "safety, health and happiness."

While Article II seems to provide a self-executing right, Article IX of the Montana Constitution mandates the legislature to "provide for the administration and enforcement" of the "clean and healthful environment." Article IX follows the Illinois example in declaring public policy, but also mandating "each person" as well as the state to protect the environment for present and future generations.[8]

Massachusetts, 1972: In 1972, Massachusetts voters placed into their constitution an environmental rights provision. The Massachusetts provision, Article 97, has its own space in the state document and was placed there in part to obtain a degree of certainty that takings by the state for environmental purposes would not otherwise be directed unless two-thirds of the Massachusetts General Court agreed. In this way, the commonwealth used its constitutional processes to address a specific issue in substantive detail. In its detail and the narrowness of the policy area addressed, Article 97 has some characteristics akin to positive law and illustrates a common state practice in which the constitution is used to raise higher hurdles for the passage of legislation than would otherwise be required.

The environmental rights section is similar to the provisions of the other states, but borrows heavily from Pennsylvania. The article protects "natural, scenic, historic and aesthetic qualities" as Pennsylvania had done the year before. Its innovative content is "freedom from excessive and unnecessary noise," a protection that had not previously appeared in a state constitution. Article 97 also protects a right of conservation and utilization of agricultural, mineral and other resources, in a variant of the more common right to access provisions. The Massachusetts provision is interesting for its mix of positive and higher law elements, and its typically state characteristic of both borrowing language from other initiatives and offering new language at the same time.

Hawaii, 1978: Hawaii's Article XI represents that state's constitutional orientation to environmental protection. The article was one of 32 provisions drafted by the 1978 constitutional convention, the second comprehensive updating of the state's document since statehood in 1958. Borrowing on the successful ratification strategy used to approve 22 out of 23 provisions from the 1968 constitutional convention, all 32 provisions drafted in 1978 were submitted separately to the people and all 32 were approved.[9]

Article 11 approaches the protection of the environment in a comprehensive manner, sub-dividing environmental protection into several headings, which include broad public trustee categories of conservation and management of natural resources along with marine and water resources, nuclear energy, public land banking and agricultural lands.[10] A separate section in Article XI devoted to environmental rights states that not only does each person have the right to "a clean and healthful environment," but also that any person has the right to enforce those protections against any public or private entity subject to reasonable limitations as provided by law. As in Montana, people in Hawaii have a private right to bring suit pertinent to the self-executing language of this section.

Rhode Island, 1987: The Rhode Island provision is found in the constitution's Declaration of Rights and Privileges, and was inserted by constitutional amendment in 1987. Rhode Island's environmental bill of right provision illustrates that each state that has opted for an environmental provision in its constitution has a unique constitutional tradition. The Rhode Island article is very detailed, encompassing an access right for swimmers and gatherers of seaweed, as well as imposing responsibility on the state to protect the natural environment by regulation and planning. The state as a trustee and steward of the environment for the people is clearly written into this provision, which relies on its execution by the state "to adopt all means necessary and proper by law to protect the natural environment. ..." The provision is quite unique in granting access to the "rights of fishery and the privileges of the shore," relying on the entitlements of the King Charles Charter that preceded the Rhode Island Constitution of 1842 and the common usages of the state. Rhode Island's bill of rights reference in the state constitution may be of 20th century origin, but its protections are rooted in hundreds of years of fishing and shore rights for its people.

Discussion

The active yet limited process invoked by environmentalists during the last third of the 20th century provides insight into one of the unique processes of political change in the United States—enlarging the rights of people by placing them in the state's constitution. In selecting state constitutional change as the mode of enlarging power in a state political system, individuals and groups must work within a state's constitutional tradition and political culture. That tradition and culture invariably are intertwined with a state's previous constitutions, particular political and historical traditions, and geopolitical developments. In selecting state constitutions as their target for environmental rights, supporters of a healthier environment hoped to establish a center of constitutional power in their respective documents that they could draw upon to repel assaults by those who would use raw political power in the states to provide unbridled development, hasty easements and takings that would despoil natural environments and endanger the health of the state's citizenry. The relative ease of the amendment process in the states, compared to fighting entrenched political interests at the federal level, offered supporters a way to write their values in the state's fundamental document.

This analysis demonstrates how environmentalists of the 1970s wrote these provisions in the frame of a higher law rather than positive or statutory law tradition. Their aim was to establish the protection of the environment not just in terms of concrete and immediate issues in the physical environment, but also on a larger community scale protecting the health and well-being of both present and future generations. While they hoped constitutional values would translate into a basis of higher political power, environmental advocates had other purposes in mind, too.

In the six states studied, it appears the framers of these amendments believed that even if the language in most cases would not support unilateral private action against serial environmental abusers, they would remind lawmakers, judges, political activists and the attentive public that the right to a clean and healthy environment is one of the most fundamental rights to which people are entitled. While these reminders might be considered merely hortatory, they also provide policy guidance to legislators, executives and courts who are encouraged to provide reasonable regulation and implementation by law in light of their public trust to take good care of the environment for future generations.

The environmental rights movement moved within the contours of the state constitutional traditions. Its legacy tells a good deal about why state constitutions were and are still important in the protection of the broader human values that are written into some of our national founding documents. The argument that the dignity of people cannot be separated from their place of habitat and that habitat must be healthy is a simple but powerful idea. That some states chose to write them into constitutions and not just into statutes

is no accident—the provisions were intended to provide authoritative advice and counsel to political decision-makers. We maintain that state constitutions are still an excellent place in which to articulate fundamental rights.

In comparing the national constitutional tradition with the state traditions, it becomes clear why environmentalists worked within the state tradition. As noted, the federal tradition is one in which a constitutional amendment is exceedingly rare because of the difficulties in the adoption process and in building a national consensus. Within the states, constitution-making processes vary considerably, but in general the states have developed more sensitive and diverse mechanisms for democratic control than exists at the national level. States are regular users of their constitutional revision processes, whether it is a legislative proposal and popular referendum, citizen initiative or even a constitutional convention.

After the Bill of Rights, amendments at the federal level have dealt with procedures such as the voting age, prohibition, or vice presidential succession. Federal amendments have responded to political crises that were percolating up from the states such as the popular election of senators or the right to vote for women. Federal provisions are also usually self-executing or if they are not, as in the case of the civil war amendments, they may have enforcement clauses. Had there been a federal environmental rights amendment it would have had to have gone through all of these stages: relative consensus in the states, extraordinary majority by proposal and ratification, most likely an enforcement clause, and certainly judicial interpretation.

Environmentalists approached the state constitutional revision process differently. Their first intent was to place protection of the environment in the state constitution's bill of rights to clothe it with inalienability. The Hawaii provision, for example, says each person has the right to a clean and healthful environment. The second and most important intent was to write language that would allow environmental protection to be the right of any person should they so choose to be its champion in the courts. Thus, the Illinois provision states, "Each person may enforce this right against any party, governmental or private."

An additional distinction between the federal and state constitutional models is that the state provisions reflect the particular circumstances and interests that were unique to the state; in this sense, they reflect the variety of regional concerns. In

Pennsylvania, the framers were concerned about leaving not only the environment, but also historic sites in good stead for future generations. In Rhode Island, access to the shoreline for swimming and fishing were important values, and in Massachusetts, where land is often at a premium, those who wrote the constitutional provision wanted to avoid having land taken for environmental purposes used for other ends unless extraordinary majorities of the General Court would agree.

While the state provisions are short and do not have excessive detail—fitting more into a higher law framework associated with the more modern constitutions of the latter part of the 20th century and the very early documents—they are not like the much more crisis-driven amendments the federal constitution has seen. It is fair to say the incremental amendment process that characterizes bill of rights provisions in the state constitutions illustrates the point that states have exercised considerable imagination as they have faced new problems and absorbed the wisdom generated by new social movements.

Notes

[1] The complete texts of the six state provisions are included in the Appendix.

[2] Franklin L. Kury, "Pennsylvania's Environmental Bill of Rights 25 Years Old," available at *http://www.dep.state.pa.us/dep/Rachel-Carson/Kury.htm.*

[3] See Appendix.

[4] John C. Dernbach, "Taking the Pennsylvania Constitution Seriously When It Protects the Environment: Part 1— An Interpretive Framework for Article 1, Section 27," 103 Dick. L. Rev. 693 (1999); Marcy Smorey-Giger, "The Effect of the Environmental Rights Amendment: How Article 1, Section 27 of the Pennsylvania Constitution Has Impacted Environmental Law in Pennsylvania," *Juris: The Duquesne University School of Law News Magazine*, 35, 1 (2001) available at *http:www.Juris.Duq.edu/winter2001/effect.htm.* See *Commonwealth v. National Gettysburg Battlefield Tower*, Inc., 311 A, 2d.588 (Pa. 1973); and *Payne v. Kassab* 312 A.2d 86 (Pa. Commw. Ct. 1973).

[5] *The Book of the States*: 1972.

[6] See *Model State Constitution*, 6th eds. 1968. New York, NY: National Municipal League.

[7] A copy of the Montana State Constitution's bill of rights as ratified in 1972 can be found at *http://www.harbornet.com/rights/Montana.txt.*

[8] See appendix for the entire article. The entire Montana Constitution can be viewed at *http://www.mcvedfund.org/constitution.htm* which is the home page of the Montana Voters Education Fund.

[9] Albert L. Sturm, "State Constitutions and Constitutional Revision: 1978–79 and the 1970s." *The Book of the States.* (Lexington Kentucky: The Council of State Governments) p. 11.

[10] Provision found in appendix. Entire Hawaii State Constitution can be viewed at *http://www.hawaii.gov/Irb/* which is the home page of the Hawaii Legislative Reference Bureau.

About the Authors

Art English is Professor of Political Science Emeritus at the University of Arkansas at Little Rock. His research has appeared in the *American Review of Politics*, *The Arkansas Lawyer*, *The Journal of Politics*, and *State and Local Government Review* among others. He has won University, College, and Community awards for public service.

John J. Carroll is distinguished Professor of Political Science Emeritus at the University of Massachusetts at Dartmouth where he served as Director of Advising Services.. His research has appeared in *The Western Political Quarterly*, *Legislative Politics Quarterly*, and *National Civic Review* among others.

Chapter Two

FEDERALISM AND INTERGOVERNMENTAL RELATIONS

State-Federal Relations:
Obstructive or Constructive Federalism?

By John Kincaid

The 2014 mid-term elections magnified the polarization between the political parties in Washington, D.C., and between blue and red states. In that respect, the elections signaled continuity in American federalism. Despite their congressional victories, lacking the presidency, Republicans are not in a position to effect major intergovernmental change. Increased Republican strength in the states will heighten state-federal conflicts over core Republican issues, while predominantly Democratic states generally will support federal policies endorsed by President Barack Obama. Whether one regards this state of affairs as obstructive or constructive federalism depends on one's point of view.

The 2014 elections strengthened the Republicans' right wing and the Democrats' left wing.

Republicans control both chambers in 30 state legislatures, Democrats control 11 and eight are split. Republicans control 68 of 98 partisan legislative chambers—exceeding their previous high of 64 in 1920—and they hold a super-majority in 21. Republicans also control nonpartisan Nebraska.

Republicans control both the governorship and the legislature in 24 states, something they have not achieved since the 1920s. Democrats control seven—the lowest for Democrats since before the Civil War. Nonetheless, 19 states (e.g., Illinois, New York and Pennsylvania) remain split. Republicans have 31 governors—one short of the previous high of 32—31 lieutenant governors, 27 attorneys general and 28 secretaries of state. Republicans flipped four governorships (Arkansas, Illinois, Maryland and Massachusetts); Democrats flipped one (Pennsylvania).

Republicans likely will challenge Common Core State Standards, student testing, data sharing with the federal government and Environmental Protection Agency (EPA) policies. They probably will seek to cut state taxes, enact abortion regulations, pass right-to-work laws, limit public-sector collective bargaining, expand private-school vouchers, and enact tort reforms, drug screening of applicants for cash and nutrition assistance, and job-seeking rules for Medicaid recipients.

Other issues on Democratic and Republican state agendas include pension liabilities, infrastructure, surface transportation, corrections, immigration, electronic cigarettes, cybersecurity, ride-sharing services (e.g., Lyft and Uber), marijuana legalization, rail transport of oil, specialty drugs that increase Medicaid costs, right-to-try (experimental drugs) policies, net-metering viability, police-community relations, sex trafficking, social impact bonds and pretrial release policies.

The election results, therefore, promise more state-federal disagreements and divergence between blue and red states. Immediately after the 2014 elections, for example, liberal groups established the State Innovation Exchange for state legislators to counteract the conservative American Legislative Exchange Council.

States also might differentiate themselves even further by opting out of the Uniform Time Act of 1966, which established uniform daylight saving time. Twelve states are considering it. Arizona and Hawaii already have opted out. Some states might stay on daylight saving time and some on standard time all year, while others still will switch time twice a year.

Nationalists versus Federalists

Underlying state-federal disagreements is a long-standing debate between nationalists and federalists. When states resist certain federal policies, as in state refusals to establish a health-insurance exchange or expand Medicaid under the Affordable Care Act—also known as Obamacare—proponents of those federal policies inveigh against uncooperative or obstructive federalism.[1] In this nationalist view, the states should be administrative arms of the federal government. Opponents of federal policies endorse state resistance as constructive federalism. In this federalist view, the states are independent sovereigns rejecting unwise federal policies and protecting liberty against overweening federal power.

What complicates the federalism landscape, though, is that nationalists sometimes support uncooperative federalism, as in state legalization of marijuana, while federalists sometimes support national intrusions upon state sovereignty, such as prohibitions on states using federal-aid funds to pay for abortions.

The nationalist view was most recently pressed by former U.S. Supreme Court Justice John Paul Stevens, who advocates six constitutional amendments to negate court rulings from which he dissented.[2] The amendments would (1) overturn the court's anti-commandeering doctrine so as to require state and local officials to implement federal policies, (2) increase judicial involvement in congressional and state legislative redistricting, (3) curtail First Amendment challenges to campaign-finance laws, (4) waive state sovereign immunity so as to allow state governments to be sued for monetary damages, (5) abolish the death penalty, and (6) abolish an individual right to bear arms. Only Stevens' third and sixth proposals would augment state powers. The first and fourth would formally abolish state sovereignty; the other two would further circumscribe state autonomy.

Stevens believes states should be administrative arms of the federal government. He quotes approvingly Justice Stephen Breyer's dissent in 1997 in *Printz v. United States*: "The federal systems of Switzerland, Germany, and the European Union ... all provide that constituent states, not federal bureaucracies, will themselves implement many of the laws ... enacted by the central 'federal' body."[3]

However, Stevens does not propose constitutional amendments that would give the states the kind of clout over federal policymaking possessed by the cantons in Switzerland and the *Länder* in Germany, nor does he acknowledge Germany's 2006 constitutional reforms that emphasized decentralization. Similarly, all the federal member-states of the European Union have amended their constitutions to give their constituent states influential representation in EU deliberations affecting states' powers.

Nationalists have had the upper hand since the New Deal, but public opinion has shifted to a more federalist view during the past two decades.[4] In 2014, 72 percent of Americans trusted local government and 62 percent trusted state government a great deal or fair amount.[5] Only 24 percent trusted the federal government always or most of the time.[6] More than 71 percent believe that if the Founding Fathers returned, they would say the federal government is too big.[7] Fifty-four percent believe the federal government is a threat to individual liberty, not a protector of liberty, and 37 percent say they fear the federal government. A 2014 Reuters poll found that 24 percent of Americans strongly or somewhat support the idea of their "state peacefully withdrawing from the United States of America and the federal government."[8]

These polls suggest polarization not only between the parties, but also between the general public and many political elites.

Federal Aid and Fiscal Federalism

President Obama's budget proposal called for $3.99 trillion in spending in 2016, a 7 percent increase over 2014. Congressional Republicans will seek to scale back spending. The Congressional Budget Office projects federal deficits to grow from $467 billion (2.5 percent of GDP) in 2016 to $1.09 trillion (4 percent of GDP) by 2025, with total federal debt increasing from $13 trillion today to $21.6 trillion (79 percent of GDP) by 2025. Projections of the long-term fiscal health of the federal government and state and local governments remain bleak.

As of late 2014, 30 states still had inflation-adjusted tax receipts below their pre-recession level. States employ 620,000 fewer people than six years ago, and municipal-bond sales were at a 15-year low. But 14 states cut taxes in 2014. State and local revenues probably will grow at a rate slightly above the cost of inflation in 2015–16. Low oil prices will depress revenues in states such as Texas and Alaska. States will, however, share half of a $1.37 billion settlement over allegations that Standard & Poor's Ratings Services misled investors by giving overly optimistic ratings to residential mortgage bonds prior to the 2008 financial crisis.

Government balance sheets must now follow new rules set by the Government Accounting Standards Board, or GASB. The new accounting will highlight underfunded state and local pension liabilities.

Federal aid to state and local governments increased annually from 1987 to 2011, declined by 10 percent in 2012, but increased to $628 billion by 2015 — 15 percent higher than 2012. Aid is expected to increase by nearly 4 percent to $652 billion in 2016. However, consistent with long-term trends, 74 percent of all federal aid will be dedicated to social welfare — especially Medicaid — which, with state matching funds, is the single largest category of state spending. Aid for infrastructure, transportation, education, economic development and other nonwelfare purposes will continue a relative decline that started in 1978.[9]

The number of grants-in-aid increased from 435 in 1987 to 1,099 in 2014. Only 21 (2 percent) of those 1,099 grants were block grants, compared to 13 block grants in 1987. In the past, intergovernmental reformers advocated reductions of categorical grants, but the system has raced in the opposite direction.

Congress and presidents prefer the tighter control of state and local spending offered by categorical grants. Given that Medicaid, which is a categorical grant, accounts for more than 45 percent of all federal aid, it is clear that the federal-aid system has been distorted, though not so much by state and local government pressure. Those governments prefer to coordinate and consolidate aid. Instead, interest groups beseech Congress to create categorical grants devoted to their interests because many federal-aid programs are implemented by nonprofit and for-profit entities in what is now often described as networked or collaborative governance.

On average, in real dollars, grants were funded at $470 million each in 1987 and $480 million each in 2014. Even though federal aid has increased, federal funds—except for several huge programs like Medicaid and transportation—are spread thinly across a large number of grants.

Nevertheless, in 2014, federal aid accounted for 30.3 percent of state spending—a historically high level—primarily because of Medicaid and other social assistance.[10] Total federal spending in the states was equivalent to 19 percent of state economic activity in 2013, though the range was from 11.6 percent in Wyoming to 32.9 percent in Mississippi. Payments for individuals were 61 percent of federal spending in the states. From 2004 to 2013, federal spending in the states grew by 26 percent to $3.1 trillion in 2013.[11]

Reforming the grants-in-aid system has been impossible, mainly because no state wants to lose funds. For example, the Federal Funds Information for States recently calculated how federal aid for Medicaid would change if the federal formula accounted for cost-of-living differences, not just states' per capita income. Hawaii's current ranking of 21 would drop to 47, thus qualifying it for more federal Medicaid money. The federal formula probably will not be changed, however, because it would benefit only eight states, while making 32 states worse off.[12]

In mid-2014, U.S. Rep. Paul D. Ryan—R-Wis.—proposed to expand the federal earned income tax credit and consolidate 11 federal anti-poverty programs, including food stamps and housing assistance, into an Opportunity Grant for the states. This block grant would emphasize state-local coordination of assistance to needy families, incentives and sanctions for poor people to exit poverty, and rules to ease convicted nonviolent criminals into work. In March 2015, President Obama announced a program to give $200 million to 10 states to help food-assistance recipients find work.

The federal government also assists states through its tax code. Obama's 2016 budget proposed to expand tax-exempt private activity bonds into Qualified Public Infrastructure Bonds (QPIBs) to finance mass transit, ports, airports, water and sewer services, solid waste disposal, and other infrastructure managed mainly by private enterprises. QPIBs would have no expiration date and no annual cap on the number of bonds issued by states and localities. States' bond issuances in 2014 were about 10 percent lower than in 2013, but likely will increase in 2015.

States' Federal Priorities

The states' congressional wish list includes passage of the Marketplace Fairness Act, long-term surface-transportation funding, renewal of the Children's Health Insurance Program, deficit reduction, immigration reform, Medicaid reform, strengthened cybersecurity, more child-care and early-learning funding, state-based insurance regulation, and more National Guard funding. States do not want the federal government to eliminate the tax exemption for interest earned on municipal bonds, cut National Guard units and equipment, or increase EPA control over in-state waterways. Some governors want the National Guard to be equipped to help state and local governments defend against cyberattacks.

Polarization will limit achievement of these priorities, although the parties sometimes do act together. Dozens of House Democrats recently joined Republicans to enhance charter school access, promote natural gas exports, stop the EPA from expanding its power over domestic waterways under the Clean Water Act of 1972, increase federal rulemaking transparency, and extend, over state opposition, the Internet Tax Freedom Act through September 2015. Congress also passed, with states' support, the Workforce Innovation and Opportunity Act of 2014, which supersedes the Workforce Investment Act of 1998.

The National Association of Insurance Commissioners commended Congress for reauthorizing the Terrorism Risk Insurance Act, which backstops insurers in the event of a catastrophic terrorist attack. The program had expired for a brief time at the end of 2014 after U.S. Senator Tom Coburn—R-Okla.—objected to a provision he said deprived states of their 10th Amendment right to regulate their own insurance agents and brokers.

State Taxation of Online and Mail-Order Sales

The Marketplace Fairness Act, first proposed in 2011, is a high priority for most states, although the prospects for House passage remain slim. The act would allow every state with a sales tax to require out-of-state businesses to collect and remit the sales tax on taxable goods sold to state residents. The National Conference of State Legislatures estimates states lost $23.3 billion in revenue in 2012 from uncollected Internet sales taxes.

In March 2015, the National Governors Association urged U.S. House Speaker John Boehner—R-Ohio—to ensure House passage of the Marketplace Fairness Act. The bill passed the Senate in 2013 by 69 to 27. A competing House bill, however, would tax purchases based on the sales tax rate in the seller's home state. The Big 7 state and local government associations joined major retailers in warning Congress that the online growth of the Chinese company Alibaba—which might soon rival Amazon, eBay and Overstock—could decimate brick-and-mortar retailers.

Also in March 2015, the U.S. Supreme Court handed a small victory to online retailers who challenged a Colorado law requiring out-of-state merchants to report transactions by Colorado customers to state tax authorities. But in a concurring opinion, Justice Anthony Kennedy issued a startling statement that the court should not delay a reconsideration of *Quill*.[13] This 1992 ruling—which prohibits state taxation of out-of-state mail-order sales without congressional consent—he opined, "now harms states to a degree far greater that could have been anticipated earlier."[14] This could be a signal that some justices might wish to effect policy change in fields left fallow by Congress.

Surface Transportation

Funding predictability for transportation programs has been a long-term concern of state and local governments. Congress has not reauthorized the surface transportation program since it expired in September 2009, nor has Congress increased the motor fuel tax since 1993. Recognizing the looming insolvency of the federal Highway Trust Fund, most states cut back projects during the summer of 2014 due to funding uncertainty.

Average annual spending on transportation projects was $207 billion per year between 2007 and 2011, 40 percent of which came from the states, 36 percent from localities and 25 percent from the federal government. Between 2002 and 2011, overall spending dropped by 12 percent in real dollars, with state spending falling by 20 percent. Between 2002 and 2012, federal gas tax revenue dropped by 31 percent in real terms; state gas tax revenue fell by 19 percent.[15]

The federal surface transportation program also needs reforms. For example, the trust fund does not send more revenue to states with bigger highway systems, more highway use or lower median incomes. Instead, less urban states and states better represented on the program's four key congressional committees benefit more.[16]

K–12 Education

For nearly a decade, Congress has failed to reauthorize and re-name the No Child Left Behind Act of 2001 (NCLB), funded at $23.3 billion in 2015. Many congressional Democrats and Republicans want to scale back the federal role in K–12 education, but President Obama wants to increase it and especially retain annual testing of students in math and reading between the third and eighth grades and once in high school. Testing in some form is likely to remain in any reauthorization. Due to congressional inaction, however, 43 states operate under waivers from the NCLB.

Another major controversy linked to reauthorization is the Common Core curriculum standards developed by the National Governors Association and the Council of Chief State School Officers in 2009. Forty-six states signed onto the initiative, but five states have since voted to repeal or replace it. Initially, opposition came mostly from conservatives objecting to certain values embedded in the standards and the use of federal aid to induce state adoption. Louisiana Gov. Bobby Jindal filed suit in federal court in 2014, arguing that Common Core violates state sovereignty. Some prominent conservatives, however, such as William J. Bennett, defend the Common Core.[17] Some liberals expressed opposition, especially to the rigorous testing attached to the Common Core.

Another controversial federal policy went into effect in fall 2014. Schools are required to comply with federal nutrition standards for food and beverages sold during the school day. The standards, promulgated under the Healthy, Hunger-Free Kids Act of 2010, might require school bake sales to replace chocolate bars and cupcakes with multigrain bars and fruit cups. The federal government will provide $4.5 billion to implement the standards over five years.

In late 2014, 18 states and 234 school districts and others won competitive grants under the new Early Head Start-Child Care Partnerships and Preschool Development Grants. Grants under the first program enable Early Head Start programs to partner with local child-care centers and family child-care providers serving infants and toddlers from low-income families. Preschool Development Grants fund states to enhance and expand preschool programs in targeted communities that can serve as models for expanding preschool to all 4-year-olds from low- and moderate-income families

Children's Health Insurance Program

Funding for the Children's Health Insurance Program, also known as CHIP, will run out in September 2015. CHIP insures children in families with incomes too high to be eligible for Medicaid. The federal government pays 70 percent of CHIP's cost, which is more than what most states receive under Medicaid. Republicans are proposing changes for the program and a two-year extension. Democrats want to continue the program in its current form for another four years at a cost of about $10 billion.[18] Thirty-nine Democratic and Republican governors have petitioned Congress to extend CHIP funding.

Immigration

Immigration reform has been a long-standing state concern, and states became especially concerned about the rise in illegal child migrants in 2013–14. However, just as the parties in Congress disagree on the substance of reform, so do blue and red states.

In the face of continued federal inaction, state legislatures passed 171 laws and 117 resolutions on immigration in 2014 — 34 percent less than in 2013.

"We ask our colleagues in Washington, D.C., to learn from state legislators, who are addressing immigration in creative and bipartisan ways in our state capitols," said Nevada state Sen. Mo Denis (D), co-chair of NCSL's Task Force on Immigration and the States.[19]

Nevertheless, 26 states have joined a federal lawsuit challenging the legality of President Obama's Deferred Action for Parents of Americans and Lawful Permanent Residents program, announced in November 2014. The program allows certain aliens who arrived in the United States on or before January 1, 2010, to apply for deferred action on deportation and to seek permission to work lawfully in the United States. The program applies to certain individuals who came to the United States as children under the age of 16 or who are parents of U.S. citizens or lawful permanent resident children. The plaintiffs argue that the president exceeded the bounds of prosecutorial discretion and abdicated his constitutional duty to faithfully execute the law. A federal district court in Texas issued an order temporarily blocking the program's implementation, which was due to start in May 2015. The National League of Cities, U.S. Conference of Mayors, and 12 states filed *amicus* briefs supporting the program.

Otherwise, the U.S. Supreme court upheld a lower court ruling requiring Arizona to issue driver's licenses to young illegal immigrants exempted from deportation by President Obama.[20]

Marijuana Legalization

In December 2014, Congress enacted a continuing funding resolution stating: "None of the funds made available in this Act to the Department of Justice may be used" to prevent "States from implementing their own State laws that authorized the use, distribution, possession, or cultivation of medical marijuana."[21] A Senate bill, the Compassionate Access, Research Expansion, and Respect States (CARERS) Act, would amend the federal Controlled Substances Act to reclassify medical marijuana as a Schedule II rather than a Schedule I drug, increase cannabis availability for research, allow some interstate transport of marijuana, make it easier for physicians to authorize marijuana for veterans in states where it is legal, loosen restrictions on banks wishing to service the industry, and prevent federal prosecution of patients and physicians in the 35 states that allow some type of medical marijuana use.

The U.S. Department of Justice told U.S. attorneys in December 2014 not to prevent Indian tribes from growing or selling marijuana on tribal lands, even in states that ban marijuana.

Six Colorado sheriffs filed suit in federal court arguing that the state's legalization of marijuana violates federal law. "The Colorado Constitution," said one sheriff "mandates that all elected officials, including sheriffs, swear an oath of office to uphold both the United States as well as the Colorado Constitutions."[22]

The attorneys general of Nebraska and Oklahoma also filed suit against Colorado, arguing that marijuana brought into their states from Colorado has increased arrests and strained their budgets. Some critics label these attorneys general "fair-weather federalists" because their suit endorses an expansive Supreme Court definition of Congress' authority to regulate commerce.[23] Seven Republican Oklahoma legislators opposed the suit, contending it could undermine the 10th Amendment rights of states to govern themselves.

The Affordable Care Act

The Affordable Care Act, also known as the ACA, is facing its third major legal challenge before the U.S. Supreme Court.[24] The lawsuit contends that individuals who purchase health insurance through a federal or partnership exchange are ineligible for federal tax credits. Such credits can be given only for insurance purchased on a state-established exchange. The federal government operates exchanges in 34 states, including seven where the state carries out some functions; 13 states operate state-created exchanges; and Nevada, New Mexico and Oregon maintain federally supported state-based exchanges. Seven states filed an *amicus* brief opposing the tax credits; 22 states filed a brief supporting the credits.

In contention are four words in Section 36B of the ACA that refer to the credit subsidies being available to individuals purchasing health insurance on an exchange "established by the State." The act says that if a state refuses to establish an exchange, the federal government shall "establish and operate such Exchange within the State." The case addresses the IRS's 2012 ruling that the ACA permits tax credits for insurance obtained through exchanges established by the federal government within states.

The Obama administration maintains that the contested phrase is merely a legal term of art, which, if read in the context of the ACA as a whole, "encompasses both state-created exchanges and "exchanges that the states chose to have HHS create for them."[25] However, states did not have a real choice. Nonetheless, the court has held that judges must determine "the plain meaning of the whole statute, not of isolated sentences."[26] Elsewhere, for instance, the ACA defines a person "qualified" to buy insurance through an exchange as one who

"resides in the State that established the Exchange." Literally, the phrase suggests that no one is eligible to buy insurance through a federal or partnership exchange. The administration also contends that the court must defer to the executive branch's interpretation of an ambiguous statute. During oral arguments on the case, Justice Anthony Kennedy worried that "the states are being told either create your own exchange, or we'll send your insurance market into a death spiral."[27]

Opponents of the tax credits argue that previous versions of the ACA provided credits for individuals enrolled through federally established exchanges, but Congress removed that language. Support for the subsidies is weakened also by the statement of Jonathan Gruber, one of the ACA's consulting architects, who declared in 2012, "if you're a state and you don't set up an exchange, that means your citizens don't get their tax credits."[28] The ACA, moreover, appropriated money for state exchanges, but not federal exchanges. Because the federal government could not commandeer the states, tax credits and federal grants were incentives for states to establish exchanges.

Some ACA supporters argue that striking down the tax credits in states with a federal or partnership exchange would violate *Pennhurst's* "clear notice" rule[29] that the federal government must give states adequate advance notice before imposing new policies. The weakness of this view, though, is that the 34 states that did not establish an exchange knew more than two years beforehand that not creating an exchange could deprive their residents of the federal tax credits. Justice Samuel Alito suggested that if the court strikes down the credits, it could delay implementation of the ruling beyond the usual 25 days to the end of the tax year.

If the court voids the tax credits, about 7.5 million people could lose insurance coverage. Premium costs for policies purchased through federal exchanges could increase by 255 percent. Enrollees in the 34 states with a federal or partnership exchange would lose about $29 billion in federal subsidies in 2016 and $340 billion over 10 years. Obama could ask Congress to amend the law, but Republicans want to replace the ACA. The 34 states that lack a state-established exchange will be pressed by their residents and health-care lobbyists to create one, although given the time required for establishing an exchange, states probably could not do so in less than a year. Furthermore, all 13 states with an exchange face funding challenges to support them and are considering such solutions as requiring more people to shop on the exchange and taxing all health insurance policies. Legislators in some states have introduced bills to create a state exchange, while legislators in some other states have introduced bills to prohibit a state exchange.

States could perhaps use the federal portal until completing their own website. Nevada, New Mexico and Oregon do this. Another proposal is to create a grant for states to provide subsidies and premium assistance. The federal government also could help the states by, for example, determining applicants' eligibility.

Section 1332 of the ACA allows a state to obtain a federal waiver to implement its own health reform plan under which it can be exempt from the ACA's individual and employer mandates, essential health benefit rules, tax credits, and cost-sharing coverage subsidies. Such a state plan must be at least as affordable and comprehensive as that provided by the ACA. However, such a plan can only start in 2017. About 26 states have considered adopting an alternative to the ACA called the Health Care Compact, an interstate compact by which member states would take primary responsibility for regulating nonmilitary health care, but only nine states have enacted the compact into law.

Meanwhile, some states also have declined to adopt the ACA's consumer information provisions and have not applied for federal grants for consumer assistance centers.

Medicaid Expansion

Medicaid expansion is another ACA controversy. Federal funds will cover 100 percent of the cost of expanding Medicaid to 133 percent of the federal poverty limit through 2016, 95 percent in 2017, 94 percent in 2018, 93 percent in 2019, and 90 percent in 2020 and subsequent years. Twenty-eight states have expanded their Medicaid programs. Six Republican governors, as well as Alaska's Independent—formerly Republican—governor and the Democratic governors of Missouri and Montana have proposed Medicaid expansion, but met opposition from their legislatures. Pennsylvania's new Democratic Gov. Tom Wolf scrapped his Republican predecessor's partial Medicaid expansion in favor of a traditional ACA expansion.

To encourage expansion, the Obama administration has given waivers to several Republican states allowing Medicaid to pay premiums for private health insurance and, in Indiana, requiring some Medicaid enrollees to pay monthly premiums equal to 2 percent of their household income.

Academic research suggests decisions to expand Medicaid and establish a health-insurance exchange are unique in state policymaking because they have been motivated almost entirely by partisan politics, rather than a combination of politics and socioeconomic factors.[30]

Other Issues and Developments

In March 2015, the U.S. Department of Justice issued a scathing report on racial police practices in Ferguson, Mo., but declined to prosecute the police officer who killed an 18-year-old black man in August 2014. The federal government conducted investigations of about 25 police departments from early 2014 to mid-2015. More than a dozen city police departments have signed consent decrees to reform their policies and practices, although some departments, such as Austin, Texas, have received a clean bill of health.

The Supreme Court has been more lenient toward rough cops as in a 2014 decision holding that West Virginia police did not use excessive force when they shot at a fleeing automobile, killing the driver and a passenger.[31] But in December 2014, Obama signed the Death in Custody Reporting Act requiring states to report quarterly the deaths of people detained or arrested by state or local police.

There also has been rising criticism of the militarization of local police that was spurred by about $34 billion in federal grants for military-type equipment since 9/11, as well as the Pentagon's 1033 program, which transfers surplus weapons and other gear to police—including public school security units—some of which have created SWAT teams. The Pentagon's program was authorized by the 1990 National Defense Authorization Act. In August 2014, faced with televised images of protesters confronting militarized police with equipment more suitable for Fallujah than Ferguson, President Obama ordered a review of these programs.

The Obama administration is expected to announce new child support enforcement rules that will allow states to use child support funding for job training. The new rules also are expected to incentivize states to engage in more discretionary enforcement and forgiveness of arrears, while making it more difficult for states to determine the income of delinquent parents. For custodial parents living in poverty, support payments make up about 45 percent of their income.[32]

In 2014, the Federal Aviation Administration re-interpreted the Airport and Airway Improvement Act of 1982 in order to require state and local governments to use airline fuel tax revenue for expenses related to air travel. States must either comply with the rule or repeal the tax. Some states objected, saying only state policymakers have constitutional authority to decide how their state's tax revenue is spent.

By a 3-2 party-line vote in March 2015, the Federal Communications Commission pre-empted laws in North Carolina and Tennessee that limited cities' ability to operate their own Internet service. Chris Nelson, chairperson of the National Association of Regulatory Utility Commissioners, declared: "By asserting jurisdiction where it clearly has none, the FCC is setting itself up for wasteful and unnecessary litigation."[33] The FCC's more general 2015 decision to regulate "net neutrality" under telecommunications laws from the telephony era will spark considerable litigation and require a sorting out of federal and state regulatory authority.

U.S. Senate Majority Leader Mitch McConnell (R-Ken.) sent a letter to all the governors urging them to reject the Environmental Protection Agency's proposed rule to require power plants to reduce carbon dioxide.[34] Under the rule, likely to be final in summer 2015, states would have to submit compliance plans by 2016 or possibly be required to comply with a federal "model rule"[35] that could shut down many coal-fired plants. The rule would mandate carbon dioxide reductions ranging from 72 percent in Washington to 11 percent in North Dakota. The reduction levels would be contingent on the EPA's estimates of what each state can attain by reducing consumption, changing fuels and improving efficiency.

A dozen states filed lawsuits to block the rule. They received support from Harvard University's constitutional scholar, Laurence H. Tribe, who argues that the EPA lacks authority to promulgate the rule and that the federal government cannot, in any event, commandeer the states to enforce such a rule.[36] Congress cannot thwart the rules until they are final.

Alabama's Supreme Court in March 2015 defied a federal court ruling and prohibited the issuance of marriage licenses to same-sex couples. Anticipating that the Supreme Court might legalize gay marriage this year, more than a dozen states are considering "conscience protection" bills that would, among other things, allow businesses and individuals to refuse certain services to same-sex couples. Texas has such a law, and Arkansas and

Indiana enacted such laws in 2015. Four federal appeals courts encompassing 21 states have struck down state bans on gay marriage.

Because exporting is important for most state economies, 31 governors signed a letter in 2014 urging congressional leaders not to end funding of the Export-Import Bank.

Six states filed suit in federal court to overturn California's ban on the sale of eggs produced by hens kept in cramped "battery" cages. About 95 percent of all eggs are produced in such cages. Michigan, Oregon and Washington have enacted laws requiring more space for hens. Ohio has banned new battery cages. Several other states are considering similar legislation.

In February 2015, a federal judge struck down Maine's two-year-old law that allowed residents to buy prescription drugs from some foreign pharmacies. The law was the first in the country.

In November 2014, a federal appeals court struck down an effort by Arizona and Kansas to require the federal government to add citizenship documentation requirements to the federal voter registration form. The ruling relied heavily on 2013 U.S. Supreme Court ruling that state voting laws are pre-empted when deemed to be in conflict with the National Voter Registration Act of 1993.[37] In March 2015, however, the U.S. Supreme Court declined to hear a challenge to Wisconsin's voter ID law.

Supreme Court Rulings

The U.S. Supreme Court continues to play a major role in state-federal relations.

Final Rulings

In 2014, the court ruled that some government workers who are not union members are not required to pay union dues,[38] struck down overall limits on individuals' contributions to candidates and political parties,[39] upheld a Michigan voter initiative banning affirmative action admissions to the state's universities,[40] struck down a Massachusetts's law on buffer zones around abortion clinics,[41] required police to get warrants to search cellphones of detained people,[42] and ruled that a corporation "closely held" by a religious family cannot be compelled to pay for workers' contraception coverage. It is not clear yet whether the latter ruling will override "contraception equity" laws in 28 states.

The court overturned a nearly 20-year precedent when it held federal agencies need not engage in notice-and-comment rulemaking pursuant to the Administrative Procedure Act before changing a rule that interprets a legislative rule.[43] This decision will make it more difficult for state and local governments to influence federal agency policy when agencies want to change an interpretive rule.

In January 2015, the court ruled that, under the Religious Land Use and Institutionalized Persons Act of 2000, a Muslim inmate of an Arkansas prison could grow a half-inch beard.[44]

In February 2015, the justices ruled that a state licensing board controlled by "active market participants" is immune from antitrust laws only if its state government supervises it actively.[45] The case arose in 2006 after North Carolina's dentist-controlled board prohibited spas, salons and other businesses from offering teeth whitening services. States are concerned that the court did not define "actively supervised," and they believe this mandate will be costly and will limit gubernatorial and legislative discretion in making board appointments.

This case reflected a rising attack on state licensing practices deemed to restrict competition. For example, 47 states have enacted laws making it easier for spouses of military personnel who move into the state to practice an occupation, such as massage therapy or dental hygiene, they practiced with a license in other states.

In March 2015, the court decided that Alabama's legislature misinterpreted the U.S. Voting Rights Act and behaved unconstitutionally by using race too rigidly in 2012 to produce legislative districts with excessively large numbers of black voters,[46] even though the U.S. Department of Justice previously had approved the racial gerrymandering plan under the preclearance rule of the U.S. Voting Rights Act. The Supreme Court struck down the use of this rule in 2013.[47]

The State and Local Legal Center supported Amazon in a case where the court held that the Fair Labor Standards Act does not require workers to be paid for time spent waiting to undergo security screenings.[48]

In a victory for state campaign-finance regulation, the court upheld Florida's ban on judicial candidates personally soliciting campaign donations.[49] Thirty states ban this. Eleven of those states and the Conference of Chief Justices filed *amicus* briefs supporting Florida's rule.

Pending Rulings

The State and Local Legal Center also filed an *amicus* brief supporting a city's right to impose more restrictions on temporary signs giving direc-

tions to a church event than on signs conveying political or ideological messages.[50]

The court will decide whether an independent redistricting commission created by Arizona voters in 2000 violates the U.S. Constitution's provision that "the Times, Places and Manner of holding Elections for Senators and Representatives, shall be prescribed in each State by the Legislature thereof."[51] The case was brought by members of the Arizona legislature, who argued that voters lack authority to transfer power from the legislature to an unelected citizens commission. The legislature is excluded from the congressional redistricting process. (The lawsuit did not challenge the commission's authority to redistrict state legislative seats.)

The constitutional clause regarding elections does not say the rules shall be prescribed by each state. The clause uses the word "legislature" in a manner consistent with all other references to state legislatures in the Constitution. Supporters of the commission contend that the state constitution defines the legislative power as including the people acting by initiative. A ruling in favor of the legislature could jeopardize other state election laws enacted by initiative, such as residency rules, voter ID and primary elections rules. California is the only other state that has an independent commission established via initiative. The NCSL filed an *amicus* brief supporting the Arizona legislature. The court also will decide whether Florida makes it too easy for juries to recommend executions of convicted criminals.[52] In 2014, the court found Florida's fixed cutoff of a 70 IQ score to be too rigid in the absence of an ability to present additional evidence on a defendant's mental capacity.[53]

The justices will decide whether Texas' rejection of a specialty license plate for the Sons of Confederate Veterans violated the organization's free-speech rights.[54] Nine states issue such plates. The court faces a difficult choice. If it upholds Texas, what neutral, rational criteria will govern states' rejection decisions? If the court rules against Texas, will states be able to maintain specialty plates and the revenues derived from them in the face of groups wanting plates to celebrate Nazism or Al Qaeda terrorism?

In another case, the court might decide to strike down the "disparate impact" rule promulgated under the Fair Housing Act of 1968.[55] The rule does not require plaintiffs to prove intent to discriminate; they need only demonstrate that an allegedly discriminatory practice affects a particular minority group more than other groups.

Seventeen states and 21 cities filed *amicus* briefs supporting disparate impact.

In a case with broad implications for state tax powers, the court will decide whether a state must provide a credit against its own taxes for taxes a resident pays on income earned in other states. Maryland provides such a credit against its state income tax, but not against the piggyback tax the state collects for its 23 counties and Baltimore city.[56] The State and Local Legal Center filed an *amicus* brief arguing if Maryland is required to provide a dollar-for-dollar tax credit, a resident with substantial out-of-state income would pay significantly less for local services than a neighbor earning the same income in state, even though both benefit equally from local services.

Finally, in a potentially blockbuster cultural case, the justices will rule on four same-sex marriage cases in order to resolve differences among federal appeals courts.[57] The court might overturn all state statutory and constitutional bans on gay marriage.

Conclusion

An important question for the states is whether disagreements among the states and state resistance to federal policies will prompt stronger forms of program nationalization, including more centralized federal leadership and mandates.[58] This is not a foregone conclusion, but the federal system has become increasingly majoritarian in the sense that state policies tend to survive only when they enjoy national majority support, as in the case of marijuana legalization. When state policies, such as same-sex marriage bans, lose national majority support, they are usually overridden by federal action. States can be laboratories of democracy so long as they are not deemed, as comic John Stewart put it, "meth labs of democracy."

Another concern for states is that state houses since 2003 have lost more than one-third of the newspaper reporters who report full time on legislative affairs.[59] Although the public trusts state governments much more than the federal government, diminished media coverage could make it more difficult for citizens to see and appreciate the positive work of state governments.

Notes

[1] Jessica Bulman-Pozen and Heather Gerken, "Uncooperative Federalism," *Yale Law Journal* 118 (May 2009): 1256–1310.

[2] John Paul Stevens, *Six Amendments: How and Why We Should Change the Constitution* (Boston: Little, Brown, 2014).

[3] Ibid., p. 30, quoting *Printz v. United States*, 521 U.S. 898, 976 (1997).

[4] John Samples and Emily Atkins, "Public Attitudes toward Federalism," Policy Analysis, No. 759, Cato Institute, September 23, 2014.

[5] Justin McCarthy, "Americans Still Trust Local Government More Than State," Gallup, September 22, 2014, *http://www.gallup.com/poll/176846/americans-trust-local-government-state.aspx*, accessed March 17, 2015.

[6] Pew Research Center, "Public Trust in Government: 1958–2014," November 13, 2014, *http://www.people-press.org/2014/11/13/public-trust-in-government/*, accessed March 17, 2015.

[7] Rasmussen Reports, "37% of Voters Fear the Federal Government," April 18, 2014, *http://www.rasmussenreports.com/public_content/politics/general_politics/april_2014/37_of_voters_fear_the_federal_government*, accessed March 16, 2015.

[8] Jim Gaines, "One in four Americans want their state to secede from the U.S., but Why?" Reuters, September 19, 2014, *http://blogs.reuters.com/jamesrgaines/2014/09/19/one-in-four-americans-want-their-state-to-secede-from-the-u-s-but-why/*, accessed March 16, 2015.

[9] John Kincaid, "The Rise of Social Welfare and Onward March of Coercive Federalism," *Networked Governance: The Future of Intergovernmental Management*, eds., Jack W. Meek and Kurt Thurmaier (Los Angeles: Sage/CQ Press, 2011), pp. 8–38.

[10] National Association of State Budget Officers, *The Fiscal Survey of States, Fall 2014* (Washington, DC: NASBO, 2014), p. 1.

[11] The Pew Charitable Trusts, "Federal Spending in the States, 2004–2013," December 2, 2014, *http://www.pewtrusts.org/en/research-and-analysis/issue-briefs/2014/12/federal-spending-in-the-states*, accessed December 3, 2014.

[12] Liz Farmer, "States Where Government Aid Goes the Furthest," August 28, 2014, *http://www.governing.com/topics/finance/gov-states-where-dollar-goes-furthest.html*, accessed March 3, 2015.

[13] *Quill Corp. v. North Dakota*, 504 U.S. 298 (1992).

[14] *Direct Marketing Association v. Brohl*, No. 13-1032 (2015).

[15] Fiscal Federalism Initiative, "Intergovernmental Challenges in Surface Transportation Funding," The Pew Charitable Trusts, September 23, 2014.

[16] Pengyu Zhu and Jeffrey R. Brown, "Donor states and done states: investigating geographic redistribution of the US federal-aid highway program 1974–2008," *Transportation* 40 (1): 203–227.

[17] William J. Bennett, "The Conservative Case for Common Core," *The Wall Street Journal*, Sepetmber 11, 2014, p. A11.

[18] Hillary Rodham Clinton and Bil Frist, "Save the Chil-

dren's Insurance," *The New York Times*, February 13, 2015, p. A27.

[19] National Conference of State Legislatures, "Year-End Immigration Report Finds States Enacted Laws on Wide Range of Issues," Press Release, January 7, 2015, *http://www.ncsl.org/press-room/states-pass-171-immigration-laws-in-2014.aspx*, accessed March 23, 2015.

[20] *Brewer v. Arizona Dream Act Coalition*, No. 14A625 (2014).

[21] H.R. 83, Consolidated and Further Continuing Appropriations Act, Sec. 538 (December 16, 2014).

[22] Quoted in Kirk Mitchell and John Ingold, "New lawsuit: Sheriffs from Colorado, elsewhere challenge Amendment 64," *The Denver Post*, March 5, 2015.

[23] See *Gonzales v. Raich*, 545 U.S. 1 (2005).

[24] *King v. Burwell*, No. 14-114 (2015).

[25] David Cole, "Can They Crush Obamacare?" *The New York Review of Books* 62:5 (March 19, 2015): 14.

[26] *Beecham v. United States*, 511 U.S. 368, 372 (1994).

[27] Quoted in Robert Pear, "Some Justices Cite 2012 Argument Against Health Care Law as Defense for It Now," *The New York Times*, March 9, 2015, p. A9.

[28] Quoted in Charles M. Blow, "Partisanship Breaks the Government," *The New York Times*, November 17, 2014, p. A25.

[29] *Pennhurst State School and Hospital v. Halderman*, 451 U.S. 1 (1981).

[30] Charles Barrilleaux and Carlisle Rainey, "The Politics of Need: Examining Governors' Decisions to Oppose the 'Obamacare' Medicaid Expansion," *State Politics & Policy Quarterly* 14 (December 2014): 437–460.

[31] *Plumhoff v. Rickard*, 134 S. Ct. 2012 (2014).

[32] Robert Doar, "Making It Easier to Skip Paying Child Support," *The Wall Street Journal*, March 10, 2015, p. A13.

[33] Quoted in Drew FitzGerald, "FCC Tests Authority Over States," *The Wall Street Journal*, March 2, 2015, p. B5.

[34] Coral Davenport, "McConnell Wants States' Help Against an Obama 'War on Coal'," *The New York Times*, March 20, 2015, pp. A1, A20, and Mitch McConnell, "States should reject Obama mandate for clean-power regulations," *The Lexington Herald-Leader*, March 3, 2015, p. A17.

[35] Coral Davenport, "For States That Don't File Carbon-Cutting Plans, E.P.A. Will Impose 'Model Rule'." *The New York Times*, January 8, 2015, p. A14.

[36] Laurence H. Tribe, "The Clean Power Plan Is Unconstitutional," *The Wall Street Journal*, December 23, 2014, p. A13.

[37] *Arizona v. The Inter Tribal Council of Arizona*, 133 S. Ct. 2247 (2013).

[38] *Harris v. Quinn*, 134 S. Ct. 2618 (2014).

[39] *McCutcheon v. Federal Election Commission*, 134 S. Ct. 1434 (2014).

[40] *Schuette v. BAMN*, 134 S. Ct. 1623 (2014).

[41] *McCullen v. Coakley*, 134 S. Ct. 2518 (2014).

[42] *Riley v. California*, 134 S. Ct. 2473 (2014).

[43] *Perez v. Mortgage Bankers Association*, 2015 U.S. LEXIS 1740 (2015).

[44] *Holt v. Hobbs*, 135 S. Ct. 853 (2015).

[45] *North Carolina State Board of Dental Examiners v. Federal Trade Commission,* 2015 U.S. LEXIS 1502.

[46] *Alabama Legislative Black Caucus v. Alabama*, 2015 U.S. LEXIS 2122 (2015).

[47] *Shelby County v. Holder*, 133 S. Ct. 2612 (2013).

[48] *Integrity Staffing Solutions, Inc. v. Busk*, 135 S. Ct. 513 (2014).

[49] *Williams-Yulee v. Florida Bar*, No. 13-1499 (2015).

[50] *Reed v. Town of Gilbert, Arizona*, No. 13-502 (2015).

[51] *Arizona State Legislature v. Arizona Independent Redistricting Commission*, No. 13-1314 (2015).

[52] *Hurst v. Florida*, 14-7505 (2015).

[53] *Hall v. Florida*, 572 U.S. ____ (2014).

[54] *Walker v. Texas Division, Sons of Confederate Veterans*, No. 14-144 (2015).

[55] *Texas Department of Housing and Community Affairs v. Inclusive Communities Project*, No. 13-1371 (2015).

[56] *Comptroller of the Treasury of Maryland v. Brian Wynne*, No. 13-485 (2015).

[57] *Obergefell v. Hodges, Bourke v. Beshear, DeBoer v. Snyder*, and *Tanco v. Haslam*.

[58] Paul L. Posner and Timothy J. Conlan, "The Future of Federalism in a Polarized Country," *Governing*, February 4, 2014, *http://www.governing.com/columns/smart-mgmt/col-states-polarized-politics-variable-speed-federalism.html,* accessed March 11, 2015, and Abigail R. Moncrieff and Jonathan Dinerstein, "Will Uncooperative Federalism Survive NFIB?" *Montana Law Review* (forthcoming).

[59] Christine Haughney, "Pew Study Finds a Sharp Drop in Reporters at Statehouses," *The New York Times*, July 11, 2014, p. B2.

About the Author

John Kincaid is the Robert B. and Helen S. Meyner Professor of Government and Public Service and Director of the Meyner Center for the Study of State and Local Government, Lafayette College, Easton, Pennsylvania. He has written the state-federal relations chapter for *The Book of the States* since 2004. He is former editor of *Publius: The Journal of Federalism*; former executive director of the U.S. Advisory Commission on Intergovernmental Relations; co-editor of *Constitutional Origins, Structure, and Change in Federal Countries* (2005), editor of *Federalism* (4 vols. 2011), and editor of a special issue of *Publius: The Journal of Federalism* (2014).

Trends in State-Local Relations

By Joseph F. Zimmerman

The 10th Amendment to the U.S. Constitution reserves powers to states in three broad spheres — a sphere most commonly controlled by local governments, a sphere controlled by state governments, and a shared state and local government sphere. Each state historically followed the English Common Law Ultra Vires Rule, *and the state legislature exercised plenary powers over its political subdivisions.*

Local governments in many states in the 19th century resented the state legislature's enactment of "ripper laws," changing the structure and/or powers of individual local governments. Voters in 41 states responded by ratifying constitutional amendments prohibiting the state legislature to enact a special law for a named local government unless the concerned local governing body requested its enactment. Nevertheless, legislative abuses continued and resulted in constitutional amendments establishing an *Imperio in Imperium* (a federal system within a state) with the state legislature devolving authority to all general purpose governments over their respective structure, property and local affairs.

Continued legislative abuses in the late 19th century generated a new type of constitutional home rule amendment directing the state legislature to devolve upon general purpose local governments adopting a new charter all powers capable of devolution except civil relations and the definition and punishment of a felony.[1]

The discretionary authority of most general-purpose local governments has changed relatively little since 2012. Many state legislatures continue to impose mandates and restraints on general-purpose local governments including state financial control boards for general purpose governments experiencing fiscal stress.

State-Local Legal Relations

These relations are exceptionally complex in a number of states. Constitutional provisions, statutes, state administrative rules and regulations, and court decisions determine the nature of state-local relations in various local government functional areas. Occasionally, a constitutional amendment devolves additional discretionary authority to general local governments. Here are some recent examples.

The state of Washington Supreme Court in January 2014 ruled the system for financing public education unconstitutional. The court on Sept. 11, 2014, held the state legislature in contempt for lack of progress in developing a detailed plan for state funding of public education, but delayed punishment until after the 2015 legislative session. The estimated cost to change the public education financing system is a minimum of $4 billion biennially.

The Texas attorney general in 2014 issued opinion No. Ga-1078 pertaining to city ordinances banning the use of plastic bags by business firms. The opinion concluded such an ordinance (1) may run afoul of state law if the city adopted it for solid waste management purposes, and (2) a city probably is prohibited from assessing a fee on the sale or the use of a replacement bag.

The Texas First District Court of Appeals in 2013 reversed a trial court order invalidating a Houston air pollution ordinance by holding its provisions on registration and fee requirements were not inconsistent with state laws. The New York Court of Appeals in 2014 opined, by a 5 to 2 vote, general purpose local governments possess the legal authority to employ zoning ordinances to prohibit oil and gas drilling and fracking. More than 170 cities, towns and villages in the state banned or imposed a moratorium on fracking.

The Pennsylvania Supreme Court in 2014 invalidated a section of State Act 13 forbidding cities, townships and boroughs to use zoning to determine where fracking will be allowed. The New York Court of Appeals, the state's highest court, in 2014 opined general-purpose local governments possess land use authority to prohibit oil and gas operations within their respective borders. The 2014 Minnesota State Legislature prohibited electronic cigarette use in buildings owned or operated by political subdivisions.

Local Government Structural Changes

The Dallas, Texas, Independent School Board of Trustees on June 27, 2014, appointed a 15-member commission to draft a home-rule school district charter. The California State Legislature in 2012 eliminated all redevelopment agencies. Texas Proposition 7 of 2013 authorizes each home rule municipality to add a procedure to its charter to fill a vacancy on its governing body.

Section 7-3-173 of the *Montana Code* required each local government to adopt a resolution placing the question of conducting a local government review on the ballot at the primary election on June 3, 2014. The resolution mandated a specification of the number of elected commission members and the dollar amount or number of mills that would be permanently levied to fund the study commission.

New York Gov. Andrew M. Cuomo in 2014 announced local government citizen reorganization empowerment grant awards to municipalities for the planning and the implementation of village dissolutions. The awards are part of the state's local government efficiency program.

California Gov. Jerry Brown in 2014 signed into law three bills creating local government agencies responsible for overseeing extraction of groundwater and replacing the state policy of permitting landowners generally to extract water beneath their respective land. The local agencies will prevent overdrafts of water. Approximately 40 percent of the water consumed in the state in a normal year is groundwater and the amount increases during droughts.

The Illinois General Assembly in 2013 enacted Senate Bill 1585 allowing a dissolution referendum in a township in Cook County that is seven miles square and substantially coterminous with a municipality whose governing body exercises township board powers or has at least one member on the township board. The legislature in 2014 enacted a statute authorizing 1 percent of the voters in a fire protection district to petition for a referendum to determine whether the district should be dissolved and to add its territory to an adjoining district.

Local Government Authority

States continue to modify the authority of local governments as illustrated by changes in Georgia and Iowa.

Georgia Senate Bill 318 of 2014 authorizes the governing body of a city or county where the sale of alcoholic beverages is lawful for on-premises consumption to adopt a resolution or an ordinance authorizing the sale of on-premises consumption of alcohol from 12:30 p.m. to midnight on any Sunday during the St. Patrick's Day holiday.

Georgia Senate Bill 288 of 2014 requires each local government to submit for approval a watershed protection plan that includes watershed protection standards and procedures to the state Department of Natural Resources. Senate Bill 290 clarifies that a local government may appoint more than one person to serve as a dog control officer. If a local animal control board or board of health has not been designated by the jurisdiction, a dog owner who receives a notice of classification as the owner of a dangerous dog may request a hearing before the Probate Court. Georgia House Bill 384 requires each local governing authority that permits motorized carts upon public streets must erect signs warning motorists that such carts are authorized for use on public streets.

Georgia Senate Bill 284 of 2012 modernizes the state law on land banks and provides tools for land banks to address tax delinquent and abandoned property. Georgia House Bill 297 of 2012 expands the coverage of the open meeting law to include all offices in a county or a city, broadens the definition of a public record to include data and data fields, and requires cities and counties to make electronic copies available to citizens, or if the requestor prefers, printouts of electronic records or data from database fields used by the city or county.

Georgia Gov. Nathan Deal, utilizing a relatively new power, in 2013 removed six members of the DeKalb County School Board in response to a Southern Association of Colleges and Schools report on infighting by board members, questionable staff hiring practices, and a $16 million debt. Tennessee in 2012 initiated the removal of pupils from public schools with the lowest student test scores and graduation rates, and placing them in a special state-operated achievement school district. Most of these schools are run by charter operators and engage in frequent testing and data analysis.

The 2013 Iowa State Legislature—in Senate File 427—exempted cities with a population less than 15,000 from the requirement to adopt the uniform plumbing code and the international mechanical code. The 2014 legislature—in House File 2366—clarified the law surrounding city elections relative to filling vacancies in the city council by placing a vacant seat on the next city election ballot. The legislature also enacted a law—House File 2289—prohibiting the state and its subdivisions from using drones.

State-Local Fiscal Relations

The Center on Budget and Policy Priorities reported states in 2014 provided less funding per pupil for kindergarten through 12th grade than was provided six years earlier. Thirty-five states provided less funding, including 14 states that reduced funding by more than 10 percent.

The California Commission on State Mandates noted voters approved Proposition 1A of 2004 requiring the state for the first time to suspend a mandate if it did not fund it during any budget cycle. Sixty mandates were suspended during the 2013–14 fiscal year, including three suspended for the first time—domestic violence background checks, identity theft and voter identification procedures.

The Illinois Local Government Consolidation Commission, established in 2011, in 2013 issued a report urging the review of all state mandates. In 2014, the commission released a report recommending (1) identifying differences between possibly duplicated local governments, (2) investigating districts and authorities with power to establish and maintain police forces, (3) making consolidation and cooperation among local governments easier, (4) standardizing state statutes governing sanitary districts, (5) amending the state statute governing certain special districts to allow for the annexation, disconnection or dissolution of the units of government, (6) monitoring the progress of Public Act 098-0126 to determine whether DuPage County can be used as a model for how counties can promote consolidation statewide, (7) exploring how the state can encourage cooperation by providing information and resources, and (8) reviewing all state mandates to ensure they are not unnecessary burdens on the various local governments and the taxpayers.

In a related action, the voters in Evanston, Ill., approved a nonbinding referendum to dissolve its coterminous township. Illinois Public Act 098-0127 of 2013 authorized Evanston voters to determine whether the municipality of Evanston should assume the duties and functions of the coterminous township. Voters in Evanston Township on March 18, 2014, approved the dissolution proposal by an approximate two-to-one margin and township operations ceased on April 30, 2014.

The New York State Legislature in 2013 created a state Fiscal Restructuring Board with authority to provide each fiscally distressed municipality with a blueprint for recovery and up to $5 million in state loans and/or grants if the municipality agrees to implement the blueprint. The New York Mandate

Relief Council in December 2013 reported the state legislature established a new pension tier expected to reduce pension costs by $80 billion over 30 years, and commenced a state takeover of the growth in the local share of Medicaid costs, thereby saving counties and New York City an estimated $1.2 billion over five years.

Former Virginia Gov. Bob McDonnell's Task Force for Local Government Mandate Review issued a 2013 interim report recommending (1) exploration of the creation of an intergovernmental roundtable in each state agency to foster communications and mutual problem-solving by the state and its local governments; (2) reinstatement of the first day introduction requirement for each bill with a local government fiscal impact; and (3) establishment of a process whereby local governments or school divisions representing 35 percent of the state's population could petition the Commission on Local Government to review bills or budget amendments that would impact unfunded or underfunded mandates on local governments or school divisions.

The League of Minnesota Cities reported the proportion of cities reporting an improved ability to meet financial needs increased from 51 percent in 2012 to 71.2 percent in 2013. The League of Oregon Cities issued a report in 2014, "Oregon Property Tax Capitalization: Evidence from Portland," revealing the state property tax "structure is significantly affecting home sales in Portland." The Wisconsin Legislative Fiscal Bureau in 2014 released a report on "unfunded mandates and items that would restrict local control enacted by the 2011–2012 legislative session" involving more than 60 laws.

The Maine Municipal Association in 2014 issued a highly critical *Municipal Priorities Paper* focusing primarily on state reductions in financial assistance for local governments. The paper alleges the state legislature, in its first session in 2013, "broke a number of longstanding agreements and arrangements with local government in an unprecedented way." Chapter 2 focuses on the increased property tax burden, notes voters had directed the state legislature to appropriate funds to pay 55 percent of the cost of K–12 public education, and reports the legislature in 2012 "is again 10 full percentage points—nearly $200 million a year—short of compliance."

Chapter 4 of the paper reports the state government has retreated from investments in transportation infrastructure, and cites the action by the

2013 state legislature reducing the local share of the state's transportation related budget to 9 percent. The focus of Chapter 5 is state mandates, and highlights the fact, "the state constitution was amended by the voters to make the enactment or promulgation of an unfunded state mandate illegal and unenforceable unless a supermajority of the lawmakers … knowingly and expressly support the mandate without funding." The report admits there has been a reduction in the number of enacted mandates to a low of 11 in 2013–14.

The Manhattan Institute for Policy Research in 2013 issued a report, *Defeating Fiscal Distress: A State Responsibility*, offering four recommendations for state government action. The report suggests states with strong public sector unions should grant mandate relief to local governments in matters of personnel spending, strengthen existing oversight policies toward local finances, develop strong and general intervention policies before cases of fiscal distress arise, allow local governments to file for Chapter 9 municipal bankruptcy only as a last resort, and appoint a state-appointed authority to guide municipalities through bankruptcy.

The Pew Charitable Trusts released in 2013 a report — *The State Role in Local Government Financial Control* — focusing on the stages of municipal financial difficulty: distress, crisis and bankruptcy, the reasons states may intervene in local government problems, and state approaches to intervention. Nineteen states have laws relative to state oversight of the finances of local governments. Fourteen of the states allow the receiver, state agency or control board to approve proposed bond sales and/or renegotiate the terms of the bonds on behalf of a municipality. Seven states allow interveners to reduce labor costs in distressed cities by renegotiating union labor contracts. Ten states grant interveners the power to increase existing taxes or to levy new taxes. The receiver in Central Falls, R.I., used this power to increase local taxes by 4 percent in each of five years. State laws in Michigan, Nevada and Tennessee permit an intervener to disincorporate or dissolve a municipality and consolidate it with a neighboring municipality.

A number of governors declared a financial emergency in a municipality and appointed an emergency manager for the unit. An example is Pontiac, Mich., where the governor in 2009 appointed the first of three emergency managers who successfully improved the fiscal health of the city to the point where Gov. Rick Snyder in 2013 determined there no longer was a need for an emergency manager, and appointed a transition advisory board with authority over city spending. In a related development, New Jersey Gov. Chris Christie announced in 2013 the state was assuming control of the Camden public school system because of the poor performance of students.

Bankruptcies

Municipal bankruptcies were common during the Great Depression, and threats of bankruptcies increased in the 1970s. The New York State Legislature responded to municipal fiscal distress by establishing a state finance control board for each of the following cities and one county: New York City in 1975, Yonkers in 1978, Troy in 1995, Buffalo in 2003, and Nassau County in 2000. New York State Comptroller Thomas P. DiNapoli in 2014 reported Buffalo's financial condition has improved, but 10 counties, 17 towns and one village are fiscally stressed with low fund balances, operating deficits and limited cash on hand. The city of Mechanicville, for example, had only 10 percent of the needed cash and issued short-term notes to obtain additional cash.

The number of municipalities declaring fiscal distress or bankruptcies continued to increase in the 21st century. In 2012, San Bernardino, Calif., became the third city in the state to seek bankruptcy court protection; Vallejo in 2008 and Stockton in 2013 sought such protection. A number of officials of the city of Harrisburg, Pa., favored seeking U.S. Bankruptcy Court protection, but the 2013 Pennsylvania State Legislature enacted a statute that made the city ineligible to seek such protection. The state appointed a receiver for the city who developed a plan for selling or leasing city assets to raise revenue to restore financial stability.

Michigan Gov. Rick Snyder on March 14, 2013, appointed a bankruptcy lawyer as the emergency manager for Detroit, and the city on July 18, 2013, sought bankruptcy protection under Chapter 9 of the U.S. Bankruptcy Act; it is the largest city in the nation to declare bankruptcy. The city in 2014 sought U.S. Bankruptcy Court Judge Steven W. Rhodes' approval of the city's plan to eliminate in excess of $7 billion of the city's estimated $18 billion debt and to devote approximately $1.5 billion to improving city services. A number of creditors, including retired city employees and a bond insurance company, supported the city's plan. The mayor and the city council regained most of their powers to make decisions on Sept. 25, 2014, but the emergency manager remains in office and retains authority over bankruptcy issues. Detroit's bankruptcy also has a major impact on numerous municipalities as the city supplies water to approximately 40 percent of the state's population. Twelve other cities and school districts in Michigan are under state financial oversight.

Can bankruptcies of local governments be prevented? The answer clearly is yes, as revealed by the experience of North Carolina since the Great Depression of the 1930s. The state legislature in 1931 created the state Local Government Commission with authority to approve or reject proposed borrowing by local governments. The result is the highest credit ratings for these governments by the three credit rating agencies. Although the Tennessee State Legislature did not adopt the North Carolina approach, Tennessee requires local governments seeking to borrow money to have debt management policies based on specific state guidelines.

Legal Services

The New Jersey State Comptroller in 2013 released a 38-page report that found many local governments failed to control excessive and improper payments for legal services. One township paid an attorney a salary for a no-work job and was unable to identify any services he provided. Two local governments paid their respective legal counsel for routine clerical and administrative work that should have been performed free of charge under the attorney's contract. A township paid a law firm at the attorney rate of $150 per hour for administrative work performed by a secretary, such as receiving messages and photocopying documents. The report also cited a series of billing errors that cost taxpayers thousands of dollars. Several local government officers admitted they had not conducted a substantive review of legal bills they received and paid.

Retiree Health Care and Non-Pension Benefits

The Massachusetts General Court (state legislature) in 2011 established the Massachusetts Special Commission to Study Retiree Health Care and Other Non-Pension Benefits because of concerns about the ability to maintain the health care financing system. The unfunded liability for state and local governments was approximately $46 billion and annual spending to provide health benefits exceeds

$1 billion. Municipalities are responsible for a proportionally larger share of increased retiree health care costs, in comparison to pensions, because they are responsible for proving health benefits to retired teachers who participate in the state teachers public employees systems for benefits.

The commission submitted its recommendations to the governor and the general court in 2013, but made no recommendation relative to accidental disability retirements. Selected recommendations follow. (1) Municipalities should adopt the Commonwealth's policy of providing prorated credit for part-time service based on the number of hours employees work each week. (2) The minimum age at which former employees become eligible for retiree health care should be increased by five years. (3) The minimum years of service for eligibility to receive retiree health care benefits should be increased from 10 to 20 years. (4) Benefits should be prorated based on the each retiree's years of service. (5) Current retirees should be exempt from the benefit design changes listed above. (6) Accidental disability retirements should be exempt from the proposed benefit design changes. (7) Municipal retirees' contributions should be frozen for three years. (8) When determining eligibility for retiree health benefits, municipalities should credit part-time service. (9) Municipalities should put their health plans out to competitive bidding to lower costs. (10) Municipalities should contribute not less than a 50 percent premium for future surviving spouses.

Notes

[1] Jefferson B. Fordham, *Model Constitutional Provisions for Municipal Home Rule* (Chicago: American Municipal Association, 1953).

About the Author

Joseph F. Zimmerman is a professor of political science at Rockefeller College of the State University of New York at Albany. He is the author of more than seventy books and numerous articles.

The Supreme Court and the States:
Beyond Same-Sex Marriage and the Affordable Care Act

By Lisa Soronen

While the same-sex marriage and Affordable Care Act cases are the most significant of the U.S. Supreme Court's 2014–15 term in general and specifically affecting states, other cases will significantly impact states too. The court will decide three tax cases, a Medicaid reimbursement case, two redistricting cases and a Fair Housing disparate impact case.

Practically speaking, only two Supreme Court decisions this term will receive any significant fanfare. Every American likely will know someone personally affected by either decision and both cases will affect the states. By the end of June 2015, the court will decide whether there is a federal constitutional right to same-sex marriage and whether the federal exchanges operating in 34 states may offer subsidized health insurance coverage under the Affordable Care Act.

Someone who cares about Supreme Court cases that affect the states should not be so distracted by these blockbusters to miss the many other cases of importance to states this term. Among other issues, including three tax cases, the court will decide whether states can be sued for providing inadequate Medicaid reimbursement, whether state legislatures can be excluded from the redistricting process and whether disparate impact claims may be brought under the Fair Housing Act.

In reviewing four consolidated cases from the Sixth Circuit, the court will decide in *Obergefell v. Hodges* two issues regarding same-sex marriage. First, whether the 14th Amendment requires states to allow same-sex marriages. Second, whether the 14th Amendment requires a state to recognize a same-sex marriage lawfully performed out-of-state. After numerous federal circuit courts of appeals decided the first question affirmatively, the Sixth Circuit answered both questions negatively. The Sixth Circuit reasoned that none of the couples' arguments "makes the case for constitutionalizing the definition of marriage and for removing the issue from the place it has been since the founding: in the hands of state voters."

The issue in *King v. Burwell* is whether tax credits for low- and middle-income health insurance purchasers are available under the Affordable Care Act (ACA) if insurance is purchased on a federal exchange rather than a state exchange. Only 16 states and the District of Columbia have established their own exchanges. The ACA makes tax credits available to those who buy health insurance on exchanges "established by the State." The IRS interpreted that language to include insurance purchased on federal exchanges. The Fourth Circuit upheld the revenue service's interpretation, concluding that "established by the State" is ambiguous, when read in combination with other sections of the ACA, and could include federal exchanges. The "board policy goals of the Act," also persuaded the court that the IRS's interpretation was permissible.

In *Armstrong v. Exceptional Child Center* the Court held 5-4 that Medicaid providers cannot rely on the Supremacy Clause or equity to sue states to enforce a Medicaid reimbursement statute. 42 U.S.C. §1396a(a)(30)(A) requires state Medicaid plans to assure that Medicaid providers are reimbursed at rates "consistent with efficiency, economy, and quality of care" while "safeguard[ing] against unnecessary utilization of ... care and services." Medicaid providers sued Idaho claiming that its reimbursement rates for rehabilitation services were lower than §(30)(A) permits. The Court first rejected the argument that the Supremacy Clause creates a private right of action. "It instructs courts what to do when state and federal law clash, but is silent regarding who may enforce federal laws in court, and in what circumstances they may do so." The Court also rejected the providers' argument that equity should permit their case to proceed. First, the statute provided a remedy for a state's breach—Health and Human Services may withhold funds—suggesting Congress intended no other remedies. Second, it would be difficult for a court to fashion a remedy in this case—a reimbursement rate—given the broad and unspecific language of §(30)(A).

In a provision added by citizen initiative, the Arizona Constitution entirely removes congressional redistricting authority from the Arizona State Legislature and places it in an unelected commission. In *Arizona State Legislature v. Arizona Independent Redistricting Commission*, the court will decide whether this violates the U.S. Constitution's Elections Clause, which requires that the time, place and manner of congressional elections be prescribed in each state by the "Legislature thereof." The Arizona district court ruled against the Arizona Legislature, reasoning that the Supreme Court previously held in two cases that a state may allow state bodies other than the legislature to redistrict. A dissenting judge didn't disagree with this, but pointed out that in those cases the state legislature still was able to participate in the redistricting process "in some very significant and meaningful capacity." While the use of redistricting commissions is popular for drawing state legislative district lines, only Arizona and California have mandated them for congressional redistricting.

In *North Carolina State Board of Dental Examiners v. FTC*, the Supreme Court held 6-3 that if the majority of state board members are active market participants, antitrust immunity applies only if the state actively supervises the board. The North Carolina State Board of Dental Examiners is a state agency principally charged with licensing dentists. Six of its eight members must be actively practicing, licensed dentists. After the board issued cease-and-desist letters to nondentist teeth whitening service providers, the Federal Trade Commission charged it with violating federal antitrust law. In *Parker v. Brown*, the court held that states receive state-action immunity from federal antitrust law when acting in their sovereign capacity. According to the court, nonsovereign entities controlled by active market participants receive state-action immunity only if the challenged restraint is clearly articulated in state policy and the policy is actively supervised by the state. Without active supervision, the court reasoned, agencies, boards and commissions made up of a majority of market participants may act in their own interest rather than the public interest. Here, the parties assumed the clear articulation requirement was met and agreed the board wasn't actively supervised by the state. So the court denied the board state-action immunity.

Michigan v. Environmental Protection Agency challenges a 2012 Environmental Protection Agency regulation intended to limit mercury and other emissions from mostly coal-fired power plants. Before regulating emissions from electric utilities, the Clean Air Act requires the EPA administrator to find that regulation is "appropriate and necessary" based on a public health hazards study. The question in this case is whether EPA unreasonably refused to consider costs in making its determination that regulation was appropriate. The D.C. Circuit agreed with the EPA that it was not required to consider costs. "Appropriate" isn't defined in the relevant section of the Clean Air Act and dictionary definitions of the term don't mention costs. Throughout the Clean Air Act, "Congress mentioned costs explicitly where it intended EPA to consider them." States are involved in this case on both sides.

The court has accepted a case for the third time involving the issue of whether disparate-impact claims can be brought under the Fair Housing Act. The Inclusive Communities Project sued the Texas Department of Housing and Community Affairs, claiming it was disproportionately approving Low Income Housing Tax Credits in minority-concentrated neighborhoods and disproportionately disapproving them in predominately white neighborhoods so as to maintain segregated housing patterns. It remains to be seen if *Texas Department of Housing and Community Affairs v. The Inclusive Communities Project* will settle like its predecessors, *Mt. Holly v. Mt. Holly Citizens in Action* and *Magner v. Gallagher*. The 11 federal circuits that have decided this issue all have held that disparate-impact claims are actionable.

The Railroad Revitalization and Regulatory Reform Act (4-R Act) prohibits state and local governments from imposing taxes that discriminate against railroads. Railroads and other commercial and industrial taxpayers in Alabama pay a four percent sales tax on diesel fuel, trucks pay a 19-cents per gallon excise tax and no sales tax, and water carriers pay no tax. CSX claimed Alabama violated the 4-R Act by requiring railroads to pay sales tax on diesel fuel and exempting its competitors (even though railroads paid less in sales tax than trucks paid in excise tax). In *Alabama Department of Revenue v. CSX Transportation** the Court held 7-2 that railroads can be compared to their competitors (rather than other commercial and industrial taxpayers) when determining whether a tax is discriminatory under the 4-R Act. Competitors are a "similarly situated" class "since discrimination in favor of that class most obviously frustrates the purpose of the 4-R Act," including restoring financial stability to railroads and fostering competition between railroads and other modes of transportation. Because "[t]here is simply no discrimination when there are roughly comparable taxes" different taxes paid by railroads and their competitors must be compared. And the justifications Alabama offered for why water carriers don't pay any tax on diesel fuel must be examined when determining if railroads have been discriminated against.

In 1992 in *Quill Corp. v. North Dakota*, the Court held that states cannot require retailers with no in-state physical presence to collect use tax. Since 2010, Colorado has required remote sellers to inform Colorado purchasers annually of their purchases and send the same information to the Colorado Department of Revenue. Direct Marketing Association sued Colorado in federal court claiming these requirements are unconstitutional under Quill. The Court held unanimously in *Direct Marketing Association v. Brohl** that the Tax Injunction Act (TIA) does not bar a federal court from deciding this case. Per the TIA, that federal courts may not "enjoin, suspend or restrain the assessment, levy or collection of any tax under State law" where a remedy is available in state court. The TIA was modelled on the Anti-Injunction Act, which concerns federal taxes. According to the Court, "the Federal Tax Code has long treated information gathering as a phase of tax administration that occurs before assessment, levy, or collection." And, while DMA's lawsuit sought to "limit, restrict, or hold back" tax collection in Colorado, it did not "restrain" tax collection in the narrow sense — by stopping it.

In *Comptroller v. Wynne*, the court will determine whether the U.S. Constitution requires states to offer a credit to its residents for all income taxes paid to another jurisdiction. The Wynnes of Howard County, Md., received S-corporation income that was generated and taxed in numerous states. Maryland law allowed them to receive a tax credit against their Maryland state taxes, but not their Maryland county taxes. Maryland's highest state court held that offering no credit against their county taxes violated the dormant Commerce Clause, which denies states the power to unjustifiably discriminate against or burden interstate commerce. If every state imposed a county tax without a credit, interstate commerce would be disadvantaged. Taxpayers who earn income out of state would be "systematically taxed at higher rates relative to taxpayers who earn income entirely within their home state."

In *Alabama Legislative Black Caucus v. Alabama* the Supreme Court held 5-4 that when determining whether unconstitutional racial gerrymandering occurred — if race was a "predominant motivating factor" in creating districts — one-person-one-vote should be a background factor. And Section 5 of the Voting Rights Act (VRA) does not require a covered jurisdiction to maintain a particular percent of minority voters in minority-majority districts. The Alabama Legislative Black Caucus sued Alabama claiming by adding more minority voters to majority-minority districts than were needed for minorities to elect a candidate of their choice Alabama engaged in unconstitutional racial gerrymandering. The Court concluded that one-person-one-vote should be taken as a given and not be weighed with other nonracial factors (compactness, contiguity, incumbency protection, etc.) because the predominance analysis is about "whether the legislature 'placed' race 'above traditional districting considerations in determining which persons were placed in appropriately apportioned districts.'" Section 5 does not require covered jurisdictions to maintain a particular percent of minority voters in majority-minority districts. Instead, it requires that a minority's ability to elect a preferred candidate be maintained. State legislatures must have a "strong basis in evidence" to support their race-based choices when redistricting.

In *Walker v. Texas Division*, Sons of Confederate Veterans, the Texas Department of Motor Vehicles Board rejected the Texas Division of the Sons of Confederate Veterans' application for a specialty license plate featuring images of the Confederate flag. The Fifth Circuit agreed with Texas' Sons of Confederate Veterans that its First Amendment rights had been violated. The speech in this case was private, applying the "reasonable observer test" test from *Pleasant Grove City, Utah v. Summum*, 555 U.S. 467 (2009), where the court held that monuments in a public park are government speech. While governments have historically used monuments "to speak to the public" in parks, a reasonable observer would understand that specialty plates are private speech because "states have not traditionally used license plates to convey a particular message to the public." The board engaged in viewpoint discrimination because it "discriminated against Texas SCV's view that the Confederate flag is a symbol of sacrifice, independence, and Southern heritage."

In the 2008 case of *Baze v. Rees*, the court approved a three-drug method for lethal injections: sodium thiopental to induce unconsciousness so pain is not felt when the second and third drugs cause paralysis and cardiac arrest. In *Glossip v. Gross*, the court will decide whether Oklahoma's use of midazolam instead of sodium thiopental violates the Eighth Amendment because it cannot reliably produce a deep, coma-like unconsciousness to prevent the substantial pain caused by the second and third drugs. The death row inmates in this case claim that midazolam poses a substantial risk that they will experience severe pain because it has a "ceiling effect"—at a certain dose it will have no greater effect—and can cause "paradoxical reactions" such as agitation. The district court rejected these concerns, relying on expert testimony that midazolam at the high dose used in executions, regardless of a ceiling effect, "will have the effect of shutting down any individual's awareness of pain" and that a paradoxical effect is rare and occurs most frequently at a low therapeutic dose.

So far the Supreme Court's current term has been a mixed bag for the states. *Armstrong is a significant win*. Had the Supreme Court ruled otherwise, the Supremacy Clause would have provided a cause of action for every federal statute that arguably conflicts with state law. *North Carolina State Board of Dental Examiners* is a significant loss for the states because it reduces the authority of state legislatures and governors to compose state agencies, boards and commissions as they may prefer. *Alabama Department of Revenue* and *DMA* might be fairly described—in total—as a draw for state government but for Justice Kennedy's concurrence in *DMA*, almost certainly prompted by the SLLC's *amicus* brief, that the "legal system should find an appropriate case for this Court to reexamine *Quill*."

Editor's Note

For updates on decisions of the U.S. Supreme Court's 2014–2015 term, please visit *The Book of the States* page in CSG's Knowledge Center:
http://knowledgecenter.csg.org/kc/category/content-type/content-type/book-states

About the Author

Lisa Soronen is the executive director of the State and Local Legal Center. In this role, she files *amicus curiae* briefs to the United States Supreme Court on behalf of members of the Big Seven, including CSG, in cases affecting state and local government.

Table 2.1
SUMMARY OF STATE INTERGOVERNMENTAL EXPENDITURES: 1944–2013
(In thousands of dollars)

Fiscal year	Total	To Federal government (a)	To local governments			For specified purposes				
			Total	For general local government support	Education	Public welfare	Highways	Health	Miscellaneous and combined
1944	$1,842,000	…	$1,842,000	$274,000	$861,000	$368,000	$298,000	…	$41,000
1946	2,092,000	…	2,092,000	357,000	953,000	376,000	339,000	…	67,000
1948	3,283,000	…	3,283,000	428,000	1,554,000	648,000	507,000	…	146,000
1950	4,217,000	…	4,217,000	482,000	2,054,000	792,000	610,000	…	279,000
1952	5,044,000	…	5,044,000	549,000	2,523,000	976,000	728,000	…	268,000
1953	5,384,000	…	5,384,000	592,000	2,737,000	981,000	803,000	…	271,000
1954	5,679,000	…	5,679,000	600,000	2,930,000	1,004,000	871,000	…	274,000
1955	5,986,000	…	5,986,000	591,000	3,150,000	1,046,000	911,000	…	288,000
1956	6,538,000	…	6,538,000	631,000	3,541,000	1,069,000	984,000	…	313,000
1957	7,440,000	…	7,440,000	668,000	4,212,000	1,136,000	1,082,000	…	342,000
1958	8,089,000	…	8,089,000	687,000	4,598,000	1,247,000	1,167,000	…	390,000
1959	8,689,000	…	8,689,000	725,000	4,957,000	1,409,000	1,207,000	…	391,000
1960	9,443,000	…	9,443,000	806,000	5,461,000	1,483,000	1,247,000	…	446,000
1962	10,906,000	…	10,906,000	839,000	6,474,000	1,777,000	1,327,000	…	489,000
1963	11,885,000	…	11,885,000	1,012,000	6,993,000	1,919,000	1,416,000	…	545,000
1964	12,968,000	…	12,968,000	1,053,000	7,664,000	2,108,000	1,524,000	…	619,000
1965	14,174,000	…	14,174,000	1,102,000	8,351,000	2,436,000	1,630,000	…	655,000
1966	16,928,000	…	16,928,000	1,361,000	10,177,000	2,882,000	1,725,000	…	783,000
1967	19,056,000	…	19,056,000	1,585,000	11,845,000	2,897,000	1,861,000	…	868,000
1968	21,950,000	…	21,950,000	1,993,000	13,321,000	3,527,000	2,029,000	…	1,080,000
1969	24,779,000	…	24,779,000	2,135,000	14,858,000	4,402,000	2,109,000	…	1,275,000
1970	28,892,000	…	28,892,000	2,958,000	17,085,000	5,003,000	2,439,000	…	1,407,000
1971	32,640,000	…	32,640,000	3,258,000	19,292,000	5,760,000	2,507,000	…	1,823,000
1972	36,759,246	…	36,759,246	3,752,327	21,195,345	6,943,634	2,633,417	…	2,234,523
1973	40,822,135	…	40,822,135	4,279,646	23,315,651	7,531,738	2,953,424	…	2,741,676
1974	45,941,111	341,194	45,599,917	4,803,875	27,106,812	7,028,750	3,211,455	…	3,449,025
1975	51,978,324	974,780	51,003,544	5,129,333	31,110,237	7,136,104	3,224,861	…	4,403,009
1976	57,858,242	1,179,580	56,678,662	5,673,843	34,083,711	8,307,411	3,240,806	…	5,372,891
1977	62,459,903	1,386,237	61,073,666	6,372,543	36,964,306	8,756,717	3,631,108	…	5,348,992
1978	67,287,260	1,472,378	65,814,882	6,819,438	40,125,488	8,585,558	3,821,135	…	6,463,263
1979	75,962,980	1,493,215	74,469,765	8,224,338	46,195,698	8,675,473	4,148,573	…	7,225,683
1980	84,504,451	1,746,301	82,758,150	8,643,789	52,688,101	9,241,551	4,382,716	…	7,801,993
1981	93,179,549	1,872,980	91,306,569	9,570,248	57,257,373	11,025,445	4,751,449	…	8,702,054
1982	98,742,976	1,793,284	96,949,692	10,044,372	60,683,583	11,965,123	5,028,072	…	9,228,542
1983	100,886,902	1,764,821	99,122,081	10,364,144	63,118,351	10,991,847	5,277,447	…	9,442,292
1984	108,373,188	1,722,115	106,651,073	10,744,740	67,484,926	11,923,430	5,686,834	…	10,811,143
1985	121,571,151	1,963,468	119,607,683	12,319,623	74,936,970	12,673,123	6,019,069	…	13,658,898
1986	131,966,258	2,105,831	129,860,427	13,383,912	81,929,467	14,214,613	6,470,049	…	13,862,386
1987	141,278,672	2,455,362	138,823,310	14,245,089	88,253,298	14,753,727	6,784,699	…	14,786,497
1988	151,661,866	2,652,981	149,008,885	14,896,991	95,390,536	15,032,315	6,949,190	…	16,739,853
1989	165,415,415	2,929,622	162,485,793	15,749,681	104,601,291	16,697,915	7,376,173	…	18,060,733

See footnotes at end of table.

SUMMARY OF STATE INTERGOVERNMENTAL EXPENDITURES: 1944–2013—Continued
(In thousands of dollars)

Fiscal year	Total	To Federal government (a)	To local governments		For specified purposes				
			Total	For general local government support	Education	Public welfare	Highways	Health	Miscellaneous and combined
1990	175,027,632	3,243,634	171,783,998	16,565,106	109,438,131	18,403,149	7,784,316	…	19,593,296
1991	186,398,234	3,464,364	182,933,870	16,977,032	116,179,860	20,903,400	8,126,477	…	20,747,101
1992	201,313,434	3,608,911	197,704,523	16,368,139	124,919,686	25,942,234	8,480,871	…	21,993,593
1993	214,094,882	3,625,051	210,469,831	17,690,986	131,179,517	31,339,777	9,298,624	…	20,960,927
1994	225,635,410	3,603,447	222,031,963	18,044,015	135,861,024	30,624,514	9,622,849	…	27,879,561
1995	240,978,128	3,616,831	237,361,297	18,996,435	148,160,436	30,772,525	10,481,616	…	28,926,886
1996	252,079,335	3,896,667	248,182,668	20,019,771	156,954,115	31,180,345	10,707,338	10,790,396	18,530,703
1997	264,207,209	3,839,942	260,367,267	21,808,828	164,147,715	35,754,024	11,431,270	11,772,189	15,453,241
1998	278,853,409	3,515,734	275,337,675	22,693,158	176,250,998	32,327,325	11,648,853	12,379,498	20,037,843
1999	308,734,917	3,801,667	304,933,250	25,495,396	192,416,987	35,161,151	12,075,195	13,611,228	26,173,293
2000	327,069,829	4,021,471	323,048,358	27,475,363	208,135,537	40,206,513	12,473,052	15,067,156	19,690,737
2001	350,326,546	4,290,764	346,035,782	31,693,016	222,092,587	41,926,990	12,350,136	16,518,461	21,454,592
2002	364,789,480	4,370,330	360,419,150	28,927,053	227,336,087	47,112,496	12,949,850	20,816,777	23,276,887
2003	382,781,397	4,391,095	378,390,302	30,766,480	240,788,692	49,302,737	13,337,114	20,241,742	23,953,537
2004	388,559,152	4,627,356	383,931,796	29,718,225	249,256,844	42,636,305	14,008,581	19,959,396	28,352,445
2005	405,925,287	4,620,167	401,305,120	28,320,648	263,625,820	48,370,718	14,500,232	17,515,138	28,972,564
2006	432,265,206	6,502,059	425,763,147	30,486,739	280,090,982	48,409,237	15,495,306	18,144,795	33,136,088
2007	459,742,295	4,670,648	455,071,647	31,207,955	301,062,065	56,899,141	14,881,789	20,067,198	30,953,499
2008	478,530,574	4,765,734	473,764,840	32,035,268	315,424,647	57,730,369	16,549,366	20,342,928	31,682,262
2009	490,887,391	4,894,977	485,992,414	30,421,570	324,374,036	58,741,316	16,492,780	21,019,353	34,943,359
2010	485,557,187	4,339,166	481,218,021	27,821,681	317,389,500	58,858,443	18,043,061	18,274,329	40,831,007
2011	496,832,436	4,295,922	492,536,514	27,577,126	330,482,270	56,678,841	17,243,590	18,745,863	41,808,824
2012	481,883,230	4,157,695	477,725,535	27,289,870	317,839,562	55,913,067	17,787,581	19,350,451	39,545,004
2013	488,782,863	3,392,576	485,390,287	28,412,169	324,995,548	55,565,254	18,158,521	20,242,808	38,015,987

Source: U.S. Census Bureau, Census of Governments: Finance (years ending in '2' and '7'), and Annual Survey of State Government Finances (remaining years). For information on sampling and nonsampling errors and definitions, see http://www.census.gov/govs/state/how_data_collected.html. Data users who create their own estimates from this table should cite the U.S. Census Bureau as the source of the original data only.

Note: Detail may not add to total due to rounding.
Key:
… — Not available.
(a) Represents primarily state reimbursements for the supplemental security income program.

Table 2.2
STATE INTERGOVERNMENTAL EXPENDITURES, BY STATE: 2001–2013
(In thousands of dollars)

State	2013	2012	2011	2010	2009	2008	2007	2006	2005	2004	2003	2002	2001
United States	$488,782,863	$481,883,230	$496,832,436	$485,557,187	$490,887,391	$478,530,574	$459,742,295	$432,265,206	$405,925,287	$388,559,152	$382,196,570	$364,847,087	$350,874,185
Alabama	6,476,073	6,563,313	6,800,787	6,604,013	6,535,634	6,720,814	6,088,940	5,759,949	5,281,804	4,164,719	4,074,005	4,095,562	3,892,653
Alaska	2,032,061	1,897,331	1,723,023	1,655,467	1,616,689	1,487,649	1,365,793	1,217,110	1,145,032	1,049,706	1,091,391	1,055,596	986,921
Arizona	8,209,708	8,023,697	8,668,387	9,179,514	9,618,970	10,320,506	10,341,643	9,063,746	8,028,519	7,556,518	6,936,753	6,902,301	6,439,144
Arkansas	4,937,560	5,047,345	5,151,981	5,057,598	4,698,889	4,392,340	4,300,048	4,039,533	3,886,756	3,212,815	3,210,582	3,071,214	2,941,918
California	95,069,461	85,425,616	91,501,553	90,530,131	94,909,240	94,872,980	93,537,044	88,317,088	80,948,431	80,132,150	84,468,847	74,687,370	69,747,365
Colorado	6,291,390	6,105,130	6,334,861	6,513,704	6,403,127	5,912,545	5,683,332	5,621,254	5,187,797	4,860,577	4,666,350	4,295,239	3,909,362
Connecticut	4,908,546	4,614,954	4,485,808	4,846,870	4,316,376	4,193,874	3,802,923	3,727,280	3,534,857	3,313,737	3,030,485	3,734,962	3,252,917
Delaware	1,271,359	1,161,381	1,293,106	1,235,608	1,205,247	1,172,083	1,157,652	1,129,736	983,773	922,710	903,476	822,544	788,160
Florida	17,809,542	17,340,127	19,725,217	18,478,449	17,677,928	19,703,095	19,680,891	19,402,818	17,475,959	15,285,893	14,460,722	14,053,858	15,010,631
Georgia	10,361,359	10,223,211	10,600,099	10,747,620	10,816,572	10,415,395	10,515,856	9,991,603	9,548,675	9,331,174	9,016,458	8,644,827	8,383,261
Hawaii	220,844	194,791	207,988	177,624	159,452	137,771	138,054	157,863	147,201	134,452	125,434	130,387	124,448
Idaho	1,981,659	1,956,717	2,036,312	2,022,896	2,077,028	2,037,507	1,931,829	1,606,232	1,519,654	1,496,785	1,449,076	1,407,058	1,363,445
Illinois	15,549,167	15,866,914	15,711,057	15,530,746	15,034,787	14,585,898	14,079,487	13,946,155	14,212,820	13,303,609	13,369,662	13,090,976	12,770,065
Indiana	9,292,344	9,313,044	9,265,386	9,705,254	8,214,991	7,976,702	8,184,884	7,817,176	7,876,764	7,963,397	6,760,945	6,556,774	7,052,415
Iowa	4,753,646	4,804,976	5,151,627	4,528,319	4,660,802	4,142,960	3,892,136	3,881,967	3,642,335	3,529,971	3,442,552	3,326,499	3,284,057
Kansas	4,057,504	3,953,778	4,208,664	4,176,958	4,314,940	4,214,475	3,869,984	3,594,505	3,281,217	3,123,152	2,925,220	2,971,413	2,953,527
Kentucky	4,802,691	5,029,106	5,069,137	5,078,845	4,769,871	4,700,971	4,526,996	4,384,427	3,915,278	3,963,425	3,693,634	3,620,967	3,620,278
Louisiana	6,241,308	6,387,767	6,580,164	6,658,397	6,505,389	6,022,791	6,175,010	5,654,409	4,588,748	4,410,251	4,329,053	4,168,290	3,800,785
Maine	1,238,618	1,286,233	1,301,692	1,346,639	1,325,723	1,335,469	1,272,764	1,217,377	1,093,027	1,049,160	1,051,164	1,009,582	976,233
Maryland	8,641,281	8,380,215	8,124,451	8,592,779	8,654,935	8,509,003	7,568,283	6,916,136	5,679,626	5,632,520	5,358,342	5,235,506	5,003,670
Massachusetts	9,401,248	9,291,231	8,826,190	9,107,483	8,890,500	8,840,769	8,909,899	7,231,774	7,271,036	5,393,684	6,435,841	6,283,972	6,886,054
Michigan	19,249,754	19,021,267	19,878,322	19,410,018	19,656,877	19,519,271	19,395,333	19,409,591	19,307,932	19,035,055	19,851,778	19,067,058	18,145,167
Minnesota	12,975,915	10,833,320	11,102,449	10,427,657	11,199,230	11,188,797	10,686,237	10,867,738	10,108,813	9,638,153	9,618,471	8,271,462	8,196,532
Mississippi	5,053,070	5,138,081	5,253,307	5,272,442	5,156,650	5,111,703	5,086,220	4,826,721	4,005,786	3,880,446	3,665,580	3,456,588	3,354,226
Missouri	5,771,802	5,877,847	5,948,493	6,227,955	5,936,688	5,743,498	5,559,734	5,386,306	5,489,120	5,260,101	5,159,094	5,073,185	4,802,371
Montana	1,373,069	1,316,548	1,352,917	1,334,478	1,276,112	1,318,649	1,175,674	1,088,009	1,005,091	955,378	938,000	910,845	863,553
Nebraska	2,170,630	2,170,016	2,306,692	2,192,338	2,064,173	1,981,940	1,793,817	1,721,265	1,659,130	1,695,613	1,784,749	1,820,137	1,684,159
Nevada	4,214,581	4,120,103	3,905,016	3,703,574	3,864,223	3,860,236	3,826,539	3,667,299	3,272,860	2,948,274	2,648,660	2,495,552	2,271,654
New Hampshire	1,300,770	1,226,012	1,191,097	1,261,454	1,278,589	1,451,976	1,408,445	1,385,014	1,224,831	1,278,988	1,283,091	1,178,642	1,040,566
New Jersey	11,102,269	11,789,109	11,167,301	11,877,592	11,135,809	10,927,571	10,671,445	11,060,423	10,642,426	10,565,755	8,997,417	9,320,357	9,081,634
New Mexico	4,500,634	4,450,387	4,325,766	4,322,463	4,766,207	4,363,063	4,160,932	3,745,083	3,617,407	3,234,697	2,951,823	2,768,420	2,561,979
New York	56,236,537	57,406,012	59,697,916	54,318,363	55,107,082	52,820,634	50,527,547	45,615,561	43,731,212	44,112,115	40,874,514	38,982,253	34,712,602
North Carolina	13,172,640	13,514,695	13,633,379	13,429,946	13,562,079	13,152,908	12,499,778	11,721,637	11,637,674	10,226,422	10,356,152	9,450,766	9,309,537
North Dakota	1,632,316	1,643,402	1,300,989	1,245,686	933,974	805,351	741,535	735,705	701,125	613,513	606,096	585,521	569,034
Ohio	16,517,064	17,932,406	18,488,325	18,348,743	18,963,232	18,080,744	18,042,563	17,347,300	16,368,355	15,730,201	15,249,395	15,052,078	14,594,220
Oklahoma	4,213,211	4,230,427	4,477,819	4,546,446	4,506,456	4,391,706	4,014,883	3,871,758	3,711,117	3,669,052	3,395,494	3,377,045	3,486,043
Oregon	5,495,337	5,657,912	5,774,682	5,864,882	5,703,775	5,640,993	5,047,346	4,947,578	4,764,615	4,637,052	4,071,501	4,212,673	4,027,505
Pennsylvania	18,834,325	18,526,116	19,944,576	18,871,434	19,144,305	17,826,902	17,058,314	13,650,400	13,307,866	12,061,035	11,943,470	12,787,590	13,120,752
Rhode Island	1,170,440	1,143,486	1,074,302	1,193,600	1,002,915	1,067,849	1,076,589	998,505	908,479	865,956	828,198	749,034	711,439
South Carolina	5,454,008	5,312,018	5,585,665	5,369,519	5,520,979	5,719,235	4,870,680	4,699,299	4,245,394	4,159,942	4,155,920	4,241,010	4,168,449

See footnotes at end of table.

STATE INTERGOVERNMENTAL EXPENDITURES, BY STATE: 2001–2013—Continued
(In thousands of dollars)

State	2013	2012	2011	2010	2009	2008	2007	2006	2005	2004	2003	2002	2001
South Dakota	740,104	753,622	774,778	737,190	707,862	679,868	652,117	633,891	608,209	566,853	514,949	506,347	480,960
Tennessee	7,074,682	7,181,421	7,104,790	6,664,828	6,797,935	6,516,598	6,034,661	5,910,319	5,705,768	5,301,665	4,952,923	4,477,936	4,582,883
Texas	27,590,295	29,860,716	29,665,803	27,461,315	29,252,364	26,089,474	21,919,511	19,785,626	17,489,900	17,032,016	17,332,957	16,680,780	17,204,468
Utah	3,069,082	3,029,283	3,106,230	3,027,680	3,120,527	3,050,173	2,601,367	2,384,402	2,189,527	2,112,921	2,165,151	2,170,884	2,100,657
Vermont	1,501,657	1,636,024	1,552,853	1,518,129	1,532,766	1,340,755	1,415,922	1,357,660	1,266,715	981,307	938,085	918,858	919,865
Virginia	11,255,705	11,653,818	11,489,163	10,959,394	11,894,394	11,260,089	10,585,635	10,019,166	9,720,411	8,820,012	8,352,635	8,369,313	7,869,121
Washington	9,777,797	9,530,116	9,346,712	9,798,444	10,043,789	9,143,766	8,602,204	7,820,778	7,443,361	6,911,826	6,785,341	6,806,350	6,576,757
West Virginia	2,469,535	2,618,032	2,533,582	2,382,633	2,232,558	2,131,100	2,074,429	2,067,829	2,004,862	1,942,069	1,544,758	1,453,707	1,535,961
Wisconsin	9,637,247	9,741,343	10,428,954	10,253,124	10,199,520	9,881,119	9,620,506	9,560,976	9,200,766	9,285,137	9,478,166	9,523,191	8,895,941
Wyoming	1,681,018	1,702,814	1,653,068	1,760,946	1,919,231	1,769,009	1,568,884	1,301,223	1,337,226	1,207,193	952,705	974,608	818,841

Source: U.S. Census Bureau, Census of Governments: Finance (2002, 2007, and 2012), and Annual Survey of State Government Finances (remaining years). For information on sampling and nonsampling errors and definitions, see *http://www.census.gov/govs/state/how_data_collected.html.* Data users who create their own estimates from this table should cite the U.S. Census Bureau as the source of the original data only. Data in this table are based on information from public records and contain no confidential data. Although the data in this table come from a census of governmental units and are not subject to sampling error, the census results may contain nonsampling error. Additional information

on nonsampling error, response rates, and definitions may be found within the survey methodology and technical documentation, *http://www2.census.gov/govs/state/13_methodology.pdf.*

Note: Includes payments to the federal government, primarily state reimbursements for the supplemental security income program. The statistics reflect state government fiscal years that end on June 30, except for four states with other ending dates: Alabama and Michigan (September 30), New York (March 31), and Texas (August 31).

Additional Note: Detail may not add to total due to rounding.

Table 2.3
STATE INTERGOVERNMENTAL EXPENDITURES, BY FUNCTION AND BY STATE: 2013
(In thousands of dollars)

State	Total	General local government support	Education	Public welfare	Highways	Health	Miscellaneous and combined
				Specified functions			
United States	$488,782,863	$28,412,169	$324,995,548	$55,565,254	$18,158,521	$20,242,808	$41,408,563
Alabama........................	6,476,073	206,798	4,786,505	112,719	207,478	41,229	1,121,344
Alaska............................	2,032,061	53,137	1,195,250	89,495	2,779	137,916	553,484
Arizona..........................	8,209,708	2,011,941	4,875,144	278,934	710,416	87,688	245,585
Arkansas........................	4,937,560	277,404	4,260,638	0	178,732	952	219,834
California	95,069,461	2,376,481	49,676,956	28,188,143	4,095,287	7,215,873	3,516,721
Colorado........................	6,291,390	128,595	4,296,969	834,531	380,378	100,908	550,009
Connecticut...................	4,908,546	392,295	3,677,030	348,399	2,878	283,133	204,811
Delaware	1,271,359	0	1,113,944	9,883	5,741	19,933	121,858
Florida...........................	17,809,542	1,770,457	13,917,786	79	586,460	63	1,534,697
Georgia..........................	10,361,359	0	9,239,380	388,976	115,367	222,511	395,125
Hawaii............................	220,844	165,122	0	382	0	12,821	42,519
Idaho..............................	1,981,659	214,682	1,577,707	0	124,622	3,684	60,964
Illinois...........................	15,549,167	1,814,068	8,985,799	1,622,677	792,103	169,917	2,164,603
Indiana...........................	9,292,344	673,655	7,638,130	45,234	800,244	29,131	105,950
Iowa	4,753,646	142,694	3,303,997	119,944	456,311	116,153	614,547
Kansas	4,057,504	149,485	3,511,730	1,822	205,305	49,563	139,599
Kentucky........................	4,802,691	0	4,042,320	117,689	187,793	134,554	320,335
Louisiana.......................	6,241,308	195,942	4,418,515	141,231	55,495	0	1,430,125
Maine.............................	1,238,618	119,936	1,011,583	17,221	23,633	100	66,145
Maryland	8,641,281	119,927	6,327,270	0	157,612	852,949	1,183,523
Massachusetts	9,401,248	955,227	6,819,860	285,033	206,756	16,625	1,117,747
Michigan........................	19,249,754	1,098,498	13,017,254	2,890,755	1,134,573	134,834	973,840
Minnesota......................	12,975,915	1,303,389	9,360,135	487,296	1,096,853	84,448	643,794
Mississippi....................	5,053,070	578,259	3,125,051	428,653	337,191	53,206	530,710
Missouri.........................	5,771,802	199,438	5,137,864	1,764	184,907	1,623	246,206
Montana	1,373,069	145,613	915,953	36,917	17,683	14,446	242,457
Nebraska........................	2,170,630	482,439	1,451,769	43,167	8,119	52,895	132,241
Nevada...........................	4,214,581	1,136,976	2,768,853	141,069	87,815	16,247	63,621
New Hampshire	1,300,770	58,805	1,042,021	142,280	34,897	2,342	20,425
New Jersey.....................	11,102,269	1,249,362	7,704,621	980,027	191,983	27,472	948,804
New Mexico	4,500,634	1,301,539	2,997,241	0	43,854	7,642	150,358
New York........................	56,236,537	424,416	28,887,650	9,543,635	15,668	6,413,944	10,951,224
North Carolina..............	13,172,640	197,036	10,539,476	1,569,013	237,665	144,075	485,375
North Dakota.................	1,632,316	313,359	849,565	17,196	138,155	8,106	305,935
Ohio...............................	16,517,064	1,461,936	10,923,197	1,536,390	794,746	544,559	1,256,236
Oklahoma......................	4,213,211	113,309	3,427,884	43,901	380,645	83,754	163,718
Oregon...........................	5,495,337	190,526	3,657,321	635,121	443,229	157,121	412,019
Pennsylvania	18,834,325	234,928	12,164,335	1,990,320	694,614	1,116,494	2,633,634
Rhode Island.................	1,170,440	57,248	1,005,225	78,446	18,605	7	10,909
South Carolina..............	5,454,008	1,661,651	3,411,496	87,346	93,287	38,989	161,239
South Dakota.................	740,104	30,649	569,147	7,904	44,401	6,585	81,418
Tennessee	7,074,682	287,580	5,078,822	849,978	157,729	82,786	617,787
Texas	27,590,295	172,407	24,815,359	515,372	240,870	339,412	1,506,875
Utah...............................	3,069,082	0	2,872,425	22,480	81,107	45,185	47,885
Vermont.........................	1,501,657	0	1,473,024	0	52,640	0	-24,007
Virginia..........................	11,255,705	1,001,724	6,805,350	584,083	535,328	392,596	1,936,624
Washington....................	9,777,797	118,744	7,546,421	7,128	657,272	627,462	820,770
West Virginia.................	2,469,535	108,276	2,018,529	39,353	13,038	58,498	231,841
Wisconsin	9,637,247	2,233,452	5,676,785	283,102	600,627	284,107	559,174
Wyoming	1,681,018	482,764	1,076,262	166	23,050	8,270	90,506

Source: U.S. Census Bureau, 2013 Annual Survey of State Government Finances.

Note: Data users who create their own estimates using these data should cite only the U.S. Census Bureau as the source of the original data. Data in this table are based on information from public records and contain no confidential data. Although the data in this table come from a census of governmental units and are not subject to sampling error, the census results may contain nonsampling error. Additional information on nonsampling error, response rates, and definitions may be found within the survey methodology *http://www2.census.gov/govs/state/13_methodology. pdf* and technical documentation.

Additional Note: Detail may not add to total due to rounding.

Table 2.4
STATE INTERGOVERNMENTAL EXPENDITURES, BY TYPE OF RECEIVING GOVERNMENT AND BY STATE: 2013
(In thousands of dollars)

State	Total intergovernmental expenditure	Federal	School districts	Other local governments
United States	$488,782,863	$3,392,576	$263,177,928	$222,212,359
Alabama	6,476,073	0	4,772,486	1,703,587
Alaska	2,032,061	0	0	2,032,061
Arizona	8,209,708	0	4,863,961	3,345,747
Arkansas	4,937,560	18	4,260,638	676,904
California	95,069,461	2,775,752	46,390,472	45,903,237
Colorado	6,291,390	3,005	4,272,693	2,015,692
Connecticut	4,908,546	0	36,930	4,871,616
Delaware	1,271,359	956	1,107,792	162,611
Florida	17,809,542	0	13,592,090	4,217,452
Georgia	10,361,359	0	9,239,380	1,121,979
Hawaii	220,844	0	0	220,844
Idaho	1,981,659	382	1,577,707	403,570
Illinois	15,549,167	0	8,926,732	6,622,435
Indiana	9,292,344	8,950	7,638,105	1,645,289
Iowa	4,753,646	24,812	3,303,868	1,424,966
Kansas	4,057,504	0	3,511,730	545,774
Kentucky	4,802,691	1,751	4,042,320	758,620
Louisiana	6,241,308	0	4,415,418	1,825,890
Maine	1,238,618	0	0	1,238,618
Maryland	8,641,281	5,811	0	8,635,470
Massachusetts	9,401,248	0	1,142,934	8,258,314
Michigan	19,249,754	202,983	13,004,555	6,042,216
Minnesota	12,975,915	13,613	9,338,113	3,624,189
Mississippi	5,053,070	0	3,103,894	1,949,176
Missouri	5,771,802	0	5,137,864	633,938
Montana	1,373,069	68,036	915,828	389,205
Nebraska	2,170,630	303	1,451,769	718,558
Nevada	4,214,581	43,057	2,768,851	1,402,673
New Hampshire	1,300,770	3,308	170,902	1,126,560
New Jersey	11,102,269	0	5,673,830	5,428,439
New Mexico	4,500,634	19,000	2,997,241	1,484,393
New York	56,236,537	0	15,547,705	40,688,832
North Carolina	13,172,640	0	0	13,172,640
North Dakota	1,632,316	0	849,565	782,751
Ohio	16,517,064	0	10,923,197	5,593,867
Oklahoma	4,213,211	9,929	3,417,884	785,398
Oregon	5,495,337	54,786	3,655,869	1,784,682
Pennsylvania	18,834,325	0	11,567,331	7,266,994
Rhode Island	1,170,440	129,162	60,501	980,777
South Carolina	5,454,008	18,204	3,367,230	2,068,574
South Dakota	740,104	0	569,147	170,957
Tennessee	7,074,682	0	303,949	6,770,733
Texas	27,590,295	1,390	24,582,015	3,006,890
Utah	3,069,082	0	2,870,958	198,124
Vermont	1,501,657	0	1,473,024	28,633
Virginia	11,255,705	0	24,392	11,231,313
Washington	9,777,797	1,312	7,546,300	2,230,185
West Virginia	2,469,535	4,404	2,007,711	457,420
Wisconsin	9,637,247	0	5,676,785	3,960,462
Wyoming	1,681,018	0	1,076,262	604,756

Source: U.S. Census Bureau, 2013 Annual Survey of State Government Finances.

Note: Data users who create their own estimates using these data should cite only the U.S. Census Bureau as the source of the original data. Data in this table are based on information from public records and contain no confidential data. Although the data in this table come from a census of governmental units and are not subject to sampling error, the census results may contain nonsampling error. Additional information on non-sampling error, response rates, and definitions may be found within the survey methodology *http://www2.census.gov/govs/state/13_methodology. pdf* and technical documentation *http://www2.census.gov/govs/state/ statetechdoc2013.pdf.*

Additional Note: Detail may not add to total due to rounding.

Table 2.5
STATE INTERGOVERNMENTAL REVENUE FROM FEDERAL AND LOCAL GOVERNMENTS: 2013
(In thousands of dollars)

State	Total intergovernmental revenue	From federal government					From local governments				
		Total (a)	Education	Public welfare	Health & hospitals	Highways	Total (a)	Education	Public welfare	Health & hospitals	Highways
United States	$551,464,163	$513,478,951	$84,408,057	$307,610,126	$25,794,434	$41,431,014	$37,985,212	$3,266,668	$28,062,951	$1,185,097	$2,057,104
Alabama	8,338,033	8,226,967	1,617,012	4,773,253	248,645	789,850	111,066	11,187	0	35,205	46,168
Alaska	2,754,412	2,747,308	339,906	1,168,655	104,566	458,856	7,104	5,748	0	0	0
Arizona	10,580,523	10,166,478	1,711,418	6,687,404	326,336	831,892	414,045	11,255	304,888	65,319	6,456
Arkansas	5,724,598	5,689,390	801,886	3,297,154	126,098	584,654	35,208	34,629	0	404	0
California	58,096,373	54,827,525	10,277,690	35,518,804	2,268,814	3,277,021	3,268,848	237,947	1,356,873	8,291	741,014
Colorado	6,508,932	6,427,852	1,412,272	2,329,076	1,375,934	742,791	81,080	15,889	215	0	19,518
Connecticut	5,962,699	5,949,159	496,231	3,826,344	210,581	533,242	13,540	1,130	0	0	0
Delaware	1,996,011	1,929,185	237,438	1,143,896	99,474	211,245	66,826	62,910	0	0	0
Florida	23,880,229	23,506,254	4,406,907	13,359,266	1,900,559	2,090,984	373,975	10,130	0	279,942	0
Georgia	14,619,221	14,323,163	3,079,313	7,073,816	1,434,300	1,359,809	296,058	252,234	0	0	11,977
Hawaii	2,331,449	2,326,602	624,748	1,084,066	69,923	159,063	4,847	0	0	0	0
Idaho	2,541,438	2,522,766	379,866	1,310,994	229,954	306,062	18,672	345	13,236	0	5,043
Illinois	17,312,790	16,973,577	3,167,335	9,902,223	592,377	1,516,860	339,213	14,760	243,725	0	64,615
Indiana	11,267,810	11,192,452	1,712,086	7,039,516	278,939	1,110,281	75,358	9,815	22,824	2,994	38,578
Iowa	5,991,401	5,915,221	993,140	3,505,067	174,449	460,512	76,180	394	42,544	8,454	13,447
Kansas	3,845,073	3,788,962	790,747	1,880,823	284,174	415,551	56,111	19,878	78	983	32,320
Kentucky	8,083,482	8,047,093	1,307,298	4,900,886	293,812	694,374	36,389	20,170	0	0	0
Louisiana	10,660,261	10,592,657	1,378,099	5,539,233	347,567	861,383	67,604	20,390	0	2,905	2,271
Maine	2,830,353	2,821,145	273,128	1,852,027	80,768	231,265	9,208	0	0	50	6,305
Maryland	10,325,181	9,952,960	1,664,398	5,139,420	1,237,251	709,449	372,221	48,731	28,366	121,788	24,849
Massachusetts	13,706,498	13,233,244	1,573,978	7,815,079	690,661	669,273	473,254	12,977	0	0	4,838
Michigan	18,007,780	17,829,882	3,256,553	10,180,474	1,358,966	908,455	177,898	9,427	67,583	45,316	19,551
Minnesota	9,315,259	9,141,995	1,354,823	6,257,462	244,286	601,092	173,264	22,119	74,886	21	64,548
Mississippi	7,649,292	7,509,589	1,073,919	4,671,168	196,145	581,465	139,703	3,628	204	4	107,315
Missouri	10,497,449	10,188,272	1,281,738	5,734,532	1,395,472	954,875	309,177	1,335	227,827	14,051	42,066
Montana	2,161,997	2,158,227	289,552	957,523	126,650	463,116	3,770	9	646	0	1,614
Nebraska	3,212,304	3,154,670	220,738	2,236,135	59,625	363,498	57,634	33,217	347	98	20,596
Nevada	3,080,240	2,844,973	573,181	1,470,300	142,451	350,773	235,267	31,403	153,290	11,380	28,152
New Hampshire	1,883,424	1,659,853	239,779	769,128	28,895	153,145	223,571	4,310	179,004	0	29,554
New Jersey	14,471,986	13,755,548	2,017,443	6,996,729	453,955	848,794	716,438	272,480	0	85,012	211,304
New Mexico	5,416,068	5,228,141	740,798	3,486,139	180,584	433,818	187,927	59,341	0	128,586	0
New York	71,682,137	46,272,851	4,813,154	32,456,517	1,307,685	1,830,124	25,409,286	185,440	24,467,044	54,061	17,427
North Carolina	15,769,950	15,470,808	2,393,962	9,852,503	672,692	1,184,730	299,142	112,535	123,182	5,733	25,912
North Dakota	1,572,480	1,529,135	266,536	591,528	20,645	367,180	43,345	1	8,586	3,595	20,287
Ohio	21,113,847	20,482,575	2,705,082	14,310,434	433,821	1,593,734	631,272	25,119	344,242	64,775	59,696
Oklahoma	7,159,511	7,028,733	1,013,833	3,501,139	1,381,690	558,808	130,778	1,141	511	1,890	33,952
Oregon	8,003,252	7,987,139	1,255,641	5,138,896	468,597	384,064	16,113	11,591	0	0	0
Pennsylvania	21,412,638	21,219,116	3,272,854	14,276,610	472,266	1,758,508	193,522	170,779	0	798	13,935
Rhode Island	2,369,822	2,331,473	312,734	1,178,035	235,746	271,075	38,349	0	0	0	0
South Carolina	7,202,824	6,698,952	1,393,650	3,846,495	270,486	635,098	503,872	88,111	280,799	5,730	68,406

See footnotes at end of table.

STATE INTERGOVERNMENTAL REVENUE FROM FEDERAL AND LOCAL GOVERNMENTS: 2013—Continued
(In thousands of dollars)

State	Total intergovernmental revenue	From federal government					From local governments				
		Total (a)	Education	Public welfare	Health & hospitals	Highways	Total (a)	Education	Public welfare	Health & hospitals	Highways
South Dakota..............	1,605,537	1,575,212	266,179	599,105	99,401	327,850	30,325	12,592	0	7,750	9,650
Tennessee	10,900,626	10,819,977	1,589,313	6,997,488	301,976	979,223	80,649	24,087	1,796	4,640	33,889
Texas........................	37,580,061	36,844,736	7,844,603	21,705,368	1,267,301	3,208,960	735,325	616,700	5,402	112,827	0
Utah..........................	4,304,061	4,298,917	889,027	2,404,604	202,281	433,542	5,144	4,997	0	0	0
Vermont.....................	1,872,013	1,869,831	270,364	1,060,200	58,112	264,720	2,182	0	0	0	2,036
Virginia.....................	9,959,041	9,412,343	2,001,991	4,979,265	448,855	1,423,807	546,698	397,946	0	62,039	67,940
Washington................	10,030,961	9,737,429	2,360,158	4,380,144	1,138,010	948,447	293,532	151,728	0	24,929	53,683
West Virginia.............	4,325,052	4,230,663	552,811	2,545,476	163,333	439,555	94,389	4,843	0	0	0
Wisconsin	9,228,907	8,952,020	1,489,040	5,492,779	245,373	783,832	276,887	14,407	114,853	23,242	95,940
Wyoming	2,318,877	2,085,931	423,405	386,948	43,953	364,309	232,946	216,863	0	2,285	12,252

Source: U.S. Census Bureau, 2013 Annual Survey of State Government Finances.

Note: Data users who create their own estimates using these data should cite only the U.S. Census Bureau as the source of the original data. Data in this table are based on information from public records and contain no confidential data. Although the data in this table come from a census of governmental units and are not subject to sampling error, the census results may contain nonsampling error. Additional information on nonsampling error, response rates, and definitions may be found within the survey methodology *http://www2.census.gov/govs/state/13_methodology.pdf* and technical documentation *http://www2.census.gov/govs/state/statetechdoc2013.pdf.*

Additional Note: Detail may not add to total due to rounding.

Key:

(a) Total includes other types of intergovernmental revenue not shown separately in this table.

Chapter Three

STATE LEGISLATIVE BRANCH

The 2014 Legislative Elections

By Tim Storey

The 2014 election resulted in Republican dominance of state legislative control unmatched in nearly a century. Riding a surge of disaffection with a president in the sixth year of office, combined with low, midterm voter turnout among Democrats, Republicans won big. They also continued to benefit from a built in redistricting advantage stemming from the 2010 election success by the party. Essentially, everything went one direction in the 2014 election — the direction of the Grand Old Party.

The GOP gained more than 300 legislative seats nationwide in November 2014, giving the party control of 30 statehouses and 4,100 of the nation's 7,383 legislative seats. That is the most seats since 1920 and the most legislative chambers in the history of the Republican Party.

The 2014 election was a GOP landslide in *nearly* every sense of the word. However, the numerical gains for the party were not overly impressive because Republicans were so successful in 2010, and to a lesser degree in 2012. There simply were not enough seats in play to make large seat gains. In the 2010 election, Republicans added more than 720 legislative seats to their ranks.

Republican success in state elections in 2014 came as no surprise. Midterm elections almost always spell trouble for the party holding the White House. With Democratic incumbent President Barack Obama at the midpoint of his final term in 2014, Republican strategists knew it was only a question of how high they could go. In the 29 midterm election cycles since 1902 — including 2014 — the party of the president has lost legislative seats in 27 of them. That's an abysmal winning percentage of only 7 percent.

Or, from the opposite perspective, the party not residing at 1600 Pennsylvania Ave., wins seats in state legislatures in midterms 93 percent of the time. Even though many Democratic state legislative candidates tried to distance themselves from President Obama while on the campaign trail and amid talk about an improving U.S. economy, they couldn't overcome one of the most consistent historic trends in all of American politics. In only two midterm elections has the party in the White House added to its legislative numbers. In 1934, at the height of the Great Depression, voters backed Franklin Roosevelt's Democrats. And in 2002 as the nation continued to react to the attacks of September 11th the previous year, Republicans gained 177 legislative seats in George W. Bush's first midterm.

Record GOP Control of Legislative Chambers

There are 99 state legislative chambers in the 50 states. Nebraska voters changed their constitution in 1934, making the state the only one in the nation with a unicameral legislature. Nebraska's constitutional amendment also mandated that candidates for The Unicameral, as it is now called, run in nonpartisan elections. So, there are 98 partisan legislative chambers in the U.S. After their sweep in the 2014 elections, Republicans have the majority in two-thirds of those partisan chambers — an unprecedented high water mark for the party of Lincoln.

In 2014, Republicans won enough seats from Democrats in specific states to add 11 legislative chambers to their side. Democrats did not switch any Republican chambers to their control. This was an echo of 2010, when Republicans shifted 22 chambers to their column and lost none.

No legislative bodies are currently tied, which is relatively unusual. Typically, there will be one or two chambers in the country that wind up with even numbers of Democrats and Republicans every two years. For almost 30 years — 1984 until 2012 — at least one chamber was tied.

More Partisan Metrics

Regular legislative elections were held in 46 states in 2014 for 6,049 of the 7,383 legislative seats. Louisiana, Mississippi, New Jersey and Virginia hold legislative elections in odd-numbered years. In four states — Kansas, Minnesota, New Mexico and South Carolina — the senates were not up. All senators in those states were elected to four-year terms in 2012.

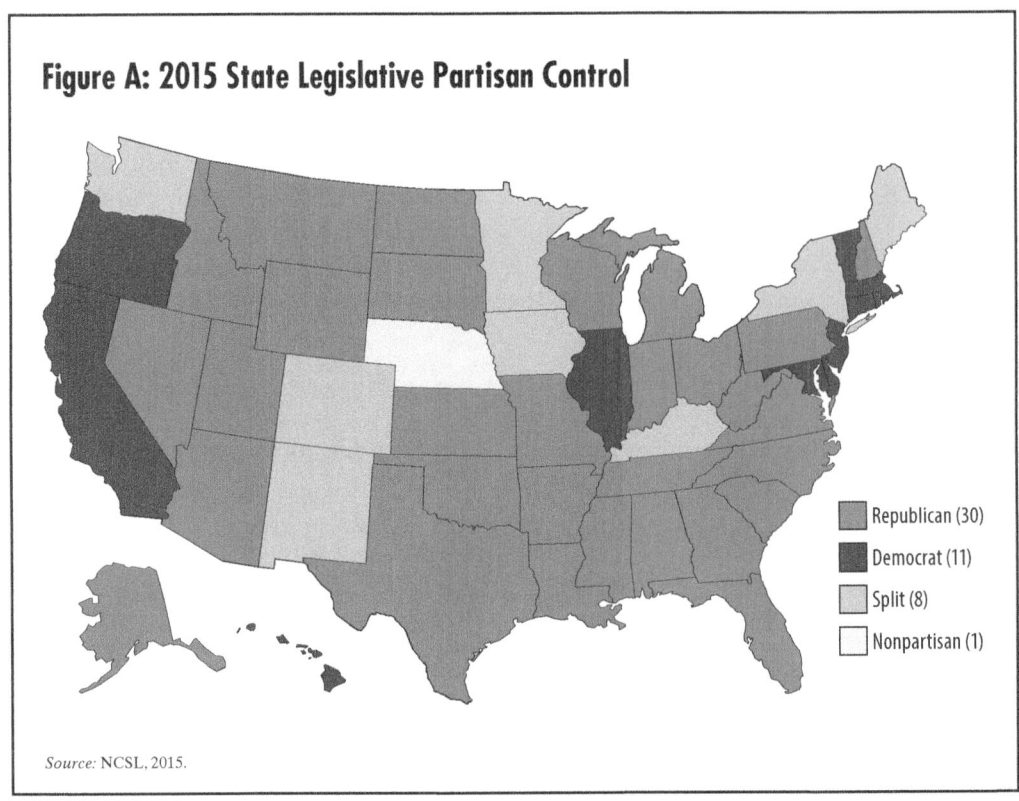

Figure A: 2015 State Legislative Partisan Control

Republican (30)
Democrat (11)
Split (8)
Nonpartisan (1)

Source: NCSL, 2015.

Republicans control both chambers of the legislature in 30 states, up from 27 states in 2014 before the election. Conversely, Democrats control the legislature in only 11 states, a drop from 19 pre-election. The two parties have shared control of the legislature in eight states, with one party holding the senate and the other one having the house. The number of divided states remains relatively low, although up from the historic low of four between the 2012 and 2014 elections. It has been more than 10 years since the number of divided states was in double digits.

Republicans added nearly 320 legislative seats to their bottom line in 2014. When legislative sessions began in January of 2015, there were 4,125 state legislators who were elected as Republicans, the most Republican legislators in nearly a century. There were 4,363 Republican legislators after the 1920 election when Warren Harding became president. The most legislative seats ever held by either party happened in 1974, when 5,100 of the nation's legislators—68.1 percent—were Democrats. Republicans now control 56.5 percent of the partisan seats in state legislatures.

Third party state legislators make up only 0.4 percent of all legislative seats; 30 legislators are neither Democrats nor Republicans. The Vermont House accounts for nearly half of the 30 third party lawmakers in the country, where six are progressives and six are independent.

Regional Overview

The post-2014 partisan legislative map is decidedly red in hue in every region of the country. The only blue on the map, where Democrats remain in charge of the whole legislature, shows up almost entirely in states that border the Atlantic and Pacific oceans. Vermont and Illinois are the only Democratic states without a saltwater coastline. Republicans expanded their ranks in every region of the nation in 2014. They added seats in Southern states where they are the strongest for the fourth consecutive election cycle.

The relatively swift increase of Republican dominance in Southern states is nothing short of remarkable. Prior to the 1990 election, only 25 percent of legislators in the South were Republican. Democrats held the majority of every legislative body south of the Mason-Dixon Line. Since 1982, Republicans have increased their numbers of legislative seats in the South in every single election cycle except for 2006. They now control 62.5 percent of Southern legislative seats. More importantly, every chamber in the region, except for the Kentucky House, has a GOP majority and leader. Many pundits thought Republicans were poised to win the Kentucky House in their 2014 sweep, yet Democrats didn't lose a single seat in the chamber, making it a rare bright spot for the party.

Table A: Republican Percent of Seats Held by Region, 2015

East	44.4%
South	62.5%
Midwest	63.3%
West	56.1%

Source: NCSL, 2015.

Chambers that Flipped

In every two-year election cycle, an average of 13 legislative chambers shift party control. Typically, one party claims the bulk of the switches, and the less fortunate party snags a couple, thus having a silver lining. As in the 2010 cycle, all the chambers shifted in one direction in 2014, from D to R. Republicans won control in 11 chambers; two short of the average. Not only did Democrats not gain in chambers in 2014, they lost seats in the vast majority of chambers where seats were up. Democrats managed to add seats to their column in only 13 chambers. Republicans boosted their ranks by at least one seat in 64 chambers.

Republicans saw their largest gains in the 400-member New Hampshire House, a chamber that has become very competitive over the past few elections, with a majority control shift in four of the past five elections. Republicans flipped more than 60 seats to win back the Granite State House of Representatives after losing it in 2012.

Republicans seized both chambers in West Virginia, giving them control of the state's legislature for the first time since the 1920s. On Election Day, Republicans won a whopping 20 additional seats in the House, giving them a comfortable majority of 64 to 36. They tied the senate at 17 seats each. On the day after the election, a Democratic senator

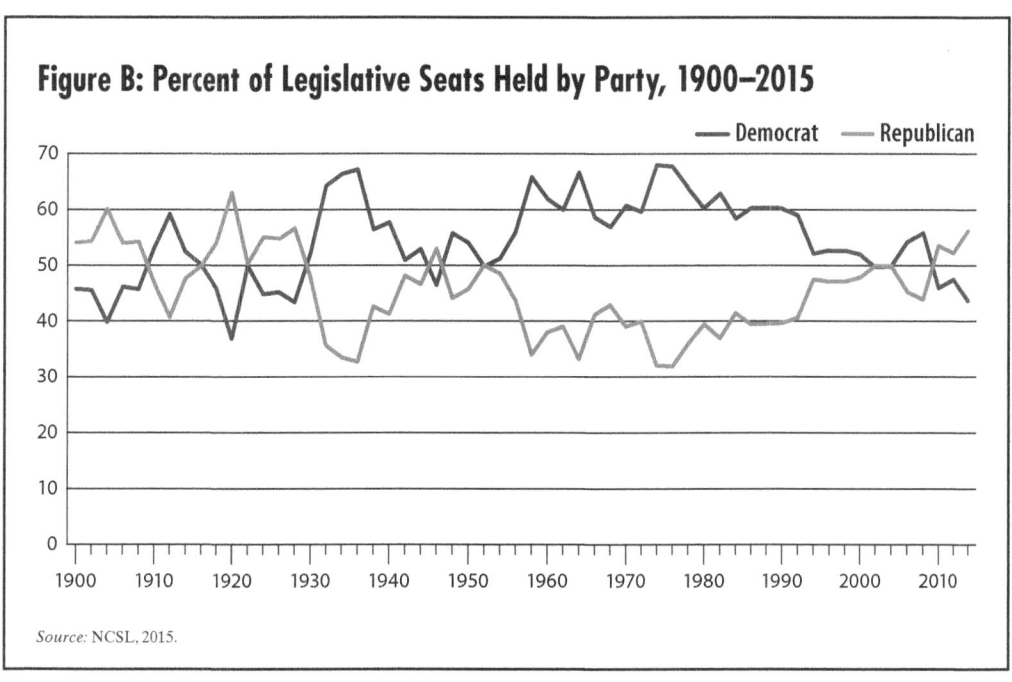

Figure B: Percent of Legislative Seats Held by Party, 1900–2015

— Democrat   — Republican

Source: NCSL, 2015.

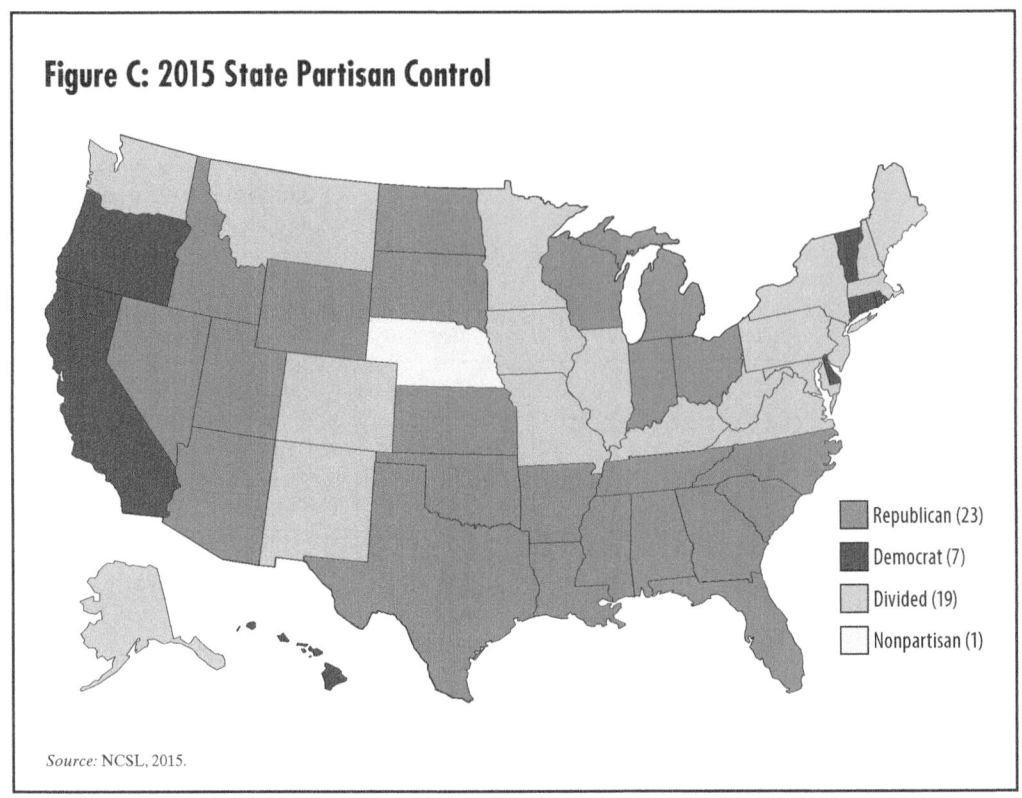

Figure C: 2015 State Partisan Control

Republican (23)

Democrat (7)

Divided (19)

Nonpartisan (1)

Source: NCSL, 2015.

changed party affiliation to the GOP, giving the party the senate majority for the first time since 1932.

Nevada was another state where both chambers went from Democrat to Republican. In the Nevada Senate, Republicans needed to win only one seat to convert the 10 Republicans-11 Democrats minority to an 11 Republicans-10 Democrats majority, and they pulled it off. Nevada Assembly Democrats got swamped by the GOP tide and lost a dozen seats, giving the Republicans a comfortable 27-15 majority headed into 2015.

New Mexico voters gave Republicans control of the House in the Land of Enchantment for the first time in 60 years. The post-election GOP majority was 37-33. The New Mexico Senate did not have any seats up for election in 2015.

One of the two closest legislative chambers going into the election was the Colorado Senate, where Democrats held an 18-17 majority before ballots were cast. Republicans won enough of the very close senate seats, even though they also lost a couple, and flipped the chamber back to their column—18 Republicans and 17 Democrats—after a decade in the minority.

The Minnesota House switched for the third consecutive election. Republicans gained nine seats to earn a 72-62 majority.

Like the Minnesota House, the Maine Senate has been one of the biggest legislative battlegrounds in recent years, having changed hands seven times since 1994. In 2014, Republicans seized control again after losing it two years ago.

In the New York and Washington senates, Republicans had been in control since 2012 by virtue of coalitions with small groups of dissident Democrats, even though Republicans did not actually have the numerical majority of the seats. New York Republicans won back the majority advantage outright (33-30) in the Empire State, as did Washington Republicans (25-24).

Gubernatorial Elections and Overall Control of States

One of the most fascinating outcomes of the 2014 elections at the state level was that Republicans did not see a net gain in the total number of states completely run by the GOP. Headed into the 2014 election, there were 23 states where the legislature and governor were both in the hands of Republicans. Democrats controlled 15 states and 11 were divided. As noted, Republicans had a net increase of 11 legislative chambers, but their gains in governor's races were less impressive.

There were races for governor in 36 states in 2014. In six of those states, the party affiliation of the governor changed with Republicans winning back the governor's mansion from Democrats in Arkansas, Illinois, Maryland and Massachusetts. Democrats took back the governor's office in Pennsylvania; in Alaska, the governor went from being a Republican to an Independent.

With all of those changes, the number of total GOP states—legislature and governor—stayed the same at 23; however, the number of states with Democrats running the show declined from 15 to seven. There are now 19 states with divided government—eight more than before the election.

Presidents and Legislative Elections

In the four elections since 2008 with either Barack Obama on the ballot or in the White House, Democrats have suffered a net loss of 816 state legislative seats. President Obama is far from having the worst track record of the presidents who saw their party strength decline in legislatures since 1900. Presidents William Taft, Warren Harding, Herbert Hoover and Dwight Eisenhower all presided over larger, four-digit losses in their party's legislative seat strength while running for and holding the highest office in the land. President Calvin Coolidge holds the record for boosting his party's fortunes as a candidate and then president. Under Coolidge, Republicans netted 260 seats. Ronald Reagan is a close second, having netted 250 seats.

Now that President Obama has seen his last election as the Democratic Party's leader, it is interesting to consider how presidents' parties have fared in legislatures during their tenure. Presidential coattails are an oft-cited factor in state elections. Factoring the Democrat's major losses in 2014 into Obama's tally, he joins the group of 14 presidents whose parties saw significant losses in legislative seats during their time at the top. Only five presidents actually gained legislative seats when heading up the ticket or being in the White House. They were Teddy Roosevelt, Calvin Coolidge, Franklin Roosevelt, Harry Truman and Ronald Reagan.

Table B: Legislative Seats Gained/Lost under Presidents since 1900

President	Party	Elections	Net legislative seats gained/lost
Theodore Roosevelt	Republican	1900, 1902, 1904, 1906	177
William Taft	Republican	1908, 1910	-1,089
Woodrow Wilson	Democrat	1912, 1914, 1916, 1918	-547
Warren Harding	Republican	1920, 1922	-1,142
Calvin Coolidge	Republican	1924, 1926	260
Herbert Hoover	Republican	1928, 1930	-1,058
Franklin Roosevelt	Democrat	1932, 1934, 1936, 1938, 1940, 1942, 1944	1,130
Harry Truman	Democrat	1946, 1948, 1950	85
Dwight Eisenhower	Republican	1952, 1954, 1956, 1958	-1,035
John Kennedy	Democrat	1960, 1962	-414
Lyndon Johnson	Democrat	1964, 1966	-234
Richard Nixon	Republican	1968, 1970, 1972	-180
Gerald Ford	Republican	1974	-628
Jimmy Carter	Democrat	1976, 1978	-379
Ronald Reagan	Republican	1980, 1982, 1984, 1986	250
George H.W. Bush	Republican	1988, 1990	-21
Bill Clinton	Democrat	1992, 1994, 1996, 1998	-612
George W. Bush	Republican	2000, 2002, 2004, 2006	-108
Barack Obama	Democrat	2008, 2010, 2012, 2014	-816

Source: NCSL, 2015.

Conclusion

The 2014 elections saw the lowest voter turnout in decades in the United States. And many of the voters who did cast a ballot wanted to send President Obama a message that they disagreed with some of his signature policies. Republican legislative candidates almost uniformly attacked Obama's signature achievement, the Affordable Care Act.

Republicans also reaped the benefits of a substantial advantage in redistricting following the 2010 census. That redistricting edge will continue until after the 2020 census. Democrats are working hard to devote more resources to state legislative elections in 2016 so they can reverse the redistricting advantage when line drawing happens again in 2021.

Because 2016 is a presidential election year when turnout goes up dramatically, especially among the Democratic-friendly voting block, Democrats are optimistic that they can turn around their decline in legislatures and stop Republicans from eclipsing their all-time numbers of legislative seats. That peak happened in the 1920 election when Warren Harding won the White House, and over 4,350 of the nation's legislators were Republicans. Republicans will need to win about 200 more seats in 2016 to break the record. Democrats have their work cut out for them.

About the Author

Tim Storey is director of leaders services at the Denver, Colo.-based National Conference of State Legislatures. He specializes in elections and redistricting, as well as legislative organization and management. He staffed NCSL's Redistricting and Elections Committee for more than 20 years and has authored numerous articles on the topics of elections and redistricting. Every two years, he leads NCSL's StateVote project to track and analyze legislative election results. He graduated from Mars Hill College in North Carolina and received his master's degree from the University of Colorado's Graduate School of Public Affairs.

Building Trust through Civil Discourse

By Ted Celeste

"How do I begin to trust someone and believe that we can work together, after a campaign season in which we have spent all our energy beating each other up?"

—from a legislator in Next Generation Maine workshop

The half-day introductory workshop established by The National Institute for Civil Discourse entitled, "Building Trust through Civil Discourse," was an outgrowth of an effort by The Council of State Governments Midwest, which brought together two legislators from different political backgrounds and different states for a workshop at its annual regional conference in Cleveland, Ohio, in July 2012. Rep. Ted Celeste, a Democrat from Columbus, Ohio, and Rep. Scott Raecker, a Republican from Urbandale, Iowa, teamed up to facilitate this first session for legislators from the Midwest region. CSG promoted the session in its materials about the annual conference, but did not have any idea how much interest there might be in the program.

Scheduled at the end of a day filled with many policy discussions, and immediately preceding receptions and the main gala event, organizers anticipated that perhaps 25 or 30 legislators might attend. The room was set up for 50. By the time the last person filtered into the room, more than 75 people were in attendance. The response was overwhelmingly positive, and the rest, as they say, is history.

A group of Ohio legislators who attended the session met afterward and decided they would like to have a similar but extended session just for Ohio legislators. Celeste teamed up with The National Institute for Civil Discourse and CSG to prepare an extended half-day workshop for the group in December 2012. Once again, Celeste and Raecker co-facilitated the program for 15 Ohio legislators. From this early effort, the institute created a program called Next Generation, which offers the half-day workshop to legislators around the country.

In 2013, upon his departure from the Ohio legislature, Celeste put in place a plan to support and market the workshop program for the institute and to develop a strategy for building a core group of legislators who would be trained as facilitators for future workshops. During 2013, three other states held workshops—Nebraska, Pennsylvania and Washington.

The first facilitator training for the workshops was held in January 2014 at the O'Connor House

in Phoenix. Former U.S. Supreme Court Justice Sandra Day O'Connor had donated her home to the state for purposes such as this.

"NCID provides an opportunity through facilitation for legislators (and legislatures) to enhance responsible governance. It is a catalyst for building trust across ideological barriers. The facilitator training in which I participated confirmed that desire for responsible governance is strongly shared across the political spectrum. Building Trust through Civil Discourse creates the venue for legislators to identify practices that undermine good governance and to identify and act on ways to improve."

—from one of our facilitators, a Wisconsin state senator

In March 2014, 39 legislators—the largest group to participate in one of the workshops—gathered in Maine. By this time, the workshop format and agenda had been through a few revisions and participants were asked to provide advice and guidance on how to make it better. The number of interested legislators who participated in the workshop and were interested in being trained to be facilitators grew quickly. And the number of states that expressed an interest in holding a workshop also grew quickly.

"What can be done about a colleague who shows a lack of respect for the institution and only wants to belittle the members of the other party?"

—from a legislator in the
Washington Next Generation workshop

The introductory workshop is not meant to be a one-and-done exercise. It is designed to create a working document and road map for legislators in each state to address the present level of incivility in their body and plan specific steps for improvement. The goal is not to point fingers, but to join hands. The mission is to help create a more bipartisan approach to problem solving in each state.

Each workshop is unique, although all of them start with a definition of the ground rules participants will be governed by during the exercise. The environment within which the workshop is carried out is meant to create a safe place for meaningful and personal interaction. The co-facilitators, one Republican and one Democrat legislator, are trained to guide but not lead the dialogue. The session is very interactive and goal driven.

All of the participants have indicated the most powerful part of the workshop is an exercise called "The Political Journey." During this exercise, legislators are asked to think about the event or events in their lives that had the greatest impact on determining who they are today politically. Through this task and the sharing of personal stories, a level of communication is reached that only happens in a very safe space where trust and respect prevails. Many legislators have reported that this part of the workshop created a bond with a particular colleague from across the aisle that grew throughout their continued work in the legislature.

"After (the) 9/11 attack, I thought our community needed a public event to grieve, come together and begin healing. I called the mayor's office to see if one was planned. That started the planning. I asked a faith leader to speak, but he was not available and asked me to fill in. Soon I found myself speaking to hundreds of people about embracing difference as a way to heal—(the) start of my path to public service."

—from a legislator in the
Minnesota Next Generation workshop

As of May 2015, 220 legislators have participated in 12 in-state workshops. Several states have held a second workshop and many others have expressed an interest in having the workshop added to the newly elected legislators' orientation prior to the beginning of their session. Twenty-seven legislators or former legislators have been trained as facilitators.

The nature of the workshop changes in each state based on the state's particular partisan makeup, the desires of the individual members who participate and the level of interest in maintaining an ongoing effort. In many of the states, a working group has been formed that looks for additional opportunities to explore the area of increasing civil discourse. Some participants have looked to structural change, with a review of operating procedures within their caucuses and legislatures. Others have looked for ways to increase bipartisan social gatherings.

"Statesmanship in a free society entails a serious commitment to civil discourse, a willingness to listen to others, and a recognition of the common humanity of equal women and men who are partners together in this democratic experiment."

—from a Washington State representative

While each state is unique, a number of common themes arise as legislators discuss the present state of civility in their legislatures. Some items raised will not be easily overcome: the impact money plays in the process, the role the media plays in focusing on conflict, and the influence political strategists play in supporting negative campaigning. However, a number of issues raised by legislators in most of the states are areas where improvement can be more easily achieved: agreeing to disagree, but not being disagreeable; choosing your words carefully, respecting your colleagues, separating emotion from logic and listening to understand.

Civil discourse in the legislative arena is much more than just being nice. Many participants come to the workshop with the belief that the focus of the discussion will be on changing one's behavior. And indeed, a good part of the workshop is aimed at creating a safe space where discussion of an individual's personal views can be carried out without a fear of retribution or mocking. However, the work of the participants goes further than individual behavior.

"We can indeed work together and still disagree."

—from an Ohio representative at our first workshop

The goal statement introduced at the beginning of every workshop says participants are there to:

1. Deepen their appreciation for each other's commitment to public service;

2. Consider ways to improve the legislative environment; and

3. Determine how to work together to strengthen civil discourse in the legislature.

The session is designed to work toward a mutual understanding of the present state of civility within the legislature, identify what barriers there are to improvement, and prepare an action agenda to overcome those barriers and create a more civil environment. Clearly, as mentioned earlier, some of the barriers are deeply embedded in the political system and change will come very slowly, if at all. However, a number of suggestions have achievable goals and have been frequently mentioned in all of the states where workshops have been held.

One of the most common suggestions for improvement is the need for more opportunities for bipartisan social interaction. Legislators often have been isolated within their party's caucus events and have little time to spend with legislators from across the aisle. Indeed, in many states this is frowned upon. There are many reasons given for the lack of bipartisan discourse, but a genuine desire exists for creating more opportunities for it to occur.

Where it is allowed, bipartisan joint lead cosponsorship of legislation has been mentioned as another area that can be expanded to improve the level of civil discourse. Several participants in the workshops have joined with their counterparts on the other side of the aisle—whom they met and interacted with in the workshops—to create legislation of common interest. In several cases, this has led to multiple pieces of new legislation.

Another suggestion made during several workshops was introducing a program to visit the district of a colleague from the other party. Perhaps even holding a town meeting in that district to learn firsthand from the constituents in another's district. This has generated interest from outside advocacy groups to the extent that they are prepared to help facilitate such events.

"I enjoyed the workshop very much. I thought we did well. It became clear that we still have a ways to go. To me, there needs to be a core group going forward that focuses on creating events where people can mingle and get to know each other. I heard a lot of good ideas and if I am lucky enough to return, will take this on as Next Generation a mission."

—from a convenor of the first Maine workshop

The introductory workshop has generated much interest in states where it has been held, and more states are considering bringing it to their legislatures. Additional modules have been developed that are aimed at the particular interests of skill development identified by the workshop participants. These include value-based negotiating skills training, conflict management tools, advanced inquiry skills and improv games for problem solving.

Much of the The National Institute for Civil Discourse's work with state legislators has been developed with the thought in mind that states are the training ground for our national political leaders. More than 50 percent of our U.S. representatives and senators come from state houses around the country. The Next Generation program for legislators will continue to develop modules for in-state workshops and provide the network of trained legislators to move up to the next level of service. Armed with the tools of effective communication skills and a stronger sense of finding common ground, this new generation of national leaders will be well positioned to help change the dysfunctional culture found today in Congress.

As some observers watch the unfolding of this effort, expressing skepticism and concern that the process is meant to eliminate strong partisan political beliefs and can lead to participants finding challenges for their seats from the extremes in their parties, more and more pressure is coming from the public and the press to find ways to find common ground and solve the difficult problems facing our states and nation.

"Finally, some Ohio politicians are talking about creating civility, instead of practicing incivility"

—editorial from the August 27, 2013 issue of The (Cleveland) Plain Dealer

About the Author

Former State Rep. **Ted Celeste** is the founder and director of Next Generation, a project of the National Institute for Civil Discourse, where Celeste serves as the Director of State Programs. His goal is to inspire and support state legislators who want to promote greater understanding and better decision-making. As part of a bi-partisan team, Celeste has facilitated training for the CSG Midwest Conference and the Colorado, Maine, Massachusetts, Minnesota, Ohio, Pennsylvania, Nebraska, Vermont and Washington State Legislatures. He has also presented at the CSG BILLD leadership program in Madison, and the National CSG annual meeting in Kansas City.

Celeste served in the Ohio Legislature from 2007–2012. Known for working effectively "across the aisle" whether he was in the majority or the minority, he has lived his belief in respectful dialogue. One of the only candidates for state office who insisted on running a positive campaign, he won each of his 3 races with a comfortable majority in a swing district. He was recognized for his emphasis on civil dialogue with the John Glenn Public Policy Institute's Outstanding Public Service Award in 2011.

Table 3.1
NAMES OF STATE LEGISLATIVE BODIES AND CONVENING PLACES

State or other jurisdiction	Both bodies	Upper house	Lower house	Convening place
Alabama	Legislature	Senate	House of Representatives	State House
Alaska	Legislature	Senate	House of Representatives	State Capitol
Arizona	Legislature	Senate	House of Representatives	State Capitol
Arkansas	General Assembly	Senate	House of Representatives	State Capitol
California	Legislature	Senate	Assembly	State Capitol
Colorado	General Assembly	Senate	House of Representatives	State Capitol
Connecticut	General Assembly	Senate	House of Representatives	State Capitol
Delaware	General Assembly	Senate	House of Representatives	Legislative Hall
Florida	Legislature	Senate	House of Representatives	The Capitol
Georgia	General Assembly	Senate	House of Representatives	State Capitol
Hawaii	Legislature	Senate	House of Representatives	State Capitol
Idaho	Legislature	Senate	House of Representatives	State Capitol
Illinois	General Assembly	Senate	House of Representatives	State House
Indiana	General Assembly	Senate	House of Representatives	State House
Iowa	General Assembly	Senate	House of Representatives	State Capitol
Kansas	Legislature	Senate	House of Representatives	State Capitol
Kentucky	General Assembly	Senate	House of Representatives	State Capitol
Louisiana	Legislature	Senate	House of Representatives	State Capitol
Maine	Legislature	Senate	House of Representatives	State House
Maryland	General Assembly	Senate	House of Delegates	State House
Massachusetts	General Court	Senate	House of Representatives	State House
Michigan	Legislature	Senate	House of Representatives	State Capitol
Minnesota	Legislature	Senate	House of Representatives	State Capitol
Mississippi	Legislature	Senate	House of Representatives	State Capitol
Missouri	General Assembly	Senate	House of Representatives	State Capitol
Montana	Legislature	Senate	House of Representatives	State Capitol
Nebraska	Legislature	(a)		State Capitol
Nevada	Legislature	Senate	Assembly	Legislative Building
New Hampshire	General Court	Senate	House of Representatives	State House
New Jersey	Legislature	Senate	General Assembly	State House
New Mexico	Legislature	Senate	House of Representatives	State Capitol
New York	Legislature	Senate	Assembly	State Capitol
North Carolina	General Assembly	Senate	House of Representatives	State Legislative Building
North Dakota	Legislative Assembly	Senate	House of Representatives	State Capitol
Ohio	General Assembly	Senate	House of Representatives	State House
Oklahoma	Legislature	Senate	House of Representatives	State Capitol
Oregon	Legislative Assembly	Senate	House of Representatives	State Capitol
Pennsylvania	General Assembly	Senate	House of Representatives	Main Capitol Building
Rhode Island	General Assembly	Senate	House of Representatives	State House
South Carolina	General Assembly	Senate	House of Representatives	State House
South Dakota	Legislature	Senate	House of Representatives	State Capitol
Tennessee	General Assembly	Senate	House of Representatives	State Capitol
Texas	Legislature	Senate	House of Representatives	State Capitol
Utah	Legislature	Senate	House of Representatives	State Capitol
Vermont	General Assembly	Senate	House of Representatives	State House
Virginia	General Assembly	Senate	House of Delegates	State Capitol
Washington	Legislature	Senate	House of Representatives	State Capitol
West Virginia	Legislature	Senate	House of Delegates	State Capitol
Wisconsin	Legislature	Senate	Assembly (b)	State Capitol
Wyoming	Legislature	Senate	House of Representatives	State Capitol
Dist. of Columbia	Council of the District of Columbia	(a)		Council Chamber
American Samoa	Legislature	Senate	House of Representatives	Maota Fono
Guam	Legislature	(a)		Congress Building
No. Mariana Islands	Legislature	Senate	House of Representatives	Civic Center Building
Puerto Rico	Legislative Assembly	Senate	House of Representatives	The Capitol
U.S. Virgin Islands	Legislature	(a)		Capitol Building

Source: The Council of State Governments, Directory I—Elective Officials 2010.
Key:
(a) Unicameral legislature. Except in the District of Columbia, members go by the title Senator.
(b) Members of the lower house go by the title Representative.

Table 3.2
LEGISLATIVE SESSIONS: LEGAL PROVISIONS

State or other jurisdiction	Regular sessions				Special sessions		
	Legislature convenes			Limitation on length of session (a)	Legislature may call	Legislature may determine subject	Limitation on length of session
	Year	Month	Day				
Alabama	Annual	Jan. Mar. Feb.	2nd Tues. (b) 1st Tues. (c) 1st Tues. (d)(e)	30 L in 105 C	No	Yes (f)	12 L in 30 C
Alaska	Annual	Jan.	3rd Tues. (g)	121 C; 90 Statutory (g)	By petition, 2/3 members, each house	Yes	30 C
Arizona	Annual	Jan.	2nd Mon.	(h)	By petition, 2/3 members, each house	Yes	None
Arkansas	Annual	Jan. Feb.	2nd Mon. 2nd Mon.	60 C (i) 30 C (i)	No	No	None (j)
California	Biennium (k)	Jan.	1st Mon. (d)	None	No	No	None
Colorado	Annual	Jan.	No later than 2nd Wed.	120 C	By petition, 2/3 members, each house	Yes (l)	None
Connecticut	Annual	Jan. (odd years) Feb. (even years)	Wed. after 1st Mon. (odd years) Wed. after 1st Mon. (even years)	(m)	By petition, majority, each house (n)	Yes	None
Delaware	Biennium	Jan.	2nd Tues.	June 30	Joint call, presiding officers, both houses	Yes	None
Florida	Annual	Mar.	1st Tues after 1st Mon. (o)	60 C (i)	Joint call, presiding officers, both houses or by petition	Yes	20 C (zz)
Georgia	Annual	Jan.	2nd Mon.	40 L	By petition, 3/5 members, each house	No (p)	40 L
Hawaii	Annual	Jan.	3rd Wed.	60 L (i)	By petition, 2/3 members, each house (uu)	Yes	30 L (i)
Idaho	Annual	Jan.	Mon. on or nearest 9th day	None	No	No	20 C
Illinois	Biennium	Jan.	2nd Wed.	None (q)	Joint call, presiding officers, both houses; Governor also may call	Yes	None
Indiana	Annual	Jan.	2nd Mon. (r)	odd–61 C or Apr. 29; even–30 C or Mar. 14	No	Yes	30 L or 40 C
Iowa	Annual	Jan.	2nd Mon.	None	By petition, 2/3 members, each house	Yes	None
Kansas	Annual	Jan.	2nd Mon.	odd–None; even–90 C (i)	Petition to governor of 2/3 members, each house	Yes	None
Kentucky	Annual	Jan.	1st Tues. after 1st Mon.	even–60 L; odd–30 L (s)	No	No	None
Louisiana	Annual	Mar. (even years) Apr. (odd years)	2nd Mon. (even and odd years)	even–60 L in 85 C; odd–45 L in 60 C	By petition, majority, each house	Yes	30 C
Maine	(t)	Dec. (even years) Jan. (subsequent even year)	1st Wed. (quadrennial election year) Wed. after 1st Tues.	Calendar days set by statute (u)	Joint call, presiding officers of both houses with the consent of a majority of the members of each political party	Yes	None
Maryland	Annual	Jan.	2nd Wed.	90 C	By petition, majority, each house	Yes	30 C
Massachusetts	Biennium	Jan.	1st Wed.	(v)	By petition (w)	Yes	None
Michigan	Annual	Jan.	2nd Wed.	None	No	No	None
Minnesota	Biennium	Jan.	1st Tues. after 1st Mon.(odd years)	120 L	No (x)	Yes	None
Mississippi	Annual	Jan.	Tues. after 1st Mon.	125 C (y); 90 C (y)	No	No	None

See footnotes at end of table.

LEGISLATIVE SESSIONS: LEGAL PROVISIONS — Continued

State or other jurisdiction	Regular sessions				Special sessions		
	Legislature convenes			Limitation on length of session (a)	Legislature may call	Legislature may determine subject	Limitation on length of session
	Year	Month	Day				
Missouri...........	Annual	Jan.	Wed. after 1st Mon.	May 30	By petition, 3/4 members, each house	Yes (l)	30 C (z)
Montana............	Biennial–odd year	Jan.	1st Mon. (vv)	90 L	By petition, majority, each house (ww)	Yes	None
Nebraska..........	Annual	Jan.	Wed. after 1st Mon.	odd–90 L; even–60 L	By petition, 2/3 members, each house	Yes	None
Nevada.............	Biennial–odd year	Feb.	1st Mon.	120 C	By petition, 2/3 members, each house	Yes (aa)	20 C (aa)
New Hampshire	Annual	Jan.	Wed. after 1st Tues.	45 L	By petition, (xx)	Yes	15 L (bb)
New Jersey	Biennium	Jan.	2nd Tues. of even year	None	By petition, majority, each house (cc)	Yes	None
New Mexico	Annual	Jan.	3rd Tues.	odd–60 C; even–30 C	By petition, 3/5 members, each house (l)	Yes (l)	30 C
New York	Annual	Jan. (dd)	Wed. after 1st Mon.	None	By petition, 2/3 members, each house	Yes (l)	None
North Carolina......	(cc)	Jan.	3rd Wed. after 2nd Mon. (odd years)	None	By petition, 3/5 members, each house	Yes	None
North Dakota........	Biennial–odd year	Jan.	First Tues. after the 3rd day in Jan.	80 L in the biennium	No	Yes	None
Ohio................	Biennium	Jan.	1st Mon. (gg)	None	Joint call, presiding officers, both houses	Yes	None
Oklahoma...........	Annual	Feb.	1st Mon.	last Fri. in May	By petition, 2/3 members, each house	Yes	None
Oregon..............	Annual	Feb.	1st Mon.	(ff)	By petition, majority, each house	Yes	None
Pennsylvania	Biennium (hh)	Jan.	1st Tues.	None	Governor may call	No	None
Rhode Island.........	Annual	Jan.	1st Tues.	None	Joint call, presiding officers, both houses	Yes	None
South Carolina......	Biennium	Jan.	2nd Tues.	(ii)	By vote, 2/3 members, each house	Yes	None
South Dakota........	Annual	Jan.	2nd Tues.	odd–40 L; even–40 L	By petition, 2/3 members, each house	Yes (jj)	None
Tennessee	Biennium (kk)	Jan.	2nd Tues.	90 L (ll)	By petition, 2/3 members, each house	Yes	30 L (ll)
Texas...............	Biennial–odd year	Jan.	2nd Tues.	140 C	No	Yes	30 C
Utah................	Annual	Jan.	4th Mon.	45 C	No	No	30 C
Vermont............	Annual (yy)	Jan.	Wed. after 1st Mon. (yy)	None	No	Yes	None
Virginia.............	Annual	Jan.	2nd Wed.	odd–30 C (i); even–60 C (i)	(tt)	Yes	None (mm)
Washington.........	Annual	Jan.	2nd Mon.	odd–105 C; even–60 C	By vote, 2/3 members, each house	Yes	30 C
West Virginia.......	Annual	Jan	2nd Wed.	60 C (i)	By petition, 3/5 members, each house	Yes (l)	None
Wisconsin	Biennium	Jan.	1st Mon.	None	(nn)	No	None
Wyoming	Biennium	Jan. (odd years); Feb. (even years)	2nd Tues. (odd years); 2nd Mon. (even years)	odd–40 L; even–20 L; biennium–60 L	By petition, majority members, each house	Yes	20 L (aaa)
Dist. of Columbia...	(oo)	Jan.	2nd day	None	...	...	...
American Samoa ...	Annual	Jan. / July	2nd Mon. / 2nd Mon.	45 L / 45 L	No	No	None
Guam...............	(pp)	Jan.	2nd Mon.	None (pp)	Only the governor may call	No	None (pp)

See footnotes at end of table.

LEGISLATIVE SESSIONS: LEGAL PROVISIONS—Continued

State or other jurisdiction	Regular sessions				Special sessions		
	Legislature convenes			Limitation on length of session (a)	Legislature may call	Legislature may determine subject	Limitation on length of session
	Year	Month (rr)	Day (d)(rr)				
No. Mariana Islands	Annual	(rr)	(d)(rr)	90 L (qq)	Upon request of presiding officers, both houses	Yes (j)	10 C
Puerto Rico	Annual (rr)	Jan. / Aug.	2nd Mon. / 3rd Mon.	5 mo. / 4 mo.	No	No	20 C
U.S. Virgin Islands	Annual	Jan. (ss)	2nd Mon. (ss)	None	No, governor calls	No	None

Source: The Council of State Governments' survey November 2014 and state websites 2015.

Key:

Annual—holds legislative sessions every year.

Biennial—odd year—holds legislative sessions every other year.

Biennium—holds legislative sessions in a two-year term of activity.

C—Calendar day

L—Legislative day (in some states called a session day or workday; definition may vary slightly, however, generally refers to any day on which either house of legislature is in session).

(a) Applies to each year unless otherwise indicated.

(b) General election year (quadrennial election year).

(c) In first year after quadrennial election.

(d) Legal provision for organizational session prior to stated convening date. Alabama—in the year after quadrennial election, second Tuesday in January for 10 C. California—in the even-numbered general election year, first Monday in December for an organizational session, recess until the first Monday in January of the odd-numbered year. No. Mariana Islands—in year after general election, second Monday in January.

(e) In second and third years of quadrennium.

(f) By 2/3 vote each house.

(g) Convening date is statutory. Length of session is 121 calendar days, 90 by statute.

(h) No constitutional or statutory provision; however, by legislative rule regular sessions shall be adjourned sine die no later than Saturday of the week during which the 100th day from the beginning of each regular session falls. The Speaker/President may by declaration authorize the extension of the session for a period not to exceed seven additional days. Thereafter the session can be extended only by a majority vote of the House/Senate.

(i) Session may be extended by vote of members in both houses. Arkansas—2/3 vote to extend up to 75 days; 3/4 vote to go beyond 75 days. Even-year fiscal session may be extended one time only by a 3/4 vote, with the extention no more than 15 C days. Florida—3/5 vote, session may be extended by vote of members in each house. Hawaii—petition of 2/3 membership for maximum 15-day extension. Kansas—2/3 vote. Virginia—2/3 vote for 30 C extension. West Virginia—may be extended by the governor.

(j) After governor's business has been disposed of, members may remain in session up to 15 C days by a 2/3 vote of both houses.

(k) Regular sessions begin after general election, in December of even-numbered year. In California, in the even-numbered general election year, first Monday in December for an organizational session, recess until the first Monday in January of the odd-numbered year.

(l) Only if legislature convenes itself. In New York, special sessions may also be called by the governor. Legislature may determine subject only if it has convened itself. In New Mexico, special sessions may only be called by the governor and subjects are limited to issues included in governor's proclamation; extraordinary session may only be called by the legislature and have no limitations on subject.

(m) Odd-numbered years—not later than Wednesday after first Monday in June; even-numbered years—not later than Wednesday after first Monday in May.

(n) Adoption of a joint resolution by a majority of each house.

(o) A regular session of the legislature shall convene on the first Tuesday after the first Monday of each odd-numbered year, and on the first Tuesday after the first Monday in March, or such other date as may be fixed by law, of each even-numbered year.

(p) If three-fifths of the General Assembly certifies to governor that an emergency exists, governor must convene a special session for all purposes.

(q) Constitution encourages adjournment by May 31.

(r) Legislators may reconvene at any time after organizational meeting; however, second Monday in January is the final date by which regular session must be in process.

(s) During the odd-year session, the members convene for four days, then break until February.

(t) Regular session begins after general election in even-numbered years. Session which begins in December of general election year runs into the following year (odd-numbered); second session begins in next even-numbered year. The second session is limited to budgetary matters; legislation in the governor's call; emergency legislation; legislation referred to committee for study.

(u) Statutory adjournment for the First Regular Session (beginning in December of even-numbered years and continuing into the following odd-numbered year) is the third Wednesday of June; statutory adjournment for the Second Regular Session (beginning in January of the subsequent even-numbered year) is the third Wednesday in April. The statutes provide for up to two extensions of up to five legislative days each for each session.

(v) Legislative rules say formal business must be concluded by Nov. 15th of the 1st session in the biennium, or by July 31st of the 2nd session for the biennium.

(w) Joint rules provide for the submission of a written statement requesting special session by a specified number of members of each chamber.

(x) Special session is called by the governor.

(y) 90 C sessions every year, except the first year of a gubernatorial administration during which the legislative session runs for 125 C.

(z) 30 C if called by legislature; 60 C if called by governor.

(aa) Legislature may determine the subject if it calls itself into special session. Special sessions are limited to 20 calendar days except in cases of impeachment of state and judicial officers or expulsion of a member of the Legislature.

(bb) Limitation is on legislative pay and mileage.

(cc) Or by joint call, presiding officers, both houses.

(dd) Regular sessions begin on the first Wednesday following the first Monday of the new legislative term (commencing the first of the year), and lasts until the legislature completes its business and adjourns sine die. However, over the past several years, both houses have adopted the tactic of declaring a recess at the call of the leaders, in order to facilitate easy recall of the legislature to override vetoes, etc. Over time the custom has become to formally adjourn both houses just before the new session opens. This leads to the rather interesting convention that when the governor calls the legislature into session, it is considered "special" or "executive," even though the regular session is ongoing.

LEGISLATIVE SESSIONS: LEGAL PROVISIONS — Continued

(ee) Legal provision for session in odd-numbered year; however, legislature may divide, and in practice has divided, to meet in even-numbered years as well.

(ff) The Oregon Constitution establishes a maximum of 160 calendar days for an odd-year regular session and a maximum of 35 calendar days for an even-year regular session. Each regular session may be extended in five-day increments by the affirmative vote of two-thirds of the members of each house.

(gg) Unless Monday is a legal holiday; in second year, the General Assembly convenes on the same date.

(hh) Sessions are two years and begin on the 1st Tuesday of January of the odd-numbered year. Session ends on November 30 of the even-numbered year. Each calendar year receives its own legislative number.

(ii) The regular session ends the first Thursday in June; it can be extended with a two-thirds majority vote.

(jj) Legislators must address topic for which the special session was called.

(kk) Each General Assembly convenes for a First and Second Regular Session over a two-year period.

(ll) 90 legislative days over a two-year period. During special sessions members will be paid up to 30 legislative days; further days will be without pay or per diem.

(mm) No limitation, but the convening of the new General Assembly following an election would by operation end the special session.

(nn) The Legislature may call itself into Extraordinary Session on any subject by a majority vote of the organizing committees of each house, by joint resolution, or by a petition of a majority of each house. Only the governor may call a special session.

(oo) Each Council period begins on January 2 of each odd-numbered year and ends on January 1 of the following odd-numbered year.

(pp) Legislature meets on the first Monday of each month following its initial session in January. One legislative day or one special session day may become several calendar days. Special sessions may address only one subject.

(qq) 60 L before April 1 and 30 L after July 31.

(rr) Legislature meets twice a year. During general election years, the legislature only convenes on the January session.

(ss) The legislature convenes in January on the second Monday; March, June and September, the third Wednesday.

(tt) The Constitution provides that the governor must call a special session upon "application" of 2/3 of the members of each house.

(uu) Governor may call both houses of the legislature or the Senate alone into special session. Also, upon a 2/3 affirmative vote, the Senate may call itself into special session to consider judicial nominations.

(vv) If the first Monday falls on New Years Day, the Legislature convenes on the first Wednesday.

(ww) Majority of the total Legislature; i.e., 76 members of the combined 100-member House and 50-member Senate.

(xx) Petition filed with Secretary of State signed by not less than 50 members of House (not more than 10 from the same county) and not less than eight members of the Senate.

(yy) Constitutionally the sessions are convened biennially in the odd year. Since the late 1960s a second-year adjourned session has been held. Adjourned session date is legislatively set or a date during the first 10 days of January.

(zz) Session may be extended by 3/5 vote Per s. 11.011, Florida Statutes, if 20 percent of the members of the Legislature certify in writing that conditions warrant convening a special session. The Department of State shall, within seven days after receiving the required number of certificates, poll the members. Upon affirmative vote of 3/5 of the members of both houses, the Department of State shall fix the day and hour for convening the special session.

(aaa) Twenty legislative days if Legislature calls themselves. Unlimited if governor calls special session.

Table 3.3
THE LEGISLATORS: NUMBERS, TERMS, AND PARTY AFFILIATIONS: 2015

State or other jurisdiction	Senate						House/Assembly						Senate and House/ Assembly totals
	Democrats	Republicans	Other	Vacancies	Total	Term	Democrats	Republicans	Other	Vacancies	Total	Term	
State and territory totals	882	1,100	16	4	2,069*	...	2,378	3,066	34	4	5,502	...	7,571*
State totals.....................	833	1,082	4	4	1,972*	...	2,350	3,036	21	4	5,411	...	7,383*
Alabama..........................	8	26	1 (b)	...	35	4	33	72	...	...	105	4	140
Alaska.............................	6	14	...	...	20	4	16	23	...	1	40	2	60
Arizona...........................	13	17	...	...	30	2	24	36	...	...	60	2	90
Arkansas.........................	11	23	...	1	35	4	36	64	...	...	100	2	135
California	26	14	...	...	40	4	52	28	...	...	80	2	120
Colorado.........................	17	18	...	...	35	4	34	31	...	...	65	2	100
Connecticut....................	21	15	...	...	36	2	87	64	...	...	151	2	187
Delaware	12	9	...	...	21	4	25	16	...	...	41	2	62
Florida............................	14	25	...	1	40	4	38	80	...	2	120	2	160
Georgia...........................	18	38	...	...	56	2	59	120	1 (b)	...	180	2	236
Hawaii.............................	24	1	...	...	25	4	43	8	...	...	51	2	76
Idaho..............................	7	28	...	...	35	2	14	56	...	...	70	2	105
Illinois............................	39	20	...	...	59	(a)	71	47	...	...	118	2	177
Indiana............................	10	40	...	...	50	4	29	71	...	...	100	2	150
Iowa	26	23	...	1	50	4	43	57	...	...	100	2	150
Kansas	8	32	...	...	40	4	28	97	...	...	125	2	165
Kentucky	11	26	...	1	38	4	54	46	...	...	100	2	138
Louisiana........................	13	26	...	...	39	4	44	59	2 (b)	...	105	4	144
Maine..............................	14	21	...	...	35	2	79	68	4 (c)	...	151	2	186
Maryland	33	14	...	...	47	4	91	50	...	...	141	4	188
Massachusetts	34	6	...	...	40	2	125	35	...	...	160	2	200
Michigan.........................	12	26	...	...	38	4	47	63	...	...	110	2	148
Minnesota.......................	39 (d)	28	...	...	67	4	62 (d)	72	...	...	134	2	201
Mississippi.....................	20	32	...	...	52	4	56	66	...	...	122	4	174
Missouri..........................	9	25	...	...	34	4	44	118	...	1	163	2	197
Montana	21	29	...	...	50	4	41	59	...	...	100	2	150
Nebraska	..Nonpartisan election..			...	49	4	.............................Unicameral						49
Nevada............................	10	11	...	...	21	4	17	25	...	...	42	2	63
New Hampshire	14	10	...	...	24	2	160	239	1 (b)	...	400	2	424
New Jersey	24	16	...	...	40	4 (f)	48	32	...	...	80	2	120
New Mexico	25	17	...	...	42	4	33	37	...	...	70	2	112
New York.........................	31	32	...	...	63	2	106	44	...	...	150	2	213
North Carolina...............	16	34	...	...	50	2	46	74	...	...	120	2	170
North Dakota..................	15	32	...	...	47	4	23	71	...	...	94	4	141
Ohio	10	23	...	...	33	4	34	65	...	...	99	2	132
Oklahoma.......................	8	40	...	...	48	4	29	72	...	...	101	2	149
Oregon............................	18	12	...	...	30	4	35	25	...	...	60	2	90
Pennsylvania	20	30	...	...	50	4	84	119	...	...	203	2	253
Rhode Island...................	32	5	1 (b)	...	38	2	63	11	1 (b)	...	75	2	113
South Carolina...............	18	28	...	...	46	4	46	78	...	...	124	2	170
South Dakota..................	8	27	...	...	35	2	12	58	...	...	70	2	105
Tennessee	6	27	...	...	33	4	26	73	...	...	99	2	132
Texas	11	20	...	...	31	4	52	98	...	...	150	2	181
Utah	5	24	...	...	29	4	12	63	...	...	75	2	104
Vermont..........................	19	9	2 (q)	...	30	2	85	53	12 (g)	...	150	2	180
Virginia...........................	19	21	...	...	40	4	32	68	...	...	100	2	140
Washington.....................	24	25	...	...	49	4	51	47	...	...	98	2	147
West Virginia..................	16	18	...	...	34	4	36	64	...	...	100	2	134
Wisconsin	14	19	...	...	33 (h)	4	36	63	...	...	99 (h)	2	132
Wyoming	4	26	...	...	30	4	9	51	...	...	60	2	90
Dist. of Columbia (i)	11	0	2 (b)	...	13	4	.............................Unicameral.............................						13
American Samoa	.........Nonpartisan election..........				18 (j)	4	.........Nonpartisan election				20 (j)	2	38
Guam	9	6	...	...	15	2	.............................Unicameral						15
No. Mariana Islands	...	4	5 (k)	...	9	4	...	7	13 (b)	...	20	2	29
Puerto Rico	18 (m)	8 (n)	1 (l)	...	27 (p)	4	28 (m)	23 (n)	...	...	51 (p)	4	78
U.S. Virgin Islands.........	11	...	4 (o)	...	15	2	.............................Unicameral.............................						15

See footnotes at end of table.

THE LEGISLATORS: NUMBERS, TERMS, AND PARTY AFFILIATIONS: 2015—Continued

Source: The Council of State Governments, January 2015.

*Note: Senate and combined body (Senate and House/Assembly) totals include Unicameral legislatures.

Key:

... — Does not apply

(a) The entire Senate comes up for election in every year ending in "2" with districts based on the latest decennial Census. Senate districts are divided into three groups. One group elects senators for terms of four years, four years and two years;the second group for terms of four years, two years and four years; the third group for terms of two years, four years, and four years.

(b) Independent.

(c) Two unenrolled and two tribal representatives.

(d) Democratic-Farmer-Labor.

(e) Independence Party.

(f) All 40 Senate terms are on a ten year cycle which is made up of a two-year term, followed by two consecutive four-year terms, beginning after the decennial census.

(g) Independent (6); Progressive (6).

(h) All House seats contested in even-numbered years; In the Senate 17 seats contested in gubernatorial years; 16 seats contested in presidential years.

(i) Council of the District of Columbia.

(j) Senate: senators are not elected by popular vote, but by county council chiefs. House: 21 seats; 20 are elected by popular vote and one appointed, non-voting delegate from Swains Island.

(k) Senate: Covenant (1); Independent (4). House: Covenant (2); Independent (11).

(l) Puerto Rican Independence Party.

(m) Popular Democratic Party.

(n) New Progressive Party.

(o) Independent (3); Independent Citizens Movement (1).

(p) Constitutionally, the Senate consists of 27 seats and the House consists of 51 seats. However, extra at-large seats can be granted to the opposition to limit any party's control to 2/3.

(q) Progressive Party.

Table 3.4
MEMBERSHIP TURNOVER IN THE LEGISLATURES: 2014

State or other jurisdiction	Senate			House/Assembly		
	Total number of members	Number of membership changes	Percentage change of total	Total number of members	Number of membership changes	Percentage change of total
Alabama	35	6	17	105	28	27
Alaska	20	2	10	40	7	18
Arizona	30	8	27	60	20	33
Arkansas	35	4	11	100	41	41
California	40	11	28	80	27	34
Colorado	35	10	29	65	21	14
Connecticut	36	8	22	151	32	2
Delaware	21	1	5	41	5	12
Florida	40	0	0	120	25	21
Georgia	56	10	18	180	14	8
Hawaii	25	3	12	51	7	14
Idaho	35	4	11	70	15	21
Illinois	59	2	3	118	17	14
Indiana	50	8	16	100	9	9
Iowa	50	5	10	100	12	12
Kansas	40	0	0	125	19	7
Kentucky	38	6	16	100	11	11
Louisiana	39	0	0	105	0	0
Maine	35	15	43	151	67	44
Maryland	47	11	23	141	57	40
Massachusetts	40	5	13	160	20	13
Michigan	38	10	26	110	44	40
Minnesota	67	0	0	134	25	19
Mississippi	52	1	2	122	0	0
Missouri	34	6	18	163	33	20
Montana	50	17	34	100	36	36
Nebraska	49	18	37	............Unicameral............		
Nevada	21	3	14	42	17	40
New Hampshire	24	5	21	400	161	40
New Jersey	40	0	0	80	0	0
New Mexico	42	0	0	70	17	24
New York	63	9	14	150	19	13
North Carolina	50	9	18	120	16	13
North Dakota	47	4	9	94	12	13
Ohio	33	3	9	99	27	27
Oklahoma	48	10	21	101	22	22
Oregon	30	2	7	60	15	25
Pennsylvania	50	8	16	203	27	13
Rhode Island	38	3	8	75	14	19
South Carolina	46	1	2	124	13	10
South Dakota	35	11	31	70	22	31
Tennessee	33	7	21	99	16	16
Texas	31	5	16	150	24	16
Utah	29	3	10	75	15	20
Vermont	30	4	13	150	35	23
Virginia	40	1	3	100	0	0
Washington	49	4	8	98	13	13
West Virginia	34	10	29	100	33	33
Wisconsin	33	6	18	99	25	25
Wyoming	30	3	10	60	14	23
Dist. of Columbia	13	3	23	............Unicameral............		
American Samoa	18	N.A.	N.A.	20	10	50
Guam	15	4	27	............Unicameral............		
No. Mariana Islands	9	6	67	18	8	44
Puerto Rico	27	0	0	51	0	0
U.S. Virgin Islands	15	7	47	............Unicameral............		

Source: The Council of State Governments, January, 2015.

Table 3.5
THE LEGISLATORS: QUALIFICATIONS FOR ELECTION

State or other jurisdiction	House/Assembly					Senate				
	Minimum age	U.S. citizen (years) (a)	State resident (years) (b)	District resident (years)	Qualified voter (years)	Minimum age	U.S. citizen (years) (a)	State resident (years) (b)	District resident (years)	Qualified voter (years)
Alabama	21	⋮	3 (c)	1	⋮	25	⋮	3 (c)	1	⋮
Alaska	21	★	3	1	★	25	★	3	1	★
Arizona	25	★	3	1	⋮	25	★	3	1	⋮
Arkansas	21	★	2	1	★	25	★	2	1	★
California	18	3	3	1	★	18	3	3	1	★
Colorado	25	★	1	1	★	25	★	1	1	★
Connecticut	18	★	★	★	★	18	★	★	★	★
Delaware	24	★	3	1	★	27	★	3 (c)	1	★
Florida	21	⋮	2	2	⋮	21	⋮	2	2	⋮
Georgia	21	★	2 (o)	1	★	25	★	2 (c)	1	★
Hawaii	18	★	3	★	★	18	★	3	★	★
Idaho	21	★	1	1	★	21	★	1	1	★
Illinois	21	★	2	2 (d)	⋮	21	2	2	2 (d)	⋮
Indiana	21	★	2	1	★	25	2	2	1	★
Iowa	21	★	1	60 days	⋮	25	★	1	60 days	⋮
Kansas	18	★	★(c)	★	★	18	★	★(c)	★	★
Kentucky	24	★	2 (c)	1	★	30	★	6 (c)	1	★
Louisiana	18	5	2	1	★	18	5	2	1	★
Maine	21	⋮	1	3 mo.	⋮	25	⋮	1	3 mo.	⋮
Maryland	21	⋮	1 (c)	6 mo. (e)	⋮	25	★	1 (c)	6 mo. (e)	⋮
Massachusetts	18	U	⋮	1	★	18	⋮	5	5	★
Michigan	21	★	★	(f)	★	21	★	★	(f)	★
Minnesota	18	⋮	1	6 mo.	★	21	⋮	1	6 mo.	★
Mississippi	21	⋮	4 (c)	2	★	25	⋮	4 (c)	2	★
Missouri	24	★	★	1	2	30	★	★	1	3
Montana	18	⋮	1	6 mo. (g)	U	18	⋮	1	6 mo. (g)	⋮
Nebraska	U	U	U	U	U	21	★	★(c)	1	★
Nevada	21	★	1 (c)	30 days (h)	★	21	★	1 (c)	30 days (h)	★
New Hampshire	18	⋮	2 (c)	1	★	30	⋮	7 (c)	1	★
New Jersey	21	★	2 (c)	1	★	30	★	2 (c)	1	★
New Mexico	21	★	★	★	★	25	★	★	★	★
New York	18	★	5	1 (i)	★	18	★	5	1 (i)	★
North Carolina	21	⋮	⋮	1	⋮	25	⋮	2	1	⋮
North Dakota	18	⋮	1	★	★	18	⋮	1	★	★
Ohio	18	★	30 days	1 (o)	★	18	★	30 days	1 (o)	★
Oklahoma	21	★	★(c)	★	★	25	★	★(c)	★	★
Oregon	21	★	⋮	1	★	21	★	★	1	★
Pennsylvania	21	★	4 (c)	1	⋮	25	⋮	4 (c)	1	⋮
Rhode Island	18	★	30 days	30 days	★	18	★	30 days	30 days	★
South Carolina	21	⋮	⋮	★(j)	⋮	25	⋮	⋮	★(j)	⋮

See footnotes at end of table.

THE LEGISLATORS: QUALIFICATIONS FOR ELECTION—Continued

State or other jurisdiction	House/Assembly					Senate				
	Minimum age	U.S. citizen (years) (a)	State resident (years) (b)	District resident (years)	Qualified voter (years)	Minimum age	U.S. citizen (years) (a)	State resident (years) (b)	District resident (years)	Qualified voter (years)
South Dakota	21	★	2	★	★	21	★	2	★	★
Tennessee	21	★	(c)	1	★	30	★	3	1	★
Texas	21	★	2	1	★	26	★	5	1	★
Utah	25	★	3 (c)	6 mo.	. . .	25	★	3 (c)	6 mo.	. . .
Vermont	18	★	2	1	. . .	18	★	2	1	. . .
Virginia	21	★	★	★	★	21	★	★	★	★
Washington	18	★	1 (c)	. . .	★	18	★	5 (c)	. . .	★
West Virginia	18	1	1	1	★	25	5	5 (c)	1	★
Wisconsin	18	★	★ (c)	★ (k)	★ (k)	25	★	★ (c)	★ (k)	★ (k)
Wyoming	21	★	★ (c)	1	★	25	★	★ (c)	1	★
Dist. of Columbia	U	U	U	U	U	18	★ (l)	1	★	★
American Samoa	25	★ (l)	5	1	U	30 (m)	★	5	1	. . .
Guam	U	U	U	U	U	25	. . .	5	. . .	★
No. Mariana Islands	21	. . .	3	(f)	★	25	. . .	5	(f)	★
Puerto Rico	25	★	2	1 (n)	. . .	30	★	2	1 (n)	. . .
U.S. Virgin Islands	U	U	U	U	U	21	. . .	3 (c)	3	★

Source: The Council of State Governments survey, November 2014 and state websites 2015.

Note: Many state constitutions have additional provisions disqualifying persons from holding office if they are convicted of a felony, bribery, perjury or other infamous crimes.

Key:

U — Unicameral legislature; members are called senators, except in District of Columbia.

★ — Formal provision; number of years not specified.

. . . — No formal provision.

(a) In some states candidate must be a U.S. citizen to be an elector, and must be an elector to run.

(b) In some states candidate must be a state resident to be an elector, and must be an elector to run.

(c) State citizenship requirement. In Tennessee—must be a citizen for three years.

(d) In the first election after a redistricting, a candidate may be elected from any district that contains a part of the district in which (s)he resided at the time of redistricting, and may be re-elected if a resident of the district (s)he represents for 18 months before re-election.

(e) If the district was established for less than six months, residency is length of establishment of district.

(f) Must be a qualified voter of the district; number of years not specified.

(g) Shall be a resident of the county if it contains one or more districts or if the district contains all or parts of more than one county.

(h) 30 days prior to close of filing for declaration of candidacy.

(i) After redistricting, candidate must have been a resident of the county in which the district is contained for one year immediately preceding election.

(j) At the time of filing.

(k) Twenty-eight days prior to election.

(l) Or U.S. national.

(m) Must be registered matai.

(n) The district legislator must live in the municipality he/she represents.

(o) One year unless absent from the district on the public business of the United States or Ohio.

Table 3.6
SENATE LEADERSHIP POSITIONS: METHODS OF SELECTION

State or other jurisdiction	President	President pro tem	Majority leader	Assistant majority leader	Majority floor leader	Assistant majority floor leader	Majority whip	Majority caucus chair	Minority leader	Assistant minority leader	Minority floor leader	Assistant minority floor leader	Minority whip	Minority caucus chair
Alabama (b)	(a)	ES	(h)						(h)					
Alaska	ES		EC				EC	EC	EC	EC			EC	EC
Arizona	ES	AP	EC				EC		EC	EC			EC	EC
Arkansas	ES	ES	EC				EC	EC	EC				EC	EC
California	(a)	ES	EC				EC	EC	EC				EC	EC
Colorado	ES	ES	EC	EC			EC	EC	EC	EC			EC	EC
Connecticut (c)	(a)	ES	AP	AP	AP	AP	AP	AP	EC	AL	AL	AL	AL	AL
Delaware	ES	ES	EC		AP		AP	AP	EC				AL	EC
Florida (mm)	EC/ES	ES	AP	AL	AP		EC		EC	AL			AL	AL
Georgia	(a)	ES	EC	AL			EC	EC	EC				EC	EC
Hawaii (d)	ES	ES(c)	EC		EC		EC	EC(f)	EC		EC		EC	EC
Idaho	(a)	(a)	EC	EC			AP/3	AP	EC	AL/5	EC	(h)	AL	AL
Illinois	ES	AP	AP	AP/5	AT	AT	AT	AP	EC		EC	(h)	(h)	EC
Indiana	(a)	ES					EC	EC	EC	EC			EC	EC
Iowa	ES	ES	EC	EC	EC		EC	EC	EC	EC			EC	EC
Kansas	ES	ES(e)	EC	EC	EC		EC	EC	EC	EC	EC		EC	EC
Kentucky (i)	ES	ES(e)	EC	EC	EC		EC	EC	EC	EC	EC		EC	EC
Louisiana	ES	ES												
Maine (ll)	ES	ES	EC	EC	(j)	(j)	(k)		EC(o)	EC	(l)	(l)	(m)	
Maryland	ES	ES	AP(n)	AP(n)	(n)	(n)	AP		EC(o)	EC	(o)		EC	EC
Massachusetts	EC	ES	AP	AP	EC(j)		EC	(p)	EC	EC	EC(l)		EC	(p)
Michigan (q)	(a)	ES(r)	EC	EC	EC	EC	EC	EC	EC	EC	EC	EC	EC	EC
Minnesota	ES	ES	EC	EC	EC	EC	EC	EC	EC	EC	EC	EC	EC	EC
Mississippi	(a)	AP	EC		EC	EC	AL		EC	EC			AL	EC
Missouri	(a)	ES			EC	EC	EC		EC	EC	EC		EC	EC
Montana	ES	ES	EC		EC(j)		EC	EC	EC	EC	EC(l)		EC	EC
Nebraska (U)(g)	(a)	ES(r)	EC					(p)	EC					(p)
Nevada (s)	(a)	ES			EC		EC	EC	EC	EC	EC		EC	EC
New Hampshire	ES	AP	AP		EC		EC	EC	EC	EC	EC		AL	AL
New Jersey	ES	ES	MA	MA	MA	MA	MA	MA	MI	MI	MI	MI	MI	MI
New Mexico	(a)	ES	EC(t)		EC(t)		EC	EC(t)	EC(t)	EC	EC		EC	EC
New York (u)	(a)	ES	(v)		AT(v)	AT(v)	AT(v)	AT(v)	EC(v)	ES	AT(v)	AT(v)	AT(v)	AL(v)
North Carolina	(a)	ES	EC		EC		EC	EC	EC	EC	EC		EC	EC
North Dakota	(a)	ES	EC	EC	ES		AL	EC	EC	AL			AL	EC
Ohio (w)(x)	ES(x)	ES	EC	MA	ES		ES	EC	ES(x)	ES			ES	MI
Oklahoma	(a)	ES	EC	EC	EC	EC	EC	EC	EC	EC	EC	EC	EC	EC
Oregon	ES	ES	EC	EC	EC	EC	EC	EC	EC	EC	EC	EC	EC	EC
Pennsylvania	ES	ES	EC	EC	EC	EC	EC	EC	EC	EC	EC	EC	EC	EC
Rhode Island (y)	ES	ES	EC	AL	EC		AL	EC	EC	AL			AL	EC
South Carolina	(a)	ES	EC		EC		AL	EC	EC	ES			AL	EC
South Dakota	(a)	ES	EC	EC	EC		EC	EC	EC	EC	EC		EC	EC
Tennessee	ES	AP	EC		EC		EC	EC	EC	EC	EC		EC	EC
Texas	(a)	ES												
Utah	ES	AL(z)	EC	EC	EC(z)	EC(z)	EC	EC	EC	EC	EC(z)	EC(z)	EC	EC(z)
Vermont	(a)	ES	EC		EC(aa)	EC(aa)	EC(aa)	EC(aa)	EC(aa)	EC	EC(aa)	EC(aa)	EC(aa)	EC(aa)

See footnotes at end of table.

SENATE LEADERSHIP POSITIONS: METHODS OF SELECTION—Continued

State or other jurisdiction	President	President pro tem	Majority leader	Assistant majority leader	Majority floor leader	Assistant majority floor leader	Majority whip	Majority caucus chair	Minority leader	Assistant minority leader	Minority floor leader	Assistant minority floor leader	Minority whip	Minority caucus chair
Virginia	(a)	ES	EC (bb)	...	EC (bb)	EC	EC	EC	EC	...	EC	EC	EC	EC
Washington (cc)	(a)	ES	EC	EC	EC	EC	EC	EC	EC	EC	EC	EC	EC	EC
West Virginia	ES	AP	AP	...	...	...	AP	...	EC	...	...	...	AL	...
Wisconsin	ES (dd)	EC	EC	EC	...	...	...	EC	EC	EC	...	...	...	EC
Wyoming	ES	ES (e)	...	...	EC	...	...	EC	EC	...	EC	...	EC	EC
Dist. of Columbia (U)	(ee)	(ff)	...	...	...	...	...	...	...	...	...	...	...	...
American Samoa	ES	ES	...	...	...	...	...	...	...	...	...	...	...	...
Guam (U)(gg)	ES (r)	ES (e)	EC	EC	EC (ii)	EC	EC	...	EC	EC	EC	EC	EC	...
No. Mariana Islands	ES (hh)	...	(hh)	...	ES (ii)	...	...	(kk)	EC (p)	...	EC (jj)	...	...	(p)
Puerto Rico	ES (p)	EC	EC	...	EC (jj)	EC	...	...	EC (p)	...	...	...	...	...
U.S. Virgin Islands (U)	ES	...	ES	...	...	...	...	...	ES	...	...	...	...	ES

Source: The Council of State Governments' survey, November 2014 and state websites 2015.

Note: In some states, the leadership positions in the Senate are not empowered by the law or by the rules of the chamber, but rather by the party members themselves. Entry following slash indicates number of individuals holding specified position.

Key:
ES — Elected or confirmed by all members of the Senate.
EC — Elected by party caucus.
AP — Appointed by president.
AT — Appointed by president pro tempore.
AL — Appointed by party leader.
MA — Elected by majority party.
MI — Elected by minority party.
(U) — Unicameral legislative body.
... — Position does not exist or is not selected on a regular basis.

(a) Lieutenant governor is president of the Senate by virtue of the office.
(b) Majority leader elected by the members of the majority party. Minority leader elected by members of the minority party. Additional leadership positions: deputy president pro tempore- appointed by Committee on Assignments and Dean of Senate- appointed by Committee on Assignments.
(c) Other position titles and methods of selection are as follows: chief deputy president pro tem (AT), deputy president pro tem (AT), assistant president pro tem (AT), Senate minority leader pro tem (AL), deputy Senate minority leader pro tem (AL), chief deputy minority leader (AL)
(d) Additional positions of president emeritus and majority policy leader (EC) exist.
(e) Official title is vice president. In Guam, vice speaker.
(f) Official title is majority caucus leader.
(g) Additional positions appointed by the majority leader: Senate Finance Committee chair, vice president pro tem, Majority Program Development Committee Chair, Majority Steering Committee chair, two assistant majority leaders, various deputies and assistants. Additional positions appoint by the minority leader: Senate Finance Committee ranking member, Minority Policy Committee chair, Minority Program Development chair, three additional minority leaders, various deputies and assistants.
(h) Appointed by minority leader.
(i) In each chamber, the membership elects chief clerk; assistant clerk; enrolling clerk; sergeant-at-arms; doorkeeper; janitor; cloakroom keeper; and pages.
(j) Same position as majority leader.

(k) Same position as assistant majority leader.
(l) Same position as assistant minority leader.
(m) Same position as assistant minority leader.
(n) Majority leader also serves as majority floor leader; deputy majority leader is official title and serves as assistant majority floor leader. There is also an assistant deputy majority leader, a majority whip, deputy majority whip, and two assistant majority whips.
(o) Minority leader also serves as the minority floor leader.
(p) President and minority floor leader are also caucus chairs. In Puerto Rico, president and minority leader. In Oregon, majority leader and minority leader.
(q) Senate Rule 1.104 provides that the president pro tempore (ES), assistant president pro tempore (ES), and the associate president pro tempore (ES) are elected by a majority of the Senate.
(r) Official title is speaker. In Guam the Speaker is elected on the Floor by majority and minority members on Inauguration Day.
(s) Additional leadership positions: Assistant Majority and Minority Whips, elected by caucus.
(t) Majority leader also serves as majority floor leader. Minority leader also serves as minority floor leader.
(u) Additional positions appointed by the Republican Conference leader include: Senate Finance Committee chair, Republican Conference vice president, Republican Conference deputy whip, assistant Senate Republican Conference whip, et.al. Additional positions appointed by the Democratic Conference leader include: Senate Finance Committee ranking Democratic member, deputy Democratic Conference whip, assistant Democratic Conference whip, et al.
(v) The position of majority leader does not exist. The Senate Majority Coalition is headed by the Majority Coalition leaders (the Republican Conference leader and the Independent Democratic Conference leader), appointed by the president pro tem. Majority floor leader bares the title deputy Republican conference leader for legislative operations; there is also a deputy Independent Democratic Conference leader for legislative operations. Majority whip bares the title Republican Conference whip; there is also an Independent Democratic Conference whip. Majority Caucus chair bares the title chair, Senate Republican Conference whip. Minority leader bares the title Democratic Conference leader. Assistant Minority Leader bares the title deputy Democratic Conference leader. Minority floor leader bares the title assistant Democratic Conference leader for floor operations. Assistant minority floor leader bares the title deputy Democratic Conference leader for floor operations. Minority whip bares the title Democratic Conference whip. Minority Caucus chair bares the title chair, Democratic Conference.
(w) While the entire membership actually votes on the election of leaders, selections generally have been made by the members of each party prior to the date of this formal election.

SENATE LEADERSHIP POSITIONS: METHODS OF SELECTION—Continued

(x) In Ohio president acts as majority leader and caucus chair; minority leader also acts as minority caucus chair; the fourth ranking minority leadership position is assistant minority whip (ES).

(y) Additional positions include deputy president pro tempore.

(z) President pro tem appointed by party leader via Legislative Rules, SR1-3-103. Official title for majority floor leader is known as the assistant majority whip; the assistant minority floor leader is known as the assistant minority whip and the minority caucus chair is known as minority caucus manager.

(aa) Majority leader serves as majority floor leader and majority caucus chair. Assistant majority leader serves as assistant majority floor leader and majority whip. Minority leader serves as minority floor leader and minority caucus chair. Assistant minority leader serves as assistant minority floor leader and minority whip.

(bb) Majority party and Minority party in Senate elects caucus officers.

(cc) Washington Senate also has the leadership position of vice-president pro tem.

(dd) Caucus nominee elected by whole membership.

(ee) Chair of the Council, which is an elected position.

(ff) Appointed by the chair; official title is chair pro tem.

(gg) Additional positions include: Parliamentarian, elected by majority caucus and Senior Senator, elected by majority caucus.

(hh) Speaker also serves as majority leader.

(ii) Official title is floor leader.

(jj) Official title is alternate floor leader.

(kk) Official title is caucus chair.

(ll) Secretary of the Senate and Assistant Secretary of the Senate, both elected by the Senate membership.

(mm) All positions other than president, president pro tempore and majority leader are party caucus designations.

Table 3.7
HOUSE/ASSEMBLY LEADERSHIP POSITIONS: METHODS OF SELECTION

State or other jurisdiction	Speaker	Speaker pro tem	Majority leader	Assistant majority leader	Majority floor leader	Assistant majority floor leader	Majority whip	Majority caucus chair	Minority leader	Assistant minority leader	Minority floor leader	Assistant minority floor leader	Minority whip	Minority caucus chair
Alabama	EH	EH	EC						EC				EC	EC
Alaska	EH		EC				EC		EC				EC	EC
Arizona	EH	AS	EC		EC		EC		EC		EC	EC	EC	EC
Arkansas	EH	AS	EC				EC		EC				EC	EC
California	EH	AS	EC	AS	AS	AS	AS	EC	EC	AL	AL	AL	AL	EC
Colorado (a)	EH	AS	EC	EC (b)			EC	EC	EC	EC	EC	EC	EC	EC
Connecticut (b)	EH	AS (b)	EC	EC (b)			AS	AS	EC	AL	AL	AL	AL	AL
Delaware	EH	EH	AS		AS	AS	EC		EC		AL		AL	EC
Florida	EH	EH	AS	AS (ee)			AS (ee)		EC	EC (ee)	AL		AL (ee)	AL (ee)
Georgia	EH	EH	EC		EC		EC	EC	EC	EC	EC	EC	EC	EC
Hawaii (c)	EH	EH (d)	EC	EC	EC	EC	EC	EC	EC	EC	EC	EC	EC	EC
Idaho	EH	EH	AS	AS (e)			EC	AS (e)	EC	(c)	AL		AL	EC (e)
Illinois	EH	AL	AS	AL	AL	AL	AL	AL	EC	AL	AL	AL	AL	AL (e)
Indiana	EH	AL	EC	EC	EC	EC	EC	EC	EC	EC	EC	EC	EC	EC
Iowa	EH	EH	EC				EC		EC				EC	EC
Kansas (f)	EH	EH	EC	EC	EC	EC	EC	EC	EC	EC	EC	EC	EC	EC
Kentucky (g)	EH	EH	EC	EC	EC	EC	EC	EC	EC	EC	EC	EC	EC	EC
Louisiana	EH	EH	AS	AL	AL		AL						AL	
Maine (bb)	EH	AS (h)	EC (h)	EC (h)	(h)	(h)	(h)	(h)	(h)	(h)	(h)	(h)	(h)	(k)
Maryland (cc)	EH	EH (i)	AS (j)	AS (j)	EC	AS	AS	(k)	EC (l)	EC	EC (l)	EC (l)	EH	(k)
Massachusetts	EC	EH	AS	AS		EC	EC	EC	EC	AL	EC	AL	EC	
Michigan (n)	EH	EH	EC	EC	EC	EC	EC	EC	EC	EC	EC	EC	EC	EC
Minnesota	EH	AS	EC	EC				EC	EC	AL	EC	EC	EC	
Mississippi	EH	EH	EC				EC		EC				EC	EC
Missouri	EH	EH	EC	EC	EC	EC	EC	EC	EC	EC	EC	EC	EC	EC
Montana	EH	EH				(o)			EC			EC		
Nebraska														
Nevada	EH	EH (d)	AS	AS (dd)	EC	EC	EC		EC	AL (dd)	EC	EC	EC	EC
New Hampshire	EH	AS (d)	MA	MA	MA	MA	MA	MA	MI	MI	MI	MI	MI	MI
New Jersey	EH	EH	MA	MA	MA	MA	MA	MA	MI	MI	MI	MI	MI	MI
New Mexico	EH	EH	EC	AS	EC (m)		EC	EC	EC (m)	EC	EC	EC	EC	EC
New York (p)	EH	AS	EC	AS	EC		AS	AS (q)	EC	AS	EC	AL	AL	AL (q)
North Carolina	EH	EH	EC	EC			EC	EC	EC	EC	EC	EC	EC	EC
North Dakota	EH	EH	EC	EC			EC	EC	EC	EC	EC		EC	EC
Ohio (r)	EH (k)	EH	EC	EC		EH	EH	EC	EH (k)	EH			EH	
Oklahoma	EH	EH	AS	AS	AS	AS	AS	EC	AL	EC	AL	AL	EH	EC
Oregon	EH	EH	EC	EC	EC	EC	EC	EC	EC	EC	EC	EC	AL	EC
Pennsylvania	EH	EH	EC	EC	EC	EC	EC	EC	EC	EC	EC	EC	EC	EC
Rhode Island	EH	EH	EC	AL	EC	EC	AL	EC	EC	AL	EC	EC	AL	EC
South Carolina	EH	EH	EC	EC			EC	EC	EC	EC	EC			
South Dakota	EH	EH	EC	EC	EC	EC	EC	EC	EC	EC	EC	EC	EC	EC
Tennessee	EH	EH	EC	EC	EC	EC	EC	EC	EC	EC	EC	EC	EC	AL (q)
Texas	EH	AS	EC	EC (s)			EC (s)	EC (s)	EC (s)	EC (s)	EC (s)	EC (s)	EC (s)	EC (s)
Utah	EH	AS	EC	EC	EC	EC	EC	EC	EC	EC	EC	EC	EC	EC
Vermont	EH		EC	EC	(t)	(t)	(t)	(t)	(t)	(t)	(t)	(t)	(t)	(t)

See footnotes at end of table.

HOUSE/ASSEMBLY LEADERSHIP POSITIONS: METHODS OF SELECTION—Continued

State or other jurisdiction	Speaker	Speaker pro tem	Majority leader	Assistant majority leader	Majority floor leader	Assistant majority floor leader	Majority whip	Majority caucus chair	Minority leader	Assistant minority leader	Minority floor leader	Assistant minority floor leader	Minority whip	Minority caucus chair
Virginia (u)	EH	EH	EC (v)	EC (v)	EC (v)	...	EC	EC	EC (w)	EC (w)	EC (w)	EC (w)	AL	EC
Washington	EH	EH	EC	EC	EC	EC	EC	EC	EC	EC	EC	EC	EC	EC
West Virginia	EH	AS	AS	AS	...	...	AS	AS	AS	AS	...	...	...	AS
Wisconsin	EH (x)	EH (x)	EC	EC	...	...	EC	EC	EC	EC	...	...	EC	EC
Wyoming	EH	EH	...	...	EC	...	EC	EC	EC	EC	EC	...	EC	EC
Dist. of Columbia	EH	EH (d)	...	...	...	...	...	(o)	...	...	...	...	...	...
American Samoa	EH	EH (d)	...	...	...	...	...	(o)	...	...	...	...	...	...
Guam	EH (y)	EH (d)	(y)	...	EH (z)	...	...	(o)	...	EC	...	EC	...	(k)
No. Mariana Islands	EH (k)	EH (d)	EC	...	EC (aa)	...	...	...	EC	...	EC	...	...	(k)
Puerto Rico														
U.S. Virgin Islands								(o)						

Source: The Council of State Governments' survey, November 2014 and state websites 2015.

Note: In some states, the leadership positions in the House are not empowered by the law or by the rules of the chamber, but rather by the party members themselves.

Key:
EH — Elected or confirmed by all members of the House.
EC — Elected by party caucus.
AS — Appointed by speaker.
AL — Appointed by party leader.
MA — Elected by majority party.
MI — Elected by minority party.
... — Position does not exist or is not selected on a regular basis.

(a) Additional positions include deputy majority whip (EC) and assistant majority caucus chair (EC).
(b) Official titles: speaker pro tem—deputy speaker; assistant majority leader—deputy majority leader.
(c) Other positions in Hawaii include speaker emeritus, majority policy leader (EC) and minority leader emeritus.
(d) Official title is deputy speaker. In Hawaii, American Samoa and Puerto Rico, vice speaker.
(e) The two deputy majority leaders appointed by the speaker are among eight assistant majority leaders; and the two deputy Republican (minority) leaders appointed by the Republican (minority) leader are among the eight assistant leaders.
(f) Additional positions include minority agenda chair (EC) and minority policy chair (EC).
(g) In each chamber, the membership elects chief clerk; assistant chief clerk; enrolling clerk; sergeant-at-arms; doorkeeper; janitor; cloakroom keeper; and pages.
(i) There is also a deputy speaker pro tem.
(j) Majority leader also serves as majority floor leader. Official title of assistant majority leader is deputy majority leader. There are also an assistant majority floor leader, majority whip, chief deputy majority whips, and deputy majority whips.
(k) Speaker and minority leader are also caucus chairs.
(l) Minority leader also serves as the minority floor leader. There are also a minority whip, assistant minority leader, a chief deputy minority whip, an assistant minority whip, and several deputy minority whips.
(m) Majority leader also serves as majority floor leader; minority leader also serves as minority floor leader.
(n) Other positions include: two associate speakers pro tempore (EH); majority caucus chair (EC); assistant majority whip (EC); assistant associate minority floor leader (EC); minority assistant caucus chair (EC); assistant minority whip (EC).

(o) Unicameral legislature; see entries in Table 3.6, "Senate Leadership Positions—Methods of Selection."
(p) Additional majority positions appointed by the speaker: deputy speaker, assistant speaker, deputy majority leader, Ways and Means Committee chair, Democratic Program Committee chair, Democratic Steering Committee chair, various deputies and assistants. Additional minority positions appointed by the minority leader: deputy minority leader, Ways and Means Committee ranking member, Republican Steering Committee chair, Republican Program Committee chair, various deputies and assistants.
(q) Official titles: the majority caucus chair is majority conference chair; minority caucus chair is minority conference chair.
(r) While the entire membership actually votes on the election of leaders, selections generally have been made by the members of each party prior to the date of this formal election. Additional positions include assistant majority whip, the 6th ranking majority leadership position (EH) and assistant minority whip, the 4th ranking minority leadership position (EH).
(s) Assistant majority leader is known as majority assistant whip; assistant minority floor leader known as minority assistant whip; minority caucus chair known as minority caucus manager.
(t) Majority leader also serves as majority floor leader; assistant majority leader also serves as assistant majority floor leader and majority whip; minority leader also serves as minority floor leader; assistant minority leader also serves as assistant minority floor leader and minority whip.
(u) The majority caucus also has a secretary, who is appointed by the speaker; the minority caucus has 2 vice-chairs, 1 vice-chair/treasurer and an interim sergeant-at-arms.
(v) The title of majority leader is not used in Virginia; the title is majority floor leader.
(w) The title of minority leader is not used in Virginia; the title is minority floor leader.
(x) Caucus nominee elected by whole membership.
(y) Speaker also serves as majority leader.
(z) Official title is floor leader.
(aa) Official title is alternate floor leader.
(bb) Clerk of the House and Assistant Clerk of the House, both elected by the House leadership.
(cc) There is a parliamentarian for the majority appointed by the Speaker and a minority parliamentarian elected by the minority party caucus.
(dd) Assistant majority leader official title is deputy majority leader. Assistant minority leader official title is deputy minority leader. Additional position is deputy majority whip (AS).
(ee) The position of assistant majority leader is known as deputy majority leader. In addition to a majority whip, deputy whips are also appointed by the speaker. The position of assistant minority leader is known as minority leader pro tem. In addition to a minority whip, deputy whips are appointed by the party leader. There is no minority caucus chair—instead there is a policy chair.

Table 3.8
METHOD OF SETTING LEGISLATIVE COMPENSATION

State	Method
Alabama	Constitutional Amendment 57
Alaska	Compensation Commission; Alaska Stat. §24.10.100, §24.10.101; §39.23.200 thru 39.23.260
Arizona	Compensation Commission Send to a Public Vote Arizona Revised Statutes 41-1103 and 41-1904
Arkansas	Amendment 70, Ark. Stat. Ann. §10-2-212 et seq.
California	State Constitution—Art. III, §8, which establishes a compensation commission.
Colorado	Colorado Stat. 2-2-307 (1)
Connecticut	Conn. Gen. Stat. Ann. §2-9a; The General Assembly takes independent action pursuant to recommendations of a compensation commission.
Delaware	Del. Code Ann. Title 29, §710 et seq.; §§3301–3304; Are implemented automatically if not rejected by resolution.
Florida	Florida Statutes §11.13(1); statute provides members same percentage increase as state employees.
Georgia	Ga. Code Ann. §45-7-4 and §28-1-8
Hawaii	Hawaii State Constitution Article XVI §3.5; Legislative Salary Commission recommendations take effect unless rejected by concurrent resolution.
Idaho	Idaho Code 67-406a and 406b; Citizen's Committee on Legislative Compensation makes recommendations that the legislature can reduce or reject, but not increase.
Illinois	25 ILCS 120—Compensation Review Act and 25 ILCS 115—General Assembly Compensation Act
Indiana	IC 2-3-1-1: An amount equal to 18% of the annual salary of a judge under IC 33-38-5-6, as adjusted under IC 33-38-5-8.1.
Iowa	Iowa Code Ann. §2.10; Iowa Code Ann. §2A.1 thru 2A.5
Kansas	Kan. Stat. Ann. §46-137a et seq.; §75-3212
Kentucky	Kentucky Rev. Stat. Ann. §6.226-229. The Kentucky committee has not met since 1995; the most recent pay raise was initiated and passed by the General Assembly.
Louisiana	La. Rev. Stat. 24:31 & 31.1
Maine	Maine Constitution Article IV, part third, §7 and 3 MRSA, §2 and 2-A. Increase in compensation is presented to the legislature as legislation; the legislature must enact and the governor must sign into law. Takes effect only for subsequent legislatures.
Maryland	Article III, §15. Commission meets before each four-year term of office and presents recommendations to the General Assembly for action. Recommendations may be reduced or rejected.
Massachusetts	Massachusetts Gen. Laws Ann. ch. 3, §§9, 10. In 1998, the voters passed a legislative referendum that, starting with the 2001 session, members will receive an automatic increase or decrease according to the median household income for the commonwealth for the following two-year period.
Michigan	Article IV §12. Compensation Commission recommends legislature by majority vote; must approve or reduce for change to be effective for the session immediately following the next general election.
Minnesota	Minn. Stat. Ann §3.099 et seq.; §15A.082; The Council submits salary recommendations to the presiding officers by May 1 in odd numbered years.
Mississippi	Miss. Code Ann. 5-1-41
Missouri	Art. III, §§16, 34; Mo. Ann. Stat. §21.140; Recommendations are adjusted by legislature or governor if necessary.
Montana	Mont. Laws 5-2-301; Tied to executive broadband pay plan.
Nebraska	Neb. Const. Art. III, §7; Neb. Rev. Stat. 50-123.01
Nevada	§218.210–§218.225
New Hampshire	Art. XV, part second
New Jersey	Article IV Sec. IV 7, 8; NJSA 52:10A-1; NJSA 52:14-15.111–114
New Mexico	Art. IV. §10; 2-1-8 NMSA
New York	Constitution—Art. 3, §6; Consolidated Laws of NY—Legislative Law, Section 5
North Carolina	N.C.G.S. 120-3
North Dakota	NDCC 54-03-10 and 54-03-20
Ohio	Art. II, §31; Ohio Rev. Code Ann. title 1 ch. 101.27 thru 101.272
Oklahoma	Okla. Stat. Ann. title 74, §291 et seq.; Art V, §21; Title 74, §291.2 et seq.; Legislative Compensation Board
Oregon	Or. Rev. Stat. §171.072
Pennsylvania	Pa. Cons. Stat. Ann. 46 PS §5; 65 PS §366.1 et seq.; Legislators receive annual cost of living increase that is tied to the Consumer Price Index.
Rhode Island	Art. VI, §3

See footnotes at end of table.

METHOD OF SETTING LEGISLATIVE COMPENSATION — Continued

State	Method
South Carolina	S.C. Code Ann. 2-3-20 and the annual General Appropriations Act
South Dakota	Art. III, §6 and Art. XXI, §2; S.D. Codified Laws Ann. §20402 et seq.
Tennessee	Art. II, §23; Tenn. Code Ann. §3-1-106 et seq.
Texas	Art. III, §24; In 1991, a constitutional amendment was approved by voters to allow Ethics Commission to recommend the salaries of members. Any recommendations must be approved by voters to be effective. The provision has yet to be used.
Utah	Art. VI, §9; Utah Code Ann. §36-2-2, et seq.
Vermont	Vt. Stat. Ann. title 32, §1051 and §1052
Virginia	Art. IV, §5; Va. Code Ann. §30-19.11 thru §30-19.14
Washington	Article II §§23 and 43.03.060, Washington Rev. Code Ann. §43.03.028. The salary commission sets salaries of the legislature and other state officials based on market study and input from citizens.
West Virginia	Art. 6, §33; W. Va. Code §4-2A-1 et seq.; Submits by resolution and must be concurred by at least four members of the commission. The Legislature must enact the resolution into law and may reduce, but shall not increase, any item established in such resolution.
Wisconsin	Wisconsin Statutes §§20.923 and 230.12, created by Chapter 90, Laws of 1973, and amended by 1983 Wisconsin Acts 27 and 33. Generally, compensation is determined as part of the state compensation plan for non-represented employees and is approved by vote of the joint committee on employment relations.
Wyoming	Wyo. Stat. §28-5-101 thru §28-5-105

Source: National Conference of State Legislatures, 2015.

Table 3.9
LEGISLATIVE COMPENSATION AND LIVING EXPENSE ALLOWANCES DURING SESSIONS

State	Salaries — Regular sessions			Mileage cents per mile	Session per diem rate
	Per-diem salary	Limit on days	Annual salary		
Alabama	…	…	$42,849 (a)	10¢/mile for a single roundtrip per session. 57.5¢/mile interim cmte. attendance.	Alabama Legislators no longer receive a set per diem rate while in session. Legislators are reimbursed for in-state travel expenses which include mileage and per diem in accordance with rates and procedures applicable to state employees. All out-of-district reimbursable travel must be for official business and in the interests of the state or in the performance of official duties, as approved by the applicable Presiding Officer.
Alaska	…	…	$50,400	56¢/mile for approved travel.	$223 or $249/day (depending on the time of year) tied to the federal rate. Legislators who reside in the Capitol area receive 75% of the Federal rate.
Arizona	…	…	$24,000	44.5¢/mile on actual miles.	$35/day for the first 120 days of the regular session and for special sessions and $10/day thereafter. Members residing outside Maricopa County receive an additional $25/day for the first 120 days of the regular session and for special sessions and an additional $10/day thereafter (V). Set by statute.
Arkansas	…	…	$39,400	56¢/mile.	$150/day (V) plus mileage; tied to the federal rate.
California	…	…	$97,197	53¢/mile.	$168/day for each day in session.
Colorado	…	…	$30,000	50¢/mile. State reimbursement rate is 90% of federal rate.	$99/day for members living outside Denver (V). Set by the legislature; $45/day for members who live 50 or fewer miles from the Capitol.
Connecticut	…	…	$28,000	57.5¢/mile.	No per diem is paid.
Delaware	…	…	$44,541	40¢/mile set by Del. Code Ann. Title 29 §7102.	No per diem is paid.
Florida	…	…	$29,697	44.5¢/mile for business travel.	$129/day based on the number of days in session. Travel vouchers are filed to substantiate.
Georgia	…	…	$17,342	50¢/mile Ga. Code Ann. §50-19-7 sets rate of reimbursement at the same mileage rate established by the U.S. General Services Administration.	$173/day (U); set by the Legislative Services Committee.
Hawaii	…	…	$59,004	Members can file a claim for mileage reimbursement based on the federal mileage reimbursement rate.	$150/day for members living outside Oahu during session; $10/day for members living on Oahu.
Idaho	…	…	$16,684	One roundtrip per week at state rate.	$129/day for members establishing a second residence in Boise; $49/day if no second residence is established and up to $25/day travel (V). Set by the compensation commission.
Illinois	…	…	$67,836 — Members are required to forfeit one day of compensation per month.	39¢/mile.	$111 per session day.

See footnotes at end of table.

LEGISLATIVE COMPENSATION AND LIVING EXPENSE ALLOWANCES DURING SESSIONS — Continued

State	Salaries — Regular sessions — Per-diem salary	Salaries — Regular sessions — Annual salary	Limit on days	Mileage cents per mile	Session per diem rate
Indiana	…	$24,140.16	…	56/mile.	$159/day (U); tied to the federal rate.
Iowa	…	$25,000	…	39/mile.	$148/day (U); $111/day for Polk County legislators (U). Set by the legislature to coincide with the federal rate. State mileage rates apply.
Kansas	$88.66/day (C)	…	…	56/mile, set by Dept. of Admin.	$129/day.
Kentucky	$188.22/day	…	…	55.5/mile.	$141.90/day.
Louisiana	…	$16,800 plus additional $6,000/year (U) expense allowance.	…	56/mile; tied to the federal rate.	$150/day (U); tied to the federal rate.
Maine	…	$14,074/year for first regular session; $9,982/year for second regular session. (b)	…	44/mile.	$38/day for lodging, or mileage and tolls in lieu of housing (at a rate of $0.44/mile up to $38/day) plus $32/day for meals. Set by statute.
Maryland	…	$45,207	…	57.5/mile. $500 annual allowance for in-district travel as taxable income, members may decline the allowance.	Meals: $45/day; mileage: $.575/mile; lodging: $100/day.
Massachusetts	…	$60,032	…	Between $10–$100 reimbursed per trip, determined by distance from the State House.	From $10/day–$100/day, depending on distance from State House (V) set by the legislature.
Michigan	…	$71,685	…	56/mile.	$10,800/year expense allowance for session and interim (V); set by the compensation commission.
Minnesota	…	$31,141	…	House: during session, members can request up to 1 roundtrip/week if they live more than 50 miles from the Capitol; $100–$1,650/month for mileage reimbursement for travel in the legislative district during interim. Senate: a reasonable allowance.	$86/day for senators and $66/day for representatives.
Mississippi	…	$10,000	…	Determined by Federal Register and Legislature.	$129/day.
Missouri	…	$35,915	…	37/mile.	$103.20/day (U); tied to the federal rate. Verification of per diem is by roll call.
Montana	$82.64 (L)	…	…	56/mile, based on IRS rate; reimbursement for actual mileage traveled in connection with legislative business.	$112.85/day (U).
Nebraska	…	$12,000	…	56/mile; tied to federal rate.	$129/day for members residing 50 miles or more from the Capitol; $46/day for members inside the 50-mile radius.

See footnotes at end of table.

LEGISLATIVE COMPENSATION AND LIVING EXPENSE ALLOWANCES DURING SESSIONS—Continued

State	Salaries Regular sessions Per-diem salary	Limit on days	Annual salary	Mileage cents per mile	Session per diem rate
Nevada	$146.29/day (c)	Max. of 60 days of session.	...	Federal rate, currently 56/mile.	$152/per day.
New Hampshire	...	...	$200/2-year term	Roundtrip home to the State House at 38/mile for the first 45 miles and 19/mile thereafter, or members will be reimbursed for actual expenses and mileage will be paid at the maximum IRS mileage rate.	No per diem is paid.
New Jersey	...	...	$49,000	None.	No per diem is paid.
New Mexico	...	...	...	55/mile; tied to the federal rate.	$165/day (V); tied to the federal rate.
New York	...	...	$79,500	Varies (V) tied to Federal GSA rate—currently 55.5/mile.	$172/full day (including overnight); $61/partial day.
North Carolina	...	...	$13,951	29/mile, 1 roundtrip/week during session; 1 roundtrip for attendance at interim cmte. mtgs.	$104/day (U) set by statute. $0.29/mile set by statute. Monthly expense allowance: $559/month, member; $666/month.
North Dakota	$167/day during legislative sessions (C)	...	...	56/mile; 1 roundtrip/week during session.	Lodging reimbursement up to $1,569 per month (V).
Ohio	...	...	$60,584	52/mile; 1 roundtrip/week from home to the State House for legislators outside Franklin County only.	No per diem is paid.
Oklahoma	...	...	$38,400	56/mile; tied to the federal rate.	$160/day (U): tied to federal rate.
Oregon	...	...	$23,052	56/mile.	$129/day (U): tied to federal rate
Pennsylvania	...	...	$85,339	56/mile; tied to the federal rate.	$159/day.
Rhode Island	...	...	$15,171—Per Article VI, Section 3 of the Rhode Island Constitution, the rate of compensation is adjusted annually to reflect changes in the cost of living.	56.5/mile to and from session.	No per diem is paid.
South Carolina	...	...	$10,400	Current IRS rate.	$140/day for meals and housing for each statewide session day and committee meeting; tied to the federal rate.
South Dakota	$129/day for interim committees	...	$6,000/session	37/mile for 1 roundtrip from Pierre to home each weekend; one trip is also paid at 5/mile. During the interim, 37/mile for scheduled committee meetings.	$129/legislative day (U); set by the legislature.

See footnotes at end of table.

LEGISLATIVE COMPENSATION AND LIVING EXPENSE ALLOWANCES DURING SESSIONS—Continued

State	Salaries			Mileage cents per mile	Session per diem rate
	Regular sessions				
	Per-diem salary	Annual salary	Limit on days		
Tennessee	...	$20,884	...	47/mile.	$198/legislative day (U); tied to federal rate.
Texas	...	$7,200	...	50/mile set by General Appropriations bill; an allowance for single, twin and turbo engines of $1.24/mile is also given.	$190/day (U); set by ethics commission.
Utah	$273/day (C)	...	...	56/mile, roundtrip from home to Capitol.	Up to $100 plus tax/calendar day (V) for lodging reimbursement, tied to in-state travel reimbursement lodging rate for Salt Lake City metropolitan area; up to $39/date meal reimbursement (V), tied to in-state travel meal reimbursement rates (includes tax and tips).
Vermont	...	$676.56/week during legislative session only.	...	Federal mileage rate, now about 56/mile; state employee reimbursement rate.	$110/day for lodging (overnight stay) or $61/day for meals and mileage if commuting.
Virginia	...	$18,000/year for Senate; $17,640/year for House.	...	56/mile.	$180/day for senators; $179/day for House members.
Washington	...	$42,106	...	56/mile	$120/day.
West Virginia	...	$20,000	...	48.5/mile based on Dept of Admin. travel regulations.	$131/day during session (U); set by compensation commission.
Wisconsin	...	$50,950	...	51/mile; 1 roundtrip/week to the Capitol	Wisconsin Senate—Current authorized amount is up to $88 per day ($44 per day for legislators living in Dane County). This rate is 64% of the maximum per diem rate for Madison. Wisconsin Assembly—Current authorized amount is up to $138 per day for members staying overnight on legislative business, and up to $69 per day when conducting legislative business and not staying overnight. The maximum number of per diem that can be claimed per year is 153 days. This overnight rate is the maximum allowed of the per diem rate for Madison.
Wyoming	$150/day during session	...	...	55/mile.	$109/day (V), including travel days for those outside of Cheyenne; set by the legislature.

Source: National Conference of State Legislatures, 2015.

Key:
C — Calendar day
L — Legislative day
(U) — Unvouchered
(V) — Vouchered
... — Not applicable

(a) Alabama legislators receive a taxable compensation equal to the Alabama median annual household income, as ascertained and adjusted yearly by the State Personnel Board. The State Personnel Board met on Oct. 22, 2014, and set the median annual household income amount. This current median annual household amount went into effect on November 5, 2014 and is effective until December 31, 2015.

(b) Annual cost of living adjustments apply. In addition, legislators receive a constituent service allowance ($2,000/year for Senators and $1,500/year for Representatives).

(c) The members of the 78th Regular Session pledged to voluntarily take a 2.3 percent reduction of their salaries for the session. The reduction does not apply to those who did not vote in favor of the voluntary reduction.

Table 3.10
LEGISLATIVE COMPENSATION: OTHER PAYMENTS AND BENEFITS

State	Legislator's compensation for office supplies, district offices and staffing	Phone allowance	Transportation offered to legislators	Insurance benefits				
				Health	Dental	Vision	Disability insurance	Life insurance benefits
Alabama	None, although annual appropriation to certain positions may be so allocated.	Yes (a)	None	S.A., O.P.	S.A., O.P.	N.A.	N.A.	N.A.
Alaska	Senators receive up to $20,000/y and representatives receive up to $16,000/y for postage per their choice for postage, stationery and other legislative expenses. Staffing allowance determined by rules and presiding officers, depending on time of year.	Yes (a)	None	S.P.P.	S.P.P.	O.P.: unless included in Health Ins.	Optional: if selected is included in health insurance.	Small policy available; additional is optional at legislator's expense.
Arizona	None.	(g)	(b)	S.P.P., S.A.	S.A., O.P.	S.A., O.P.	S.P.P.	State pays 15K policy; additional amount is paid by legislator.
Arkansas	Legislators receive a maximum reimbursement of $14,400/y for legislative expenses. Committee chairs, vice chairs, and standing subcommittee chairs may claim additional reimbursement up to $3,600/y.	No	None	S.P.P. (cc)	O.P.	O.P. (cc)	O.P.– Supplemental	State pays for $30K as part of the health plan; additional is optional at legislator's expense.
California	Assembly members have a base allowance of $263,000/y to cover these expenses. Senate member expenses are paid directly and maintained by the Senate Rules Committee.	No	(c)	S.P.P. (dd)	(dd)	(dd)	Assembly members do not have disability insurance coverage; senators are covered by a long-term disability insurance policy.	$250,000 term policy for the Assembly: members pay 18% of the premium plus the taxable value on coverage above $50,000. Senators are eligible for up to $250,000 term coverage: members pay 18% of the age-based premium plus the taxable value on coverage above $50,000.
Colorado	None.	Yes (a)	None	S.P.P.– Amount differs according to plan selected.	S.P.P.– Amount differs according to plan selected.	N.A.	N.A.	State pays full amount for $50,000 policy; additional is optional at legislator's expense.
Connecticut	Senators receive $5,500/y and representatives receive $4,500/y in unvouchered expense allowance.	Yes (d)	None	S.P.P.	S.P.P.	Some health insurance plans include discounts on eyewear.	O.P.	O.P.
Delaware	Office supplies are distributed out of the general House supply budget.	Yes (a)	None	S.P.P.	O.P.	O.P.	N.A.	O.P.

See footnotes at end of table.

LEGISLATIVE COMPENSATION: OTHER PAYMENTS AND BENEFITS — Continued

State	Legislator's compensation for office supplies, district offices and staffing	Phone allowance	Transportation offered to legislators	Insurance benefits Health	Dental	Vision	Disability insurance	Life insurance benefits
Florida	Senate: $2,921/m for district office expenses; House: $2,482/m for district office expenses.	No	(e)	Legislators pay $50/m for individual coverage and $180/m for family coverage.	S.P.	O.P.	S.P.	S.P.
Georgia	Legislators have $7,000/y reimbursable expense account. If the member requests and provides receipts, the member is reimbursed for personal services, office equipment, rent, supplies, transportation, telecommunications, etc.	No	None	S.A., S.P.P.	O.P.	O.P.	S.P.P.	S.P.P.
Hawaii	No district offices. The allocation for session staffing is approximately $5,000–$8,000/m for the January–April legislative session.	(r)	(f)	S.P.P.— Same options as legislative employees.	S.P.P.— Same options as legislative employees.	S.P.P.— Same options as legislative employees.	S.P.P.	S.P.P.— Same options as legislative employees.
Idaho	$1,875/y for unvouchered constituent expense. No staffing allowance.	No	None	S.P.P.	S.P.P.	S.P.P.	S.P.P.	S.P.P.
Illinois	Senators receive $83,063/y and representatives $69,409/y for office expenses, including district offices and staffing.	No	None	S.P.P.	S.P.P.	S.P.P.	S.P.	S.P.P.
Indiana	These expenses come out of one main Senate budget. No district offices.	No	None	S.A.	S.A.	S.A.	Legislators are not offered disability insurance.	S.A.
Iowa	$300/m to cover district constituency postage, travel, telephone and other expenses. No staffing allowance.	No	None	S.P.P.	S.P.P.	N.A.	S.P.	State pays first $20,000, additional at legislator expense.
Kansas	Allowed $7,083/y which is taxable income for the legislators. Staffing allowances vary for leadership, which has its own budget. Legislators provided with secretaries during session only.	Yes	None	S.P.P.	S.P., legislator pays dependent portion.	O.P.	S.P.	150% of annual salary if part of KPERS. Additional insurance is optional at legislator's expense.
Kentucky	$1,788.51/y for district expenses during interim.	No	(h)	S.A.	O.P.	O.P.	O.P.	State pays $20,000; additional is optional at legislator's expense.

See footnotes at end of table.

LEGISLATIVE COMPENSATION: OTHER PAYMENTS AND BENEFITS—Continued

State	Legislator's compensation for office supplies, district offices and staffing	Phone allowance	Transportation offered to legislators	Insurance benefits				
				Health	Dental	Vision	Disability insurance	Life insurance benefits
Louisiana	Allowed $500/m. Senators and representatives receive an additional $1,500/m supplemental allowance for vouchered office expenses, rent, and travel mileage in district. Senators and Representatives staff allowance $2,000/m starting salary up to $3,000/m with annual increases.	Yes (i)	None	S.P.P.—State pays 50% and legislator pays 50%.	S.P.P.—State pays 50% and legislator pays 50%; Senators pay 100%.	O.P.	O.P.	S.P.P.—State pays 50% and legislator pays 50%.
Maine	None. However, supplies for staff offices are provided and paid for out of general legislative account.	No	None	S.A.—The state pays 95% or 100% of legislator coverage and 50% of dependent coverage.	S.A., O.P.—State pays 100% of legislators' coverage.	O.P.	N.A.	Legislators are eligible for a group life insurance program with coverage in amount equal to legislators' salary; plan is 100% legislator-paid.
Maryland	$18,265/y for normal expenses of an office with limits on postage, telephone and publications. Legislators must use $5,800 for clerical services. Senators receive one administrative assistant and session secretary.	No	None	S.A.—The state pays 80–85% depending on the plan selected; legislator pays 20% for PPO, 17% for POS or 15% for HMO.	S.A., O.P.—The state pays 50%.	Covered under the medical plan.	N.A.	Term insurance; optional at legislator's expense.
Massachusetts	Allowed $7,200/y for office expenses.	No	None	S.P.P. (State currently pays 80%.)	S.P.P.	S.P.P.	O.P.	$5,000 policy provided; Additional up to 8 times salary at legislator's expense.
Michigan	$51,900 per majority senator for office budget and $51,900 for minority senator for office budget.	Yes (a)	None	Health, vision, life, cancer, prescription, offered via cafeteria plan.			N.A.	Offered at different levels as part of cafeteria plan.
Minnesota	Supplies provided in Capitol. In the House, staffing is provided centrally. Senators have one legislative assistant and are given $75/w for interns. No district offices.	Yes (j)	(k)	The state pays 100% for single coverage and 90% of family coverage.	The state pays 81% for single coverage and 60% for family coverage.	S.A.	O.P., STD, LTD—Optional life for member, spouse, and child; AD&D and long-term care.	State pays premium for benefit of $35,000.
Mississippi	$1,500/m out of session.	No	None	S.P.—Legislator only premiums.	O.P.	O.P.	O.P.	S.P.P.
Missouri	$700/m to cover all reasonable and necessary business expenses.	Yes (l)	None	S.P.P.	O.P.	O.P.	S.P.	S.P.—Additional amounts are optional at legislator's expense.
Montana	None.	Yes (m)	(x)	S.P.—Dependents are not covered.	S.P.—Dependents are legislators' responsibility.	O.P.	N.A.	State pays $14,000 term policy. Additional at legislator's expense.

See footnotes at end of table.

LEGISLATIVE COMPENSATION: OTHER PAYMENTS AND BENEFITS — Continued

State	Legislator's compensation for office supplies, district offices and staffing	Phone allowance	Transportation offered to legislators	Insurance benefits Health	Dental	Vision	Disability insurance	Life insurance benefits
Nebraska	No allowance; however, each member is provided with two full-time capitol staff year-round.	Yes (a)	None	O.P.	O.P.	O.P.	O.P.	O.P.
Nevada	None.	Yes— $2,800/y allowance	(n)	O.P.	O.P.	O.P.	O.P.	O.P.
New Hampshire	None.	No	None	O.P.	O.P.	N.A.	N.A.	N.A.
New Jersey	Allowed $1,250 for office supplies. Equipment and furnishings supplied through a district office program and there is $110,000/y for district office personnel. State provides stationery for each legislator and $10,000 for postage stamps.	No	(o)	S.A.—Members appointed or elected after 5/21/10 are not eligible for coverage.	S.A.—Members appointed or elected after 5/21/10 are not eligible for coverage.	S.A.—Members appointed or elected after 5/21/10 are not eligible for coverage.	Temporary disability insurance is not available to members. Some members have permanent disability options available through their pension plan; those not eligible for pension are offered long-term disability insurance unless they are already retired from a public pension plan.	Members enrolled in the pension plan have up to three times the annual salary. Members enrolled in the defined contribution plan have one and a half times the annual salary. Members not covered by either plan have no death benefit.
New Mexico	None.	No	None	N.A.	N.A.	N.A.	N.A.	N.A.
New York	Staff allowance (district and Capitol) is set by the majority leader for majority members and by the minority leader for minority members. Geographic location, seniority and leadership responsibilities will cause variations.	Yes (a)	(p)	S.P.P.	S.P.	S.P.	S.P.	O.P.
North Carolina	Non-leaders receive $6,708/y for any legislative expenses not otherwise provided. Full-time secretarial assistance is provided during session.	Yes (q)	None	The state pays the full amount for the PPO 70/30 plan. For the 80/20 plan, legislators pay a variety of rates depending on participation in wellness activities. Optional family coverage for both plans is at legislators' expense.	O.P.	O.P.	O.P.	O.P.

See footnotes at end of table.

LEGISLATIVE COMPENSATION: OTHER PAYMENTS AND BENEFITS — Continued

State	Legislator's compensation for office supplies, district offices and staffing	Phone allowance	Transportation offered to legislators	Insurance benefits				
				Health	Dental	Vision	Disability insurance	Life insurance benefits
North Dakota	None.	No	None	S.P.	O.P.	O.P.	O.P.	State pays for $1,300 term life policy.
Ohio	None.	Yes (a)	None	S.P.P.–The state pays 85%, and legislators pay 15%.	S.P.	S.P.	N.A.	State pays for an amount equal to salary. Member may purchase a supplemental policy, which is also offered to state employees.
Oklahoma	Each member is given a $1,500/y allotment. This may be spent on electronic communications such as cell phone bills as well as office expenses.	Yes (s)	None	Allowance ranging from $608.57 for legislator only to $1,596.95/m for family.	S.A.	S.A.	S.A.	S.A.
Oregon	$36,367/y for session staffing and $2,692.80 for services and supplies. For interim periods, legislators receive $68,538/biennium to spend as they choose. They also receive an additional $450–$750/m during interim only, as a district allowance, depending on geographic size of district.	Yes (t)	None	S.A., S.P.P.	S.A., S.P.P.	S.A., S.P.P.	O.P., S.A.	O.P., S.A.
Pennsylvania	Staffing is determined by leadership.	No	(u)	Medical/hospital, dental, vision, Rx. Legislators pay 1% of salary toward benefits.			Legislators are not eligible for disability insurance.	A group life policy is for up to the amount of salary.
Rhode Island	None.	No	None	S.A.	S.A.	S.A.	O.P.	O.P.
South Carolina	Senate $3,400/y for postage, stationery and telephone. House $1,800/y for telephone and $600/y for postage. Legislators also receive $1,000/m for in district expenses that is treated as income.	Yes (aa)	None	S.P.P.	S.P.P.	N.A.	S.P.P.	S.P.P.
South Dakota	None.	Yes (v)	None	N.A.	N.A.	N.A.	S.P. for accidental death/dismemberment ins. only.	N.A.
Tennessee	Allowed $1,000/m for expenses in district (U).	Yes (w)	None	State pays 80%, legislator pays 20%.	O.P.	N.A.	N.A.	State pays $15,000; Legislator pays $7,000.
Texas	Approved allowance for staff salaries, supplies, stationery, postage, district office rental, telephone expense, etc. Senate and House allocations are not the same.	No	None	S.P., S.A.	O.P.	Included in health coverage.	O.P.	O.P.

See footnotes at end of table.

LEGISLATIVE COMPENSATION: OTHER PAYMENTS AND BENEFITS — Continued

State	Legislator's compensation for office supplies, district offices and staffing	Phone allowance	Transportation offered to legislators	Insurance benefits				
				Health	Dental	Vision	Disability insurance	Life insurance benefits
Utah............	None.	Yes (bb)	None	S.P.P.—Similar to state employees.	S.P.P.—Similar to state employees.	Optional group discounts; similar to state employees.	S.P.	S.P.
Vermont............	None.	Yes	None	O.P.	N.A.	N.A.	N.A.	N.A.
Virginia............	Legislators receive $1,250/m and leadership receives $1,750/m office expense allowance. Legislators receive a staffing allowance of $56,000/y; leadership receives $79,879/y.	Yes	None	S.P.P.	S.P.P.	S.P.P.	S.P.—only permanent disability retirement through retirement system.	S.P.P.
Washington............	Senate—$7,800/y for legislative expenses, for which the legislator has not been otherwise entitled to reimbursement. No staffing allowance.	Yes (a)	None	S.A.	S.A.	Included in medical.	S.P.P.	S.P.P.
West Virginia.........	None.	Yes	None	O.P.	O.P.	O.P.	N.A.	O.P.
Wisconsin	$15,000/two-year session in the Assembly. No available staffing at district office. $45,000/two-year period for office expenses. $191,700/two-year period for staffing allowance.	(y)	None	S.P.P.—Single or family coverage with premiums from $84/m to $576/m; 26 health insurance carriers offer plans across the state.	Some HMOs offer coverage.	N.A.	O.P.	Legislators may have up to five times their salary as life insurance under group term coverage. Spouses and dependents may be covered at lower levels. Premiums for legislators vary with salary and age.
Wyoming	$750/quarter through the constituent service allowance.	Yes (z)	None	N.A.	N.A.	N.A.	N.A.	N.A.

Source: National Conference of State Legislatures, 2014.
Key:
(U) — Unvouchered. (V) — Vouchered. d — day. m — month. w — week. y — year.
N.A. — Not available.
S.P. — State pays full amount. S.P.P. — State pays portion and legislator pays portion.
S.A. — Same as state employees. O.P. — Optional at legislator's expense.
(a) Official state business only.
(b) Access to motor pool for approved legislative travel.
(c) One round-trip flight for each week of session; Use of a pool car for those members who fly to Sacramento.
(d) Official business only; charges for personal calls are reimbursed by legislator.
(e) Rental cars for official business.
(f) Round-trip airfare for non-Oahu legislators to travel from their home island to the Capitol on Oahu.
(g) Phone cards allowed for certain districts; none used at this time.
(h) State cars are available but not assigned to members.
(i) District office line with one extension.
(j) House members: $75/month communications allowance. Senators: $200/month communications allowance. Senators: $200/month communications allowance.
reimbursement.
(k) Car rental is available with prior approval.
(l) Phone cards issued but expenditures deducted from monthly expense allowance.
(m) Leadership positions only.
(n) Motor pool or private car. Legislative police shuttle to/from Reno airport.
(o) Automobiles for some top leadership positions.

(p) Top leadership has access to vehicles.
(q) Allowance of $2,275 for postage, stationery and telephone.
(r) Senate members may claim cell phone service expenses related to official legislative business, paid from the member's annual allowance for legislative expenses.
(s) $1,500/year for electronic communications such as cell phone bills as well as office expenses.
(t) State-provided office and district office phone for legislative business only.
(u) Mileage basis or vehicle from Department of General Services fleet.
(v) Telephone allowance: $600/6 months for legislators and $900/6 months for leadership.
(w) Phone cards.
(x) Limited access to state-owned cars.
(y) Members' office expenses, including phone expense, are limited to the amount of each legislator's office budget, as established by the committees on Senate and Assembly organization.
(z) Phone card for official business only with a $2,000 limit during 2 years.
(aa) Senate: $3,400/year for postage, stationery and telephone. House: $1,800/year for telephone and $1,100/year for postage.
(bb) State-paid mobile phone or reimbursement for personal phone at same rate as state-paid plan.
(cc) Health: The state pays $410 monthly; legislators pay the balance depending on the plan chosen. Vision: Vision screening with co-pay, once/2 years with health plan; additional coverage optional at legislators' expense.
(dd) Health: The state pays a portion (20% less than the contribution paid for state managerial employees); legislators pay a portion. Dental: Legislators pay 18% of the basic dental premium; enhanced coverage is available at an additional cost to the member. Vision: Legislators pay 18% of the basic vision premium; enhanced coverage is available at an additional cost to the member.

The Council of State Governments **91**

Table 3.11
ADDITIONAL COMPENSATION FOR SENATE LEADERS

State	Presiding officer	Majority leader	Minority leader	Other leaders and committee chairs
Alabama	$2/day plus $1,500/mo. expense allowance.	None	None	None
Alaska	$500/year	None	None	None
Arizona	Generally approved for additional interim per diem.	Generally approved for additional interim per diem.	Generally approved for additional interim per diem.	None
Arkansas	None	None	None	None
California	$109,584/year for the Senate president pro tem.	$102,437/year for the majority floor leader.	$109,584/year for the minority leader.	$102,437/year for the second ranking minority leader.
Colorado	All leaders receive $99/day salary during interim when attending to matters pertaining to the General Assembly.			None
Connecticut	$10,689/year	$8,835/year	$8,835/year	$6,446/year each for the dep. min. and maj. ldrs.; $4,241/year each for the asst. maj. and min. ldrs. and maj. and min. whips.
Delaware	$19,983/year	$12,376/year	$12,376/year	Leaders: Maj. and min. whips $7,794/year.
Florida	$11,484/year	None	None	None
Georgia	None	$200/mo.	$200/mo.	$400/mo. for the pres. pro tem; $200/mo. for the admin. floor leader; $100/mo. for the asst. admin. floor leader.
Hawaii	$7,500/year salary differential for the presiding officer.	None	None	None
Idaho	$3,754/year salary differential for the presiding officer.	None	None	None
Illinois	$27,477/year	$20,649/year	$27,477/year	$20,649/year each for the dep. min. ldr., asst. maj. and min. ldrs., and maj. and min. caucus chairs.
Indiana	$7,000/year	$5,500/year for the majority floor leader.	$6,000/year for the minority floor leader.	$3,000/year for the asst. pres. pro tem; $3,500/year for the asst. maj. floor ldr.; $1,500/year each for the maj. and min. floor ldrs. emeritus; $5,500/year for the maj. caucus chair; $1,000/year each for the asst. maj. caucus chair and asst. min. whip; $4,000/year for the maj.whip; $2,000/year each for the asst. maj. whip, co-min. whip, and asst. min. caucus chair; $5,000/year each for the asst. min. floor ldr. and min. caucus chair.
Iowa	$11,593/year	$11,593/year	$11,593/year	$1,243/year for the president pro tem.
Kansas	$14,039.22/year	$12,665.64/year	$12,665.64/year	$7,165.34/year each for asst. maj. and min. ldrs. and vice pres.
Kentucky	$47.35/day	$37.40/day	$37.40/day	$28.66/day each for maj. and min. caucus chairs and whips.
Louisiana	$32,000/year	None	None	$24,500/year for pres. pro tem.
Maine	150% of base salary/year	125% of base salary/year	112.5% of base salary/year	None
Maryland	$13,511/year	None	None	None
Massachusetts	$35,000/year	$22,500/year	$22,500/year	$15,000/year each for asst. maj. and min. ldrs. (and 2nd and 3rd assistant), pres. pro tem.
Michigan	$4,962/year	$23,400/year	$19,800/year	$10,800/year for the maj. floor ldr.; $9,000/year for the min. floor ldr.

See footnotes at end of table.

ADDITIONAL COMPENSATION FOR SENATE LEADERS — Continued

State	Presiding officer	Majority leader	Minority leader	Other leaders and committee chairs
Minnesota	None	Additional compensation is 40% of base salary.	Additional compensation is 40% of base salary.	$4,152/year each for the asst. maj. ldr., and tax and finance cmte. chairs.
Mississippi	$60,000/year total salary for the lt. gov.; $15,000/year for the pres. pro tem.	None	None	None
Missouri	None	None	None	None
Montana	$5/day during session.	None	None	None
Nebraska	None	None	None	None
Nevada	$900/year	$900/year	$900/year	$900/year for pres. pro tem.
New Hampshire	$50/two-year term	None	None	None
New Jersey	1/3 above annual salary.	None	None	None
New Mexico	None	None	None	None
New York	$41,500/year	$34,500/year	$34,500/year	$13,000–$34,000/year for 24 other leaders.
North Carolina	$38,151/year plus $1,413/month expense allowance.	$17,048/year plus $666/month expense allowance.	$17,048/year plus $666/month expense allowance.	$21,739/year plus $10,032/year expense allowance for the deputy pro tem.
North Dakota	None	$15/day during legislative sessions; $325 per month during term of office.	$15/day during legislative sessions; $325 per month during term of office.	$10/day during legislative sessions for asst. ldrs.
Ohio	$94,437.36/year for the president.	$86,164.76/year for the pres. pro tem; $81,163.21/year for the maj. flr. ldr.; $76,168.69/year for the maj. whip.	$86,164.76/year for the min. ldr.	Compensation for committee leadership (See committee chair table).
Oklahoma	$17,932/year	$12,364/year	$12,364/year	None
Oregon	$21,596/year additional salary for the president.	None	None	None
Pennsylvania	$47,136/year	$37,710/year	$37,710/year	$27,942/year each for maj. and min. whips; $17,422/year each for maj. and min. caucus chairs; $11,506/year each for maj. and min. caucus secretaries, policy chairs and caucus admins.
Rhode Island	Senate president receives double the annual rate for senators.	None	None	None
South Carolina	Lt. gov. holds this position.	None	None	President pro tem, $11,000/year.
South Dakota	None	None	None	None
Tennessee	$60,609/year base salary	None	None	None
Texas	None	None	None	None
Utah	$3,000/year	$2,000/year	$2,000/year	$2,000/year each for maj. and min. whips and asst. maj. and min. whips.

See footnotes at end of table.

ADDITIONAL COMPENSATION FOR SENATE LEADERS — Continued

State	Presiding officer	Majority leader	Minority leader	Other leaders and committee chairs
Vermont	$61,776/year for the lt. gov. who holds this position.	None	None	None
Virginia	None	$200/day only for days that official meetings are attended.	$200/day only for days that official meetings are attended.	President pro tem $200/day only for days that official meetings are attended.
Washington	Lt. gov. holds this position.	$50,106/year ($8,000/year addition to base salary).	$46,106/year ($4,000/year addition to base salary).	None
West Virginia	$150/day during session.	$50/day during session.	$50/day during session.	$150/day for the chair of Finance and Judiciary, up to 30 days, when the legislature is not in session or meeting for interims. $150/day for up to six more people named by the presiding officer, for up to 30 days, when the legislature is not in session or meeting for interims.
Wisconsin	None	None	None	None
Wyoming	$3/day during session; $978/month when not in session.	$600/month when not in session.	$600/month when not in session.	None

Source: National Conference of State Legislatures, 2015.

Table 3.12
ADDITIONAL COMPENSATION FOR HOUSE/ASSEMBLY LEADERS

State	Presiding officer	Majority leader	Minority leader	Other leaders and committee chairs
Alabama	$2/day plus $1,500/month expense allowance.	None	None	None
Alaska	$500/year	None	None	None
Arizona	Generally approved for additional interim per diem.	Generally approved for additional interim per diem.	Generally approved for additional interim per diem.	None
Arkansas	None	None	None	None
California	$109,584/year each for the speaker of the Assembly and pro tem of the Senate.	$102,437/year	$109,584/year	$102,437/year for the 2nd ranking min. ldrs.
Colorado	All leaders receive $99/day salary during interim when in attendance at committee or leadership matters.			
Connecticut	$10,689/year	$8,835/year	$8,835/year	$6,446/year each for the dep. spkr., dep. maj. and min. ldrs., asst. maj. and min. ldrs.; $4,241/year each for the maj. and min. whips.
Delaware	$19,893/year	$12,376/year	$12,376/year	$7,794/year each for the maj. and min. whips.
Florida	$11,484/year	None	None	None
Georgia	$6,811/month	$200/month	$200/month	$200/month for the gov.'s floor ldr.; $100/month for the asst. floor ldr.; $400/month for the spkr. pro tem.
Hawaii	$7,500/year salary differential for the presiding officer.	None	None	None
Idaho	$4,000/year	None	None	None
Illinois	$27,477/year	$23,300/year	$27,477/year	$19,791/year each for the dep. maj. and min. ldrs.; $18,066/year each for the asst. maj. and min. ldrs. and maj. and min. conference chairs.
Indiana	$7,000/year	$5,500/year	$6,000/year	$5,000/year each for the spkr. pro tem and maj. caucus chair; $4,500/year for the min. caucus chair; $3,500/year each for the asst. min. floor ldr. and maj. whip; $1,000/year for the asst. maj. floor ldr.; $1,500/year for the min. whip.
Iowa	$11,593/year	$11,593/year	$11,593/year	$1,243/year for the spkr. pro tem.
Kansas	$14,039.22/year	$12,665.64/year	$12,665.64/year	$7,165.34/year each for the asst. maj. and min. ldrs. spkr. pro tem.
Kentucky	$47.35/day	$37.40/day	$37.40/day	$28.66/day each for the maj. and min. caucus chairs and whips.
Louisiana	$32,000/year (a)	None	None	$24,500/year (a) for the spkr. pro tem.
Maine	150% of base salary	125% of base salary	112.5% of base salary	None
Maryland	$13,000/year	None	None	None
Massachusetts	$35,000/year	$22,500/year	$22,500/year	$15,000/year each for the asst. maj. and min. ldrs. (and second and third assistants) and spkr. pro tem.
Michigan	$27,000/year	Position does not exist.	$22,000/year	$5,513/year for the spkr. pro tem; $10,000/year for the min. floor ldr.; $12,000/year for the maj. floor ldr.

See footnotes at end of table.

ADDITIONAL COMPENSATION FOR HOUSE/ASSEMBLY LEADERS — Continued

State	Presiding officer	Majority leader	Minority leader	Other leaders and committee chairs
Minnesota	40% of base salary	40% of base salary	40% of base salary	None
Mississippi	$60,000 (a)	None	None	$15,000/year for the spkr. pro tem.
Missouri	$208.34/month	$125/month	$125/month	None
Montana	$5/day during session.	None	None	None
Nebraska	None	None	None	None
Nevada	$900/year	$900/year	$900/year	$900/year for the spkr. pro tem.
New Hampshire	$50/two-year term	None	None	None
New Jersey	1/3 above annual base salary.	None	None	None
New Mexico	None	None	None	None
New York	$41,500/year	$34,500/year	$34,500/year	$9,000–$25,000/year for 31 leaders
North Carolina	$38,151/year and $16,956/year expense allowance.	$17,048/year and $7,992/year expense allowance.	$17,048/year and $7,992/year expense allowance.	$21,739/year and $10,032/year expense allowance for the spkr. pro tem.
North Dakota	$15/day during legislative session.	$15/day during legislative session, $325/month during term of office.	$15/day during legislative session, $325/month during term of office.	$10/day for asst. ldrs. during legislative sessions.
Ohio	$94,437.36/year for the spkr.	$86,165/year for the spkr. pro tem; $81,163/year for the maj. floor ldr.; $76,169/year for the asst. maj. floor ldr.; $71,173/year for the maj. whip; $66,175/year for the asst. maj. whip.	$86,164.76/year for the min. ldr.	Compensation for committee leadership
Oklahoma	$17,932/year	$12,364/year	$12,364/year	$12,364/year for the spkr. pro tem.
Oregon	$22,596/year in additional salary for the speaker.	None	None	None
Pennsylvania	$46,022/year	$36,819/year	$36,819/year	$27,942/year each for the maj. and min. whips; $17,422/year each for the maj. and min. caucus chairs; $11,506/year each for the maj. and min. caucus secretaries, policy chairs and administrators.
Rhode Island	Speaker of the House receives double annual rate for representatives.	None	None	None
South Carolina	$11,000/year	None	None	$3,600/year for the spkr. pro tem.
South Dakota	None	None	None	None
Tennessee	$60,609/year	None	None	None
Texas	None	None	None	None
Utah	$3,000/year	$2,000/year	$2,000/year	$2,000/year each for the whips and asst. whips.
Vermont	$730.66/week during session plus an additional $11,296/year salary.	None	None	None

See footnotes at end of table.

ADDITIONAL COMPENSATION FOR HOUSE/ASSEMBLY LEADERS — Continued

State	Presiding officer	Majority leader	Minority leader	Other leaders and committee chairs
Virginia	$8,000/year in addition to base salary.	$4,000/year in addition to base salary.	$4,000/year in addition to base salary.	None
Washington	$8,000/year	None	$4,000/year	None
West Virginia	$150/day for the speaker when attending to legislative business.	$50/day during session.	$50/day during session.	$150/day for the chairman of Finance and Judiciary, up to 30 days, when the legislature is not in session or meeting for interims. $150/day for up to six more people named by the presiding officer, for up to 30 days, when the legislature is not in session or meeting for interims.
Wisconsin	$25/month	None	None	None
Wyoming	$3/day during session; $918/month when not in session.	$600/month when not in session.	$600/month when not in session.	None

Source: National Conference of State Legislatures, 2015.
(a) Total annual salary for this position.

Table 3.13
STATE LEGISLATIVE RETIREMENT BENEFITS

State or other jurisdiction	Participation	Plan name	Requirements for regular retirement	Employee contribution rate	Benefit formula
Alabama	None available				
Alaska	Optional	Public Employees Retirement System	Age 60 with 10 yrs.	Employee 6.75%	2% (first 10 yrs.); or 2.25% (second 10 yrs.); or 2.5% over 20 yrs. x average salary over 5 highest consecutive yrs. x yrs. of service.
Arizona	Mandatory—except that officials subject to term limits may opt out for a term of office.	Elected Officials Retirement System	Age 65, 5+ yrs. service; age 62, 10+ yrs. service; or 20 yrs. service; earlier retirement with an actuarial reduction of benefits. Vesting at 5 yrs.	Employee 7%	4% x years of credited service x highest 3 yr. average in the past 10 yrs. The benefit is capped at 80% of FAS. An elected official may purchase service credit in the plan for service earned in a non-elected position by buying it at an actuarially-determined amount.
Arkansas	Optional. Those elected before 7/1/99 may have service covered as a regular state employee but must have 5 years of regular service to do so.	Arkansas Public Employees Retirement System	Age 65, 10 yrs. service; or age 55, 12 yrs. service; or any age, 28 yrs. service; any age if serving in the General Assembly on 7/1/79; any age if in elected office on 7/1/79 with 17 and 1/2 yrs. of service. As a regular employee, age 65, 5 yrs. service, or any age and 28 yrs. Members of the contributory plan established in 2005 must have a minimum of 10 yrs. legislative service if they have only legislative state employment.	Non-contributory plan in effect for those elected before 2006. For those elected then and thereafter, a contributory plan that requires 5% of salary.	For service that began after 7/1/99: 2.07% x FAS x years of service. FAS based on three highest consecutive years or service. For service that began after 7/1/91: $35 x years of service equals monthly benefit. For contributory plan, 2% x FAS x years of service.
California	Legislators elected after 1990 are not eligible for retirement benefits for legislative service.				
Colorado	Mandatory	Either Public Employees' Retirement Association or State Defined Contribution Plan. A choice is not irrevocable.	PERA: age 65, 5 yrs. service; age 50, 30 yrs. service; when age + service equals 80 or more (min. age of 55). DCP: no age requirement and vested immediately	Employee: 8%	PERA: 2.5% x FAS x yrs. of service, capped at 100% of FAS. DCP benefit depends upon contributions and investment returns.
Connecticut	Mandatory	State Employees Retirement System Tier IIA	Age 60, 25 yrs. credited service; age 62, 10–25 yrs. credited service; age 62.5 yrs. actual state service. Reduced benefit available with earlier retirement ages.	2%	(.0133 x avg. annual salary) + (.005 x avg. annual salary in excess of "breakpoint" x credited service up to 35 years. 2003—$36,400 2007—$46,000 2004—$38,600 2008—$48,800 2005—$40,900 2009—$51,700 2006—$43,400 After 2009—increase breakpoint by 6% per year rounded to nearest $100.

See footnotes at end of table.

STATE LEGISLATIVE RETIREMENT BENEFITS — Continued

State or other jurisdiction	Participation	Plan name	Requirements for regular retirement	Employee contribution rate	Benefit formula
Delaware	Mandatory	State Employees Pension Plan	Age 60, 5 yrs. credited service	3% of total monthly compensation in excess of $6,000	2% times FAS times years of service before 1997 + 1.85% times FAS times years of service from 1997 on. FAS = average of highest 3 years.
Florida	Optional. Elected officials may opt out and may choose between DB and DC plans.	Florida Retirement System	Vesting in DB plan, 6 years; in DC plan, 1 year. DB plan: Age 62 with 6 years; 30 years at any age. DC plan: any age	No employee contribution. Employer contribution for 2004–2005 for legislators is 12.49% of salary.	DB plan: 3% x years of creditable service x average final compensation (average of highest 5 yrs). DC plan: Dependent upon investment experience.
Georgia	Optional: Choice when first elected.	Georgia Legislative Retirement System	Vested after 8 yrs.: age 62, with 8 yrs. of service; age 60 with reduction for early retirement.	Employee rate 3.75% + $7 month	$36 per month for each year of service.
Hawaii	Mandatory	Public Employees Retirement System; elected officials' plan	Age 55 with 5 years of service; any age with 10 years service. Vesting at 5 years.	Main plan is non-contributory; 7.8% for elected officials' plan for annuity.	3.5 x yrs. of service as elected official x highest average salary plus annuity based on contributions as an elected official. Highest average salary = average of 3 highest 12-month periods as elected official.
Idaho	Mandatory		Age 65 with 5 yrs. service; reduced benefit at age 55 with 5 yrs. of service.	6.97%	Avg. monthly salary for highest 42 consecutive months x 2% x months of credited service.
Illinois	Optional	General Assembly Retirement System	Age 55, 8 yrs. service; or age 62, 4 yrs. service	8.5% for retirement; 2% for survivors; 1% for automatic increases; 11.5% total	3% of each of 1st 4 yrs.; 3.5% for each of next 2 yrs.; 4% for each of next 2 yrs.; 4.5% for each of the next 4 yrs.; 5% for each yr. above 12.
Indiana	DB plan is optional for those serving on April 30, 1989. Defined contribution plan is optional for those serving on April 30, 1989 and mandatory for those elected or appointed since April 30, 1989.	Legislator's Retirement System and Defined Benefit (DB) Plan and Defined Contribution Plan (DC).	DB plan: Vesting at 10 yrs. Age 65 with 10 yrs. of legislative service; or if no longer in the legislature, these options apply: at least 10 yrs. service; no state salary; at age 55+ Rule of 85 applies; or age 60 with 15 yrs. of service. Early retirement with reduced benefit. Immediate vesting in the DC plan.	DC plan: 5% employee, 20% state (of taxable income). DB plan and employer contributions funded by appropriation.	DB benefit plan monthly benefit: Lesser of (a) $40 x years of General Assembly service completed before November 8, 1989 or (b) 1/12 of the average of the three highest consecutive years of General Assembly service salary. DC plan: numerous options for withdrawing accumulations in accord with IRS regulations. Loans are available. A participant in both plans may receive a benefit from both plans.
Iowa	Optional	Public Employees Retirement System	Age 65; age 62 with 20 yrs. service Rule of 88; reduced benefit at 55 with at least 4 years of service.	3.7% individual	2% times FAS times years of service for first 30 years, + 1% times FAS times years in excess of 30 but no more than 5 in excess of 30. FAS is average of 3 highest years.
Kansas	Optional	Public Employees Retirement System	Age 65, age 62 with 10 yrs. of service or age plus yrs. of service equals 85 pts.	4% of salary. (4% annualized salary for Legislators).	3 highest yrs. x 1.75% x yrs. service divided by 12.

See footnotes at end of table.

STATE LEGISLATIVE RETIREMENT BENEFITS—Continued

State or other jurisdiction	Participation	Plan name	Requirements for regular retirement	Employee contribution rate	Benefit formula
Kentucky	Optional. Those who opt out are covered by the state employees' plan	Kentucky Legislator's Retirement Plan	Age 65 with five years of service; any age with 30 years of service, and intermediate provisions. Early retirement with reduced benefits.	5% of creditable compensation, set by law at $27,500; not the same as actual salary. Revised to be payable on compensation reported on W-2 forms beginning in 2005.	2.75% of FAS (based on creditable compensation) x years of service. FAS is the average monthly earnings for the 60 months preceding retirement.
Louisiana	None available				
Maine	Mandatory	Maine State Retirement Plan	Age 60 (if 10 yrs. of service on 7/1/93) and age 62 (if less than 10 yrs. of service on 7/1/93). Reduced benefit available for earlier retirement.	7.65% legislators; employer contribution is actuarially determined.	2% of average final compensation (the average of the 3 high salary years) times years of service.
Maryland	Optional	State Legislator's Pension Plan	Age 60, with 8 yrs.; age 50, 8+yrs creditable service (early reduced retirement)	5% of annual salary	3% of legislative salary for each yr. of service up to a max. of 22 yrs. 3 months. Benefits are recalculated when legislative salaries are changed.
Massachusetts	Optional after each election or re-election to the General Court.	State Retirement System legislator's plan	Age 55 with 6 years service; unreduced benefit at 65. Vesting at 6 yrs. Reduced benefits for retirement before age 65.	9%. Some legislators are grandfathered at lower rates.	2.5 times years of service times FAS. FAS = average of highest 36 months. Service credit is allowed for membership in other Massachusetts retirement plans.
Michigan	Optional	Legislative Retirement System (DB) for legislators elected before 3/31/97. Others may join the state defined contribution plan.	Age 55, 5 yrs. or age plus service equals 70	7%–13% for DB plan. For the DC plan, the state contributes 4% of salary. Members may contribute up to 3% of salary. The state will match the member's contribution in addition to the state 4% contribution.	For DB plans, various provisions, depending on when service started. For the DC plan, benefits depend upon contributions and earnings.
Minnesota	Mandatory	Legislators Retirement Plan before 7/1/97; Defined Contribution Plan (DCP) since then.	LRP: Age 62, 6 yrs. service and fully vested. DCP: age 55 and vested immediately. LRP members do not have Social Security coverage. DCP members have Social Security coverage.	LRP: 9% DCP: 4% from member, 6% from state.	2.7% x high 5 yr. avg. salary x length of service (yrs.) DCP benefit depends upon contributions and investment return.
Mississippi	Mandatory	Legislators' plan within the Public Employees' Retirement System	Age 60 with 4 or more years of service, or 25 years of service.	Regular: 7.25%; state 9.75% to 10.75% effective July 1, 2005; Supplement for legislative service: 3%/6.33%.	Legislators who qualify for regular state retirement benefits also automatically qualify for the legislators' supplemental benefits. Regular: 2% times FAS times years of service up to and including 25 years of service + 2.5% times FAS times service in excess of 25 years FAS is based on the high 4 years. Supplement: 1% times FAS times years of legislative service through 25 years, + 1.25% times FAS times years of service in excess of 25.

See footnotes at end of table.

STATE LEGISLATIVE RETIREMENT BENEFITS — Continued

State or other jurisdiction	Participation	Plan name	Requirements for regular retirement	Employee contribution rate	Benefit formula
Missouri..........	Mandatory	Missouri State Employee Retirement System	Age 55; three full biennial assemblies (6 years) or Rule of 80. Vesting at 6 years of service.	Non-contributory	Monthly pay divided by 24 x years of creditable service, capped at 100% of salary. Benefit is adjusted by the percentage increase in pay for an active legislator.
Montana	Optional	Public Employees Retirement System. Either a DB or a DC plan is available.	Vesting at 5 years Age 60 with at least 5 years service; age 65 regardless of years of service; or 30 years of service regardless of age	6.9% for DB plan. Employer contribution of 4.19% plus employee contribution of 6.9 % for DC plan.	DB plan: 1/56 times years of service times FAS. Early retirement with reduced benefits is available. DC plan: Employee contributions and earnings are immediately vested. Employer contributions and earnings are vested after 5 years.
Nebraska	None available				
Nevada	Mandatory; but Chapter 380, Laws of 2005, allows legislators to withdraw from the system at will. The decision is final.	Legislator's Retirement System	Age 60, 10 yrs. service	15% of session salary	Number of years x $25 = monthly allowance
New Hampshire	None available				
New Jersey	Mandatory	Public Employees' Retirement System	Age 60; no minimum service requirement. Early retirement with no benefit reduction with 25 years of service. Vesting at 8 years.	5% of salary	3% x Final Average Salary x years of service. FAS = higher of three highest years or three final years. Benefit is capped at 2/3 of FAS, Other formulas apply if a legislator also has other service covered by the Public Employee Retirement System.
New Mexico	Optional	Legislative Retirement Plan	Plans 1A and 1B: Age 65 with 5 years of service; 64/8; 63/11; 60/12; or any age with 14 years of service. Plan 2: 65 with five years of service or at any age with 10 years of service.	Plan 1A: $100 per year for service after 1959 Plan 1B: $200 per year (now closed to new enrollments). Plan 2: $500/year	Plan 1A: $250 per year of service. Plan 1B: $500 per year of service after 1959. Plan 2: 11 percent of the IRS per diem rate in effect on December 31st of the year a legislator retires x 60 x the years of credited service. For a legislator who retired in 2003 the benefit would be $957 per year of credited service. Annual 3% COLA.
New York..........	Mandatory	New York State and Local Retirement System	Age 62 with 5 years of service; 55 with 30 years; reduced benefit available at 55/5. Vesting at 5 years.	3% for first 10 years of membership (Tier 4 provisions).	Tier 4: For less than 20 yrs. of service, pension = 1/60th for (1.66%) of final average salary (FAS) x years of service; for 20 years service, pension = 1/50th (2%) of FAS x years of service; each year of service beyond 39, pension = 3/200th (1.5%) of FAS.
North Carolina..........	Mandatory	Legislative Retirement System	Age 65 with 5 years of service; reduced benefit available at earlier ages.	7%	Highest annual compensation x 4.02% x years of service.
North Dakota..........	None available				
Ohio..........	Optional	Public Employees Retirement System	Age 60 with 5 years service or 55 with 25 years service or at any age with 30 years service.	8.5% of gross salary. A 10% contribution rate for legislators will be phased in over three years starting in 2006.	2.2% of final average salary times years of service up to and through 30 years of service. 2.5% starting with the 31st year of service and every year thereafter.

See footnotes at end of table.

STATE LEGISLATIVE RETIREMENT BENEFITS—Continued

State or other jurisdiction	Participation	Plan name	Requirements for regular retirement	Employee contribution rate	Benefit formula
Oklahoma	Legislators may retain membership as regular public employees if they have that status when elected; one time option to join Elected Officials' Plan.	Public Employee Retirement System, as regular member or elected official member. [Information here is for the Elected Officials' Plan.]	Elected Officials' Plan: Age 60 with 6 years service, vesting at 6 years.	Optional contribution of 4.5%, 6%, 7.5%, 8.5%, 9%, or 10% of total compensation.	Avg. participating salary x length of service x computation factor depending on optional contributions ranging from 1.9% for a 4.5% contribution to 4% for a 10% contribution.
Oregon	Optional	Public Employee Retirement System legislator plan	Age 55, 30+ yrs. service, 5 years vesting.	16.317% of subject wages	1.67% x yrs. service and final avg. monthly salary.
Pennsylvania	Optional	State Employees' Retirement System	Age 50, 3 yrs. service, any age with 35 years of service; early retirement with reduced benefit.	7.5%	3% x final avg. salary x credited yrs. of service (x withdrawal factor if under regular retirement age—50 for legislators).
Rhode Island	Legislators elected after January 1995 are ineligible for retirement benefits based on legislative service. (a)				
South Carolina	Mandatory, but members may opt out six months after being sworn into office.	South Carolina Retirement System	Age 60, 8 yrs. service; 30 yrs. of service regardless of age.	10%	4.82% of annual compensation x yrs. service.
South Dakota	None available				
Tennessee	Optional		Age 55, 4 yrs. service	5.43%	$70 per month x yrs. service with a $1,375 monthly cap.
Texas	Optional	Employee Retirement System: Elected Class Members	Age 60, 8 yrs. service; age 50, 12 yrs. service. Vesting at 8 years.	8%	2.3% x district judge's salary x length of service, with the monthly benefit capped at the level of a district judge's salary, and adjusted when such salaries are increased. Various annuity options are available. Military service credit may be purchased to add to elective class service membership. In July 2005, a district judge's salary was set at $125,000, a year.
Utah	Mandatory	Governors' and Legislators' Retirement Plan	Age 62 with 10 years and an actuarial reduction; age 65 with 4 years of service for full benefits.	Non-contributory	$24.80/month (as of July 2004) x years of service; adjusted semi-annually according to consumer price index up to a maximum increase of 2%.
Vermont	None available. Deferred compensation plan available.				
Virginia	Mandatory		Age 50, 30 yrs. service (unreduced); age 55, 5 yrs. service; age 50, 10 yrs. service (reduced).	8.91% of creditable compensation	1.7% of average final compensation x yrs. of service.

See footnotes at end of table.

STATE LEGISLATIVE RETIREMENT BENEFITS—Continued

State or other jurisdiction	Participation	Plan name	Requirements for regular retirement	Employee contribution rate	Benefit formula
Washington	Optional. If before an election the legislator belonged to a state public retirement plan, he or she may continue in that by making contributions. Otherwise the new legislator may join PERS Plan 2 or Plan 3.	See column to left. PERS Plan 2 is a DB plan. PERS Plan 3 is a hybrid DB/DC plan.	PERS Plan 2: Age 65 with 5 years of service credit. Plan 3: Age 65 with 10 years of service credit for the DB side of the plan; immediate benefits (subject to federal restrictions) on the DC side of the plan. The member may choose various options for investment of contributions to the DC plan.	PERS Plan 2: Employee contribution of 2.43% for 2002. Estimated at 3.33% for 2005–2007. Plan 3: No required member contribution for the DB component. The member may contribute from 5% to 15% of salary to the DC component.	PERS Plan 2: 2% x years of service credit x average final compensation. Plan 3: DB is 1% x service credit years x average final compensation. DC benefit depends upon the value of accumulations.
West Virginia	Optional		Age 55, if yrs. of service + age equal 80.	4.5% gross income	2% of final avg. salary x yrs. service. Final avg. salary is based on 3 highest yrs. out of last 10 yrs.
Wisconsin	Mandatory		Age 62 normal; age 57 with 30 years of service.	2.6% of salary in 2003, adjusted annually	Higher benefit of formula (2.165% x years of service x salary for service before 2000; 2% x years of service x salary for service 2000 and after) or money-purchase calculation.
Wyoming	None available				
Dist. of Columbia	Mandatory		Age 62, 5 yrs. service; age 55, 30 yrs. service; age 60, 20 yrs. service.	Before 10/1/87, 7%; after 10/1/87, 5%	Multiply high 3 yrs. average pay by indicator under applicable yrs. or months of service.
Puerto Rico	Optional	Retirement System of the Employees of the Government of Puerto Rico	After 1990, age 65 with 30 years of service.	8.28%	1.5% of average earnings multiplied by the number of years of accredited service.
Guam	Optional		Age 60, 30 yrs. service; age 55, 15 yrs. service	5% or 8.5%	An amount equal to 2% of avg. annual salary for each of the first 10 yrs. of credited service and 2.5% of avg. annual salary for each yr. or part thereof of credited service over 10 yrs.
U.S. Virgin Islands	Optional		Age 60, 10 yrs. service	8%	At age 60 with at least 10 yrs. of service, at 2.5% for each yr. of service or at any time with at least 30 yrs. service.

Source: National Conference of State Legislatures, January 2006 and updated January 2009.
Notes: This table shows the retirement plans effective for state legislators elected in 2003, 2004 and thereafter. In general the table does not include information on closed plans, plans that continue in force for some legislators who entered the plans in previous years, but which have been closed to additional members. The information in this table was updated for all states and Puerto Rico in 2004 and updated for 2005 state legislation. Information for the District of Columbia, Guam and the Virgin Islands dates from 2002.

Key:
N.A. — Information not available.
None available — No retirement benefit provided.
(a) Constitution has been amended effective 1/95. Any legislator elected after this date is not eligible to join the State Retirement System, but will be compensated for $10,000/yr. with cost of living increases to be adjusted annually.

Table 3.14
BILL PRE-FILING, REFERENCE AND CARRYOVER

State or other jurisdiction	Pre-filing of bills allowed (b)	Bills referred to committee by: Senate	Bills referred to committee by: House/ Assembly	Bill referral restricted by rule (a) Senate	Bill referral restricted by rule (a) House/ Assembly	Bill carryover allowed (c)
Alabama	★(d)	(e) (f)	Speaker (f)	L, M	L, M	...
Alaska	★	President	Speaker	L, M	L, M	★
Arizona	★	President	Speaker	L	L	...
Arkansas	★	President (g)	Speaker	L	L	...
California	★(h)	Rules Cmte.	Rules Cmte.	L	L	★(h)
Colorado	★	President	Speaker	(i)	(i)	...
Connecticut	★	Pres. Pro Tempore	Speaker	M	M	...
Delaware	★	Pres. Pro Tempore	Speaker	L	L	★
Florida	★	President	Speaker	L, M	M	...
Georgia	★	President (f)	Speaker	...	...	★
Hawaii	(j)	(j)	Speaker	...	...	★
Idaho	...	President (e)	Speaker	(qq)	(qq)	...
Illinois	★	Cmte. on Assignments	Rules Cmte.	(k)	(k)	★
Indiana	★(l)	Pres. Pro Tempore	Speaker	(m)	...	...
Iowa	★	President	Speaker	M	M	★
Kansas	★	President	Speaker	L (n)	L (n)	★
Kentucky	★	Cmte. on Cmtes.	Cmte. on Cmtes.	L, M	L, M	...
Louisiana	★	President (o)	Speaker (o)	L	L	...
Maine	★	Secy. of Senate	Clerk of House	(p)	(p)	★(rr)
Maryland	★	President (q)	Speaker (q)	L	L	...
Massachusetts	★	Clerk	Clerk	M	M	★
Michigan	...	Majority Ldr.	Speaker	(uu)	(uu)	★
Minnesota	★(r)	President	Speaker	L, M	L, M	★(r)
Mississippi	★	President (e)	Speaker	L	L	...
Missouri	★	Pres. Pro Tempore	Speaker	L	L	...
Montana	★	President	Speaker	L (tt)	L (tt)	...
Nebraska	★	Reference Cmte. (s)	U	L	U	★(t)
Nevada	★	President (u)	Speaker (u)	L (v)	...	...
New Hampshire	★	President	Speaker	M	M	★(ss)
New Jersey	★	President	Speaker	L, M	L, M	★
New Mexico	★	(w)	Speaker	L	L, M	...
New York	★	Minority Coalition leaders	Speaker	L,M	L, M	★
North Carolina	...	Rules Chair	Speaker	M	M	★
North Dakota	★	Majority Leader	Speaker	L	L	...
Ohio	★(y)	Reference Cmte.	Rules & Reference Cmte.	L (z)	L, M (aa)	★(bb)
Oklahoma	★	Majority Leader	Speaker	L	L	★(cc)
Oregon	★	President	Speaker	(dd)	(ee)	...
Pennsylvania	(x)	President Pro Tempore	Chief Clerk	M	M	...
Rhode Island	★	President	Speaker	M	M	★
South Carolina	★	President	Speaker	M	M	★(ff)
South Dakota	★	President Pro Tempore	Speaker	L	L	...
Tennessee	★	Speaker	Speaker	L, M	L, M	★(gg)
Texas	★	President	Speaker	L	L	...
Utah	★	President	Speaker	L	L	...
Vermont	(hh)	President	Speaker	L, M	L, M	★
Virginia	★	Clerk	Clerk (ii)	L, M (jj)	(kk)	★(ll)
Washington	★	(mm)	Speaker	L	L	★
West Virginia (nn)	★	President	Speaker	L, M	L, M	...
Wisconsin	...	President	Speaker	L, M	L, M	★(oo)
Wyoming	★	President	Speaker	L	L	...
American Samoa	...	...	...	...	...	...
Guam	★	Cmte. on Calendar Chairs	U	L, M (pp)	U	★
No. Mariana Islands	★	President	Speaker	L	L	...
Puerto Rico	...	President	Secretary	M	M	★
U.S. Virgin Islands	...	Senate President in Pro-Forma meeting	U	L	U	★

See footnotes at end of table.

BILL PRE-FILING, REFERENCE AND CARRYOVER — Continued

Sources: The Council of State Governments' survey, November 2014 and update from state websites 2015.

Key:

★ — Yes

... — No

L — Rules generally require all bills be referred to the appropriate committee of jurisdiction.

M — Rules require specific types of bills be referred to specific committees (e.g., appropriations, local bills).

U — Unicameral legislature.

(a) Legislative rules specify all or certain bills go to committees of jurisdiction.

(b) Unless otherwise indicated by footnote, bills may be introduced prior to convening each session of the legislature. In this column only: ★ — pre-filing is allowed in both chambers (or in the case of Nebraska, in the unicameral legislature); ... — pre-filing is not allowed in either chamber.

(c) Bills carry over from the first year of the legislature to the second (does not apply in Alabama, Arkansas, Montana, Nevada, North Dakota, Oregon and Texas, where legislatures meet biennially). Bills generally do not carry over after an intervening legislative election.

(d) Except between the end of the last regular session of the legislature in any quadrennium and the organizational session following the general election and special sessions.

(e) Lieutenant governor is the president of the Senate.

(f) Senate bills by president with concurrence of president pro tem. House bills by president pro tem with concurrence of president, if no concurrence, referred to majority leader for assignment.

(g) Senate chief counsel makes recommendations to the presiding officer.

(h) Bills may be drafted prior to session, but may not be introduced until the first day of session. Bills introduced in the first year of the regular session and passed by the house of origin on or before the January 31st constitutional deadline in the second year are carryover bills.

(i) In either house, state law requires any bill which affects the sentencing of criminal offenders and which would result in a net increase of imprisonment in state correctional facilities must be assigned to the appropriations committee of the house in which it was introduced. In the Senate, a bill must be referred to the Appropriations Committee if it contains an appropriation from the state treasury or the increase of any salary. Each bill which provides that any state revenue be devoted to any purpose other than that to which it is devoted under existing law must be referred to the Finance Committee.

(j) Prefiling allowed in the House by rule, seven calendar days before the commencement of the regular session, in even-numbered years. Senate allows prefiling of bills as determined on a year-to-year basis. Senate bills are referred to committee by the members of the majority leadership appointed by the President.

(k) In even-numbered years, the Committee on Assignments (Senate) or Rules Committee (House) is to refer to substantive committees only appropriation bills implementing the budget, and bills deemed by the Committee on Assignments (Senate) or Rules Committee (House) to be of an emergency nature or of substantial importance to the operation of government.

(l) Only in the Senate.

(m) At the discretion of President Pro Tempore.

(n) Appropriation bills are the only "specific type" mentioned in the rules to be referred to either House Appropriation Cmte. or Senate Ways and Means.

(o) Subject to approval or disapproval. Louisiana—majority members present.

(p) Maine Joint Rule 308 sections 1,2,3, "All bills and resolves must be referred to committee, except that this provision may be suspended by a majority vote in each chamber."

(q) The President and Speaker may refer bills to any of the standing committees or the Rules Committees, but usually bills are referred according to subject matter.

(r) Pre-filing of bills allowed prior to the convening of the 2nd year of the biennium. Bill carryover allowed if in second year of a two-year session.

(s) The Nebraska Legislature's Executive Board serves as the Reference Committee.

(t) Bills are carried over from the 90-day session beginning in the odd-numbered year to the 60-day session, which begins in even-numbered year. Bills that have not passed by the last day of the 60-day session are all indefinitely postponed by motion on the last day of the session. The odd-numbered year shall be carried forward to the even-numbered year.

(u) In the Senate any member may make a motion for referral, but committee referrals are under the control of the Majority Floor Leader. In the House any member may make a motion for referral, and a chart is used to guide bill referrals based on statutory authority of committee, but committee referrals are under the control of the Majority Floor Leader.

(v) Rules do not require specific types of bills be referred to specific committees.

(w) Sponsor subject to approval of the body.

(x) Only in the Senate.

(y) Senate Rule 33: Between the general election and the time for the next convening session, a holdover member or member-elect may file bills for introduction in the next session with the Clerk's office. Those bills shall be treated as if they were bills introduced on the first day of the session. House Rule 61: Bills introduced prior to the convening of the session shall be treated as if they were bills introduced on the first day of the session. Between the general election and the time for the next convening session, a member-elect may file bills for introduction in the next session with the Clerk's office. The Clerk shall number such bills consecutively, in the order in which they are filed, beginning with the number "1."

(z) Senate Rule 35: Unless a motion or order to the contrary, bills are referred to the proper standing committee. All Senate bills and resolutions referred by the Committee on Reference on or before the first day of April in an even-numbered year shall be scheduled for a minimum of one public hearing.

(aa) House Rule 37: All House bills and resolutions introduced, in compliance with House Rules, on or before the fifteenth day of May in an even -numbered year shall be referred to a standing select, or special committee, and shall be scheduled for a minimum of one public hearing. House Rule 65: All bills carrying an appropriation shall be referred to the Finance and Appropriations Committee for consideration and report before being considered the third time.

(bb) Bills carry over between the first and second year of each regular annual session, but not to the next biennial 2-year General Assembly.

(cc) A legislature consists of two years. Bills from the first session can carry over to the second session only. 2015 will begin a new Legislature, the 55th, and no bills from 2014 will carry over to 2015.

(dd) The President can refer bills to any standing or special committee and may also attach subsequent referrals to other committees following action by the first committee.

(ee) Rules specify bills shall be referred by the Speaker to any standing or special committee and may also attach subsequent referrals to other committees following action by the first committee.

(ff) Allowed during the first year of the two year session.

(gg) Bills and resolutions introduced in the First Regular Session may carry over to the Second Regular Session (odd-numbered year to even-numbered year) only.

(hh) Bills are drafted prior to session but released starting first day of session.

(ii) Under the direction of the speaker.

(jj) Jurisdiction of the committees by subject matter is listed in the Rules.

(kk) The House Rules establish jurisdictional committees. The Speaker refers legislation to those committees as he deems appropriate.

(ll) Even-numbered year session to odd-numbered year session.

(mm) By the floor leader.

(nn) Prefiling allowed only in the house in even-numbered years.

(oo) From odd-year to even-year, but not between biennial sessions.

(pp) Substantive resolutions referred to sponsor for public hearing.

(qq) Bills may be referred to any appropriate committee (Senate Rule 14). Bills may be referred to any standing committee (House Rule 43).

(rr) Allowed between session in a biennium, not to subsequent legislatures.

(ss) Referred bills may be held in committee and acted on during second year session.

(tt) President and Speaker have broad discretion.

(uu) Senate Rule 3.203 a) The Senate Majority Leader shall refer all bills and joint resolutions to a standing committee no later than one (1) Senate legislative day after being submitted to the Secretary of the Senate. The presiding officer shall announce the reference of all bills and joint resolutions. ... c) The Senate Majority Leader may change the original referral of a bill or resolution by oral notice to the Senate or written communication submitted to the Secretary of the Senate before the end of session on the next Senate legislative day following the day of the original referral. Notices of the written communication shall be announced by the Secretary of the Senate during session and both oral and written notifications shall be printed in the Journal. House Rule 41: (4) The Speaker shall refer all bills and joint resolutions to a standing committee no later than one House legislative day after being submitted to the Clerk. (5) The Speaker may change the original referral of a bill or resolution by written communication submitted to the Clerk before the end of session on the next House legislative day following the day of the original referral. Notice of the referral shall be announced by the Clerk and printed in the Journal.

Table 3.15
TIME LIMITS ON BILL INTRODUCTION

State or other jurisdiction	Time limit on introduction of bills	Procedures for granting exception to time limits
Alabama	House: no limit. Senate: 24th legislative day of regular session (a).	House: N.A. Senate: Unanimous vote to suspend rules.
Alaska	35th C day of 2nd regular session.	Introduction by committee or by suspension of operation of limiting rule.
Arizona	House: 29th day of regular session; 10th day of special session. Senate: 22nd day of regular session; 10th day of special session.	House: Permission of rules committee. Senate: Permission of rules committee.
Arkansas	55th day of regular session (50th day for appropriations bills). Retirement and health care legislation affecting licensures shall be introduced during the first 15 days.	2/3 vote of membership of each house for appropriations bills and all others except retirement and health care legislation affecting licensures which require 3/4 vote of the membership of each house.
California	Deadlines established by the Joint Rules Committee adpoted in each session.	Approval of Rules Committee and 3/4 vote of membership.
Colorado	House: 22nd C day of regular session. Senate: 17th C day of regular session.	Committees on delayed bills may extend deadline.
Connecticut	10 days into session in odd-numbered years, 3 days into session in even-numbered years (b).	2/3 vote of members present.
Delaware	House: no limit. Senate: no limit.	
Florida	House: noon of the first day of regular session. Senate: noon first day of regular session (h).	House: No exception as such; if neeed, one would be granted by waiving the rule by 2/3 vote on the floor. Senate: Existence of an emergency reasonably compelling consideration notwithstanding the deadline.
Georgia	Only for specific types of bills	
Hawaii	Actual dates established during session.	Majority vote of membership.
Idaho	House: 20th day of session for personal bills; 36th day of session for all committees; beyond that only privileged cmtes. Senate: 12th day of session for personal bills; 36th day of session for all committees; beyond that only privileged cmtes.	House and Senate: speaker/president pro tempore may designate any standing committee to serve as a privileged committee temporarily.
Illinois	House: determined by speaker. Senate: determined by senate president.	House: The speaker may set deadlines for any action on any category of legislative measure, including deadlines for introduction of bills. Senate: At any time, the president may set alternative deadlines for any legislative action with written notice filed with the secretary.
Indiana	House: Mid-January. Senate: Date specific—set in Rules, different for long and short session. Mid-January.	House: 2/3 vote. Senate: If date falls on weekend/Holiday—extended to next day. Sine die deadline set by statute, does not change.
Iowa	House: Friday of 5th week of 1st regular session; Friday of 2nd week of 2nd regular session. Senate: Friday of 5th week of 1st regular session; Friday of 2nd week of 2nd regular session.	House: Majority. Senate: Constitutional majority.
Kansas	Actual dates established in the Joint Rules of the House and Senate every two years when the joint rules are adopted.	Resolution adopted by majority of members of either house may make specific exceptions to deadlines.
Kentucky	House: No introductions during the last 14 L days of odd-year session, during last 22 L days of even-year session. Senate: No introductions during the last 14 L days of odd-year session, during last 20 L days of even-year session.	None.
Louisiana	House: 10th C day of odd year sessions and 23rd C day of even-year sessions. Senate: 10th C day of odd year sessions and 23rd C day of even-year sessions.	None.
Maine	House: Cloture dates established by the Legislative Council. Senate: Cloture dates established by the Legislative Council.	House: Bills filed after cloture date must be approved by a majority of the Legislative Council. Senate: Appeals heard by Legislative Council. Six votes required to allow introduction of legislation.

See footnotes at end of table.

TIME LIMITS ON BILL INTRODUCTION — Continued

State or other jurisdiction	Time limit on introduction of bills	Procedures for granting exception to time limits
Maryland	House and Senate: No introductions during the last 35 days of regular session, unless 2/3 of the elected members of a chamber vote yes. Additional limitations involve committee action. Senate bills introduced after the 24th calendar day must be referred to the Senate Rules Committee and also Senate bills introduced after the 10th calendar day on behalf of the administration, i.e. the governor, must be referred to the Senate Rules Committee. House bills introduced during the last 59 calendar days (after the 31st day) are referred to the House Rules Committee. The Senate Rules and House Rules contain further provisions concerning the requirements for forcing legislation out of these committees.	House: 2/3 vote of elected members of each house.
Massachusetts	1st Wednesday in December even-numbered years. 1st Wednesday in November odd-numbered years.	2/3 vote of members present and voting.
Michigan	No limit.	
Minnesota	No limit.	
Mississippi	14th C day in 90-day session; 49th C day in 125-day session (e).	2/3 vote of members present and voting.
Missouri	House: 60th L day of regular session. Senate: March 1.	Majority vote of elected members each house; governor's request for consideration of bill by special message.
Montana	Introduction of bills & resolutions: 10th L day if requested prior to convening or 2 days after receipt of finished bill draft after session convenes, whichever is earlier. Requests for general bills and resolutions: 12th L day; revenue bills: 17th L day; committee bills and resolutions: 36th L day; appropriations bills: 45th L day; interim study resolutions: 60th L day; committee revenue bills and bill proposing referenda: 62nd L day; committee bills implementing provision of a general appropriation act: 67th L day; resolutions confirming governor appointees or bill amending/repealing administrative rule: no deadline.	2/3 vote of members.
Nebraska	10th L day of any session (f).	3/5 vote of elected membership.
Nevada	Actual dates established at start of session.	Waiver granted by majority leader of the Senate and speaker of the Assembly acting jointly.
New Hampshire	Determined by rules.	2/3 vote of members present.
New Jersey	No limit.	
New Mexico	House: 15 days in short session/even years, 30 days in long session/odd years. Senate: 15 days in short session/even years, 30 days in long session/odd years.	None. Statutory limit for legislators; governor not limited and can send bill with message.
New York	Assembly: For unlimited introduction of bills, the final day is the last Tuesday in May of the 2nd year of the legislative term. Senate: Determined by the Majority Conference leaders, but no earlier than 1st Tuesday in March; except introduction by agencies is March 1, for all other program bills it is 1st Tuesday in April.	Assembly: Introduction by Rules Cmte., by message from the Senate, or with consent of the speaker, by members elected at a special election who take office on or after the 1st Tues. in May. Senate: Introduction by Rules Committee after 2nd Friday in June, or by message from the Assembly.
North Carolina	Actual dates established during session.	Senate: 2/3 vote of membership present and voting shall be required.
North Dakota	Proposed limits for 2015 session; House: January 19. Senate: January 26.	2/3 vote of the floor or by approval of Delayed Bills Committee.
Ohio	No limit.	
Oklahoma	Time limit set in rules.	2/3 vote of membership.
Oregon	House: 17th C day of odd-year session. All measures must be presession filed for even-year session. Senate: 17th C day of odd-year session. All measures must be presession filed for even-year session.	House: Bills approved by the Rules Cmte.: appropriation or fiscal measures sponsored by the Cmte. on Ways and Means; member priority requests (limited to 5 measures for odd-year session, none for even-year session). Senate: Measures approved by the Senate president: appropriation or fiscal measures sponsored by the Cmte. on Ways and Means; member priority requests (limited to 5 measures for odd-year session, none for even-year session).

See footnotes at end of table.

TIME LIMITS ON BILL INTRODUCTION — Continued

State or other jurisdiction	Time limit on introduction of bills	Procedures for granting exception to time limits
Pennsylvania..................	No limit.	
Rhode Island	Second week of February for Public Bills.	Sponsor must give one legislative day's notice.
South Carolina	House: Prior to April 15 of the 2nd yr. of a two-yr. legislative session; May 1 for bills first introduced in Senate. Rule 5.12. Senate: May 1 of regular session for bills originating in House. Rule 47.	House: 2/3 vote of members present and voting. Senate: 2/3 vote of members present and voting.
South Dakota	Individual bills: 40-day session: 15th L day; 35-day session: 10th L day. Committee bills: 40-day session: 16th L day; 35-day session: 11th L day. If a session calendar is adopted for a period of 36 days to 39 days, the legislative deadlines for the 35-day session shall be increased by the number of days by which the length of the session calendar exceeds 35 days.	2/3 approval of members-elect.
Tennessee........................	General bills, 10th L day of regular session (g).	Unanimous approval by Delayed Bills Committee.
Texas................................	60th C day of regular session, except for local bills, emergency appropriations and all emergency matters submitted by the governor in special message to the legislature.	4/5 vote of members present and voting.
Utah.................................	12 p.m. on 11th day of session.	Motion for request must be approved by a constitutional majority vote.
Vermont	House: 1st session — last day of February; 2nd session — last day of January. Senate: 1st session — 70 day limit; 2nd session — 25 C days before start of session.	Approval by Rules Committee.
Virginia	Set by joint procedural resolution adopted at the beginning of the session (usually the second Friday of the session is the last day to introduce legislation that does not have any earlier deadline).	As provided in the joint procedural resolution (usually unanimous consent or at written request of the governor).
Washington	Until 10 days before the end of session unless 2/3 vote of elected members of each house.	2/3 vote of elected members of each house.
West Virginia	Senate and House: 41st C day	2/3 vote of members present.
Wisconsin	No limit.	
Wyoming	House: 15th L day of session in odd-numbered years. 5th L day in even-numbered years. Senate: 12th L day of session in odd-numbered years. 5th L day in even-numbered years	2/3 vote of elected members.
American Samoa	House: After the 25th L day of the fourth Regular Session. Senate: After the 15th L day.	
Guam...............................	Public hearing on bill must be held no more than 120 days after date of bill introduction.	
No. Mariana Islands.......	No limit.	
Puerto Rico	1st session — within first 125 days; 2nd session — within first 60 days.	None.
U.S. Virgin Islands	No limit.	

Source: The Council of State Governments' survey, November 2014 and updates from state websites 2015.

Key:
C — Calendar   L — Legislative
(a) Not applicable to local bills, advertised or otherwise.
(b) Specific dates set in Joint Rules.
(c) Not applicable to appropriations bills.
(d) Not applicable to local bills and joint resolutions.
(e) Except Appropriation and Revenue bills (51st/86th C day) and Local and Private bills (83rd/118th C day).

(f) Except appropriations bills and bills introduced at the request of the governor, bills can be introduced during the first 10 legislative days of the session. Appropriation bills and bills introduced at the request of the governor can be introduced at any time during the session.
(g) Local bills have no cutoff.
(h) Not applicable to joint resolutions, local bills (which have no deadline), claim bills (deadline is Aug. 1 of the year preceding consideration or within 62 days of a senator's election), committee bills, trust fund bills and public records exemptions linked to timely filed bills.

Table 3.16
ENACTING LEGISLATION: VETO, VETO OVERRIDE AND EFFECTIVE DATE

State or other jurisdiction	Governor may item veto appropriation bills		Days allowed governor to consider bill (a)			Votes required in each house to pass bills or items over veto (c)	Effective date of enacted legislation (d)
	Amount	Other (b)	During session — Bill becomes law unless vetoed	After session — Bill becomes law unless vetoed	Bill dies unless signed		
Alabama	★(e)	…	6 (f)	20P	10A	Majority of elected body	Date signed by governor, unless otherwise specified.
Alaska	★	★	15	10A		2/3 elected (g)	90 days after enactment or the specified effective date.
Arizona	★	…	5	10A		2/3 elected (h)	90 days after adjournment.
Arkansas	★	…	5	20A		Majority elected	91st day after adjournment.
California	★(i)	…	12 (j)	30A		2/3 elected	(k)
Colorado	…	(l)	10P (ggg)	30A (m)		2/3 elected	90 days after adjournment. (n)
Connecticut	…	…	5	15P	(o)	2/3 elected	Oct. 1, unless otherwise specified.
Delaware	…	…	10P	10P	30A	3/5 elected	Immediately or enactment clause.
Florida	★	★	7 (ddd)	15P (m)		2/3 members each house	60 days after adjournment since die or on specified date.
Georgia	★	★	6	40A		2/3 elected	Unless other date specified, July 1 for generals, date signed by governor for locals.
Hawaii (q)	★(r)	…	10 (s)	45A (s)(p)	10P (p)	2/3 elected	Immediately or on the prospective date stated in the legislation.
Idaho	★	★	5	10P		2/3 present	July 1
Illinois	★	…	60 (m)	60P (m)		3/5 elected (g)	Usually Jan. 1 of next year. (t)
Indiana	…	…	7	7P		Majority elected	(u)
Iowa	★	★	3		30A	2/3 elected	July 1, unless otherwise specified. Effective date for bills which become law on or after July 1, 45 days after approval, unless otherwise specified.
Kansas	★	★	10 (m)	90A	10P	2/3 membership	Upon publication or specified date after publication.
Kentucky	★	…	10			Majority elected	90 days after adjournment sine die. Unless the bill contains an emergency clause or special effective date.
Louisiana (q)	★	★	10 (m)	20P (m)		2/3 elected	Aug. 1
Maine	★	★	10		(v)	2/3 elected	90 days after adjournment unless enacted as an emergency.
Maryland	★(w)	★	6 (x)	30P (y)	(z)	3/5 elected (aa)	June 1 (bb)
Massachusetts	★	★	10	10P	10A	2/3 present	90 days after enactment.
Michigan	★	★	14		14P	2/3 elected and serving	Immediate effect if vote of 2/3 elected and serving. 90 days after adjournment, if immediate effect not given.
Minnesota	★	(i)	3P	14A, 3P	3A, 14P	2/3 elected — 90 House; 45 Senate	Aug. 1 (cc)
Mississippi	★	…	5	15P (dd)		2/3 elected	July 1 unless specified otherwise.
Missouri	★	…	15	45A		2/3 elected	Aug. 28 (ee)
Montana (q)	★	★	10 (m)	25A (m)		2/3 present	Oct. 1 (cc)
Nebraska	★	★	5	5A, 5P	(ff)	3/5 elected	90 days following adjournment sine die. Unless bill contains an emergency clause.
Nevada	…	…	5 (gg)	10A (gg)		2/3 elected	Oct. 1, unless measure stipulates a different date.
New Hampshire	…	…	5	5P		2/3 present	60 days after enactment, unless otherwise noted.
New Jersey	★	…	45			2/3 elected	Dates usually specified.
New Mexico	★	★	3 (hh)		20A	2/3 present	90 days after adjournment unless other date specified. General appropriations acts or emergency clauses passed by 2/3 present take effect immediately.
New York	★	…	10 (ii)	(ii)	30A	2/3 votes in each house	20 days after enactment.
North Carolina	…	…	10	30A		3/5 elected	60 days after adjournment.
North Dakota	★	…	3	15A		2/3 elected	(jj)
Ohio	★	★	10	10P	10A	3/5 elected (kk)	91st day after filing with secretary of state. (ll)

See footnotes at end of table.

ENACTING LEGISLATION: VETO, VETO OVERRIDE AND EFFECTIVE DATE—Continued

State or other jurisdiction	Governor may item veto appropriation bills		Days allowed governor to consider bill (a)			Votes required in each house to pass bills or items over veto (c)	Effective date of enacted legislation (d)
			During session	After session			
	Amount	Other (b)	Bill becomes law unless vetoed	Bill becomes law unless vetoed	Bill dies unless signed		
Oklahoma	★	...	5 (mm)		15A (mm)	2/3 elected	90 days after adjournment unless specified in the bill.
Oregon	★	...	5	30A (s)		2/3 present	Jan. 1st of following year. (nn)
Pennsylvania	★	★	10	30A		2/3 majority	60 days after signed by governor.
Rhode Island	...	...	6	10P (oo)	(oo)	3/5 present	Immediately (pp)
South Carolina	★	...	5	(qq)		2/3 vote of the members present and voting	Date of signature.
South Dakota	★	...	5 (rr)	15P (rr)		2/3 elected	July 1
Tennessee	★	...	10	(ss)	(ss)	Constitutional majority	40 days after enactment unless otherwise specified.
Texas	★	...	10	20A		2/3 elected	90 days after adjournment unless otherwise specified.
Utah	★	...	10P	20A		2/3 elected	60 days after adjournment of the session at which it passed.
Vermont	...	...	5	5A	(fff)	2/3 present	July 1 unless otherwise specified.
Virginia	★	★(tt)	7 (m)	30A (uu)		2/3 present (vv)	July 1 (ww)
Washington	★	★	5	20A		2/3 present	90 days after adjournment.
West Virginia	...	(i)	5	15A (xx)		Majority elected	90 days after enactment.
Wisconsin	...	★(ccc)	6	6P		2/3 present	Day after publication date unless otherwise specified.
Wyoming	★	★	3	15A		2/3 elected	Specified in act.
American Samoa	★	...	10	30A		2/3 elected	60 days after adjournment. (yy)
Guam	★	★	10	10P	30P (zz)	10 votes to override	Immediately (bbb)
No. Mariana Islands	★	...	40 (m)(aaa)			2/3 elected	Upon signing by the governor.
Puerto Rico	★	★	10	10P	30P	2/3 elected	Specified in act.
U.S. Virgin Islands	★(ccc)	★(ccc)	10	10P	30A	2/3 elected	Immediately

Source: The Council of State Governments' survey, November 2014 and state websites January 2015.

Key:
★ — Yes
... — No
A — Days after adjournment of legislature.
P — Days after presentation to governor.
(a) Sundays excluded, unless otherwise indicated.
(b) Includes language in appropriations bill.
(c) Bill returned to house of origin with governor's objections.
(d) Effective date may be established by the law itself or may be otherwise changed by vote of the legislature. Special or emergency acts are usually effective immediately.
(e) The governor may line item distinct items or item veto amounts in appropriation bills, if returned prior to final adjournment.
(f) Except bills presented within five days of final adjournment, Sundays are included.
(g) Different number of votes required for revenue and appropriations bills. Alaska—3/4 elected. Illinois—Only the usual majority of members elected is required to restore a reduced item.
(h) Several specific requirements of 3/4 majority.
(i) Line item veto.
(j) For a bill to become law during session, if 12th day falls on a Saturday, Sunday, or holiday, the period is extended to the next day that is not a Saturday, Sunday, or holiday.
(k) For legislation enacted in regular sessions: January 1 of the following year. Urgency legislation: immediately upon chaptering by Secretary of State. Legislation enacted in Special Session: 91st day after adjournment of the special session at which the bill was passed.

(l) The governor may not line-item veto any portion of any bill (including appropriation clauses in bills) other than line items in the Long Appropriations Bill. The governor may line-item veto individual lines in the Long Appropriations Bill. In those instances, the governor must line-item veto the entire amount of any item; an item is an indivisible sum of money dedicated to a single purpose.
(m) Sundays included.
(n) An act takes effect on the date stated in the act, or if no date is stated in the act, then upon signature of the governor. If no safety clause on a bill, the bill takes effect 90 days after sine die if no referendum petition has been filed. The state constitution allows for a 90 day period following adjournment when petitions may be filed for bills that do not contain a safety clause.
(o) Bill enacted if not signed /vetoed within time frames.
(p) The governor must notify the legislature 10 days before the 45th day of his intent to veto a measure on that day. The legislature may convene at or before noon on the 45th day after adjournment to consider the vetoed measure. If the legislature fails to reconvene, the bill does not become law. If the legislature reconvenes, it may pass the measure over the governor's veto or it may amend the law to meet the governor's objections. If the law is amended, the governor must sign the bill within 10 days after it is presented to him in order for it to become law.
(q) Constitution withholds right to veto constitutional amendments proposed by the legislature.
(r) Governor can also reduce amounts in appropriations bills. In Hawaii, governor can reduce items in executive appropriations measures, but cannot reduce or item veto amounts appropriated for the judicial or legislative branches.
(s) Except Sundays and legal holidays. In Hawaii, except Saturdays, Sundays, holidays and any days in which the legislature is in recess prior to its adjournment. In Oregon, if the governor does not sign the bill within 30 days after adjournment, it becomes law without the governor's signature, Saturdays and Sundays are excluded.

ENACTING LEGISLATION: VETO, VETO OVERRIDE AND EFFECTIVE DATE—Continued

(t) Effective date for bills which become law on or after July 1: A bill passed after May 31 cannot take effect before June 1 of the following year unless it states an earlier effective date and is approved by 3/5 of the members elected to each house.

(u) Varies with date of the veto.

(v) "If the bill or resolution shall not be returned by the governor within 10 days (Sundays excepted) after it shall have been presented to the governor, it shall have the same force and effect as if the governor had signed it unless the Legislature by their adjournment prevent its return, in which case it shall have such force and effect, unless returned within 3 days after the next meeting of the same Legislature which enacted the bill or resolution; if there is no such next meeting of the Legislature which enacted the bill or resolution, the bill or resolution shall not be a law." (excerpted from Article IV, Part Third, Section 2 of the Constitution of Maine).

(w) The governor cannot veto the budget bill but may exercise a total veto or item veto on a supplementary appropriations bill. In practice this means the governor may strike items in the annual general capital loan bill. Occasionally the governor will also veto a bond bill or a portion of a bond bill.

(x) If a bill is presented to the governor in the first 83 days of session, the governor has only six days (not including Sunday) to act before the bill automatically becomes law.

(y) All bills passed at regular or special sessions must be presented to the governor no later than 20 days after adjournment. The governor has a limited time to sign or veto a bill after it is presented. If the governor does not act within that time, the bill becomes law automatically; there is no pocket veto. The time limit depends on when the presentment is made. Any bill presented in the last 7 days of the 90-day session or after adjournment must be acted on within 30 days after presentment. Bills vetoed after adjournment are returned to the legislature for reconsideration at the next meeting of the same General Assembly.

(z) The governor has a limited time to sign or veto a bill after it is presented. If the governor does not act within that time, the bill becomes law automatically; there is no pocket veto. The time limit depends on when the presentment is made.

(aa) Vetoed bills are returned to the house of origin immediately after that house has organized at the next regular or special session. When a new General Assembly is elected and sworn in, bills vetoed from the previous session are not returned. These vetoed bills are not subject to any further legislative action.

(bb) Unless otherwise provided, June 1 is the effective date for bond bills, July 1 for budget, tax and revenue bills. By custom October 1 is the usual effective date for other legislation. If the bill is an emergency measure, it may take effect immediately upon approval by the governor or at a specified date prior to June 1. For vetoed legislation, 30 days after the veto is overridden or on the date specified in the bill, whichever is later. An emergency bill passed over the governor's veto takes effect immediately.

(cc) Different date for fiscal legislation. Minnesota—July 1. Montana—Appropriations effective July 1 unless otherwise specified in bill; revenue bills effected July 1 unless otherwise specified in bill, often next Jan. 1.

(dd) Bills vetoed after adjournment are returned to the legislature for reconsideration. Mississippi—returned within three days after the beginning of the next session.

(ee) If bill has an emergency clause, it becomes effective upon governor's signature.

(ff) Bills are carried over from the 90-day session beginning in the odd-numbered year to the 60-day session, which begins in even-numbered years. Bills that have not passed by the last day of the 60-day session are all indefinitely postponed by motion on the last day of the session.

(gg) The day of delivery and Sundays are not counted for purposes of calculating these periods.

(hh) Except bills going up in the last three days of session, for which the governor has 20 days.

(ii) If the legislature adjourns during the governor's consideration of a 10-day bill, the bill shall not become law without the governor's approval.

(jj) August 1 after filing with the secretary of state. Appropriations and tax bills July 1 after filing with secretary of state, or date set in legislation by Legislative Assembly, or by date established by 3/5 of the members elected to each house.

(kk) The exception covers such matters as emergency measures and court bills that originally required a 2/3 majority for passage. In those cases, the same extraordinary majority vote is required to override a veto.

(ll) Emergency, current appropriation, and tax legislation effective immediately. The General Assembly may also enact an uncodified section of law specifying a desired effective date that is after the constitutionally established effective date.

(mm) During session the governor has 5 days (except Sunday) to sign or veto a bill or it becomes law automatically. After Session a bill becomes a pocket veto if not signed 15 days after sine die.

(nn) Unless emergency declared or date specific in text of measure, which must be at least 90 days after adjournment sine die unless emergency is declared. Emergency cannot be declared in bills regulating taxation or exemption.

(oo) Bills become effective without signature if not signed or vetoed.

(pp) Date signed, date received by Secretary of State if effective without signature, date that veto is overridden, or other specified date.

(qq) Two days after the next meeting.

(rr) During a session, a bill becomes law if a governor signs it or does not act on it withing five days, not including Saturdays, Sundays or holidays. If the legislature has adjourned or recessed or is within five days of a recess or an adjournment, the governor has 15 days to act on the bill. If he does not act, the bill becomes law.

(ss) Adjournment of the legislature is irrelevant; the governor has 10 days to act on a bill after it is presented to him or it becomes law without his signature.

(tt) If part of the item.

(uu) The governor has thirty days after adjournment of the legislature to act on any bills. The Constitution of Virginia provides that: "If the governor does not act on any bill, it shall become law without his signature."

(vv) Must include majority of elected members.

(ww) Unless a different date is stated in the bill. Special sessions—first day of fourth month after adjournment.

(xx) Five days for supplemental appropriation bills.

(yy) Laws required to be approved only by the governor. An act required to be approved by the U.S. Secretary of the Interior only after it is vetoed by the governor and so approved takes effect 40 days after it is returned to the governor by the secretary.

(zz) After Legislature adjourns sine die at end of two-year term.

(aaa) Twenty days for appropriations bills.

(bbb) U.S. Congress may annul.

(ccc) May item veto language or amounts in a bill that contains two or more appropriations.

(ddd) The governor has seven days, Sundays included, to act on presented bills while the Legislature is in session. If the Legislature adjourns sine die during the seven-day period or takes a recess of more than 30 days, the governor has 15 consecutive days from the date of presentation to act on the bill(s).

(eee) Governor may partially veto words or numbers in the case of appropriation bills.

(fff) Three days subsequent to presentation following adjournment in even-numbered years.

(ggg) Ten calendar days after receipt of bill. When the governor receives bills within the last 10 days of session, the governor has 30 days to act on the bills.

Table 3.17
LEGISLATIVE APPROPRIATIONS PROCESS: BUDGET DOCUMENTS AND BILLS

State or other jurisdiction	Budget document submission							Budget bill introduction		
	Legal source of deadline		Submission date relative to convening							
	Constitutional	Statutory	Prior to session	Within one week	Within two weeks	Within one month	Over one month	Same time as budget document	Another time	Not until committee review of budget document
Alabama	★	★	(a)	...	...	...	...	★	...	...
Alaska	★	★	...	(a)	...	...	...	★	...	...
Arizona	...	★	★	...	...	...	...	...	...	★
Arkansas	...	★	★	...	...	...	...	...	...	★
California	★	...	...	...	...	(a)	...	★(b)	...	...
Colorado	...	★	★(a)	...	...	...	...	...	76th day by rule	...
Connecticut	...	★	...	...	...	(a)	...	★	...	...
Delaware	...	...	...	...	...	...	...	...	...	★
Florida	★	★	★	...	...	...	...	...	...	★
Georgia	★	...	...	(a)	...	...	...	★	...	...
Hawaii	...	★	30 days	...	...	...	...	...	★	...
Idaho	...	★	...	★	...	...	...	...	...	★
Illinois	...	★	...	...	...	...	★(a)	...	★(c)	...
Indiana	...	★	...	...	...	...	...	...	★	...
Iowa	...	★	...	...	...	(a)	...	...	...	★(d)
Kansas	...	★	...	...	★(e)	...	...	...	★	...
Kentucky	★	...	...	...	(a)	...	...	★	...	...
Louisiana	...	★	(f)	(f)	...	...	...	(g)	...	...
Maine	...	★	...	(a)	...	...	...	★	...	...
Maryland	★	...	...	★(e)	...	...	...	★(h)	...	...
Massachusetts	...	★	...	...	...	★	...	★	...	...
Michigan	...	★	...	...	...	★	...	★	...	...
Minnesota	...	★	...	...	...	(a)	...	...	...	★
Mississippi	...	★	★	...	...	...	...	...	★	...
Missouri	★	...	...	...	...	★	...	...	...	★
Montana	...	★	★	...	...	...	...	...	★	...
Nebraska	...	★	★	...	...	★	...	★(i)	...	...
Nevada	★	...	(a)	...	...	...	...	...	...	★
New Hampshire	...	★	...	...	...	(a)	...	★	...	...
New Jersey	...	★	...	...	...	...	...	...	...	★
New Mexico	...	★	...	...	...	(a)	...	...	★	...
New York	★	...	...	...	★(a)	...	...	...	★(j)	...
North Carolina	...	...	...	...	...	...	...	★	...	...
North Dakota	...	★	(k)	...	...	...	...	...	★(k)	...
Ohio	...	★	...	...	...	★(d)(e)	...	★(x)	...	...
Oklahoma	★	★	...	★	...	...	...	...	★	...
Oregon	...	★	★	...	...	...	★(l)	★(m)	...	★
Pennsylvania	★	...	...	...	...	...	★	...	...	★
Rhode Island	...	★	...	...	...	...	★	...	★	...
South Carolina	...	★	...	★	...	...	...	...	...	★
South Dakota	...	★	...	...	...	...	★(o)	...	★(p)	...
Tennessee	...	★	...	...	★(a)(e)	★(a)(e)	...	★	...	...
Texas	...	★	...	(n)	...	...	...	★(q)	...	...
Utah	...	★(t)	(a)	...	...	...	...	...	...	★
Vermont	...	★	(s)	...	...	...	...	...	...	★
Virginia	...	★	Dec. 20	...	...	...	...	★	...	...
Washington	★(t)	...	(u)	...	...	...	...	★	★	...
West Virginia	★	...	...	★	...	...	...	★	...	...
Wisconsin	...	★	...	...	...	★(v)	...	★	...	...
Wyoming	...	★	Dec. 1	...	...	...	...	...	...	★
American Samoa	...	★	★	...	...	...	...	★	...	...
Guam	...	★	...	...	...	★(w)	...	★	...	...
No. Mariana Islands	★	★	April 1	...	...	...	...	...	★	★
Puerto Rico	...	★	...	...	...	★	...	...	...	★
U.S. Virgin Islands	...	★	May 30	...	...	...	...	...	★	...

See footnotes at end of table.

LEGISLATIVE APPROPRIATIONS PROCESS: BUDGET DOCUMENTS AND BILLS — Continued

Source: The Council of State Governments' survey, November 2014 and state web sites, January 2015.

Key:

★ — Yes

... — No

(a) Specific time limitations: Alabama—five days; Alaska—December 15, 4th legislative day; California—January 10; Connecticut—not later than the first session day following the third day in February, in each odd numbered year; Colorado—presented by November 1 to the Joint Budget Committee; Georgia—first five days of session; Illinois—Third Wednesday in February; Iowa—no later than February 1; Kentucky—10th legislative day; Maine—The Governor shall transmit the budget document to the Legislature not later than the Friday following the first Monday in January of the first regular legislative session. ... A Governor-elect elected to a first term of office shall transmit the budget document to the Legislature not later than the Friday following the first Monday in February of the first regular legislative session (Maine Revised Statutes, Title 5, Chapter 149, Section 1666); Minnesota—by the 4th Tuesday in January each odd-numbered year; Nevada—no later than 14 days before commencement of regular session; New Hampshire—by February 15; New Mexico—by January 1 each year; New York—The executive budget must be submitted by the governor to the legislature by the 2nd Tuesday following the opening of session (or February 1 for the first session following a gubernatorial election); Tennessee—on or before February 1 for sitting governor; Utah—Must submit to the legislature by the calendared floor time on the first day of the annual session.

(b) Budget and Budget Bill are annual—to be submitted within the first 10 days of each calendar year.

(c) Deadlines for introducing bills in general are set by Senate president and House speaker.

(d) Executive budget bill is introduced and used as a working tool for committee.

(e) Later for first session of a new governor; Kansas—21 days; Maryland—10 days after; New Jersey—February 15; Ohio—by March 15; Tennessee—March 1;

(f) The governor shall submit his executive budget to the Joint Legislative Committee on the budget no later than 45 days prior to each regular session; except that in the first year of each term, the executive budget shall be submitted no later than 30 days prior to the regular session. Copies shall be made available to the entire legislature on the first day of each regular session.

(g) Bills appropriating monies for the general operating budget and ancillary appropriations, bills appropriating funds for the expenses of the legislature and the judiciary must be submitted to the legislature for introduction no later than 45 days prior to each regular session, except that in the first year of each term, such appropriation bills shall be submitted no later than 30 days prior to the regular session.

(h) Appropriations bill other than the budget bill (supplementary) may be introduced at any time. They must provide their own tax source and may not be enacted until the budget bill is enacted.

(i) Governor's budget bill is introduced and serves as a working document for the Appropriations Committee. The governor must submit the budget proposal by January 15 of each odd-numbered year. (Neb. Rev.Stat. sec.81–125). The statute extends this deadline to February 1 for a governor who is in his first year of office.

(j) Submission of the governor's budget bills to the legislature occurs with submission of the executive budget.

(k) Legislative Council's Budget Section hears the executive budget recommendations during legislature's December organizational session. Budget bill introduction one week after governor's budget message.

(l) By December 1st of even-numbered year unless new governor is elected; if new governor is elected, then February 1st of odd-numbered year.

(m) Legislature often introduces other budget bills during legislative session that are not part of the governor's recommended budget.

(n) The Legislative Budget Board is required to submit a copy of the budget of estimated appropriations to the governor and members of the legislature not later than the fifth day after session convenes. The baord is required to submit a copy of the general appropriations bill not later than the seventh day after session convenes.

(o) It is usually over a month. The budget must be delivered to the Legislature not later than the first Tuesday after the first Monday in December.

(p) It must be introduced no later than the 16th legislative day.

(q) State law does not specify a special deadline for filing the General Appropriations Act, but it is generally filed soon after the Legislative Budget Board submits the budget document.

(r) Legislative rules require budget bills to be introduced by the 43rd day of the session.

(s) Third Tuesday each year.

(t) And Rules.

(u) For fiscal period other than biennium, 20 days prior to first day of session.

(v) Last Tuesday in January. A later submission date may be requested by the governor.

(w) Usually January before end of current fiscal year.

(x) Bill may actually be officially introduced a few days later; it is usually not immediately introduced upon the presentation of the governor's budget.

Table 3.18
FISCAL NOTES: CONTENT AND DISTRIBUTION

State or other jurisdiction	Intent or purpose of bill	Cost involved	Projected future cost	Proposed source of revenue	Fiscal impact on local government	Other	All	Available on request	Bill sponsor	Members	Chair only	Fiscal staff	Executive budget staff
Alabama	★	★	...	★	★	★(a)	...	★	★	...	...	...	...
Alaska	...	★	★	★	...	...	★	★	★	...	...	★	★
Arizona	★	★	★	★	★	★	★	★	★	★	...	★	★
Arkansas (b)	...	★	★	...	★	★	★	...	...	...	...	...	...
California	★	★	★	★	★	...	★	...	...	...	...	★	★
Colorado	★	★	★	★	★	...	★	...	...	...	...	...	...
Connecticut	★	★	★	★	★	...	(c)	...	...	...	...	...	...
Delaware	...	★	...	...	★	...	★	...	...	...	...	...	...
Florida	★	★	★	★	★	★	★	...	...	...	...	★	...
Georgia	...	★	★	...	★	...	★	★	...	...	...	...	...
Hawaii	...	...	...	...	...	★(hh)	...	...	...	...	...	...	...
Idaho	★	★	★	★	★	★(d)	★	...	...	...	...	(e)	(e)
Illinois	...	★	★	★	★	...	★(f)	★	★	...	...	...	...
Indiana	★	★	★	★	★	...	★	...	...	...	...	★	★
Iowa	★	★	★	★	★	...	............................(g)............................
Kansas	★	★	★	★	★	...	★	★	★	...	★	★	★
Kentucky	★	★	★	★	★	★	...	★	★	★	...	★	...
Louisiana	...	★	★	...	★	...	★	★	...	...	★(h)	...	...
Maine	...	★	★	★	★	...	...	★(i)	★	...	...	★	★
Maryland	★	★	★	★	★	★(j)	...	...	★(k)	...	...	...	...
Massachusetts	...	★(l)	★	...	...	★	★	...	...	...	★	...	...
Michigan	★	★	★	★	★	★(m)	★(n)	...	...	...	...	...	...
Minnesota	★	★	★	★	★	...	...	...	★	...	★	★	★
Mississippi	...	★	★	★	...	...	...	...	★(o)	...	...	...	...
Missouri	★	★	★	★	★	...	...	...	★	★	...	...	★
Montana	...	★	★	...	★	★(p)	★	...	...	...	...	★	★
Nebraska	...	★	★	★	★	...	★	★	...	...	...	★	★
Nevada	...	★	★	★	★	...	★(kk)	...	...	...	...	...	...
New Hampshire (ii)	★	★	...	★	★	...	...	★	...	★	...	★	★
New Jersey	...	★	...	★	★	...	★	...	...	...	...	★	★
New Mexico	★	★	★	★	★	...	★	...	...	★	...	(q)	(q)
New York	★	★	★	...	★	★(r)	...	★	★	★	...	★	...
North Carolina	...	★	★	...	★	★	(s)	...	...	...	...	...	...
North Dakota	...	...	★	★	★	★(t)	(u)	★	...	...	...	★	★
Ohio	★	★	★	★	★	...	(v)	★	★	...	...	★	...
Oklahoma	★	★	★	★	...	...	...	★	★	...	★	★	★
Oregon	★	★	★	★	★	...	★	...	...	...	...	★	★
Pennsylvania	...	★	★	★	★	...	...	★	...	★	...	★	...
Rhode Island	★	★	★	★	★	...	...	★	...	★	...	★	★
South Carolina	★	★	★	★	★	...	...	★	...	(w)	...	★	★
South Dakota	...	★	★	★	★	...	...	★	...	...	...	...	...
Tennessee	★	★	★	...	★	...	★	★	★	...	...	...	...
Texas	...	★	★	★	★	★(x)	★	★	★	(jj)	...	...	...
Utah	...	★	★	★	★	★(y)	★	★	★	...	★	★	★
Vermont	............................(z)............................	...	★	...	★	...	...
Virginia	★	★	★	★	★	★(aa)	(bb)	...	★	...	★	★(cc)	...
Washington	...	★	★	★	★	★(dd)	★	★	★	★	★	★	...
West Virginia	...	★	★	★	★	...	...	...	...	★	...	...	...
Wisconsin	...	★	★	★	★	...	(ee)	...	...	...	...	(ee)	...
Wyoming	...	★	★	★	...	...	★	...	...	...	...	...	...
Guam	...	★	...	...	★	★(ff)	★	...	...	★	★	★	...
No. Mariana Islands	★	★	★	★	★	★	...	...	...	★	★	★	...
Puerto Rico	★	...	...	...	...	............................(gg)............................
U.S. Virgin Islands	★	★	...	★	...	...	★	...	...	...	...	...	...

See footnotes at end of table.

FISCAL NOTES: CONTENT AND DISTRIBUTION — Continued

Source: The Council of State Governments survey, November 2014.

Note: A fiscal note is a summary of the fiscal effects of a bill on government revenues, expenditures and liabilities.

Key:

★ — Yes

... — No

(a) Fiscal notes included on final passage calendar.

(b) Only retirement, corrections, revenue, tax and local government bills require fiscal notes. During the past session, fiscal notes were provided for education.

(c) The fiscal notes are printed with the bills favorably reported by the committees.

(d) Statement of purpose.

(e) Attached to bill, so available to both fiscal and executive budget staff.

(f) A summary of each fiscal note is attached to the summary of its bill in the printed Legislative Synopsis and Digest, and on the General Assembly's website. Fiscal notes are prepared for the sponsor and attached to the bill on file with the House Clerk or Senate Secretary.

(g) Fiscal notes are available to everyone.

(h) Prepared by the Legislative Fiscal Office when a state agency is involved and prepared by Legislative Auditor's office when a local board or commission is involved; copies sent to House and Senate staff offices respectively.

(i) Distributed to members of the committee of reference; also available on the Legislature's website.

(j) A fiscal note is now known as a fiscal and policy note to better reflect the contents. Fiscal and policy notes also identify any mandate on local government and include analyses of the economic impact on small businesses.

(k) In practice fiscal and policy notes are prepared on all bills and resolutions prior to a public hearing on the bills/resolutions. After initial hard copy distribution to sponsor and committee, the note is released to member computer system and thereafter to the legislative website.

(l) Fiscal notes are prepared only if cost exceeds $100,000 or matter has not been acted upon by the Joint Committee on Ways and Means.

(m) Other relevant data.

(n) At present, fiscal information is part of the bill analysis on the legislative website.

(o) And committee to which bill referred.

(p) Mechanical defects in bill.

(q) Fiscal impact statements prepared by Legislative Finance Committee staff are available to anyone on request and on the legislature's website.

(r) Fiscal notes are required for retirement bills, bills enacting or amending tax expenditures, and all bills increasing or decreasing state revenues, or affecting appropriation or expenditure of state monies.

(s) Fiscal notes are posted on the Internet and available to all members.

(t) Notes required only if impact is $5,000 or more. Bills impacting workforce safety and insurance benefits or premiums have actuarial statements as do bills proposing changes in state and local retirement systems.

(u) Fiscal notes are available online to anyone from the legislative branch website.

(v) Fiscal notes are prepared for bills before being voted on in any standing committee or floor session. Fiscal notes for all introduced bills are posted on the Web. They are also distributed to the committees in which the bills are heard.

(w) Fiscal impact statements on proposed legislation are prepared by the Revenue and Fiscal Affairs Office and sent to the House or Senate standing committeee that requested the impact. All fiscal impacts are posted on the Revenue and Fiscal Affairs website.

(x) Some bills may also require the preparation of one or more of the following fiscal impact statements: an actuarial impact statement, a criminal justice policy impact statement, an equalized education funding impact statement, a higher education impact statement, an open government impact statement, an impact statement regarding the economic effect of tax changes, a tax/fee equity note, or a water development policy impact statement.

(y) Fiscal notes are to include cost and revenue estimates on all bills that anticipate direct impact on state government, local government, residents, and businesses.

(z) Fiscal notes are not mandatory and their content will vary.

(aa) Technical amendments, if needed. Fiscal notes do not provide statements or interpretations of legislative intent for legal purposes. A summary of the stated objective, effect, and impact may be included.

(bb) Fiscal impact statements are widely available because they are also posted on the Internet shortly after they are distributed. The Joint Legislative Audit Review Commission (JLARC) also prepares a review of the fiscal impact statement if requested by a standing committee chair. The review statement is also available on the Internet.

(cc) Legislative budget directors.

(dd) Impact on private sector.

(ee) The fiscal estimate is printed as an appendix to the bill; anyone that has a copy of the bill has a copy of the fiscal estimate.

(ff) Fiscal impact on local economy.

(gg) The Legislature of Puerto Rico does not prepare fiscal notes, but upon request the economics unit could prepare one. The Department of Treasury has the duty to analyze and prepare fiscal notes.

(hh) Hawaii does not require the submission of fiscal notes.

(ii) Whenver possible, fiscal notes appear at end of introduced version of bill.

(jj) After a bill has been set for hearing, the Legislative Budget Board distributes the fiscal note to the committee clerk and the sponsor of the bill. In the House, the fiscal note must be attached to the affected bill before a public hearing on the bill may be held, and Senate practice is for a copy of the fsical note to be provided to the committee members before a final vote on a bill in committee is taken. If the bill is reported from committee, the fiscal note is attached to the bill as part of the committee report when it is printed and distributed to the legislators. Fiscal notes are publicly available online for bills that have been voted out of committee.

(kk) Fiscal notes requested by the Legislative Counsel Bureau are posted on the Legislature's website.

Table 3.19
BILL AND RESOLUTION INTRODUCTIONS AND ENACTMENTS:
2014 REGULAR SESSIONS

State	Duration of session**	Introductions Bills	Introductions Resolutions*	Enactments/Adoptions Bills	Enactments/Adoptions Resolutions*	Measures vetoed by governor (a)(b)	Length of session
Alabama	Jan. 14–Apr. 3, 2014	1,103	678	268	189	5	30L
Alaska	Jan. 21–Apr. 25, 2014	604	143	189	84	2	N.A.
Arizona	Jan. 13–Apr. 24, 2014	1,205	113	280	35	25	101C
Arkansas	Feb 10–Mar. 19, 2014	309	34	300	10	0	N.A.
California	Jan. 6–Nov. 30, 2014	1,977	275	932	73	143	118 L(c)
Colorado	Jan. 8–May 8, 2014	621	77	426	35	5	120C
Connecticut	Feb. 5–May 7, 2014	1,073 (d)	181	258	117	7	92C
Delaware	Jan. 14–Jun. 30, 2014	695	130	443	. . .	1	40L
Florida	Mar. 4–M ay 2, 2014	1,758	126	255	2	1 (a)	60C
Georgia	Jan. 13–Mar. 20, 2014	1,591	3,443	670	3,000	15	N.A.
Hawaii	Jan. 15–May 1, 2014	2,312	704	245	188	7	60L
Idaho	Jan. 6–Mar. 20, 2014	542	66	357	43	. . .	74C
Illinois	Jan. 13–May 31, 2014	4,026	1,188	1,125	N.A.	. . .	57L
Indiana	Jan. 7–Mar. 13, 2014	865	305	224	243	0	N.A.
Iowa	Jan. 13–May. 2, 2014	1,256 (e)	69	141	48 (f)	2	110C
Kansas	Jan. 13–May 30, 2014	569	23	142	12	2	79C
Kentucky	Jan. 7–Apr. 15, 2014	820	99	139	7	1	59L
Louisiana	Mar. 10–Jun. 2, 2014	1,951	838	546	768	14	60L
Maine	Jan. 8–Apr. 17, 2014	1,865	N.A.	753	109	128	N.A.
Maryland	Jan. 8–Apr. 7, 2014	2,672	21	657	2	154 (m)	90C
Massachusetts	Jan. 8–Jul. 31, 2014	6,988	4,546	704	N.A.	5	N.A.
Michigan	Jan. 8–Dec. 18, 2014	3,271	851	857	618	24	N.A.
Minnesota	Feb. 25–May 16, 2014	2,483	N.A.	168	. . .	1	44L
Mississippi	Jan. 7–Apr. 6, 2014	2,654	237	392	182	. . .	90C
Missouri	Jan. 8–May 16, 2014	1,517	158	142	64	20	N.A.
Montana	No regular session in 2014						
Nebraska (U)	Jan. 8–Apr. 17, 2014	460	239	185	135	2	60L
Nevada	No regular session in 2014						
New Hampshire	Jan. 8–Sep. 17, 2014	905	27	330	6	4	23L
New Jersey	Jan. 14–Dec. 31, 2014	6,849	819	117	141	52	N.A.
New Mexico	Jan. 21–Feb. 20, 2014	696	40	8,081	4	10	31C
New York	Jan. 8, 2014–Jan. 7, 2015	15,972	N.A.	479	3,805	42	365C
North Carolina	May 14–Oct. 20, 2014	384	26	122	8	1	99C
North Dakota	No regular session in 2014						
Ohio	Jan. 2–Dec. 30, 2014 (g)	418	45	136	19	. . .	123L(h)
Oklahoma	Feb. 3–May 23, 2014	2,233	191	427	97	33	64L
Oregon	Feb. 3–Mar. 9, 2014	247	19	121	13	0	64L
Pennsylvania	Jan. 6–Nov. 30, 2014	4,061	1,601	204	1,361	(j)	69L(i)
Rhode Island	Jan. 7–Jun. 21, 2014	4,914	N.A.	1,488	N.A.	15	N.A.
South Carolina	Jan. 9–Aug. 27, 2014 (k)	642	624	203	4	76	68L(1)
South Dakota	Jan. 14–Mar. 31, 2014	449	49	248	27	1	38L
Tennessee	Jan. 14–Apr. 17, 2014	2,417	1,319	N.A.	N.A.	. . .	N.A.
Texas	No regular session in 2014						
Utah	Jan. 27–Mar. 13, 2014	710	74	437	46	3	45C
Vermont	Jan. 7–May 9, 2014	1,211	119	222	88	N.A.	106C
Virginia	Jan. 8–Mar. 8, 2014	3,864	1,798	862	1,523	10	N.A.
Washington	Jan. 13–Mar. 13, 2014	1,345	27	225	8	4	60C
West Virginia	Jan. 8–Mar. 8, 2014	1,876	301	201	82	8	60C
Wisconsin	Jan. 7, 2013–Apr. 1, 2014	1,627	251	380	107	1	72L
Wyoming	Feb. 10–Mar. 6, 2014	225	4	132	3	. . .	19L
No. Mariana Islands		289	185	71	5		120C

See footnotes at end of table.

BILL AND RESOLUTION INTRODUCTIONS AND ENACTMENTS:
2014 REGULAR SESSIONS — Continued

Source: The Council of State Governments' survey of legislative agencies and state Web sites, November 2014 and February 2015.

*Includes Joint and Concurrent resolutions.

**Actual adjournment dates are listed regardless of constitutional or statutory limitations. For more information on provisions, see Table 3.2, "Legislative Sessions: Legal Provisions."

Key:

C — Calendar day.

L — Legislative day (in some states, called a session or workday; definition may vary slightly; however, it generally refers to any day on which either chamber of the legislature is in session).

U — Unicameral legislature.

N.A. — Not available.

(a) Line item or partial vetoes: California — 5; Florida — 1; Hawaii — 1; Idaho — 1; Iowa — 6; Kansas — 7; Kentucky — 3; Louisiana — 8; Minnesota — 1; New Mexico — 6; New York — 3; Ohio — 2; South Carolina — 76 line item vetos on state appropriations bill; Utah — 1; Washington — 13; Wisconsin — 3; Wyoming — 1.

(b) Number of vetoes overridden: Nebraska — 5; Oklahoma — 2; South Carolina — 55 (53 of those are on the line item vetos on state appropriations bill).

(c) Assembly only; 120 legislative days in Senate

(d) There is some redundancy in the numbers because committee bills are based on proposed bills, which are introduced by individual legislators at the beginning of the session. The total number, 1,073, breaks down as: 831 (Raised Bills); 16 (Committee Bills); 226 (Proposed Bills).

(e) Bill introductions total includes 415 filed study bills.

(f) Simple resolution enactments.

(g) House only. Senate adjourned on 12/18.

(h) Senate only; 113 legislative days in House.

(i) House only; 61 legislative days in Senate.

(j) The senate sued Gov. Corbett in Pennsylvania Commonwealth Court on November 11, 2014 on his veto of portions of the Fiscal Code.

(k) House only; Senate adjourned on 6/19.

(l) House only; 78 legislative days in Senate.

(m) All but one were duplicative bills.

Table 3.20
BILL AND RESOLUTION INTRODUCTIONS AND ENACTMENTS:
2014 SPECIAL SESSIONS

State or other jurisdiction	Duration of session**	Introductions		Enactments/adoptions		Measures vetoed by governor	Length of session
		Bills	Resolutions*	Bills	Resolutions*		
Alabama......................			No special session in 2014				
Alaska.........................			No special session in 2014				
Arizona.......................	May 27 - May 29, 2014	2	0	2	0	0	2C
Arkansas.....................	Jun. 30 - Jul. 2, 2014	10	4	8	0	0	3C
California	Apr. 24 - Nov. 30, 2014 (a)	0	2	0	0	0	20L (a)
Colorado.....................			No special session in 2014				
Connecticut................			No special session in 2014				
Delaware	Jul. 1, 2014	0	0	0	0	0	1L
	Oct. 8, 2014 (c)	0	0	0	0	0	2L
Florida	Aug. 7 - Aug. 11, 2014	5	3	1	0	0	5C
Georgia.......................			No special session in 2014				
Hawaii........................	Oct. 22 - 23, 2014 (b)	0	1	0	1	0	2L
Idaho..........................			No special session in 2014				
Illinois.......................			No special session in 2014				
Indiana.......................			No special session in 2014				
Iowa...........................			No special session in 2014				
Kansas			No special session in 2014				
Kentucky			No special session in 2014				
Louisiana....................			No special session in 2014				
Maine.........................			No special session in 2014				
Maryland			No special session in 2014				
Massachusetts			No special session in 2014				
Michigan.....................			No special session in 2014				
Minnesota...................			No special session in 2014				
Mississippi	April 2, 2014	1	N.A.	1	N.A.	0	1C
	May 8, 2014	1	N.A.	1	N.A.	0	1C
Missouri.....................			No special session in 2014				
Montana			No special session in 2014				
Nebraska (U)			No special session in 2014				
Nevada........................	Sep. 10 - 11, 2014	4	7	4	7	0	2C
New Hampshire			No special session in 2014				
New Jersey	July 31 - Aug. 4, 2014	2	0	2	0	0	5C
New Mexico			No special session in 2014				
New York....................			No special session in 2014				
North Carolina...........			No special session in 2014				
North Dakota.............			No special session in 2014				
Ohio...........................			No special session in 2014				
Oklahoma...................			No special session in 2014				
Oregon.......................			No special session in 2014				
Pennsylvania			No special session in 2014				
Rhode Island..............			No special session in 2014				
South Carolina...........			No special session in 2014 (e)				
South Dakota.............			No special session in 2014				
Tennessee			No special session in 2014				
Texas..........................			No special session in 2014				
Utah...........................			No special session in 2014				
Vermont......................			No special session in 2014				
Virginia......................	Mar. 24, 2014 - Jan. 13, 2015	26	468	5	448	0	N.A.
Washington................			No special session in 2014				
West Virginia..............	Mar. 14, 2014	14	0	9	0	0	1L
	May 19 - 21, 2014	12	0	6	0	0	3C
Wisconsin	Jan. 23 - Mar. 20, 2014	4	0	2	0	0	18L
Wyoming			No special session in 2014				
No. Mariana Islands ..	May 1 - Jul. 31, 2014	0	0	0	0	0	6C

See footnotes at end of table.

BILL AND RESOLUTION INTRODUCTIONS AND ENACTMENTS:
2014 SPECIAL SESSIONS — Continued

Source: The Council of State Governments' survey of state legislative agencies, November 2014.

*Includes Joint and Concurrrent resolutions.

**Actual adjournment dates are listed regardless of constitutional or statutory limitations. For more information on provisions, see Table 3.2, "Legislative Sessions: Legal Provisions."

Key:

N.A. — Not available.

C — Calendar day.

L — Legislative day (in some states, called a session or workday; definition may vary slightly; however, it generally refers to any day on which either chamber of the legislature is in session).

U — Unicameral legislature.

(a) Assembly convened on April 24 and Senate convened on April 28. Assembly was in session for 20 legislative days; Senate was in session for two legislative days.

(b) The special session only involved the Senate exercising its constitutional authority to confirm judicial nominations.

(c) Only the Senate came in during the Oct. 8 session for judicial confirmations.

(d) Called by Governor's Proclamation — "to respond to the ruling of the United State's Supreme Court in *Alleyne v. United States.*"

(e) Senate and House returned under the terms of the Sine Die Resolution adopted by both bodies to address gubernatorial vetoes. Senate returned on 6/19/14 and the House returned on 6/17/14 and 8/27/14.

Table 3.21
STAFF FOR INDIVIDUAL LEGISLATORS

State or other jurisdiction	Senate Capitol Personal	Senate Capitol Shared	Senate District	House/Assembly Capitol Personal	House/Assembly Capitol Shared	House/Assembly District
Alabama	YR	YR/2	(a)	YR	YR/10	(a)
Alaska (b)	YR/SO	...	YR	YR/SO	...	YR
Arizona	YR (c)	...	...	...	YR (c)	...
Arkansas	...	YR	...	...	YR (d)	...
California	YR	...	YR	YR	...	YR
Colorado	SO (e)	YR (e)	...	SO (e)	YR (e)	...
Connecticut (f)	YR/36	...	...	...	YR/38	...
Delaware	....(g)..					
Florida	YR (h)	...	YR (h)	YR (h)	...	YR (h)
Georgia	...	YR/3, SO/68	...	...	YR/25, SO/113	...
Hawaii (nn)	YR/2+	...	...	YR/1+	...	...
Idaho	...	SO, YR (i)	...	...	SO, YR (i)	...
Illinois	YR (j)	YR (j)	YR (j)	YR (j)	YR (j)	YR (j)
Indiana	...	YR/2 (k)	...	...	YR	...
Iowa	SO/1 (oo)	...	(oo)	SO/1 (oo)	...	(oo)
Kansas	SO/1	...	...	(l)	SO/3	...
Kentucky	...	YR (m)	...	...	YR (m)	...
Louisiana	(n)	YR (o)	YR (n)	(n)	YR (o)	YR (n)
Maine	YR, SO (p)	YR/27, SO/7	YR	...	YR (q)	...
Maryland	YR, SO (r)	...	YR (r)	YR (r)	SO (r)	YR (r)
Massachusetts	YR	...	...	YR	...	...
Michigan	YR (s)	...	...	YR/2 (s)	...	...
Minnesota	YR (t)	Varies	...	YR/3	Varies	...
Mississippi	...	YR	...	...	YR	...
Missouri	YR	YR	...	YR	YR	...
Montana	...	SO	...	...	SO	...
Nebraska	YR (u)	...	...	...................Unicameral........................		
Nevada	SO (pp)	YR	...	SO (pp)	YR	...
New Hampshire	...	YR	...	...	YR	...
New Jersey	YR (h)	...	YR (h)	YR (h)	...	YR (h)
New Mexico	SO/1	...	...	...	SO/2	...
New York	YR (w)	...	YR (w)	YR (w)	...	YR (w)
North Carolina	YR (x)	YR	...	YR (x)	YR	...
North Dakota	...	SO (v)	...	...	SO (v)	...
Ohio	YR/2 (y)	...	(z)	YR/1 (aa)	...	(z)
Oklahoma	YR/1 (bb)	YR (bb)	...	YR (bb)	YR/1 (bb)	...
Oregon	YR (cc)	YR	YR (dd)	YR (cc)	YR	YR (dd)
Pennsylvania	YR	...	YR	YR	...	YR
Rhode Island	...	YR (ee)	...	...	YR (ee)	...
South Carolina	...	YR/2	...	YR/4	...	...
South Dakota	(ff)	(ff)	...	(ff)	(ff)	...
Tennessee	YR/1	...	...	(gg)	YR/1	...
Texas	YR/6 (hh)	...	...	YR/3 (hh)	...	...
Utah	SO (ii)	YR /5-8(ii)	...	SO (ii)	...	...
Vermont	YR/1 (jj)	...	...	YR/1 (jj)	...	...
Virginia	SO/1 (kk)	...	(kk)	SO (kk)	SO/2	(kk)
Washington	YR/1	...	IO/1	YR/1	...	YR/1
West Virginia	SO	...	...	...	SO/17	...
Wisconsin	YR (ll)	YR	YR (ll)	YR (ll)	YR	YR (ll)
Wyoming	...	...	...	...	...	...
American Samoa	...	...	...	...	...	...
Guam	...	...	...	...................Unicameral........................		
No. Mariana Islands	YR (mm)	(mm)	...	YR (mm)	(mm)	(ll)
Puerto Rico	YR (mm)	...	...	YR (mm)	...	...
U.S. Virgin Islands	YR (mm)	...	...	...................Unicameral........................		

See footnotes at end of table.

STAFF FOR INDIVIDUAL LEGISLATORS — Continued

Source: The Council of State Governments' survey, November 2014.

Note: For entries under column heading "Shared," figures after slash indicate approximate number of legislators per staff person, where available.

Key:

. . . — Staff not provided for individual legislators.

YR — Year-round.

SO — Session only.

IO — Interim only.

(a) Six counties have local delegation offices with shared staff.

(b) The number of staff per legislator varies depending on their position.

(c) Representatives share a secretary with another legislator; however, House leadership and committee chairs usually have their own secretarial staff. All legislators share professional research staff.

(d) The legislators share 21 staff people; 4.76 legislators per staff person.

(e) Senate: Personal – There is no limit on the number of paid aides and unpaid interns or volunteers, though each Senator has a limit of 420 aide hours for use each session and an additional 100 hours for use at any time during the fiscal year. Shared — 18 session-only employees are employed by the Senate: 2 each by the majority and the minority and 14 by the non-partisan staff. 17 year-round employees are employed Senate and House. By the Senate: 8 by the majority, 5 by the minority and 4 by the non-partisan staff. There are also 4 session-only employees in the bill room who are jointly managed by the Colorado Senate and House. House: Personal — Full time staff consists of 6 majority caucus staff; 5 minority caucus staff; 6 nonpartisan chief clerk's staff. Shared — 65 House legislators share all staff. Full time staff consists of 6 majority caucus staff; 5 minority caucus staff; 6 chief clerk's non-partisan staff. The Colorado session only staff consists of 3 majority caucus staff; 2 minority caucus staff; 23 chief clerk's non-partisan staff.

(f) The numbers are for staff assigned to specific legislators. There is additional staff working in the leadership offices that also support the rank and file members.

(g) Staffers are a combination of full time, part time, shared, personal, etc. and their assignments change throughout the year.

(h) Personal and district staff are the same. In Florida, district employees may travel to the capitol for sessions (two district employees in the Senate and one district employee in the House).

(i) In the Senate, Idaho has one year-round full-time and two part-time year-round employees, with 60 additional employees during the session. The House has one full-time and one part-time person year round and 38 additional people during session.

(j) Each senator has one secretary and two House members share a secretary. Partisan staffers also help legislators with many issues as well as staffing committees. Most senators and representatives have one or two district office employees, paid from a separate allowance for that purpose.

(k) Leadership has one legislative assistant. During session, college interns are hired to provide additional staff — one for every two members. Leadership has one intern.

(l) One clerical staff person for three individual House members is the norm. Chairpersons are provided their own individual clerical staff person.

(m) The General Assembly is provided professional and clerical staff services by a centralized, non-partisan staff, with the exception of House and Senate leadership which employs partisan staff. No district staff provided.

(n) Each legislator may hire as many assistants as desired, but pay from public funds ranges from $2,000 to $3,000 per month per legislator. Assistant(s) generally work in the district office but may also work at the capitol during the session.

(o) The six caucuses are assigned one full-time position each (potentially 24 legislators per one staff person).

(p) President's office: six year round; Majority office: 7 year round, 1 session only; Secretary's office: nine year round, five session only.

(q) The 151 House members do not have individual staff. There are 21 people who work year round in the two partisan offices, 12 of whom are legislative aides who primarily work directly with legislators.

(r) Senators have one year round administrative aide and one session only secretary. Delegates have one part-time year round administrative aide and a shared session only secretary. Legislators may increase staff and also hire student interns if their district office funds are used.

(s) Senate — majority, 2–6 staff per legislator; minority — 2–3 staff per legislator. House — 2 staff per legislator.

(t) One to two staff persons per legislator.

(u) Two to five staff persons per legislator.

(v) Secretarial staff; in North Dakota, leadership only.

(w) House/party leaders determine allowances/funds for members once allocations are made. Members have considerable independence in hiring personal and committee staffs.

(x) Part time during interim.

(y) Some leadership offices have more.

(z) Some legislators maintain district offices at their own expense.

(aa) Some offices have more.

(bb) Senate: Pro Tem — 6 staff persons; Senate minority leader — 1 staff person. House — year round one to five, majority party only; minority party one staff person per legislator. Committee, fiscal and legal staffs are available to legislators on a year round basis.

(cc) Two staff persons per legislator during session.

(dd) Senate — Equivalent of one full-time staff. House — 1 during interim.

(ee) The General Assembly has a total of 280 full time positions, 267 full-time shared staff and additional 13 full-time positions for the House.

(ff) The non-partisan Legislative Research Council serves all members of both houses year round. Committee secretaries and legislative interns and pages provide support during the sessions.

(gg) Several House members have year-round personal staff. It depends on seniority, duties (such as committee chairs), and committee assignments.

(hh) Average staff numbers are from staff member totals from each chamber.

(ii) Most legislators are assigned one student intern during session who is temporarily employed by OLRGC. Some legislators provide their own personal intern (volunteer or financial arrangements are made between them). Senate shared staff: 5–8. In the fall of 2014, the Senate hired four full-time constituent services staff to take care of administrative matters and constituent inquiries year round. Three were hired for 24 majority members, one for five minority members.

(jj) No personal staff except one administrative assistant for the Speaker and one for the Senate Pro Tempore.

(kk) Senate — One administrative assistant (secretary) provided to the members during the session by the Clerk's offices. Members also receive a set dollar allowance to hire additional legislative assistants who may serve year round at the capitol and in the district. House — Members also receive a set dollar allowance to hire additional legislative assistants who may serve year round at the capitol and in the district.

(ll) Staffing levels vary according to majority/minority status and leadership or committee responsibilities. Members may assign staff to work in the district office.

(mm) Individual staffing and staff pool arrangements are at the discretion of the individual legislator.

(nn) Each senator has the authority to hire at least two full-time, year-round staff. Each representative has the authority to hire at least one full-time, year-round staff. Depending on leadership or committee chair assignment, additional staff positions may be authorized.

(oo) One clerk provided in capitol. District/Caucus — 11 staff persons for Republicans and 9 staff persons for Democrats.

(pp) Senate — Majority Leader, 3 staff; Minority Leader, 2 staff; Other Seantors 1 staff per legislator. Secretarial staff. House — 1 staff per legislator. Secretarial staff; Leadership positions are assigned additional staff

Table 3.22
STAFF FOR LEGISLATIVE STANDING COMMITTEES

State or other jurisdiction	Committee staff assistance				Source of staff services **							
	Senate		House/Assembly		Joint central agency (a)		Chamber agency (b)		Caucus or leadership		Committee or committee chair	
	Prof.	Cler.	Prof.	Cler.	Prof.	Cler.	Prof.	Cler.	Prof.	Cler.	Prof.	Cler.
Alabama	●	★	●	★	B	B	B	B	...	...	...	...
Alaska	★	★	★	★	B	B	...	...	...	...	B	B
Arizona	★	★	★	★	B	B	B	B	B	B	B	B
Arkansas	★	★	★	★	B	B	B	B	...	...	...	...
California	★	★	★	★	B	B	B	B	B	B	B	B
Colorado	★	...	★	...	B	...	B	B	B	B (c)	...	...
Connecticut	...	★	...	★	B	...	...	...	...	B	...	B
Delaware	...	★	...	★	B	...	B	...	B	...	...	B
Florida	★	★	★	★	B	B	B	B	B	B	B	B
Georgia	●	★	●	★	B	B	B	B	B	B	B	...
Hawaii	★	★	★	★	B	B	B	B	B	B	B	B
Idaho	...	★	...	★	B (d)	B (d)	B	B	...	B (e)	...	...
Illinois	★	★	★	★	...	...	B	B	B	B	...	...
Indiana	★	...	...	...	...	...	S	...	S	...	...	...
Iowa	★	...	★	...	B	...	(f)	B	B	...	...	B
Kansas	★	★	★	★	B	B (g)	B	B	B	B	B	B
Kentucky	★	★	★	★	B	B	...	...	B (h)	B (h)	...	...
Louisiana	★(i)	★	★(i)	★	B	B	B	B	B	B	B (j)	B (j)
Maine	★(k)	★(k)	★(k)	★(k)	B	B	B	B	B	B	...	B
Maryland	★(l)	★ (l)	★(l)	★(l)	B	B	...	...	...	...	...	...
Massachusetts	★	★	★	★	...	...	...	...	...	...	...	...
Michigan	★	★	★	★	B	...	B	B	B	S	...	...
Minnesota	★	★	★	★	...	...	B	H	S	B	B	B
Mississippi	●	★	●	★	...	...	B	B	...	...	B	B
Missouri	★	...	★	...	B	...	B	...	S	S	B	...
Montana	★	★	★	★	B	...	...	B	...	...	...	...
Nebraska	★	★	U	U	(m)	...	(m)	...	(m)	...	S	S
Nevada	★	★	★	★	B	...	...	...	...	...	...	...
New Hampshire	★	★	★	★	B	B	B	B	...	S	...	S
New Jersey	★	★	★	★	B	B	B	B	...	...	...	...
New Mexico	★	★	★	★	...	...	B	B	...	...	...	...
New York	★	★	★	★	...	...	B	B	B	B	B	B
North Carolina	★	★(n)	★	★(n)	B	...	...	...	...	...	...	B (n)
North Dakota	●	★	●	★	B	B	...	...	...	...	...	...
Ohio	★	★	★	★	B	...	...	...	B	...	B	B
Oklahoma	★	★	★	★	...	...	B	B	S	...	B	B
Oregon	★	★	★	★	B	B	B	B	B	B	B	B
Pennsylvania	★	★	★	★	B	B	B	B	B	B	B	B
Rhode Island	●	★	●	★	B	B	...	B	...	...	B	...
South Carolina	★	★	★	★	B	B	B	B	B	B	B	B
South Dakota	★	★	★	★	B	...	...	(l)	...	(l)	...	(l)
Tennessee	★	★	★	★	B	...	B	B	...	...	...	B
Texas	★	★	★	★	B	B	B	B	...	...	B	B
Utah	★	★(r)	★	★(r)	B	B	...	B	B (s)	B	...	...
Vermont	★	●	★	●	B	B	...	...	...	...	...	...
Virginia	★	★	★	★	B	...	B	B	...	...	(o)	(o)
Washington	★	★	★	★	...	...	B	B	B	B	B	B
West Virginia	★	★	★	★	B	B	B	B	B	B	B	B
Wisconsin	★	★	★	★	B	...	...	...	...	...	(p)	B
Wyoming	...	★	...	★	B	...	...	B	...	...	...	...
American Samoa	●	★	●	★	B	B	B	B	...	...	B	...
Guam	★	★	U	U	...	...	S	S	...	...	...	...
No. Mariana Islands	★	★	★	★	B (q)	B (q)	B (q)	B (q)	B (q)	B (q)	B (q)	B (q)
Puerto Rico	★	★	★	★	B (q)	B (q)	B (q)	B (q)	B (q)	B (q)	B (q)	B (q)
U.S. Virgin Islands	★	★	U	U	S (q)	S (q)	S (q)	S (q)	S (q)	S (q)	S (q)	S (q)

See footnotes at end of table.

STAFF FOR LEGISLATIVE STANDING COMMITTEES — Continued

Source: The Council of State Governments' survey, November 2014.

** — Multiple entries reflect a combination of organizations and location of services.

Key:

★ — All committees

● — Some committees

... — Services not provided

B — Both chambers

H — House

S — Senate

U — Unicameral

(a) Includes legislative council or service agency or central management agency.

(b) Includes chamber management agency, office of clerk or secretary and House or Senate research office.

(c) Senate—there is secretarial staff for both majority and minority offices for the Senate in the Capitol. Most of the clerical work is done by caucus staff.

House—the clerical and secretarial staff for the House is more centralized and is supervised by the Clerk of the House.

(d) Professional staff and clerical support is provided via the Legislative Services Office, a non-partisan office serving all members on a year round basis.

(e) Leadership in each party hire their respective support staff.

(f) The Senate secretary and House clerk maintain supervision of committee clerks.

(g) Senators and House chairpersons select their secretaries and notify the central administrative services agency; all administrative employee matters handled by the agency.

(h) Leadership employs partisan staff to provide professional and clerical services. However, all members, including leadership are also served by the centralized, non-partisan staff.

(i) House Appropriations and Senate Finance Committees have Legislative Fiscal Office staff at their hearings.

(j) Staff are assigned to each committee but work under the direction of the chair.

(k) Standing committees are joint House and Senate committees.

(l) The clerical support comes from employees who are hired to work only during the legislative sessions. They are employees of either the House or the Senate, and are not part of the central agency.

(m) Professional services are not provided, except that the staff of the Legislative Fiscal Office serves the Appropriations Committee. Individual senators are responsible for the process of hiring their own staff.

(n) Member's personal secretary serves as a clerk to the committee or subcommittee that the member chairs.

(o) The House Appropriations Committee and the Senate Finance Committees have their own staff. The staff members work under the direction of the chair.

(p) Standing committees are staffed by subject specialist from the Joint Legislative Council.

(q) In general, the legislative service agency provides legal and staff assistance for legislative meetings and provides associated materials. Individual legislators hire personal or committee staff as their budgets provide and at their own discretion.

(r) Clerical staff not assigned to Rules Cmtes.

(s) Refers only to Chief Deputy of the Senate and Chief of Staff in the House.

Table 3.23
STANDING COMMITTEES: APPOINTMENT AND NUMBER

State or other jurisdiction	Committee members appointed by:		Committee chairpersons appointed by:		Number of standing committees during regular 2014 session		
	Senate	House/Assembly	Senate	House/Assembly	Senate	House/Assembly	Joint
Alabama	(w)	S	(w)	S	25	25	5
Alaska	CC	CC	CC	CC	10	10	11
Arizona	P	S	P	S	13	18	16
Arkansas	(a)	(b)	(a)	S	9	10	24
California	CR	S	CR	S	22	30	7
Colorado	MjL	S	MjL	S	10	11	6
Connecticut	CC	CC	CC	CC	22 (c)	22 (c)	22 (c)
Delaware	PT	S	PT	S	24	25	3
Florida	P	S	P	S	20	9	5
Georgia	CC	S	CC	S	30	38	1
Hawaii	P	S	P	(d)	16	19	. . .
Idaho	PT (f)	S	PT	S	10	14	3
Illinois	P, MnL	S, MnL	P	S	21	32	3
Indiana	PT	S	PT	S	20	20	. . .
Iowa	MjL, MnL	S	MjL	S	17	19	1
Kansas	(g)	S	P	S	15	23	19
Kentucky	CC	CC	CC	CC	15	19	15
Louisiana	P	S (h)	P	S	17	17	2
Maine	P	S	P	S	17	6	(i)
Maryland	P	S	P	S	5	7	19
Massachusetts	P	S	P	S	7	9	27
Michigan	MjL	S	MjL	S	22	23	. . .
Minnesota	CR	S	S	S	13	28	. . .
Mississippi	P	S	P	S	43	46	2
Missouri	PT (j)	S	PT	S	18	43	20
Montana	CC	S	CC	S	16	16	1
Nebraska	CC	U	E	U	14	U	U
Nevada	MjL €	S	MjL	S	. . .	. . .	. . .
New Hampshire	P (k)	S (k)	P (k)	S (k)	11	21	. . .
New Jersey	CC	CC	CC	CC	16	23	5
New Mexico	CC	S	CC	S	9 (l)	16 (l)	. . .
New York	PT	S	PT	S	37	37	. . .
North Carolina	PT	S	PT	S	17	20	. . .
North Dakota	CC	CC	CC	CC	11	12 (n)	. . .
Ohio	P (m)	S (m)	P (m)	S (m)	17	17	. . .
Oklahoma	PT (e)	S	PT	S	16	21	. . .
Oregon	P	S	P	S	12	16	8
Pennsylvania	PT	S	PT	S	22	27	. . .
Rhode Island	P	S	P	S	10	11	3
South Carolina	(o)	S	(p)	E	15	11	. . .
South Dakota	PT	S	PT	S	13	13	1
Tennessee	S	S	S	S	9	14	15
Texas	P	S (q)	P	S	18	38	1
Utah	P	S	P	S	11	14	0
Vermont	CC	S	CC	S	11	14	13
Virginia	E	S	(r)	S	11	14	. . .
Washington	CC	CC	CC (s)	CC (t)	15	23	7
West Virginia	P	S	P	S	18	18	5
Wisconsin	MjL	S	MjL	S	18	44	10
Wyoming	P	S	P	S	12	12	12
Dist. of Columbia	(u)	U	(u)	U	14	U	U
American Samoa	P	S	E	S	16	20	. . .
Guam	(v)	U	(v)	U	12	U	U
No. Mariana Islands	P	S	P	S	8	8	. . .
Puerto Rico	P	S	P	S	23	30	. . .
U.S. Virgin Islands	E	U	E	U	10	U	U

See footnotes at end of table.

STANDING COMMITTEES: APPOINTMENT AND NUMBER — Continued

Source: The Council of State Governments' survey, November 2014.
Key:
CC — Committee on Committees
CR — Committee on Rules
E — Election
MjL — Majority Leader
MnL — Minority Leader
P — President
PT — President pro tempore
S — Speaker
U — Unicameral Legislature
... — None reported.
(a) Selection process based on seniority.
(b) Members of the standing committees shall be selected by House District Caucuses with each caucus selecting five members for each "A" standing committee and five members for each "B" standing committee.
(c) Substantive standing committees are joint committees. There are also three joint statutory committees.
(d) By resolution with members of majority party designating the chair, vice-chairs and majority party members of committees, and members of minority party designating minority party members.
(e) Minority Leader selects minority members.
(f) Committee members appointed by the Senate leadership under the direction of the president pro tempore, by and with the Senate's consent.
(g) Committee on Organization, Calendar and Rules.
(h) Speaker appoints only 12 of the 19 members of the Committee on Appropriations.
(i) There are currently 16 Joint Standing Committees, two Joint Select Committees, and a joint Government Oversight Committee.

(j) Senate minority committee members chosen by minority caucus, but appointed by president pro tempore.
(k) Senate president and House speaker consult with minority leaders.
(l) Senate: includes eight substantive committees and one procedural committee. House: includes 12 substantive committees and three procedural committees.
(m) The minority leader may recommend for consideration minority party members for each committee.
(n) The House had a Constitutional Revision Committee.
(o) Appointment based on seniority (Senate Rule 19D).
(p) Appointed by seniority which is determined by tenure within the committee rather than tenure within the Senate. Also, chair is based on the majority party within the committee (Senate Rule 19E).
(q) For each standing substantive committee of the House, except for the appropriations committee, a maximum of one-half of the membership, exclusive of chair and vice-chair, is determined by seniority; the remaining membership of the committee is determined by the speaker.
(r) Senior member of the majority party on the committee is the chair.
(s) Recommended by the Committee on Committees, approved by the president, then confirmed by the Senate.
(t) Recommended by the Committee on Committees, then confirmed by the House.
(u) Chair of the Council.
(v) Members are appointed by the Chairperson; Chairperson is elected during majority caucus prior to inauguration.
(w) Committee on Assignments.

Table 3.24
RULES ADOPTION AND STANDING COMMITTEES: PROCEDURE

State or other jurisdiction	Constitution permits each legislative body to determine its own rules	Committee meetings open to public*		Specific, advance notice provisions for committee meetings or hearings	Voting/roll call provisions to report a bill to floor
		Senate	House/Assembly		
Alabama..............	★	★	★	Senate: 4 hours, if possible. House: 24 hours, except Rules and Local Legislations Committee. Exceptions after 27th legislative day and special sessions.	Senate: final vote on a bill, except a local bill, is recorded. House: recorded vote if requested by member of committee and sustained by one additional committee member.
Alaska..............	...	★	★	For meetings, by 4:00 p.m. on the preceding Thurs.; for first hearings on bills, 5 days.	Roll call vote on any measure taken upon request by any member of either house.
Arizona..............	★	★	★	Senate: Written agenda for each regular and special meeting containing all bills, memorials and resolutions to be considered shall be distributed to each member of the committee and to the Secretary of the Senate at least five days prior to the committee meeting. House: The committee chair shall prepare an agenda and distribute copies to committee members, the Information Desk and the Chief Clerk's Office by 4 p.m. each Wednesday for all standing committees meeting on Monday of the following week and 4 p.m. each Thursday for all standing committees meeting on any day except Monday of the following week.	Senate: roll call vote. House: roll call vote.
Arkansas..............	★	★	★	Senate: 2 days (anytime with 2/3's vote of the committee). House: 18 hours (2 hours with 2/3's vote of the committee).	Senate: roll call votes are recorded. House: report of committee recommendation signed by committee chair.
California	★	★	★	Senate: advance notice provisions exist and are published in the agendas of each house. House: public notice is published in the agendas of each house. (h)	Senate: roll call. House: roll call.
Colorado..............	★	★	★	Senate: Final action on a measure is prohibited unless notice is posted one calendar day prior to its consideration. The prohibition does not apply if the action receives a majority vote of the committee. House: Meeting publicly announced while the House is in actual session as much in advance as possible.	Senate: final action by recorded roll call vote. House: final action by recorded roll call vote.
Connecticut	★	★	★	Senate: 1 day notice for meetings, 5 days notice for hearings. House: 1 day notice for meetings, 5 days notice for hearings.	Senate: roll call required. House: roll call required.
Delaware	★	★	★	Senate: agenda released 1 day before meetings. House: agenda released 4 days before meetings.	Senate: results of all committee reports are recorded. House: results of all committee reports are recorded.
Florida	★	★	★	Senate: during session—3 weekdays for first 40 days, 4 hours thereafter. House: 2 days for first 45 days, 1 day thereafter.	Senate: vote on final passage is recorded. House: vote on final passage is recorded.
Georgia..............	★	★	★	Senate: a list of committee meetings shall be posted by 10:00 a.m. the preceding Friday. House: none.	Senate: bills can be voted out by voice vote or roll call. House: bills can be voted out by voice vote or roll call.

See footnotes at end of table.

RULES ADOPTION AND STANDING COMMITTEES: PROCEDURE — Continued

State or other jurisdiction	Constitution permits each legislative body to determine its own rules	Committee meetings open to public*		Specific, advance notice provisions for committee meetings or hearings	Voting/roll call provisions to report a bill to floor
		Senate	House/Assembly		
Hawaii	★	★(a)	★(a)	Senate: 72 hours before 1st referral committee meetings, 48 hours before subsequent referral committee. House: 48 hours.	Senate: a quorum of committee members must be present before voting. House: a quorum of committee members must be present before voting.
Idaho	★	★(a)	★(a)	Senate: none. House: per rule; chair provides notice of next meeting dates and times to clerk to be read prior to adjournment each day of session.	Senate: bills can be voted out by voice vote or roll call. House: bills can be voted out by voice vote or roll call.
Illinois	★	★(b)	★(b)	Senate: 6 days. House: 6 days.	Senate: votes on all legislative measures acted upon are recorded. House: votes on all legislative matters acted upon are recorded.
Indiana	★	★	★	Senate: 48 hours. House: prior to adjournment of the meeting day next preceding the meeting or announced during session.	Senate: committee reports—do pass; do pass amended, reported out without recommendation. House: majority of quorum; vote can be by roll call or consent.
Iowa	★	★	★	Senate: yes, but can be suspended. House: yes, but can be suspended.	Senate: final action by roll call. House: committee reports include roll call on final disposition.
Kansas	★	★	★	Senate: none. House: none.	Senate: vote recorded upon request of member. House: total for and against actions recorded.
Kentucky	★	★	★	Senate: none. House: none.	Senate: each member's vote recorded on each bill. House: each member's vote recorded on each bill.
Louisiana	★	★(a)	★(a)	Senate: no later than 1:00 p.m. the preceding day. House: no later than 4:00 p.m. the preceding day.	Senate: any motion to report an instrument is decided by a roll call vote. House: any motion to report an instrument is decided by a roll call vote.
Maine	★	★	★	Senate and House: must be advertised two weekends in advance.	Senate and House: recorded vote is required to report a bill out of committee.
Maryland	★	★	★	Senate: none. (c) House: none. (c)	Senate: the final vote on any bill is recorded. House: the final vote on any bill is recorded.
Massachusetts	★	★	★	Senate: 48 hours for public hearings. House: 48 hours for public hearings.	Senate: voice vote or recorded roll call vote at the request of two committee members. House: recorded vote upon request by a member.
Michigan	★	★	★	Senate and House: Notice shall be published in the journal in advance of a hearing. Notice of a special meeting shall be posted at least 18 hours before a meeting. Special provisions for conference committees.	Senate: committee reports include the vote of each member on any bill. House: the daily journal reports the roll call on all motions to report bills.
Minnesota	★	★	★	Senate: 3 days. House: 3 days.	Senate: not needed. House: not needed.

See footnotes at end of table.

RULES ADOPTION AND STANDING COMMITTEES: PROCEDURE—Continued

State or other jurisdiction	Constitution permits each legislative body to determine its own rules	Committee meetings open to public*		Specific, advance notice provisions for committee meetings or hearings	Voting/roll call provisions to report a bill to floor
		Senate	House/ Assembly		
Mississippi	★	★	★	Senate: none. House: none.	Senate: bills are reported out by voice vote or recorded roll call vote. House: bills are reported out by voice vote or recorded roll call vote.
Missouri	★	★	★	Senate: 24 hours. House: 24 hours.	Senate: yeas and nays are reported in journal. House: bills are reported out by a recorded roll call vote.
Montana	★	★	★	Senate: 3 legislative days or as circumstances require. House: 3 legislative days or as circumstances require.	Senate: every vote of each member is recorded and made public. House: every vote of each member is recorded and made public.
Nebraska	★	★	U	7 calendar days notice before hearing a bill.	In executive session, majority of the committee must vote in favor of the motion made.
Nevada	★	★	★	Senate: by rule—"adequate notice" shall be provided. (d) House: by rule—"adequate notice" shall be provided. (d)	Senate: recorded vote is taken upon final committee action on bills. House: recorded vote is taken upon final committee action on bills.
New Hampshire	★	★	★	Senate: 4 days. House: no less than 4 days.	Senate: committees report bills out by recorded roll call votes. House: committees report bills out by recorded roll call votes.
New Jersey	★	★	★	Senate: 5 state working days. House: 5 days.	Senate: the chair reports the vote of each member present on a motion to report a bill. House: the chair reports the vote of each member present on motions with respect to bills.
New Mexico	★	★	★	Senate: none. House: none.	Senate: vote on the final report of the committee taken by yeas and nays. Roll call vote upon request. House: vote on the final report of the committee taken by yeas and nays. Roll call vote upon request.
New York	★	★(a)	★(a)	Senate: 1 week for hearings. Rules require that notice be given for public hearings, but the rules are silent as to how long. House: 1 week for hearings, Thursday of prior week for meetings.	Senate: majority vote required. House: majority vote required.
North Carolina	(f)	★	★	Senate: none. (e) House: none. (e)	Senate: no roll call vote may be taken in any committee. House: roll call vote taken on any question when requested by member and sustained by one-fifth of members present.
North Dakota	★	★	★	Senate: hearing schedule printed Friday mornings. House: hearing schedule printed Friday mornings.	Senate: included with minutes from standing committee. House: included with minutes from standing committee.

See footnotes at end of table.

RULES ADOPTION AND STANDING COMMITTEES: PROCEDURE — Continued

State or other jurisdiction	Constitution permits each legislative body to determine its own rules	Committee meetings open to public*		Specific, advance notice provisions for committee meetings or hearings	Voting/roll call provisions to report a bill to floor
		Senate	House/ Assembly		
Ohio................	★	★	★	Senate: Rule 21 At least two days preceding the day bills or joint resolutions to propose a constitutional amendment are to be given a first hearing, the clerk shall post in the clerk's office schedule of such bills and joint resolutions in each standing committee or subcommittee with the exception of the standing Committee on Rules. In case of necessity, the notice of hearing may be given in a shorter period than two days by such reasonable method as shall be prescribed by the Committee on Rules. House: Rule 36(a) The chairman of a standing committee, subcommittee, select committee or joint committee, not later than five days before a meeting of the committee, shall give due notice of the meeting. (b) If, however, an emergency requires consideration of a matter at a meeting, and the matter has not been stated in the notice of the meeting, the chair may revise or supplement the notice at any time before or during the meeting to include the matter and the matter may be then considered as the emergency requires.	Senate: Rule 24 The affirmative votes of a majority of all members of a committee shall be necessary to report or to postpone further consideration of bills or resolutions. Every member present shall vote, unless excused by the chair. At discretion of chair the roll call may be continued for a vote by any member who was present at the prior meeting, but no later than 10:00 a.m. of next calendar day. House: Rule 40(b) The affirmative votes of a majority of all members constituting a committee shall be necessary to report a bill or resolution out of committee, and a record of every vote shall be kept by the committee. The affirmative vote of a majority of all the members constituting the committee shall be necessary to agree to any motion to recommend for passage or to postpone indefinitely further consideration of bills or resolutions, and a record of such vote shall be kept by the committee. Every member present shall vote unless excused by the committee. The affirmative votes of a majority of all members of a committee shall be necessary to report or to postpone further consideration of bills or resolutions. Every member present shall vote, unless excused by the chair. Rule 41(a) No proxy vote shall be valid. Nor shall any member vote except while sitting in committee in actual session, unless the member shall have first been present and recorded as such during actual session before the vote is taken, and by motion the roll call on a motion to recommend a bill or resolution for passage is continued for a vote by any member who is temporarily absent from the meeting until the adjournment thereof, which shall be not later than 12:00 noon one day following the committee meeting.
Oklahoma............	★	★	★	Senate: 48 hours notice. House: 3 days notice.	Senate: roll call vote. House: roll call vote.
Oregon................	★	★	★	Senate: At least 48 hrs. notice except at the end of session when President invokes 1-hour notice when adjournment sine die is imminent. House: First public hearing on a measure must have at least 72 hours notice, all other meetings at least 48 hours notice except in case of emergency.	Senate: affirmative roll call vote of majority of members of committee and recorded in committee minutes. House: affirmative roll call vote of majority of members of committee and recorded in committee minutes.
Pennsylvania	★	★	★	Senate: written notice to members containing date, time, place and agenda. House: written notice to members containing date, time, place and agenda.	Senate: a majority vote of committee members. House: a majority vote of committee members.
Rhode Island..........	★	★	★	Senate: notice required. House: notice required.	Senate: majority vote of the members present. House: majority vote of the members present.

See footnotes at end of table.

RULES ADOPTION AND STANDING COMMITTEES: PROCEDURE — Continued

State or other jurisdiction	Constitution permits each legislative body to determine its own rules	Committee meetings open to public*		Specific, advance notice provisions for committee meetings or hearings	Voting/roll call provisions to report a bill to floor
		Senate	House/ Assembly		
South Carolina	★	★	★	Senate: 24 hours. House: 24 hours.	Senate: favorable report out of committee (majority of committee members voting in favor). House: favorable report out of committee (majority of committee members voting in favor).
South Dakota	★	★	★	Senate and House: at least one legislative day must intervene between the date of posting and the date of consideration in both houses.	Senate and House: a majority vote of the members-elect taken by roll call is needed for final disposition on a bill. This applies to both houses.
Tennessee	★	★	★	Senate: 6 days. House: 72 hours.	Senate: majority referral to Calendar and Rules Committee, majority of Calendar and Rules Committee referral to floor. House: majority referral to Calendar and Rules Committee, majority of Calendar and Rules Committee referral to floor.
Texas	★	★	★	Senate: 24 hours. House: The House requires five calendar days notice before a public hearing at which testimony will be taken, and two hours notice or an announcement from the floor before a formal meeting (testimony cannot be taken at a formal meeting). 24-hour advance notice is required during special session.	Senate: bills are reported by recorded roll call vote. House: committee reports include the record vote by which the report was adopted, including the vote of each member.
Utah	★	★	★	Senate: not less than 24 hours public notice. House: not less than 24 hours public notice.	Senate: voice vote accepting the recommendation of the committee. House: voice vote accepting the recommendation of the committee.
Vermont	★	★	★	Senate: none. House: none.	Senate: vote is recorded for each committee member for every bill considered. House: vote is recorded for each committee member for every bill considered.
Virginia	★	★(a)	★(a)	Senate: none. House: none.	Senate: recorded vote, except resolutions that do not have a specific vote requirement under the Rules. In these cases, a voice vote is sufficient. House: vote of each member is taken and recorded for each measure.
Washington	★	★	★	Senate: 5 days. House: 5 days.	Senate: bills reported from a committee carry a majority report which must be signed by a majority of the committee. House: every vote to report a bill out of committee is by yeas and nays; the names of the members voting are recorded in the report.
West Virginia	★	★	★	Senate: none. House: none.	Senate: majority of committee members voting. House: majority of committee members voting.
Wisconsin	★	★	★	Senate: Monday noon of the preceding week. House: Monday noon of the preceding week.	Senate: number of ayes and noes, and members absent or not voting are reported. House: number of ayes and noes are recorded.
Wyoming	★	★	★	Senate: by 3:00 p.m. of previous day. House: by 3:00 p.m. of previous day.	Senate: bills are reported out by recorded roll call vote. House: bills are reported out by recorded roll call vote.

See footnotes at end of table.

RULES ADOPTION AND STANDING COMMITTEES: PROCEDURE — Continued

State or other jurisdiction	Constitution permits each legislative body to determine its own rules	Committee meetings open to public*		Specific, advance notice provisions for committee meetings or hearings	Voting/roll call provisions to report a bill to floor
		Senate	*House/ Assembly*		
American Samoa	★	★(g)	★(g)	Senate: at least 3 calendar days in advance. House: at least 3 calendar days in advance.	Senate/House: There are four methods of ascertaining the decision upon any matter: by raising of hands; by secret ballot, when authorized by law; by rising; and by call of the members and recorded by the Clerk of the vote of each.
Guam	★		U	5 days prior to public hearings.	Majority vote of committee members.
No. Mariana Islands...	★	★	★	Senate: 3 days. House: 1 day.	Senate and House: majority.
Puerto Rico............	★	★	★	Senate: Must be notified every Thurs, one week in advance. House: 24 hours advanced notice, no later than 4:00 p.m. previous day.	Senate: bills reported from a committee carry a majority vote. House: bills reported from a committee carry a majority vote by referendum or in an ordinary meeting.
U.S. Virgin Islands...	★	★	U	7 calendar days.	Bills must be reported to floor by Rules Committee.

Source: The Council of State Governments' survey, November 2014.

Key:
★ — Yes
* — Notice of committee meetings may also be subject to state open meetings laws; in some cases, listed times may be subject to suspension or enforceable only to the extent "feasible" or "whenever possible."
U — Unicameral.

(a) Certain matters may be discussed in executive session. (Other states permit meetings to be closed for various reasons, but their rules do not specifically mention "executive session.")

(b) A session of a house or one of its committees can be closed to the public if two-thirds of the members elected to that house determine that the public interest so requires. A meeting of a joint committee or commission can be closed if two-thirds of the members of both houses so vote.

(c) General directive in the Senate and House rules to the Department of Legislative Services to compile a list of the meetings and to arrange for distribution which in practice is done on a regular basis.

(d) Senate: This rule may be suspended for emergencies by a two-thirds vote of appointed committee members. House: This rule may be suspended for emergencies by a majority vote of appointed committee members. In the Assembly this rule does not apply to committee meetings held on the floor during recess or conference committee meetings.

(e) If public hearing, five calendar days.

(f) Not referenced specifically, but each body publishes rules.

(g) Unless privileged information is being discussed with counsel or the security of the territory is involved.

(h) For bill hearings, the first committee of reference has a four-day notice and the second committee of reference has a two-day notice. Informational hearings have a four-day notice. No public notice is required for resolutions or special session bills.

Table 3.25
LEGISLATIVE REVIEW OF ADMINISTRATIVE REGULATIONS: STRUCTURES AND PROCEDURES

State or other jurisdiction	Type of reviewing committee	Rules reviewed	Time limits in review process
Alabama	Joint bipartisan, standing committee	P	If not approved or disapproved within 35 days of filing, rule is approved. If disapproved by committee, rule suspended until adjournment of the next regular session or until legislature by resolution revokes suspension. Rule takes effect upon final adjournment unless committee's disapproval is sustained by legislature. The committee may approve a rule.
Alaska	Joint bipartisan, standing committee and Legislative Affairs Agency review of proposed regulations.	P,E	. . .
Arizona	Joint bipartisan	P,E	. . .
Arkansas	Joint bipartisan	P,E	. . .
California	Standing committee	P,E	The Legislature may study and make recommendations regarding existing or proposed regulations. Comprehensive regulation review conducted by independent executive branch agency.
Colorado	Joint bipartisan	E	Rules continue unless the annual legislative Rule Reviews Bill discontinues a rule. The Rule Reviews Bill is effective upon the governor's signature.
Connecticut	Joint bipartisan, standing committee	P	Submittal of proposed regulation shall be on the first Tuesday of month; after first submittal committee has 65 days after date of submission to review/take action on revised regulation. Second submittal: 35 days for committee to review/take action on revised regulation.
Delaware	Joint bipartisan, standing committee	P,E (j)	. . .
Florida	Joint bipartisan	P,E	. . .
Georgia	Standing committee	P	The agency notifies the Legislative Counsel 30 days prior to the effective dates of proposed rules.
Hawaii	Legislative agency	P,E	The legislative reference bureau assists agencies to comply with a uniform format of style. This does not affect the status of rules.
Idaho	Germane joint subcommittees	P	Germane joint subcommittees vote to object or not object to a rule. They cannot reject a proposed rule directly, only advise an agency which may choose to adopt a rule subject to review by the full legislature. The legislature as a whole reviews rules during the first three weeks of session to determine if they comport with state law. The Senate and House may reject rules via resolution adopted by both. Rules imposing fees must be approved or are deemed approved unless rejected. Temporary rules expire at the end of session unless extended by concurrent resolution.
Illinois	Joint bipartisan	P,E	An agency proposing non-emergency regulations must allow 45 days for public comment. At least five days after any public hearing on the proposal, the agency must give notice of the proposal to the Joint Committee on Administrative Rules, and allow it 45 days to approve or object to the proposed regulations.
Indiana	Joint bipartisan	P	. . .
Iowa	Joint bipartisan	P,E	. . .
Kansas	Joint bipartisan	P	Agencies must give a 60-day notice to the public and the Joint Committee of their intent to adopt or amend specific rules and regulations, a copy of which must be provided to the committee. Within the 60-day comment period, the Joint Committee must review and comment, if it feels necessary, on the proposals. Final rules and regulations which differ in subject matter or in any material respect from the rules and regulations originally proposed or which are not a logical outgrowth of the rules and regulations originally proposed must be resubmitted to the Joint Committee as part of new rulemaking.
Kentucky	Joint bipartisan statutory committee	P,E	45 days.

See footnotes at end of table.

LEGISLATIVE REVIEW OF ADMINISTRATIVE REGULATIONS: STRUCTURES AND PROCEDURES — Continued

State or other jurisdiction	Type of reviewing committee	Rules reviewed	Time limits in review process
Louisiana (b)............	Standing committee	P	All proposed rules and fees are submitted to designated standing committees of the legislature. If a rule or fee is unacceptable, the committee sends a written report to the governor. The governor has 10 days to disapprove the committee report. If both Senate and House committees fail to find the rule unacceptable, or if the governor disapproves the action of a committee within 10 days, the agency may adopt the rule change. (d)
Maine.........................	Joint bipartisan, standing committee	P (i)	One legislative session.
Maryland..................	Joint bipartisan	P,E	Proposed regulations are submitted for review at least 15 days before publication. Publication triggers 45-day review period which may be extended by the committee, but if agreement cannot be reached, the governor may instruct the agency to modify or withdraw the regulation, or may approve its adoption.
Massachusetts (b).....	Public hearing by agency	P	In Massachusetts, the General Court (Legislature) may by statute authorize an administrative agency to promulgate regulations. The promulgation of such regulations are then governed by Chapter 30A of the Massachusetts General Laws. Chapter 30A requires 21-day notice to the public of a public hearing on a proposed regulation. After public hearing the proposed regulation is filed with the state secretary who approves it if it is in conformity with Chapter 30A. The state secretary maintains a register entitled "Massachusetts Register" and the regulation does not become effective until published in the register. The agency may promulgate amendments to the regulations following the same process.
Michigan....................	Joint bipartisan	P	Joint Committee on Administrative Rules (JCAR) has 15 session days in which to consider the rule and to object to the rule by filing a notice of objection. If no objection is made, the rules may be filed and go into effect. If JCAR does formally object, bills to block the rules are introduced in both houses of the legislature simultaneously by the committee chair and placed directly on the Senate and House calendars for action. If the bills are not enacted by the legislature and presented to the governor within 15 session days, the rules may be filed with the secretary of state take effect. Between legislative sessions the committee can meet and suspend rules promulgated during the interim between sessions.
Minnesota..................	Joint bipartisan, standing committee	P,E	Minnesota Statute Sec. 3.842, subd. 4a
Mississippi................	............................(a)............................	. . .	Administrative Regulations are not reviewed by the Mississippi Legislature.
Missouri....................	Joint bipartisan, standing committee	P,E	The committee must disapprove a final order of rulemaking within 30 days upon receipt or the order of rulemaking is deemed approved.
Montana....................	Germane joint bipartisan committees	P	Prior to adoption.
Nebraska...................	Standing committee	P	If an agency proposes to repeal, adopt or amend a rule or regulation, it is required to provide the Executive Board Chair with the proposal at least 30 days prior to the public hearing, as required by law. The Executive Board Chair shall provide to the appropriate standing committee of the legislature, the agency proposal for comment.
Nevada.......................	Ongoing statutory committee (Legislative Commission)	P	Proposed regulations are either reviewed at the Legislative Commission's next regularly scheduled meeting (if the regulation is received more than 10 working days before the meeting), or they are referred to the Commission's Subcommittee to Review Regulations. If there is no objection to the regulation, then the Commission will "promptly" file the approved regulation with the secretary of state. If the Commission or its subcommittee objects to a regulation, then the Commission will "promptly" return the regulation to the agency for revision. Within 60 days of receiving the written notice of objection to the regulation, the agency must revise the regulation and return it to the Legislative Counsel. If the Commission or its subcommittee objects to the revised regulation, the agency shall continue to revise and resubmit it to the Commission or subcommittee within 30 days after receiving the written notice of objection to the revised regulation.

See footnotes at end of table.

LEGISLATIVE REVIEW OF ADMINISTRATIVE REGULATIONS: STRUCTURES AND PROCEDURES — Continued

State or other jurisdiction	Type of reviewing committee	Rules reviewed	Time limits in review process
New Hampshire	Joint bipartisan	P	Under APA, for regular rulemaking, the joint committee of administrative rules has 45 days to review a final proposed rule from an agency, Otherwise the rule is automatically approved. If JLCAR makes a preliminary or revised objection, the agency has 45 days to respond, and JLCAR has another 50 days to decide to vote to sponsor a joint resolution, which suspends the adoption process. JLCAR may also, or instead, make a final objection, which shifts the burden of proof in court to the agency. There is no time limit on making a final objection. If no JLCAR action in the 50 days to vote to sponsor a joint resolution, the agency may adopt the rule.
New Jersey	Joint bipartisan	P,E	The legislature must pass and transmit a concurrent resolution to the gov. and head of the agency which promulgated or proposed the regulation. Agency has 30 days from receipt of concurrent resolution to amend or withdraw the regulation or proposed regulation. If the agency does not respond in a manner satisfactory to Legislature, the Legislature may, at least 20 calendar days after a transcript of the legislative hearing concerning the regulation is placed on the desks of the members in open session, pass another concurrent resolution, this one invalidating the regulation.
New Mexico	.... (g)		
New York	Joint bipartisan commission	P,E	. . .
North Carolina	Rules Review Commission; Public membership appointed by legislature	P,E	The Rules Review Commission must review a permanent rule submitted to it on or before the 20th of the month by the last day of the next month. The commission must review a permanent rule submitted to it after the 20th of the month by the last day of the second subsequent month.
North Dakota	Interim committee	E	The Administrative Rules Committee meets in each calendar quarter to consider rules filed in previous 90 days.
Ohio	Joint bipartisan	P,E (h)	The committee's jurisdiction is 65 days from date of original filing plus an additional 30 days from date of re-filing. Rules filed with no changes, pursuant to the five-year review, are under a 90-day jurisdiction.
Oklahoma	Standing committee (c)	P,E	The legislature has 30 legislative days to review proposed rules. The legislature reviews all agency rules submitted prior to April 1st. Any rules submitted after April 1st are to be reviewed the next legislative session.
Oregon	Office of Legislative Counsel	E	Agencies must copy Legislative Counsel within 10 days of rule adoption.
Pennsylvania	Joint bipartisan, standing committee	P	Time limits decided by the president pro tempore and speaker of the House.
Rhode Island	.... (a)		
South Carolina	Standing committee (e)	P	General Assembly has 120 days to approve or disapprove. If not disapproved by joint resolution before 120 days, regulation is automatically approved. It can be approved during 120-day review period by joint resolution.
South Dakota	Joint bipartisan	P	Rules must be adopted within 75 days of the commencement of the public hearing; emergency rules must be adopted within 30 days of the date of the publication of the notice of intent. Many other deadlines exist; see SDCL 1-26-4 for further details.
Tennessee	Joint bipartisan	P	All permanent rules take effect 90 days after filing with the secretary of state. Emergency rules take effect upon filing with the secretary of state and may be effective for not longer than 180 days.
Texas	Standing committee	P,E	No time limit.
Utah	.... (f)	P,E	Except as provided in Subsection (2)(b), every agency rule that is in effect on February 28 of any calendar year expires May 1 of that year unless it has been reauthorized by the legislature. (UCA 63G-3-502)
Vermont	Joint bipartisan	P	The Joint Legislative Committee on Rules must review a proposed rule within 30 days of submission to the committee.

See footnotes at end of table.

LEGISLATIVE REVIEW OF ADMINISTRATIVE REGULATIONS: STRUCTURES AND PROCEDURES — Continued

State or other jurisdiction	Type of reviewing committee	Rules reviewed	Time limits in review process
Virginia......................	Joint bipartisan, standing committee	P	Standing committees and the Joint Commission on Administrative Rules may object to a proposed or final adopted rule before it becomes effective. This delays the process for 21 days and the agency must respond to the objection. In addition or as an alternative, standing committees and the Commission may suspend the effective date of all or a part of a final regulation until the end of the next regular session, with the concurrence of the governor.
Washington...............	Joint bipartisan	P,E	If the committee determines that a proposed rule does not comply with legislative intent, it notifies the agency, which must schedule a public hearing within 30 days of notification. The agency notifies the committee of its action within seven days after the hearing. If a hearing is not held or the agency does not amend the rule, the objection may be filed in the state register and referenced in the state code. The committee's powers, other than publication of its objections, are advisory.
West Virginia.............	Joint bipartisan	P,E	...
Wisconsin	Joint bipartisan, standing committee	P,E	The standing committee in each house has 30 days to conduct its review for a proposed rule. If either objects the Joint Committee for the Review of Administrative Rules has 30 days to introduce legislation in each house overturning the rules. After 40 days the bills are placed on the calendar. If either bill passes, the rules are overturned. If they fail to pass, the rules go into effect.
Wyoming	Joint bipartisan	P,E	An agency shall submit copies of adopted, amended or repealed rules to the legislative service office for review within five days after the date of the agency's final action adopting, amending or repealing those rules. The legislature makes its recommendations to the governor who within 15 days after receiving any recommendation, shall either order that the rule be amended or rescinded in accordance with the recommendation or file in writing his objections to the recommendation.
American Samoa	Standing committee	E	...
Guam	Standing committee	P	45 Calendar days
Puerto Rico..............	....(a)..		
U.S. Virgin Islands	....(a)..		

Source: The Council of State Governments' survey, November 2014.
Key:
P — Proposed rules
E — Existing rules
... — No formal time limits
(a) No formal rule review is performed by both legislative and executive branches.
(b) Review of rules is performed by both legislative and executive branches.
(c) House has a standing committee to which all rules are generally sent for review. In the Senate rules are sent to standing committee which deals with that specific agency.
(d) If the committees of both houses fail to find a fee unacceptable, it can be adopted. Committee action on proposed rules must be taken within 5 to 30 days after the agency reports to the committee on its public hearing (if any) and whether it is making changes on proposed rules.

(e) Submitted by General Assembly for approval.
(f) Created by statute (63G-3-501).
(g) No formal review is performed by legislature. Periodic review and report to legislative finance committee is required of certain agencies.
(h) The Committee reviews proposed new, amended, and rescinded rules. The Committee participates in a five-year review of every existing rule.
(i) Major substantive Rules (as designated by the Legislature) are subject to legislative review and approval; Routine Technical Rules are not subject to any formal legislative review and approval process.
(j) The chair of a standing committee can call a hearing to review the rule during the interim. The Joint Sunset Committee can order a review of an agency's rules during regular session.

Table 3.26
LEGISLATIVE REVIEW OF ADMINISTRATIVE RULES/REGULATIONS: POWERS

State or other jurisdiction	Reviewing committee's powers			Legislative powers
	Advisory powers only (a)	No objection constitutes approval of proposed rule	Committee may suspend rule	Method of legislative veto of rules
Alabama	...	★	★	If not approved or disapproved within 35 days of filing, rule is approved. If disapproved by committee, rule suspended until adjournment, next regular session or until legislature by resolution revokes suspension. Rule takes effect upon final adjournment unless committee's disapproval is sustained by legislature. The committee may approve a rule.
Alaska	★	...	(b)	Constitution and Statute
Arizona	★	N.A.	N.A.	N.A.
Arkansas	★	...	...	...
California	★(cc)	...	...	Statute
Colorado	...	★	...	Rules that the General Assembly has determined should not be continued are listed as exceptions to the continuation.
Connecticut	...	★	...	Statute CGS 4-170 (d) and 4-171; (c)
Delaware	★(ff)	...	...	N.A.
Florida	★(ee)	...	...	Statute
Georgia	...	★	...	Resolution (d)
Hawaii	★	...	...	...
Idaho	...	★	...	Concurrent resolution. All rules are terminated one year after adoption unless the legislature reauthorizes the rule.
Illinois	...	(e)	★(f)	(f)
Indiana	★	...	...	(g)
Iowa	...	...	(h)	By constitutional majority vote of each house, by concurrent resolution, with approval of governor not required.
Kansas	★	...	...	Statute
Kentucky	(x)	(y)	(z)	Enacting legislation to void. (z)
Louisiana	...	★	(i)	Concurrent resolution to suspend, amend or repeal adopted rules or fees. Proposed rules and emergency rules exist (i).
Maine	★(aa)	★(bb)	...	(j)
Maryland	★(k)	...	...	...
Massachusetts	...	...	...	The legislature may pass a bill which would supersede a regulation if signed into law by the governor.
Michigan	...	...	(l)	Joint Committee on Rules has 15 session days to approve the filing of a notice of objection. The filing of the notice of objection starts another 15-day session period that stays the rules and causes committee members to introduce legislation in both houses of the legislature for enactment and presentment to the governor. Any member of the legislature, pursuant to statute, can introduce a bill at a session, which in effect amends or rescinds a rule.
Minnesota	★	...	...	(m)
Mississippi			(n)	
Missouri	...	★	★	Concurrent resolution passed by both houses of the General Assembly.
Montana	...	...	★(o)	Statute
Nebraska	★	★	...	...
Nevada	N.A.	★	★	Proposed regulations are either reviewed at the Legislative Commission's next regularly scheduled meeting (if the regulation is received more than three working days before the meeting), or they are referred to the Commission's Subcommittee to Review Regulations. If there is no objection to the regulation, then the Commission will "promptly" file the approved regulation with the Secretary of State. If the Commission or its subcommittee objects to a regulation, then the Commission will "promptly" return the regulation to the agency for revision. Within 60 days of receiving the written notice of objection to the regulation, the agency must revise the regulation and return it to the Legislative Counsel. If the Commission or its subcommittee objects to the revised regulation, the agency shall continue to revise and resubmit it to the Commission or subcommittee within 30 days after receiving the written notice of objection to the revised regulation.

See footnotes at end of table.

LEGISLATIVE REVIEW OF ADMINISTRATIVE RULES/REGULATIONS: POWERS — Continued

State or other jurisdiction	Reviewing committee's powers			Legislative powers
	Advisory powers only (a)	No objection constitutes approval of proposed rule	Committee may suspend rule	Method of legislative veto of rules
New Hampshire	★	(q)	. . .	(r)
New Jersey	★	. . .	. . .	(s)
New Mexico	N.A.	N.A.	N.A.	No formal mechanism exists for legislative review of administrative rules.
New York....................	★	. . .	. . .	Reviewing commission's powers are advisory; it may, via its chair, introduce legislation with regard to agency rulemaking.
North Carolina..........	★	★	★	. . .
North Dakota.............	. . .	★(t)	. . .	The Administrative Rules Committee can void a rule.
Ohio	★	. . .	. . .	Concurrent resolution. Committee recommends to the General Assembly that a rule be invalidated. The General Assembly invalidates a rule through adoption of concurrent resolution.
Oklahoma..................	★(p)	★(p)	★(p)	The legislature may disapprove (veto) proposed rules by concurrent or joint resolution. A concurrent resolution does not require the governor's signature. Existing rules may be disapproved by joint resolution. A committee may not disapprove; only the full legislature may do so. Failure of the legislature to disapprove constitutes approval. Pursuant to HB 2055 enacted in 2013, legislature shall adopt omnibus resolution approving all proposed permanent rules except those listed in resolution which are to be disapproved.
Oregon.......................	★	★	(dd)	By passing statute that overrides terms of rule.
Pennsylvania	. . .	★	★	Upon vote of General Assembly.
Rhode Island.............	. . . . (n)			
South Carolina..........	. . .	★	. . .	. . .
South Dakota............	. . .	★	★	The Interim Rules Review Committee may, by statute, suspend rules that have not become effective yet by an affirmative vote of the majority of the committee.
Tennessee	. . .	. . .	★	The Government Operations committee of either house may stay a permanent rule for up to 60 days, and may request an agency to repeal, amend or withdraw. In accordance with statutorily imposed termination dates, all permanent rules filed in one calendar year expire on June 30 of the subsequent year unless the general assembly enacts legislation to extend the rules to a date certain or indefinitely.
Texas.........................	★	. . .	. . .	N.A.
Utah...........................	★	. . .	. . .	All rules must be reauthorized by the legislature annually. This is done by omnibus legislation, which also provides for the sunsetting of specific rules listed in the bill.
Vermont.....................	. . . . (u)			Statute
Virginia......................	. . .	. . .	(v)	The General Assembly must pass a bill enacted into law to directly negate the administrative rule.
Washington................	★	★	★	N.A.
West Virginia.............	★	. . .	. . .	(w)
Wisconsin	. . .	★	★	The standing committee in each house has 30 days to conduct its review for a proposed rule. If either objects the Joint Committee for the Review of Administrative Rules has 30 days to introduce legislation in each house overturning the rules. After 40 days the bills are placed on the calendar. If either bill passes, the rules are overturned. If they fail to pass, the rules go into effect.
Wyoming	★	★	. . .	Action must be taken by legislative order adopted by both houses before the end of the next succeeding legislative session to nullify a rule.
American Samoa				The enacting clause of all bills shall be: Be it by the Legislature of American Samoa, and no law shall be except by bill. Bills may originate in either house, and may be amended or rejected by the other. The governor may submit proposed legislation to the Legislature for consideration by it. He may designate any such proposed legislation as urgent, if he so considers it.
Guam	N.A.	N.A.	N.A.	Legislation to disapprove rules and regulations.
No. Mariana Islands...	★	★	★	
U.S. Virgin Islands	. . . . (n)			

See footnotes at end of table.

LEGISLATIVE REVIEW OF ADMINISTRATIVE RULES/REGULATIONS: POWERS — Continued

Source: The Council of State Governments' survey, November 2014.

Key:

★ — Yes

. . . — No

N.A. — Not applicable

(a) This column is defined by those legislatures or legislative committees that can only recommend changes to rules but have no power to enforce a change.

(b) Authorized, although constitutionally questionable.

(c) Disapproval of proposed regulations may be sustained, or reversed by action of the General Assembly in the ensuing session. The General Assembly may by resolution sustain or reverse a vote of disapproval.

(d) The reviewing committee must introduce a resolution to override a rule within the first 30 days of the next regular session of the General Assembly. If the resolution passes by less than a two-thirds majority of either house, the governor has final authority to affirm or veto the resolution.

(e) The Administrative Procedure Act is not clear on this point, but implies that the Joint Committee should either object or issue a statement of no objections.

(f) Joint Committee on Administrative Rules can send objections to issuing agency. If it does, the agency has 90 days from then to withdraw, change, or refuse to change the proposed regulations. If the Joint Committee determines that proposed regulations would seriously threaten the public good, it can block their adoption. Within 180 days the Joint Cmte., or both houses of the General Assembly, can "unblock" those regulations; if that does not happen, the regulations are dead.

(g) None — except by passing statute.

(h) Committee may delay or suspend object to rules, and has authority to approve emergency filed rules.

(i) If the committee determines that a proposed rule is unacceptable, it submits a report to the governor who then has 10 days to accept or reject the report. If the governor rejects the report, the rule change may be adopted by the agency. If the governor accepts the report, the agency may not adopt the rule. Emergency rules become effective upon adoption or up to 60 days after adoption as provided in the rule, but a standing committee or governor may void the rule by finding it unacceptable within 2 to 61 days after adoption and reporting such finding to agency within four days.

(j) No veto allowed. If Legislature wishes to stop a rule from being adopted, it must enact appropriate legislation prohibiting the agency from adopting the rule.

(k) Except for emergency regulations which require committee approval for adoption.

(l) Committee can suspend rules during interim.

(m) The Legislative Commission to Review Administrative Rules (LCRAR) ceased operating, effective July 1, 1996. The Legislative Coordinating Commission (LCC) may review a proposed or adopted rule. Contact the LCC for more information. See Minn. Stat. 3.842, subd. 4a.

(n) No formal mechanism for legislative review of administrative rules. In Virginia, legislative review is optional.

(o) A rule disapproved by the reviewing committee is reinstated at the end of the next session if a joint resolution in the legislature fails to sustain committee action.

(p) Pursuant to HB 2055 enacted in 2013, the legislature shall adopt omnibus resolution approving all proposed permanent rules except those listed in resolution which are to be disapproved. Full legislature may suspend rules.

(q) Failure to object or approve within 45 days of agency filing of final proposal constitutes approval.

(r) The legislature may permanently block rules through legislation. The vote to sponsor a joint resolution suspends the adoption of a proposed rule for a limited time so that the full legislature may act on the resolution, which would then be subject to governor's veto and override.

(s) Article V, Section IV, par. 6 of the NJ Constitution, as amended in 1992, says the legislature may review any rule or regulation to determine whether the rule or regulation is consistent with legislative intent. The legislature transmits its objections to existing or proposed rules or regulations to the governor and relevant agency via concurrent resolutions. The legislature may invalidate or prohibit an existing or proposed rule from taking effect by a majority vote of the authorized membership of each house, in compliance with constitutional provisions.

(t) Unless formal objections are made or the rule is declared void, rules are considered approved.

(u) JLCAR may recommend that an agency amend or withdraw a proposal. A vote opposing rule does not prohibit its adoption but assigns the burden of proof in any legal challenge to the agency.

(v) Standing committees and The Joint Commission on Administrative Rules may suspend the effective date of all or a part of a final regulation until the end of the next regular legislative session with the concurrence of the governor.

(w) State agencies have no power to promulgate rules without first submitting proposed rules to the legislature via a statute authorizing the agency to promulgate the rule. If the legislature during a regular session disapproves all or part of any legislative rule, the agency may not issue the rule nor take action to implement all or part of the rule unless authorized to do so. However, the agency may resubmit the same or a similar proposed rule to the committee.

(x) The promulgating agency's proposed language may be amended upon agreement of the committee and the promulgating agency.

(y) The committee does not approve or disapprove administrative regulations. It reviews them and can propose amendments that will be made, if the promulgating agency agrees to the amendment.

(z) The committee may make a finding of deficiency. If that happens, a letter is sent to the governor requesting the governor's determination whether the administrative regulation should be withdrawn, withdrawn and amended, or put into effect notwithstanding the finding of deficiency. The finding itself does not stop the rule from going into effect. If the governor determines that the administrative regulation should go into effect notwithstanding the finding of deficiency, the General Assembly will usually address that issue in its next regular session, either by its own finding that the administrative regulation found deficient is null, void, and unenforceable, or by amending the authorizing statute to restrict the need for the administrative regulation.

(aa) Committee makes recommendations on Major Substantive Rules, but approval or disapproval is by the full Legislature (the instrument used is a resolve).

(bb) Under very specific circumstances the answer is yes with respect to Major Substantive Rules: if the rules are submitted in accordance with the timelines established by law, and the Legislature fails to act on them, the rules may be adopted as if the Legislature approved them.

(cc) Executive branch agency has more than advisory power.

(dd) Negative rule determinations are made public and remain on website until rule is modified to comply with statutory authority, statute is modified to establish validity of rule or court case upholds validity of rule.

(ee) Joint Administrative Procedures Committee, with approval of the president and speaker, may seek judicial review of validity or invalidity of rules.

(ff) A standing committee can recommend a special session to consider committee's recommendations.

Table 3.27
SUMMARY OF SUNSET LEGISLATION

State	Scope	Preliminary evaluation conducted by	Other legislative review	Other oversight mechanisms in law	Phase-out period	Life of each agency (in years)	Other provisions
Alabama	C	Dept. of Examiners of Public Accounts	Standing Cmtes.	Perf. audit	No later than Oct. 1 of the year following the regular session or a time as may be specified in the Sunset bill.	(Usually 4)	Schedules of licensing boards and other enumerated agencies are repealed according to specified time tables.
Alaska	C	...	...	...	1/y	...	...
Arizona	C	Budget & Audit Cmte.	Joint Cmte.	...	6/m	10	...
Arkansas	D	...	...	...	...	...	...
California	S	Jt. Legis. Sunset Review Cmte. (a)	...	Perf. eval.	...	Established by the Legislature	...
Colorado	R	Dept. of Regulatory Agencies	Legis. Cmtes. of Reference	Bills need adoption by the legislature.	1/y	Up to 15	State law provides certain criteria that are used to determine whether a public need exists for an entity or function to continue and that its regulation is the least restrictive regulation consistent with the public interest.
Connecticut	S	Committee of cognizance of program entity being reviewed.	Further review conducted by Legis. Program Review and Investigations Cmte. upon request of cmte. of cogninzance.	Programs or entities must be affirmatively re-established by the legislature.	1/y (b)	10	(c)
Delaware	C	Agencies under review submit reports to Del. Sunset Comm. based on criteria for review and set forth in statute. Comm. staff conducts separate review.	...	Perf. audit	Dec. 31 of next succeeding calendar year	4	Yearly sunset review schedules must include at least nine agencies. If the number automatically scheduled for review or added by the General Assembly is less than a full schedule, additional agencies shall be added in order of their appearance in the Del. Code to complete the review schedule.
Florida	S (f)	...	...	...	...	...	...
Georgia	R	Dept. of Audits	Standing Cmtes.	Perf. audit	...	...	A performance audit of each regulatory agency must be conducted upon the request of the Senate or House standing committee to which an agency has been assigned for oversight and review. (d)
Hawaii	R	Legis. Auditor	Standing Cmtes.	Perf. eval.	None	Established by the legislature	Schedules various professional and vocational licensing programs for repeal. Proposed new regulatory measures must be referred to the Auditor for sunrise analysis.

See footnotes at end of table.

SUMMARY OF SUNSET LEGISLATION—Continued

State	Scope	Preliminary evaluation conducted by	Other legislative review	Other oversight mechanisms in law	Phase-out period	Life of each agency (in years)	Other provisions
Idaho..............	S (e)	...	...	...	...	...	...
Illinois............	R,S	Governor's Office of Mgmt. and Budget	Cmte. charged with re-enacting law	(g)	...	Usually 10	...
Indiana............	S	Non-partisan staff units	Interim cmte. formed to review	...	...	...	Smaller program review process now in place after about a dozen years of formal sunset program.
Iowa					No Program		
Kansas............	(h)	...	...	...	...	...	...
Kentucky.........	R	Administrative Regulation Review Subcommittee	Joint committee with subject matter jurisdiction.	Perf. Eval.	...	...	...
Louisiana.........	C	Standing cmtes. of the two houses with subject matter jurisdiction.	...	Perf. eval.	1/y	Up to 6	Act provides for termination of a department and all offices in a department. Also permits committees to select particular agencies or offices for more extensive evaluation. Provides for review by Jt. Legis. Cmte. on Budget of programs that were not funded during the prior fiscal year for possible repeal.
Maine..............	S (w)	Joint standing cmte. of jurisdiction.	Office of Program Evaluation and Government Accountability	...	...	Generally 10 years	...
Maryland..........	R	Dept. of Legislative Services	Standing Cmtes.	Perf. eval.	...	Varies (usually 10)	...
Massachusetts					No Program		
Michigan...........	(e)	...	...	...	...	...	...
Minnesota.........	S (y)	...	...	...	1/y	...	(aa)
Mississippi........	(i)	...	...	...	...	...	...
Missouri	R	Oversight Division of Cmte. on Legislative Research	...	...	...	6, not to exceed total of 12	...
Montana	(e)	...	...	...	...	...	...
Nebraska	D (e)(j)	...	...	...	...	...	...

See footnotes at end of table.

SUMMARY OF SUNSET LEGISLATION—Continued

State	Scope	Preliminary evaluation conducted by	Other legislative review	Other oversight mechanisms in law	Phase-out period	Life of each agency (in years)	Other provisions
Nevada	C (e)(x)	Sunset Subcommittee	Legislative Commission, Full Legislature	...	...	...	...
New Hampshire	(k)	...	...	...	...	...	...
New Jersey	(e)	...	...	...	...	...	...
New Mexico	S	Legis. Finance Cmte.	...	Public hearing before termination	1/y	6	...
New York	(e)	...	...	...	...	...	...
North Carolina	(l)	...	...	...	...	...	...
North Dakota				No Program			
Ohio	C (m)	Sunset Review Cmte.	...	Perf. eval.	(n)	6	...
Oklahoma	S, D	Senate: Standing Cmtes. with jurisdiction over sunset bills House: Joint Cmtes. with jurisdiction over sunset bills	Appropriations and Budget Cmte.	...	1/y	6	...
Oregon	D (o)	...	(o)	(o)	...	...	...
Pennsylvania	R	Leadership Cmte.	...	...	...	Varies	...
Rhode Island	(p)	...	No	...	...	...	...
South Carolina	(q)	...	...	Perf. eval.	1/y	...	...
South Dakota	(r)	...	...	...	...	...	...
Tennessee	C	Office of the Comptroller	Government Operations Committees	...	1/y	Up to 6 years	...
Texas	S	Sunset Advisory Commission staff	...	...	1/y	12	...
Utah	S	Interim cmtes, then Legislative Mgmt. Cmte.	Standing cmtes. as amendments may be made to bill	...	(v)	(v)	...

See footnotes at end of table.

SUMMARY OF SUNSET LEGISLATION — Continued

State	Scope	Preliminary evaluation conducted by	Other legislative review	Other oversight mechanisms in law	Phase-out period	Life of each agency (in years)	Other provisions
Vermont	(s)	Legis. Council staff	Senate and House Government Operations Cmtes.	...	...	...	...
Virginia	S (e)	...	...	...	...	...	Sunset provisions vary in length. The only standard sunset required by law is on bills that create a new advisory board or commission in the executive branch of government. The legislation introduced for these boards and commissions must contain a sunset provision to expire the entity after three years.
Washington	D	...	...	Perf. eval.	1/y	...	...
West Virginia	S	Jt. Cmte. on Govt. Operations	Performance Evaluation and Research Division	Perf. audit	1/y	6	Jt. Cmte. on Govt. Operations composed of five House members, five Senate members and five citizens appointed by governor. Agencies may be reviewed more frequently.
Wisconsin	(e)	...	...	...	...	...	...
Wyoming	D (t)	Program evaluation staff who work for Management Audit Cmte.	...	Perf. eval. (u)	...	...	...
No. Mariana Islands		No	No	Perf. eval.	1/y		

Source: The Council of State Governments' survey, November 2014.

Key:

C — Comprehensive — requires all statutory agencies to be subject to a sunset review once per review cycle.

R — Regulatory — review focus is on regulatory and licensing agencies and bureaus.

S — Selective — selective implementation and reviews are concentrated on entities such as occupational licensing and administrative agencies such as highway, health and education departments.

D — Discretionary — sunset review board has the ability to select which entities will face review.

d — day

m — month

y — year

... — Not applicable

(a) Jt. Legis. Sunset Review Cmte. — Review by the Jt. Legislative Sunset Review Cmte. of professional and vocational licensing boards, pursuant to Government Code 9147.7. Sunset clauses are included in other selected programs and legislation.

(b) Upon termination a program shall continue for one year to conclude its affairs.

(c) Process conducted in accordance with Chapter 28 of Connecticut General Statutes.

(d) The automatic sunsetting of an agency every six years was eliminated in 1992. The legislature must pass a bill in order to sunset a specific agency.

(e) While they have not enacted sunset legislation in the same sense as the other states with detailed information in this table, the legislatures in Idaho, Michigan, Minnesota, Montana, Nebraska, Nevada, New Jersey, New York, Virginia and Wisconsin have included sunset clauses in selected programs or legislation.

(f) Comprehensive agency sunset review and repeal was repealed in 2011. Florida does have Open Government Sunset Review or public records and meetings exemptions.

(g) Governor is to read GOMB report and make recommendations to the General Assembly every even-numbered year.

(h) Sunset legislation terminated July 1992. Legislative oversight of designated state agencies, consisting of audit, review and evaluation, continues.

(i) Sunset Act terminated December 31, 1984. House and Senate Rules are available at *bills.status.la.state.ms.us.* New Rules were adopted in January 2012.

(j) Sunset legislation is discretionary, meaning that senators are free to offer sunset legislation or attach termination dates to legislative proposals. There is no formal sunset commission. Nebraska. Revised Statutes section 50-1303 directs the Legislature's Government, Military and Veteran's Committee to conduct an evaluation of any board, commission, or similar state entity. The review must include, among other things, a recommendation as to whether the board, commission, or entity should be terminated, continued or modified.

(k) New Hampshire's Sunset Committee was repealed July 1, 1986.

(l) North Carolina's sunset law terminated on July 30, 1981. Successor vehicle, the Legislative Committee on Agency Review, operated until June 30, 1983.

(m) There are statutory exceptions.

SUMMARY OF SUNSET LEGISLATION—Continued

(n) Authority for latest review (SB 171 of the 129th General Assembly) expires December 31, 2016.

(o) Sunset legislation was repealed in 1993. No general law sunsetting rules or agencies. Oversight mechanisms, including auditing, reporting or performance measures, are discretionary but may be included in specific bills as determined by legislature.

(p) No standing sunset statutes or procedures at this time.

(q) Law repealed by 1998 Act 419, Part II, Sect. 35E.

(r) South Dakota suspended sunset legislation in 1979. A later law directing the Executive Board of the Legislative Research Council to establish one or more interim committees each year to review state agencies was repealed in 2012.

(s) Sunsets are at the legislature's discretion. Their structure will vary on an individual basis.

(t) Wyoming repealed sunset legislation in 1988.

(u) The program evaluation process evolved out of the sunset process, but Wyoming currently does not have a scheduled sunset of programs.

(v) Default is ten years, although years may be decreased by legislative decisions.

(w) Sometimes programs or agencies are subject to sunset provisions; this is entirely ad hoc as the Legislature determines appropriate. There is a general law, however, called State Government Evaluation Law that provides for regular reviews of agencies and boards by committee of jurisdiction; the committees can recommend termination (sunset) but, again, this is ad hoc.

(x) The 2011 Nevada Legislature created the Sunset Subcommittee of the Legislative Commission with the enactment of Senate Bill 251 (Chapter 480, Statutes of Nevada). The Subcommittee is to conduct reviews of all boards and commissions not provided for in the Nevada Constitution or created by Executive Order of the governor, and is charged with determining whether those entities should be terminated, modified, consolidated, or continued. The Subcommittee must review each entity no less often than once every 10 years. After making it's initial recommendations no later than June 30, 2012, the Subcommittee must submit all subsequent recommendations to the Legislative Commission on or before June 30 of each even-numbered year. The Legislative Commission may accept or reject the recommendations in whole or part and may then request that legislation be drafted for consideration by the full Legislature.

(y) While they have not enacted sunset legislation in the same sense as the other states with detailed information in this table, the legislatures in Minnesota have included sunset clauses in selected programs or legislation.

Chapter Four

STATE EXECUTIVE BRANCH

The State of the State Addresses: More Comfortable, Still Cautious[1]

By Keegan Smith and Katherine Willoughby

Mixed messages of the current economy keep at bay a full recovery from the Great Recession that officially ended in June 2009. The drop in oil prices has put money in consumers' pockets, but these consumers seem wary of returning it into circulation, with many using the extra cash to pay off or reduce personal debt. In some ways, governors are similarly disposed as they map the policy and budget way forward for their respective states. Several chief executives are asking for more stringent laws, constitutional requirements, for budget balance or regarding the payment of debt, to keep their states on a path toward fiscal sustainability. Watch words this year include "cautious optimism" and "continuous improvement."

Party control of governors did not shift significantly with the November 2014 elections. In fact, Republicans supplemented their stronghold on state executives, increasing to 31 the number of states with GOP governors.[2] States with Democratic governors decreased by three for a total of 18. Four states—Arkansas, Illinois, Maryland and Massachusetts—now have Republican governors. Pennsylvania elected Democratic Gov. Tom Wolf, and Alaskans elected the lone Independent governor of the American states, Bill Walker.[3]

Just as the Republican Party extended its dominance of state gubernatorial seats, the party's dominance of state legislatures was further cemented following the 2014 elections. The GOP now controls both chambers in 30 legislatures, compared to 11 controlled by Democrats. Republicans have majorities in 33 state houses and 34 state senates, while Democrats have majorities in 16 houses and 14 senates.[4] Although the number of states (23) in which both the executive and legislative branches are controlled by the GOP remained constant from 2014 to 2015, the number of states under unified Democratic control was halved. The Democratic Party currently controls both branches of government in just seven states. There are 19 states in which the chief executive faces a state legislature that is either controlled by an opposing political party or is split across the chambers. Party control of the states in 2015 includes:

- 23 with a Republican governor and Republican legislature;

- One with a Republican governor and a unicameral, nonpartisan legislature;

- Three with a Republican governor, Republican house and Democratic senate;

- Four with a Republican governor and a Democratic legislature;

- One with an Independent governor and a Republican legislature;

- Six with a Democratic governor and a Republican legislature;

- Five with a Democratic governor, Democratic house and Republican senate; and

- Seven with a Democratic governor and Democratic legislature.[5]

Speeches Impact State Success

Governors use state of the state addresses to communicate their budget and policy agendas to state legislators and the public, generally. Numerous personal and institutional factors—as well as political party, term of office and the economy—affect how successful governors are in realizing these agendas as they are guided through state legislatures.[6] The outcome, in turn, influences state economics.

Recent research has focused on gubernatorial "verbal style" and its influences on a governor's success with his or her budget and policy objectives.[7] Robert Crew Jr. and Christopher Lewis determined that "words matter" on the part of governors in their communications with legislatures. Specifically, chief executives who generate expressions of "enthusiasm, activity, and realism" in conveying their agendas are more likely to realize legislative success.[8]

Table A:
Issues Expressed by Governors in State of the State Addresses, 2011–2015

Issue expressed by governors	2011 percentage of governors mentioning the issue (N=47)	2012 percentage of governors mentioning the issue (N=43)	2013 percentage of governors mentioning the issue (N=49)	2014 percentage of governors mentioning the issue (N=42)	2015 percentage of governors mentioning the issue (N=44)
Education	93.6%	95.3%	100.0%	95.2%	90.9%
Economic development/jobs	87.2	90.7	77.6	83.3	81.8
Tax/revenue initiative	70.2	81.4	71.4	66.7	72.7
Transportation/roads/bridges	46.8	48.8	46.9	50.0	68.2
Safety/corrections	38.3	55.8	67.3	73.8	63.6
Natural resources/energy	44.7	65.1	57.1	59.5	61.4
Health care	72.3	55.8	79.6	73.8	59.1
Performance/accountability	83.0	55.8	30.6	33.3	56.8
Surplus/deficit/rainy day funds/reserves	34.0	60.5	32.7	54.8	36.4
Local government	17.0	25.6	14.3	26.2	36.4
Ethics reform	8.5	7.0	16.3	14.3	20.5
Transparency	2.1	25.6	12.2	26.2	11.4
Debt reduction	8.5	7.0	6.1	16.7	6.8
Borders/illegal immigrants	8.5	11.6	8.2	7.1	6.8
Pensions/OPEBs	36.2	32.6	18.4	21.4	4.6
Average number of issues expressed by governors	8	7	6	7	7
Numbrt of issues expressed by at least 66 percent of governors	5	3	5	5	4

Source: Content analysis of 2011 state of state addresses conducted by Byungwoo Cho, MPA candidate; content analysis of 2012 state of state addresses conducted by Megan Phillips, MPA candidate and Sarah Beth Gehl, Ph.D. candidate, Public Policy; content analysis of 2013 state of state addresses conducted by Sarah Beth Gehl, Ph.D. candidate, Public Policy; content analysis of 2014 and 2015 state of state addresses conducted by Keegan Smith, MPA candidate, all students of the Andrew Young School of Policy Studies, Georgia State University, Atlanta.

Other researchers have examined the tone of gubernatorial state of state speeches to determine any specific effects of these talks on the actions of firms and economic development within state borders. Art Durnev, Larry Fauver and Nandini Gupta coded American governors' state addresses from 2002 to 2010, examining a total of 388 speeches to score degree of optimism on the part of governors in relaying their messages.[9] These scholars compared the speeches, calculating net optimism as the "number of optimistic words less the number of pessimistic words per 500 words of text."[10] Then, they analyzed the association of these scores with investment and employment of firms located in the states. Their comparison of speeches according to level of optimism showed governors in Nevada, Georgia and Vermont as delivering the most optimistic speeches, while governors in California, South Dakota and Pennsylvania delivered the least optimistic ones for the period of the study. Their findings indicated a statistically significant, positive market response to speeches with highly optimistic tones. Greater certainty expressed by governors in articulating a way forward and specificity about proposed budget and policy actions also are associated with positive firm investment responses. Additionally, firms engaged in state contracts "significantly increase investments if the budget-related parts of the speeches are more optimistic."[11] Speeches that are more pessimistic elicit no response from investors. These findings suggest speeches have their greatest impact during periods of economic uncertainty. "These results do not change even controlling for firm, political speech, and state characteristics."[12]

Although the overall tone of addresses this year remains somewhat subdued, many governors seem comfortable in verbally mapping out their budget and policy goals as the "new normal" becomes simply "normal" in terms of state finances. For example, in his final state of the state address, Kentucky Gov. Steve Beshear channeled optimism and enthusiasm, referencing his state's "tremendous momentum" throughout the course of the speech. This governor railed defiantly against "mainstream media," "inflammatory rhetoric" and "negative dialogue," calling instead for "collaborative leadership" among policymakers. "It's easy to get caught up in this negative dialogue, ... to believe that such rancor is mandatory and to conclude that consensus and collaboration are cardinal sins. But that's not what being a leader is about." Beshear framed his different budget and policy initiatives as opportunities "to keep the momentum going." The governor ended his speech on an upbeat note, claiming confidently, "Kentucky is back and we're not going to let up now."

On the other hand, new Maryland Gov. Larry Hogan presented a much bleaker picture of his state, declaring upfront that Maryland's economy was "floundering." In spite of describing his state as one of considerable assets, Hogan lamented that Maryland is not as strong as it "could or should be." This governor cites polling data that finds, "nearly half of all Marylanders would leave the state if they could" and he details his concerns by specifying Maryland's economic weaknesses, explaining how the state is "third in the nation in foreclosures and dead last in manufacturing." Commenting on his upcoming budget negotiations with the Maryland General Assembly, Hogan engaged an assertive tone to drive home his aversion to raising taxes as the answer for spending needs, declaring that, "If ever Maryland needed a dose of honesty, it's now." His address concentrated heavily on tax relief to individuals and businesses, and programmatic reforms to address poorly performing areas, especially the environment (Maryland's Chesapeake Bay "received a D+ on a recent report card") and health (Maryland has a "heroin epidemic"). The Kentucky and Maryland addresses provide good examples of the characterization of words and tones explained by the scholars.

Gubernatorial Agendas in 2015

Table A presents analysis of governors' state of state speeches for the past five years, indicating the proportion of governors mentioning specific issues as relevant to their budget and policy agendas in the 2016 fiscal year and beyond. This year, at least two-thirds of governors addressed four policy areas—education, jobs, taxes and transportation. Of these issues, transportation made the greatest leap in gubernatorial interest from being discussed by 50 percent of governors in 2014 to consideration by 68.2 percent in 2015.

Our examination of state of the state addresses in 2014 characterized issues as perennial (addressed consistently year-to-year), cyclical (addressed more or less across years) or temporal (addressed in a punctuated manner across years) in nature.[13] This year, education remained a perennial issue for governors; it is a concern of more than 90 percent of governors. This is not surprising, given the predominant portion of state budgets made up of education spending, as well as its consistent linkages by governors to a well-performing state.

Economic development and jobs remained a perennial issue as well—more than 80 percent of governors again this year are pushing their budget and policy goals in this area. Taxes and revenues remained cyclical in interest—with a bit more or less than an average of 72.5 percent of governors discussing their ideas for generating new revenues or tax changes across the past five years. Gubernatorial consideration of budget balance and rainy day funds is cyclical, too. This makes sense given the nature of balance and fund use—drawing down funds in one period necessitates replenishment in the next.

Governors' interest in transparency is also cyclical, spiking in 2012 and again in 2014, then settling back in 2013 and 2015. Other perennial issues or those shifting to perennial include debt reduction (after a punctuation last year, 6.8 percent of governors specifically mention this in 2015), natural resources and energy (after a punctuation in 2012, the proportion of governors mentioning this issue has hovered around 58 percent), and illegal immigration (the proportion of governors discussing this issue has averaged 8.4 percent in the past five years).

Interest in transportation spiked this year, perhaps indicative of a shift from a perennial policy issue of moderate interest to a temporal one of stronger concern. Most governors highlighting this issue lamented that past investments just have not been enough to keep up with state transportation needs. South Dakota Gov. Dennis Daugaard spoke for many regarding transportation funding when he said, "the slow-motion disappearance of the [federal] Highway Trust Fund" calls into question any state "waiting for the federal government to act." He reminded his state's residents of the funds necessary to meet the goal of "80 percent of pavements in excellent or good condition at any given time." Other governors also specified state investment to combat decay, expansion and maintenance of highways, roads and/or bridges—including those from Georgia, Idaho, Indiana, Iowa, Kentucky, Michigan, New Mexico, New York, North Carolina, South Dakota, Texas, West Virginia and Wyoming. Texas Gov. Greg Abbott referenced his own personal experience when he stated, "it's a sad day in Texas when a guy in a wheelchair can move faster than traffic on our congested roads. ... My budget adds more than $4 billion a year to build more roads in Texas without raising taxes, fees, tolls or debt."

Some governors called for investment in ports and/or airports—those in Georgia, New York, Pennsylvania and Virginia—while others pointed to commuter rail needs—including governors from Hawaii, New Hampshire and New York. Governors in several states discussed strategic, regional or local transportation investment—Indiana, Maryland, Montana and North Carolina—and a few envisioned "world class" integrated, multimodal transportation systems—chief executives in New York, Pennsylvania and Washington. Illinois Gov. Bruce Rauner attacked his state's bidding process, calling for a "restructuring of bidding for construction projects at every level of government." Missouri Gov. Jay Nixon encouraged the development of improved linkages of source funding to transportation infrastructure in order to better connect "state goods and global markets."

Among the issues listed in Table A, the greatest spike in interest by governors in 2015 occurred with performance and accountability, a temporal issue that indicates high variability across years. This year, a majority—57 percent—of governors are discussing performance and accountability, up 24 percent from last year. Most of these governors discuss general management efficiencies like "going paperless," reorganizations and/or process streamlining, reforming state contracting and/or program improvements—Hawaii, Illinois, Michigan, Mississippi, Nebraska, New Hampshire, New Jersey, South Dakota and Wisconsin. North Carolina Gov. Pat McCrory asked for focused study of workers' compensation costs to ferret out abuse in order to "pay legitimate claims." Tennessee Gov. Bill Haslam wants to link state employee pay raises to performance *and* market adjustments, "rewarding employees like the private sector does, on their performance and results, not just on seniority." He also suggested pairing this with increased manage-

ment flexibility and discretion. Kansas Gov. Sam Brownback encouraged reform to the selection of state Supreme Court judges.

Governors mentioned numerous performance and accountability improvements related to public schools. New Mexico Gov. Susana Martinez pressed for tossing aside "comfortable notions" that all teachers should be treated similarly" by pairing excellent teachers with "struggling ones" to enhance teaching performance. Nevada Gov. Bryan Sandoval advanced better pay for performance laws related to teachers, increased support for their professional development and "calling out" under-performing schools. Ohio Gov. John Kasich suggests a similar "crackdown on charter school sponsors involved with failing schools." Vermont Gov. Peter Shumlin agreed that consistently poor-performing schools should be closed. New York Gov. Andrew Cuomo described a residency program to encourage a pipeline of able teachers. He offered up full tuition to state university graduates who commit to five years teaching in New York schools. Pennsylvania Gov. Tom Wolf asked for a fair funding formula for local school districts, while Utah Gov. Gary Herbert stressed the need for a 10-year strategic education plan that sets benchmarks for education performance.

Other state activities mentioned by governors as ripe for performance and accountability initiatives include higher education in Oklahoma, campaign finance and election reform in Kansas and Maryland, childcare facilities in Kentucky, and public private partnerships in Virginia. Michigan Gov. Rick Snyder suggested that the state legislature prepare fiscal notes with proposed legislation, "so we can see the budgetary impact and how to be more efficient."

Most of the other issues listed in Table A can be characterized as temporal, indicating moderate to dramatic shifts in gubernatorial interest across years. The interest of governors in safety and corrections seems to have built for the past four years (by 2014, 74 percent of governors discussed this issue in their addresses), only to drop off in 2015 (64 percent of governors mentioned safety and corrections plans this year). Most governors (80 percent) addressed their state's health care plans in 2013, the year before implementation of the federal Affordable Care Act. By 2015, while still a majority, just 59 percent of chief executives include a discussion of health care in their speeches.

Compared to 2011, the proportion of governors addressing the functioning and fiscal health of local governments this year has more than doubled. This could be attributable to the building pressures on local governments to improve and increase public service delivery and infrastructure maintenance in the face of declining federal, as well as state, financial support. Many of the governors discussing local government this year offered up ideas to boost the fiscal sustainability of this level of government, including: targeted spending and/or "growth tools" to economically challenged communities in Delaware, Kansas and Wyoming; strengthening localities via greater control of school funding, consolidation, employee empowerment zones, and/or reducing unfunded state mandates in Illinois, Nevada, Texas, Utah and West Virginia; allowing localities to vote for local sales taxes targeted to local projects in Kentucky; development of a local financial performance scorecard in Michigan; reforming municipal courts in Missouri; through local infrastructure projects in New Hampshire, North Carolina and South Dakota; and by reforming local education funding in Ohio.

Narrow and Broad Agendas

Of the 15 budget and policy issues defined here, governors considered, on average approximately seven issues, though there is great variability among the chief executives in agenda items addressed. In 2015, Connecticut Gov. Dan Malloy focused almost exclusively on transportation. He highlighted the economic consequences of his state's underfunded transportation infrastructure. Malloy estimated Connecticut's deficit and overly congested roads and bridges cost the state $4.2 billion a year. He offered specific project proposals to remedy the state's transportation woes, identified locations for new commuter rail stations in addition to calling out particular highways in need of widening. This governor made it clear that he was unwilling to raise any new revenues, however, unless such funds would be directly tied to funding transportation infrastructure:

"Today, I am proposing that Connecticut create a secure transportation lock box that will ensure every single dollar raised for transportation is spent on transportation, now and into the future. ... Send me a bill that accomplishes these goals and I will sign it immediately. Until that legislation is passed and signed, I will veto any attempt to levy additional sources of new revenue for transportation."

On the other end of the spectrum, Texas Gov. Greg Abbott offered a much more expansive address to Texans, tackling 13 policy issues during the course of his speech. Addressing more issues—of those defined here—than any other governor in 2015, Abbott provided some fairly basic policy initiatives, regarding debt reduction, "my budget requires most state agencies to reduce their general revenue spending by 3 percent." His educational plan calls for "additional funding for schools that adopt high-quality pre-k programs," expansion of community colleges "that serve as the gateway to better jobs," and tamping down on the "spiraling cost of higher education so more Texans can reap the rewards that come from college." Abbott was more explicit regarding other policy proposals—he discussed specific improvements to the state's border security and a detailed transportation funding plan, offering:

"My budget adds more than $4 billion a year to build more roads in Texas without raising taxes, fees, tolls or debt. This funding comes from three places: One is the funding received from Proposition 1. Two, it ends diversions of state highway funds—tax dollars paid for roads should be spent on roads. Third, my plan constitutionally dedicates one-half of the existing motor vehicle sales tax to fund roads."

Governors and State Finances

In 2015 and the near term, modest growth is perhaps the best way to describe the fiscal situation in states. The National Association of State Budget Officers' —also known as NASBO—fall 2014 *Fiscal Survey of the States* concludes, "overall, states are in a better position than they were a few years ago, but as the economy continues along a trajectory of slow growth, fiscal challenges are likely to persist."[14] Revenue growth in the 2014 fiscal year was 1.3 percent, but is projected to trend upward to 3.1 percent in 2015. State general fund expenditures are higher in 2015 than in 2014, although total state spending growth is tepid. According to NASBO, the general fund spending acceleration of 4.9 percent in 2014 gives way to weaker growth this year of 3.1 percent. Despite improving revenues and employment rates, NASBO noted, poor growth in wages may freeze the ability of states to break out from fiscal doldrums.[15]

Chief executives of states in stronger fiscal positions were more likely than others to use their state of the state address to push for moderate investment to begin tackling long-term liabilities, such as underfunded infrastructure. For instance, governors in Michigan and Georgia used their speeches to propose further investments in transportation projects. After highlighting the state's improved fiscal position, Georgia Gov. Nathan Deal discussed his plans for transportation investments to ensure sustained economic growth:

"It's estimated that truck traffic out of the [Savannah] port will increase by 50 percent in less than 10 years. We have to be ready to meet that need. Without Plan C, a new strategy for transportation investment, we will be forced to go to Plan D, which is to do nothing. If that is our plan, then our roads will slowly slip into disrepair, the safety of our citizens will be jeopardized and our economy will be stagnated by increased congestion."

Governors in Florida, Nebraska, New York, North Dakota and Ohio viewed their states' revenue growth and improved fiscal footing as an opportunity to cut taxes to further advance state economies. Ohio Gov. John Kasich described his commitment to this approach succinctly, "I believe the most important thing that we can do to plan ahead is to continue strengthening Ohio's economy by further cutting taxes." South Carolina Gov. Nikki Haley explained that the state's growing economy is not the result of raising taxes. She proclaimed to veto any "straight up increase in the gas tax." Haley also is looking to cut the state's income tax "by nearly 30 percent over the next decade."

However, governors in other states face substantive drops in revenues. At least 16 states are struggling with budget gaps as revenues continue to fall short.[16] The precarious nature of his state's budget has led even the self-described "lifelong conservative" Alabama Gov. Robert Bentley to call for multiple different tax increases, bemoaning in his address that:

"We cannot put off solving these problems anymore. We cannot cut our way out of this. There is nothing more conservative than paying your debts and getting your financial house in order. And by keeping spending at a reasonable level we will actually save money, and potentially create a surplus in the General Fund in future years."

The decline in oil prices has had a significant, negative effect on revenue projections for oil-rich states, including North Dakota, Oklahoma and Texas. North Dakota Gov. Jack Dalrymple specifically mentioned increasing "state support to oil and gas producing counties by an additional $1 billion" to help these governments manage. Still, perhaps no state has been hit quite as hard as Alaska. This state relies on crude oil production for 90 percent of its operating budget.[17] Gov. Bill Walker in his speech discussed Alaska's dire fiscal status, given a $3.5 billion deficit and the rapid rate at which the state is burning through its savings. He explained that, "the price of oil has dropped by more than 50 percent over the past six months. This has moved us from a $7 million-per-day deficit just six months ago to a $10 million-per-day deficit today."

Conclusion

Politically in 2015, almost half of states are totally red, under GOP hold in both the executive and legislative branches; just seven states are unified Democratic. Economically, states have vastly different challenges. Governors in some states with stronger balance sheets are calling for investment, while others believe such circumstance offers a chance for tax relief. On the other end of the spectrum, oil rich states are in a fiscal scramble. For example, Alaska's governor emphasized the need for his state "to hold off on projects to assess their overall costs and benefit to the state."

On average, governors this year addressed seven of the 15 issues studied here—the mean considered by chief executives for the past five years. At least two-thirds of governors lay out their education, jobs, taxes and transportation agendas. Of these top issues, transportation realized the biggest jump in interest by governors, a punctuation of concern about a normally perennial issue of moderate interest. Federal foot-dragging on funding, in combination with aging infrastructure, seemed to push state chief executives to present their plans to address the safety, building, maintenance and economic development components related to transportation. Of all issues examined, performance and accountability, a temporal one, realized the greatest surge in interest by governors in 2015. Perhaps because of the mixed economic picture, many state chief executives realize the need for pressure on enhanced accountability and continuous improvement.

In addition to political rhetoric, addresses like gubernatorial state of state speeches communicate futures as uplifting, grim or somewhere in between. Research has determined that upbeat addresses are more likely to spur positive economic investment within state borders. Greater specificity of a vision forward also spurs positive private investment response. Examination of state of the state speeches in 2015 finds a broad range in the level of optimism expressed, number of issues addressed and amount of detail provided by governors for their plans. It remains to be seen if 2016 state economies will realize the effects of these various words and tones.

Notes

[1] Governors report annually or biennially to their legislatures regarding the fiscal condition of their state, commonwealth or territory. They often use their address to lay out their policy and budget agendas for their upcoming or continuing administration. The 2015 state of the state addresses were accessed from Jan. 1 – March 30, 2015, via *www.nga.org*, *www.stateline.org*, *www.nasbo.org* or the state government's homepage. This research considers the 44 states with transcripts available at these sites as of March 30, 2015. Governors from Arkansas, Louisiana, Massachusetts, Minnesota, Oregon and Rhode Island did not give their state of state address by March 30, 2015. (Governor John Kitzhaber of Oregon, who had won a fourth term as governor in that state in November 2014, resigned Feb. 18, 2015, amid controversies related to his fiancée, her work and state activities.) All quotes and data presented here are from the addresses accessed on these websites, unless otherwise noted. To conduct a content analysis of governors' state of state addresses, as in the past, topics were considered addressed if the chief executive specifically discussed them as relevant to state operations and the budget *going forward*. The governor needed to relay that the function, activity or issue is an important item in next year's—fiscal 2016—budget and policy direction. Just mentioning a state function or policy area like health care in a speech did not classify the issue as an agenda item addressed by a governor. Further, a review by a governor of his or her past accomplishments in any particular issue area did not count in this content analysis.

[2] National Governors Association. (2015). *Current Governors by State, Party Affiliation, and Terms in Office*. Accessed on March 1, 2015, via *http://www.nga.org/files/live/sites/NGA/files/pdf/GOVLIST.PDF*.

[3] National Governors Association, 2015.

[4] National Conference of State Legislatures. (2015). *2015 State and Legislative Partisan Composition*. Accessed on March 1, 2015, via *http://www.ncsl.org/Portals/1/Documents/Elections/Legis_Control_2015_Feb4_11am.pdf*.

[5] National Conference of State Legislatures, 2015.

[6] Kousser, T. and Phillips, J.H. (2012). *The Powers of American Governors: Winning on Budgets, Losing on Policy*. Cambridge University Press. See also, Ferguson, M.R. (2003). "Chief Executive Success in the Legislative Arena." *State Politics and Policy Quarterly*. June, 3(2), 158–182.

[7] Crew, Jr., R.E. and Lewis, C. (2011). "Verbal Style, Gubernatorial Strategies, and Legislative Success." *Political Psychology*. August, 32(4), 623–642.

[8] Crew, Jr. and Lewis, 2011.

[9] Durney, A., Fauver, L. and Gupta, N. (2013). "Political Speech and Economic Outcomes: Running the Numbers." *ISB Insight*. October-December, 1(1), 8–14.

[10] Durney, Fauver and Gupta, 2013, 9.

[11] Durney, Fauver and Gupta, 2013, 11.

[12] Durney, Fauver and Gupta, 2013, 12–13.

[13] Smith, K. and Willoughby, K. (2014). "The State of the State Addresses: Holding Steady in the New Normal," in Audrey S. Wall, ed. *The Book of the States*. Vol. 46 (Lexington, KY: The Council of State Governments), 134–135.

[14] National Association of State Budget Officers. (2014). *Fiscal Survey of the States* (Fall). Accessed on March 1, 2015, via *http://www.nasbo.org/publications-data/fiscal-survey-of-the-states*.

[15] National Association of State Budget Officers, 2014, 41–42.

[16] Wilson, R. (2014). "Even Amid Recovery, State Budgets Bleed Red Ink." *The Washington Post*. (December 12). Accessed on April 15, 2015, via *http://www.washingtonpost.com/blogs/govbeat/wp/2014/12/12/even-amid-recovery-state-budgets-bleed-red-ink/*.

[17] Krohn, J. and McManmon, R. (2015). "Oil Price Decline Leads to Lower Tax Revenues in Top Oil-producing States." U.S. Energy Information Administration. (March 12). Accessed on April 16, 2015, via *http://www.eia.gov/todayinenergy/detail.cfm?id=20332#*.

About the Authors

Keegan Smith is a graduate student in the master of public administration program in the Department of Public Management and Policy at Georgia State University in Atlanta.

Katherine Willoughby is professor of public management and policy in the Andrew Young School of Policy Studies at Georgia State University in Atlanta. Her research concentrates on state and local government budgeting and financial management, public policy development and public organization theory. Willoughby has conducted extensive research in the area of state and local government budgeting as well as comparative budgeting, with a concentration on performance budgeting and management.

Gubernatorial Elections, Campaign Costs and Winning Governors of 2014[1]

By Thad Beyle and Jennifer M. Jensen

There were many issues facing governors in 2014. Even as the stock market rebounded and state budgets grew at a moderate pace, unemployment and underemployment remained high. Public discontent with government has been indiscriminate in its focus, levied at not only politicians in Washington, but also those in state capitals. This led to political fallout from voters as they vented their anger and frustration on elected leaders on Election Day.

Thirty-six states had gubernatorial elections in 2014. Midway through a presidential term is the quadrennial bumper crop of political campaigns.

Open Seat Races

Seven states had open seat gubernatorial primaries in 2014. Four of these states—Arizona, Arkansas, Maryland and Nebraska—had governors facing term limits. Three states had incumbent governors who were not term limited and did not run for re-election.

One incumbent governor who opted against a re-election campaign was Deval Patrick of Massachusetts. Patrick, a Democrat, had highs and lows during his eight years in office, but completed his second gubernatorial term with strong approval ratings and would have been competitive for a third term. While the former governor might be considering a 2016 presidential bid, Patrick declared in 2013 that he would not be a candidate in the next presidential election. Some pundits say the former U.S. assistant attorney general might be positioning himself for the U.S. attorney general post should a fellow Democrat win the White House.

Another governor who declined to run, Rhode Island Gov. Lincoln Chafee, had served in the U.S. Senate as a Republican and served his first gubernatorial term as an Independent, ultimately joining the Democratic Party in 2013, more than halfway through his term as governor. Lacking both popularity and party support, Chafee declined to run for a second term. Finally, Texas Republican Rick Perry announced in July 2013 that he would not run for re-election in 2014. Perry took office in December 2000, assuming the governorship when then-governor George W. Bush resigned in advance of becoming president of the United States; he was subsequently elected to full gubernatorial terms in 2002, 2006 and 2010.

An eighth state, Hawaii, had an open-seat general election when incumbent Gov. Neil Abercrombie lost in the Democratic primary election.

Of these eight states, Hawaii and Rhode Island saw a Democratic candidate in 2014 succeed a Democratic predecessor. Four states saw Republicans maintain control of the governorship—Arizona, Arkansas, Nebraska and Texas.

Only two states with an open gubernatorial seat saw a partisan change with the 2014 election. Both Maryland and Massachusetts—each typically considered solidly Democratic states in presidential elections—had a Republican candidate replace an outgoing Democrat. Massachusetts saw a very tight race between Republican businessman Charlie Baker and state Attorney General Martha Coakley. Baker bested Coakley by approximately 40,000 votes out of more than 2.1 million votes cast. This was Coakley's second time losing a statewide election that many had predicted she would win. In 2010, she was the Democratic candidate in the special election to fill the late Ted Kennedy's seat in the U.S. Senate, but lost to Scott Brown in an upset. In Maryland, Republican businessman Larry Hogan won the seat previously held by Martin O'Malley.

Incumbent Governors Seeking Re-election

Incumbent governors sought to win a new term in 29 states and won in 25 states. Democratic incumbents sought another term in 10 states and won in eight states[2] while two incumbents lost in Hawaii and Illinois. Republican incumbents sought another term in 19 states and won in 17 states.[3]

The party candidates winning these 36 races were 24 Republicans (66.7 percent),[4] 11 Democrats (30.6 percent)[5] and one Independent (2.8 percent).[6] Democrats won six of the nine races in the Northeast, while the Republicans won only three. However, Republicans dominated the remaining regions, winning seven in both the South and in the Midwest.

Table A: Gubernatorial Elections: 1970–2014

Year	Number of races	Democratic winner Number	Democratic winner Percent	Eligible to run Number	Eligible to run Percent	Actually ran Number	Actually ran Percent	Won Number	Won Percent	Lost Number	Lost Percent	Lost In primary	Lost In general election
1970	35	22	63%	29	83%	24	83%	16	64%	8	36%	1 (a)	7 (b)
1971	3	3	100	0	...	...	...	...	...	...	...	...	...
1972	18	11	61	15	83	11	73	7	64	4	36	2 (c)	2 (d)
1973	2	1	50	1	50	1	100	...	...	1	100	1 (e)	...
1974	35	27 (f)	77	29	83	22	76	17	77	5	24	1 (g)	4 (h)
1975	3	3	100	2	66	2	100	2	100	...	...	...	...
1976	14	9	64	12	86	8	67	5	63	3	33	1 (i)	2 (j)
1977	2	1	50	1	50	1	100	1	100	...	...	...	...
1978	36	21	58	29	81	23	79	16	73	7	30	2 (k)	5 (l)
1979	3	2	67	0	...	...	...	...	...	...	...	...	...
1980	13	6	46	12	92	12	100	7	58	5	42	2 (m)	3 (n)
1981	2	1	50	0	...	...	...	...	...	...	...	...	...
1982	36	27	75	33	92	25	76	19	76	6	24	1 (o)	5 (p)
1983	3	3	100	1	33	1	100	...	...	1	100	1 (q)	...
1984	13	5	38	9	69	6	67	4	67	2	33	...	2 (r)
1985	2	1	50	1	50	1	100	1	100	...	...	...	...
1986	36	19	53	24	67	18	75	15	83	3	18	1 (s)	2 (t)
1987	3	3	100	2	67	1	50	...	...	1	100	1 (u)	...
1988	12	5	42	9	75	9	100	8	89	1	11	...	1 (v)
1989	2	2	100	0	...	...	...	...	...	...	...	...	...
1990	36	19 (w)	53	33	92	23	70	17	74	6	26	...	6 (x)
1991	3	2	67	2	67	2	100	...	...	2	100	1 (y)	1 (z)
1992	12	8	67	9	75	4	44	4	100	...	...	...	...
1993	2	0	0	1	50	1	100	...	...	1	100	...	1 (aa)
1994	36	11 (bb)	31	30	83	23	77	17	74	6	26	2 (cc)	4 (dd)
1995	3	1	33	2	67	1	50	1	100	...	...	...	...
1996	11	7	64	9	82	7	78	7	100	...	...	...	...
1997	2	0	0	1	50	1	100	1	100	...	...	...	...
1998	36	11 (ee)	31	27	75	25	93	23	92	2	8	...	2 (ff)
1999	3	2	67	2	67	2	100	2	100	...	...	...	...
2000	11	8	73	7	88	6	86	5	83	1	17	...	1 (gg)
2001	2	2	100	0	...	...	...	...	...	...	...	...	...
2002	36	14	39	22	61	16	73	12	75	4	25	...	4 (hh)
2003	4 (ii)	1	25	2	50	2	100	...	...	2	100	...	2 (jj)
2004	11	6	55	11	100	8	73	4	50	4	50	2 (kk)	2 (ll)
2005	2	2	100	1	50	...	...	...	...	...	...	...	...
2006	36	20	56	31	86	27	87	25	93	2	7	1 (mm)	1 (nn)
2007	3	1	33	3	100	2	67	1	50	1	50	...	1 (oo)
2008	11	7	64	9	82	8	89	8	100	...	...	...	...
2009	2	0	0	1	50	1	100	...	...	1	100	...	1 (pp)
2010	37	13	35	22	60	14	64	11	79	3	21	1 (qq)	2 (rr)
2011	4	2	50	3	75	3	100	3	100	0	0	0	0
2012	12	7	58	8	67	7	88	7	100	...	...	...	...
2013	2	1	50	1	50	1	50	1	50	0	0	0	0
2014	36	13	36	31	86	29	81	26	72.2	3	8	1 (a)	2 (b)
Totals:													
Number	626	330		477		378		293		85		22	63
Percent	100	52.7		76.2		79.6		77.5		22.5		25.9	74.1

Source: The Council of State Governments, *The Book of the States, 2012,* (Lexington, KY: The Council of State Governments, 2012), 204, updated.

Key:
(a) Albert Brewer, D-Ala.; Neil Abercrombie, D-Hawaii.
(b) Keith Miller, R-Alaska; Winthrop Rockefeller, R-Ark.; Claude Kirk, R-Fla.; Don Samuelson, R-Idaho; Norbert Tieman, R-Neb.; Dewey Bartlett, R-Okla.; Frank Farrar, R-S.D.; Sean Parnell, R-Alaska; Tom Corbett, R-Penn.
(c) Walter Peterson, R-N.H.; Preston Smith, D-Texas.
(d) Russell Peterson, R-Del.; Richard Ogilvie, R-Ill.
(e) William Cahill, R-N.J.
(f) One independent candidate won: James Longley of Maine.

(g) David Hall, D-Okla.
(h) John Vanderhoof, R-Colo.; Francis Sargent, R-Mass.; Malcolm Wilson, R-N.Y.; John Gilligan, D-Ohio.
(i) Dan Walker, D-Ill.
(j) Sherman Tribbitt, D-Del.; Christopher 'Kit' Bond, R-Mo.
(k) Michael Dukakis, D-Mass.; Dolph Briscoe, D-Texas.
(l) Robert F. Bennett, R-Kan.; Rudolph G. Perpich, D-Minn.; Meldrim Thompson, R-N.H.; Robert Straub, D-Ore.; Martin J. Schreiber, D-Wis.
(m) Thomas L. Judge, D-Mont.; Dixy Lee Ray, D-Wash.
(n) Bill Clinton, D-Ark.; Joseph P. Teasdale, D-Mo.; Arthur A. Link, D-N.D.

Footnotes are continued on the next page.

Table A: Gubernatorial Elections: 1970–2014, Footnotes Continued

(o) Edward J. King, D-Mass.
(p) Frank D. White, R-Ark.; Charles Thone, R-Neb.; Robert F. List, R-Nev.; Hugh J. Gallen, D-N.H.; William P. Clements, R-Texas.
(q) David Treen, R-La.
(r) Allen I. Olson, R-N.D.; John D. Spellman, R-Wash.
(s) Bill Sheffield, D-Alaska.
(t) Mark White, D-Texas; Anthony S. Earl, D-Wis.
(u) Edwin Edwards, D-La.
(v) Arch A. Moore, R-W.Va.
(w) Two Independent candidates won: Walter Hickel (Alaska) and Lowell Weiker (Conn.). Both were former statewide Republican office holders.
(x) Bob Martinez, R-Fla.; Mike Hayden, R-Kan.; James Blanchard, D-Mich.; Rudy Perpich, DFL-Minn.; Kay Orr, R-Neb.; Edward DiPrete, R-R.I.
(y) Buddy Roemer, R-La.
(z) Ray Mabus, D-Miss.
(aa) James Florio, D-N.J.
(bb) One Independent candidate won: Angus King of Maine.
(cc) Bruce Sundlun, D-R.I.; Walter Dean Miller, R-S.D.

(dd) James E. Folsom Jr., D-Ala.; Bruce King, D-N.M.; Mario Cuomo, D-N.Y.; Ann Richards, D-Texas.
(ee) Two Independent candidates won: Angus King of Maine and Jesse Ventura of Minnesota.
(ff) Fob James, R-Ala.; David Beasley, R-S.C.
(gg) Cecil Underwood, R-W.Va.
(hh) Don Siegelman, D-Ala.; Roy Barnes, D-Ga.; Jim Hodges, D-S.C.; and Scott McCallum, R-Wis.
(ii) The California recall election and replacement vote of 2003 is included in the 2003 election totals and as a general election for the last column.
(jj) Gray Davis, D-Calif.; Ronnie Musgrove, D-Miss.
(kk) Bob Holden, D-Mo.; Olene Walker, R-Utah, lost in the pre-primary convention.
(ll) Joe Kernan, D-Ind.; Craig Benson, R-N.H.
(mm) Frank Murkowski, R-Alaska.
(nn) Robert Ehrlich, R-Md.
(oo) Ernie Fletcher, R-Ky.
(pp) Jon Corzine, D-N.J.
(qq) Jim Gibbons, R-Nev.
(rr) Chet Culver, D-Iowa; Ted Strickland, D-Ohio.

Plurality Winners

While third-party candidates for governor are commonplace, most do not garner enough votes to affect the outcomes of general elections, let alone win office. In 2014, however, there were 10 races where the winner of the general election did not receive a majority of all votes cast, which speaks to the significance of third-party candidates in this election cycle.[7]

Nearly one-third of governors were elected or re-elected without the support of the majority of voters in their states. More governors were elected without a majority vote in 2014 than in any election in the past 100 years.[8] In a few cases, third-party or unaffiliated candidates garnered enough votes that their presence on the ballot could have affected the final outcome of the election. Colorado is a case in point. Incumbent Democrat John Hickenlooper won the general election with 49.1 percent of the vote and Republican Robert Beauprez won 46.2 percent of the vote. The remaining vote was divided between a Green Party candidate, a Libertarian Party candidate, and two other candidates. A shifting of votes from these third-party candidates could have affected the outcome of the election.

An independent won in Alaska when former Valdez mayor Bill Walker—a candidate in the Republican gubernatorial primary in 2010—teamed with former Juneau mayor Byron Mallett, a Democrat, to form a winning unity ticket against incumbent Republican Sean Parnell. In 2014, Mallett had been a Democratic gubernatorial candidate in his own right. When Walker dropped his Republican affiliation in August 2013, he took advantage of the fact that third party candidates have somewhat better odds in Alaska than in other states, and the fact that the Democratic Party did not field its own candidate helped him win with 48 percent of the vote.

Recapping the Most Competitive Races

Historically, the two major parties have had roughly equal control of American governorships over time. Democratic candidates held an edge in 330 of the 626 gubernatorial elections—or 52.7 percent—that have occurred between 1970 and 2014. In 229 of these races—36.6 percent—the outcome led to a party shift in the governor's office. Party shifts have played out over the years so that neither of the two major parties has held an edge for more than 40 years in gubernatorial elections.

There are cycles in these shifts; whoever wins the most recent presidential election seems to have a negative effect on their party's gubernatorial races in elections in the following two years. After the election of Democrat Barack Obama as president in 2008, Democrats won only 13 of the 39 gubernatorial races in 2009 and 2010—just 33.3 percent. Following Obama winning a second term in 2012, Democrats won only 12 of the 38 governor races in 2013 and 2014—31.6 percent.

The strong Republican showing in the 2014 gubernatorial elections likely reflected a national political mood that manifested itself on the 2014 congressional elections as well. Obama's approval

Table B: Total Cost of Gubernatorial Elections: 1977–2014 (in thousands of dollars)

Year	Number of races	Total campaign costs		Average cost per state
		Actual $	2014$ (a)	(2014$)(b)
1977	2	$12,312	$47,336	$23,668
1978	36 (c)	102,342	365,638	10,157
1979	3	32,744	105,050	35,017
1980	13	35,634	100,746	7,750
1981	2	24,648	63,168	31,584
1982	36	181,832	438,890	12,191
1983	3	39,966	93,466	31,155
1984	13	47,156	105,731	8,133
1985	2	18,859	40,829	20,415
1986	36	270,605	575,143	15,976
1987	3	40,212	82,452	27,484
1988	12 (d)	52,208	102,812	8,568
1989	2	47,902	89,991	44,995
1990	36	345,493	615,742	17,104
1991	3	34,564	59,114	19,705
1992	12	60,278	100,080	8,340
1993	2	36,195	58,351	29,175
1994	36	417,873	656,826	18,245
1995	3	35,693	54,560	18,187
1996	11 (e)	68,610	101,871	9,261
1997	2	44,823	65,055	32,528
1998	36	470,326	672,182	18,672
1999	3	16,276	22,757	7,586
2000	11	97,098	131,125	11,920
2001	3	70,400	92,607	30,869
2002	36	841,427	1,089,649	30,268
2003	4 (f)	69,939	88,564	22,141
2004	11	112,625	138,889	12,626
2005	2	131,996	157,438	78,719
2006	36	727,552	840,712	23,353
2007	3	93,803	105,385	35,128
2008	11	118,912	128,651	11,696
2009	2	92,911	100,001	50,000
2010	37 (g)	920,735	983,586	26,583
2011	4 (h)	45,934	47,570	11,893
2012	12 (i)	144,044	146,149	12,179
2013	2	84,746	84,746	42,373
2014	36	704,300	704,300	19,564

Sources: Thad Beyle and The Council of State Governments.
Key:
N.A. — Not available.
(a) Developed from the table "Historic Consumer Price Index for All Urban Consumers (CPI-U)," created by the Bureau of Labor Statistics for the U.S. Department of Labor. Each year's expenditures are converted into the 2014$ value of the dollar by dividing those $ expenditures by the percent of that year's CPI-U value to control for the effect of inflation or recession over the period.
(b) Average cost per state is the result of dividing the 2014$ total campaign expenditures by the number of elections held that year.
(c) The expenditure data of 1978 are a particular problem as the two sources compiling data on this year's elections did so in differing ways that excluded some candidates. The result is that the numbers for 1978 under-represent the actual costs of these elections by some unknown amount. The sources are: Rhodes Cook and Stacy West, "1978 Advantage," *CQ Weekly Report*,(1979): 1757–1758, and *The Great Louisiana Spendathon* (Baton Rouge: Public Affairs Research Council, March 1980).
(d) As of the 1986 election, Arkansas switched to a four-year term for the governor, hence the drop from 13 to 12 for this off-year.
(e) As of the 1994 election, Rhode Island switched to a four-year term for the governor, hence the drop from 12 to 11 for this off-year.
(f) In 2003, there was a special recall and replacement election held in California in which voters elected to recall incumbent Gov. Gray Davis (D) from office and replace him with Gov. Arnold Schwarzenegger (R), hence the fourth election in this off-year instead of the normal three.
(g) In 2010, Utah held a special election to elect Gov. Gary Herbert (R) to the position which he had been appointed to in 2009. In 2009, then Lt. Gov. Herbert succeeded to the office of governor after Jon Huntsman (R) left to become U.S. ambassador to China. Under Utah law, voters must agree that a succeeding governor can hold the role until the next regularly scheduled election.
(h) In 2011, West Virginia held a special election to elect Gov. Earl Ray Tomblin (D) to the position he had been appointed to in 2010. Tomblin was appointed governor upon the resignation of Gov. Joe Manchin (D), who won a seat in the U.S. Senate. West Virginia law requires a special election must be held in the case of a gubernatorial succession.
(i) In 2012, Wisconsin held a special recall and replacement election focused on Gov. Scott Walker (R). Walker received 53 percent of the vote and was not recalled. In North Dakota, the law has been changed so that candidates no longer have to report the amount of $ expenditures made in the campaign.

ratings hit the lowest point of his presidency as the 2014 elections loomed. Republicans had a net gain of 12 seats in the U.S. House of Representatives in November, leaving Democrats with 188 congressional seats—the fewest they have controlled since 1949. Democrats also lost control of the U.S. Senate.

What is surprising about the number of Republican wins in 2014, however, is that Republicans had this strong finish even though quite a large proportion of campaigns remained close until the end. Many candidates won with very narrow margins. In fact, the gubernatorial campaigns were where the political excitement was in 2014. More than one-third of the gubernatorial races in 2014 were considered competitive—meaning, if not complete tossups, races where each candidate had a significant chance to win, even as Nov. 6 drew close. The 2014 gubernatorial elections were more competitive than their statewide election brethren, the 2014 U.S. Senate races.

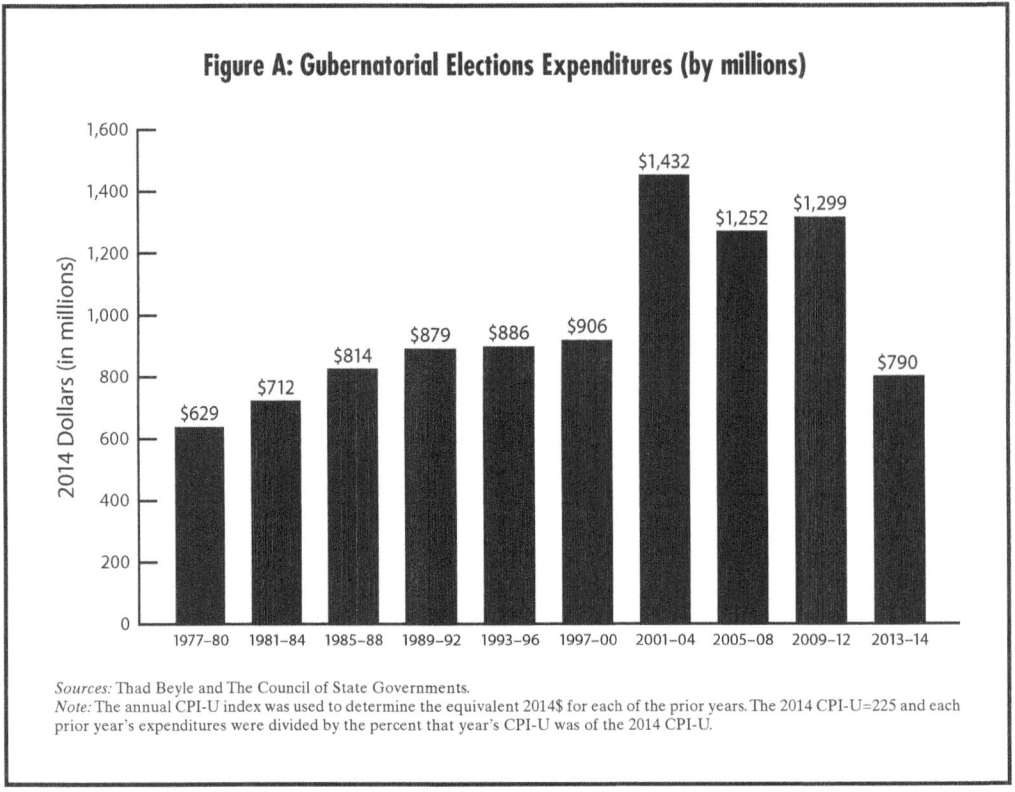

Figure A: Gubernatorial Elections Expenditures (by millions)

Y-axis: 2014 Dollars (in millions)

Values by period:
- 1977–80: $629
- 1981–84: $712
- 1985–88: $814
- 1989–92: $879
- 1993–96: $886
- 1997–00: $906
- 2001–04: $1,432
- 2005–08: $1,252
- 2009–12: $1,299
- 2013–14: $790

Sources: Thad Beyle and The Council of State Governments.
Note: The annual CPI-U index was used to determine the equivalent 2014$ for each of the prior years. The 2014 CPI-U=225 and each prior year's expenditures were divided by the percent that year's CPI-U was of the 2014 CPI-U.

Despite the number of competitive races, however, the final outcomes showed the impact of the aforementioned Republican wave. The road to victory may have been rocky; six of the 13 races that *The New York Times* had labeled tossups produced winners who took office with a plurality rather than a majority of support. But in the end, most Republican incumbents who were threatened were able to hold their seats, Democratic incumbents who were threatened were unable to hold theirs, and open seat races were more likely to produce a Republican winner. As for the safe races, every Republican-favored race produced a win for the Republican candidate.

Recapping 13 races widely seen as especially competitive:

- Alaska: As discussed above, Republican Sean Parnell couldn't hold his seat and lost to an Independent. There were state budget problems due to falling oil prices, and Independent candidate Bill Walker argued that Parnell's tax cuts made the situation worse. Former Republican Gov. Sarah Palin didn't help Parnell when she endorsed his opponent.

- Colorado: As mentioned above, neither major party candidate received a majority vote, and Democrat John Hickenlooper was re-elected. Republican Beau Beauprez, a former congressman, rancher and community banker who was seen by many in his party as their best hope in the general election, did not receive a place on the primary ballot at the state party convention. He subsequently petitioned his way on the ballot and won the Republican primary against four other major candidates. Democratic incumbent John Hickenlooper was popular in the state, but suffered in the polls as the election approached—perhaps affected by his signing of gun control and marijuana legalization bills into law, and changing his position on the death penalty.

- Connecticut: Due to the economy in Connecticut in 2014 not rebounding as well as some other states, incumbent Democrat Dan Malloy was in one of the most competitive races in the country. This was a rematch of the 2010 battle between Malloy and Republican Tom Foley for governor. A statistical dead heat heading into Election Day, Malloy was re-elected by a 3 percent margin.

Table C: Cost of Gubernatorial Campaigns, Most Recent Elections, 2011–2014

State	Year	Winner	Point margin	All candidates (2014$)	Cost per vote (2014$)	Spent (2014$)	Percent of all expenditures	Vote percent
				Total campaign expenditures		*Winner*		
Alabama	2014	R★	+27.26	$7,990,363	6.77	$6,769,778	84.7%	63.6%
Alaska	2014	I★★★	+2.22	1,791,047	6.40	847,593	47.3	48.1
Arizona	2014	R#	+11.90	20,471,454	13.59	7,910,241	38.6	53.5
Arkansas	2014	R#	+12.96	15,950,408	18.79	5,883,158	38.9	55.5
California	2014	D★	+20.00	13,772,803	18.82	5,945,649	43.7	60.0
Colorado	2014	D★	+3.14	10,619,170	5.20	5,463,070	51.5	49.2
Connecticut	2014	D★	+2.82	16,892,137	15.46	6,735,418	39.9	51.4
Delaware	2012	D★	+40.64	1,958,861	4.92	1,656,189	96.5	69.3
Florida	2014	R★	+1.08	22,872,029	3.84	10,447,966	45.7	48.2
Georgia	2014	R★	+7.86	10,739,159	4.21	1,588,830	14.8	52.8
Hawaii	2014	D#	+12.30	9,173,312	25.04	2,029,646	22.1	49.0
Idaho	2014	R★	+15.35	6,559,929	6.70	2,143,926	32.5	54.9
Illinois	2014	R★	+3.92	102,434,649	28.16	65,426,075	63.9	50.3
Indiana	2012	R#	+2.89	20,535,517	7.97	13,085,571	65.7	49.5
Iowa	2014	R★	+21.80	10,516,834	9.31	8,577,632	81.6	59.0
Kansas	2014	R★	+3.70	7,121,660	8.19	2,268,612	31.9	49.8
Kentucky	2011	D★	+20.4	15,514,696	18.62	12,081,847	80.3	55.7
Louisiana	2011	R★	+47.9	9,050,900	8.85	8,675,274	98.8	65.8
Maine	2014	R★	+4.77	7,897,902	12.92	1,906,350	24.1	47.7
Maryland	2014	R#	+3.80	24,496,947	14.17	4,929,224	20.1	51.0
Massachusetts	2014	R#	2.88	21,606,838	10.00	6,762,699	31.3	48.5
Michigan	2014	R★	5.74	21,812,323	6.91	14,498,509	66.5	51.7
Minnesota	2014	D★	+5.56	5,451,188	2.76	3,039,926	55.8	50.1
Mississippi	2011	R#	+22.1	12,216,185	13.67	7,856,360	66.3	61.1
Missouri	2012	D★	+12.1	27,018,238	9.90	15,512,314	59.2	54.7
Montana	2012	D#	+1.56	4,656,165	9.53	1,708,031	36.7	48.9
Nebraska	2014	R#	+17.51	14,760,429	27.35	7,059,254	47.8	57.2
Nevada	2014	R★	+46.89	3,617,676	6.61	3,513,555	97.1	70.6
New Hampshire	2014	D★	+9.08	3,341,358	6.87	1,472,416	44.1	52.5
New Jersey	2013	R★	+22.1	27,040,070	12.75	19,820,437	75.6	60.3
New Mexico	2014	R★	+14.44	12,486,204	24.35	8,501,999	88.5	57.2
New York	2014	D★	+13.97	59,541,778	15.59	52,663,635	88.5	54.3
North Carolina	2012	R#	+11.49	17,398,973	3.90	11,161,800	66.2	54.7
North Dakota	2012	R★	+28.79	(a)	(a)	(a)	(a)	(a)
Ohio	2014	R★	+30.96	20,166,455	6.60	16,640,931	82.5	63.8
Oklahoma	2014	R★	+14.80	5,987,244	7.26	4,317,938	72.1	55.8
Oregon	2014	D★	+5.76	8,106,083	5.51	5,006,085	61.8	49.9
Pennsylvania	2014	D#	+9.86	75,887,787	21.70	31,364,073	41.3	54.9
Rhode Island	2014	D#	+4.50	13,488,998	41.62	6,284,440	46.6	40.7
South Carolina	2014	R★	+14.46	15,110,615	12.12	7,887,670	52.2	55.9
South Dakota	2014	R★	+45.04	1,857,606	6.70	1,506,034	81.1	70.5
Tennessee	2014	R★	+47.73	4,272,410	3.16	4,246,999	99.4	70.7
Texas	2014	R#	+20.32	78,983,336	16.74	49,460,752	67.6	59.2
Utah	2012	R★	+40.5	2,755,320	2.74	2,150,305	80.5	68.3
Vermont	2014	D★	+1.26	1,264,972	6.55	961,469	76.0	46.8
Virginia	2013	D#	+2.52	60,353,635	26.93	32,417,401	53.4	47.8
Washington	2012	D#	+3.4	24,559,984	8.00	11,484,573	48.2	51.5
West Virginia	2012	D★	+4.85	6,897,808	10.38	3,376,110	50.5	50.5
Wisconsin	2014	R★	+5.74	46,336,867	19.22	29,673,716	52.9	52.9
Wyoming	2014	R★	+31.52	4,118,264	24.53	626,707	49.2	52.5

Source: Thad Beyle, Jennifer Jensen, Aaron Luedtke and The Council of State Governments.

Note: All dollar figures are in equivalent 2014$.

Key:
D — Democrat
I — Independent
R — Republican
— Open seat
★ — Incumbent ran and won.
★★ — Incumbent ran and lost in party primary.
★★★ — Incumbent ran and lost in general election.

(a) Data unavailable due to a change in North Dakota's campaign contribution reporting requirements. They are no longer required to file the $ expenditures by candidates, but must file data on contributions of $200 or more received by candidates.

Table D: Women Governors in the States

Governor	State	Year elected or succeeded to office	How woman became governor	Tenure of service	Previous offices held	Last elected position held before governorship
Phase I — From initial statehood to adoption of the 19th Amendment to U.S. Constitution (1920)						
No women elected or served as governor						
Phase II — Wives of former governors elected governor, 1924–1966						
Nellie Tayloe Ross (D)	Wyoming	1924	E	1/1925–1/1927	F	...
Miriam "Ma" Ferguson (D)	Texas	1924	E	1/1925–1/1927 1/1933–1/1935	F	...
Lurleen Wallace (D)	Alabama	1966	E	1/1967–5/1968	F	...
Phase III — Women who became governor on their own merit, 1970 to date						
Ella Grasso (D)	Connecticut	1974	E	1/1975–12/1980	SH, SOS, (a)	(a)
Dixy Lee Ray (D)	Washington	1976	E	1/1977–1/1981	(b)	...
Vesta M. Roy (R)	New Hampshire	1982	S (c)	12/1982–1/1983	(d)	(d)
Martha Layne Collins (D)	Kentucky	1983	E	12/1983–12/1987	(e), LG	LG
Madeleine M. Kunin (D)	Vermont	1984	E	1/1985–1/1991	SH, LG	LG
Kay A. Orr (R)	Nebraska	1986	E	1/1987–1/1991	T	T
Rose Mofford (D)	Arizona	1988	S (f)	4/1988–1/1991	SOS	SOS
Joan Finney (D)	Kansas	1990	E	1/1991–1/1995	T	T
Barbara Roberts (D)	Oregon	1990	E	1/1991–1/1995	(g), C, SH, SOS	SOS
Ann Richards (D)	Texas	1990	E	1/1991–1/1995	C, T	T
Christy Whitman (R)	New Jersey	1993	E	1/1994–1/2001	(h)	(h)
Jeanne Shaheen (D)	New Hampshire	1996	E	1/1997–1/2003	(d)	(d)
Jane Dee Hull (R)	Arizona	1997	S (i)	9/1997–1/2003	(j), SOS	SOS
Nancy P. Hollister (R)	Ohio	1998	S (k)	12/1998–1/1999	LG	LG
Ruth Ann Minner (D)	Delaware	2000	E	1/2001–1/2009	SH, SS, LG	LG
Judy Martz (R)	Montana	2000	E	1/2001–1/2005	LG	LG
Sila Calderón (Pop D)	Puerto Rico	2000	E	1/2001–1/2005	M	M
Jane Swift (R)	Massachusetts	2001	S (l)	4/2001–1/2003	SS, LG	LG
Janet Napolitano (D)	Arizona	2002	E	1/2003–1/2009	(m), AG	AG
Linda Lingle (R)	Hawaii	2002	E	12/2002–12/2010	C, M (n)	M
Kathleen Sebelius (D)	Kansas	2002	E	1/2003–1/2009	SH, (o)	(o)
Jennifer Granholm (D)	Michigan	2002	E	1/2003–1/2011	(p), AG	AG
Olene Walker (R)	Utah	2003	S (q)	11/2003–1/2005	SH, LG	LG
Kathleen Blanco (D)	Louisiana	2003	E	1/2004–1/2008	SH, LG	LG
M. Jodi Rell (R)	Connecticut	2004	S (r)	7/2004–1/2011	SH, LG	LG
Christine Gregoire (D)	Washington	2004	E	1/2005–1/2013	AG	AG
Sarah Palin (R)	Alaska	2006	E	1/2007–7/2009	M (s)	M
Beverly Perdue (D)	North Carolina	2008	E	1/2009–1/2013	SH, SS, LG	LG
Jan Brewer (R)	Arizona	2009	S (t)	1/2009–	C, SH, SS, SOS	SOS
Susana Martinez (R)	New Mexico	2010	E	1/2011–	(u)	(u)
Mary Fallin (R)	Oklahoma	2010	E	1/2011–	(a)	(a)
Nikki Haley (R)	South Carolina	2010	E	1/2011–	SH	SH
Maggie Wood Hassan (D)	New Hampshire	2012	E	1/2013–	SS	SS
Gina Raimondo (D)	Rhode Island	2014	E	1/2015–	ST	ST
Kate Brown (D)	Oregon	2015	S (v)	2/2015–	SH, SS, SOS	SOS

Sources: National Governors Association website, *www.nga.org*, and individual state government websites.

Key:
S — Succeeded to office upon death, resignation or removal of the incumbent governor.

AG — Attorney general
C — City council or county commission
E — Elected governor
F — Former first lady
LG — Lieutenant governor
M — Mayor
SH — State House member
SOS — Secretary of state
SS — State Senate member
T — State treasurer

(a) Congresswoman.
(b) Ray served on the U.S. Atomic Energy Commission from 1972 to 1975 and was chair of the AEC from 1973 to 1975.
(c) Roy as state Senate president succeeded to office upon the death of Gov. Hugh Gallen.
(d) State Senate president.
(e) State Supreme Court clerk.
(f) Mofford as secretary of state became acting governor in February 1988 and governor in April 1988 upon the impeachment and removal of Gov. Evan Mecham.
(g) Local school board member.
(h) Whitman was a former state utilities official.
(i) Hull as secretary of state became acting governor when Gov. Fife Symington resigned. Elected to full term in 1998.
(j) Speaker of the state House.

(k) Hollister as lieutenant governor became governor when Gov. George Voinovich stepped down to serve in the U.S. Senate.
(l) Swift as lieutenant governor succeeded Gov. Paul Celluci who resigned after being appointed ambassador to Canada. Was the first governor to give birth while serving in office.
(m) U.S. attorney.
(n) Lingle was mayor of Maui for two terms, elected in 1990 and 1996.
(o) Insurance commissioner.
(p) Federal prosecutor.
(q) Walker as lieutenant governor succeeded to the governorship upon the resignation of Gov. Mike Leavitt in 2003.
(r) Rell as lieutenant governor succeeded to the governorship upon the resignation of Gov. John Rowland in 2004.
(s) Palin was a two-term Mayor of Wasilla, Alaska, and had unsuccessfully sought the lieutenant governor's office in 2002. In 2008, Palin was nominated to be the vice presidential candidate on the Republican ticket with U.S. Sen. John McCain.
(t) Brewer as secretary of state succeeded to the governorship upon the resignation of Gov. Janet Napolitano in January 2009 after her confirmation as head of the U.S. Department of Homeland Security. Brewer then won a full term in the 2010 election.
(u) District Attorney – Dona Ana County, N.M.
(v) Kate Brown as secretary of state succeded to the governorship upon the resignation of Gov. John Kitzhaber in February 2015 after allegations of criminal wrongdoing involving the role his fiancée, Cylvia Hayes, held in his office.

Table E: 2011–2014 Governors' Race Winners by Party and Margin

Democratic winners				Republican winners				Independent winners			
State	Election Year	Percent of win	Point margin	State	Election Year	Percent of win	Point margin	State	Election Year	Percent of win	Point margin
Delaware	2012	69.3	+40.7	Nevada	2014	70.6	+46.7	Alaska	2014	48.1	+2.2
California	2014	59.8	+19.6	South Dakota	2014	70.5	+45.0				
Vermont	2012	57.8	+22.2	Tennessee	2014	70.3	+47.5				
Kentucky	2011	55.9	+20.4	Utah	2012	68.4	+40.6				
Pennsylvania	2014	54.9	+9.9	Louisiana	2011	65.8	+47.9				
Missouri	2012	54.8	+12.3	Alabama	2014	64.0	+28.0				
New York	2014	54.3	+14.0	Ohio	2014	63.6	+30.6				
New Hampshire	2012	52.6	+12.1	North Dakota	2012	63.3	+28.8				
New Hampshire	2014	52.5	+9.1	Wyoming	2014	62.6	+33.8				
Washington	2012	51.5	+3.0	Mississippi	2011	61.1	+22.1				
Connecticut	2014	51.0	+3.0	New Jersey	2013	60.3	+22.1				
West Virginia	2012	50.4	+4.7	Texas	2014	59.2	+20.3				
Minnesota	2014	49.8	+5.6	Iowa	2014	59.0	+21.8				
Oregon	2014	49.8	+5.8	New Mexico	2014	57.2	+14.5				
Colorado	2014	49.2	+3.4	Nebraska	2014	57.2	+17.9				
Hawaii	2014	49.0	+12.3	South Carolina	2014	55.9	+14.5				
Montana	2012	48.8	+1.6	Oklahoma	2014	55.8	+14.8				
Virginia	2013	47.8	+2.5	Arkansas	2014	55.5	+13.0				
Vermont	2014	43.4	+1.3	North Carolina	2012	54.7	+11.5				
Rhode Island	2014	40.7	+4.5	Arizona	2014	53.5	+11.9				
				Idaho	2014	53.5	+14.9				
				Georgia	2014	53.0	+8.0				
				Wisconsin	2014	52.3	+5.7				
				Michigan	2014	52.2	+5.8				
				Maryland	2014	51.0	+3.8				
				Illinois	2014	50.3	+3.9				
				Kansas	2014	50.0	+4.0				
				Massachusetts	2014	48.5	+1.9				
				Florida	2014	48.1	+1.0				
				Maine	2014	48.0	+5.0				

Source: Thad Beyle.

Overall Results by Victory Point Margin: Party and Region

Point margin	Number of states	Number of Republicans	Number of Democrats	Number of Independents	East	South	Midwest	West
10+ points	29	21	8	0	5	9	6	9
5–10 points	8	4	4	0	3	1	3	1
0–5 points	15	6	8	1	7	2	2	4
Totals:	52	31	20	1	15	12	11	14

Source: Thad Beyle.

Foley—a businessman who served as ambassador to Ireland under President George W. Bush and worked previously in the U.S. departments of State and Defense—lost to Malloy by only 6,200 votes in 2010. Malloy was mayor of Stamford before his election as governor.

- Florida: Incumbent Rick Scott bested former governor Charlie Crist in this rematch of the 2010 gubernatorial election. This was the second time

Scott beat Crist with a margin of fewer than two percentage points. Witnessing a campaign with vigorous negative attacks on both sides, voters seemed unenthusiastic about either choice. Scott accused Crist of being a political flip-flopper; Crist attacked Scott—a former health care executive— for cuts to education, for spending his own wealth on his campaigns, and for the Medicare fraud at a hospital that was part of Scott's health care chain.

Table F: New Governors Elected Each 4-Year Period, 1970–2014 (a)

Year	Number of gubernatorial elections	New Governors		Incumbents Running			
		Won	Percent	Number	Won	Lost	Percent Lost
1970	35	19	54%	24	16	8	36%
1971	3	3	100	...	...	...	...
1972	18	11	61	11	7	4	36
1973	2	2	100	1	...	1	100
1974	35	18	51	22	17	5	24
1975	3	1	33	2	2	...	...
1976	14	9	64	8	5	3	33
1977	2	1	50	1	1	...	...
1978	36	20	56	23	16	7	30
1979	3	3	100	...	...	...	...
1980	13	6	46	12	7	5	42
1981	2	2	100	...	...	...	...
1982	36	17	47	25	19	6	24
1983	3	3	100	1	...	1	100
1984	13	9	69	6	4	2	33
1985	2	1	50	1	1	...	...
1986	36	21	58	18	15	3	18
1987	3	3	100	1	...	1	100
1988	12	4	33	9	8	1	11
1989	2	2	100	...	...	...	...
1990	36	19	53	23	17	6	26
1991	3	3	100	2	...	2	100
1992	12	8	67	4	4	...	...
1993	2	1	50	1	...	1	100
1994	36	19	53	23	17	6	26
1995	3	2	67	1	1	...	...
1996	11	4	36	7	7	...	...
1997	2	1	50	1	1	...	...
1998	36	13	36	25	23	2	8
1999	3	1	33	2	2	...	...
2000	11	6	55	6	5	1	17
2001	2	2	100	...	...	...	...
2002	36	24	67	16	12	4	25
2003 (b)	4	4	100	2	...	2	100
2004	11	7	64	8	4	4	50
2005	2	2	100	...	...	...	...
2006	36	9	25	27	25	2	7
2007	3	2	67	2	1	1	50
2008	11	3	24	8	8	...	...
2009	2	2	100	1	...	1	100
2010	37	26	70	14	11	3	21
2011	4	1	25	3	3	...	...
2012 (c)	12	5	42	7	7	...	...
2013	2	1	50	1	1	...	...
2014	36	10	28	29	26	3	10
Totals:	626	332	53	378	293	85	23

Source: Thad Beyle.
Key:
(a) Table A: Gubernatorial Elections: 1970–2010, *The Book of the States, 2011* (Lexington, KY: The Council of State Governments, 2011), 128.
(b) In 2003, there was a recall and replacement election vote in California in which the incumbent Gov. Gray Davis (D) was recalled and Republican Arnold Schwarzenegger was elected as his replacement.
(c) In June 2012, a recall and replacement election was held in Wisconsin. Gov. Scott Walker (R) won 53 percent of the votes cast and was not recalled.

- Georgia: The biggest question as the 2014 election grew close was not whether Republican incumbent Nathan Deal would be the largest vote-getter in the general election—he had maintained a small but consistent lead in the polls for months—but whether he would get 50 percent of the vote. He did so, thus avoiding a runoff election to secure his next four years in office. Deal beat Democrat Jason Carter, a sitting state senator and grandson of former President (and former Georgia governor) Jimmy Carter, and Libertarian Andrew Hunt, founder and former CEO of a technology company.

- Illinois: Incumbent Democrat Pat Quinn lost his seat to Republican business executive Bruce Rauner. Quinn was elevated to governor in 2009 when incumbent Rod Blagojevich was impeached, and then narrowly elected in his own right in 2010. The 2014 race was one of the most closely watched this season. At different points in the campaign, each candidate was ahead in the polls. With a competitive race and major media markets, this was an extremely expensive race.

- Kansas: Incumbent Republican Sam Brownback was re-elected with 49.8 percent of the vote. State House Minority Leader Paul Davis won 46.1 percent of the vote, and Libertarian Keen Umbehr took 4 percent of the vote. Brownback, a former U.S. senator and a very conservative Republican, has been a divisive leader in a party of moderate and conservative Republicans. In his first term as governor, he enacted significant tax cuts and followed a conservative social agenda. In a surprising move, more than 100 Republican officials endorsed his Democratic opponent in July 2014, saying they could not support Brownback's cuts in education and other services. All this made for quite a horse race, though Brownback was able to win a second term.

- Maryland: Sitting Lt. Gov. Anthony Brown faced Republican businessman Paul Hogan for an open seat. Hogan took 51.3 percent of the vote. Tax hikes signed into law by Gov. Martin O'Malley, a Democrat, gave Hogan an opening in this traditionally Democratic state. Early polls in election season indicated that Brown had a comfortable lead, and Brown was viewed as the strong favorite through much of the campaign. The national winds made it difficult for Democrats, however, and Brown's role overseeing the implementation of the Affordable Care Act may have hurt him.

- Maine: Republican incumbent Paul LePage held his seat against Democratic Congressman Mike Michaud, winning 48.2 percent of the vote in the general election. This was considered a competitive race in large part because LePage was more conservative than the typical Maine Republican. LePage had managed to win office when two other candidates split the Democratic vote in a competitive three-way race in 2010. Michaud was hurt in 2014 by the candidacy of Independent Eliot Cutler, who had narrowly lost to LePage in the 2010 three-way race. Urged by others to withdraw as the 2014 general election neared and it became clear that he would not win, Cutler stayed on the ballot but released his supporters from voting for him, ultimately receiving 8.4 percent of the vote.

- Michigan: Rick Snyder won re-election over Democrat Mark Schauer, a former congressman. Snyder withstood attacks on his significant cuts to education, ultimately winning 51 percent of the vote in what most experts predicted would be a close election. Snyder had won his first gubernatorial election by a wide margin, but drew criticism for his budget cuts and for signing "right to work" legislation in 2012, which effectively banned unions from requiring workers to pay dues and substantially weakened the power of unions in the state.

- Rhode Island: Democrat Gina Raimondo beat Republican Allan Fung, mayor of Cranston, by five points in an election where third-party candidate Bob Healey took 21 percent of the vote. Raimondo, a former Rhodes Scholar, received national attention for her overhaul of Rhode Island's public pension system, which was one of the most underfunded in the country. Her focus on the state's weak economy and her fiscal management helped her get the plurality she needed to win.

- Vermont: In another race without a majority winner, Democratic incumbent Peter Shumlin won 46.4 percent of the vote, compared to 45.1 percent of the vote for Republican Scott Milne. Libertarian Dan Feliciano received 4.4 percent of the general election vote, and four other third-party candidates write-in candidates together drew more than 4 percent of the vote. With no majority winner, the race went to the Democratically controlled legislature, which in January elected Shumlin to his third term by a 110-69 vote. The legislature has voted for the top vote-getter in every plurality election in more than 150 years. Shumlin was also a plurality winner in his 2010 gubernatorial election.

- Wisconsin: Wisconsin's electorate has deeply divided about its incumbent governor, Republican Scott Walker. Throughout his time as governor, political polls have reported very few "Don't know/Don't care/Refuse to answer" responses to questions about approval for Walker. Thus the campaign between Walker and his Democratic opponent, Madison school board member

Mary Burke, was as much a referendum on Walker as a statement about his opponent. Walker, who was first elected governor in 2010 and who faced a contentious recall battle in 2012 following his successful effort to enact "right to work" legislation in the state, saw the same results in 2014 that he did in his previous two elections: bitterly fought but ultimately successful.

The Characteristics of the Governors

The governors elected in the most recent cycle of gubernatorial elections—2011 through 2014—who were either holding office or facing election in November 2014, took several routes to the office. Twenty of these governors previously held elected nonstatewide offices. These include:

- Seven former members of Congress: Washington Gov. Jay Inslee, a Democrat; and Arkansas Gov. Asa Hutchinson, Georgia Gov. Nathan Deal, Indiana Gov. Mike Pence, Louisiana Gov. Bobby Jindal, Ohio Gov. John Kasich and Oklahoma Gov. Mary Fallin, all Republicans.

- Six mayors or former mayors: Alaska Gov. Bill Walker, Valdez, an Independent; Colorado Gov. John Hickenlooper, Denver, and Connecticut Gov. Dannel Malloy, Stamford—both Democrats; and Maine Gov. Paul LePage, Waterville; North Carolina Gov. Pat McCrory, Charlotte; and Tennessee Gov. Bill Haslam, Knoxville—all Republicans.

- Five state legislators: South Carolina Gov. Nikki Haley, a Republican state representative; Hawaii Gov. David Ige, a Democratic state senator; New Hampshire Gov. Maggie Wood Hassan, a Democratic senate majority leader; Vermont Gov. Peter Shumlin and West Virginia Gov. Earl Ray Tomblin, both Democratic state senate leaders.

- Two county officials: New Mexico Gov. Susana Martinez, district attorney; and Wisconsin Gov. Scott Walker, county CEO—both Republicans.

Eight governors followed paths to the governorship that did not include political experience in the legislative or executive political arena. These include:

- Three former federal attorneys or judges: New Jersey Gov. Chris Christie, a former U.S. attorney; Nevada Brian Sandoval, a former federal district court judge; and Wyoming Gov. Matt Mead, a former U.S. attorney—all Republicans.

- Four businessmen: Florida Gov. Rick Scott, a health care company executive; Michigan Gov. Rick Snyder, a venture capitalist in computers; Nebraska Gov. Peter Ricketts, partner in a family business (Ameritrade)—all Republicans; and Virginia Gov. Terry McAuliffe, a diverse businessman, a Democrat and a former Democratic National Committee chair.

- One doctor: Alabama Gov. Robert Bentley, a dermatologist and a Republican.

In the past 516 gubernatorial races held between 1977 and 2014, candidates held a variety of statewide political offices prior to seeking the governor's office. Among the candidates were 119 lieutenant governors (33 won); 110 attorneys general (31 won); 37 secretaries of state (eight won); 33 state treasurers (10 won); and 20 state auditors or comptrollers (three won). Looking at these numbers from a bettor's point of view, the odds of a lieutenant governor being elected governor stand at 3.5-to-1; an attorney general at 3.6-to-1; a secretary of state at 4.6-to-1; a state treasurer at 3.3-to-1; and a state auditor or comptroller at 6.7-to-1.

Five women won governorships in 2014. Four women won their second terms in 2014: Maggie Hassan in New Hampshire; Susana Martinez in New Mexico; Mary Fallin in Oklahoma; and Nikki Haley in South Carolina. In 2014, Gina Raimondo won her first term in Rhode Island.

Cost of Gubernatorial Elections

Table B presents data on the total cost of gubernatorial elections from 1977 to 2014. These data show the rhythm of gubernatorial elections in each four-year cycle, a rhythm reflecting the fact that there are more states with gubernatorial races in some years than in others.

In the past few years, we have seen a disruption of what has been the consistent growth in the amount of money spent in gubernatorial elections during the four-decade period considered. Over most of this 37-year period, we have seen only a few drops between comparable years in the cycles. These declines usually were tied to relatively uncontested races when an incumbent was successful in his or her re-election bid.

The money spent on gubernatorial campaigns has been increasing, but we are seeing a shift in who is spending that money. The 2010 U.S. Supreme Court decision in *Citizens United v. the Federal Election Commission* paved the way for the explosion of 527 groups, "super-PACs" which do not make contributions directly to political parties or candidates for office, and thus can accept unlimited contributions from individuals, unions and corporations. This has funneled campaign funding to groups such as the Democratic Governors Association, the Republican Governors Association and other groups that spend heavily on gubernatorial campaigns, and away from the gubernatorial campaigns themselves.

Notes

[1] The authors thank Aaron Luedtke for his research assistance.

[2] Democratic incumbent winners were in California, Colorado, Connecticut, Minnesota, New Hampshire, New York, Oregon, Vermont. Two incumbent Democrats who lost their bids were in Hawaii—primary election, and Illinois—general election.

[3] Republican incumbent winners were in Alabama, Florida, Georgia, Idaho, Iowa, Kansas, Maine, Michigan, Nevada, New Mexico, Ohio, Oklahoma, South Carolina, South Dakota, Tennessee, Wisconsin and Wyoming. Two incumbent Republicans who lost their bids were in Alaska —General election, and Pennsylvania—General election.

[4] Republicans won in Alabama, Arkansas, Arizona, Florida, Georgia, Idaho, Illinois, Iowa, Kansas, Maine, Maryland, Massachusetts, Michigan, Nebraska, Nevada, New Mexico, Ohio, Oklahoma, South Carolina, South Dakota, Tennessee, Texas, Wisconsin and Wyoming.

[5] Democrats won in California, Colorado, Connecticut, Hawaii, Minnesota, New Hampshire, New York, Oregon, Pennsylvania, Rhode Island and Vermont.

[6] An Independent won in Alaska.

[7] Races that yielded a winner with a plurality, rather than a majority, of the general election vote were in Arizona, Arkansas, Colorado, Florida, Hawaii, Maine, Massachusetts, Oregon, Rhode Island and Vermont.

[8] Chikshi, Niraj. 2014. "More governors have won without majority support in the 2010s than in any decade in the past century." *Washington Post Online* December 10. *http://wapo.st/12tS7Z5*. Accessed March 10, 2015.

About the Authors

Thad L. Beyle is a professor emeritus of political science at the University of North Carolina at Chapel Hill. After being an undergraduate and master's student at Syracuse University, he received his doctorate at the University of Illinois. He spent a year in the North Carolina governor's office in the mid-1960s, followed by two years with Terry Sanford's "A Study of American States" project at Duke University. He also has worked with the National Governors Association in several capacities on gubernatorial transitions.

Jennifer M. Jensen is deputy provost for academic affairs and associate professor of political science at Lehigh University. She earned her bachelor's degree from the University of Michigan and her master's and doctorate from the University of North Carolina at Chapel Hill. She has worked in the U.S. House of Representatives and in governmental relations. Her most recent research focuses on governors in the intergovernmental arena.

Table 4.1
THE GOVERNORS, 2015

State or other jurisdiction	Name and party	Length of regular term in years	Date of first service	Present term ends	Number of previous terms	Term limits	Joint election of governor and lieutenant governor (a)	Official who succeeds governor	Birthdate	Birthplace
Alabama	Robert Bentley (R)	4	1/2011	1/2019	1	2-4	No	LG	2/3/1943	AL
Alaska	Bill Walker (I)	4	12/2014	12/2018	…	2-4	Yes	LG	4/16/1951	AK
Arizona	Doug Ducey (R)	4	1/2015	1/2019	…	2-4	(b)	SS	4/9/1964	OH
Arkansas	Asa Hutchinson (R)	4	1/2015	1/2019	…	2A	No	LG	12/3/1950	AR
California	Edmund Gerald "Jerry" Brown (D)	4	1/1975 (c)	1/2019	2 (c)	2A (c)	No	LG	4/7/1938	CA
Colorado	John Hickenlooper (D)	4	1/2011	1/2019	1	2-4	Yes	LG	2/7/1952	PA
Connecticut	Dan Malloy (D)	4	1/2011	1/2019	1	…	Yes	LG	7/21/1955	CT
Delaware	Jack Markell (D)	4	1/2009	1/2017	1	2A	No	LG	11/26/1960	DE
Florida	Rick Scott (R)	4	1/2011	1/2019	1	2A	Yes	LG	12/2/1952	IL
Georgia	Nathan Deal (R)	4	1/2011	1/2019	1	2-4	No	LG	8/25/1942	GA
Hawaii	David Ige (D)	4	12/2014	12/2018	…	2-4	Yes	LG	6/26/1938	NY
Idaho	C.L. "Butch" Otter (R)	4	1/2007	1/2019	2	…	No	LG	5/3/1942	ID
Illinois	Bruce Rauner (R)	4	1/2015	1/2019	…	2A	Yes	LG	12/16/1948	IL
Indiana	Mike Pence (R)	4	1/2013	1/2017	…	2-12	Yes	LG	6/7/1959	IN
Iowa	Terry Branstad (R)	4	1/1983 (d)	1/2019	5 (d)	…	Yes	LG	11/17/1946	IA
Kansas	Sam Brownback (R)	4	1/2011	1/2019	1	2-4	Yes	LG	9/12/1956	KS
Kentucky	Steven L. Beshear (D)	4	12/2007	12/2015	1	2-4	Yes	LG	9/21/1944	KY
Louisiana	Bobby Jindal (R)	4	1/2008	1/2016	1	2-4	No	LG	6/10/1971	LA
Maine	Paul LePage (R)	4	1/2011	1/2019	1	2-4	(b)	PS	10/9/1948	ME
Maryland	Larry Hogan (R)	4	1/2015	1/2019	…	2-4	Yes	LG	1/18/1963	MD
Massachusetts	Charlie Baker (R)	4	1/2015	1/2019	…	…	Yes	LG	7/31/1956	IL
Michigan	Rick Snyder (R)	4	1/2011	1/2019	1	2A	Yes	LG	8/19/1958	MI
Minnesota	Mark Dayton (D)	4	1/2011	1/2019	1	…	Yes	LG	1/26/1947	MN
Mississippi	Phil Bryant (R)	4	1/2012	1/2016	…	2A	Yes	LG	12/9/1954	MS
Missouri	Jay Nixon (D)	4	1/2009	1/2017	1	2A	No	LG	2/13/1956	MO
Montana	Steve Bullock (D)	4	1/2013	1/2017	…	2-16	Yes	LG	4/11/1966	MT
Nebraska	Pete Ricketts (R)	4	1/2015	1/2019	…	2-4	Yes	LG	5/12/1948	NE
Nevada	Brian Sandoval (R)	4	1/2011	1/2019	1	2A	No	LG	8/5/1963	CA
New Hampshire	Maggie Hassan (D)	2	1/2013	1/2017	1	…	(b)	PS	2/27/1958	MA
New Jersey	Chris Christie (R)	4	1/2010	1/2018	1	2-4	Yes	LG	9/6/1962	NJ
New Mexico	Susana Martinez (R)	4	1/2011	1/2019	1	2-4	Yes	LG	7/14/1959	TX
New York	Andrew Cuomo (D)	4	1/2011	1/2019	1	…	Yes	LG	12/6/1957	NY
North Carolina	Pat McCrory (R)	4	1/2013	1/2017	…	2-4	No	LG	10/17/1956	VA
North Dakota	Jack Dalrymple (R)	4	12/2010 (e)	12/2016	1	…	Yes	LG	10/16/1948	MN
Ohio	John Kasich (R)	4	1/2011	1/2019	1	2-4	Yes	LG	5/13/1952	PA
Oklahoma	Mary Fallin (R)	4	1/2011	1/2019	1	2-A	No	LG	12/9/1954	MO
Oregon	Kate Brown (D)	4	2/2015 (f)	1/2019	… (f)	2-12	(b)	SS	3/5/1947	WA
Pennsylvania	Tom Wolf (D)	4	1/2015	1/2019	…	2-4	Yes	LG	6/17/1949	PA
Rhode Island	Gina Raimondo (D)	4	1/2015	1/2019	…	2-4	No	LG	3/26/1953	RI
South Carolina	Nikki Haley (R)	4	1/2011	1/2019	1	2-4	No	LG	1/20/1972	SC

See footnotes at end of table.

THE GOVERNORS, 2015 — Continued

State or other jurisdiction	Name and party	Length of regular term in years	Date of first service	Present term ends	Number of previous terms	Term limits	Joint election of governor and lieutenant governor (a)	Official who succeeds governor	Birthdate	Birthplace
South Dakota	Dennis Daugaard (R)	4	1/2011	1/2019	1	2-4	Yes	LG	6/11/1953	SD
Tennessee	Bill Haslam (R)	4	1/2011	1/2019	1	2-4	No	SpS (g)	8/23/1952	TN
Texas	Greg Abbott (R)	4	1/2015	1/2019	…	…	No	LG	3/4/1950	TX
Utah	Gary Herbert (R)	4	8/2009 (h)	1/2017	2	…	Yes	LG	5/7/1947	UT
Vermont	Peter Shumlin (D)	2	1/2011	1/2017	2	…	No	LG	3/24/1956	VT
Virginia	Terry McAuliffe (D)	4	1/2014	1/2018	…	1-4	No	LG	2/9/1957	NY
Washington	Jay Inslee (D)	4	1/2013	1/2017	…	…	No	LG	2/9/1951	WA
West Virginia	Earl Ray Tomblin (D)	4	11/2010 (i)	1/2017	1	2-4	(b)	PS (g)	3/15/1952	WV
Wisconsin	Scott Walker (R)	4	1/2011	1/2019	1	…	Yes	LG	11/2/1967	CO
Wyoming	Matt Mead (R)	4	1/2011	1/2019	1	2-16	(b)	SS	3/11/1962	WY
American Samoa	Lolo Matalasi Moliga (I)	4	1/2013	1/2017	…	2-4	Yes	LG	1949	AS
Guam	Eddie Calvo (R)	4	1/2011	1/2019	1	2-4	Yes	LG	8/29/1961	Guam
No. Mariana Islands	Eloy Inos (C)	4	2/2013 (j)	1/2019	1	2A	Yes	LG	11/27/1945	CNMI
Puerto Rico	Alejandro García Padilla (PDP)	4	1/2013	1/2017	…	…	(b)	SS	8/3/1971	PR
U.S. Virgin Islands	Kenneth Mapp (I)	4	1/2015	1/2019	…	2-4	Yes	LG	11/13/1957	USVI

Source: The Council of State Governments, June 2015.

Key:
C — Covenant
D — Democrat
I — Independent
PDP — Popular Democratic Party
R — Republican
LG — Lieutenant Governor
SS — Secretary of State
PS — President of the Senate
SpS — Speaker of the Senate
… — Not applicable
2A — Two terms, absolute.
2-4 — Two terms, re-eligible after four yrs.
2-12 — Two terms, eligible for eight out of 12 yrs.
2-16 — Two terms, eligible for eight out of 16 yrs.
1-4 — One term, re-eligible after four yrs.
(a) The following also choose candidates for governor and lieutenant governor through a joint nomination process: Florida, Kansas, Maryland, Minnesota, Montana, North Dakota, Ohio, Utah, American Samoa, Guam, No. Mariana Islands and U.S. Virgin Islands.
(b) No lieutenant governor.
(c) Gov. Brown previously served two terms as governor of California from 1975–1983. He was elected again in November 2010 and in November 2014 and is now serving his fourth and final term. California instituted absolute term-limits of two four-year terms for the office of governor in 1990.

Those who served as governor prior to that date are eligible for re-election. Gov. Brown is now limited to completing his current term.
(d) Gov. Branstad was first elected in 1983 and served for four terms until 1999. He was elected to a 5th term in November 2010 and 6th, and final, in 2014.
(e) Lt. Gov. Dalrymple was sworn in on December 21, 2010 to complete Gov. Hoeven's term as governor of North Dakota after Hoeven was elected to the Senate.
(f) Oregon Secretary of State Kate Brown became governor on February 18, 2015, following Gov. John Kitzhaber's resignation. A special gubernatorial election will be held in November 2016 to fill the position for the final two years of Gov. Kitzhaber's term.
(g) Official bears the additional title of "lieutenant governor."
(h) Lt. Gov. Gary Herbert was sworn in as governor on August 10, 2009 after Gov. Huntsman resigned to accept President Obama's appointment as Ambassador to China. Utah law states that a replacement governor elevated in a term's first year will face a special election at the next regularly scheduled general election, November 2010, instead of serving the remainder of the term. Gov. Herbert was elected to serve a full term in Nov. 2012.
(i) Senate President Earl Ray Tomblin was sworn in as governor on November 15, 2010 after Gov. Manchin was elected in the November election to fill Sen. Robert Byrd's seat. He was elected to a full term in November 2012.
(j) Northern Mariana Islands Lt. Gov. Eloy S. Inos became governor on Feb. 20, 2013, completing the unexpired term of Gov. Benigno Fitial following his resignation. Gov. Fitial was serving a five-year second term in office as governor instead of the normal four-year term. This was due to Senate Legislative Initiative 16-11, which changed future general elections to even-numbered years. Gov. Inos was elected in 2014 to a regular 4-year term.

Table 4.2
THE GOVERNORS: QUALIFICATIONS FOR OFFICE

State or other jurisdiction	Minimum age	State citizen (years)	U.S. citizen (years) (a)	State resident (years) (b)	Qualified voter (years)
Alabama........................	30	7	10	7	★
Alaska...........................	30	★	7	7	★
Arizona.........................	25	5	10	. . .	. . .
Arkansas.......................	30	★	★	7	★
California	18	. . .	5	5	★
Colorado.......................	30	. . .	★	2	. . .
Connecticut	30	6 months	★	★	★
Delaware	30	. . .	12	6	. . .
Florida	30	★	. . .	7	7
Georgia.........................	30	. . .	15	6	. . .
Hawaii...........................	30	. . .	5	5	★
Idaho............................	30	2	★	2	. . .
Illinois..........................	25	3	★	3	★
Indiana.........................	30	. . .	5	5	★
Iowa	30	2	2	2	★
Kansas	. . .	. . .	. . .	. . .	. . .
Kentucky	30	6	. . .	6	. . .
Louisiana......................	25	5	5	5	★
Maine............................	30	. . .	15	5	. . .
Maryland	30	. . .	(c)	5	5
Massachusetts	. . .	. . .	. . .	7	. . .
Michigan.......................	30	. . .	★	★	4
Minnesota.....................	25	. . .	★	1	★
Mississippi	30	★	20	5	★
Missouri........................	30	. . .	15	10	. . .
Montana	25	★	★	2	★
Nebraska	30	5	5	5	. . .
Nevada..........................	25	2	. . .	2	★
New Hampshire	30	. . .	. . .	7	. . .
New Jersey	30	. . .	20	7	. . .
New Mexico	30	. . .	★	5	★
New York.......................	30	. . .	★	5	. . .
North Carolina..............	30	. . .	5	2	★
North Dakota................	30	. . .	★	5	★
Ohio..............................	18	. . .	★	★	★
Oklahoma......................	31	. . .	10	10	(d)
Oregon..........................	30	. . .	★	3	. . .
Pennsylvania	30	★	★	7	★
Rhode Island	18	30 days	30 days	30 days	30 days
South Carolina..............	30	5	5	5	. . .
South Dakota................	18	★	★	★	★
Tennessee	30	7	★	. . .	. . .
Texas	30	. . .	★	5	. . .
Utah..............................	30	5	3	5	★
Vermont........................	. . .	. . .	. . .	4	. . .
Virginia.........................	30	★	★	★	5
Washington...................	18	. . .	★	★	★
West Virginia................	30	5	★	1	★
Wisconsin	18	★	★	★	★
Wyoming	30	★	★	5	★
American Samoa	35	. . .	★	5	. . .
Guam	30	. . .	5	5	★
No. Mariana Islands	35	. . .	★	10	★
Puerto Rico...................	35	5	5	5	. . .
U.S. Virgin Islands.......	30	. . .	5	5	★

Sources: The Council of State Governments' survey of governors' offices, December 2014, and state websites, May 2015.

Key:

★ — Formal provision; number of years not specified.

. . . — No formal provision.

(a) In some states you must be a U.S. citizen to be an elector, and must be an elector to run.

(b) In some states you must be a state resident to be an elector, and must be an elector to run.

(c) *Crosse v. Board of Supervisors of Elections* 243 Md. 555, 221 A.2d 431 (1966) — opinion rendered indicated that U.S. citizenship was, by necessity, a requirement for office.

(d) In order to file as a candidate for nomination by a political party to any state or county office, a person must have been a registered voter of that party for the six-month period preceding the first day of the filing perod (26 O.S.§. 5 - 105A - A).

Table 4.3
THE GOVERNORS: COMPENSATION, STAFF, TRAVEL AND RESIDENCE

State or other jurisdiction	Salary	Governor's office staff (a)	Access to state transportation			Receives travel allowance	Reimbursed for travel expenses	Official residence
			Automobile	Airplane	Helicopter			
Alabama	(c)	40	★	★	★	...	★(b)	★
Alaska	145,000	71	★	★	...	...	★(b)	★
Arizona	95,000	29 (f)	★	★	...	...	★(b)	...
Arkansas	87,759	67	★	★	...	...	★	★
California	177,467	81	★	...	...	...	(d)	...
Colorado	90,000	50	★	★	...	★	★	(e)
Connecticut	150,000	27	★	...	...	...	...	(e)
Delaware	171,000	32	★	...	...	...	...	★
Florida	130,273	256 (f)	★	★(j)	...	(b)	(b)	★
Georgia	139,339	56 (f)	★	★	★	...	...	★
Hawaii	146,628	56	★	...	...	★	★	★
Idaho	121,975	18	★	★	...	★(b)	...	...
Illinois	177,412	99	★	★	★	★	(d)	★
Indiana	111,688	34	★	★	★	★(b)	★(b)	★
Iowa	130,000	17	★	...	...	...	★	★
Kansas	99,636	24	★	★	★	...	★	★
Kentucky	151,643 (c)	80	★	★	★	...	★(b)	★
Louisiana	130,000	93 (f)	★	★	★	...	★	★
Maine	70,000	21	★	...	...	★	★	★
Maryland	150,000	85 (f)	★	★	★	(b)	(b)	★
Massachusetts	151,800	approx. 60	★	...	★	★(b)	★(b)	...
Michigan	159,300 (c)	76	★	★	★	(b)	(b)	★(e)
Minnesota	123,427	37	★	★	★	...	★	★
Mississippi	122,160	29	★	★(k)	...	...	★	★
Missouri	133,821	22	★	★	...	(b)	(d)	★
Montana	108,167	58 (f)	★	★	★	...	★	★
Nebraska	105,000	9	★	★	...	★	★	★
Nevada	149,730	18 (f)	★	★	...	(b)	★(b)	★
New Hampshire	113,834	19	★	...	...	(b)	(d)	(e)
New Jersey	175,000	128	★	...	★	★	★(b)	★
New Mexico	110,000	33	★	★	★	...	★	★
New York	179,000 (c)	180	★	★	★	...	★	★
North Carolina	142,265	68	★	★	...	★	★	★
North Dakota	125,330	17	★	★	...	...	★	★
Ohio	148,886	60	★	★	★	(b)	(d)	(e)
Oklahoma	147,000	34	★	★	...	...(b)	★(b)	★
Oregon	98,600	65 (f)	★	...	...	★(b)	★(b)	★
Pennsylvania	190,823 (c)	68	★	★	...	...	★(b)	★
Rhode Island	129,210	37.5	★	...	★	...	★	...
South Carolina	106,078	16	★	★	...	...	★	★
South Dakota	107,121	21.5	★	★	...	...	★	★
Tennessee	184,632 (c)	37	★	★	★	★(b)	(d)	★
Texas	150,000	277	★	★	★	...	★	★
Utah	109,470	23	★	★	★	...	★	★
Vermont	145,538 (c)	14	★	★	...	★	...	...
Virginia	175,000	36	★	★	★	...	★	★
Washington	166,891	36	★	★	...	(b)	(d)	★
West Virginia	150,000	56	★	★	★	(b)	(d)	★
Wisconsin	147,328	25	★	★	...	...	(d)	★
Wyoming	105,000	25	★	★	...	...	★(b)	★
American Samoa	90,000	23	★	...	...	(b)	...	★
Guam	130,000	42	★	...	...	$218/day	...	★
No. Mariana Islands	70,000	16	★	...	...	(b)	...	★
Puerto Rico	70,000	28	★	(g)	(g)	...	★	★
U.S. Virgin Islands	150,000	84	★	...	...	...	★	★

See footnotes at end of table.

THE GOVERNORS: COMPENSATION, STAFF, TRAVEL AND RESIDENCE — Continued

Sources: The Council of State Governments' survey of governors' offices, December 2014, and state websites, May 2015.

Key:

★ — Yes

. . . — No

N.A. — Not available.

(a) Definitions of "governor's office staff" vary across the states — from general office support to staffing for various operations within the executive office.

(b) Travel expenses.

Alabama — According to state policy.

Alaska — $42/day per diem plus actual lodging expenses.

American Samoa — $105,000. Amount includes travel allowance for entire staff.

Arizona — Receives up to $59/day for meals based on location; receives per diem for lodging out of state; default $34/day for meals and $60/day lodging in state.

Florida — The Executive Office of the Governor allocates an annual budget for the governor's travel expenses. Gov. Scott is not reimbursed for personally incurred travel expenses. The Executive Office of the Governor pays the governor's travel expenses directly (hotel accommodations, meals, etc.) out of funds allocated for travel.

Guam — The amount varies based on destination but averages $218 per day.

Idaho — Travel allowance included in office budget.

Indiana — Statute allows $12,000 but due to budget cuts the amount has been reduced to $9,800 and reimbursed for actual expenses for travel/lodging.

Kentucky — Mileage at same rate as other state officials.

Maryland — Travel allowance included in office budget.

Massachusetts — As necessary.

Michigan — The governor is provided a $54,000 annual expense allowance, as determined by the State Officers Compensation Commission in 2010. "Expense allowance" is for normal, reimbursable personal expenses such as food, lodging, and travel costs incurred by an individual in carrying out the responsibilities of state office.

Missouri — Amount includes travel allowance for entire staff. Amount not available.

Nevada — Amount includes travel allowance for entire staff. The following figures include travel expenses for governor and staff, $28,982 in state; $12,767 out of state. Reimbursed for travel expenses per GSA/Conus rate.

New Hampshire — Travel allowance included in office budget.

New Jersey — Reimbursement may be provided for necessary expenses.

Northern Mariana Islands — Travel allowance included in office budget. Governor has a "contingency account" that can be used for travel expenses and expenses in other departments or other projects.

Ohio — Set administratively.

Oklahoma — Reimbursed for actual and necessary expenses.

Oregon — $1,000 a month for expenses, not specific to travel. Reimbursed for actual travel expenses.

Pennsylvania — Reimbursed for reasonable expenses.

Tennessee — Travel allowance included in office budget.

Washington — Travel allowance included in office budget.

West Virginia — Included in general expense account.

Wyoming — $99/day or actual.

(c) Governor's salary:

Alabama — Gov. Robert Bentley is not accepting his salary, $120,395 until the unemployment rate in Alabama drops.

Kentucky — Reflects a voluntary 10 percent salary reduction.

Michigan — Gov. Rick Snyder returns all but $1.00 of his salary.

New York — Gov. Andrew Cuomo has reduced his salary by 5 percent.

Tennessee — Gov. Haslam returns his salary to the state.

Vermont — Governor has taken a voluntary 3 percent reduction in the annual salary set in statue.

(d) Information not provided.

(e) Governor's residence: Many governors are choosing to live in their own residences even when an official residence is provided.

Colorado — The governor chooses to live in his private home and allow cabinet members who live farther away to occupy the governor's mansion.

Connecticut — Provided by the Department of Administrative Services.

Michigan — Constitution mandates official residence in Lansing.

New Hampshire — The current governor does not occupy the official residence.

Ohio — The governor chooses not to live in the state-provided housing.

(f) Governor's staff:

Arizona — There are 29 members of the governor's executive staff, not including administrative staff.

Florida — There are 256 full-time employees. Those are broken into the following areas: Executive Direction and Support Services — 104 positions; Systems Development and Design — 48 positions; Office of Policy and Budget — 104 positions.

Georgia — Full-time employees — 56 and 2 part-time employees.

Louisiana — Full-time employees — 93, part-time (non-student) — 21, students — 25.

Maryland — Full-time employees — 85 and 1 part-time employee.

Montana — Including 16 employees in the Office of Budget and Program Planning.

Nevada — Currently 18. Maximum permitted is 23.

Oregon — Of this total, 45 are true governor's staff and 20 are on loan for agency staff.

Vermont — Voluntary 5 percent salary reduction.

(g) The Governor's office pays for access to an airplane or helicopter with a corporate credit card and requests a refund of those expenses with the corresponding documentation to the Dept. of Treasury.

(h) Provided for security reasons as determined by the state police.

(i) When not in use by other state agencies.

(j) Gov. Scott does not utilize a state-owned airplane, but instead uses his personal aircraft.

(k) Only for official business.

Table 4.4
THE GOVERNORS: POWERS

State or other jurisdiction	Budget making power — Full responsibility	Budget making power — Shares responsibility	Item veto power — Governor has item veto power on all bills	Item veto power — Governor has item veto power on appropriations only	Item veto power — Governor has no item veto power	Item veto — 2/3 legislators present or 3/5 elected to override	Item veto — majority legislators elected to override	Authorization for reorganization through executive order (a)
Alabama	★(b)		★				★	★
Alaska	★			★		★		★
Arizona	★(b)			★			(c)	. . .
Arkansas		★		★			★	★
California	★(b)			★		★		★(d)
Colorado		★		★		★		★
Connecticut		★	★			★		★(e)
Delaware	★(b)		★			★		★
Florida		★		★		★		★
Georgia	★			★		(c)		★
Hawaii	★(x)(f)			★		★		★
Idaho	★		★			★		★
Illinois		★	★			★		★
Indiana		★			★			★
Iowa	★			★		★		★
Kansas	★		★			★		★
Kentucky	★(b)			★		★		★
Louisiana	★	★		★			★(g)	★(h)
Maine	★		★				★	★
Maryland	★			★		★		★
Massachusetts	★		★				★(g)	★(d)
Michigan	★(i)			★(j)		★(g)		★
Minnesota		★		★			★(g)	★(l)
Mississippi		★(k)		★		★		★
Missouri	★(b)			★		★		★
Montana	★			★		★(g)		★(m)
Nebraska	★			★		★(n)		★
Nevada	★(b)				★			★(o)
New Hampshire	★(b)				★			. . .
New Jersey	★(b)			★			★(g)	★(p)
New Mexico	★			★		★		★
New York	★	★	★			★		★
North Carolina		★			★			★
North Dakota	★	★		★		★		★(q)
Ohio	★	★		★		★		★
Oklahoma		★		★			★(g)	★(r)
Oregon	★			★		★		★
Pennsylvania		★		★		★		. . .
Rhode Island		★			★			★
South Carolina		★		★		★		. . .

See footnotes at end of table.

THE GOVERNORS: POWERS—Continued

State or other jurisdiction	Budget making power — Full responsibility	Shares responsibility	Governor has item veto power on all bills	Governor has item veto power on appropriations only	Item veto power — Governor has no item veto power	Item veto— 2/3 legislators present or 3/5 elected to override	Item veto— majority legislators elected to override	Authorization for reorganization through executive order (a)
South Dakota	★	...	...	★	...	★(s)	...	★
Tennessee	...	★	...	★	...	...	★	★
Texas	...	★	...	★	...	★	...	...
Utah	★	...	...	...	★	★	...	★
Vermont	...	...	...	★	...	...	...	★
Virginia	★	...	★(t)	...	...	★	...	★
Washington	★	...	★(t)	...	...	★	...	...
West Virginia	★	...	...	★	...	★	...	...
Wisconsin	★(b)	...	...	★(u)	...	★	...	...
Wyoming	...	★	★	...	...	★	...	...
American Samoa	★	★	★	...	...	...	...	★
Guam	...	...	★	...	...	★	...	★
No. Mariana Islands	...	★	...	★	...	★	...	...
Puerto Rico	...	★	...	★	...	★	...	★(v)
U.S. Virgin Islands	★	...	★	★	...	...	...	★

Source: The Council of State Governments' survey of governors' offices, December 2014.

Key:

★ — Yes; provision for.

... — No; not applicable.

(a) For additional information on executive orders, see Table 4.5.

(b) Full responsibility to propose; legislature adopts or revises and governor signs or vetoes.

(c) 2/3 of members to which each house is entitled are required to override veto.

(d) Authorization for reorganization provided for in state constitution.

(e) Governor cannot create a budgeted agency but may "direct such action by the several budgeted agencies as will, in his judgment, effect efficiency and economy in the conduct of the affairs of the state government."

(f) Governor must list objections.

(g) 2/3 of elected legislators of each house to override.

(h) Only for agencies and offices within the Governor's Office.

(i) Governor has sole authority to propose annual budget. No money may be paid out of state treasury except in pursuance of appropriations made by law.

(j) Governor may veto any distinct item or items appropriating money in any appropriations bill.

(k) Governor has the responsibility of presenting a balanced budget. The budget is based on revenue estimated by the Governor's office and the Legislative Budget Committee.

(l) Statute provides for reorganization by the Commissioner of Administration with the approval of the governor.

(m) The office of the governor shall continuously study and evaluate the organizational structure, management practices, and functions of the executive branch and of each agency. The governor shall, by executive order or other means within the authority granted to him, take action to improve the manageability of the executive branch.

(n) 3/5 majority required to override line item veto.

(o) Only as to commissions, boards and councils.

(p) Executive reorganization plans can be disapproved by majority vote in both houses of the legislature.

(q) Executive Order must be approved by the legislature if changes affect existing law.

(r) The governor has the authority, through state statute, to enact executive orders that create agencies, boards and commissions; and reassigns agencies, boards and commissions to different cabinet secretaries. However, in order for the continued operation of any agency created by executive order the state legislature must approve legislation that allows the agency to continue to operate; if not, the agency cannot continue operation beyond sine die adjournment of the legislature for the session.

(s) Requires 2/3 of legislators elected to override.

(t) Governor has veto power of selections for nonappropriations and item veto in appropriations.

(u) In Wisconsin, governor has "partial" veto over appropriation bills. The partial veto is broader than item veto.

(v) Only if it is not prohibited by law.

Table 4.5
GUBERNATORIAL EXECUTIVE ORDERS: AUTHORIZATION, PROVISIONS, PROCEDURES

State or other jurisdiction	Authorization for executive orders	Provisions — Civil defense disasters, public emergencies	Provisions — Energy emergencies and conservation	Provisions — Other emergencies	Provisions — Executive branch reorganization plans and agency creation	Provisions — Create advisory, coordinating, study or investigative committees/commissions	Provisions — Respond to federal programs and requirements	Provisions — State personnel administration	Provisions — Other administration	Procedures — Filing and publication procedures	Procedures — Subject to administrative procedure act	Procedures — Subject to legislative review
Alabama	S,I, Case Law	★	★	★						★		★
Alaska	C	★(a)	★(a)	(a)	★(a)	★(a)	★(a)	★(a)	★(a)	★		
Arizona	I	★	★	★	★	★	★	★		★		★
Arkansas	S,I, Common Law	★(a)	★(a)	★(a)	★(a)	★(a)	★(a)	★(a)	★(a)	★(b)		
California	I (q)	★	★	★	★	★	★	★	★		★	
Colorado	C	★	★	★	★	★	★	★				
Connecticut	C,S	★	★	★	★	★	★	★	★	(b)		
Delaware	C	★	★	★	★	★	★	★		(b)		★
Florida	C,S	★	★	★	★	★	★	★		★	★	
Georgia	S,I (d)	★	★	★	★	★	★	★		★		
Hawaii	C,S, Common Practice	★	★	★	★	★	★	★		★		★
Idaho	S	★	★	★	★	★	★	★		★		★
Illinois	C,S	★	★	★	★(limited)	★	★	★		★		★
Indiana	C,S, Case Law (f)	★	★	★								
Iowa		★	★	★	★	★	★	★	(g)	★		★(h)
Kansas	C,S	★	★	★	★	★	★	★	★(j)(k)(l)	★(b)	★	★
Kentucky	C,S	★	★	★(i)	★	★	★	★		★(b)	★	★(o)
Louisiana	C,S (m)	★	★	★	★	★	★	★			★	
Maine	I	★	★(a)	★	★	★	★	★				
Maryland	C,S	★	★	★	★	★	★	★	★(n)		★	★(o)
Massachusetts	C,S	★	★	★	★	★	★	★		★		
Michigan	C	★	★	★	★(p)	★	★	★	★(r)	★(p)		
Minnesota	S	★	★	★	★	★	★	★	(r)(bb)	★(b)		
Mississippi	C,S, Common Law	★	★	★	★	★	★	★		(s)	(s)	★(o)
Missouri	C,S, Common Law	★	★	★	★	★	★	★	★(o)	★(o)		★(o)(t)
Montana	S,I, Common Law	★	★	★	★	★	★	★		★		
Nebraska	C,S	★	★	★	★	★	★	★			★	
Nevada	S,I	★	★	★	★	★	★	★		★		
New Hampshire	S	★(a)	★(a)	★	★	★	★	★	★(k)(u)	★(c)	★	★(o)
New Jersey	C,S,I	★	★	★	★	★	★	★	★(u)	★	★	
New Mexico	C,S	★	★	★	★	★	★	★		★		
New York	C,S	★	★	★	★	★	★	★		★		
North Carolina	C,S	★	★	★	★	★	★	★	★	★		
North Dakota	S,I	★	★	★	★	★	★		(l)(r)(u)(w)(x)(y)			★(v)
Ohio	S,I (z)	★	★	★	★	★	★	★		★		
Oklahoma	C	★	★	★	(aa)	★	★	★				
Oregon	I	★	★	★(n)(bb)(cc)(dd)	★	★	★	★	★(dd)	★	(s)	
Pennsylvania	C,S	★	★	★	★	★	★	★		★(b)(bb)		
Rhode Island	I, Case Law	★	★	★	★	★	★	★		★		★
South Carolina	S	★	★	★	★	★	★	★		★		

See footnotes at end of table.

GUBERNATORIAL EXECUTIVE ORDERS: AUTHORIZATION, PROVISIONS, PROCEDURES—Continued

State or other jurisdiction	Authorization for executive orders	Provisions								Procedures		
		Civil defense emergencies, public disasters	Energy emergencies and conservation	Other emergencies	Executive branch reorganization plans and agency creation	Create advisory, coordinating, study or investigative committees/commissions	Respond to federal programs and requirements	State personnel administration	Other administration	Filing and publication procedures	Subject to administrative procedure act	Subject to legislative review
South Dakota	C	★	★	★	★	★	★	★	★	★	…	…
Tennessee	S	★	★	★	★	★	★	★	★	★(b)	…	…
Texas	C,S,I	★	★	★	★	★	★	★	★	…	…	…
Utah	S,I	★	★	…	★	★	★	★	★	…	…	…
Vermont	S,I	★	★	★	★(ee)	★	★	★	★	…	…	★(ff)
Virginia	S	★	…	…	…	★	★	★	★	…	…	…
Washington	S	★	★	★	…	★	★	★	★	…	★	…
West Virginia	C,S	★	★	★	…	★	★	★	★	…	…	…
Wisconsin	C,S	…	…	…	…	★	★	★	★	★	…	…
Wyoming	(gg)	…	…	…	…	…	…	…	…	…	…	…
American Samoa	C,S	★	★	★	★	★	★	★	★	★(hh)	★(hh)	…
Guam	C	★	★	…	(ii)	★	★	★	★	★	…	…
No. Mariana Islands	C	★	★	★	…	…	★	…	★	…	…	…
Puerto Rico	C,S,I, Case Law	★	★	★	★	★	★	…	★	(jj)	…	…
U.S. Virgin Islands	S	★	…	★	★	★	★	★	★	…	…	…

Source: The Council of State Governments' survey of governors' offices, December 2014.

Key:
C — Constitutional
S — Statutory
I — Implied
★ — Formal provision.
… — No formal provision.

(a) Broad interpretation of gubernatorial authority. In Arizona, the governor is authorized to make executive orders in all of these areas and situations so long as there is not a conflicting statute in place.
(b) Executive orders must be filed with secretary of state or other designated officer.
(c) In addition to filing and publication procedures—Executive Orders are countersigned by and filed with the secretary of state and published.
(d) Implied from Constitution.
(e) Some implied.
(f) Constitution, statute, implied, case law, common law.
(g) Executive clemency.
(h) Only for EROs. When an ERO is submitted the legislature has 30 days to veto the ERO or it becomes law.
(i) To give immediate effect to state regulation in emergencies.
(j) To control administration of state contracts and procedures.
(k) To impound or freeze certain state matching funds.
(l) To reduce state expenditures in revenue shortfall.
(m) Inherent.
(n) To control procedures for dealing with public.
(o) Reorganization plans and agency creation.
(p) Executive reorganizations not effective if rejected by both houses of legislature within 60 calendar days. Executive orders reducing appropriations not effective unless approved by appropriations committees of both houses of legislature.

(q) Authorization implied from constitution and statute as recognized by 63 Ops. Cal. Atty. Gen. 583.
(r) To assign duties to lieutenant governor, issue writ of special election.
(s) Governor is exempt from the Administrative Procedures Act and filing and administrative procedures Miss. Code Ann. § 25-43-102 (1972).
(t) Reorganization plans and agency creation and for meeting federal program requirements. To administer and govern the armed forces of the state.
(u) To administer and govern the armed forces of the state.
(v) Must submit to the secretary of state who must compile, index and publish Executive Orders. Copies must also be sent to president of the Senate, speaker of House and principal clerk of each chamber.
(w) To suspend certain officials and/or other civil actions.
(x) To designate game and wildlife areas or other public areas.
(y) Appointive powers.
(z) Executive authority implied except for emergencies which are established by statute.
(aa) The governor has the authority, through state statute, to enact executive orders that: create agencies, boards and commissions; and reassigns agencies, boards and commissions to different cabinet secretaries. However, in order for the continued operation of any agency created by executive order the state legislature must approve legislation that allows the agency to continue to operate; if not, the agency cannot continue operation beyond sine die adjournment of the legislature for the session.
(bb) Filing.
(cc) For fire emergencies.
(dd) To transfer funds in an emergency.
(ee) Subject to legislative approval when inconsistent with statute.
(ff) Only if reorganization order filed with the legislature.
(gg) No specific authorization granted, general authority only.
(hh) If executive order fits definition of rule.
(ii) Can reorganize, but not create.
(jj) Executive Orders are filed in the Department of State.

Table 4.6
STATE CABINET SYSTEMS

State or other jurisdiction	Authorization for cabinet system				Criteria for membership			Number of members in cabinet (including governor)	Frequency of cabinet meetings	Open cabinet meetings
	State statute	State constitution	Governor created	Tradition in state	Appointed to specific office (a)	Elected to specified office (a)	Gubernatorial appointment regardless of office			
Alabama	★	★	★	★	★	...	...	23	Quarterly	...
Alaska	...	...	★	...	★	...	★	19	Gov.'s discretion	★(b)
Arizona	...	...	★	...	★	...	★	36	Monthly	...
Arkansas	...	...	★	...	★	...	...	47	Monthly	...
California	...	★	★	...	★	...	★	11	Every two weeks	...
Colorado	★	...	★	...	...	...	★	21	Monthly	...
Connecticut	★(k)	...	...	...	...	...	★	14	Gov.'s discretion	...
Delaware	★	...	...	...	★	...	★	19	Gov.'s discretion	...
Florida	★	★	...	...	...	★	...	4	Bi-weekly	★
Georgia	....(d)...									
Hawaii	★	...	...	...	★	★	...	22	Monthly	...
Idaho	★	★	...	...	...	...	★	39	Gov.'s discretion	...
Illinois	★	★	...	...	...	...	...	18	N.A.	...
Indiana	...	...	★	...	...	...	★	16	Bi-monthly	...
Iowa	★	★	★	★	★	...	...	30	Monthly	...
Kansas	...	★	...	...	...	...	★	14	Bi-weekly	...
Kentucky	...	★	★	...	★	...	★	10	Weekly	...
Louisiana	★	...	★	★	★	...	...	16	Monthly	...
Maine	...	★	...	★	...	...	★	16	Monthly	...
Maryland	★	...	...	...	★	...	...	25	Every other week	...
Massachusetts	...	★	...	...	★	...	...	10	Bi-weekly	...
Michigan	...	★	★	...	★	★	(e)	22	Gov.'s discretion	...
Minnesota	...	...	★	...	★	...	...	25	Quarterly	...
Mississippi	....(d)...									
Missouri	★	...	...	★	★	...	...	17	Gov.'s discretion	...
Montana	★	★	...	...	★	...	...	19	Monthly	★
Nebraska	...	...	★	★	★	...	★	30	Monthly	...
Nevada	...............................(d)...............................							21	At call of the governor	...
New Hampshire	....(d)...									
New Jersey	★	★	...	...	★	...	...	23	Gov.'s discretion	...
New Mexico	★	★	...	★	★	...	...	29	Gov.'s discretion	...
New York	...	...	...	★	...	...	★	75	Gov.'s discretion	...
North Carolina (f)	★	★	★	...	...	...	★	9	Monthly	...
North Dakota	...	...	★	...	★	...	★	18	Monthly	★
Ohio	★	...	...	...	★	...	...	24	Gov.'s discretion	★
Oklahoma	...	★	...	...	...	...	★	16 (h)	Monthly	...
Oregon	....(d)...									
Pennsylvania	★	★	★	...	★(i)	...	★	28	Gov.'s discretion	★
Rhode Island	...	...	...	★	...	...	★	24	Gov.'s discretion	...
South Carolina	★	★	...	...	★(i)	...	...	15	Monthly	★
South Dakota	★	★	...	...	★	...	...	19	Monthly	...
Tennessee	...	★	...	...	★	...	...	29	Monthly	...
Texas	....(d)...									
Utah	...	★	★	...	★	...	★	24	Monthly, weekly during legislative session	...
Vermont	★	★	...	...	★	...	...	12	Gov.'s discretion	...
Virginia	★	...	★	★	★	...	★(j)	15	Weekly	...
Washington	...	...	★	...	★	...	...	25	Monthly	...
West Virginia	...	...	★	★	★	...	...	10	Weekly	...
Wisconsin	...	★	...	...	★	...	...	16	Gov.'s discretion	★
Wyoming	...	...	★	...	...	...	★	20	Monthly	...
American Samoa	★	★	...	...	★	...	★	16	Gov.'s discretion	★
Guam	...	...	★	...	★	...	...	55	Bi-monthly	...
No. Mariana Islands	...	★	...	...	★	...	...	17	Gov.'s discretion	★
Puerto Rico	★	★	...	...	...	...	★	10 (c)	Every 6 weeks	...
U.S. Virgin Islands	★	...	...	...	★	...	...	21	Monthly	★

See footnotes at end of table.

STATE CABINET SYSTEMS — Continued

Source: The Council of State Governments' survey of governors' offices, December 2014.

Key:

★ — Yes

... — No

N.A. — Not available.

(a) Individual is a member by virtue of election or appointment to a cabinet-level position.

(b) Except when in executive session.

(c) The Constitutional Cabinet has 10 members including the governor. There are other members of the Cabinet provided by statute.

(d) No formal cabinet system. In Nevada, the cabinet is traditionally comprised of directors, chairpersons and leaders of Nevada's top agencies, departments, institutions and the National Guard, in addition to the lt. governor.

(e) Membership determined by governor. Some officers formally designated as cabinet members by executive order.

(f) The Governor's Cabinet consists of eight department heads who have responsibility for the majority of the executive branch. They are appointed by the governor and report to the governor. There are 10 members of the Council of State, a body of independently elected statewide officials who oversee certain areas of the executive branch.

(g) Frequency of meetings may fluctuate with governor's schedule.

(h) State statute allows for 15 cabinet members. With the governor included there are 16 members.

(i) With the consent of the Senate.

(j) Appointed by the governor and confirmed by each house.

(k) Governor's cabinet is specified in statute, but no longer in use. Governor directs department heads through commissioners' meetings and subject matter groups called clusters.

Table 4.7
THE GOVERNORS: PROVISIONS AND PROCEDURES FOR TRANSITION

State or other jurisdiction	Legislation pertaining to gubernatorial transition	Appropriation available to gov-elect ($)	Gov-elect's participation in state budget for coming fiscal year	Gov-elect to hire staff to assist during transition	State personnel to be made available to assist gov-elect	Office space in buildings to be made available to gov-elect	Acquainting gov-elect staff with office procedures and routine office functions	Transfer of information (files, records, etc.)
Alabama	...	...	★	●	●	●	●	●
Alaska	●	●	...	●	●	●	●	★
Arizona	...	...	★	...	●	●	●	●
Arkansas	●	10,000	...	...	...	...	...	...
California	★	450,000	★	★	★	★	●	●
Colorado	★	10,000	★	★	★	★	●	★
Connecticut	★	★	★	★	★	★	★	★
Delaware	★	15,000	●	★	●	●	●	●
Florida	★	(b)	●	★	●	★	●	●
Georgia	★	50,000	●	★	★	★	●	★
Hawaii	★	50,000	★	★	●	★	●	●
Idaho	★	15,000	★	★	★	★	★	★
Illinois	...	...	...	★	...	★	★	★
Indiana	★	40,000	...	...	...	★	★	★
Iowa	●	100,000	★	●	●	●	●	★
Kansas	★	150,000 (c)	★	★	★	★	★	★
Kentucky	★	200,000	★	★	★	★	★	★
Louisiana	★	65,000 ●	★	★	...	★	...	●
Maine	●	5,000	★	●	●	●	●	●
Maryland	★	●	...	★	★	★	★	●
Massachusetts	●	●	●	...	●	●	●	●
Michigan	●	$1.5 million ●	...	●	●	●	●	●
Minnesota	★	(e)	★	★	★	★	●	★
Mississippi	●	★(f)	★	★	★	★	★	★
Missouri	★	100,000	★	★	●	★	●	●(g)
Montana	★	★	★	★	★	★	★	★
Nebraska	★	85,288	★	...	★	★	★	★
Nevada	★	Reasonable amount	★	★	...	★	...	★
New Hampshire	★	75,000	★	★	★	★	★	...
New Jersey	★	★(j)	●	★	★	★	●	★
New Mexico	★	(k)	★	★	★	★	★	★
New York	...	...	...	...	★	★	★	★
North Carolina	★	★(l)	...	★	●	★	★	★
North Dakota	●	10,000	(m)	(n)	●	...	●	★
Ohio	★	Unspecified (o)	●	★	●	...	●	★
Oklahoma	●	●	★	●	●	★	●	●
Oregon	★	★	★	★	★	★	★	★
Pennsylvania	★	...	...	★	●	●	●	...
Rhode Island	★	Adequate funds	...	★	★	●	●	●
South Carolina	...	●	●	●	●	●	●	●
South Dakota	★	...	...	...	...	...	...	...
Tennessee	★	★	●	★	★	★	●	●
Texas	●	●	●	●	●	●	●	●
Utah	★	★(p)	★	★	★	★	★	★
Vermont	●	★(q)	★	...	★	...	...	...
Virginia	★	★(h)	★	★	★	★	★	★
Washington	★	★	●	★	●	★	●	●
West Virginia	...	●	...	●	...	●	●	●
Wisconsin	★	Unspecified	★	★	★	★	★	★
Wyoming	●	...	●	●	●	●	●	●
American Samoa	...	Unspecified	★(i)	★	●	●	★	●
Guam	★	(t)	...	...	★	★	★	●
No. Mariana Islands	★	Unspecified	...	★	★	★	★	★
Puerto Rico	★	...	★	★	★	★	★	★
U.S. Virgin Islands	★	100,000	...	★	★	★	★	★

See footnotes at end of table.

THE GOVERNORS: PROVISIONS AND PROCEDURES FOR TRANSITION — Continued

Source: The Council of State Governments' survey of governors' offices, December 2015.

Key:

... — No provisions or procedures.

★ — Formal provisions or procedures.

● — No formal provisions, occurs informally.

N.A. — Not applicable.

(a) Varies.

(b) Section 14.057, Florida Statute provides: Governor-elect; establishment of operating fund. — (1) There is established an operating fund for the use of the Governor-elect during the period dating from the certification of his or her election by the Elections Canvassing Commission to his or her inauguration as Governor. The Governor-elect during this period may allocate the fund to travel, expenses, his or her salary, and the salaries of the Governor-elect's staff as he or she determines. Such staff may include, but not be limited to, a chief administrative assistant, a legal adviser, a fiscal expert, and a public relations and information adviser. The salary of the Governor-elect and each member of the Governor-elect's staff during this period shall be determined by the Governor-elect, except that the total expenditures chargeable to the state under this section, including salaries, shall not exceed the amount appropriated to the operating fund. The Executive Office of the Governor shall supply to the Governor-elect suitable forms to provide for the expenditure of the fund and suitable forms to provide for the reporting of all expenditures therefrom. The Chief Financial Officer shall release moneys from this fund upon the request of the Governor-elect properly filed.

(c) Transition funds are used by both the incoming and outgoing administrations.

(d) Amount to be determined.

(e) 1.5% of amount appropriated for the fiscal year to the Governor's office.

(f) Miss. Code Ann. § 7-1-101 provides as follows: the governor's office of general services shall provide a governor-elect with office space and office equipment for the period between the election and inauguration. A special appropriation to the governor's office of general services is hereby authorized to defray the expenses of providing necessary staff employees and for the operation of the office of governor-elect during the period between the election and inauguration. The department of finance and administration shall make available to a governor-elect and his designated representatives information on the following: (a) all information and reports used in the preparation of the budget report; and (b) all information and reports on projected income and revenue estimates for the state.

(g) Activity is traditional and routine, although there is no specific statutory provision.

(h) Determined every 4 years.

(i) Can submit reprogramming or supplemental appropriation measure for current fiscal year.

(j) No specific amount — necessary services and facilities.

(k) Legislature required to make appropriation; no dollar amount stated in legislation.

(l) Governor receives $80,000 and lieutenant governor receives $10,000.

(m) Responsible for submitting budget for coming biennium.

(n) Governor usually hires several incoming key staff during transition.

(o) Determined in budget.

(p) Appropriated by legislature at the time of transition.

(q) Governor-elect entitled to 70% of Governor's salary.

(t) Appropriations given upon the request of governor-elect.

Table 4.8
IMPEACHMENT PROVISIONS IN THE STATES

State or other jurisdiction	Governor and other state executive and judicial officers subject to impeachment	Legislative body which holds power of impeachment	Vote required for impeachment	Legislative body which conducts impeachment trial	Chief justice presides at impeachment trial (a)	Vote required for conviction	Official who serves as acting governor if governor impeached (b)	Legislature may call special session for impeachment
Alabama	★	H	maj. mbrs.	S	★	majority of elected mbrs.	LG	★
Alaska	★	S	2/3 mbrs.	H	(c)	2/3 mbrs.	LG	★
Arizona	★(d)	H	maj. mbrs.	S	★(e)	2/3 mbrs.	SS	★
Arkansas	★	H	maj. mbrs.	S	...	2/3 mbrs.	LG	...
California	★	S	...	S	...	2/3 mbrs.	LG	...
Colorado	★	H	maj. mbrs.	S	...	2/3 mbrs.	LG	★
Connecticut	★	H	maj. mbrs.	S	★(f)	2/3 mbrs. must be present	LG	★
Delaware	★	H	2/3 mbrs.	S	★	2/3 mbrs.	LG	...
Florida	★	H	2/3 mbrs.	S	★(g)	2/3 mbrs. present (h)	LG (i)	★
Georgia	★(l)	H	...	S	★(e)	2/3 mbrs.	...	★(j)
Hawaii	★	H	2/3 mbrs.	S	...	2/3 mbrs.	LG	...
Idaho	★	H	2/3 mbrs.(k)	S	★	2/3 mbrs.	LG	★
Illinois	★	H	2/3 mbrs.	S	★	2/3 mbrs.	LG	★
Indiana	★(l)	H	2/3 mbrs.	S	...	2/3 mbrs.	LG	★
Iowa	★	H	maj. mbrs.	S	...	majority of elected mbrs.	LG	★
Kansas	★	H	(m)	S	★	2/3 mbrs.	LG	...
Kentucky	★	H	...	S	...	2/3 mbrs. present	LG	...
Louisiana	★	H	(n)	S	...	(n)	LG	★
Maine	★	H	2/3 mbrs. present	S	...	2/3 mbrs. present	PS	★
Maryland	★	H	maj. mbrs.	S	...	2/3 mbrs.	LG	★
Massachusetts	★	H	maj. mbrs.	S	...	2/3 mbrs.	LG	★
Michigan	★	H	maj. mbrs.	S	★	2/3 mbrs.	LG	...
Minnesota	★	H	maj. mbrs.	S	...	2/3 mbrs. present	LG	...
Mississippi	★	H	2/3 mbrs. present	S	★(r)	2/3 mbrs. present (s)	LG	(u)
Missouri	★	H	...	(t)	(t)	(t)	LG	...
Montana	★	H	2/3 mbrs.	S	★	2/3 mbrs.	LG	★
Nebraska	★(d)	S (v)	maj. mbrs.	(w)	(w)	(w)	LG	...
Nevada	★	H	maj. mbrs.	S	★	2/3 mbrs.	LG	...
New Hampshire	★	H	...	S	★	...	PS	...
New Jersey	★	H	maj. mbrs.	S	...	2/3 mbrs. present	LG	★(aa)
New Mexico	★	H	maj. mbrs.	S	★(p)	2/3 mbrs.	LG	★
New York	★	H	maj. mbrs.	S	★	2/3 mbrs. present	LG	★
North Carolina	★	H	2/3 mbrs.	S	★(x)	2/3 mbrs. present	LG	★
North Dakota	★(d)	H	maj. mbrs.	S	★	2/3 mbrs.	LG	...
Ohio	★	H	maj. mbrs.	S	...	2/3 mbrs. present	LG	...
Oklahoma	★	S	maj. mbrs.	H and S	★	2/3 mbrs. present	LG	★
Oregon			......(y)......					
Pennsylvania	★	H	...	S	...	2/3 maj. mbrs.	LG	...
Rhode Island	★	H	2/3 maj. mbrs.	S	★	2/3 maj. mbrs.	LG	★
South Carolina	★	H	2/3 mbrs.	S	★	2/3 mbrs.	LG	...

See footnotes at end of table.

IMPEACHMENT PROVISIONS IN THE STATES—Continued

State or other jurisdiction	Governor and other state executive and judicial officers subject to impeachment	Legislative body which holds power of impeachment	Vote required for impeachment	Legislative body which conducts impeachment trial	Vote required for conviction	Chief justice presides at impeachment trial (a)	Official who serves as acting governor if governor impeached (b)	Legislature may call special session for impeachment
South Dakota	★	H	maj. mbrs.	S	2/3 mbrs.	★	LG	★
Tennessee	★	H	maj. mbrs.	S	2/3 mbrs. (z)	★	PS	★
Texas	★	H (o)	maj. mbrs.	S	2/3 mbrs. present	...	LG	★
Utah	★	H	2/3 mbrs.	S	2/3 mbrs.	★(f)	LG	★
Vermont	★	H	2/3 mbrs.	S	2/3 mbrs.	...	LG	...
Virginia	★	H	maj. mbrs.	S	2/3 mbrs. present	...	LG	★
Washington	★(d)	H	maj. mbrs.	S	2/3 mbrs.	★	LG	...
West Virginia	★	H	...	S	2/3 mbrs.	★	PS	★
Wisconsin	★	H	maj. mbrs.	S	2/3 mbrs.	★	LG	...
Wyoming	★	H	maj. mbrs.	S	2/3 mbrs.	★	SS	★
Dist. of Columbia							...	...
American Samoa	(q)	H	2/3 mbrs.	S (p)	2/3 mbrs.	★	...	...
Guam				(p)				
No. Mariana Islands	★	H	2/3 mbrs.	S	2/3 mbrs.	...	LG	★
Puerto Rico	★	H	2/3 mbrs.	S	3/4 mbrs.	★	SS	
U.S. Virgin Islands				(p)				

Source: The Council of State Governments' survey of governors' offices, December 2014.

Key:

★ — Yes; provision for.
... — Not specified, or no provision for.
H — House or Assembly (lower chamber).
S — Senate.
LG — Lieutenant Governor.
PS — President or Speaker of the Senate.
SS — Secretary of State.

(a) Presiding justice of state court of last resort. In many states, provision indicates that chief justice presides only on occasion of impeachment of governor.

(b) For provisions on official next in line of succession if governor is convicted and removed from office, refer to Chapter 4, "The Governors."

(c) An appointed Supreme Court justice presides.

(d) With exception of certain judicial officers. In Arizona and Washington—justices of courts not of record. In Nevada—justices of the peace. In North Dakota—county judges, justices of the peace, and police magistrates.

(e) Should the Chief Justice be on trial, or otherwise disqualified, the Senate shall elect a judge of the Supreme Court to preside.

(f) Only if Governor is on trial.

(g) Except in a trial of the chief justice, in which case the governor shall preside.

(h) An officer impeached by the house of representatives shall be disqualified from performing any official duties until acquitted by the senate, and, unless impeached, the governor may by appointment fill the office until completion of the trial.

(i) Governor may appoint someone to serve until the impeachment procedures are final.

(j) Special sessions of the General Assembly shall be limited to a period of 40 days unless extended by 3/5 vote of each house and approved by the Governor or unless at the expiration of such period an impeachment trial of some officer of state government is pending, in which event the House shall adjourn and the Senate shall remain in session until such trial is completed.

(k) No person shall be convicted without the concurrence of two-thirds of there senators elected. When the governor is impeached, the chief justice shall preside.

(l) Judges not included.

(m) No statute, simple majority is the assumption.

(n) Concurrence of 2/3 of the elected senators.

(o) House votes on articles of impeachment; Senate presides over impeachment trial to remove official.

(p) Removal of elected officials by recall procedure only.

(q) Governor, lieutenant governor.

(r) When the governor is tried; if Chief Justice is unable to preside, the next longest serving justice shall preside.

(s) No person shall be convicted without concurrence of 2/3 of all senators present. Miss Const. 1890 Art. IV § 52.

(t) All impeachments are tried before the state Supreme Court, except that the governor or a member of the Supreme Court is tried by a special commission of seven eminent jurists to be elected by the Senate. A vote of 5/7 of the court of special commission is necessary to convict.

(u) It is implied but not addressed directly in Miss Const. 1890 Art. IV §§ 49-53.

(v) Unicameral legislature; members use the title "senator."

(w) Court of impeachment is composed of chief justice and supreme court. A vote of 2/3 present of the court is necessary to convict.

(x) Chief Justice presides if it is the Governor or Lieutenant Governor; otherwise, the President of the Senate presides.

(y) No provision for impeachment. Public officers may be tried for incompetence, corruption, malfeasance, or delinquency in office in same manner as criminal offenses.

(z) Vote of 2/3 of members sworn to try the officer impeached.

(aa) In the event of simultaneous vacancies in both the offices of Governor and Lieutenant Governor resulting from any cause, the President of the Senate shall become Governor until a new Governor or Lieutenant Governor is elected and qualifies.

Table 4.9
CONSTITUTIONAL AND STATUTORY PROVISIONS FOR
NUMBER OF CONSECUTIVE TERMS OF ELECTED STATE OFFICIALS
(All terms are four years unless otherwise noted)

State or other jurisdiction	Governor	Lt. Governor	Secretary of state	Attorney general	Treasurer	Auditor	Comptroller	Education	Agriculture	Labor	Insurance
Alabama	2 C	2 C	2 C	2 C	2 C	2 C	...	2 C	2 C	...	...
Alaska	2 C	2	(a)	...	(b)	...	...	...	...	...	...
Arizona	2 C	(c)	2	2	2	...	...	2	...	...	...
Arkansas	2 T	2 T	2 T	2 T	2 T	2 T	...	...	...	...	...
California	2 T	2 T	2 T	2 T	2 T	...	2 T	2 T	...	...	2 T
Colorado	2 C	2 C	2 C	2 C	2 C	...	...	...	...	...	...
Connecticut	N	N	N	N	N	...	N	...	...	...	...
Delaware	2 T	2 T	...	N	N	N	...	...	...	...	N
Florida	2 C	2 C	N	2 C	2 C (d)	...	2 C (d)	N	2 C	...	2 C (d)
Georgia	2 C	N	N	N	...	...	...	N	N	N	N
Hawaii	2 C	2 C	(a)	...	...	...	...	...	...	...	...
Idaho	N	N	N	N	N	...	2 C	N	...	...	...
Illinois	N	N	N	N	N	...	N	...	...	...	...
Indiana	2 (e)	N	2 (e)	...	2 (e)	2 (e)	(f)	...	...	...	...
Iowa	N	N	N	N	N	N	...	...	N	...	...
Kansas	2 C	2 C	N	N	N	...	...	...	...	...	N
Kentucky	2 C	2 C	2 C	2 C	2 C	2 C	...	...	2 C	2 C	...
Louisiana	2 C	N	N	N	N	...	...	N	N	...	N
Maine	2 C	(g)	...	...	...	...	...	...	...	...	...
Maryland	2 C	N	...	N	...	...	N	...	...	...	...
Massachusetts	N	N	N	N	N	N	...	...	...	...	...
Michigan	2 T	2 T	2 T	2 T	...	...	...	...	...	...	...
Minnesota	N	N	N	N	...	N	...	...	...	...	(h)
Mississippi	2 T	2 T	N	N	N	N	...	...	...	...	...
Missouri	2 T	N	N	N	2 T	N	...	...	...	...	...
Montana	2 (i)	2 (i)	2 (i)	2 (i)	...	2 (i)	...	2 (i)	...	...	...
Nebraska	2 C	2 C	N	N	2 C	N	...	...	...	...	...
Nevada	2 T	2 T	2 T	2 T	2 T	...	2 T	...	...	...	...
New Hampshire	N (j)	...	...	...	...	...	...	...	...	...	...
New Jersey	2 C	2 C	...	...	...	...	...	...	...	...	...
New Mexico	2 C	2 C	2 C	2 C	2 C	2 C	...	...	...	...	...
New York	N	N	...	N	...	N (k)	N	...	...	...	...
North Carolina	2 C	2 C	N	N	N	N	...	N	N	N	N
North Dakota	N	N	N	N	N	N	...	N	N	N	N
Ohio	2 C	2 C	2 C	2 C	2 C	2 C	...	...	...	...	...
Oklahoma	2 (l)	2 (l)	...	2 (l)	2 (l)	2 (l)	...	2 (l)	...	2 (l)	2 (l)
Oregon	2 (e)	(m)	2 (e)	N	2 (e)	...	...	...	...	...	...
Pennsylvania	2 C	2 C	...	2 C	2 C (n)	2 C	...	...	...	...	...
Rhode Island	2 C	2 C	2 C	2 C	2 C	...	...	...	...	...	...
South Carolina	2 C	2 C	N	N	N	...	N	N	N	...	...
South Dakota	2 C	2 C	2 C	2 C	2 C	2 C	...	2 C	...	...	...
Tennessee	2 C	(f)	...	(o)	...	...	...	...	...	...	...
Texas	N	N	N	...	N	(k)	...	N	...	N	...
Utah	N	N	(a)	N	N	N	...	...	...	...	...
Vermont	N (j)	N (j)	N (j)	N (j)	N (j)	N (j)	...	...	...	...	...
Virginia	1 C	N	...	N	...	...	...	...	...	...	...
Washington	N	N	N	N	N	N	...	N	...	...	...
West Virginia	2 C	N (g)	N	N	N	...	N	...	N	...	...
Wisconsin	N	N	N	N	N	...	...	N	...	...	...
Wyoming	2 (i)	(m)	N	...	N	N	...	N	...	...	...
Dist. of Columbia	N (p)	...	...	...	...	...	...	...	...	...	...
American Samoa	2 C	2 C	(a)	...	...	...	(q)	...	...	...	...
Guam	2 C	2 C	(a)	2 C	...	2 C	(r)	...	...	...	...
No. Mariana Islands	2 T	2 T	...	...	...	2 T	(q)	...	...	...	(h)
Puerto Rico	N	(m)	...	...	...	...	...	...	...	...	...
U.S. Virgin Islands	2 C	2 C	(k)	...	(c)	...	(c)	...	...	...	(a)

See footnotes at end of table.

CONSTITUTIONAL AND STATUTORY PROVISIONS FOR
NUMBER OF CONSECUTIVE TERMS OF ELECTED STATE OFFICIALS — Continued
(All terms are four years unless otherwise noted)

Source: The Council of State Governments, June 2015.

Note: All terms last four years unless otherwise noted. Footnotes specify if a position's functions are performed by an official under a different title.

Key:

N — No provision specifying number of terms allowed.

C — Consecutive Terms

T — Total Terms

. . . — Position is appointed or elected by governmental entity (not chosen by the electorate).

(a) Lieutenant Governor performs this function.

(b) Deputy Commissioner of Department of Revenue performs function.

(c) Finance Administrator performs function.

(d) Chief Financial Officer performs this function as of January 2003.

(e) Eligible for eight years out of any period of twelve years.

(f) State auditor performs this function.

(g) President or Speaker of the Senate is next in line of succession to the governorship. In Tennessee and West Virginia, Speaker of the Senate has the statutory title " Lieutenant Governor."

(h) Commerce administrator performs this function.

(i) Eligible for eight out of sixteen years.

(j) Two-year term.

(k) Comptroller performs this function.

(l) Limited to 8 years per office during a lifetime.

(m) Secretary of State is next in line to the governorship.

(n) Treasurer must wait four years before being eligible for the office of auditor general.

(o) Term is 8 years; attorney general is appointed by the state Supreme Court.

(p) Mayor.

(q) State treasurer performs this function.

(r) General services administrator performs function.

Table 4.10
SELECTED STATE ADMINISTRATIVE OFFICIALS: METHODS OF SELECTION

State or other jurisdiction	Governor	Lieutenant governor	Secretary of state	Attorney general	Treasurer	Adjutant general	Administration	Agriculture	Auditor	Banking
Alabama	CE	CE	CE	CE	CE	G	G	SE	CE	GS
Alaska	CE	CE	(a-1)	GB	AG	GB	GB	AG	L	AG
Arizona	CE	(a-2)	CE	CE	CE	GS	GS	GS	L	GS
Arkansas	CE	CE	CE	CE	CE	G	G	BG	CE	GS
California	CE	CE	CE	CE	CE	GS	...	G	GB	GS
Colorado	CE	CE	CE	CE	CE	GS	GS	GS	L	A
Connecticut	CE	CE	CE	CE	CE	GE	GE	GE	L	GE
Delaware	CE	CE	GS	CE	CE	GS	(c)	GS	CE	GS
Florida	CE	CE	GS	CE	CE	GS	GS	CE	L	CE
Georgia	CE	CE	CE	CE	B	G	G	CE	(d)	G
Hawaii	CE	CE	...	GS	GS	GS	...	GS	CL	AG
Idaho	CE	CE	CE	CE	CE	GS	GS	GS	...	(a-24)
Illinois	CE	CE	CE	CE	CE	GS	GS	GS	CL	GS
Indiana	CE	CE	CE	SE	CE	G	G	LG	CE	G
Iowa	CE	CE	CE	CE	CE	GS	GS	CE	CE	GS
Kansas	CE	CE	CE	CE	CE	GS	GS	GS	N.A.	GS
Kentucky	CE	CE	CE	CE	CE	G	...	CE	CE	G
Louisiana	CE	CE	CE	CE	CE	GS	GS	CE	GS	GS
Maine	CE	(e)	CL	CL	CL	GLS	GLS	GLS	L	GLS
Maryland	CE	CE	GS	CE	CL	G	GS	GS	N.A.	AG
Massachusetts	CE	CE	CE	CE	CE	G	G	CG	CE	G
Michigan	CE	CE	CE	CE	CE	GS	GS	GS	CL	GS
Minnesota	CE	CE	CE	CE	(a-24)	GS	GS	GS	CE	A
Mississippi	CE	CE	CE	CE	CE	GE	GS	SE	CE	GS
Missouri	CE	CE	CE	CE	CE	GS	GS	GS	CE	GS
Montana	CE	CE	CE	CE	GS	GS	GS	GS	CE	A
Nebraska	CE	CE	CE	CE	CE	GS	GS	GS	CE	GS
Nevada	CE	CE	CE	CE	CE	G	G	BG	...	A
New Hampshire	CE	(e)	CL	GC	CL	GC	GC	GC	...	GC
New Jersey	CE	CE	GS (f)	GS	GS	GS	...	BG	(g)	GS
New Mexico	CE	CE	CE	CE	CE	G	(a-26)	A	CE	N.A.
New York	CE	CE	GS	CE	GS	G	G	GS	(a-14)	GS
North Carolina	CE	CE	CE	CE	CE	A	G	CE	CE	G
North Dakota	CE	CE	CE	CE	CE	G	...	CE	CE	GS
Ohio	CE	CE	CE	CE	CE	G	GS	GS	CE	A
Oklahoma	CE	CE	GS	CE	CE	GS	GS	GS	CE	GS
Oregon	CE	(a-2)	CE	SE	CE	G	GS	GS	SS	...
Pennsylvania	CE	CE	GS	CE	CE	GS	G	GS	CE	GS
Rhode Island	SE	SE	CE	SE	SE	GS	GS	GS	LS	GS
South Carolina	CE	CE	CE	CE	CE	CE	B	CE	B	A
South Dakota	CE	CE	CE	CE	CE	GS	GS	GS	L	AB
Tennessee	CE	CL (e)	CL	CT	CL	G	G	G	(a-14)	G
Texas	CE	CE	G	CE	(a-14)	G	A	SE	L	B
Utah	CE	CE	(a-1)	CE	CE	GS	GS	GS	CE	GS
Vermont	CE	CE	CE	SE	CE	SL	GS	GS	CE	GS
Virginia	CE	CE	GB	CE	GB	GB	GB	GB	SL	B
Washington	CE	CE	CE	CE	CE	G	G	G	CE	G
West Virginia	CE	(e)	CE	CE	CE	GS	GS	CE	CE	GS
Wisconsin	CE	CE	CE	CE	CE	G	GS	GS	LS	A
Wyoming	CE	(a-2)	CE	GS	CE	G	GS	GS	CE	AG
American Samoa	CE	CE	(a-1)	GB	GB	N.A.	GB	GB	N.A.	N.A.
Guam	CE	CE	...	CE	CS	GS	GS	GS	CE	GS
No. Mariana Islands	CE	CE	...	GS	CS	...	G	...	GB	C
Puerto Rico	CE	...	GS	GS	GS	GS	...	GS	GS	GS
U.S. Virgin Islands	SE	SE	(a-1)	GS	GS	GS	GS	GS	GS	LG

Source: The Council of State Governments' survey of state personnel agencies and state websites, April 2015.

Key:
N.A. — Not available.
... — No specific chief administrative official or agency in charge of function.
CE — Constitutional, elected by public.
CL — Constitutional, elected by legislature.
SE — Statutory, elected by public.
SL — Statutory, elected by legislature.
L — Selected by legislature or one of its organs.
CT — Constitutional, elected by state court of last resort.
CP — Competitve process.

Appointed by:
G — Governor
GS — Governor..................Senate (in Neb., unicameral legislature)
GB — Governor ....Both houses
GE — Governor ....Either house
GC — Governor ....Council
GD — Governor.................Departmental board
GLS — Governor ....Appropriate legislative committee and Senate
GOC — Governor and Council or cabinet
LG — Lieut. Governor
LGS — Lieut. Governor......Senate
AT — Attorney General
ATS — Attorney General ...Senate
SS — Secretary of State

Approved by:

SELECTED STATE ADMINISTRATIVE OFFICIALS: METHODS OF SELECTION — Continued

State or other jurisdiction	Budget	Civil rights	Commerce	Community affairs	Comptroller	Consumer affairs	Corrections	Economic development	Education	Election admin.
Alabama	CS	...	G	G	CS	CS	G	(a-12)	B	CS
Alaska	G	GB	GB	(a-12)	AG	(a-13)	GB	(a-13)	GD	AG
Arizona	L	N.A.	B	N.A.	A	N.A.	GS	B	CE	(a-2)
Arkansas	AG	N.A.	N.O.	N.A.	N.O.	N.O.	B	GS	BG	B
California	(a-24)	...	...	GS	CE	G	GS	...	CE	G
Colorado	G	A	...	A	A	AT	GS	G	AB	CS
Connecticut	CS	GE	GE	GE	CE	GE	GE	GE	BG	CS
Delaware	GS	CG	(a-2)	...	CG	AT	GS	GS	GS	GS
Florida	G	A	N.A.	A	CE	A	GS	GS	B	A
Georgia	G	G	B	B	CE	G	GD	B	CE	A
Hawaii	GS	B	GS	...	GS	A	GS	GS	B	B
Idaho	GS	B	GS	...	CE	(a-3)	B	(a-12)	CE	(a-2)
Illinois	G	GS	GS	(a-12)	CE	(a-3)	GS	(a-12)	B	B
Indiana	G	G	G	G	(a-8)	AT	G	G	CE	(b)
Iowa	GS	GS	GS	A	...	ATS	GS	GS	GS	SS
Kansas	G	B	GS	C	C	AT	GS	C	B	(a-2)
Kentucky	G	B	G	G	CG	AT	G	GC	B	B
Louisiana	CS	B	GS	G	GS	A	GS	GS	BG	A
Maine	A	B	(a-17)	(a-17)	A	GLS	GLS	GLS	GLS	SS
Maryland	GS	G	GS	...	CE	A	GS	GS	B	B
Massachusetts	CG	G	G	G	G	G	CG	G	B	CE
Michigan	GS	B	GS	...	CS	...	GS	...	B	(b)
Minnesota	(a-24)	GS	GS	(a-17)	(a-24)	A	GS	GS	GS	(a-2)
Mississippi	GS	...	SE	A	(a-6)	A	GS	GS	BS	A
Missouri	AGS	B	GS	A	A	CE	GS	GS	B	SS
Montana	G	CP	GS	CP	CP	CP	GS	G	CE	SS
Nebraska	A	B	GS	A	A	CE	GS	GS	B	A
Nevada	(a-5)	G	G	...	CE	A	G	G	G	(b)
New Hampshire	GC	CS	GC	N.O.	AGC	AGC	GC	AGC	B	CL
New Jersey	GS	A	(a-17)	GS	GS	A	GS	G	GS	A
New Mexico	G	N.A.	(a-17)	N.A.	N.A.	AT	GS	GS	GS	CE
New York	G	GS	GS	GS	CE	GS	GS	GS	B	B
North Carolina	(a-24)	A	G	A	G	(i)	G	A	CE	G
North Dakota	A	G	G	...	A	AT	G	N.A.	CE	SS
Ohio	GS	B	GS	A	GS	A	GS	GS	B	CE
Oklahoma	A	B	GS	(i)	A	B	B	GS	CE	L
Oregon	A	A	GS	G	A	GS	GS	GS	SE	A
Pennsylvania	G	B	G	G	G	AT	GS	GS	GS	AG
Rhode Island	A	B	GS	...	A	SE	GS	GS (j)	B	B
South Carolina	A	B	GS	N.A.	CE	B	GS	(a-12)	CE	B
South Dakota	CP	CP	(a-44)	(a-48)	(a-40)	AT	GS	GS	GS	SS
Tennessee	A	G	G	G	SL	A	G	G	G	A
Texas	G	B	G	G	CE	(i)	B	G	B	(b)
Utah	G	A	GS	GS	AG	GS	GS	A	B	A
Vermont	CG	AT	GS	CG	CG	AT	CG	CG	GS	CE
Virginia	GB	AT	GB	GB	GB	A	GB	B	GB	GB
Washington	G	I	G	(a-12)	(a-10)	CE	G	(a-12)	CE	(a-2)
West Virginia	CS	GS	GS	B	(a-8)	(a-13)	GS	(a-13)	B	(a-2)
Wisconsin	A	A	N.A.	...	A	A	GS	CS	CE	B
Wyoming	AG	CS	GS	N.A.	(a-8)	SS	GS	(a-12)	CE	A
American Samoa	GB	N.A.	GB	(a-12)	(a-4)	(a-3)	A	(a-12)	GB	G
Guam	GS	...	GS	...	CS	CS	GS	B	B	GS
No. Mariana Islands	G	A	GS	GS	C	GS	C	C	B	B
Puerto Rico	G	N.A.	GS	N.A.	GB	GS	GS	GS	GS	N.A.
U.S. Virgin Islands	GS	GS	GS	GS	(a-24)	GS	GS	GS	GS	B

Appointed by:
C — Cabinet Secretary
CG — Cabinet Secretary........Governor
A — Agency head
AB — Agency head................Board
AG — Agency head................Governor
AGC — Agency head.............Governor and Council
AGS — Agency head.............Senate
ALS — Agency head..............Appropriate legislative committee
ASH — Agency head..............Senate president and House speaker
B — Board or commission
BG — Board ....Governor
BGS — Board ....Governor and Senate
BS — Board or commission....Senate
BA — Board or commission...Agency head
CS — Civil Service
LS — Legislative Committee..Senate

Approved by:

(a) Chief administrative official or agency in charge of function:
(a-1) Lieutenant governor.
(a-2) Secretary of state.
(a-3) Attorney general.
(a-4) Treasurer.
(a-5) Adjutant general.
(a-6) Administration.
(a-7) Agriculture.
(a-8) Auditor.
(a-9) Banking.
(a-10) Budget.
(a-11) Civil rights.
(a-12) Commerce.
(a-13) Community affairs.
(a-14) Comptroller.
(a-15) Consumer affairs.
(a-16) Corrections.

SELECTED STATE ADMINISTRATIVE OFFICIALS: METHODS OF SELECTION—Continued

State or other jurisdiction	Emergency management	Employment services	Energy	Environmental protection	Finance	Fish & wildlife	General services	Health	Higher education	Highways
Alabama	G	CS	CS	B	G	CS	CS	B	B	G
Alaska	AG	AG	(k)	GB	AG	GB	AG	AG	B	GB
Arizona	G	A	A	GS	(a-14)	B	A	GS	B	A
Arkansas	GS	G	N.O.	BG/BS	(a-6)	B	GS	BG	BG	BS
California	GS	GS	G	GS	G	G	GS	GS (b)	B (b)	(a-49)
Colorado	A	A	G	A	A	A	A	GS	GS	GS
Connecticut	GE	A	GE	GE	GE	CS (b)	GE	GE	BG	GE
Delaware	CG	CG	CG	(a-35)	GS	CG	CG	CG	B	(a-49)
Florida	G	GS	A	GS	CE	B	GS	GS	B	GOC
Georgia	G	A	CE	BG	G	A	A	A	B	B
Hawaii	A	CS	CS	CS	(q)	CS	GS	GS	B	CS
Idaho	A	GS	AGS	GS	GS	B	A	GS	B	(a-49)
Illinois	GS	GS	(a-42)	GS	(a-10)	(a-35)	(a-6)	GS	B	(a-49)
Indiana	G	G	LG	G	G	A	(a-6)	G	G	(a-49)
Iowa	GS	GS	GS	A	A	A	A	GS	...	A
Kansas	(b)	GS	B	C	N.A.	CS	GS	GS	B	(a-49)
Kentucky	AG	AG	AG	G	G	G	...	CG	B	CG
Louisiana	GS	A	CS	GS	GS	GS	GS	GS	B	GS
Maine	A	A	(a-38)	GLS	(a-6)	GLS	A	GLS	N.A.	(a-49)
Maryland	AG	A	G	GS	GS	...	(a-6)	GS	G	AG
Massachusetts	G	CG	CG	CG	G	CG	G	CG	B	G
Michigan	GS	CS	CS	GS	GS	(b)	GS	GS	...	(a-49)
Minnesota	GS	A	A	GS	GS	A	(a-6)	GS	B	GS
Mississippi	GS	GS	A	GS	(a-6)	GS	...	BS	BS	(a-49)
Missouri	A	A	G	A	AGS	(b)	A	GS	B	(a-49)
Montana	CP	CP	CP	GS	CP	GS	CP	GS	CP	GS
Nebraska	GS	A	GS	GS	(b)	A	A	GS	B	(a-49)
Nevada	A	A	G	A	(a-14)	GD	...	(b)	B	(a-49)
New Hampshire	G	GC	G	GC	(a-6)	BGS	GC	AGC	B	(a-49)
New Jersey	GS	A	A	GS	GS	B	(b)	GS	B	A
New Mexico	GS	(a-32)	GS	GS	GS	A	GS	GS	GS	A
New York	GS	GS	B	GS	CE	GS	G	GS	B	GS
North Carolina	G	G	A	G	G	G	G	G	B	A
North Dakota	A	G	A	A	A	G	A	G	B	(a-49)
Ohio	AG	GS	GS	GS	A (b)	A	A	GS	B	GS
Oklahoma	GS	B	GS	B	GS	B	GS	B	B	B
Oregon	AG	GS	G	B	(a-4)	B	(a-6)	A	B	A
Pennsylvania	G	AG	AG	GS	G	B	GS	GS	AG	AG
Rhode Island	G	GS	A	GS	GS	GS	GS	GS	B (b)	GS
South Carolina	A	B	A	(b)	B	B	A	GS	B	B
South Dakota	A	A	(a-42)	(a-35)	GS	GS	(a-6)	GS	B	A
Tennessee	A	G	A	G	G	B	G	G	B	(a-49)
Texas	A	B	...	B	(a-14)	B	B	BG	B	(a-49)
Utah	A	GS	A	GS	AG	A	A	GS	B	(a-49)
Vermont	AG	GS	GS	CG	CG	CG	CG	CG	...	(a-49)
Virginia	GB	GB	A	GB	GB	B	GB	GB	B	GB
Washington	A	G	(a-23)	G	G	G	(a-6)	G	N.A.	(a-49)
West Virginia	GS	GS	GS	GS	(a-6)	CS	C	GS	B	GS
Wisconsin	A	GS	A	A	A	A	GS	A	N.A.	A
Wyoming	G	GS	G	GS	N.A.	GD	AG	GS	GB	GS
American Samoa	G	A	GB	GB	(a-4)	GB	G	GB	(a-18)	(a-49)
Guam	GS	GS	G	GS	GS	GS	CS	GS	B	GS
No. Mariana Islands	G	C	C	G	GS	C	GS	GS	B	C
Puerto Rico	N.A.	GS	N.A.	N.A.	G	N.A.	GS	GS	N.A.	GS
U.S. Virgin Islands	GS	GS	GS	GS	GS	GS	GS	GS	GS	GS

(a-17) Economic development.
(a-18) Education (chief state school officer).
(a-19) Election administration.
(a-20) Emergency management.
(a-21) Employment Services.
(a-22) Energy.
(a-23) Environmental protection.
(a-24) Finance.
(a-25) Fish and wildlife.
(a-26) General services.
(a-27) Health.
(a-28) Higher education.
(a-29) Highways.
(a-30) Information systems.
(a-31) Insurance.
(a-32) Labor.
(a-33) Licensing.

(a-34) Mental health.
(a-35) Natural resources.
(a-36) Parks and recreation.
(a-37) Personnel.
(a-38) Planning.
(a-39) Post audit.
(a-40) Pre-audit.
(a-41) Public library development.
(a-42) Public utility regulation.
(a-43) Purchasing.
(a-44) Revenue.
(a-45) Social services.
(a-46) Solid waste management.
(a-47) State police.
(a-48) Tourism.
(a-49) Transportation.
(a-50) Welfare.

SELECTED STATE ADMINISTRATIVE OFFICIALS: METHODS OF SELECTION — Continued

State or other jurisdiction	Information systems	Insurance	Labor	Licensing	Mental health & retardation	Natural resources	Parks & recreation	Personnel	Planning	Post audit
Alabama	CS	G	G	...	G	G	CS	B	(a-12)	LS
Alaska	AG	AG	GB	AG	AG	GB	AG	AG	...	(a-8)
Arizona	A	GS	BS	...	B	GS	GS	A	(a-10)	...
Arkansas	GS	GS	GS	N.A.	A	G	GS	AG	N.A.	L
California	G	CE	AG	G	(b)	GS	GS	GS	...	...
Colorado	G	BA	GS	A	A	GS	A	A	G	(a-8)
Connecticut	GE	GE	GE	CS	GE (b)	CS	CS	GE	A	(a-8)
Delaware	GS	CE	GS	CG	CG (b)	GS	CG	CG	CG	(a-8)
Florida	N.A.	GOC	GS	A	A	GS	A	A	A	CE
Georgia	GD	CE	CE	A	BG	BG	A	GS	(a-10)	(a-8)
Hawaii	CS	AG	GS	CS	G	GS	CS	GS	CS	CS
Idaho	(a-6)	GS	GS	GS	...	B	B	GS	...	(a-14)
Illinois	(a-6)	GS	GS	(a-9)	(a-45)	GS	(a-35)	(a-6)	...	(a-8)
Indiana	G	G	G	G	A	G	A	G	...	G
Iowa	A	GS	GS	...	A	GS	A	A	...	...
Kansas	G	SE	GS	B	C	GS	CS	C	N.A.	L
Kentucky	G	G	G	...	CG	G	CG	G	G	CE
Louisiana	A	CE	GS	...	GS	GS	LGS	B	CS	CL
Maine	A	GLS	GLS	A	(a-45)	GLS	(a-35)	A	N.A.	N.A.
Maryland	A	GS	GS	A	A (b)	GS	A	A	GS	N.A.
Massachusetts	C	G	G	G	CG (b)	CG	CG	CG	G	CE
Michigan	GS	GS	GS	GS	CS	GS	CS	CS	...	CL
Minnesota	GS	A	GS	A	GS (b)	GS	A	(a-24)	N.A.	(a-8)
Mississippi	BS	SE	...	...	B	GS	GS	B	A	(a-8)
Missouri	A	GS	GS	A	BS	GS	A	G	AGS	CE
Montana	G	CE	GS	CP	CP	GS	CP	CP	G	L
Nebraska	GS	GS	GS	A	GS	GS	B	A	GS	(a-8)
Nevada	G	A	A	...	(b)	G	A	G	...	...
New Hampshire	GC	GC	GC	GC	AGC	GC	AGC	AGC	...	(a-14)
New Jersey	A	GS	GS	...	A (b)	A	A	GS	A	...
New Mexico	GS	G	GS	G	...	GS	N.A.	GD	N.A.	(a-8)
New York	G	GS	GS	(b)	(b)	(a-23)	GS	GS	GS	(a-14)
North Carolina	G	CE	CE	...	A	G	A	G	N.A.	(a-8)
North Dakota	G	CE	G	...	A	...	G	A	...	A
Ohio	G	GS	A	...	GS (b)	GS	A	A	GS	CE
Oklahoma	A	CE	CE	...	B	(a-48)	(a-48)	GS	...	...
Oregon	A	GS	SE	GS	A	GOC	B	A	...	SS
Pennsylvania	G	GS	GS	AG	G	GS	A	G	G	(a-8)
Rhode Island	A	A	GS	CS	GS	GS	GS	A	A	N.A.
South Carolina	A	GS	GS	GS	B(b)	B	GS	A	AB	B
South Dakota	GS	A	GS	...	GS	GS	A	GS	...	(a-8)
Tennessee	A	G	G	A	G	G	A	G	A	SL
Texas	B	G	B	B	B	B	B	...	G	L
Utah	GS	GS	GS	AG	AB	GS	AG	GS	G	(a-8)
Vermont	CG	GS	GS	SS	CG	GS	CG	CG	...	(a-8)
Virginia	B	B	GB	GB	GB	GB	GB	GB	(a-10)	(a-8)
Washington	G	SE	G	G	(a-45)	CE	G	G	(a-10)	N.A.
West Virginia	C	GS	GS	...	(a-27)	(a-25)	(a-25)	C	(a-17)	LS
Wisconsin	A	GS	GS	GS	A	GS	A	GS	...	(a-8)
Wyoming	GS	GS	AG	CS	AG	G	GS	AG	G	AG
American Samoa	(a-49)	G	N.A.	N.A.	(a-45)	AG	GB	A	(a-12)	G
Guam	GS	GS	GS	GS	GS	GS	GS	GS	GS	CE
No. Mariana Islands	C	CS	C	B	C	GS	C	GS	G	GS
Puerto Rico	N.A.	N.A.	GS	N.A.	N.A.	GS	GS	GS	GS	N.A.
U.S. Virgin Islands	G	SE	GS	GS	GS	GS	GS	GS	G	L

(b)
California—Health—Responsibilities shared between Director of Health Care Services and Director of Public Health, both (GS).

California—Higher education—Responsibilities shared between Chancellor of California Community Colleges (B) and California Postsecondary Education Commission (B).

California—Mental Health and Retardation—Responsibilities shared between Director of Mental Health (GS) and Director of Developmental Services (A).

Connecticut—Fish and Wildlife—Responsibilities shared between Director of Wildlife, Director of Inland Fisheries and Director of Marine Fisheries (CS).

Connecticut—Mental Health and Retardation—Responsibilities shared between Commissioner of Mental Health (GE) and Commissioner of Retardation (GE).

Delaware—Mental Health and Retardation—Responsibilities shared between Director, Division of Substance Abuse and Mental Health

Department of Health and Social Services (CG); and Director, Division of Developmental Disabilities Services, same department (CG).

Delaware—Social Services—Responsibilities shared between Secretary of Health and Social Services (GS); and Acting Secretary, Department of Services of Children, Youth and their Families (GS).

Hawaii—Finance—Responsibilities shared between Director of Budget and Finance (GS) and the Comptroller (GS).

Indiana—Election Administration—Responsibilities shared between Co-Directors.

Kansas—Emergency Management—Responsibilities shared between Adjutant General (GS) and Deputy Director (C).

Maryland—Mental Health and Retardation—Responsibilities shared between Executive Director, Mental Hygiene Administration (A); and Director, Developmental Disabilities Administration, Department of Health and Mental Hygiene (A).

Massachusetts—Mental Health and Retardation—Responsibilities shared between Commissioner, Department of Mental Retardation (CG);

SELECTED STATE ADMINISTRATIVE OFFICIALS: METHODS OF SELECTION — Continued

State or other jurisdiction	Pre-audit	Public library development	Public utility regulation	Purchasing	Revenue	Social services	Solid waste mgmt.	State police	Tourism	Transportation	Welfare
Alabama	(a-14)	B	SE	CS	G	B	CS	G	G	(a-29)	(a-45)
Alaska	...	AG	GB	AG	GB	GB	AG	AG	AG	GB	AG
Arizona	N.A.	SS	B	A	GS	GS	A	GS	GS	GS	GS
Arkansas	N.A.	B	GS	AG	AG	GS	N.A.	BG	AG	BS	(a-45)
California	(a-14)	...	GS	(a-26)	BS	BS	G	GS	...	GS	AG
Colorado	(a-14)	BA	CS	CS	GS	GS	CS	A	CS	GS	GS
Connecticut	CE	CS	GB	CS	GE	GE	CS	GE	GE	GE	GE
Delaware	(a-8)	CG	CG	(a-26)	G	GS (b)	B	CG	CG	GS	CG
Florida	CE	A	B	A	GOC	GS	A	GOC	N.A.	GS	A
Georgia	(a-8)	AB	CE	A	GS	GD	A	BG	A	A	A
Hawaii	CS	B	GS	GS	GS	GS	CS	...	B	GS	CS
Idaho	(a-14)	B	GS	(a-6)	GS	(a-27)	...	GS	GS	B	A
Illinois	(a-14)	SS	GS	(a-6)	GS	GS	(a-23)	GS	(a-12)	GS	GS
Indiana	CE	G	G	A	G	G	A	G	LG	G	(a-45)
Iowa	CS	B	GS	A	GS	GS	CS	GS	CS	GS	A
Kansas	CS	GS	B	C	GS	GS	C	GS	C	GS	C
Kentucky	...	G	G	G	G	G	AG	G	G	G	(a-45)
Louisiana	A	BGS	BS	A	GS	GS	GS	GS	LGS	GS	GS
Maine	(a-14)	B	G	CS	A	GLS	CS	A/GLS	(a-17)	GLS	(a-45)
Maryland	A	A	GS	A	A	GS	A	GS	A	GS	(a-45)
Massachusetts	CE	B	G	CG	CG	CG	CG	CG	CG	G	CG
Michigan	...	...	GS	CS	CS	GS	CS	GS	...	GS	GS
Minnesota	(a-8)	N.A.	G (b)	A	GS	GS (b)	GS	A	A	GS	GS (b)
Mississippi	(a-8)	B	GS	A	GS	GS	A	GS	A	B	GS
Missouri	A	B	GS	A	GS	GS	A	GS	A	B	A
Montana	L	CP	CE	CP	GS	GS	GS	CP	CP	GS	GS
Nebraska	A	B	B	A	GS	GS	A	GS	B	GS	GS
Nevada	...	(b)	G	A	G	G	...	GD	B	B	(b)
New Hampshire	(a-14)	AGC	GC	CS	GC	GC	AGC	AGC	AGC	GC	AGC
New Jersey	...	...	GS	GS	A	GS	A	GS	A	GS	A
New Mexico	N.A.	N.A.	G	N.A.	GS	N.A.	N.A.	GS	GS	GS	N.A.
New York	CE	B	GS	G	GS	GS	GS	GS	GS	GS	GS
North Carolina	(a-8)	A	G	A	G	A	A	G	A	G	A
North Dakota	...	...	CE	A	CE	G	A	G	G	G	G
Ohio	GS	B	BG	A	GS	(b)	A	GS	LG	A	GS
Oklahoma	A	B	(b)	A	GS	GS	A	A	B	B	GS
Oregon	(a-10)	B	GS	A	GS	GS	B	GS	A	GS	GS
Pennsylvania	(a-4)	G	GS	AG	GS	GS	AG	GS	A	GS	GS
Rhode Island	(a-14)	A	GS	A	GS	GS (b)	(h)	G	GS (j)	GS	GS
South Carolina	(a-14)	B	B	A	GS	GS	BS	B	GS	GS	GS
South Dakota	CE	A	CE	A	GS	GS	A	A	GS	GS	(a-45)
Tennessee	A	A	SE	A	G	G	A	G	G	G	G
Texas	(a-14)	A	B	A	(a-14)	(i)	A	B	A	B	BG
Utah	AG	A	A	A	BS	GS	A	A	A	GS	GS
Vermont	(a-24)	CG	BGS	CG	CG	GS	CG	GS	CG	GS	CG
Virginia	(a-14)	B	(b)	A	GB	GB	(a-23)	GB	G	GB	(a-45)
Washington	(a-4)	(a-2)	G	(a-6)	G	G	G	G	N.A.	G	(a-34)
West Virginia	(a-8)	B	GS	CS	GS	(a-27)	B	GS	GS	(a-29)	(a-27)
Wisconsin	A	A	GS	A	GS	A	A	A	GS	GS	A
Wyoming	(a-8)	AG	G	CS	GS	GS	AG	AG	AG	(a-29)	(a-45)
American Samoa	(a-4)	(a-18)	N.A.	A	(a-4)	GB	GB	GB	(a-12)	(a-29)	N.A.
Guam	GS	(i)	GS	GS	GS	GS	GS	GS	B	...	GS
No. Mariana Islands	G	B	B	C	C	C	A	GS	GB	CS	A
Puerto Rico	N.A.	N.A.	GS	GS	GS	N.A.	N.A.	GS	GS	GS	N.A.
U.S. Virgin Islands	GS	GS	G	GS	GS	G	GS	GS	GS	GS	GS

and Commissioner, Department of Mental Health, Executive Office of Human Services (CG).

Michigan — Fish and Wildlife — Responsibilities shared between Director (GS), Chief of Fisheries (CS) and Chief of Wildlife (CS).

Michigan — Election Administration — Responsibilities shared between Secretary of State (CE); and Director, Bureau of Elections (CS).

Minnesota — Human/Social Services, Mental Health and Retardation and Welfare are under the Commissioner of Human Services (GS).

Minnesota — Public Utility Regulation — Responsibilities shared between the five Public Utility Commissioners (G).

Missouri — Fish and Wildlife — Responsibilities shared between Administrator, Division of Fisheries, Department of Conservation; Administrator, Division of Wildlife, same department (AB).

Nebraska — Finance — Responsibilities shared between State Tax Commissioner, Department of Revenue (GS); Administrator, Budget Division (A) and the Auditor of Public Accounts (CE).

Nevada — Election Administration — Responsibilities shared between Secretary of State (CE), Deputy Secretary of State (SS), Chief Deputy Secretary of State (A).

Nevada — Health — Responsibilities shared between Director of Health and Human Services (G) and Division Administrator, Health (AG).

Nevada — Mental Health and Retardation — Responsibilities shared between Director of Health and Human Services (G) and Division Administrator, MHDS (G).

Nevada — Public Library — Responsibilities shared between Director, Dept. of Tourism and Cultural Affairs (G) and Division Administrator of Library and Archives (A).

Nevada — Welfare — Responsibilities shared between Director of Health and Human Services (G) and Division Administrator, Welfare and Support Services (AG).

New Jersey — General Services — Responsibilities shared between Director, Division of Purchase and Property, Dept. of the Treasury (GS),

SELECTED STATE ADMINISTRATIVE OFFICIALS: METHODS OF SELECTION — Continued

and Director, Division of Property Management and Construction, Dept. of the Treasury (A).

New Jersey — Mental Health and Retardation — Responsibilities shared between Director, Division of Mental Health Services, Dept. of Human Services (A) and Director, Division of Developmental Disabilities, Dept. of Human Services (A).

New York — Licensing — Responsibilities shared between Secretary of State (GS) and Commissioner of State Education Department (B).

New York — Mental Health and Retardation — Responsibilities shared between Commissioner, Office of Mental Health, and Commissioner, Office of Mental Retardation and Developmental Disabilities, both (GS).

Ohio — Finance — Responsibilities shared between Assistant Director, Office of Budget and Management (A) and Deputy Director, same office (A).

Ohio — Mental Health and Retardation — Responsibilities shared between Director, Dept. of Developmental Disabilities (GS) and Director, Department of Mental Health (GS).

Ohio — Social Services — Responsibilities shared between Director, OH Dept. of Job and Family Services (GS), Superintendent of Dept. of Education (B), Executive Director of Rehabilitation Services Commission (B), Director of Dept. of Aging (GS).

Oklahoma — Public Utility Regulation — Responsibilities shared between General Administrator Public Utility Division, Corporation Commission (B); and 3 Commissioners, Corporation Commission (SE).

Rhode Island — Higher Education — This employee serves in a dual role as Commissioner of Higher Education and as the president of the Community College of Rhode Island.

Rhode Island — Social Services — This position is filled by two employees one, Stephen Costantino, is the Commissioner, Office of Health and Human Services; Sandra Powell serves as the Director of Human Services and reports to the Commissioner, Office of Health and Human Services.

South Carolina — Environmental Protection — Responsibilities shared between Commissioner (BS) and the Director (B).

South Carolina — Mental Health and Retardation — Responsibilities shared between Director of Disabilities and Special Needs (B) and Director of Mental Health (B).

Texas — Election Administration — Responsibilities shared between Secretary of State (G); and Division Director of Elections, Elections Division, Secretary of State (A).

Virginia — Public Utility Regulation — No single position. Functions are shared between Communication, Energy Regulation and Utility and Railroad Safety, all (B).

(c) Department abolished July 1, 2005; responsibilities transferred to office of Management and Budget, General Services and Department of State.

(d) Appointed by the House and approved by the Senate.

(e) In Maine, New Hampshire, Tennessee and West Virginia, the presidents (or speakers) of the Senate are next in line of succession to the governorship. In Tennessee and West Virginia, the speaker of the Senate bears the statutory title of lieutenant governor.

(f) The governor has assigned the role of secretary of state (GS) to the lieutenant governor, with no additional salary.

(g) The New Jersey State Constitution states: "The State Auditor shall be appointed by the Senate and General Assembly in joint meeting for a term of five years and until his successor shall be appointed and qualify." So it is a Constitutional Officer, but is appointed, not elected by the legislature.

(h) Solid waste is managed by the Rhode Island Resource Recovery Corporation (RIRRC). Although not a department of the state government, RIRRC is a public corporation and a component of the State of Rhode Island for financial reporting purposes. To be financially self-sufficient, the agency earns revenue through the sale of recyclable products, methane gas royalties and fees for its services.

(i) Method not specified.

(j) The Rhode Island Economic Development Corporation is a quasi-public agency.

(k) The authority is a public corporation of the state and a body corporate and politic constituting a political subdivision within the Department of Commerce, Community, and Economic Development, but with separate and independent legal existence.

Table 4.11
SELECTED STATE ADMINISTRATIVE OFFICIALS: ANNUAL SALARIES

State or other jurisdiction	Governor	Lieutenant governor	Secretary of state	Attorney general	Treasurer	Adjutant general	Admin.	Agriculture	Auditor	Banking
Alabama	$0 (d)	$69,503	$85,248	$168,002	$85,248	$91,014	$0	$84,655	$85,248	$157,380
Alaska	145,000	115,000	(a-1)	137,712	151,044	137,712	137,712	124,488	145,296	115,632
Arizona	95,000	(a-2)	70,000	90,000	70,000	146,000	165,000	105,040	141,986	124,950
Arkansas	87,759	42,315	54,848	73,132	54,848	117,506	155,626	N.A.	54,848	139,161
California	177,467	133,100	133,100	154,150	141,973	182,004	...	199,173	183,852	153,120
Colorado	90,000	68,500	68,500	80,000	68,500	146,040	146,040	146,040	140,000	128,004
Connecticut	150,000	110,000	110,000	110,000	110,000	162,617	160,000	118,000	(c)	138,535
Delaware	171,000	79,053	128,090	145,707	113,874	122,321	...	119,540	109,032	111,916
Florida	130,273	124,851	141,000	128,972	128,972	157,252	141,000	128,972	135,000	128,972
Georgia	139,339	91,609	130,690	137,791	181,250	186,157	145,000	121,557	159,215	136,788
Hawaii	146,628	143,028	...	143,028	143,028	221,672	(c)	136,212	136,212	112,752
Idaho	120,785	42,275	102,667	124,000	102,667	140,899	95,201	120,702	...	(a-24)
Illinois	177,412	135,669	156,541	156,541	135,669	109,463	142,339	133,273	149,005	135,081
Indiana	111,688	88,543	76,892	92,503	76,892	138,633	130,000	137,500	76,892	120,000
Iowa	130,000	103,212	103,212	123,669	103,212	173,270	154,300	103,212	103,212	113,300
Kansas	99,636	54,000	86,003	98,901	86,003	106,392	120,000	110,000	N.A.	105,000
Kentucky	151,643 (d)	118,217	118,217	118,217	118,217	139,456	...	118,217	118,217	127,260
Louisiana	130,000	115,000	115,000	115,000	115,000	193,398	204,402	115,000	132,620	145,000
Maine	70,000	(h)(e)	77,792	103,750	70,658	108,930	108,930	108,930	91,250	102,419
Maryland	150,000	125,000	87,500	125,000	125,000	130,560 (b)	138,374 (b)	130,050 (b)	...	117,751 (b)
Massachusetts	151,800	122,058	130,916	130,552	127,916	172,062	161,522	131,802	134,952	141,254
Michigan	159,300 (d)	111,510	112,410	112,410	174,204	123,036	169,125	150,000	163,200	145,000
Minnesota	123,427	80,226	92,581	117,270	(a-24)	171,413	144,435	144,435	104,195	122,720
Mississippi	122,160	60,000	90,000	108,960	90,000	124,443	140,174	90,000	90,000	137,720
Missouri	133,821	86,484	107,746	116,437	107,746	91,524	125,712	121,705	107,746	102,243
Montana	108,167	86,362	88,099	115,817	107,610	116,349	107,610	107,610	88,099	107,610
Nebraska	105,000	75,000	85,000	95,000	85,000	103,837	135,000	111,459	85,000	100,000
Nevada	149,573	63,648	102,898	141,086	102,898	117,030	127,721	117,030	...	97,901
New Hampshire	121,896	(e)	105,930	117,913	105,930	105,930	117,913	100,171	...	105,929
New Jersey	175,000	141,000	(a-1)	141,000	141,000	141,000	...	141,000	141,793	141,000
New Mexico	110,000	85,000	85,000	95,000	85,000	193,787	126,250	125,000	85,000	90,900
New York	179,000 (d)	151,500	120,800	151,500	N.A.	120,800	172,482	120,800	151,500	127,000
North Carolina	142,265	125,676	125,676	125,676	125,676	105,901	129,000	125,676	125,676	N.A.
North Dakota	125,330	97,295	99,698	147,996	94,148	190,524	...	102,418	99,698	117,372
Ohio	148,886	78,041	109,986	109,986	109,986	90,896	127,400	116,397	109,985	100,485
Oklahoma	147,000	114,713	140,000	132,825	114,713	172,062	85,000	87,005	114,713	151,907
Oregon	98,600	(a-2)	77,000	82,220	77,000	176,568	194,224	145,308	157,800	...
Pennsylvania (f)	190,823*	160,289*	137,392*	158,764	158,764	137,392*	152,666	137,392*	158,764	137,392*
Rhode Island (g)	129,210	108,808	108,808	115,610	108,808	94,769	149,512	(a-23)	140,050	101,598
South Carolina	106,078	46,545	92,007	92,007	92,007	92,007	185,517	92,007	104,433	104,134
South Dakota	107,121	(h)	85,629	107,009	85,629	109,272	98,345	102,907	115,348	97,525
Tennessee	184,632 (d)	62,652 (e)	190,260	179,640	190,260	158,556	190,260	158,556	190,260	158,556
Texas	150,000	7,200 (i)	125,880	150,000	(a-14)	143,340	...	137,500	212,850	237,000 (j)
Utah	109,470	104,000	(a-1)	98,509	104,000	104,686	119,891	113,048	104,000	116,667
Vermont	145,538	61,776	98,280	116,917	95,285	102,877	127,026	127,026	98,280	110,302
Virginia	175,000	36,321	155,849	150,000	162,214	132,890	156,629	160,394	173,530	157,538
Washington	166,891	97,000	116,950	151,718	125,000	172,062	147,012	125,400	116,950	125,400
West Virginia	150,000	(e)	95,000	95,000	95,000	125,000	95,000	95,000	95,000	75,000
Wisconsin	147,328	77,795	69,936	142,966	69,936	127,502	128,026	122,415	115,496	N.A.
Wyoming	105,000	(a-2)	92,000	153,614	92,000	131,429	146,656	N.A.	92,000	102,224
Guam	130,000	85,000	...	105,286	52,492	68,152	88,915	60,850	100,000	88,915
No. Mariana Islands	70,000	65,000	...	80,000	40,800 (b)	...	54,000	40,800 (b)	80,000	40,800 (b)
Puerto Rico	70,000	...	125,000	N.A.	N.A.	N.A.	N.A.	N.A.	N.A.	N.A.
U.S. Virgin Islands	150,000	75,000	(a-1)	76,500	76,500	85,000	76,500	76,500	76,500	75,000

Sources: The Council of State Governments' survey of state personnel agencies and state websites, February 2015.
Key:
N.A. — Not available.
... — No specific chief administrative official or agency in charge of function.
(a) Chief administrative official or agency in charge of function:
(a-1) Lieutenant governor.
(a-2) Secretary of state.
(a-3) Attorney general.
(a-4) Treasurer.
(a-5) Adjutant general.
(a-6) Administration.
(a-7) Agriculture.
(a-8) Auditor.

(a-9) Banking.
(a-10) Budget.
(a-11) Civil rights.
(a-12) Commerce.
(a-13) Community affairs.
(a-14) Comptroller.
(a-15) Consumer affairs.
(a-16) Corrections.
(a-17) Economic development.
(a-18) Education (chief state school officer).
(a-19) Election administration.
(a-20) Emergency administration.
(a-21) Employment Services.
(a-22) Energy.
(a-23) Environmental protection.

SELECTED STATE ADMINISTRATIVE OFFICIALS: ANNUAL SALARIES — Continued

State or other jurisdiction	Budget	Civil rights	Commerce	Community affairs	Comptroller	Consumer affairs	Corrections	Economic development	Education	Election admin.
Alabama	$177,266	...	$162,232	$91,014	$138,305	$72,686	$71,712	$91,014	$250,000	$72,686
Alaska	190,008	161,088	137,712	(a-12)	125,988	(a-12)	137,712	(a-12)	137,712	130,716
Arizona	N.A.	N.A.	250,000	N.A.	123,587	N.A.	168,000	250,000	85,000	70,000
Arkansas	101,077	N.O.	N.O.	N.A.	N.O.	N.O.	149,017	119,839	231,177	72,427
California	(a-24)	...	...	132,384	141,973	183,852	243,360	...	154,150	128,520
Colorado	156,465	124,572	...	137,280	126,540	124,728	150,000	150,000	225,000	117,600
Connecticut	152,626	110,000	170,000	187,000	110,000	127,500	160,000	170,000	185,000	132,804
Delaware	147,870	79,754	(a-2)	...	147,870	122,268	147,870	128,090	160,645	81,628
Florida	135,000	98,000	N.A.	116,000	128,972	103,583	160,000	141,000	276,000	97,250
Georgia	155,000	105,202	125,000	147,000	N.A.	130,000	149,000	169,500	127,500	86,700
Hawaii	143,028	101,688	136,212	...	136,212	109,728	136,212	136,212	200,000	80,004
Idaho	122,990	67,787	149,385	...	102,667	(a-3)	139,984	(a-12)	102,667	(a-2)
Illinois	150,000	115,613	142,339	(a-12)	135,669	(a-3)	150,228	(a-12)	203,445	121,648
Indiana	120,000	103,000	(a-17)	110,000	(a-8)	99,639	130,000	163,000	92,503	(c)
Iowa	136,500	97,460	105,000	98,592	121,284	128,890	147,846	154,300	147,000	108,550
Kansas	130,000	76,476	103,000	N.A.	115,000	90,000	125,000	108,529	170,000	(a-2)
Kentucky	146,216	123,713	139,244	114,609	106,152	86,928	94,258	250,000	227,250	77,735
Louisiana	136,261	85,634	320,000	78,000	204,402	106,080	136,719	320,000	275,000	115,003
Maine	92,206	70,803	(a-17)	(a-17)	95,846	98,488	108,930	108,930	108,930	89,523
Maryland	166,082 (b)	110,699 (b)	155,000 (b)	...	125,000	121,005 (b)	166,082 (b)	155,000 (b)	195,000	109,372 (b)
Massachusetts	120,000	134,688	161,522	145,000	176,624	145,000	150,000	161,522	161,522	130,916
Michigan	149,350	145,000	150,000	...	138,978	...	146,450	...	195,238	(c)
Minnesota	(a-24)	139,464	144,435	(a-17)	(a-24)	112,424	149,427	149,427	149,427	(a-2)
Mississippi	(a-6)	...	90,000	130,000	(a-6)	82,000	132,761	183,000	300,000	75,000
Missouri	103,525	81,305	121,200	104,838	96,746	116,437	121,705	121,200	187,776	91,044
Montana	107,609	79,441	107,610	70,298	104,510	75,092	107,610	102,743	104,635	95,550
Nebraska	153,071	85,932	125,000	95,000	106,120	95,000	179,999	145,000	210,000	89,383
Nevada	(a-6)	87,773	127,721	...	102,898	74,367	127,721	N.A.	124,908	(c)
New Hampshire	105,930	80,971	114,554	...	106,575	100,171	117,913	87,423	114,553	(a-2)
New Jersey	133,507	120,000	(a-17)	141,000	141,000	136,000	141,000	186,600	141,000	115,000
New Mexico	95,950	N.A.	123,725	N.A.	N.A.	83,891	123,725	123,725	126,250	85,000
New York	175,000	109,800	120,800	120,800	151,500	127,000	N.A.	1 (d)	N.A.	(k)
North Carolina	(a-24)	99,446	136,000	...	156,159	N.A.	N.A.	...	125,676	106,000
North Dakota	126,696	96,408	152,700	...	126,696	127,440	128,724	124,572	113,498	50,400
Ohio	150,405	96,408	121,950	90,002	150,405	76,502	127,400	128,502	192,504	109,986
Oklahoma	99,000	N.A.	126,508	N.A.	120,000	112,350	160,000	N.A.	124,373	105,665
Oregon	150,276	107,004	160,176	149,231	127,884	160,176	168,184	157,032	225,300	127,368
Pennsylvania (f)	165,008	135,609	155,365	129,605	144,861	123,600	152,657*	145,025*	152,657*	120,001
Rhode Island (g)	154,151	81,363	(a-9)	N.A.	119,343	(a-3)	145,644	185,000 (l)	203,000	137,573
South Carolina	128,060	N.A.	162,640	N.A.	92,007	106,762	154,879	(a-12)	92,007	90,281
South Dakota	69,080	46,446	(a-44)	(a-48)	(a-40)	54,020	109,272	126,756	113,097	53,000
Tennessee	142,476	116,964	180,000	180,000	190,260	...	158,556	180,000	200,004	121,560
Texas	150,000	98,400	...	142,430	150,000	128,670	260,000	151,500	215,000	(c)
Utah	138,715	94,515	133,619	65,998	(a-24)	(a-12)	122,345	130,041	225,014	105,830
Vermont	105,061	100,006	127,026	90,646	105,061	100,006	110,302	90,646	127,026	98,280
Virginia	162,470	80,558	163,642	128,772	162,344	110,514	153,000	288,995	202,419	106,080
Washington	(a-24)	104,491	151,704	(a-12)	(a-24)	(a-3)	163,056	(a-12)	127,772	(a-2)
West Virginia	98,616	N.A.	95,000	95,000	(a-8)	(a-13)	80,000	(a-13)	230,000	(a-2)
Wisconsin	126,228	97,933	...	...	N.A.	N.A.	127,514	...	121,307	107,112
Wyoming	130,000	79,674	140,000	N.A.	(a-8)	130,220	141,413	(a-12)	92,000	98,940
Guam	88,915	...	88,915	...	83,400	55,341	67,150	82,025	82,025	61,939
No. Mariana Islands	54,000	49,000	52,000	52,000	40,800 (b)	52,000	40,800 (b)	45,000	80,000	53,000
Puerto Rico	N.A.	N.A.	N.A.	N.A.	N.A.	N.A.	N.A.	N.A.	N.A.	N.A.
U.S. Virgin Islands	76,500	60,000	76,500	(c)	76,500	76,500	76,500	85,000	76,500	135,000

(a-24) Finance.
(a-25) Fish and wildlife.
(a-26) General services.
(a-27) Health.
(a-28) Higher education.
(a-29) Highways.
(a-30) Information systems.
(a-31) Insurance.
(a-32) Labor.
(a-33) Licensing.
(a-34) Mental health.
(a-35) Natural resources.
(a-36) Parks and recreation.
(a-37) Personnel.

(a-38) Planning.
(a-39) Post audit.
(a-40) Pre-audit.
(a-41) Public library development.
(a-42) Public utility regulation.
(a-43) Purchasing.
(a-44) Revenue.
(a-45) Social services.
(a-46) Solid waste management.
(a-47) State police.
(a-48) Tourism.
(a-49) Transportation.
(a-50) Welfare.

SELECTED STATE ADMINISTRATIVE OFFICIALS: ANNUAL SALARIES — Continued

State or other jurisdiction	Emergency mgmt.	Employment services	Energy	Environ. protection	Finance	Fish & wildlife	General services	Health	Higher education	Highways
Alabama	$124,200	$88,543	$97,766	$152,618	$177,266	$113,479	$97,766	$282,446	$206,184	$169,000
Alaska	129,156	112,992	180,000	137,712	130,716	137,712	(a-43)	137,712	320,000	168,684
Arizona	N.A.	115,861	63,000	141,750	(a-14)	160,000	121,800	N.A.	300,000	159,814
Arkansas	97,354	147,186	N.O.	132,250	(a-6)	137,729	132,473	217,603	168,129	170,300
California	183,852	153,120	140,016	183,852	183,852	157,704	139,092	(c)	(c)	(a-49)
Colorado	105,000	117,504	130,000	144,876	126,540	144,876	130,404	215,000	146,040	138,000
Connecticut	170,000	148,000	139,000	139,000	187,000	(c)	160,000	170,000	380,000	175,000
Delaware	91,215	96,566	98,570	(a-35)	147,870	99,040	108,671	170,483	109,801	(a-49)
Florida	141,000	141,000	N.A.	150,000	128,972	140,737	141,000	141,000	200,000	150,000
Georgia	122,004	88,456	116,452	175,000	148,000	113,000	N.A.	175,000	497,000	120,000
Hawaii	118,500	86,364 (b)	86,364 (b)	86,364 (b)	(c)	86,364 (b)	(a-14)	136,212	375,000	N.A.
Idaho	122,532	119,995	86,174	115,960	106,890	132,600	...	151,569	126,048	(a-49)
Illinois	128,920	142,339	(a-42)	133,273	(a-10)	(a-35)	(a-6)	150,228	150,000	(a-49)
Indiana	135,000	150,000	75,000	120,943	142,000	81,421	(a-6)	160,500	163,001	(a-49)
Iowa	112,070	147,000	(a-17)	119,704	124,946	124,946	124,946	133,900	...	155,709
Kansas	(c)	108,000	71,600	105,019	115,000	73,320	114,000	190,000	197,000	(a-49)
Kentucky	83,514	76,125	139,244	103,929	139,244	125,000	...	172,847	360,000	119,236
Louisiana	135,200	108,621	96,637	137,197	204,402	123,614	204,402	236,001	350,000	170,000
Maine	77,230	N.A.	(a-38)	108,930	(a-6)	108,930	95,846	115,877	N.A.	(a-49)
Maryland	127,500 (b)	116,485 (b)	130,050 (b)	(b)	166,082 (b)	...	(a-6)	166,082 (b)	127,500 (b)	159,858
Massachusetts	142,875	161,522	115,920	135,000	161,522	120,000	138,338	140,000	226,194	160,473
Michigan	150,000	132,600	115,260	150,000	149,350	(c)	...	151,000	...	(a-49)
Minnesota	154,398	N.A.	125,112	149,427	154,398	125,112	(a-6)	149,427	385,762	154,398
Mississippi	107,868	135,315	140,000	129,347	(a-6)	126,668	...	230,000	300,000	139,700
Missouri	98,483	94,510	101,000	104,011	103,525	(c)	96,746	121,709	172,205	170,076
Montana	91,925	105,164	103,445	120,528	104,510	107,610	93,786	107,610	303,143	(a-49)
Nebraska	103,837	105,506	100,000	122,700	(c)	104,262	110,142	152,645	177,000	146,370
Nevada	97,901	127,721	106,904	123,783	(a-14)	117,030	...	(c)	23,660 (d)	(a-49)
New Hampshire	105,930	105,930	80,971	114,554	(a-10)	100,171	(a-6)	100,171	79,664	(a-49)
New Jersey	132,300	N.A.	100,000	141,000	133,507	105,783	(c)	141,000	141,000	123,500
New Mexico	125,000	113,827	106,050	113,827	126,250	103,000	106,050	123,725	126,250	N.A.
New York	N.A.	N.A.	120,800	136,000	151,500	136,000	136,000	N.A.	N.A.	136,000
North Carolina	98,352	137,619	82,494	119,000	(d)	129,575	129,000	143,000	525,000	162,080
North Dakota	104,688	115,000	152,700	119,964	126,696	121,968	183,108	194,364	291,000	(a-49)
Ohio	100,901	127,400	128,502	127,920	(c)	104,270	85,010	141,170	159,515	127,400
Oklahoma	95,000	115,110	114,000	123,013	171,833	123,032	85,000	194,244	394,983	(a-49)
Oregon	107,004	160,176	141,432	145,308	(a-4)	145,308	(a-6)	168,156	165,372	157,789
Pennsylvania (f)	135,003	135,512	127,942	152,657*	165,008	(c)	145,025*	152,657*	N.A.	145,272
Rhode Island (g)	88,177	130,152	75,154	108,460	(a-44)	(a-23)	(a-6)	134,975	265,000 (c)	(a-49)
South Carolina	99,910	N.A.	111,055	(c)	185,517	129,877	116,000	154,879	150,480	153,010
South Dakota	82,089	65,317	(a-42)	(a-35)	131,127	113,643	(a-6)	117,420	356,378	100,247
Tennessee	N.A.	152,256	140,484	168,708	190,260	168,708	159,996	176,868	175,392	158,556
Texas	165,200	165,320	...	175,940	(a-14)	180,000	142,570	210,000	191,930	(a-49)
Utah	87,651	137,280	109,595	120,473	129,688	115,669	116,355	137,280	N.A.	(a-49)
Vermont	91,187	103,834	110,302	105,976	105,061	89,877	104,354	124,467	...	107,910
Virginia	120,383	153,000	94,248	179,117	165,592	135,547	152,104	191,465	187,960	198,450
Washington	172,062	151,704	145,000	145,000	163,056	141,012	147,012	144,324	N.A.	(a-49)
West Virginia	65,000	75,000	81,900	95,000	(a-6)	75,000	80,004	85,512	N.A.	120,000
Wisconsin	105,231	112,213	102,011	127,514	126,228	127,514	128,026	125,599	525,000	(c)
Wyoming	95,286	146,302	112,000	124,238	N.A.	143,427	112,500	194,488	165,000	150,130
Guam	68,152	73,020	55,303	60,850	88,915	60,850	60,528	74,096	195,000	88,915
No. Mariana Islands	45,000	40,800 (b)	45,000	58,000	54,000	40,800 (b)	54,000	80,000	80,000	40,800 (b)
Puerto Rico	N.A.	N.A.	N.A.	N.A.	N.A.	N.A.	N.A.	N.A.	N.A.	N.A.
U.S. Virgin Islands	71,250	76,500	69,350	76,500	76,500	76,500	76,500	76,500	76,500	65,000

(b) Salary ranges, top figure in ranges follow:

Hawaii: Employment Services, $124,596; Energy, $124,596; Environmental Protection, $124,596; Fish and Wildlife, $124,596; Highways,124,596; Information Systems, 124,596; Licensing, $118,680; Parks and Recreation, $124,596; Post-Audit, $124,596; Pre-Audit, $124,596; Solid Waste Management, $118,680; Welfare, $136,164.

Maryland: For these positions the salary in the chart is the actual salary and the following are the salary ranges: Adjutant General, $107,196–$143,270; Administration, $107,196–$143,270; Agriculture, $107,196–$143,270; Banking, $73,341–$117,751; Budget, $124,175–$166,082; Civil Rights, $86,161–$115,000; Commerce, $124,175–$166,082; Consumer Affairs, $78,233–$125,743; Corrections, $124,175–$166,082; Economic Development, $124,175–$166,082; Elections Administration, $86,161–$115,000; Emergency Management, $99,637–$133,112; Work-force Development, $92,640–$123,708; Energy, $99,637–$133,112; Environmental Protection, $115,356–$154,235; Finance, $124,175–$166,082; Health, $124,175–$166,082; Higher Education, $115,356–$154,235; Information Services, $124,175–$166,082; Insurance, $124,175–$166,082; Labor, $124,175–$166,082; Licensing, $86,161–$115,000; Mental Health shared duties, $143,767–$237,562 (actual, $211,632) and $92,640–$123,708 (actual, $120,870); Natural Resources, $115,356–$154,235; Parks and Recreation, $86,161–$115,000; Personnel, $99,637–$133,112; Planning, $107,196–$143,270; Pre-Audit, $92,640–$123,708; Public Library, $86,161–$115,000; Purchasing, $80,160–$106,940; Revenue, $92,460–$123,708; Social Services, $124,175–$166,082; Solid Waste Management, $86,161–$115,000; State Police, $124,175–$166,082; Tourism, $92,640–$123,708; Transportation, $124,175–$166,082; Welfare, $124,175–$166,082.

SELECTED STATE ADMINISTRATIVE OFFICIALS: ANNUAL SALARIES — Continued

State or other jurisdiction	Info. systems	Insurance	Labor	Licensing	Mental health	Natural resources	Parks & recreation	Personnel	Planning	Post audit
Alabama	$177,266	$91,014	$139,859	...	$152,618	$141,000	$100,198	$168,622	(a-12)	$241,695
Alaska	119,988	119,988	137,712	105,492	98,796	137,712	124,488	125,988	...	(a-8)
Arizona	115,500	115,500	132,372	...	110,000	N.A.	159,952	131,250	N.A.	...
Arkansas	136,000	130,820	128,850	N.O.	134,224	111,639	122,188	105,494	N.O.	183,603
California	175,000	141,973	183,852	153,000	(c)	183,852	135,000	167,004	...	...
Colorado	156,000	120,000	146,040	125,004	133,116	146,040	144,876	126,540	138,000	(a-8)
Connecticut	158,000	143,000	148,000	114,914	(c)	150,720	151,230	160,000	141,600	(a-8)
Delaware	160,645	109,032	119,540	106,500	(c)	128,090	99,039	118,252	95,658	(a-8)
Florida	N.A.	134,158	141,000	71,400	N.A.	150,000	114,000	111,000	116,000	128,972
Georgia	135,000	120,394	121,570	86,700	180,000	155,227	113,000	128,748	(a-10)	(a-8)
Hawaii	86,364 (b)	112,752	136,212	82,272 (b)	124,344	136,212	86,364 (b)	136,212	N.A.	86,364 (b)
Idaho	(a-6)	102,273	(a-21)	83,116	...	129,771	91,561	99,548	...	(a-14)
Illinois	(a-6)	135,081	124,090	(a-9)	(a-45)	133,273	(a-35)	(a-6)	...	(a-8)
Indiana	115,000	105,000	105,000	100,000	107,990	115,000	84,445	115,000	...	104,000
Iowa	137,197	106,623	112,070	...	124,130	128,890	(a-25)	124,405	...	...
Kansas	120,000	86,003	108,000	65,153	75,000	111,490	111,490	92,000	N.A.	115,296
Kentucky	137,865	101,220	139,244	...	120,336	101,220	112,110	139,244	150,206	118,217
Louisiana	150,000	115,000	137,000	...	230,090	129,210	45,652	133,827	112,227	N.A.
Maine	102,419	102,419	108,930	108,930	(a-45)	108,930	(a-35)	95,846	N.A.	N.A.
Maryland	166,082 (b)	(b)	158,974 (b)	100,581 (b)	(b)(c)	148,778 (b)	115,000 (b)	117,416 (b)	124,848 (b)	N.A.
Massachusetts	176,864	N.A.	110,363	122,035	(c)	161,522	143,872	157,678	161,522	(a-8)
Michigan	169,125	145,000	150,000	150,000	138,978	150,000	125,569	138,978	...	(a-8)
Minnesota	149,427	122,720	144,435	108,618	(a-45)	154,398	125,112	(a-24)	N.A.	(a-8)
Mississippi	173,209	90,000	...	...	165,223	129,347	126,668	119,657	97,128	(a-8)
Missouri	111,605	121,705	121,705	96,213	115,522	121,705	111,605	96,746	103,525	107,746
Montana	123,871	88,099	107,610	105,213	107,877	107,610	104,342	98,622	102,743	127,362
Nebraska	137,303	121,399	125,000	75,762	110,000	117,772	128,902	99,324	135,000	85,000
Nevada	117,030	117,030	97,901	...	(c)	127,721	107,465	107,465	...	...
New Hampshire	117,913	105,930	105,930	105,930	105,930	114,554	91,965	88,933	...	(a-14)
New Jersey	140,000	130,000	141,000	...	(c)	125,000	110,000	141,000	95,000	...
New Mexico	113,827	114,000	113,827	101,000	...	106,050	96,604	105,000	76,198	85,000
New York	163,200	127,000	N.A.	(c)	(c)	136,000	127,000	120,800	1	151,500
North Carolina	156,066	125,676	125,676	...	110,000	129,000	118,815	140,000	N.A.	125,676
North Dakota	158,892	99,696	96,408	...	110,052	...	107,052	108,000	...	109,800
Ohio	124,758	150,405	90,397	(m)	(c)	127,400	98,800	104,000	128,502	109,554
Oklahoma	160,000	126,713	105,053	...	173,318	126,508	126,508	120,000	...	...
Oregon	182,568	163,247	77,000	N.A.	150,276	N.A.	145,308	136,344	...	157,800
Pennsylvania (f)	150,006	137,392*	152,657*	N.A.	139,248	145,025*	135,609	154,661	145,018	(a-8)
Rhode Island (g)	137,604	(a-9)	(a-21)	(n)	143,206	(a-23)	(a-23)	146,165	115,891	N.A.
South Carolina	127,462	130,000	124,973	124,973	(c)	129,877	120,379	120,493	N.A.	101,361
\South Dakota	120,200	85,000	103,000	N.A.	103,809	109,272	90,690	109,272	N.A.	(a-8)
Tennessee	166,476	158,556	152,256	116,988	158,556	168,708	84,792	158,556	N.A.	(a-14)
Texas	180,285	175,000	165,900	175,000	200,000	175,940	180,000	...	150,000	(a-8)
Utah	133,619	112,153	104,686	116,355	122,013	130,042	113,568	117,250	(a-10)	(a-8)
Vermont	117,146	110,302	103,834	88,005	120,515	127,275	97,802	104,853	...	(a-8)
Virginia	160,650	156,848	124,225	135,000	175,000	155,849	144,276	141,689	162,470	173,530
Washington	151,704	116,950	148,500	141,552	(a-45)	124,050	124,224	163,056	(a-24)	N.A.
West Virginia	110,503	92,500	70,000	...	(a-27)	(a-25)	(a-25)	(a-17)	(a-17)	N.A.
Wisconsin	122,413	119,864	96,697	112,725	112,725	127,514	109,035	112,213	...	(a-8)
Wyoming	146,230	122,900	90,436	68,179	(c)	117,834	105,683	110,704	139,860	103,247
Guam	88,915	88,915	73,020	88,915	75,208	60,850	60,850	88,915	88,915	100,000
No. Mariana Islands	45,000	40,800 (b)	45,000	45,360	40,800 (b)	52,000	40,800 (b)	60,000	45,000	80,000
Puerto Rico	N.A.	N.A.	N.A.	N.A.	N.A.	N.A.	N.A.	N.A.	N.A.	N.A.
U.S. Virgin Islands	71,250	75,000	76,500	76,500	70,000	76,500	76,500	76,500	76,500	55,000

Northern Mariana Islands: $49,266 top of range applies to the following positions: Treasurer, Banking, Comptroller, Corrections, Employment Services, Fish and Wildlife, Highways, Insurance, Mental Health and Retardation, Parks and Recreation, Purchasing, Social/Human Services, Transportation.

(c) Responsibilities shared between:

California — Health — Responsibilities shared between Director of Health Care Services, $182,016 and Director, Department of Public Health $226,400.

California — Higher Education — Responsibilities shared between Chancellor of California Community Colleges, $208,548 and California Post Secondary Education Commission Director, $140,004.

California — Mental Health — Responsibilities shared between Director of Mental Health, $173,352 and Director of Developmental Services, $173,352.

Connecticut — Auditor — Responsibilities shared between John C. Geragosian, $158,676 and Robert M. Ward, $163,744.

Connecticut — Fish and Wildlife — Responsibilities shared between Director of Wildlife, $137,388, Director of Inland Fisheries, $121,558 and Director of Marine Fisheries, $136,328.

Connecticut — Mental Health — Responsibilities shared between Commissioner, Mental Health, $147,800 and Commissioner, Retardation, $150,000.

Delaware — Mental Health — Responsibilities shared between Director, Division of Substance Abuse and Mental Health, Department of Health and Social Services, $144,213 and Director, Division of Developmental Disabilities Service, same department, $115,419.

Delaware — Social Services — Function split between two cabinet positions: Secretary, Dept. of Health and Social Services : $147,870 and Secretary, Dept. of Svcs. for Children, Youth and their Families, $133,241.

SELECTED STATE ADMINISTRATIVE OFFICIALS: ANNUAL SALARIES — Continued

State or other jurisdiction	Pre-audit	Public library dvpmt.	Public utility reg.	Purchasing	Revenue	Social services	Solid waste mgmt.	State police	Tourism	Trans-portation	Welfare
Alabama	(a-14)	$95,000	$103,490	$95,359	$91,014	$140,000	$105,403	$149,000	$91,014	(a-29)	(a-45)
Alaska	...	130,716	130,716	102,084	137,712	(a-27)	107,616	137,712	125,988	137,712	125,988
Arizona	(a-14)	64,161	154,320	121,800	152,250	215,250	96,000	175,000	110,250	136,500	215,250
Arkansas	N.A.	109,715	125,493	101,078	138,534	161,037	N.A.	117,610	95,114	(a-29)	(a-45)
California	(a-14)	...	138,324	(a-26)	170,076	213,924	150,204	238,332	...	173,352	183,852
Colorado	(a-14)	112,543	114,948	99,600	146,040	150,000	136,488	135,000	100,000	151,840	150,000
Connecticut	(a-14)	134,640	137,686	140,844	170,000	170,000	139,395	170,000	133,900	175,000	170,000
Delaware	(a-8)	84,307	104,500	(a-26)	125,103	(c)	163,000	166,245	93,223	138,945	115,522
Florida	128,972	83,000	131,036	N.A.	129,000	140,000	114,013	134,875	N.A.	141,000	100,932
Georgia	(a-8)	N.A.	116,452	135,300	158,000	171,600	80,187	140,000	125,000	187,979	137,940
Hawaii	86,364 (b)	N.A.	118,500	116,172	136,212	136,212	82,272 (b)	...	N.A.	136,212	94,428 (b)
Idaho	(a-14)	96,636	95,899	(a-6)	88,908	(a-27)	...	117,707	(a-12)	178,942	121,305
Illinois	(a-14)	100,511	134,022	(a-6)	142,339	150,228	(a-23)	132,566	(a-12)	150,228	142,339
Indiana	76,892	...	114,902	80,000	123,720	165,000	97,929	135,910	90,000	137,500	(a-45)
Iowa	108,555	137,197	125,008	103,126	152,955	154,300	(a-23)	128,890	99,570	147,014	124,946
Kansas	80,829	85,000	99,292	114,000	107,990	105,000	86,965	91,017	82,961	110,000	N.A.
Kentucky	...	91,947	122,488	90,142	122,849	105,922	80,537	112,466	111,353	139,244	(a-45)
Louisiana	124,384	111,280	137,904	134,992	250,000	129,995	102,000	134,351	111,280	170,000	113,723
Maine	(a-14)	77,792	126,714	70,096	102,419	115,877	75,795	102,419	(a-17)	108,930	(a-45)
Maryland	110,000 (b)	115,000 (b)	150,000	(b)	120,026 (b)	(b)	114,167 (b)	166,082 (b)	114,444 (b)	166,082 (b)	(a-45)
Massachusetts	(a-8)	116,725	139,986	138,338	155,318	137,692	135,000	229,451	138,338	159,135	119,324
Michigan	...	...	140,000	136,071	125,709	151,000	119,808	150,000	...	146,450	151,000
Minnesota	(a-8)	N.A.	(c)	120,806	154,398	154,398	149,427	121,514	122,270	154,398	(a-34)
Mississippi	(a-8)	90,000	108,850	60,000	122,296	130,000	81,909	138,115	85,748	139,700	130,000
Missouri	96,746	85,344	106,625	96,746	121,705	121,704	73,225	108,768	95,950	170,076	98,784
Montana	127,362	96,264	98,125	93,786	107,610	107,610	120,528	102,775	93,340	107,610	107,610
Nebraska	106,120	101,598	115,267	110,142	117,772	200,000	73,297	113,838	83,847	146,370	200,000
Nevada	...	(c)	123,783	97,901	127,721	127,721	(a-23)	127,721	117,030	127,721	(c)
New Hampshire	(a-14)	91,965	111,687	75,410	117,913	121,896	100,171	105,930	91,965	117,913	100,171
New Jersey	...	...	125,301	130,000	128,000	(c)	108,128	132,300	90,000	141,000	127,200
New Mexico	90,228	N.A.	90,000	91,910	106,050	126,250	87,929	125,000	106,050	113,827	123,725
New York	151,500	N.A.	127,000	136,000	N.A.	N.A.	136,000	N.A.	1	136,000	N.A.
North Carolina	(a-8)	109,068	139,849	113,000	129,000	112,601	106,000	119,815	N.A.	136,000	N.A.
North Dakota	...	...	102,418	93,168	108,202	166,152	99,840	107,820	119,004	155,328	166,152
Ohio	150,405	99,902	124,509	85,010	127,400	(c)	81,037	130,000	100,006	99,341	127,400
Oklahoma	(a-14)	85,850	(c)	95,700	123,126	185,000	108,792	111,133	126,508	139,000	185,000
Oregon	(a-10)	108,660	149,667	97,044	152,508	176,568	N.A.	152,508	N.A.	176,193	176,568
Pennsylvania (f)	(a-4)	N.A.	145,241	130,015	145,025*	152,657*	127,942	145,025*	89,213	152,657*	152,657*
Rhode Island (g)	(a-14)	124,420	125,071	121,409	156,876	(c)	(o)	148,937	(a-17)	130,000	(a-45)
South Carolina	92,007	N.A.	171,683	112,602	139,167	154,879	162,578	153,010	120,379	156,220	(a-45)
South Dakota	85,629	77,167	99,864	57,429	103,809	108,150	96,198	100,247	102,881	109,272	(a-45)
Tennessee	135,384	126,840	152,256	N.A.	158,556	158,556	121,800	188,148	158,556	158,556	158,556
Texas	(a-14)	140,000	128,780	170,530	(a-14)	210,000	N.A.	183,500	118,100	273,000	260,000
Utah	(a-24)	113,256	107,256	(a-26)	75,587	123,219	115,544	116,355	112,855	158,121	(a-45)
Vermont	105,061	93,080	135,366	104,354	102,586	127,026	105,976	117,936	90,043	127,026	110,302
Virginia	162,344	144,276	(c)	120,000	148,144	147,000	179,117	173,897	164,305	163,642	147,000
Washington	(a-4)	(a-2)	128,160	(a-6)	145,000	163,056	(a-23)	151,704	N.A.	163,056	(a-45)
West Virginia	(a-8)	72,000	90,000	105,648	95,000	(a-27)	79,700	85,000	93,504	99,999	(a-27)
Wisconsin	(a-8)	116,410	120,002	100,485	122,925	124,457	109,035	107,806	110,175	127,512	102,013
Wyoming	(a-8)	99,942	125,145	72,868	121,407	136,795	111,600	120,056	133,326	(a-29)	(a-45)
Guam	88,915	55,303	1,200	88,915	88,915	74,096	88,915	74,096	88,591	...	74,096
No. Mariana Islands	54,000	45,000	80,000	40,800 (b)	45,000	40,800 (b)	54,000	54,000	70,000	40,800 (b)	52,000
Puerto Rico	N.A.	N.A.	N.A.	N.A.	N.A.	N.A.	N.A.	108,000	N.A.	N.A.	N.A.
U.S. Virgin Islands	76,500	53,350	54,500	76,500	76,500	76,500	76,500	76,500	76,500	65,000	76,500

Hawaii — Administration — There is no one single agency for Administration. The functions are divided among the Director of Budget and Finance, Director of Human Resources Development and the Comptroller.

Hawaii — Finance — Responsibilities shared between Director of Budget and Finance, $143,028 and Comptroller, $136,212.

Indiana — Elections Administration — Responsibilities shared between Co-Directors Brad King, $79,129 and Trent Deckard, $78,554.

Kansas — Emergency Management — Responsibilities shared between Adjutant General, $106,392 and deputy director, $72,000.

Maryland — Mental Health — Responsibilities shared between Executive Director of Mental Hygiene Administration, $211,632 and Director of Developmental Disabilities Administration, $120,870.

Massachusetts — Mental Health — Responsibilities shared between Commissioners Marcia Fowler, $155,407 and Elin M. Howe, $153,511.

Michigan — Elections Administration — Responsibilities shared between Secretary of State Ruth Johnson, $112,410 and Bureau Director Christopher Thomas, $125,709.

Michigan — Fish and Wildlife — Responsibilities shared between Chief of Fisheries, $115,803 and Chief of Wildlife, $114,897.

Minnesota — Public Utility Regulation — Responsibilities shared between five commissioners with salaries of $124,530 for each.

Missouri — Fish and Wildlife — Responsibilities shared between Administrator, Division of Fisheries, Department of Conservation, $101,352; Administrator, Division of Wildlife, same department, $85,368.

SELECTED STATE ADMINISTRATIVE OFFICIALS: ANNUAL SALARIES — Continued

Nebraska—Finance—Responsibilities shared between Auditor of Public Accounts, $85,000; Director of Administration, $153,071, and State Tax Commissioner-$117,772.

Nevada—Elections Administration—Responsibilities shared between Secretary of State, $102,898, Deputy Secretary of State for Elections, $107,465 and Chief Deputy Secretary of State, $117,030.

Nevada—Health and Welfare—Responsibilities shared between Director, Health and Human Services, $127,721 and Division Administrator, $123,783.

Nevada—Mental Health—Responsibilities shared between Director, Health and Human Services, $127,721 and Division Administrator, $123,783.

Nevada—Public Library Development—Responsibilities shared between Director, Department of Tourism and Cultural Affairs, $117,030 and Division Administrator, Library and Archives, $97,901.

New Jersey—General Services—Responsibilities shared between Acting Director, Division of Purchase and Property, Dept. of the Treasury, $130,000 (acting) and Director, Division of Property Management and Construction, Dept. of the Treasury, $120,000.

New Jersey—Mental Health—Responsibilities shared between Assistant Commissioner Lynn Kovich, Division of Mental Health Services, Dept. of Human Services, $128,000 and position of Deputy Commissioner Elizabeth Shea, Division of Developmental Disabilities, Dept. of Human Services, $128,000.

New Jersey—Social Services—Responsibilities shared between Commissioner, Department of Human Services, $141,000 and Commissioner, Department of Children and Families, $141,000.

New York—Licensing—Responsibilities shared between Commissioner, State Education Department and Secretary of State, Department of State, $120,800.

New York—Mental Health—Responsibilities shared between Commissioner of Office of Mental Retardation and Developmental Disabilities, and Commissioner of Office of Mental Health.

Ohio—Finance—Responsibilities shared between Assistant Director of Budget and Management, $134,056 and Deputy Director, Office of Budget and Management, $106,413.

Ohio—Mental Health—Responsibilities shared between Director of Dept. of Mental Retardation and Developmental Disabilities, $126,090 and Director, Dept. of Mental Health, $116,397.

Ohio—Social Services—Responsibilities shared between Director, Dept. of Job and Family Services, $127,400, Superintendent of Dept. of Education, $192,504, Executive Director of Rehabilitation Services Commission, $108,992 and Director of Dept. of Aging, $119,808.

Oklahoma—Public Utility Regulation—Responsibilities shared between three Commissioners, $116,713, $114,713 and $114,713 and General Administrator, $104,000.

Pennsylvania—Fish and Wildlife—Responsibilities shared between Executive Director of (Fish), $135,609 and Executive Director (Game), $135,609.

Rhode Island—Higher Education—Serves a dual role as Commissioner of Higher Education and as the President of the Community College of Rhode Island.

Rhode Island—Social Services—Responsibilities shared between Commissioner, Office of Health and Human Services, $141,828 and Director of the Dept. of Human Service, $129,627, and reports to the Commissioner, Office of Health and Human Services.

South Carolina—Environmental Protection—Responsibilities shared between Commissioner Catherine Templeton $162,578 (BS) and Director Alvin Taylor $129,877 (B).

South Carolina—Mental Health—Responsibilities shared between Director for Disabilities and Special Needs, $139,967 and Director of Mental Health, 166,692.

Texas—Elections Administration—Responsibilities shared between Secretary of State, $125,880; and Division Director, $122,390.

U.S. Virgin Islands—Community Affairs—Responsibilities for St. Thomas, $74,400; St. Croix, $76,500; St. John, $74,400.

Virginia—Public Utility Regulation—Functions shared between Communications, William Irby, $157,577; Energy Regulation, William F. Stephens, $157,538; Utility and Railroad Safety, Massoud Tahamtani, $154,629.

Wisconsin—Highways—Function currently split among various divisions, and the department is also currently going through a reorganization. The department secretary has overall responsibility.

Wyoming—Mental Health—Responsibilities shared between State Hospital, William Sexton, $150,000 and Life Resource Center, Richard Dunkley, $96,648.

(d) These individuals have voluntarily taken no salary or a reduced salary:

Alabama—Gov. Robert Bentley is not accepting his salary, $120,395 until the unemployment rate in Alabama drops.

Kentucky—Gov. Beshear takes a voluntary 10% cut in his salary.

Michigan—Gov. Rick Snyder returns all but $1.00 of his salary.

Nevada—Higher Education—Chancellor Dan Klaich—elected to receive a lower wage than authorized.

New York—Governor Andrew Cuomo has reduced his salary by 5 percent.

North Carolina—State Budget Officer Art Pope chose not to receive pay for performing the duties of State Budget Director.

Tennessee—Governor Haslam returns his salary to the state.

(e) In Maine, New Hampshire, Tennessee and West Virginia, the presidents (or speakers) of the Senate are next in line of succession to the governorship. In Tennessee and West Virginia, the speaker of the Senate bears the statutory title of lieutenant governor.

(f) The Pennsylvania entries with asterisks denote that 1.7 percent of the officeholders' salary is being repaid as part of the management pay freeze.

(g) A number of the employees receive a stipend for their length of service to the State (known as a longevity payment). This amount can vary significantly among employees and, depending on state turnover, can show dramatic changes in actual salaries from year to year.

(h) $63,654, Part-time

(i) Lieutenant governor receives additional pay when serving as acting governor.

(j) This agency is now a self-directed state agency.

(k) The statutory salary for each of the four members of the Board of Elections is $25,000, including the two co-chairs, Douglas A. Kellner and James A. Walsh.

(l) The Rhode Island Economic Development Corporation is a quasi-public agency.

(m) Numerous licensing boards, too many to list.

(n) Varies by department.

(o) Solid waste is managed by the Rhode Island Resource Recovery Corporation (RIRRC). Although not a department of the state government, RIRRC is a public corporation and a component of the State of Rhode Island for financial reporting purposes. To be financially self-sufficient, the agency earns revenue through the sale of recyclable products, methane gas royalties and fees for it services.

Lt. Governors Impact States

By Julia Nienaber Hurst

A well-structured office of lieutenant governor gives a state a competitive advantage and increases governance efficiency. Thorough succession laws contribute to smooth transitions of governance when needed. Lieutenant governors impact states every day in all issue areas and by leading parts of government. Governors, lieutenant governors and legislators have roles to ensure the office of lieutenant governor is positioned to propel a state forward.

Lieutenant governors play a vital role in state government beyond gubernatorial succession. Many preside over state senates, lead divisions of government or sit on the governor's cabinets. All are the second-highest ranking official of their state or territory and succeed to governor if the office is vacated.

While roles beyond succession vary, the nation's lieutenant governors directly impact states in profound ways. The design of the office of lieutenant governor—from the method by which a lieutenant governor is elected to the official's portfolio of work—can give a state a competitive advantage and make states more efficient and effective.

Higher Office

Every lieutenant governor shares one common duty —the responsibility to succeed to governor should a vacancy occur. Federal directives say continuity of government planning, including gubernatorial succession, is an essential security objective for states. Between Jan. 1, 2000, and Dec. 31, 2009, 22 gubernatorial successions occurred. Yet, gaps in succession law exist and can reduce the efficiency of the office of lieutenant governor for a state.

A gubernatorial succession statute should ensure a sufficiently deep and clearly delineated line of succession, clarity on transition resources for successors, a thorough definition of incapacity covering location, physicality, functionality and temporary incapacitation; and congruous succession plans in cases of impeachment and recall. Incapacity may occur when a governor leaves the state, leaves the country, is in a war zone, is unconscious, is too physically ill to perform duties; or is unwilling, unable or ill-advised to perform certain required duties. In 2008, for example, the Illinois state attorney general queried whether former-Gov. Rod Blagojevich should be ruled "temporarily incapacitated'" so he could not appoint a U.S. senator after he was arrested for corruption regarding the appointment.

As of March 1, 2015, nine sitting governors had served first as lieutenant governor or as first in line of gubernatorial succession, including the governors of Iowa, Kentucky, Mississippi, North Dakota, Oklahoma, South Dakota, Utah and West Virginia. National Lieutenant Governors Association (NLGA) research shows the office of lieutenant governor has a greater success rate of its occupants becoming governor than any other local, state or Congressional office. In 2010, the University of Virginia Center for Politics found that in the past quarter-century, twice as many lieutenant governors than attorneys general became governor. The office of lieutenant governor is unquestionably a successful springboard to higher office.

Work Portfolios

In daily service, lieutenant governors impact states and territories in all areas, from economic development and public health to education and intergovernmental affairs. More than half the nation's seconds-in-command have powers in both the legislative and executive branches by presiding over state senates. The office of lieutenant governor may derive duties from the constitution, the governor, the legislature or through personal initiative. This makes the office of lieutenant governor a robust office that can be shaped to advance a state's competitiveness and aid its efficiency and effectiveness. The following is a snapshot of some duties performed by various lieutenant governors.

Economic Development

By statute, Washington Lt. Gov. Brad Owen chairs the bicameral Legislative Committee on Economic Development and International Relations. The Louisiana lieutenant governor directs the Department of Culture, Recreation and Tourism, industries that account for more than 1 in every 10 jobs in that state. Nevada Lt. Gov. Mark Hutchison chairs the Commission on Tourism, is vice chair of the state board of transportation and is a member of the

Governor's Office of Economic Development. Several lieutenant governors focus on small business. Rhode Island Lt. Gov. Dan McKee chairs the Small Business Advocacy Council and Oklahoma Lt. Gov. Todd Lamb is the state Small Business Advocate, as designated by the governor. Others promote international trade. For example, Wisconsin Lt. Gov. Rebecca Kleefisch led a state mission to China and North Dakota Lt. Gov. Drew Wrigley chairs the state's International Trade Office. All these lieutenant governors have additional duties.

Public Health

Through personal initiative, Georgia Lt. Gov. Casey Cagle launched the Lieutenant Governor's Healthy Kids Challenge, a public-private partnership enrolling schools to encourage children to make healthy lifestyle decisions. Connecticut Lt. Gov. Nancy Wyman chairs the state's health exchange, health information technology efforts and the Governor's Health Cabinet. Michigan Lt. Gov. Brian Calley has chaired the state Mental Health and Wellness Commission and the Mental Health Diversion Council. By statute, Missouri Lt. Gov. Peter Kinder is the state's official Senior Advocate and he serves on the following boards: the Rx Plan Commission, the Personal Independence Commission and the Minority Older Individuals Commission. Kansas Lt. Gov. Jeff Colyer led a transformation of that state's Medicaid system, and in Ohio and the U.S. Virgin Islands, the lieutenant governor is director of the insurance department. All have additional duties.

Education

Oklahoma Lt. Gov. Todd Lamb led the state Commission on School Security and Iowa Lt. Gov. Kim Reynolds co-chairs the Governor's STEM Advisory Council. By statute, the North Carolina lieutenant governor serves on the state Board of Education and the state Board of Community Colleges, while the California lieutenant governor serves as a University of California Regent and as a California State University system trustee. The Colorado lieutenant governor currently also serves as director of the Department of Higher Education. All have additional duties.

Intergovernmental Affairs

Many lieutenant governors serve in intergovernmental capacities, from being state liaison to military affairs to serving as ombudsman to localities. Alabama Lt. Gov. Kay Ivey chairs the Job Creation and Military Stability Commission and Pennsylvania Lt. Gov. Mike Stack chairs a military base commission. Indiana Lt. Gov. Sue Ellspermann manages the Office of Defense Development and South Dakota Lt. Gov. Matt Michels oversees the departments of the Military, Veterans' Affairs and Tribal Relations. Massachusetts Lt. Gov. Karyn Polito serves as the administration's primary liaison to localities and Illinois Lt. Gov. Evelyn Sanguinetti chairs the state Rural Affairs Council. New Mexico Lt. Gov. John Sanchez is statutorily ombudsman for the state, helping constituents with agencies of government. All have additional duties.

This listing of duties is not comprehensive or all encompassing, but rather provides examples of how the office of lieutenant governor may be shaped in each state.

Election Methods

The method of election of a lieutenant governor may impact the role the office plays. Only five states use an official other than lieutenant governor to succeed the governor. In Arizona, Oregon and Wyoming, the second-in-command is the secretary of state. In Maine and New Hampshire, this official is the senate president. In 2015, legislative measures were advanced in Arizona and Maine to create an office of lieutenant governor. It is possible in most states to change or add the title "lieutenant governor" to the official who is second-in-command. This is the case in Tennessee and West Virginia.

A lieutenant governor may be elected with the governor as a team in the general election or may be elected separately. In some cases, the governor and lieutenant governor are elected separately in the primary and are paired in the general election, sometimes called "an arranged marriage." The method of election may impact how an office of lieutenant governor is structured in a state.

Conclusion

Lieutenant governors impact states daily from leading senates or divisions of government to all aspects of constituent life, from education and jobs to public health. These roles may be impacted by methods of election, clarity of succession law; and actions taken by governors, legislators and lieutenant governors themselves in shaping portfolios of work. The office of lieutenant governor is unquestionably a springboard to the office of governor and adds to the efficiency of a state or territory.

About the Author

Julia Nienaber Hurst has more than 20 years of state government experience as a lobbyist, legislative chief of staff and association executive. She is executive director of the National Lieutenant Governors Association, also known as NLGA. See *www.nlga.us*.

Table 4.12
THE LIEUTENANT GOVERNORS, 2015

State or other jurisdiction	Name and party	Method of selection	Length of regular term in years	Date of first service	Present term ends	Number of previous terms	Joint election of governor and lieutenant governor (a)
Alabama	Kay Ivey (R)	CE	4	1/2011	1/2019	1	No
Alaska	Byron Mallott (I)	CE	4	12/2014	12/2018	...	Yes
Arizona	......(b)						
Arkansas	Tim Griffin (R)	CE	4	1/2015	1/2019	...	No
California	Gavin Newsom (D)	CE	4	1/2011	1/2019	1	No
Colorado	Joseph Garcia (D)	CE	4	1/2011	1/2019	1	Yes
Connecticut	Nancy Wyman (D)	CE	4	1/2011	1/2019	1	Yes
Delaware	Vacant (m)	CE	4	...	...	...	No
Florida	Carlos Lopez-Cantera (R)	CE	4	2/2014 (k)	1/2019	(k)	Yes
Georgia	Casey Cagle (R)	CE	4	1/2007	1/2019	2	No
Hawaii	Shan Tsutsui (D)	CE	4	1/2013 (e)	12/2018	(e)	Yes
Idaho	Brad Little (R)	CE	4	1/2009 (c)	1/2019	(c)	No
Illinois	Evelyn Sanguinetti (R)	CE	4	1/2015	1/2019	...	Yes
Indiana	Sue Ellspermann (R)	CE	4	1/2013	1/2017	...	Yes
Iowa	Kim Reynolds (R)	CE	4	1/2011	1/2019	1	Yes
Kansas	Jeff Colyer (R)	CE	4	1/2011	1/2019	1	Yes
Kentucky	Crit Luallen (D)	CE	4	11/2014 (l)	12/2015	...	Yes
Louisiana	Jay Dardenne (R)	CE	4	11/2010 (d)	1/2016	1	No
Maine	......(b)						
Maryland	Boyd Rutherford (R)	CE	4	1/2015	1/2019	...	Yes
Massachusetts	Karyn Polito (R)	CE	4	1/2015	1/2019	...	Yes
Michigan	Brian Calley (R)	CE	4	1/2011	1/2019	1	Yes
Minnesota	Tina Smith (D)	CE	4	1/2015	1/2019	...	Yes
Mississippi	Tate Reeves (R)	CE	4	1/2012	1/2016	...	No
Missouri	Peter Kinder (R)	CE	4	1/2005	1/2017	2	No
Montana	Angela McLean (D)	CE	4	2/2014 (j)	1/2017	...	Yes
Nebraska	Mike Foley (R)	CE	4	1/2015	1/2019	...	Yes
Nevada	Mark Hutchison (R)	CE	4	1/2015	1/2019	...	No
New Hampshire	......(b)						
New Jersey	Kim Guadagno (R)	CE	4	1/2010	1/2018	1	Yes
New Mexico	John Sanchez (R)	CE	4	1/2011	1/2019	1	Yes
New York	Kathy Hochul (D)	CE	4	1/2015	1/2019	...	Yes
North Carolina	Dan Forest (R)	CE	4	1/2013	1/2017	...	No
North Dakota	Drew Wrigley (R)	CE	4	12/2010 (f)	12/2018	1	Yes
Ohio	Mary Taylor (R)	SE	4	1/2011	1/2019	1	Yes
Oklahoma	Todd Lamb (R)	CE	4	1/2011	1/2019	1	No
Oregon	......(b)						
Pennsylvania	Mike Stack (D)	CE	4	1/2015	1/2019	...	Yes
Rhode Island	Dan McKee (D)	SE	4	1/2015	1/2019	...	No
South Carolina	Henry McMaster (R)	CE	4	1/2015	1/2019	...	No
South Dakota	Matt Michels (R)	CE	4	1/2011	1/2019	1	Yes
Tennessee	Ron Ramsey (R)	(g)	2	1/2007	1/2017	4 (g)	No
Texas	Dan Patrick (R)	CE	4	1/2015	1/2019	...	No
Utah	Spencer J. Cox (R)	CE	4	10/2013 (h)	1/2017	...	Yes
Vermont	Phil Scott (R)	CE	2	1/2011	1/2017	2	No
Virginia	Ralph Northam (D)	CE	4	1/2014	1/2018	...	No
Washington	Brad Owen (D)	CE	4	1/1997	1/2017	4	No
West Virginia	Bill Cole (R)	(i)	2	1/2015	...	...	No
Wisconsin	Rebecca Kleefisch (R)	CE	4	1/2011	1/2019	1	Yes (n)
Wyoming	......(b)						
American Samoa	Lemanu Peleti Mauga (D)	CE	4	1/2013	1/2017	...	Yes
Guam	Ray Tenorio (R)	CE	4	1/2011	1/2019	1	Yes
No. Mariana Islands	Ralph Torres (R)	CE	4	1/2015	1/2019	...	Yes
Puerto Rico	......(b)						
U.S. Virgin Islands	Osbert Potter (I)	SE	4	1/2015	1/2019	...	Yes

See footnotes at end of table.

THE LIEUTENANT GOVERNORS, 2015—Continued

Source: The Council of State Governments, January 2015.

Key:

CE — Constitutional, elected by public.

SE — Statutory, elected by public.

. . . — Not applicable.

(a) The following also choose candidates for governor and lieutenant governor through a joint nomination process: Florida, Kansas, Maryland, Minnesota, Montana, North Dakota, Ohio, Utah, American Samoa, Guam, No. Mariana Islands, and U.S. Virgin Islands. For additional information see The National Lieutenant Governors Association website at *http://www.nlga.us.*

(b) No lieutenant governor.

(c) Brad Little was appointed by Gov. Otter and confirmed by the state senate after Lt. Gov. Ritsch won the U.S. Senate seat.

(d) Lt. Gov. Dardenne won a special election in Nov. 2010 to replace Lt. Gov. Mitch Landrieu after he left to become New Orleans mayor.

(e) Senate President Shan Tsutsui was sworn in as Hawaii's lieutenant governor on January 3, 2013. Gov. Abercrombie named Lt. Gov. Schatz as the replacement for U.S. Sen. Daniel Inouye who died on Dec. 17, 2012. Under Hawaii law, the senate president has the choice whether to become lieutenant governor.

(f) Lt. Gov. Drew Wrigley was appointed by Gov. Jack Dalrymple, who moved from the office of lieutenant governor to governor when Gov. John Hoeven resigned to become a U.S. senator.

(g) In Tennessee, the president of the senate and the lieutenant governor are one in the same. The legislature provided in statute the title of lieutenant governor upon the senate president. The senate president serves two-year terms, elected by the Senate on the first day of the first session of each two-year legislative term.

(h) Lt. Gov. Spencer J. Cox was appointed to the office of lieutenant governor in Oct. 2013 after Lt. Gov. Greg Bell resigned to return to the private sector.

(i) In West Virginia, the president of the senate and the lieutenant governor are one in the same. The legislature provided in statute the title of lieutenant governor upon the senate president. The senate president serves two-year terms, elected by the Senate on the first day of the first session of each two-year legislative term.

(j) Angela McLean was sworn in on Feb. 17, 2014 after Lt. Gov. John Walsh was appointed to fill a vacant U.S. Senate seat.

(k) Carlos Lopez-Cantera was appointed lt. governor on Feb. 3, 2014 after Lt. Gov. Jennifer Carroll resigned Mar. 12, 2013 amid charges of misconduct.

(l) Crit Luallen was appointed lt. governor by Gov. Beshear on Nov. 6, 2014 after Lt. Gov. Jerry Abramson resigned to serve President Obama as deputy assistant to the president and director of intergovernmental affairs.

(m) Lt. Gov. Matthew Denn resigned Jan. 6, 2015, upon taking the oath of office to serve as Delaware's attorney general, a position he was elected to during the Nov. 4, 2014 general election. The office of lieutenant governor will remain vacant until the 2016 elections after the General Assembly's failed attempt to pass legislation providing a method to choose a new lt. governor in the event of a vacancy. The current successor is the Secretary of State Jeffrey Bullock.

(n) The governor and lt. governor are elected on a joint ticket at the November general election. However, they run on separate party primary ballots in the August primary election.

Table 4.13
LIEUTENANT GOVERNORS: QUALIFICATIONS AND TERMS

State or other jurisdiction	Minimum age	State citizen (years)	U.S. citizen (years) (a)	State resident (years) (b)	Qualified voter (years)	Length of term (years)	Maximum consecutive terms allowed
Alabama	30	7	10	7	...	4	2
Alaska	30	7	7	7	★	4	2
Arizona	...(c)...						
Arkansas	30	7	★	7	...	4	2
California	18	★	★	5	★	4	2
Colorado	30	...	★	2	...	4	2
Connecticut	30	★	★	★	★	4	...
Delaware	30	★	12	6	★	4	2
Florida	30	★	★	7	★	4	2
Georgia	30	★	15	6	★	4	2
Hawaii	30	5	★	5	★	4	2
Idaho	30	...	★	2	...	4	...
Illinois	25	...	★	3	...	4	...
Indiana	30	★	★	★	★	4	2
Iowa	30	...	2	2	...	4	...
Kansas	...	...	...	...	...	4	2
Kentucky	30	6	★	★	★	4	2
Louisiana	25	5	5	5	...	4	...
Maine	...(c)...						
Maryland	30	★	★	★	★	4	2
Massachusetts	...	★	★	★	★	4	...
Michigan	30	★	★	4	4	4	2 (d)
Minnesota	25	...	★	1	...	4	...
Mississippi	30	...	20	5	★	4	2
Missouri	30	10	15	10	...	4	...
Montana	25	2	★	2	...	4	2 (e)
Nebraska	30	5	★	5	★	4	2
Nevada	25	2	★	2	★	4	2
New Hampshire	...(c)...						
New Jersey	30	...	20	7	...	4	2
New Mexico	30	★	★	5	★	4	2
New York	30	★	★	5	★	4	...
North Carolina	30	...	5	2	...	4	2
North Dakota	30	5	...	...	...	4	...
Ohio	18	...	★	★	★	4	2
Oklahoma	31	10	★	★	★	4	...
Oregon	...(c)...						
Pennsylvania	30	★	★	7	★	4	2
Rhode Island	18	★	★	★	★	4	2
South Carolina	30	5	5	5	★	4	2
South Dakota	21	2	★	2	★	4	2
Tennessee (f)	30	★	★	3	1	2	...
Texas	30	...	★	5	...	4	...
Utah	30	★	★	★	★	4	...
Vermont	18	4	★	4	★	2	...
Virginia	30	...	★	5	5	4	...
Washington	18	★	★	★	★	4	...
West Virginia (g)	25	1	1	1	★	2	...
Wisconsin	18	★	★	★	★	4	...
Wyoming	...(c)...						
American Samoa	35	(h)	★	5	★	4	2
Guam	30	...	5	5	★	4	2
No. Mariana Islands	35	★	★	★	★	4	2
Puerto Rico	...(c)...						
U.S. Virgin Islands	30	...	5	5	5	4	2

Sources: The Council of State Government's survey of lieutenant governors' offices, November 2014 and state websites, January 2015.

Note: This table includes constitutional and statutory qualifications.

Key:

★ — Formal provision; number of years not specified.

... — No formal provision.

(a) In some states you must be a U.S. citizen to be an elector, and must be an elector to run.

(b) In some states you must be a state resident to be an elector, and must be an elector to run.

(c) No lieutenant governor.

(d) In 1993 a constitutional limit of two lifetime terms in the office was enacted.

(e) Eligible for eight out of 16 years.

(f) In Tennessee, the speaker of the Senate, elected from Senate membership, has statutory title of "lieutenant governor."

(g) In West Virginia, the president of the Senate and the lieutenant governor are one in the same. The legislature provided in statute the title of lieutenant governor upon the Senate president. The Senate president serves two-year terms, elected by the Senate on the first day of the first session of each two-year legislative term.

(h) Must be a U.S. national.

Table 4.14
LIEUTENANT GOVERNORS: POWERS AND DUTIES

State or other jurisdiction	Presides over Senate	Appoints committees	Breaks roll-call ties	Assigns bills	Authority for governor to assign duties	Member of governor's cabinet or advisory body	Serves as acting governor when governor out of state	Other duties (a)
Alabama	★	...	★	★	...	...	★(b)	...
Alaska	...	...	...	...	★	★	...	(c)
Arizona	...............................(d)...............................							
Arkansas	★	...	★	...	...	...	★	...
California	★	...	★	...	★	...	★	(c)
Colorado	...	...	...	...	★	★	★	(c)
Connecticut	★	...	★	...	★	★	★	...
Delaware	★	...	★	...	...	★	...	(c)
Florida	...	...	...	...	★	...	★	...
Georgia	★	★	...	★	★	★	...	(c)
Hawaii	...	...	...	...	★	...	★	(c)
Idaho	★	...	★	...	★	...	★	...
Illinois	...	...	...	...	★	★	...	(c)
Indiana	★	...	★	...	...	...	★	(c)
Iowa	...	(e)	...	...	★	(f)	(g)	...
Kansas	...	...	...	...	...	★	...	...
Kentucky	...	...	...	...	★	...	(h)	(c)
Louisiana	...	...	...	...	★	★	★	...
Maine	...............................(i)...............................							
Maryland	...	...	...	...	...	★	★	...
Massachusetts	...	★	...	...	★	★	★	(c)
Michigan	★	...	★	...	★	★	★(j)	(c)
Minnesota	...	...	...	...	★	...	★	(c)
Mississippi	★	★	★	★	...	...	★	(c)
Missouri	★	...	★	...	★	...	★	(c)
Montana	...	...	...	...	★	★	★	...
Nebraska	★(k)	...	...	...	...	...	★	...
Nevada	★	...	★(l)	...	...	...	★	...
New Hampshire	...............................(i)...............................							
New Jersey	...	...	...	...	★	★	★	(c)
New Mexico	★	...	★	...	...	★	★	...
New York	★	...	★(m)	...	★	★	★	...
North Carolina	★	...	★	...	★	★	★	(c)
North Dakota	★	...	...	...	★	★	★	...
Ohio	...	...	...	...	★	★	...	...
Oklahoma	★(n)	...	★	...	...	...	★	(c)
Oregon	...............................(d)...............................							
Pennsylvania	★	...	★	...	...	...	...	...
Rhode Island	...	...	...	...	...	...	...	(c)
South Carolina	★	★	★	★	...	★	★	(c)
South Dakota	★	...	★	...	★	★	★	(c)
Tennessee	★	★	★	★	...	...	...	...
Texas	★	★	★	★	...	...	★	...
Utah	...	...	...	...	...	★	...	(c)
Vermont	★	★(o)	★	★(o)	...	★	★	...
Virginia	★	...	★	...	...	★	...	...
Washington	★	★	★	...	...	...	★	...
West Virginia	★	★	...	★	...	...	...	(c)
Wisconsin	...	...	...	...	★	★	...	(c)
Wyoming	...............................(d)...............................							
American Samoa	...	...	...	...	...	...	★	...
Guam	(k)	...	...	...	★	★	★	...
No. Mariana Islands	...	...	...	...	...	★	★	(c)
Puerto Rico	...............................(d)...............................							
U.S. Virgin Islands	...	...	...	...	★(f)	★	★	...

See footnotes at end of table.

LIEUTENANT GOVERNORS: POWERS AND DUTIES — Continued

Source: The Council of State Governments' survey of lieutenant governors' offices, November 2014.

Key:

★ — Provision for responsibility.

. . . — No provision for responsibility.

(a) Lieutenant governors may obtain duties through gubernatorial appointment, statute, the Constitution, direct democracy action, or personal initiative. Hence, an exhaustive list of duties is not maintained, but this chart provides examples which are not all inclusive.

(b) The lieutenant governor performs the duties of the governor in the event of the governor's death, impeachment, disability, or absence from the state for more than 20 days.

(c) Alaska—The lieutenant governor bears these additional responsibilities: Alaska Historical Commission Chair; Alaska Workforce Investment Board; supervise the Division of Elections: supervise the certification process for citizen ballot initiative and referenda; provide constituent care and communications; lend support to governor's legislative and administrative initiatives; review, sign and file regulations; publish the Alaska Administrative Code and the Online Public Notice System; commission notaries public; regulate use of State Seal, co-chair Alaska Criminal Justice Working Group; member of Clemency Advisory Cmte.; represent Alaska in the Aerospace States Association (ASA), the National Association of Secretaries of State and the National Lieutenant Governors' Association; Arctic Winter Games; Experimental Program to Stimulate Competitive Research (EPSCoR), Chair.

California—Lieutenant governor also sits on the UC Board of Regents and the CSU Board of Trustees, serves as the chair of the Commission for Economic Development, chair of the State Lands Commission, member of the Ocean Protection Council, and as a member of the California Emergency Council.

Colorado—Additional responsibilities include: director of the Colorado Department of Higher Education and chair of the Colorado Commission of Indian Affairs (by statute).

Delaware—Serves as President of the Board of Pardons.

Georgia—The lieutenant governor, by statute, is responsible for board, commission and committee appointments. In addition the lieutenant governor appoints conference committees, rules on germaneness, and must sign all acts of the General Assembly.

Hawaii—Also serves as Secretary of State.

Illinois—The lt. governor serves on or chairs several bodies according to statute and executive order including the: Illinois River Coordinating Council, Mississippi River Coordinating Council, Wabash and Ohio River Coordinating Council, Interagency Military Base Support and Economic Development Committee, Illinois Discharged Service Member Task Force, Governor's Rural Affairs Council, IL Farmers Market Task Force, Illinois Local Food, Farms, and Jobs Council, Commission to End Hunger, Illinois Main Street, Housing Task Force, Commission to Eliminate Poverty, Illinois Broadband Deployment Council, ISBE/ROE Service Evaluation Committee, Charitable Trust Stabilization Committee.

Indiana—Serves as Secretary of Agriculture and Rural Development. Oversees six state agencies: Department of Agriculture, Office of Community and Rural Affairs, Office of Defense Development, Office of Tourism Development, Indiana Small Business Development Center and the Indiana Housing and Community Development Authority.

Kentucky—In addition to the duties set forth by the Kentucky Constitution, state law also gives the lieutenant governor the responsibility to act as chair, or serve as a member, on various boards and commissions. Some of these include: the State Property and Buildings Commission, Kentucky Turnpike Authority, Kentucky Council on Agriculture, Board of the Kentucky Housing Corporation and the Appalachian Development Council. The governor also has the power to give the lieutenant governor other specific job duties.

Massachusetts—The lieutenant governor is a member of, and presides over, the Governor's Council, an elected body of 8 members which approves all judicial nominations.

Michigan—The lieutenant governor serves as a member of the State Administrative Board; and represents the governor and the state at selected local, state, and national meetings. In addition the governor may delegate additional responsibilities.

Minnesota—Serves as the Chair of the Capitol Area Architectural and Planning Board Committee.

Mississippi—The lieutenant governor also appoints chairs of standing committees, appoints conferees to committees and is a member of the Legislative Budget Committee, chair of this committee every other year.

Missouri—Other duties of the lieutenant governor include: Official Senior Advocate for State of Missouri and Advisor to Department of Elementary and Secondary Education on early childhood education and Parents-as-Teachers program. The lieutenant governor also serves on

the following boards and commissions: Board of Fund Commissioners; Board of Public Buildings; Governor's Advisory Council for Veterans Affairs (chair); Missouri Community Service Commission; Missouri Development Finance Board; Missouri Housing Development Commission; Missouri Rural Economic Development Council; Missouri Rural Economic Development Council; Missouri Senior Rx Program (chair); Missouri Tourism Commission (vice-chair); Personal Independence Commission (co-chair); Second State Capitol Commission; Statewide Safety Steering Committee; Veteran's Benefits Awareness Task Force (chair); Special Health, Psychological, and Social Needs of Minority Older Individuals Commission; Mental Health Task Force (chair); Missouri Energy Task Force.

New Jersey—The lieutenant governor will serve as the head of a principal department or other executive or administrative agency or delegate duties of the office of governor or both. (Lt. Gov. Guadagno is currently appointed as secretary of state.)

North Carolina—Serves as a voting member on the State Board of Education. Serves on the State Board of Economic Development. Serves on the State Community College Board. Serves as Chairman of the Energy Policy Council. Serves on the Military Affairs Commission. Serves as Chair of the eLearning Commission.

Oklahoma—Lieutenant governor also serves on 10 boards and commissions: Tourism and Recreation Commission, Indian Cultural and Educational Authority, State Board of Equalization, School Land Commission, the Oklahoma Capitol Improvement Authority, the Oklahoma Archives and Records Commission, the Oklahoma Film and Music Advisory Commission, CompSource Oklahoma Board of Managers, the Commissioners of the Land Office, and the Oklahoma Linked Deposit Review Board.

Rhode Island—Serves as Chair of a number of Advisory Councils including issues related to Emergency Management, Long-term Care and Small Business. Each year submits a legislative package to the General Assembly.

South Carolina—The lieutenant governor heads the State Office on Aging; appoints members and chairs the South Carolina Affordable Housing Commission.

South Dakota—The lieutenant governor also serves as the Chair of the Workers Compensation Advisory Commission and as a member of the Constitutional Revision Commission.

Utah—The lieutenant governor serves as Chief Election Officer (statutory); Chair of the Lieutenant Governor's Commission on Volunteers (statutory); Chair of the Lieutenant Governor's Commission on Civic and Character Education (statutory); Chair of the Utah Capitol Preservation Board (statutory).

West Virginia—The president of the Senate and the lieutenant governor are one in the same. The legislature provided in statute the title of lieutenant governor upon the Senate president. The Senate President serves 2-year terms, elected by the Senate on the first day of the first session of each two-year legislative term.

Northern Mariana Islands—The lieutenant governor is charged with overseeing administrative functions.

(d) No lieutenant governor; secretary of state is next in line of succession to governorship.

(e) Appoints all standing committees. Iowa—appoints some special committees.

(f) Presides over cabinet meetings in absence of governor.

(g) Only in emergency situations.

(h) The Kentucky Constitution specifically gives the lieutenant governor the power to act as governor, in the event the governor is unable to fulfill the duties of office.

(i) No lieutenant governor; Senate president or speaker is next in line of succession to governorship.

(j) As defined in the state constitution, the lieutenant governor performs gubernatorial functions in the governor's absence. In the event of a vacancy in the office of governor, the lieutenant governor is first in line to succeed to the position.

(k) Unicameral legislative body. In Guam, that body elects own presiding officer.

(l) Except on final passage of bills and joint resolutions.

(m) With respect to procedural matters, not legislation.

(n) May preside over the Senate when desired.

(o) Appoints committees with the Pres. Pro Tem and one Senator on Committee on Committees. Committee on Committees assigns bills.

(p) In the event of a vacancy in the office of governor resulting from the death, resignation or removal of a governor in office, or the death of a governor-elect, or from any other cause, the lieutenant governor shall become governor, until a new governor is elected and qualifies.

To Share or Not to Share:
Should Ballot "Selfies" be Banned Inside the Voting Booth?

By Kay Stimson

Voters who want to share a selfie with their marked ballot on Election Day need to think twice. Many states make it a crime to take photos or videos in the voting booth, and at least one state has adopted strict new penalties for sharing your ballot selfie via social media. States with such bans say the laws are necessary to ensure ballot secrecy and discourage vote selling, but election officials say the prohibitions are tough to enforce. In an era where more and more voters have smartphones, states are grappling with just how smart it is to ban ballot selfies.

From the campaign trail all the way to the White House, the world of politics is filled with those who enjoy sharing "selfies," self-taken photos snapped with a mobile phone or tablet computer. Facebook, Twitter, Instagram, Tumblr and Snapchat are just a few of the online applications where they can be found. But there is one area of government where the selfie craze is fueling new controversy—inside the voting booth.

At least two-thirds of all states have made it illegal to photograph or film a marked ballot, according to the Digital Media Law Project. However, few states have updated their laws to address social media sharing and what is permissible.

One notable exception is New Hampshire, where Secretary of State Bill Gardner championed an update to state law that specifically bans posting photos of a completed ballot on the Internet using social media or other means. Violators risk a felony charge and a $1,000 fine.

Dave Scanlan, New Hampshire's deputy secretary of state, said the new law, implemented in 2014, is necessary to prevent the use of digital technology to carry out vote rigging or voter coercion schemes.

"State legislatures around the country were very successful in implementing balloting reforms designed to throttle back vote buying, coercion and intimidation schemes that were rampant in the mid to late 1800s. Those reforms, including general prohibitions against showing one's marked ballot, have withstood the test of time. Modern technology, however, threatens to let the show-me-your-ballot genie back out of the bottle."

However, not everyone agrees that the state interest in banning ballot selfies is of the highest concern. Opponents of the law contend that it has a chilling effect on what people can share about their political views in the Internet age.

The law has led to a high-profile lawsuit from the New Hampshire Civil Liberties Union representing three voters who posted ballot selfies—including a state legislator and a candidate for state office. Some New Hampshire legislators want to repeal the ballot selfie ban altogether.

Ethan Wilson, a legal clerk who has researched and written about the issue for the National Conference of State Legislatures, thinks the ACLU has a strong case.

"Core political speech is protected speech under the First Amendment, and essentially articulating how you voted for someone or some measure could be construed as political speech," Wilson said. "Sharing a picture of your ballot online is one way to do that."

Threatening Democracy?

At the core of the argument is the notion of whether taking a selfie of one's own marked ballot is an act of political free speech or a potential gateway to fraud and high-tech vote buying.

"This is an unusual issue," noted Louisiana Secretary of State Tom Schedler, who serves as president-elect of the National Association of Secretaries of State. "When we are talking about photography in a polling place, there is a need to weigh the fundamental right to freedom of speech against the secrecy and the integrity of the ballot."

Schedler pointed out that many laws banning cameras in the polling place were adopted to protect voters. Allowing the posting of ballots online could make it easier for an unscrupulous person to intimidate, bribe or harass someone into voting for a particular candidate by requiring them to prove it with photographic evidence.

Sound far-fetched? In testifying before the New Hampshire State Legislature, Zandra Rice

Hawkins, executive director of Granite State Progress, cited several modern-day scenarios where it could happen, including a church were a congregant doesn't share the same political views as other members and a union that endorses a candidate other than the one someone wants to support.[1]

Think about the Starbucks #RaceTogether campaign, where a well-meaning CEO set off a firestorm of public controversy by urging employees to dive into conversations about race relations with customers and share their dialogue online. Without ballot selfie bans in place, who's to say something similar couldn't happen under the guise of encouraging dialogue about political participation? Could a culture of disclosure interfere with a voter's exercise of personal choice?

"You absolutely have the right to engage in as much free speech as you want to beyond the boundary marked by the 'No Electioneering' signs," wrote state Rep. Timothy Horrigan in testimony before New Hampshire's House Election Law Committee. "However, the space inside that boundary is a secure space where the debate stops and the secret balloting begins."

Policing the Internet

Even if the courts side with New Hampshire's ban on ballot selfies, election officials are quick to point out that most state laws remain unclear about social media sharing. Many of the states with photo and video bans in the polling place adopted their laws well before the introduction of smartphones. Ohio's statute, for example, merely prohibits voters from displaying their ballots "with the apparent intention of letting it be known how the elector is about to vote," or "exhibiting any ticket or ballot the elector intends to cast."[2]

Plus, there are major challenges to enforcement. In an age where sharing via social media is common, most voters are not aware that ballot-sharing photos or videos are against the law. During the November 2014 general election, millions of people posted selfies with their "I Voted" stickers and photographs of their ballots. In Chicago, election officials took to Twitter to urge voters to retract their ballot selfies and familiarize themselves with the photography restrictions that were in place at polling sites.

"For a lot of states where the practice is banned by law, it is a matter of voter education and outreach," said Michelle Shafer, an independent communications consultant who works with election officials on technology issues. "Prohibitions against photos and videos of ballots are rooted in decades-old practices to prevent corruption in elections, but today's younger voters don't always understand the connection. The message needs to be that it's not necessary or appropriate. I mean, would the same people sharing ballot selfies post their IRS filings to show how much they paid in taxes?"

Monitoring social media postings for violators is also no simple endeavor. In states like Oregon and Washington, where voting is largely conducted by mail and people often fill out their ballots at home, the challenges are even steeper. Without poll workers to inform voters about ballot sharing rules, election administrators could face some major burdens.

"Who is going to do this [enforce restrictions] in a local elections office that is already overburdened with other elections responsibilities, lacking in IT capabilities and staffed by people who aren't necessarily proficient in social media?" asked Shafer. "Where will the dollars for training and staffing come from to monitor and enforce the law?"

In fact, no one interviewed for this article could identify an instance where someone actually was prosecuted for violating a state ban on ballot photography.

Decriminalizing Selfies

As states grapple with options for keeping up with advances in social media—and the related desire to share every notable moment in the day—some officials want to keep the #ballotselfie hashtag going. A new law in Utah gives voters the lawful right to snap photos of their own ballot and a similar proposal was introduced in Illinois.

"Though it may seem silly to some, young voters in particular are fond of sharing ballot photos as a way of demonstrating civic pride and identifying with political candidates or a cause," said Bryant Jackson-Green, criminal justice policy analyst for the Illinois Policy Institute. "As the saying goes, a picture is worth a thousand words; expressing your political stances and participation in the political process with a photograph is an effective way to speak out about your values."[3]

Case in point: Beyoncé. The megastar performer made news in 2012 when she posted her ballot on Instagram for millions to see. While forced to defend herself over the legality of the move, some media outlets also recognized the positive message that Beyoncé was sending to young fans about doing their civic duty.

Which begs the question, are legislators who support ballot selfies promoting the use of social sharing for collective good? What if posting photos on Instagram or Twitter serves as a catalyst for identifying—and addressing—problems or issues that confuse or disenfranchise voters? Could they actually serve as a new form of election protection?

The states moving to allow ballot selfies may prove to be the testing grounds for this question.

Snapshot of the Future

For now, the jury is out on taking a photo of your ballot, but one thing is clear: selfies are a mainstay of modern life. A February 2014 survey by the Pew Research Center revealed that at least 55 percent of all young adults ages 18 to 33 have posted a selfie online. Kim Kardashian published her own book of selfies.

Thanks to social media, anyone with a smartphone can broadcast your (selfie). Collective notions about personal privacy are rapidly shifting in digital life. As a whole new generation of selfie-sticks, viral videos and insta-sharing shape the political landscape, could this new era of connectedness affect assumptions about the need for restrictions on ballot secrecy?

"Thanks to the Internet, younger generations have a very different notion of privacy and what kinds of things should be protected or kept personal," said Schedler, Louisiana's secretary of state. "For now, election officials need to educate voters on what is at stake when they are thinking about sharing their marked ballot with friends or followers. Let's leave it up to the courts and the legislatures to figure out what that is."

Adds New Hampshire's Deputy Secretary Dave Scanlan, "Bottom line on this issue is to make sure we maintain an election system where every voter can vote their conscience, free from peer pressure, intimidation and the temptation to sell a vote. Can this be accomplished by permitting the sharing of marked ballots through social media? If the courts and state legislatures don't get this right, it could be a significant step backwards."

Notes

[1] Rice Hawkins, Zandra. "Statement on NH New Hampshire House Voting Down HB 404, Ballot Selfies." *Granite State Progress*, 4 Mar. 2015. Web. 11 Mar. 2015.

[2] "3599.20 Prohibitions concerning Ballots Generally." *Ohio Revised Code, Title [35] XXXV Elections, Chapter 3599: Offenses and Penalties.* State of Ohio, 12 Dec. 1997. Web. 28 Feb. 2015. *http://codes.ohio.gov/orc/3599.20.*

[3] Jackson-Green, Bryant. "Should Voting-Booth Selfies be a Crime?" *Illinois Policy Institute.* Illinois Policy, 11 Nov 2014. Web. 28 Feb. 2015.

About the Author

Kay Stimson is director of communications and special projects for the National Association of Secretaries of State in Washington, D.C. A former television news reporter who covered the state legislatures in Maryland and South Carolina, she often focuses on writing about state and federal policy issues for lawmakers.

Table 4.15
THE SECRETARIES OF STATE, 2015

State or other jurisdiction	Name and party	Method of selection	Length of regular term in years	Date of first service	Present term ends	Number of previous terms	Maximum consecutive terms allowed by constitution
Alabama	John Merrill (R)	E	4	1/2015	1/2019	...	2
Alaska				...(a)...			
Arizona	Michele Reagan (R)	E	4	1/2015	1/2019	...	2
Arkansas	Mark Martin (R)	E	4	1/2011	1/2019	1	2
California	Alex Padilla (D)	E	4	1/2015	1/2019	...	2
Colorado	Wayne Williams (R)	E	4	1/2015	1/2019	...	2
Connecticut	Denise Merrill (D)	E	4	1/2011	1/2019	1	...
Delaware	Jeffrey Bullock (D)	A (c)	4	1/2009	...	...	...
Florida	Kenneth Detzner (R) (e)	A	4	2/2012	...	(e)	2
Georgia	Brian Kemp (R)	E (d)	4	1/2010 (d)	1/2019	(d)	...
Hawaii				...(a)...			
Idaho	Lawerence Denney (R)	E	4	1/2015	1/2019	...	...
Illinois	Jesse White (D)	E	4	1/1999	1/2019	4	...
Indiana	Connie Lawson (R) (f)	E	4	3/2012 (f)	1/2019	(f)	2
Iowa	Paul Pate (R)	E	4	12/2014	12/2018	...	...
Kansas	Kris Kobach (R)	E	4	1/2011	1/2019	1	...
Kentucky	Alison Lundergan Grimes (D)	E	4	12/2011	12/2015	...	2
Louisiana	Tom Schedler (R)	E (g)	4	11/2010	1/2016	...	...
Maine	Matt Dunlap (D)	L	2	1/2005 (m)	1/2017	(m)	4 (h)
Maryland	John Wobensmith (R)	A	...	1/2015	...	...	...
Massachusetts	William Francis Galvin (D)	E	4	1/1995	1/2019	5	...
Michigan	Ruth Johnson (R)	E	4	1/2011	1/2019	1	2
Minnesota	Steve Simon (DFL)	E	4	1/2015	1/2019	...	...
Mississippi	C. Delbert Hosemann Jr. (R)	E	4	1/2008	1/2016	1	...
Missouri	Jason Kander (D)	E	4	1/2013	1/2017	...	...
Montana	Linda McCulloch (D)	E	4	1/2009	1/2017	1	(i)
Nebraska	John Gale (R)	E	4	12/2000 (j)	1/2019	(j)	...
Nevada	Barbara Cegavske (R)	E	4	1/2015	1/2019	...	2
New Hampshire	William Gardner (D)	L	2	12/1976	12/2016	19	...
New Jersey				...(a)(k)...			
New Mexico	Dianna Duran (R)	E	4	12/2010	12/2018	1	2
New York	Cesar Perales (D)	A	...	5/2011	...	...	...
North Carolina	Elaine Marshall (D)	E	4	1/1997	1/2017	4	...
North Dakota	Alvin A. Jaeger (R)	E	4	1/1993	12/2018	5	...
Ohio	Jon Husted (R)	E	4	1/2011	1/2019	1	2
Oklahoma	Chris Benge (R) (n)	A	4	11/2013 (n)	1/2019	(n)	...
Oregon	Jeanne Atkins (D)	E	4	3/2015	1/2017	...	2
Pennsylvania	Pedro Cortes (D)	A	...	1/2003 (b)	...	(b)	...
Rhode Island	Nellie Gorbea (D)	E	4	1/2015	1/2019	...	2
South Carolina	Mark Hammond (R)	E	4	1/2003	1/2019	3	...
South Dakota	Shantel Krebs (R)	E	4	1/2015	1/2019	...	2
Tennessee	Tre Hargett (R)	L	4	1/2009	1/2017	1	...
Texas	Nandita Berry (R)	A	...	1/2014	...	...	...
Utah				...(a)...			
Vermont	Jim Condos (D)	E	2	1/2011	1/2017	2	...
Virginia	Levar Stoney (D)	A	...	1/2010	...	...	...
Washington	Kim Wyman (R)	E	4	1/2013	1/2017	...	...
West Virginia	Natalie Tennant (D)	E	4	1/2009	1/2017	1	...
Wisconsin	Douglas LaFollette (D)	E	4	1/1974 (l)	1/2019	10 (l)	...
Wyoming	Ed Murray (R)	E	4	1/2015	1/2019	...	...
American Samoa				...(a)...			
Guam				...(a)...			
No. Mariana Islands				...(a)...			
Puerto Rico	David Bernier (PDP)	A	...	1/2013	1/2017	...	...
U.S. Virgin Islands				...(a)...			

See footnotes at end of table.

THE SECRETARIES OF STATE, 2015—Continued

Source: The Council of State Governments, February 2015.

Key:

E — Elected by voters.
A — Appointed by governor.
L — Elected by legislature.
... — No provision for.

(a) No secretary of state; lieutenant govenor performs functions of this office. See Tables 4.12 through 4.14.

(b) Cortes served as secretary of the commonwealth from 2003 to 2010. He was appointed as secretary by Gov. Tom Wolf in January 2015.

(c) Appointed by the governor and confirmed by the Senate.

(d) Gov. Perdue appointed Brian Kemp on January 8, 2010 to replace Karen Handel after she resigned to run for the office of governor. Kemp was elected to a full term in the 2010 general election and re-elected in 2014.

(e) Detzner was appointed in February 2012. He served previously in 2003 as the office transitioned from an elected position to an appointed one.

(f) Lawson was appointed March 16, 2012 to fill the position left vacant when Charlie White was dismissed Feb. 4, 2012 after his conviction on felony charges. She was elected to a full term in 2014.

(g) Schedler was appointed and sworn in as secretary of state on Nov. 22, 2010 after Jay Dardenne was elected to serve as lieutenant governor.

(h) Statutory term limit of four consecutive two-year terms.

(i) Eligible for eight out of 16 years.

(j) Gale was appointed by Gov. Mike Johanns in December 2000 upon the resignation of Scott Moore. He was elected to full four-year terms in November 2002, 2006, 2010 and again in 2014.

(k) The secretary of state of New Jersey is an appointed position. Gov. Christie appointed Lt. Gov. Kim Guadagno to serve as secretary of state for this term of office.

(l) LaFollette was first elected in 1974 and served a four-year term. He was elected again in 1982 and has been re-elected since. The present term ends in 2019.

(m) Secretary Matthew Dunlap previously served as Secretary of State from 2005 to 2010. He was elected by the Legislature to serve again in January 2013 and re-elected in January 2015.

(n) Benge was appointed by Gov. Mary Fallin on November 8, 2013.

Table 4.16
SECRETARIES OF STATE: QUALIFICATIONS FOR OFFICE

State or other jurisdiction	Minimum age	U.S. citizen (years) (a)	State resident (years) (b)	Qualified voter (years)	Method of selection to office
Alabama	25	7	5	★	E
Alaska	. . .	. . .	. . . (c) . . .		
Arizona	25	10	5	. . .	E
Arkansas	18	★	★	★	E
California	18	★	★	★	E
Colorado	25	★	2	. . .	E
Connecticut	18	★	★	★	E
Delaware	. . .	. . .	. . .	. . .	A
Florida	. . . . (d)				A
Georgia	25	10	4	★	E
Hawaii	. . . . (c)				
Idaho	25	★	2	★	E
Illinois	25	★	3	. . .	E
Indiana	. . .	. . .	★	. . .	E
Iowa	18	★	. . .	. . .	E
Kansas	. . .	. . .	. . .	. . .	E
Kentucky	30	★	★	★	E
Louisiana	25	5	5	★	E
Maine	. . .	. . .	. . .	. . .	(e)
Maryland	. . .	. . .	. . .	. . .	A
Massachusetts	18	★	5	★	E
Michigan	18	★	★	★	E
Minnesota	21	★	1	★	E
Mississippi	25	★	5	★	E
Missouri	. . .	★	★	2	E
Montana	25	★	2	★	E
Nebraska	★	★	★	★	E
Nevada	25	2	2	. . .	E
New Hampshire	18	★	★	★	(e)
New Jersey	18	★	★	★	A
New Mexico	30	★	5	★	E
New York	18	★	★	. . .	A
North Carolina	21	★	★	★	E
North Dakota	25	★	5	5	E
Ohio	18	★	★	★	E
Oklahoma	31	★	★	10	A
Oregon	18	★	★	★	E
Pennsylvania	. . .	. . .	. . .	. . .	A
Rhode Island	18	★	30 days	★	E
South Carolina	. . .	★	★	★	E
South Dakota	. . .	. . .	. . .	. . .	E
Tennessee	. . .	. . .	. . .	. . .	(e)
Texas	18	★	. . .	. . .	A
Utah	. . . . (c)				
Vermont	18	★	★	★	E
Virginia	. . .	. . .	. . .	. . .	A
Washington	18	★	★	★	E
West Virginia	. . .	★	★	★	E
Wisconsin	18	★	★	★	E
Wyoming	25	★	1	★	E
American Samoa	. . . . (c)				
Guam	. . . . (c)				
No. Mariana Islands	. . . . (c)				
Puerto Rico	. . .	5	5	. . .	A
U.S. Virgin Islands	. . . . (c)				

Source: The Council of State Governments' survey of secretaries of state offices, December 2014.

Key:
★ — Formal provision; number of years not specified.
. . . — No formal provision.
A — Appointed by governor.
E — Elected by voters.
(a) In some states you must be a U.S. citizen to be an elector, and must be an elector to run.

(b) In some states you must be a state resident to be an elector, and must be an elector to run.
(c) No secretary of state.
(d) As of January 1, 2003, the office of Secretary of State shall be an appointed position (appointed by the governor). It will no longer be a cabinet position, but an agency head and the Department of State shall be an agency under the governor's office.
(e) Chosen by joint ballot of state senators and representatives. In Maine and New Hampshire, every two years. In Tennessee, every four years.

Table 4.17
SECRETARIES OF STATE: ELECTION AND REGISTRATION DUTIES

State or other jurisdiction	Election								Registration				
	Chief election officer	Determines ballot eligibility of political parties	Receives initiative and/or referendum petition	Files certificate of nomination or election	Supplies election ballots or materials to local officials	Files candidates' expense papers	Files other campaign reports	Conducts voter education programs	Registers charitable organizations	Registers corporations (a)	Processes and/or commissions notaries public	Registers securities	Registers trade names/marks
Alabama	★	★	...	★	...	★	★	★	★	★	★	...	★
Alaska (b)	★	★	★	★	★	...	...	★	...	...	★	...	...
Arizona	★	★	★	★	...	★	★	★	★	...	★	...	★
Arkansas	★	★	★	★	...	★	★	★	...	★	★	...	★
California	★(c)	★	...	★	★	★	★	★	★(d)	★	★	...	★
Colorado	★	★	★	★	...	★	★	★	★	★	★	...	★
Connecticut	★	★	...	★	★	...	...	★	★	★	★	...	★
Delaware	...	...	...	(e)	...	...	(f)	...	★(g)	★	★	...	★
Florida (v)	★	★	★	★	...	★	★	...	★	...	★	★	★
Georgia	★	★	...	★	★	★	★	★	★	★	...	★	★
Hawaii (b)	...	...	...	...	...	...	...	...	...	...	...	...	...
Idaho	★	★	★	★	★	★	★	★	...	★	★	...	★
Illinois	...	...	★	(h)	...	...	...	...	...	★	★	★	★
Indiana (i)	★	★	...	★	★	★	★	★	★	★	★	★	★
Iowa	★	★	...	★	...	...	...	★	★	★	★	...	★
Kansas	★	★	...	★	★	★	...	★	★	★	★	...	★
Kentucky	★	★	...	★	...	...	...	★	★	★	★	...	★
Louisiana	★	★	...	★	★	...	...	★	★	★	★	...	★
Maine	★	★	★	★	★	...	...	★	...	★	★	...	★
Maryland	★	★	...	★	...	...	...	★	...	★	★	...	★
Massachusetts	★	★	★	★	★	(f)	(f)	★	...	★	★	★	★
Michigan	★	★	★	★	...	★	★	★	...	...	★	...	...
Minnesota	★	★	...	★	★	...	...	★	★	★	★	...	★
Mississippi	★	★	★	★	...	★	★	★	★	★	★	...	★
Missouri	★	★	★	★	...	...	...	★	★	★	★	★	★
Montana	★	★	★	★	★	...	...	★	★	★	★	...	★
Nebraska	★	★	★	★	★	...	...	★	★	★	★	...	★
Nevada (j)	★	★	★	★	★	★	★	★	★	★	★	★	★
New Hampshire	★	★	...	★	★	★	★	...	★	★	★	★	★
New Jersey	★	★	★	★	★	★	★	★	★	★	★	...	★
New Mexico	★	★	...	★	...	★	★	★	★	★	★	...	★
New York	...	...	...	...	...	...	...	...	★	★	★	...	★
North Carolina (k)	...	...	...	...	...	...	...	...	★	★	★	★	★
North Dakota	★	★	★	★	★	★	★	★	★	★	★	...	★
Ohio (l)	★	★	★	★(m)	★	...	★	★	...	★	★	...	★
Oklahoma	...	...	★	...	...	...	...	...	★	★(n)	★	...	★
Oregon	★	★	★	★	★	★	★	★	★	...	★	★	★
Pennsylvania	★	★	...	★	...	...	★	★	★	★	★	★	★
Rhode Island (o)	★	★	...	★	★	...	...	★	...	★	★	...	★
South Carolina	...	...	...	...	...	...	...	...	★	★(p)	★	...	★
South Dakota	★	★	★	★	...	★	★	★	...	★	★	...	★
Tennessee (q)	...	★	...	★	★	...	...	★	★	★	★	...	★
Texas	★	★	...	★	★	...	...	★	...	★	★	...	★
Utah (b)	★	★	★	★	★	★	★	★	★	★	...	...	★
Vermont (r)	★	...	...	★	★	★	...	★	★	★	★	...	★
Virginia	...	...	...	...	...	...	...	...	...	...	...	...	...
Washington	★	★	★	★	...	...	...	★	★	★	...	★	★
West Virginia	★	★	...	★	...	★	★	★	★	★	★	...	★
Wisconsin (s)	...	...	...	...	...	...	...	...	...	...	★	...	★
Wyoming	★	★	★	★	(t)	★	★	★	★	★	★	★	★
American Samoa (b)	...	...	...	★	...	★	★	★	★	★	★	...	...
Guam (b)	...	...	...	...	...	...	...	...	...	...	...	...	...
Puerto Rico	...	...	...	...	...	...	...	...	★	★	★	★	★
U.S. Virgin Islands (b)	...	...	...	...	...	...	...	...	★	★(u)	★	...	★

See footnotes at end of table.

SECRETARIES OF STATE: ELECTION AND REGISTRATION DUTIES — Continued

Source: The Council of State Governments' survey of secretaries of state offices, December 2014.

Key:

★ — Responsible for activity.

. . . — Not responsible for activity.

(a) Unless otherwise indicated, office registers domestic, foreign and non-profit corporations.

(b) No secretary of state. Duties indicated are performed by lieutenant governor. In Hawaii, election-related responsibilities have been transferred to an independent Chief Election Officer. In U.S. Virgin Islands election duties are performed by Supervisor of Elections.

(c) Other election duties include: tallying votes from all 58 counties, testing and certifying voting systems for use by local elections officials, maintaining statewide voter registration database, publishing state Voter Information Guide.

(d) This office does not register charitable trusts, but does register charitable organizations as nonprofit corporations; also limited partnerships, limited liability corporations, and domestic partners, Advanced Health Care Directives, and administers the Safe at Home mail forwarding program.

(e) Files certificates of election for publication purposes only; does not file certificates of nomination.

(f) Federal candidates only.

(g) Incorporated organizations only.

(h) Office issues document, but does not receive it.

(i) Additional registration duties include securities enforcement and auto dealer registration and enforcement.

(j) Additional registration duties include: Issues annual State Business License, registers Domestic Partnerships, registers advanced directives for health care.

(k) Other election duties: administers the Electoral College. Other registration duties: Maintains secure online registry of advance health care directives.

(l) Supplies poll worker training materials to county boards of elections; certifies official form of the ballot to county board of elections.

(m) Issues certificate of nomination or election to all statewide candidates and U.S. Representatives.

(n) Certifies U.S. Congressional election results to Washington, D.C. Also registers partnerships, limited liability companies and limited liability partnerships.

(o) Additional registration duties include: Non-resident landlord appointment of agent for service and Uniform Commercial Code.

(p) Also registers the Cable Franchise Authority.

(q) Appoints the Coordinator of Elections who performs the election duties indicated above, and also prepares the elections manual and elections handbook for use by state officials. Also registers athlete agents, as well as individuals and entities seeking exemption from Tennessee's workers' compensation requirements.

(r) Additional registration duties include: registers temporary officiants for civil marriages.

(s) Additional registration duties include: Issues authentications and apostilles.

(t) Materials not ballots.

(u) Both domestic and foreign profit; but only domestic non-profit.

(v) Additional registration duties include: registers fictitious names and other types of business entities.

Table 4.18
SECRETARIES OF STATE: CUSTODIAL, PUBLICATION AND LEGISLATIVE DUTIES

State or other jurisdiction	Custodial				Publication					Legislative			
	Archives state records and regulations	Files state agency rules and regulations	Administers uniform commercial code provisions	Files other corporate documents	State manual or directory	Session laws	State constitution	Statutes	Administrative rules and regulations	Opens legislative sessions (a)	Enrolls or engrosses bills	Retains copies of bills	Registers lobbyists
Alabama	...	...	★	★	...	★	★	★	...	...	★	★	...
Alaska (b)	...	★	...	...	...	...	★	...	★	★	...	★	...
Arizona	★	★	★	...	...	...	★	...	★	...	...	★	★
Arkansas (c)	★	★	★	★	...	★	...	...	★	...	...	★	★
California	★	★	★	★	★	...	...	...	...	...	(d)	...	★
Colorado	...	★	★	★	...	...	★	...	★	...	...	★	★
Connecticut	★(e)	★	★	★	★	...	...	...	★(v)	S	...	★	★
Delaware	★	★	★	★	...	...	...	...	...	...	...	...	...
Florida (u)	★	★	★	★	...	★	★	★	★	...	...	...	...
Georgia	★	★	...	...	★	...	★	...	★	...	...	...	...
Hawaii (b)	...	★	...	...	...	★	...	...	...	...	...	★	...
Idaho	...	...	★	...	★	★	★	...	...	...	...	★	★
Illinois	★	★	★	★	★	★	★	...	★	H	...	★	★
Indiana	(n)	...	★	★	...	...	...	...	...	H	...	(n)	...
Iowa	★	...	★	★	...	★	★	...	...	★	...	★	★
Kansas (s)	...	★	★	★	★	★	...	(o)	★	★	...	★	★
Kentucky	★	...	★	★	...	★	...	...	...	...	★	★	...
Louisiana	★	...	★	★	...	...	★	★	...	...	★	★	(f)
Maine	★	★	★	★	...	...	★	...	★	...	...	...	...
Maryland	...	★	...	...	...	★	...	...	(g)	...	★	★	...
Massachusetts	★	★	★	★	★	★	★	★	★	...	★	★	★
Michigan	★	★	★	...	...	★	★	★	★	...	...	...	★
Minnesota	★	★	★	★	★	...	...	...	...	H	...	★	...
Mississippi	★	★	★	★	★	★	★	★	★	H	...	(p)	★
Missouri	★(h)	★	★	★	★	...	★	...	★	H	...	★	...
Montana	★	★	★	★	...	...	★	...	★	H	★	★	...
Nebraska	★	★	★	★	...	...	...	...	★	...	...	★	...
Nevada	★	★	★	★	...	...	...	...	★	...	...	★	...
New Hampshire	★	...	★	★	★	...	...	...	...	...	★	★	★
New Jersey	★	...	...	...	...	...	★	...	...	...	...	★	...
New Mexico	...	★	★	★	★	★	★	★	★	H	...	★	★
New York	...	★	★	...	★	...	★	...	★	...	...	★	...
North Carolina (t)	★	★	★	...	★	...	★	...	...	...	★	★	★
North Dakota	...	...	★	★	...	...	...	...	...	...	...	★	★
Ohio (i)	...	★	★	★	★	★	★	...	...	...	...	★	...
Oklahoma (j)	...	★	...	★	...	...	...	...	★	...	...	★	...
Oregon	★	★	★	★	★	...	...	...	...	...	...	★	...
Pennsylvania	...	...	★	★	...	...	...	...	...	...	★	★	...
Rhode Island (k)	★	★	★	★	★	...	★	...	...	...	...	★	★
South Carolina	...	...	★	★	...	...	...	...	...	...	...	★	...
South Dakota	★	★	★	★	...	...	...	★	★	H	...	★	★
Tennessee	★(q)	★	★	★	★(l)	★	...	★	★	...	...	...	...
Texas	...	★	★	★	...	★	...	...	★	H	...	★	...
Utah (b)	...	...	...	...	...	...	...	...	...	...	...	★	★
Vermont (m)	★	★	★	★	★	★	★	...	★	H	...	★	...
Virginia	...	...	...	...	★	...	...	...	...	...	...	...	★
Washington	★	...	...	★	★	...	★	...	...	...	★	★	...
West Virginia	★	★	★	★	...	...	...	...	★	...	...	★	...
Wisconsin	★	...	...	...	★	...	...	...	...	...	...	...	...
Wyoming	★	★	★	★	★	...	★	...	...	H	...	★	★
American Samoa (b)	...	★	...	★	...	★	★	...	★	...	...	...	...
Guam (b)	...	...	...	...	...	...	...	★	...	...	...	...	...
Puerto Rico	...	★	★	★	...	★	★	★	★	...	...	...	...
U.S. Virgin Islands (b)	...	★	★	★	...	...	...	...	...	...	★	★	...

See footnotes at end of table.

SECRETARIES OF STATE: CUSTODIAL, PUBLICATION AND LEGISLATIVE DUTIES — Continued

Sources: The Council of State Governments' survey of secretaries of state offices, December 2014.

Key:

★ — Responsible for activity.

... — Not responsible for activity.

(a) In this column only: ★—Both houses; H—House; S—Senate.

(b) No secretary of state. Duties indicated are performed by lieutenant governor.

(c) Additional custodial duties for the Arkansas Secretary of State include serving as the caretaker for the Arkansas State Capitol Building and Grounds, including all custodial duties, HVAC system, building maintenance, historic preservation and conducting tours.

(d) Office does not enroll or engross bills but does chapter bills that are signed into law and retains final chaptered copies.

(e) The secretary of state is keeper of public records, but the state archives is a department of the Connecticut State Library.

(f) Only registers political pollsters.

(g) Code of Maryland regulations.

(h) Also responsible for the State Library.

(i) Additional publication duties include: elections statistics, official roster of federal, state, and county officers and official roster of township and municipal officers. Additional legislative duties include: Distributing laws to specified state and local government agencies.

(j) Other custodial duties include: Effective Financing Statements identifying farm products that are subject to a security interest, UCC and mortgage documents pertaining to transmitting utilities and also railroads and files open meeting notices.

(k) Additional duties include administering oaths of office to general officers and legislators.

(l) The Division of Publications of the Office of the Secretary of State also publishes the following: The Tennessee Blue Book, Board and Commission vacancies, and Executive Orders and Proclamations.

(m) Additional custodial duties include: records management and certifying vital records.

(n) The Secretary of State's office receives and authenticates Bills and Enrolled Acts, but does not keep or maintain them. Shortly after the end of each session, they are sent to state archives for public access.

(o) Responsible for distribution only.

(p) Chapters and indexes all signed bill and chamber and concurrent resolutions.

(q) The Division of Records Management of the Office of the Secretary of State assists state agencies in the appropriate utilization, disposition, retention and destruction of state records.

(s) Additionally, the secretary of state publishes the Kansas Register and opens legislative reorganization meetings.

(t) Other publication duties include: Publishes state board and commission meeting notices online. Other legislative duties include: The Secretary of State is responsible for the certification of election results before legislators take the oath of office at the opening of each session of the General Assembly.

(u) Files other types of business entity and cable franchise documents, records federal tax liens and judgment liens and issues apostilles.

(v) The regulations function is being developed and will be fully implemented in 2015.

Table 4.19
THE ATTORNEYS GENERAL, 2015

State or other jurisdiction	Name and party	Method of selection	Length of regular term in years	Date of first service	Present term ends	Number of previous terms	Maximum consecutive terms allowed
Alabama	Luther Strange (R)	E	4	1/2011	1/2019	1	2
Alaska	Craig W. Richards (R)	A	...	12/2014	...	0	...
Arizona	Mark Brnovich (R)	E	4	1/2015	1/2019	0	2
Arkansas	Leslie Rutledge (R)	E	4	1/2015	1/2019	0	2
California	Kamala Harris (D)	E	4	1/2011	1/2019	1	2
Colorado	Cynthia Coffman (R)	E	4	1/2015	1/2019	0	2
Connecticut	George Jepsen (D)	E	4	1/2011	1/2019	1	★
Delaware	Matthew Denn (D)	E	4	1/2015	1/2019	0	★
Florida	Pam Bondi (R)	E	4	1/2011	1/2019	1	2
Georgia	Sam Olens (R)	E	4	1/2011	1/2019	1	★
Hawaii	Doug Chin (D)	A	4 (a)	1/2015	1/2019	0	...
Idaho	Lawrence Wasden (R)	E	4	1/2003	1/2019	3	★
Illinois	Lisa Madigan (D)	E	4	1/2003	1/2019	3	★
Indiana	Greg Zoeller (R)	E	4	1/2009	1/2017	1	★
Iowa	Tom Miller (D)	E	4	1/1979 (b)	1/2019	8 (b)	★
Kansas	Derek Schmidt (R)	E	4	1/2011	1/2019	1	★
Kentucky	Jack Conway (D)	E	4	12/2007	12/2016	1	2
Louisiana	James D. Caldwell (R)	E	4	1/2008	1/2016	1	★
Maine	Janet T. Mills (D)	L (c)	2	1/2011	...	1 (d)	4
Maryland	Brian Frosh (D)	E	4	1/2015	1/2019	0	★
Massachusetts	Maura Healey (D)	E	4	1/2015	1/2019	0	...
Michigan	Bill Schuette (R)	E	4	1/2011	1/2019	1	2
Minnesota	Lori Swanson (D)	E	4	1/2007	1/2019	2	★
Mississippi	Jim Hood (D)	E	4	1/2004	1/2016	2	★
Missouri	Chris Koster (D)	E	4	1/2009	1/2017	1	★
Montana	Tim Fox (R)	E	4	1/2013	1/2017	0	2
Nebraska	Doug Peterson (R)	E	4	1/2015	1/2019	0	★
Nevada	Adam Laxalt (R)	E	4	1/2015	1/2019	0	2
New Hampshire	Joseph A. Foster (D)	A	4	5/2013	1/2017	0	...
New Jersey	John Jay Hoffman (R) (e)	A	4	6/2013 (e)	(e)	0	...
New Mexico	Hector Balderas (D)	E	4	1/2015	1/2019	0	2 (f)
New York	Eric Schneiderman (D)	E	4	1/2011	1/2019	1	★
North Carolina	Roy Cooper (D)	E	4	1/2001	1/2017	3	★
North Dakota	Wayne Stenehjem (R)	E	4 (g)	1/2001	12/2019	3 (g)	★
Ohio	Mike Dewine (R)	E	4	1/2011	1/2019	1	2
Oklahoma	Scott Pruitt (R)	E	4	1/2011	1/2019	1	★
Oregon	Ellen F. Rosenblum (D)	E	4	6/2012 (i)	1/2017	0	★
Pennsylvania	Kathleen Kane (D (h)	E	4	1/2013 (h)	1/2017	0	2
Rhode Island	Peter Kilmartin (D)	E	4	1/2011	1/2019	1	2
South Carolina	Alan Wilson (R)	E	4	1/2011	1/2019	1	★
South Dakota	Martin J. Jackley (R)	E	4	9/2009 (j)	1/2019	2	2 (f)
Tennessee	Herbert Slatery (R)	(k)	8	10/2014	8/2022	0	...
Texas	Ken Paxton (R)	E	4	1/2015	1/2019	0	★
Utah	Sean Reyes (R)	E	4	12/2013	1/2017	0	★
Vermont	William H. Sorrell (D)	E	2	5/1997 (l)	1/2017	7 (l)	★
Virginia	Mark Herring (D)	E	4	1/2014	1/2018	0	(m)
Washington	Bob Ferguson (D)	E	4	1/2013	1/2017	0	★
West Virginia	Patrick Morrisey (R)	E	4	1/2013	1/2017	0	★
Wisconsin	Brad Schimel (R)	E	4	1/2015	1/2019	0	★
Wyoming	Peter Michael (R)	A	...	7/2013	...	0	...
Dist. of Columbia	Karl Racine (D)	A	...	1/2015	1/2019	0	...
American Samoa	Talauega Eleasalo V. Ale (D)	A	4	1/2014	...	1	...
Guam	Elizabeth Barrett-Anderson (R)	E	4	1/2015	1/2019	0	...
No. Mariana Islands	Edward Manibusan (I)	A	4	11/2015	...	0	...
Puerto Rico	Cesar Miranda Rodriguez (PPD/D)	A	4	1/2014	...	0	...
U.S. Virgin Islands	James S. Carroll III (Acting)	A	4	5/2015	...	0	...

See footnotes at end of table.

THE ATTORNEYS GENERAL, 2015—Continued

Sources: National Association of Attorneys General and The Council of State Governments, January 2015.

Key:

★ — No provision specifying number of terms allowed.

... — No formal provision, position is appointed or elected by governmental entity (not chosen by the electorate).

A — Appointed by the governor.

E — Elected by the voters.

L — Elected by the legislature.

N.A. — Not available.

(a) Term runs concurrently with the governor.

(b) Attorney General Miller was elected in 1978, 1982, 1986, 1994, 1998, 2002, 2006, 2010 and 2014.

(c) Chosen biennially by joint ballot of state senators and representatives.

(d) Janet Mills previously served as Attorney General from Jan. 2001 through Jan. 2011.

(e) On June 6, 2013, Gov. Christie appointed Attorney General Jeff Chiesa to fill the Senate seat left vacant by Sen. Frank Lautenberg's death. Chiesa will hold the seat on an interim basis until a special election can be held on Oct 16, 2013. Currently John Jay Hoffman, former Executive Assistant Attorney General is serving as Acting Attorney General.

(f) After two consecutive terms, must wait four years and/or one full term before being eligible again.

(g) The term of the office of the elected official is four years, except that in 2004 the attorney general was elected for a term of two years.

(h) Appointed to fill Tom Corbett's unexpired term after he was elected to Pennsylvania governor's office in May 2011.

(i) Rosenblum was appointed by Gov. Kitzhaber on June 29, 2012 to fill the term left vacant when AG John Kroger resigned to become President of Reed College. She was elected in Nov. 2012 to a full term.

(j) Appointed September 4, 2009 to fill Larry Long's unexpired term. AG Long resigned to accept a state judgeship.

(k) Appointed by judges of state Supreme Court.

(l) Appointed to fill unexpired term in May 1997. He was elected in 1998 to his first full term.

(m) Provision specifying individual may hold office for an unlimited number of terms.

(n) Must be confirmed by the Senate.

Table 4.20
ATTORNEYS GENERAL: QUALIFICATIONS FOR OFFICE

State or other jurisdiction	Minimum age	U.S. citizen (years) (a)	State resident (years) (b)	Qualified voter (years)	Licensed attorney (years)	Membership in the state bar (years)	Method of selection to office
Alabama	25	7	5	★	...	...	E
Alaska	18	★	...	...	★	★	A
Arizona	25	10	5	★	5	...	E
Arkansas	...	...	★	★	...	...	E
California	18	★	★	★	★	5	E
Colorado	27	★	2	★	★	...	E
Connecticut	18	★	★	★	10	10	E
Delaware	...	...	...	...	...	...	E
Florida	30	★	7	★	★	5	E
Georgia	25	10	4	★	7	7	E
Hawaii	...	1	1	...	★	(d)	A
Idaho	30	★	2	...	★	★	E
Illinois	25	★	3	★	★	★	E
Indiana	...	2	2	★	5	...	E
Iowa	18	★	★	...	...	...	E
Kansas	...	...	...	...	...	...	E
Kentucky	30	...	2 (e)	...	8	2	E
Louisiana	25	★	5	★	★	★	E
Maine	...	...	...	...	★	★	(f)
Maryland	...	★(g)	★	★	★	10	E
Massachusetts	18	...	5	★	...	★	E
Michigan	18	★	★	...	★	★	E
Minnesota	21	★	30 days	★	...	...	E
Mississippi	26	★	5	★	5	★	E
Missouri	...	★	1	...	...	...	E
Montana	25	★	2	...	5	★	E
Nebraska	...	...	★	...	...	...	E
Nevada	25	★	2	★	...	...	E
New Hampshire	...	★	★	...	★	★	A (h)
New Jersey	18	...	★	...	...	...	A
New Mexico	30	★	5	★	★	...	E
New York	30	★	5	...	(i)	...	E
North Carolina	21	★	★	★	★	(i)	E
North Dakota	25	★	5	★	★	★	E
Ohio	18	★	★	★	...	...	E
Oklahoma	31	★	★	10	...	...	E
Oregon	18	★	★	★	...	...	E
Pennsylvania	30	★	...	...	★	...	E
Rhode Island	18	...	...	...	★	★	E
South Carolina	...	★	30 days	★	★	★	E
South Dakota	18	★	★	★	(i)	(i)	E
Tennessee	...	...	...	...	...	...	(j)
Texas	...	...	...	...	(i)	(i)	E
Utah	25	★	5 (e)	★	★	★	E
Vermont	18	★	★	★	...	...	E
Virginia	30	★	1 (k)	★	...	5 (k)	E
Washington	18	★	★	★	★	★	E
West Virginia	25	...	5	★	...	...	E
Wisconsin	...	★	★	...	...	...	E
Wyoming	...	★	★	★	4	4	A (l)
Dist. of Columbia	...	...	★	...	★	★	A
American Samoa	...	...	(c)	...	(i)	(i)	A
Guam	...	...	...	...	...	...	A
No. Mariana Islands	...	...	3	...	5	...	A
Puerto Rico	...	★	...	...	★	★	A
U.S. Virgin Islands	...	...	★	★	★	★	A

Sources: The Council of State Governments' survey of attorneys general, state constitutions and statutes, January 2015.

Key:

★ — Formal provision; number of years not specified.

. . . — No formal provision.

A — Appointed by governor.

E — Elected by voters.

(a) In some states you must be a U.S. citizen to be an elector, and must be an elector to run.

(b) In some states you must be a state resident to be an elector, and must be an elector to run.

(c) No statute specifically requires this, but the State Bar Act can be interpreted as making this a qualification.

(d) No period specified; all licensed attorneys are members of the state bar.

(e) State citizenship requirement.

(f) Chosen biennially by joint ballot of state senators and representatives.

(g) *Crosse v. Board of Supervisors of Elections* 243 Md. 555, 221 A.2d 431 (1966)–opinion rendered indicated that U.S. citizenship was, by necessity, a requirement for office.

(h) Appointed by the governor and confirmed by the governor and the executive council.

(i) Implied.

(j) Appointed by state supreme court.

(k) Same as qualifications of a judge of a court of record.

(l) Must be confirmed by the Senate.

Table 4.21
ATTORNEYS GENERAL: PROSECUTORIAL AND ADVISORY DUTIES

State or other jurisdiction	Authority in local prosecutions: Authority to initiate local prosecutions	Authority in local prosecutions: May intervene in local prosecutions	Authority in local prosecutions: May assist local prosecutor	Authority in local prosecutions: May supersede local prosecutor	Issues advisory opinions (a): To state executive officials	Issues advisory opinions (a): To legislators	Issues advisory opinions (a): To local prosecutors	Issues advisory opinions (a): On the constitutionality of bills or ordinances	Reviews legislation (b): Prior to passage	Reviews legislation (b): Before signing
Alabama	A	A,D	A,D	A	★	★	★	...	★	...
Alaska	(c)	(c)	(c)	(c)	★	★	...	★	★	★
Arizona	A	A	A,B	A,F	★	★	★	★	(u)	(u)
Arkansas	...	...	D	...	★	★	★	★	...	...
California	A,B,C,D,E,F	A,B,C,D,E,F	A,B,C,D,E,F	A,B,C,D,E,F,G	★	★	★	★	(v)	(v)
Colorado	A,F	B	D,F	B	★	★	★	★	★	★
Connecticut	...	...	...	...	★	(d)	...	★	(e)	(e)
Delaware	A (f)	(f)	(f)	(f)	★	★	...	★	★(g)	★(g)
Florida	F	...	D	...	★	★	★	...	...	...
Georgia	B,D,F,G	...	A,D	...	★	★	★	...	...	...
Hawaii	A,B,C,D,E	A,B,C,D,E	A,B,C,D,E	A,B,C,D,E	★	★	...	★(h)	★	★
Idaho	B,D,F	...	D	...	★	★(a)	★	★	★	★
Illinois	D,F	D,G	D	G	★	★	★	...	(i)	(i)
Indiana	F	...	D	...	★	★	★	★	...	...
Iowa	D,F	D,F	D,F	D,E,F	★	★	★	...	(j)	(j)
Kansas	A,B,C,D,F	A,D	D	A,F	★	★	★	★	...	...
Kentucky	D,F,G	B,D,G	D	B	★	★	★	★	...	...
Louisiana	D,E,G	D,E,G	D,E,G	E,G	★	★	★	...	★	★
Maine	A	A	A	A	★	★	...	★	★	★
Maryland	B,F	D	D	...	★	★	★	★	★	★
Massachusetts	A	A	A,D	A	★	★(k)	★	★	(l)	(l)
Michigan	A	A	A	A	★	★	★	★	...	...
Minnesota	B,F	B,D,G	A,B,D,G	B	★	★(k)	★	...	...	(l)
Mississippi	A,D,F	D,F	A,D,F	D,F	★	★	★	...	...	...
Missouri	B,F,G	F	B,F	G	★	★	★	...	(l)	(l)
Montana	D	E	E	E	★	★(m)	★	...	...	...
Nebraska	A,D	A,D	A,D,E,F	...	★	★	★	★	...	...
Nevada	D,F,G	D	...	...	★	...	★	★	...	...
New Hampshire	A,E,F	A,E,F	A,D,E,F	A,E,F	★	★	★	...	(n)	(n)
New Jersey	A,B,C,D	A,B,C,D	A,B,C,D	A,B,C,D	★	★	★	★	★	★
New Mexico	B,D,E,F	D,E,F	A,B,D,E,F	D,E,F,G	★	★	★	★	★	★
New York	B,F	B,D,F	D	B	★	★(k)	★	★	★	★
North Carolina	...	D	D	...	★	★	★	★	★	...
North Dakota	A,D,E,F,G	A,D,E,G	A,B,D,E,F,G	A,D,E,G	★	★	★	★	...	...
Ohio	F	D	D	F	★	(m)	★	...	...	...
Oklahoma	A,B,C,D,E,F,G	A,B,C,D,E,F,G	A,B,C,D,E,F,G	A,B,C,D,E,F,G	★	★	★	★	★	★
Oregon	B,D,F	B,D	B,D	B	★	★	★	...	...	★
Pennsylvania	A,D,F	D,F	D,F	...	★	...	...	...	...	...
Rhode Island	A	A	A	A	★	★	...	...	...	...
South Carolina	A	A	A	A	★	(q)	★	★	...	...
South Dakota	A,B,D,E,F (p)	D,G	A,B,D,E	D,F	★	★	★	...	★	...
Tennessee	D,F,G	D,G	D	...	★	★	★	★	...	...
Texas	D,F	F	D,F	D,F	★	★	★	★	...	...
Utah	A,B,D,E,F,G	E,G	D,E	E	★	★(q)	★	★	★(l)	★(l)
Vermont	A	A	A	G	★	★	★	★	★	★
Virginia	B,F	B,D,F	B,D,F	B	★	★	★	★	★	★
Washington	B,D,G	B,D,G	B,D,G	B,D,G	★	★	★	...	(o)	(o)
West Virginia	(r)	...	...	...	★	★	★	★	...	...
Wisconsin	B,C,D,F	B,C,D	D	B	★	★	★	★	(e)	(e)
Wyoming	B,D,F	B,D	B,D	G	★	★	★	★(h)	★	★
Dist. of Columbia	F	D	D	F	★	★	(s)	★	★	★
American Samoa	A (t)	(t)	(t)	(t)	★	...	(t)	(e)	(l)	(l)
Guam	A	A	A	A	★	★	★	★	(l)	B
No. Mariana Islands	A (t)	(t)	(t)	(t)	★	★	...	★	...	...
Puerto Rico	A	(t)	(t)	(t)	★	★	...	★	★	★
U.S. Virgin Islands	A (t)	(t)	(t)	(t)	★	...	...	★	★	★

See footnotes at end of table.

ATTORNEYS GENERAL: PROSECUTORIAL AND ADVISORY DUTIES — Continued

Sources: The Council of State Governments' survey of attorneys general, state constitutions and statutes, January 2015.

Key:

A — On own initiative.

B — On request of governor.

C — On request of legislature.

D — On request of local prosecutor.

E — When in state's interest.

F — Under certain statutes for specific crimes.

G — On authorization of court or other body.

★ — Has authority in area.

. . . — Does not have authority in area.

(a) Also issues advisory opinions to: Alabama — Designated heads of state departments, agencies, boards, and commissions; local public officials; and political subdivisions. Hawaii — Judges/judiciary as requested. Idaho — to whole legislature, either house, or any member. Kansas — to counsel for local units of government. Montana — county and city attorneys, city commissioners. Wisconsin — corporation counsel.

(b) Also reviews legislation: Alabama — when requested by the governor. Alaska — after passage. Arizona — at the request of the legislature. Kansas — upon request of legislator, no formal authority.

(c) The attorney general functions as the local prosecutor.

(d) To legislative leadership.

(e) Informally reviews bills or does so upon request.

(f) The attorney general prosecutes all criminal offenses in Delaware.

(g) Also at the request of agency or legislature.

(h) Bills, not ordinances.

(i) Review and track legislation that relates to the Office of Attorney General and the office mission.

(j) No requirements for review.

(k) To legislature as a whole not individual legislators.

(l) Only when requested by governor or legislature.

(m) To either house of legislature, not individual legislators.

(n) Provides information when requested by the Legislature. Testifies for or against bills on the Attorney General's own initiative.

(o) May review legislation at request of clients or legislature.

(p) Certain statutes provide for concurrent jurisdiction with local prosecutors.

(q) Only when requested by legislature.

(r) Can be involved in local at request of local prosecutors. If requested by local authority, can participate in criminal prosecutions.

(s) The office of attorney general prosecutes local crimes to an extent. The office's Legal Counsel Division may issue legal advice to the office's prosecutorial arm. Otherwise, the office does not usually advise the OUSA, the district's other local prosecutor.

(t) The attorney general functions as the local prosecutor.

(u) Reviews enacted legislation only when there is a compelling need.

(v) May review legislation at any time but does not have a de jure role in approval of bills as to form or constitutionality; California has a separate Legislative Counsel to advise the legislature on bills.

Table 4.22
ATTORNEYS GENERAL: CONSUMER PROTECTION ACTIVITIES, SUBPOENA POWERS AND ANTITRUST DUTIES

State or other jurisdiction	May commence civil proceedings	May commence criminal proceedings	Represents the state before regulatory agencies (a)	Administers consumer protection programs	Handles consumer complaints	Subpoena powers (b)	Antitrust duties
Alabama	★	★	★	★	★	●	A,B,C
Alaska	★	. . .	★	★	★	★	A,B,C,D
Arizona	★	. . .	. . .	★(c)	★	★	A,B,C,D
Arkansas	★	. . .	★	★	★	●	A,B
California	★	★	★	★	★	★	A,B,C,D
Colorado	★	★	★	★	★	●	A,C,D
Connecticut	★	(d)	★	★	★	●	A,B,D
Delaware	★	★	★	★	★	★	A,B,D
Florida	★	. . .	. . .	★	★	★	A,B,D
Georgia	★	★	★	. . .	. . .	●	A,B
Hawaii	★	★	★	. . .	★	★	A,B,C,D
Idaho	★	. . .	★	★	★	★	A,B,D
Illinois	★	. . .	★	★	★	●	A,B,C
Indiana	★	. . .	★	★	★	★	A,B
Iowa	★	★	★	★	★	★	B,C
Kansas	★	★	★	★	★	★	B,C,D
Kentucky	★	★	★	★	★	★	A,B,C,D
Louisiana	★	★	★	★	★	★	A,B,C
Maine	★	★	★	★	★	★	A,B,C
Maryland	★	★(e)	★	★	★	★	B,C,D
Massachusetts	★	★	★	★	★	★	A,B,C,D
Michigan	★	★	★	★	★	★	A,B,C,D
Minnesota	★	. . .	★	★	★	●	A,B,C
Mississippi	★	★	. . .	★	★	★	A,B,C,D
Missouri	★	★	★	★	★	★	A,B,C,D
Montana	★	★	. . .	★	★	. . .	A,B
Nebraska	★	★	★	★	★	★	A,B,C,D
Nevada	★	★	★	★	★	●	A,B,C,D
New Hampshire	★	★	★	★	★	★	A,B,C,D
New Jersey	★	★	★	★	★	★	A,B,C,D
New Mexico	★	★	★	★	★	★	A,B,C (g)
New York	★	★	★	★	★	★	A,B,C,D
North Carolina	★	★(f)	★	★	★	★	A,B,C,D
North Dakota	★	. . .	★	★	★	★	A,B,D
Ohio	★	★	★	★	★	★	A,B,C,D
Oklahoma	★	★	★	★	★	★	A,B,C,D
Oregon	★	★(f)	★	★	★	●	A,B,C,D
Pennsylvania	★	★	★	★	★	★	A,B
Rhode Island	★	★	. . .	★	★	★	A,B,C
South Carolina	★(a)	★(h)	★	. . .	(i)	●	A,B,C,D
South Dakota	★	★	★	★	★	★	A,B,C
Tennessee	★	(e)(f)	(f)	. . .	. . .	★	B,C,D
Texas	★	. . .	. . .	★	★	●	A,B,D
Utah	★(j)	★	★(j)	. . .	★(k)	●	A (l),B,C,D (l)
Vermont	★	★	★	★	★	★	A,B,C
Virginia	★	(f)	★	★(k)	★(k)	●	A,B,C,D
Washington	★	. . .	★	★	★	★	A,B,D
West Virginia	★	. . .	★	★	★	★	A,B,D
Wisconsin	★	★	★	★	★	●	A,B,C (g)
Wyoming	★	. . .	★	★	★	●	A,B
Dist. of Columbia	★	★(m)	★	★	★	★	A,B,C,D
American Samoa	★	★	★	★	★	. . .	. . .
Guam	★	★	★	★	★	●	A,B,C,D
No. Mariana Islands	★	★	★	★	★	★	A,B
Puerto Rico	★	★	. . .	. . .	. . .	★	A,B,C,D
U.S. Virgin Islands	★	★	★	★	★	●	A

See footnotes at end of table.

ATTORNEYS GENERAL: CONSUMER PROTECTION ACTIVITIES, SUBPOENA POWERS AND ANTITRUST DUTIES — Continued

Sources: The Council of State Governments' survey of attorneys general, state constitutions and statutes, January 2015.

Key:

A — Has parens patriae authority to commence suits on behalf of consumers in state antitrust damage actions in state courts.

B — May initiate damage actions on behalf of state in state courts.

C — May commence criminal proceedings.

D — May represent cities, counties and other governmental entities in recovering civil damages under federal or state law.

★ — Has authority in area.

... — Does not have authority in area.

(a) May represent state on behalf of: the "people" of the state; an agency of the state; or the state before a federal regulatory agency.

(b) In this column only: ★ broad powers and ● limited powers.

(c) The 49th Legislature, first regular session, established a statutory scheme that provided for a mortgage recovery fund to pay those harmed by dishonest loan originators. The attorney general is now authorized to try to recover from the dishonest loan originators the money that the fund paid out (See ARS 6-991.15).

(d) In certain cases only.

(e) May commence criminal proceedings with local district attorney.

(f) To a limited extent.

(g) May represent other governmental entities in recovering civil damages under federal or state law.

(h) When permitted to intervene.

(i) On a limited basis because the state has a separate consumer affairs department.

(j) Attorney general has exclusive authority.

(k) Attorney general handles legal matters only with no administrative handling of complaints.

(l) Opinion only, since there are no controlling precedents.

(m) In antitrust, not criminal proceedings.

Table 4.23
ATTORNEYS GENERAL: DUTIES TO ADMINISTRATIVE AGENCIES AND OTHER RESPONSIBILITIES

State or other jurisdiction	Serves as counsel for state	Appears for state in criminal appeals	Issues official advice	Interprets statutes or regulations	Conducts litigation: On behalf of agency	Conducts litigation: Against agency	Prepares or reviews legal documents	Represents the public before the agency	Involved in rule-making	Reviews rules for legality
Alabama	A,B,C (a)	★(a)	★	★	★	★	(b)	(b)	★	★
Alaska	A,B,C	★	★	★	★	★	★	★	★	★
Arizona	A,B,C	★	★	★	★	★	★	...	★	★
Arkansas	A,B,C	★	★	★	★	★	★	★	...	...
California	A,B,C	★	★	★	★	...	★	...	★	★
Colorado	A,B,C	★	★	★	★	★	★	★	★	★
Connecticut	A,B,C	(b)	★	★	★	★	★	★	★	★
Delaware (f)	A,B,C	★	★	★	★	★(g)	★	★	★	★
Florida	A,B,C	★	★	★	★	...	★	...	...	...
Georgia	A,B,C	★	★	★	★	...	★	...	...	★
Hawaii	A,B,C	★	★	★	★	★	★	★	★	★
Idaho	A,B,C	★(a)	★	★	★	★	★	★	★	★
Illinois	A,B,C	★	...	★	★	...	★	...	...	...
Indiana	A,B,C	★	★	★	★	...	★	...	★	★
Iowa	A,B,C	★	★	★	★	★	★	★	★	★
Kansas	A,B,C	★	★	★	★	★	★	...	★	★
Kentucky	A,B,C	★	★	★	★	...	...	★	...	★
Louisiana	A,B,C	...	★	★	★	...	★	★	★	★
Maine	A,B,C	★	★	★	★	...	★	...	...	★
Maryland	A,B,C	★	★	★	★	(b)	★	★	★	★
Massachusetts	A,B,C	(b)(c)(d)	★	★	★	★	★	★	★	★
Michigan	A,B,C	★	★	★	★	★	★	★	★	★
Minnesota	A,B,C	(c)(d)	★	★	(a)	★	★	★	★	★
Mississippi	A,B,C	...	★	★	★	...	★	...	...	...
Missouri	A,B,C	★	★	★	★	...	★	...	★	...
Montana (h)	A,B	...	★	★	★	...	★	...	...	...
Nebraska	A,B,C	★	★	★	★	★	★	...	...	...
Nevada	A,B,C	★	★	★	★	...	★	...	★	★
New Hampshire	A,B,C	★	★	★	★	...	★	★	★	...
New Jersey	A,B,C	★	★	★	★	...	★	...	★	★
New Mexico	A,B,C	★	★	★	★	★	★	★	★	★
New York	A,B,C	(b)	...	★	★	(b)	★	(b)	...	...
North Carolina	A,B,C	★	★	★	★	★	★	(b)	★	★
North Dakota	A,B,C	★	★	★	★	★	★	...	★	★
Ohio	A,B,C	★	★	...	★	...	★	...	...	...
Oklahoma	A,B,C	★	★	★	★	★	★	★	★	★
Oregon	A,B	★	★	★	★	...	★	...	★	★
Pennsylvania	A,B	...	...	...	★	...	★	...	...	★
Rhode Island	A,B,C	★	★	★	★	★	★	...	...	...
South Carolina	A,B,C	★(d)	(a)	★	★	(b)	★	...	★	★
South Dakota	A,B,C	★	★	★	★	★	★	...	...	...
Tennessee	A,B,C	★	★	★	★	...	★	(e)	(e)	★
Texas (i)	A,B,C	★	★	★	★	★	★	★(m)	★	...
Utah	A,B,C	★(a)	★	★	★	★	★	(b)	★	★
Vermont	A,B,C	★	★	★	★	★	★	★	★	★
Virginia	A,B,C	★	★	★	★	★	★	★	★	★
Washington	A,B,C	★(k)	★	★	★	★	★	★	★	★
West Virginia	A,B,C	★	★	★	★	★	★	...	(l)	(l)
Wisconsin	A,B,C	★	★	★	★	(b)	(b)	(b)	(b)	(b)
Wyoming	A,B,C	★	★	★	★	★	★	...	★	★
Dist. of Columbia	A,B	★(j)	★	★	★	...	★	...	★	★
American Samoa	A,B,C	★(a)	★	★	★	...	★	...	★	★
Guam	A,B,C	★	★	★	(d)	★	★	(b)	★	★
No. Mariana Islands	A,B,C	★	★	★	★	★	★	...	★	★
Puerto Rico	A,B,C	★	★	★	★	...	★	...	★	★
U.S. Virgin Islands	A,B	★	★	★	★	★	★	★	...	★

See footnotes at end of table.

ATTORNEYS GENERAL: DUTIES TO ADMINISTRATIVE AGENCIES AND OTHER RESPONSIBILITIES — Continued

Sources: The Council of State Governments' survey of attorneys general, state constitutions and statutes, January 2015.

Key:

A — Defend state law when challenged on federal constitutional grounds.

B — Conduct litigation on behalf of state in federal and other states' courts.

C — Prosecute actions against another state in U.S. Supreme Court.

★ — Has authority in area.

... — Does not have authority in area.

(a) Attorney general has exclusive jurisdiction.

(b) In certain cases only to prepare or review legal documents and represent the public before the agency.

(c) When assisting local prosecutor in the appeal.

(d) Can appear on own discretion.

(e) Consumer Advocate Division represents the public in utility rate making hearings and rule making proceedings.

(f) Except as otherwise provided by statute, the Attorney General represents all state agencies and officials.

(g) Rarely.

(h) Most state agencies are represented by agency counsel who do not answer to the attorney general. The attorney general does provide representation for agencies in conflict situations and where the agency requires additional or specialized assistance.

(i) Other administrative duties include representing one state agency before another state agency.

(j) However, OUSA handles felony cases and most major misdemeanors.

(k) Limited to federal death penalty habeas corpus.

(l) On request of agency. Office acts as legal counsel to any state agency on request and that can include reviewing legislation and drafting rules and regulations.

(m) Represents the public before an agency only in energy rate cases.

Table 4.24
THE TREASURERS, 2015

State or other jurisdiction	Name and party	Method of selection	Length of regular term in years	Date of first service	Present term ends	Maximum consecutive terms allowed by constitution
Alabama	Young Boozer (R)	E	4	1/2011	1/2019	2
Alaska (a).................	Pamela Leary	A	Governor's Discretion	12/2009	...	...
Arizona.....................	Jeff DeWitt (R)	E	4	1/2015	1/2019	2
Arkansas..................	Dennis Milligan (R)	A	4	1/2015	1/2019	2
California	John Chiang (D)	E	4	1/2015	1/2019	2
Colorado...................	Walker Stapleton (R)	E	4	1/2011	1/2019	2
Connecticut..............	Denise L. Nappier (D)	E	4	1/1999	1/2019	★
Delaware	Ken Simpler (R)	E	4	1/2015	1/2019	★
Florida (b)..............	Jeff Atwater (R)	E	4	1/2011	1/2019	2
Georgia.....................	Steve McCoy	A	Pleasure of the Board	11/2011	...	...
Hawaii (c)................	Wesley Machida (D)	A	Governor's Discretion	12/2014	...	...
Idaho.........................	Ron G. Crane (R)	E	4	1/1999	1/2019	★
Illinois......................	Mike Frerichs (D)	E	4	1/2015	1/2019	★
Indiana.....................	Kelly Mitchell (R)	E	4	1/2015	1/2019	(d)
Iowa..........................	Michael L. Fitzgerald (D)	E	4	1/1983	1/2019	★
Kansas	Ron Estes (R)	E	4	1/2011	1/2019	★
Kentucky	Todd Hollenbach (D)	E	4	12/2007	12/2015	2
Louisiana..................	John N. Kennedy (R)	E	4	1/2000	1/2016	★
Maine........................	Teresea M. Hayes	L	2	1/2015	...	4
Maryland	Nancy K. Kopp (D)	L	4	2/2002	...	★
Massachusetts	Deb Goldberg (D)	E	4	1/2015	1/2019	★
Michigan...................	Kevin Clinton	A	Governor's Discretion	10/2013	...	...
Minnesota (e)............	Myron Frans	A	Governor's Discretion	1/2015	...	...
Mississippi...............	Lynn Fitch (R)	E	4	1/2012	1/2016	★
Missouri....................	Clint Zweifel (D)	E	4	1/2009	1/2017	2
Montana	Mike Kadas	A	Governor's Discretion	1/2013	...	...
Nebraska	Don Stenberg (R)	E	4	1/2011	1/2019	2
Nevada	Dan Schwartz (R)	E	4	1/2015	1/2019	2
New Hampshire	William Dwyer	L	2	1/2015	...	★
New Jersey	Andrew P. Sidamon-Eristoff	A	Governor's Discretion	2/2010	...	...
New Mexico	Tim Eichenberg (D)	E	4	1/2015	1/2019	2
New York...................	Eric Mostert	A	Governor's Discretion	N.A.	...	...
North Carolina..........	Janet Cowell (D)	E	4	1/2009	1/2017	★
North Dakota............	Kelly L. Schmidt (R)	E	4	1/2005	1/2017	★
Ohio	Josh Mandel (R)	E	4	1/2011	1/2019	2
Oklahoma..................	Ken Miller (R)	E	4	1/2011	1/2019	★
Oregon......................	Ted Wheeler (D) (f)	E	4	3/2010	1/2017	2
Pennsylvania............	Chris Craig (i)	E	4	1/1/2015 (i)	...	2
Rhode Island.............	Seth Magaziner (D)	E	4	1/2015	1/2019	2
South Carolina..........	Curtis Loftis (R)	E	4	1/2011	1/2019	★
South Dakota............	Richard Sattgast (R)	E	4	1/2011	1/2019	2
Tennessee	David H. Lillard Jr.	L	2	1/2009	...	...
Texas (g)..................	Glenn Hegar (R)	E	4	1/2015	1/2019	★
Utah..........................	Richard K. Ellis (R)	E	4	1/2009	1/2017	★
Vermont....................	Elizabeth Pearce (D)	E	2	1/2011	1/2017	★
Virginia.....................	Manju Ganeriwala	A	Governor's Discretion	1/2009	...	...
Washington...............	James L. McIntire (D)	E	4	1/2009	1/2017	★
West Virginia............	John D. Perdue (D)	E	4	1/1997	1/2017	★
Wisconsin	Mattt Adamczyk (R)	E	4	1/2015	1/2019	★
Wyoming	Mark Gordon (R)	E	4	11/2012 (h)	1/2019	2
American Samoa	Falema'o Pili	A	4	12/2008	...	...
Dist. of Columbia	Jeffrey Barnette	A	Pleasure of CFO	6/2008	N.A.	...
Guam	Rosita Fejeran	CS	...	N.A.	...	...
No. Mariana Islands...	Antoinette S. Calvo	A	4	N.A.	N.A.	...
Puerto Rico..............	Juan Zaragoza	A	4	N.A.	N.A.	...
U.S. Virgin Islands	Valdamier Collens	A	4	N.A.	N.A.	...

Source: The Council of State Governments, May 2015.
Key:
★ — No provision specifying number of terms allowed.
... — No formal provision, position is appointed or elected by governmental entity (not chosen by the electorate).
A — Appointed by the governor. (In the District of Columbia, the Treasurer is appointed by the Chief Financial Officer. In Georgia, position is appointed by the State Depository Board.)
E — Elected by the voters.   CS — Civil Service.
L — Elected by the legislature.   N.A. — Not available.
(a) The Deputy Commissioner of Department of Revenue performs this function.
(b)The official title of the office of state treasurer is Chief Financial Officer.

(c) The Director of Finance performs this function.
(d) Eligible for eight out of any period of twelve years.
(e) The Commissioner of Management and Budget performs this function.
(f) Wheeler was appointed as state treasurer in March 2010 and served as an interim designee. He was elected by Oregon voters in November 2010 and again in November 2012 to a full four-year term.
(g) The Comptroller of Public Accounts performs this function.
(h) Gordon was appointed as state treasurer in October 2012 after the death of Joseph Meyer.
(i) Christopher Craig is the interim office holder. He assumed the office on January 30, 2015, replacing Rob McCord (D), who resigned effective earlier the same day following a federal investigation into campaign finance violations. Investigators found that McCord pressured potential contributors in his failed gubernatorial run in 2014. Craig will serve until Gov. Wolf selects a replacement for the remaining two years of McCord's elected term.

Table 4.25
TREASURERS: QUALIFICATIONS FOR OFFICE

State or other jurisdiction	Minimum age	U.S. citizen (years)	State resident (years)	Qualified voter (years)
Alabama	25	7	5	...
Alaska	...	...	...	...
Arizona	25	10	5	★
Arkansas	21	★	★	...
California	18	★	★	★
Colorado	25	★	2	★
Connecticut	18	★	★	★
Delaware	18	★	★	★
Florida	30	★	7	★
Georgia	...	★	★	...
Hawaii	...	★	1	...
Idaho	25	2	2	...
Illinois	25	★	3	...
Indiana	...	★	★	★
Iowa	18	...	★	★
Kansas	...	...	...	...
Kentucky	30	2	2	★
Louisiana	25	5	5	★
Maine	...	★	★	...
Maryland	...	...	...	...
Massachusetts	...	...	...	...
Michigan	...	...	...	...
Minnesota	...	...	...	...
Mississippi	25	★	★	★
Missouri	30	15	10	★
Montana	...	...	...	...
Nebraska	...	★	★	★
Nevada	25	2	2	★
New Hampshire	...	...	...	...
New Jersey	...	...	★	...
New Mexico	30	★	5	★
New York	...	...	...	...
North Carolina	21	★	1	...
North Dakota	25	★	★	★
Ohio	18	★	★	★
Oklahoma	31	10	10	★
Oregon	18	...	★	...
Pennsylvania	...	...	...	...
Rhode Island	18	★	★	★
South Carolina	...	★	★	★
South Dakota	...	...	...	...
Tennessee	...	...	...	...
Texas	18	★	★	...
Utah	25	...	5	★
Vermont	...	★	★	...
Virginia	...	...	...	...
Washington	18	★	...	★
West Virginia	18	★	★	★
Wisconsin	18	★	★	★
Wyoming	25	★	★	★
Dist. of Columbia	...	★	...	...

Source: National Association of State Treasurers, January 2014.
Key:
★ — Formal provision; number of years not specified.
... — No formal provision.
N.A. — Not applicable.
(a) Five years immediately preceding the date of qualification for office.

Table 4.26
RESPONSIBILITIES OF THE TREASURER'S OFFICE

State or other jurisdiction	Cash management	Banking services	Investment of retirement funds	Investment of trust funds	Deferred compensation	Management of bonded debt	Bond issuance	Debt service	Arbitrage	Unclaimed property	Archives for disbursement of documents	College savings	Collateral programs	Local government investment pool	Other
Alabama	★	★	...	...	...	★	...	★	...	★	...	★	★	...	...
Alaska	★	★	★	★	...	...	★	★	★	★	...	...	...	...	...
Arizona	★	★	...	★	...	...	...	...	...	...	...	...	...	★	...
Arkansas	★	★	★	...	...	...	...	...	...	...	...	★	...	★	...
California	★	★	...	★	...	★	★	★	★	...	...	★	★	★	...
Colorado	★	★	...	...	...	★	★	...	...	★	...	...	...	...	...
Connecticut	★	★	★	★	...	★	★	★	★	★	...	★	...	★	(a)
Delaware	★	★	...	...	★	...	★	★	★	...	...	...	★	★	(b)
Florida	★	★	...	★	★	...	...	...	...	★	...	...	★	...	(c)
Georgia	★	★	...	★	...	...	...	★	...	...	...	...	★	★	(d)
Hawaii	★	★	★	★	...	...	★	★	...	★	...	★	...	...	...
Idaho	★	★	...	...	...	★	...	...	...	★	...	★	...	★	...
Illinois	★	★	★	...	...	...	...	★	★	★	...	★	...	★	...
Indiana	★	★	...	★	...	★	...	...	...	...	★	★	...	★	...
Iowa	★	★	★	★	...	★	★	★	★	★	...	★	★	...	...
Kansas	★	★	...	...	...	...	...	...	...	★	...	★	...	...	(e)
Kentucky	★	★	...	...	...	...	...	★	★	★	★	...	...	...	...
Louisiana	★	★	...	★	...	★	★	★	★	★	...	...	★	...	(f)
Maine	★	★	...	★	...	★	★	★	★	★	...	★	...	...	(g)
Maryland	★	★	...	...	...	★	★	★	★	★	...	...	★	★	...
Massachusetts	★	★	★	★	★	★	★	★	...	★	...	★	...	...	...
Michigan	★	★	★	★	...	★	★	★	★	★	...	★	...	...	...
Minnesota	★	★	...	...	...	★	★	★	...	...	...	...	...	...	...
Mississippi	★	★	★	★	...	★	...	★	★	★	...	★	★	★	...
Missouri	★	★	...	★	...	...	...	★	...	★	...	★	...	...	(h)
Montana	★	★	...	...	...	★	★	★	★	...	...	...	...	...	...
Nebraska	★	★	...	...	...	...	...	...	...	★	...	★	...	...	(i)
Nevada	★	★	...	...	...	★	★	★	...	★	...	★	★	★	...
New Hampshire	★	★	...	★	...	★	★	★	★	★	...	★	...	...	...
New Jersey	★	★	★	★	★	★	★	★	★	★	...	...	...	★	...
New Mexico	★	★	★	★	...	...	...	★	...	...	★	...	...	★	...
New York	★	★	★	★	...	...	...	...	...	★	...	...	...	★	...
North Carolina	★	★	★	★	...	★	★	★	★	★	...	★	...	★	...
North Dakota	★	...	★	...	...	...	...	...	...	...	...	...	...	...	(j)
Ohio	★	★	...	...	...	★	★	★	★	...	...	...	★	★	...
Oklahoma	★	★	...	...	...	...	...	...	...	★	...	★	★	...	...
Oregon	★	★	★	★	★	★	★	★	★	...	...	★	★	★	...
Pennsylvania	★	★	★	★	...	...	★	★	★	★	...	★	...	★	...
Rhode Island	★	★	★	★	...	...	★	★	★	★	...	★	★	★	...
South Carolina	★	★	★	★	...	★	★	★	★	★	...	★	★	★	...
South Dakota	★	★	★	★	...	...	...	...	...	★	...	...	★	...	(k)
Tennessee	★	★	★	...	★	...	...	...	...	★	...	★	★	★	...
Texas	★	★	...	...	...	★	...	...	...	★	...	★	★	★	(l)
Utah	★	★	...	★	★	★	★	★	★	★	...	...	...	★	...
Vermont	★	★	★	★	★	★	★	★	★	★	...	...	...	...	...
Virginia	★	★	...	★	...	★	★	★	★	★	...	...	★	★	(m)
Washington	★	★	...	...	...	★	★	★	★	★	...	★	★	★	...
West Virginia	★	★	...	★	★	...	...	★	...	★	...	★	★	★	...
Wisconsin	...	...	...	...	...	...	...	...	...	★	...	...	...	★	...
Wyoming	★	★	...	★	...	★	★	★	★	★	...	...	★	★	(n)
Dist. of Columbia	★	★	★	★	★	★	★	★	★	★	...	★	★	...	...

Source: The National Association of State Treasurers, January 2014.
Key:
★ — Responsible for activity.
... — Not responsible for activity.
N.A. — Data not available.
(a) Second Injury Fund.
(b) General Fund account reconcilement; Disbursements—2004.
(c) State Accounting Disbursement, Fire Marshall, Insurance and Banking Consumer Services, Insurance Rehabilitation.
(d) Merchant Card Services.
(e) Municipal bond servicing.

(f) Social Security for Section 218 Agreements—2004.
(g) Municipal Revenue Sharing.
(h) Investment of all State funds.
(i) Nebraska Child Support Payment Center, Long-Term Care Savings Plan.
(j) Financial Literacy.
(k) Treasurer is a member of the trust and retirement investment programs—2004.
(l) Tax Administration/Collection/Estimating.
(m) Risk Management.
(n) Several other legislatively designated programs.

Table 4.27
THE STATE AUDITORS, 2015

State or other jurisdiction	State agency	Agency head	Title	Legal basis for office	Method of selection	Term of office	U.S. citizen	State resident	Maximum consecutive terms allowed
Alabama	Department of Examiners of Public Accounts	Ronald L. Jones	Chief Examiner	S	LC	7 yrs.	★	...	None
Alaska	Division of Legislative Audit	Kris Curtis	Legislative Auditor	C,S	L	(a)	...	...	None
Arizona	Office of the Auditor General	Debra K. Davenport	Auditor General	S	LC	5 yrs.	★	★	None
Arkansas	Division of Legislative Audit	Roger A. Norman	Legislative Auditor	S	LC	Indefinite	★	★	None
California	Bureau of State Audits	Elaine M. Howle	State Auditor	S	G	4 yrs.	★	...	None
Colorado	Office of the State Auditor	Dianne E. Ray	State Auditor	C,S	LC	5 yrs.	★	★	None
Connecticut	Office of the Auditors of Public Accounts	John C. Geragosian and Robert M. Ward	State Auditors	S	L	4 yrs.	...	...	None
Delaware	Office of the Auditor of Accounts	R. Thomas Wagner Jr.	Auditor of Accounts	C	E	4 yrs.	★	★	None
Florida	Office of the Auditor General	David W. Martin	Auditor General	C,S	L	(a)	...	...	None
Georgia	Department of Audits and Accounts	Greg S. Griffin	State Auditor	S	L	Indefinite	...	★	None
Hawaii	Office of the Auditor	Jan K. Yamane	State Auditor	C	L	8 yrs.	...	...	None
Idaho	Legislative Services Office— Legislative Audits	April J. Renfro	Division Manager	S	LC	(b)	...	...	None
Illinois	Office of the Auditor General	William G. Holland	Auditor General	C,S	L	10 yrs.	...	...	None
Indiana	State Board of Accounts	Paul D. Joyce	State Examiner	S	G	4 yrs.	★	...	None
Iowa	Office of the Auditor of State	Mary Mosiman	Auditor of State	C,S	E	4 yrs.	★	★	None
Kansas	Legislative Division of Post Audit	Scott E. Frank	Legislative Post Auditor	S	LC	(b)	...	...	None
Kentucky	Office of the Auditor of Public Accounts	Adam Edelen	Auditor of Public Accounts	C,S	E	4 yrs.	★	★	2
Louisiana	Office of the Legislative Auditor	Daryl G. Purpera	Legislative Auditor	C,S	L	(a)	...	...	None
Maine	Department of Audit	Pola A. Buckley	State Auditor	S	L	4 yrs.	...	...	2
Maryland	Office of Legislative Audits	Thomas J. Barnickel III	Legislative Auditor	S	ED	(a)	...	...	None
Massachusetts	Office of the Auditor of the Commonwealth	Suzanne M. Bump	Auditor of the Commonwealth	C,S	E	4 yrs.	★	★	None
Michigan	Office of the Auditor General	Doug Ringler	Auditor General	C	L	8 yrs.	...	★	None
Minnesota	Office of the Legislative Auditor	James R. Nobles	Legislative Auditor	S	L	6 yrs.	...	★	None
Mississippi	Office of the State Auditor	Rebecca Otto	State Auditor	C	E	4 yrs.	★	★	None
Missouri	Office of the State Auditor	Stacey E. Pickering	State Auditor	C	E	4 yrs.	★	★	None
	Office of the State Auditor	Nicole Galloway	State Auditor	C,S	E	4 yrs.	★	★	None
Montana	Legislative Audit Division	Tori Hunthausen	Legislative Auditor	C,S	LC	4 yrs.	...	★	None
Nebraska	Office of the Auditor of Public Accounts	Charlie Janssen	Auditor of Public Accounts	C	E	4 yrs.	★	★	None
Nevada	Legislative Counsel Bureau, Audit Division	Paul Townsend	Legislative Auditor	S	LC	Indefinite	...	★	None
New Hampshire	Office of the Legislative Budget Assistant	Jeffry A. Pattison	Legislative Budget Assistant	S	LC	2 yrs.	...	...	None
New Jersey	Office of the State Auditor	Stephen M. Eells	State Auditor	C,S	L	5 yr. term and until successor is appointed	★	...	None
	Office of the State Comptroller	Marc Larkins	Acting State Comptroller	S	G	6 yrs.	...	...	
New Mexico	Office of the State Auditor	Tim Keller	State Auditor	C,S	E	4 yrs.	★	★	2
New York	Office of the State Comptroller, State Audit Bureau	Thomas P. DiNapoli	State Comptroller	C,S	E	4 yrs.	★	★	2
North Carolina	Office of the State Auditor	Beth A. Wood	State Auditor	C	E	4 yrs.	★	★	None
North Dakota	Office of the State Auditor	Robert R. Peterson	State Auditor	C,S	E	4 yrs.	...	★	None
Ohio	Office of the Auditor of State	Dave Yost	Auditor of State	C,S	E	4 yrs.	★	★	2

See footnotes at end of table.

THE STATE AUDITORS, 2015—Continued

State or other jurisdiction	State agency	Agency head	Title	Legal basis for office	Method of selection	Term of office	U.S. citizen	State resident	Maximum consecutive terms allowed
Oklahoma	Office of the State Auditor and Inspector	Gary Jones	State Auditor and Inspector	C,S	E	4 yrs.	★	★	None
Oregon	Division of Audits	Gary Blackmer	Director	C,S	SS	(c)	…	…	None
Pennsylvania	Department of the Auditor General	Eugene DePasquale	Auditor General	C,S	E	4 yrs.	…	…	2
	Legislative Finance and Budget Cmte.	Philip R. Durgin	Executive Director	S	LC	(b)	…	…	None
Rhode Island	Office of the Auditor General	Dennis E. Hoyle	Auditor General	S	LC	(b)	…	…	None
South Carolina	Legislative Audit Council	Earle Powell	Director	S	LC	4 yrs.	…	…	None
	Office of the State Auditor	Richard H. Gilbert Jr.	Interim State Auditor	S	SB	Indefinite	…	…	None
South Dakota	Department of Legislative Audit	Martin L. Guindon	Auditor General	S	L	8 yrs.	…	…	None
Tennessee	Comptroller of the Treasury, Dept. of Audit	Justin P. Wilson	Comptroller of the Treasury	C,S	L	2 yrs.	…	…	None
Texas	Office of the State Auditor	John Keel	State Auditor	S	LC	(b)	…	…	None
Utah	Office of the State Auditor	John Dougall	State Auditor	C,S	E	4 yrs.	★	★	None
Vermont	Office of the State Auditor	Douglas R. Hoffer	State Auditor	C	E	2 yrs.	…	★	None
Virginia	Office of the Auditor of Public Accounts	Martha S. Mavredes	Auditor of Public Accounts	C,S	L	4 yrs.	…	…	None
Washington	Office of the State Auditor	Jan Jutte	State Auditor	C,S	E	4 yrs.	★	★	None
West Virginia	Legislative Auditor's Office	Aaron Allred	Legislative Auditor	S			…	★	
Wisconsin	Legislative Audit Bureau	Joe Chrisman	State Auditor	S	LC	(b)	…	…	None
Wyoming	Department of Audit	Jeffrey C. Vogel	Director	S	GC	6 yrs.	…	…	None
Dist. of Columbia	Office of the D.C. Auditor	Yolanda Branche	District of Columbia Auditor	S					
American Samoa	AS Territorial Auditor Office	Liua Fatuesi	Territorial Auditor						
Guam	Office of the Public Auditor	Doris Flores Brooks	Public Auditor	S	E	4 yrs.	★	★	None
No. Mariana Islands	Office of the Public Auditor	Michael Pai	Public Auditor	C,S	GL	6 yrs.	N.A.	N.A.	2
Puerto Rico	Office of the Comptroller	Yesmin M. Valdivieso-Galib	Comptroller	C	GL	10 yrs.	★	★	1

Sources: *Auditing in the States: A Summary*, 2013 edition, The National Association of State Auditors, Comptrollers and Treasurers. Updated March 2015)

Key:
★ — Provision for.
… — No provision for.
E — Elected by the public.
L — Appointed by the legislature.
G — Appointed by the governor.
SS — Appointed by the secretary of state.
LC — selected by legislative committee, commission or council.
ED — appointed by the executive director of legislative services.

GC — Appointed by governor, secretary of state and treasurer.
GL — Appointed by the governor and confirmed by both chambers of the legislature.
SB — Appointed by state budget and control board.
C — Constitutional.
S — Statutory.
N.A. — Not applicable.
(a) Serves at the pleasure of the legislature.
(b) Serves at the pleasure of a legislative committee.
(c) Serves at the pleasure of the secretary of state.

Table 4.28
STATE AUDITORS: SCOPE OF AGENCY AUTHORITY

State or other jurisdiction	Authority to audit all state agencies	Authority to audit local governments	Authority to obtain information	Authority to issue subpoenas	Authority to specify accounting principles for local governments	Investigations Agency investigates fraud, waste, abuse, and/or illegal acts	Agency operates a hotline
Alabama	★	...	★	★	★(a)	★	...
Alaska	★	...	★	★	...	★	...
Arizona	★	...	★	...	...	★	...
Arkansas	★	★	★	★	...	★	...
California	★	★	★	★	...	★	★
Colorado	★	★	★	★	★	★	...
Connecticut	★	...	★	...	...	★	★
Delaware	★	★	★	★	...	★	★
Florida	(b)	★	★	...	...	★	...
Georgia	★	...	★	★	★	★	...
Hawaii	★	★	★	★	...	★	★
Idaho	★	...	★	...	...	★	...
Illinois	★	...	★	★	(c)	★	★
Indiana	★	★	★	★	★	★	...
Iowa	★	★	★	★	...	★	...
Kansas	★	★	★	...	...	...	...
Kentucky	★	★	★	★	...	★	★
Louisiana	★	★	★	★	★	★	★
Maine	★	★	★	★	★	★	★
Maryland	★(b)	(d)	★	...	★	★	★
Massachusetts	★	★	★	★	...	★	★
Michigan	★	...	★	★	...	★	...
Minnesota							
Legislative Auditor	★	...	★	★	...	★	...
State Auditor	(e)	★	★	★	★	★	...
Mississippi	★	...	★	★	★	★	★
Missouri	★	...	★	★	...	★	★
Montana	★	...	★	...	...	★	★
Nebraska	★	★	★	...	★	★	★
Nevada	★	★	★	...	...	★	...
New Hampshire	...	...	★	...	...	★	...
New Jersey							
State Auditor	★	...	★	...	...	★	...
State Comptroller	★	★	★	★	...	★	★
New Mexico	★	★	★	★	★	★	★
New York	★	★	★	★	★	★	★
North Carolina	★	...	★	★	...	★	★
North Dakota	(f)	★	★	...	★	★	...
Ohio	★	★	★	★	★	★	★
Oklahoma	★	★	★	★	...	★	★
Oregon	★	...	★	★	★	★	★
Pennsylvania	(g)	★	★	★	...	★	★
Rhode Island	★	...	★	★	★	★	...
South Carolina							
Legislative Audit Council	★	...	★	...	...	★	...
State Auditor	(h)	...	★	...	...	★	...
South Dakota	★	★	★	★	...	★	...
Tennessee	★	★	★	★	★	★	★
Texas	★	(i)	★	...	...	★	★
Utah	(j)	★	★	★	★	★	★
Vermont	★	★	★	★	(k)	★	★
Virginia	★	...	★	...	★	★	...
Washington	★	★	★	★	★	★	★
West Virginia	★	...	★	★	...	★	★
Wisconsin	★	...	★	★	...	★	★
Wyoming	★	★	★	★	...	★	...
Guam	★	★	★	★	★	★	★
No. Mariana Islands	★	N.A.	★	★	★	★	N.A.
Puerto Rico	★	★	★	★	...	★	★

See footnotes at end of table.

STATE AUDITORS: SCOPE OF AGENCY AUTHORITY — Continued

Source: Auditing in the States, 2012 Edition, The National Association of State Auditors, Comptrollers and Treasurers. Update 2015.

Key:

★ — Provision for responsibility.

... — No provision for responsibility.

N.A. — Not available.

(a) Municipalities not covered.

(b) The legislature or legislative branch is excluded from audit authority.

(c) Audits of local governments conducted as directed by the General Assembly.

(d) Local school systems only.

(e) State agencies are audited by the Office of Legislative Auditor.

(f) The Bank of North Dakota is excluded.

(g) The legislative and judicial branches are excluded from audit authority.

(h) State's public colleges and universities and a few agencies are excluded from audit authority.

(i) The state auditor can conduct an audit or investigation of any entity receiving funds from the state; also, certain political subdivisions of the state.

(j) State Retirement and Workers' Compensation Fund are excluded from audit authority.

(k) Local governments not receiving state money.

Table 4.29
STATE AUDITORS: TYPES OF AUDITS

State or other jurisdiction	Financial statement	Single audit	Attestation engagements	Compliance only	Economy and efficiency	Program	Sunset	Performance measures	IT	Accounting and review services	Other audits
Alabama	★	★							★		
Alaska	★	★	★	★	★	★		★	★		
Arizona	★	★	★	★	★	★	★		★	★	(a)
Arkansas	★	★	★			★			★		(b)
California	★	★		★	★	★		★	★		
Colorado	★	★			★	★		★	★		(c)
Connecticut	★	★		★	★	★		★	★		(d)
Delaware		★	★	★	★				★		
Florida	★	★	★	★	★	★			★		(e)
Georgia	★	★	★	★	★	★	★	★	★	★	
Hawaii	★	★							★		
Idaho	★	★	★		★	★		★	★	★	(f)
Illinois	★	★	★	★			★	★	★	★	
Indiana	★	★	★	★	★	★			★		
Iowa		★		★					★		
Kansas	★	★	★	★	★	★		★	★	★	(g)
Kentucky	★	★	★	★	★	★		★	★		
Louisiana	★	★		★	★	★	★		★		
Maine	★							★	★		
Maryland		★		★	★	★		★	★		(h)
Massachusetts		★	★	★	★	★		★	★	★	
Michigan	★	★	★		★	★		★	★		
Minnesota											
Legislative Auditor	★	★			★	★		★	★		(i)
State Auditor	★	★						★	★		(j)
Mississippi	★	★	★		★	★		★	★		
Missouri	★	★		★	★	★		★	★		
Montana	★	★	★	★	★	★		★	★		
Nebraska	★	★	★					★	★		
Nevada				★	★	★		★	★		(k)
New Hampshire	★	★		★	★	★		★			
New Jersey											
State Auditor	★	★	★	★	★	★			★		
State Comptroller				★				★	★		(l)
New Mexico	★	★	★		★	★		★	★	★	
New York	★	★		★	★	★		★	★		(m)
North Carolina	★	★		★	★	★		★	★		
North Dakota	★	★		★		★			★		
Ohio	★		★	★	★	★		★	★	★	

See footnotes at end of table.

STATE AUDITORS: TYPES OF AUDITS — Continued

State or other jurisdiction	Financial statement	Single audit	Attestation engagements	Compliance only	Economy and efficiency	Program	Sunset	Performance measures	IT	Accounting and review services	Other audits
Oklahoma	★	★	★	...	★	★	...	...	★	...	(n)
Oregon	★	★	★	★	★	★	...	...	★	★	...
Pennsylvania	★	★	★	★	★	★	...	...	★	...	...
Rhode Island	★	★	★	★	...	★	...	...	★	...	...
South Carolina											
Legislative Audit Council	...	...	...	...	...	★	...	...	...	...	...
State Auditor	★	★	★	...	★	...	...	...	...	...	...
South Dakota	★	★	★	...	...	...	...	...	...	★	...
Tennessee	★	★	★	★	★	★	★	★	★	★	...
Texas	★	★	★	...	...	...	...	★	★	...	...
Utah	★	★	★	...	...	...	...	★	...	★	(o)
Vermont	★	★	...	★	★	★	...	★	★	★	...
Virginia	★	★	★	...	...	★	...	★	★	...	(p)
Washington	...	★	★	★	★	★	...	★	★	★	...
West Virginia	★	...	...	★	...	...	...	...	...	...	(q)
Wisconsin	...	★	...	...	★	★	...	...	...	...	...
Wyoming	★	...	...	★	★	...	...	★	...	...	...
Guam	...	...	...	...	★	★	...	...	...	...	...
No. Mariana Islands	★	★	★	...	★	★	...	...	★	★	...
Puerto Rico	...	...	...	★	...	...	...	...	...	...	...

Sources: Auditing in the States: A Summary, 2012 edition. The National Association of State Auditors, Comptrollers and Treasurers and state constitutions and statutes. Updated March 2014.

Key:

★ — Provision for responsibility.

... — No provision for responsibility.

N.A. — Not available.

(a) Internal control and compliance reviews; financial compliance reports; special reports; investigative reports.

(b) Investigations, assessments related to high risk.

(c) Agreed-upon procedures.

(d) Delaware contracts out financial statement and IT audits.

(e) Desk reviews.

(f) Agreed-upon procedures.

(g) Investigative or forensic audits.

(h) Privatization audits.

(i) Internal control and compliance audits.

(j) Agreed-upon procedures.

(k) Internal control reviews.

(l) School district forensic audits.

(m) Internal control reviews; studies.

(n) Investigations (reviews).

(o) Special projects, feasibility studies.

(p) Cash receipts audits at local courts.

(q) Legislative research and performance audits.

Table 4.30
THE STATE COMPTROLLERS, 2015

State	Agency or office	Name	Title	Legal basis for office	Method of selection	Approval or confirmation, if necessary	Length of term	Elected comptroller's maximum consecutive terms	Civil service or merit system employee
Alabama	Office of the State Comptroller	Thomas L. White Jr.	State Comptroller	S	(c)	AG	(b)	...	★
Alaska	Division of Finance	Scot Arehart	Division Director	S	(d)	AG	(a)	...	★
Arizona	General Accounting Office	D. Clark Partridge	State Comptroller	S	(d)	AG	(b)	...	...
Arkansas	Dept. of Finance and Administration	Larry Walther	Chief Fiscal Officer, Director	S	G	...	(a)	...	...
	Office of the State Auditor	Andrea Lea	State Auditor	C					
California	Office of the State Controller	Betty Yee (D)	State Controller	C	E	...	4 yrs.	2 terms	...
	Department of Finance	Todd Jerue	Chief Operating Officer						
Colorado	Department of Personnel and Administration	Bob Jaros	State Controller	S	(d)	AG	(g)	...	★
Connecticut	Office of the Comptroller	Kevin P. Lembo (D)	Comptroller	C	E	...	4 yrs.	unlimited	...
Delaware	Dept. of Finance	Kristopher Knight	Director, Division of Accounting	S	G	AS	(a)	...	...
Florida	Dept. of Financial Services	Jeff Atwater	Chief Financial Officer	C,S	E	...	4 yrs.	2 terms	...
Georgia	State Accounting Office	Alan Skelton	State Accounting Officer	S	G	...	(a)	...	...
Hawaii	Dept. of Accounting and General Services	Douglas Murdock	State Comptroller	S	G	AS	4 yrs.	...	...
Idaho	Office of State Controller	Brandon Woolf	State Controller	C	E	...	4 yrs.	2 terms	...
Illinois	Office of the State Comptroller	Leslie Munger (R)	State Comptroller	C	E	...	4 yrs.	unlimited	...
Indiana	Office of the Auditor of State	Suzanne Crouch	Auditor of State	C	E	...	4 yrs.	2 terms	...
Iowa	State Accounting Enterprise	Calvin McKelvogue	Chief Operating Officer	S	(g)	AS	(a)	...	...
Kansas	Office of Management, Analysis and Standards	DeAnn Hill	Director	S	(d)	...	(b)	...	★
Kentucky	Office of the Controller	Edgar C. Ross	Controller	S	(f)	AG	(i)	...	...
Louisiana	Division of Administration	John McLean	Director	S	G	...	(a)	...	...
Maine	Office of the State Controller	Douglas Cotnoir	State Controller	C	(f)	AG	(i)	...	...
Maryland	Office of the Comptroller of the Treasury	Peter Franchot (D)	State Comptroller	C	E	...	4 yrs	unlimited	...
Massachusetts	Office of the Comptroller	Thomas Shack, III	Comptroller	S	G	...	4 yrs	...	★
Michigan	Office of Financial Management	Michael J. Moody	Director	S	SBD	SBD	(k)	...	...
Minnesota	Department of Finance	Myron Frans	Commissioner	S	G	AS	(a)	...	...
Mississippi	Department of Finance and Administration	Diane Langham	Director, Office of Fiscal Management	C,S	G	...	(a)	...	...
Missouri	Division of Accounting	Stacy Neal	Director of Accounting	S	(d)	...	(g)	...	...
Montana	State Accounting Division	Cody Pearce	Administrator	S	(m)	...	(b)	...	★
Nebraska	Accounting Division	Wes Mohling	State Accounting Administrator	S	(d)	...	(b)	...	...
Nevada	Office of the State Controller	Ron Knecht (R)	State Controller	C,S	E	...	4 yrs.	2 terms	...
New Hampshire	Department of Administration	Gerard Murphy	State Comptroller	S	G	...	4 yrs.	...	...
New Jersey	Office of Management and Budget	Charlene M. Holzbaur	State Comptroller	S	G	AS	(a)	...	★

See footnotes at end of table.

THE STATE COMPTROLLERS, 2015—Continued

State	Agency or office	Name	Title	Legal basis for office	Method of selection	Approval or confirmation, if necessary	Length of term	Elected comptroller's maximum consecutive terms	Civil service or merit system employee
New Mexico	Dept. of Finance and Administration, Financial Control Division	Ronald Spilman	State Controller	S	G	...	(a)	...	★
New York	Office of the State Comptroller	Thomas P. DiNapoli	State Comptroller	C,S	E	...	4 yrs.	unlimited	...
North Carolina	Office of the State Controller	Linda Combs	State Controller	S	G	GA	7 yrs.	...	...
North Dakota	Office of Management and Budget	Pam Sharp	Director	S	G	...	(a)	unlimited	...
Ohio	Office of Budget and Management	Timothy S. Keen	Director	S	G	AS	(a)	...	...
Oklahoma	Office of State Finance	Lynne Bajema	State Comptroller	S	(c)	...	(h)	...	...
Oregon	Chief Financial Office	Robert Hamilton	Manager, Statewide Accounting and Reporting	S	(d)	AG	(g)	...	...
Pennsylvania	Office of the Budget/Comptroller Operations	Anna Maria Kiehl	Chief Accounting Officer	S	SBD	AG	(a)	...	...
Rhode Island	Office of Accounts and Control	Marc Leoncetti	State Controller	S	(d)	...	(b)	...	★
South Carolina	Office of the Comptroller General	Richard Eckstrom (R)	Comptroller General	C,S	E	...	4 yrs.	unlimited	...
South Dakota	Office of the State Auditor	Steve Barnett (R)	State Auditor	C	E	...	4 yrs.	2 terms	...
Tennessee	Division of Accounts	Mike Corricelli	Chief of Accounts	S	(f)	...	(b)	...	...
Texas	Office of the Comptroller of Public Accounts	Glenn Hegar (R)	Comptroller of Public Accounts	C,S	E	...	4 yrs.	unlimited	...
Utah	Division of Finance	John C. Reidhead	Director	S	(d)	AG	(g)	...	...
Vermont	Department of Finance and Management	James Reardon	Commissioner	S	G	AS	(a)	...	...
Virginia	Department of Accounts	David A. Von Moll	State Comptroller	S	G	GA	(a)	...	...
Washington	Office of Financial Management	David Schumacher	Director	C	G	...	(a)	...	...
West Virginia	Office of the State Auditor	Glen B. Gainier III (D)	State Auditor	C	E	...	4 yrs.	unlimited	...
	Finance Division, Office of the State Comptroller	Ross Taylor	State Comptroller and Finance Director	S	(d)	AG	AG	...	...
Wisconsin	State Controller's Office	Jeffrey Anderson	State Controller	S	CS	...	(b)	unlimited	★
Wyoming	Office of the State Auditor	Cynthia Cloud	State Auditor	C	E	...	4 yrs.	2 terms	...

Sources: Comptrollers: Technical Activities and Functions, 2012 edition, National Association of State Auditors, Comptrollers and Treasurers. Updated April 2015.

Key:
★ — Yes, provision for.
... — No provision for.
C — Constitutional.
S — Statutory.
N.A. — Not applicable.
E — Elected by the public.
G — Appointed by the governor.
CS — Civil Service.
AG — Approved by the governor.
AS — Approved/confirmed by the Senate.
SBD — Approved by state budget director.
GA — Confirmed by the General Assembly.
SDB — Confirmed by State Depository Board.

(a) Serves at the pleasure of the governor.
(b) Indefinite.
(c) Appointed by the director of the Dept. of Finance (merit system position).
(d) Appointed by the head of the Department of Administration or Administrative Services.
(e) Appointed by the head of the Finance Department or agency.
(f) Appointed by the head of Financial and Administrative Services.
(g) Serves at the pleasure of the head of the Department of Administration or Administrative Services.
(h) Serves at the pleasure of the head of the Finance Department or agency.
(i) Serves at the pleasure of the head of Financial and Administrative Services.
(j) Appointed by the governor for a term coterminous with the governor.
(k) Two-year renewable contractual term; classified executive service.
(l) As of July 1, 2005, the responsibility for accounting and financial reporting in Georgia was transferred to the newly created State Accounting Office.
(m) Classified position.

Table 4.31
STATE COMPTROLLERS: QUALIFICATIONS FOR OFFICE

State	Minimum age	U.S. citizen (years)	State resident (years) (a)	Education years or degree	Professional experience and years	Professional certification and years	Other qualifications	No specific qualifications for office
Alabama	★	★	★	★, B.S.	★, 10 yrs.	(b)	...	...
Alaska	...	...	...	...	...	...	...	★
Arizona	...	★, 1 yr.	★, 1 yr.	★, B.S.	★, 7–10 yrs.	★(c)	...	...
Arkansas	30	...	...	...	★	...	...	...
California	★	...	...	...	...	...	...	...
Colorado	...	...	...	★(d)	★, 6 yrs.	★, CPA	...	...
Connecticut	...	...	★	...	...	...	...	...
Delaware	...	...	...	...	...	...	...	★
Florida	30	...	★, 7 yrs.	...	...	...	...	...
Georgia	...	...	...	...	...	...	...	★
Hawaii	...	...	30 days	...	...	...	...	★
Idaho	25	(e)	★, 2 yrs.	...	...	...	...	...
Illinois	25	★	★, 3 yrs.	...	...	...	...	...
Indiana	...	...	★(e)	...	...	...	...	...
Iowa	...	...	...	...	...	...	...	★
Kansas	...	...	...	...	...	...	...	★
Kentucky	...	...	...	...	...	...	(f)	★
Louisiana	...	...	...	...	...	...	...	★
Maine	...	...	...	...	...	...	(g)	★
Maryland	18	★	★	...	...	...	...	...
Massachusetts	...	...	...	★(h)	★, 7 yrs.	...	...	...
Michigan	...	...	...	★(i)	★, 2 yrs.	(i)	(i)	...
Minnesota	...	...	...	...	...	...	...	★
Mississippi	...	...	...	★(h)	★, 10 yrs.	★, CPA	(j)	...
Missouri	...	...	...	...	...	...	...	★
Montana	...	...	...	★(k)	★, 10 yrs.	★, CPA	...	★
Nebraska	...	...	...	★(l)	★(m)	★, CPA	...	...
Nevada	25	★	★, 2 yrs.	...	...	...	...	...
New Hampshire	...	...	...	...	...	...	(n)	★
New Jersey	...	...	...	...	...	...	...	★
New Mexico	30	★	5	N.A.	N.A.	N.A.	N.A.	N.A.
New York	30	★	★(o)	...	...	...	...	...
North Carolina	...	...	...	★(p)	★	...	★(p)	...
North Dakota	...	...	...	...	...	...	...	★
Ohio	...	...	...	...	...	...	...	...
Oklahoma	...	★	★	★	★, 5 yrs.	...	...	★
Oregon	...	...	...	...	...	...	...	★
Pennsylvania	...	...	...	...	...	...	...	★
Rhode Island	...	★	★	★(q)	...	★, CPA	...	...
South Carolina	18	...	...	...	...	...	...	...
South Dakota	★	★	★, 1 yr.	...	...	...	...	...
Tennessee	...	...	...	★	★, 7 yrs.	★, CPA	...	...
Texas	18	★(e)	★, 1 yr.	...	...	...	...	...
Utah	...	★	...	★	★, 6 yrs.	★, CPA	...	...
Vermont	...	...	...	...	...	...	...	★
Virginia	...	...	...	...	...	...	...	★
Washington	★	★, Whole life	★	★	★	★	...	...
West Virginia Office of State Auditor	25	★	★	...	...	...	...	...
Division of Finance, Office of State Comptroller	...	★	★	★, B.S., B.A.	★, 4 yrs.	...	...	...
Wisconsin	...	...	...	★, B.S.	...	★, CPA	...	...
Wyoming	★	★	★	...	...	...	...	...

Sources: The National Association of State Auditors, Comptrollers and Treasurers, January 2014, and The Council of State Governments, January 2015.

Key:
★ — Formal provision.　... — No formal provision.
N.A. — Not applicable.
(a) 18 yrs. at time of election or appointment and a citizen of the state.
(b) One of the following CPA, CIA, CPM, CGFM or CGFO.
(c) Any of those mentioned or CFE, CPM, etc.
(d) 5 yrs. or college degree.
(e) Years not specified.
(f) The Kentucky Revised Statutes state that "The state controller shall be a person qualified by education and experience for the position and held in high esteem in the accounting community."
(g) There are no educational or professional mandates, yet the appointed official is generally qualified by a combination of experience and education.

(h) Master's degree. For Massachusetts an advanced degree in accounting, auditing, financial management, business administration or public administration (M.G.L.C. 7A, S.1).
(i) Bachelor's degree, no professional certification required, but CPA certification is considered desirable. Financial management experience, knowledge of GAAP and good communication skills are other qualifications.
(j) The executive director (a) shall be a certified public accountant; or (b) shall possess a master's degree in business, public administration or a related field; or (c) shall have at least 10 yrs. experience in management in the private or public sector and a minimum of 5 yrs. experience in high level management with a documented record of management.
(k) Bachelor's degree in accounting.
(l) 4-yr. degree with concentration in accounting.
(m) 3 yrs. directing the work of others.
(n) Education and relevant experience.
(o) Five preceding elections.
(p) Qualified by education and experience for the position.
(q) Master's degree in accounting or business administration.

Table 4.32
STATE COMPTROLLERS: DUTIES, RESPONSIBILITIES AND FUNCTIONS

State	Disbursements	Payroll	Pre-audit	Post-audit	Operating the financial management system	Financial reporting
Alabama	★	★	★	...	★	★
Alaska	★	★	...	...	★	★
Arizona	N.A.	N.A.	N.A.	N.A.	N.A.	N.A.
Arkansas	N.A.	N.A.	N.A.	N.A.	N.A.	N.A.
California	N.A.	N.A.	N.A.	N.A.	N.A.	N.A.
Colorado	★	★	★	...	★	★
Connecticut	N.A.	N.A.	N.A.	N.A.	N.A.	N.A.
Delaware	★	...	★	★	★	★
Florida	★	★	★	★	★	★
Georgia	...	★	...	...	★	★
Hawaii	★	★	★	★	...	★
Idaho	★	★	...	...	★	★
Illinois	★	★	★	★	★	★
Indiana	N.A.	N.A.	N.A.	N.A.	N.A.	N.A.
Iowa	★	★	★	★	★	★
Kansas	N.A.	N.A.	N.A.	N.A.	N.A.	N.A.
Kentucky	★	...	★	...	★	★
Louisiana	★	★	...	...	★	★
Maine	★	★	★	★	★	★
Maryland	★	★	★	★	★	★
Massachusetts	★	★	★	★	★	★
Michigan	...	★	...	...	★	★
Minnesota	N.A.	N.A.	N.A.	N.A.	N.A.	N.A.
Mississippi	★	★	★	★	★	★
Missouri	★	★	★	...	★	★
Montana	★	...	...	...	★	★
Nebraska	★	★	★	...	★	★
Nevada	★	...	...	...	★	★
New Hampshire	★	★	★	★	...	★
New Jersey	★	★	...	★	★	★
New Mexico	★	★	★	★	★	★
New York	★	★	★	★	★	★
North Carolina	★	★	...	...	★	★
North Dakota	★	★	...	...	★	★
Ohio	★	...	★	★	★	★
Oklahoma	★	★	★	★	★	★
Oregon	...	★	...	...	★	★
Pennsylvania	★	★	★	★	★	★
Rhode Island	★	★	★	★	★	★
South Carolina	★	★	...	★	★	★
South Dakota	...	...	...	★	★	★
Tennessee	★	★	★	★	★	★
Texas	★	★	★	★	★	★
Utah	★	★	...	★	★	★
Vermont	N.A.	N.A.	N.A.	N.A.	N.A.	N.A.
Virginia	★	★	★	★	★	★
Washington	N.A.	N.A.	N.A.	N.A.	N.A.	N.A.
West Virginia	★	★	★	★	★	...
Wisconsin	★	★	★	★	★	★
Wyoming	★	★	...	...	★	★

See footnotes at end of table.

STATE COMPTROLLERS: DUTIES, RESPONSIBILITIES AND FUNCTIONS — Continued

State	Debt management	Investment management	Internal control oversight	Transparency	Quality assurance	Enterprise Resource Planning System responsibility	Other
Alabama	...	...	...	★	...	...	...
Alaska	...	...	...	★	...	...	(a)
Arizona	N.A.	N.A.	N.A.	N.A.	N.A.	N.A.	N.A.
Arkansas	N.A.	N.A.	N.A.	N.A.	N.A.	N.A.	N.A.
California	N.A.	N.A.	N.A.	N.A.	N.A.	N.A.	N.A.
Colorado	★	...	★	★	★	...	(b)
Connecticut	N.A.	N.A.	N.A.	N.A.	N.A.	N.A.	N.A.
Delaware	...	...	★	★	★	★	(c)
Florida	...	★	...	★	...	...	(d)
Georgia	...	...	...	...	...	★	(e)
Hawaii	...	...	...	★	...	...	...
Idaho	...	...	...	★	...	...	...
Illinois	...	...	...	★	★	...	...
Indiana	N.A.	N.A.	N.A.	N.A.	N.A.	N.A.	N.A.
Iowa	...	...	...	...	...	★	(f)
Kansas	N.A.	N.A.	N.A.	N.A.	N.A.	N.A.	N.A.
Kentucky	★	★	...	★	...	★	...
Louisiana	...	...	...	★	...	★	(g)
Maine	...	...	★	★	★	★	...
Maryland	...	...	...	★	★	...	(h)
Massachusetts	...	...	★	...	...	...	...
Michigan	...	...	★	...	...	...	...
Minnesota	N.A.	N.A.	N.A.	N.A.	N.A.	N.A.	N.A.
Mississippi	★	...	★	★	★	★	...
Missouri	★	...	★	★	...	★	(i)
Montana	...	...	...	...	★	★	(j)
Nebraska	...	...	★	★	★	★	...
Nevada	...	...	...	★	...	...	...
New Hampshire	...	...	★	★	...	...	...
New Jersey	...	...	...	...	...	...	(k)
New Mexico	...	...	★	★	...	...	...
New York	★	★	...	...	...	...	...
North Carolina	...	...	★	★	★	★	...
North Dakota	...	...	...	★	...	★	...
Ohio	★	...	★	...	...	...	(l)
Oklahoma	...	...	...	★	★	...	...
Oregon	...	...	...	★	★	...	...
Pennsylvania	...	...	★	★	★	★	(m)
Rhode Island	...	...	...	★	...	...	...
South Carolina	...	...	...	★	...	...	...
South Dakota	...	...	★	★	...	...	...
Tennessee	★	...	...	★	★	...	(n)
Texas	...	★	★	★	★	★	...
Utah	★	...	★	★	★	★	(o)
Vermont	N.A.	N.A.	N.A.	N.A.	N.A.	N.A.	N.A.
Virginia	...	...	★	★	★	...	...
Washington	N.A.	N.A.	N.A.	N.A.	N.A.	N.A.	N.A.
West Virginia	...	...	...	...	...	...	(p)
Wisconsin	...	...	★	★	★	★	...
Wyoming	...	...	...	...	...	...	...

Source: The National Association of State Auditors, Comptrollers and Treasurers, March 2014.

Key:
★ — Formal provision.
. . . . — No formal provision.
N.A. — Not available.
(a) Data warehouse, enterprise travel office, and one-card program.
(b) Some of the functions are shared with the Office of Information Technology.
(c) Payroll compliance (not processing).
(d) State treasury—deposit security and funds management, risk management, and unclaimed property.
(e) Building shared service center for payroll, A/P and travel.
(f) Income offsets, CMIA & SWCAP and 1099 reporting.

(g) Planning and budgeting, and facility planning and control (capital outlay).
(h) Tax collection, tax compliance, and revenue estimates.
(i) State Social Security administrator.
(j) Treasury—deposits and recons, local government audit and reporting, and Social Security administrator.
(k) Accounting and grants management, cash management and cash accounting.
(l) Accounting and shared services.
(m) Employee travel.
(n) Policy development, technical accounting training, CMIA and certain banking relationships.
(o) Data warehouse, loan servicing, central budget and accounting.
(p) Financial audits, securities administration and land commissioner.

Chapter Five

STATE JUDICIAL BRANCH

Voter Identification in the Courts

By Justin Levitt

Every state has a system for asking voters to show that they are who they say they are. The most restrictive of such laws have drawn court challenge. This litigation is as varied as the voter ID regimes: cases have proceeded on different facts in different contexts, under different legal theories.

In a polarized environment, changes to election procedures with a perceived partisan skew are often highly controversial. Few recent changes have been more prominent in this respect than those regarding voter identification regulations. And predictably, as voter identification regimes have changed, litigation has followed.

A voter identification system is really just a set of procedures to ensure that voters are who they say they are. Most of the recent changes in state law concern the identification of voters who show up in person at the polls. Despite widespread recognition that absentee voting has posed more of a problem historically, few states have changed the process for absentee voters.

Federal Law

Federal law sets a baseline for voter identification. Under the Help America Vote Act of 2002, any new voter who registers to vote by mail must have her identity confirmed in one of two ways.[1] First, election officials may be able to match driver's license numbers or Social Security digits on the registration form to other data systems to confirm that the individual on the form is who she says she is. If the numbers cannot be matched, then before the citizen's ballot can be counted, the voter must provide documentation: a photo ID card, utility bill, bank statement, government check, paycheck, or government document with the voter's name and address. Perhaps because this regime allows voters to confirm their identity in several different ways, it has never been challenged in court.

State Laws

Beyond the federal baseline, every state has some means to ensure that voters are who they say they are. Some states compare signatures from the registration form to a voter's entry in the poll book. Some ask for a document from a fairly extensive list. Some ask for a government-issued photo ID from those who have one, and require a special affidavit from those who do not. In some states,

similarly, voters without a qualifying ID card will be asked to vote a provisional ballot, which is counted if the voter's signature on a sworn attestation of identity matches the signature on his or her registration form.

And a few states effectively require all voters beyond a few discrete carve-outs—for example, those with a religious objection or those who are legally indigent—to present a current government-issued photo ID. A citizen without such a card will not be able to cast a valid ballot. Even within this category, there is variety: some accept some student IDs, for example, and some do not.

These more restrictive laws are at the heart of the current controversy.[2] Though most citizens have the ID required by each state, many in the more restrictive regimes do not—and these citizens without are at the center of the legal and policy battle. Indiana and Georgia passed photo-ID-only laws in 2005; Missouri followed in 2006; Kansas, Tennessee, Texas and Wisconsin in 2011; Mississippi and Pennsylvania in 2012; and Arkansas, North Carolina and Virginia in 2013.[3]

In the Courts

Court challenges have followed in each state above, other than Mississippi and Virginia. Laws have been invalidated in Arkansas, Missouri and Pennsylvania; sustained against particular attacks in Indiana and Tennessee (though others have followed); and blocked (at least temporarily, but perhaps only temporarily) in Georgia, Texas and Wisconsin. Several cases are pending.

But that simple recounting of successful, unsuccessful and partially successful challenges masks substantial diversity in the litigation. Different courts are not, by and large, evaluating the same facts under the same cause of action to arrive at different results.

Instead, the impact of voter ID laws differs from state to state; the available legal claims differ from state to state; and even the quality of lawyering and litigation strategy differs from state to state. Differing outcomes sometimes reflect disagreement among judges—but they also reflect litigation under different conditions and with different legal theories. Moreover, the success or failure of particular allegations often depends as much on the particular evidence presented to a court as on the abstract merit of the claims themselves. The U.S. Supreme Court has rejected one claim that one state's voter ID law violated one constitutional doctrine—but that is not the same as deciding that voter ID laws are constitutional.

Claims Based on Implementation

One set of claims has aimed not at the ultimate validity of ID laws, but at their rollout: too fast, too sloppy, too little information. Courts in Georgia and Pennsylvania pressed pause, giving states time to ensure that education and implementation were uniform; a North Carolina federal court declined to do so. In Pennsylvania, the court ultimately determined that the state would be unable to adequately implement the law as written at any point.[4]

Claims Based on Legislative Power

Other claims concern the legislature's authority to enact rules like ID requirements. Most states' constitutions expressly authorize the legislature to regulate the election process—and some specify the election-related topics that a legislature may regulate. Litigation has proceeded on the premise that these authorization clauses are exclusive: if the state constitution does not expressly authorize legislative regulation of ID, the legislature may not regulate ID. State supreme courts in Georgia, Indiana and Tennessee have dismissed such claims, though the Arkansas Supreme Court struck down the state's ID law on this basis.[5]

Claims Based on Partisan Motive

Still another type of claim attacks the alleged partisan motivation of the legislature in enacting the new laws. These allegations have flavored existing cases, but have not yet been the centerpiece of any lawsuit.[6] The Supreme Court has strongly resisted legal challenges along these lines in other electoral arenas as long as a plausible alternative purpose exists. And related, but distinct, claims of undue partisan effect have found even less hospitable legal homes.

Claims Based on Racial Discrimination

Another set of claims attacks the newer ID laws as abridging the right to vote on account of race or ethnicity. ID laws are not inherently racist; neither are literacy tests, poll taxes, registration purges or

district lines. But any tool can be abused. Even without intent to disenfranchise based on race, an ID law that interacts with the legacy of racial discrimination in other arenas to create a disparate racial impact may, in certain circumstances, create liability under the federal Voting Rights Act.

The racial and ethnic impact of the more restrictive ID laws is not uniform: the communities most affected in Kansas are different from those in Tennessee. Nor is the political or historical environment the same from state to state with respect to the enactment of a new regulation of the franchise. Both the Constitution and the Voting Rights Act are profoundly sensitive to local context; liability in one area need not imply liability in a different area, even for a law that looks very similar in the statute books. In areas where new laws have a more dramatically skewed demographic impact, or where there exists a more profound history of discrimination or present evidence of misconduct, these claims are more likely to resonate.

Claims of intentional racial discrimination under the Constitution are quite difficult to prove; claims under the Voting Rights Act are subject to a standard that is still a work in progress for ID laws. Most early cases under the Voting Rights Act were based on direct, and directly discriminatory, outright denials of the vote; later cases built a jurisprudence concerning redistricting. Neither line of cases fits the current ID controversies particularly well, which means that courts are just now working through the applicable standards.

The race-based claims that have succeeded are quite recent and are now proceeding through an appellate process. A federal judge struck down Texas' ID law as the product of intentional race discrimination and as a Violation of the Voting Rights Act; that decision is now on appeal.[7] In Wisconsin, a federal judge found a violation of the Voting Rights Act due to disparate impact that was in part the legacy of discrimination in other arenas; an appeals panel rejected the claim, with a significantly narrower conception of the Voting Rights Act.[8]

Claims Based on Unequal Treatment

Still another set of claims is premised on the assertion that the newer ID laws treat similarly situated voters differently, in an unconstitutional fashion. Some of these challenges concern the differential treatment of absentee voters and voters at the polls; others concern the differential treatment of students.[9] To date, none has succeeded, though various claims are pending.

Claims Based on Impermissible Cost

A further set of claims attacks the newer ID laws as imposing an impermissible cost or other property requirement, either under state constitutions or under federal statutory and constitutional prohibitions of a poll tax. Even when government-issued ID cards are available without charge, there may be travel time and effort to procure them, or a monetary cost to procure the underlying documents necessary to apply for the cards. This sort of claim was rejected in Tennessee and is pending in North Carolina. A federal court has struck Texas' ID law on this basis, but the case is on appeal.[10]

Claims Based on Undue Burden

A final set of claims is both the most common and the most varied. The federal Constitution and many state constitutions require that electoral regulations' burdens be justified. The greater the burden, the more justification is necessary.

Proof of burden sufficient to satisfy a court has been difficult to come by. Most challenges to more restrictive ID laws have attempted to stop the laws before they take effect. It is tricky to find people who have already been blocked from voting by a law that is still in the future, and in Georgia, Indiana and Tennessee, these challenges have failed; in Wisconsin, a challenge that succeeded at the trial court was rejected on appeal.[11] The Indiana case—one of the first challenges to restrictive ID laws in the country—was thin on empirical support and became the claim that the Supreme Court ultimately rejected. The Wisconsin case had substantially more factual development.

Other cases have turned to proxy estimates of harm, like local statistics attempting to assess the number of citizens without valid ID, and testimony speaking to the difficulties facing those without ID as they try to get an ID. In Missouri and Pennsylvania, for example, state courts found that ID laws created a burden insufficiently justified by the ostensible interest in preventing voters from impersonating others at the polls. A federal court similarly struck down Texas' new ID law, but the case is now on appeal.[12]

Cases Modifying Voter ID Statutes

The cases above resulted in injunctions against the implementation of restrictive ID laws, rejections of claims for injunctions, or temporary injunctions that were later dissolved. But a review of voter ID in the courts would not be complete without an acknowledgment of litigation that reshaped ID

requirements rather than providing a thumbs-up or thumbs-down.

South Carolina passed a new voter ID law in 2011, when it was still subject to a preclearance regime requiring federal approval before implementing any electoral change. In the course of litigation, South Carolina officials explained that voters with a government-issued photo ID would be required to show it, but any voter with a "reasonable impediment" to obtaining photo ID could cast a valid ballot after completing an affidavit; virtually any reason will suffice.[13] And in Wisconsin, litigation in state court concerning the cost of ID forced the state Department of Transportation to issue a photo ID to citizens without any underlying documentation of their identity, if procuring that documentation otherwise would require paying a fee.[14]

Notes

[1] 52 U.S.C. § 21083(b).

[2] There have been fewer court challenges to identification laws permitting citizens to vote a valid ballot at the polls even if they do not possess (and cannot readily obtain) a particular government-issued photo ID card, or to aspects of ID laws that apply only to certain subpopulations seeking to vote at the polls. Challenges to a Michigan requirement that voters either show photo ID or complete an affidavit were rejected by the state Supreme Court, In re Request for Advisory Opinion Regarding Constitutionality of 2005 PA 71, 740 N.W.2d 444 (Mich. 2007); challenges to an Arizona requirement that voters either show photo ID or two non-photo pieces of identification were rejected by the 9th Circuit Court of Appeals, *Gonzalez v. Arizona*, 677 F.3d 383 (9th Cir. 2012); and challenges to a Colorado requirement that voters show identification mirroring the Help America Vote Act were rejected by a state trial court, *Colo. Common Cause v. Davidson*, No. 04CV7709, 2004 WL 2360485 (Colo. Dist. Ct. 2004). Challenges to an Ohio law requiring various forms of voter identification were resolved by consent decree. Consent Decree, *Northeast Ohio Coalition for the Homeless v. Blackwell*, No. 2:06-cv-00896 (S.D. Ohio Nov. 1, 2006); Consent Decree, *Northeast Ohio Coalition for the Homeless v. Brunner*, No. 2:06-cv-00896 (S.D. Ohio April 19, 2010). And a challenge to Oklahoma's law (requiring a government-issued photo ID card, registration card, or match of voter information) is still pending. *Gentges v. Oklahoma State Election Board*, 319 P.3d 674 (Okla. 2014).

With respect to subpopulations, for example, a federal court in Ohio struck down a state requirement that naturalized citizens, but not others, show proof of their citizenship. *Boustani v. Blackwell*, 460 F. Supp. 2d 822 (N.D. Ohio 2006). A federal court in Minnesota similarly struck down limits on tribal ID cards not applicable to other forms of ID cards. *ACLU of Minn. v. Kiffmeyer*, No. 04-CV-4653, 2004 WL 2428690 (D. Minn. 2004).

[3] Some municipalities have passed their own voter ID

regulations as well, for municipal elections only. For example, Albuquerque, New Mexico, requires voters at the polls to show a photo ID card, but allows for several private ID cards (like a student ID, debit card, insurance card, union card, or professional association card) in addition to government-issued ID cards. In 2008, the law was upheld against a challenge on several grounds. *ACLU of New Mexico v. Santillanes*, 546 F.3d 1313 (10th Cir. 2008).

[4] *Common Cause/Georgia v. Billups*, 406 F.Supp.2d 1326 (N.D. Ga. 2005); *Common Cause/Georgia v. Billups*, 439 F.Supp.2d 1294 (N.D. Ga. 2006); *League of Women Voters of N.C. v. North Carolina*, 769 F.3d 224 (4th Cir. 2014); *Applewhite v. Pennsylvania*, No. 330 M.D. 2012, 2012 WL 4497211 (Pa. Comm. Ct. 2012); *Applewhite v. Pennsylvania*, No. 330 M.D. 2012, 2014 WL 184988 (Pa. Comm. Ct. 2014).

[5] *Democratic Party of Georgia, Inc. v. Perdue*, 707 S.E.2d 67 (Ga. 2011); *League of Women Voters of Indiana, Inc. v. Rokita*, 929 N.E.2d 758 (Ind. 2010); *City of Memphis v. Hargett*, 414 S.W.3d 88 (Tenn. 2013); *Martin v. Kohls*, 444 S.W.3d 844 (Ark. 2014).

[6] Memorandum Opinion and Order, *Green Party of Tenn. v. Hargett*, No. 2:13-cv-224 (E.D. Tenn. Feb. 20, 2014).

[7] Opinion, *Veasey v. Perry*, No. 13-cv-00193, 2014 WL 5090258 (S.D. Tex. Oct. 9, 2014).

[8] *Frank v. Walker*, 768 F.3d 744 (7th Cir. 2014), *reversing* 17 F. Supp. 3d 837 (E.D. Wis. 2014).

[9] *League of Women Voters of Indiana, Inc. v. Rokita*, 929 N.E.2d 758 (Ind. 2010); *City of Memphis v. Hargett*, 414 S.W.3d 88 (Tenn. 2013).

[10] Order on Parties' Motions for Judgment on the Pleadings, *Currie v. North Carolina*, No. 13-CVS-1419 (N.C. Super. Ct. Feb. 24, 2015); *City of Memphis v. Hargett*, 414 S.W.3d 88 (Tenn. 2013); Opinion, *Veasey v. Perry*, No. 13-cv-00193, 2014 WL 5090258 (S.D. Tex. Oct. 9, 2014).

[11] *Common Cause/Georgia v. Billups*, 554 F.3d 1340 (11th Cir. 2009); *Democratic Party of Georgia, Inc. v. Perdue*, 707 S.E.2d 67 (Ga. 2011); *Crawford v. Marion County Election Board*, 553 U.S. 181 (2008); *League of Women Voters of Indiana, Inc. v. Rokita*, 929 N.E.2d 758 (Ind. 2010); *City of Memphis v. Hargett*, 414 S.W.3d 88 (Tenn. 2013); *Frank v. Walker*, 768 F.3d 744 (7th Cir. 2014), *reversing* 17 F. Supp. 3d 837 (E.D. Wis. 2014).

[12] *Weinschenk v. Missouri*, 203 S.W.3d 201 (Mo. 2006) (en banc); *Applewhite v. Pennsylvania*, No. 330 M.D. 2012, 2014 WL 184988 (Pa. Comm. Ct. 2014); Opinion, *Veasey v. Perry*, No. 13-cv-00193, 2014 WL 5090258 (S.D. Tex. Oct. 9, 2014).

[13] *South Carolina v. United States*, 898 F. Supp. 2d 30 (D.D.C. 2012) (three-judge court).

[14] *Milwaukee Branch of the NAACP v. Walker*, 851 N.W.2d 262 (Wis. 2014).

About the Author

Justin Levitt, Professor of Law at Loyola Law School, Los Angeles, is a national expert in the law of democracy. He has testified before federal and state legislative bodies and courts, and his research has been widely cited, including by the U.S. Supreme Court. He has represented and advised officials of both major parties and voters seeking to compel officials to comply with their legal obligations.

The Modern Grand Jury*

By Gordon Griller and Greg Hurley

Grand juries historically were responsible for formally charging felony defendants in federal courts and in many state courts. Their role has changed very little to the present. However, recent events have caused some to question whether they are still a necessary component of those systems. The article below addresses the pros and cons of the modern grand jury process, as well as describing its historical roots.

Historically, the grand-jury system began in England in the 12th century to guard against unfair prosecution during the reign of English kings, concurrent with the decline of the "divine right of kings" as feudal lords and barons gained power.[1] Grand juries, composed of 25 freemen—mostly barons and later property owners—operated as self-regulating, autonomous bodies charged with investigating alleged wrongdoing and, if found, charging and delivering the accused to the courts for adjudication.

Today, the Fifth Amendment to the U.S. Constitution states, "No person shall be held to answer for a capital, or otherwise infamous crime, unless on a presentment or indictment of a Grand Jury." Rule 7 of the Federal Rules of Criminal Procedure extends the protections afforded to criminal defendants by requiring the use of a grand jury in the charging process for any federal crime that is punishable "by imprisonment for more than one year." As a practical matter, that means grand juries are required in the charging process of all federal felony cases.

However, there is no requirement under the U.S. Constitution or federal law that mandates states to use grand juries in their felony-charging process. Although a number of state constitutions and statutes require a grand-jury indictment to dispose of a felony charge, by trial or by a guilty plea, these states may allow a defendant to waive the right to have his or her case presented to a grand jury. Such waivers are relatively rare. Additionally, waivers of this nature are almost exclusively done pursuant to a plea agreement, often when the proposed plea is to a crime that was not charged in a pending indictment.

In addition to states requiring an indictment for all felony cases, four states require a grand jury indictment in specific situations.[2] In Louisiana and Rhode Island, a defendant has the right to require a grand jury indictment in capital cases or cases

with a possible life sentence. In Florida, this right extends only to capital cases, and in Minnesota, which does not have a death penalty, the right exists for cases with a possible life sentence.

Pros and Cons of Grand Juries in Criminal Cases

Critics of the modern grand-jury process aver that grand juries now have almost no true independence. They argue that over the past two centuries the executive and legislative branches, often feeling the brunt of grand jury investigations and indictments themselves, narrowed the jury's independence through laws, statutes and legal convention. They further note that grand juries are almost completely dependent to make decisions based on the evidence that is presented by the prosecuting attorney. The prosecutor, therefore, has the ability to sculpt the decision of the grand jury by manipulating the evidence that is presented to them. This can be done by presenting exculpatory evidence in specific cases, such as cases in which a law enforcement officer was involved in killing or seriously injuring a citizen.

Supporters of the modern grand jury system note that although this may be a practical reality in many circumstances, grand jurors have a number of powers to counteract the impact of the prosecutor. First, they can question witnesses and they can compel those witnesses to produce documents or other evidence for their review. Second, they can subpoena witnesses without the consent of the prosecution. Those witnesses can be compelled to provide testimony subject to the Fifth Amendment's right to remain silent, and witnesses can be incarcerated for contempt of court if they fail to do so. When exercised appropriately, these tools afford grand jury members the ability to investigate facts and theories of crimes that may go beyond anything that was contemplated in the presentation of the prosecutor.

Grand jury proceedings are secret, and testimony before a grand jury can only lawfully be released under very specific situations. In a limited number of cases, the secret nature of the proceeding may encourage noncooperative witnesses to be candid. The secrecy also protects some defendants by keeping the facts of their cases from appearing in the media—facts that may be inadmissible at trial—which reduces exposure of these facts to prospective jurors. However, the secrecy makes it impossible for members of the public to be sure that the prosecutor zealously presented any given case to the grand jury, which is their ethical obligation. Public uncertainty was undoubtedly a significant part of the sensation that justice had not been served by the grand jury in Ferguson, Mo., when the jury declined to indict police officer Darren Wilson in connection with his shooting of Michael Brown.

Many state systems do not use a grand jury to bring charges in felony cases. In those states, the prosecution merely files the charging document with the court and defendants are tried on that document. On the one hand, a prosecutor who wants to avoid bringing a defendant to trial, whether that is justifiable or not, has the ability in these systems to merely refuse to file the charges with the court. Although the prosecutor conceivably could be disciplined for failing to zealously prosecute the case, or could be removed from office, there is no practical way to navigate around the prosecutorial monopoly for a given case.

The grand jury process in many states eliminates the prosecutorial monopoly over the charging process. A number of states authorize "citizen presentments" to the grand jury. Citizen presentments allow a member of the public to gain access to the grand jury to present evidence of a felony and seek an indictment. This is a useful tool for a member of the public that feels the prosecutor is neglecting or abusing his or her position through inaction on a case. For example, a citizen may petition a circuit court in West Virginia to gain access to the grand jury. If the trial judge determines the conduct the citizen wishes to present is a felony, state law requires the citizen be given access to present the case. From a broader perspective, this procedure allows members of the public at large to have greater trust and confidence in the system, knowing that a felony charge may be obtained without the assistance of the prosecution.

However, prosecutors also can use a grand jury to insulate themselves from making a particularly difficult or unpopular decision regarding charging in a specific case or class of cases. Consider, for example, a prosecutor's office that has a policy of presenting all incidents involving a police officer shooting a citizen, whether or not there is any reason to believe the officer's actions were criminal in nature. This policy certainly would relieve the prosecution of its burden to decide whether to charge a law enforcement officer. It also would eliminate hostility between the prosecution and law enforcement, regardless of the determination of the grand jury. This policy might even be in the best interest of justice, but only if the public could be sure that the prosecution zealously presented the best case against the officer. However, due to the secrecy related to grand jury proceedings, the public has no way to know that.

Another possible benefit of the grand jury system is the didactic value for members of the grand jury. As members of grand juries are typically selected from randomized lists of the public, most members will have very little knowledge of the criminal activity occurring in their jurisdiction, other than high-profile crimes reported by the media. Through their grand jury experience, they quickly become aware of the magnitude and volume of criminal activity that impacts the courts, law enforcement, social services, etc. Although grand jury proceedings are secret and grand jurors are instructed not to discuss them, they are not precluded from discussing the nature of criminal activity locally in a general sense.

Proposed Grand Jury Reforms for Police Shooting Cases

So, what is the solution? Do the benefits of the grand jury outweigh some of the problematic features? While it is difficult to answer these questions, U.S. Rep. Hank Johnson of Georgia has filed House Resolution 429, or the "Grand Jury Reform Act."[3] In a press release dated Jan. 21, 2015, he noted:

> The bill requires the appointment of a special prosecutor to conduct an investigation and present the results to a judge in a probable cause hearing, open to the public, whenever a police officer kills an individual while acting in the line of duty. Passage of this bill would help restore trust in our justice system, while ensuring a fair process for all parties.[4]

To achieve compliance, the bill, if enacted, would use as leverage federal funds the states receive under subpart 1 of part E of 21 title I of the Omnibus Crime Control and Safe Streets Act 22 of 1968 (42 U.S.C. 3750 et seq.). A noncompliant state would be ineligible to receive funding under this provision in the future.

New York Gov. Andrew Cuomo announced a similar initiative for his state.[5] Under his plan, an independent monitor would be appointed to review cases in which a grand jury has declined to indict a police officer that killed an unarmed citizen. The Cuomo plan also would make the grand jury process less secretive. The plan would require district attorneys submit a public report in these cases, which would identify the facts of the case and summarize the testimony provided by each witness to the grand jury.

Both the reform efforts advocated by Johnson and Gov. Cuomo apply to a small portion of all the cases handled by grand juries nationally. Additionally, these concepts have one thing in common: if enacted they both would effectively create a two-tiered grand jury system. One system would apply to police officers involved in killing a citizen and the other for everyone else. Although these suggested plans are clearly being proposed to improve the public's view of the grand jury as a fair and equitable process, if enacted, they may have the opposite impact.

Conclusion

The grand jury process historically has been a component of the criminal justice system at the federal level and in a number of states. At the federal level, the U.S. Constitution mandates its use for the most serious of crimes. It is also mandated by many state constitutions. The grand jury is also interwoven into both the legal culture and the criminal procedure in jurisdictions that mandate its use for felony cases. As such, it is unlikely that the grand jury process will cease to exist.

However, reinvigorating grand jury systems to have the vitality and independence they historically had certainly should be a goal. One easy way to accomplish this is to ensure that individual grand jurors fully understand their rights and powers as grand jurors, for example, by explaining to them that they have the right to question witnesses, to subpoena witnesses, and to demand production of documents and other evidence. Jurors also should be allowed to exercise these rights without interference from the prosecution.[6]

If grand jurors regularly exercise these rights, this would help the institution once again be a partner in the justice system rather than being an archaic relic. It also, over time, would improve the public's trust in grand jury systems.

Notes

*The National Center for State Courts does not take a position on whether using grand juries in the felony-charging process is beneficial to the criminal justice system, needs reform or should be eliminated.

[1] Article 61 in the Magna Carta, signed by King John in 1215, called for 25 barons to sit as a body to oversee the actions and acts of the king to ensure they did not violate the "liberties of the people."

[2] W. R. LaFave, Criminal Procedure, Fifth Edition (2009), at 775.

[3] The Grand Jury Reform Act, *http://hankjohnson.house. gov/sites/hankjohnson.house.gov/files/documents/Grand_Jury_Reform_Act_2015.pdf.*

[4] Press release date January 21, 2015 from U.S. Representative Hank Johnson's website, *http://hankjohnson.house. gov/press-release/rep-johnson-re-introduces-grand-jury-reform-act.*

[5] The Huffington Post, January 22, 2015, *http://hankjohnson.house.gov/press-release/rep-johnson-re-introduces-grand-jury-reform-act.*

[6] New York Unified Courts Grand Juror Handbook, at 10 ("When the grand jury directs the prosecutor to call a witness, that request must be honored"), see *http://www. nyjuror.gov/pdfs/hb_Grand.pdf.* See also the Illinois Courts Grand Juror Handbook, at *http://www.state.il.us/court/CircuitCourt/Jury/GrandJuror.asp.*

About the Authors

Gordon Griller is a principal court management consultant at the National Center for State Courts. He joined NCSC in 2006 after a 30-year career as a trial court administrator in Minneapolis and Saint Paul, Minn. and Phoenix. As a consultant, he works with numerous courts nationwide in such areas as delay reduction, process re-engineering, operational improvements, leadership, and governance. He graduated from the University of Minnesota with a bachelor's in political science and a master's in public administration.

Greg Hurley is a senior knowledge management analyst at the National Center for State Courts, where he has worked since 2007. He is also a member of the Center for Jury Studies, which is a component of NCSC. He publishes a weekly newsletter called the *Jur-E Bulletin*, which contains information and stories for jury managers and judges. He graduated from Widener School of Law in Harrisburg, Pa., with a juris doctorate in 1996. He graduated from the University of Connecticut in 1991 with a bachelor's in Russian studies.

Table 5.1
STATE COURTS OF LAST RESORT

State or other jurisdiction	Name of court	Justices chosen (a) At large	Justices chosen (a) By district	No. of judges (b)	Term (in years) (c)	Method of selection [Chief justice]	Term of office for chief justice
Alabama	S.C.	★		9	6	Partisan election	6 years
Alaska	S.C.	★		5	10	By court	3 years
Arizona	S.C.	★		5	6	By court	6 years
Arkansas	S.C.	★		7	8	Non-partisan popular election	8 years
California	S.C.	★		7	12	Gubernatorial appointment with consent of Commission on Judicial Appointments	12 years
Colorado	S.C.	★		7	10	By court	10 years
Connecticut	S.C.	★		7	8	Gubernatorial appointment with consent of the Legislature	8 years
Delaware	S.C.	★		5	12	Gubernatorial appointment from judicial nominating commission with consent of the Legislature	12 years
Florida	S.C.	★(d)	★(d)	7	6	By court	2 years
Georgia	S.C.	★		7	6	By court	6 years
Hawaii	S.C.	★		5	10	Gubernatorial appointment from judicial nominating commission with consent of the Senate	10 years
Idaho	S.C.	★		5	6	By court	4 years
Illinois	S.C.	★(e)	★(e)	7	10	By court	3 years
Indiana	S.C.	★		5	10	Judicial nominating commission	2 years
Iowa	S.C.	★		7	8	By court	8 years
Kansas	S.C.	★		7	6	Rotation by seniority	Duration of service
Kentucky	S.C.		★	7	8	By court	4 years
Louisiana	S.C.		★	7	10	By seniority of service	Duration of service
Maine	S.J.C.	★		7	7	Appointed by governor with consent of the Legislature	7 years
Maryland	C.A.		★	7	10	Appointed by governor	To age 70
Massachusetts	S.J.C.	★		7	To age 70	Gubernatorial appointment with approval of elected executive council	To age 70
Michigan	S.C.	★		7	8	By court	8 years
Minnesota	S.C.	★		7	6	Non-partisan popular election	Duration of service
Mississippi	S.C.		★(g)	9	8	By seniority of service	Duration of service
Missouri	S.C.	★		7	12	By court	2 years
Montana	S.C.	★		7	8	Non-partisan popular election	8 years
Nebraska	S.C.	★(h)	★(h)	7	6	Gubernatorial appointment from judicial nominating commission	Duration of service
Nevada	S.C.	★		7	6	Rotation by seniority	(i)
New Hampshire	S.C.	★		5	To age 70	Rotation by seniority	To age 70
New Jersey	S.C.	★		5	7 / To age 70 (j)	Gubernatorial appointment with consent of the Senate	7 years, plus tenure, to age 70
New Mexico	S.C.	★		5	8	By court	2 years
New York	C.A.	★		7	14	Gubernatorial appointment from judicial nominating commission with consent of the Senate	14 years
North Carolina	S.C.	★		7	8	Non-partisan popular election	8 years
North Dakota	S.C.	★		5	10	By Supreme and District Court judges	5 years
Ohio	S.C.	★		7	6	Popular election (k)	6 years

See footnotes at end of table.

STATE COURTS OF LAST RESORT—Continued

State or other jurisdiction	Name of court	Justices chosen (a) At large	By district	No. of judges (b)	Term (in years) (c)	Method of selection	Chief justice Method of selection	Term of office for chief justice
Oklahoma	S.C.		★	9	6	By court		2 years
	C.C.A.		★	5	6	By court		1 year
Oregon	S.C.	★		7	6	By court		6 years
Pennsylvania	S.C.	★		7	10	Seniority		To age 70
Rhode Island	S.C.	★		5	Life	Gubernatorial appointment from judicial nominating commission with consent of the Legislature		Hold office during good behavior
South Carolina	S.C.	★		5	10	Legislative appointment		10 years
South Dakota	S.C.	★(l)		5	8	By court		4 years
Tennessee	S.C.	★		5	8	By court		2 years
Texas	S.C.	★		9	6	Partisan election		6 years
	C.C.A.	★		9	6	Partisan election		6 years
Utah	S.C.	★		5	10	By court		4 years
Vermont	S.C.	★		5	6	Gubernatorial appointment from judicial nominating commission with consent of the Legislature		6 years
Virginia	S.C.	★		7	12	By court		4 years
Washington	S.C.	★		9	6	By court		To age 75
West Virginia	S.C.A.	★		5	12	By court		1 year
Wisconsin	S.C.	★		7	10	Seniority		Until declined
Wyoming	S.C.	★		5	8	By court		4 years
Dist. of Columbia	C.A.	★		9	15	Judicial nominating commission appointment		4 years
Puerto Rico	S.C.	★		9	To age 70	Gubernatorial appointment with consent of the Legislature		To age 70

Sources: S. Strickland, R. Schauffler, R. LaFountain and K. Holt, eds. State Court Organization. Last updated January 9, 2015. National Center for State Courts. www.ncsc.org/sco.

Key:
★ — Yes
S.C. — Supreme Court
S.C.A. — Supreme Court of Appeals
S.J.C. — Supreme Judicial Court
C.A. — Court of Appeals
C.C.A. — Court of Criminal Appeals
(a) See Table 5.6, entitled, "Selection and Retention of Appellate Court Judges," for more detail.
(b) Number includes chief justice.
(c) The initial term may be shorter. See Table 5.6, entitled, "Selection and Retention of Appellate Court Judges," for more detail.

(d) Elected statewide, but each of 5 regional appellate districts entitled to at least one justice.
(e) Three justices chosen from First District (Cook County), rest from other districts.
(g) Three justices chosen from each of three districts.
(h) Chief justice chosen statewide; associate judges chosen by district.
(i) The senior justice in commission is the Chief Justice, and in case the commissions of two or more of the justices bear the same date, the justices shall determine by lot who is the Chief Justice.
(j) All judges are subject to gubernatorial reappointment and consent by the Senate after an initial seven-year term; thereafter, they may serve until mandatory retirement at age 70.
(k) Party affiliation is not included on the ballot in the general election, but candidates are chosen through partisan primary nominations.
(l) Initially chosen by district; retention determined statewide.

Table 5.2
STATE INTERMEDIATE APPELLATE COURTS AND GENERAL TRIAL COURTS: NUMBER OF JUDGES AND TERMS

State or other jurisdiction	Intermediate appellate court			General trial court		
	Name of court	2014 No. of judges	Term (years)	Name of court	2014 No. of judges	Term (years)
Alabama	Court of Criminal Appeals	5	6	Circuit Court	144	6
	Court of Civil Appeals	5	6			
Alaska	Court of Appeals	3	8	Superior Court	42	6
Arizona	Court of Appeals	22	6	Superior Court	174	4 (a)
				Tax Court	1	
Arkansas	Court of Appeals	12	8	Circuit Court	121	6
California	Courts of Appeal	96	12	Superior Court	1,695	6
Colorado	Court of Appeals	22	8	District Court	168 (b)	6
				Denver Juvenile Court	3	6
				Denver Probate Court	1	6
Connecticut	Appellate Court	9	8	Superior Court	165	8
Delaware	…	…	…	Superior Court	21	12
				Court of Chancery	5	12
Florida	District Courts of Appeals	61	6	Circuit Court	599	6
Georgia	Court of Appeals	12	6	Superior Court	209	4
Hawaii	Intermediate Court of Appeals	6	10	Circuit Court	31	10
Idaho	Court of Appeals	4	6	District Court	45	4
Illinois	Appellate Court	54	10	Circuit Court	916 (c)	6
Indiana	Court of Appeals	15	10	Superior Court, Probate Court and Circuit Court	315	6
	Tax Court	1	10			
Iowa	Court of Appeals	9	6	District Court	337 (d)	6
Kansas	Court of Appeals	14	4	District Court	248 (e)	4
Kentucky	Court of Appeals	14	8	Circuit Court	94	8
				Family Court	51	8
Louisiana	Courts of Appeal	53	10	District Court	218	6
				Juvenile and Family Court	18	6
Maine	…	…	…	Superior Court	17	7
				District Court	36	7
Maryland	Court of Special Appeals	12	10	Circuit Court	157	15
Massachusetts	Appeals Court	28	To age 70	Superior Court	80	To age 70
Michigan	Court of Appeals	28	6	Circuit Court	218	6
				Court of Claims	4	6
Minnesota	Court of Appeals	19	6	District Court	280	6
Mississippi	Court of Appeals	10	8	Circuit Court	53	4
Missouri	Court of Appeals	32	12	Circuit Court	334 (f)	6 (g)
Montana	…	…	…	District Court	46 (h)	6
				Water Court	5	4
				Workers' Compensation Court	1	6
Nebraska	Court of Appeals	6	6	District Court	55	6
Nevada	…	…	…	District Court	82	6
New Hampshire	…	…	…	Superior Court	22	To age 70
New Jersey	Appellate Division of Superior Court	33	7 / To age 70 (i)	Superior Court	409	7 / To age 70 (i)

See footnotes at end of table.

STATE INTERMEDIATE APPELLATE COURTS AND GENERAL TRIAL COURTS: NUMBER OF JUDGES AND TERMS — Continued

State or other jurisdiction	Intermediate appellate court			General trial court		
	Name of court	2014 No. of judges	Term (years)	Name of court	2014 No. of judges	Term (years)
New Mexico	Court of Appeals	10	8	District Court	75	6
New York	Appellate Division of Supreme Court	55	5 (j)	Supreme Court	269	14
	Appellate Terms of Supreme Court	11	Duration of term	County Court	127	10
North Carolina	Court of Appeals	15	8	Superior Court	112 (k)	8 (l)
North Dakota	Temporary Court of Appeals	3	1 (m)	District Court	44	6
Ohio	Courts of Appeals	69	6	Court of Common Pleas	384	6
Oklahoma	Court of Civil Appeals	12	6	District Court	241 (n)	4 (o)
Oregon	Court of Appeals	13	6	Circuit Court	173	6
				Tax Court	1	6
Pennsylvania	Superior Court	23	10	Court of Common Pleas	449 (p)	10
	Commonwealth Court	9	10			
Rhode Island	...	...	...	Superior Court	25 (q)	Life
South Carolina	Court of Appeals	9	6	Circuit Court	47	6
South Dakota	...	...	...	Circuit Court	41	8
Tennessee	Court of Appeals	12	8	Chancery Court	34	8
	Court of Criminal Appeals	12	8	Circuit Court	83	8
				Criminal Court	33	8
				Probate Court	2	8
Texas	Courts of Appeals	80	6	District Court	458	4
Utah	Court of Appeals	7	6	District Court	75	6
Vermont	...	...	...	Superior Court	32	6
Virginia	Court of Appeals	11	8	Circuit Court	158	8
Washington	Courts of Appeal	22	6	Superior Court	189	4
West Virginia	...	...	...	Circuit Court	70	8
Wisconsin	Court of Appeals	16	6	Circuit Court	249	6
Wyoming	...	...	...	District Court	23	6
Dist. of Columbia	...	...	...	Superior Court	62	15
Puerto Rico	Court of Appeals	39	16	Court of First Instance	338 (r)	12 (s)

Sources: S. Strickland, R. Schauffler, R. LaFountain and K. Holt, eds. *State Court Organization.* Last updated January 9, 2015. National Center for State Courts. *www.ncsc.org/sco.*

Key:

... — Court does not exist in jurisdiction or not applicable.

(a) Unless rotated to a different court by the presiding judge.

(b) Judges also serve Water Court.

(c) 514 Circuit Court Judges and 378 Associate Judges.

(d) 146 of these are part-time judicial magistrates.

(e) Includes both district judges and district magistrate judges.

(f) The number of Circuit Court judges includes associate judges.

(g) Associate Circuit judges serve a term of four years.

(h) Three of these judges serve the Water Court.

(i) Followed by tenure. All judges are subject to gubernatorial reappointment and consent by the Senate after an initial seven-year term; thereafter, they may serve until mandatory retirement at age 70.

(j) Or duration.

(k) The number of Superior Court judges includes special judges.

(l) Special judges serve a term of four years.

(m) Assignments are for a specified time, not to exceed one year or the completion of one or more cases on the docket of the Supreme Court.

(n) The number of District Court judges includes associate judges and special judges.

(o) District and associate judges serve four-year terms; special judges serve at pleasure.

(p) Includes both active and senior judges.

(q) The number of judges includes magistrates.

(r) The number of Court of First Instance judges includes Municipal Division judges.

(s) Municipal judges serve a term of eight years.

Table 5.3
QUALIFICATIONS OF JUDGES OF STATE APPELLATE COURTS AND GENERAL TRIAL COURTS

State or other jurisdiction	Residency requirement				Minimum age		Legal credentials	
	State		Local					
	A	T	A	T	A	T	A	T
Alabama	1 yr.	1 yr.	...	1 yr.	...	18	10 years state bar	5 years state bar
Alaska	5 yrs.	5 yrs.	...	...	...	...	8 years practice	5 years practice
Arizona	5/10 yrs. (a)	5 yrs.	(b)	1 yr.	30	30	(c)	(d)
Arkansas	...	...	★	...	...	...	8 years practice	6 years licensed in state
California	★	...	...	...	...	...	10 years state bar	10 years state bar
Colorado	★	★	...	★	...	...	5 years state bar	5 years state bar
Connecticut	★	★	...	...	...	...	Licensed attorney	Member of the bar
Delaware	★	★	...	★	...	...	"Learned in law"	"Learned in law"
Florida	★	★	★(f)	★(g)	...	...	10 years state bar	5 years state bar
Georgia	★	3 yrs.	...	must reside within court circuit	...	30	7 years state bar	7 years state bar
Hawaii	★	★	...	...	...	30	10 years state bar	10 years state bar
Idaho	2 yrs.	1 yr.	...	...	30	...	10 years state bar	10 years state bar
Illinois	★	★	★	★	...	...	Licensed attorney	Law degree
Indiana	★	1 yr.	...	★	...	...	10 years state bar (h)	Licensed attorney
Iowa	★	★	...	★	...	...	Licensed attorney	Admitted to state bar
Kansas	...	5 yrs.	...	...	30	30	10 years active and continuous practice (i)	5 years state bar
Kentucky	2 yrs.	2 yrs.	2 yrs.	2 yrs.	...	...	8 years state bar and licensed attorney	8 years state bar
Louisiana	1 yrs.	1 yrs.	1 yrs.	1 yrs.	...	...	10 years state bar	8 years state bar
Maine	...	...	...	...	...	...	"Learned in law"	1 year state bar
Maryland	5 yrs.	5 yrs.	6 mos.	6 mos.	30	30	State bar member	State bar member
Massachusetts	...	...	...	...	...	...	...	State bar member
Michigan	★	★	...	...	...	...	State bar member and 5 years practice	State bar member
Minnesota	30 days	30 days	...	30 days	...	...	Licensed attorney	Licensed attorney
Mississippi	5 yrs.	5 yrs.	★(j)	...	30	26	5 years state bar	5 years practice
Missouri	9 yrs. (k)	3 yrs. (k)	...	1 yr. (k)	30	30	State bar member	State bar member
Montana	2 yrs.	2 yrs.	...	...	...	...	5 years state bar	5 years state bar
Nebraska	3 yrs.	★	★	★	30	30	5 years practice	5 years practice
Nevada	2 yrs.	2 yrs.	...	...	25	25	State bar member (l)	2 years state bar member and 10 years practice
New Hampshire	...	...	...	...	...	...	10 years practice	State bar member
New Jersey	★	(m)	...	(m)	...	...	Admitted to practice in state for at least 10 years	10 years practice of law
New Mexico	3 yrs.	3 yrs.	...	★	35	35	10 years practice	6 years active practice
New York	★	★	...	...	...	18	10 years state bar	10 years state bar
North Carolina	...	★	...	(n)	...	...	State bar member	State bar member
North Dakota	★	★	...	★	...	...	License to practice law	State bar member
Ohio	★	★	...	★	...	...	6 years practice	6 years practice
Oklahoma	★	(o)	1 yr.	★	30	...	5 years state bar	(p)
Oregon	3 yrs.	3 yrs.	...	1 yr.	...	...	State bar member	State bar member
Pennsylvania	1 yr.	★	...	1 yr.	...	21	State bar member	State bar member
Rhode Island	...	...	...	...	21	...	License to practice law	State bar member
South Carolina	5 yrs.	5 yrs.	...	(q)	32	32	8 years state bar	8 years state bar
South Dakota	★	★	★	★	...	...	State bar member	State bar member
Tennessee	5 yrs.	5 yrs.	★(r)	1 yr.	35/30 (s)	30	License to practice law	License to practice law
Texas	★	...	...	2 yrs.	35	25	(t)	(u)
Utah	5 yrs.	3 yrs.	...	★	30	25	State bar member	State bar member
Vermont	...	...	...	...	...	...	5 years state bar	5 years state bar
Virginia	...	★	...	★	...	...	5 years state bar	5 years state bar
Washington	1 yr.	1 yr.	1 yr.	1 yr.	...	...	State bar member	State bar member
West Virginia	5 yrs.	★	...	...	30	30	10 years state bar	5 years state bar
Wisconsin	28 days	28 days	28 days	28 days	...	18	5 years state bar	5 years state bar
Wyoming	3 yrs.	2 yrs.	...	...	30	28	9 years practice	Law degree
Dist. of Columbia	N.A.	N.A.	90 days	90 days	...	...	5 years practice	5 years state bar (v)
Puerto Rico	5 yrs.	...	...	...	...	...	10 years practice	7 years state bar

See footnotes at end of table.

QUALIFICATIONS OF JUDGES OF STATE APPELLATE COURTS
AND GENERAL TRIAL COURTS — Continued

Sources: S. Strickland, R. Schauffler, R. LaFountain, and K. Holt, eds. *State Court Organization.*National Center for State Courts. May 13, 2014. *www.ncsc.org/sco.*

Key:

A — Judges of courts of last resort and intermediate appellate courts.

T — Judges of general trial courts.

★ — Provision; length of time not specified.

... — No specific provision.

N.A. — Not applicable.

(a) For court of appeals, five years.

(b) No local residency requirement stated for Supreme Court. Local residency of 3 years required for Court of Appeals.

(c) Supreme Court—ten years state bar, Court of Appeals—five years state bar.

(d) Admitted to the practice of law in Arizona for five years.

(e) Court of Appeals minimum age is 30.

(f) The candidate must be a resident of the district at the time of the original appointment.

(g) Circuit court judge must reside within the territorial jurisdiction of the court.

(h) In the Supreme Court and the Court of Appeals, five years service as a general jurisdiction judge may be substituted.

(i) Relevant legal experience, such as being a member of a law faculty or sitting as a judge, may qualify under the 10-year requirement.

(j) Must reside within the district.

(k) At the appellate level must have been a state voter for nine years. At the general trial court level must have been a state voter for three years and resident of the circuit for one year.

(l) Minimum of two years state bar member and at least 15 years of legal practice.

(m) Restricted Superior court judgeships require residence within the particular county of assignment at time of appointment and reappointment.

(n) Resident judges of the Superior Court are required to have local residency, but special judges are not.

(o) District and associate judges must be state residents for six months if elected, and associate judges must be county residents.

(p) District Court: judges must be a state bar member for four years or a judge of a court of record. Associate judges must be a state bar member for two years or a judge of a court of record.

(q) Circuit judges must be county electors and residents of the circuit.

(r) Supreme Court: One justice from each of three divisions and two seats at large; no more than two may be from any grand division. Court of Appeals and Court of Criminal Appeals: Must reside in the grand division served.

(s) Thirty-five for Supreme Court, 30 for Court of Appeals and Court of Criminal Appeals.

(t) Ten years practicing law or a lawyer and judge of a court of record at least 10 years.

(u) District Court: judges must have been a practicing lawyer or a judge of a court in this state, or both combined, for four years.

(v) Superior Court: Judge must also be an active member of the unified District of Columbia bar and have been engaged, during the five years immediately preceding the judicial nomination, in the active practice of law as an attorney in the District, been on the faculty of a law school in the District, or been employed by either the United States or District of Columbia government.

Table 5.4
COMPENSATION OF JUDGES OF APPELLATE COURTS AND GENERAL TRIAL COURTS

State or other jurisdiction	Appellate courts						General trial courts	Salary
	Court of last resort	Chief Justice salaries	Associate Justice salaries	Intermediate appellate court	Chief/Presiding salaries	Judges salaries		
Eastern Region								
Connecticut	Supreme Court	$194,750	$180,205	Appellate Court	$178,210	$169,245	Superior courts	$162,751
Delaware	Supreme Court	200,631	191,860	...	...	...	Superior courts	180,233
Maine	Supreme Judicial Court	149,406	129,230	...	...	...	Superior courts	121,118
Maryland	Court of Appeals	190,600	171,600	Court of Special Appeals	158,800	158,800	Circuit courts	149,600
Massachusetts	Supreme Judicial Court	181,239	175,984	Appellate Court	170,358	165,087	Superior courts	159,694
New Hampshire	Supreme Court	157,209	152,476	...	...	...	Superior courts	143,018
New Jersey	Supreme Court	192,795	185,482	Appellate division of	175,534	175,534	Superior courts	165,000
New York	Court of Appeals	198,600	192,500	Appellate divisions of	177,900	177,900	Supreme courts	174,000
Pennsylvania	Supreme Court	206,032	200,205	Superior Court	194,728	188,903	Courts of common pleas	173,791
Rhode Island	Supreme Court	185,946	169,041	...	...	...	Superior courts	152,191
Vermont	Supreme Court	149,200	142,396	...	...	...	Superior/District/Family	135,369
Regional averages		182,401	171,907		175,922	172,578		156,070
Midwestern Region								
Illinois	Supreme Court	216,542	216,542	Court of Appeals	203,806	203,806	Circuit courts	187,018
Indiana	Supreme Court	161,524	161,524	Court of Appeals	157,014	157,017	Circuit courts	134,112
Iowa	Supreme Court	178,538	170,544	Court of Appeals	159,885	154,556	District courts	143,897
Kansas	Supreme Court	139,310	135,905	Court of Appeals	134,750	131,518	District courts	120,037
Michigan	Supreme Court	164,610	164,610	Court of Appeals	151,441	151,441	Circuit courts	139,919
Minnesota	Supreme Court	172,012	156,375	Court of Appeals	154,712	147,346	District courts	138,318
Nebraska	Supreme Court	160,540	160,540	Court of Appeals	152,513	152,513	District courts	148,500
North Dakota	Supreme Court	152,246	147,996	...	...	...	District courts	135,611
Ohio	Supreme Court	150,850	141,600	Court of Appeals	132,000	132,000	Courts of common pleas	121,350
South Dakota	Supreme Court	131,131	129,131	...	...	...	Circuit courts	120,612
Wisconsin	Supreme Court	153,942	145,942	Court of Appeals	137,681	137,681	Circuit courts	129,887
Regional averages		161,931	157,337		153,756	151,986		138,115
Southern Region								
Alabama	Supreme Court	161,601 (a)	149,589 (b)	Court of Criminal Appeals	145,828 (c)	144,982 (d)	Circuit courts	140,372 (c)
Arkansas	Supreme Court	162,200	162,200	Court of Appeals	154,140	154,140	Chancery courts	146,080
Florida	Supreme Court	167,210	167,210	District Court of Appeals	166,186	166,186	Circuit courts	(f)
Georgia	Supreme Court	140,504	135,504	Court of Appeals	133,044	130,044	Superior courts	124,620
Kentucky	Supreme Court	170,525	162,404	Court of Appeals	159,695	152,091	Circuit courts	146,262
Louisiana	Supreme Court	137,195	132,390	Court of Appeals	127,854	124,939	District courts	120,085
Mississippi	Supreme Court	176,295	168,636	Court of Appeals	154,176	154,176	Chancery courts	145,343
Missouri	Supreme Court	143,623	139,896	Court of Appeals	137,682	134,109	Circuit courts	126,875
North Carolina	Supreme Court	147,000	137,655	Court of Appeals	132,825	130,410	Superior courts	131,835
Oklahoma	Supreme Court	151,317	144,111	Court of Appeals	142,670	140,508	District courts	136,905
South Carolina	Supreme Court	181,980	176,988	Court of Appeals	173,604	171,108	Circuit courts	165,204
Tennessee	Supreme Court	170,500	168,000	Court of Appeals	176,177	173,177	Chancery courts	(h)
Texas	Supreme Court	200,552	188,949	Court of Appeals	(e)	(g)	District courts	162,878
Virginia	Supreme Court (i)			Court of Appeals (j)			Circuit courts	126,000
West Virginia	Supreme Court	136,000	136,000	...			Circuit courts	139,372
Regional averages		160,464	154,967		150,323	147,989		

See footnotes at end of table.

COMPENSATION OF JUDGES OF APPELLATE COURTS AND GENERAL TRIAL COURTS — Continued

State or other jurisdiction	Appellate courts						General trial courts	Salary
	Court of last resort	Chief Justice salaries	Associate Justice salaries	Intermediate appellate court	Chief/Presiding salaries	Judges salaries		
Western Region								
Alaska	Supreme Court	198,768	198,192	Court of Appeals	187,236	187,236	Superior courts	183,252
Arizona	Supreme Court	160,000	155,000	Court of Appeals	150,000	150,000	Superior courts	145,000
California	Supreme Court	236,307	225,342	Court of Appeals	219,710	211,260	Superior court	184,610
Colorado	Supreme Court	161,151	157,710	Court of Appeals	154,933	151,463	District courts	145,219
Hawaii	Supreme Court	218,112	210,312	Intermediate Court	198,588	194,724	Circuit courts	189,456
Idaho	Supreme Court	137,000	135,000	Court of Appeals	132,000	130,000	District courts	124,000
Montana	Supreme Court	126,269	124,949	...	...	...	District courts	117,600
Nevada	Supreme Court	170,000	170,000	...	...	...	District courts	160,000
New Mexico	Supreme Court	133,174	131,174	Court of Appeals	126,516	124,616	District courts	118,385
Oregon	Supreme Court	133,556	130,688	Court of Appeals	130,688	127,820	Circuit courts	119,468
Utah	Supreme Court	152,150	150,150	Court of Appeals	145,300	143,300	District courts	136,500
Washington	Supreme Court	167,505	167,505	Court of Appeals	159,455	159,455	Superior courts	151,809
Wyoming	Supreme Court	165,000	165,000	...	...	...	District courts	150,000
Regional averages		165,749	162,585		160,443	157,987		148,100
Regional averages w/o California		163,831	160,868		145,205	140,788		144,179

Source: National Center for State Courts, July 1, 2014.

Note: Compensation is shown rounded to the nearest thousand, and is reported according to most recent legislation, even though laws may not yet have taken effect. There are other non-salary forms of judicial compensation that can be a significant part of a judge's compensation package. It should be noted that many of these can be important to judges or attorneys who might be interested in becoming judges or justices. These include retirement, disability, and death benefits, expense accounts, vacation, holiday, and sick leave and various forms of insurance coverage.

Key:
(a) Salary range is between $161,002–$201,252.
(b) Salary range is between $160,003–$200,007.
(c) Salary range is between $159,503–$199,378.
(d) Salary range is between $159,003–$198,753.
(e) Salary range is between $119,949–$149,936.
(f) Salary range is between $120,252–$190,492.
(g) Salary range is between $154,000–$163,000.
(h) Salary range is between $140,000–$158,000.
(i) Plus $13,500 in lieu of travel, lodging, and other expenses.
(j) Plus $6,500 in lieu of travel, lodging, and other expenses.

Table 5.5
SELECTED DATA ON COURT ADMINISTRATIVE OFFICES

State or other jurisdiction	Title	Established	Appointed by (a)	Salary
Alabama	Administrative Director of Courts	1971	CJ (b)	(g)
Alaska	Administrative Director	1959	CJ (b)	$196,192
Arizona	Administrative Director of Courts	1960	SC	(h)
Arkansas	Director, Administrative Office of the Courts	1965	CJ (c)	113,729
California	Administrative Director of the Courts	1960	JC	(i)
Colorado	State Court Administrator	1959	SC	154,933
Connecticut	Chief Court Administrator (d)	1965	CJ	187,148
Delaware	Director, Administrative Office of the Courts	1971	CJ	135,078
Florida	State Courts Administrator	1972	SC	135,999
Georgia	Director, Administrative Office of the Courts	1973	JC	144,473
Hawaii	Administrative Director of the Courts	1959	CJ (b)	129,073
Idaho	Administrative Director of the Courts	1967	SC	130,000
Illinois	Administrative Director of the Courts	1959	SC	203,806
Indiana	Executive Director, Division of State Court Administration	1975	CJ	124,070
Iowa	Court Administrator	1971	SC	154,000
Kansas	Judicial Administrator	1965	CJ	120,037
Kentucky	Administrative Director of the Courts	1976	CJ	124,620
Louisiana	Judicial Administrator	1954	SC	152,091
Maine	Court Administrator	1975	CJ	121,118
Maryland	State Court Administrator	1955	CJ (b)	146,881
Massachusetts	Chief Justice for Administration and Management	1978	SC	170,358
Michigan	State Court Administrator	1952	SC	157,452
Minnesota	State Court Administrator	1963	SC	160,003
Mississippi	Court Administrator	1974	SC	92,960
Missouri	State Courts Administrator	1970	SC	124,472
Montana	State Court Administrator	1975	SC	98,800
Nebraska	State Court Administrator	1972	CJ	132,000
Nevada	Director, Office of Court Administration	1971	SC	123,788
New Hampshire	Director of the Administrative Office of the Court	1980	SC	122,324
New Jersey	Administrative Director of the Courts	1948	CJ	175,534
New Mexico	Director, Administrative Office of the Courts	1959	SC	131,165
New York	Chief Administrator of the Courts	1978	CJ	180,400
North Carolina	Director, Administrative Office of the Courts	1965	CJ	129,259
North Dakota	Court Administrator (h)	1971	CJ	134,724
Ohio	Administrative Director of the Courts	1955	SC	(l)
Oklahoma	Administrative Director of the Courts	1967	SC	130,410
Oregon	Court Administrator	1971	SC	(m)
Pennsylvania	Court Administrator	1968	SC	188,903
Rhode Island	State Court Administrator	1969	CJ	(n)
South Carolina	Director of Court Administration	1973	CJ	132,292
South Dakota	State Court Administrator	1974	SC	110,272
Tennessee	Director	1963	SC	171,108
Texas	Administrative Director of the Courts (i)	1977	SC	157,920
Utah	Court Administrator	1973	SC	136,500
Vermont	Court Administrator	1967	SC	135,369
Virginia	Executive Secretary to the Supreme Court	1952	SC	173,177
Washington	Administrator for the Courts	1957	SC (e)	138,516
West Virginia	Administrative Director of the Supreme Court of Appeals	1975	SC	145,000
Wisconsin	Director of State Courts	1978	SC	137,681
Wyoming	Court Coordinator	1974	SC	115,000
Dist. of Columbia	Executive Officer, Courts of D.C.	1971	(f)	199,910
American Samoa	Administrator/Comptroller	N.A.	N.A.	N.A.
Guam	Administrative Director of Superior Court	N.A.	CJ	N.A.
No. Mariana Islands	Director of Courts	N.A.	N.A.	N.A.
Puerto Rico	Administrative Director of the Courts	1952	CJ	N.A.
U.S. Virgin Islands	Court/Administrative Clerk	N.A.	N.A.	N.A.

Source: National Center for State Courts, July 1, 2014.
Note: Compensation shown is rounded to the nearest thousand, and is reported according to most recent legislation, even though laws may not yet have taken effect. Other information from State Court Administrator web sites.
Key:
SC — State court of last resort.
CJ — Chief justice or chief judge of court of last resort.
JC — Judicial council.
N.A. — Not available.
    (a) Term of office for all court administrators is at pleasure of appointing authority.

(b) With approval of Supreme Court.
(c) With approval of Judicial Council.
(d) Administrator is an associate judge of the Supreme Court.
(e) Appointed from list of five submitted by governor.
(f) Joint Committee on Judicial Administration.
(g) Salary range is between $100,197 and $152,618.
(h) Salary range is between $109,000 and $197,000.
(i) Salary range is between $192,084 and $211,272.
(j) Salary range is between $109,704 and $148,123.
(l) Salary range is between $125,000 and $145,000.
(m) Salary range is between $103,056 and 167,784.
(n) Salary range is between $126,600 and $140,356.

Table 5.6
SELECTION AND RETENTION OF APPELLATE COURT JUDGES

State or other jurisdiction	Name of court	Type of court	Method of selection		Method of retention	Geographic basis for selection
			Unexpired term	Full term		
Alabama	Supreme Court	SC	GU	PE	PE	SW
	Court of Civil Appeals	IA	GU	PE	PE	SW
	Court of Criminal Appeals	IA	GU	PE	PE	SW
Alaska	Supreme Court	SC	GN	GN	RE (a)	SW
	Court of Appeals	IA	GN	GN	RE (a)	SW
Arizona	Supreme Court	SC	GN	GN	RE	SW
	Court of Appeals	IA	GN	GN	RE	DS
Arkansas	Supreme Court	SC	GU	NP	NP	SW
	Court of Appeals	IA	GU	NP	NP	DS
California	Supreme Court	SC	GU	GU	RE	SW
	Courts of Appeal	IA	GU	GU	RE	DS
Colorado	Supreme Court	SC	GN	GN	RE	SW
	Court of Appeals	IA	GN	GN	RE	SW
Connecticut	Supreme Court	SC	GNL	GNL	GNL	SW
	Appellate Court	IA	GNL	GNL	GNL	SW
Delaware	Supreme Court	SC	GNL	GNL	GNL	SW
Florida	Supreme Court	SC	GN	GN	RE	DS and SW (b)
	District Courts of Appeal	IA	GN	GN	RE	DS
Georgia	Supreme Court	SC	GN	NP	NP	SW
	Court of Appeals	IA	GN	NP	NP	SW
Hawaii	Supreme Court	SC	GNL	GNL	JN	SW
	Intermediate Court of Appeals	IA	GNL	GNL	JN	SW
Idaho	Supreme Court	SC	GN	NP	NP	SW
	Court of Appeals	IA	GN	NP	NP	SW
Illinois	Supreme Court	SC	CS	PE	RE	DS
	Appellate Court	IA	SC	PE	RE	DS
Indiana	Supreme Court	SC	GN	GN	RE	SW
	Court of Appeals	IA	GN	GN	RE	DS
	Tax Court	IA	GN	GN	RE	SW
Iowa	Supreme Court	SC	GN	GN	RE	SW
	Court of Appeals	IA	GN	GN	RE	SW
Kansas	Supreme Court	SC	GN	GN	RE	SW
	Court of Appeals	IA	GL	GL	RE	SW
Kentucky	Supreme Court	SC	GN	NP	NP	DS
	Court of Appeals	IA	GN	NP	NP	DS
Louisiana	Supreme Court	SC	CS (c)	PE (d)	PE (d)	DS
	Courts of Appeal	IA	SC (c)	PE (d)	PE (d)	DS
Maine	Supreme Judicial Court	SC	GL	GL	GL	SW
Maryland	Court of Appeals	SC	GNL	GNL	RE	DS
	Court of Special Appeals	IA	GNL	GNL	RE	DS
Massachusetts	Supreme Judicial Court	SC	(e)	GNE (f)	(g)	SW
	Appeals Court	IA	(e)	GNE (f)	(g)	SW
Michigan	Supreme Court	SC	GU	PE (h)	PE (h)	SW
	Court of Appeals	IA	GU	PE (h)	PE (h)	DS
Minnesota	Supreme Court	SC	GU	NP	NP	SW
	Court of Appeals	IA	GU	NP	NP	SW
Mississippi	Supreme Court	SC	GU	NP	NP	DS
	Court of Appeals	IA	GU	NP	NP	DS
Missouri	Supreme Court	SC	GN	GN	RE	SW
	Court of Appeals	IA	GN	GN	RE	DS
Montana	Supreme Court	SC	GNL	NP	NP (i)	SW
Nebraska	Supreme Court	SC	GN	GN	RE	SW and DS (j)
	Court of Appeals	IA	GN	GN	RE	DS
Nevada	Supreme Court	SC	GN	NP	NP	SW

See footnotes at end of table.

SELECTION AND RETENTION OF APPELLATE COURT JUDGES — Continued

State or other jurisdiction	Name of court	Type of court	Method of selection		Method of retention	Geographic basis for selection
			Unexpired term	Full term		
New Hampshire	Supreme Court	SC	GE	GE	(k)	SW
New Jersey	Supreme Court	SC	GL	GL	GL	SW
	Superior Court, Appellate Div.	IA	GL	GL (l)	GL (l)	SW
New Mexico	Supreme Court	SC	GN	PE	RE	SW
	Court of Appeals	IA	GN	PE	RE	SW
New York	Court of Appeals	SC	GNL	GNL	GNL	SW
	Supreme Court, Appellate Div.	IA	GN	GN	GN	SW (m)
North Carolina	Supreme Court	SC	GU	NP	NP	SW
	Court of Appeals	IA	GU	NP	NP	SW
North Dakota	Supreme Court	SC	GN (n)	NP	NP	SW
	Temporary Court of Appeals	IA	(w)	SC (x)	(w)	SW
Ohio	Supreme Court	SC	GU	PE (o)	PE (o)	SW
	Courts of Appeals	IA	GU	PE (o)	PE (o)	DS
Oklahoma	Supreme Court	SC	GN	GN	RE	DS
	Court of Criminal Appeals	SC	GN	GN	RE	DS
	Court of Civil Appeals	IA	GN	GN	RE	DS
Oregon	Supreme Court	SC	GU	NP	NP	SW
	Court of Appeals	IA	GU	NP	NP	SW
Pennsylvania	Supreme Court	SC	GL	PE	RE	SW
	Superior Court	IA	GL	PE	RE	SW
	Commonwealth Court	IA	GL	PE	RE	SW
Rhode Island	Supreme Court	SC	GN	GN	(p)	SW
South Carolina	Supreme Court	SC	LA	LA	LA	SW
	Court of Appeals	IA	LA	LA	LA	SW
South Dakota	Supreme Court	SC	GN	GN	RE	DS and SW (q)
Tennessee	Supreme Court	SC	GN	GN	RE	SW
	Court of Appeals	SC	GN	GN	RE	SW
	Court of Criminal Appeals	IA	GN	GN	RE	SW
Texas	Supreme Court	SC	GU	PE	PE	SW
	Court of Criminal Appeals	SC	GU	PE	PE	SW
	Courts of Appeals	IA	GU	PE	PE	DS
Utah	Supreme Court	SC	GNL	GNL	RE	SW
	Court of Appeals	IA	GNL	GNL	RE	SW
Vermont	Supreme Court	SC	GNL	GNL	LA	SW
Virginia	Supreme Court	SC	GU (r)	LA	LA	SW
	Court of Appeals	IA	GU (r)	LA	LA	SW
Washington	Supreme Court	SC	GU	NP	NP	SW
	Courts of Appeals	IA	GU	NP	NP	DS
West Virginia	Supreme Court of Appeals	SC	GU (s)	PE	PE	SW
Wisconsin	Supreme Court	SC	GU	NP	NP	SW
	Court of Appeals	IA	GU	NP	NP	DS
Wyoming	Supreme Court	SC	GN	GN	RE	SW
District of Columbia	Court of Appeals	SC	(t)	(t)	(t)	SW (u)
Puerto Rico	Supreme Court	SC	GL	GL	(v)	SW
	Court of Appeals	IA	GL	GL	GL	SW

See footnotes at end of table.

SELECTION AND RETENTION OF APPELLATE COURT JUDGES — Continued

Sources: S. Strickland, R. Schauffler, R. LaFountain and K. Holt, eds. *State Court Organization.* Last updated January 9, 2015. National Center for State Courts. *www.ncsc.org/sco.*

Key:
SC — Court of last resort
IA — Intermediate appellate court
N/S — Not stated
N.A. — Not applicable
AP — At pleasure
CS — Court selection
DS — District
DU — Duration of service
GE — Gubernatorial appointment with approval of elected executive council
GL — Gubernatorial appointment with consent of the legislature
GN — Gubernatorial appointment from judicial nominating commission
GNE — Gubernatorial appointment from judicial nominating commission with approval of elected executive council
GNL — Gubernatorial appointment from judicial nominating commission with consent of the legislature
GU — Gubernatorial appointment
ID — Indefinite
JN — Judicial nominating commission appoints
LA — Legislative appointment
NP — Non-partisan election
PE — Partisan election
RE — Retention election
SC — Court of last resort appoints
SCJ — Chief justice/judge of the court of last resort appoints
SN — Seniority
SW — Statewide

(a) A judge must run for a retention election at the next election, immediately following the third year from the time of initial appointment.

(b) Five justices are selected by region (based on the District Courts of Appeal) and two justices are selected statewide.

(c) The person selected by the Supreme Court is prohibited from running for that judgeship; an election is held within one year to serve the remainder of the term.

(d) Louisiana uses a blanket primary, in which all candidates appear with party labels on the primary ballot. The two top vote getters compete in the general election.

(e) There are no expired judicial terms. A judicial term expires upon the death, resignation, retirement, or removal of an incumbent.

(f) The Executive (Governor's) Council is made up of nine people elected by geographical area and presided over by the lieutenant governor.

(g) There is no retention process. Judges serve during good behavior to age 70.

(h) Candidates may be nominated by political parties and are elected on a nonpartisan ballot.

(i) If the justice/judge is unopposed, a retention election is held.

(j) Chief justices are selected statewide while associate justices are selected by district.

(k) There is no retention process. Judges serve during good behavior to age 70.

(l) All Superior Court judges, including Appellate Division judges, are subject to gubernatorial reappointment and consent by the Senate after an initial seven-year term. Among all the judges, the chief justice designates the judges of the Appellate Division.

(m) The presiding judge of each Appellate Division must be a resident of the department.

(n) The governor may appoint from a list of names or call a special election at his discretion.

(o) Party affiliation is not included on the ballot in the general election, but candidates are chosen through partisan primary nominations.

(p) There is no retention process. Judges serve during good behavior for a life tenure.

(q) Initial selection is by district, but retention selection is statewide.

(r) Gubernatorial appointment is for interim appointments.

(s) Appointment is effective only until the next election year; the appointee may run for election to any remaining portion of the unexpired term.

(t) Initial appointment is made by the president of the United States and confirmed by the Senate. Six months prior to the expiration of the term of office, the judge's performance is reviewed by the tenure commission. Those found "well qualified" are automatically reappointed. If a judge is found to be "qualified"the president may nominate the judge for an additional term (subject to Senate confirmation). If the president does not wish to reappoint the judge, the District of Columbia Nomination Commission compiles a new list of candidates.

(u) The geographic basis of selection is the District of Columbia.

(v) There is no retention process. Judges serve during good behavior to age 70.

(w) The Supreme Court may provide for the assignment of active or retired district court judges, retired justices of the Supreme Court, and lawyers, to serve on three-judge panels.

(x) There is neither a retention process nor unexpired terms. Assignments are for a specified time, not to exceed one year or the completion of one or more cases on the docket of the Supreme Court.

Table 5.7
SELECTION AND RETENTION OF TRIAL COURT JUDGES

State or other jurisdiction	Name of Court	Types of court	Method of selection Unexpired term	Method of selection Full term	Method of retention	Geographic basis for selection
Alabama	Circuit	GJ	GU (a)	PE	PE	Circuit
	District	LJ	GU (a)	PE	PE	County
	Municipal	LJ	MU	MU	RA	Municipality
	Probate	LJ	GU	PE	PE	County
Alaska	Superior	GJ	GN	GN	RE (b)	State (c)
	District	LJ	GN	GN	RE (d)	District
	Magistrate's Division	N.A.	PJ	PJ	PJ	District
Arizona	Superior	GJ	GN (e)	GN or NP (f)	NP or RE (f)	County
	Justice of the Peace	LJ	CO	PE	PE	Precinct
	Municipal	LJ	CC (g)	CC (g)	CC (g)	Municipality
Arkansas	Circuit	GJ	GU (h)	NP	NP	Circuit
	District	LJ	GU	NP	NP	District
	City	LJ	LD	LD	LD	City
California	Superior	GJ	GU	NP	NP (i)	County
Colorado	District	GJ	GN	GN	RE	District
	Denver Probate	GJ	GN	GN	RE	District
	Denver Juvenile	GJ	GN	GN	RE	District
	Water	GJ	SC (j)	SC (j)	RE	District
	County	LJ	GN	GN (k)	RE	County
	Municipal	LJ	MU	MU	RA	Municipality
Connecticut	Superior	GJ	GNL	GNL	GNL	State
	Probate	LJ	PE	PE	PE	District
Delaware	Superior	GJ	GNL	GNL	GNL	State
	Chancery	LJ	GNL	GNL	GNL	State
	Justice of the Peace	LJ	GNL (l)	GNL (l)	GU	County
	Family	LJ	GNL	GNL	GNL	County
	Common Pleas	LJ	GNL	GNL	GNL	County
	Alderman's	LJ	LD	CC	LD	Town
Florida	Circuit	GJ	GN	NP	NP	Circuit
	County	LJ	GN	NP	NP	County
Georgia	Superior	GJ	GN	NP	NP	Circuit
	Juvenile	LJ	CS (m)	CS (m)	CS (m)	County/Circuit
	Civil	LJ	GU	PE	PE	County
	State	LJ	GU	NP	NP	County
	Probate	LJ	GU	PE (n)	PE (n)	County
	Magistrate	LJ	LD	LD (o)	LD (o)	County
	Municipal/of Columbus	LJ	MA	Elected	Elected	Municipality
	County Recorder's	LJ	LD	LD	LD	County
	Municipal/City of Atlanta	LJ	MU	MU	LD	Municipality
Hawaii	Circuit	GJ	GNL	GNL	JN	State
	District	LJ	SCJ (p)	SCJ (p)	JN	Circuit
Idaho	District	GJ	GN	NP	NP	District
	Magistrate's Division	LJ	JN (q)	JN (q)	RE	County
Illinois	Circuit	GJ	SC	PE	RE	Circuit/County (r)
	Associate Division	N.A.	SC	PE	RE	Circuit/County (r)
Indiana	Superior	GJ	GU	PE (s)	PE (s)	County
	Circuit	GJ	GU	PE (t)	PE (t)	County
	Probate	GJ	GU	PE	PE	County
	County	LJ	GU	PE	PE	County
	City	LJ	GU	PE	PE	Municipality
	Town	LJ	GU	PE	PE	Municipality
	Small Claims/Marion County	LJ	GU	PE	PE	Township
Iowa	District	GJ	GN (u)	GN (u)	RE (u)	District
Kansas	District	GJ	GN and PE (v)	GN and PE (v)	RE and PE (v)	District
	Municipal	LJ	MU	MU	MU	City
Kentucky	Circuit	GJ	GN	NP	NP	Circuit
	District	LJ	GN	NP	NP	District
Louisiana	District	GJ	SC (w)	PE	PE	District
	Juvenile and Family	GJ	SC (w)	PE	PE	District
	Justice of the Peace	LJ	SC (w)	PE (x)	PE	Ward
	Mayor's	LJ	MA	LD	LD	City
	City and Parish	LJ	SC (w)	PE	PE	Ward

See footnotes at end of table.

SELECTION AND RETENTION OF TRIAL COURT JUDGES — Continued

State or other jurisdiction	Name of Court	Types of court	Method of selection Unexpired term	Method of selection Full term	Method of retention	Geographic basis for selection
Maine	Superior	GJ	GL	GL	GL	State
	District	GJ	GL	GL	GL	State and District (y)
	Probate	LJ	GU	PE	PE	County
Maryland	Circuit	GJ	GNL	GNL	NP	County
	District	LJ	GNL	GNL	RA	District
	Orphan's	LJ	GU	PE (z)	PE (z)	County
Massachusetts	Superior	GJ	(aa)	GNE (bb)	(cc)	State
	District	LJ	(aa)	GNE (bb)	(cc)	State
	Probate and Family	LJ	(aa)	GNE (bb)	(cc)	State
	Juvenile	LJ	(aa)	GNE (bb)	(cc)	State
	Housing	LJ	(aa)	GNE (bb)	(cc)	State
	Boston Municipal	LJ	(aa)	GNE (bb)	(cc)	State
	Land	LJ	(aa)	GNE (bb)	(cc)	State
Michigan	Circuit	GJ	GU	NP	NP	Circuit
	Claims	GJ	GU	NP	NP	Circuit
	District	LJ	GU	NP	NP	District
	Probate	LJ	GU	NP	NP	District and Circuit
	Municipal	LJ	LD	NP	NP	City
Minnesota	District	GJ	GN	NP	NP	District
Mississippi	Circuit	GJ	GU	NP	NP	District
	Chancery	LJ	GU	NP	NP	District
	County	LJ	GU	NP	NP	County
	Municipal	LJ	LD	LD	LD	Municipality
	Justice	LJ	LD	PE	PE	District in County
Missouri	Circuit	GJ	GU and GN (dd)	PE and GN (ee)	PE and RE (ff)	Circuit/County (gg)
	Municipal	LJ	LD	LD	LD	City
Montana	District	GJ	GN	NP	NP	District
	Workers' Compensation	GJ	GN	GN	RA	State
	Water	GJ	SCJ (hh)	SCJ (hh)	SCJ (ii)	State
	Justice of the Peace	LJ	CO	NP	NP	County
	Municipal	LJ	MU	NP	NP	City
	City	LJ	CC	NP	NP	City
Nebraska	District	GJ	GN	GN	RE	District
	Separate Juvenile	LJ	GN	GN	RE	District
	County	LJ	GN	GN	RE	District
	Workers' Compensation	LJ	GN	GN	RE	District
Nevada	District	GJ	GN	NP	NP	District
	Justice	LJ	CO	NP	NP	Township
	Municipal	LJ	CC	NP	NP	City
New Hampshire	Superior	GJ	GE	GE	(jj)	State
	District	LJ	GE	GE	(jj)	District
	Probate	LJ	GE	GE	(jj)	County
New Jersey	Superior	GJ	GL	GL	GL	County
	Tax	LJ	GL	GL	GL	State
	Municipal	LJ	MA or MU (kk)	MA or MU (kk)	MU	Municipality
New Mexico	District	GJ	GN	PE	RE	District
	Magistrate	LJ	GU	PE	PE	County
	Metropolitan/Bernalillo County	LJ	GN	PE	RE	County
	Municipal	LJ	MU	PE	PE	City
	Probate	LJ	CO	PE	PE	County
New York	Supreme	GJ	GL	PE	PE	District
	County	GJ	GL	PE	PE	County
	Claims	GJ	GNL	GNL	GU	State
	Surrogates'	LJ	GNL	PE	PE	County
	Family	LJ	GNL and MU (ll)	PE and MU (ll)	PE and MU (ll)	County and NYC
	District	LJ	(mm)	PE	PE	District
	City	LJ	Elected	Elected	LD	City
	NYC Civil	LJ	MA (nn)	PE	PE	City
	NYC Criminal	LJ	MA	MA	MA	City
	Town and Village Justice	LJ	LD	LD	LD	Town or Village
North Carolina	Superior	GJ	GU	NP	NP	District
	District	LJ	GU	NP	NP	District

See footnotes at end of table.

SELECTION AND RETENTION OF TRIAL COURT JUDGES — Continued

State or other jurisdiction	Name of Court	Types of court	Method of selection Unexpired term	Full term	Method of retention	Geographic basis for selection
North Dakota	District	GJ	GN	NP	NP	District
	Municipal	LJ	MA	NP	NP	City
Ohio	Common Pleas	GJ	GU	PE (oo)	PE (oo)	County
	Municipal	LJ	GU	PE (oo)	PE (oo)	County/City
	County	LJ	GU	PE (oo)	PE (oo)	County
	Claims	LJ	SCJ	SCJ	SCJ	N.A.
	Mayor's	LJ	Elected	PE	PE	City/Village
Oklahoma	District	GJ	GN (pp)	NP (pp)	NP (pp)	District
	Municipal Not of Record	LJ	MM	MM	MM	Municipality
	Municipal of Record	LJ	MU	MU	MU	Municipality
	Workers' Compensation	LJ	GN	GN	GN	State
	Tax Review	LJ	SCJ	SCJ	SCJ	District
Oregon	Circuit	GJ	GU	NP	NP	District
	Tax	GJ	GU	NP	NP	State
	County	LJ	CO	NP	NP	County
	Justice	LJ	GU	NP	NP	County
	Municipal	LJ	CC	CC/Elected	CC/Elected	(qq)
Pennsylvania	Common Pleas	GJ	GL	PE	RE	District
	Philadelphia Municipal	LJ	GL	PE	RE	City/County
	Magisterial District Judges	LJ	GL	PE	PE	District
	Philadelphia Traffic	LJ	GL	PE	RE	City/County
Rhode Island	Superior	GJ	GN	GN	(rr)	State
	Workers' Compensation	LJ	GN	GN	(rr)	State
	District	LJ	GN	GN	(rr)	State
	Family	LJ	GN	GN	(rr)	State
	Probate	LJ	CC	CC or MA	RA	Town
	Municipal	LJ	CC	CC or MA	CC or MA	Town
	Traffic Tribunal	LJ	GN	GN	(rr)	State
South Carolina	Circuit	GJ	LA and GN (ss)(tt)	LA and GN (tt)	LA and GL (tt)	Circuit and State (tt)
	Family	LJ	LA	LA	LA	Circuit
	Magistrate	LJ	GL	GL	GL	County
	Probate	LJ	GU	PE	PE	County
	Municipal	LJ	CC	CC	CC	District
South Dakota	Circuit	GJ	GN	NP	NP	Circuit
	Magistrate	LJ	PJS	PJS	PJS	Circuit
Tennessee	Circuit	GJ	GU	PE (uu)	PE	District
	Chancery	GJ	GU	PE (uu)	PE	District
	Criminal	GJ	GU	PE (uu)	PE	District
	Probate	GJ	(vv)	PE (uu)	PE	District
	Juvenile	LJ	(vv)	PE (uu)	PE	County
	Municipal	LJ	LD	LD (uu)	LD	Municipality
	General Sessions	LJ	MU	PE (uu)	PE	County
Texas	District	GJ	GL	PE	PE	District
	Constitutional County	LJ	CO	PE	PE	County
	Probate	LJ	CO	PE	PE	County
	County at Law	LJ	CO	PE	PE	County
	Justice of the Peace	LJ	CO	PE	PE	Precinct
	Municipal	LJ	CC	LD	LD	Municipality
Utah	District	GJ	(ww)	GNL	RE	District
	Justice	LJ	MM (xx)	MM (xx)	RE and RA (yy)	County/Municipality
	Juvenile	LJ	(ww)	GNL	RE	District
Vermont	Superior (zz)	GJ	GNL	GNL	LA	State
	Judicial Bureau	LJ	PJ	PJ	AP	State
Virginia	Circuit	GJ	GU	LA	LA	Circuit
	District	LJ	CS (aaa)	LA	LA	District
Washington	Superior	GJ	GU	NP	NP	County
	District	LJ	CO	NP	NP	District
	Municipal	LJ	CC	MA/CC	MA/CC (bbb)	Municipality
West Virginia	Circuit	GJ	GU	PE	PE	Circuit
	Magistrate	LJ	PJ	PE	PE	County
	Municipal	LJ	LD	LD	LD	Municipality
	Family	LJ	GU	PE	PE	Circuit

See footnotes at end of table.

SELECTION AND RETENTION OF TRIAL COURT JUDGES — Continued

State or other jurisdiction	Name of Court	Types of court	Method of selection		Method of retention	Geographic basis for selection
			Unexpired term	Full term		
Wisconsin	Circuit	GJ	GU	NP	NP	District
	Municipal	LJ	MU (ccc)	NP	NP	Municipality
Wyoming	District	GJ	GN	GN	RE	District
	Circuit	LJ	GN	GN	RE	Circuit
	Municipal	LJ	MA	MA	LD	Municipality
Dist. of Columbia	Superior	GJ	(ddd)	(ddd)	(ddd)	State (eee)
Puerto Rico	First Instance	GJ	GL	GL	GL	State

Sources: S. Strickland, R. Schauffler, R. LaFountain and K. Holt, eds. *State Court Organization.* Last updated January 9, 2015. National Center for State Courts. *www.ncsc.org/sco.*

Key:
GJ — General jurisdiction court
LJ — Limited jurisdiction court
N/S — Not stated
N.A. — Not applicable
AP — At pleasure
CA — Court administrator appointment
CC — City or town council/commission appointment
CO — County board/commission appointment
CS — Court selection
DU — Duration of service
GE — Gubernatorial appointment with approval of elected executive council
GL — Gubernatorial appointment with consent of the legislature
GN — Gubernatorial appointment from judicial nominating commission
GNE — Gubernatorial appointment from judicial nominating commission with approval of elected executive council
GNL — Gubernatorial appointment from judicial nominating commission with consent of the legislature
GU — Gubernatorial appointment
JN — Judicial nominating commission appoints
LA — Legislative appointment
LD — Locally determined
MA — Mayoral appointment
MC — Mayoral appointment with consent of city council
MM — Mayoral appointment with consent of governing municipal body
MU — Governing municipal body appointment
NP — Non-partisan election
PE — Partisan election
PJ — Presiding judge of the general jurisdiction court appoints
PJS — Presiding judge of the general jurisdiction court appoints with approval of the court of last resort
RA — Reappointment
RE — Retention election
SC — Court of last resort appoints
SCJ — Chief justice/judge of the court of last resort appoints
(a) The counties of Baldwin, Jefferson, Lauderdale, Madison, Mobile, Shelby, Talladega, and Tuscaloosa use gubernatorial appointment from the recommendations of the Judicial Nominating Commission.
(b) A judge must run for retention at the next election immediately following the third year from the time of the initial appointment.
(c) Judges are selected on a statewide basis, but run for retention on a district-wide basis.
(d) Judges must run for retention at the first general election held more than one year after appointment.
(e) Maricopa and Pima counties use the gubernatorial appointment from the Judicial Nominating Commission process. The method for submitting names for the other 13 counties varies.
(f) Maricopa and Pima counties use the gubernatorial appointment from the Judicial Nominating Commission process. The other 13 counties hold non-partisan elections.
(g) Municipal court judges are usually appointed by the city or town council except in Yuma, where judges are elected.
(h) The office can be held until December 31 following the next general election and then the judge must run in a non-partisan election for the remainder of the term.
(i) If unopposed for reelection, incumbent's name does not appear on the ballot unless a petition was filed not less than 83 days before the election date indicating that a write-in campaign will be conducted for the office.

An unopposed incumbent is not declared elected until the election date. This is for the general election; different timing may apply for the primary election (see Elec. Code §8203).
(j) Judges are chosen by the Supreme Court from among District Court judges.
(k) The mayor appoints Denver County Court judges.
(l) The Magistrate Screening Commission recommends candidates.
(m) Juvenile Court judges are appointed by Superior Court judges in all but one county, in which juvenile judges are elected. Associate judges (formerly referees) must be members of the state bar or law school graduates. They serve at the pleasure of the judge(s).
(n) Probate judges are selected in non-partisan elections in 66 of 159 counties.
(o) Magistrate judges are selected in non-partisan elections in 41 of 159 counties.
(p) Selection occurs by means of Chief Justice appointment from the Judicial Nominating Commission with consent of the Senate.
(q) The Magistrate Commission consists of the administrative judge, three mayors and two electors appointed by the governor, and two attorneys (nominated by the district bar and appointed by the state bar). There is one commission in each district.
(r) There exists a unit less than county in Cook County.
(s) Non-partisan elections are used in the Superior Courts in Allen and Vanderburgh counties. Nominating commissions are used in St. Joseph County and in some courts in Lake County. In those courts that use the nominating commission process for selection; retention elections are used as the method of retention.
(t) Non-partisan elections are used in the Circuit Courts in Vanderburgh County.
(u) This applies to district judges only. Associate judges are selected by the district judges and retention is by a retention election. Magistrates are selected and retained by appointment from the County Judicial Magistrate Nominating Commission. The County Judicial Magistrate Nominating Commission consists of three members appointed by the county board and two elected by the county bar, presided over by a District Court judge.
(v) Seventeen districts use gubernatorial appointment from the Judicial Nominating Commission for selection and retention elections for retention. Fourteen districts use partisan elections for selection and retention.
(w) Depending on the amount of time remaining, selection may be by election following a Supreme Court appointment.
(x) Louisiana uses a blanket primary in which all candidates appear with party labels on the primary ballot. The top two vote getters compete in the general election.
(y) At least one judge who is a resident of the county in which the district lies must be appointed from each of the 13 districts.
(z) Two exceptions are Hartford and Montgomery counties where Circuit Court judges are assigned.
(aa) There are no expired judicial terms. A judicial term expires upon the death, resignation, retirement, or removal of an incumbent.
(bb) The Executive (Governor's) Council is made up of eight people elected by geographical area and presided over by the lieutenant governor.
(cc) There is no retention process. Judges serve during good behavior to age 70.
(dd) Gubernatorial appointment occurs in partisan circuits; gubernatorial appointment from Judicial Nominating Commission takes place in non-partisan circuits.
(ee) Partisan elections occur in some circuits; gubernatorial appointment from the Judicial Nominating Commission with a non-partisan election takes place in others.
(ff) Partisan elections take place in some circuits; retention elections occur in other circuits.
(gg) Associate circuit judges are selected on a county basis.

SELECTION AND RETENTION OF TRIAL COURT JUDGES — Continued

(hh) Selection occurs through chief justice appointment from Judicial Nominating Commission.

(ii) Other judges are designated by the District Court judges.

(jj) There is no retention process. Judges serve during good behavior to age 70.

(kk) In multi-municipality, joint, or countywide municipal courts, selection is by gubernatorial appointment with consent of the Senate.

(ll) Mayoral appointment occurs in New York City.

(mm) The appointment is made by the County Chief Executive Officer with confirmation by District Board of Supervisors.

(nn) Housing judges are appointed by the chief administrator of the courts.

(oo) Party affiliation is not included on the ballot in the general election, but candidates are chosen through partisan primary nominations.

(pp) This applies to District and associate judges; special judges are selected by the district judges.

(qq) The geographic basis for selection is the municipality for those judges that are elected. Judges that are either appointed or are under contract may be from other cities.

(rr) There is no retention process. Judges serve during good behavior for a life tenure.

(ss) The governor may appoint a candidate if the unexpired term is less than one year.

(tt) In addition to Circuit Court judges, the Circuit Court has masters-in-equity whose jurisdiction is in matters referred to them in the Circuit Court. Masters-in-equity are selected by gubernatorial appointment from the Judicial Merit Selection Commission, retained by gubernatorial appointment with the consent of the Senate, and the geographic basis for selection is the state.

(uu) Each county legislative body has the discretion to require elections to be non-partisan.

(vv) The selection method used to fill an unexpired term is established by a special legislative act.

(ww) There are no expired terms; each new judge begins a new term.

(xx) Appointment is by the local government executive with confirmation by the local government legislative body (may be either county or municipal government).

(yy) County judges are retained by retention election; municipal judges are reappointed by the city executive.

(zz) Effective 2011, the Family, District, Environmental and Probate Courts were combined into the Superior Court.

(aaa) Circuit Court judges appoint.

(bbb) Full-time municipal judges must stand for non-partisan election.

(ccc) A permanent vacancy in the office of municipal judge may be filled by temporary appointment of the municipal governing body or jointly by the governing bodies of all municipalities served by the judge.

(ddd) The Judicial Nomination Commission nominates for presidential appointment and Senate confirmation. Not less than six months prior to the expiration of the term of office, the judge's performance is reviewed by the Commission on Judicial Disabilities and Tenure. A judge found "well qualified" is automatically reappointed for a new term of 15 years; a judge found "qualified" may be renominated by the president (and subject to Senate confirmation). A judge found "unqualified" is ineligible for reappointment or if the president does not wish to reappoint a judge, the Nomination Commission compiles a new list of candidates.

(eee) The geographic basis for selection is the District of Columbia.

Table 5.8
JUDICIAL DISCIPLINE: INVESTIGATING AND ADJUDICATING BODIES

State or other jurisdiction	Investigating body	Adjudicating body	Appeals from adjudication are filed with:	Final disciplining body	Point at which reprimands are made public
Alabama	Judicial Inquiry Committee	Court of the Judiciary	Court of Last Resort	Court of the Judiciary	Filing of the complaint with the Court of the Judiciary
Alaska	Committee on Judicial Conduct	Supreme Court	Court of Last Resort	Supreme Court	Filing of recommendation with Supreme Court
Arizona	Commission on Judicial Conduct	Commission on Judicial Conduct	Court of Last Resort	Supreme Court	Within 15 days of formal charges being brought, unless a motion for reconsideration is filed
Arkansas	Judicial Discipline and Disability Committees	Commission	Court of Last Resort	Supreme Court	At disposition of case
California	Commission on Judicial Performance	Commission on Judicial Performance	Court of Last Resort	Commission on Judicial Performance	Upon commission determination (a)
Colorado	Commission on Judicial Discipline	Commission on Judicial Discipline	No appeal	Supreme Court	Adjudication
Connecticut	Judicial Review Council	Judicial Review Council; Supreme Court (b)	Court of Last Resort	Supreme Court	Public censure is issued at between 10 and 30 days after notice to the judge, provided that if the judge appeals there is an automatic stay of disclosure
Delaware	Preliminary Committee of the Court on the Judiciary	Court on the Judiciary	No appeal	Court on the Judiciary	Upon issuance of opinion and imposition of sanction
Florida	Judicial Qualifications Commission	Judicial Qualifications Commission (b)	No appeal	Supreme Court	Filing of formal charges by Committee with Supreme Court Clerk
Georgia	Judicial Qualifications Commission	Supreme Court	No appeal	Supreme Court	Formal Hearing
Hawaii	Commission on Judicial Conduct	Commission on Judicial Conduct	No appeal	Supreme Court	Imposition of public discipline by Supreme Court
Idaho	Judicial Council	Supreme Court	Court of Last Resort	Supreme Court	Filing with the Supreme Court
Illinois	Judicial Inquiry Board	Courts Commission	No appeal	Courts Commission	Filing of decision by Courts Commission
Indiana	Commission on Judicial Qualifications	Supreme Court	Court of Last Resort	Supreme Court	After disciplinary charges are filed and case is tried or agreed resolution is accepted by Supreme Court
Iowa	Judicial Qualifications Commission	Judicial Qualifications Commission	Court of Last Resort	Supreme Court	Referral by the commission to the Supreme Court recommending formal sanction
Kansas	Commission on Judicial Qualifications	Supreme Court	Court of Last Resort	Supreme Court	Reprimand is published if approved by Supreme Court
Kentucky	Judicial Conduct Commission	Judicial Conduct Commission	Court of Last Resort	Judicial Conduct Commission	Once the judge has responded to the formal charges
Louisiana	Judiciary Commission	Supreme Court	No appeal	Supreme Court	The lodging of the record of proceedings and a recommendation by the Judiciary Commission to the Supreme Court
Maine	Committee on Judicial Responsibility and Disability	Supreme Judicial Court	No appeal	Supreme Court	Filing of report to Supreme Judicial Court
Maryland	Commission on Judicial Disabilities	Commission on Judicial Disabilities	Court of Last Resort	Court of Appeals	Unless confidential, upon filing of a response (or expiration of the time for filing a response) with the Commission
Massachusetts	Commission on Judicial Conduct	Supreme Judicial Court	No appeal	Supreme Judicial Court	Supreme Judicial Court

See footnotes at end of table.

JUDICIAL DISCIPLINE: INVESTIGATING AND ADJUDICATING BODIES—Continued

State or other jurisdiction	Investigating body	Adjudicating body	Appeals from adjudication are filed with:	Final disciplining body	Point at which reprimands are made public
Michigan	Judicial Tenure Commission	Supreme Court	Court of Last Resort	Supreme Court	Filing of formal complaint by commission with Supreme Court or upon filing in the Supreme Court a consent resolution to a matter
Minnesota	Board on Judicial Standards	Supreme Court	No appeal	Supreme Court	Filing of formal charges by committee with Supreme Court
Mississippi	Commission on Judicial Performance	Supreme Court	No appeal	Supreme Court	Recommendation of Commission to Supreme Court
Missouri	Commission on Retirement, Removal and Discipline	Commission on Retirement, Removal and Discipline	Court of Last Resort	Supreme Court	Filing of recommendation by Committee to Supreme Court
Montana	Judicial Standards Commission	Supreme Court	No appeal	Supreme Court	Filing of record by Committee with Supreme Court
Nebraska	Commission on Judicial Qualification	Supreme Court	No appeal	Supreme Court	Commission may issue a public reprimand
Nevada	Commission on Judicial Discipline	Commission on Judicial Discipline	Court of Last Resort	Commission on Judicial Discipline	Discretion of the Commission, upon filing of report by Committee and service upon judge
New Hampshire	Supreme Court Committee on Judicial Conduct	Supreme Court	No appeal	Supreme Court	On issuance of reprimand
New Jersey	Advisory Committee on Judicial Conduct	Supreme Court	No appeal	Supreme Court	When reprimand is filed by Supreme Court
New Mexico	Judicial Standards Commission	Supreme Court	No appeal	Supreme Court	Upon recommendation of Commission to Supreme Court
New York	Commission on Judicial Conduct	Commission on Judicial Conduct	Court of Last Resort	Commission on Judicial Conduct and Court of Appeals	After a hearing at which a judge is admonished, censured, removed or retired, and after the judge is served
North Carolina	Judicial Standards Commission	Supreme Court	No appeal	Supreme Court	Public imposition of disciplinary action by the Supreme Court
North Dakota	Commission on Judicial Conduct	Supreme Court	No appeal	Supreme Court	At formal hearing
Ohio	Office of Disciplinary Counsel	Board of Commissioners on Grievance and Discipline	Court of Last Resort	Supreme Court	Adjudication
Oklahoma	Court on the Judiciary Trial Division Council	Court on the Judiciary Trial Division; Council on Judicial Complaints	Court on the Judiciary Division; no appeal from Council on Judicial Complaints	Court on the Judiciary Appellate Division	Filing with clerk of the appellate court
Oregon	Commission on Judicial Fitness and Disability	Supreme Court	No appeal	Supreme Court	Allegations become public when the commission issues a notice of public hearing
Pennsylvania	Judicial Conduct Board	Court of Judicial Discipline	Court of Last Resort	Supreme Court	Once a final decision has been made
Rhode Island	Commission on Judicial Tenure and Discipline	Supreme Court	No appeal	Supreme Court	Unless private, after the commission files its recommendation with the Chief Justice
South Carolina	Commission on Judicial Conduct	Supreme Court	No appeal	Supreme Court	Adjudication
South Dakota	Judicial Qualifications Commission	Supreme Court	No appeal	Supreme Court	Filing with the Supreme Court
Tennessee	Board of Judicial Conduct	Board of Judicial Conduct	Court of Last Resort	General Assembly	Filing formal charges with Board of Judicial Conduct
Texas	State Commission on Judicial Conduct	State Commission on Judicial Conduct (d)	Court of Last Resort	Special Court of Review	When issued by the Commission

See footnotes at end of table.

JUDICIAL DISCIPLINE: INVESTIGATING AND ADJUDICATING BODIES — Continued

State or other jurisdiction	Investigating body	Adjudicating body	Appeals from adjudication are filed with:	Final disciplining body	Point at which reprimands are made public
Utah	Judicial Conduct Commission	Judicial Conduct Commission (e)	Court of Last Resort	Supreme Court	10 days after filing appeal
Vermont	Judicial Conduct Board	Supreme Court	Court of Last Resort	Supreme Court	Supreme Court
Virginia	Judicial Inquiry and Review Commission	Supreme Court	Court of Last Resort	Supreme Court	Filing of formal complaint by Commission with Supreme Court
Washington	Commission on Judicial Conduct	Commission on Judicial Conduct	Supreme Court	Supreme Court	At termination of proceeding in CJC
West Virginia	Judicial Investigation Commission	Judicial Hearing Board	Court of Last Resort	Supreme Court of Appeals	Upon decision by Supreme Court of Appeals
Wisconsin	Judicial Commission	Supreme Court	No appeal	Supreme Court	Filing of formal complaint with Supreme Court
Wyoming	Commission on Judicial Conduct and Ethics	Supreme Court	No appeal	Supreme Court or Special Supreme Court	Upon the recommendation of the Conduct and Ethics Commission and Order of the Supreme Court
Dist. of Columbia	Commission on Judicial Disabilities and Tenure	Commission on Judicial Disabilities and Tenure	Chief Justice of U.S. Supreme Court	Commission on Judicial Disabilities and Tenure	Public reprimands are issued with the judge's consent; orders of involuntary removal become public upon filing with the D.C. Court of Appeals
Puerto Rico	Judicial Discipline Commission	Supreme Court	No appeal	Supreme Court	Filing of formal complaint to the Judicial Discipline Commission

Sources: S. Strickland, R. Schauffler, R. LaFountain and K. Holt, eds. *State Court Organization.* Last updated January 9, 2015. National Center for State Courts. *www.ncsc.org/sco.*

Key:
N.A. — Not applicable
(a) Public admonishments or public censures are sent to the judge describing the improper conduct and stating the findings made by the commission; these notices are made available to the press and the general public.

(b) For suspensions in excess of one year or removal from office, the Judicial Review Council makes a recommendation and the Supreme Court makes the decision.
(c) The Judicial Qualifications Commission investigates and makes recommendations to the Supreme Court for discipline or removal. Commission has the authority to issue sanctions, but recommendations of removal must be brought before the Supreme Court.
(d) Decision by the Conduct Commission cannot be implemented until reviewed and approved by the Supreme Court.

Chapter Six

ELECTIONS

Clarion Call: Voter Registration Modernization

By Tammy Patrick

The Presidential Commission on Election Administration made several recommendations in its report to the President which draw attention to the need to modernize voter registration in the United States. This article highlights the recommendations which have been demonstrated by states to be successful policies while also addressing existing federal laws governing the registration of voters.

Chances are that in most states, there are not many services being provided to the public that are executed in the same basic way they were 100 years ago—with the exception of how we register our voters.

In more than half the states, any time residents want to register to vote or update their existing registration they still are required to complete a paper form and return it to their local election administrator either in person or by mail. However, the nation's population is becoming more mobile over time and that creates a challenge with ensuring that voter registration rolls remain accurate. A recent study found that as many as 8 percent of voter registration records nationally were inaccurate—voters had either moved or were no longer eligible. In some states, that number was as high as 15 percent of voter registration records.[1]

The U.S. Census Bureau reports that 12 percent of the population moves each year.[2] Couple the transient nature of our voting population with commonly held beliefs by voters that their registration is mobile and will follow them automatically when they update their information with the post office or the department of motor vehicles,[3] and the situation becomes dire.

In the 2012 general election, survey data showed that more than 5 million voters waited for longer than an hour to vote. In some parts of the country, the wait to vote was upward of seven hours.[4] President Obama declared in his 2013 State of the Union address that he was creating the Presidential Commission on Election Administration to "fix that." The commission conducted meetings and hearings all across the country with election administrators, academics, usability experts, stakeholders and the voters themselves. The foundation of America's democracy is the registration process, and the commission found that our foundation is crumbling.

The presidential commission made a number of recommendations that will help remedy the situation. First, enforce existing laws such as the National Voter Registration Act—also known as Motor Voter—and the Help America Vote Act. Secondly, modernize the voter registration system, such as online voter registration. Lastly, expand data-sharing programs, both *intra*state and *inter*state.

The Law

National Voter Regisration Act

42 U.S. Code § 1973gg–2(a)(1)

The National Voter Registration Act calls for two very specific requirements with which many states don't currently comply. First, a voter registration application at the Department of Motor Vehicles may be *"made simultaneously* with an application for a motor vehicle driver's license" and can require no duplication of information that is provided by the applicant on the driver's license application. This means states simply providing a voter registration form are not in compliance with federal law. Information provided by the applicant that is shared in the two processes (name, address, date of birth, etc.) must auto-populate the voter registration application and cannot require duplicative effort by the voter.

The voter registration act clearly states *"each State motor vehicle driver's license application* (including any renewal application) submitted to the appropriate State motor vehicle authority under State law *shall serve as an application for voter registration* with respect to elections for Federal office unless the applicant fails to sign the voter registration application" and that *"an application for voter registration submitted … shall be considered as updating any previous voter registration* by the applicant."

This brings us to the second failing of compliance. In many states, the modification of an existing voter registration record with information provided to the Department of Motor Vehicles occurs as an "opt-in" process rather than the default outlined in the National Voter Registration Act. The law states that, "*Any change of address form submitted in accordance with State law for purposes of a State motor vehicle driver's license shall serve as notification of change of address for voter registration* with respect to elections for federal office for the registrant involved unless the registrant states on the form that the change of address *is not for voter registration purposes.*"

Nationally, less than a third of all new voter registration applications come through the DMV according to the Election Assistance Commission National Voter Registration Act survey.[5] Yet, interactions by the public with the DMV occur practically synonymously with triggering life events: moves, name changes, etc. In seven states and the District of Columbia, more than half of the registrations come from the DMV. States that are compliant with the federal voter registration law see better results.

Help America Vote Act
42 USC 15483.(a)(1)(A)(iv)
When the Help America Vote Act was passed in 2002, the vision was that all states would have a single voter registration list that would be used in conjunction with other state agency lists. HAVA specifies "the computerized list shall be coordinated with other agency databases within the State."

The Help America Vote Act provides specific instruction for the DMV to collaborate with the chief state election official. "The chief State election official and the official responsible for the State motor vehicle authority of a State shall enter into an agreement to match information in the database of the statewide voter registration system with information in the database of the motor vehicle authority to the extent required to enable each such official to verify the accuracy of the information provided on applications for voter registration."

The Good News

There are solutions to these problems that perfectly balance access and integrity, outreach and security, and make better use of public resources while meeting voter expectations. The basic mod-ernizations states should be considering is to offer online voter registration integrated with other state systems—such as the DMV—and utilizing technology to capitalize on efficiencies that can be gained by such integration, both with *intra*state list comparisons as well as *inter*state compacts.

Arizona was the first state to offer online voter registration to its residents in 2002. The Arizona Department of Motor Vehicles, at that time, began offering address updates and modifications online. Election officials believed that to maintain compliance with the National Voter Registration Act, it was essential to expand the voter registration efforts to coincide with this modernization at the DMV.

Arizona's integration of online voter registration has had many benefits during the ensuing 13 years. A 2007 study conducted in Maricopa County found that for every application submitted through the online network rather than by a paper form, the county saved 80 cents in putting that voter on the rolls. There have been additional savings in time and materials; annual printing costs for voter registration forms have decreased by an average of 85 percent. Although the cost of instituting online voter registration is about $250,000, the cost savings is considerable and investments are quickly recovered. California recovered its invested money after the first month online voter registration was in service.

States already offering online voter registration have the ability to improve and capitalize on their existing infrastructure. Washington state expanded its online system to be adaptable to endless registration points—National Voter Registration Act agencies, voter registration drives, etc.—via the simple creation of URL extensions to its official website. This low-cost solution not only allows for tracking of NVRA compliance, but also performance reporting for registration drives and is more secure because reports only contain the personal information allowed under state law.

Michigan and Delaware are two states that have exemplary programs for their NVRA compliance with the DMV. The seamless integration of applicant information and data transmission between the state agencies results in the highest performance in the nation.

As states modernize their various agency system infrastructures or expand their services online, it is critical that their voter registration requirements be built into the system from the beginning. The efficiencies found in integrating processes benefits other state agencies as well as the elections office. In Delaware, the DMV was able to shave 60 seconds—or two-thirds of their processing time—off of their customer interaction designated for voter registration activities.[6] Lines can form at the polls on Election Day when voter registration lists are inaccurate. Integrating registration responsibilities at the DMV not only helps with that problem, but also has the added benefit of reducing transaction time and thus reducing lines at the DMV—something with which every state struggles.

Good list maintenance doesn't end at the state line. There are two programs that currently assist with identifying voters who have moved out of state and potentially could be registered in two locations. The first is the Interstate Voter Registration Cross Check—commonly known as the Kansas Cross Check—and the Election Registration Information Center, also known as ERIC. The former is a one-to-one comparison of two states' voter registration lists that occurs after each federal general election. The latter is a sophisticated data-matching program that takes a state's voter registration list, its DMV lists, the U.S. Postal Service's National Change of Address list and the National Death Index and provides potential duplicate registrations, not only from one state to the other, but also within a state. The ERIC reports also identify potentially eligible but unregistered voters that the election administrators are required to reach out to, and are run on an ongoing basis. ERIC was developed by IBM, with funding by the Pew Center on the States, in consultation with election administrators from more than a dozen states. It is now run completely by the state consortium.

States that have joined the ERIC program have experienced a reduction in their provisional voting, have identified duplicate registrations within their states as well as in the other member states, and have registered voters well before the traditional rush that occurs in the last days before the registration deadline for a federal election. A study of the pioneer states in ERIC found:

- **Total voter registration:** ERIC states showed a net improvement in registration of 1.23 percentage points over non-ERIC states.

- **New voter registration:** ERIC states showed a net improvement in new registrations of 0.87 percentage points over non-ERIC states.

- **Voter turnout:** ERIC states showed a net increase in voter turnout of 2.36 percentage points over non-ERIC states.

- **Provisional ballots:** ERIC states showed a smaller increase in the use of provisional ballots. ERIC states also showed less growth in the rejection of provisional ballots.

- **Not registering:** ERIC states showed improvements over non-ERIC states in numbers of residents who did not register to vote because they missed deadlines or did not know where or how to register.

- **Not voting:** ERIC states showed a net improvement in the percentage of people not voting due to registration problems.

- **Voter file errors:** State officials are finding the data ERIC makes available enables them to make valuable corrections to birthdates and other fields in voter files.[7]

States participating in ERIC and in the Interstate Voter Registration Cross Check, those who have implemented online voter registration and instituted intrastate data sharing programs, are both "blue" states and "red" states. Voter registration enjoys not only bipartisan support, but also nonpartisan support. The Presidential Commission on Election Administration recommended these administrative solutions because of this very fact. The National Conference of State Legislatures advises, "allowing citizens to register to vote online has proven to be astoundingly cost effective in some cases, and has improved accuracy in our nation's voter rolls. It's also a rare issue in elections administration that appeals to Democrats and Republicans alike."[8]

The tools necessary to modernize the foundation of our democratic process exist and some states are taking advantage and taking action. The question remains, is your state one of them?

Notes

[1] Stephen Ansolabehere and Eitan Hersh, Voter Registration: The Process and Quality of Lists, in *The Measure of American Elections*, Table 1 (Barry C. Burden and Charles Stewart III eds.)

[2] Press Release, U.S. Census Bureau, Census Bureau Reports National Mover Rate Increases After a Record Low in 2011 (Dec. 10, 2012), available at *http://www.census.gov/newsroom/releases/archives/mobility_of_the_population/cb12-240.html*.

[3] Pew Center on the States presentation at National Conference of State Legislatures Dec. 11, 2014, Improving Motor Voter: "nearly 1 in 3 respondents was unaware that they could register to vote at a motor vehicle agency" and "About 1 in 4 mistakenly believe that if they move, election officials or the U.S. Postal Service automatically update

their registration." *http://www.ncsl.org/documents/forum/forum_2014/NCSL_Dec11.pdf.*

[4]Charles Stewart III, Final Report: 2012 Survey of the Performance of American Elections 124 (Draft of Feb. 25, 2013).

[5]*www.eac.gov.*

[6]Presentation by Elaine Manlove, Delaware Elections Director at National Conference of State Legislatures Winter Legislative Conference in Washington, D.C., Dec. 11, 2014. Pew Center on the States report Measuring Motor Voter *http://www.pewtrusts.org/~/media/Assets/2014/05/06/MeasuringMotorVoter.pdf.*

[7]Bland, G., and Burden, B.C. (December 2013). Electronic Registration Information Center (ERIC) stage 1 evaluation report to the Pew Charitable Trusts. Research Triangle Park, NC: RTI International.

[8]See Online Voter Registration: the Bipartisan Trend in Elections, NCSL.ORG (Nov. 12, 2013), *http://www.ncsl.org/research/elections-and-campaigns/online-voter-registration-webinar.aspx.*

About the Author

Tammy Patrick is a Senior Advisor of the Democracy Project with the Bipartisan Policy Center, focusing on implementation of the recommendations of the Presidential Commission on Election Administration (PCEA). Former Federal Compliance Officer for Maricopa County Elections Department for 11 years, Ms. Patrick was tasked with serving more than 1.9 million registered voters in the greater Phoenix Valley. She collaborates with community and political organizations to create a productive working relationship with the goal of voter participation. In May of 2013 she was selected by President Obama to serve as a Commissioner on the Presidential Commission on Election Administration (*www.supportthevoter.gov*) which has led to the position at the Bipartisan Policy Center to further the work of the PCEA.

Electronic Ballot Return for Military and Overseas Voters—Experiences in Alaska, Arizona and Washington

By Kamanzi Kalisa

Over a decade ago, States began to explore the use of electronic technology in the U.S. military and overseas voting process. This article explores the varying policy solutions and technology platforms administered by Alaska, Arizona and Washington as well as emerging federal requirements affecting U.S. military and overseas voters.

Introduction

The Presidential Commission on Election Administration was created following President Obama's 2013 State of the Union message to improve the administration of U.S. elections. In a January 2014 report, the commission outlined their scope: "The United States runs its elections unlike any other country in the world. Responsibility for elections is entrusted to local officials in approximately 8,000 different jurisdictions. In turn, they are subject to general oversight by officials most often chosen through a partisan appointment or election process. The point of contact for voters in the polling place is usually a temporary employee who has volunteered for one-day duty and has received only a few hours of training. These defining features of our electoral system, combined with the fact that Americans vote more frequently on more issues and offices than citizens anywhere else, present unique challenges for the effective administration of elections that voters throughout the country expect and deserve. This Report focuses not only on the problem of election administration for all voters, but also the effect of administrative failures on discrete populations such as voters with disabilities, those with limited English proficiency, and military and overseas voters."

Over a decade ago, States began to explore the use of electronic technology in the U.S. military and overseas ballot submission and ballot return process. This article explores the varying policy solutions and technology platforms administered by Alaska, Arizona and Washington as well as emerging federal requirements affecting U.S. military and overseas voters; specifically, the implementation of electronic ballot return systems.

Historical Background

Election administration policy in the United States has been a top policy issue dating back to the controversial 2000 U.S. presidential election. Following that election, Congress passed the 2002 Help America Vote Act, which authorized $3.86 billion for improvements to various components of elections technology.[1] The act also mandated establishing the U.S. Election Assistance Commission, an independent, bipartisan agency to study and share election administration research and innovation.[2]

For decades, many members of the U.S. military and their dependents experienced problems navigating the overseas voting process. The primary problem was that insufficient time was provided for an overseas voter's ballot to be delivered and returned in time to be counted. Military and overseas voters are a relatively mobile and transient population, some of whom reside in remote areas of the world.

The Federal Voting Assistance Program at the U.S. Department of Defense carries out many of the responsibilities mandated by the Uniformed and Overseas Citizens Absentee Voting Act of 1986, which was later amended by the Military and Overseas Voter Empowerment Act of 2009—also known as the MOVE Act. These federal laws attempted to solve absentee voting issues experienced by overseas voters. The acts required states to:

- Permit U.S. citizens abroad to register and vote by absentee ballot;
- Eliminate the requirement for notarization of overseas ballots;
- Make voter registration and applications for absentee ballots available electronically;
- Accept the Federal Write-In Absentee Ballot in case state ballots do not arrive in time; and
- Make provisions to have ballots available for sending to overseas and military voters at least 45 days before the scheduled Election Day.[3]

The MOVE Act specifically requires states to provide blank absentee ballots to overseas voters in at least one electronic format (email, fax or an online delivery system) at least 45 days before an election.

Federal law allows ballot return to be a state discretionary issue. Returning voted overseas ballots by mail continues to be the primary option, and in 19 states this is the only option. Two states—Alaska and Arizona—allow overseas voters to return ballots via email, fax or web upload. Twenty-three states and the District of Columbia allow overseas voters to return ballots by email or fax.

Alaska, Arizona and Washington are three states that have gone beyond MOVE Act requirements by allowing their military and overseas voters to submit their absentee ballots electronically.

Alaska

In 2012, Alaska implemented a web-based ballot delivery system designed by a third-party vendor that was first used in the 2012 general election and provides Alaskan overseas voters an electronic ballot return tool. In order to use this system, Alaskan overseas voters must have online access through a standard platform (desktop, laptop, tablet, etc.), a scanner and a printer.

Once the voter has marked their ballot electronically, they must then upload that ballot as a digital file (PDF, TIFF or JPEG) onto the web-based system. They are then required to complete and print a voter certificate and sign it by hand, providing an identifier and having it witnessed by someone 18 years of age or older. The accompanying voter certificate must be uploaded to Alaska's Clarity eBallot Delivery Voting System as a digital file.

Ballots delivered to the Alaska Elections Division through the Clarity eBallot Delivery Voting System must be received on or before 8 p.m. Alaska Standard Time on Election Day. The requirements for voting with this method are the same for both overseas and Alaskan stateside voters, except that overseas voters are allowed to apply for an electronic delivered ballot at any time during the calendar year and have their ballot available beginning 45 days prior to Election Day. Stateside voters may not apply and receive an electronic delivered ballot until 15 days prior to Election Day.

In the system's first election, the 2012 general election, 2,305 voters requested their ballot be delivered through the web-based system, 1,600 were returned and 1,508 of the ballots were counted. In the 2014 general election, 1,794 voters requested their ballot be delivered through the web-based system, 1,295 were returned and 1,205 were counted. One of the benefits of Alaska's electronic ballot return system is rooted in the system's accessibility, as many military and civilian overseas voters do not have reliable mail service or access to a fax machine. Alaskan election officials maintain that the system's intent is to provide another method for the state's voters to ensure, inasmuch as possible, that all voters have the opportunity to cast a ballot.

Arizona

In 2004, the Arizona secretary of state's office implemented a web-based system allowing military and overseas voters the opportunity to register to vote, request an early ballot, and/or obtain information on upcoming elections. The military and overseas voter could only return a *voted* ballot by mail or fax.

In 2008, the Arizona Legislature passed House Bill 2213, allowing uniformed and overseas voters the option of returning a ballot by other electronic means. In response to this legislation, the secretary of state developed internally in 2014 the Arizona Ballot Scan and Upload System. This system requires an Arizona overseas voter to have access to a computer with Internet access, scanner and printer. An overseas voter receives their ballot and prints it out, along with their official affidavit form that requires their signature. After the voter marks and scans this material into their computer, they log on to the Arizona Ballot Scan and Upload System with a specific user identification and password—provided separately from the secretary of state's system when they requested their ballot—to upload their voted ballot and affidavit.

These overseas voters' ballots and accompanying affidavits are processed by county election administrators similar to other absentee ballots, validating the voter registration and verifying the signature before forwarding the ballots for tabulation. In the 2008 general election, 208 ballots were returned electronically and counted. In the 2010 general election, 36 ballots were returned electronically and counted. In the 2012 general election, 126 ballots were returned electronically and counted. In the 2014 general election, 29 ballots were returned electronically and counted.

In coordination with a third-party vendor, Arizona conducted a pilot program in 2014 that allowed their overseas voters to return a voted ballot electronically without the use of a scanner. For the 2014 general election, 430 ballots were returned electronically without the use of a scanner. Due to performance issues, the electronic ballot delivery return system has been discontinued.

The Arizona Ballot Scan and Upload System costs $1,500 annually. The pilot program cost $586,000 for the installation and the first year of maintenance. Had the state extended this pilot project, it would have spent $117,200-$128,920 for yearly maintenance.

Washington

In 2011, Washington House Bill 1080 was signed into law allowing overseas voters to return their ballots electronically by 8 p.m. on Election Day. Because Washington is one of the few majority vote-by-mail states, the Washington secretary of state's office created an online ballot delivery tool, "MyBallot," which is available to all Washington voters.

Washington's overseas voters can receive their ballot electronically or by mail; once they've completed voting they are required to physically sign and attach a voter declaration form. If voters are unable to return their ballot by mail, they can return the ballot by fax, email or any other method available to them. The most common method to return ballots electronically is by using a scanner to create an electronic copy of their ballot, but in lieu of a scanner, voters can use a camera to take pictures of their ballot and signed declaration form and send those images to their county auditor. Any ballot that is returned electronically is duplicated by county election officials onto a ballot that can be scanned by that county's tabulation system.

In the 2012 general election, 34,754 ballots were returned electronically and counted. In the 2014 general election, 10,229 ballots were returned electronically and counted. Some Washington counties have contracted with select election management software solution companies for online ballot delivery solutions to complement MyBallot.

Current Outlook

Technology is critical to ensuring military and overseas voters can effectively participate in U.S. elections. The complexity and speed of emerging technologies move at such a record pace that a growing number of election officials and voters either want new voting technology systems or improvements to existing technology that would enhance their jurisdiction's overseas voting performance. This evaluation process is taking place against the backdrop of voters demanding easier, multiple and often times electronic platforms to access registration and voting; changing federal, state and local statutes and standards; and budgetary restraints that often force technology applications to reduce costs, offset staffing layoffs and furloughs.

The security and accuracy of electronic ballot return systems remain a high risk and concern for states as well. Merle King, associate professor of Information Systems and the executive director for the Center for Election Systems at Kennesaw State University said every voting system—including the Alaska, Arizona and Washington electronic ballot return systems—incorporates some measure of risk.

"There is no guarantee that any deployed system will function perfectly," King said. "We have seen high-performing systems developed by small innovators, new to the elections market space, and we have also seen certified systems produced by large, established firms fail. Each system has to be evaluated on its own merits—especially one that is breaking new ground.

"The responsibility of a state or local jurisdiction regarding voting systems is to ensure that it captures voter intent and tabulates results, accurately, securely and with full accessibility, according to federal and state statutes. One way that jurisdictions attempt to achieve these goals is by using U.S. Election Assistance Commission certified systems."

Notes

[1] The Help America Vote Act and Election Administration: Overview and Issues Kevin J. Coleman Analyst in Elections Eric A. Fischer Senior Specialist in Science and Technology December 17, 2014.

[2] The Help America Vote Act and Election Administration: Overview and Issues Kevin J. Coleman Analyst in Elections Eric A. Fischer Senior Specialist in Science and Technology December 17, 2014.

[3] *http://www.gpo.gov/fdsys/pkg/PLAW-111publ84/html/PLAW-111publ84.htm.*

About the Author

Kamanzi Kalisa joined CSG in 2014. As director of CSG's Overseas Voting Initiative, Kalisa works with the U.S. Department of Defense's Federal Voting Assistance Program through a four-year, $3.2 million cooperative agreement to improve the overseas voting process for U.S. citizens living abroad—uniformed services personnel, their voting-age dependents and overseas civilians. CSG's Overseas Voting initiative provides the U.S. Department of Defense with collaborative management, research services, and product development and dissemination to state and local governments regarding innovative military and overseas voting technologies and policies.

Prior to joining CSG, Kalisa served as the director of the Help America Vote Act program for Georgia's Office of the Secretary of State, distributing federal funds to improve election administration for local jurisdictions in the state. Kalisa holds a bachelor's degree in political science from Tufts University and a master's degree in public administration from the Andrew Young School of Policy Studies at Georgia State University.

Table 6.1
STATE EXECUTIVE BRANCH OFFICIALS TO BE ELECTED: 2015–2019

State or other jurisdiction	2015	2016	2017	2018	2019
Alabama				G,LG,AG,AR,A,SS,T	
Alaska				G,LG	
Arizona		(a)		G,AG,SS,SP,T (a)	
Arkansas				G,LG,AG,A,SS,T (b)	
California				G,LG,AG,C,CI,SS,SP,T (c)	
Colorado				G,LG,AG,SS,T	
Connecticut				G,LG,AG,C,SS,T	
Delaware		G,LG,CI		AG,A,T	
Florida				G,LG,AG,AR,CFO	
Georgia				G,LG,AG,AR,CI,SS,SP (d)	
Hawaii				G,LG	
Idaho				G,LG,AG,C,SS,SP,T	
Illinois				G,LG,AG,C,SS,T	
Indiana		G,LG,AG,SP		A,SS,T	
Iowa				G,LG,AG,AR,A,SS,T	
Kansas				G,LG,AG,CI,SS,T	
Kentucky	G,LG,AG,AR,A,SS,T				G,LG,AG,AR,A,SS,T
Louisiana	G,LG,AG,AR,CI,SS,T				G,LG,AG,AR,CI,SS,T
Maine (e)					
Maryland					
Massachusetts				G,LG,AG,A,SS,T	
Michigan		(f)		G,LG,AG,SS (f)	
Minnesota				G,LG,AG,A,SS	
Mississippi	G,LG,AG,AR,A,CI,SS,T				G,LG,AG,AR,A,CI,SS,T
Missouri		G,LG,AG,SS,T		A	
Montana		G,LG,AG,A,SS,SP			
Nebraska				G,LG,AG,A,SS,T	
Nevada				G,LG,AG,C,SS,T	
New Hampshire		G		G	
New Jersey			G,LG		
New Mexico				G,LG,AG,A,SS,T (g)	
New York				G,LG,AG,C	
North Carolina		G,LG,AG,AR,A,CI,SS,SP,T (h)			
North Dakota		G,LG,A,CI,SP,T (i)		AG,AR,SS (i)(j)	
Ohio				G,LG,AG,A,SS,T	
Oklahoma		(k)		G,LG,AG,A,CI,SP,T (k)	
Oregon		G,AG,SS,T (l)		G (m)	
Pennsylvania		AG,A,T		G,LG	
Rhode Island				G,LG,AG,SS,T	
South Carolina				G,LG,AG,AR,C,SS,SP,T (n)	
South Dakota		(o)		G,LG,AG,A,SS,SP,T (o)	
Tennessee				G	
Texas		(p)		G,LG,AG,AR,C (p)	
Utah		G,LG,AG,A,T			
Vermont		G,LG,AG,A,SS,T		G,LG,AG,A,SS,T	

See footnotes at end of table.

STATE EXECUTIVE BRANCH OFFICIALS TO BE ELECTED: 2015–2019—Continued

State or other jurisdiction	2015	2016	2017	2018	2019
Virginia	…	…	G,LG,AG	…	…
Washington	…	G,LG,AG,A,CI,SS,SPT (q)	…	…	…
West Virginia	…	G,AG,AR,A,SS,T	…	…	…
Wisconsin	…	…	SP	G,LG,AG,SS,T	…
Wyoming	…	…	…	G,A,SS,SPT	…
American Samoa	…	G,LG	…	G,LG,AG	…
Guam	…	A	…	G,LG	…
No. Mariana Islands	…	G	…	G,LG	…
Puerto Rico	…	…	…		…
U.S. Virgin Islands	…	…	…	G,LG	…
Totals for year:					
Governor	3	14	2	39	3
Lieutenant Governor	3	10	2	33	3
Attorney General	3	10	1	31	3
Agriculture	3	2	0	7	3
Auditor	2	9	0	15	2
Chief Financial Officer	0	0	0	1	0
Comptroller	0	0	0	9	0
Comm. of Insurance	2	4	0	4	2
Secretary of State	3	7	0	26	3
Supt. of Public Inst. or Comm. of Education	0	5	1	8	0
Treasurer	3	9	0	24	3

Sources: The Council of State Governments' survey and state election administration offices and websites, February 2015.

Note: This table shows the executive branch officials up for election in a given year. Footnotes indicate other offices (e.g., commissioners of labor, public service, etc.) also up for election in a given year. The data contained in this table reflect information available at press time.

Key:

… — No regularly scheduled elections of state executive officials.
G — Governor
LG — Lieutenant Governor
AG — Attorney General
AR — Agriculture
A — Auditor
C — Comptroller/Controller
CFO — Chief Financial Officer
CI — Commissioner of Insurance
SS — Secretary of State
SP — Superintendent of Public Instruction or Commissioner of Education
T — Treasurer

(a) Corporation commissioners (5)—4-year terms, 2016—3 seats, 2018—2 seats. State Mine Inspector—4-year term, 2018 election.
(b) Commissioner of State Lands.
(c) Four (4) Board of Equalization members are elected to serve 4-year concurrent terms. The State Controller is the 5th member of the Board.

(d) Commissioner of Labor.
(e) The Maine legislature elects constitutional officers (AG,SS,T) for 2-year terms; the auditor was elected by the legislature in 2012 and serves a 4-year term.
(f) Michigan State University trustees (8)—8-year terms, 2016—2, 2018—2, 2020—2, 2022—2. University of Michigan regents (8)—8-year terms, 2016—2, 2018—2, 2020—2, 2022—2. Wayne State University governors (8)—8-year terms, 2016—2, 2018—2, 2020—2, 2022—2. State Board of Education (8)—8-year terms, 2016—2, 2018—2, 2020—2, 2022—2.
(g) Commissioner of Public Lands—4-year term, 2014, 2018.
(h) Commissioner of Labor.
(i) Public Service Commissioners (3)—6-year terms, 2016—1, 2018—1, 2020—1.
(j) Tax Commissioner.
(k) Corporation Commissioners (3)—6-year terms, 2016—1, 2018—1, 2020—1; Commissioner of Labor—2014, 4-year term.
(l) Gov. John Kitzhaber resigned on February 13, 2015. Secretary of State Kate Brown will serve as interim governor. In November 2016, voters will select a candidate to fill the remaining two years of Kitzhaber's term.
(m) Commissioner of the Bureau of Labor and Industries.
(n) Adjutant General—4-year term.
(o) The title is Commissioner of Schools and Public Lands; Public Utility Commissioners (3)—6-year terms, 2016—1, 2018—1, 2020—1.
(p) Commissioner of General Land Office—4-year term, 2018; railroad commissioners (3)—6-year terms, 2016—1, 2018—1, 2020—1.
(q) Commissioner of Public Lands.

Table 6.2
STATE LEGISLATURE MEMBERS TO BE ELECTED: 2015–2019

State or other jurisdiction	Total legislators Senate	Total legislators House/Assembly	2015 Senate	2015 House/Assembly	2016 Senate	2016 House/Assembly	2017 Senate	2017 House/Assembly	2018 Senate	2018 House/Assembly	2019 Senate	2019 House/Assembly
Alabama	35	105	...	...	...	...	...	...	35	105	...	...
Alaska	20	40	...	...	10	40	...	...	10	40	...	...
Arizona	30	60	...	...	30	60	...	...	30	60	...	...
Arkansas	35	100	...	...	17	100	...	...	18	100	...	...
California	40	80	...	...	20 (a)	80	...	...	20 (b)	80	...	...
Colorado	35	65	...	...	17	65	...	...	18	65	...	...
Connecticut	36	151	...	...	36	151	...	...	36	151	...	...
Delaware	21	41	...	...	11	41	...	...	10	41	...	...
Florida	40	120	...	...	20 (a)	120	...	...	20 (b)	120	...	...
Georgia	56	180	...	...	56	180	...	...	56	180	...	...
Hawaii	25	51	...	...	13	51	...	...	12	51	...	...
Idaho	35	70	...	...	35	70	...	...	35	70	...	...
Illinois	59	118	...	...	20 (c)	118	...	...	20 (c)	118	...	...
Indiana	50	100	...	...	25	100	...	...	25	100	...	...
Iowa	50	100	...	...	25 (b)	100	...	...	25 (a)	100	...	...
Kansas	40	125	...	...	40	125	...	...	40	125	...	...
Kentucky	38	100	...	...	19 (a)	100	...	...	19 (b)	100	...	...
Louisiana	39	105	39	105	...	...	...	...	...	...	39	105
Maine	35	151 (d)	...	...	35	151	...	...	35	151	...	...
Maryland	47	141	...	...	35	151	...	...	47	141	...	...
Massachusetts	40	160	...	...	40	160	...	...	40	160	...	...
Michigan	38	110	...	...	...	110	...	...	38	110	...	...
Minnesota	67	134	...	...	67	134	...	...	...	134	...	...
Mississippi	52	122	52	122	...	...	...	...	...	...	52	122
Missouri	34	163	...	...	17 (a)	163	...	...	17 (b)	163	...	...
Montana	50	100	...	...	25	100	...	...	25	100	...	...
Nebraska	49	U	...	...	25 (a)	U	...	...	24 (b)	U	...	...
Nevada	21	42	...	...	10	42	...	...	11	42	...	...
New Hampshire	24	400	...	...	24	400	...	...	24	400	...	...
New Jersey	40	80	...	80	...	...	40	80	...	...	...	80
New Mexico	42	70	...	...	42	70	...	...	...	70	...	...
New York	63	150	...	...	63	150	...	...	63	150	...	...
North Carolina	50	120	...	...	50	120	...	...	50	120	...	...
North Dakota	47	94	...	...	23 (b)	47 (b)	...	...	24 (a)	47 (a)	...	...
Ohio	33	99	...	...	16 (b)	99	...	...	17 (a)	99	...	...
Oklahoma	48	101	...	...	24 (a)	101	...	...	24 (b)	101	...	...
Oregon	30	60	...	...	15	60	...	...	15	60	...	...
Pennsylvania	50	203	...	...	25 (a)	203	...	...	25 (b)	203	...	...
Rhode Island	38	75	...	...	38	75	...	...	38	75	...	...
South Carolina	46	124	...	...	46	124	...	...	...	124	...	...

See footnotes at end of table.

STATE LEGISLATURE MEMBERS TO BE ELECTED: 2015–2019—Continued

State or other jurisdiction	Total legislators		2015		2016		2017		2018		2019	
	Senate	House/Assembly	Senate	House/Assembly	Senate	House/Assembly	Senate	House/Assembly	Senate	House/Assembly	Senate	House/Assembly
South Dakota	35	70	…	…	35	70	…	…	35	70	…	…
Tennessee	33	99	…	…	16 (b)	99	…	…	17 (a)	99	…	…
Texas	31	150	…	…	16	150	…	…	15	150	…	…
Utah	29	75	…	…	15	75	…	…	14	75	…	…
Vermont	30	150	…	…	30	150	…	…	30	150	…	…
Virginia	40	100	40	100	…	…	…	100	…	…	40	100
Washington	49	98	…	…	25	98	…	…	24	98	…	…
West Virginia	34	100	…	…	17	100	…	…	17	100	…	…
Wisconsin	33	99	…	…	16 (b)	99	…	…	17 (a)	99	…	…
Wyoming	30	60	…	…	15 (b)	60	…	…	15 (a)	60	…	…
Dist. of Columbia	13	U	…	…	6	U	…	…	7	U	…	…
American Samoa	18	20 (e)	…	…	(e)	20 (e)	…	…	(e)	20 (e)	…	…
Guam	15	U	…	…	15	U	…	…	15	U	…	…
No. Marianas Islands	9	20	3	20	…	…	3	20	…	…	3	20
Puerto Rico	27	51 (f)	…	…	27 (f)	51	…	…	…	U	…	…
U.S. Virgin Islands	15	U	…	…	15	U	…	…	15	U	…	…
State Totals	1,972	5,411	131	407	1,164	4,711	40	180	1,130	4,957	131	407
Totals	2,071	5,502	134	427	1,227	4,782	43	200	1,167	4,977	134	427

Source: The Council of State Governments, February 2015.

Note: This table shows the number of elections in a given year. The data compiles in this table reflect information avaible at press time. See Chapter 3.3 table entitled, "The Legislators: Numbers, Terms, and Party Affiliations," for specific information on legislative terms.

Key:
… – No regularly scheduled elections
U – Unicameral legislature
(a) Odd-numbered Senate districts.
(b) Even-numbered Senate districts.
(c) The Illinois Senate operates on a ten-year election cycle. All 59 senators are elected in each year ending with a "2" (following redistricting following the decennial census). Senate districts are then divided into three groups. Each group of senators is elected to one of the following schedules: terms of four years, four years and two years; terms of two years, four years and four years; and terms of four years, two years and four years.

(d) In addition, there are three nonvoting members representing the Penobscot Nation, the Passama-quoddy Tribe and the Houlton Band of Maliseet Indians.

(e) In American Samoa, Senators are not elected by popular vote. They are selected by the county council of chiefs. House: 21 seats; 20 are elected by popular vote and one appointed, non-voting delegate from Swains Island.

(f) The Senate consists of 27 members, 2 per electoral district, and 11 elected according to the different districts' proportion of population. Two extra seats are granted in each house to the opposition if necessary to limit any party's control to two thirds.

Table 6.3
METHODS OF NOMINATING CANDIDATES FOR STATE OFFICES

State or other jurisdiction	Methods of nominating candidates
Alabama	Primary election; however, the state executive committee or other governing body of any political party may choose instead to hold a state convention for the purpose of nominating candidates. Submitting a petition to run as an independent or third-party candidate or an independent nominating procedure.
Alaska	Primary election. Petition for no-party candidates.
Arizona	Candidates who are members of a recognized party are nominated by an open primary election. Candidates who are not members of a recognized political party may file petitions to appear on the general election ballot. A write-in option is also available.
Arkansas	Primary election, convention and petition.
California	Primary election or independent nomination procedure.
Colorado	Primary election, convention or by petition.
Connecticut	Convention/primary election. Major political parties hold state conventions (convening not earlier than the 68th day and closing not later than the 50th day before the date of the primary) for the purpose of endorsing candidates. If no one challenges the endorsed candidate, no primary election is held. However, if anyone (who received at least 15 percent of the delegate vote on any roll call at the convention) challenges the endorsed candidate, a primary election is held to determine the party nominee for the general election.
Delaware	Pr-imary election for Democrats and primary election and convention for Republicans.
Florida	Primary election. Minor parties may nominate their candidate in any manner they deem proper.
Georgia	Primary election.
Hawaii	Primary election.
Idaho	Primary election and convention. New political parties hold a convention to nominate candidates to be placed on a general election ballot.
Illinois	Primary election. The primary election nominates established party candidates. New political parties and independent candidates go directly to the general election file based on a petition process.
Indiana	Primary election, convention and petition. The governor is chosen by a primary. All other state officers are chosen at a state convention, unless the candidate is an independent. Any party that obtains between 2 percent and 8 percent of the vote for secretary of state may hold a convention to select a candidate.
Iowa	Primary election, convention and petition.
Kansas	Candidates for the two major parties are nominated by primary election. Candidates for minor parties are nominated for the general election at state party conventions. Independent candidates are nominated for the general election by petition.
Kentucky	Primary election. A slate of candidates for governor and lieutenant governor that receives the highest number of its party's votes but which number is less than 40 percent of the votes cast for all slates of candidates of that party, shall be required to participate in a runoff primary with the slate of candidates of the same party receiving the second highest number of votes.
Louisiana	Candidates may qualify for any office they wish, regardless of party affiliation, by completing the qualifying document and paying the appropriate qualifying fee; or a candidate may file a nominating petition.
Maine	Primary election or non-party petition.
Maryland	Primary election, convention and petition. Unaffiliated candidates or candidates affiliated with non-recognized political parties may run for elective office by collecting the requisite number of signatures on a petition. The required number equals 1 percent of the number of registered voters eligible to vote for office. Only recognized non-principal political parties may nominate its candidate by a convention in accordance with its by laws (at this time, Maryland has four non-principal parties: Libertarian, Green, Constitution and Populist.)
Massachusetts	Primary election.
Michigan	Governor, state house, state senate use primary election. Lieutenant governor runs as the running mate to gubernatorial candidate, not separately, and is selected through the convention process Secretary of state and attorney general candidates are chosen at convention. Nominees for State Board of Education, University of Michigan Regents, Michigan State University Trustees and Wayne State University Governors are nominated by convention. Minor parties nominate candidates to all partisan offices by convention.
Minnesota	Primary election. Candidates for minor parties or independent candidates are by petition. They must have the signatures of 2,000 people who will be eligible to vote in the next general election.
Mississippi	Primary election, petition (for independent candidates), independent nominating procedures (third-party candidate).
Missouri	Primary election.
Montana	Primary election and independent nominating procedure.
Nebraska	Primary election.
Nevada	Primary election. Independent candidates are nominated by petition for the general election. Minor parties nominated by petition or by party.
New Hampshire	Primary election. Minor parties by petition.

See footnotes at end of table.

METHODS OF NOMINATING CANDIDATES FOR STATE OFFICES — Continued

State or other jurisdiction	Methods of nominating candidates
New Jersey	Primary election. Independent candidates are nominated by petition for the general election.
New Mexico	Statewide candidates petition to go to convention and are nominated in a primary election. District and legislative candidate petition for primary ballot access.
New York	Primary election/petition.
North Carolina	Primary election. Newly recognized parties just granted access submit their first nominees by convention. All established parties use primaries.
North Dakota	Convention/primary election. Political parties hold state conventions for the purpose of endorsing candidates. Endorsed candidates are automatically placed on the primary election ballot, but other candidates may also petition their name on the ballot.
Ohio	Primary election, petition and by declaration of intent to be a write-in candidate.
Oklahoma	Primary election.
Oregon	Primary election. Minor parties hold conventions.
Pennsylvania	Primary election, and petition. Nomination petitions filed by major party candidates to access primary ballot. Nomination papers filed by minor party and independent candidates to access November ballot.
Rhode Island	Primary election.
South Carolina	Primary election for Republicans and Democrats; party conventions held for minor parties. Candidates can have name on ballot via petition.
South Dakota	Convention, petition and independent nominating procedure.
Tennessee	Primary election/petition.
Texas	Primary election/convention. Minor parties without ballot access nominate candidates for the general election after qualifying for ballot access by petition.
Utah	Convention, primary election and petition.
Vermont	Primary election. Major parties by primary, minor parties by convention, independents by petition.
Virginia	Primary election, convention and petition.
Washington	Primary election.
West Virginia	Primary election, convention, petition and independent nominating procedure.
Wisconsin	Primary election/petition. Candidates must file nomination papers (petitions) containing the minimum number of signatures required by law. Candidates appear on the primary ballot for the party they represent. The candidate receiving the most votes in each party primary goes on to the November election.
Wyoming	Primary election.
Dist. of Columbia	Primary election. Independent and minor party candidates file by nominating petition.
American Samoa	Individual files petition for candidacy with the chief election officer. Petition must be signed by statutorily-mandated number of qualified voters.
Guam	Individual files petition for candidacy with the chief election officer. Petition must be signed by statutorily-mandated number of qualified voters.
No. Mariana Islands	Candidates are all nominated by petition. Candidates seeking the endorsement of recognized political parties must also include in their submitted petition submission a document signed by the recognized political parties' chairperson/president and secretary attesting to such nomination. Recognized political parties may, or may not, depending on their by-laws and party rules conduct primaries separate from any state election agency participation.
Puerto Rico	Primary election and convention.
U.S. Virgin Islands	Primary election.

Source: The Council of State Governments' survey of state websites, March 2015.
Note: The nominating methods described here are for state offices; procedures may vary for local candidates. Also, independent candidates may have to petition for nomination.

Table 6.4
ELECTION DATES FOR NATIONAL AND STATE ELECTIONS
(Formulas and dates of state elections)

State or other jurisdiction	National (a) Primary	National (a) General	State (b) Primary	State (b) Runoff	State (b) General	Type of primary (c)
Alabama	March, 2nd T March 8, 2016	Nov.,★ Nov. 8, 2016	June, 1st T June 4, 2018	6th T AP July 17, 2018	Nov.,★ Nov. 6, 2018	Open
Alaska	(d) NA	Nov.,★ Nov. 8, 2016	Aug., 3rd T Aug. 16, 2016	...	Nov.,★ Nov. 8, 2016	Partially Closed
Arizona	T following March 15 March 22, 2016	Nov.,★ Nov. 8, 2016	10th T Prior Aug. 30, 2016	...	Nov.,★ Nov. 8, 2016	Partially Closed
Arkansas	T 3 wks. prior to runoff May 24, 2016	Nov.,★ Nov. 8, 2016	T 3 wks. prior to runoff May 24, 2016	June, 2nd T June 14, 2016	Nov.,★ Nov. 8, 2016	Open
California	June,★ June 7, 2016	Nov.,★ Nov. 8, 2016	June,★ June 7, 2016	...	Nov.,★ Nov. 8, 2016	Top Two
Colorado	Rep: Feb. 2, 2016* (d)(e) Dem: Feb. 2, 2016*	Nov.,★ Nov. 8, 2016	June, last T June 28, 2016	...	Nov.,★ Nov. 8, 2016	Partially Closed
Connecticut	April, Last T April 26, 2016	Nov.,★ Nov. 8, 2016	Aug., 2nd T Aug. 9, 2016	...	Nov.,★ Nov. 8, 2016	Partially Closed
Delaware	April, 4th T April 26, 2016	Nov.,★ Nov. 8, 2016	Sept., 2nd T after 1st M Sept. 13, 2016	...	Nov.,★ Nov. 8, 2016	Closed
Florida	(d)(f) March 15, 2016	Nov.,★ Nov. 8, 2016	10th T prior to General Aug. 30, 2016	...	Nov.,★ Nov. 8, 2016	Closed
Georgia	(g) March 1, 2016*	Nov.,★ Nov. 8, 2016	24th T prior to General May 24, 2016	9th T AP July 26, 2016	Nov.,★ Nov. 8, 2016	Open
Hawaii	Rep: March 8, 2016* (d) Dem: March 12, 2016*	Nov.,★ Nov. 8, 2016	Aug., 2nd S Aug. 13, 2016	...	Nov.,★ Nov. 8, 2016	Open
Idaho	(d) NA	Nov.,★ Nov. 8, 2016	May, 3rd T May 17, 2016	...	Nov.,★ Nov. 8, 2016	Partially Closed
Illinois	March, 3rd T March 15, 2016	Nov.,★ Nov. 8, 2016	March, 3rd T March 15, 2016	...	Nov.,★ Nov. 8, 2016	Partially Open
Indiana	May,★ May 3, 2016	Nov.,★ Nov. 8, 2016	May,★ May 3, 2016	...	Nov.,★ Nov. 8, 2016	Partially Open
Iowa	(d) Jan. 18, 2016*	Nov.,★ Nov. 8, 2016	June,★ June 7, 2016	...	Nov.,★ Nov. 8, 2016	Partially Open
Kansas	(d)(h) NA	Nov.,★ Nov. 8, 2016	Aug., 1st T Aug. 2, 2016	...	Nov.,★ Nov. 8, 2016	Closed
Kentucky	May, 1st T after 3rd M May 17, 2016	Nov.,★ Nov. 8, 2016	May, 1st T after 3rd M May 19, 2015	...	Nov.,★ Nov. 3, 2015	Closed
Louisiana	March, 1st S March 5 2016	Nov.,★ Nov. 8, 2016	Oct., 2nd to last S (i) Oct. 24, 2015	...	Nov., 4th S AP (i) Nov. 21, 2015	Top Two
Maine	(d) NA	Nov.,★ Nov. 8, 2016	June, 2nd T June 14, 2016	...	Nov.,★ Nov. 8, 2016	Closed

See footnotes at end of table.

ELECTION DATES FOR NATIONAL AND STATE ELECTIONS
(Formulas and dates of state elections)

State or other jurisdiction	National (a)		State (b)			Type of primary (c)
	Primary	General	Primary	Runoff	General	
Maryland	April, 1st T / April 5, 2016	Nov.★ / Nov. 8, 2016	June, last T / June 26, 2018	...	Nov.★ / Nov. 6, 2018	Partially Closed
Massachusetts	March, 1st T / March 1, 2016	Nov.★ / Nov. 8, 2016	7th T Prior / Sept. 20, 2016	...	Nov.★ / Nov. 8, 2016	Partially Closed
Michigan	March, 2nd T / March 8, 2016	Nov.★ / Nov. 8, 2016	Aug.,★ / Aug. 2, 2016	...	Nov.★ / Nov. 8, 2016	Open
Minnesota	(d)(j) / March 1, 2016	Nov.★ / Nov. 8, 2016	Aug., 2nd T / Aug. 9, 2016	...	Nov.★ / Nov. 8, 2016	Open
Mississippi	March, 2nd T / March 8, 2016	Nov.★ / Nov. 8, 2016	Aug.,★ / Aug. 4, 2015	3rd T AP / Aug. 25, 2015	Nov.★ / Nov. 3, 2015	Partially Open
Missouri	March, 2nd T after 1st M / March 15, 2016	Nov.★ / Nov. 8, 2016	Aug.,★ / Aug. 2, 2016	...	Nov.★ / Nov. 8, 2016	Open
Montana	June,★ / June 7, 2016	Nov.★ / Nov. 8, 2016	June,★ / June 7, 2016	...	Nov.★ / Nov. 8, 2016	Open
Nebraska	May, 1st T after 2nd M / May 10, 2016	Nov.★ / Nov. 8, 2016	May, 1st T after 2nd M / May 10, 2016	...	Nov.★ / Nov. 8, 2016	Top Two
Nevada	(d) / Feb. 13, 2016*	Nov.★ / Nov. 8, 2016	June, 2nd T / June 14, 2016	...	Nov.★ / Nov. 8, 2016	Closed
New Hampshire	(k) / Jan. 26, 2016*	Nov.★ / Nov. 8, 2016	Sept., 2nd T / Sept. 13, 2016	...	Nov.★ / Nov. 8, 2016	Partially Closed
New Jersey	June,★ / June 7, 2016	Nov.★ / Nov. 8, 2016	June,★ / June 2, 2015	...	Nov.★ / Nov. 3, 2015	Closed
New Mexico	June,★ / June 7, 2016	Nov.★ / Nov. 8, 2016	June,★ / June 7, 2016	...	Nov.★ / Nov. 8, 2016	Closed
New York	Feb., 1st T / Feb. 2, 2016	Nov.★ / Nov. 8, 2016	Sept.,1st T after 2nd M / Sept. 13, 2016	...	Nov.★ / Nov. 8, 2016	Closed
North Carolina	Tues. after South Carolina primary / Feb. 23, 2016*	Nov.★ / Nov. 8, 2016	May,★ / May 3, 2016	7 wks. AP / June 21, 2016	Nov.★ / Nov. 8, 2016	Partially Closed
North Dakota	(d)(l) / NA	Nov.★ / Nov. 8, 2016	June, 2nd T / June 14, 2016	...	Nov.★ / Nov. 8, 2016	Open
Ohio	March,★ / March 8, 2016	Nov.★ / Nov. 8, 2016	March,★ / March 8, 2016 (m)	...	Nov.★ / Nov. 8, 2016	Partially Open
Oklahoma	March, 1st T / March 1, 2016	Nov.★ / Nov. 8, 2016	June, last T / June 28, 2016	Aug., 4th T / Aug. 23, 2016	Nov.★ / Nov. 8, 2016	Partially Closed
Oregon	May, 3rd T / May 17, 2016	Nov.★ / Nov. 8, 2016	May, 3rd T / May 17, 2016	...	Nov.★ / Nov. 8, 2016	Partially Closed

See footnotes at end of table.

ELECTION DATES FOR NATIONAL AND STATE ELECTIONS
(Formulas and dates of state elections)

State or other jurisdiction	National (a) Primary	National (a) General	State (b) Primary	State (b) Runoff	State (b) General	Type of primary (c)
Pennsylvania	April, 4th T April 26, 2016	Nov., ★ Nov. 8, 2016	April, 4th T April 26, 2016 (n)	...	Nov., ★ Nov. 8, 2016	Closed
Rhode Island	April, 4th T April 26, 2016	Nov., ★ Nov. 8, 2016	Sept., 2nd T after 1st M Sept. 13, 2016	...	Nov., ★ Nov. 8, 2016	Partially Closed
South Carolina	(d) Feb. 20, 2016*	Nov., ★ Nov. 8, 2016	June, 2nd T June 14, 2016	2nd T AP June 28, 2016	Nov., ★ Nov. 8, 2016	Partially Open
South Dakota	June, ★ June 7, 2016	Nov., ★ Nov. 8, 2016	June, ★ June 7, 2016	10th T AP (o) Aug. 16, 2016	Nov., ★ Nov. 8, 2016	Partially Closed
Tennessee	March, 1st T March 1, 2016	Nov., ★ Nov. 8, 2016	Aug., 1st TH Aug. 4, 2016	...	Nov., ★ Nov. 8, 2016	Partially Open
Texas	March, 1st T March 1, 2016	Nov., ★ Nov. 8, 2016	March, 1st T March 1, 2016	May, 4th T May 24, 2016	Nov., ★ Nov. 8, 2016	Partially Open
Utah	(p) NA	Nov., ★ Nov. 8, 2016	June, 4th T June 28, 2016	...	Nov., ★ Nov. 8, 2016	Partially Closed
Vermont	March, 1st T March 1, 2016	Nov., ★ Nov. 8, 2016	Aug., 2nd T Aug. 9, 2016	...	Nov., ★ Nov. 8, 2016	Open
Virginia	March, 1st T March 1, 2016	Nov., ★ Nov. 8, 2016	June, 2nd T June 9, 2015	...	Nov., ★ Nov. 8, 2016	Partially Open
Washington	May, 4th T (q) May 24, 2016	Nov., ★ Nov. 8, 2016	Aug., 1st T Aug. 2, 2016	...	Nov., ★ Nov. 3, 2015	Top Two
West Virginia	May, 2nd T May 10, 2016	Nov., ★ Nov. 8, 2016	May, 2nd T May 10, 2016	...	Nov., ★ Nov. 8, 2016	Partially Closed
Wisconsin	April, 1st T April 5, 2016	Nov., ★ Nov. 8, 2016	Aug., 2nd T Aug. 9, 2016	...	Nov., ★ Nov. 8, 2016	Open
Wyoming	(d) NA	Nov., ★ Nov. 8, 2016	Aug., 1st T after 3rd M Aug. 16, 2016	...	Nov., ★ Nov. 8, 2016	Closed
Dist. of Columbia	April, 1st T April 5, 2016	Nov., ★ Nov. 8, 2016	April, 1st T April 5, 2016	...	Nov., ★ Nov. 8, 2016	Closed
American Samoa	(d) NA	Nov., ★ Nov. 8, 2016	(r) ...	NA	Nov., ★ Nov. 8, 2016	(r)
Guam	(d) NA	Nov., ★ Nov. 8, 2016	Aug., last S Aug. 27, 2016	...	Nov., ★ Nov. 8, 2016	NA
No. Marianas Islands	(d) NA	Nov., ★ Nov. 8, 2016	(r) ...	14 days following certification of results	Nov., ★ Nov. 8, 2016	(r)
Puerto Rico	NA NA	Nov., ★ Nov. 8, 2016	March, 3rd SU March 20, 2016	...	Nov., ★ Nov. 8, 2016	NA
U.S. Virgin Islands	(d) NA	Nov., ★ Nov. 8, 2016	Aug., 1st S Aug. 6, 2016	...	Nov., ★ Nov. 8, 2016	Closed

See footnotes at end of table.

ELECTION DATES FOR NATIONAL AND STATE ELECTIONS
(Formulas and dates of state elections)

Sources: The Council of State Governments, March 2015. National Conference of State Legislatures. "Primary Elections."

Note: This table describes the basic formulas for determining when national and state elections will be held. For specific information on a particular state, the reader is advised to contact the state election administration office. All dates provided are based on the state election formula and dates are subject to change.

Key:
★ — First Tuesday after first Monday.
. . . — No provision.
M — Monday.
T — Tuesday.
TH — Thursday.
S — Saturday.
SN — Sunday.
Prior — Prior to general election.
AP — After primary.
* — Tentative. Confirmed date not available at press time.
NA — Not available at press time.

(a) National refers to presidential elections.

(b) State refers to election in which a state executive official or legislator is to be elected. See Table 6.1, State Executive Branch Officials to be Elected, and Table 6.2, State Legislature Members to be Elected.

(c) Open (11 states): Voters can privately select which party's ballot to vote, regardless of party affiliation. Closed (11 states and Washington, D.C.): Voters must be registered members of the party to vote its primary ballot.

Partially Open (9 states): Voters can choose in which primary to vote but that choice is not private. In certain states, a voter's primary ballot selection may be regarded as a form of registration with the corresponding party.

Partially Closed (15 states): Unaffiliated voters may participate in any party's primary. Members of a political party are not allowed to cross over and vote in a different political party's primary.

Top Two primaries (4 states): All voters in California and Washington receive one ballot with candidates from all parties listed together. The top two finishers face each other at the general election. Louisiana has a similar election type but its primary is held in November with a runoff election in December if no candidate garners 50 percent or more of the vote. Nebraska uses a single primary ballot to elect lawmakers to its nonpartisan legislature.

(d) The dates for presidential caucuses are set by the political parties.

(e) The state parties have the option of choosing either the first Tuesday in March (March 1, 2016) date called for in the statute or moving up to the first Tuesday in February (Feb. 2, 2016).

(f) Under Florida law, the presidential preference primary shall be held on the first Tuesday that the rules of the major political parties provide for state delegations to be allocated without penalty.

(g) The secretary of state has the authority to set the date of the presidential primary election. Currently held in March, the presidential primary could be held as late as June 14.

(h) Kansas has not held a presidential primary since 1992, because the Legislature has not appropriated money for that purpose. However, state statute grants the Kansas secretary of state the option of choosing a date that either coincides with at least 5 other states' delegate selection events or is on the first Tuesday in April or before.

(i) Louisiana has an open primary which requires all candidates, regardless of party affiliation, to appear on a single ballot. If a candidate receives over 50 percent of the vote in the primary, that candidate is elected to the office. If no candidate receives a majority vote, then a single election is held between the two candidates receiving the most votes. For national elections, the first vote is held on the first Saturday in October of even-numbered years with the general election held on the first Tuesday after the first Monday in November. For state elections, the election is held on the second to last Saturday in October with the runoff being held on the fourth Saturday after first election.

(j) Parties must notify the secretary of state's office in writing prior to Dec. 1 the year preceding the date of the election of their intentions to hold a preference primary election. Unless the chairs of the two major political parties jointly propose a different date, the caucuses are held on the first Tuesday in February.

(k) The secretary of state selects a date for the primary, which must be 7 days or more immediately preceding the date on which any other state holds a similar election.

(l) On one designated day, following presidential nominating contests in the states of Iowa and New Hampshire and prior to the first Wednesday in March in every presidential election year, every political party entitled to a separate column may conduct a presidential preference caucus. Before August 15 of the odd-numbered year immediately preceding the presidential election year, the secretary of state shall designate the day after consulting with and taking recommendations from the two political parties casting the greatest vote for president of the United States at the most recent general elections when the office of president appeared on the ballot.

(m) Primary elections shall be held on the first Tuesday after the first Monday in May of each year except in years in which a presidential primary election is held. In years in which a presidential primary election is held, all primary elections shall be held on the first Tuesday after the first Monday in March except as otherwise authorized by a municipal or county charter.

(n) The third Tuesday in May is Primary Election Day in Pennsylvania except in presidential election years when the primary is held on the fourth Tuesday in April.

(o) South Dakota only holds runoffs for the offices of U.S. senator, U.S. representative and governor.

(p) In 2015, the Utah legislature failed to pass a bill (HB 329) to allocate $3 million to move the primary from June to March. As a result, the presidential primary is scheduled for the same date as the June state primary date. However, it is too late under both Republican and Democratic party rules, making the state "out of compliance," meaning the parties could suffer penalties from the national parties. The Republicans now plan to hold a caucus. Democrats are currently considering an online presidential primary vote.

(q) The Washington Legislature voted to suspend the 2012 presidential primary for budgetary reasons, replacing it with caucuses. The primary is expected to return in 2016.

(r) American Samoa and the Northern Mariana Islands do not conduct primary elections. Instead, the law provides for a runoff when none of the candidates receives more than 50% of the vote.

Table 6.5
POLLING HOURS: GENERAL ELECTIONS

State or other jurisdiction	Polls open	Polls close	Notes on hours (a)
Alabama	7 a.m.	7 p.m.	Polling places located in the Eastern Time Zone may be open from 7 a.m. to 7 p.m. ET.
Alaska	7 a.m.	8 p.m.	
Arizona	6 a.m.	7 p.m.	
Arkansas	7:30 a.m.	7:30 p.m.	
California	7 a.m.	8 p.m.	
Colorado	7 a.m.	7 p.m.	
Connecticut	6 a.m.	8 p.m.	
Delaware	7 a.m.	8 p.m.	
Florida	7 a.m.	7 p.m.	
Georgia	7 a.m.	7 p.m.	
Hawaii	7 a.m.	6 p.m.	
Idaho	8 a.m.	8 p.m.	Clerk has the option of opening all polls at 7 a.m. Idaho is in two time zones—MT and PT.
Illinois	6 a.m.	7 p.m.	
Indiana	6 a.m.	6 p.m.	For those counties on Central time, polling places will observe these times in Central time.
Iowa	7 a.m.	9 p.m.	
Kansas	7 a.m.	7 p.m.	Counties may open the polls earlier and close them later. Several western counties are in the Mountain Time Zone.
Kentucky	6 a.m.	6 p.m.	Counties may be either in Eastern or Central Time Zones.
Louisiana	6 a.m.	8 p.m.	
Maine	Between 6 and 10 a.m.	8 p.m.	Applicable opening time depends on variables related to the size of the precinct.
Maryland	7 a.m.	8 p.m.	
Massachusetts	7 a.m.	8 p.m.	Some municipalities may open their polls as early as 5:45 a.m.
Michigan	7 a.m.	8 p.m.	Eastern Time Zone and Central Time Zone
Minnesota	7 a.m.	8 p.m.	A few polling places in small townships located outside the eleven-county metropolitan area may open as late as 10 a.m.
Mississippi	7 a.m.	7 p.m.	
Missouri	6 a.m.	7 p.m.	
Montana	7 a.m.	8 p.m.	A polling place having fewer than 400 registered electors must be open from at least noon to 8 p.m. or until all registered electors in any precinct have voted, at which time that precinct in the polling place must be closed immediately.
Nebraska	7 a.m. MT / 8 a.m. CT	7 p.m. MT / 8 p.m. CT	
Nevada	7 a.m.	7 p.m.	
New Hampshire	No later than 11 a.m.	No earlier than 7 p.m.	Polling hours vary from town to town.
New Jersey	6 a.m.	8 p.m.	
New Mexico	7 a.m.	7 p.m.	
New York	6 a.m.	9 p.m.	
North Carolina	6:30 a.m.	7:30 p.m.	
North Dakota	Between 7 and 9 a.m.	Between 7 and 9 p.m.	Polling locations cannot open earlier than 7 a.m. and must be open by 9 a.m., with the exception of those precincts in which fewer than 75 votes were cast in the last General Election, which must open no later than noon. All polling locations must remain open until 7 p.m. and close no later than 9 p.m.
Ohio	6:30 a.m.	7:30 p.m.	
Oklahoma	7 a.m.	7 p.m.	

See footnotes at end of table.

POLLING HOURS: GENERAL ELECTIONS — Continued

State or other jurisdiction	Polls open	Polls close	Notes on hours (a)
Oregon	7 a.m.	8 p.m.	Official dropsites open 8 hours or more and until 8 p.m. for depositing cast ballots. County Clerks office open 7 a.m.–8 p.m. for issuing and depositing ballots
Pennsylvania	7 a.m.	8 p.m.	
Rhode Island	Between 7 and 9 a.m	8 p.m.	Polls open at 9 a.m. in special elections.
South Carolina	7 a.m.	7 p.m.	
South Dakota	7 a.m.	7 p.m.	
Tennessee	8 a.m. (may be earlier)	7 p.m. CT / 8 p.m. ET	Polling places must be open a minimum of ten continuous hours, but no more than 13 hours. In any county having a population of not less than 120,000, all polling places must open by 8 a.m., but nothing prevents an earlier opening time at the discretion of the county election commission.
Texas	7 a.m.	7 p.m.	
Utah	7 a.m.	8 p.m.	
Vermont	Between 5 and 10 a.m.	7 p.m.	The opening time for polls is set by local boards of civil authority.
Virginia	6 a.m.	7 p.m.	
Washington	NA	NA	Washington votes by mail. The ballot must be postmarked no later than Election Day; or returned to a designated ballot drop box by 8 p.m. on Election Day; or returned in person to the county elections department by 8 p.m. on Election Day.
West Virginia	6:30 a.m.	7:30 p.m.	
Wisconsin	7 a.m.	8 p.m.	
Wyoming	7 a.m.	7 p.m.	
Dist. of Columbia	7 a.m.	8 p.m.	
American Samoa	6 a.m.	6 p.m.	
Guam	7 a.m.	8 p.m.	
No. Mariana Islands	7 a.m.	7 p.m.	
Puerto Rico	9 a.m.	5 p.m.	
U.S. Virgin Islands	7 a.m.	7 p.m.	

Sources: The Council of State Governments and state websites, September 2014.
Note: Hours for primary, municipal and special elections may differ from those noted.

(a) In all states, voters standing in line when the polls close are allowed to vote; however, provisions for handling those voters vary across jurisdictions.

Table 6.6
VOTER REGISTRATION INFORMATION

State or other jurisdiction	Closing date for registration before general election (days)	Same-day registration	Online registration	Residency requirements (a)	Registration in other places prohibited (b)	Provision regarding mental competency
Alabama	14	...	...	S	★	★
Alaska	30	(c)	...	S, D, 30	★	★
Arizona	29	...	★	S, C, 29	...	★
Arkansas	30	...	...	S, 30	★	★
California	15	★(d)	★	S	...	★
Colorado	22 by mail, 8 online, Election Day in person	★	★	S, 22	★	...
Connecticut	14 by mail, 7 in person, Election Day	★	★	S, T	★	★
Delaware	24	...	★	S	★	★
Florida	29	...	...	S	...	★
Georgia	28	...	★	S, C	...	★
Hawaii	30 (e)	★(e)	★(f)	S	★	★
Idaho	25 or Election Day	★	...	S, C, 30	...	...
Illinois	27 (g)	★	★	S, P, 30	★	...
Indiana	29	...	★	S, P, 30	...	...
Iowa	10 or Election Day	★	★(f)	S	★	★
Kansas	21	...	★	S	★	...
Kentucky	29	...	...	S, P, 28	★	★
Louisiana	30	...	★	S, Parish, 30	★	★
Maine	21 by mail, up to Election Day in person	★	...	S, M	★	★
Maryland	21 (h)	(h)	★	S, 21	★	★
Massachusetts	20	...	★(f)	S	...	★
Michigan	30	...	★(i)	S, M, 30	★	...
Minnesota	21 or Election Day	★	★	S, 20	...	★
Mississippi	30	...	...	S, T, 30	★	★
Missouri	28	...	★	S	...	★
Montana	30 by mail or up to Election Day in person	★	...	S, 30	★	★
Nebraska	17 by mail, 10 in person	...	★(f)	S, 30	★	★
Nevada	31 by mail, 21 in person or online	...	★	S, C, 30; P, 10	★	★
New Hampshire	10 or Election Day	★	...	S	★	...
New Jersey	21	...	...	S, C, 30	★	★
New Mexico	28	...	(j)	S	...	★
New York	25	...	★	S, P, 30	★	★
North Carolina	25 (k)	(k)	...	S, C, 30	★	...
North Dakota	(l)	(l)	(l)	S, P, 30	(l)	...
Ohio	30 (m)	(m)	(j)	S, 30	★	★
Oklahoma	24	...	...	S	...	★
Oregon	21	...	★	S	★	★
Pennsylvania	30	...	...	S, D, 30	★	...
Rhode Island	30 (c)	★(c)	...	S, T	★	★
South Carolina	30	...	★	S, C, P	★	★
South Dakota	15	...	...	S	★	★
Tennessee	30	...	...	S	★	★
Texas	30	...	...	S, C	...	★
Utah	30 by mail, 8 in person, 7 online (n)	...	★	S, 30	★	★
Vermont	6	...	...	S, C	...	...
Virginia	22	...	★	S	★	★
Washington	30 by mail, 8 in person	...	★	S, 30	★	★
West Virginia	21	...	★(f)	S, T, 30	★	★
Wisconsin	20 by mail, 4 in person, or Election Day	★	...	S, P, 28	...	★
Wyoming	14 or Election Day	★	...	S, P	...	★
Dist. of Columbia	30 by mail, 15 in person, Election Day	★	...	D, 30	★	★
American Samoa	30	...	...	D, T	★	...
Guam	10	...	...	T	★	★
No. Mariana Islands	60	...	...	T, 120	★	★
Puerto Rico	50	...	...	T (o)	...	★
U.S. Virgin Islands	30	...	...	T, P, 90	★	★

See footnotes at end of table.

VOTER REGISTRATION INFORMATION — Continued

Source: The Council of State Governments survey of state election websites, March 2015.

Key:

★ — Provision exists

. . . — No state provision.

(a) Key for residency requirements: S — State, C — County, D — District, M — Municipality, P — Precinct, T — Town. Numbers represent the number of days before an election for which one must be a resident.

(b) State provision prohibiting registration or claiming the right to vote in another state or jurisdiction.

(c) Election-day registration is available in presidential election years, but voters who do so can vote only for the offices of President and Vice President, not in state or local races.

(d) California's same-day registration will take effect on January 1 of the year following the year in which the Secretary of State certifies that the state has a statewide voter registration database that complies with the requirements of the federal Help America Vote Act of 2002. Secretary of State Debra Bowen said in February 2014 that the state will not meet the legal requirements to implement the law until 2016 or later.

(e) In 2014 Hawaii lawmakers passed legislation (HB 2590) to allow voters to register at early voting sites beginning in 2016 or at their assigned polling places on Election Day starting in 2018.

(f) Not yet implemented: Hawaii, passed in 2012; Iowa, approved by the Voter Registration Commission; Massachusetts, passed in 2014; Nebraska, passed in 2014; West Virginia, passed in 2013.

(g) Registration closes 27 days before a general election. Illinois also has a "grace period" registration that extends registration from the normal close of registration up through the 3rd day before the election.

Once registered, this voter may cast a ballot during this "Grace Period" at the election authority's office or at a location specifically designated for this purpose by the election authority, or by mail, at the discretion of the election authority.

(h) Beginning January 1, 2016, Maryland voters will be able to register and vote on the same day at early voting locations, but not on Election Day.

(i) An online system allows voters to change their address for both their drivers license and voter registration at the same time. Michigan law requires that the same address be on record for both.

(j) In New Mexico and Ohio, a registered voter can update an existing registration record online, but new applications must still be made on paper.

(k) In 2014, the North Carolina legislature eliminated voters' ability to register and vote on the same day at early voting locations. Registered voters may still update their name and address on their voter registration at an Early Voting site.

(l) No voter registration.

(m) In 2014, the Ohio Legislature passed a bill that eliminates the ability of voters to register during the six early voting days referred to as "Golden Week," when people could both register to vote and cast an in-person absentee ballot.

(n) Must be postmarked 30 days before an election. Voters can register in-person up to 8 days before the election, and may register online up to 7 days before the election. However, these voters will not be eligible to participate in early voting, and must vote on election day.

(o) Voters must have a permanent residence in Puerto Rico to be a qualified elector.

Table 6.6a
VOTER INFORMATION

State or other jurisdiction	Vote by mail (a)	Early voting allowed (b)	Voter ID required (c)	Photo ID required	Persons eligible for absentee voting (d)	Permanent absentee status available (e)	Absentee votes signed by witness or notary (f)	Voting rights revoked	Method/ process or provision for restoration (g)
					Absentee voting			*Provisions for felons*	
Alabama	No	Yes	Yes	Yes (h)	Excuse required	...	N or 2 W	★	B
Alaska	★(i)	Yes	Yes (j)	No	No excuse required	...	N or 1 W	★	C
Arizona		Yes	Yes	No	No excuse required	★	...	★	B
Arkansas		Yes	Yes	No (k)	Excuse required	...	...	★	C
California		Yes	No	No	No excuse required	★	...	★	C
Colorado	★(l)	Yes	Yes	No	No excuse required	★	...	★	C
Connecticut		No	Yes	No	Excuse required	...	...	★	C
Delaware		No	Yes	No	Excuse required	...	...	★	C
Florida		Yes	Yes	Yes	No excuse required	...	...	★	A
Georgia		Yes	Yes	Yes	No excuse required	...	...	★	C
Hawaii		Yes	Yes	Yes	No excuse required	★	...	★	C
Idaho		Yes	Yes	Yes (m)	No excuse required	...	...	★	C
Illinois		Yes	No	No	No excuse required	...	...	★	C
Indiana		Yes	Yes	Yes	Excuse required	...	...	★	C
Iowa		Yes	No	No	No excuse required	...	...	★	A
Kansas		Yes	Yes	Yes	No excuse required	...	...	★	C
Kentucky		No	Yes	No	Excuse required	...	...	★	A
Louisiana		Yes	Yes	Yes	Excuse required	...	N or W	★	C
Maine		Yes	No	No	No excuse required	...	...	...	N/A
Maryland		Yes	No	No	No excuse required	...	...	★	C
Massachusetts		No	No	No	Excuse required	...	...	★	C
Michigan		No	Yes	Yes	Excuse required	...	...	★	C
Minnesota		Yes	No	No	No excuse required	...	N or W (n)	★	C
Mississippi		No	Yes	Yes	Excuse required	...	N (o)	★	B
Missouri		No	Yes	No	Excuse required	...	N (p)	★	C
Montana		Yes	Yes	No	No excuse required	★	...	★	C
Nebraska		Yes	No	No	No excuse required	...	...	★	C
Nevada		Yes	No	No	No excuse required	...	...	★	B
New Hampshire		No	Yes	Yes	Excuse required	...	...	★	C
New Jersey		No	No	No	No excuse required	★	...	★	C
New Mexico		Yes	No	No	No excuse required	...	...	★	C
New York		No	No	No	Excuse required	...	...	★	C
North Carolina		Yes	No	No (q)	No excuse required	...	N or 2 W	★	C
North Dakota		Yes	Yes	No	No excuse required	...	...	★	C
Ohio		Yes	Yes	No	No excuse required	...	...	★	C
Oklahoma		Yes	Yes	No (r)	No excuse required	...	N (s)	★	C
Oregon	★(t)	N/A	No	No	No excuse required	★	...	★	C
Pennsylvania		No	No (u)	No (u)	Excuse required	...	...	★	C
Rhode Island		No	Yes	Yes	Excuse required	...	N or 2W (v)	★	C
South Carolina		No	Yes	No (w)	Excuse required	...	W (x)	★	C
South Dakota		Yes	Yes	Yes	No excuse required	...	(y)	★	C
Tennessee		Yes	Yes	Yes	Excuse required	...	...	★	B
Texas		Yes	Yes	Yes	Excuse required	...	...	★	C
Utah		Yes	Yes	No	No excuse required	★	...	★	C
Vermont		Yes	No	No	No excuse required	...	...	...	N/A
Virginia		No	Yes	Yes	Excuse required	...	W	★	B
Washington	★(z)	N/A	No	No	No excuse required	★	...	★	C
West Virginia		Yes	No	No	Excuse required	...	...	★	C
Wisconsin		Yes	No	No	No excuse required	...	W	★	C
Wyoming		Yes	No	No	No excuse required	...	...	★	B
Dist. of Columbia		Yes	No	No	No excuse required	★	...	★	C
American Samoa		No	No	No	Excuse required	...	...	★	C
Guam		No	No	No	Excuse required	...	N	★	C
No. Mariana Islands		No	No	No	Excuse required	...	N	★	C
Puerto Rico		Yes	Yes	No	Excuse required	...	(aa)	...	N/A
U.S. Virgin Islands		No	Yes	No	Excuse required	...	Affidavit	★	C

See footnotes at end of table.

VOTER INFORMATION — Continued

Sources: The Council of State Governments survey of state election websites, March 2015. The Sentencing Project, "Felony Disenfranchisement," *http://www.sentencingproject.org/template/page.cfm?id=133*.

Key:

★ — Provision exists.

. . . — No state provision.

N/A — Not Applicable.

(a) Three states — Colorado, Oregon, and Washington — conduct elections by mail. All registered voters are automatically mailed a ballot in advance of Election Day. Alaska is the first state to allow all voters — not just those covered by the federal Uniformed and Overseas Citizens Absentee Voting Act (UOCAVA) — to submit an absentee ballot electronically. Civilian voters must apply for an electronic ballot beginning 15 days before the election.

(b) Early voting is usually done in person on the same equipment as that used on Election Day. An excuse is not required.

(c) Voter identification laws include both photo or non-photo identification requirements.

(d) Typical excuses include some or all of the following: absent on business; senior citizen; disabled persons; not absent, but prevented by employment from voting; out of state on Election Day; out of precinct on Election Day; absent for religious reasons; students; temporarily out of jurisdiction.

(e) State allows voters to be added to the permanent absentee voter list, in which an absentee ballot will be automatically sent for each election. No excuse is required. This does not include states that allow certain voters to be added to the list, including permanently disabled or ill voters, the elderly, uniformed service members and their families, or people who live outside the United States.

(f) Absentee votes must be signed by, N — Notary or W — Witness. Numbers indicated the number of signatures required.

(g) A — permanent disenfranchisement for all offenders; states that permanently disenfranchise all or some felons may allow felons to apply, on an individual basis, to the state for an exemption that will restore their voting rights. B — permanent disenfranchisement for some offenders; in these states, felons who commit certain felonies are permanently disenfranchised. C — voting rights restored after completion of some or all of sentence; 20 states (Alaska, Ark., Ga., Idaho, Kans., La., Md., Minn., Mo., Nebr., N.J., N.M., N.C., Okla., S.C., S.D., Texas, Wash., W. Va., Wis.) restore rights after completion of entire sentence, including parole and probation; 13 states (Hawaii, Ill., Ind., Mass., Mich., Mont., N.H., N.D., Ohio, Ore., Pa., R.I., Utah) plus the District of Columbia restore rights after completion of prison sentence, allowing parolees and probationers to vote; 4 states (Calif., Colo., Conn., N.Y.) restore rights after completion of prison time and parole, allowing probationers to vote.

(h) Photo identification is not required if two election officials can sign sworn statements saying they know the voter.

(i) Alaska is the first state to allow all voters — not just those covered by the federal Uniformed and Overseas Citizens Absentee Voting Act (UOCAVA) — to submit an absentee ballot electronically. Civilian voters must apply for an electronic ballot beginning 15 days before the election.

(j) An election officer may waive the identification requirement if the election officials knows the identity of the voter.

(k) In October 2014, the Arkansas Supreme Court struck down a state law that requires voters to show photo identification before casting a ballot, ruling the requirement unconstitutional.

(l) While all registered voters are automatically mailed a ballot prior to the election, the state also operates in-person voting sites.

(m) A registered voter must either present a photo ID or sign a Personal Identification Affidavit. After signing the Affidavit, the voter will be issued a ballot to be tabulated with all other ballots.

(n) Unless the witness is a notary, the witness must also be a registered Minnesota voter.

(o) Disabled voters do not need to have an absentee ballot notarized, but it must be witnessed.

(p) All absentee ballots must be notarized with the exception of the following: Missouri residents outside the U.S., including military on active duty and their immediate family members; permanently disabled voters and those voting absentee due to illness or physical disability; and caregivers.

(q) Photo identification will be required starting in 2016.

(r) A Voter Identification Card issued by the County Election Board is the only valid proof of identity that does not include a photograph.

(s) All absentee ballots must notarized with the following exceptions: Physically incapacitated voters and voters who care for physically incapacitated persons (ballot affidavit must be witnessed by two people); voters in a nursing home; overseas voters.

(t) State conducts election by mail. All registered voters are automatically mailed a ballot in advance of Election Day.

(u) In 2012, the legislature enacted a law requiring voters to show photo identification. However, in 2014 a state judge struck down the law.

(v) All absentee ballots must be notarized or signed by two witnesses with the following exceptions: military and overseas voters.

(w) If a voter has a reasonable impediment to obtaining photo identification, he or she may vote a provisional ballot after showing a non-photo voter registration card. State law defines a reasonable impediment as any valid reason, beyond a person's control, that creates an obstacle to obtaining Photo ID. Some examples include: religious objection to being photographed; disability or illness; work schedule; lack of transportation; lack of birth certificate; family responsibilities; election within short time frame of implementation of photo ID law (January 1, 2013); and any other obstacle a person finds reasonable.

(x) All absentee ballots must be notarized or signed by one witness, with the exception of qualified voters under the Uniformed and Overseas Citizens Absentee Voters Act.

(y) Absentee ballot applications (not absentee ballots) are required to be notarized unless a copy of the voter's photo identification is also submitted.

(z) State conducts election by mail. All registered voters are automatically mailed a ballot in advance of Election Day. Only Pierce County offers in-person voting.

(aa) Absentee ballot applications (not absentee ballots) are required to be certified by various officials, depending on the reason for voting absentee, such as a college registrar, employer, or medical official.

Table 6.7
VOTING STATISTICS FOR GUBERNATORIAL ELECTIONS

State or other jurisdiction	Date of last election	Primary election Republican	Primary election Democrat	Primary election 3rd Party	Primary election Independent	Primary election Total votes	General election Republican	Percent	Democrat	Percent	3rd Party	Percent	Independent and Write-in	Percent	Total votes
Alabama	2014	434,525	180,658	0	0	615,183	750,231	63.6	427,787	36.2	0	0.0	2,395	0.0	1,180,413
Alaska	2014	106,648	46,427(a)	0	0	153,075	128,435	45.9	8,985(b)	3.2	6,987	2.5	135,551(b)	48.4	279,958
Arizona	2014	539,690	271,276(c)	4,739	0	815,705	805,062	53.4	626,921	41.6	72,769	4.8	1,664	0.1	1,506,416
Arkansas	2014	179,225	153,343	0	0	332,568	470,429	55.4	352,115	41.5	26,408	3.1	0	0.0	848,952
California (d)	2014	1,729,985	2,391,810	119,579	91,654	4,333,028	2,929,213	40.0	4,388,368	60.0	0(d)	0.0	0	0.0	7,317,581
Colorado	2014	384,749	214,403(c)	0	0	599,152	938,195	46.0	1,006,433	49.3	96,946	4.7	0	0.0	2,041,574
Connecticut	2014	79,426	(c)	0	0	79,426	526,295(e)	48.2	554,314(c)	50.7	0	0.0	12,164	1.1	1,092,773
Delaware	2012	(c)	(c)	0	0	0	113,793	28.6	275,993	69.3	8,369	2.1	0	0.0	398,155
Florida	2014	949,144	837,796	0	0	1,786,940	2,865,343	48.1	2,801,198	47.1	223,356	3.8	61,664	1.0	5,951,561
Georgia	2014	596,218	304,243(c)	0	0	900,461	1,345,237	52.7	1,144,794	44.9	60,185	2.4	432	0.0	2,550,648
Hawaii	2014	43,052	233,179	2,526	0	278,757	135,775	37.1	181,106	49.5	49,329	13.5	0	0.0	366,210
Idaho	2014	155,310	25,638	0	0	180,948	235,378	53.2	169,595	38.3	25,627	5.8	11,668	2.6	442,268
Illinois	2014	819,710	447,318	0	0	1,267,028	1,833,627	50.4	1,681,343	46.2	121,534	3.3	1,186	0.0	3,637,690
Indiana	2012	554,412(c)	207,365(c)	0	0	761,777	1,275,424	49.5	1,200,016	46.6	101,868	4.0	21	0.0	2,577,329
Iowa	2014	162,589	72,382	0	0	234,971	666,023	59.0	420,778	37.3	41,140	3.6	1,093	0.1	1,129,034
Kansas	2014	263,594	66,357(c)	0	0	329,951	433,196	49.8	401,100	46.1	35,206	4.0	0	0.0	869,502
Kentucky	2011	142,108	(c)	0	0	142,108	294,034	35.3	464,245	55.7	0	0.0	74,860	9.0	833,139
Louisiana (f)	2011	673,239	288,161	12,528	49,235	1,023,163	(f)		(f)		(f)		(f)		(f)
Maine	2014	50,856(c)	56,286(c)	0	0	107,142	294,519	48.2	265,114	43.4	51,515	8.4	79	0.0	611,227
Maryland	2014	214,935	485,093	0	0	700,028	884,400	51.2	818,890	47.4	25,382	1.5	303	0.0	1,728,975
Massachusetts	2014	156,580	540,733	0	0	697,313	1,044,573	48.4	1,004,408	46.5	71,814	3.3	37,531	1.7	2,158,326
Michigan	2014	617,720(c)	513,263(c)	0	0	1,130,983	1,607,399	50.9	1,479,057	46.9	70,025	2.2	50	0.0	3,156,531
Minnesota	2014	184,110	191,259	5,822	0	381,191	879,257	44.5	989,113	50.1	106,241	5.4	795	0.0	1,975,406
Mississippi	2011	289,788	412,530(c)	0	0	702,318	544,851	61.0	348,617	39.0	0	0.0	0	0.0	893,468
Missouri	2012	557,406	314,158	2,500	0	874,064	1,160,265	42.5	1,494,056	54.8	73,509	2.7	53	0.0	2,727,883
Montana	2012	88,561	136,060	0	0	224,621	228,879	47.3	236,450	48.9	18,160	3.8	0	0.0	483,489
Nebraska	2014	221,020	65,620(c)	402(c)	0	287,042	308,751	57.2	211,905	39.3	19,001	3.5	0	0.0	539,657
Nevada	2014	117,510(h)	72,521(h)	0	0	190,031	386,340	70.6	130,722	23.9	14,536	2.7	15,751(h)	2.9	547,349
New Hampshire	2014	41,976	113,273	0	0	155,249	230,610	47.4	254,666	52.4	0	0.0	907	0.2	486,183
New Jersey	2013	223,761	197,171	0	0	420,932	1,278,932	60.3	809,978	38.2	29,172	1.4	2,784	0.1	2,120,866
New Mexico	2014	64,413(c)	125,371	0	0	189,784	293,443	57.2	219,362	42.8	0	0.0	0	0.0	512,805
New York	2014	(c)	574,350	0	0	574,350	1,536,879(i)	40.2	2,069,480(i)	54.2	206,349	5.4	6,719	0.2	3,819,427
North Carolina	2012	897,137	934,287	0	0	1,831,424	2,440,707	54.6	1,931,580	43.2	94,652	2.1	1,356	0.0	4,468,295
North Dakota	2012	95,483(c)	52,238(c)	664	0	148,385	200,525	63.1	109,048	34.3	7,974	2.5	267	0.1	317,814
Ohio	2014	559,671(c)	440,253	674	0	1,000,598	1,944,848	63.6	1,009,359	33.0	101,706	3.3	0	0.0	3,055,913
Oklahoma	2014	264,894	(c)	0	0	264,894	460,298	55.8	338,239	41.0	0	0.0	26,294	3.2	824,831
Oregon	2014	248,552	301,875	0	0	550,427	648,542	44.1	733,230	49.9	81,298	5.5	6,654	0.5	1,469,724
Pennsylvania	2014	(c)	1,920,355	0	0	1,920,355	1,575,511	45.1	1,920,355	54.9	0	0.0	0	0.0	3,495,866
Rhode Island	2014	31,929	128,095	0	0	160,024	117,428	36.2	131,899	40.7	69,278	21.4	5,450	1.7	324,055
South Carolina	2014	(c)	(c)	0	0	0	696,645	55.9	516,166	41.4	21,060	1.7	12,432	1.0	1,246,303

See footnotes at end of table.

VOTING STATISTICS FOR GUBERNATORIAL ELECTIONS BY REGION — Continued

State or other jurisdiction	Date of last election	Primary election					General election								
		Republican	Democrat	3rd Party	Independent	Total votes	Republican	Percent	Democrat	Percent	3rd Party	Percent	Independent and Write-in	Percent	Total votes
South Dakota	2014	74,213	27,594	0	0	101,807	195,477	70.5	70,549	25.4	0	0.0	11,377	4.1	277,403
Tennessee	2014	651,247	228,025	0	0	879,272	951,796	70.3	309,237	22.8	45,150	3.3	47,545	3.5	1,353,728
Texas	2014	1,337,875	554,014	0	0	1,891,889	2,796,547	59.3	1,835,596	38.9	85,063	1.8	1,062	0.0	4,718,268
Utah	2012	(j)	(j)	3,333	0	3,333	688,592	68.4	277,622	27.6	40,307	4.0	3	0.0	1,006,524
Vermont	2014	16,010	19,828	263	0	36,101	87,075	45.1	89,509	46.4	10,101	5.2	6,402	3.3	193,087
Virginia	2013	(j)	(c)	(j)	0	0	1,013,354	45.2	1,069,789	47.8	146,084	6.5	11,087	0.5	2,240,314
Washington	2012	665,925	709,987	23,498	10,457	1,409,867	1,488,245	48.5	1,582,802	51.5	0	0.0	0	0.0	3,071,047
West Virginia	2012	104,090	202,068	0	0	306,158	303,291	45.6	335,468	50.5	25,696	3.9	0	0.0	664,455
Wisconsin	2014	240,102(c)	312,106	141	0	552,349	1,259,706	52.3	1,122,913	46.6	0	0.0	27,695	1.1	2,410,314
Wyoming	2014	97,884	15,799(c)	0	0	97,884	99,700	59.4	45,752	27.3	4,040	2.4	18,385	11.0	167,877
American Samoa	2012	(k)	(k)	(k)	(k)	(k)	2,521	19.3	4,315(k)	33.1	0	0.0	6,217(k)	0.0	13,053
Guam	2014	11,034(c)	7,330(c)	0	0	18,364	22,512	63.9	12,712	36.1	0	0.0	0	0.0	35,224
No. Mariana Islands	2014	(l)	(l)	(l)	(l)	(l)	541	3.9	6,342	46.0	0	0.0	6,915	0.0	13,798
Puerto Rico	2012	(c)	(c)	(c)	0	0	884,775	47.1	896,060	47.7	82,834	4.4	13,510	0.0	1,877,179
U.S. Virgin Islands	2014	N/A	9,962	0	0	9,962	0	0.0	10,173(m)	39.2	0	0.0	15,802(l)	0.0	25,975

Source: The Council of State Governments' survey of state elections websites, February 2015.

Key:

N/A — Not Applicable

(a) In 2014, the Democratic Primary featured candidates from the Democratic Party and the Libertarian Party.

(b) In a move endorsed by the Alaska Democratic Party, independent gubernatorial candidate Bill Walker and Democratic candidate Byron Mallott joined forces in a self-proclaimed "unity" ticket to challenge — and ultimately defeat — incumbent Republican Gov. Sean Parnell. Walker, a Republican who petitioned onto the ballot as an independent, headed the ticket, while the Democratic candidate Mallott ran as the lieutenant governor. This move required Hollis French, the Democratic lieutenant governor candidate, and Craig Fleener, Walker's former running mate, to resign from their respective ballots. As a result, there were no Democratic candidates for governor for the first time in state history. The unity ticket received 134,658 votes. Write-in votes totaled 893.

(c) Candidate ran unopposed.

(d) California became an open primary state after passage of Proposition 14 in the June 2010 election. The top two vote getters in primary races for congressional, state legislative and statewide offices, regardless of political party, will be in a face-off in the general election.

(e) Republican vote total includes 22,297 votes from the Independent party. Democratic vote total includes 24,762 from the Working Families Party.

(f) Louisiana has an open primary which requires all candidates, regardless of party affiliation, to appear on a single ballot. If a candidate receives over 50 percent of the vote in the primary, he is elected to the office. If no candidate receives a majority vote, then a single election is held between the two candidates receiving the most votes. In the October 22, 2011 primary election Governor Bobby Jindal

(R) received 65.8 percent of the vote, the four Democrats received 28.2 percent of the vote and the other five candidates received the remaining 6 percent of the vote. No runoff election was required.

(g) In the Democratic primary in Mississippi, a runoff was held because no candidate received more than 50% of the vote. The vote total in the runoff election was 323,284.

(h) Nevada voters have the option to select "None of These Candidates." If the "None of These Candidates" option receives the most votes in an election, the actual candidate who receives the most votes wins the election. In the Democratic primary, the "None of These Candidates" option received the most votes (21,725 or 30%). The winner of the primary — Robert Goodman — received 17,691 votes (25%). In the Republican primary, 3,509 voters selected that option. The "None of These Candidates" option received 15,751 votes in the general election.

(i) Democratic vote includes 73,266 from the Independence Party, 51,052 from the Women's Equality Party, and 120,446 from the Working Families Party. The Republican vote includes 239,266 from the Conservative Party and 50,242 from the Stop Common Core Party.

(j) Candidate nominated by convention.

(k) There are no primaries. Instead, the law provides for a runoff when none of the candidates receives more than 50% of the vote. In the general election, a runoff was held. The vote total in the runoff election was 12,553, with the Independent candidate Lolo Letalu Matalasi Moliga defeating the Democratic candidate, winning with 52.9% of the vote.

(l) There are no primaries. Instead, the law provides for a runoff when none of the candidates receives more than 50% of the vote.

(m) In the general election in the U.S. Virgin Islands, a runoff was held because no candidate received more than 50% of the vote. The vote total in the runoff election was 25,396, with the Independent candidate Kenneth Mapp winninng with 62.7% of the vote.

Table 6.8
VOTER TURNOUT FOR PRESIDENTIAL ELECTIONS BY REGION: 2004, 2008 AND 2012
(In thousands)

State or other jurisdiction	2012 Voting age population (a)	2012 Number registered	2012 Number voting (b)	2008 Voting age population (a)	2008 Number registered	2008 Number voting (b)	2004 Voting age population (a)	2004 Number registered	2004 Number voting (b)
U.S. Total	234,564	153,161	129,140	227,719	189,391	128,628	208,247	170,937	122,501
Alabama	3,647	2,556	2,074	3,504	2,841	2,100	3,252	2,597	1,883
Alaska	523	361	300	501	496	326	460	472	313
Arizona	4,763	2,812	2,299	4,668	2,987	2,321	3,800	2,643	2,038
Arkansas	2,204	1,376	1,069	2,134	1,686	1,087	1,951	1,686	1,055
California	27,959	15,356	13,039	27,169	23,209	13,214	22,075	16,557	12,589
Colorado	3,804	2,635	2,570	3,668	3,209	2,401	3,246	2,890	2,130
Connecticut	2,757	1,760	1,558	2,682	2,210	1,645	2,574	1,823	1,579
Delaware	692	470	414	659	602	391	594	554	376
Florida	14,799	9,102	8,474	14,207	11,248	8,358	12,539	10,301	7,610
Georgia	7,196	4,767	3,898	7,013	5,266	3,924	6,080	4,249	3,285
Hawaii	1,056	547	437	997	691	454	873	647	429
Idaho	1,139	745	652	1,091	862	655	996	798	613
Illinois	9,701	6,425	5,242	9,653	7,790	5,578	9,519	7,499	5,274
Indiana	4,876	3,270	2,625	4,758	4,515	2,751	4,420	4,163	2,468
Iowa	2,318	1,745	1,582	2,276	2,076	1,537	2,212	2,107	1,522
Kansas	2,126	1,467	1,160	2,079	1,750	1,751	2,038	1,694	1,188
Kentucky	3,316	2,303	1,797	3,237	2,907	1,827	3,012	2,819	1,796
Louisiana	3,415	2,498	1,994	3,213	2,945	1,961	3,249	2,923	1,957
Maine	1,054	787	725	1,037	1,000	731	1,042	957	741
Maryland	4,421	2,888	2,707	4,259	3,429	2,632	3,922	3,070	2,396
Massachusetts	5,129	3,759	3,184	5,016	4,220	3,103	4,931	3,973	2,927
Michigan	7,540	5,620	4,731	7,624	7,471	5,044	7,541	7,164	4,839
Minnesota	4,020	3,085	2,937	3,937	3,200	2,910	3,823	2,977	2,828
Mississippi	2,212	1,794	1,286	2,150	1,873	1,290	2,014	1,865	1,140
Missouri	4,563	3,384	2,757	4,453	4,181	2,925	4,297	4,194	2,731
Montana	766	553	484	738	668	490	680	596	450
Nebraska	1,367	901	794	1,328	1,157	801	1,257	1,160	778
Nevada	2,036	1,176	1,015	1,905	1,208	968	1,580	1,094	830
New Hampshire	1,029	752	711	1,017	864	708	991	856	684
New Jersey	6,727	4,326	3,638	6,622	5,379	3,868	6,669	5,009	3,612
New Mexico	1,541	978	784	1,469	1,193	830	1,318	1,105	756
New York	15,053	8,887	7,117	14,884	12,031	7,675	14,206	11,837	7,448
North Carolina	7,254	5,295	4,505	6,843	6,226	4,311	6,453	5,527	3,501
North Dakota	523	383 (c)	323	496	(c)	317	487	(c)	316
Ohio	8,806	6,076	5,581	8,715	8,163	5,698	8,604	7,973	5,426
Oklahoma	2,822	1,806	1,335	2,717	2,184	1,463	2,515	2,143	1,464
Oregon	2,965	2,086	1,789	2,884	2,154	1,828	2,665	2,120	1,837
Pennsylvania	9,910	6,795	5,742	9,646	8,730	5,995	9,404	8,367	5,770
Rhode Island	829	552	446	824	701	470	803	709	437
South Carolina	3,545	2,479	1,964	3,347	2,554	1,921	3,214	2,315	1,618
South Dakota	611	454	364	599	508	382	573	502	395
Tennessee	4,850	3,210	2,459	4,685	3,978	2,600	4,284	3,532	2,437
Texas	18,280	10,749	7,994	17,281	13,575	8,077	16,071	13,098	7,411
Utah	1,893	1,138	1,017	1,828	1,433	905	1,522	1,278	928
Vermont	497	357	299	489	454	325	490	445	312
Virginia	6,147	4,210	3,854	5,885	5,044	3,724	5,194	4,528	3,195
Washington	5,143	3,533	3,126	4,932	3,630	3,037	4,596	3,508	2,883
West Virginia	1,466	982	670	1,424	1,212	713	1,406	1,169	744
Wisconsin	4,347	3,318	3,071	4,280	3,405	2,983	4,119	2,957 (c)	2,997
Wyoming	428	268	251	397	276	255	370	246	244
Dist. of Columbia	501	385	294	475	427	267	435	384	228

Sources: U.S. Congress, Clerk of the House, Statistics of the Presidential and Congressional Election, 2004, 2008, 2012. U.S. Census Bureau, Resident Population of Voting Age and Percent Casting Votes—States, as of July 1, 2010. U.S. Census Bureau, Table 4a: Reported Voting and Registration of the Citizen Voting-Age Population, for States: November 2012. U.S. Census Bureau, Current Population Survey, December 2008. The Council of State Governments' survey of election officials, January 2009, January 2005.

Key:
(a) Estimated population, 18 years old and over. Includes armed forces in each state, aliens, and institutional population.
(b) Number voting is number of ballots cast in presidential race.
(c) No statewide registration required.

2014 Ballot Propositions

By John G. Matsusaka

Voters looked favorably on ballot propositions in 2014, approving 67 percent of the 158 measures they decided. Marijuana advocates scored important victories in Alaska, Oregon and Washington, D.C., and minimum wage advocates continued their unbroken run of successful measures in five more states.

Overview

Voters decided 158 propositions in 2014, with 146 appearing on the Nov. 4 ballot. The total number of propositions was down 15 percent from the 186 propositions in 2012, well below the recent high point of 235 propositions in 1998, and the lowest total in an even-numbered year in the 21st century. The approval rate of 67 percent matches the approval rate in 2002 and 2004, which are the highest in the 21st century.

The propositions were distributed across 42 states. The most active state was Louisiana, where voters approved six of 14 proposed constitutional amendments. Other busy states were North Dakota, with nine propositions, and Missouri and New Mexico, both with eight propositions.

Most propositions (111) were placed on the ballot by state legislatures. These "legislative measures" were mostly bond proposals and constitutional amendments, both of which require popular approval in many states. Forty propositions were placed on the ballot by citizen petition; of these, 35 were "initiatives," meaning proposals of new laws, while five were "referendums," meaning proposals to repeal laws passed by the legislature. There were also five advisory propositions, one proposition placed on the ballot by a state commission and one proposition calling for a constitutional convention that was required by the state constitution. See Table A for a summary of propositions by state and type in 2014, Table B for a year-by-year breakdown of ballot proposition activity since 2000, and Table C for a complete list of propositions decided in 2014.

Initiative Trends

Typically, the most visible and controversial propositions are initiatives. Initiatives usually attract the lion's share of campaign contributions as well. Advocates view the initiative process as an important supplement to representative democracy that allows citizens to counteract the influence of special interests on elected officials, while opponents view the process as increasing the influence of wealthy and organized interest groups that can fund petition drives and the subsequent election campaigns.

The initiative, together with the referendum and recall, were quintessential Progressive-era reforms. South Dakota was the first state to adopt the process, in 1898, followed by Utah in 1900 and Oregon in 1902. By 1918, 19 states had adopted the process, and adoption has continued at the rate of about one state every 20 years. Mississippi was the last state to adopt the initiative process, in 1992, bringing the total number of states that allow initiatives to 24.[1] The initiative process is widely available in states west of the Mississippi, but it is not a purely Western phenomenon. Some initiative states are in the Northeast (Maine, Massachusetts), South (Arkansas, Florida), and Central regions (Michigan, Ohio).

The total count of 35 initiatives in 2014 was down 30 percent from the 50 initiatives in 2012, and the lowest total in an even-numbered year since 1974, when only 19 initiatives reached the ballot. The number of initiatives in 2014 also was well below the peak number of 93 in 1996 during the last big initiative wave. The approval rate for initiatives in 2014 was 46 percent, above the long run historical average of 40 percent.

Initiative use overall appears to be waning from its peak in the mid-1990s for reasons that are not immediately apparent. Figure A shows the number of initiatives by decade, beginning in 1904 when the first initiatives appeared on the ballot in Oregon. Initiatives were common in the first four decades of the 20th century, particularly in the Progressive era that preceded the Great Depression. Many initiatives during this period were fueled by tensions between the new urban majorities in

Table A: State-by-State Totals for 2014

State	Initiatives	Legislative measures	Referendums	Advisory	Other	Total	Issues
Alabama (a)	...	6 (6)	...	...	...	6 (6)	Sharia Law; right to bear arms; right to hunt and fish
Alaska (b)	3 (3)	...	1 (1)	...	...	4 (4)	Legalized marijuana; minimum wage
Arizona	...	2 (2)	...	...	1 (0)	3 (2)	State enforcement of federal health plan
Arkansas	2 (1)	3 (3)	...	...	...	5 (4)	Alcohol sales in counties; minimum wage
California (c)	3 (1)	4 (4)	1 (0)	...	...	8 (5)	$7.72 billion bonds; rainy day fund; health insurance rates
Colorado	4 (1)	...	...	...	...	4 (1)	GMO food; abortion ban; wagering on horse races
Connecticut	...	1 (1)	...	...	...	1 (1)	Absentee voting
Florida	2 (1)	1 (0)	...	...	...	3 (1)	Medical marijuana
Georgia	...	3 (0)	...	...	...	3 (0)	Income tax limit
Hawaii	...	5 (3)	...	...	...	5 (3)	Bonds; mandatory retirement for judges
Idaho	...	1 (0)	...	...	...	1 (0)	Legislative approval of executive rules
Illinois	...	2 (2)	...	3 (3)	...	5 (5)	Victims' rights; minimum wage; school spending
Kansas	...	1 (1)	...	...	...	1 (1)	Charitable gambling
Louisiana	...	14 (6)	...	...	...	14 (6)	Health care trust funds
Maine	1 (0)	6 (6)	...	...	...	7 (6)	Hunting ban; bonds
Maryland	...	2 (2)	...	...	...	2 (2)	Transportation trust fund
Massachusetts	4 (2)	...	...	...	...	4 (2)	Casino gambling; mandatory sick leave; bottle deposit
Michigan (d)	...	1 (1)	2 (0)	...	...	3 (1)	Wolf hunting; endangered species
Mississippi	...	1 (1)	...	...	...	1 (1)	Right to hunt and fish
Missouri (e)	1 (0)	8 (5)	...	...	...	8 (5)	Right to farm; right to guns; sales tax surcharge; teachers
Montana	...	2 (0)	...	...	...	2 (0)	Voter registration deadline
Nebraska	1 (1)	...	...	...	...	1 (1)	Minimum wage
Nevada	1 (0)	2 (1)	...	...	...	3 (1)	Business tax increase; minerals taxes
New Jersey	...	2 (2)	...	...	...	2 (2)	Denial of bail
New Mexico	...	8 (8)	...	...	...	8 (8)	Bonds; school bond elections
New York	...	3 (3)	...	...	...	3 (3)	$2 billion bonds; independent redistricting
North Carolina	...	1 (1)	...	...	...	1 (1)	Jury trials
North Dakota (f)	4 (0)	5 (2)	...	...	...	9 (2)	Pharmacy ownership; initiative restrictions
Ohio (g)	...	1 (1)	...	...	...	1 (1)	$1.875 billion bonds for transporation and water
Oklahoma	...	3 (3)	...	...	...	3 (3)	Homestead tax exemptions
Oregon	4 (2)	2 (1)	1 (0)	...	...	7 (3)	Marijuana legalization; $4.3 billion bonds; GMO food
Rhode Island	...	6 (5)	...	...	1 (0)	7 (5)	Casino authorization; bond issues
South Carolina	...	2 (2)	...	...	...	2 (2)	Charitable raffles
South Dakota	2 (2)	1 (1)	...	...	...	3 (3)	Minimum wage; gambling; health insurance
Tennessee	...	4 (4)	...	...	...	4 (4)	Public funding of abortion; income tax limit
Texas	...	1 (1)	...	...	...	1 (1)	Rainy day fund
Utah	...	3 (3)	...	...	...	3 (3)	Lieutenant governor; tax commission membership
Virginia	...	1 (1)	...	...	...	1 (1)	Property tax exemption for soldiers
Washington	3 (2)	...	...	2 (2)	...	5 (4)	Gun purchase background checks; school spending
West Virginia	...	1 (1)	...	...	...	1 (1)	Tax break for Boy Scout camp
Wisconsin	...	1 (1)	...	...	...	1 (1)	Gas tax revenue
Wyoming	...	1 (0)	...	...	...	1 (0)	Nonresident trustees for state university
Total	35 (16)	111 (84)	5 (1)	5 (5)	2 (0)	158 (106)	

Source: Initiative & Referendum Institute (www.iandrinstitute.org).

Note: The table reports the total number of propositions during 2014. Except as noted below, all propositions appeared on the ballot on Nov. 4. The main entry is the number of propositions appearing; the number approved is in parentheses. For advisory measures in Washington, the proposition is classifed as "approved" if the recommendation was to maintain the existing law. For referendums, "approved" means that voters approved the law in question. The "other" category includes an Arizona proposition placed on the ballot by a state commission and a Rhode Island proposition mandated by the state constitution.

Key:

(a) One Alabama proposition appeared on the July 15 ballot.

(b) The Alaska referendum appeared on the Aug. 19 ballot.

(c) Two California legislative measures appeared on the June 3 ballot; both were approved.

(d) Michigan had one legislative statute that was approved on the Aug. 5 primary election ballot.

(e) Missouri had five amendments on the Aug. 5 ballot, of which three were approved.

(f) North Dakota voters approved on legislative amendment on June 10.

(g) Ohio's Issue 1 appeared on the May 6 ballot.

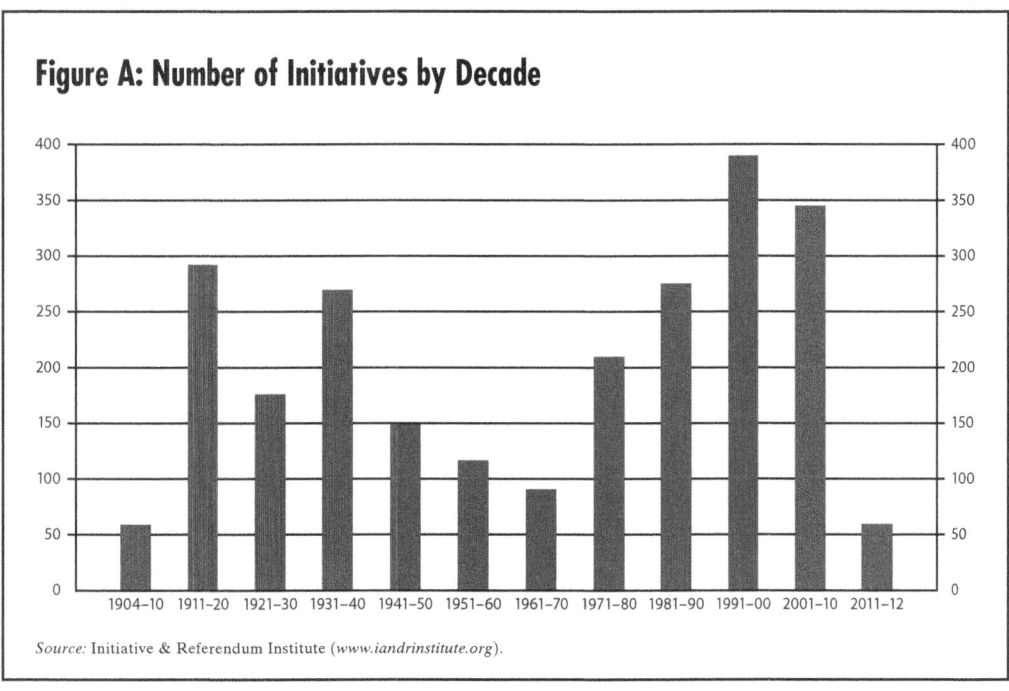

Figure A: Number of Initiatives by Decade

Source: Initiative & Referendum Institute (*www.iandrinstitute.org*).

many states and the rural interests that still controlled state legislatures because district lines were not regularly redrawn to accommodate population changes. Initiative activity tailed off in the middle decades of the 20th century, with a trough of only 89 measures from 1961 to 1970. Beginning in the late 1970s, initiative use picked up again, following California's Proposition 13 in 1978 that set off a national tax revolt. Each successive decade after Proposition 13 set a new record for the number of initiatives, peaking with 394 from 1991 to 2000. Voters have decided 96 initiatives so far in the current decade, well below the pace in the preceding two decades.

In terms of individual states, Oregon remains the overall leader, having voted on 367 initiatives since adopting the process in 1902. California is a close second with 357 initiatives since adopting the process in 1911. Rounding out the top five are Colorado with 224, North Dakota with 192, and Washington with 174. Initiative activity remains particularly high in the Western half of the country. East of the Mississippi River, Arkansas has voted on 123 initiatives, the most of any state. In the 21st century, California leads with 88 initiatives, followed by 64 in Oregon, 49 in Colorado and 46 Washington. These patterns highlight that the West Coast, particularly the Pacific states, have become

the country's clear leaders in the practice of direct democracy to the point that citizen lawmaking is seen as a central feature of the political process in those states.

Multistate Issues

Every year, some issues appear on the ballot in multiple states. This may happen as a result of a coordinated campaign by an interest group, or more often, as individual states respond to a common event, such as a court ruling, or learn from each other. Multistate issues can take on a life of their own and spread across the country if they meet with voter approval initially and reveal unexpected popular support for an issue. For this reason, multistate issues are worth watching as possible leading indicators of national trends.

Marijuana

Perhaps the biggest ballot proposition story of the year was the approval of initiatives to legalize recreational use of marijuana in Alaska, Oregon and Washington, D.C. Alaska's Measure 2, which legalized possession of 1 ounce of marijuana and manufacture and sale of the drug, was approved by a margin of 53-47; Oregon's Measure 91, which legalized possession of up to 4 ounces of marijuana and charged the state with regulating the sale of

Table B: Number of Ballot Propositions by Year Since 2000

Year	All	Initiatives	Referendums	Legislative	Other
2000	239	76	6	151	6
2001	39	4	0	35	0
2002	224	51	5	164	4
2003	68	7	0	61	0
2004	176	64	3	108	1
2005	45	18	1	26	0
2006	226	79	4	142	1
2007	43	2	2	39	0
2008	168	68	6	90	4
2009	32	5	3	24	0
2010	184	46	4	130	4
2011	34	10	2	22	0
2012	187	48	14	122	3
2013	31	3	0	23	5
2014	158	35	5	111	7
2000–2014	1,854	516	55	1,248	35

Source: Initiative & Referendum Institute (*www.iandrinstitute.org*).
Note: "Other" includes propositions placed on the ballot by commissions, constitutions, or statutes.

the drug, was approved by a margin of 56-44; and the District of Columbia's Initiative 71, which legalized possession of up to 2 ounces of marijuana and called on the city council to regulate sales, was approved by a huge margin, 70-30.

Coming on the heels of successful legalization initiatives in Colorado and Washington in 2012 — and the medical marijuana campaigns that have legalized marijuana for medical uses in almost half of the states—the status of marijuana has been transformed in just a few years. The country (or at least parts of the country) appears to be moving in a libertarian direction on marijuana.

Even the solitary setback for marijuana advocates in 2014 reveals growing support for legalization. In Florida, Amendment 2, which would have permitted use of marijuana for medical purposes, received 58 percent of the votes in favor, but it failed to gain approval because the state requires 60 percent approval for constitutional amendments. The remarkable success rate for legalization initiatives so far is likely to encourage proponents to try to expand the legalization beachhead, with the remaining West Coast state of California a natural next step.

The legal status of the various laws permitting marijuana use is somewhat ambiguous. The initiatives all conflict with federal law that still criminalizes possession and sale of the drug, and federal law is nominally supreme. Federal authorities, however, have not tried to enforce federal law in the states that have approved legalization, so there appears to be a willingness to defer to state law in these cases. The District of Columbia is a more complicated case because of Congress' oversight role. Following passage of the initiative, Congress responded by prohibiting use of public funds to regulate marijuana. The status quo appears to be that possession and use is permitted in the city, but sales are not permitted.

The tendency for a successful initiative in one state to stimulate similar initiatives in other states has been often noted, with California's tax-cutting Proposition 13 the most famous example. The spillovers, which usually happen in adjoining states, appear to happen for two reasons. A successful vote in one state demonstrates the existence of an electoral constituency for an issue, which encourages interested groups to organize and fund a campaign. A successful initiative also has a demonstration effect once the policy is implemented.[2]

A primary concern in the minds of many citizens is the possibility that marijuana legalization will spur crime and create a population of addicts. In the few years since the first legalization, these fears have not come to bear in the adopting states; if this pattern continues, support is likely to grow for legalization in other states and nationally.

Minimum Wage

Voters in five states—Alaska, Arkansas, Illinois, Nebraska and South Dakota—approved proposals to increase the minimum wage. None of the elections were close, with an average margin of victory of 26 percent. The unbroken run of success for state-level minimum wage propositions in the 21st

Table C: Complete List of Statewide Ballot Propositions in 2014

State	Type	Result	Short description
Alabama			
Amendment 1 (July 15)	L/CA	Approved 67-33	Allows cotton producers to opt out of promotion program.
Amendment 1	L/CA	Approved 72-28	Prohibits courts from recognizing Sharia Law.
Amendment 2	L/CA	Approved 51-49	$50 million bond issue for national guard armories
Amendment 3	L/CA	Approved 72-28	Declares right to bear arms.
Amendment 4	L/CA	Approved 56-44	Requires 2/3 vote for school boards to increase spending.
Amendment 5	L/CA	Approved 80-20	Declares right to hunt and fish.
Alaska			
Ballot Measure 1 (Aug. 19)	R/ST	Approved 53-47	Approves law increasing oil and gas severance taxes.
Ballot Measure 2	I/ST	Approved 53-47	Legalizes recreational marijuana.
Ballot Measure 3	I/ST	Approved 70-30	Increases minimum wage.
Ballot Measure 4	I/ST	Approved 66-34	Requires legislative approval of sulfide mine.
Arizona			
Prop 122	L/CA	Approved 51-49	Declares state may refuse to enforce federal programs.
Prop 303	L/ST	Approved 78-22	Permits terminally ill patients to use experimental treatments.
Prop 304	Com/ST	Failed 32-68	Increases legislator salaries.
Arkansas			
Issue 1	L/CA	Approved 59-41	Allows legislature to reject administrative rules.
Issue 2	L/CA	Approved 53-47	Sets petition signature thresholds for insufficiencies to be corrected.
Issue 3	L/CA	Approved 52-48	Limits lobbying, establishes commission to set legislator salaries.
Issue 4	I/CA	Failed 43-57	Legalizes alcohol sales in all counties.
Issue 5	I/ST	Approved 66-34	Increases minimum wage.
California			
Prop 41 (June 3)	L/ST	Approved 65-35	$600 million bond issue for low income veteran housing
Prop 42 (June 3)	L/CA	Approved 62-38	Eliminates requirement for state reimbursement of local government
Prop 1	L/ST	Approved 67-33	$7.12 billion bond issue for water projects
Prop 2	L/CA	Approved 69-31	Increases rainy day fund.
Prop 45	I/ST	Failed 41-59	Allows insurance commissioner to set health insurance rates
Prop 46	I/ST	Failed 33-67	Requires drug testing of physicians
Prop 47	I/ST	Approved 60-40	Reduces sentences for certain crimes
Prop 48	R/ST	Failed 39-61	Reverses approval of tribal off-reservation casino
Colorado			
Amendment 67	I/CA	Failed 35-65	Defines "personhood" to outlaw abortion.
Amendment 68	I/CA	Failed 30-70	Permits gambling on horse races.
Prop 104	I/ST	Approved 70-30	Requires school district negotiations with unions to be public.
Prop 105	I/ST	Failed 35-65	Requires labeling of GMO food.
Connecticut			
Const. Amendment	L/CA	Failed 48-52	Enables absentee voting.
Florida			
Amendment 1	I/CA	Approved 75-25	Funds land acquisition trust fund.
Amendment 2	I/CA	Failed 58-42 (a)	Allows medical use of marijuana.
Amendment 3	L/CA	Failed 48-52	Allows governor to fill short-term judicial vacancies.
Georgia			
Const. Amendment 1	L/CA	Approved 74-26	Prohibits increase in income tax.
Const. Amendment 2	L/CA	Approved 70-30	Additional penalties for reckless driving.
Referendum Question A	L/ST	Approved 74-26	Tax exemption for student housing.

See footnotes at end of table.

Table C: Complete List of Statewide Ballot Propositions in 2014, continued

State	Type	Result	Short description
Hawaii			
Const. Amendment	L/CA	Approved 88-12	Requires list of judicial nominees to be disclosed.
Const. Amendment	L/CA	Approved 55-45	Authorizes bonds for agriculture.
Const. Amendment	L/CA	Failed 23-77	Increases mandatory retirement age for judges from 70 to 80 years.
Const. Amendment	L/CA	Failed 45-55	Allows public funding of early childhood education.
Const. Amendment	L/CA	Approved 69-31	Authorizes bonds for dams and reservoirs.
Idaho			
HJR 2	L/CA	Failed 49-51	Allows legislature to reject agency rules.
Illinois			
CA 8.1	L/CA	Approved 78-22	Establishes rights for crime victims.
CA 8	L/CA	Approved 71-29	Declares right to vote.
Statewide Advisory Question	L/Adv	Approved 67-33	Increases minimum wage.
Statewide Advisory Question	L/Adv	Approved 66-34	Requires provision of birth control in health insurance plans.
Statewide Advisory Question	L/Adv	Approved 64-36	Requires more funding for school districts.
Kansas			
Constitutional Amendment	L/CA	Approved 75-25	Permits charitable raffles.
Louisiana			
Amendment 1	L/CA	Approved 56-44	Creates state medical assistance trust fund.
Amendment 2	L/CA	Approved 56-44	Creates hospital stabilization fund.
Amendment 3	L/CA	Failed 36-64	Allows designated agents to assist in tax sales.
Amendment 4	L/CA	Failed 32-68	Allows state funds to be used to capitalize infrastructure bank.
Amendment 5	L/CA	Failed 42-58	Removes mandatory retirement age for judges.
Amendment 6	L/CA	Approved 51-49	Permits Orleans Parish to increase property taxes.
Amendment 7	L/CA	Approved 74-26	Property tax exemption for disabled veterans.
Amendment 8	L/CA	Approved 57-43	Establishes artificial reef development fund.
Amendment 9	L/CA	Failed 47-53	Exempts disabled homeowners from certifying income.
Amendment 10	L/CA	Approved 54-46	Provides 18-month redemption period for tax sale property.
Amendment 11	L/CA	Failed 30-70	Increases number of executive departments.
Amendment 12	L/CA	Failed 41-59	Dedicates two positions on wildlife commission to specific parishes.
Amendment 13	L/CA	Failed 41-59	Authorizes New Orleans to sell specified property.
Amendment 14	L/CA	Failed 41-59	Prohibits tax legislation in even-numbered years.
Maine			
Question 1	I/ST	Failed 47-53	Limits bear hunting methods.
Question 2	L/ST	Approved 60-40	$8 million bond issue for laboratory at state university.
Question 3	L/ST	Approved 62-38	$4 million bond issue for loans to small businesses.
Question 4	L/ST	Approved 63-37	$10 million bond issue for cancer research center.
Question 5	L/ST	Approved 51-49	$3 million bond issue for biological lab.
Question 6	L/ST	Approved 65-35	$10 million bond issue for water projects.
Question 7	L/ST	Approved 59-41	$7 million bond issue for marine businesses.
Maryland			
Question 1	L/CA	Approved 82-18	Prohibits transfers from transportation fund.
Question 2	L/CA	Approved 81-19	Allows spending for special county elections.
Massachusetts			
Question 1	I/ST	Approved 53-47	Eliminates inflation indexing of gas tax.
Question 2	I/ST	Failed 27-73	Expands beverage container deposit law.
Question 3	I/ST	Failed 40-60	Prohibits casino gambling and wagering on dog races.
Question 4	I/ST	Approved 59-41	Mandates that employees receive 40 hours of sick time annually.

See footnotes at end of table.

Table C: Complete List of Statewide Ballot Propositions in 2014, continued

State	Type	Result	Short description
Michigan			
Proposal 14-1 (Aug. 5)	L/ST	Approved 69-31	Adjusts tax on mobile business assets.
Proposal 14-1	R/ST	Failed 45-55	Authorizes open hunting season for wolves.
Proposal 14-2	R/ST	Failed 36-64	Authorizes hunting of currently protected animals.
Mississippi			
Initiative Measure 1	L/CA	Approved 88-12	Establishes right to hunt and fish.
Missouri			
Const. Amendment 1 (Aug. 5)	L/CA	Approved 50.1-49.9	Establishes right to farm and ranch.
Const. Amendment 5 (Aug. 5)	L/CA	Approved 61-39	Declares right to keep and bear arms.
Const. Amendment 7 (Aug. 5)	L/CA	Failed 41-59	Temporary sales tax increase.
Const. Amendment 8 (Aug. 5)	L/CA	Failed 45-55	Creates lottery program with revenue for veterans.
Const. Amendment 9 (Aug. 5)	L/CA	Approved 75-25	Protects electronic communication from searches.
Const. Amendment 2	L/CA	Approved 72-28	Makes criminal history admissable in sex crime cases.
Const. Amendment 3	I/CA	Failed 24-76	Requires teachers to be assessed based on performance.
Const. Amendment 6	L/CA	Failed 30-70	Allows pre-election voting.
Const. Amendment 10	L/CA	Approved 57-43	Restricts governors' budget authority.
Montana			
C-45	L/CA	Failed 48-52	Changes name of two state offices.
LR-126	L/ST	Failed 43-57	Changes date of close of voter registration.
Nebraska			
Initiative Measure 425	I/ST	Approved 59-41	Increases minimum wage.
Nevada			
Ballot Question 1	L/CA	Approved 54-46	Creates court of appeals.
Ballot Question 2	L/CA	Failed 49.7-50.3	Allows taxes on minerals and mining.
Ballot Question 3	I/ST	Failed 21-79	2% tax on business profits.
New Jersey			
Public Question 1	L/CA	Approved 62-38	Allows courts to deny bail.
Public Question 2	L/CA	Approved 65-35	Increases tax revenue dedicated to environment.
New Mexico			
Const. Amendment 1	L/CA	Approved 58-42	Separates school elections from other election days.
Const. Amendment 2	L/CA	Approved 65-35	Requires student on state board of regents.
Const. Amendment 3	L/CA	Approved 62-38	Allows legislature to set filing date for judge elections.
Const. Amendment 4	L/CA	Approved 59-41	Allows "urban counties".
Const. Amendment 5	L/CA	Approved 53-47	Regulates investment of land grant fund.
Bond Question A	L/ST	Approved 65-35	$17 million bond issue for elderly facilities.
Bond Question B	L/ST	Approved 63-37	$11 million bond issue for libraries.
Bond Question C	L/ST	Approved 60-40	$141 million bond issue for schools.
New York			
Proposal 1	L/CA	Approved 58-42	Establishes independent redistricting commission.
Proposal 2	L/CA	Approved 77-23	Allows legislative bills to be in electronic form.
Proposal 3	L/ST	Approved 62-38	$2 billion bond issue for schools.
North Carolina			
Const. Amendment	L/CA	Approved 53-47	Allows defendents to waive right to jury trial.

See footnotes at end of table.

Table C: Complete List of Statewide Ballot Propositions in 2014, continued

State	Type	Result	Short description
North Dakota			
Const. Measure 1 (June 10)	L/CA	Approved 54-46	Allows less time for initiative petitions.
Const. Measure 1	L/CA	Failed 36-64	Declares right to life (bans abortion).
Const. Measure 2	L/CA	Approved 76-24	Prohibits mortgage taxes.
Const. Measure 3	L/CA	Failed 25-75	Creates full time higher education commission.
Const. Measure 4	L/CA	Failed 43-57	Prohibits initiatives from appropriating funds.
Ohio			
Issue 1 (May 6)	L/CA	Approved 65-35	$1.875 million bond authorization for roads and water.
Oklahoma			
State Question 769	L/CA	Approved 69-31	Allows officials to hold military positions.
State Question 770	L/CA	Approved 90-10	Expands tax break for veterans.
State Question 771	L/CA	Approved 90-10	Creates tax break for spouses of veterans.
Oregon			
Measure 86	L/CA	Failed 43-57	$4.3 billion bond issue for college scholarships.
Measure 87	L/CA	Approved 58-42	Permits judges to work for state universities.
Measure 88	R/ST	Failed 34-66	Allows issuance of driver card to illegal immigrants.
Measure 89	I/CA	Approved 64-36	Guarantees equality of rights based on sex.
Measure 90	I/ST	Failed 32-68	Creates "top two" primary.
Measure 91	I/ST	Approved 56-44	Legalizes recreational marijuana.
Measure 92	I/ST	Failed 49.9-50.1	Requires labeling of GMO food.
Rhode Island			
Question 1	L/CA	Failed 56-44 (b)	Authorizes casino in Newport.
Question 2	L/CA	Approved 68-32	Requires local voter approval to relocate casinos.
Question 3	X	Failed 45-55	Calls a constitutional convention.
Question 4	L/ST	Approved 64-36	$125 million bond issue for college of engineering.
Question 5	L/ST	Approved 61-39	$35 million bond issue for arts.
Question 6	L/ST	Approved 60-40	$35 million bond issue for mass transit.
Question 7	L/ST	Approved 71-29	$53 million bond issue for water projects and zoo.
South Carolina			
Amendment 1	L/CA	Approved 83-17	Allows nonprofits to run raffles.
Amendment 2	L/CA	Approved 56-44	Makes adjutant general appointed rather than elected.
South Dakota			
Const. Amendment Q	L/CA	Approved 57-43	Allows casino gambling in Deadwood.
Initiated Measure 17	I/ST	Approved 62-38	Requires health insurance to include all willing providers.
Initiated Measure 18	I/ST	Approved 55-45	Increases minimum wage.
Tennessee			
Amendment 1	L/CA	Approved 53-47	Declares state is not required to fund abortions.
Amendment 2	L/CA	Approved 61-39	Allows governor to appoint judges to fill vacancies.
Amendment 3	L/CA	Approved 66-34	Prohibits income taxes.
Amendment 4	L/CA	Approved 70-30	Allows charitable lotteries.
Texas			
Const. Amendment	L/CA	Approved 80-20	Redirects oil and gas revenue to rainy day fund.
Utah			
Amendment A	L/CA	Failed 40-60	Eliminates bipartisan requirement for tax commission.
Amendment B	L/CA	Approved 56-44	Shortens term of appointed lieutenant governor.
Amendment C	L/CA	Failed 34-66	Allows legal counsels for three state offices.

See footnotes at end of table.

Table C: Complete List of Statewide Ballot Propositions in 2014, continued

State	Type	Result	Short description
Virginia			
Const. Amendment	L/CA	Approved 87-13	Property tax exemption for spouses of veterans.
Washington			
I-1351	I/ST	Approved 51-49	Increases state education spending.
I-591	I/ST	Failed 45-55	Limits state-required background checks to buy guns.
I-594	I/ST	Approved 59-41	Extends firearm background checks.
Advisory Vote 8	Adv/ST (c)		Maintain 54-46 Maintain or repeal tax break for marijuana farming.
Advisory Vote 9	Adv/ST (c)		Maintain 55-45 Maintain or repeal higher leasehold excise taxes.
West Virginia			
Amendment 1	L/CA	Approved 62-38	Tax break for Boy Scout camp.
Wisconsin			
Question 1	L/CA	Approved 80-20	Prevents diversion of gas tax from transportation.
Wyoming			
Const. Amendment A	L/CA	Failed 30-70	Allows nonresident trustees for state university.

Source: Initiative & Referendum Institute.
Note: An advisory vote is classified as "approved" if the majority recommendation is to maintain the existing law.
  Additional Note: A referendum is classified as "approved" if the challenged law was retained.

Key:
I — initiative   ST — statute
L — legislative measure   Adv — advisory
Com — commission   X — constitution
CA — constitutional amendment
(a) Florida amendments require 60% approval to pass.
(b) Rhode Island's Question 1 required approval in the city of Newport, which it did not receive.
(c) Washington requires advisory votes on legislative tax increases.

century now extends to 15 and includes both traditionally liberal and conservative states. At the local level, voters in Oakland and San Francisco also approved increases in the minimum wage. With voters displaying a healthy appetite for increasing the minimum wage, we can expect to see a continuing flow of similar proposals in the next few years.

Prior to Nov. 4, there was much discussion whether the minimum wage initiatives would attract Democratic voters to polls and help Democratic candidates in other elections. Democrats did not do particularly well in any of the minimum wage states, suggesting that spillover effects were minor or nonexistent. This reinforces the observation that ballot propositions have their own dynamics and rarely spill over into candidate elections in a material way. The absence of spillovers could be because the issue is not important enough to attract nonvoters to the polls, or because its appeal cuts across party lines and attracts both Democrats and Republicans. The large majorities in favor suggest minimum wage increases appeal to voters of both parties.

GMO Foods

One of the more interesting recent trends has been the emergence of genetically modified food as an issue in ballot proposition campaigns. These propositions are being promoted by groups opposed to genetically modified food; they do not seek to ban such food, but rather to require its labeling at the point of sale. The campaigns have been built around the idea that consumers have right to know what is "in" their food, but the long run hope apparently is that consumers will refuse to purchase GMO products, driving them from the market.

Voters rejected two GMO labeling initiatives in 2014. Colorado's Prop 105 was turned down by a large margin, 35-65, while Oregon's Measure 92 was defeated by a mere 837 votes out of total 1.5 million cast. These defeats follow the rejection of GMO labeling initiatives in 2012 in California (49-51) and in 2013 in Washington (49-51). (The first such initiative was Oregon's Measure 27 in 2002 that was crushed 30-70.) These losses came after initial opinion polls suggested strong support for the initiatives; it was only after intense campaigns that enough voters shifted their views to cause a defeat.

Opponents of these initiatives have outspent supporters, often by substantial margins. For example, supporters in Oregon spent about $11 million compared to $20 million spent by opponents. Most of the money on both sides has come from businesses with commercial interests at stake. In Oregon, "yes" funding came from Dr. Bronner's Magic Soaps, an organic soap supplier, while much "no" funding came from Monsanto, DuPont, Pepsico, Coca-Cola and other food companies. In addition to heavy negative campaigning, voters appear to have been swayed by editorial opinions. Most newspapers in the initiative states have come out against GMO labeling, sometimes based on the risk of driving up food prices, but also based on questions about the underlying science and whether GMO foods ought to be demonized.

While the most recent results give GMO-labeling proponents a perfect record of futility, having lost all five elections, they may be poised for a breakthrough win in the near future. This possibility is suggested by the extremely narrow nature of the losses in California, Oregon and Washington, which suggest that opinion is divided closely enough that under the right conditions, GMO labeling can win. At the same time, even if GMO labelers achieve a success in the near future, because of the difficulty they are having in states that should be the most receptive to this idea, the potential for the idea to spread across the rest of the country seems limited.

Taxes

Tax issues are the most common subject of ballot propositions historically. Fifteen tax-related measures were on the ballot this year. Voters across the nation showed an aversion to new taxes and a willingness to grant exemptions to narrowly targeted groups, such as spouses of veterans who die in the line of duty. Four states approved tax limitation amendments: Georgia voters approved 74-26 an amendment that prohibits any future increase in income tax rates; Tennessee voters approved 67-33 an amendment that bans state and local income or payroll taxes; North Dakota voters approved 76-24 an amendment to prohibit real estate transfer taxes; and Massachusetts voters approved 53-47 a proposal to stop indexing the gas tax. Nevada voters rejected 21-79 a proposal to impose a 2 percent tax on business profits, with the revenue dedicated to schools.

Bond Issues

Many states require voter approval before state bonds can be issued. After a lull following the recession, legislatures are increasingly willing to request bond authorization from the voters, and voters seem amenable to taking on more debt. In 2014, legislatures placed 19 bond measures before the voters in nine states, with an aggregate value of $16.4 billion. Voters responded by approving all but one proposal, for a total of $12.1 billion.

The biggest proposal was California's Proposition 1, which authorized a hefty $7.12 billion for water projects; it was decisively approved by a 67-33 margin. Three other hefty bond proposals passed: New York voters approved $2 billion for capital projects in schools; Ohio voters approved $1.875 billion for transportation and water projects; and California voters approved $600 million for housing for low-income veterans. Alabama (1), Maine (6), New Mexico (3), and Rhode Island (4) also approved one or more bond propositions each, mostly for smaller projects.

The only loser was Oregon's Measure 86, which would have allowed the state to borrow $4.3 billion to subsidize tuition for college students; voters rejected the measure by a 43-57 margin. Not only did Measure 86 propose an enormous amount of borrowing given the population of the state, but it also deviated from traditional budgeting principles that debt should be used for long-lived capital expenditures, not to fund transfers.

Gambling

Another issue that was contested in multiple states in 2014 was gambling, with a total of 10 gambling-related propositions appearing in nine states. Voters in Kansas, South Carolina and Tennessee amended their constitutions to allow charitable and other nonprofit organizations to operate games of chance for small-scale fundraising. Voters in Rhode Island and South Dakota approved proposals to allow existing gambling operations—Newport Grand and Deadwood City, respectively—to offer a full menu of casino games. Gambling proposals fared worse in Colorado and Massachusetts, where proposals to allow wagering on dog races were rejected by large margins; and in Missouri, where voters rejected a proposal to add a new state lottery program with revenue dedicated to veterans programs. In California, voters repealed a gaming compact that would have allowed an Indian tribe to establish a casino outside the borders of its traditional reservation.

Notes

[1] For detailed information on initiative adoption and provisions and a discussion of pros and cons about the process, see John G. Matsusaka, *For the Many or the Few: The Initiative, Public Policy, and American Democracy* (University of Chicago Press, 2004) and M. Dane Waters, *Initiative and Referendum Almanac* (Carolina Academic Press, 2003).

[2] For rigorous evidence on how initiatives diffuse policy, with respect to tax-and-expenditure limits, see Ellen Moule and Nichlas W. Weller, "Learning in Laboratories of Democracy: The Diffusion of Political Information via Direct Democracy in the U.S. States," *State Politics and Policy Quarterly*, 2011.

About the Author

John G. Matsusaka is the Charles F. Sexton Chair in American Enterprise in the Marshall School of Business, Gould School of Law, and Department of Political Science, and executive director of the Initiative & Referendum Institute, all at the University of Southern California. He is the author of *For the Many or the Few: The Initiative, Public Policy, and American Democracy* (University of Chicago Press, 2004).

Chapter Seven

STATE FINANCE

State Budgets in 2014 and 2015: Spending and Revenue Growth Remains Limited, As States Experience Slow Growth

By Brian Sigritz

Fiscal conditions for states were somewhat mixed in the 2014 fiscal year as state general fund revenue growth declined due to the impact of the federal fiscal cliff, while total state spending growth accelerated due to increased federal Medicaid funds from the Affordable Care Act. The number of states making midyear budget cuts remained low and states maintained stable rainy day fund levels. In the 2015 fiscal year, states are expecting both revenue and spending to grow slowly, but below the historical rate of growth. It is likely that budget proposals for the 2016 fiscal year and beyond will remain mostly cautious with limited spending growth.

State fiscal conditions in the 2014 fiscal year were somewhat of a mixed bag.

On the one hand, states experienced much slower revenue growth than the prior year. State general fund revenues grew only 1.3 percent in the 2014 fiscal year, compared to 7.1 percent in 2013.[1] The main reason for the strong revenue growth in the 2013 fiscal year and the slow growth in 2014 was due to the impact of the federal "fiscal cliff." In 2013, states experienced temporary gains in revenues as taxpayers took actions to avoid scheduled higher federal taxes; in the 2014 fiscal year, states did not experience the same one-time gains.

While state general fund revenues experienced much slower growth in the 2014 fiscal year, total state expenditures—or spending from all fund sources—grew much more sharply. In 2014, total state spending—general funds, other state funds, bonds and federal funds combined—grew 5.7 percent, compared to 2.2 percent in 2013. The accelerated growth in total state spending largely was due to increased federal expenditures, as federal funds to states grew 7.6 percent in the 2014 fiscal year mainly as a result of the Medicaid expansion under the Affordable Care Act. In contrast, in both 2013 and 2012 federal funds to states declined by 1.8 percent and 9.8 percent respectively due to the wind down of spending from the American Recovery and Reinvestment Act, or stimulus.[2]

In the 2015 fiscal year, states are expected to return to their recent trend of slow but steady growth. State general fund revenues and general fund spending are both projected to grow at 3.1 percent. This would be the fifth consecutive year of modest general fund spending growth, following

back-to-back declines in 2009 and 2010. However, all five years of spending increases have been below states' historical average of 5.5 percent.[3]

In examining other indicators of state fiscal health, it is likely state rainy day fund levels will remain healthy and around their totals of the past several years, and that the number of states making midyear budget cuts will remain well below the level experienced during the past economic downturn. While most states have experienced stable fiscal conditions so far in the 2015 fiscal year, some have experienced revenue difficulties, most notably oil-producing states due to a drop in worldwide oil prices. Looking forward, it is likely that spending plans for 2016 and beyond will remain mostly cautious, with limited growth and an emphasis on ensuring budgets are structurally balanced and sustainable in the future.

The Current State Fiscal Condition

Revenues in the 2014 Fiscal Year

Revenue growth slowed considerably in the 2014 fiscal year compared to the prior year. Whereas total state general fund revenues grew 7.1 percent in 2013, state revenues only grew 1.3 percent in 2014.[4] Additionally, 2014 saw 20 states with revenues coming in below original projections, five on target and 25 higher than projections.[5] This contrasts with 2013, when only seven states experienced revenues coming in below projections, six on target and 37 higher than projections.[6]

The primary reason for the slowdown in the 2014 fiscal year was related to the federal "fiscal cliff." In 2013, states experienced temporary gains in revenues as taxpayers took actions to avoid scheduled higher federal taxes; states did not experience the same one-time gains in 2014. Additionally, revenue collections may have been hampered by winter storms in early 2014. On a quarterly basis, the Rockefeller Institute of Government reported that state revenues grew 4.1 percent in first quarter of the 2014 fiscal year (July–September 2013), increased 2.1 percent in the second quarter, declined 0.9 percent in the third quarter and decreased 2.1 percent in the fourth quarter.[7]

The impact of the federal fiscal cliff also was seen when examining individual revenue sources. Income taxes experienced the most severe slowdowns in 2014, with personal income taxes growing only 0.9 percent and corporate income taxes increasing 0.7 percent. Sales taxes, on the other hand, grew 4.9 percent.[8] Overall state revenues increased $9.7 billion in 2014, from $716.4 billion to $725.9 billion.[9]

Revenues in the 2015 Fiscal Year

Revenue growth is projected to increase in the 2015 fiscal year, but remain slow and below the historical average. Total state general fund revenues are projected to grow 3.1 percent, the same percentage as total state general fund spending growth.[10] Since 1979, general fund revenues have increased 5.5 percent on average according to the National Association of State Budget Officers' *Fiscal Survey of States*. Overall, general fund revenues are projected to grow by $22.2 billion in 2015, from $725.9 billion to $748.3 billion, with sales taxes increasing by $9.2 billion (4.0 percent), personal income taxes growing by $14.6 billion (4.7 percent), and corporate income taxes increasing by $778 million (1.7 percent).[11]

Through the first half of 2015, revenue growth has been near projections for most states. According to the Rockefeller Institute of Government, state revenues grew 2.8 percent during the first quarter of the 2015 fiscal year (July–September 2014), and preliminary figures show 6.4 percent growth in the second quarter of 2015 (October–December 2014).[12] According to data collected by National Association of State Budget Officers — also known as NASBO — in the fall of 2014, 26 states were seeing revenues coming in on target for 2015, with 10 lower and seven higher — not all states were able to report data.[13] While most states have seen stable revenue growth so far in 2015, some have experienced significant revenue difficulties, most notably oil-producing states due to a drop in worldwide oil prices.

Tax and Fee Changes in the 2015 Fiscal Year

States enacted $2.3 billion in net tax and fee decreases for the 2015 fiscal year, with 21 states enacting a net decrease and 10 states enacting net increases. Similar to 2015, in 2014 states enacted $2.1 billion in net tax and fee decreases, with 23 states enacting decreases and 12 enacting increases. Emerging from the economic downturn, states have now enacted net tax and fee decreases in four out of the past five years. States with the largest net tax and fee decreases in 2015 include, in order of largest to smallest decrease, Texas, New York, Florida, Minnesota, Wisconsin, Arkansas and Indiana, while states with the largest net increases include, in order of the increase, Oregon, Delaware, New Hampshire and Colorado. It should be noted that while states enacted a large number of tax and fee decreases in 2015, the net decrease only represents 0.3 percent of overall general fund revenue.

In the 2015 fiscal year, personal income taxes saw the largest enacted decrease, reduced by $747 million. Much of that decline came from actions taken, in order of decrease, by Minnesota and Wisconsin. The second largest decline was in "other taxes" at $698 million, with much of it attributed to Texas. Additional revenue sources that experienced a net decrease include fees (-$427 million); sales taxes (-$248 million); corporate income (-$207 million); and alcohol (-$200,000). Revenue sources that experienced a net increase include motor fuels ($33 million), and cigarettes and tobacco ($8 million).[14]

State Spending in 2014

Total state spending,[15] or expenditures from all fund sources, grew by 5.7 percent in the 2014 fiscal year, compared to 2.2 percent growth in 2013. The accelerated growth in total state spending largely was due to increased federal expenditures, as federal funds to states grew 7.6 percent in 2014 mainly as a result of Medicaid expansion under the Affordable Care Act. In contrast, in both 2013 and 2012 federal funds to states declined by 1.8 percent and 9.8 percent respectively due to the wind down of spending from the American Recovery and Reinvestment Act, or stimulus. In fact, the reduction in federal funds in 2012 was so significant that total state spending declined for the first time in the 27-year history of NASBO's *State Expenditure Report*. State funds[16] growth has been much steadier over the past three years, increasing 3.8 percent in 2012, 4.1 percent in 2013, and 4.8 percent in 2014.[17]

The recovery act and the Affordable Care Act also contributed to shifts in the distribution of funding sources for state expenditures. Over a two-year period from fiscal years 2008 and 2010, general funds shrank from representing 45.9 percent of total state expenditures to 38.1 percent, while federal funds rose from 26.3 percent to 34.9 percent. However, due to the expiration of recovery act funds, general funds started to once again make up a larger component of total state expenditures. By 2013, general funds accounted for 40.9 percent of total state expenditures, federal funds 29.8 percent, other state funds 27.3 percent, and bonds 2.1 percent. In 2014, it is estimated that federal funds will grow to 30.3 percent of total state spending, while general funds will decline slightly to 40.5 percent. The increase in federal funds in 2014 was almost solely due to additional Medicaid dollars.[18]

Looking in greater detail at the 2014 fiscal year, total state expenditures—general funds, federal funds, other state funds and bonds combined—grew by an estimated 5.7 percent to $1.79 trillion.[19] Medicaid remained the largest category of total state spending in 2014, representing 25.8 percent. Other categories of total state expenditures include elementary and secondary education (19.5 percent), higher education (10.1 percent), transportation (7.7 percent), corrections (3.1 percent), public assistance (1.4 percent), and "all other" (32.4 percent). As recently as 2008, elementary and secondary education represented a larger share of total state expenditures than Medicaid.[20]

General fund spending is estimated to be $723.8 billion in the 2014 fiscal year, a 4.8 percent increase from 2013. General funds typically receive their revenue from broad-based state taxes, such as sales and personal income. All program areas saw at least some general fund spending growth in 2014, with the exception of public assistance, which declined 2.6 percent. Transportation, which receives few general fund dollars, grew fastest at 33.4 percent, followed by Medicaid (5.8 percent), K–12 (5.0 percent), higher education (4.7 percent), corrections (4.1 percent), and all other (3.8 percent).[21]

Elementary and secondary education remained the largest category of general fund expenditures in the 2014 fiscal year, accounting for 35 percent. Medicaid represented 19.1 percent and higher education accounted for 9.4 percent. Combined, education (both K–12 and higher education) and Medicaid comprised 64 percent of total state general fund spending. Other categories of general fund spending included corrections (6.8 percent), public assistance (1.4 percent), transportation (0.9 percent), and all other (27.4 percent).[22]

Federal fund spending is estimated to be $541.2 billion in 2014, amounting to 7.6 percent more than the 2013 fiscal year. While federal Medicaid funds to states increased $41.8 billion, or 17.8 percent, in 2014, all other federal funds to states are estimated to have declined $3.4 billion, or 1.3 percent.[23] By far, Medicaid accounted for the largest share of state spending from federal funds at 51.0 percent in 2014, with elementary and secondary education at 9.9 percent and transportation at 7.7 percent, representing the next largest shares.[24]

State Spending in 2015

According to appropriated budgets, general fund expenditures are expected to increase by 3.1 percent in the 2015 fiscal year, the fifth consecutive year of modest general fund spending growth following back-to-back declines in 2009 and 2010. Despite increases in 2015, general fund spending growth is projected to once again remain below the 37-year historical average of 5.5 percent.[25] In total, general fund expenditures are estimated to be $751.6 billion in 2015, a $22.7 billion increase from the prior year. Forty-three states enacted a 2015 budget with general fund spending levels above 2014, with 29 states reporting general fund expenditure growth between 0 and 4.9 percent, and 14 states reporting growth greater than 5 percent. Although the vast majority of states enacted 2015 budgets with general fund spending growth, in 11 states general fund spending levels remain below 2008.[26]

Budget Cuts

A clear indicator of the current improvement in state fiscal conditions is that the amount of mid-year budget cuts has sharply declined since the Great Recession. During the midst of the economic downturn, 41 states made net midyear cuts in 2009 totaling $31.3 billion, and 39 states made midyear cuts in 2010 totaling $18.3 billion, demonstrating the widespread impact of the recession. However, the number of states making net midyear cuts began to decline in 2011, with 19 states making cuts of $7.4 billion, eight states making cuts of $1.7 billion in 2012, 11 states making cuts of $1.3 billion in 2013, and eight states making cuts of $1.0 billion in 2014. The largest program areas of net mid-year cuts in the 2014 fiscal year include K–12 (nine states), public assistance (seven states), Medicaid (seven states), and corrections (seven states).[27]

Through December 2014, seven states had made net midyear budget cuts in 2015 totaling $852 million. The largest cuts to date were seen in Missouri

($512 million), Indiana ($129 million), and Maryland ($79 million).[28]

Balances

Total balances include both ending balances as well as the amounts in states' budget stabilization (or rainy day) funds. Combined, these reserves reflect the funds states may use to respond to unforeseen circumstances after budget obligations have been met. Forty-eight states have either a budget stabilization fund or a rainy day fund, with about three-fifths of the states having limits on the size of these funds.[29] Total balances peaked in the 2006 fiscal year at $69 billion — 11.5 percent of general fund expenditures — and had declined to $32.5 billion, or 5.2 percent of expenditures, by 2010.

States have begun to replenish their reserves, although they have not returned to pre-recession levels. Total balance levels greatly increased in the 2013 fiscal year as revenues outpaced projections in many states due partly to the impact of the federal fiscal cliff, leading to budget surpluses and bringing total balances to $67 billion — or 9.6 percent of general fund expenditures. In 2014, total balances declined slightly to $62.7 billion, or 8.9 percent of expenditures; and in 2015, it is projected that total balances will once again decline to $53.1 billion, or 7.3 percent of expenditures. While total balances are projected to decline for the second consecutive year, it is largely because states are forecasting smaller ending balances. States' rainy day fund levels have remained relatively consistent during the past three years at $40.0 billion in 2013, $43.8 billion in 2014, and $42.5 billion in 2015.[30]

Looking Ahead

Most states have experienced significant economic improvements since the end of the Great Recession, including business expansions, lower unemployment and some increased consumer spending. The overall improvement in state economies has led to more stable fiscal conditions, with most budgets including modest revenue growth, moderate increases in state spending and rainy day fund levels at or near historical averages.

However, state spending has been constrained as a result of such factors as slow revenue growth, the decline in the price of oil, federal uncertainty, continued pressures from long-term obligations, and efforts to limit the size of state government. It is expected that in the 2016 fiscal year and beyond, much of the additional state spending will be directed toward core services such as education,

health care, corrections and transportation, while other areas of the budget will in many instances see flat spending growth or spending reductions. Looking forward, it is likely that budget proposals will remain mostly cautious, with limited spending growth and an emphasis on ensuring that budgets are structurally balanced and sustainable in the future.

Notes

[1] National Association of State Budget Officers, *The Fiscal Survey of States* (December 2014), 41.

[2] National Association of State Budget Officers, *Summary: NASBO State Expenditure Report*, (November 20, 2014), 1.

[3] *The Fiscal Survey of States* (December 2014), 7, 41.

[4] See note 1 above.

[5] *The Fiscal Survey of States* (December 2014), 42.

[6] *The Fiscal Survey of States* (December 2013), 41.

[7] Nelson A. Rockefeller Institute of Government, *State Revenue Report*, (February 2015), 5.

[8] *The Fiscal Survey of States* (December 2014), 45.

[9] *The Fiscal Survey of States* (December 2014), 5–6.

[10] See note 3 above.

[11] *The Fiscal Survey of States* (December 2014), 44–45.

[12] Nelson A. Rockefeller Institute of Government, *State Revenue Report*, (February 2015), 1, 5.

[13] *The Fiscal Survey of States* (December 2014), 42.

[14] *The Fiscal Survey of States* (December 2014), 46–49.

[15] Total state spending consists of general funds, other state funds, bonds, and federal funds combined.

[16] State funds are general funds and other state funds combined, excluding bonds.

[17] See note 2 above.

[18] *Summary: NASBO State Expenditure Report*, (November 20, 2014), 2.

[19] National Association of State Budget Officers, *State Expenditure Report* (November 2014), 8.

[20] *State Expenditure Report* (November 2014), 10–11.

[21] *State Expenditure Report* (November 2014), 7–8.

[22] *State Expenditure Report* (November 2014), 11.

[23] *State Expenditure Report* (November 2014), 1.

[24] See note 22 above.

[25] *The Fiscal Survey of States* (December 2014), 2.

[26] *The Fiscal Survey of States* (December 2014), 1, 3.

[27] *The Fiscal Survey of States* (June 2014), 8–10.

[28] *The Fiscal Survey of States* (December 2014), 8.

[29] National Association of State Budget Officers, *Budget Processes in the States*, (Summer 2008), 67–69.

[30] *The Fiscal Survey of States* (December 2014), 58–59.

About the Author

Brian Sigritz is the director of State Fiscal Studies at the National Association of State Budget Officers, also known as NASBO. He received his master's of public administration from the George Washington University and his bachelor's degree from St. Bonaventure University. Prior to working at NASBO, Sigritz worked for the Ohio Senate and the Ohio House of Representatives.

Table 7.1
FISCAL 2013 STATE GENERAL FUND, ACTUAL
(In millions of dollars)

State	Beginning balance	Revenues	Adjustments	Total resources	Expenditures	Adjustments	Ending balance	Budget stabilization fund
Total....................	$22,265	$716,396	...	$742,051	$694,535	...	$38,982	$41,286
Alabama* (a)	60	7,263	146	7,468	7,164	0	304	14
Alaska (b)	0	6,932	60	6,992	7,783	187	-978	16,332
Arizona (c)..................	397	8,153	1,008	9,558	8,463	200	896	454
Arkansas......................	0	4,728	0	4,728	4,728	0	0	0
California* (d)	-1,615	99,915	499	98,800	96,562	-290	2,527	1,573
Colorado* (e)..............	796	8,555	0	9,351	7,912	-7	1,446	373
Connecticut (f)............	0	19,405	-221	19,184	19,026	-19	177	271
Delaware*	565	3,730	0	4,294	3,659	0	636	199
Florida	1,509	26,095	0	27,604	24,712	0	2,892	709
Georgia* (g).................	551	18,296	363	19,210	18,310	0	900	717
Hawaii..........................	275	6,234	0	6,510	5,666	0	844	24
Idaho (h)	100	2,790	-113	2,777	2,697	0	80	135
Illinois (i)...................	40	34,376	1,987	36,403	30,292	5,957	154	0
Indiana (j)	1,803	14,756	34	16,593	14,247	918	1,428	515
Iowa (k)	0	6,769	572	7,341	6,413	0	928	611
Kansas (l)	503	6,341	0	6,844	6,135	0	709	0
Kentucky (m)	90	9,450	267	9,807	9,527	156	123	122
Louisiana (n)...............	0	8,277	253	8,530	8,369	0	161	444
Maine (o).....................	42	3,048	116	3,206	3,082	117	8	60
Maryland (p)	551	14,885	171	15,607	15,105	0	502	700
Massachusetts*	1,990	33,779	0	35,769	33,894	0	1,874	1,557
Michigan (q)................	979	9,958	-899	10,038	8,851	0	1,187	506
Minnesota* (r)	1,795	18,656	0	20,451	18,739	0	1,712	656
Mississippi (s).............	53	4,940	-100	4,894	4,744	96	54	32
Missouri (t)	204	8,083	185	8,471	8,024	0	447	277
Montana	452	2,078	3	2,533	1,997	-2	538	0
Nebraska (u)................	499	4,047	-142	4,404	3,589	0	815	384
Nevada (v)...................	336	3,301	0	3,636	3,289	47	300	85
New Hampshire* (w)...	23	1,437	0	1,460	1,257	121	82	9
New Jersey (x)	444	31,432	-110	31,765	31,455	0	310	0
New Mexico* (y)..........	713	5,784	0	6,497	5,826	20	651	651
New York* (z)..............	1,787	58,783	0	60,570	58,960	0	1,610	1,306
North Carolina............	351	20,603	0	20,954	20,631	0	324	651
North Dakota (aa).......	1,294	2,331	305	3,930	2,353	181	1,396	584
Ohio (bb).....................	974	29,559	0	30,532	27,893	0	2,639	482
Oklahoma (cc)	107	6,331	-27	6,411	6,276	3	133	535
Oregon (dd)	48	7,225	-47	7,226	6,739	0	487	69
Pennsylvania (ee)	659	27,397	202	28,258	27,731	-13	541	0
Rhode Island (ff)	115	3,324	-96	3,344	3,216	24	104	172
South Carolina* (gg) ...	956	6,390	0	7,346	6,200	100	1,046	388
South Dakota (hh).......	0	1,258	58	1,316	1,291	1	24	135
Tennessee (ii)...............	819	12,034	-44	12,809	11,458	551	800	356
Texas (jj)	-78	48,572	-2,172	46,322	40,816	0	5,506	6,170
Utah (kk).....................	157	5,329	108	5,594	5,127	119	348	403
Vermont (ll)	0	1,345	0	1,345	1,323	22	0	74
Virginia........................	1,350	16,666	0	18,016	17,136	0	880	440
Washington (mm)	-380	15,783	244	15,647	15,479	0	168	270
West Virginia (nn)	611	4,104	96	4,811	4,271	28	512	915
Wisconsin (oo).............	342	14,086	683	15,111	14,333	19	759	0
Wyoming (pp)	0	1,788	0	1,788	1,788	0	0	927
Puerto Rico.................	0	0	0	0	0	0	0	0

See footnotes at end of table.

FISCAL 2013 STATE GENERAL FUND, ACTUAL — Continued
(In millions of dollars)

Source: National Association of State Budget Officers.

Note: NA Indicates data not available. *In these states, the ending balance includes the balance in the budget stabilization fund.

Key:

... — Not applicable

(a) Revenue Adjustments include one-time revenues of $145.8M.

(b) Revenues: 2014 Spring Revenue Source Book. Revenue Adjustments: Fiscal Summary Anticipated Reappropriations and Carry-forward. Expenditures: Fiscal Summary – Pre Transfer Authorization (Operating + Capital + Supplemental). Ending Balance: 2013 CAFR SBR draw of $776.4 Million. Adjustments Fiscal Summary transfers Rainy Day fund = SBR + CBR balance 2013 CAFR.

(c) Adjustments to revenue include revenues from the temporary 1% sales tax increase and budget transfers. Adjustments to expenditures include the transfer of revenue into the rainy day fund.

(d) Represents adjustments to the Beginning Fund Balance. This consists primarily of adjustments made to K–12 and HHS spending, and major taxes.

(e) A total of $1,073.5M was transferred to the State Education Fund per HB12-1338 at year end after the statutory reserve of 5% was fully funded.

(f) Revenue adjustments include $220.8 million reserved for use in future fiscal years. Expenditure adjustments include miscellaneous adjustments of $0.7 million, and net adjustments of $18 million due to carry-forward of appropriations. The reported rainy day fund balance includes the ending balance.

(g) Beginning and ending balances reflect the total Revenue Shortfall Reserve balance as reported in the Budgetary Compliance Report. Adjustments to Revenues include surplus from state agencies and other funds collected by the State Treasury. Final Rainy Day Fund balance reflects the ending balance less the 1% mid-term adjustment for K–12 enrollment appropriated during FY 2014.

(h) Transfers included: $111,269,300 to the Budget Stabilization Fund; $500,000 to the Constitutional Defense Fund; and $200,000 to the Legislative Legal Defense Fund. Deficiency Warrants included: $349,400 to the Pest Control Fund; $6,013,200 for fire suppression; and $28,100 to the Hazardous Substances Emergency Response Fund. Transfer in included: $3,033,300 for the Catastrophic Health Care Fund; $2,014,900 from the Consumer Protection Fund; and $500,000 in miscellaneous adjustments.

(i) Revenue adjustments include statutory transfers in. Expenditure adjustments include statutory transfers out, including but not limited to debt service payments, and pay-down of accounts payable during fiscal year.

(j) Revenue adjustments include prior year adjustments; transfer to the Rainy Day Fund; and PTRC and homestead credit adjustments. Expense adjustments include reversions from distributions, capital, and reconciliations; 2012 appropriations; HEA 1072-2011 loans; payback of loans for charter schools; bond defeasance; IPS and Gary tuition support settlement; transfer to the Preneed Consumer Settlement Fund; and distributions to pensions funds and the automatic taxpayer refund. The Rainy Day Fund balance reflects $370.1M in the Counter-Cyclical Revenue and Economic Stabilization Fund and $145M in the Medicaid Contingency and Reserve Account.

(k) Revenue adjustments include $572.1 million of residual funds transferred to the General Fund after the Reserve Funds were filled to their statutorily set maximum amounts. The Ending balance of the General Fund is transferred in the current fiscal year to the Reserve Funds in the subsequent fiscal year. After the Reserve Funds are at their statutorily set maximum amounts, the remainder of the funds is transferred back to the General Fund in that subsequent fiscal year.

(l) Kansas does not have a "Rainy Day" fund. However, the balanced budget provision of the constitution requires revenues to finance the approved budget.

(m) Revenue includes $101.7 million in Tobacco Settlement funds. Adjustment for Revenues includes $156.4 million that represents appropriation balances carried over from the prior fiscal year, and $109.2 million from fund transfers into the General Fund. Adjustment to Expenditures represents appropriation balances forwarded to the next fiscal year.

(n) Revenues adjustments — Includes carryforward balances $13.7; Transfer of $239.3 from various funds.

(o) Revenue and Expenditure adjustments reflect legislatively authorized transfers.

(p) The Maryland General Assembly passed a revenue package during the 2012 Special Session. For FY 2013 only, the majority of revenue generated through this legislation was deposited in a special fund known as the Budget Restoration Fund. These numbers include the Budget Restoration Fund. Revenue adjustments include $12.8 million in transfers from tax credit reserves, a $157.0 million transfer from the Budget Restoration Fund, and a $1.0 million transfer from other funds.

(q) Fiscal 2013 revenue adjustments include the impact of federal and state law changes (-$394.9 million); revenue sharing payments to local government units (-$370.6 million); deposits from state restricted funds ($6.7 million); and deposit to the rainy day fund (-$140.0 million). Total expenditures include $582.6 million in one-time spending financed from one-time revenues.

(r) Ending balance includes cash flow account of $350 million and budget reserve account of $656.5 million.

(s) State statute requires 2% of the revenue estimate plus beginning cash (excluding reappropriated amounts) be set aside prior to legislative appropriations. At fiscal year close, the 2% is recombined with any remaining revenue balance and distributed to other funds as required by statute, leaving an amount equal to 1% of the appropriations retained in the General Fund.

(t) Revenue adjustments include transfers from other funds into the general revenue fund.

(u) Revenue adjustments are transfers between the General Fund and other funds. Per Nebraska law, includes a transfer of $104.8 million to the Cash Reserve Fund (Rainy Day Fund) of the amount the prior year's net General Fund receipts exceeded the official forecast. Among others, also includes a $110 million transfer from the General Fund to the Property Tax Credit Cash Fund as well as a $78 million transfer to the General Fund from the Cash Reserve Fund (Rainy Day Fund) for budget stabilization.

(v) Expenditure adjustments are restricted transfers.

(w) Revenue Adjustments: $121.3 million moved to the Education Trust Fund. Total Expenditures: Includes $9.3 million of GAAP and Other Adjustments.

(x) Budget vs. GAAP entries, transfers to other funds.

(y) $20 million contingent liability for special education funding Maintenance of Effort.

(z) The ending balance includes $1.3 billion in rainy day reserve funds, $77 million reserved to cover costs of potential retroactive labor settlements with certain unions, $93 million in a community projects fund, $113 million reserved for debt reduction, and $21 million reserved for litigation risks.

(aa) Revenue adjustments are a $305.0 million transfer from the property tax relief fund into the general fund. Expenditure adjustments include $181.0 million transfer from the general fund into the budget stabilization fund and miscellaneous adjustments/transfers.

(bb) FY 2013 expenditures include a $235 million transfer to the Budget Stabilization Fund (Rainy Day Fund) from the FY 2012 surplus ending balance. FY 2013 expenditures include both transfers out of the General Revenue Fund and encumbrances (obligations) in place at the end of FY 2013.

(cc) Revenue adjustment represents the difference in cash flow. $2.7 million expenditure adjustment is amount deposited into the Rainy Day fund from surplus revenues.

(dd) Revenue adjustment is a statutory transfer to local governments for local property tax relief where income taxes from new jobs exceeds amount of local property tax relief and a statutory dedication of some corporate taxes to RDF. RDF Balance is traditional RDF (primarily GF) and Education Stability Fund (primarily Lottery Funds). Each fund may include donations.

(ee) Revenue adjustments include a $13.5 million adjustment to the beginning balance and $188.7 million in prior year lapses. Expenditure adjustment reflects $13.3 million in current year lapses. The year-end transfer to the Rainy Day Fund (25% of the ending balance) was suspended for FY 2013.

(ff) Adjustments to revenues reflect a transfer of $103.2 million to the Budget Reserve Fund plus a reappropriation of $7.7 million. Expenditure adjustments of $23.6 million reflect transfers to the retirement fund, the Information Technology Investment Fund, and the State Fleet Revolving Loan Fund totaling $16.5 million and reappropriations of $7.1 million.

FISCAL 2013 STATE GENERAL FUND, ACTUAL — Continued
(In millions of dollars)

(gg) Ending Balance = 5% General Reserve ($281.6) + 2% Capital Reserve ($106.1) + Surplus Contingency Reserve ($277.2) + Agency Appropriation Balances Carried Forward to Next FY ($381.1); Expenditure Adjustments include FY 11–12 Capital Reserve Funds transferred to State agencies.

(hh) Adjustments in Revenues: $29.9 million addition to revenue is from one-time receipts; $27.8 million addition to revenue is obligated cash carried forward from FY 2012 for FY 2013 expenses. Adjustments to Expenditures: $1.0 million is obligated cash that will be carried forward for FY 2014 expenses. The ending balance of $24.2 million is cash that is obligated to the Budget Reserve fund the following fiscal year. This $24.2 million is not included in the total rainy day fund balance of $134.7 million.

(ii) Adjustments (Revenues) $70.5 million transfer from debt service fund unexpended appropriations. -$50.0 million transfer to Rainy Day Fund. -$64.3 million transfer to dedicated revenue reserves. Total -$43.8 million Adjustments (Expenditures) $183.3 million transfer to capital outlay projects fund. $141.2 million transfer to state office buildings and support facilities fund. $4.1 million transfer to debt service fund. $222.3 million transfer to reserves for unexpended appropriations. Total $550.9 million. Ending Balance: $679.4 million reserve for appropriations 2013–2014. $119.8 million unappropriated budget surplus at June 30, 2013. $0.5 million undesignated balance. Total $799.7 million.

(jj) Adjustment is net of set aside for transfer to Rainy Day Fund (-$2,514.823 m). In addition, the Comptroller adjustment to general fund dedicated account balances (+$343.0 m).

(kk) Includes transfers from previous year balance, to/from Rainy Day Fund, and special revenue funds.

(ll) Adjustments equal net transfer effect out of General Fund.

(mm) Fund transfers between General Fund and other accounts, and balancing to the final audited ending balance.

(nn) Fiscal Year 2013 Beginning balance includes $476.9 million in Reappropriations, Unappropriated Surplus Balance of $101.9 million, and FY 2012 13th month expenditures of $31.9 million. Expenditures include Regular, Surplus and Reappropriated funds and $31.9 million of 31-day prior year expenditures. Revenue adjustments are prior year redeposits and special revenue expirations. Expenditure adjustment represents the amount transferred to the Rainy Day Fund. The ending balance is mostly the historically carried forward reappropriation amounts that will remain and be reappropriated to the next fiscal year, the 13th month expenditures and unappropriated surplus balance.

(oo) Revenue adjustments include Designated Balance, $72.4; Tribal Gaming, $25.9; and Other Revenue, $584.9. Expenditure adjustments include Designation for Continuing Balances, $18.8.

(pp) Wyoming budgets on a biennial basis. To arrive at annual figures certain assumptions and estimates were required.

Table 7.2
FISCAL 2014 STATE GENERAL FUND, PRELIMINARY ACTUAL
(In millions of dollars)

State	Beginning balance	Revenues	Adjustments	Resources	Expenditures	Adjustments	Ending balance	Budget stabilization fund
Total................................	$37,648	$726,051	...	$764,142	$728,884	...	$28,161	$45,091
Alabama (a)	304	7,328	204	7,836	7,522	314	0	328
Alaska (b)	0	5,304	35	5,339	7,323	-270	-1,714	15,033
Arizona (c)....................	896	8,338	153	9,386	8,812	0	574	455
Arkansas.......................	0	4,944	0	4,944	4,944	0	0	0
California* (d)	2,528	102,185	-636	104,077	100,711	-537	3,903	2,948
Colorado* (e)...............	373	8,929	2	9,304	8,742	6	557	411
Connecticut (f).............	0	17,608	-408	17,200	16,980	-29	248	519
Delaware*	636	3,573	0	4,209	3,794	0	414	202
Florida	2,892	26,583	0	29,475	27,152	0	2,323	925
Georgia* (g)..................	900	19,168	28	20,097	19,109	0	988	796
Hawaii...........................	844	6,096	0	6,940	6,275	0	665	83
Idaho (h)	80	2,818	-70	2,828	2,784	0	45	161
Illinois (i)......................	154	34,616	2,152	36,922	30,811	6,037	74	0
Indiana (j)	1,428	14,660	22	16,110	14,553	520	1,036	969
Iowa (k).........................	0	6,489	679	7,168	6,462	0	707	650
Kansas (l)	709	5,986	0	6,696	5,999	0	697	0
Kentucky (m)	123	9,621	302	10,046	9,864	102	80	77
Louisiana (n)................	0	8,337	64	8,401	8,401	0	-0	445
Maine (o).......................	8	3,075	132	3,214	3,200	2	13	68
Maryland (p)................	502	15,106	78	15,686	15,539	0	148	764
Massachusetts*	1,874	35,711	0	37,585	36,176	0	1,409	1,259
Michigan (q).................	1,187	9,876	-1,419	9,644	9,207	0	437	396
Minnesota* (r)..............	1,712	19,304	0	21,016	19,678	0	1,338	661
Mississippi (s)..............	54	5,403	-108	5,348	5,041	266	41	110
Missouri (t)	447	8,003	124	8,574	8,352	0	222	270
Montana	538	2,077	-2	2,613	2,188	1	424	0
Nebraska (u).................	815	4,106	-456	4,465	3,791	0	674	719
Nevada (v).....................	300	3,257	0	3,557	3,280	9	268	28
New Hampshire* (w)...	82	1,323	0	1,405	1,252	124	29	9
New Jersey (x)	310	31,229	1,535	33,074	32,774	0	300	0
New Mexico* (y)...........	651	6,062	0	6,713	6,027	108	579	579
New York* (z)...............	1,610	61,868	0	63,478	61,243	0	2,235	1,481
North Carolina.............	351	20,153	0	20,504	20,234	0	269	651
North Dakota (aa).......	1,396	2,586	342	4,324	3,237	0	1,087	584
Ohio (bb)......................	2,639	29,233	0	31,872	30,595	0	1,277	1,478
Oklahoma (cc)	133	6,330	37	6,500	6,500	0	-0	535
Oregon (dd)	487	7,635	-166	7,955	7,925	0	30	206
Pennsylvania (ee)	541	27,502	433	28,476	28,597	-202	81	0
Rhode Island (ff)	104	3,436	-99	3,441	3,336	37	68	177
South Carolina* (gg) ...	1,046	6,552	0	7,599	6,329	106	1,163	408
South Dakota (hh).......	24	1,354	98	1,476	1,442	24	10	139
Tennessee (ii)	800	12,140	208	13,148	12,535	341	273	456
Texas (jj)	5,505	49,232	-3,413	51,325	47,649	0	3,676	6,656
Utah (kk)......................	348	5,247	41	5,636	5,420	0	216	401
Vermont (ll)	0	1,388	8	1,396	1,386	10	-0	71
Virginia.........................	880	18,084	0	18,964	18,959	0	5	688
Washington (mm)........	168	16,353	-69	16,452	16,089	0	363	414
West Virginia (nn)	512	4,106	8	4,626	4,208	6	412	956
Wisconsin (oo)..............	759	13,948	606	15,313	14,674	122	517	0
Wyoming (pp)	0	1,787	0	1,787	1,787	0	0	926
Puerto Rico..................	0	0	0	0	0	0	0	0

See footnotes at end of table.

FISCAL 2014 STATE GENERAL FUND, PRELIMINARY ACTUAL — Continued
(In millions of dollars)

Source: National Association of State Budget Officers.

*In these states, the ending balance includes the balance in the budget stabilization fund.

... — Not applicable.

(a) Revenue Adjustments include one-time revenues of $145.8M, a tobacco settlement of $46.4M, and an insurance settlement of $12M. Expenditure Adjustments include Rainy Day payments of $260.4M, $35M, and $18.4M. Per Code Section 29-9-4, the ending balance of the ETF shall be used to repay the Rainy Day Account.

(b) Revenues: 2014 Spring Revenue Source Book 4/7/2014. Revenue Adjustments: Fiscal Summary Anticipated Reappropriations and Carry-forward 5/1/14. Expenditure: Fiscal Summary – Pre Transfer Authorization (Operating + Capital + Supplemental) 5/1/14 Ending Balance: Fiscal Summary expected draw from SBR. 5/1/14 Adjustments Fiscal Summary Rainy Day fund = SBR + CBR balance as per OMB 10-year plan.

(c) Adjustments to revenue include revenues from the budget transfers.

(d) Represents adjustments to the Beginning Fund Balance. This consists primarily of adjustments made to K–12 and HHS spending, and major taxes.

(e) A total of $120.6M was transferred to other funds in priority order, leaving the 5% GF reserve of $410.9M plus $25.0M pursuant to HB14-1339, HB14-1342, and SB14-223.

(f) Revenue adjustments include release of reserved fund balance of $190.8 million, $598.5 million for GAAP conversion bonds, and $0.5 million reserved for future fiscal years. Expenditure adjustments include $2.2 million in miscellaneous adjustments, and $26.5 million in net adjustments due to carry-forward of appropriations. The reported rainy day fund balance includes the ending balance.

(g) Figures are preliminary and are subject to change pending final audit. Rainy Day Fund balance reflects preliminary balance less the required 1% FY 2015 midterm appropriation for K–12 enrollment. Final Rainy Day Fund balance will be higher pending the lapse of current year surplus from state agencies.

(h) Transfers included: $26,375,800 to the Budget Stabilization Fund; $3,000,000 to the Business Jobs Development Fund; $15,000,000 to the Water Resources Board; $10,000,000 to the Permanent Building Fund; $10,000,000 to the Public Education Stabilization Fund; and $2,000,000 to the Higher Education Stabilization Fund. Deficiency Warrant transfers included: $38,700 to the Hazardous Substances Emergency Response Fund; $10,379,600 for fire suppression; and $1,456,700 to the Pest Control Fund. Transfers in included: $6,430,800 from the Catastrophic Health Care Fund and $1,581,700 in miscellaneous adjustments.

(i) Revenue adjustments include statutory transfers in. Expenditure adjustments include statutory transfers out, including but not limited to debt service payments, and pay-down of accounts payable during fiscal year.

(j) Revenue adjustments include PTRC and homestead credit adjustments HEA 1072-2011 loan repayments, and a transfer from the Mine Subsidence Fund. Expenditure adjustments include reversions from distributions, capital, and reconciliations; the cost of a 13th check for pension recipients; transfer to the Major Moves 2020 trust fund; transfer to the tuition reserve fund; and state agency and university line item capital projects. The Rainy Day Fund balance reflects $373.9M in the Counter-Cyclical Revenue and Economic Stabilization Fund, $445M in the Medicaid Contingency and Reserve Account, and $150M in the State Tuition Reserve Fund.

(k) Revenue adjustments include an estimated $679.3 million of residual funds transferred to the General Fund after the Reserve Funds are filled to their statutorily set maximum amounts. The Ending balance of the General Fund is transferred in the current fiscal year to the Reserve Funds in the subsequent fiscal year. After the Reserve Funds are at their statutorily set maximum amounts, the remainder of the funds is transferred back to the General Fund in that subsequent fiscal year.

(l) Kansas does not have a "Rainy Day" fund. However, the balanced budget provision of the constitution requires revenues to finance the approved budget.

(m) Revenue includes $159.4 million in Tobacco Settlement funds. Adjustment for Revenues includes $156.4 million that represents appropriation balances carried over from the prior fiscal year, and $145.7 million from fund transfers into the General Fund. Adjustment to Expenditures represents appropriation balances forwarded to the next fiscal year.

(n) Revenues adjustments — Includes transfer of $63.5 from various funds.

(o) Revenue and Expenditure adjustments reflect legislatively authorized transfers.

(p) Includes $16.1 million for tax credit reimbursements and $61.8 million in transfers from other funds.

(q) Fiscal 2014 revenue adjustments include the impact of federal and state law changes (-$557.0 million); revenue sharing payments to local government units (-$396.6 million); deposits from state restricted funds ($176.1 million); deposit to the rainy day fund (-$75.0 million); deposit to the Roads and Risks Reserve Fund (-$230.0 million), and general fund revenue dedicated for roads(-$336.6 million). Total expenditures include $803.1 million in one-time spending financed from one-time revenues.

(r) Ending balance includes cash flow account of $350 million, budget reserve account of $661 million, and stadium reserve of $37.4 million.

(s) State statute requires 2% of the revenue estimate plus beginning cash (excluding reappropriated amounts) be set aside prior to legislative appropriations. At fiscal year close, the 2% is recombined with any remaining revenue balance and distributed to other funds as required by statute, leaving an amount equal to 1% of the appropriations retained in the General Fund.

(t) Revenue adjustments include transfers from other funds into the general revenue fund.

(u) Revenue adjustments are transfers between the General Fund and other funds. Per Nebraska law, includes a transfer of $285.3 million to the Cash Reserve Fund (Rainy Day Fund) of the amount the prior year's net General Fund receipts exceeded the official forecast and an additional $49.4 million transferred from the General Fund to the Cash Reserve Fund to set aside additional funds as a result of increasing General Fund revenues. Among others, also includes a $113 million transfer from the General Fund to the Property Tax Credit Cash Fund.

(v) Expenditure adjustments are restricted transfers. 2014 data is budgeted rather than preliminary actual.

(w) Revenue Adjustments: $102.0 million is estimated to be moved to the Education Trust Fund and $0.7 million to the Fish and Game Fund. Total Expenditures: Anticipated to include $20.8 million of GAAP and Other Adjustments.

(x) Balances targeted to be lapsed and transfers to other funds.

(y) $31.7 million contingent liability for cash reconciliation from FY 13 audit, $16 million contingent liability for PED Maintenance of Effort, $60.2 million for contingent liability for Medicaid receivables.

(z) The ending balance includes approximately $1.5 billion in rainy day reserve funds, $45 million reserved to cover costs of potential retroactive labor settlements with certain unions, $87 million in a community projects fund, $500 million reserved for debt reduction, $21 million reserved for litigation risks, and $101 million in undesignated fund balance to be used for gap-closing purposes in FY 2015.

(aa) Revenue adjustments are a $341.8.0 million transfer from the property tax relief fund into the general fund.

(bb) FY 2014 expenditures include encumbrances or obligations incurred in FY 2014 that will be disbursed in FY 2015. Expenditures also include a transfer out of $995.9 million to the state's Budget Stabilization (Rainy Day) Fund.

(cc) Revenue amounts are based upon reconciled, but yet uncertified, FY 2014 collections; Revenue adjustment represents the difference in cash flow for the year; there was no expenditure adjustment, since no Rainy Day Fund deposit was made.

(dd) Revenue adjustment transfers prior biennium ending GF balance to Rainy Day Fund (which can be up to 1% of total biennial budget appropriation less GF reversions and statutorily authorized carry-forward amounts for the Legislative and Judicial branches); estimated cost of Tax Anticipation Notes; statutory dedication of some corp. taxes to RDF; plus statutory transfer to local governments for local property tax relief.

(ee) Revenue adjustments include a $6 million adjustment to the beginning balance, $425.1 million in prior year lapses, and $1.5 million in legislative lapses. Expenditure adjustment reflects $201.6 million in current year lapses. The year-end transfer to the Rainy Day Fund (25% of the ending balance) was suspended for FY 2014. The $0.1 million increase in the Rainy Day Fund balance resulted from a distribution of a legal settlement.

(ff) Adjustments to revenues reflect a transfer of $106.2 million to the Budget Reserve Fund plus a reappropriation of $7.1 million. Expenditure adjustments of $37.1 million reflects transfers to the retirement fund ($19.7 million) and the Accelerated Depreciation Fund ($10.0 million) and reappropriations of $7.4 million.

(gg) Ending Balance = 5% General Reserve ($292.9) + 2% Capital Reserve ($114.9) + Surplus Contingency Reserve ($265.6) + Agency

FISCAL 2014 STATE GENERAL FUND, PRELIMINARY ACTUAL — Continued
(In millions of dollars)

Appropriation Balances Carried Forward to Next FY ($489.9); Expenditure Adjustments include FY 12–13 Capital Reserve Funds transferred to State agencies.

(hh) The beginning balance of $24.2 million and adjustment to expenditures reflects the prior year's ending balance that is transferred to the rainy day fund. Adjustment to revenue of $98.2 million is from one-time receipts. The ending balance of $9.9 million is cash that is obligated to the Budget Reserve fund the following fiscal year. This $9.9 million is not included in the total rainy day fund balance of $139.3 million.

(ii) Adjustments (Revenues) $82.0 million transfer from debt service fund unexpended appropriations. $41.7 million transfer from Strategic Health-Care Programs Reserves. $5.3 million transfer from Tobacco MSA Settlement Reserve. $153.7 million transfer from Agency Reserves. $0.6 million transfer from System Development Fund. $5.0 million transfer from TennCare Maintenance of Trust Fund. $20.0 million TennCare reversion. -$100.0 million transfer to Rainy Day Fund. Total $208.3 million. Adjustments (Expenditures) $164.9 million transfer to capital outlay projects fund. $170.8 million transfer to state office buildings and support facilities fund. $3.8 million transfer to debt service fund. $1.0 million transfer to reserves for dedicated revenue appropriations. Total $340.5 million. Ending Balance $5.0 million Reserve for 2014–2015 appropriation – Univ. of Tennessee Super Computer. $0.9 million Reserve for 2014–2015 appropriation – Dept. of Safety study. $266.7 million unappropriated budget surplus at June 30, 2014. Total $272.6 million.

(jj) Adjustment is net of set aside for transfer to Rainy Day Fund (-$1,383.5m) and the State Highway Fund 6 (-$1,383.4m). In addition, the Comptroller adjustment to general fund dedicated account balances (-$646.1m).

(kk) Includes transfers from previous year balance, to/from Rainy Day Fund, and special revenue funds.

(ll) Adjustments equals net transfer effect in/out of General Fund.

(mm) Fund transfers between General Fund and other accounts, and changes made by the 2014 Legislature.

(nn) Fiscal Year 2014 Beginning Balance includes $456.2 million in Reappropriations, Unappropriated Surplus Balance of $11.8 million, and FY 2013 13th month expenditures of $44.1 million. Expenditures include Regular, Surplus and Reappropriated funds and $44.1 million of 31-day prior year expenditures. Revenue adjustments are prior year redeposits and special revenue expirations. Expenditure adjustment represents the amount transferred to the Rainy Day Fund. The ending balance is mostly the historically carried forward reappropriation amounts that will remain and be reappropriated to the next fiscal year, the 13th month expenditures and unappropriated surplus balance.

(oo) Revenue adjustments include Designated Balance, $18.8; and Other Revenue, $587.1. Expenditure adjustments include Designation for Continuing Balances, $122.4.

(pp) Wyoming budgets on a biennial basis. To arrive at annual figures certain assumptions and estimates were required.

Table 7.3
FISCAL 2015 STATE GENERAL FUND, APPROPRIATED
(In millions of dollars)

State or other jurisdiction	Beginning balance	Revenues	Adjustments	Resources	Expenditures	Adjustments	Ending balance	Rainy day fund balance
Total................................	$29,229	$748,290	. . .	$777,881	$751,626	. . .	$18,293	$42,466
Alabama (a)	0	7,734	166	7,900	7,662	109	129	437
Alaska (b)	0	4,523	0	4,523	5,839	68	-1,384	11,371
Arizona (c)	574	8,752	54	9,379	9,272	0	108	455
Arkansas.......................	0	5,047	0	5,047	5,047	0	0	0
California (d)*	3,903	105,488	0	109,391	107,987	0	1,404	2,056
Colorado* (e)...............	436	9,601	17	10,053	9,333	0	720	570
Connecticut.................	0	17,458	0	17,458	17,458	0	0	520
Delaware* (f)................	414	3,949	0	4,363	3,864	0	500	213
Florida	2,323	27,565	0	29,888	28,299	0	1,589	1,139
Georgia* (g)..................	988	19,746	0	20,734	19,746	0	N/A	N/A
Hawaii...........................	665	6,202	0	6,867	6,439	0	428	91
Idaho (h)	44	2,962	-2	3,005	2,936	0	69	161
Illinois (i)......................	74	33,039	1,895	35,008	29,373	5,561	74	0
Indiana (j)	1,036	15,092	0	16,128	14,870	211	1,048	1,122
Iowa (k)	0	6,850	652	7,502	6,982	0	520	696
Kansas (l)	697	5,975	0	6,672	6,301	0	371	0
Kentucky (m)	81	9,901	337	10,318	10,124	112	82	98
Louisiana (n)................	0	8,683	0	8,683	8,758	-76	1	470
Maine (o)......................	13	3,247	50	3,310	3,184	125	1	68
Maryland (p).................	127	15,992	26	16,145	16,061	0	83	783
Massachusetts*	1,409	38,107	0	39,516	38,285	0	1,232	1,218
Michigan (q).................	437	10,268	-902	9,804	9,801	0	3	509
Minnesota* (r)..............	1,338	19,788	0	21,126	19,910	0	1,216	811
Mississippi (s)..............	41	5,460	0	5,501	5,501	0	0	395
Missouri (t)	252	8,590	131	8,972	8,755	0	218	233
Montana	424	2,137	0	2,561	2,199	0	362	0
Nebraska (u)	674	4,221	-235	4,660	4,106	312	242	708
Nevada (v).....................	268	3,341	0	3,610	3,339	9	262	0
New Hampshire* (w) ..	36	1,430	0	1,466	1,358	99	9	9
New Jersey	300	32,295	0	32,595	32,207	0	388	0
New Mexico* (x)..........	579	6,294	0	6,872	6,202	0	670	670
New York* (y)...............	2,235	62,962	0	65,197	63,142	0	2,055	1,481
North Carolina.............	269	21,001	0	21,271	21,082	186	2	652
North Dakota (z)	1,087	2,320	520	3,927	3,473	0	454	584
Ohio (aa)	1,700	30,779	0	32,479	31,847	0	632	1,478
Oklahoma (bb)	0	6,595	0	6,595	6,403	0	192	N/A
Oregon (cc)	30	8,266	-55	8,241	7,990	0	251	386
Pennsylvania (dd)	81	28,956	0	29,036	29,027	2	7	3
Rhode Island (ee)........	59	3,493	-107	3,446	3,445	0	1	178
South Carolina* (ff) ...	1,163	6,660	0	7,824	6,738	115	971	447
South Dakota (gg)	10	1,392	0	1,402	1,392	10	0	149
Tennessee (hh).............	273	12,493	-36	12,730	12,585	141	4	492
Texas (ii)......................	3,676	50,208	-2,660	51,225	48,661	0	2,564	8,070
Utah (jj)	216	5,447	19	5,682	5,675	0	7	401
Vermont (kk)	0	1,448	1	1,448	1,440	8	0	72
Virginia.........................	5	18,973	0	18,979	18,973	0	6	938
Washington (ll)	363	16,816	-68	17,111	16,640	0	471	583
West Virginia (mm)	412	4,254	0	4,666	4,270	0	397	860
Wisconsin (nn).............	517	14,725	559	15,800	15,883	-19	-64	0
Wyoming (oo)	0	1,765	0	1,765	1,765	0	0	890
Puerto Rico..................	0	0	0	0	0	0	0	0

See footnotes at end of table.

FISCAL 2015 STATE GENERAL FUND, APPROPRIATED — Continued
(In millions of dollars)

Source: National Association of State Budget Officers.

Key:

* In these states, the ending balance includes the balance in the budget stabilization fund.

NA — Indicates data are not available.

... — Not applicable

(a) Revenue Adjustments include one-time revenues of $145.8M and a transfer of $20M. Expenditure Adjustments include a Rainy Day payment of $109.2M.

(b) Revenues: Fiscal Summary Revenue Estimate 5/1/14. Revenue Adjustments: Fiscal Summary Anticipated Reappropriations and Carry-forward 5/1/14. Expenditure: Fiscal Summar — Pre Transfer Authorization (Operating + Capital + Supplemental) 5/1/14. Ending Balance: 2015 Expected SBR draw. LFD Fiscal Summary 5/1/14. Expenditure Adjustments Fiscal Summary. Rainy Day fund = SBR + CBR balance as per OMB 10-year plan.

(c) Adjustments to revenue include revenues from the budget transfers.

(d) Ending balance excludes $1,606.4 million that was transferred to the Budget Stabilization Account for "rainy day" purposes.

(e) A balance of $150.6M in excess of the 6.5% statutory reserve of $569.9M is estimated as of June 2014, per the OSPB forecast.

(f) Figures based on enacted FY 2015 General Fund appropriations and revenue estimates contained in SJR 14 of the 147th General Assembly. Revenue adjustments from the June 2014 DEFAC Fiscal Year 2015 revenue forecast include a $16 million increase to the General Fund by adjusting the Farmland Preservation and Open Space programs annual funding from $10 million each to $2 million each, an additional $4.0 million increase to the General Fund by adjusting the Energy Efficiency Investment Fund annual funding from $5 million to $1 million, and an increase of $40 million by waiving the earmark of Abandoned Property funds to the Transportation Trust Fund. General Fund revenues will be reduced by $1 million by increasing the earmark of Insurance Premiums taxes on health insurance policies that is dedicated to emergency medical services from 0.015% to 0.02% of total premiums.

(g) Georgia does not project future fund balances.

(h) Transfers include: $1,000,000 to the Constitutional Defense Fund; $101,200 to the Permanent Building Fund; $400,000 to the Wolf Control Fund; and $225,800 to the Time-Sensitive Emergencies Registry Fund.

(i) Revenue adjustments include statutory transfers in. Expenditure adjustments include statutory transfers out, including but not limited to debt service payments, and pay-down of accounts payable during fiscal year.

(j) Expenditure adjustments include reversions from distributions, capital, and reconciliations; the cost of a 13th check for pension recipients; transfer to the tuition reserve fund; and state agency and university line item capital projects. The Rainy Day Fund balance reflects $376.9M in the Counter-Cyclical Revenue and Economic Stabilization Fund, $445M in the Medicaid Contingency and Reserve Account, and $300M in the State Tuition Reserve Fund.

(k) Revenue adjustments include an estimated $651.6 million of residual funds transferred to the General Fund after the Reserve Funds are filled to their statutorily set maximum amounts. The Ending balance of the General Fund is transferred in the current fiscal year to the Reserve Funds in the subsequent fiscal year. After the Reserve Funds are at their statutorily set maximum amounts, the remainder of the funds is transferred back to the General Fund in that subsequent fiscal year. FY2015 Revenues are based upon the October 2014 Revenue Estimating Conference estimates.

(l) Kansas does not have a "Rainy Day" fund. However, the balanced budget provision of the constitution requires revenues to finance the approved budget.

(m) Revenue includes $99.7 million in Tobacco Settlement funds. Adjustment for Revenues includes $112.1 million that represents appropriation balances carried over from the prior fiscal year, and $224.5 million from fund transfers into the General Fund. Adjustment to Expenditures represents appropriation balances forwarded to the next fiscal year.

(n) Expenditure adjustments—Includes a $75.7 state general fund reduction as authorized by Act 15 of the 2014 legislative session .

(o) Revenue and Expenditure adjustments reflect legislatively authorized transfers.

(p) Includes $24.8 million for tax credit reimbursements and $1.0 million in transfers from other funds. Also, the FY 2015 enacted was

projected to be $127 million; however, with the actual fund balance closing at $147.6 million in FY 2014, the FY 2015 fund balance will be higher.

(q) Fiscal 2015 revenue adjustments include the impact of federal and state law changes (-$445.4 million); revenue sharing payments to local government units (-$468.0 million); deposits from state restricted funds ($390.7 million); deposit to the rainy day fund (-$94.0 million); and general fund dedicated for roads (-$285.0 million). Total expenditures include $495.3 million in one-time spending financed from one-time revenues.

(r) Ending balance includes cash flow account of $350 million, budget reserve account of $811 million, and stadium reserve of $23.4 million.

(s) Legislation was passed to suspend the statutory 2% set aside of revenue estimate prior to legislative appropriations for FY 2015 and changed the normal distribution of ending cash balances to insure the Rainy Day Fund was at its statutory requirement.

(t) Revenue adjustments include transfers from other funds into the general revenue fund and $33.4 from collection initiatives. The enacted revenue estimate, if met, would be insufficient to cover budget expenses. The above expenditures assume expenditure reductions.

(u) Revenue adjustments are transfers between the General Fund and other funds. Per Nebraska law, includes an estimated transfer of $96.7 million to the Cash Reserve Fund (Rainy Day Fund) of the amount the prior year's net General Fund receipts are estimated to exceed the official forecast. Among others, also includes a $138 million transfer from the General Fund to the Property Tax Credit Cash Fund. Expenditure adjustments are reappropriations ($307.2 million) of unexpended balance of appropriations from the prior year plus $5 million reserved for potential deficit appropriations.

(v) Expenditure adjustments are restricted transfers.

(w) Revenue Adjustments: The FY 2015 Enacted Budget anticipates moving $99.2 million to the Education Trust Fund.

(x) FY15 figures reflect the FY15 budget appropriation as passed during the 2014 Legislative Session.

(y) The ending balance includes approximately $1.5 billion in rainy day reserve funds, $53 million reserved to cover costs of potential retroactive labor settlements with certain unions, $500 million reserved for debt reduction, and $21 million reserved for litigation risks.

(z) Revenue adjustments are a $520.0 million transfer from the strategic investment and improvements fund to the general fund.

(aa) FY 2015 estimated expenditures include encumbrances or obligations that are estimated to be incurred in FY 2015 but not disbursed until FY 2016 or some future year.

(bb) Revenue and expenditure adjustments cannot be calculated at this time; nor can we calculate the final balance of the Rainy Day Fund at year-end.

(cc) Revenue adjustment is estimated cost of Tax Anticipation Notes; a transfer to RDF; and statutory transfer to local governments for local property tax relief.

(dd) Expenditure adjustment reflects a transfer of $2.4 million (25% of ending balance) to the Rainy Day Fund.

(ee) Adjustments to revenues reflect a transfer of $106.6 million to the Budget Reserve Fund.

(ff) Ending Balance = 5% General Reserve ($319.5) + 2% Capital Reserve ($127.8) + Surplus Contingency Reserve ($33.5) + Agency Appropriation Balances Carried Forward to Next FY ($489.9); Expenditure Adjustments include FY13–14 Capital Reserve Funds transferred to State agencies.

(gg) The beginning balance of $9.9 million and adjustment to expenditures reflects the prior year's ending balance which is transferred to the rainy day fund.

(hh) Adjustments (Revenues) -$35.5 million transfer to Rainy Day Fund. Total -$35.5 million. Adjustments (Expenditures) $123.3 million transfer to capital outlay projects fund. $13.1million transfer to state office buildings and support facilities fund. $3.8 million transfer to debt service fund. $1.0 million transfer to reserves for dedicated revenue appropriations. Total $141.2 million. Ending Balance $4.4 million undesignated balance. Total $4.4 million.

(ii) Adjustment is net of set aside for transfer to Rainy Day Fund (-$1,327m) and State Highway Fund 6 (-$1,326.9m). In addition, the Comptroller adjustment to general fund dedicated account balances (+$5.6m).

(jj) Includes transfers from previous year balance, to/from Rainy Day Fund, and special revenue funds.

FISCAL 2015 STATE GENERAL FUND, APPROPRIATED — Continued
(In millions of dollars)

(kk) Adjustments equals net transfer effect in/out of General Fund.

(ll) Fund transfers between General Fund and other accounts, and changes made by the 2014 Legislature.

(mm) Fiscal Year 2015 Beginning balance includes $378.2 million in Reappropriations, Unappropriated Surplus Balance of $18.3 million, and FY 2014 13th month expenditures of $15.9 million. Expenditures include Regular, Surplus and Reappropriated funds and $15.9 million of 31 day prior year expenditures. Revenue adjustments are prior year redeposits and special revenue expirations. Expenditure adjustment represents the amount anticipated to be transferred to the Rainy Day Fund. The ending balance is mostly the historically carried forward reappropriation amounts that will remain and be reappropriated to the next fiscal year, the 13th month expenditures & any unappropriated surplus balance.

(nn) Revenue adjustments include Tribal Gaming, $23.5 and Other Revenue, $535.2. Expenditure adjustments include Transfers, $169.6; Lapses, -$317.7; Biennial Spend Ahead, -$4.4; and Compensation Reserves of $133.1. The transfer amount includes the amount needed to reflect the biennial transfer requirement.

(oo) Wyoming budgets on a biennial basis. To arrive at annual figures certain assumptions and estimates were required.

Table 7.4
FISCAL 2014 STATE TAX COLLECTIONS COMPARED WITH PROJECTIONS
USED IN ADOPTING FISCAL 2014 BUDGETS
(In millions of dollars)

State or other jurisdiction	Sales tax		Personal income tax		Corporate income tax		Revenue collection (a)
	Original estimate	Current estimate	Original estimate	Current estimate	Original estimate	Current estimate	
Total (b)......................	$229,469	$230,438	$305,879	$311,352	$47,111	$46,581	–
Alabama........................	2,108	2,070	3,155	3,212	359	359	L
Alaska............................	NA	NA	NA	NA	644	552	T
Arizona	3,998	3,986	3,447	3,462	683	575	T
Arkansas........................	2,208	2,173	3,101	3,111	429	440	H
California (c)................	22,983	22,759	60,827	66,522	8,508	8,107	H
Colorado	2,255	2,373	5,381	5,699	657	721	H
Connecticut..................	4,044	4,101	8,809	8,719	724	782	T
Delaware	NA	NA	1,173	1,188	203	102	L
Florida..........................	19,205	19,708	NA	NA	2,285	2,043	H
Georgia..........................	5,053	5,170	9,005	8,966	817	944	H
Hawaii	3,142	2,826	1,790	1,745	82	87	L
Idaho.............................	1,148	1,146	1,320	1,329	194	188	H
Illinois..........................	7,385	7,610	16,073	16,301	2,897	3,317	H
Indiana..........................	7,088	6,926	5,163	4,899	900	1,054	L
Iowa	2,665	2,642	3,947	3,972	625	550	L
Kansas	2,455	2,446	2,525	2,218	410	399	L
Kentucky	3,173	3,131	3,689	3,749	365	475	L
Louisiana......................	2,657	2,610	2,786	2,812	340	280	T
Maine............................	1,158	1,156	1,381	1,406	170	183	H
Maryland	4,224	4,143	7,959	7,774	823	761	L
Massachusetts	5,494	5,496	12,949	13,202	1,843	2,049	H
Michigan (d).................	7,331	7,285	8,269	8,206	407	308	L
Minnesota.....................	4,817	5,041	8,649	9,647	1,165	1,284	H
Mississippi	1,946	1,955	1,668	1,667	465	677	H
Missouri	1,933	1,925	5,644	5,404	465	396	L
Montana	68	63	1,039	1,063	154	148	H
Nebraska	1,500	1,525	2,039	2,061	265	307	H
Nevada..........................	970	968	NA	NA	NA	NA	L
New Hampshire	NA	NA	NA	NA	350	344	L
New Jersey	8,929	8,856	13,039	12,050	2,663	2,640	L
New Mexico	2,571	2,502	1,217	1,250	342	205	H
New York.......................	11,733	11,786	42,543	42,961	6,375	6,046	H
North Carolina.............	5,456	5,567	10,518	10,272	1,075	1,357	L
North Dakota................	1,149	1,213	383	514	185	239	H
Ohio..............................	9,197	9,166	7,850	8,065	812	794	H
Oklahoma......................	2,031	1,959	2,103	2,028	482	307	L
Oregon..........................	NA	NA	6,535	6,628	488	495	H
Pennsylvania	9,229	9,130	11,728	11,437	2,482	2,502	L
Rhode Island................	907	916	1,103	1,116	117	115	H
South Carolina.............	2,473	2,517	2,846	2,921	248	288	H
South Dakota...............	805	823	NA	NA	NA	NA	H
Tennessee	7,288	7,274	202	239	2,136	1,855	L
Texas	26,659	27,386	NA	NA	NA	NA	H
Utah..............................	2,155	2,131	2,749	2,782	285	283	H
Vermont........................	360	354	668	671	96	95	L
Virginia.........................	3,261	3,067	11,452	11,253	905	758	T
Washington...................	8,003	8,205	NA	NA	NA	NA	H
West Virginia................	1,269	1,222	1,862	1,770	230	204	L
Wisconsin.....................	4,498	4,628	7,295	7,061	962	967	L
Wyoming	490	505	NA	NA	NA	NA	H
Puerto Rico..................	0	0	0	0	0	0	0

See footnotes at end of table.

FISCAL 2014 STATE TAX COLLECTIONS COMPARED WITH PROJECTIONS USED IN ADOPTING FISCAL 2014 BUDGETS — Continued
(In millions of dollars)

Source: National Association of State Budget Officers.

Note: Unless otherwise noted, original estimates reflect the figures used when the fiscal 2014 budget was adopted, and current estimates reflect preliminary actual tax collections.

Key:

H — Revenues higher than estimates.

L — Revenues lower than estimates.

T — Revenues on target.

NA — Indicates data are not available because, in most cases, these states do not have that type of tax.

(a) Refers to whether fiscal 2014 revenues from all sources (includes sales, personal income, corporate income, excise, and motor vehicle and all other taxes and fees) were higher than, lower than, or on target with original estimates.

(b) Totals include only those states with data for both original and current estimates for fiscal 2014.

(c) Fiscal 2014 revenues were higher compared to projection in the 2013–14 Budget Act.

(d) Fiscal 2014 revenues were lower than projections as of July 2014.

Table 7.5
COMPARISON OF TAX COLLECTIONS IN FISCAL 2013, FISCAL 2014, AND ENACTED FISCAL 2015
(In millions of dollars)

State or other jurisdiction	Sales tax			Personal income tax			Corporate income tax		
	Fiscal 2013	Fiscal 2014	Fiscal 2015	Fiscal 2013	Fiscal 2014	Fiscal 2015	Fiscal 2013	Fiscal 2014	Fiscal 2015
Total (a)	$219,760	$230,438	$239,598	$308,657	$311,352	$325,955	$46,272	$46,581	$47,359
Alabama	2,022	2,070	2,120	3,103	3,212	3,294	349	359	387
Alaska	N.A.	N.A.	N.A.	N.A.	N.A.	N.A.	547	552	591
Arizona	3,842	3,986	4,208	3,398	3,462	3,697	662	575	671
Arkansas	2,125	2,173	2,208	3,144	3,111	3,173	431	440	450
California	20,482	22,759	23,823	64,484	66,522	70,238	7,783	8,107	8,910
Colorado (b)	2,212	2,373	2,475	5,596	5,699	6,113	636	721	775
Connecticut	3,897	4,101	4,167	8,719	8,719	9,265	743	782	704
Delaware	N.A.	N.A.	N.A.	1,140	1,188	1,226	188	102	212
Florida	18,418	19,708	20,681	N.A.	N.A.	N.A.	2,081	2,043	2,264
Georgia	5,277	5,170	5,259	8,772	8,966	9,537	797	944	847
Hawaii	2,945	2,826	3,057	1,736	1,745	1,912	101	87	69
Idaho	1,110	1,146	1,233	1,284	1,329	1,403	199	188	207
Illinois	7,354	7,610	7,810	16,539	16,301	14,844	3,177	3,317	3,071
Indiana	6,796	6,926	7,442	4,978	4,899	5,419	968	1,054	869
Iowa	2,548	2,642	2,753	4,084	3,972	4,291	555	550	610
Kansas	2,525	2,446	2,527	2,931	2,218	2,519	371	399	425
Kentucky	3,022	3,131	3,150	3,723	3,749	3,977	401	475	463
Louisiana (c)	2,582	2,610	2,696	2,754	2,812	2,932	336	280	351
Maine (d)	1,037	1,156	1,240	1,522	1,406	1,447	172	183	178
Maryland	4,068	4,143	4,350	7,691	7,774	8,469	818	761	781
Massachusetts	5,164	5,496	5,789	12,831	13,202	14,021	1,822	2,049	1,993
Michigan	7,154	7,285	7,549	8,270	8,206	8,506	660	308	468
Minnesota (e)	4,760	5,041	5,145	9,013	9,647	9,860	1,281	1,284	1,372
Mississippi	1,911	1,955	2,045	1,650	1,667	1,736	524	677	666
Missouri	1,872	1,925	1,978	5,489	5,404	5,918	416	396	416
Montana	62	63	68	1,048	1,063	1,015	178	148	155
Nebraska	1,475	1,525	1,536	2,102	2,061	2,208	276	307	263
Nevada	923	968	1,023	N.A.	N.A.	N.A.	N.A.	N.A.	N.A.
New Hampshire	N.A.	N.A.	N.A.	N.A.	N.A.	N.A.	345	344	357
New Jersey	8,455	8,856	9,332	12,109	12,050	12,627	2,536	2,640	2,820
New Mexico	2,398	2,502	2,665	1,241	1,250	1,280	267	205	289
New York	11,232	11,786	12,113	40,227	42,961	43,735	6,253	6,046	5,438
North Carolina	5,294	5,567	6,244	10,953	10,272	10,885	1,192	1,357	1,095
North Dakota	1,166	1,213	1,324	616	514	415	187	239	193
Ohio (f)	8,445	9,166	9,914	9,508	8,065	8,717	790	794	833
Oklahoma	1,901	1,959	2,034	2,057	2,028	2,129	452	307	375
Oregon	N/A	NA	NA	6,268	6,628	7,122	453	495	543
Pennsylvania	8,894	9,130	9,477	11,371	11,437	12,033	2,423	2,502	2,501
Rhode Island	879	916	940	1,086	1,116	1,157	132	115	119
South Carolina	2,448	2,517	2,590	2,844	2,921	3,013	351	288	304
South Dakota	776	823	851	N.A.	N.A.	N.A.	N.A.	N.A.	N.A.
Tennessee (g)	7,012	7,274	7,515	233	239	264	2,021	1,855	1,904
Texas	25,842	27,386	27,638	N.A.	N.A.	N.A.	N/A	NA	NA
Utah (h)	2,038	2,131	2,200	2,852	2,782	2,913	338	283	311
Vermont	347	354	367	661	671	739	95	95	93
Virginia	3,220	3,067	3,211	11,340	11,253	12,350	797	758	817
Wisconsin	7,687	8,205	8,405	N/A	N.A.	N.A.	N.A.	N.A.	N.A.
West Virginia	1,255	1,222	1,318	1,796	1,770	1,905	242	204	206
Washington	4,410	4,628	4,607	7,497	7,061	7,651	925	967	994
Wyoming	481	505	521	N.A.	N.A.	N.A.	N.A.	N.A.	N.A.
Puerto Rico	0	0	0	0	0	0	0	0	0

See footnotes at end of table.

COMPARISON OF TAX COLLECTIONS IN FISCAL 2013, FISCAL 2014, AND ENACTED FISCAL 2015—Continued
(In millions of dollars)

Source: National Association of State Budget Officers.

Note: Unless otherwise noted, fiscal 2014 figures reflect actual tax collections, 2014 figures reflect preliminary actual tax collections estimates, and fiscal 2015 figures reflect the estimates used in enacted budgets.

Key:

N.A. — Indicates data are not available because, in most cases, these states do not have that type of tax.

(a) Totals include only those states with data for all years.

(b) Reported actual fiscal 2013 collections and preliminary actual fiscal 2014 collections are from OSPB June 2014. Appropriated fiscal 2015 collections are from OSPB March 2014.

(c) Reported collections for fiscal 2014 and fiscal 2015 are from REC May 2014.

(d) Reported collections for fiscal 2015 are from the March 2014 Revenue Forecasting Committee report.

(e) Reported collections from fiscal 2013, 2014 and 2015 are from May 2014, July 2014 and May 2014 respectively.

(f) Ohio no longer has a corporate income tax, but instead a privilege of doing business tax on gross receipts.

(g) Sales tax, personal income tax, and corporate income tax are shared with local governments. Corporate income tax includes franchise tax.

(h) Reported sales tax collections include all state sales taxes, not just those used for the general fund.

Table 7.6
TOTAL STATE EXPENDITURES: CAPITAL INCLUSIVE
(In millions of dollars)

State	Actual fiscal 2011					Actual fiscal 2012					Estimated fiscal 2013				
	General fund	Federal funds	Other state funds	Bonds	Total	General fund	Federal funds	Other state funds	Bonds	Total	General fund	Federal funds	Other state funds	Bonds	Total
Total..................	$661,932	$511,945	$444,468	$35,385	$1,653,730	$690,515	$502,737	$461,156	$35,134	$1,689,542	$723,796	$541,151	$483,034	$37,295	$1,785,276
Alabama (a)............	7,380	9,439	7,455	324	24,598	7,121	9,482	7,693	224	24,520	7,835	9,288	6,770	495	24,388
Alaska.................	7,400	3,017	1,322	50	11,789	7,262	2,730	1,296	550	11,838	7,053	2,971	1,567	0	11,591
Arizona................	8,414	12,299	6,783	585	28,081	8,714	12,008	6,946	629	28,297	8,848	12,837	7,220	629	29,534
Arkansas...............	4,582	6,278	9,693	135	20,688	4,755	6,082	10,405	203	21,445	4,865	6,511	11,212	155	22,743
California..............	86,405	73,063	33,853	6,104	199,425	96,562	70,431	37,724	6,715	211,432	100,711	81,059	39,528	8,689	229,987
Colorado...............	7,311	7,691	13,775	0	28,777	7,948	7,423	13,664	0	29,035	8,684	7,756	13,847	0	30,287
Connecticut............	18,782	2,631	3,439	2,656	27,508	19,026	2,613	3,712	2,501	27,852	17,045	5,501	3,893	2,962	29,401
Delaware...............	3,592	1,777	3,388	185	8,942	3,659	1,783	3,281	439	9,162	3,794	1,903	3,459	452	9,608
Florida................	23,054	24,570	13,971	1,395	62,990	24,490	24,272	14,340	869	63,971	26,690	25,416	21,445	689	74,240
Georgia................	17,240	12,469	10,802	632	41,143	18,019	13,046	10,571	808	42,444	19,121	11,834	10,424	850	42,229
Hawaii.................	5,511	1,932	3,285	766	11,494	5,666	1,912	3,271	735	11,584	6,275	2,148	3,337	825	12,585
Idaho..................	2,504	2,383	1,349	33	6,269	2,691	2,648	1,342	10	6,691	2,789	2,814	1,741	28	7,372
Illinois...............	29,291	14,007	14,426	2,122	59,846	30,309	15,472	17,552	1,954	65,287	30,740	19,964	19,652	2,382	72,738
Indiana................	13,579	9,272	3,344	0	26,195	14,189	10,357	3,625	0	28,171	14,553	9,978	2,729	0	27,260
Iowa...................	6,010	6,551	6,072	229	18,862	6,299	5,727	7,398	107	19,531	6,641	6,122	7,316	71	20,150
Kansas.................	6,098	4,153	3,737	408	14,396	6,135	3,890	3,529	415	13,969	6,026	3,511	5,132	381	15,050
Kentucky...............	9,334	8,687	7,628	0	25,649	9,426	8,001	8,246	0	25,673	9,705	9,614	9,516	0	28,835
Louisiana..............	8,359	10,616	7,793	320	27,088	8,421	10,241	8,277	378	27,317	8,612	11,091	9,071	373	29,147
Maine..................	3,087	2,649	2,309	61	8,106	3,041	2,563	2,059	16	7,679	3,150	2,696	2,180	63	8,089
Maryland...............	13,281	9,951	9,452	1,156	33,840	14,951	9,058	9,906	962	34,877	15,119	11,811	8,909	1,135	36,974
Massachusetts..........	25,826	16,157	13,303	1,827	57,113	26,771	15,530	13,459	1,781	57,541	29,018	15,135	12,734	2,173	59,060
Michigan...............	8,619	17,549	20,844	275	47,287	8,882	17,424	20,766	326	47,398	9,828	20,632	20,777	235	51,472
Minnesota..............	16,580	8,170	4,855	609	30,214	18,739	8,435	5,090	810	33,074	19,678	9,492	6,183	780	36,133
Mississippi............	4,526	7,590	5,566	353	18,035	4,736	7,755	5,237	784	18,512	4,888	8,197	5,591	257	18,933
Missouri...............	7,938	7,539	7,887	0	23,364	8,022	7,209	7,712	0	22,943	8,348	7,208	7,622	0	23,178
Montana................	1,764	2,131	2,024	0	5,919	1,947	2,115	1,978	0	6,040	2,041	2,149	1,998	0	6,188
Nebraska...............	3,445	2,988	3,443	0	9,876	3,589	3,014	3,559	0	10,162	3,792	2,817	3,933	0	10,542
Nevada.................	3,062	2,554	1,977	29	7,622	3,182	2,918	2,756	41	8,897	3,278	2,823	2,625	19	8,745
New Hampshire..........	1,280	1,650	1,965	81	4,976	1,266	1,604	2,060	87	5,017	1,253	1,703	2,122	71	5,149
New Jersey.............	30,379	10,998	5,911	1,358	48,646	31,202	12,041	6,194	1,374	50,811	32,511	13,566	7,063	1,225	54,365
New Mexico.............	5,464	5,790	3,121	0	14,375	5,651	5,799	3,246	0	14,696	5,893	6,126	4,207	0	16,226
New York...............	56,489	40,311	32,843	3,861	133,504	58,960	38,574	32,305	3,258	133,097	61,243	41,171	31,672	3,440	137,526
North Carolina.........	20,195	14,513	14,562	652	49,922	20,230	12,691	9,953	231	43,105	21,082	12,850	9,914	383	44,229
North Dakota...........	2,223	1,884	1,902	11	6,020	2,220	1,536	1,950	6	5,712	3,237	1,590	1,949	17	6,793
Ohio...................	26,395	13,144	16,370	2,013	57,922	27,439	12,647	15,996	2,186	58,268	28,902	13,046	17,141	2,133	61,222
Oklahoma...............	6,575	7,122	7,088	146	20,931	6,991	6,923	7,372	144	21,430	7,101	7,425	7,620	155	22,301
Oregon.................	6,925	7,753	12,007	329	27,014	5,957	7,451	12,263	132	25,803	7,925	8,090	12,250	158	28,423
Pennsylvania...........	27,031	24,177	32,159	1,379	84,746	27,717	23,945	32,916	800	85,378	28,492	23,810	33,899	1,265	87,466
Rhode Island...........	3,110	2,599	2,000	198	7,907	3,216	2,520	1,973	157	7,866	3,289	2,543	1,970	79	7,881
South Carolina.........	5,517	9,284	7,164	123	22,088	6,200	7,800	8,208	0	22,208	6,329	6,993	8,116	0	21,438

See footnotes at end of table.

TOTAL STATE EXPENDITURES: CAPITAL INCLUSIVE — Continued
(In millions of dollars)

State	Actual fiscal 2011					Actual fiscal 2012					Estimated fiscal 2013				
	General fund	Federal funds	Other state funds	Bonds	Total	General fund	Federal funds	Other state funds	Bonds	Total	General fund	Federal funds	Other state funds	Bonds	Total
South Dakota..........	1,207	1,507	939	35	3,688	1,291	1,494	1,278	35	4,098	1,442	1,420	1,227	21	4,110
Tennessee (b)	11,685	12,806	5,674	254	30,419	12,093	12,532	5,565	301	30,491	13,465	13,231	5,367	266	32,329
Texas (c)	44,549	32,324	14,886	1,308	93,067	42,645	30,884	18,159	1,556	93,244	49,394	34,676	15,979	1,197	101,246
Utah..........	4,742	3,588	3,039	453	11,822	5,011	3,446	3,734	488	12,679	5,317	3,644	3,946	481	13,388
Vermont..........	1,277	1,831	1,853	56	5,017	1,352	1,695	1,845	73	4,965	1,389	1,771	1,993	116	5,269
Virginia..........	16,986	9,212	15,890	1,284	43,372	18,833	9,546	16,191	1,167	45,737	18,052	9,568	17,071	908	45,599
Washington..........	15,279	8,049	8,136	1,711	33,175	15,479	8,100	8,785	1,632	33,996	15,867	9,102	9,304	1,683	35,956
West Virginia..........	4,144	4,064	13,611	78	21,897	4,283	4,075	13,885	77	22,320	4,256	4,412	15,142	78	23,888
Wisconsin	13,381	10,572	17,371	0	41,324	14,042	10,815	17,912	0	42,769	14,634	11,006	19,253	0	44,893
Wyoming (d)	2,455	1,547	1,748	0	5,750	3,709	2,354	3,069	0	9,132	3,031	2,082	2,532	0	7,645

Source: National Association of State Budget Officers, State Expenditure Report (Fiscal 2012-2014).

Note: "State funds" refers to general funds plus other state fund spending. State spending from bonds is excluded. "Total funds" refers to funding from all sources-general fund, federal funds, other state funds and bonds. Small dollar amounts, when rounded, cause an aberration in the percentage increase. In these instances, the actual dollar amounts should be consulted to determine the exact percentage increase. Medicaid reflects provider taxes, fees, assessments, donations and local funds in Other State Funds.

Key:

(a) Amounts shown in fiscal years 2013 and 2013 are based on actual expenditures during these years, regardless of the year appropriated. Fiscal 2014 amounts shown are equal to actual expenditures through nine months and then annualized for the year.

(b) Tennessee collects personal income tax on income from dividends on stocks and interest on certain bonds. Tax revenue estimates do not include federal funds and other departmental revenues. However, federal funds and other departmental revenues are included in the budget as funding sources for the general fund, along with state tax revenues.

(c) Data are compiled from multiple sources, such as agency annual financial reports, Texas Comptroller publications, the General Appropriations Act, and Legislative Budget Board online resources. Methodologies employed by these sources may differ somewhat between each other and across time. In addition, the report was compiled according to NASBO methodologies.

(d) Part of Wyoming's yearly variation in expenditure totals is due to the fact that the state budgets on a two year cycle.

Table 7.7
ELEMENTARY AND SECONDARY EDUCATION EXPENDITURES, BY STATE
(In millions of dollars)

State	Actual fiscal 2012					Actual fiscal 2013					Estimated fiscal 2014				
	General fund	Federal funds	Other state funds	Bonds	Total	General fund	Federal funds	Other state funds	Bonds	Total	General fund	Federal funds	Other state funds	Bonds	Total
Total	$229,800	$54,985	$34,583	$2,936	$322,304	$241,169	$51,683	$39,493	$2,474	$334,819	$253,206	$53,577	$39,198	$2,576	$348,557
Alabama (a)	3,909	969	183	0	5,061	3,773	967	273	0	5,013	4,017	1,388	187	0	5,592
Alaska	1,292	233	54	0	1,579	1,364	209	43	0	1,616	1,379	228	43	0	1,650
Arizona	3,375	1,169	533	89	5,166	3,465	1,123	590	88	5,266	3,621	1,078	674	87	5,460
Arkansas	2,000	615	765	0	3,380	2,056	519	767	0	3,342	2,103	519	815	0	3,437
California	32,102	6,261	122	1,216	39,701	37,979	6,307	127	872	45,285	38,830	6,647	79	1,060	46,616
Colorado (b)	2,833	656	3,781	0	7,270	3,015	614	3,918	0	7,547	3,153	594	4,169	0	7,916
Connecticut	2,769	556	3	506	3,834	2,880	484	10	563	3,937	3,039	476	2	628	4,145
Delaware	1,156	244	659	138	2,197	1,194	211	681	141	2,227	1,243	208	700	168	2,319
Florida	8,264	2,204	767	20	11,255	9,448	2,098	787	1	12,334	10,034	1,961	841	0	12,836
Georgia (c)	7,061	2,241	331	232	9,865	7,380	2,353	334	167	10,234	7,601	2,011	318	239	10,169
Hawaii	1,458	284	56	0	1,798	1,444	287	63	0	1,794	1,537	303	49	0	1,889
Idaho	1,241	293	77	0	1,611	1,299	243	80	0	1,622	1,328	237	89	0	1,654
Illinois	6,739	2,029	35	0	8,803	6,539	2,128	34	0	8,701	6,687	3,007	77	0	9,771
Indiana	7,277	1,231	135	0	8,643	7,452	1,057	171	0	8,680	7,625	980	120	0	8,725
Iowa	2,694	435	44	0	3,173	2,731	444	31	0	3,206	2,866	460	69	0	3,395
Kansas	3,077	471	166	0	3,714	3,092	479	171	0	3,742	2,964	468	367	0	3,799
Kentucky	4,129	919	32	0	5,080	4,141	846	34	0	5,021	4,202	797	35	0	5,034
Louisiana	3,341	1,104	863	0	5,308	3,370	1,042	847	0	5,259	3,526	1,115	783	0	5,424
Maine	1,046	16	0	0	1,062	1,087	202	8	0	1,297	1,150	194	30	0	1,374
Maryland (d)	5,709	980	121	0	6,810	5,552	969	437	0	6,958	5,691	1,110	408	0	7,209
Massachusetts (e)	5,161	1,173	4	0	6,338	5,407	1,004	5	0	6,416	5,622	1,259	5	0	6,886
Michigan	102	1,907	10,383	0	12,392	312	1,743	10,841	0	12,896	185	1,915	11,372	0	13,472
Minnesota	6,616	779	44	1	7,440	8,865	745	44	1	9,655	8,473	785	42	3	9,303
Mississippi	1,993	795	328	0	3,116	2,011	705	324	0	3,040	2,068	760	400	0	3,228
Missouri	2,770	1,086	1,425	0	5,281	2,914	957	1,358	0	5,229	2,922	943	1,426	0	5,291
Montana	629	173	115	0	917	697	162	77	0	936	721	163	86	0	970
Nebraska	1,047	395	66	0	1,508	1,088	328	72	0	1,488	1,142	303	77	0	1,522
Nevada	1,116	251	431	0	1,798	1,214	384	382	0	1,980	1,286	259	422	0	1,967
New Hampshire	0	208	956	7	1,171	0	199	959	14	1,172	0	178	954	1	1,133
New Jersey	11,110	869	18	0	11,997	11,754	856	20	0	12,630	12,499	818	15	0	13,332
New Mexico	2,366	421	1	0	2,788	2,455	414	1	0	2,870	2,556	414	2	0	2,972
New York	18,508	4,908	3,009	17	26,442	19,070	3,407	3,164	16	25,657	19,279	3,927	3,310	17	26,533
North Carolina	7,580	1,438	549	0	9,567	8,784	1,420	502	0	10,706	9,146	1,420	502	0	11,068
North Dakota	620	154	56	0	830	660	141	57	0	858	838	113	73	0	1,024
Ohio (f)	6,530	2,239	814	474	10,057	6,831	2,000	751	312	9,894	7,128	1,912	1,045	201	10,286
Oklahoma	2,357	755	338	0	3,450	2,368	662	444	0	3,474	2,269	667	555	0	3,491
Oregon	2,967	661	164	0	3,792	2,527	560	593	0	3,680	3,351	593	182	0	4,126
Pennsylvania	9,258	2,430	618	0	12,306	9,705	2,423	618	0	12,746	9,971	2,507	617	0	13,095
Rhode Island	861	235	27	0	1,123	928	214	29	1	1,172	941	173	33	2	1,149
South Carolina	1,995	824	690	0	3,509	2,264	890	749	0	3,903	2,416	901	735	0	4,052

See footnotes at end of table.

ELEMENTARY AND SECONDARY EDUCATION EXPENDITURES, BY STATE—Continued
(In millions of dollars)

State	Actual fiscal 2012					Actual fiscal 2013					Estimated fiscal 2014				
	General fund	Federal funds	Other state funds	Bonds	Total	General fund	Federal funds	Other state funds	Bonds	Total	General fund	Federal funds	Other state funds	Bonds	Total
South Dakota........	358	169	3	0	530	402	173	3	0	578	401	168	5	0	574
Tennessee............	4,046	1,261	63	0	5,370	4,160	1,165	89	0	5,414	4,359	1,258	84	0	5,701
Texas	18,026	4,778	3,530	14	26,348	14,726	4,954	5,902	3	25,585	18,503	4,780	4,044	3	27,330
Utah	2,409	469	37	0	2,915	2,534	433	30	0	2,997	2,534	481	76	3	3,091
Vermont	337	137	1,077	8	1,559	357	121	1,103	8	1,589	376	116	1,173	7	1,672
Virginia...............	4,979	1,358	607	0	6,944	5,254	1,029	645	0	6,928	5,302	967	678	0	6,947
Washington..........	6,789	887	126	191	7,993	6,735	856	109	264	7,964	7,207	798	400	137	8,542
West Virginia.......	1,950	369	16	23	2,358	1,969	346	14	23	2,352	1,970	340	14	23	2,347
Wisconsin	5,841	848	230	0	6,919	5,915	782	238	0	6,935	7,145	875	253	0	8,273
Wyoming	7	98	131	0	236	2	28	964	0	994	0	3	763	0	766

Source: National Association of State Budget Officers, State Expenditure Report (Fiscal 2012–2014).

Note: Small dollar amounts, when rounded, cause an aberration in the percentage increase. In these instances, the actual dollar amounts should be consulted to determine the exact percentage increase.

Key:

(a) Federal funds received directly by local school systems are not reported at the state budget level.

(b) School personnel are paid at the school district level—state costs for employer contributions to employee pensions and health benefits only reflect Colorado Department of Education personnel. Funds library-related programs across the state.

(c) Estimated federal funds expenditures in FY 2014 reflect amounts as appropriated in the annual appropriations act. The Georgia State Constitution allows for federal funds to be "continuously appropriated" throughout the fiscal year and additional federal funds are amended into the budget with approval of the Governor's Office of Planning and Budget as they become available during the fiscal year.

(d) In fiscal 2013, other state funds growth is due to the increased use of lottery funds to finance education local aid.

(e) Figures reflect K-12 education, the Michigan Department of Education, adult education and pre-school. Employer contributions to current employees' pensions and health benefits are reported for Department of Education employees and partially excluded for employees of K-12 schools. Effective for fiscal 2013, state funds partially offset employer-paid retirement obligations for employees of K-12 schools. Fiscal 2012 figures are adjusted from the 2012 published survey to remove $459 million School Aid Fund revenue support for higher education spending inadvertently reported under elementary and secondary education. Actual ARRA expenditures will be recorded with the fiscal 2014 annual financial report.

(f) Debt service appropriations for school construction is no longer included in the elementary and secondary education category.

Table 7.8
MEDICAID EXPENDITURES BY STATE
(In millions of dollars)

State	Actual fiscal 2012				Actual fiscal 2013				Estimated fiscal 2014			
	General fund	Federal funds	Other state funds	Total	General fund	Federal funds	Other state funds	Total	General fund	Federal funds	Other state funds	Total
Total	$127,133	$224,980	$38,960	$391,073	$130,706	$234,168	$48,857	$413,731	$138,321	$275,966	$46,166	$460,453
Alabama (a)	575	3,795	1,257	5,627	595	3,820	1,171	5,586	638	3,932	1,126	5,696
Alaska	566	798	5	1,369	605	836	7	1,448	677	966	10	1,653
Arizona	2,078	5,782	576	8,436	2,069	5,756	606	8,431	2,019	6,160	650	8,829
Arkansas	630	3,142	652	4,424	736	3,180	595	4,511	818	3,802	404	5,024
California	15,228	26,446	1,378	43,052	15,008	28,507	9,608	53,123	16,726	39,991	5,920	62,637
Colorado (b)	1,693	2,591	1,686	5,970	1,844	2,805	1,736	6,385	2,092	3,492	1,626	7,210
Connecticut (c)	5887	0	0	5887	6060	0	0	6060	3638	2992	0	6630
Delaware	637	784	0	1,421	707	870	0	1,577	662	1,001	0	1,663
Florida	4,010	10,929	4,330	19,269	4,721	11,823	3,788	20,332	5,277	13,562	4,272	23,111
Georgia (d)	2,641	5,599	335	8,575	2,755	5,915	363	9,033	2,853	5,700	386	8,939
Hawaii	606	807	0	1,413	796	877	0	1,673	844	1,090	0	1,934
Idaho	399	1,063	242	1,704	467	1,241	168	1,876	475	1,335	214	2,024
Illinois	4,372	6,189	2,390	12,951	4,811	7,620	3,098	15,529	4,833	9,635	3,337	17,805
Indiana	1,717	4,716	745	7,178	1,883	5,950	956	8,789	1,815	6,225	679	8,719
Iowa	903	2,068	733	3,704	987	2,140	749	3,876	1,157	2,450	665	4,272
Kansas	1,122	1,510	51	2,683	1,100	1,425	58	2,583	1,209	1,627	52	2,888
Kentucky	1,319	4,090	373	5,782	1,267	3,923	436	5,626	1,267	5,042	449	6,758
Louisiana	1,289	4,474	588	6,351	1,425	4,721	704	6,850	1,726	4,700	848	7,274
Maine (e)	661	1,443	230	2,334	737	1,517	255	2,509	747	1,767	267	2,781
Maryland (f)	2,740	3,617	826	7,183	2,758	3,893	974	7,625	2,897	4,816	860	8,573
Massachusetts (g)	3,679	6,752	0	10,431	3,782	6,998	0	10,780	4,668	7,244	0	11,912
Michigan (g)	2,324	8,198	2,016	12,538	2,330	8,194	1,990	12,514	2,278	9,829	2,174	14,281
Minnesota	4,163	4,422	68	8,653	4,007	4,032	7	8,046	4,276	4,962	233	9,471
Mississippi	73	3,182	1,050	4,305	316	3,627	891	4,834	468	3,427	743	4,638
Missouri	1,719	4,245	2,224	8,188	1,664	4,238	2,308	8,210	1,834	4,378	2,270	8,482
Montana	230	675	91	996	235	736	110	1,081	255	714	86	1,055
Nebraska	683	935	31	1,649	784	1,003	35	1,822	817	1,006	34	1,857
Nevada (b)	535	1,008	392	1,935	546	1,165	310	2,021	555	1,452	299	2,306
New Hampshire	470	584	133	1,187	511	605	169	1,285	546	660	175	1,381
New Jersey (i)	3,777	5,667	1,074	10,518	3,718	5,546	1,092	10,356	3,904	6,888	1,050	11,842
New Mexico	849	2,562	229	3,640	868	2,560	250	3,678	864	3,010	263	4,137
New York	9,783	24,478	4,996	39,257	10,602	23,421	4,769	38,792	10,981	24,237	4,754	39,972
North Carolina	3,517	7,535	1,172	12,224	3,404	8,433	1,093	12,930	3,689	8,433	1,100	13,222
North Dakota	306	419	5	730	355	421	6	782	392	458	7	857
Ohio (j)	11,686	4,269	790	16,745	12,030	4,102	878	17,010	13,571	6,317	2,053	21,941
Oklahoma	1,205	2,924	605	4,734	1,343	2,931	646	4,920	1,420	3,095	695	5,210
Oregon	1,219	3,094	598	4,911	923	3,476	1,111	5,510	1,331	4,592	788	6,711
Pennsylvania	7,620	12,245	2,364	22,229	7,945	12,372	2,632	22,949	8,253	13,174	2,829	24,256
Rhode Island	919	995	10	1,924	939	1,004	11	1,954	1,013	1,214	12	2,239
South Carolina	640	3,426	719	4,785	688	3,519	683	4,890	746	3,909	773	5,428

See footnotes at end of table.

MEDICAID EXPENDITURES BY STATE—Continued
(In millions of dollars)

State	Actual fiscal 2012				Actual fiscal 2013				Estimated fiscal 2014			
	General fund	Federal funds	Other state funds	Total	General fund	Federal funds	Other state funds	Total	General fund	Federal funds	Other state funds	Total
South Dakota	287	487	0	774	316	500	0	816	351	515	0	866
Tennessee (k)	2,792	6,007	534	9,333	2,787	6,121	491	9,399	3,213	6,548	300	10,061
Texas	10,686	16,987	1,654	29,327	10,190	17,483	1,845	29,518	10,880	22,263	1,011	34,154
Utah	380	1,356	329	2,065	380	1,435	369	2,184	316	1,597	620	2,533
Vermont (l)	242	716	309	1,267	295	775	334	1,404	281	830	333	1,444
Virginia	3,569	3,465	0	7,034	3,862	3,772	0	7,634	3,934	3,961	0	7,895
Washington (m)	1,951	2,162	111	4,224	1,764	1,993	280	4,037	1,899	3,330	327	5,556
West Virginia	543	1,978	243	2,764	375	2,143	490	3,008	518	2,612	404	3,534
Wisconsin	1,954	4,070	797	6,821	2,144	4,435	762	7,341	2,411	4,709	1,044	8,164
Wyoming	259	294	19	572	272	309	23	604	287	317	24	628

Source: National Association of State Budget Officers, State Expenditure Report (Fiscal 2012–2014).

Note: States were asked to report Medicaid expenditures as follows: General funds: all general funds appropriated to the Medicaid agency and any other agency which are used for direct Medicaid matching purposes under Title XIX. Other state funds: other funds and revenue sources used as Medicaid match, such as local funds and provider taxes, fees, donations, assessments (as defined by the Centers for Medicare and Medicaid Services). Federal Funds: all federal matching funds provided pursuant to Title XIX. The states were asked separately to detail the amount of provider taxes, fees, donations, assessments and local funds reported as Other State Funds.

(a) Fiscal 2012 through fiscal 2014 Other State Funds includes provider taxes in the amounts of $342 million, $356 million, and $382 million, respectively.

(b) CHIP is included in "Medicaid" expenditures, all part of the Department of Health Care Policy and Financing.

(c) In fiscal 2012 and fiscal 2013, Medicaid was "gross funded" with federal funds deposited directly to the State Treasury. Beginning in fiscal 2014, the Medicaid appropriation in the Department of Social Services (DSS) is "net funded" while other Medicaid expenditures remain gross funded. With the exception of enhanced FMAP available for certain populations and services, Connecticut's FMAP is 50%. Includes Medicaid expenditures for administrative services organizations and fiscal intermediaries in DSS. Excludes state portion of Qualified Medicare Beneficiaries and School Based Child Health as those expenditures are netted out of federal Medicaid reimbursement. Also excludes provider taxes, which are deposited directly to the State Treasury.

(d) State general funds paid by other agencies to the state Medicaid agency are reflected as state general funds rather than other funds.

(e) Medicaid Other State Funds provider taxes are: fiscal 2012 $151.2 million; fiscal 2013 $153.3 million; fiscal 2014 $168.1 million.

(f) There was a slight change in the methodology used to calculate Medicaid compared to prior years. The CHIP figures for this year are slightly higher due to CHIP expenditures being accounted for in all State agencies, not just the Medical Care Programs Administration.

(g) Fiscal 2012 general fund spending includes Medicare Part D payments of $178 million inadvertently excluded for the 2013 survey. Increased spending in fiscal 2014 is primarily due to implementation of the Healthy Michigan Plan. Other state funds include local funds of $73.0 million and provider taxes of $959.0

million for fiscal 2012; local funds of $96.5 million and provider taxes of $948.0 million for fiscal 2013; and local funds of $99.6 million and provider taxes of $833.3 million for fiscal 2014. Federal revenue support includes federal ARRA/FMAP funding of $31.5 million for fiscal 2012. Actual ARRA expenditures will be recorded with the fiscal 2014 annual financial report. Public health and community and institutional care for mentally and developmentally disabled persons are partially reported in the Medicaid totals.

(h) CHIP medical expenditures are included in Medicaid totals. Starting in 2014, CHIP staff is included in All Other Expenditures. Before 2014, CHIP staff was included in Medicaid totals as well.

(i) Medicaid Other State Funds: FY12/FY13/FY14 (in millions): Nursing Home Provider Tax $121/$134/$126; Other Assessments/Taxes/Fees $572/$571/$559. Beginning in FFY14, CHIP parents were moved to Medicaid (Title XIX).

(j) Previously Medicaid totals only included expenditures by the Department of Job and Family Services; however, now the category includes expenditures from other agencies.

(k) Regarding premium revenue: fiscal 2012 totals $291 million, fiscal 2013 totals $302 million, and fiscal 2014 totals $368 million. Certified Public Expenditures – Local fund from Hospitals: fiscal 2012 totals $374 million, fiscal 2013 totals $378 million, and fiscal 2014 totals $275 million. Nursing Home Tax: fiscal 2012 totals $82 million, fiscal 2013 totals $83 million, and fiscal 2014 totals $82 million. ICF/ MR 6 percent Gross Receipts Tax: fiscal 2012 totals $11 million, fiscal 2013 totals $14 million, and fiscal 2014 totals $11 million. Intergovernmental Transfers: fiscal 2012 totals $70 million, fiscal 2013 totals $70 million, and fiscal 2014 totals $100 million.

(l) The breakdown of local funds, etc. included in Other State Funds is as follows for fiscal 2012: provider tax $144,415,197; employee assessment $11,168,000; local match provided by schools $16,151,589; tobacco litigation settlement funds $36,978,473; other $100,859,035. The breakdown is as follows for fiscal 2013: provider tax $148,638,656; employee assessment $11,886,600; local match provided by schools $17,758,156; tobacco litigation settlement funds $31,343,693, other $124,012,725. The breakdown is as follows for estimated fiscal 2014: provider tax $154,109,028; employee assessment $12,995,400; local match provided by schools $19,206,889; tobacco litigation settlement funds $35,975,693, other $110,272,870.

(m) Declines in general fund Medicaid spending is partly attributable to Medicaid caseloads falling below previous levels in recent years, however there is an expectation that with the Affordable Care Act, caseloads will increase because of efforts to insure as many citizens as possible.

The Economic Recovery Continues, but State Finances Remain Weak

By Donald J. Boyd and Lucy Dadayan

The slow economic recovery, a fall-off in capital gains and a reluctance to raise taxes have combined to depress state tax revenue compared to past recoveries. States have had to make room for Medicaid spending driven by recession-induced enrollment increases. The result has been years of cuts in infrastructure spending, government employment, education and other areas, which in turn appear to have created pent-up demand, pressure to restore some cuts and a reluctance to cut spending much further.

The national economic recovery has been underway for six years, yet some states have announced budget shortfalls recently and several are even contemplating tax increases. Why are state finances so weak in the midst of recovery and what does it mean for state policy choices?

This economic recovery has been slower than past recoveries.

Employment is one of the most important economic indicators for state budget officials. It is a broad measure of the overall economy, and it plays a major role in determining wages subject to state

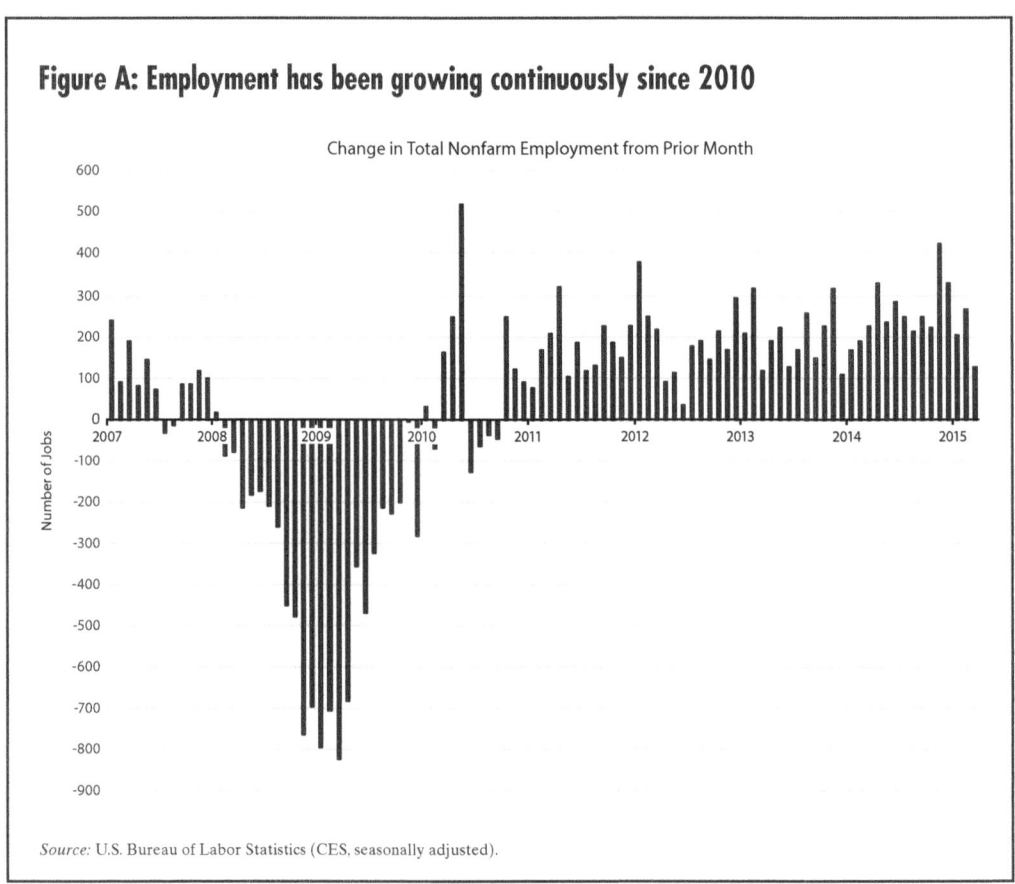

Figure A: Employment has been growing continuously since 2010

Change in Total Nonfarm Employment from Prior Month

Source: U.S. Bureau of Labor Statistics (CES, seasonally adjusted).

Figure B: Employment Is below where it was in past recoveries

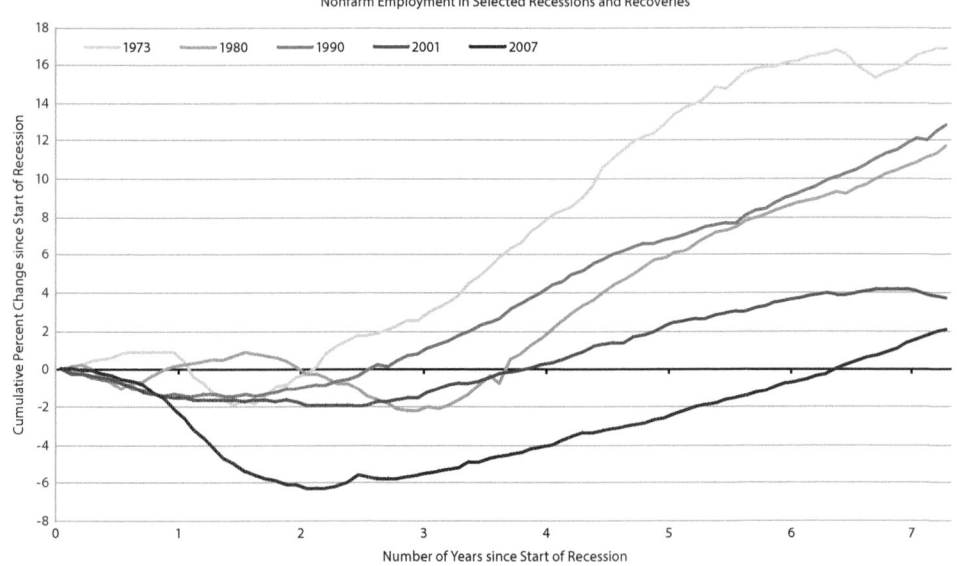

Nonfarm Employment in Selected Recessions and Recoveries

Source: U.S. Bureau of Labor Statistics (CES, seasonally adjusted).

Figure C: Inflation-adjusted consumer expenditures are far below expenditure levels in prior recoveries

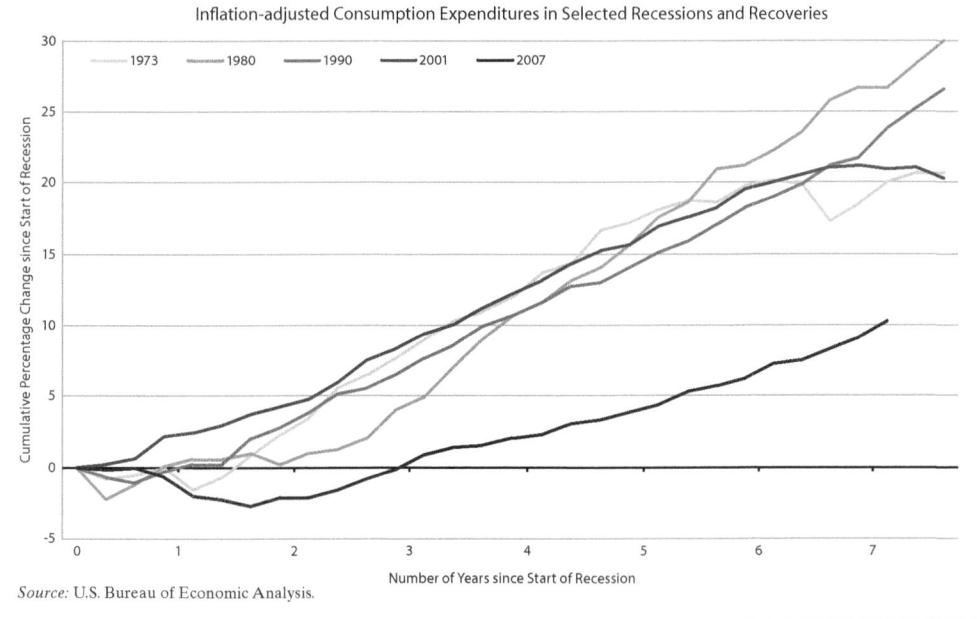

Inflation-adjusted Consumption Expenditures in Selected Recessions and Recoveries

Source: U.S. Bureau of Economic Analysis.

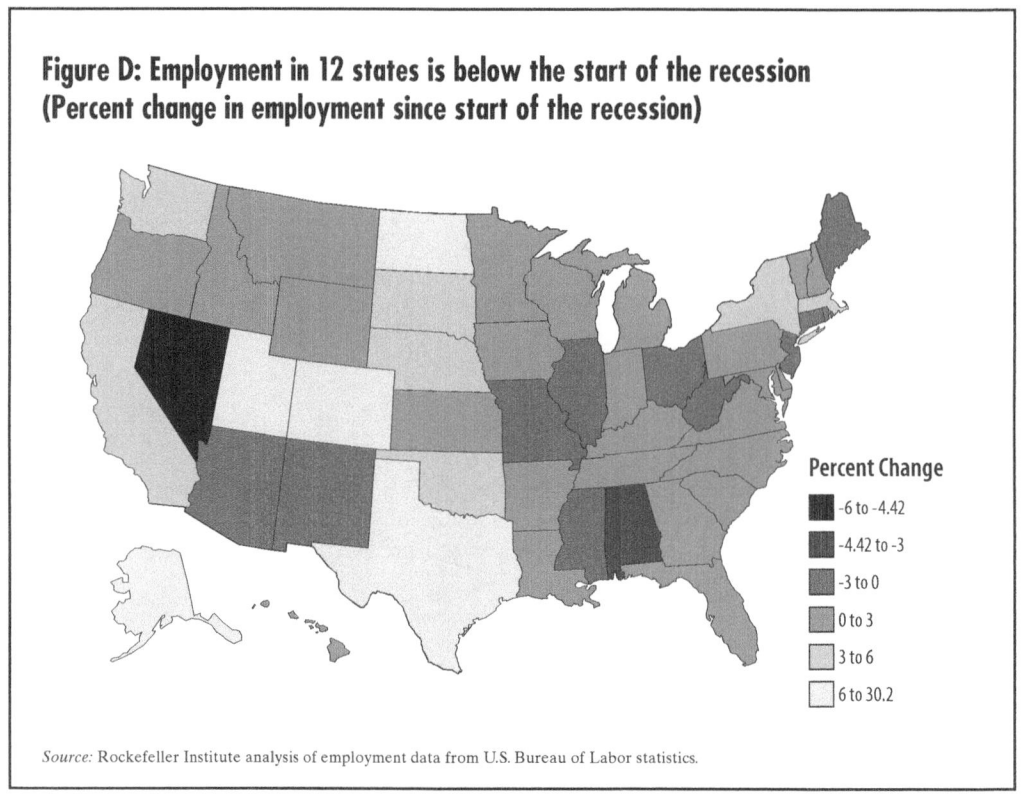

Figure D: Employment in 12 states is below the start of the recession
(Percent change in employment since start of the recession)

Percent Change
- -6 to -4.42
- -4.42 to -3
- -3 to 0
- 0 to 3
- 3 to 6
- 6 to 30.2

Source: Rockefeller Institute analysis of employment data from U.S. Bureau of Labor statistics.

income taxes and in supporting consumer purchases subject to state sales taxes. Employment has been recovering continuously since late 2010 with occasional slowing and acceleration.

While the extended employment recovery has been welcome news for states, it is slow by historical standards. Seven years after the start of the recession, employment is only 2 percent above its prior peak, compared to 3.7 percent at this point after the 2001 recession, and more than 12 percent for each of the three prior recessions.[1]

Consumer expenditures are important to state sales taxes, but the consumption recovery has been slower than the employment recovery relative to past recessions. Seven years after the recession's start, inflation-adjusted consumption is only 10 percent above its prior peak, compared to more than 20 percent for each of four major previous recessions.

The national data mask growth in some states and decline in others. Employment ranges from 30 percent above the recession's start in North Dakota—which benefited from an oil boom since gone bust—to 4.4 percent below in Nevada, which

was devastated by the recession but is now recovering, although it hasn't reached its prior peak. Employment in 12 states remains below the pre-recession peak of seven years ago.

The tax revenue recovery is slower than previous tax recoveries.

The weak economic recovery has caused tax revenue to be weak by historical standards. Seven years after the start of the recession, inflation-adjusted state government tax revenue is only 5 percent above pre-recession revenue, whereas in four major preceding recoveries, inflation-adjusted state tax revenue by this point ranged from 15 to 25 percent above pre-recession revenue.[2]

The corporate income tax, which plays a minor role in most states' revenue structures, is more than 15 percent below its 2007 level. The sales tax has been the weakest of the major taxes, reflecting the slow growth in consumption. The personal income tax, while stronger than the sales tax, has been held back by a huge decline in capital gains, which has recovered only partially. Other taxes have grown substantially, reflecting legislated increases

Figure E: Seven years after the recession started, tax revenue is only 5 percent above the prior peak and is far lower than in past recoveries

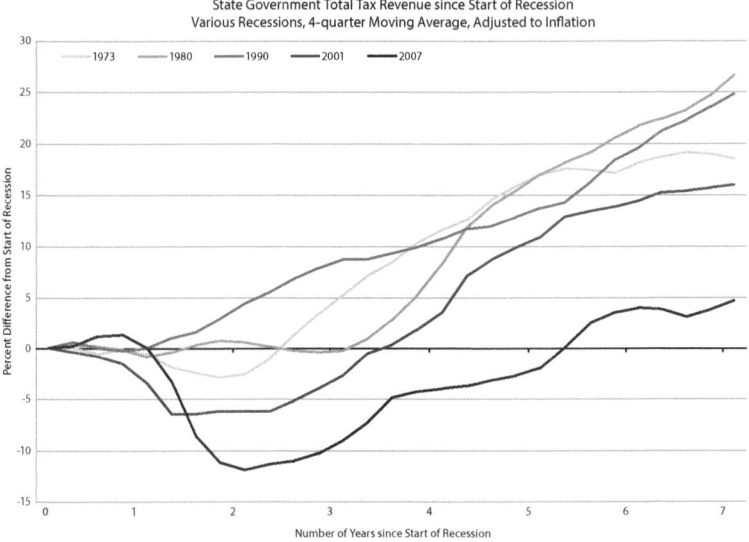

Source: Rockefeller Institute analysis of U.S. Census Bureau tax data.

Figure F: The sales tax is barely above pre-recession levels, the income tax is up only 4 percent, and the corporate income tax is 16 percent below its prior peak

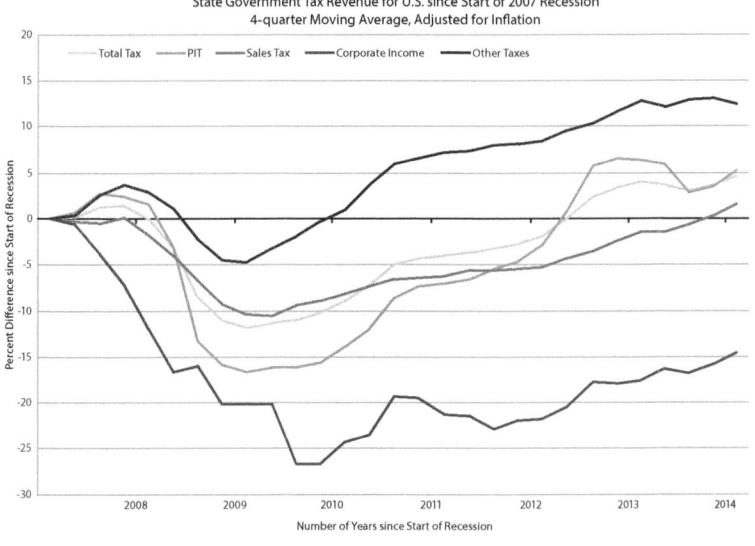

Source: Rockefeller Institute analysis of U.S. Census Bureau tax data.

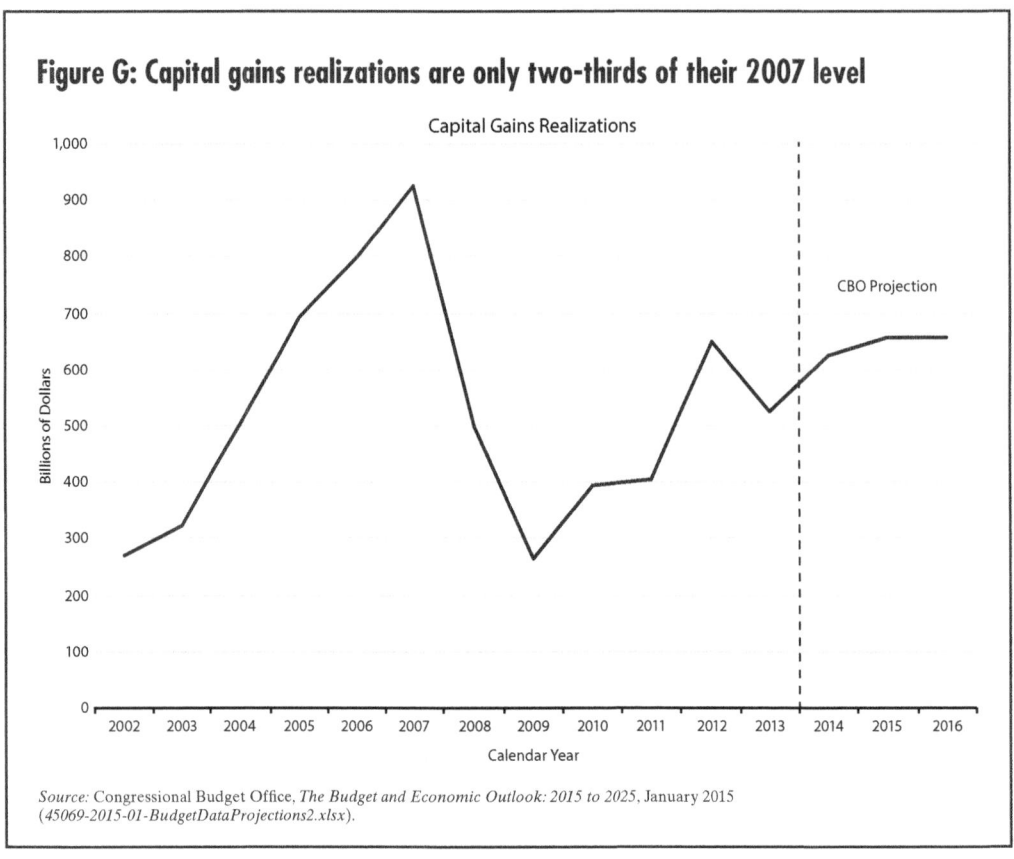

Figure G: Capital gains realizations are only two-thirds of their 2007 level

Capital Gains Realizations

CBO Projection

Billions of Dollars

Calendar Year

Source: Congressional Budget Office, *The Budget and Economic Outlook: 2015 to 2025*, January 2015 (*45069-2015-01-BudgetDataProjections2.xlsx*).

in taxes on cigarettes, motor fuel and other items. Figure F shows the path of revenue by tax type since the start of the recession.

State income taxes have been affected acutely by capital gains, which do not appear in traditional measures of the economy. Between 2007 and 2009, capital gains fell by 72 percent. They have since more than doubled, gyrating substantially in 2012 and 2013 as taxpayers moved money between tax years in response to expected and actual changes in federal tax rates.[3] Despite increases in 2010 through 2014, capital gains remain about a third below its 2007 peak, contributing to the relatively low level of the personal income tax.

In 2012, approximately three-quarters of net capital gains were claimed by the one-quarter of 1 percent of tax filers who had adjusted gross income of $1 million or more.[4] Thus, virtually all capital gains are taxed at the highest rates unless a state has a tax-rate preference for gains; decisions by relatively few taxpayers can have a large impact on state tax revenue. This volatility has been a source

of frustration to many state revenue forecasters and a cause of budget forecasting errors.[5]

State fortunes have varied, reflecting differences in economies, tax structures and tax policy choices. Inflation-adjusted tax revenue is up by 2.1 percent in the median state in the seven years since the start of the recession, but it ranges from a near-tripling in North Dakota to a decline of 57 percent in Alaska. North Dakota revenue was driven upward by its oil boom, while declines in Alaskan oil production and cuts in petroleum taxes drove Alaska tax revenue down. Inflation-adjusted tax revenue remains lower than its level at the start of the recession in 21 states, with Southeastern states faring particularly poorly (Figure H). It is not easy for elected officials to bring budgets in line with revenue that is lower than it was seven years ago.

Little support for tax increases.

Although the Great Recession drove state tax revenue down more than any other recession since the Great Depression, it did not lead to the larg-

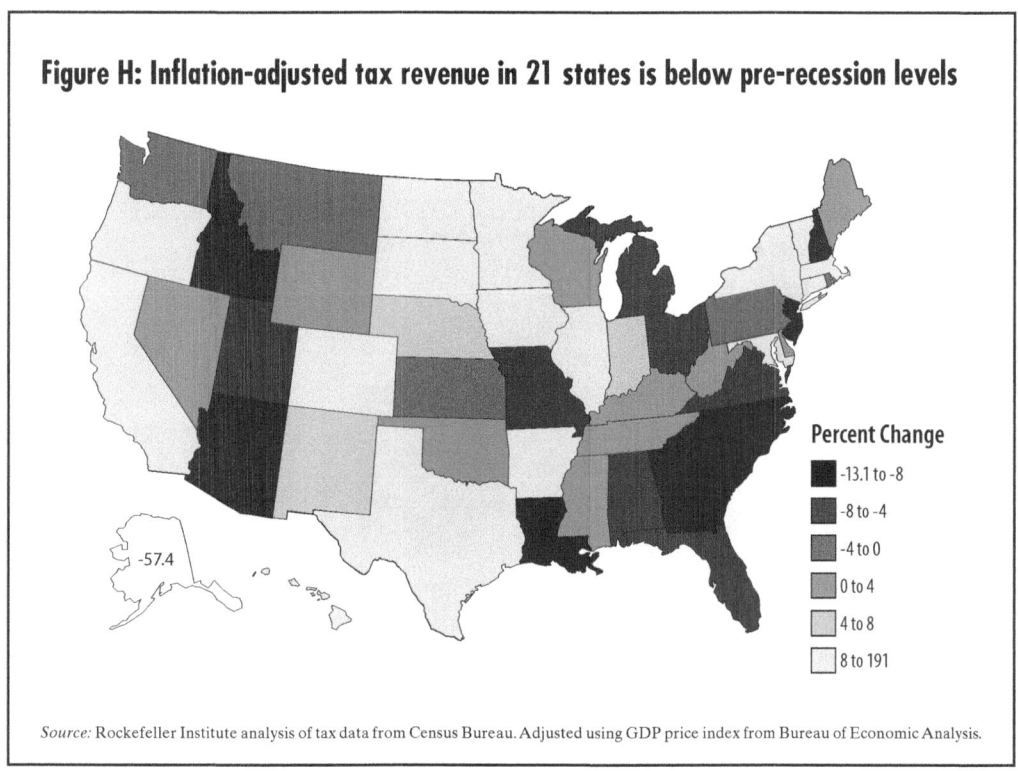

Figure H: Inflation-adjusted tax revenue in 21 states is below pre-recession levels

Percent Change
- -13.1 to -8
- -8 to -4
- -4 to 0
- 0 to 4
- 4 to 8
- 8 to 191

-57.4

Source: Rockefeller Institute analysis of tax data from Census Bureau. Adjusted using GDP price index from Bureau of Economic Analysis.

est tax increases. Table A shows state government legislated tax changes for boom and bust periods of the past 25 years, adjusted for inflation.[6] States raised taxes by $33 billion in the five years of greatest response to this recession, 38 percent less than the $54 billion raised in response to the 1990 recession.

The recent increases were greater than the $24 billion raised after the much milder and briefer 2001 recession, but that doesn't tell the full story. Very few states raised taxes significantly in the recent recession, with the top three — California, Illinois and New York — accounting for 81 percent of the total, compared to 50 percent for the top three responses to the 1991 recession. The next 47 states raised taxes by $12.1 billion in the 2001 response, versus only $6.4 billion in the 2007 response. Thus, large tax increases actually were more common after the mild 2001 recession than after the deep 2007 recession. This declining reliance on large tax increases is shown in Figure I.

Elected officials and the electorate have become extremely reluctant to rely on tax increases to close budget gaps. Public opinion polls and recent state government behavior do suggest that Americans are more likely to support taxes for transportation purposes.[7]

Spending pressures continue, but their character is changing.

A sea change in state and local government spending

The U.S. Bureau of Economic Analysis publishes estimates of aggregate state and local government spending on social benefits, approximately 80 percent of which is Medicaid; consumption, which includes spending for services such as teachers, police, firefighters and administrators; and investment, including construction spending on infrastructure, buildings and other investments. Investment data include gross investment expenditures and net investment after allowing for "capital consumption" to reflect the fact that assets generally are used up over time (e.g., roads and bridges deteriorate in quality). The bureau does not regularly break state and local government expenditure data into state government spending and local government spending.

Figure J shows inflation-adjusted social benefit, consumption and investment spending from 2000

Figure I: Large tax increases were far less common in response to the Great Recession than they were in response to the severe 1990 recession, or even the mild 2001 recession

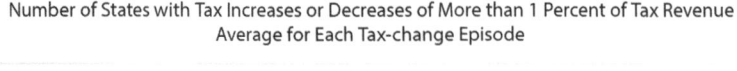

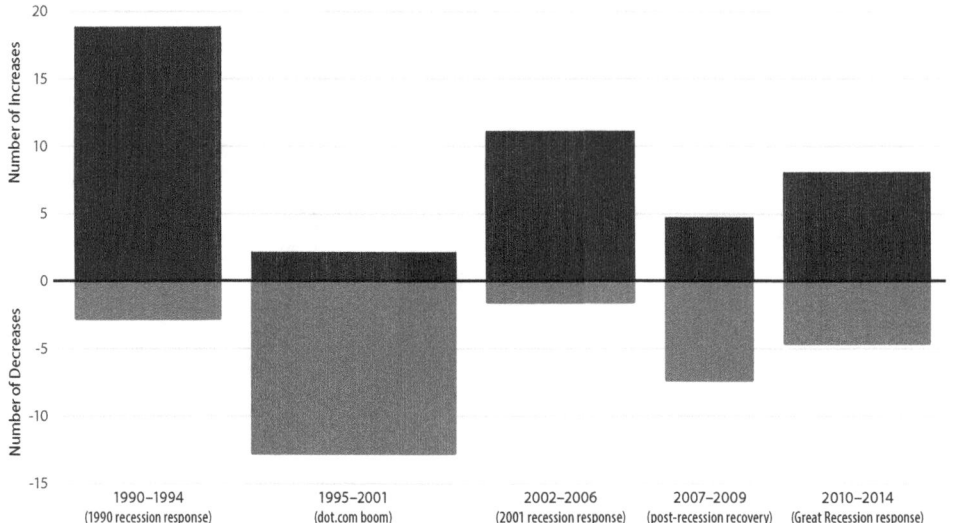

Number of States with Tax Increases or Decreases of More than 1 Percent of Tax Revenue
Average for Each Tax-change Episode

Sources: Rockefeller Institute analysis of tax-change data from National Association of State Budget Officers (NASBO) and tax revenue data from U.S. Census Bureau.

Table A: States raised taxes higher in response to the 1991 recession than they did in response to the 2001 and 2007 recessions

Legislated changes in state tax revenue, boom and bust episodes

| | | | | | Other taxes | | | | |
State fiscal years	Personal income tax	General sales tax	Corporate income tax	Total	Tobacco	Motor fuel	Alcohol	All other taxes	Total taxes
1990–1994 (1990 recession response)	$15,222	$14,339	$5,889	$18,713	$2,918	$5,435	$955	$9,405	$54,163
1995–2001 (dot.com boom)	-25,428	-2,620	-5,637	-11,927	1,597	768		-14,291	-45,613
2002–2006 (2001 recession response)	3,137	7,127	2,922	11,072	7,216	299	143	3,413	24,258
2007–2009 (post-recession recovery)	-4,060	1,312	1,869	-1,296	1,668	-30	14	-2,947	-2,176
2010–2014 (Great Recession response)	20,896	5,847	375	6,303	2,326	2,704	123	1,150	33,421

Sources: Rockefeller Institute analysis of data from the National Governors Association, *Fiscal Survey of the States* (various years) and from state websites.

Figure J: State and local spending on investment spending has declined sharply, consumption spending has leveled off, and socal benefit spending is rising

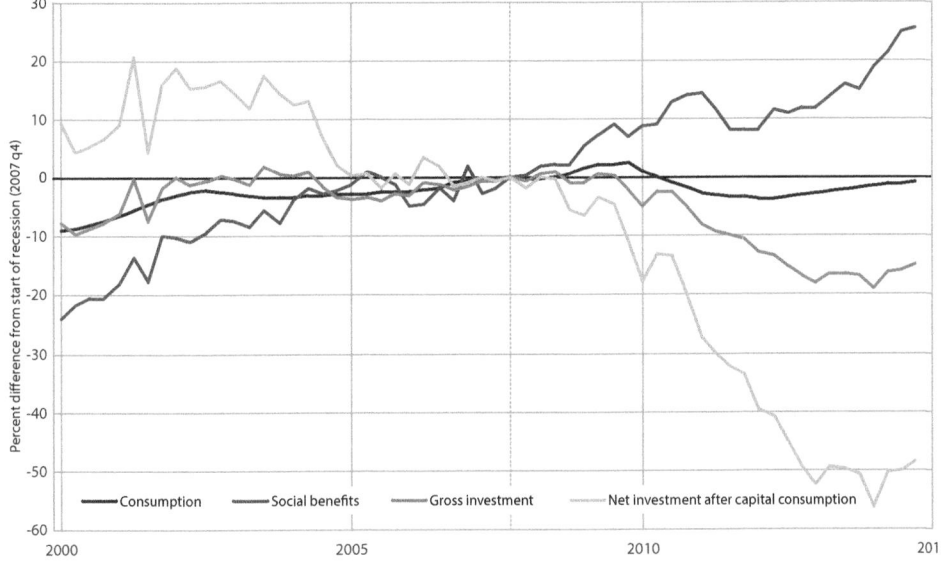

State and Local Government Inflation-adjusted Expenditure on Consumption, Social Benefits, and Investment Relative to Start of Recession (Marked by Dashed Vertical Line)

Source: Rockefeller Institute analysis of data from U.S. Bureau of Economic Analysis. Various tables, adjusted for inflation using category-specific prices indexes.

Table B: State and local government construction spending has declined since the recession's start

State and local government construction spending, adjusted for inflation Billions of 2014 dollars at annual rates, seasonally adjusted	Fourth quarter of:			
	2007	2014	$ change	% change
Total state and local construction	**$306.8**	**$256.5**	**-$50.3**	**-16.4%**
Transportation-related construction	**110.5**	**114.3**	**$3.7**	**3.4**
Pavement and other highway and street construction, excluding bridges	56.9	53.7	-$3.2	-5.6
Bridges	26.9	30.0	$3.1	11.4
Mass transit	4.3	7.6	$3.3	77.5
Other transportation (e.g., airport runways, and bus, rail and air passenger terminals)	22.5	23.1	$0.6	2.5
Education	**90.6**	**60.1**	**-$30.5**	**-33.7**
Primary and secondary education	63.2	34.4	-$28.8	-45.5
Higher education and other education	27.4	25.7	-$1.7	-6.3
Waste disposal and water supply	**42.3**	**35.9**	**-$6.4**	**-15.1**
Sewage and waste disposal (including waste water)	26.5	23.1	-$3.5	-13.1
Water supply	15.7	12.8	-$2.9	-18.5
Power (e.g., power plants and facilities for gathering storage, transmission, and distribution of electricity, oil and gas)	**13.2**	**10.3**	**-$2.9**	**-21.9**
Amusement and recreation (e.g., parks, camps, sports facilities, convention centers)	**11.7**	**8.9**	**-$2.8**	**-23.7**
Health care (primarily hospitals)	**8.1**	**6.2**	**-$1.9**	**-23.9**
Public safety	**9.7**	**6.2**	**-$3.6**	**-36.9**
Police stations, sherrifs' offices and related construction	1.6	1.7	$0.1	5.3
Fire stations, rescue squads, jails, prisons, other public safety	8.1	4.5	-$3.7	-45.2
All other construction	**20.6**	**14.7**	**-$5.9**	**-28.7**

Source: Rockefeller Institute analysis of data from the Census Bureau's Value of Construction Put in Place Survey (*http://www.census. gov/construction/c30/xls/s&lsatime.xls*). Data converted to quarterly and adjusted for inflation using the GDP price index from the U.S. Bureau of Economic Analysis.

Table C: States cut spending in most areas other than Medicaid and higher education

State government inflation-adjusted expenditures in billions of 2013 dollars	2003	2008	2013	$ change 2003–08	$ change 2008–13	% change 2003–08	% change 2008–13
General expenditures	**$1,432.4**	**$1,622.4**	**$1,683.2**	**$190.0**	**$60.8**	**13.3%**	**3.7%**
Education	**505.9**	**589.0**	**599.2**	**83.1**	**10.1**	**16.4**	**1.7**
Elementary and secondary education	289.7	331.5	318.4	41.8	-13.1	14.4	-3.9
Higher education and other education	216.2	257.5	280.7	41.3	23.2	19.1	9.0
Health and public welfare services	**496.0**	**567.4**	**649.9**	**71.4**	**82.5**	**14.4**	**14.5**
Medical vendor payments (primarily Medicaid)	260.8	310.1	399.1	49.4	89.0	18.9	28.7
Health and hospitals (generally excluding Medicaid)	109.1	124.5	130.7	15.5	6.2	14.2	5.0
Children's services, social services, cash assistance, low-income energy assistance, homeless services and other public welfare	126.1	132.7	120.0	6.6	-12.7	5.2	-9.6
Other major functions	**197.5**	**215.2**	**202.7**	**17.7**	**-12.5**	**9.0**	**-5.8**
Highways	105.5	115.7	112.2	10.2	-3.6	9.7	-3.1
Police and corrections	61.9	68.3	63.5	6.4	-4.8	10.3	-7.0
Natural resources, plus parks and recreation	30.1	31.1	27.0	1.1	-4.1	3.6	-13.3
Administration, interest and all other	**233.0**	**250.8**	**231.5**	**17.8**	**-19.4**	**7.6**	**-7.7**
Finance, judiciary, legislatures and other administration	54.0	57.6	52.8	3.5	-4.8	6.5	-8.3
Interest on debt	38.5	48.2	46.1	9.7	-2.1	25.3	-4.3
All other general expenditures	140.5	145.0	132.6	4.5	-12.5	3.2	-8.6
Exhibit: Amounts distributed within categories above							
Higher education, medical vendor payments and health and hospitals	586.1	692.2	810.5	106.1	118.4	18.1	17.1
Expenditures other than for higher education, medical vendor payments and health and hospitals	846.4	930.3	872.6	83.9	-57.6	9.9	-6.2
Salaries and wages	225.7	247.3	259.6	21.6	12.3	9.6	5.0
Capital outlays	104.4	116.0	108.7	11.6	-7.3	11.1	-6.3
Pension contributions	24.1	39.3	45.9	15.2	6.7	63.1	16.9

Source: Rockefeller Institute analysis of data from the Census Bureau's Value of Construction Put in Place Survey (*http://www.census. gov/construction/c30/xls/s&lsatime.xls*). Data converted to quarterly and adjusted for inflation using the GDP price index from the U.S. Bureau of Economic Analysis.

through 2014, relative to the fourth quarter of 2007 when the recession began.[8] Real gross investment fell by 15 percent since the start of the recession and net investment declined more than 45 percent. Social benefit spending has risen by about 25 percent, while consumption spending on many of the bread-and-butter services of government has declined slightly. This is a dramatic change from the previous five years.

Much of the recent decline in investment spending appears to reflect a decline in school building construction (see next section) rather than traditional infrastructure investment. Spending on transportation and water infrastructure, a large majority of infrastructure spending, has been relatively stable at about 2.5 percent of gross domestic product since the early 1980s.[9] Nonetheless, the recent sharp shift in investment expenditures indicates a very substantial change in state and local government spending.

Sharp declines in construction spending, particularly for school buildings.

According to U.S. Census Bureau data, inflation-adjusted state and local government construction spending declined by $48 billion at annual rates— 15.6 percent—between the fourth quarters of 2007 and 2014. Spending declined, or increased only negligibly, in every category other than bridges and mass transit (Table B).

Spending on primary and secondary education buildings accounted for more than half of the decline. This may reflect changing demographics. Growth in the number of primary and secondary education pupils slowed from 0.8 percent annually in 1996–2006 to 0.1 percent annually in 2006–13. High school enrollment also has declined for five consecutive years. The National Center for Education Statistics projects that the number of pupils will rise 0.6 percent annually from 2015 through 2023.[10]

Declines in most spending other than Medicaid.

State governments cut spending in most functional areas. Table C shows inflation-adjusted state government expenditures in 2008 before the federal stimulus package took effect, five years later in 2013 (latest available year), and five years earlier. The third from right column shows the dollar change in spending between 2008 and 2013, reflecting policy choices states made in response to the recession. The "Exhibit" block at the bottom shows selected groupings of expenditures included above.

Total general expenditures rose $190 billion — 13.3 percent — between 2003 and 2008, and then slowed as states responded to the recession, rising $60.8 billion — 3.7 percent — between 2008 and 2013.

Spending on higher education, medical vendor payments — similar in concept to Medicaid — and health and hospitals rose by $118.4 billion, or 17.1 percent, between 2008 and 2013; all other spending declined by $57.6 billion, or 6.2 percent. Pension contributions, while small relative to state budgets in aggregate, accounted for substantial spending growth in both periods.[11]

Spending on higher education includes spending from state support and from tuition and fees. Even though state governments cut their direct support in response to the recession, public higher education institutions raised tuition and fee revenue to help meet increased demand.[12, 13]

Medicaid expenditures were driven upward primarily by recession-related increases in enrollment.[14] Medicaid is largely an entitlement and as a practical matter, states needed to fund the spending at the expense of cuts elsewhere or higher taxes. States had substantial assistance early in the recession from the federal stimulus package.

States cut inflation-adjusted spending in almost every other significant area, despite growth in student enrollment and populations served by government programs.

States cut employment as they reduced spending. According to data from the U.S. Bureau of Labor Statistics, in the past five and a half years, states have cut non-education employment by 5.8 percent, compared with an increase in past recoveries of 18.7 percent for the typical, or median, recovery.[15]

More-detailed Census Bureau data show that between 2009 and 2013, states increased employment in higher education and health, but cut employment in other areas by 6.5 percent. Almost every major area was cut. The largest cuts were

to corrections at 10.4 percent, which may reflect changes in workload. The state prisoner population peaked in 2009, then fell 3.4 percent by 2013, reflecting changes in policies for sentencing, parole and probation, among other things.[16]

Special circumstances in many states.

A surprising number of states face special circumstances, most of which are contributing to fiscal stress. Some states face several of the stresses described below.

Connecticut, Kansas and New Jersey are struggling with the aftermath of well-publicized income tax revenue shortfalls at the end of the 2014 fiscal year that threw their 2015 budgets out of balance. Efforts to balance these budgets relied disproportionately on non-recurring revenue, in turn creating difficulties for their 2016 budgets.

Kansas cut taxes sharply in 2012 and 2013. In addition to the April 2014 income tax shortfall, it has had several rounds of subsequent significant revenue shortfalls. It faces difficult choices about the extent to which it should cut spending or modify elements of the tax cuts.

Illinois, Kentucky, New Jersey and Pennsylvania are struggling to accommodate increasing pension contributions that are required due to investment shortfalls and years of contribution underpayments.[17]

Falling oil prices are a threat to the finances of several oil producing states, either directly through their impact on severance taxes, or through their impact on the broader state economy. Alaska, Louisiana, New Mexico and Oklahoma are addressing revenue shortfalls or slowing revenue growth related to the drop in the price of oil. While North Dakota and Texas are also oil-rich states, the falling oil prices have had less impact on these states. Texas has a wider and more diverse economy and is not solely reliant on the energy sector. And in North Dakota, the general fund is well insulated from the fluctuations of oil price and production. By law, only $300 million of oil tax revenue is allowed to flow through to the general fund. The rest of the oil and gas tax collections are distributed to oil producing counties and tribes, as well as to several constitutional and statutory funds.

Looking ahead

State finances are tied closely to the economy. Major economic forecasters expect that the national economy will continue to improve throughout 2015 and 2016; inflation will be low, but gradually

Table D: The Congressional Budget Office projects continued economic improvement in a low-inflation environment, with gradually rising interest rates

Economic forecast for selected variables (Congressional Budget Office, January 2015)

	Calendar years			
	2014	*2015*	*2016*	*2017*
Growth rates (percentage change)				
Real GDP (inflation-adjusted)	2.3%	2.9%	3.0%	2.7%
Employment	1.8	1.9	1.3	1.0
Consumer prices (CPI-U)	1.7	1.1	2.2	2.3
Personal income	3.9	4.3	4.8	4.9
Wages	4.3	4.3	4.7	4.7
Non-wage personal income	3.2	4.0	4.1	5.0
Capital gains (not included in personal income)	18.5	5.2	0.2	2.1
Rates (percent)				
Unemployment rate	6.2	5.6	5.4	5.3
3-month Treasury bill	0.0	0.2	1.2	2.6
10-year Treasury note	2.6	2.8	3.4	3.9

Sources: Congressional Budget Office, *The Budget and Economic Outlook: 2015 to 2025*, January 2015, *www.cbo.gov/publication/49892*.
(Files: 45066-2015-01-EconomicDataProjections2.xlsx and 45069-2015-01-BudgetDataProjections2.xlsx)

rising, and interest rates will rise slightly.[18] The Congressional Budget Office's January 2015 forecast is in line with this consensus (see Table D).[19]

This forecast suggests relatively slow growth in tax revenue.

Income taxes generally grow faster than the economy. As incomes rise due to inflation and productivity increases, more income is taxed at higher rates. Capital gains and other financial market income can alter income tax growth substantially, but CBO forecasts that capital gains will grow only slightly faster than income in 2015, and more slowly in later years.[20]

Retirement income — including federally taxable portions of pensions, Social Security income and IRA distributions — is another potential source of faster growth. It has been driven upward by an aging population and, in the case of IRA distributions, growth in financial assets. Between 2007 and 2012 wages grew by 7 percent, but these income sources grew by 35 percent.[21] However, most states exempt some of this federally taxable income in an apparent effort to lure seemingly footloose senior citizens, despite the absence of evidence that state income tax breaks affect elderly migration.[22, 23] Illinois, arguably the most fiscally stressed state, exempts all retirement income from tax, including IRA distributions.[24]

General sales taxes have been growing more slowly than the economy for more than 40 years.[25]

This is a result of the difficulty in taxing services and of collecting tax on Internet sales, among other things. Slow sales tax growth is likely to continue.

Selective sales taxes and licenses — such as taxes on cigarettes, motor fuel and alcohol — usually are based on the quantity of the good sold (for example, 15 cents per gallon of gas or $3 per pack of cigarettes), rather than on the sales price. Two of the largest selective sales taxes, motor fuel taxes and cigarette taxes, have long-term downward trends. Fuel economy improvements have led to declines in gasoline consumption, while cigarette consumption has declined in response to government efforts to reduce smoking. In aggregate, these taxes generally decline except when increased legislatively.

Income, general sales, and selective sales and license taxes account for nearly 90 percent of state taxes. The current economic environment suggests that slow growth is likely for these taxes.

Conclusion

The slow economic recovery, a fall-off in capital gains and a reluctance to raise taxes have combined to depress state tax revenue compared to past recoveries. States also have had to make room for Medicaid spending driven by recession-induced enrollment increases. The result has been years of cuts in infrastructure spending, government employment, education and other areas, which in turn appear to have created pent-up demand, pressure to restore some cuts, and reluctance to cut spending much further.

These pressures have been exacerbated by special circumstances in many states — circumstances that mostly increase fiscal stress. Several states need to increase pension contributions significantly to pay now for services delivered in the past, driven by years of shirking and by investment income shortfalls. A few states are struggling to live within the confines of large tax cuts. Other states face pressures to find revenue to fund transportation. Many oil producing states are finding their economies out of phase with the national recovery, facing new revenue shortfalls while most other states' revenue has stabilized.

The net result of these forces has been budget shortfalls in several states and fiscal stress in many.

Looking forward, mainstream economic forecasts for 2015 for the U.S. as a whole call for low inflation, with nominal income growth in the 4 to 5 percent range. Absent booming financial markets or other special factors, income and sales tax revenue growth for the U.S. is unlikely to fall far outside the 4 to 5 percent range — on the high side in the case of income taxes and on the low side in the case of sales taxes. This is not likely to be enough to restore spending cuts, fund infrastructure expansion, pay for Medicaid growth and cover the costs of past promises. States face difficult choices in the midst of growth.

Notes

[1] The recovery from the 2001 recession was historically weak but, employment did get more than 4 percent above its prior peak. Seven years after the start of that recession, employment was again heading downward, reflecting the onset of the Great Recession. The graph does not show the 1981 recession separately; rather, it is included in the period after the 1980 recession.

[2] We use the four-quarter moving average of tax revenue, adjusted for inflation with the gross domestic product price index from the U.S. Bureau of Economic Analysis. As with our analysis of economic recoveries, we treat the 1981 recession as part of the 1980 recession.

[3] We have written about these gyrations and the incentives that caused them in several state revenue reports during the relevant time period, available at *http://www.rockinst.org/government_finance/*.

[4] Authors' calculations from Table 2. Individual Income and Tax Data, by State and Size of Adjusted Gross Income, Tax Year 2012, Statistics of Income, Internal Revenue Service, 12in54cm.xlsx, *http://www.irs.gov/file_source/pub/irs-soi/12in54cm.zip* and *http://www.irs.gov/file_source/pub/irs-soi/12in54cmcsv.csv*.

[5] "States' Revenue Estimating: Cracks in the Crystal Ball" (Pew Center on the States and Rockefeller Institute of Government, March 2011). Donald J. Boyd and Lucy Dadayan, *State Tax Revenue Forecasting Accuracy* (The Nelson A. Rockefeller Institute of Government, September 2014), *http://216.7.28.163/pdf/government_finance/state_revenue_report/2014-09-30-Revenue_Forecasting_Accuracy.pdf*. Managing Volatile Tax Collections in State Revenue Forecasts (The Pew Charitable Trusts and the Nelson A. Rockefeller Institute of Government, March 2015), *http://www.pewtrusts.org/~/media/Assets/2015/03/StateRevenueForecastingReportARTFINALv4web.pdf?la=en*.

[6] The table is based on data reported in the *Fiscal Survey of the States*, compiled annually by the National Association of State Budget Officers and the National Governors Association, supplemented with information from state sources for selected large actions taken outside of the survey periods. We have divided years into episodes of response to boom and bust based upon clear patterns in the data. We adjusted for inflation using the gross domestic product price index from the U.S. Bureau of Economic Analysis.

[7] Asha W. Agrawal and Hilary Nixon, "What Do Americans Think about Federal Transportation Tax Options? Results from Year Five of a National Survey," Mineta Transportation Institute, no. Report 12–36 (June 2014), *http://works.bepress.com/cgi/viewcontent.cgi?article=1005&context=hilary_nixon*.

[8] The data are adjusted for inflation using price indexes specific to each category. Price indexes were chosen based on conversations with staff of the BEA.

[9] Much of the decline in real state and local government infrastructure spending in the late 2000s and early 2010s was not a decline in "effort" by state and local governments, but rather reflected increases in the prices of goods and services needed to build and maintain infrastructure. (See *Public Spending on Transportation and Water Infrastructure, 1956 to 2014* (Congressional Budget Office, March 2015).) According to CBO, real transportation and water infrastructure capital spending fell 23 percent from 2003 to 2014 when adjusted for inflation using input price indexes. However, when adjusted using the GDP price index, real infrastructure spending actually rose by 11 percent (authors' calculations). Put differently, state and local governments were trying harder, but getting less for their money due to input price increases.

[10] Authors' analysis of data in Table 203.10 of the 2013 Digest of Education Statistics, National Center for Education Statistics.

[11] Pension contributions vary greatly around the country. In general they are a larger share of local government budgets than state budgets, and in some states they are increasingly important.

[12] Spending on higher education includes spending from tuition and fees as well as from direct support.

[13] Michael Mitchell, Vincent Palacios, and Michael Leachman, "States Are Still Funding Higher Education below Pre-Recession Levels," Center on Budget and Policy Priorities, 2014, *http://www.cbpp.org/files/5-1-14sfp.pdf*.

[14] Rachel Garfield et al., *Trends in Medicaid Spending Leading up to ACA Implementation* (Kaiser Commission on Medicaid and the Uninsured, February 2015), *http://files.kff.org/attachment/issue-brief-trends-in-medicaid-spending-leading-up-to-aca-implementation*.

[15] Authors' analysis of Current Employment Statistics from the U.S. Bureau of Labor Statistics.

[16] For prisoner statistics, see E. Ann Carson, *Prisoners in 2013* (U.S. Bureau of Justice Statistics, September 2014).

[17] For pension contribution underpayments see Chris Mier, *Twelfth Annual Public Pension Funding Review* (Loop Capital Markets, September 2014).

[18] See *http://projects.wsj.com/econforecast/* and *http://www.philadelphiafed.org/research-and-data/real-time-center/survey-of-professional-forecasters/* for surveys of major forecasters, and see *http://online.wsj.com/public/resources/documents/wsjecon0315.xls* for the latest forecasts available at this writing.

[19] We use the CBO forecast because it is a well-regarded high-quality forecast developed from an internally consistent model, and because CBO publishes details that are useful for analysis of tax revenue. It is not necessarily likely to be more or less accurate than other forecasts. *The Wall Street Journal* and the Philadelphia Federal Reserve Bank surveys report averages of major forecasts, and thus their reported numbers are not produced by a single internally consistent model. This makes them less useful for revenue analysis than the CBO forecast.

[20] For useful discussions of these issues see D.J. Boyd and L. Dadayan, "Revenue Declines Less Severe, But States' Fiscal Crisis Is Far From Over," *State Revenue Report* (The Nelson A. Rockefeller Institute of Government, April 2010); David L. Sjoquist, Andrew V. Stephenson, and Sally Wallace, "The Impact of Tax Revenue from Capital Gains Realizations on State Income Tax Revenue and Budget Conditions," *Public Budgeting and Finance*, Winter 2011; and Norton Francis and Sarah Gault, *Federal Tax Policy Uncertainty and State Revenue Estimates*, State and Local Finance Initiative (Urban Institute, March 2015), *http://www.urban.org/UploadedPDF/2000125-federal-tax-policy-uncertainty-and-state-tax-revenue-estimates.pdf*.

[21] Authors' calculations from Table 2. Individual Income and Tax Data, by State and Size of Adjusted Gross Income, Statistics of Income, Internal Revenue Service, various years, and *http://www.irs.gov/file_source/pub/irs-soi/12in54cmcsv.csv*.

[22] Karen Smith Conway and Jonathan C. Rork, "No Country for Old Men (or Women)—Do State Tax Policies Drive Away the Elderly?," *National Tax Journal* 65, no. 2 (2012): 313–56.

[23] Karen Smith Conway and Jonathan C. Rork, "State Income Tax Preferences for the Elderly," *Andrew Young School of Policy Studies Research Paper Series*, no. 07–20 (2007), *http://papers.ssrn.com/sol3/papers.cfm?abstract_id=989660*. Ron Snell, *State Personal Income Taxes on Pensions and Retirement Income: Tax Year 2010* (National Conference of State Legislatures, February 2011), *http://www.ncsl.org/documents/ fiscal/taxonpensions2011.pdf*.

[24] Note that exemptions for IRA distributions appear to be less common than exemptions for pension or Social Security income.

[24] Jeffrey R. Brown, *Including Retirement Income in the Illinois Income Tax Base*, Illinois Budget Policy Toolbox (University of Illinois Institute of Government and Public Affairs, February 27, 2014).

[25] John L. Mikesell, "The Disappearing Retail Sales Tax," *State Tax Notes*, March 5, 2012.

About the Authors

Donald J. Boyd is a senior fellow at the Rockefeller Institute of Government and the former director of the Institute's State and Local Government Finance research group. Boyd has over three decades of experience analyzing state and local fiscal issues, and has written or co-authored many of the program's reports on the fiscal climate in the 50 states. His previous positions include executive director of the State Budget Crisis Task Force created by former Federal Reserve Board Chairman Paul Volcker and former New York Lieutenant Governor Richard Ravitch, director of the economic and revenue staff for the New York State Division of the Budget, and director of the tax staff for the New York State Assembly Ways and Means Committee. Boyd holds a Ph.D. in managerial economics from Rensselaer Polytechnic Institute.

Lucy Dadayan is a senior policy analyst at the Rockefeller Institute and contributed to the work of the State Budget Crisis Task Force throughout its first phase. Dadayan holds a Ph.D in Informatics from the University of Albany.

Table 7.9
STATE TAX AMNESTY PROGRAMS, 1982–Present

State or other jurisdiction	Amnesty period	Legislative authorization	Major taxes covered	Accounts receivable included	Collections ($ millions) (a)	Installment arrangements permitted (b)
Alabama	1/20/84–4/1/84	No (c)	All	No	3.2	No
	2/1/09–5/15/09	Yes	Ind. Income, Corp. Income, Business, Sales and Use	N.A.	8.1	N.A.
Arizona	11/22/82–1/20/83	No (c)	All	No	6.0	Yes
	1/1/02–2/28/02	Yes	Individual income	No	N.A.	No
	9/1/03–10/31/03	Yes	All (t)	N.A.	73.0	Yes
	5/1/09–6/1/09	N.A.	All	N.A.	32.0	N.A.
	9/1/15–10/31/15	Yes	N.A.	N.A.	N.A.	N.A.
Arkansas	9/1/87–11/30/87	Yes	All	No	1.7	Yes
	7/1/04–12/31/04	Yes	All	N.A.	N.A.	No
California	12/10/84–3/15/85	Yes	Individual income	Yes	154.0	Yes
		Yes	Sales	No	43.0	Yes
	2/1/05–3/31/05	Yes	Income, Franchise, Sales	N.A.	N.A.	Yes
Colorado	9/16/85–11/15/85	Yes	All	No	6.4	Yes
	6/1/03–6/30/03	N.A.	All	N.A.	18.4	Yes
	10/1/11–11/15/11	Yes	All	No	N.A.	No
Connecticut	9/1/90–11/30/90	Yes	All	Yes	54.0	Yes
	9/1/95–11/30/95	Yes	All	Yes	46.2	Yes
	9/1/02–12/2/02	N.A.	All	N.A.	109.0	N.A.
	5/1/09–6/25/09	Yes	All	No	40.0	No
	9/16/13–11/15/13	Yes	All	Yes	193.5	No
Delaware	9/1/09–10/30/09	Yes	All	Yes	N.A.	Yes
Florida	1/1/87–6/30/87	Yes	Intangibles	No	13.0	No
	1/1/88–6/30/88	Yes (d)	All	No	8.4 (d)	No
	7/1/03–10/31/03	Yes	All	N.A.	80.0	N.A.
	7/1/10–9/30/10	Yes	All	Yes	N.A.	Yes
Georgia	10/1/92–12/5/92	Yes	All	Yes	51.3	No
Hawaii	5/27/09–6/26/09	N.A.	All	No	14.0	No
Idaho	5/20/83–8/30/83	No (c)	Individual income	No	0.3	No
Illinois	10/1/84–11/30/84	Yes	All (u)	Yes	160.5	No
	10/1/03–11/17/03	Yes	All	N.A.	532.0	N.A.
	10/1/10–11/8/10	Yes	All	Yes	314 (y)	No
Indiana	9/15/05–11/15/05	N.A.	All	N.A.	255.0	Yes
Iowa	9/2/86–10/31/86	Yes	All	Yes	35.1	N.A.
	9/4/07–10/31/07	Yes	All	Yes	N.A.	N.A.
Kansas	7/1/84–9/30/84	Yes	All	No	0.6	No
	10/1/03–11/30/03	Yes	All	Yes	53.7	N.A.
	9/1/10–10/15/10	Yes	All	Yes	N.A.	No
Kentucky	9/15/88–9/30/88	Yes (c)	All	No	100.0	No
	8/1/02–9/30/02	Yes (c)	All	No	100.0	No
	10/1/12–11/30/12	Yes	All	Yes	N.A.	N.A.
Louisiana	10/1/85–12/31/85	Yes	All	No	1.2	Yes (f)
	10/1/87–12/15/87	Yes	All	No	0.3	Yes (f)
	10/1/98–12/31/98	Yes	All	No (q)	1.3	No
	9/1/01–10/30/01	Yes	All	Yes	192.9	No
	9/1/09–10/31/09	Yes	All	N.A.	303.7	N.A.
	9/23/13–11/22/13	Yes	All	Yes	435.0	No
	10/15/14–11/14/14	Yes	All	Yes	N.A.	Yes
Maine	11/1/90–12/31/90	Yes	All	Yes	29.0	Yes
	9/1/03–11/30/03	Yes	All	N.A.	37.6	N.A.
	9/1/09–11/30/09	Yes	All	Yes	16.2	No
Maryland	9/1/87–11/2/87	Yes	All	Yes	34.6 (g)	No
	9/1/01–10/31/01	Yes	All	Yes	39.2	No
	9/1/09–10/31/09	Yes	Income, Withholding, Sales and Use	Yes	9.6	Yes
Massachusetts	10/17/83–1/17/84	Yes	All	Yes	86.5	Yes (h)
	10/1/02–11/30/02	Yes	All	Yes	96.1	Yes
	1/1/03–2/28/03	Yes	All	Yes	11.2	N.A.
	4/1/10–6/1/10	Yes	All	Yes	32.6	No
	9/2/14–10/31/14	Yes	All	Yes	N.A.	No
	3/16/15–5/15/15	Yes	Corporate	Yes	N.A.	No

See footnotes at end of table.

STATE TAX AMNESTY PROGRAMS, 1982–Present — Continued

State or other jurisdiction	Amnesty period	Legislative authorization	Major taxes covered	Accounts receivable included	Collections ($ millions) (a)	Installment arrangements permitted (b)
Michigan	5/12/86–6/30/86	Yes	All	Yes	109.8	No
	5/15/02–6/30/02	Yes	All	Yes	N.A.	N.A.
	5/15/11–6/30/11	Yes	All	Yes	76.0	No
Minnesota	8/1/84–10/31/84	Yes	All	Yes	12.1	No
Mississippi	9/1/86–11/30/86	Yes	All	No	1.0	No
	9/1/04–12/31/04	Yes	All	No	7.9	No
Missouri	9/1/83–10/31/83	No (c)	All	No	0.9	No
	8/1/02–10/31/02	Yes	All	Yes	76.4	N.A.
	8/1/03–10/31/03	Yes	All	Yes	20.0	N.A.
Nebraska	8/1/04–10/31/04	Yes	All	No	7.5	No
Nevada	2/1/02–6/30/02	N.A.	All	N.A.	7.3	N.A.
	7/1/08–10/28/08	No	Sales, Business, License	Yes	N.A.	No
	7/1/10–10/1/10	Yes	All	Yes	N.A.	No
New Hampshire	12/1/97–2/17/98	Yes	All	Yes	13.5	No
	12/1/01–2/15/02	Yes	All	Yes	13.5	N.A.
New Jersey	9/10/87–12/8/87	Yes	All	Yes	186.5	Yes
	3/15/96–6/1/96	Yes	All	Yes	359.0	No
	4/15/02–6/10/02	Yes	All	Yes	276.9	N.A.
	5/4/09–6/15/09	Yes	All	N.A.	725.0	N.A.
	10/1/14–11/17/14	N.A.	All	Yes	N.A.	No
New Mexico	8/15/85–11/13/85	Yes	All (i)	No	13.6	Yes
	8/16/99–11/12/99	Yes	All	Yes	45.0	Yes
	6/7/10–9/30/10	Yes	All	No	N.A.	Yes
New York	11/1/85–1/31/86	Yes	All (j)	Yes	401.3	Yes
	11/1/96–1/31/97	Yes	All	Yes	253.4	Yes (o)
	11/18/02–1/31/03	Yes	All	Yes	582.7	Yes (s)
	10/1/05–3/1/06	N.A.	Income, Corporate	N.A.	349.0	N.A.
	1/15/10–3/15/10	Yes	All	Yes	56.5	No
New York City	10/20/03–1/23/04	Yes	All (v)	Yes (w)	N.A.	No
North Carolina	9/1/89–12/1/89	Yes	All (k)	Yes	37.6	No
North Dakota	9/1/83–11/30/83	No (c)	All	No	0.2	Yes
	10/1/03–1/31/04	Yes	N.A.	N.A.	6.9	N.A.
Ohio	10/15/01–1/15/02	Yes	All	No	48.5	No
	1/1/06–2/15/06	Yes	All	No	63.0	No
Oklahoma	7/1/84–12/31/84	Yes	Income, Sales	Yes	13.9	No (l)
	8/15/02–11/15/02	N.A.	All (r)	Yes	N.A.	N.A.
	9/15/08–11/14/08	Yes	All	Yes	81.0	Yes
Oregon	10/1/09–11/19/09	Yes	Personal, Corporate, Inheritance	N.A.	N.A.	N.A.
Pennsylvania	10/13/95–1/10/96	Yes	All	Yes	N.A.	No
	4/26/10–6/18/10	Yes	All	Yes	261.0	No
Rhode Island	10/15/86–1/12/87	Yes	All	No	0.7	Yes
	4/15/96–6/28/96	Yes	All	Yes	7.9	Yes
	7/15/06–9/30/06	N.A.	All	Yes	6.5	Yes
	9/2/12–11/15/12	Yes	All	Yes	22.3	Yes
South Carolina	9/1/85–11/30/85	Yes	All	Yes	7.1	Yes
	10/15/02–12/2/02	Yes	All	Yes	66.2	N.A.
South Dakota	4/1/99–5/15/99	Yes	All	Yes	0.5	N.A.
Texas	2/1/84–2/29/84	No (c)	All (m)	No	0.5	No
	3/11/04–3/31/04	No (c)	All (m)	No	N.A.	No
	6/15/07–8/15/07	No (c)	All (m)	No	100	No
	6/12/12–8/17/12	No (c)	All (m)	No	100	No
Vermont	5/15/90–6/25/90	Yes	All	Yes	1 (e)	No
	7/20/09–8/31/09	Yes	All	N.A.	2.2	N.A.
Virginia	2/1/90–3/31/90	Yes	All	Yes	32.2	No
	9/2/03–11/3/03	Yes	All	Yes	98.3	N.A.
	10/7/09–12/5/09	Yes	All	Yes	102.1	No

See footnotes at end of table.

STATE TAX AMNESTY PROGRAMS, 1982–Present — Continued

State or other jurisdiction	Amnesty period	Legislative authorization	Major taxes covered	Accounts receivable included	Collections ($ millions) (a)	Installment arrangements permitted (b)
Washington....................	2/1/11–4/30/11	Yes	All		Yes	346.0	No
West Virginia................	10/1/86–12/31/86	Yes	All		Yes	15.9	Yes
	9/1/04–10/31/04	Yes	All		N.A.	10.4	Yes
Wisconsin	9/15/85–11/22/85	Yes	All		Yes (n)	27.3	Yes
	6/15/98–8/14/98	Yes	All		Yes	30.9	N.A.
Dist. of Columbia	7/1/87–9/30/87	Yes	All		Yes	24.3	Yes
	7/10/95–8/31/95	Yes	All (p)		Yes	19.5	Yes (p)
	8/2/10–9/30/10	Yes	All (p)		Yes	N.A.	No
No. Mariana Islands	9/30/05–3/30/06	Yes	All		N.A.	N.A.	N.A.

Source: The Federation of Tax Administrators, March 2015.

Key:

N.A. — Not available.

(a) Where applicable, figure includes local portions of certain taxes collected under the state tax amnesty program.

(b) "No" indicates requirement of full payment by the expiration of the amnesty period. "Yes" indicates allowance of full payment after the expiration of the amnesty period.

(c) Authority for amnesty derived from pre-existing statutory powers permitting the waiver of tax penalties.

(d) Does not include intangibles tax and drug taxes. Gross collections totaled $22.1 million, with $13.7 million in penalties withdrawn.

(e) Preliminary figure.

(f) Amnesty taxpayers were billed for the interest owed, with payment due within 30 days of notification.

(g) Figure includes $1.1 million for the separate program conducted by the Department of Natural Resources for the boat excise tax.

(h) The amnesty statute was construed to extend the amnesty to those who applied to the department before the end of the amnesty period, and permitted them to file overdue returns and pay back taxes and interest at a later date.

(i) The severance taxes, including the six oil and gas severance taxes, the resources excise tax, the corporate franchise tax, and the special fuels tax were not subject to amnesty.

(j) Availability of amnesty for the corporation tax, the oil company taxes, the transporation and transmissions companies tax, the gross receipts oil tax and the unincorporated business tax restricted to entities with 500 or fewer employees in the United States on the date of application. In addition, a taxpayer principally engaged in aviation, or a utility subject to the supervision of the State Department of Public Service was also ineligible.

(k) Local taxes and real property taxes were not included.

(l) Full payment of tax liability required before the end of the amnesty period to avoid civil penalties.

(m) Texas does not impose a corporate or individual income tax. In practical effect, the amnesty was limited to the sales tax and other excises.

(n) Waiver terms varied depending upon the date the tax liability was assessed.

(o) Installment arrangements were permitted if applicant demonstrated that payment would present a severe financial hardship.

(p) Does not include real property taxes. All interest was waived on tax payments made before July 31, 1995. After this date, only 50% of the interest was waived.

(q) Exception for individuals who owed $500 or less.

(r) Except for property and motor fuel taxes.

(s) Multiple payments could be made so long as the required balance was paid in full no later than March 15, 2003.

(t) All taxes except property, estate and unclaimed property.

(u) Does not include the motor fuel use tax.

(v) All NYC taxes administered by the NYC Dept. of Finance are covered except for Real Estate Tax. NYC Sales and Use Tax and NYC Resident Personal Income Tax also are not covered because they are administered by the NYC Dept. of Taxation and Finance.

(w) Taxpayers under audit as of 3/10/03 are ineligible; Taxpayers with an existing installment agreement are ineligible; Taxpayers under criminal investigation are ineligible; Taxpayers party to an administrative or court proceding must withdraw as a condition.

(x) The Massachusetts Department of Revenue was required to hold an amnesty to end before June 30, 2010.

(y) In Illinois, the 2010 Amnesty called collected a total of $717 million, $314 million for the state GF and the rest for local governments

Table 7.10a
STATE EXCISE TAX RATES
(As of January 1, 2015)

State or other jurisdiction	General sales and gross receipts tax (percent)	Cigarettes (cents per pack of 20)	Distilled spirits	
			Excise tax rate ($ per gallon)	Sales taxes applied
Alabama	4.0	42.5 (e)	(j)	Yes
Alaska	none	200	12.8 (l)	...
Arizona	5.6	200	3	Yes
Arkansas	6.5	115	2.5 (l)	Yes
California	7.5 (b)	87	3.3 (l)	Yes
Colorado	2.9	84	2.28	Yes
Connecticut	6.35	340	5.4 (l)	Yes
Delaware	none	160	3.75 (l)	...
Florida	6.0	133.9 (f)	6.5 (l)	Yes
Georgia	4.0	37	3.79 (l)	Yes
Hawaii	4.0	320	5.98	Yes
Idaho	6.0	57	(j)	Yes
Illinois	6.25	198 (e)	8.55 (l)	Yes
Indiana	7.0	99.5	2.68 (l)	Yes
Iowa	6.0	136	(j)	Yes
Kansas	6.15	79	2.5 (l)	...
Kentucky	6.0	60 (g)	1.92 (l)	Yes
Louisiana	4.0	36	2.50	Yes
Maine	5.5	200	(j)	Yes
Maryland	6.0	200	1.5 (l)	Yes
Massachusetts	6.25	351	4.05 (l)	...
Michigan	6.0	200	(j)	Yes
Minnesota	6.875	290 (h)	5.03 (l)	...
Mississippi	7.0	68	(j)	Yes
Missouri	4.225	17 (e)	2	Yes
Montana	none	170	(j)	...
Nebraska	5.5	64	3.75	Yes
Nevada	6.85 (a)	80	3.6 (l)	Yes
New Hampshire	none	178	(j)	...
New Jersey	7.0	270	5.5	Yes
New Mexico	5.125	166	6.06	Yes
New York	4.0	435 (e)	6.44 (l)	Yes
North Carolina	4.75	45	(j)	Yes (k)
North Dakota	5.0	44	2.5 (l)	...
Ohio	5.75	125	(j)	Yes
Oklahoma	4.5	103	5.56 (l)	Yes
Oregon	none	131	(j)	...
Pennsylvania	6.0	160	(j)	Yes
Rhode Island	7.0	350	5.40	Yes
South Carolina	6.0	57	2.72 (l)	Yes
South Dakota	4.0	153	3.93 (l)	Yes
Tennessee	7.0	62 (e)(g)	4.4 (l)	Yes
Texas	6.25	141	2.4 (l)	Yes
Utah	5.95 (c)	170	(j)	Yes
Vermont	6.0	275	(j)(l)	...
Virginia	5.3 (d)	30 (e)	(j)	Yes
Washington	6.5	302.5	14.27 (l)(m)	...
West Virginia	6.0	55	(j)	Yes
Wisconsin	5.0	252	3.25 (l)	Yes
Wyoming	4.0	60	(j)	Yes
Dist. of Columbia	5.75	250 (i)	1.5 (l)	...

See footnotes at end of table.

STATE EXCISE TAX RATES — Continued
(As of January 1, 2015)

Source: Compiled by The Federation of Tax Administrators from various sources, January 2015.

Key:

... — Tax is not applicable.

(a) Nevada sales tax rate scheduled to decrease to 6.5% on July 1, 2015.

(b) The tax rate may be adjusted annually according to a formula based on balances in the unappropriated general fund and the school foundation fund.

(c) Includes statewide tax of 1.25 percent levied by local governments in Utah. Food sales subject to local taxes.

(d) Includes statewide 1.0% tax levied by local governments in Virginia.

(e) Counties and cities may impose an additional tax on a pack of cigarettes: in Alabama, 1¢ to 25¢; Illinois, 10¢ to $4.18; Missouri, 4¢ to 7¢; New York City, $1.50; Tennessee, 1¢; and Virginia, 2¢ to 15¢.

(f) Florida's rate includes a surcharge of $1 per pack.

(g) Dealers pay an additional enforcement and administrative fee of 0.1¢ per pack in Kentucky and 0.05¢ in Tennessee.

(h) In addition, Minnesota imposes an in lieu cigarette sales tax determined annually by the Department. The current rate is 52.6¢ through Dec. 31, 2015.

(i) In addition, District of Columbia imposes an in lieu cigarette sales tax calculated every March 31. The current rate is 40¢.

(j) In 17 states, the government directly controls the sales of distilled spirits. Revenue in these states is generated from various taxes, fees, price mark-ups, and net liquor profits.

(k) General sales tax applies to on-premise sales only.

(l) Other taxes in addition to excise taxes for the following states: Alaska, under 21% — $2.50/gallon; Arkansas, under 5% — $0.50/gallon, under 21% — $1.00/gallon, $0.20/case, 3% off- and 14% on-premise retail taxes; California, over 50% — 6.6/gallon; Connecticut, under 7% — $2.46/gallon; Delaware, 25% or less — $2.30/gallon; Florida, under 17.259% — $2.25/gallon, over 55.780% — $9.53/gallon; Georgia, $0.83/gallon local tax; Illinois, under 20% — $1.39/gallon, $2.68/gallon in Chicago and $2.00/gallon in Cook County; Indiana, under 15% — $0.47/gallon; Kansas, 8% off- and 10% on-premise retail taxes; Kentucky, under 6% — $0.25/gallon, $0.05/case and 11% wholesale tax; Maryland, 9% sales tax; Massachusetts, under 15% — $1.10/gallon, over 50% alcohol — $4.05/gallon, 0.57% on private club sales; Minnesota, $0.01/bottle (except miniatures) and 9% sales tax; Nevada, 5% to 14% — $0.70/gallon, 15% to 22% — $1.30/gallon; New York, under 24% — $2.54/gallon, additional $1.00/gal. in New York City; North Dakota, 7% state sales tax; Oklahoma, 13.5% on-premise; South Carolina, $5.36/case and 9% surtax, additional 5% on-premise tax; South Dakota, under 14% — $0.93/gallon, 2% wholesale tax; Tennessee, 15% on-premise, under 7% — $1.10/gallon; Texas, 6.7% on-premise and $0.05/drink on airline sales; Vermont, 10% on-premise sales tax; Wisconsin, $0.03/gallon administrative fee; Dist. of Columbia, 9% off- and on-premise sales taxes.

(m) Washington privatized liquor sales effective June 1, 2012.

Table 7.10b
STATE EXCISE TAX RATES
(As of January 1, 2015)

State or other jurisdiction	General sales and gross receipts tax (percent)	Motor fuel excise tax rates (cents per gallon)		
		Gasoline	Diesel	Gasohol
Alabama (e)(f)................	4.0	18	19	18
Alaska...........................	none	8	8	8
Arizona (e)...................	5.6	19	27	19
Arkansas (e)................	6.5	21.8	22.8	21.8
California (e)	7.5 (b)	42.5	38	42.5
Colorado......................	2.9	22	20.5	20
Connecticut (e)...........	6.35	25	54.5	25
Delaware (e)	none	23	22	23
Florida (e)(g)	6.0	28.525	31.6	28.525
Georgia (e)..................	4.0	19.3	21.3	19.3
Hawaii (e)(f)	4.0	17	17	17
Idaho (e)(j)	6.0	26	26	26
Illinois (e)(f)	6.25	20.1	22.6	20.1
Indiana (e)...................	7.0	18	16	18
Iowa (e)	6.0	22	23.5	20
Kansas (e)	6.15	25.03	27.03	25.03
Kentucky (e)(h)..........	6.0	27.6	24.6	27.6
Louisiana (e)...............	4.0	20.125	20.125	20.125
Maine (i)......................	5.5	30	31.2	30
Maryland (i)	6.0	30.3	31.5	30.3
Massachusetts	6.25	24	24	24
Michigan (e).................	6.0	19	15	19
Minnesota (e)(i)	6.875	28.6	28.6	28.6
Mississippi (e)	7.0	18.4	18.4	18.4
Missouri (e).................	4.225	17.3	17.3	17.3
Montana	none	27	27.75	27
Nebraska (e)(i)............	5.5	26.5	25.9	26.5
Nevada (e)(f)	6.85 (a)	23.805	27.75	23.805
New Hampshire (e)	none	23.825	23.825	23.825
New Jersey (e)	7.0	14.5	17.5	14.5
New Mexico (e)	5.125	18.875	22.875	18.875
New York (e)................	4.0	25.8	24.05	25.8
North Carolina (e)(h)..	4.75	37.75	37.75	37.75
North Dakota..............	5.0	23	23	23
Ohio (e)........................	5.75	28	28	28
Oklahoma (e)..............	4.5	17	14	17
Oregon (f)	none	30	30	30
Pennsylvania (e)	6.0	50.5	64.2	50.5
Rhode Island (e).........	7.0	33	33	33
South Carolina (e)......	6.0	16.75	16.75	16.75
South Dakota (e)(f).....	4.0	24	24	24
Tennessee (e)(f)..........	7.0	21.4	18.4	21.4
Texas...........................	6.25	20	20	20
Utah............................	5.95 (c)	24.5	24.5	24.5
Vermont (e)(i)..............	6.0	31.97	32	31.97
Virginia (e)(f)	5.3 (d)	16.2	20.2	16.2
Washington (e)............	6.5	37.5	37.5	37.5
West Virginia (e).........	6.0	34.6	34.6	34.6
Wisconsin (e)	5.0	32.9	32.9	32.9
Wyoming (e)	4.0	24	24	24
Dist. of Columbia (e) ..	5.75	23.5	23.5	23.5

See footnotes at end of table.

STATE EXCISE TAX RATES — Continued
(As of January 1, 2015)

Source: Compiled by The Federation of Tax Administrators from various sources, January 2015.

Note: The tax rates listed are fuel excise taxes collected by distributor/supplier/retailers in each state. Additional taxes may apply to motor carriers. Carrier taxes are coordinated by the International Fuel Tax Association.

Key:

... — Tax is not applicable.

(a) Nevada sales tax rate scheduled to decrease to 6.5% on July 1, 2015.

(b) The tax rate may be adjusted annually according to a formula based on balances in the unappropriated general fund and the school foundation fund.

(c) Includes statewide tax of 1.25 percent levied by local governments in Utah. Food sales subject to local taxes.

(d) Includes statewide 1.0% tax levied by local governments in Virginia.

(e) Other taxes and fees; Alabama—inspection fee; Arizona—diesel rate specified is the fuel use tax rate on large trucks, leaking underground storage tax (LUST), small vehicles are subject to 18 cents tax rate; Arkansas—environmental fee; California—includes pre-paid sales tax, gasoline subject to 2.25% sales tax, diesel subject to 9.25% sales tax; Connecticut—additional 8.1% petroleum tax; Delaware—additional 0.9% GRT; Florida—sales tax added to excise; Georgia—sales tax added to excise; Hawaii—sales tax additional; Idaho—clean water tax; Illinois—carriers pay an additional surcharge equal to 19.3 cent for gasoline and 21.0 cents for diesel, sales tax additional, environmental fee and leaking underground storage tax (LUST); Indiana—carriers pay an additional surcharge equal to 11 cents, sales tax additional; Iowa—environmental fee; Kansas—environmental and inspection fees; Kentucky—carriers pay

an additional surcharge equal to 2% for gasoline and 4.7% for diesel, environmental fee; Louisiana—inspection fee; Michigan—sales tax additional; Minnesota—inspection fee; Mississippi—environmental fee; Missouri—inspection and load fees; Nebraska—petroleum fee; Nevada—inspection fee and cleanup fee; New Hampshire—oil discharge cleanup fee; New Jersey—petroleum fee; New Mexico—petroleum loading fee; New York—petroleum tax, sales tax additional; North Carolina—inspection tax; Oklahoma—environmental fee; Pennsylvania—oil franchise tax only; Rhode Island—leaking underground storage tank (LUST); South Carolina—inspection fee and leaking underground storage tank (LUST); South Dakota—inspection fee; Tennessee—petroleum tax and environmental fee; Vermont—cleanup fee and transportation fee; Virginia—large trucks pay an additional 3.5 cents for diesel and 12.6 cents for gasoline. Actual rates are 6% for diesel and 5.1% gasoline; Washington—0.5% privilege tax; West Virginia—sales tax added to excise; Wisconsin—petroleum inspection fee; Wyoming—license tax.

(f) Tax rates do not include local option taxes. In AL, 1 to 3 cents; HI, 8.8 to 18.0 cents; IL, 5 cents in Chicago and 6 cents in Cook county (gasoline only); NV, 4.0 to 9.0 cents; OR, 1 to 3 cents; SD and TN, 1 cent; and VA 2.1%.

(g) Local taxes for gasoline and gasohol vary from 11.1 cents to 19.1 cents. Includes inspection fee, SCETS and additional local tax.

(h) Tax rate is based on the average wholesale price and is adjusted quarterly. The actual rates are: KY, 9%; and NC, 17.5¢ + 7%.

(i) Portion of the rate is adjustable based on maintenance costs, sales volume, cost of fuel to state government, or inflation.

(j) Tax rate is reduced by the percentage of ethanol used in blending (reported rate assumes the max. 10% ethanol).

Table 7.11
STATE SALES TAX RATES AND FOOD AND DRUG EXEMPTIONS
(As of January 1, 2015)

State or other jurisdiction	Tax rate (percentage)	Exemptions		
		Food (a)	Prescription drugs	Nonprescription drugs
Alabama	4.0		★	
Alaska	none			
Arizona	5.6	★	★	
Arkansas	6.5	1.5% (f)	★	
California	7.5 (b)	★	★	
Colorado	2.9	★	★	
Connecticut	6.35	★	★	
Delaware	none			
Florida	6.0	★	★	★
Georgia	4.0	★(f)	★	
Hawaii	4.0		★	
Idaho	6.0		★	
Illinois	6.25	1%	1%	1%
Indiana	7.0	★	★	
Iowa	6.0	★	★	
Kansas	6.15		★	
Kentucky	6.0	★	★	
Louisiana	4.0	★(f)	★	
Maine	5.5	★	★	
Maryland	6.0	★	★	★
Massachusetts	6.25	★	★	
Michigan	6.0	★	★	
Minnesota	6.875	★	★	★
Mississippi	7.0		★	
Missouri	4.225	1.225%	★	
Montana	none		★	
Nebraska	5.5	★	★	
Nevada	6.85 (c)	★	★	
New Hampshire	none			
New Jersey	7.0	★	★	★
New Mexico	5.125	★	★	
New York	4.0	★	★	★
North Carolina	4.75	★(f)	★	
North Dakota	5.0	★	★	
Ohio	5.75	★	★	
Oklahoma	4.5		★	
Oregon	none			
Pennsylvania	6.0	★	★	★
Rhode Island	7.0	★	★	
South Carolina	6.0	★	★	
South Dakota	4.0		★	
Tennessee	7.0	5.0%	★	
Texas	6.25	★	★	★
Utah	5.95 (d)	1.75% (f)	★	
Vermont	6.0	★	★	★
Virginia	5.3 (e)	2.5% (e)	★	★
Washington	6.5	★	★	
West Virginia	6.0	★	★	
Wisconsin	5.0	★	★	
Wyoming	4.0	★	★	
Dist. of Columbia	5.75	★	★	★

Source: Compiled by FTA from various sources. January 2015.
Key:
★—Indicates exempt from tax, blank indicates subject to general sales tax rate.
(a) Some states tax food, but allow a rebate or income tax credit to compensate poor households. They are: Hawaii, Idaho, Kansas, Oklahoma and South Dakota.
(b) The tax rate may be adjusted annually according to a formula based on balances in the unappropriated general fund and the school foundation fund.

(c) Nevada sales tax rate scheduled to decrease to 6.5% on July 1, 2015.
(d) Includes statewide tax of 1.25 percent levied by local governments in Utah. Food sales subject to local taxes.
(e) Includes statewide 1.0% tax levied by local governments in Virginia.
(f) Food sales subject to local taxes. Includes a statewide 1.25% tax levied by local governments in Utah.

Table 7.12
STATE INDIVIDUAL INCOME TAXES
(Tax rates for tax year 2015—as of January 1, 2015)

State or other jurisdiction	Tax rate range (in percents) Low	High	Number of brackets	Income brackets Lowest	Highest	Personal exemptions Single	Married	Dependents	Federal income tax deductible
Alabama	2.0	- 5.0	3	500 (b)	- 3,001 (b)	1,500	3,000	500 (e)	★
Alaska				(No state income tax)					...
Arizona	2.59	- 4.54	5	10,000 (b)	- 150,001 (b)	2,100	4,200	2,100	...
Arkansas (a)	0.9	- 6.9	6	4,299	- 35,100	26 (c)	52 (c)	26 (c)	...
California (a)	1.0	12.3 (f)	9	7,749 (b)	- 519,687 (b)	108 (c)	216 (c)	333 (c)	...
Colorado	4.63		1	Flat rate		4,000 (d)	8,000 (d)	4,000 (d)	...
Connecticut	3.0	- 6.7	6	10,000 (b)	- 250,000 (b)	14,500 (g)	24,000 (g)	0	...
Delaware	0.0	- 6.6	7	2,000	- 60,001	110 (c)	220 (c)	110 (c)	...
Florida				(No state income tax)					...
Georgia	1.0	- 6.0	6	750 (h)	- 7,001 (h)	2,700	5,400	3,000	...
Hawaii (w)	1.4	- 11.00	12	2,400 (b)	- 200,001 (b)	1,040	2,080	1,040	...
Idaho (a)	1.6	- 7.4	7	1,429 (b)	- 10,718 (b)	4,000 (d)	8,000 (d)	4,000 (d)	...
Illinois	3.75		1	Flat rate		2,000	4,000	2,000	...
Indiana	3.3		1	Flat rate		1,000	2,000	2,500 (i)	...
Iowa (a)	0.36	- 8.98	9	1,539	- 69,255	40 (c)	80 (c)	40 (c)	★
Kansas	2.7	- 4.6 (j)	2	15,000 (b)		2,250	4,500	2,250	...
Kentucky	2.0	- 6.0	6	3,000	- 75,001	20 (c)	40 (c)	20 (c)	...
Louisiana	2.0	- 6.0	3	12,500 (b)	- 50,001 (b)	4,500 (k)	9,000 (k)	1,000	★
Maine (a)	0.0	- 7.95	3	5,200 (b)	- 20,900 (b)	3,900	7,800	3,900	...
Maryland	2.0	- 5.75	8	1,000 (l)	- 250,000 (l)	3,200	6,400	3,200	...
Massachusetts (a)	5.15		1	Flat rate		4,400	8,800	1,000	...
Michigan (a)	4.25		1	Flat rate		3,950	7,900	3,950	...
Minnesota (a)	5.35	- 9.85	4	25,070 (m)	- 154,951 (m)	4,000 (d)	8,000 (d)	4,000 (d)	...
Mississippi	3.0	- 5.0	3	5,000	- 10,001	6,000	12,000	1,500	...
Missouri	1.5	- 6.0	10	1,000	- 9,001	2,100	4,200	1,200	★(n)
Montana (a)	1.0	- 6.9	7	2,800	- 17,100	2,280	4,560	2,280	★(n)
Nebraska (a)	2.46	- 6.84	4	3,050 (b)	- 39,640 (b)	130 (c)	260 (c)	130 (c)	...
Nevada				(No state income tax)					...
New Hampshire				(State income tax of 5% on dividends and interest income only.)					...
New Jersey	1.4	- 8.97	6	20,000 (o)	- 500,000 (o)	1,000	2,000	1,500	...
New Mexico	1.7	- 4.9	4	5,500 (p)	- 16,001 (p)	4,000 (d)	8,000 (d)	4,000 (d)	...
New York	4.0	- 8.82	8	8,200 (b)	- 1,029,250 (b)	0	0	1,000	...
North Carolina	5.75		1	Flat rate		None			...
North Dakota (a)	1.22	- 3.22	5	37,450 (q)	- 411,500 (q)	4,000 (d)	8,000 (d)	4,000 (d)	...
Ohio (a)	0.528	5.333	9	5,200	- 208,000	2,200 (r)	4,400 (r)	1,700 (r)	...
Oklahoma	0.5	- 5.25	7	1,000 (s)	- 8,701 (s)	1,000	2,000	1,000	...
Oregon (a)	5.0	- 9.9	4	3,350 (b)	- 125,000 (b)	194 (c)	388 (c)	194 (c)	★(n)
Pennsylvania	3.07		1	Flat rate		None			...
Rhode Island (a)	3.75	- 5.99	3	60,550	- 137,650	3,850	7,700	3,850	...
South Carolina (a)	0.0	- 7.0	6	2,910	- 14,550	4,000 (d)	8,000 (d)	4,000 (d)	...
South Dakota				(No state income tax)					...
Tennessee		-(State income tax 6% on dividends and interest income only.)–				1,250	2,500	0	...
Texas				(No state income tax)					...
Utah	5.0		1	Flat rate		(t)	(t)	(t)	...
Vermont (a)	3.55	- 8.95	5	37,450 (u)	- 411,500 (u)	4,000 (d)	8,000 (d)	4,000 (d)	...
Virginia	2.0	- 5.75	4	3,000	- 17,001	930	1,860	930	...
Washington				(No state income tax)					...
West Virginia	3.0	- 6.5	5	10,000	- 60,000	2,000	4,000	2,000	...
Wisconsin (a)	4.0	- 7.65	4	11,090 (v)	- 244,270 (v)	700	1,400	700	...
Wyoming				(No state income tax)					...
Dist. of Columbia (w)	4.0	- 8.95	4	10,000	- 350,000	1,675	3,350	1,675	...

See footnotes at end of table.

STATE INDIVIDUAL INCOME TAXES — Continued
(Tax rates for tax year 2015 — as of January 1, 2015)

Source: The Federation of Tax Administrators from various sources, January 2015.

Key:

★ — Yes

... — No

(a) Seventeen states have statutory provision for automatically adjusting to the rate of inflation the dollar values of the income tax brackets, standard deductions, and/or personal exemptions. Massachusetts, Michigan, and Nebraska index the personal exemption only. Oregon does not index the income brackets for $125,000 and over. Maine has suspended indexing for 2014 and 2015.

(b) For joint returns, taxes are twice the tax on half the couple's income.

(c) The personal exemption takes the form of a tax credit instead of a deduction.

(d) These states use the personal exemption amounts provided in the federal Internal Revenue Code.

(e) In Alabama, the per-dependent exemption is $1,000 for taxpayers with state AGI of $20,000 or less, $500 with AGI from $20,001 to $100,000, and $300 with AGI over $100,000.

(f) California imposes an additional 1% tax on taxable income over $1 million, making the maximum rate 13.3% over $1 million.

(g) Connecticut's personal exemption incorporates a standard deduction. An additional tax credit is allowed ranging from 75% to 0% based on state adjusted gross income. Exemption amounts are phased out for higher income taxpayers until they are eliminated for households earning over $71,000.

(h) The Georgia income brackets reported are for single individuals. For married couples filing jointly, the same tax rates apply to income brackets ranging from $1,000, to $10,000.

(i) In Indiana, includes an additional exemption of $1,500 for each dependent child.

(j) Kansas tax rates are scheduled to decrease on 1/1/2016. New rates will range from 2.4% to 4.6%.

(k) The amounts reported for Louisiana are a combined personal exemption-standard deduction.

(l) The income brackets reported for Maryland are for single individuals. For married couples filing jointly, the same tax rates apply to income brackets ranging from $1,000, to $300,000.

(m) The income brackets reported for Minnesota are for single individuals. For married couples filing jointly, the same tax rates apply to income brackets ranging from $36,650 to $258,261.

(n) The deduction for federal income tax is limited to $5,000 for individuals and $10,000 for joint returns in Missouri and Montana, and to $6,350 for all filers in Oregon.

(o) The New Jersey rates reported are for single individuals. For married couples filing jointly, the tax rates also range from 1.4% to 8.97%, with seven brackets and the same high and low income ranges.

(p) The income brackets reported for New Mexico are for single individuals. For married couples filing jointly, the same tax rates apply to income brackets ranging from $8,000 to $24,000.

(q) The income brackets reported for North Dakota are for single individuals. For married couples filing jointly, the same tax rates apply to income brackets ranging from $62,600 to $411,500.

(r) Ohio provides an additional tax credit of $20 per exemption.

(s) The income brackets reported for Oklahoma are for single persons. For married persons filing jointly, the same tax rates apply to income brackets ranging from $2,000, to $15,000.

(t) Utah provides a tax credit equal to 6% of the federal personal exemption amounts (an applicable standard deduction).

(u) Vermont's income brackets reported are for single individuals. For married taxpayers filing jointly, the same tax rates apply to income brackets ranging from $62,600, to $411,500.

(v) The Wisconsin income brackets reported are for single individuals. For married taxpayers filing jointly, the same tax rates apply income brackets ranging from $14,790 to $325,700.

(w) Tax rates in the District of Columbia and Hawaii are scheduled to decrease for tax year 2016.

Table 7.13
STATE PERSONAL INCOME TAXES: FEDERAL STARTING POINTS
(As of January 1, 2015)

State or other jurisdiction	Relation to Internal Revenue Code	Federal tax base used as a starting point to calculate state taxable income
Alabama	. . .	. . .
Alaska	————————— No state income tax —————————	
Arizona	1/1/2014	Adjusted gross income
Arkansas	. . .	. . .
California	1/1/2009	Adjusted gross income
Colorado	Current	Taxable income
Connecticut	Current	Adjusted gross income
Delaware	Current	Adjusted gross income
Florida	————————— No state income tax —————————	
Georgia	1/1/2014	Adjusted gross income
Hawaii	12/31/2013	Adjusted gross income
Idaho	1/1/2014	Taxable income
Illinois	Current	Adjusted gross income
Indiana	1/1/2013	Adjusted gross income
Iowa	1/1/2014	Adjusted gross income
Kansas	Current	Adjusted gross income
Kentucky	1/1/2014	Adjusted gross income
Louisiana	Current	Adjusted gross income
Maine	12/31/2013	Adjusted gross income
Maryland	Current	Adjusted gross income
Massachusetts	1/1/2005	Adjusted gross income
Michigan	Current (a)	Adjusted gross income
Minnesota	3/26/2014	Taxable income
Mississippi	. . .	. . .
Missouri	Current	Adjusted gross income
Montana	Current	Adjusted gross income
Nebraska	Current	Adjusted gross income
Nevada	————————— No state income tax —————————	
New Hampshire	————————— On interest and dividends only —————————	
New Jersey	. . .	. . .
New Mexico	Current	Adjusted gross income
New York	Current	Adjusted gross income
North Carolina	12/31/2013	Adjusted gross income
North Dakota	Current	Taxable income
Ohio	3/22/2013	Adjusted gross income
Oklahoma	Current	Adjusted gross income
Oregon	1/3/2013	Taxable income
Pennsylvania	. . .	. . .
Rhode Island	Current	Adjusted gross income
South Carolina	12/31/2013	Taxable income
South Dakota	————————— No state income tax —————————	
Tennessee	————————— On interest and dividends only —————————	
Texas	————————— No state income tax —————————	
Utah	Current	Adjusted gross income
Vermont	1/1/2014	Taxable income
Virginia	1/2/2013	Adjusted gross income
Washington	————————— No state income tax —————————	
West Virginia	12/31/2013	Adjusted gross income
Wisconsin	12/31/2010	Adjusted gross income
Wyoming	————————— No state income tax —————————	
Dist. of Columbia	Current	Adjusted gross income

Source: Compiled by the Federation of Tax Administrators from various sources. January 2015.

Key:
. . . — State does not employ a federal starting point.
Current — Indicates state has adopted the Internal Revenue Code as currently in effect. Dates indicate state has adopted IRC as amended to that date.
(a) Michigan's taxpayers can choose to use either current or 1/1/1996 federal law.

Table 7.14
RANGE OF STATE CORPORATE INCOME TAX RATES
(For tax year 2015, as of January 1, 2015)

State or other jurisdiction	Tax rate (percent)	Tax brackets Lowest	Tax brackets Highest	Number of brackets	Financial institution tax rates (percent) (a)	Federal income tax deductible
Alabama	6.5	--------- Flat Rate ---------		1	6.5	★
Alaska	0 - 9.4	25,000	222,000	10	0 - 9.4	...
Arizona	6.5 (b)	--------- Flat Rate ---------		1	6.5 (b)	...
Arkansas	1.0 - 6.5	3,000	100,001	6	1.0 - 6.5	...
California	8.84 (c)	--------- Flat Rate ---------		1	10.84 (c)	...
Colorado	4.63	--------- Flat Rate ---------		1	4.63	...
Connecticut	7.5 (d)	--------- Flat Rate ---------		1	7.5 (d)	...
Delaware	8.7	--------- Flat Rate ---------		1	8.7-1.7 (e)	...
Florida	5.5 (f)	--------- Flat Rate ---------		1	5.5 (f)	...
Georgia	6.0	--------- Flat Rate ---------		1	6.0	...
Hawaii	4.4 - 6.4 (g)	25,000	100,001	3	7.92 (g)	...
Idaho	7.4 (h)	--------- Flat Rate ---------		1	7.4 (h)	...
Illinois	7.75 (i)	--------- Flat Rate ---------		1	7.75 (i)	...
Indiana	7.0 (j)	--------- Flat Rate ---------		1	8.0 (j)	...
Iowa	6.0 - 12.0	25,000	250,001	4	5.0	★(k)
Kansas	4.0 (l)	--------- Flat Rate ---------		1	2.25 (l)	...
Kentucky	4.0 - 6.0	50,000	100,001	3	(a)	...
Louisiana	4.0 - 8.0	25,000	200,001	5	4.0 - 8.0	★
Maine	3.5 - 8.93	25,000	250,000	4	1.0 (m)	...
Maryland	8.25	--------- Flat Rate ---------		1	8.25	...
Massachusetts	8.0 (n)	--------- Flat Rate ---------		1	9.0 (n)	...
Michigan	6.0	--------- Flat Rate ---------		1	(a)	...
Minnesota	9.8 (o)	--------- Flat Rate ---------		1	9.8 (o)	...
Mississippi	3.0 - 5.0	5,000	10,001	3	3.0 - 5.0	...
Missouri	6.25	--------- Flat Rate ---------		1	7.0	★(k)
Montana	6.75 (p)	--------- Flat Rate ---------		1	6.75 (p)	...
Nebraska	5.58 - 7.81	100,000		2	(a)	...
Nevada	--- No corporate income tax---					
New Hampshire	8.5 (q)	--------- Flat Rate ---------		1	8.5 (q)	...
New Jersey	9.0 (r)	--------- Flat Rate ---------		1	9.0 (r)	...
New Mexico	4.8 - 6.9 (s)	500,000	1 million	3	4.8 - 6.9 (s)	...
New York	7.1 (t)	--------- Flat Rate ---------		1	7.1 (t)	...
North Carolina	5.0 (u)	--------- Flat Rate ---------		1	6.0 (u)	...
North Dakota	1.48 - 4.53	25,000	50,001	3	7.0 (b)	★
Ohio	--- (v) ---					...
Oklahoma	6.0	--------- Flat Rate ---------		1	6.0	...
Oregon	6.6 - 7.6 (w)	1 million			6.6 - 7.6 (w)	...
Pennsylvania	9.99	--------- Flat Rate ---------		1	(a)	...
Rhode Island	7.0 (c)	--------- Flat Rate ---------		1	7.0 (c)	...
South Carolina	5.0	--------- Flat Rate ---------		1	4.5 (x)	...
South Dakota	------------------No corporate income tax----------------------				6.0-0.25 (b)	...
Tennessee	6.5	--------- Flat Rate ---------		1	6.5	...
Texas	--- (y) ---					...
Utah	5.0 (c)	--------- Flat Rate ---------		1	5.0 (c)	...
Vermont	6.0 - 8.5 (c)	10,000	25,000	3	(a)	...
Virginia	6.0	--------- Flat Rate ---------		1	6.0	...
Washington	--- No corporate income tax---					
West Virginia	6.5	--------- Flat Rate ---------		1	6.5	...
Wisconsin	7.9	--------- Flat Rate ---------		1	7.9	...
Wyoming	--- No corporate income tax---					
Dist. of Columbia	9.4 (c)	--------- Flat Rate ---------		1	9.4 (c)	...

See footnotes at end of table.

RANGE OF STATE CORPORATE INCOME TAX RATES — Continued
(For tax year 2015, as of January 1, 2015)

Source: Compiled by the Federation of Tax Administrators from various sources January 2015.

Key:

★ — Yes

. . . — No

(a) Rates listed are the corporate income tax rate applied to financial institutions or excise taxes based on income. Some states have other taxes based upon the value of deposits or shares.

(b) Arizona minimum tax is $100. Tax rate is scheduled to decrease to 5.5% in tax year 2016.

(c) Minimum tax is $800 in California, $100 in District of Columbia, $50 in North Dakota (banks), $500 in Rhode Island, $200 per location in South Dakota (banks), $100 in Utah, $250 in Vermont.

(d) Connecticut's tax is the greater of the 7.5% tax on net income, a 0.31% tax on capital stock and surplus (maximum tax of $1 million), or $250 (the minimum tax). Plus, an additional 20% surtax applies for tax years 2012 and 2016.

(e) The Delaware Bank marginal rate decreases over 4 brackets ranging from $20 to $650 million in taxable income. Building and loan associations are taxed at a flat 8.7%.

(f) An exemption of $50,000 is allowed. Florida's Alternative Minimum Tax rate is 3.3%.

(g) Hawaii taxes capital gains at 4%. Financial institutions pay a franchise tax of 7.92% of taxable income (in lieu of the corporate income tax and general excise taxes).

(h) Idaho's minimum tax on a corporation is $20. The $10 Permanent Building Fund Tax must be paid by each corporation in a unitary group filing a combined return. Taxpayers with gross sales in Idaho under $100,000, and with no property or payroll in Idaho, may elect to pay 1% on such sales (instead of the tax on net income).

(i) The Illinois rate of 7.75% is the sum of a corporate income tax rate of 5.25% plus a replacement tax of 2.5%.

(j) The Indiana tax rate is scheduled to decrease to 6.5% on July 1, 2015.

(k) 50% of the federal income tax is deductible.

(l) In addition to the flat 4% corporate income tax, Kansas levies a 3.0% surtax on taxable income over $50,000. Banks pay a privilege tax of 2.25% of net income, plus a surtax of 2.125% (2.25% for savings and loans, trust companies, and federally chartered savings banks) on net income in excess of $25,000.

(m) The state franchise tax on financial institutions is either (1) the sum of 1% of the Maine net income of the financial institution for the taxable year, plus 8¢ per $1,000 of the institution's Maine assets as of the end of its taxable year, or (2) 39¢ per $1,000 of the institution's Maine assets as of the end of its taxable year.

(n) Business and manufacturing corporations pay an additional tax of $2.60 per $1,000 on either taxable Massachusetts tangible property or taxable net worth allocable to the state (for intangible property corporations). The minimum tax for both corporations and financial institutions is $456.

(o) In addition, Minnesota levies a 5.8% tentative minimum tax on Alternative Minimum Taxable Income.

(p) Montana levies a 7% tax on taxpayers using water's edge combination. The minimum tax per corporation is $50; the $50 minimum applies to each corporation included on a combined tax return. Taxpayers with gross sales in Montana of $100,000 or less may pay an alternative tax of 0.5% on such sales, instead of the net income tax.

(q) New Hampshire's 8.5% Business Profits Tax is imposed on both corporations and unincorporated associations with gross income over $50,000. In addition, New Hampshire levies a Business Enterprise Tax of 0.75% on the enterprise base (total compensation, interest and dividends paid) for businesses with gross income over $150,000 or base over $75,000.

(r) In New Jersey small businesses with annual entire net income under $100,000 pay a tax rate of 7.5%; businesses with income under $50,000 pay 6.5%. The minimum Corporation Business Tax is based on New Jersey gross receipts. It ranges from $500 for a corporation with gross receipts less than $100,000, to $2,000 for a corporation with gross receipts of $1 million or more.

(s) New Mexico tax rates are scheduled to decrease for tax year 2016.

(t) New York's general business corporate rate shown. Corporations may also be subject to a capital stocks tax, which is being phased out through 2021. A minimum tax ranges from $25 to $200,000, depending on receipts ($250 minimum for banks). Certain qualified New York manufacturers pay 0%. Small business taxpayers in New York pay rates of 6.5%, 7.1% and 4.35% on 3 brackets of entire net income up to $390,000.

(u) In North Carolina financial institutions are also subject to a tax equal to $30 per one million in assets. Tax rate is scheduled to decrease to 4% in tax year 2016, if certain revenue targets are met.

(v) Ohio no longer levies a tax based on income (except for a particular subset of corporations), but instead imposes a Commercial Activity Tax (CAT) equal to $150 for gross receipts sitused to Ohio of between $150,000 and $1 million. Banks continue to pay a franchise tax of 1.3% of net worth. For those few corporations for whom the franchise tax on net worth or net income still applies, a litter tax also applies.

(w) Oregon's minimum tax for C corporations depends on the Oregon sales of the filing group. The minimum tax ranges from $150 for corporations with sales under $500,000, up to $100,000 for companies with sales of $100 million or above.

(x) South Carolina taxes savings and loans at a 6% rate.

(y) Texas imposes a Franchise Tax, otherwise known as margin tax, imposed on entities with more than $1,030,000 total revenues at rate of 1%, or 0.5% for entities primarily engaged in retail or wholesale trade, on lesser of 70% of total revenues or 100% of gross receipts after deductions for either compensation or cost of goods sold.

Table 7.15
STATE SEVERANCE TAXES: 2015

State	Title and application of tax (a)	Rate
Alabama	Iron Ore Mining Tax	$.03/ton.
	Forest Products Severance Tax	Varies by species and ultimate use.
	Oil and Gas Conservation & Regulation of Production Tax	2% of gross value at point of production, of all oil and gas produced. 1% of the gross value (for a 5-year period from the date production begins) for well, for which the initial permit issued by the Oil and Gas Board is dated on or after July 1, 1996, and before July 1, 2002, except a replacement well for which the initial permit was dated before July 1, 1996; 1.66% gross proceeds from offshore production greater than 8,000 ft. below sea level.
	Oil and Gas Privilege Tax on Production	8% of gross value at point of production; 4% of gross value at point of incremental production resulting from a qualified enhanced recovery project; 4% if wells produce 25 bbl. or less oil per day or 200,000 cu. ft. or less gas per day; 6% of gross value at point of production for certain on-shore and off-shore wells. A 50% rate reduction for wells permitted by the oil and gas board on or after July 1, 1996, and before July 1, 2002, for 5 years from initial production, except for replacement wells for which the initial permit was dated before July 1, 1996; 3.65% gross proceeds from offshore production greater than 8,000 ft. below sea level;
	Coal and Lignite Severance Tax	$.20/ton in addition to coal severance tax. In 2012, state legislature extended through 2021.
	Local Solid Minerals Tax	Varies by county for sand, clay, gravel, granite, shale, and other products.
Alaska	Uniform Natural Minerals Tax	$.10/ton.
	Cost Recovery Fisheries Assessment (b)	Elective; currently no assessments in place.
	Dive Fishery Management Assessment (b)	Elective; currently 7% of value for select dive fishery species in select management regions.
	Fisheries Business Tax	Tax based on unprocessed value of fishery resources processed in or exported from the state. 1% of value for shore-based processing in developing fisheries; 3% of value for floating processing in developing fisheries or shore-based processing in established fisheries; 4.5% of value for salmon cannery processing in established fisheries; 5% of value for floating processing in established fisheries.
	Fishery Resource Landing Tax	Tax based on unprocessed value of fishery resources processed outside and first landed in the state. 1% of value for developing fisheries; 3% of value for established fisheries.
	Mining License Tax	Up to 7% of net income and royalties received in connection with mining properties and activities in Alaska. New mining operations other than sand and gravel exempt for 3 ½ years after production begins.
	Alaska Oil Production Tax	Alaska will impose a base rate of 35 percent on oil companies' net profits in the state, replacing a 25 percent base rate that increased by 0.4 percentage points for every $1 above a net wellhead price of $30.
	Salmon Enhancement Tax (b)	Elective; 2% or 3% of value for salmon sold in or exported from select aquaculture regions.
	Seafood Development Tax (b)	Elective; currently 1% of value for select commercial fish species in select seafood development regions.
	Seafood Marketing Assessment (b)	Elective; currently 0.5% of value for all commercial fish species exported from, landed or processed in-state.
Arizona	Severance Tax	2.5% of net severance base for mining (metalliferous minerals); $1.51/1,000 board ft. ($2.13 for ponderosa pine) for timbering. 3.125% for oil and gas production and nonmetal mining.
Arkansas	Natural Resources Severance Tax	Separate rate for each substance. Timber $0.178/ton (pine), all other $0.125/ton.
	Oil and Gas Conservation Tax	Natural gas 1.25%, 1.5%, and 5% depending on well classification; crude oil 4% to 5% depending on production levels.
	Oil and Gas Conservation Assessment	Maximum 43 mills/bbl. of oil and 9 mills per MCF produced of gas.
California	Oil and Gas Production Assessment	Rate determined annually by Department of Conservation to fund agency operations; no state severance tax.
	Lumber Tax	The Lumber Tax was enacted in Sept. 2012. Retailers are required to impose a 1% tax on lumber sold in California.
Colorado	Severance Tax (c)	Taxable years commencing prior to July 1, 1999, 2.25% of gross income exceeding $11 million for metallic minerals and taxable years commencing after July 1, 1999, 2.25% of gross income exceeding $19 million for metallic minerals; on or after July 1, 1999, $.05/ton for each ton exceeding 625,000 tons each quarter for molybdenum ore; 2% to 5% based on gross income for oil, gas, CO_2, and coalbed methane; after July 1, 1999, $.36/ton adjusted by the producers' prices index for each ton exceeding 300,000 tons each quarter for coal; and 4% of gross proceeds on production exceeding 15,000 tons per day for oil shale.
	Oil and Gas Conservation Levy (d)	0.07% charge on all oil, natural gas, and CO_2 produced.

See footnotes at end of table.

STATE SEVERANCE TAXES: 2015—Continued

State	Title and application of tax (a)	Rate
Florida	Oil, Gas and Sulfur Production Tax	5% of gross value for small well oil, and 8% of gross value for all other, and an additional 12.5% for escaped oil; tiered formula for tertiary oil; the gas base rate ($0.171) times the gas base adjustment rate each fiscal year for gas; and the sulfur base rate ($2.43) times the sulfur base rate adjustment each fiscal year for sulfur.
	Solid Minerals Tax (e)	8% of the value of the minerals severed; heavy minerals (rate computed annually at $1.34/ton plus times the surchage rate currently at 2.57) and phosphate rock (rate computed annually at a base rate of $1.61/ton plus $1.38 surcharge adjustment).
Idaho	Mine License Tax	1% of net value.
	Oil and Gas Production Tax	Maximum of 5 mills/bbl. of oil and 5 mills/50,000 cu. ft. of gas. Current conservation rate is 5 mills (.005).
	Additional Oil and Gas Production Tax	2.5% of market value at site of production.
Illinois	Oil and Gas Production Assessment (f)	0.1% fee per well of gross revenue for oil and natural gas.
	Timber Fee	4% of purchase price. (g)
Indiana	Petroleum Severance Tax (h)	1% of value or $.24 per barrel for oil or $.03 per 1,000 cu. ft. of gas, whichever is greater.
Kansas	Severance Tax (i)	8% of gross value of oil and gas, less property tax credit of 3.67%; $1/ton of coal.
	Oil Inspection Fee/barrel (i)	$0.015/barrel.
	Oil and Gas Conservation Tax	91.00 mills/bbl. crude oil or petroleum marketed or used each month; 12.9 mills/1,000 cu. ft. of gas sold or marketed each month.
	Mined-Land Conservation & Reclamation Tax	$50, plus per ton fee of between $.03 and $.10.
Kentucky	Oil Production Tax	4.5% of market value.
	Coal Severance Tax	4.5% of gross value, less transportation expenses; $0.50/ton minimum for extraction and processing.
	Natural Resource Severance Tax	4.5% of gross value, less transportation expenses.
Louisiana	Natural Gas Severance Tax (j)	The natural gas severance tax rate effective July 1, 2014 through June 30, 2015 has been set at 16.3 cents per thousand cubic feet (MCF) measured at a base pressure of 15.025 pounds per square inch absolute and at the temperature base of 60 degrees Fahrenheit. This tax rate is set each year by multiplying the natural gas severance tax base rate of 7 cents per MCF by the "gas base rate adjustment" determined by the Secretary of the Department of Natural Resources in accordance with R.S. 47:633(9)(d)(i). The "gas base rate adjustment" is a fraction, of which the numerator is the average of the New York Mercantile Exchange (NYMEX) Henry Hub settled price on the last trading day for the month, as reported in *The Wall Street Journal* for the previous 12-month period ending on March 31, and the denominator is the average of the monthly average spot market prices of gas fuels delivered into the pipelines in Louisiana as reported by the Natural Gas Clearing House for the 12-month period ending March 31, 1990 (1.7446 $/MMBTU). Based on this computation, the Secretary of the Department of Natural Resources has determined the natural gas severance "gas base rate adjustment" for April 1, 2013, through March 31, 2014, to be 232.34 percent. Applying this gas base rate adjustment to the base tax rate of 7 cents per MCF produces a tax rate of 16.3 cents per MCF effective July 1, 2014, through June 30, 2015. The reduced natural gas severance tax rates provided for in R.S. 47:633(9)(b) and (c) remain the same.
	Oil/Condensate Severance Tax (j)	Value on a per barrel basis (42 gallons) the rates are: full-rate, 12.5%; incapable oil rate, 6.25%; stripper oil rate, 3.25%; reclaimed oil, 3.25%; produced water full-rate, 10%; produced water incapable oil rate, 5.0%; produced water stripper oil rate, 2.5%.
	Timber Severance Tax (j)	Louisiana Revised Statute 47:633 imposes a severance tax on timber and pulpwood based on the trees and timber 2.25% of current stumpage value determined by state commission; pulpwood 5% of current stumpage value; current average stumpage market value determined annually on the second Monday of December by the Louisiana Forestry Commission Effective for 2015, the timber values to be used to determine the severance tax on timber are as follows: Pine Sawtimber, Value Per Ton $31.68, Tax Rate 2.25%, Tax Per Ton $0.71; Hardwood Sawtimber, Value Per Ton $35, Tax Rate 2.25%, Tax Per Ton $0.79; Pine Chip-n-Saw, Value Per Ton $16.50, Tax Rate 2.25%, Tax Per Ton $0.37; Pulpwood Pine, Value Per Ton $8.76, Tax Rate 5.00%, Tax Per Ton $0.44; Pulpwood Hardwood, Value Per Ton $10.50, Tax Rate 5.00%, Tax Per Ton $0.53.
	Mineral Severance Tax (j)	Various fees on a per ton basis for products like sulphur, salt, marble, stone, sand, lignit, and others.
	Oil Field Site Restoration Fee	Rate varies according to type of well and production.
	Freshwater Mussel Tax	5% of revenues from the sale of whole freshwater mussels, at the point of first sale.

See footnotes at end of table.

STATE SEVERANCE TAXES: 2015—Continued

State	Title and application of tax (a)	Rate
Maine	Mining Excise Tax	The greater of a tax on facilities and equipment or a tax on gross proceeds.
Maryland	Mine Reclamation Surcharge	$.15/ton of coal removed by open-pit, strip or deep mine methods. Of the $.15, $.06 is remitted to the county from which the coal was removed.
Michigan	Gas and Oil Severance Tax	5% (gas), 6.6% (oil) and 4% (oil from stripper wells and marginal properties) of gross cash market value of the total production. Maximum additional fee of 0.82% of gross cash market value on all oil and gas (2015 fee).
Minnesota	Taconite and Iron Sulfides	$2.56 per ton of concentrates or pellets (rate indexed to inflation by law).
	Direct Reduced Iron (k)	$2.56 per ton of concentrates plus an additional $.03 per ton for each 1% that the iron content exceeds 72%.
Mississippi	Oil and Gas Severance Tax	6% of value at point of gas production; 3% of gross value of occluded natural gas from coal seams at point of production for well's first five years; also, maximum 35 mills/bbl. oil or 4 mills/1,000 cu. ft. gas (Oil and Gas Board maintenance tax). 6% of value at point of oil production; 3% of value at production when enhanced oil recovery method used.
	Timber Severance Tax	Varies depending on type of wood and ultimate use.
	Salt Severance Tax	3% of value of entire production in state.
Montana	Coal Severance Tax	Varies from 3% to 15% depending on quality of coal and type of mine.
	Metalliferous Mines License Tax (l)	Progressive rate, taxed on amounts in excess of $250,000. For concentrate shipped to smelter, mill or reduction work, 1.81%. Gold, silver or any platinum group metal shipped to refinery, 1.6%.
	Oil or Gas Conservation Tax	Maximum 0.3% on the market value of each barrel of crude petroleum oil or 10,000 cu. ft. of natural gas produced, saved and marketed or stored within or exported from the state. (m)
	Oil and Natural Gas Production Tax	Varies from 0.5% to 14.8% according to the type of well and type of production.
	Miscellaneous Minerals License Tax	$.05/ton.
	Cement License Tax (n)	$.22/ton of cement, $.05/ton of cement, plaster, gypsum or gypsum products.
	Resource Indemnity Trust Tax	$25 plus 0.5% of gross value greater than $5,000. For talc, $25 plus 4% of gross value greater than $625. For coal, $25 plus 0.40% of gross value greater than $6,250. For vermiculite, $25 plus 2% of gross value greater than $1,250. For limestone, $25 plus 10% of gross value greater than $250. For industrial garnets, $25 plus 1% of gross value greater than $2,500.00.
Nebraska	Oil and Gas Severance Tax	3% of value of nonstripper oil and natural gas; 2% of value of stripper oil.
	Oil and Gas Conservation Tax	Two percent of value of stripper oil. Maximum 15 mills/$1 of value at wellhead, as of January 1, 2000. (f)
	Uranium Tax	2% of gross value over $5 million. The value of the uranium severed subject to tax is the gross value less transportation and processing costs.
Nevada	Minerals Extraction Tax	Between 2% and 5% of net proceeds of each geographically separate extractive operation, based on ratio of net proceeds to gross proceeds of whole operation.
	Oil and Gas Conservation Tax	$50/mills/bbl. of oil and 50 mills/50,000 cu. ft. of gas.
New Hampshire	Refined Petroleum Products Tax	0.1% of fair market value.
	Excavation Tax	$.02 per cubic yard of earth excavated.
	Timber Tax	10% of stumpage value at the time of cutting. Not assessed under the general property tax but rather is taxed by municipalities.
New Mexico	Resources Excise Tax (o)	Potash .5%, molybdenum .125%, all others .75% of value.
	Severance Tax (o)	Copper .5%, timber .125% of value. Pumice, gypsum, sand, gravel, clay, fluorspar and other non-metallic minerals, .125% of value. Gold, silver .20%; Lead, zinc, thorium, molybdenum, manganese, rare earth and other .125% of value.
	Oil and Gas Severance Tax	3.75% of value of oil, other liquid hydrocarbons, natural gas and carbon dioxide.
	Oil and Gas Emergency School Tax	3.15% of value of oil, other liquid hydrocarbons and carbon dioxide. 4% of value of natural gas.
	Natural Gas Processor's Tax	$0.0220/Mmbtu tax on volume.
	Oil and Gas Ad Valorem Production Tax	Varies, based on property tax in district of production.
	Oil and Gas Conservation Tax (p)	0.19% of value.
North Carolina	Oil and Gas Conservation Tax	Maximum 5 mills/barrel of oil and 0.5 mill/1,000 cu. ft. of gas.
	Primary Forest Product Assessment Tax	$.50/1,000 board ft. for softwood sawtimber, $.40/1,000 board ft. for hardwood sawtimber, $.20/cord for softwood pulpwood, $.12/cord hardwood pulpwood.

See footnotes at end of table.

STATE SEVERANCE TAXES: 2015—Continued

State	Title and application of tax (a)	Rate
North Dakota	Oil Gross Production Tax	5% of gross value at well.
	Gas Gross Production Tax	$.04/1,000 cu.ft. of gas produced (the rate is subject to a gas rate adjustment each fiscal year). Through June 30, 2013, the rate was $.0982 per mcf.
	Coal Severance Tax	$.375/ton plus $.02/ton. (q)
	Oil Extraction Tax	6.5% of gross value at well (with exceptions due to production volumes and and production incentives for enhanced recovery projects).
Ohio	Resource Severance Tax	$.10/bbl. of oil; $.025/1,000 cu. ft. of natural gas; $.04/ton of salt; $.02/ ton of sand, gravel, limestone and dolomite; $.10/ton of coal; and $0.01/ ton of clay, sandstone or conglomerate, shale, gypsum or quartzite.
Oklahoma	Oil, Gas and Mineral Gross Production Tax and Petroleum Excise Tax (r)	Rate: 0.75% levied on asphalt and metals. 7% (if greater than $2.10 mcf) 4% (if greater than $1.75 mcf, but less than $2.10 mcf) 1% (if less than $1.75 mcf) casinghead gas and natural gas as well as 0.95% being levied on crude oil, casinghead gas and natural gas. Oil Gross Production Tax is now a variable rate tax, beginning with January 1999 production, at the following rates based on the average price of Oklahoma oil: a) If the average price equals or exceeds $17/bbl, the tax shall be 7%; b) If the average price is less than $17/bbl, but is equal to or exceeds $14/bbl, the tax shall be 4%; c) If the average price is less than $14/bbl, the tax shall be 1%.
Oregon	Forest Products Harvest Tax	$3.5316/1,000 board ft. harvested from public and private land—through Dec. 31, 2013.
	Oil and Gas Production Tax	6% of gross value at well.
	STF Severance Tax— Eastern Oregon Forestland Option	$4.03/1,000 board ft. harvested from land under the Small Tract Forestland Option—through Dec. 31, 2015.
	STF Severance Tax— Western Oregon Forestland Option	$5.18/1,000 board ft. harvested from land under the Small Tract Forestland Option—through Dec. 31, 2015.
Pennsylvania	Natural Gas Severance Tax	Annual $50,000 per-well fee. Local fees and taxes determined by county.
South Carolina	Forest Renewal Tax	Softwood products: 50 cents per 1,000 board feet or 20 cents per cord. Hardwood products: 25 cents per 1,000 board feet or 7 cents per cord.
South Dakota	Precious Metals Severance Tax	$4 per ounce of gold severed plus additional tax depending on price of gold; 10% on net profits or royalties from sale of precious metals, and 8% of royalty value.
	Energy Minerals Severance Tax (s)	4.5% of taxable value of any energy minerals.
	Conservation Tax	2.4 mills of taxable value of any energy minerals.
Tennessee	Oil and Gas Severance Tax	3% of sales price.
	Coal Severance Tax (t)	$1.00/ton (effective 7/17/13).
	Mineral Tax	Up to $0.15 per ton, rate set by county legislative body.
Texas	Natural Gas Production Tax	7.5% of market value of gas. Condensate Production Tax: 4.6% of market value of gas.
	Crude Oil Production Tax	4.6% of market value or $.046/bbl.
	Sulphur Production Tax	$1.03/long ton or fraction thereof.
	Cement Production Tax	$0.55 per ton or $.0275/100 lbs. or fraction of 100 pounds of taxable cement.
	Oil-Field Cleanup Regulatory Fees	5/8 of $.01/barrel; 1/15 of $.01/1,000 cubic feet of gas. (u)
	Oyster Sales Fee	$1 per 300 lb. barrel of oysters taken from Texas waters.
Utah	Mining Severance Tax	2.6% of taxable value for metals or metalliferous minerals sold or otherwise disposed of.
	Oil and Gas Severance Tax	3% of value for the first $13 per barrel of oil, 5% from $13.01 and above; 3% of value for first $1.50/mcf, 5% from $1.51 and above; and 4% of taxable value of natural gas liquids.
	Oil and Gas Conservation Fee	.002% of market value at wellhead.
Virginia	Forest Products Tax	$1.15 per 1,000 feet B.M. of pine lumber and 1,000 board feet of pine logs. $0.475 collected per cord of pine pulpwood.
	Coal Surface Mining Reclamation Tax	Varies depending on balance of Coal Surface Mining Reclamation Fund.
Washington	Uranium and Thorium Milling Tax (tax reported as inactive)	$0.05/per pound.
	Enhanced Food Fish Tax	0.09% to 5.62% of value (depending on species) at point of landing.
	Timber Excise Tax	5% of stumpage value for harvests on public and private lands.

See footnotes at end of table.

STATE SEVERANCE TAXES: 2015 — Continued

State	Title and application of tax (a)	Rate
West Virginia...............	Natural Resource Severance Taxes	Coal: State rate is greater of 5% or $.75 per ton (4.65% for state purposes and .35% for distribution to local governments). Special state rates for coal from new low seam mines. For seams between 37" and 45" the rate is greater of 2% or $.75/ton (1.65% for state purposes and .35% for distribution to local governments). For seams less than 37" the rate is greater of 1% or $.75/ton (.65% for state purposes and .35% for distribution to local governments). For coal from gob, refuse piles, or other sources of waste coal, the rate is 2.5% (distributed to local governments). Additional tax for workers' compensation debt reduction is $.56/ton. Two special reclamation taxes at $.07/clean ton and $.02/clean ton. Limestone or sandstone, quarried or mined, and other natural resources: 5% of gross value. Natural gas: 5% of gross value (10% of net tax distributed to local governments), additional tax for workers' compensation debt reduction is $.047/mcf of natural gas produced. Oil: 5% of gross value (10% of net tax distributed to local governments). Sand, gravel or other mineral products not quarried or mined: 5% of gross value. Timber: 1.22%, additional tax for workers' compensation debt reduction is 2.78%.
Wisconsin	Mining Net Proceeds Tax	Progressive net proceeds tax ranging from 3% to 15% is imposed on the net proceeds from mining metalliferous minerals. The tax brackets are annually adjusted for inflation based on the change in the GNP deflator.
	Oil and Gas Severance Tax	7% of market value of oil or gas at the mouth of the well.
	Forest Crop Law Severance Tax	10% of stumpage.
	Managed Forest Law Yield Tax	5% yield tax. This tax will be waived for the first five years of most MFL land.
Wyoming	Severance Taxes	Severance Tax is defined as an excise tax imposed on the present and continuing privilege of removing, extracting, severing or producing any mineral in this state. Except as otherwise provided by W.S. 39-14-205. The total Severance Tax on crude oil, lease condensate or natural gas shall be six percent (6%). Stripper oil is taxed at four percent (4%). Surface coal is taxed at seven percent (7%). Underground coal is taxed at three and three-fourths percent (3.75%). Trona is taxed at four percent (4%). Bentonite, sand and gravel, and all other minerals are taxed at two percent (2%). Tertiary Oil (4%). Natural Gas (6%). Uranium (4%).

Source: The Council of State Governments, 2015.
Note: Severance tax collection totals may be found in the Chapter 7 table entitled "State Government Revenue, By Type of Tax."
Key:
(a) Application of tax is same as that of title unless otherwise indicated by a footnote.
(b) Tax rates and applicability for these severance taxes determined by a vote of the appropriate association within the seafood industry, by the Alaska Seafood Marketing Institute, or by the Department of Revenue. Proceeds from these elective assessments are customarily appropriated for benefit of the seafood industry.
(c) Metallic minerals, molybdenum ore, coal, oil shale, oil, gas, CO_2, and coalbed methane. Petroleum Profits Tax (PPT) was changed in 2007.
(d) As of July 1, 2007, set at .0007 mill/$1.
(e) Clay, gravel, phosphate rock, lime, shells, stone, sand, heavy minerals and rare earths.
(f) Fee sunsets in 2018 under state law.
(g) Buyer deducts amount from payment to grower; amount forwarded to Department of Natural Resources.
(h) Petroleum, oil, gas and other hydrocarbons. Oil inspection fee rate based on Department of Revenue factsheet.
(i) Coal, oil and gas, based on Department of Revenue information.
(j) Oil inspection fee rate based on Department of Revenue factsheet.
(k) Coal, oil and gas, based on Department of Revenue information.
(l) Production is considered commercial when it exceeds 50,000 tons annually. There is a six-year phase-in of the tax. In years one and two, the rate is zero. In year three, it is 25% of the statutory rate and 50% and 75% in years four and five respectively. An Aggregate Materials Tax

is imposed by resolution of county boards. It is not required that any county impose the tax, which is $.10/cubic yard or $.07/ton on materials produced in the county.
(m) Metals, precious and semi-precious stones and gems.
(n) The maximum rate of 0.3% is split between the Oil or Gas Conservation Tax and the Oil, Gas and Coal Natural Resource Account Fund. Currently the Oil or Gas Conservation Tax is .18% and the Oil, Gas and Coal Natural Resource Account Fund tax rate is .08%.
(o) Cement and gypsum or allied products.
(p) Natural resources except oil, natural gas, liquid hydrocarbons or carbon dioxide.
(q) Oil, coal, gas, liquid hydrocarbons, geothermal energy, carbon dioxide and uranium.
(r) Rate reduced by 50% if burned in cogeneration facility using renewable resources as fuel to generate at least 10% of its energy output. Coal shipped out of state is subject to the $.02/ton tax and 30% of the $.375/ton tax. The coal may be subject to up to the $.375/ton tax at the option of the county in which the coal is mined.
(s) Asphalt and ores bearing lead, zinc, jack, gold, silver, copper or petroleum or other crude oil or other mineral oil, natural gas or casinghead gas and uranium ore.
(t) Any mineral fuel used in the production of energy, including coal, lignite, petroleum, oil, natural gas, uranium and thorium.
(u) Counties and municipalities also authorized to levy severance taxes on sand, gravel, sandstone, chert and limestone at a rate up to $.15/ton.
(v) Fees will not be collected when Oil-Field Cleanup Fund reaches $20 million, but will again be collected when fund falls below $10 million.

Table 7.16
STATE GOVERNMENT TAX REVENUE, BY SELECTED TYPES OF TAX: 2013
(In thousands of dollars)

State	Total taxes	Sales and gross receipts	Licenses	Individual income	Corporation net income	Severance	Property taxes	Death and gift	Documentary and stock transfer	Other
United States	$847,077,345	$393,764,504	$55,460,732	$309,524,489	$45,015,768	$16,493,397	$13,053,517	$4,882,887	$6,376,472	$2,505,579
Alabama	9,267,567	4,708,518	490,430	3,202,520	382,202	119,424	322,300	18	42,155	0
Alaska	5,132,811	249,586	135,720	0	630,941	4,016,966	99,598	0	0	0
Arizona	13,471,690	8,206,708	412,769	3,397,707	662,026	29,829	762,651	0	0	0
Arkansas	8,586,407	4,019,203	356,920	2,649,577	402,874	80,862	1,022,066	92	30,190	24,623
California	133,184,246	48,074,580	8,743,748	66,809,000	7,462,000	37,732	1,982,208	0	0	74,978
Colorado	11,245,662	4,279,544	637,707	5,528,485	652,180	147,732	0	14	0	0
Connecticut	16,189,525	6,776,058	453,112	7,811,949	572,628	30	0	421,065	151,624	3,059
Delaware	3,346,316	487,202	1,259,277	1,130,501	309,644	0	0	20,161	138,358	1,173
Florida	35,377,566	29,315,741	1,993,965	0	2,071,710	47,050	360	0	1,948,450	0
Georgia	17,794,152	7,408,422	744,401	8,772,227	797,255	0	61,052	0	10,795	0
Hawaii	6,092,893	3,932,220	230,189	1,735,718	123,661	0	0	14,886	56,219	0
Idaho	3,579,093	1,773,270	306,627	1,292,562	200,340	6,224	0	70	0	0
Illinois	38,729,322	14,719,741	2,583,108	16,538,662	4,462,627	0	61,806	309,376	54,002	0
Indiana	16,930,731	10,298,491	699,373	4,976,375	781,585	2,421	7,008	165,478	0	0
Iowa	8,374,376	3,608,991	798,137	3,436,758	428,554	0	0	86,785	15,151	0
Kansas	7,620,282	3,742,916	382,944	2,956,588	384,553	73,806	79,475	0	0	0
Kentucky	10,815,954	5,110,456	462,726	3,722,964	646,875	269,786	558,377	41,326	3,444	0
Louisiana	9,223,829	4,974,642	369,930	2,739,983	252,430	834,116	52,686	42	0	0
Maine	3,884,450	1,779,873	260,918	1,531,504	171,987	0	38,636	79,083	22,449	0
Maryland	18,118,191	7,347,048	805,292	7,693,324	952,092	0	750,927	234,552	145,753	189,203
Massachusetts	23,901,047	7,455,326	945,922	12,876,192	1,888,449	0	4,795	313,395	219,465	197,503
Michigan	24,936,087	12,298,069	1,464,607	8,126,352	895,183	70,236	1,879,024	293	202,323	0
Minnesota	21,031,809	8,289,780	1,184,465	8,950,755	1,363,128	54,343	821,799	159,115	208,424	0
Mississippi	7,402,725	4,571,294	530,010	1,755,424	415,980	104,692	24,122	21	0	1,182
Missouri	11,139,394	4,791,043	549,473	5,380,651	377,258	8	29,896	175	10,815	75
Montana	2,644,610	558,961	320,858	1,045,500	170,999	282,356	262,313	0	0	3,623
Nebraska	4,718,944	2,197,988	130,762	2,101,694	275,563	4,064	148	0	8,725	0
Nevada	7,026,626	5,468,363	586,801	0	0	290,448	235,143	0	59,261	386,610
New Hampshire	2,349,693	945,290	252,442	99,027	553,197	0	400,369	0	99,368	0
New Jersey	29,076,881	12,198,133	1,516,432	12,108,615	2,282,055	0	4,620	623,840	343,186	0
New Mexico	5,201,576	2,651,625	255,968	1,240,945	267,457	713,998	71,583	0	0	0
New York	73,667,171	23,217,491	1,952,367	40,230,379	4,920,605	0	0	1,014,862	877,859	1,453,608
North Carolina	23,768,578	9,714,217	1,543,201	11,068,166	1,285,907	1,656	0	112,364	43,067	0
North Dakota	5,298,770	1,763,437	207,482	641,766	225,719	2,457,530	2,808	28	0	0
Ohio	27,516,947	13,822,045	3,445,620	9,869,545	262,226	12,308	0	105,203	0	0
Oklahoma	8,892,503	3,848,451	1,010,430	2,916,615	585,146	515,981	0	874	15,006	0
Oregon	9,160,887	1,369,266	923,123	6,260,161	459,744	23,305	19,893	101,831	3,564	0
Pennsylvania	33,965,626	17,106,300	2,585,202	10,777,334	2,208,163	0	55,537	812,350	395,176	25,564
Rhode Island	2,940,433	1,516,423	138,518	1,088,992	144,310	0	2,331	31,156	18,703	0
South Carolina	8,721,305	4,476,982	439,843	3,357,518	386,669	0	8,549	0	51,744	0

See footnotes at end of table.

STATE GOVERNMENT TAX REVENUE, BY SELECTED TYPES OF TAX: 2013
(In thousands of dollars) —Continued

State	Total taxes	Sales and gross receipts	Licenses	Individual income	Corporation net income	Severance	Property taxes	Death and gift	Documentary and stock transfer	Other
South Dakota	1,533,663	1,228,262	257,220	0	37,172	10,816	0	0	193	0
Tennessee	12,366,891	9,128,175	1,421,174	262,842	1,256,173	2,502	0	114,191	161,183	20,651
Texas	51,714,295	39,277,583	7,788,864	0	0	4,647,848	0	0	0	0
Utah	6,325,126	2,739,916	290,388	2,852,088	330,684	112,050	0	0	0	0
Vermont	2,878,930	983,226	106,509	663,027	105,635	0	971,718	15,387	28,747	4,681
Virginia	19,186,853	6,192,666	806,572	10,900,860	772,001	2,117	33,188	0	376,892	102,557
Washington	18,667,044	14,647,173	1,359,685	0	0	38,656	1,939,883	104,258	577,389	0
West Virginia	5,378,122	2,579,011	137,437	1,795,947	242,429	608,371	6,149	2	8,776	0
Wisconsin	16,513,692	7,088,411	1,026,823	7,227,690	955,752	6,201	148,600	304	48,016	11,895
Wyoming	2,186,054	826,387	155,241	0	0	867,933	331,899	0	0	4,594

Source: U.S. Census Bureau, 2013 Annual Survey of State Government Finances.

Note: Data users who create their own estimates using these data should cite only the U.S. Census Bureau as the source of the original data. Data in this table are based on information from public records and contain no confidential data. Although the data in this table come from a census of governmental units and are not subject to sampling error, the census results may contain nonsampling error. Addi-tional information on nonsampling error, response rates, and definitions may be found within the survey methodology, *http://www2.census.gov/govs/state/13_methodology.pdf,* and technical documentation, *http://www2.census.gov/govs/state/statetechdoc2013.pdf.*

Note: Detail may not add to total due to rounding.

Table 7.17
STATE GOVERNMENT SALES AND GROSS RECEIPTS TAX REVENUE: 2013
(In thousands of dollars)

State	Total	General sales or gross receipts	Selective sales taxes Total	Motor fuels	Insurance premiums	Public utilities	Tobacco products	Alcoholic beverages	Amusements	Pari-mutuels	Other
United States	$393,764,504	$254,792,055	$138,972,449	$40,089,067	$17,427,572	$14,356,400	$17,858,789	$6,058,633	$6,861,882	$129,610	$36,190,496
Alabama	4,708,518	2,331,676	2,376,842	530,244	297,958	737,619	120,110	174,395	93	1,557	514,866
Alaska	249,586	0	249,586	41,608	60,236	4,295	69,175	39,194	8,427	0	26,651
Arizona	8,206,708	6,472,777	1,733,931	781,426	424,369	21,013	315,428	68,684	531	234	122,246
Arkansas	4,019,203	2,837,788	1,181,415	455,914	162,962	0	237,328	50,656	36,109	3,113	235,333
California	48,074,580	33,915,885	14,158,695	5,492,850	2,242,379	676,997	868,703	357,000	0	14,088	4,506,678
Colorado	4,279,544	2,416,731	1,862,813	626,619	211,320	11,528	197,026	39,217	94,699	610	681,794
Connecticut	6,776,058	3,855,861	2,920,197	483,881	242,448	340,920	399,885	60,416	382,390	6,876	1,003,381
Delaware	487,202	0	487,202	112,616	87,512	58,866	115,191	18,412	0	79	94,526
Florida	29,315,741	20,785,507	8,530,234	2,332,191	657,710	3,045,930	1,172,500	486,278	165,804	9,150	660,671
Georgia	7,408,422	5,277,211	2,131,211	1,000,626	329,237	0	211,618	180,786	0	0	408,944
Hawaii	3,932,220	2,944,487	987,733	92,516	136,542	163,930	112,104	48,962	0	0	433,679
Idaho	1,773,270	1,324,182	449,088	244,738	72,251	1,920	49,324	8,588	0	1,195	71,072
Illinois	14,719,741	8,159,003	6,560,738	1,259,834	359,578	1,638,578	857,110	279,928	598,897	5,881	1,560,932
Indiana	10,298,491	6,793,923	3,504,568	803,376	207,800	224,212	461,637	45,053	754,248	2,543	1,005,699
Iowa	3,608,991	2,520,072	1,088,919	440,365	104,885	0	226,300	13,865	270,659	3,996	28,849
Kansas	3,742,916	2,897,033	845,883	415,352	174,531	321	98,985	119,462	391	0	36,841
Kentucky	5,110,456	3,021,794	2,088,662	838,344	139,471	67,197	260,358	121,753	184	4,843	656,512
Louisiana	4,974,642	2,825,752	2,148,890	583,025	399,551	9,680	123,497	56,879	675,249	4,660	296,349
Maine	1,779,873	1,071,886	707,987	237,675	99,693	29,599	137,952	17,518	51,162	2,068	132,320
Maryland	7,347,048	4,114,296	3,232,752	740,556	429,410	123,431	415,922	30,867	25,281	1,203	1,466,082
Massachusetts	7,455,326	5,184,312	2,271,014	651,375	403,757	23,738	558,297	77,357	2,670	1,830	551,990
Michigan	12,298,069	8,465,895	3,832,174	956,173	301,883	35,653	958,961	138,900	110,668	4,599	1,325,337
Minnesota	8,289,780	5,009,508	3,280,272	860,833	400,974	50	392,552	80,153	37,253	544	1,507,913
Mississippi	4,571,294	3,191,683	1,379,611	412,966	212,493	6,191	150,277	41,787	139,630	0	416,267
Missouri	4,791,043	3,154,531	1,636,512	701,078	274,089	0	103,734	36,119	379,828	0	141,664
Montana	558,961	0	558,961	216,155	74,667	47,861	87,935	31,743	57,295	11	43,294
Nebraska	2,197,988	1,669,380	528,608	297,483	69,248	53,887	66,049	28,936	4,229	237	8,539
Nevada	5,468,363	3,637,356	1,831,007	297,387	249,390	21,993	104,766	40,903	921,872	0	194,696
New Hampshire	945,290	0	945,290	143,132	83,547	73,141	209,555	9,682	454	677	425,102
New Jersey	12,198,133	8,454,788	3,743,345	524,557	568,484	959,009	753,562	136,066	214,859	0	586,808
New Mexico	2,651,625	1,968,571	683,054	235,375	125,836	22,334	71,420	40,980	55,281	22,270	130,886
New York	23,217,491	12,117,579	11,099,912	1,634,932	1,435,166	1,027,932	1,543,016	247,303	1,030	0	5,188,261
North Carolina	9,714,217	5,592,560	4,121,657	1,893,576	542,551	396,056	281,097	332,656	14,703	0	661,018
North Dakota	1,763,437	1,268,695	494,742	211,700	47,867	39,807	28,743	9,154	5,521	742	151,208
Ohio	13,822,045	8,626,426	5,195,619	1,704,594	504,075	1,111,197	828,703	98,279	225,439	6,246	717,086
Oklahoma	3,848,451	2,518,598	1,329,853	434,719	268,121	41,207	283,902	111,001	20,767	1,191	168,945
Oregon	1,369,266	0	1,369,266	498,778	101,569	84,131	269,344	16,294	0	2,138	397,012
Pennsylvania	17,106,300	9,243,355	7,862,945	2,046,738	790,975	1,312,254	1,074,092	336,400	1,447,200	13,149	842,137
Rhode Island	1,516,423	881,458	634,965	94,191	94,915	101,502	131,974	12,717	0	1,184	198,482
South Carolina	4,476,982	3,199,752	1,277,230	520,501	150,213	26,831	27,677	156,759	39,172	0	356,077

See footnotes at end of table.

STATE GOVERNMENT SALES AND GROSS RECEIPTS TAX REVENUE: 2013—Continued
(In thousands of dollars)

State	Total	General sales or gross receipts	Selective sales taxes								
			Total	Motor fuels	Insurance premiums	Public utilities	Tobacco products	Alcoholic beverages	Amusements	Pari-mutuels	Other
South Dakota	1,228,262	853,570	374,692	142,364	71,989	3,558	60,969	16,027	9,325	534	69,926
Tennessee	9,128,175	6,629,923	2,498,252	834,999	686,280	9,461	274,471	140,068	0	0	552,973
Texas	39,277,583	26,127,421	13,150,162	3,228,437	1,788,471	636,274	1,534,004	984,423	39,979	7,169	4,931,405
Utah	2,739,916	1,884,170	855,746	373,242	108,872	24,484	120,472	48,228	0	0	180,448
Vermont	983,226	347,273	635,953	106,840	57,517	17,272	74,270	23,159	0	0	356,895
Virginia	6,192,666	3,708,389	2,484,277	910,038	392,397	128,780	187,943	204,049	81	0	660,989
Washington	14,647,173	11,122,868	3,524,305	1,194,910	436,118	462,736	465,148	364,795	0	1,594	599,004
West Virginia	2,579,011	1,255,377	1,323,634	408,914	151,136	160,762	107,022	17,690	70,259	2,312	405,539
Wisconsin	7,088,411	4,410,130	2,678,281	968,338	176,710	368,708	632,174	57,290	243	0	474,818
Wyoming	826,387	702,623	123,764	70,986	18,419	3,555	26,505	1,802	0	145	2,352

Source: U.S. Census Bureau. 2013 Annual Survey of State Government Finances.

Note: Data users who create their own estimates using these data should cite only the U.S. Census Bureau as the source of the original data. Data in this table are based on information from public records and contain no confidential data. Although the data in this table come from a census of governmental units and are not subject to sampling error, the census results may contain nonsampling error. Additional information on nonsampling error, response rates, and definitions may be found within the survey methodology, http://www2.census.gov/govs/state/13_methodology.pdf, and technical documentation, http://www2.census.gov/govs/state/statetechdoc2013.pdf.

Note: Detail may not add to total due to rounding.

Table 7.18
STATE GOVERNMENT LICENSE TAX REVENUE: 2013
(In thousands of dollars)

State	Total license tax revenue	Motor vehicle license revenue	Occupation and business license, NEC	Corporation license	Motor vehicle operator's license	Hunting and fishing license	Public utility license	Alcoholic beverage license	Amusement license	Other license taxes
United States	$55,460,732	$2,509,665	$13,390,705	$11,414,552	$23,213,282	$1,554,995	$945,119	$692,086	$596,089	$1,144,239
Alabama	490,430	21,031	87,908	136,786	204,960	21,470	14,086	4,185	0	4
Alaska	135,720	0	40,522	0	58,822	25,569	514	1,788	1	8,504
Arizona	412,769	29,620	126,846	10,357	193,816	29,246	15,747	5,164	0	1,973
Arkansas	356,920	17,486	121,868	27,376	149,982	23,760	9,917	4,424	458	1,649
California	8,743,748	311,239	4,202,960	59,998	3,579,253	102,073	416,056	53,008	15,134	4,027
Colorado	637,707	30,945	39,378	13,175	462,676	71,096	12,140	6,734	629	934
Connecticut	453,112	42,607	155,506	27,828	209,745	5,713	686	8,803	209	2,015
Delaware	1,259,277	5,712	379,809	812,596	51,237	2,728	0	1,943	328	4,924
Florida	1,993,965	203,842	212,184	284,117	1,227,158	15,392	25,096	8,332	16,000	1,844
Georgia	744,401	49,334	133,903	39,243	457,490	23,502	0	3,512	797	36,620
Hawaii	230,189	389	30,866	1,606	175,341	488	20,111	0	0	1,388
Idaho	306,627	11,403	69,984	2,077	133,204	32,868	51,453	1,727	294	3,617
Illinois	2,583,108	103,140	430,765	345,961	1,584,922	38,472	18,262	12,289	17,658	31,639
Indiana	699,373	218,479	31,739	7,421	336,161	18,493	0	9,954	8,452	68,674
Iowa	798,137	14,237	112,333	43,938	540,619	28,719	12,033	14,564	23,997	7,697
Kansas	382,944	21,256	55,457	0	205,760	89,900	5,685	3,282	15	1,589
Kentucky	462,726	16,050	124,506	98,774	184,760	26,535	0	6,281	264	5,556
Louisiana	369,930	12,178	106,332	105,789	105,963	28,488	7,066	0	0	4,114
Maine	260,918	10,728	102,584	8,980	107,906	16,148	0	5,377	700	8,495
Maryland	805,292	34,569	208,228	92,984	450,618	15,770	0	1,266	30	1,827
Massachusetts	945,922	107,398	265,590	25,624	381,189	5,302	0	3,067	231	157,521
Michigan	1,464,607	56,672	160,987	22,736	943,486	49,326	30,696	16,118	0	184,586
Minnesota	1,184,465	44,130	321,197	8,491	668,947	55,580	752	1,966	3,141	80,261
Mississippi	530,010	37,793	96,020	149,321	151,627	17,341	14,717	2,927	17,410	42,854
Missouri	549,473	17,039	131,276	54,666	266,955	31,614	19,998	5,035	1,762	21,128
Montana	320,858	9,067	96,285	3,230	149,104	46,590	6	2,079	4,489	10,008
Nebraska	130,762	6,200	10,805	3,055	95,343	13,681	0	1,068	610	0
Nevada	586,801	21,729	230,099	65,070	162,250	10,121	0	0	92,967	4,565
New Hampshire	252,442	12,603	84,265	38,129	92,324	10,036	9,606	4,321	233	925
New Jersey	1,516,432	53,515	509,584	253,561	615,425	13,150	6,797	3,960	58,402	2,038
New Mexico	255,968	3,528	25,909	30,624	168,125	24,668	536	2,216	362	0
New York	1,952,367	145,008	226,912	60,319	1,377,900	56,643	22,842	61,225	59	1,459
North Carolina	1,543,201	112,726	232,570	575,862	581,590	16,619	0	15,915	0	7,919
North Dakota	207,482	5,135	73,437		113,651	14,087	3	347	822	0
Ohio	3,445,620	82,767	753,465	1,649,423	714,947	38,069	31,094	40,844	118,919	16,092
Oklahoma	1,010,430	15,517	115,344	44,580	649,232	19,683	5	1,224	152,863	11,982
Oregon	923,123	39,447	266,125	29,474	512,729	50,246	13,063	4,421	825	6,793
Pennsylvania	2,585,202	61,907	987,158	488,427	837,215	72,852	72,092	16,740	29,968	18,083
Rhode Island	138,518	4,991	54,000	4,719	66,202	1,668	0	73	169	6,696
South Carolina	439,843	9,449	98,299	74,208	210,000	17,346	0	12,394	1,718	16,429

See footnotes at end of table.

STATE GOVERNMENT LICENSE TAX REVENUE: 2013—Continued
(In thousands of dollars)

State	Total license tax revenue	Motor vehicle license revenue	Occupation and business license, NEC	Corporation license	Motor vehicle operator's license	Hunting and fishing license	Public utility license	Alcoholic beverage license	Amusement license	Other license taxes
South Dakota	257,220	3,739	126,781	4,504	66,660	28,140	0	785	7,628	18,983
Tennessee	1,421,174	46,945	298,207	758,051	270,469	31,380	5,995	1,320	314	8,493
Texas	7,788,864	132,626	509,681	4,824,007	1,934,422	103,912	21,659	66,463	8,069	188,025
Utah	290,388	15,244	47,700	490	195,363	28,726	0	1,936	0	929
Vermont	106,509	7,410	18,144	1,945	69,563	7,253	0	376	38	1,780
Virginia	806,572	62,311	185,964	57,191	452,626	29,503	0	12,284	102	6,591
Washington	1,359,685	91,739	280,384	30,836	509,854	43,289	18,762	257,601	6,045	121,175
West Virginia	137,437	105,877	11,887	4,858	2,456	113	304	1,392	3,483	7,067
Wisconsin	1,026,823	40,610	372,894	19,649	452,850	66,863	67,340	1,356	494	4,767
Wyoming	155,241	2,298	25,298	12,496	80,385	34,764	0	0	0	0

Source: U.S. Census Bureau, 2013 Annual Survey of State Government Finances.

Note: Data users who create their own estimates using these data should cite only the U.S. Census Bureau as the source of the original data. Data in this table are based on information from public records and contain no confidential data. Although the data in this table come from a census of governmental units and are not subject to sampling error, the census results may contain nonsampling error. Additional information on nonsampling error, response rates, and definitions may be found within the survey methodology, *http://www2.census.gov/govs/state/13_methodology.pdf*, and technical documentation, *http://www2.census.gov/govs/state/statetechdoc2013.pdf*.

Note: Detail may not add to total due to rounding.

Table 7.19
SUMMARY OF FINANCIAL AGGREGATES, BY STATE: 2013
(In millions of dollars)

State	Revenue Total	General	Utilities & liquor store	Insurance trust (a)	Expenditure Total	General	Utilities & liquor store	Insurance trust	Total debt outstanding at end of fiscal year	Total cash and security holdings at end of fiscal year
United States	$2,216,076	$1,709,786	$21,055	$485,235	$2,005,912	$1,683,170	$30,294	$292,448	$1,137,364	$3,837,747
Alabama.................	29,093	22,760	278	6,055	28,204	24,602	267	3,335	9,055	41,204
Alaska......................	14,018	12,280	17	1,721	12,215	10,707	209	1,298	6,218	80,064
Arizona...................	36,948	29,176	33	7,739	31,968	27,751	35	4,183	13,723	52,507
Arkansas.................	21,542	17,310	0	4,232	19,522	17,560	0	1,963	3,947	27,942
California	315,359	219,693	1,021	94,645	283,572	233,454	870	49,248	152,186	559,096
Colorado.................	30,987	23,129	0	7,857	28,744	23,189	16	5,539	16,309	68,213
Connecticut............	31,851	25,446	37	6,368	29,303	23,719	752	4,832	32,357	42,600
Delaware	8,908	7,794	17	1,097	8,648	7,783	135	731	5,755	13,396
Florida	95,694	74,726	24	20,944	80,436	71,098	142	9,196	37,892	196,509
Georgia...................	53,487	38,392	7	15,088	45,484	38,702	37	6,744	13,293	86,023
Hawaii....................	12,945	10,825	0	2,120	11,478	10,098	6	1,374	8,318	16,243
Idaho......................	9,391	7,340	137	1,914	8,531	7,378	104	1,049	3,648	20,044
Illinois....................	84,493	65,562	0	18,932	75,325	61,222	0	14,103	63,660	128,341
Indiana...................	38,142	33,499	0	4,643	36,794	33,450	0	3,344	22,564	59,309
Iowa.......................	23,103	18,534	259	4,310	20,518	17,902	176	2,441	6,648	40,606
Kansas	18,013	15,246	0	2,767	16,437	14,516	0	1,921	6,825	19,908
Kentucky	28,637	22,927	0	5,711	28,888	24,458	26	4,404	14,984	38,513
Louisiana................	31,238	25,255	7	5,976	32,038	27,800	5	4,233	18,589	56,742
Maine......................	9,571	7,991	9	1,571	8,950	7,877	24	1,050	5,375	17,672
Maryland	41,802	34,779	138	6,885	39,557	34,171	932	4,454	26,067	61,078
Massachusetts	55,438	46,180	784	8,474	56,773	46,360	2,289	8,123	76,161	86,423
Michigan.................	66,401	54,343	912	11,146	62,945	53,550	883	8,513	30,377	70,535
Minnesota...............	45,594	34,651	0	10,942	39,943	35,059	9	4,876	13,573	66,051
Mississippi	21,865	17,511	282	4,073	20,102	17,387	227	2,488	7,113	28,227
Missouri..................	37,529	26,662	0	10,867	30,451	26,039	0	4,412	19,308	62,864
Montana	7,982	5,768	82	2,132	7,075	6,061	83	932	3,558	17,770
Nebraska.................	11,484	9,819	0	1,665	9,881	9,184	0	696	1,847	15,789
Nevada....................	17,041	11,402	79	5,559	13,274	10,639	84	2,551	3,610	31,311
New Hampshire	8,164	6,132	589	1,443	7,420	6,207	469	744	8,763	13,889
New Jersey	67,918	53,864	989	13,065	67,363	50,052	2,777	14,533	64,264	113,531
New Mexico	17,808	14,295	0	3,513	17,200	15,015	0	2,185	7,233	46,721
New York.................	212,859	165,201	7,900	39,758	184,040	147,156	12,795	24,089	136,014	318,156
North Carolina........	60,004	47,575	0	12,430	53,626	46,103	72	7,451	19,055	101,336
North Dakota..........	8,830	8,060	0	771	6,410	5,786	0	624	1,834	20,326
Ohio........................	90,344	60,946	929	28,469	76,292	59,502	356	16,434	33,133	220,915
Oklahoma...............	26,345	20,800	602	4,943	22,920	19,579	814	2,527	9,514	40,244
Oregon....................	32,951	22,833	498	9,620	26,850	21,465	271	5,114	13,598	69,449
Pennsylvania	87,911	69,756	1,731	16,424	87,533	72,244	1,586	13,702	47,021	124,835
Rhode Island..........	8,682	6,933	33	1,715	8,189	6,563	155	1,472	9,568	15,100
South Carolina........	29,639	22,161	1,875	5,603	28,246	22,331	2,227	3,688	14,724	41,025
South Dakota..........	5,759	4,036	0	1,724	4,477	4,011	0	466	3,425	14,202
Tennessee	32,356	27,402	0	4,955	30,586	27,831	0	2,755	6,192	47,293
Texas......................	136,487	112,936	0	23,551	124,930	108,025	0	16,905	39,625	303,266
Utah........................	18,442	14,811	291	3,341	16,823	14,956	206	1,660	7,050	29,361
Vermont..................	6,296	5,635	51	610	6,018	5,608	52	358	3,330	7,476
Virginia...................	50,852	41,140	637	9,075	47,614	42,530	514	4,570	28,023	76,703
Washington.............	47,862	35,670	612	11,581	45,726	37,865	516	7,345	30,474	92,193
West Virginia...........	14,581	12,391	93	2,098	13,234	11,709	79	1,446	7,356	21,396
Wisconsin...............	45,892	32,281	0	13,611	37,525	31,878	8	5,638	23,188	87,571
Wyoming	7,574	5,929	102	1,543	5,835	5,037	88	711	1,021	27,812

See footnotes at end of table.

SUMMARY OF FINANCIAL AGGREGATES, BY STATE: 2013 — Continued
(In millions of dollars)

Source: U.S. Census Bureau, 2013 Annual Survey of State Government Finances.

Note: Data users who create their own estimates using these data should cite only the U.S. Census Bureau as the source of the original data. Data in this table are based on information from public records and contain no confidential data. Although the data in this table come from a census of governmental units and are not subject to sampling error, the census results may contain nonsampling error. Additional information on nonsampling error, response rates, and definitions may be found within the survey methodology, *http://www2.census.gov/govs/state/13_methodology.pdf*, and technical documentation, *http://www2.census.gov/govs/state/statetechdoc2013.pdf*.

Note: Detail may not add to total due to rounding. Data presented are statistical in nature and do not represent an accounting statement. Therefore, a difference between an individual government's total revenue and expenditure does not necessarily indicate a budget surplus or deficit.

Key:

(a) Within insurance trust revenue, net earnings of state0administered pension systems is a calculated statistic (the item code in the data file is X08), and thus can be positive or negative. Net earnings is the sum of earnings on investments plus gains on investments minus losses on investments. The change made in 2002 for asset valuation from book to market value in accordance with Statement 34 of the Governmental Accounting Standards Board is reflected in the calculated statistics. The statistics reflect state government fiscal years that end on June 30, except for four states with other ending dates: Alabama and Michigan (September 30), New York (March 31), and Texas (August 31).

Table 7.20
NATIONAL TOTALS OF STATE GOVERNMENT FINANCES FOR SELECTED YEARS: 2005–2013 (In thousands of dollars)

Item	2013	2012	2011	2010	2009	2008	2007	2006	2005
Revenue total	$2,216,076,231	$1,905,807,119	$2,266,850,424	$2,039,926,569	$1,133,446,448	$1,579,327,215	$1,995,259,199	$1,774,648,692	$1,642,468,017
General revenue	1,709,786,388	1,629,267,996	1,658,377,770	1,567,206,839	1,493,989,614	1,509,888,971	1,451,775,306	1,391,133,672	1,286,899,373
Taxes	847,077,345	798,586,949	762,378,532	705,929,253	713,474,529	779,716,635	757,467,232	715,973,170	650,611,855
Intergovernmental revenue	551,464,163	533,655,081	595,028,792	575,371,668	494,782,446	441,972,830	426,590,487	419,640,660	407,791,786
From Federal Government	513,478,951	514,139,109	575,788,668	555,592,308	475,661,252	419,965,984	407,263,017	398,200,459	386,313,543
Public welfare	307,610,126	296,964,692	332,256,781	315,808,952	280,281,988	240,299,037	230,623,974	224,406,166	223,248,268
Education	84,408,057	90,264,309	104,711,082	105,511,630	82,447,792	74,307,867	73,422,139	72,376,901	68,882,228
Highways	41,431,014	43,199,512	44,245,077	42,969,373	36,518,798	35,722,224	35,200,889	34,187,690	32,676,739
Employment security administration	4,647,159	4,771,326	5,174,051	4,888,356	4,455,882	3,952,385	3,932,896	4,380,567	4,412,445
Other	70,770,258	74,371,641	84,933,214	82,442,778	68,492,747	62,384,943	60,639,547	62,849,135	53,823,548
From local government	37,985,212	19,515,972	19,240,124	19,779,360	19,121,194	22,006,846	19,327,470	21,440,201	21,478,243
Charges and miscellaneous revenue	311,244,880	297,025,966	300,970,446	285,905,918	285,732,639	288,199,506	267,717,587	255,519,842	228,495,732
Liquor stores revenue	7,480,124	7,114,248	6,739,028	6,494,993	6,376,562	6,128,282	5,799,273	5,475,237	5,118,462
Utility revenue	13,574,604	13,626,445	14,991,180	15,121,578	16,471,341	16,521,947	16,735,684	15,816,555	14,628,425
Insurance trust revenue (a)	485,235,115	255,798,430	586,742,446	451,103,159	-383,391,069	46,788,015	520,948,936	362,223,228	335,821,757
Employee retirement	388,424,920	152,590,817	476,654,285	353,373,854	-449,271,197	-11,549,775	457,687,157	295,602,816	269,617,472
Unemployment compensation	74,232,787	80,109,746	87,410,032	75,037,579	41,976,470	34,359,648	34,063,242	36,863,504	35,242,919
Worker compensation	15,295,670	15,526,364	15,032,589	15,311,140	16,618,791	18,574,527	19,785,182	21,906,234	23,352,729
Other	7,281,738	7,571,503	7,645,540	7,380,586	7,284,867	5,403,615	9,413,355	7,850,674	7,608,637
Expenditure and debt redemption	2,140,494,012	2,105,861,811	2,112,703,375	2,052,749,013	1,937,658,906	1,816,831,616	1,713,047,679	1,631,438,503	1,556,924,635
Debt redemption	134,582,345	124,664,050	106,755,419	109,226,381	105,062,105	77,528,415	75,083,761	76,905,629	84,382,231
Expenditure total	2,005,911,667	1,981,197,761	2,005,947,956	1,943,522,632	1,832,596,801	1,739,303,201	1,637,963,918	1,554,532,874	1,472,542,404
General expenditure	1,683,170,060	1,648,195,648	1,654,428,735	1,593,693,957	1,560,046,263	1,508,097,761	1,426,195,280	1,349,968,143	1,278,433,682
Education	599,151,748	588,340,483	592,863,150	571,147,157	567,674,062	547,511,580	514,588,891	483,476,753	454,348,376
Intergovernmental expenditure	324,995,548	317,839,562	330,482,270	317,389,500	324,374,036	315,424,647	301,062,065	280,090,982	263,625,820
State institutions of higher education	232,678,490	230,296,706	222,760,979	214,010,622	207,010,341	197,886,661	180,960,143	169,883,923	160,884,249
Other education	366,473,258	358,043,777	370,102,171	357,136,535	360,663,721	349,624,919	333,628,748	313,592,830	293,464,127
Public welfare	519,178,293	489,162,351	494,828,803	462,430,908	438,744,629	411,662,728	393,323,467	376,675,058	368,764,661
Intergovernmental expenditure	55,565,254	55,913,067	56,678,841	58,858,443	58,741,316	57,730,369	56,899,141	54,858,307	52,935,802
Cash assistance, categorical program	28,086,238	29,222,998	28,128,920	29,280,893	28,045,391	28,083,853	30,343,357	30,310,961	32,738,159
Cash assistance, other	6,508,047	6,401,260	6,582,490	6,164,123	6,290,097	5,730,497	4,823,199	4,516,397	2,717,631
Other public welfare	484,584,008	453,538,093	460,117,393	426,985,892	404,409,141	377,848,378	358,156,911	341,847,700	333,308,871
Highways	112,174,050	115,296,570	109,397,936	111,169,808	107,286,437	107,584,368	103,511,290	100,841,813	92,816,461
Intergovernmental expenditure	18,158,521	17,787,581	17,243,590	18,043,061	16,492,780	16,549,366	14,881,789	15,495,306	14,500,232
Regular state highway facilities	104,088,029	105,496,969	101,913,730	102,742,620	98,889,122	99,047,301	95,954,560	93,964,195	86,571,074
State toll highway facilities	8,086,021	9,799,601	7,484,206	8,427,188	8,397,315	8,537,037	7,556,730	6,877,618	6,245,387
Health and hospitals	130,680,311	130,621,569	126,020,387	122,754,039	120,594,797	115,742,953	107,236,896	96,663,369	92,256,859
Hospitals	67,433,480	69,265,569	65,985,505	64,509,024	58,041,020	54,733,920	49,798,760	45,960,293	43,623,308
Health	63,246,831	61,356,000	60,034,882	58,245,015	62,553,777	61,009,033	57,438,136	50,703,076	48,633,551
Natural resources	21,345,804	22,051,093	21,989,895	21,514,767	22,605,445	22,538,841	22,053,343	20,036,460	18,822,456
Corrections	48,407,786	48,439,991	49,166,999	48,549,551	50,382,439	49,880,748	46,485,220	42,793,514	40,562,217
Financial administration	23,136,739	21,771,566	22,334,533	22,610,662	22,978,925	23,457,406	22,574,672	21,676,940	21,224,584
Employment security administration	4,846,304	5,065,317	5,214,711	5,108,615	4,520,197	4,037,994	3,975,130	4,551,037	4,259,347
Police protection	15,106,964	14,275,634	14,248,537	13,828,055	13,676,971	13,617,829	12,879,814	12,220,732	11,395,489
Interest on general debt	46,138,932	47,273,956	46,653,282	45,259,591	45,281,069	44,838,072	41,694,648	38,231,722	34,242,019
Veterans' services	523,718	470,153	515,414	476,593	423,542	399,051	375,475	992,146	294,264
Utility expenditure	24,661,698	23,724,473	25,548,643	23,864,159	26,295,576	24,578,412	24,280,280	24,922,440	21,827,440
Insurance trust expenditure	292,447,534	303,669,929	320,563,723	320,720,833	241,080,311	201,682,378	182,824,248	175,304,033	168,199,527
Employee retirement	203,454,835	190,622,956	180,712,886	166,956,051	156,708,757	148,157,101	136,241,863	127,501,115	118,332,771
Unemployment compensation	71,181,425	95,317,830	121,384,316	134,908,383	65,974,092	35,470,883	28,854,007	28,008,860	29,776,222
Other	17,811,274	17,729,143	18,466,521	18,856,399	18,397,462	18,054,394	17,728,378	19,794,058	20,090,534

See footnotes at end of table.

NATIONAL TOTALS OF STATE GOVERNMENT FINANCES FOR SELECTED YEARS: 2005–2013—Continued
(In thousands of dollars)

Item	2013	2012	2011	2010	2009	2008	2007	2006	2005
Total expenditure by character and object	2,005,911,667	1,981,197,761	2,005,947,956	1,943,522,632	1,832,596,801	1,739,303,201	1,637,963,918	1,554,532,874	1,472,542,404
Direct expenditure	1,517,128,804	1,499,314,531	1,509,115,520	1,457,965,445	1,341,709,410	1,260,772,627	1,178,221,623	1,122,267,668	1,066,617,117
Current operation	1,020,376,950	986,062,966	984,180,683	934,321,563	901,310,643	866,901,215	810,478,208	774,002,589	738,885,771
Capital outlay	114,980,312	119,668,339	115,570,769	118,010,630	116,989,763	112,695,425	110,483,120	103,253,138	95,155,295
Construction	97,778,294	102,756,659	98,061,234	100,962,250	97,929,543	92,779,391	91,190,839	85,712,794	78,049,253
Other capital outlay	17,202,018	16,911,680	17,509,535	17,048,380	19,060,220	19,916,034	19,292,281	17,540,344	17,106,042
Assistance and subsidies	40,795,280	40,078,288	39,762,087	37,561,512	35,005,215	32,657,676	30,750,791	29,564,773	28,403,006
Interest on debt	48,528,728	49,835,009	49,038,258	47,350,907	47,323,478	46,835,933	43,685,256	40,143,135	35,973,518
Insurance benefits and repayments	292,447,534	303,669,929	320,563,723	320,720,833	241,080,311	201,682,378	182,824,248	175,304,033	168,199,527
Intergovernmental expenditure	488,782,863	481,883,230	496,832,436	485,557,187	490,887,391	478,530,574	459,742,295	432,265,206	405,925,287
Cash and security holdings at end of fiscal year	3,837,746,513	3,667,671,249	3,672,783,154	3,323,047,498	3,082,511,650	3,758,006,530	3,862,584,916	3,443,236,625	3,153,795,074
Insurance trust	1,572,694,369	1,523,149,081	2,518,525,924	2,214,651,546	2,020,928,749	2,656,071,709	2,814,408,903	2,495,133,155	2,306,208,483
Unemployment fund balance	3,723,399	-11,838,923	-18,830,490	-17,632,312	9,820,731	38,489,823	39,795,912	35,053,864	27,595,746
Debt offsets	458,510,770	485,559,643	500,220,858	500,337,284	491,111,560	461,876,851	429,725,192	390,865,042	363,955,939

Source: U.S. Census Bureau, Census of Governments: Finance (2007 and 2012) and Annual Survey of State Government Finances (remaining years).

Notes: Data users who create their own estimates using these data should cite only the U.S. Census Bureau as the source of the original data. Data in this table are based on information from public records and contain no confidential data. Although the data in this table come from a census of governmental units and are not subject to sampling error, the census results may contain nonsampling error. Additional information on nonsampling error, response rates, and definitions may be found within the survey methodology and technical documentation. The statistics reflect state government fiscal years that end on June 30, except for four states with other ending dates: Alabama and Michigan (September 30), New York (March 31), and Texas (August 31). Data are released on a flow basis and will be replaced when updated data are available. For more information, see the Federal, State, and Local Governments release schedule.

Key:

(a) Within insurance trust revenue, net earnings of state-administered pension systems is a calculated statistic (the item code in the data file is X08), and thus can be positive or negative. Net earnings is the sum of earnings on investments plus gains on investments minus losses on investments. The change made in 2002 for asset valuation from book to market value in accordance with Statement 34 of the Governmental Accounting Standards Board is reflected in the calculated statistics.

Table 7.21
STATE GENERAL REVENUE, BY SOURCE AND BY STATE: 2013 (In thousands of dollars)

State	Total general revenue (a)	Taxes Total (b)	Sales and gross receipts — Total (b)	Sales and gross receipts — General	Motor fuels	Licenses — Total (b)	Motor vehicle	Individual income	Corporation net income	Intergovernmental revenue	Charges and miscellaneous general revenue
United States	$1,709,786,388	$847,077,345	$393,764,504	$254,792,055	$40,089,067	$55,460,732	$23,213,282	$309,524,489	$45,015,768	$551,464,163	$311,244,880
Alabama	22,759,645	9,267,567	4,708,518	2,331,676	530,244	490,430	204,960	3,202,520	382,202	8,338,033	5,154,045
Alaska	12,280,315	5,132,811	249,586	0	41,608	135,720	58,822		630,941	2,754,412	4,393,092
Arizona	29,176,274	13,471,690	8,206,708	6,472,777	781,426	412,769	193,816	3,397,707	662,026	10,580,523	5,124,061
Arkansas	17,310,068	8,586,407	4,019,203	2,837,788	455,914	356,920	149,982	2,649,577	402,874	5,724,598	2,999,063
California	219,692,720	133,184,246	48,074,580	33,915,885	5,492,850	8,743,748	3,579,253	66,809,000	7,462,000	58,096,373	28,412,101
Colorado	23,129,280	11,245,662	4,279,544	2,416,731	626,619	637,707	462,676	5,528,485	652,180	6,508,932	5,374,686
Connecticut	25,446,414	16,189,525	6,776,058	3,855,861	483,881	453,112	209,745	7,811,949	572,628	5,962,699	3,294,190
Delaware	7,793,920	3,346,316	487,202	0	112,616	1,259,277	51,237	1,130,501	309,644	1,996,011	2,451,593
Florida	74,725,923	35,377,566	29,315,741	20,785,507	2,332,191	1,993,965	1,227,158	0	2,071,710	23,880,229	15,468,128
Georgia	38,391,794	17,794,152	7,408,422	5,277,211	1,000,626	744,401	457,490	8,772,227	797,255	14,619,221	5,978,421
Hawaii	10,825,114	6,092,893	3,932,220	2,944,487	92,516	230,189	175,341	1,735,718	123,661	2,331,449	2,400,772
Idaho	7,340,263	3,579,093	1,773,270	1,324,182	244,738	306,627	133,204	1,292,562	200,340	2,541,438	1,219,732
Illinois	65,561,519	38,729,322	14,719,741	8,159,003	1,259,834	2,583,108	1,584,922	16,538,662	4,462,627	17,312,790	9,519,407
Indiana	33,499,152	16,930,731	10,298,491	6,793,923	803,376	699,373	336,161	4,976,375	781,585	11,267,810	5,300,611
Iowa	18,533,679	8,374,376	3,608,991	2,520,072	440,365	798,137	540,619	3,436,758	428,554	5,991,401	4,167,902
Kansas	15,245,978	7,620,282	3,742,916	2,897,033	415,352	382,944	205,760	2,956,588	384,553	3,845,073	3,780,623
Kentucky	22,926,606	10,815,954	5,110,456	3,021,794	838,344	462,726	184,760	3,722,964	646,875	8,083,482	4,027,170
Louisiana	25,255,359	9,223,829	4,974,642	2,825,752	583,025	369,930	105,963	2,739,983	252,430	10,660,261	5,371,269
Maine	7,990,979	3,884,450	1,779,873	1,071,886	237,675	260,918	107,906	1,531,504	171,987	2,830,353	1,276,176
Maryland	34,779,321	18,118,191	7,347,048	4,114,296	740,556	805,292	450,618	7,693,324	952,092	10,325,181	6,333,949
Massachusetts	46,180,318	23,901,047	7,455,326	5,184,312	651,375	945,922	381,189	12,876,192	1,888,449	13,706,498	8,572,773
Michigan	54,343,294	24,936,087	12,298,069	8,465,895	956,173	1,464,607	943,486	8,126,352	895,183	18,007,780	11,399,427
Minnesota	34,651,478	21,031,809	8,289,780	5,009,508	860,833	1,184,465	668,947	8,950,755	1,363,128	9,315,259	4,304,410
Mississippi	17,510,532	7,402,725	4,571,294	3,191,683	412,966	530,010	151,627	1,755,424	415,980	7,649,292	2,458,515
Missouri	26,662,036	11,139,394	4,791,043	3,154,531	701,078	549,473	266,955	5,380,651	377,258	10,497,449	5,025,193
Montana	5,767,554	2,644,610	558,961	0	216,155	320,858	149,104	1,045,500	170,999	2,161,997	960,947
Nebraska	9,819,327	4,718,944	2,197,988	1,669,380	297,483	130,762	95,343	2,101,694	275,563	3,212,304	1,888,079
Nevada	11,402,396	7,026,626	5,468,363	3,637,356	297,387	586,801	162,250	0	0	3,080,240	1,295,530
New Hampshire	6,132,439	2,349,693	945,290	0	143,132	252,442	92,324	99,027	553,197	1,883,424	1,899,322
New Jersey	53,863,834	29,076,881	12,198,133	8,454,788	524,557	1,516,432	615,425	12,108,615	2,282,055	14,471,986	10,314,967
New Mexico	14,295,361	5,201,576	2,651,625	1,968,571	235,375	255,968	168,125	1,240,945	267,457	5,416,068	3,677,717
New York	165,200,561	73,667,171	23,217,491	12,117,579	1,634,932	1,952,367	1,377,900	40,230,379	4,920,605	71,682,137	19,851,253
North Carolina	47,574,530	23,768,578	9,714,217	5,592,560	1,893,576	1,543,201	581,590	11,068,166	1,285,907	15,769,950	8,036,002
North Dakota	8,059,929	5,298,770	1,763,437	1,268,695	211,700	207,482	113,651	641,766	225,719	1,572,480	1,188,679
Ohio	60,945,518	27,516,947	13,822,045	8,626,426	1,704,594	3,445,620	714,947	9,869,545	262,226	21,113,847	12,314,724
Oklahoma	20,799,702	8,892,503	3,848,451	2,518,598	434,719	1,010,430	649,232	2,916,615	585,146	7,159,511	4,747,688
Oregon	22,833,016	9,160,887	1,369,266		498,778	923,123	512,729	6,260,161	459,744	8,003,252	5,668,877
Pennsylvania	69,755,731	33,965,626	17,106,300	9,243,355	2,046,738	2,585,202	837,215	10,777,334	2,208,163	21,412,638	14,377,467
Rhode Island	6,933,496	2,940,433	1,516,423	881,458	94,191	138,518	66,202	1,088,992	144,310	2,369,822	1,623,241
South Carolina	22,160,859	8,721,305	4,476,982	3,199,752	520,501	439,843	210,000	3,357,518	386,669	7,202,824	6,236,730

See footnotes at end of table.

STATE GENERAL REVENUE, BY SOURCE AND BY STATE: 2013 (In thousands of dollars) —Continued

State	Total general revenue (a)	Taxes								Intergovernmental revenue	Charges and miscellaneous general revenue
		Total (b)	Sales and gross receipts			Licenses		Individual income	Corporation net income		
			Total (b)	General	Motor fuels	Total (b)	Motor vehicle				
South Dakota	4,035,680	1,533,663	1,228,262	853,570	142,364	257,220	66,660	0	37,172	1,605,537	896,480
Tennessee	27,401,810	12,366,891	9,128,175	6,629,923	834,999	1,421,174	270,469	262,842	1,256,173	10,900,626	4,134,293
Texas	112,935,910	51,714,295	39,277,583	26,127,421	3,228,437	7,788,864	1,934,422	0	0	37,580,061	23,641,554
Utah	14,810,655	6,325,126	2,739,916	1,884,170	373,242	290,388	195,363	2,852,088	330,684	4,304,061	4,181,468
Vermont	5,635,209	2,878,930	983,226	347,273	106,840	106,509	69,563	663,027	105,635	1,872,013	884,266
Virginia	41,140,409	19,186,853	6,192,666	3,708,389	910,038	806,572	452,626	10,900,860	772,001	9,959,041	11,994,515
Washington	35,669,826	18,667,044	14,647,173	11,122,868	1,194,910	1,359,685	509,854	0	0	10,030,961	6,971,821
West Virginia	12,390,766	5,378,122	2,579,011	1,255,377	408,914	137,437	2,456	1,795,947	242,429	4,325,052	2,687,592
Wisconsin	32,280,837	16,513,692	7,088,411	4,410,130	968,338	1,026,823	452,850	7,227,690	955,752	9,228,907	6,538,238
Wyoming	5,929,052	2,186,054	826,387	702,623	70,986	155,241	80,385	0	0	2,318,877	1,424,121

Source: U.S. Census Bureau, 2013 Annual Survey of State Government Finances.

Note: Data users who create their own estimates using these data should cite only the U.S. Census Bureau as the source of the original data. Data in this table are based on information from public records and contain no confidential data. Although the data in this table come from a census of governmental units and are not subject to sampling error, the census results may contain nonsampling error. Additional information on nonsampling error, response rates, and definitions may be found within the survey methodology, http://www2.census.gov/govs/state/13_methodology.pdf, and technical documentation, http://www2.census.gov/govs/state/statetechdoc2013.pdf.

Note: Detail may not add to total due to rounding.

Key:

(a) Total general revenue equals total taxes plus intergovernmental revenue plus charges and miscellaneous revenue.

(b) Total includes other taxes not shown separately in this table.

Table 7.22
STATE EXPENDITURE, BY CHARACTER AND OBJECT AND BY STATE: 2013 (In thousands of dollars)

State	Intergovernmental expenditures	Total	Direct expenditures								Exhibit: Total salaries and wages
			Current operation	Capital outlay			Assistance and subsidies	Interest on debt	Insurance benefits and repayments		
				Total	Construction	Other					
United States	$488,782,863	$1,517,128,804	$1,020,376,950	$114,980,312	$97,778,294	$17,202,018	$40,795,280	$48,528,728	$292,447,534		$259,634,720
Alabama	6,476,073	21,727,685	15,061,164	2,358,894	1,757,651	601,243	617,154	355,035	3,335,438		4,511,760
Alaska	2,032,061	10,182,537	6,962,794	1,460,784	1,209,809	250,975	192,835	267,684	1,298,440		1,886,305
Arizona	8,209,708	23,758,373	16,816,013	1,568,048	1,230,675	337,373	691,319	500,034	4,182,959		3,283,193
Arkansas.................	4,937,560	14,584,692	10,892,041	1,073,644	963,990	109,654	518,755	137,746	1,962,506		2,981,327
California	95,069,461	188,503,030	118,110,030	9,367,080	8,171,192	1,195,888	4,285,537	7,492,325	49,248,058		28,083,907
Colorado.................	6,291,390	22,452,523	14,204,199	1,485,834	1,260,385	225,449	362,907	860,563	5,539,020		4,034,587
Connecticut............	4,908,546	24,394,169	15,752,174	1,827,444	1,491,095	336,349	547,167	1,435,495	4,831,889		4,272,596
Delaware.................	1,271,359	7,376,891	5,254,757	780,520	657,534	122,986	257,805	353,163	730,646		2,473,124
Florida....................	17,809,542	62,626,494	44,962,402	5,190,234	4,600,075	590,159	1,963,673	1,313,796	9,196,389		8,926,358
Georgia...................	10,361,359	35,122,420	24,073,754	2,659,934	2,362,882	297,052	979,446	665,293	6,743,993		5,931,608
Hawaii....................	220,844	11,256,867	8,491,719	897,975	712,640	185,335	144,068	349,062	1,374,043		2,310,366
Idaho	1,981,659	6,549,199	4,653,245	551,740	441,930	109,810	133,844	161,777	1,048,593		1,090,045
Illinois....................	15,549,167	59,775,553	36,944,818	3,962,519	3,599,768	362,751	1,262,268	3,503,179	14,102,769		8,904,708
Indiana...................	9,292,344	27,501,295	19,786,809	2,427,613	2,005,994	421,619	981,692	961,664	3,343,517		4,314,917
Iowa.......................	4,753,646	15,764,288	10,900,406	1,619,526	1,402,346	217,180	557,861	245,725	2,440,770		2,682,143
Kansas....................	4,057,504	12,379,202	8,991,368	1,089,440	910,880	178,560	162,307	215,245	1,920,842		3,644,550
Kentucky	4,802,691	24,085,092	16,123,500	1,968,741	1,698,449	270,292	896,380	692,650	4,403,821		3,969,946
Louisiana	6,241,308	25,796,270	18,265,363	1,998,074	1,721,187	276,887	451,268	849,059	4,232,506		4,050,956
Maine	1,238,618	7,711,789	5,852,116	433,151	364,216	68,935	143,592	233,066	1,049,864		756,435
Maryland.................	8,641,281	30,915,712	20,952,583	2,493,037	2,039,893	453,144	1,914,736	1,101,621	4,453,735		4,857,463
Massachusetts..........	9,401,248	47,371,526	31,853,811	3,290,261	3,068,603	221,658	840,410	3,263,912	8,123,132		6,268,290
Michigan.................	19,249,754	43,695,740	30,360,266	2,148,561	1,663,829	484,732	1,233,603	1,440,019	8,513,291		7,727,625
Minnesota...............	12,975,915	26,967,577	18,908,308	1,581,068	1,281,852	299,216	1,120,702	481,576	4,875,923		5,209,914
Mississippi..............	5,053,070	15,048,856	10,814,367	1,190,761	1,011,876	178,885	280,220	275,259	2,488,249		2,518,296
Missouri..................	5,771,802	24,679,576	17,463,592	1,457,994	1,236,785	221,209	554,905	790,713	4,412,372		3,794,857
Montana..................	1,373,069	5,702,348	3,883,434	630,469	553,929	76,540	115,506	140,943	931,996		1,026,453
Nebraska.................	2,170,630	7,710,207	5,891,144	879,194	801,046	78,148	173,474	70,011	696,384		2,372,694
Nevada....................	4,214,581	9,059,226	5,368,958	632,219	553,757	78,462	315,805	191,517	2,550,727		1,563,233
New Hampshire	1,300,770	6,119,650	4,385,046	484,826	406,241	78,585	148,436	357,212	744,130		900,538
New Jersey	11,102,269	56,260,341	34,168,935	4,102,039	3,592,902	509,137	1,292,133	2,164,380	14,532,854		10,349,020
New Mexico.............	4,500,634	12,699,840	9,093,983	872,853	810,827	62,026	259,745	288,029	2,185,230		2,662,738
New York.................	56,236,537	127,803,663	86,853,934	9,493,079	7,548,281	1,944,798	1,636,851	5,730,909	24,088,890		22,974,180
North Carolina.........	13,172,640	40,453,222	28,260,807	3,466,699	2,726,764	739,935	655,108	619,671	7,450,937		9,281,523
North Dakota...........	1,632,316	4,777,845	3,055,372	841,567	776,951	64,616	159,841	97,306	623,759		1,108,571
Ohio.......................	16,517,064	59,774,607	35,493,425	4,611,905	4,215,143	396,762	2,003,369	1,231,811	16,434,097		9,396,073

See footnotes at end of table.

STATE EXPENDITURE, BY CHARACTER AND OBJECT AND BY STATE: 2013 (In thousands of dollars)—Continued

State	Intergovernmental expenditures	Total	Direct expenditures								Exhibit: Total salaries and wages
			Current operation	Capital outlay			Assistance and subsidies	Interest on debt	Insurance benefits and repayments		
				Total	Construction	Other					
Oklahoma	4,213,211	18,707,163	13,302,644	1,883,892	1,567,708	316,184	453,666	539,565	2,527,396		3,162,736
Oregon	5,495,337	21,354,747	14,100,769	1,138,779	882,046	256,733	577,064	424,175	5,113,960		4,797,424
Pennsylvania	18,834,325	68,698,329	44,347,538	7,054,683	6,353,219	701,464	2,147,773	1,446,132	13,702,203		8,090,451
Rhode Island	1,170,440	7,018,575	4,518,481	404,000	352,174	51,826	150,354	474,116	1,471,624		1,176,761
South Carolina	5,454,008	22,791,696	15,772,341	1,663,802	1,542,292	121,510	1,017,174	650,863	3,687,516		3,596,657
South Dakota	740,104	3,736,621	2,433,676	639,183	591,828	47,355	83,929	114,194	465,639		956,329
Tennessee	7,074,682	23,511,638	17,700,839	1,618,748	1,424,748	194,000	1,172,474	264,464	2,755,113		3,766,072
Texas	27,590,295	97,339,243	68,361,537	8,045,756	6,255,591	1,790,165	2,297,935	1,729,403	16,904,612		16,384,939
Utah	3,069,082	13,753,420	9,766,636	1,324,378	1,093,409	230,969	731,866	270,687	1,659,853		2,925,621
Vermont	1,501,657	4,516,590	3,710,721	204,307	172,888	31,419	149,104	94,202	358,256		789,408
Virginia	11,255,705	36,358,360	25,953,846	3,059,704	2,545,039	514,665	1,615,558	1,159,003	4,570,249		6,777,430
Washington	9,777,797	35,948,066	22,335,778	3,380,742	2,890,088	490,654	1,597,316	1,289,645	7,344,585		10,114,009
West Virginia	2,469,535	10,764,620	7,755,238	1,074,774	916,095	158,679	234,604	253,663	1,446,341		1,868,736
Wisconsin	9,637,247	27,887,557	18,591,474	2,086,899	1,868,764	218,135	641,349	929,923	5,637,912		4,369,544
Wyoming	1,681,018	4,153,874	2,818,795	502,938	471,028	31,910	70,392	51,243	710,506		738,304

Source: U.S. Census Bureau, 2013 Annual Survey of State Government Finances.

Note: Data users who create their own estimates using these data should cite only the U.S. Census Bureau as the source of the original data. Data in this table are based on information from public records and contain no confidential data. Although the data in this table come from a census of governmental units and are not subject to sampling error, the census results may contain nonsampling error. Additional information on nonsampling error, response rates, and definitions may be found within the survey methodology. http://www2.census.gov/govs/state/13_methodology.pdf, and technical documentation, http://www2.census.gov/govs/state/statetechdoc2013.pdf.

Note: Detail may not add to total due to rounding.

Table 7.23
STATE GENERAL EXPENDITURE, BY FUNCTION AND BY STATE: 2013 (In thousands of dollars)

State	Total general expenditures (a)	Education	Public welfare	Highways	Hospitals	Natural Resources	Health	Corrections	Financial administration	Employment security administration	Police
United States	$1,683,170,060	$599,151,748	$519,178,293	$112,174,050	$67,433,480	$21,345,804	$63,246,831	$48,407,786	$23,136,739	$4,846,304	$15,106,964
Alabama	24,601,701	10,616,535	6,386,764	1,753,303	2,132,163	276,034	558,857	533,083	248,400	97,936	160,779
Alaska	10,707,194	2,806,879	2,084,000	1,152,768	79,817	331,740	348,730	335,234	233,899	48,632	166,917
Arizona	27,750,523	9,423,140	8,494,905	1,971,558	683,817	263,092	1,924,080	829,019	300,229	96,683	232,360
Arkansas	17,559,746	7,518,389	5,139,921	1,219,251	936,138	248,511	297,457	403,821	414,188	96,127	109,098
California	233,454,218	80,195,847	80,014,405	13,193,489	9,107,869	4,102,500	8,785,009	7,844,627	3,299,564	517,095	1,600,910
Colorado	23,189,078	9,478,848	5,840,287	1,448,635	710,618	321,265	1,055,306	975,698	302,682	75,354	172,792
Connecticut	23,719,309	7,019,066	7,318,979	1,056,211	1,288,711	164,033	950,351	669,700	360,713	98,246	232,639
Delaware	7,782,971	2,745,343	1,971,064	595,377	47,575	73,337	449,699	282,015	198,775	18,282	126,436
Florida	71,097,679	22,904,253	22,528,115	5,869,267	820,601	1,100,119	3,763,817	2,145,818	571,434	358,667	514,377
Georgia	38,702,490	17,337,702	11,518,235	2,170,602	948,316	454,830	1,204,357	1,487,452	487,975	63,052	319,687
Hawaii	10,098,104	3,404,040	2,098,924	409,269	799,790	113,135	494,927	200,984	109,106	5,750	34,307
Idaho	7,378,235	2,658,667	2,190,795	691,516	52,453	217,916	178,448	251,160	213,786	48,114	54,577
Illinois	61,221,951	17,272,058	20,424,637	4,969,276	1,345,563	237,443	2,240,614	1,327,176	705,952	125,536	467,598
Indiana	33,450,122	14,613,475	10,748,417	2,530,006	160,643	335,053	495,892	688,283	291,830	113,760	237,564
Iowa	17,901,551	6,469,134	5,265,106	1,658,218	1,519,773	295,335	256,786	334,893	211,928	46,577	96,322
Kansas	14,515,864	6,057,156	3,386,863	1,181,586	1,556,542	231,678	356,630	347,040	184,930	20,511	105,054
Kentucky	24,457,976	9,453,475	7,083,731	2,365,583	1,132,362	333,797	691,179	532,134	273,401	90,298	197,374
Louisiana	27,799,897	8,881,174	7,165,251	1,716,072	1,930,770	801,023	523,905	701,296	408,892	111,845	356,701
Maine	7,876,981	2,019,094	2,892,491	614,592	111,922	171,924	484,261	136,811	139,977	19,694	75,602
Maryland	34,170,869	11,398,463	10,044,675	1,949,117	517,097	447,136	2,149,504	1,396,307	934,704	57,276	550,989
Massachusetts	46,360,151	13,010,482	15,560,077	2,005,325	489,640	343,750	1,151,865	1,095,858	562,992	67,307	829,770
Michigan	53,549,642	22,972,166	14,985,940	2,419,026	3,080,402	318,918	1,329,434	1,857,508	464,546	191,770	401,026
Minnesota	35,058,976	15,026,229	11,323,904	2,464,343	265,135	607,961	431,809	514,959	354,857	91,989	382,588
Mississippi	17,386,707	5,456,159	5,816,559	1,376,640	1,131,700	291,359	403,671	376,455	175,333	80,982	112,169
Missouri	26,039,006	8,952,460	7,988,161	1,595,271	1,683,129	339,286	1,585,857	736,445	213,122	29,526	214,524
Montana	6,060,601	1,856,783	1,421,146	683,224	49,673	322,807	175,007	191,150	183,610	24,055	51,138
Nebraska	9,184,453	3,367,219	2,517,272	754,226	261,809	251,065	476,668	246,519	94,011	42,792	86,623
Nevada	10,639,400	4,365,150	2,400,389	721,780	265,446	116,153	275,542	283,918	111,986	87,305	101,604
New Hampshire	6,207,431	2,068,121	1,682,499	557,978	49,410	76,860	140,321	112,422	76,680	40,634	56,132
New Jersey	50,052,284	16,426,314	14,701,447	3,192,396	2,106,102	581,243	1,260,358	1,436,484	672,255	191,609	818,347
New Mexico	15,015,244	5,406,138	3,946,347	756,210	953,684	182,694	491,298	400,947	229,196	10,247	134,511
New York	147,156,113	41,151,716	58,009,518	4,238,973	4,750,662	423,976	9,215,195	3,438,227	2,386,721	283,741	995,306
North Carolina	46,102,728	19,250,605	12,977,012	3,688,451	2,020,269	511,455	1,368,833	1,210,318	507,385	58,332	703,083
North Dakota	5,786,402	1,931,216	943,371	1,051,899	53,709	329,500	161,118	96,683	61,813	10,586	35,210
Ohio	59,501,507	21,606,929	19,186,691	3,678,390	3,125,123	390,327	2,493,472	1,543,631	1,261,016	385,494	318,780

See footnotes at end of table.

STATE GENERAL EXPENDITURE, BY FUNCTION AND BY STATE: 2013 (In thousands of dollars)—Continued

State	Total general expenditures (a)	Education	Public welfare	Highways	Hospitals	Health	Natural Resources	Corrections	Financial administration	Employment security administration	Police
Oklahoma	19,579,099	7,321,724	6,258,083	1,802,547	258,175	861,552	231,332	569,140	407,392	52,785	233,623
Oregon	21,465,429	7,172,341	6,575,475	1,312,821	1,548,755	792,133	449,716	730,873	570,068	65,984	183,495
Pennsylvania	72,244,141	22,628,667	23,078,652	7,601,344	3,789,791	3,080,531	642,051	2,119,602	1,318,587	99,390	911,672
Rhode Island	6,562,768	1,986,630	2,394,541	318,630	66,449	158,767	59,205	182,888	131,144	20,998	71,704
South Carolina	22,331,442	8,352,080	6,050,877	923,605	1,444,046	1,011,767	196,531	490,627	366,655	71,703	183,055
South Dakota	4,011,086	1,266,106	971,649	653,007	21,930	178,414	178,255	116,535	94,118	23,154	38,321
Tennessee	27,831,207	9,810,510	10,959,849	1,752,119	404,978	672,883	291,223	889,870	302,528	90,721	232,868
Texas	108,024,926	47,479,191	30,780,705	7,536,463	5,237,650	2,774,086	1,040,736	3,701,789	833,467	206,143	799,712
Utah	14,956,224	6,874,554	3,017,968	961,772	1,180,848	390,835	172,571	310,560	245,280	13,770	143,594
Vermont	5,607,879	2,407,364	1,629,482	455,461	287	235,775	81,883	135,127	76,114	14,018	91,112
Virginia	42,529,852	15,214,402	9,855,058	3,912,825	3,598,411	1,343,432	248,919	1,706,864	538,886	137,156	559,409
Washington	37,864,966	15,582,462	8,389,040	3,183,817	2,160,922	2,185,121	861,649	954,986	414,185	203,385	356,847
West Virginia	11,708,850	4,333,893	3,526,796	1,102,651	126,185	345,537	225,833	300,693	184,365	28,088	75,101
Wisconsin	31,878,459	10,877,543	8,849,077	2,409,285	1,422,217	771,081	664,438	1,090,920	300,364	99,154	122,600
Wyoming	5,036,628	1,723,856	783,143	547,875	4,403	274,660	394,207	143,237	105,696	14,051	50,957

Source: U.S. Census Bureau, 2013 Annual Survey of State Government Finances.

Note: Data users who create their own estimates using these data should cite only the U.S. Census Bureau as the source of the original data. Data in this table are based on information from public records and contain no confidential data. Although the data in this table come from a census of governmental units and are not subject to sampling error, the census results may contain nonsampling error. Additional information on nonsampling error, response rates, and definitions may be found within the survey methodology. http://www2.census.gov/govs/state/13_methodology.pdf, and technical documentation, http://www2.census.gov/govs/state/statetechdoc2013.pdf.

Note: Detail may not add to total due to rounding.

Key:

(a) Total includes other expenditures not shown separately in this table.

Table 7.24
STATE DEBT OUTSTANDING AT END OF FISCAL YEAR, BY STATE: 2013
(In thousands of dollars)

State	Total	Long-term total	Short-term	Net long-term total (a)
United States	$1,137,363,585	$1,131,695,556	$5,668,029	$673,184,786
Alabama...................................	9,055,227	9,022,866	32,361	7,205,340
Alaska.....................................	6,218,363	6,039,975	178,388	2,381,602
Arizona....................................	13,723,166	13,674,685	48,481	9,649,947
Arkansas..................................	3,947,169	3,947,169	0	2,400,990
California	152,186,012	152,186,012	0	120,765,605
Colorado..................................	16,309,217	16,289,471	19,746	4,213,322
Connecticut..............................	32,356,807	32,355,800	1,007	17,864,967
Delaware	5,754,587	5,754,587	0	3,313,777
Florida	37,892,165	37,858,479	0	30,634,276
Georgia....................................	13,292,965	13,173,035	33,686	9,959,599
Hawaii......................................	8,318,403	8,318,403	119,930	7,519,815
Idaho.......................................	3,647,841	3,636,772	0	719,176
Illinois.....................................	63,660,340	63,648,354	11,069	33,460,534
Indiana....................................	22,564,017	22,362,681	11,986	2,710,889
Iowa	6,647,699	6,647,699	201,336	1,074,694
Kansas.....................................	6,825,293	6,765,478	0	3,697,606
Kentucky	14,983,712	14,943,682	59,815	9,064,992
Louisiana..................................	18,589,438	18,586,813	40,030	10,445,065
Maine.......................................	5,374,528	5,374,528	2,625	1,248,448
Maryland..................................	26,066,617	25,993,895	0	13,848,190
Massachusetts	76,160,503	75,929,609	72,722	42,797,116
Michigan..................................	30,377,220	30,094,468	230,894	14,961,706
Minnesota.................................	13,572,769	13,566,980	282,752	7,496,166
Mississippi................................	7,112,560	7,090,975	5,789	5,603,193
Missouri...................................	19,307,770	19,247,522	21,585	5,224,768
Montana	3,558,343	3,558,105	60,248	264,988
Nebraska..................................	1,846,583	1,845,318	238	393,202
Nevada.....................................	3,609,752	3,609,752	1,265	2,495,628
New Hampshire	8,763,339	8,713,495	0	2,890,268
New Jersey	64,264,050	64,203,722	49,844	42,754,931
New Mexico	7,232,938	7,200,981	60,328	4,153,974
New York..................................	136,014,460	135,379,542	31,957	93,627,253
North Carolina...........................	19,054,585	19,023,785	634,918	8,033,114
North Dakota.............................	1,834,319	1,823,782	30,800	743,278
Ohio..	33,132,906	32,548,652	10,537	13,341,595
Oklahoma.................................	9,514,281	9,500,592	584,254	5,962,964
Oregon.....................................	13,598,468	13,466,596	13,689	8,967,771
Pennsylvania	47,020,552	46,739,081	131,872	24,342,530
Rhode Island.............................	9,568,297	9,496,920	281,471	2,688,126
South Carolina...........................	14,723,546	14,394,263	71,377	10,293,755
South Dakota.............................	3,425,424	3,424,634	329,283	846,820
Tennessee	6,191,955	5,723,281	790	1,643,059
Texas.......................................	39,624,672	38,452,696	468,674	29,565,812
Utah..	7,049,552	7,001,324	1,171,976	4,256,379
Vermont...................................	3,330,238	3,195,300	48,228	988,749
Virginia....................................	28,022,656	27,845,516	134,938	13,514,926
Washington...............................	30,474,333	30,474,333	177,140	20,981,521
West Virginia.............................	7,355,630	7,355,630	0	3,155,400
Wisconsin	23,187,772	23,187,772	0	8,879,389
Wyoming	1,020,546	1,020,546	0	137,571

Source: U.S. Census Bureau, 2013 Annual Survey of State Government Finances.

Note: Data users who create their own estimates using these data should cite only the U.S. Census Bureau as the source of the original data. Data in this table are based on information from public records and contain no confidential data. Although the data in this table come from a census of governmental units and are not subject to sampling error, the census results may contain nonsampling error. Additional information on nonsampling error, response rates, and definitions may be found within the survey methodology, *http://www2.census.gov/govs/ state/13_methodology.pdf,* and technical documentation, *http://www2. census.gov/govs/state/statetechdoc2013.pdf.*

Note: Detail may not add to total due to rounding.

Key:
(a) Long-term debt outstanding minus long-term debt offsets.

Table 7.25
NUMBER AND MEMBERSHIP OF STATE PUBLIC-EMPLOYEE PENSION SYSTEMS
BY STATE: FISCAL YEAR 2013

State	Number of systems (a)	Membership			Total beneficiaries receiving periodic benefit payments (a)
		Total (a)	Active members (a)	Inactive members (a)	
United States........................	224	17,525,187	12,515,498	5,009,689	7,912,924
Alabama (b)	4	250,112	220,815	29,297	124,031
Alaska	4	43,099	34,607	8,492	41,613
Arizona	4	457,423	241,416	216,007	140,356
Arkansas	6	166,086	133,650	32,436	73,458
California	5	1,898,023	1,301,011	597,012	907,892
Colorado	2	407,363	207,511	199,852	109,135
Connecticut	6	132,147	117,313	14,834	83,232
Delaware	1	46,420	43,061	3,359	26,180
Florida.................................	1	617,250	514,436	102,814	346,678
Georgia	10	635,611	371,625	263,986	175,992
Hawaii	1	73,538	66,226	7,312	41,812
Idaho	2	92,698	65,585	27,113	39,032
Illinois.................................	6	791,296	471,013	320,283	334,238
Indiana	8	265,999	224,032	41,967	134,760
Iowa	4	242,765	169,762	73,003	109,527
Kansas	1	199,244	156,053	43,191	87,096
Kentucky..............................	6	333,038	213,317	119,721	138,670
Louisiana	14	285,461	191,758	93,703	156,376
Maine	1	62,142	53,191	8,951	39,302
Maryland.............................	2	247,607	195,560	52,047	139,574
Massachusetts......................	14	244,866	209,731	35,135	136,379
Michigan (b)	6	296,442	267,490	28,952	293,987
Minnesota	8	512,881	283,705	229,176	180,516
Mississippi..........................	4	293,905	162,455	131,450	93,056
Missouri	10	287,954	233,320	54,634	146,338
Montana..............................	9	76,880	52,570	24,310	36,959
Nebraska.............................	5	84,833	57,698	27,135	21,638
Nevada	2	112,851	99,079	13,772	52,509
New Hampshire	2	57,277	48,743	8,534	29,785
New Jersey...........................	7	556,915	417,287	139,628	290,677
New Mexico..........................	5	161,731	117,848	43,883	71,932
New York	2	920,902	795,146	125,756	566,257
North Carolina.....................	6	659,671	489,237	170,434	251,493
North Dakota.......................	2	41,364	31,738	9,626	16,224
Ohio....................................	5	1,258,759	652,691	606,068	429,203
Oklahoma	6	167,967	150,998	16,969	100,321
Oregon	1	208,078	163,259	44,819	125,804
Pennsylvania........................	3	541,887	395,452	146,435	332,046
Rhode Island	1	40,331	32,188	8,143	26,311
South Carolina	4	378,187	212,241	165,946	137,138
South Dakota	2	53,886	38,594	15,292	23,566
Tennessee.............................	1	247,701	215,076	32,625	127,918
Texas (b)	7	1,598,702	1,333,662	265,040	536,364
Utah....................................	6	143,488	104,072	39,416	50,663
Vermont	3	31,863	24,836	7,027	15,685
Virginia	1	460,728	340,751	119,977	169,588
Washington	6	276,100	218,129	57,971	147,887
West Virginia	1	97,039	76,503	20,536	55,847
Wisconsin	1	416,806	256,833	159,973	173,655
Wyoming..............................	6	47,871	42,224	5,647	24,224

Source: U.S. Census Bureau, 2013 Annual Survey of Public Pensions: State-Administered Defined Benefit Data.

Note: Pension obligations and Covered payroll for defined benefit pension systems are only collected at the state level.

Note: Data users who create their own estimates using these data should cite the U.S. Census Bureau as the source of the original data only. The data in this table are based on information from public records and contain no confidential data. Although the data in this table come from a census of pension systems and are not subject to sampling error, the census results do contain nonsampling error. Additional information on nonsampling error, response rates, and definitions may be found within the survey methodology, http://www2.census.gov/govs/retire/2013surveymeth.pdf.

Note: Detail may not add to total due to rounding.

Key:

(a) These categories are in whole numbers: Number of systems, Total membership, Active membership, Inactive membership, and Total beneficiaries receiving periodic benefit payments.

(b) There are exceptions to the fiscal year rule for the state pension systems in Alabama, Michigan, and Texas. For systems in these states, the fiscal year moves beyond the June 30 cutoff. The data for the survey year 2013 covers the fiscal year ending August 31, 2013 for Texas and September 30, 2013 for Alabama and Michigan. These exceptions are made to better align the data with the Survey of State Government Finances.

Table 7.26
FINANCES OF STATE PUBLIC-EMPLOYEE PENSION SYSTEMS, BY STATE: FISCAL YEAR 2013*
(In thousands of dollars)

State and level of government	Total receipts	Employee contributions	Government contributions Total	From state government	From local government	Earnings on investments (b)	Total payments	Benefits	Withdrawals	Other payments
United States.........	$434,941,171	$37,454,045	$81,751,369	$45,108,649	$36,642,720	$315,735,757	$213,432,731	$199,138,321	$4,549,283	$9,745,127
Alabama (a)	5,750,150	700,319	983,923	139,266	844,657	4,065,908	2,966,784	2,820,519	100,999	45,266
Alaska	1,904,117	165,220	552,766	438,698	114,068	1,186,131	1,017,759	983,374	13,721	20,664
Arizona	6,885,859	1,162,427	1,396,661	218,833	1,177,828	4,326,771	3,496,322	3,104,294	262,651	129,377
Arkansas................	3,934,985	187,414	781,363	305,872	475,491	2,966,208	1,501,031	1,398,813	29,515	72,703
California...............	78,109,256	6,672,210	13,637,647	5,590,748	8,046,899	57,799,399	31,995,623	30,586,445	443,716	965,462
Colorado	6,880,453	723,991	1,124,941	349,299	775,642	5,031,521	4,132,025	3,752,386	198,361	181,278
Connecticut	6,762,746	456,272	1,922,043	1,860,996	61,047	4,384,431	3,358,780	3,260,384	16,776	81,620
Delaware...............	1,177,603	59,798	262,725	252,450	10,275	855,080	556,211	524,436	4,028	27,747
Florida...................	18,586,808	830,618	1,540,775	326,497	1,214,278	16,215,415	7,133,553	6,675,112	5,034	453,407
Georgia	14,758,875	698,689	1,635,561	1,041,822	593,739	12,424,625	5,226,786	5,044,567	93,078	89,141
Hawaii...................	2,186,914	185,837	581,447	435,107	146,340	1,419,630	1,089,851	1,033,281	7,204	49,366
Idaho	1,495,690	185,102	285,966	73,484	212,482	1,024,622	741,564	692,990	0	48,574
Illinois..................	21,332,973	1,777,965	6,703,950	5,663,555	1,040,395	12,851,058	10,659,160	10,001,813	229,703	427,644
Indiana..................	3,901,420	328,909	1,939,454	1,411,411	528,043	1,633,057	2,439,116	2,161,183	98,790	179,143
Iowa.......................	3,852,756	446,996	687,600	131,750	555,850	2,718,160	1,948,060	1,838,083	43,621	66,356
Kansas	2,702,244	300,472	617,925	420,882	197,043	1,783,847	1,448,288	1,340,945	53,900	53,443
Kentucky...............	5,170,409	583,529	1,322,209	868,540	453,669	3,264,671	3,467,287	3,302,115	52,049	113,123
Louisiana	7,598,389	772,904	2,371,653	1,963,041	408,612	4,453,832	3,806,798	3,509,434	166,634	130,730
Maine	1,640,328	153,537	294,694	267,572	27,122	1,192,097	836,912	772,360	22,771	41,781
Maryland................	6,507,571	710,855	1,670,349	989,132	681,217	4,126,367	3,320,497	2,981,005	38,281	301,211
Massachusetts.......	8,078,630	1,322,192	1,791,772	1,648,406	143,366	4,964,666	4,767,425	4,487,536	113,510	166,379
Michigan (a)	10,019,605	529,062	2,547,446	773,747	1,773,699	6,943,097	6,439,267	6,327,208	38,470	73,589
Minnesota	9,641,456	826,249	958,893	201,657	757,236	7,856,314	3,765,724	3,645,120	66,418	54,186
Mississippi............	4,137,254	550,047	914,020	336,144	577,876	2,673,187	2,206,114	2,029,121	108,536	68,457
Missouri................	10,390,996	813,684	1,442,517	529,792	912,725	8,134,795	4,165,027	3,435,622	84,503	644,902
Montana.................	1,913,062	164,007	228,477	136,330	92,147	1,520,578	674,954	608,545	19,180	47,229
Nebraska................	1,577,658	200,110	239,401	74,298	165,103	1,138,147	537,510	487,299	22,068	28,143
Nevada...................	4,631,397	99,258	1,310,296	191,494	1,118,802	3,221,843	1,745,414	1,681,320	26,126	37,968
New Hampshire	1,292,486	199,413	252,582	56,986	195,596	840,491	632,181	578,593	23,191	30,397
New Jersey.............	12,036,297	1,947,855	2,939,333	2,938,827	506	7,149,109	9,065,176	8,837,414	172,094	55,668
New Mexico...........	3,634,510	476,727	590,299	370,909	219,390	2,567,484	1,838,336	1,688,343	86,830	63,163
New York	34,483,351	400,738	7,075,476	3,565,421	3,510,055	27,007,137	16,503,704	15,640,385	20,869	842,450
North Carolina......	10,159,988	1,177,328	1,545,817	1,146,481	399,336	7,436,843	5,300,897	4,772,166	142,567	386,164
North Dakota........	475,320	91,078	109,735	28,013	81,722	274,507	266,129	240,791	8,932	16,406
Ohio.......................	25,271,519	2,721,279	3,227,197	1,809,329	1,417,868	19,323,043	13,750,319	12,676,592	568,405	505,322
Oklahoma..............	4,760,323	407,659	1,134,499	731,384	403,115	3,218,165	2,021,831	1,865,374	70,394	86,063
Oregon	8,177,121	16,986	834,161	224,075	610,086	7,325,974	3,984,674	3,556,060	17,440	411,174
Pennsylvania.........	11,279,914	1,352,586	2,056,937	1,373,159	683,778	7,870,391	9,538,903	8,667,574	53,084	818,245
Rhode Island	1,333,423	171,350	373,038	227,337	145,701	789,035	935,806	902,832	11,940	21,034
South Carolina......	4,843,081	775,279	1,103,044	347,199	755,845	2,964,758	3,467,534	2,923,716	102,255	441,563
South Dakota........	1,716,293	101,679	102,377	39,625	62,752	1,512,237	466,503	401,451	25,161	39,891
Tennessee..............	4,659,363	266,831	1,010,424	388,418	622,006	3,382,108	2,003,919	1,918,704	39,518	45,697
Texas (a)................	22,117,030	3,392,018	3,980,642	1,914,478	2,066,164	14,744,370	13,094,725	12,081,519	622,663	390,543
Utah.......................	3,403,510	40,634	812,240	681,161	131,079	2,550,636	1,201,596	1,153,231	5,260	43,105
Vermont	463,736	77,251	106,030	51,370	54,660	280,455	264,615	241,760	5,707	17,148
Virginia	8,896,284	595,339	1,896,837	627,132	1,269,705	6,404,108	4,110,170	3,672,541	81,538	356,091
Washington............	8,864,319	569,028	1,177,053	1,176,065	988	7,118,238	3,547,556	3,248,120	55,079	244,357
West Virginia	2,267,394	166,909	722,743	513,017	209,726	1,377,742	1,000,339	961,668	28,734	9,937
Wisconsin..............	12,086,318	757,151	799,350	219,036	580,314	10,529,817	4,549,158	4,208,151	26,563	314,444
Wyoming................	1,189,987	141,254	155,081	38,404	116,677	893,652	444,818	416,026	21,416	7,376

See footnotes at end of table.

FINANCES OF STATE PUBLIC-EMPLOYEE PENSION SYSTEMS, BY STATE: FISCAL YEAR 2013*
(In thousands of dollars) — Continued

Source: U.S. Census Bureau, 2013 Annual Survey of Public Pensions: State-Administered Defined Benefit Data.

*Effective with the 2012 survey cycle, the Annual Survey of Public Pensions: State-Administered Defined Benefit Data revised the survey form to implement changes in asset classification. These changes apply to the categories designated as corporate stocks, corporate bonds, federal government securities, state and local government securities, and other securities. Federally-sponsored agency securities are classified under federal government securities instead of corporate bonds. Private equity, venture capital, and leverage buyouts are classified under corporate stocks instead of other securities. Due to these changes in asset classification, there are shifts in the distribution of assets from corporate bonds to federal government securities and from other securities to corporate stocks. However, since investment decisions guide the distribution of assets, we cannot calculate the exact impact that the changes in classification had on the asset distribution for 2012. As such, for the above mentioned asset categories, any data comparisons between data from 2012 to the present, and data prior to 2012 should be exercised with caution.

Notes: Pension obligations and Covered payroll for defined benefit pension systems are only collected at the state level. Data users who create their own estimates using these data should cite the U.S. Census Bureau
as the source of the original data only. The data in this table are based on information from public records and contain no confidential data. Although the data in this table come from a census of pension systems and are not subject to sampling error, the census results do contain nonsampling error. Additional information on nonsampling error, response rates, and definitions may be found within the survey methodology, *http://www2.census.gov/govs/retire/2013surveymeth.pdf.* Detail may not add to total due to rounding.

Key:

(a) There are exceptions to the fiscal year rule for the state pension systems in Alabama, Michigan, and Texas. For systems in these states, the fiscal year moves beyond the June 30 cutoff. The data for the survey year 2013 covers the fiscal year ending August 31, 2013 for Texas and September 30, 2013 for Alabama and Michigan. These exceptions are made to better align the data with the Survey of State Government Finances.

(b) The total of "net earnings" is a calculated statistic and thus can be positive or negative. Net earnings is the sum of earnings on investments plus gains on investments minus losses on investments. The change made in 2002 for asset valuation from book to market value in accordance with Statement 34 of the Governmental Accounting Standards Board is reflected in the calculated statistics.

Table 7.27
NATIONAL SUMMARY OF STATE-ADMINISTERED DEFINED BENEFIT PENSION SYSTEM FINANCES: FISCAL YEARS, 2013 AND HISTORICAL FISCAL YEARS

	Amount (in thousands of dollars)							Percentage distribution						
	2012–2013	2011–2012	2010–2011	2009–2010	2008–2009	2007–2008	2006–2007	2012–2013	2011–2012	2010–2011	2009–2010	2008–2009	2007–2008	2006–2007
Total contributions (a)	$119,205,414	$110,517,658	$105,856,548	$97,960,078	$96,896,954	$96,213,263	$87,088,833	100.0%	100.0%	100.0%	100.0%	100.0%	100.0%	100.0%
Employee contributions	37,454,045	35,932,106	34,071,682	33,163,241	33,370,232	31,905,999	29,323,427	31.4	32.5	32.2	33.9	34.4	33.2	33.7
Government contributions	81,751,369	74,585,552	71,784,866	64,796,837	63,526,722	64,307,264	57,765,406	68.6	67.5	67.8	66.1	65.6	66.8	66.3
State government contributions	45,108,649	41,932,108	39,182,364	35,646,331	34,623,278	36,019,351	31,675,999	37.8	37.9	37.0	36.4	35.7	37.4	36.4
Local government contributions	36,642,720	32,653,444	32,602,502	29,150,506	28,903,444	28,287,913	26,089,407	30.7	29.5	30.8	29.8	29.8	29.4	30.0
Earnings on investments (b)	315,735,757	81,998,680	414,042,169	291,060,107	-511,544,873	-71,743,687	402,274,323							
Total Payments	213,432,731	199,422,184	189,133,595	174,184,100	163,467,019	158,260,995	148,992,161	100.0	100.0	100.0	100.0	100.0	100.0	100.0
Benefits	199,138,321	186,352,632	176,750,586	163,430,279	153,361,522	144,796,455	131,679,736	93.3	93.4	93.5	93.8	93.8	91.5	88.4
Withdrawals	4,549,283	4,348,826	3,911,578	3,525,772	3,347,235	3,360,646	4,562,127	2.1	2.2	2.1	2.0	2.0	2.1	3.1
Other payments	9,745,127	8,720,726	8,471,431	7,228,049	6,758,262	10,103,894	12,750,298	4.6	4.4	4.5	4.1	4.1	6.4	8.6
Total cash and investment holdings	2,726,314,125	2,527,989,000	2,544,893,736	2,217,913,893	2,006,286,505	2,617,809,877	2,772,534,682	100.0	100.0	100.0	100.0	100.0	100.0	100.0
Cash and short-term investments	88,788,091	82,300,200	107,478,261	78,655,273	86,403,215	82,334,322	92,102,370	3.3	3.3	4.2	3.5	4.3	3.1	3.3
Total securities	2,241,785,872	2,031,090,549	2,032,529,139	1,826,931,429	1,643,995,517	2,160,496,945	2,379,726,742	82.2	80.3	79.9	82.4	81.9	82.5	85.8
Government securities	245,468,798	252,772,673	200,434,737	193,431,482	182,248,585	185,421,948	222,463,385	9.0	10.0	7.9	8.7	9.1	7.1	8.0
Federal government	244,239,375	252,090,042	198,835,328	192,303,212	181,511,264	184,428,997	221,263,987	9.0	10.0	7.8	8.7	9.0	7.0	8.0
United States Treasury	153,671,610	157,596,907	144,305,059	132,563,258	126,666,846	117,442,816	138,309,054	5.6	6.2	5.7	6.0	6.3	4.5	5.0
Federal agency	90,567,765	94,493,135	54,530,269	59,739,954	54,844,418	66,986,181	82,954,933	3.3	3.7	2.1	2.7	2.7	2.6	3.0
State and local government	1,229,423	682,631	1,599,409	1,128,270	737,321	992,951	1,199,398	0.0	0.0	0.1	0.1	0.0	0.0	0.0
Nongovernmental securities	1,996,317,074	1,778,317,876	1,832,094,402	1,633,499,947	1,461,746,932	1,975,074,997	2,157,263,357	73.2	70.3	72.0	73.7	72.9	75.4	77.8
Corporate bonds	314,363,670	316,668,174	359,851,358	356,974,404	339,443,955	424,661,423	363,832,211	11.5	12.5	14.1	16.1	16.9	16.2	13.1
Corporate stocks	997,525,635	931,182,599	861,927,189	767,117,342	673,984,627	940,685,027	1,055,194,290	36.6	36.8	33.9	34.6	33.6	35.9	38.1
Mortgages	8,310,181	9,613,974	10,388,104	10,649,377	11,100,929	16,221,239	16,801,440	0.3	0.4	0.4	0.5	0.6	0.6	0.6
Funds held in trust	53,403,123	35,065,839	28,787,214	36,390,628	27,783,932	36,103,622	43,943,975	2.0	1.4	1.1	1.6	1.4	1.4	1.6
Foreign and international	539,488,439	453,273,648	449,994,638	359,356,396	317,392,838	407,931,692	447,213,593	19.8	17.9	17.7	16.2	15.8	15.6	16.1
Other nongovernmental securities	83,226,026	32,513,642	121,145,899	103,011,800	92,040,651	149,471,994	230,277,848	3.1	1.3	4.8	4.6	4.6	5.7	8.3
Other investments	395,740,162	414,598,251	404,886,336	312,327,191	275,887,773	374,978,610	300,705,570	14.5	16.4	15.9	14.1	13.8	14.3	10.8
Real property	110,625,169	105,991,152	100,782,628	83,280,616	88,403,128	99,271,409	95,276,289	4.1	4.2	4.0	3.8	4.4	3.8	3.4
Miscellaneous investments	285,114,993	308,607,099	304,103,708	229,046,575	187,484,645	275,707,201	205,429,281	10.5	12.2	11.9	10.3	9.3	10.5	7.4

Source: 2007–2013 Annual Surveys of Public Pensions: State Data. Data users who create their own estimates using data from this report should cite the U.S. Census Bureau as the source of the original data only. The data in this table are based on information from public records and contain no confidential data. Although the data in this table come from a census of retirement systems and are not subject to sampling error, the census results do contain nonsampling error. Additional information on nonsampling error and response rates may be found at http://www.census.gov/govs/retire/how_data_collected.html.

Note: Detail may not add to total due to rounding.

Key:
(a) Contributions and earnings on investments are both classified as revenue. Contributions reflect actual transactions made, while earnings can be unrealized. Earnings also may be positive or negative. See note (b).
(b) The total of "net earnings" is a calculated statistic (the item code in the data file is X08), and thus can be positive or negative. Net earnings is the sum of earnings on investments plus gains on investments minus losses on investments. The change made in 2002 for asset valuation from book to market value in accordance with Statement 34 of the Governmental Accounting Standards Board is reflected in the calculated statistics.

Chapter Eight

STATE MANAGEMENT, ADMINISTRATION AND DEMOGRAPHICS

Awash in Data: Promises and Pitfalls

By Katherine Barrett and Richard Greene

The word "data" may appear to many policymakers and managers as a modern-day "open sesame," to enter the cave of well-run states. But, while gathering facts and figures is a crucial first step, actually analyzing, utilizing and communicating them is the key to progress. That's not easy.

The use of valid, timely data to effectively run a government is not a new factor in the world of the states. The first census—just 14 years after the Declaration of Independence was signed—was an indicator that the Founding Fathers understood that if this new republic couldn't count things (people in this case), it could hardly be expected to manage itself.

In the pre-computer age, of course, the utility of data was little more sophisticated than that in a Mom and Pop candy store at the time, where cash sat in the register and was supposed to match a pile of receipts kept in a nearby drawer. Even after computers began to enter the scene, simple financial data for the states was still in its infancy.

When Edward Regan took the comptroller's helm in New York state in 1978, he lamented the state of the art of the day. As he told Forbes magazine in 1980, "There [has been] no accountability. The books [have been] so loose and kept in such an undisciplined manner that governors and legislators [have not] been held responsible for their actions."[1]

While there's a wide variation between the quality of data today—both financial and performance related—and its utility, one thing has increasingly emerged as a significant trend in states: the sheer quantity of data available grows every minute of every day across the 50 states.

Consider a sunset review that recently was completed in Texas about the five agencies that make up the health and human services system: "According to informal estimates, the total volume of information maintained by system agencies could top 200 terabytes of data. For comparison, a digitized version of the Library of Congress's 17 million printed holdings would total about 136 terabytes; while all data sent from the Hubble Telescope from its first 24 years was about 100 terabytes."[2]

Meanwhile, as the review points out, Texas' health and human services now has 800 underlying data systems that have grown up over time with different standards and different data definitions.

Despite obstacles such as those cited above, the potential for the technology that permits states to gather nearly unthinkable quantities of data is huge. Some people increasingly have referred to "big data," as the science of utilizing huge quantities of data across a variety of databases to come up with better policies and practices.[3] As a result of this phenomenon, the vision of what such information can do has grown immensely.

This potential can be realized with knowledge, skills and creativity. It is not necessarily dependent on buying new expensive technology systems.

"You can simulate things that you couldn't have done in the past," said Max Arinder, executive director of Mississippi's Joint Committee on Performance Evaluation and Peer Review (PEER). "You can do some magical things."[4]

A few examples:

- In order to improve collection of child support payments, Pennsylvania in 2009 determined to provide new, real-time, information about parents' financial employment and asset history. It began to use electronic data exchanges to lessen reliance on manual data collection, improve case management and develop more sophisticated predictive abilities. That was the beginning. In 2010, the state's data exchanges were enhanced and case managers had access to reliable, relevant and current data, which allowed them to quickly determine the most effective actions for collecting child support or providing medical insurance to children. By 2011, the most recent year for which national statistics are available, Pennsylvania had been able to raise its child support collection rate to about 80 percent, compared with the 50-state average of 62.4 percent.[5]

- One audit, recently issued by the Massachusetts State Auditor's Office examined all 710,025 Medicaid claims paid for by MassHealthwithin the program designed to aid illegal immigrants with emergency treatments. Data analytics allowed the state to fully analyze every transaction processed through this program over a three-year period in a relatively short amount of time. Some 45 percent of those claims were discovered to be questionable. This was a remarkably high figure and has galvanized the state to target attention on specific issues, ameliorate them and prevent them from recurring.[6]

- Indiana attacked the problem of infant mortality with intensive data analytics in 2014, combining multiple data sets to look at the drivers of infant mortality and give policymakers information on how to best lower Indiana's above average infant mortality rates. Analysts started initially with 17 integrated data sets that came from five agencies, and public sources like the U.S. Census, and ended up concentrating on five data sets that helped analyze what population sub-groups were most at risk. Data revealed that about 65 percent of deaths occurred for mothers who had fewer than 10 prenatal visits and that younger mothers on Medicaid were most at risk of not getting the prenatal care needed.[7]

This knowledge, combined with more qualitative research, is contributing to new policy approaches that will help the state target pregnant women who may be most vulnerable to poor birth outcomes and develop ways to improve their prenatal care. For example, while the deep data dig revealed that distance to a health facility or doctor was not a factor in lowering access to prenatal care, subsequent follow-up research has suggested that helping individuals with transportation could have positive effects on increasing that care.[8]

Like others, Gary Blackmer, the director of the audit division in Oregon's Secretary of State's Office, talks about the difference in the way his office makes use of full data sets now as opposed to the sampling that occurred in the past. For example, it did some matching between lottery winners and recipients of public assistance since some of these winners now have enough cash to make it unnecessary for the public to subsidize their living costs.

"We were matching millions of records to millions of records. We worked with the Department of Human Services to make sure that what we came up with is not a keying error," said Blackmer.[9]

The auditors found about 9,000 files in which there could be problems and they pointed the department to those 9,000 files to look more closely. In the past, they would have drawn a sample of files and reached a conclusion about the number of potential problems in that sample. But they wouldn't have been able to point specifically to the problem cases to look at.

"Now, we can hand them 9,000 records in which we think there are errors," Blackmer said. "In the past, we would have said, 'There are fish out there. Go catch them.'"[10]

One key to getting more and better utility out of data is to persuade state agencies to share the information they've gathered, considering it to be a state-wide asset rather than an agency possession. Doug Robinson, executive director of the National Association of State CIOs, recommended that every state have a data management element to its architecture and that data be regarded as a major strategic asset. He said discussions need to occur at the enterprise level. This requires a major shift in thinking.

"This is an asset of the state government, not data owned by individual state agencies," he said.[11]

Getting buy-in for this concept isn't always the easiest thing in the world. Some agencies—particularly those with a great deal of private information about citizens—feel they are restrained from sharing that information with anyone outside their particular agencies. Even when there's no legislative mandate or federal regulations requiring this kind of privacy, it's often part of the ethos of the agencies themselves.

Beyond that, there's often a technological blockage to sharing data across agencies. Multiple platforms have developed over the course of years, and so there's no magic button to push to combine data from the department of mental health, say, and the department of corrections. Yet, these are exactly the kinds of agencies that can benefit from dealing with one complete database.

"The really big obstacle to using data is culture," said Catherine Lyles, Louisiana's senior auditor. "People don't understand the value of the information they collect and therefore they collect it in an inconsistent way that limits its usefulness."[12]

The Louisiana state audit performance division has been particularly active in working with agencies to help them understand how to use data more effectively.

"Agencies collect a lot of data, but they don't use it for management purposes," said Karen Leblanc, director of performance audit services in Louisiana. "We try to teach them to use the data they collect."[13]

Of course, drawing data from the agencies is only useful if the material they've gathered is reliable and that's not always the case.

"The legislature needs to make decisions, but the decisions are only as good as the information they receive," said Jan Yamane, acting auditor in Hawaii.[14]

Ohio Auditor Dave Yost says auditors must do a much better job of ensuring that the data driving decisions can be trusted. At the summer 2015 meeting of the National Association of State Auditors, Comptrollers and Treasurers, he plans to come armed to discuss the speedily evolving need to ensure data integrity.

"I think this is probably the most important emerging trend for government executives, across the board at all levels," Yost said. If data is distorted, he said, "then making decisions based on that data is worse than making decisions based on no data at all."[15]

Even as states make progress toward gathering and validating data, there's a sense of a receding shore phenomenon here. The more information states have to make good policy decisions, the more they seem to want and the greater demands policymakers are imposing on their data-crunchers. As John Turcotte, the director of the North Carolina General Assembly's division of program evaluation put it, "There is strong and sustained legislative interest in decision analytics in North Carolina and frustration with lagging capability within state government."[16]

Medicaid payment reform, for example, is built on the principle that payments be based on quality and performance. But that requires that the quality and performance information be up to the task. James Nobles, legislative auditor in Minnesota, has worked in the legislative auditor's office for 36 years and has seen many improvements in the quality and use of data.

"But our expectations get raised," Nobles said. "So there's always that gap. I think we have greater expectations that if we have big data systems and powerful computers, why can't we answer these questions more easily. There's a frustration level there."[17]

One obstacle in many states to making the highest and best use of data is a lack of a governing structure over its use.

In Maine, data governance is getting attention from both the legislative and executive branches. The Office of Program Evaluation and Government Accountability started looking into ways to move the state forward in a report they did almost 10 years ago that asked how Maine could make better use of data. It's now doing a follow up

review. One of the issues that has materialized is the role that the Office of Information Technology plays. As in many states, the technology officials see their role as supporting the technology and the tools that agencies use, and in ensuring the security of the data.

"But they clearly don't think their role includes how consistent the data is or being able to use the data," said Beth Ashcroft, director of Maine's Office of Program Evaluation and Government Accountability. "Part of our effort has been to see whether there is some place for data leadership to emerge."

Although chief information officers have everything to do with the technology that houses data, they are often quite removed from the management of the data.

"Honestly, they don't have a lot of authority in that space," said Robinson of the National Association of State CIOs.[18]

The next step for many states is to develop a governance structure; a way of bringing together groups that represent the various agencies and assigning responsibilities for data stewardship. Some states have talked about having a master data index and centralized rules for data management, but this includes many policy discussions that states have generally not successfully confronted yet.

"A lot of times, nobody has really thought about it," Ashcroft said. "Nobody has thought through proactively what kind of data we need. When the federal government requires certain data to be reported, it's fine, but beyond that it doesn't get a lot of time with folks thinking through the key things to be looking at and what kinds of different analyses we might do at the management level to help inform us. If this isn't thought through, the data isn't captured. If nobody has focused on data and the key pieces of data that need to be gathered in a consistent way, then it's weak."[19]

There are a handful of states that already are focusing more intently on these questions. Virginia and Utah, often leaders in matters of management, have been developing an enterprise approach to data. Virginia's move toward improved data governance includes developing standards and ways to manage data like an asset; they are developing data about their data.

Indiana presents a powerful example of the ways in which attention to data itself — as opposed to the technology that is used to store and access it — likely will become a greater focus of attention.

Paul Baltzell, the chief information officer for Indiana, took on that position when Gov. Mike Pence took office in January 2013. In the first months of the administration, Baltzell saw his role as many CIOs do—he was in charge of the technology and the technology infrastructure.

"We didn't really manage data," Baltzell said.[20]

But Pence had a strong belief in the importance of using data more effectively to manage government programs and policies. Shortly after he took office, the state made its first major plunge into data analytics with its study of infant mortality. Then in March 2014, Pence issued an executive order to officially create the Governor's Management and Performance Hub. The order requires agencies to provide central executive branch access to data and systems; in effect, making the data itself a property of the state enterprise, not just of any individual agency.[21]

With the importance of data as a strategic asset evolving, Baltzell's office was moved from its traditional position under the chief of staff, to the Office of Management and Budget, where it has a closer link to the governor himself.

"When you have a petabyte[22] of data, that has a value," Baltzell said. "We've taken on data management as a challenge because we believe we need to centralize and manage our data better. We believe it's an asset that is helping to leverage the M in OMB."

Following its analysis of infant mortality, Indiana officials have embarked on an effort to use data to analyze recidivism and are looking into ways that the data can help reduce child abuse and domestic violence. It's also pursuing the more typical data analytics that target a reduction in fraud.

Baltzell believes other states that want to leverage data likely will move in a similar direction, making the information aspect of information technology a much clearer focus.

"It's making us think about it," he said. "Quite honestly, before, when I talked with other CIOs, it wasn't a topic. This wasn't on my radar as CIO until we did this."

Notes

[1] Forbes Magazine, You Can't Fight City Hall if You Can't Understand it, March, 1980

[2] Texas Sunset Advisory Commission Staff Report on Health and Human Services Commission and System Issues, October 2014

[3] It's worth being cautious with the term "big data," though the definition used in this article is reasonably generic, based on telephone conversations with high-level representatives of 10 entities (eight states, one city, one university), it emerged that there is no refined and universally accepted definition of "big data."

[4] Interview by authors with Arinder, Jan. 19, 2015

[5] "2011 State by State Child Support Collections," National Conference of State Legislatures, updated January 2013, http://www.ncsl.org/research/human-services/state-by-state-data-on-child-support-collecti.aspx

[6] Office of Medicaid (MassHealth) – Review of the MassHealth Limited Program (Emergency Medical Services, Massachusetts), The Massachusetts Office of the State Auditor, Dec. 10, 2014, http://www.mass.gov/auditor/docs/2014/201313743m.pdf

[7] Hughes, Jessica, "Data Analytics Helps Indiana Change its Approach to Infant Mortality," Government Technology, Feb. 3, 2015 http://www.govtech.com/data/Data-Analytics-Helps-Indiana-Change-its-Approach-to-Infant-Mortality.html

[8] Hughes, Jessica, "Data Analytics Helps Indiana Change its Approach to Infant Mortality," Government Technology, Feb. 3, 2015 http://www.govtech.com/data/Data-Analytics-Helps-Indiana-Change-its-Approach-to-Infant-Mortality.html

[9] Interview with Gary Blackmer, Jan. 22, 2015

[10] Ibid

[11] Interview by authors, Jan. 20, 2015

[12] Author's interview, Dec. 19, 2014

[13] Authors interview, Dec. 19, 2014

[14] Authors' Interview, Dec. 10, 2014

[15] Authors' Interview, Feb. 4, 2015

[16] Authors' interview, Jan. 14, 2015

[17] Authors' interview, Jan. 6, 2015

[18] ibid

[19] ibid

[20] Author's interview, March 5, 2015

[21] ibid

[22] A petabyte (PB) is 1,000 terabytes (TB) or 1,000,000 gigabytes (GB).

About the Author

Katherine Barrett and Richard Greene are a husband and wife team who are senior fellows at the Council of State Governments; senior advisers to the Pew Charitable Trusts government performance unit, senior advisors to the Fels Institute at the University of Pennsylvania and fellows in the National Academy of Public Administration. They are also columnists for Governing Magazine and senior fellows at the Governing Institute.

Developing Uniform Measures of State Government Activity: Context, Classification and Census Bureau Data

By Elizabeth Accetta and Joseph Dalaker

The U.S. Census Bureau measures state and local government activity through the Census of Governments and related surveys. The data produced from these efforts are standardized across states and are the only nationwide dataset that allows for comparability both across states and on a national basis. Even with this standardization, the activities of 50 different state political systems present unique challenges to those who collect and use these data. We will introduce the principles by which the Census Bureau classifies governments and their activities. Additionally, through specific case studies, we will illustrate the ways states differ in their operation and in how they conduct the business of public service. Through these illustrations, we will offer a perspective that enables data users to delve into the data with a more thorough and accurate understanding, allowing them to formulate analyses more accurately.

The 10th Amendment of the U.S. Constitution, similar to Article II of the Articles of Confederation, limited the power of the federal government so as to protect state autonomy. Because of this amendment, one can think of the states as 50 autonomous governments defining their own political processes and governmental structure within their boundaries, with divergent results. Therefore, those who use the U.S. Census Bureau's statistics on governments should consider the ways in which a state government may have made different decisions about which public services get provided, how they get provided, what administrative tools are put in place to provide them and the structure of local governments within its borders.

In order to create uniform datasets on the organization, employment, and finances of state and local governments, the Census Bureau uses a system for classifying the functions, or activities, performed by governmental employees and by various financial transactions. This classification system also is supported by principles for identifying and defining which organized entities can properly be called "governments." The Census Bureau conducts legislative research, and when necessary, contacts state or local officials, to keep track of the creation of new governments, the abolition of existing governments and governmental mergers, and to determine whether certain organizational entities meet the Census Bureau's definition of a government for the purpose of measuring public sector activity. These principles enable the Census Bureau to create a uniform dataset even though

states are diverse in their organizational arrangements and in how they conduct public business.

All the same, it is wise for data users to be aware of the Census Bureau's classification principles and to appreciate the diversity among state governments. That is, data users should bear in mind how states are organized and conduct their business to understand the Census Bureau's statistics that could be misleading if not viewed in light of that larger context.

The rest of this article will discuss the diverse ways in which state governments conduct their business, with an eye toward helping the users of Census Bureau public sector data better understand how the data are affected by those differences. We begin by discussing the Census Bureau's definition of a government, which affects how we classify entities as independent governments or as dependent on another "parent" government. We then explain how the states' choices of ending dates for their fiscal years affect the way users should analyze the fiscal impact of historical events. To illustrate further, we will discuss how the different ways states establish and work with dependent agencies can affect the dollar amounts shown in a variety of fiscal transactions, and that those amounts do not always agree with the amounts reported by the state governments themselves because the Census Bureau sometimes classifies the dependent agencies differently from state authorities. Last, we illustrate how states' choices in the way they raise revenue, and how states classify that revenue, can complicate state-to-state comparisons. Through these illustrations, we hope that the reader will avoid making hasty conclusions when looking at state data, avoid treating all states identically, and instead appreciate the differences by which state governments operate and analyze Census Bureau statistics with that broader context in mind.

The Census Bureau's Criteria for Classifying Governments

The Census Bureau defines a government as follows:

A government is an organized entity which, in addition to having governmental character, has sufficient discretion in the management of its own affairs to distinguish it as separate from the administrative structure of any other governmental unit. To be defined as a government, any entity must possess all three of the attributes reflected in the foregoing definition: Existence as an organized entity, governmental character, and substantial autonomy.[1]

The three attributes are further defined in the Census Bureau's reports on Government Organization from the Censuses of Governments.[2] In brief:
Existence as an organized entity is demonstrated by:

... The presence of some form of organization and the possession of some corporate power, such as perpetual succession, the right to sue and be sued, have a name, make contracts, acquire and dispose of property, and the like. ... [S]ome entities not so specifically stated by law to be corporations [nevertheless] do have sufficient powers to be counted as governments.

The mere right to exist is not sufficient. Where a former government has ceased to operate — [that is, it] receives no revenue, conducts no activities, and has no officers at present — it is not counted as an active government.[3]

The presence of language in a state's laws describing the establishment, merger or disincorporation of a government is an important indicator of an entity's existence or lack thereof. However, quite often further research is needed to determine the entity's actual status, including, for example, contacting the local officials for information on the entity's activities and relationships with other governmental bodies.
Governmental character is a somewhat circular term when used to define governments, but nonetheless does denote that the entity must provide services, or wield authority or bear accountability that is of a public nature. The Census Bureau's reports provide examples of indicators of governmental character, any of which may be sufficient, but not all are necessary:

Governmental character exists when officers of the entity are popularly elected or are appointed by public officials. A high degree of responsibility to the public, demonstrated by requirements for public reporting or for accessibility of records to public inspection, is also taken as critical evidence of governmental character.

Governmental character is attributed to any entities having power to levy property taxes, power to issue debt for which the interest is exempt from federal taxation.... However, a lack of either of these attributes ... does not preclude a class of units from being recognized as having governmental character, if it meets the indicated requirements as to officers or public accountability. Thus, some special district governments that have no taxing powers and provide electric power or other public utility services also widely rendered privately are counted as local governments because of provisions as to their administration and public accountability.[4]

Substantial autonomy consists of two components: fiscal independence and administrative independence. As described in the Census Bureau's reports:

Fiscal independence generally derives from the power of the entity to:

- Determine its budget without review and detailed modification by other local officials or governments;

- Determine taxes to be levied for its support;

- Fix and collect charges for its services; or

- Issue debt without review by another local government.

Administrative independence is closely related to the basis for selection of the governing body of the entity. Accordingly, a public agency is counted as an independent government if it has independent fiscal powers and additionally:

- Has a popularly elected governing body;

- Has a governing body representing two or more state or local governments; or

• Even in the event its governing body is appointed, performs functions that are essentially different from those of, and are not subject to specification by, its creating government.[5]

An entity must demonstrate both fiscal independence and administrative independence to be considered a government. Census Bureau reports also provide examples of situations in which an entity may be considered to be a dependent agency of another "parent" government, owing to the makeup of its board—as being composed mainly of officials of the parent government—or provisions that its plans or budgets be reviewed and potentially altered by another government.[6]

These dependent agencies—synonymously referred to as "subordinate agencies"—can present a challenge to data users in two ways. First, the Census Bureau may consider some entities to be dependent upon—and thus part of—another government in ways the entities or parent governments themselves may not recognize or agree with. It should be kept in mind that the Census Bureau endeavors to measure public sector activity without omission or duplication, and as such, the dependent agencies need to be included with their parent government in order to measure public sector activity both completely and consistently.

Second, as discussed in the Census Bureau's report *Individual State Descriptions*, dependent agencies:

… can be involved in a wide variety of activities—school systems, universities, utilities, toll highways, hospitals, etc. …

Contrasting examples of the existence of dependent agencies are found in New York City and Chicago. Almost all local government services in New York City are classified as part of the city government. … As a result, New York City government includes over 100 dependent agencies. By contrast, many of these services in Chicago are classified as functions of independent special district governments.[7]

Cautionary Examples of Using Census Bureau Statistics on Governments

Fiscal Years

Not all governments end their fiscal years on the same date, nor can the federal government mandate to more than 90,000 governments that they end their fiscal years on a given date. As a result, there are a variety of fiscal year end dates for the governments throughout the nation. Even at the state level, there are differences in dates. For the most part, 46 of the 50 states end their fiscal year on June 30. The other four states have varying ends for their fiscal years:

• New York ends on March 31;

• Texas ends on Aug. 31; and

• Alabama and Michigan end on Sept. 30.

Due to the general differences in fiscal year end dates, to collect financial data for a given fiscal year, the Census Bureau defines a reference period for the census and surveys on government finances. The defined reference period for a survey cycle begins on July 1 of year A and ends on June 30 of year A+1. The reference period would be known as "Fiscal Year A+1." However, there are exceptions to this reference period. The states of Texas, Alabama and Michigan will include the fiscal years that extend beyond the reference period; similar instances for local governments include the District of Columbia and local school systems in Alabama, Nebraska and Texas.

Given the variation in fiscal years, a user needs to take caution when trying to use Census Bureau statistics on governments to analyze the effect of a time-specific event. A good example would be trying to analyze the government spending during and after a large-scale hurricane. A high category hurricane travels up the Gulf Coast hammering through Mississippi, Alabama and Florida, leaving the states with wind damage and flooding. How did the state governments respond to the natural disaster? How much federal money did these governments receive?

To continue the example using Figure A, let's say that the event occurred in August 2014. A user wants to compare the government spending of Mississippi, Alabama and Florida to determine how each responded to the natural disaster. Mississippi and Florida have the fiscal year end date of June 30, but Alabama's fiscal year ends on September 30.

When looking at Census Bureau government statistics for the 2014 fiscal year, and given the Census Bureau defined reference period, Mississippi and Florida would show data from their fiscal year that ended on June 30, 2014. However, the data for this reference period for Alabama would include data through their fiscal year ending on Sept. 30, 2014.

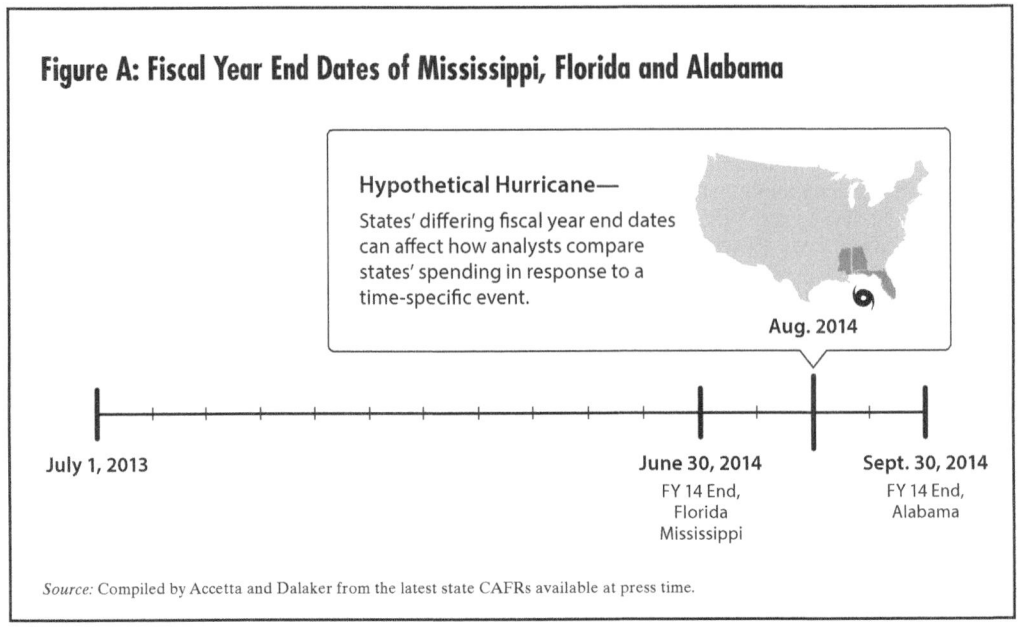

Figure A: Fiscal Year End Dates of Mississippi, Florida and Alabama

Hypothetical Hurricane—

States' differing fiscal year end dates can affect how analysts compare states' spending in response to a time-specific event.

Aug. 2014

July 1, 2013

June 30, 2014
FY 14 End,
Florida
Mississippi

Sept. 30, 2014
FY 14 End,
Alabama

Source: Compiled by Accetta and Dalaker from the latest state CAFRs available at press time.

Because of the differences in fiscal years, the effects of the hurricane in August 2014 would not be shown in the Mississippi or Florida data for the 2014 fiscal year. It would, however, be included for Alabama's data. Therefore, a comparison between the three states for a single fiscal year would not be feasible. This is important to remember. A user would have a greater benefit by looking at the impact over at least two fiscal years of data. In this case, the differences in fiscal year periods alone would have an important effect, not to mention any long-range fiscal impacts such a storm might have.

Dependent Agencies

For the purpose of Census Bureau statistics, the term "state government" refers not only to the executive, legislative and judicial branches of a given state, but it also includes those agencies, institutions, commissions and public authorities that operate separately from the central state government but where the state government maintains administrative or fiscal control over their activities, as described earlier.

Consider the following example, which illustrates how recognizing the presence of dependent agencies can help one to understand the Census Bureau's finance data. A data user looks to compare New Jersey's debt reported in the state's Comprehensive Annual Financial Report, also known as CAFR, to

what is reported for the Annual Survey of State Government Finances (shown in Table A.) The user notices that the figures do not match. Why does it appear to the user that the Census Bureau is overstating the debt for the state?

When the user adds the general obligation bonds and revenue bonds for the state in the CAFR, they come to a figure of $23.9 billion. When that user consults the Census Bureau data, they see a figure for total outstanding debt of $64.2 billion. How can the difference be so great? The Census Bureau statistics gather outstanding debt from not only the central state government—as reported in the CAFR—but also from a number of other agencies the state considers to be "legally separate entities." From the Census Bureau classification, however, these entities do not meet the criteria to be a separate, independent government and have

Table A: New Jersey Total 2013 Outstanding Long-term Debt

New Jersey State CAFR	Census Bureau Data
$23.9 billion	$64.2 billion

Source: New Jersey 2013 Comprehensive Annual Financial Report; U.S. Census Bureau 2013 Annual Survey of State Government Finances

shown either fiscal or administrative dependence, or both. Some of these agencies include such entities as the New Jersey Transit Corporation, New Jersey Turnpike Authority and New Jersey Educational Facilities Authority.

State Government Tax Revenue

When analyzing tax data, especially when comparing tax data across states, it is essential to remember that the Census Bureau's statistics on tax revenue reflect taxes a state collects from activity within the state and not necessarily from the residents of that state, because people, companies or other organizations from outside the state may be the ones performing the activities. As a result, analyses based on rankings or per capita statistics do not measure "burden," nor lend themselves as easily to apples-to-apples comparisons, in the way a data user might expect. To understand the economic impact of taxes on states, it is not enough to compare only the total taxes collected by each state—one must also understand how those taxes are collected.

As an example, the following table highlights the total taxes collected for Florida and Alaska in 2013, the population estimates for each state and the tax revenue per capita.

From this table, can a data user accurately state that the tax burden for a resident of Alaska is almost four times that of a person that lives in Florida? Not necessarily. The user should dig further into the source of the tax revenue in each state before establishing such a hypothesis.

Alaska, for instance, does not have general sales taxes or individual income taxes, but it does collect severance taxes from companies that extract oil and natural gas. Like Alaska, Florida also does not collect individual income taxes. But unlike Alaska, Florida instead relies heavily on a general sales tax, which, because of its tourist industry, is partially supported by visitors from outside Florida. In that sense, both Alaska and Florida use "exported taxes"—taxes collected from people or organizations that may reside outside their state.

State-Specific Terminology

A state's definitions of a certain activity will be set to fit their specific policy needs. As a result, we will see a variety of different terms to define the same activity or revenue. It is the responsibility of the Census Bureau to sift through the various terms and classify these activities according to standardized definitions.

For example, medical provider taxes have provided a large funding mechanism for many years. They have been used by state governments to generate the state matching funds needed to receive federal financial participation for Medicaid. The variety of names referenced across the states for this type of tax is also large. Some of the variations include:

- Hospital Assessments
- Provider Fees
- Quality Assessments
- Provider Taxes

When classifying these aforementioned assessments, fees and taxes into our own set of definitions, the Census Bureau looks beyond the terms used for the revenue and into the definition of the assessment, fee or tax. In each case, the definition included some form of per unit charge for a hospital or medical provider. For example, State Y's "Hospital Assessment Fee" is charged to hospitals at a rate of $350 per inpatient bed day. State X's "Hospital

Table B: 2013 Tax Revenue Per Capita, Alaska, Florida

	Alaska	Florida
2013 Total Tax Revenue	$5,132,811	$35,377,566
2013 Population Estimate	710,231	18,801,310
Tax Revenue Per Capita	7,227	1,881

Source: U.S. Census Bureau, 2013 Annual Survey of State Government Tax Collections; and Annual Estimates of the Resident Population: April 1, 2010 to July 1, 2013.
Note: Total tax revenues in thousands; population estimates and per capita dollars in single units.

Services Tax" is charged to hospitals at a rate of 3 percent of gross revenues. Two different terms, and two different definitions for the state, but the Census Bureau will classify them in the same tax category (Other Selective Sales and Gross Receipts Taxes).

The Census Bureau tax category "Other Selective Sales and Gross Receipts Taxes" is defined as:

Taxes on specific commodities, businesses, or services not reported separately above. For state governments, includes sales or use taxes based on sale price, where the authorizing legislation is separate from the state's general sales and use tax law.

Since that definition does not yield a starkly unambiguous explanation, one needs to look to the definition of the subcategory for "Selective Sales and Gross Receipts Taxes:"

Taxes imposed on the sale of particular commodities or services or on gross receipts. ...

Here, one sees that the definition will include taxes on *services* and *gross receipts*. So while State Y is collecting a rate per inpatient bed day—a unit of service—and State X is collecting a rate per gross revenues—or gross receipts—by the Census Bureau definition, both will be included in "Other Selective Sales and Gross Receipts Taxes."

Discussion: Using the Data

As discussed and illustrated above, the Census Bureau's data may not entirely be in accordance with the state governments' own accounts of their activities, but they do reflect a consistent approach toward creating a unified dataset that accounts for all public sector activity without omission or duplication. In order to make the best use of the data, the data user should understand the basic principles by which the Census Bureau classified governments and their activities, and in so doing, become sensitive to the differences by which governments in different jurisdictions conduct their business.

Is there any way to do better than just "becoming sensitive" to the differences among governments? That is, can the data be made completely consistent, so that all governmental units and activities can be treated as identical? The 10th Amendment to the U.S. Constitution implies that the answer is a resounding "no:"

The powers not delegated to the United States by the Constitution, nor prohibited by it to the states, are reserved to the states respectively, or to the people.

States, therefore, have been long-recognized as having the powers to organize their governmental affairs, and for setting the rules by which they, and the local governments within their purview, can operate. At this point, a careful analyst might worry that conducting valid analysis depends upon having identical units to compare and analyze. This article argues that in many cases, governments are not truly identical units.

What, then, should the analyst do to ensure that his or her work is valid? Users of statistics on governments should appreciate the diversity of state governments by framing their research with sensitivity toward the dimensions talked about in this article: the timing of fiscal years when looking at historical events; the role of agencies that the Census Bureau classifies as dependent or subordinate to the state; the degree to which revenue may be obtained from people or groups outside the state's boundaries; and the Census Bureau's classification system, which focuses on the purposes of activities rather than on specific programs, and the purposes of financial transactions rather than specific funds. To that end, two resources cited earlier can assist data users in their analysis: the publication *Individual State Descriptions*, see footnote 2; and the *Government Finance and Employment Classification Manual*, 2006 edition, see footnote 8.

Conclusion

The Census of Governments and its related programs provide a rich source of data on state and local governments in the United States, not only on the number of governments by type, but also additional detail on their organization, employment and finances. Census Bureau staff apply a standard set of criteria while classifying governments and their activities in order to provide what is perhaps the only complete and uniform set of data on the activities of governments in the United States.

In making their classification decisions, Census Bureau staff do need to be sensitive to the differences of governance among states and local governments, and the effects those differences have on the data. Similarly, data users can strengthen their analyses when they too take account of the broader context within which states provide public services, bearing in mind the examples discussed in this article.

Disclaimer: This report is released to inform interested parties of research and to encourage discussion of work in progress. The views expressed are those of the authors and not necessarily those of the U.S. Census Bureau.

Acknowledgments: The authors would like to thank Stephen D. Owens, Lisa M. Blumerman, Brigitte Wehrs, Erika Becker-Medina, Melissa Therrien, Joy Pierson, Franklin Winters, and Kevin Deardorff of the U.S. Census Bureau for their thoughtful review and comments on drafts of this paper.

Notes

[1] U.S. Census Bureau, 1957 Census of Governments, vol. 1 no. 3, *Local Government Structure*. p. 3.

[2] U.S. Census Bureau, 2012 Census of Governments, *Individual State Descriptions*, p. v *et passim*. *http://www2.census.gov/govs/cog/2012isd.pdf*, accessed 3 March 2015.

[3] Ibid.

[4] Ibid.

[5] Ibid.

[6] Ibid.

[7] Ibid., p. vii.

[8] U.S. Census Bureau, *Government Finance and Employment Classification Manual*. p. 4-12.

[9] Ibid.

About the Authors

Elizabeth Accetta is a section chief in the Public Sector Frame and Classification Branch in the U.S. Census Bureau's Economic Statistical Methods Division. She holds a Masters Degree in Public Administration from the University of Pittsburgh and a Bachelor's Degree in Economics from the University of Nevada Las Vegas.

Joseph Dalaker is a section chief in the Data User Outreach and Education Office of the U.S. Census Bureau's Economy-Wide Statistics Division. He holds a Master of Public Policy degree from the University of Michigan and a Bachelor's degree cum laude in Government and Economics from Cornell University.

Table 8.1
SUMMARY OF STATE GOVERNMENT EMPLOYMENT: 1953–2012

| | Employment (in thousands) | | | | | | Monthly payrolls (in millions of dollars) | | | Average monthly earnings of full-time employees | | |
| | Total, full-time and part-time | | | Full-time equivalent | | | | | | | | |
Year (October)	All	Education	Other	All	Education	Other	All	Education	Other	All	Education	Other
1953......................	1,082	294	788	966	211	755	278.6	73.5	205.1	289	320	278
1954......................	1,149	310	839	1,024	222	802	300.7	78.9	221.8	294	325	283
1955......................	1,199	333	866	1,081	244	837	325.9	88.5	237.4	302	334	290
1956......................	1,268	353	915	1,136	250	886	366.5	108.8	257.7	321	358	309
1957 (April)..........	1,300	375	925	1,153	257	896	372.5	106.1	266.4	320	355	309
1958......................	1,408	406	1,002	1,259	284	975	446.5	123.4	323.1	355	416	333
1959......................	1,454	443	1,011	1,302	318	984	485.4	136	349.4	373	427	352
1960......................	1,527	474	1,053	1,353	332	1,021	524.1	167.7	356.4	386	439	365
1961......................	1,625	518	1,107	1,435	367	1,068	586.2	192.4	393.8	409	482	383
1962......................	1,680	555	1,126	1,478	389	1,088	634.6	201.8	432.8	429	518	397
1963......................	1,775	602	1,173	1,558	422	1,136	696.4	230.1	466.3	447	545	410
1964......................	1,873	656	1,217	1,639	460	1,179	761.1	257.5	503.6	464	560	427
1965......................	2,028	739	1,289	1,751	508	1,243	849.2	290.1	559.1	484	571	450
1966......................	2,211	866	1,344	1,864	575	1,289	975.2	353	622.2	522	614	483
1967......................	2,335	940	1,395	1,946	620	1,326	1,105.5	406.3	699.3	567	666	526
1968......................	2,495	1,037	1,458	2,085	694	1,391	1,256.7	477.1	779.6	602	687	544
1969......................	2,614	1,112	1,501	2,179	746	1,433	1,430.5	554.5	876.1	655	743	597
1970......................	2,755	1,182	1,573	2,302	803	1,499	1,612.2	630.3	981.9	700	797	605
1971......................	2,832	1,223	1,609	2,384	841	1,544	1,741.7	681.5	1,060.2	731	826	686
1972......................	2,957	1,267	1,690	2,487	867	1,619	1,936.6	746.9	1,189.7	778	871	734
1973......................	3,013	1,280	1,733	2,547	887	1,660	2,158.2	822.2	1,336	843	952	805
1974......................	3,155	1,357	1,798	2,653	929	1,725	2,409.5	932.7	1,477	906	1023	855
1975......................	3,271	1,400	1,870	2,744	952	1,792	2,652.7	1,021.7	1,631	964	1080	909
1976......................	3,343	1,434	1,910	2,799	973	1,827	2,893.7	1,111.5	1,782	1031	1163	975
1977......................	3,491	1,484	2,007	2,903	1,005	1,898	3,194.6	1,234.4	1,960	1096	1237	1031
1978......................	3,539	1,508	2,032	2,966	1,016	1,950	3,483	1,332.9	2,150	1167	1311	1102
1979......................	3,699	1,577	2,122	3,072	1,046	2,026	3,869.3	1,451.4	2,418	1257	1399	1193
1980......................	3,753	1,599	2,154	3,106	1,063	2,044	4,284.7	1,608	2,677	1373	1523	1305
1981......................	3,726	1,603	2,123	3,087	1,063	2,024	4,667.5	1,768	2,900	1507	1671	1432
1982......................	3,747	1,616	2,131	3,083	1,051	2,032	5,027.7	1,874	3,154	1625	1789	1551
1983......................	3,816	1,666	2,150	3,116	1,072	2,044	5,345.5	1,989	3,357	1711	1850	1640
1984......................	3,898	1,708	2,190	3,177	1,091	2,086	5,814.9	2,178	3,637	1825	1991	1740
1985......................	3,984	1,764	2,220	2,990	945	2,046	6,328.6	2,433.7	3,884.9	1935	2155	1834
1986......................	4,068	1,800	2,267	3,437	1,256	2,181	6,801.4	2,583.4	4,226.9	2052	2263	1956
1987......................	4,115	1,804	2,310	3,491	1,264	2,227	7,297.8	2,758.3	4,539.5	2161	2396	2056
1988......................	4,236	1,854	2,381	3,606	1,309	2,297	7,842.3	2,928.6	4,913.7	2260	2490	2158
1989......................	4,365	1,925	2,440	3,709	1,360	2,349	8,443.1	3,175.0	5,268.1	2372	2627	2259
1990......................	4,503	1,984	2,519	3,840	1,418	2,432	9,083	3,426	5,657	2472	2732	2359
1991......................	4,521	1,999	2,522	3,829	1,375	2,454	9,437	3,550	5,887	2479	2530	2433
1992......................	4,595	2,050	2,545	3,856	1,384	2,472	9,828	3,774	6,054	2562	2607	2521
1993......................	4,673	2,112	2,562	3,891	1,436	2,455	10,288.2	3,999.3	6,288.9	2722	3034	2578
1994......................	4,694	2,115	2,579	3,917	1,442	2,475	10,666.3	4,176.8	6,489.3	2776	3073	2640
1995......................	4,719	2,120	2,598	3,971	1,469	2,502	10,926.5	4,173.3	6,753.2	2854	3138	2725
1996......................	(a)	(a)	(a)	(a)	(a)	(a)	(a)	(a)	(a)	(a)	(a)	(a)
1997 (March)........	4,733	2,114	2,619	3,987	1,484	2,503	11,413.1	4,372.0	7,041.1	2968	3251	2838
1998 (March)........	4,758	2,173	2,585	3,985	1,511	2,474	11,845.2	4,632.1	7,213.1	3088	3382	2947
1999 (March)........	4,818	2,229	2,588	4,034	1,541	2,493	12,564.1	4,957.0	7,607.7	3236	3544	3087
2000 (March)........	4,877	2,259	2,618	4,083	1,563	2,520	13,279.1	5,255.3	8,023.8	3374	3692	3219
2001 (March)........	4,985	2,329	2,656	4,173	1,615	2,559	14,136.3	5,620.7	8,515.6	3521	3842	3362
2002 (March)........	5,072	2,414	2,658	4,223	1,659	2,564	14,837.8	5,996.6	8,841.2	3657	4007	3479
2003 (March)........	5,043	2,413	2,630	4,191	1,656	2,534	15,116.4	6,154.4	8,962.0	3751	4115	3566
2004 (March)........	5,041	2,432	2,609	4,188	1,673	2,515	15,477.5	6,411.8	9,065.7	3845	4256	3631
2005 (March)........	5,078	2,459	2,620	4,209	1,684	2,525	16,061.6	6,668.9	9,392.6	3966	4390	3745
2006 (March)........	5,128	2,493	2,635	4,251	1,708	2,542	16,769.4	6,960.9	9,808.6	4098	4505	3883
2007 (March)........	5,200	2,538	2,663	4,307	1,740	2,566	17,788.7	7,418.9	10,369.9	4276	4670	4063
2008 (March)........	5,270	2,593	2,677	4,363	1,780	2,582	18,725.9	7,883.2	10,842.7	4445	4853	4222
2009 (March)........	5,346	2,649	2,697	4,408	1,814	2,594	19,424.8	8,278.6	11,146.3	4565	5007	4320
2010 (March)........	5,326	2,669	2,656	4,378	1,824	2,554	19,579.1	8,516.5	11,062.6	4620	5111	4342
2011 (March)........	5,314	2,704	2,609	4,359	1,847	2,512	19,971.9	8,813.2	11,158.6	4715	5233	4446
2012 (March)........	5,286,102	2,723,444	2,562,658	4,312,054	1,842,704	2,469,350	20,172.8	9,060.4	11,112.4	4838	5410	4501
2013 (March)........	5,282	2,733	2,549	4,306	1,855	2,451	20,501.6	9,285.8	11,215.8	4933	5525	4580

Sources: U.S. Census Bureau, Census of Governments: Employment (1957, 1962, 1967, 1972, 1977, 1982, 1987, 1992, 1997, 2002, 2007, 2012 and the Annual Survey of Public Employment and Payroll remaining years. For information on sampling and nonsampling errors and definitions, see http://www.census.gov/govs/apes/how_data_collected.html. Data users who create their own estimates from this table should cite the U.S. Census Bureau as the source of the original data only.

Note: Detail may not add to totals due to rounding.
Key:
(a) Due to a change in the reference period, from October to March, the October 1996 Annual Survey of Government Employment and Payroll was not concluded. This change in collection period was effective beginning with the March 1997 survey.

Table 8.2
EMPLOYMENT AND PAYROLLS OF STATE AND LOCAL GOVERNMENTS BY FUNCTION: MARCH 2013

Functions	All employees, full-time and part-time (in thousands)			March payrolls (in thousands of dollars)			Average March earnings of full-time employees
	Total	State government	Local government	Total	State government	Local government	
All functions..	19,086,324	5,281,933	13,804,391	$71,437,378,499	$20,501,635,364	$50,935,743,135	$4,603
Education:							
Higher education	3,157,493	2,579,522	577,971	10,300,678,826	8,678,539,202	1,622,139,624	5,551
Instructional personnel only..	1,115,732	831,687	284,045	4,706,503,328	3,851,236,843	855,266,485	7,501
Elementary/Secondary schools..	7,626,823	60,562	7,566,261	26,161,021,057	230,250,228	25,930,770,829	4,122
Instructional personnel only..	5,212,997	44,986	5,168,011	20,646,875,701	185,943,673	20,460,932,028	4,609
Libraries..	184,057	711	183,346	427,627,591	1,695,874	425,931,717	3,794
Other Education	92,650	92,650	0	377,056,124	377,056,124	0	4,462
Selected functions:							
Streets and Highways.................	509,499	222,820	286,679	2,138,995,363	998,978,406	1,140,016,957	4,399
Public Welfare	520,744	237,923	282,821	1,961,127,393	904,662,792	1,056,464,601	3,988
Hospitals.......................................	1,044,655	419,634	625,021	4,726,741,297	1,864,716,945	2,862,024,352	4,909
Police protection	969,928	105,348	864,580	5,062,607,334	583,764,806	4,478,842,528	5,662
Police Officers......................	718,716	67,626	651,090	4,189,764,113	433,586,676	3,756,177,437	6,070
Fire protection.............................	420,318	0	420,318	2,043,950,110	0	2,043,950,110	6,198
Firefighters only.....................	381,881	0	381,881	1,885,220,204	0	1,885,220,204	6,266
Natural Resources.......................	186,674	143,125	43,549	725,056,633	568,370,898	156,685,735	4,435
Correction....................................	701,969	439,240	262,729	2,977,973,773	1,859,649,330	1,118,324,443	4,324
Social Insurance	83,003	82,566	437	338,610,887	336,169,835	2,441,052	4,255
Financial Admin..........................	419,661	170,596	249,065	1,779,631,583	767,954,705	1,011,676,878	4,624
Judicial and Legal	426,855	176,284	250,571	2,049,507,101	936,641,012	1,112,866,089	5,136
Other Government Admin.........	399,848	57,793	342,055	1,183,774,647	247,760,179	936,014,468	4,593
Utilities..	512,193	36,999	475,194	2,679,237,869	232,160,902	2,447,076,967	5,539
State Liquor stores	11,283	11,283	0	27,732,808	27,732,808	0	3,356
Other and unallocable....................	1,818,671	444,877	1,373,794	6,476,048,103	1,885,531,318	4,590,516,785	4,434

Source: U.S. Census Bureau, 2013 Annual Survey of Public Employment and Payroll.

Note: Data users who create their own estimates using these data should cite the U.S. Census Bureau as the source of the original data only. The data in this table are based on information from public records and contain no confidential data. The data in this table come from a sample of governmental units and are thus subject to both sampling and nonsampling error. Additional information on nonsampling error, response rates, and definitions may be found within the survey methodology *http://www2.census.gov/govs/apes/2013_methodology.pdf.*

Additional Note: Detail may not add to total due to rounding.

Table 8.3
STATE AND LOCAL GOVERNMENT EMPLOYMENT, BY STATE: MARCH 2013

State or other jurisdiction	All employees (full-time and part-time)			Full-time equivalent employment		
	Total	State	Local	Total	State	Local
United States	19,086,324	5,281,933	13,804,391	16,062,128	4,305,701	11,756,427
Alabama	317,499	109,181	208,318	281,979	89,275	192,704
Alaska	64,086	30,812	33,274	55,423	27,287	28,136
Arizona	334,437	88,803	245,634	283,499	70,767	212,732
Arkansas	194,380	74,338	120,042	168,776	63,927	104,849
California	2,093,138	485,811	1,607,327	1,710,692	397,348	1,313,344
Colorado	339,244	102,540	236,704	276,275	77,621	198,654
Connecticut	222,606	78,847	143,759	185,888	62,775	123,113
Delaware	57,529	31,941	25,588	50,240	26,691	23,549
Florida	977,816	208,289	769,527	862,353	179,484	682,869
Georgia	581,900	162,815	419,085	512,186	128,795	383,391
Hawaii	88,651	72,138	16,513	72,413	56,767	15,646
Idaho	102,485	28,922	73,563	79,957	22,710	57,247
Illinois	787,734	153,890	633,844	645,435	127,253	518,182
Indiana	385,918	109,580	276,338	319,551	85,193	234,358
Iowa	227,384	67,351	160,033	170,714	48,553	122,161
Kansas	247,634	61,100	186,534	201,233	49,639	151,594
Kentucky	272,001	96,528	175,473	236,197	82,494	153,703
Louisiana	289,360	92,054	197,306	256,931	77,809	179,122
Maine	92,788	27,042	65,746	72,785	21,151	51,634
Maryland	334,814	90,763	244,051	298,311	85,748	212,563
Massachusetts	382,911	122,652	260,259	323,135	98,761	224,374
Michigan	544,699	185,132	359,567	433,882	143,097	290,785
Minnesota	358,935	102,633	256,302	276,267	80,681	195,586
Mississippi	212,595	65,739	146,856	192,915	58,161	134,754
Missouri	376,554	102,268	274,286	317,327	86,316	231,011
Montana	72,708	27,107	45,601	57,054	20,799	36,255
Nebraska	145,832	36,968	108,864	119,564	31,975	87,589
Nevada	126,892	34,417	92,475	102,557	27,225	75,332
New Hampshire	87,201	25,823	61,378	68,905	18,672	50,233
New Jersey	543,890	161,503	382,387	472,764	143,739	329,025
New Mexico	143,254	54,315	88,939	124,179	45,250	78,929
New York	1,321,543	271,766	1,049,777	1,172,034	239,472	932,562
North Carolina	685,667	172,912	512,755	549,488	146,387	403,101
North Dakota	63,072	25,776	37,296	45,222	19,239	25,983
Ohio	712,697	188,148	524,549	580,437	136,994	443,443
Oklahoma	242,439	84,874	157,565	208,438	66,367	142,071
Oregon	241,104	81,426	159,678	189,737	66,219	123,518
Pennsylvania	684,530	205,068	479,462	568,261	158,890	409,371
Rhode Island	57,072	23,758	33,314	48,172	18,870	29,302
South Carolina	287,097	92,645	194,452	257,548	79,088	178,460
South Dakota	62,333	18,770	43,563	46,323	14,442	31,881
Tennessee	373,291	98,630	274,661	327,858	80,704	247,154
Texas	1,588,282	365,985	1,222,297	1,422,565	316,638	1,105,927
Utah	191,928	71,322	120,606	141,798	53,870	87,928
Vermont	49,922	17,112	32,810	39,617	14,313	25,304
Virginia	528,146	162,782	365,364	439,592	125,234	314,358
Washington	396,511	137,902	258,609	320,857	106,223	214,634
West Virginia	120,863	49,582	71,281	104,612	41,101	63,511
Wisconsin	366,364	106,570	259,794	274,394	72,347	202,047
Wyoming	60,370	15,603	44,767	50,429	13,340	37,089
Dist. of Columbia	46,218		46,218	45,359		45,359

Source: 2013 Annual Survey of Public Employment and Payroll. For information on sampling and nonsampling errors and definitions, see *http://www.census.gov/govs/apes/how_data_collected.html.* Data users who create their own estimates from these tables should cite the U.S. Census Bureau as the source of the original data only.

Note: Statistics for local governments are estimates subject to sampling variation.

Table 8.4
STATE AND LOCAL GOVERNMENT PAYROLLS AND AVERAGE EARNINGS
OF FULL-TIME EMPLOYEES, BY STATE: MARCH 2013

State or other jurisdiction	Amount of payroll (in thousands of dollars)			Percentage of March payroll		Average earnings of full-time state and local government employees (dollars)		
	Total	State government	Local governments	State government	Local government	All	Education employees	Other
United States	$65,538,278,229	$18,318,070,452	$47,220,207,777	28%	72%	$4,603	$4,413	$4,811
Alabama..............	953,619,300	342,316,634	611,302,666	36%	64%	3,678	3,666	3,689
Alaska.................	269,426,352	139,431,227	129,995,125	52%	48%	5,344	4,901	5,731
Arizona...............	1,057,250,013	273,006,782	784,243,231	26%	74%	4,245	3,916	4,612
Arkansas.............	547,424,376	224,893,156	322,531,220	41%	59%	3,515	3,678	3,307
California	8,931,540,035	2,157,214,226	6,774,325,809	24%	76%	6,190	5,838	6,475
Colorado.............	1,052,670,441	292,162,691	760,507,750	28%	72%	4,598	4,240	4,950
Connecticut.........	923,515,217	335,482,797	588,032,420	36%	64%	5,739	5,562	5,972
Delaware	201,697,819	102,672,190	99,025,629	51%	49%	4,572	5,025	4,154
Florida	3,187,886,922	662,161,885	2,525,725,037	21%	79%	3,996	3,598	4,382
Georgia...............	1,683,537,503	444,730,002	1,238,807,501	26%	74%	3,544	3,647	3,404
Hawaii.................	296,054,915	221,297,591	74,757,324	75%	25%	4,424	4,213	4,612
Idaho..................	256,520,888	86,617,970	169,902,918	34%	66%	3,710	3,242	4,235
Illinois................	2,938,858,618	576,312,444	2,362,546,174	20%	80%	5,231	4,867	5,687
Indiana................	1,080,984,479	319,957,758	761,026,721	30%	70%	3,878	3,864	3,896
Iowa	665,567,606	242,623,836	422,943,770	36%	64%	4,672	4,577	4,787
Kansas	673,682,716	197,169,598	476,513,118	29%	71%	3,745	3,590	3,971
Kentucky	780,238,419	293,815,142	486,423,277	38%	62%	3,631	3,626	3,639
Louisiana............	885,178,837	307,432,185	577,746,652	35%	65%	3,754	3,658	3,844
Maine..................	242,832,243	77,986,017	164,846,226	32%	68%	3,802	3,638	4,043
Maryland	1,356,299,264	382,004,115	974,295,149	28%	72%	5,119	5,316	4,891
Massachusetts	1,498,795,287	479,683,583	1,019,111,704	32%	68%	5,222	5,038	5,449
Michigan.............	1,746,716,596	620,514,131	1,126,202,465	36%	64%	4,906	5,109	4,657
Minnesota............	1,129,947,856	364,357,968	765,589,888	32%	68%	4,911	4,762	5,096
Mississippi	584,621,670	196,541,241	388,080,429	34%	66%	3,250	3,244	3,257
Missouri..............	1,028,682,371	277,010,191	751,672,180	27%	73%	3,594	3,636	3,549
Montana	188,475,628	70,299,795	118,175,833	37%	63%	3,982	3,966	3,997
Nebraska	433,517,477	110,549,764	322,967,713	26%	74%	4,157	3,936	4,396
Nevada................	479,267,463	116,289,617	362,977,846	24%	76%	5,120	4,495	5,650
New Hampshire ...	246,422,611	71,553,178	174,869,433	29%	71%	4,306	4,195	4,465
New Jersey	2,494,771,821	799,313,465	1,695,458,356	32%	68%	5,800	5,829	5,763
New Mexico	438,283,043	179,270,406	259,012,637	41%	59%	3,875	3,785	3,976
New York.............	6,124,204,279	1,328,502,381	4,795,701,898	22%	78%	5,706	5,350	6,004
North Carolina.....	1,927,144,949	560,859,901	1,366,285,048	29%	71%	3,900	3,735	4,069
North Dakota.......	152,606,872	69,333,280	83,273,592	45%	55%	4,059	4,042	4,081
Ohio....................	2,192,960,352	560,942,450	1,632,017,902	26%	74%	4,399	4,357	4,449
Oklahoma............	672,058,166	230,564,869	441,493,297	34%	66%	3,495	3,322	3,719
Oregon................	750,630,361	272,601,542	478,028,819	36%	64%	4,745	4,505	4,950
Pennsylvania	2,337,908,383	666,318,952	1,671,589,431	29%	71%	4,639	4,761	4,500
Rhode Island........	239,878,039	96,311,141	143,566,898	40%	60%	5,429	5,377	5,486
South Carolina......	877,103,016	279,887,992	597,215,024	32%	68%	3,711	3,719	3,703
South Dakota.......	143,622,942	52,953,371	90,669,571	37%	63%	3,561	3,479	3,673
Tennessee	1,103,165,269	305,578,382	797,586,887	28%	72%	3,672	3,443	3,914
Texas...................	5,199,894,628	1,285,121,058	3,914,773,570	25%	75%	3,945	3,824	4,121
Utah....................	484,322,502	208,164,050	276,158,452	43%	57%	4,158	4,127	4,193
Vermont...............	145,376,300	64,410,893	80,965,407	44%	56%	4,220	4,076	4,450
Virginia................	1,665,322,919	483,792,718	1,181,530,201	29%	71%	4,215	4,133	4,325
Washington..........	1,435,242,012	413,925,408	1,021,316,604	29%	71%	5,512	5,332	5,633
West Virginia.......	326,833,185	138,063,498	188,769,687	42%	58%	3,430	3,675	3,131
Wisconsin	1,044,395,093	282,295,927	762,099,166	27%	73%	4,661	4,727	4,577
Wyoming	190,076,068	53,771,054	136,305,014	28%	72%	4,317	4,162	4,451
Dist. of Columbia	271,245,108	–	271,245,108	0%	100%	6,391	6,171	6,436

Source: 2013 Annual Survey of Public Employment and Payroll. For information on sampling and nonsampling errors and definitions, see http://www.census.gov/govs/apes/how_data_collected.html. Data users who create their own estimates from these tables should cite the U.S. Census Bureau as the source of the original data only.

Note: Statistics for local governments are estimates subject to sampling variation.

Table 8.5
STATE GOVERNMENT EMPLOYMENT (FULL-TIME EQUIVALENT) FOR SELECTED FUNCTIONS, BY STATE: 2013

| | | Education | | | | | | | | Selected functions | |
State	All functions	Higher education (a)	Other education (b)	Highways	Public welfare	Hospitals	Corrections	Police protection	Natural resources	Financial and other governmental administration	Judicial and legal administration
United States	4,305,701	1,721,340	133,427	218,098	233,346	390,483	435,540	103,545	130,525	219,194	171,876
Alabama...............	89,275	41,345	2,918	4,237	3,952	11,709	4,932	1,389	1,919	3,023	3,316
Alaska..................	27,287	5,911	3,391	3,182	1,918	248	2,095	671	2,447	1,863	1,497
Arizona................	70,767	31,588	3,240	2,860	5,829	618	9,758	1,901	1,544	3,168	2,300
Arkansas.............	63,927	25,982	1,469	3,379	3,953	6,799	5,532	1,224	2,080	2,705	1,395
California	397,348	161,522	4,185	19,957	3,724	41,927	51,506	10,944	14,743	29,567	6,348
Colorado.............	77,621	43,120	1,547	3,086	2,217	5,583	7,035	1,226	1,053	2,368	4,613
Connecticut.........	62,775	18,198	3,020	3,174	5,583	6,518	6,719	1,957	854	4,116	4,967
Delaware	26,691	8,428	353	1,528	1,624	1,466	2,898	1,058	529	1,230	1,760
Florida	179,484	62,139	2,971	6,362	9,015	4,049	24,551	4,128	8,101	8,506	19,350
Georgia................	128,795	58,832	3,553	4,813	8,488	7,807	17,022	2,021	3,924	4,534	3,684
Hawaii.................	56,767	10,713	25,286	877	422	4,638	2,337	0	798	1,337	2,461
Idaho...................	22,710	8,453	365	1,512	1,622	561	1,987	480	1,818	1,627	487
Illinois................	127,253	62,134	1,719	7,041	9,015	9,815	10,937	3,194	3,383	6,880	2,597
Indiana................	85,193	53,895	992	3,683	4,777	1,901	6,288	1,900	2,156	2,591	1,432
Iowa	48,553	22,488	1,078	2,203	2,729	6,777	2,969	940	1,599	1,495	2,204
Kansas	49,639	21,306	662	2,930	2,242	8,064	3,399	1,073	803	2,281	2,111
Kentucky	82,494	38,830	1,377	4,525	7,624	5,701	4,314	979	2,787	3,460	5,611
Louisiana............	77,809	27,734	4,171	4,566	5,193	10,405	5,918	1,725	4,170	4,740	1,714
Maine..................	21,151	7,332	278	2,063	2,699	455	1,152	544	1,026	1,739	748
Maryland	85,748	27,281	2,047	4,526	6,578	3,638	12,078	2,487	2,005	4,275	5,116
Massachusetts	98,761	31,383	3,333	3,135	6,815	5,462	6,937	7,882	1,149	5,826	9,107
Michigan.............	143,097	73,861	634	2,678	12,161	17,172	13,263	2,467	3,269	5,644	1,416
Minnesota............	80,681	36,616	3,916	4,532	2,848	4,254	4,126	921	2,992	5,726	3,612
Mississippi	58,161	19,547	1,516	3,394	3,033	11,701	3,250	1,239	3,094	1,959	745
Missouri..............	86,316	28,521	1,632	5,183	6,998	10,219	12,087	2,472	2,425	3,810	4,289
Montana	20,799	7,359	380	2,102	1,709	634	1,274	469	1,570	1,671	710
Nebraska	31,975	12,495	530	2,078	2,380	3,813	2,862	774	2,142	1,101	741
Nevada	27,225	9,346	127	1,734	1,826	1,294	3,580	888	854	2,624	741
New Hampshire ...	18,672	6,767	309	1,651	1,912	573	1,124	491	303	1,152	874
New Jersey	143,739	35,031	18,275	5,860	8,859	17,233	9,023	3,768	1,588	6,709	13,004
New Mexico	45,250	17,520	870	2,059	1,719	7,541	3,643	505	966	1,866	3,044
New York.............	239,472	53,728	4,642	11,084	4,411	42,888	29,582	5,782	2,912	20,173	18,801
North Carolina......	146,387	60,353	2,792	10,828	1,123	18,536	20,744	3,499	4,422	4,849	6,293
North Dakota.......	19,239	9,903	337	1,007	537	921	830	198	576	898	576
Ohio....................	136,994	72,064	1,996	6,303	2,715	15,630	13,229	2,614	2,470	7,283	2,328
Oklahoma.............	66,367	30,185	1,703	2,830	5,820	1,769	4,656	1,910	1,832	1,876	2,837
Oregon.................	66,219	23,710	653	3,668	7,504	7,915	5,068	1,334	2,546	4,955	2,923
Pennsylvania	158,890	55,266	4,673	13,745	11,171	11,084	18,384	6,562	5,767	10,105	3,053
Rhode Island........	18,870	5,658	949	741	1,222	792	1,553	304	419	1,640	1,160
South Carolina......	79,088	31,190	2,974	4,429	4,683	6,995	8,174	2,070	2,060	4,391	815
South Dakota.......	14,442	5,623	360	989	1,715	375	868	316	973	758	642
Tennessee	80,704	35,188	2,147	3,598	7,516	3,824	7,067	1,707	3,819	4,037	2,474
Texas...................	316,638	135,749	4,387	12,765	22,525	24,841	40,160	6,652	10,525	9,711	5,630
Utah....................	53,870	24,489	1,870	1,600	2,789	8,637	3,032	822	1,297	2,889	1,573
Vermont...............	14,313	4,999	447	1,058	1,408	176	1,101	632	572	1,124	679
Virginia................	125,234	56,785	2,624	7,240	2,839	14,154	13,469	3,148	2,662	4,859	3,757
Washington...........	106,223	43,577	2,102	6,807	9,610	7,387	8,376	2,183	4,798	3,843	1,938
West Virginia........	41,101	14,266	1,329	5,314	3,458	1,673	3,644	1,044	1,913	2,312	1,596
Wisconsin	72,347	38,912	1,086	1,384	2,113	3,585	9,667	759	2,045	3,024	2,263
Wyoming	13,340	4,018	212	1,798	723	726	1,340	292	826	874	544

Source: U.S. Census Bureau, 2013 Annual Survey of Public Employment and Payroll.

Note: Data users who create their own estimates using these data should cite the U.S. Census Bureau as the source of the original data only. The data in this table are based on information from public records and contain no confidential data. The data in this table come from a sample of governmental units and are thus subject to both sampling and nons-ampling error. Additional information on nonsampling error, response rates, and definitions may be found within the survey methodology, *http://www2.census.gov/govs/apes/2013_methodology.pdf.*

Key:

(a) Includes instructional and other personnel.

(b) Includes instructional and other personnel in elementary and secondary schools.

Table 8.6
STATE GOVERNMENT PAYROLLS FOR SELECTED FUNCTIONS, BY STATE: MARCH 2013
(In thousands of dollars)

| State | All functions | Education | | Selected functions | | |
		Higher education (a)	Other education (b)	Highways	Public welfare	Hospitals
United States	20,501,635,364	8,678,539,202	607,306,352	998,978,406	904,662,792	1,864,716,945
Alabama.......................	372,877,100	187,931,766	11,233,497	15,272,278	13,707,594	50,351,911
Alaska.........................	147,268,896	31,342,396	14,407,814	18,315,648	8,929,642	1,307,504
Arizona........................	303,153,071	151,331,380	11,735,017	12,549,005	20,208,164	2,602,719
Arkansas......................	240,400,803	110,452,214	5,270,088	12,452,832	12,503,484	24,680,164
California	2,508,684,591	1,024,682,437	20,062,596	141,462,910	17,112,880	319,333,601
Colorado......................	375,090,681	216,650,088	6,877,207	14,118,273	9,552,828	23,696,123
Connecticut..................	376,188,870	107,219,029	17,099,152	19,909,409	33,249,764	40,536,785
Delaware	114,446,490	41,558,265	2,059,618	5,051,963	5,549,514	4,901,998
Florida	719,696,502	315,890,005	10,246,750	26,530,496	27,243,337	13,247,556
Georgia........................	491,516,760	280,688,496	12,806,974	13,232,752	25,935,740	25,907,288
Hawaii.........................	239,511,581	50,858,596	97,288,664	3,939,410	1,608,356	24,650,127
Idaho...........................	96,857,513	35,907,182	1,845,178	5,597,118	5,778,637	1,836,449
Illinois.........................	665,950,749	289,369,335	8,814,859	42,593,862	50,036,860	52,336,209
Indiana........................	351,672,218	233,584,330	3,746,430	13,574,237	16,795,572	6,315,909
Iowa	266,073,425	122,596,396	5,754,820	11,137,171	13,349,928	43,571,834
Kansas	215,113,009	103,693,359	2,780,365	10,721,408	7,409,525	35,897,362
Kentucky	320,139,037	162,302,461	5,791,503	14,661,728	25,638,524	24,679,063
Louisiana.....................	328,789,311	124,537,930	18,187,069	17,813,025	19,511,168	40,719,188
Maine..........................	86,061,489	30,014,759	1,074,583	7,575,540	9,653,307	1,908,629
Maryland	414,505,762	146,701,918	9,927,215	21,650,250	26,565,537	15,405,627
Massachusetts	526,717,280	160,664,602	16,621,900	17,623,770	36,989,378	23,738,630
Michigan......................	736,380,513	393,193,559	3,509,645	13,911,027	54,363,890	85,426,922
Minnesota....................	415,663,318	201,480,301	20,646,850	22,466,341	10,360,939	18,687,117
Mississippi	211,429,939	85,226,613	4,979,438	9,982,482	10,236,586	36,254,136
Missouri.......................	302,628,066	120,638,539	5,355,704	17,559,804	18,210,720	32,539,661
Montana	83,873,295	29,151,641	1,559,918	9,184,402	6,210,597	2,261,559
Nebraska.....................	122,408,492	50,327,046	2,280,052	8,177,911	7,170,445	14,029,553
Nevada........................	128,100,534	48,955,491	601,161	7,376,243	6,422,071	5,813,185
New Hampshire	84,489,410	33,964,861	1,324,152	6,921,420	7,530,805	2,267,196
New Jersey	846,956,652	217,987,467	117,641,857	29,686,965	49,669,350	79,779,841
New Mexico	197,572,434	90,473,396	3,404,091	7,286,351	5,932,519	31,143,726
New York......................	1,402,155,998	304,011,737	21,807,826	60,881,425	21,672,919	231,204,207
North Carolina.............	623,005,511	288,302,080	12,407,754	41,488,682	4,074,714	76,973,346
North Dakota...............	78,524,732	39,815,087	1,285,040	5,522,340	1,758,445	2,751,367
Ohio............................	650,014,245	335,719,829	10,308,005	29,112,105	14,162,544	75,063,662
Oklahoma....................	254,728,885	125,205,705	6,141,020	10,473,303	16,487,575	5,069,953
Oregon........................	312,697,948	118,578,825	2,940,039	17,886,687	27,651,789	41,058,194
Pennsylvania	769,263,233	312,885,405	18,757,723	55,066,718	43,476,069	38,608,920
Rhode Island...............	103,361,354	28,174,643	5,282,521	3,948,299	7,204,540	4,259,008
South Carolina.............	303,577,426	142,533,519	10,782,378	14,505,366	13,150,354	21,505,179
South Dakota...............	58,273,466	25,838,395	1,297,492	3,930,545	5,849,594	1,115,327
Tennessee	332,624,894	146,487,782	8,137,689	12,705,940	24,947,428	14,094,077
Texas...........................	1,413,938,187	711,241,215	19,720,830	53,908,309	69,679,218	117,203,955
Utah............................	237,560,334	120,143,051	7,445,877	6,954,116	9,713,154	35,913,019
Vermont.......................	70,308,602	27,490,830	2,086,806	4,820,228	6,126,113	853,813
Virginia........................	551,316,837	273,553,519	12,350,994	32,926,290	11,949,137	57,243,526
Washington..................	510,577,399	217,245,458	10,075,154	35,069,998	42,188,904	34,910,564
West Virginia...............	149,730,393	64,504,198	5,464,938	16,958,399	9,082,382	4,276,074
Wisconsin	333,207,485	180,901,505	5,007,811	7,245,380	8,736,129	14,329,030
Wyoming	56,550,644	16,530,561	1,072,288	7,238,245	3,314,123	2,456,152

See footnotes at end of table.

STATE GOVERNMENT PAYROLLS FOR SELECTED FUNCTIONS, BY STATE: MARCH 2013—Continued
(In thousands of dollars)

State	Corrections	Police protection	Natural resources	Financial and other governmental administration	Judicial and legal administration
United States	1,859,649,330	583,764,806	568,370,898	1,015,714,884	936,641,012
Alabama	16,063,678	5,234,956	7,460,218	13,465,592	14,302,643
Alaska..........................	11,578,237	4,343,386	13,663,032	10,662,724	9,287,818
Arizona........................	34,527,837	9,586,337	6,351,803	12,439,260	11,399,529
Arkansas......................	16,963,043	4,566,288	6,607,536	10,220,450	5,374,812
California	361,884,040	80,395,164	81,527,077	139,079,489	41,535,513
Colorado......................	29,128,559	6,734,096	5,336,754	11,196,159	22,875,132
Connecticut.................	40,277,776	13,826,767	5,035,123	24,072,419	29,960,090
Delaware	11,587,315	6,816,742	1,985,328	4,465,357	8,200,003
Florida	77,371,535	15,749,807	26,864,318	30,576,548	77,320,304
Georgia........................	38,973,885	6,739,217	11,724,026	15,346,087	13,867,422
Hawaii..........................	9,864,294	–	3,281,214	5,223,556	10,662,714
Idaho...........................	7,909,878	2,210,023	7,839,643	6,975,436	3,965,995
Illinois.........................	61,706,246	22,850,430	14,233,190	40,286,378	22,741,371
Indiana........................	19,755,535	8,642,515	7,683,730	11,175,402	9,641,991
Iowa	14,848,996	5,361,127	8,399,278	7,509,023	12,125,727
Kansas	10,694,781	4,649,713	3,300,929	8,766,682	8,882,337
Kentucky	11,398,148	3,384,719	11,524,179	14,062,136	19,905,940
Louisiana.....................	22,957,433	9,306,289	16,964,210	19,653,149	7,535,711
Maine..........................	4,614,447	2,683,003	4,407,549	6,883,262	4,274,945
Maryland	50,820,302	12,802,401	10,023,158	20,306,556	27,634,687
Massachusetts	36,070,860	49,438,569	7,096,807	31,268,459	51,099,738
Michigan......................	65,053,205	14,672,832	15,335,580	29,945,175	9,693,926
Minnesota....................	17,803,075	4,257,622	13,878,791	31,232,786	20,091,759
Mississippi...................	8,451,445	4,973,755	9,651,913	7,442,834	4,505,313
Missouri.......................	31,862,672	9,743,436	7,745,744	13,699,098	16,907,672
Montana	5,372,789	2,138,398	6,223,664	6,414,134	3,122,624
Nebraska	9,906,131	3,560,363	7,360,879	4,227,087	3,591,644
Nevada........................	14,930,051	5,757,868	3,877,862	11,317,051	4,725,228
New Hampshire	5,065,629	2,537,814	1,386,879	5,042,175	4,544,472
New Jersey	54,076,131	28,797,792	10,153,716	35,781,983	81,386,195
New Mexico	12,215,981	2,117,567	4,032,347	7,797,469	12,234,031
New York......................	175,627,844	49,973,836	15,805,960	106,236,176	135,092,312
North Carolina.............	63,677,178	15,345,555	16,774,263	21,365,916	29,988,843
North Dakota...............	3,188,988	922,569	2,617,054	3,762,212	2,958,112
Ohio	58,916,790	13,215,290	10,595,615	38,239,874	12,265,009
Oklahoma....................	14,582,282	8,420,523	6,337,044	7,068,598	12,529,585
Oregon.........................	22,279,910	7,057,012	10,558,323	21,869,082	14,033,295
Pennsylvania	83,217,864	39,534,222	28,924,693	43,932,389	25,055,169
Rhode Island...............	9,845,559	2,279,553	2,396,294	8,908,483	6,818,054
South Carolina.............	23,313,526	7,623,186	6,346,719	15,412,094	3,978,212
South Dakota...............	2,773,772	1,246,938	3,355,430	3,207,988	2,762,976
Tennessee	20,823,050	8,200,144	14,914,834	20,952,628	26,442,972
Texas...........................	118,454,074	33,773,803	47,966,202	43,004,588	28,503,328
Utah............................	10,864,968	3,335,784	4,824,318	13,263,985	6,724,414
Vermont.......................	4,672,718	3,242,391	2,761,989	5,426,994	3,225,481
Virginia........................	42,730,880	14,537,906	12,074,643	21,446,722	17,826,312
Washington..................	35,706,728	11,651,360	21,860,664	19,419,078	10,846,480
West Virginia...............	9,475,288	4,287,334	6,784,157	7,435,096	7,378,032
Wisconsin	40,885,229	3,841,060	8,607,466	13,866,628	13,842,117
Wyoming	4,878,748	1,397,344	3,908,753	4,362,437	2,973,023

Source: U.S. Census Bureau, 2013 Annual Survey of Public Employment and Payroll.

Note: Data users who create their own estimates using these data should cite the U.S. Census Bureau as the source of the original data only. The data in this table are based on information from public records and contain no confidential data. The data in this table come from a sample of governmental units and are thus subject to both sampling and nonsampling error. Additional information on nonsampling error, response rates, and definitions may be found within the survey methodology, *http://www2.census.gov/govs/apes/2013_methodology.pdf.*

Key:
(a) Includes instructional and other personnel.
(b) Includes instructional and other personnel in elementary and secondary schools.

Table 8.7
STATE EMPLOYEES: PAID HOLIDAYS**

State or other jurisdiction	Major holidays (a)	Martin Luther King's Birthday (b)	Lincoln's Birthday	President's Day (c)	Washington's Birthday (c)	Good Friday	Memorial Day (d)	Columbus Day (e)	Veteran's Day	Day after Thanksgiving	Day before or after Christmas	Day before or after New Year's	Election Day (f)	Other (g)
Alabama	★	★(h)	...	...	★(i)	...	★	★	★	(k)	(k)	...	...	★
Alaska	★	★	...	★	...	...	★	...	★	(k)	...	...	...	★
Arizona	★	★	...	★	...	...	★	★	★	...	...	...	...	...
Arkansas	★	★(h)	...	...	★(i)	...	★	...	★	(k)	Before	...	...	★
California	★	★	...	★	...	...	★	★	★	★	...	...	...	...
Colorado	★	★	...	★	...	...	★	★	★	...	...	...	...	★
Connecticut	★	★	★	...	★	★	★	★	★	...	...	...	...	...
Delaware	★	★	...	...	★	★	★	...	★	★	...	...	★	...
Florida	★	★	...	...	...	...	★	...	★	★	...	...	...	...
Georgia	★	★	...	...	(l)	...	★	★	★	(l)	(l)	...	...	★
Hawaii	★	★	...	★	...	...	★	...	★	...	...	...	★	★
Idaho	★	★(h)	...	★	...	...	★	★	★	...	...	...	★	...
Illinois	★	★	★	...	★	...	★	★	★	★	...	...	★	...
Indiana	★	★	(m)	...	(m)	★	★	★	★	(m)	(m)	...	★	...
Iowa	★	★	...	...	...	...	★	...	★	★	...	...	...	★
Kansas	★	★	...	...	...	...	★	...	★	★	(ee)	...	...	...
Kentucky	★	★	...	...	★(n)	★	★	...	★	★	★	★	★(t)	...
Louisiana	★	★	...	...	★	★	★	...	★	...	...	...	★(u)	★
Maine	★	★	...	★	...	...	★	★	★	★	...	...	...	★
Maryland	★	★	...	★	...	...	★	★	★	★(aa)	...	...	★	★
Massachusetts	★	★	...	★	...	...	★	★	★	...	...	...	...	★
Michigan	★	★	...	★	...	...	★	...	★	★	Before	Before	★(z)	...
Minnesota	★	★	...	★	...	...	★	...	★	★	...	...	...	★
Mississippi	★	★(h)	...	...	★	...	★(v)	...	★	(k)	(k)	...	...	★
Missouri	★	★	★	...	★	...	★	★	★	...	...	...	...	★
Montana	★	★	...	★	...	...	★	★	★	...	...	...	★	...
Nebraska	★	★	...	★	...	...	★	★	★	...	...	...	...	...
Nevada	★	★	...	...	★	...	★	...	★	★(cc)	...	...	...	★
New Hampshire	★	★(h)	...	★	...	...	★	...	★	★	...	...	...	★
New Jersey	★	★	...	★	...	★	★	★	★	...	...	...	★	...
New Mexico	★	★	...	(o)	...	...	★	★	★	(o)	...	...	(w)	★
New York	★	★	(j)	...	★	...	★	★	★	...	...	...	★(j)	...
North Carolina	★	★	...	...	...	★	★	...	★	★	(x)	...	...	★
North Dakota	★	★	...	★	...	★	★	★	★	...	(p)	...	...	...
Ohio	★	★	...	★	...	...	★	★	★	...	...	...	...	...
Oklahoma	★	★	...	★	...	...	★	...	★	★	Before	...	...	...
Oregon	★	★	...	★	...	...	★	...	★	...	...	...	...	...
Pennsylvania	★	★	...	★	...	...	★	★	★	★	...	...	...	...
Rhode Island	★	★	...	...	...	...	★	★	★	...	...	...	★	★
South Carolina	★	★	...	★	...	...	★	...	★	★	Both	...	...	★
South Dakota	★	★	...	★	...	...	★	(y)	★	...	...	...	...	...
Tennessee	★	★	...	★	...	★	★	(q)	★	(q)	Before	...	...	★
Texas	★	★	...	★	...	(r)	★	...	★	★	Both	...	...	★
Utah	★	★	...	★	...	...	★	★	★	...	...	...	...	★
Vermont	★	★	...	★	...	...	★	★	★	(dd)	...	...	...	★
Virginia	★	★	...	...	★	...	★	★	★	★	(ee)	...	...	★
Washington	★	★	...	★	...	...	★	...	★	★	...	...	...	★
West Virginia	★	★	...	★	...	...	★	★	★	(hh)	(s)	(s)	★	★
Wisconsin	★	★	...	★	...	...	★	...	...	...	Before	Before	...	...
Wyoming	★	★	...	★	...	...	★	...	★	...	...	...	...	...
Dist. of Columbia	★	★	...	...	★	...	★	★	★	...	...	...	...	★
American Samoa	★	★	...	★	...	★	★	★	★	...	...	...	...	★
Guam	★	★	...	★	...	★	★	...	★	...	...	...	...	★
No. Mariana Islands	★	★	...	★	...	★	★	(ff)	★	...	...	...	...	★
Puerto Rico	★	★	...	★	...	★	★	★	★	...	Before	...	...	★
U.S. Virgin Islands	★	★	...	★	...	★	★	(gg)	★	...	★(bb)	...	...	★

See footnotes at end of table.

STATE EMPLOYEES: PAID HOLIDAYS** — Continued

**Holidays in addition to any other authorized paid personal leave granted state employees.

Source: The Council of State Governments' survey of state personnel office websites, January 2014.

Note: In some states, the governor may proclaim additional holidays or select from a number of holidays for observance by state employees. In some states, the list of paid holidays is determined by the personnel department at the beginning of each year; as a result, the number of holidays may change from year to year. Number of paid holidays may also vary across some employee classifications. If a holiday falls on a weekend, generally employees get the day preceding or following.

Key:

★ — Paid holiday granted.

. . . — Paid holiday not granted.

(a) New Year's Day, Independence Day, Labor Day, Thanksgiving Day and Christmas Day.

(b) Third Monday in January.

(c) Generally, third Monday in February; Washington's Birthday or President's Day. In some states the holiday is called President's Day or Washington-Lincoln Day. Most frequently, this day recognizes George Washington and Abraham Lincoln.

(d) Last Monday in May in all states indicated, except Vermont where holiday is observed on May 30. Generally, states follow the federal government's observance (last Monday in May) rather than the traditional Memorial Day (May 30).

(e) Second Monday in October.

(f) General election day only, unless otherwise indicated. In Indiana, primary and general election days.

(g) Additional holidays:

Alabama — Mardi Gras Day (Baldwin and Mobile counties only)(day before Ash Wednesday), Confederate Memorial Day (fourth Monday in April), Jefferson Davis' Birthday (first Monday in June).

Alaska — Seward's Day (last Monday in March), Alaska Day (October 18).

Arkansas — Employee is granted one holiday to observe his or her birthday.

California — César Chávez Day (March 31), one personal holiday (employees become eligible for a personal holiday once they have completed six months of state employment).

Colorado — State employees may have César Chávez Day (March 31) off in lieu of any other legal holiday that occurs on a weekday in the same fiscal year.

Delaware — Eligible employees are granted two floating holidays per calendar year, Return Day after 12:00 noon (second day after a general election) in Sussex County only.

Florida — Full-time employees are entitled to one personal holiday each year. Personal holidays are credited to eligible employees on July 1, and must be taken by the employee by June 30 of each year.

Georgia — Confederate Memorial Day (fourth Monday in April).

Hawaii — Prince Jonah Kuhio Kalanianaole Day (March 26), King Kamehameha I Day (June 11), Statehood Day (third Friday in August).

Iowa — State employees are granted two days of paid leave each year to be added to the vacation allowance and accrued under certain provisions.

Kansas — One discretionary holiday that can be used any time during the calendar year.

Louisiana — Mardi Gras Day (Tuesday before Ash Wednesday), Inauguration Day (every four years, in Baton Rouge only).

Maine — Patriot's Day (third Monday in April).

Maryland — Service reduction days in 2014 include May 23, August 29, November 26, December 24 and December 31. Due to budget constraints, state operations are curtailed on service reduction days.

Massachusetts — Patriot's Day (third Monday in April), Evacuation Day (March 17 — Suffolk County only), Bunker Hill Day (June 17 — Suffolk County only).

Minnesota — Regular and temporary employees with at least six months of employment shall receive one floating holiday each payroll year.

Mississippi — Confederate Memorial Day (last Monday in April).

Missouri — Harry Truman's Birthday (May 8).

Nebraska — Arbor Day (last Friday in April).

Nevada — Nevada Day (last Friday in October).

New Hampshire — Employees who are employed on a full-time basis are eligible for two floating holildays.

Rhode Island — Victory Day (second Monday in August).

South Carolina — Confederate Memorial Day (May 10).

Tennessee — New Year's Eve.

Texas — The following are partial staffing holidays: Confederate Heroes Day (January 19), Texas Independence Day (March 2), San Jacinto Day (April 21), Emancipation Day in Texas (June 19) and Lyndon Baines Johnson Day (August 27). Staff offices are scheduled to be open on partial staffing holidays and optional holidays. An employee may observe optional holidays in lieu of any partial staffing holiday on which state offices are required to be open to conduct public business. Optional holidays include César Chávez Day (March 31), Good Friday, Rosh Hashanah and Yom Kippur.

Utah — Pioneer Day (July 24).

Vermont — Town Meeting Day (first Tuesday in March), Bennington Battle Day (August 16).

Virginia — Lee-Jackson Day (Friday preceding the third Monday in January). State offices will close at noon on the day before Thanksgiving.

Washington — One additional paid holiday per calendar year.

West Virginia — West Virginia Day (June 20).

District of Columbia — District of Columbia Emancipation Day (April 16).

American Samoa — American Samoa Flag Day (April 17), Manu'a Cession Day (July 16), White Sunday (second Sunday in October).

Guam — Liberation Day (July 21), All Souls' Day (November 2) and Our Lady of Camarin Day (December 8).

Northern Mariana Islands — Commonwealth Covenant Day (March 25), Citizenship Day (November 4) and Constitution Day (December 8).

Puerto Rico — Three Kings Day (or Epiphany Day)(January 6), Birthday of Eugenio María de Hostos (second Monday in January), Birthday of Luis Muñoz Marín (February 18), Emancipation Day (March 22), Birthday of José de Diego (third Monday in April), Birthday of Don Luis Muñoz Rivera (third Monday in July), Constitution or Puerto Rico Day (July 25), Birthday of Dr. José Celso Barbosa (July 27), Discovery of Puerto Rico (November 19).

U.S. Virgin Islands — Three Kings Day (or Ephiphany Day)(January 6), Holy Thursday (Thursday before Good Friday), Transfer Day (March 31), Easter Monday (Monday after Easter), Emancipation Day (July 3), Liberty Day (or D. Hamilton Jackson Day)(November 1).

(h) In Alabama, Arkansas and Mississippi, also celebrated as Robert E. Lee's Birthday. In Idaho, also celebrated as Idaho Human Rights Day. In New Hampshire, also celebrated as Civil Rights Day.

(i) In Alabama, celebrated as George Washington's and Thomas Jefferson's Birthday. In Arkansas, celebrated as George Washington's Birthday and Daisy Gatson Bates Day.

(j) The state has designated Lincoln's birthday as a floating holiday in 2014 for state employees in certain bargaining units.

(k) At the discretion of the governor.

(l) In Georgia, Robert E. Lee's Birthday is observed on the day after Thanksgiving, and Washington's Birthday is observed on the day before Christmas.

(m) In Indiana, Lincoln's Birthday is observed on the day after Thanksgiving, and Washington's Birthday is observed on the day before Christmas.

(n) In Kentucky, half day.

(o) In New Mexico, President's Day is observed on the day after Thanksgiving.

(p) In North Dakota, state offices close at noon on Christmas Eve when it falls on Monday through Thursday.

(q) In Tennessee, at the governor's discretion Columbus Day may be observed the day after Thanksgiving.

(r) In Texas, Good Friday is an optional holiday. An employee is entitled to observe optional holidays in lieu of any partial staffing holiday in which state offices are required to be open to conduct public business.

(s) Half day on Christmas Eve and New Year's Eve (closes at noon).

(t) Tuesday after first Monday in November of presidential election years.

(u) General Election Day is a state holiday the first Tuesday after the first Monday in November in even-numbered years.

(v) Also celebrated as Jefferson Davis' Birthday.

(w) Employees are allowed up to two hours paid administrative leave to vote.

(x) Three days when Christmas Day falls on Tuesday, Wednesday or Thursday; two days when Christmas Day falls on Friday or Monday.

(y) Celebrated as Native Americans Day.

(z) First Tuesday in November, even-numbered years.

(aa) Observed as American Indian Heritage Day.

(bb) Observed as Boxing Day.

(cc) Observed as Family Day.

(dd) Most state offices will be closed the day after Thanksgiving.

(ee) A half-day holiday will be granted on the day before Christmas and a whole day granted after Christmas.

(ff) Celebrated as Commonwealth Cultural Day.

(gg) Also celebrated as V.I./P.R. Friendship Day.

(hh) Observed as Lincoln's Day.

Women in State Government: Still Far from Parity

By Susan J. Carroll

In recent years the movement of women into state-level offices has slowed after several decades of gains, and the 2014 elections did not alter this pattern. Efforts to actively recruit women for elected and appointed positions will be critical in determining what the future holds for women in state government.

In the history of our nation, women are relative newcomers among state elected and appointed officials. Women first entered state-level offices in the 1920s following passage and ratification of the 19th Amendment to the U.S. Constitution which granted women suffrage. Significant growth in the numbers of women in office, however, occurred only after the emergence of the contemporary women's movement during the late-1960s and early-1970s.

Since the mid-1970s, as data collected by the Center for American Women and Politics show,[1] women have greatly increased their numbers among elected and appointed officials in state government. Nevertheless, progress has slowed in recent years and nationwide statistics show little or no growth in the numbers of women serving in state-level offices since the turn of the century.

The 2014 elections did not appreciably improve the representation of women among state office-holders. The number of women governors remained at five immediately after the 2014 elections, with Jan Brewer (R) stepping down in Arizona and Gina Raimando (D) winning election in Rhode Island. Women fared slightly better in elections for other statewide offices, resulting in a modest increase, but the number of women statewide elected officials in 2015 continues to be lower than the record number who held these offices at the turn of the century. At the state legislative level, the number of women serving nationwide actually declined slightly, with women holding 1,786 seats in early 2015 compared with 1,791 seats before the 2014 elections. Notably, fewer women serve today than in 2010 when a record 1,809 women held legislative seats.

Governors

Since the founding of our country, only 36 women (21D, 15R) have served as state governors (Table A), and only one woman has served as governor of a U.S. territory (Puerto Rico).[2] Almost half of the states, 23, have never had a woman chief executive.

Arizona is the only state to have had four women governors as well as the only state to have had a woman succeed another as governor. New Hampshire has been governed by three different women although one of those governors—Vesta Roy—served for only seven days following the death of an incumbent. Connecticut, Kansas, Oregon, Texas and Washington each have had two women governors.

The first woman governor, Nellie Tayloe Ross of Wyoming, was selected in a special election to succeed her deceased husband in 1925. Fifteen days later a second woman, Miriam "Ma" Ferguson, was inaugurated as governor of Texas, having been elected as a surrogate for her husband, a former governor who had been impeached and consequently was barred constitutionally from running again. Ferguson's campaign slogan was "Two governors for the price of one."[3] The third woman to serve as a governor, Lurleen Wallace of Alabama, campaigned on the slogan, "Let George do it," and was similarly elected to replace a husband who was prohibited by term limits from seeking an additional term in office.[4]

The first woman elected in her own right (i.e., without following her husband) into the governorship was Ella Grasso, who presided over Connecticut from 1975 to 1980. Twenty-five of the women governors, including Grasso, who have served since the mid-1970s were elected in their own right. The other eight became governor through constitutional succession; only three of these eight were subsequently elected to full terms.

Six women (3D, 3R) serve as governors in 2015, falling short of the record nine women who served simultaneously in 2004 and again in 2007. Four women governors—Mary Fallin (R-Oklahoma), Nikki Haley (R-South Carolina), Maggie Hassan (D-New Hampshire) and Susana Martinez (R-New Mexico)—were re-elected in 2014. With the departure of Jan Brewer (R-Arizona) and the election of Gina Raimondo (D-Rhode Island),

Table A: Female Governors Throughout History

Name (Party-State)	Dates served	Special circumstances
Nellie Tayloe Ross (D-WY)	1925–1927	Won special election to replace deceased husband.
Miriam "Ma" Ferguson (D-TX)	1925–1927, 1933–1935	Inaugurated 15 days after Ross; elected as surrogate for husband who could not succeed himself.
Lurleen Wallace (D-AL)	1967–1968	Elected as surrogate for husband who could not succeed himself.
Ella Grasso (D-CT)	1975–1980	First woman elected governor in her own right; resigned for health reasons.
Dixy Lee Ray (D-WA)	1977–1981	
Vesta Roy (R-NH)	1982–1983	Elected to state senate and chosen as senate president; served as governor for seven days when incumbent died.
Martha Layne Collins (D-KY)	1984–1987	
Madeleine Kunin (D-VT)	1985–1991	First woman to serve three terms as governor.
Kay Orr (R-NE)	1987–1991	First Republican woman governor and first woman to defeat another woman in a gubernatorial race.
Rose Mofford (D-AZ)	1988–1991	Elected as secretary of state, succeeded governor who was impeached and convicted.
Joan Finney (D-KS)	1991–1995	First woman to defeat an incumbent governor.
Ann Richards (D-TX)	1991–1995	
Barbara Roberts (D-OR)	1991–1995	
Christine Todd Whitman (R-NJ)	1994–2001	Resigned to take presidential appointment as commissioner of the Environmental Protection Agency.
Jeanne Shaheen (D-NH)	1997–2003	
Jane Dee Hull (R-AZ)	1997–2003	Elected as secretary of state, succeeded governor who resigned; later elected to a full term.
Nancy Hollister (R-OH)	1998–1999	Elected lieutenant governor; served as governor for 11 days when predecessor took U.S. Senate seat and successor had not yet been sworn in.
Jane Swift (R-MA)	2001–2003	Elected as lieutenant governor, succeeded governor who resigned for an ambassadorial appointment.
Judy Martz (R-MT)	2001–2005	
Olene Walker (R-UT)	2003–2005	Elected as lieutenant governor, succeeded governor who resigned to take a federal appointment.
Ruth Ann Minner (D-DE)	2001–2009	
Jennifer M. Granholm (D-MI)	2003–2011	
Linda Lingle (R-HI)	2003–2011	
Janet Napolitano (D-AZ)	2003–2009	First woman to succeed another woman as governor; resigned to become U.S. Secretary of Homeland Security.
Kathleen Sebelius (D-KS)	2003–2009	Father was governor of Ohio. Resigned to become U.S. Secretary of Health and Human Services.
Kathleen Blanco (D-LA)	2004–2008	
M. Jodi Rell (R-CT)	2004–2011	Elected as lieutenant governor, succeeded governor who resigned.
Christine Gregoire (D-WA)	2005–2013	
Sarah Palin (R-AK)	2007–2009	Resigned.
Beverly Perdue (D-NC)	2009–2013	
Jan Brewer (R-AZ)	2009–2015	Elected as secretary of state, succeeded governor who resigned.
Mary Fallin (R-OK)	2011–present	
Nikki Haley (R-SC)	2011–present	First Asian (Indian) American woman to be elected governor.
Susana Martinez (R-NM)	2011–present	First Latina to be elected governor.
Maggie Hassan (D-NH)	2013–present	
Gina Ramaindo (D-RI)	2015–present	
Kate Brown(D-OR)	2015–present	Elected as secretary of state, succeeded governor who resigned.

Source: Center for American Women and Politics, Eagleton Institute of Politics, Rutgers University.

Figure A: Proportion of Women Among Statewide Elective Officials

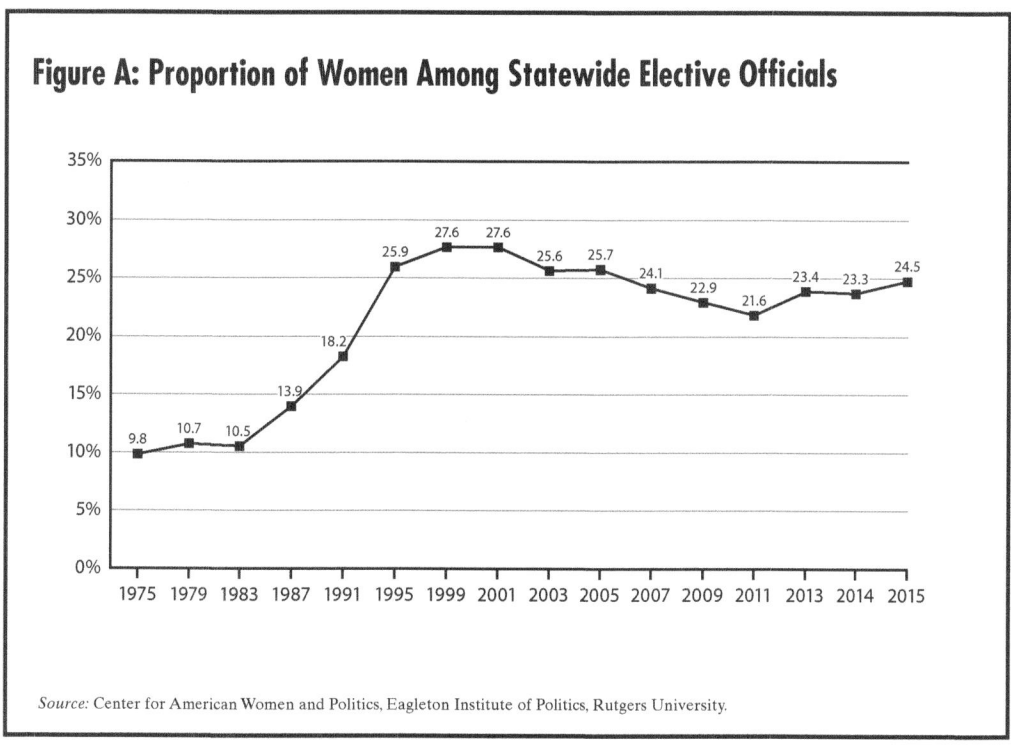

Source: Center for American Women and Politics, Eagleton Institute of Politics, Rutgers University.

the number of women governors remained at five immediately after, just as before, the 2014 elections. But then following the resignation of the governor of Oregon in early 2015, Secretary of State Kate Brown (D-Oregon) succeeded to the governorship of that state, bringing the number of women governors to six.

Martinez, a Latina, and Haley, an Indian American, are the first two women of color ever to serve as governor of a state.

Other Statewide Elected and Appointed Officials in the Executive Branch

The states vary greatly in their numbers of statewide elected and appointed officials. For example, Maine and New Hampshire have only one statewide elected official, the governor, while North Dakota, at the other extreme, has 12.

The first woman to ever hold a major statewide office was Soledad C. Chacon (D-New Mexico) who was secretary of state in New Mexico from 1923–1926;[5] Delaware, Kentucky, New York, South Dakota and Texas also had women secretaries of state in the 1920s. The first woman treasurer — Grace B. Urbahns (R-Indiana) — served during this same time period, from 1926–1932.

Several more years passed before a woman became lieutenant governor. Matilda R. Wilson (R-Michigan) served briefly as lieutenant governor of Michigan in 1940, when she was appointed to fill an expiring term. However, the first woman elected as a lieutenant governor was Consuelo N. Bailey (R-Vermont) who served from 1955–1956. An additional three decades passed before a woman became attorney general of a state; the first was Arlene Violet (R-Rhode Island) who served from 1985–1987.

As evident from Figure A, the proportion of women among statewide elective officials (including governor) has grown substantially since the early 1970s. From 1971 to 1983 the increases were small and incremental. Then, between 1983 and 2000, there was a period of significant growth. The number and proportion of women serving statewide almost tripled, reaching a record of 92 women and constituting 28.5 percent of all statewide elected officials in 2000. Since 2000, the numbers and proportions have dropped notably. Although the number of women serving in statewide elective offices actually increased as a result of the 2014 elections, fewer women, 78,[6] hold statewide offices in 2015 than in 1995 when there were 84 women.

In early 2015, women held 24.5 percent of the 318 statewide elective positions.[7] In addition to the six women governors, 13 women (5D, 8R) served as lieutenant governors in the 44 states that elect lieutenant governors in statewide elections. This is considerably fewer than the record high number of 19 women who served as lieutenant governors in 1995.

Other women statewide elected officials include: 14 secretaries of state (7D, 7R), nine chief education officials (3D, 5R, 1 nonpartisan), eight attorneys general (6D, 2R), eight state auditors (4D, 4R), seven state treasurers (4D, 3R), three corporation commissioners (3R), three public service commissioners (1D, 2R), two state comptroller/controllers (1D, 1R), one commissioner of insurance (1D), one commissioner of labor (R), one railroad commissioner (R), one agriculture and commerce commissioner (R), and one public utilities commissioner (R).

In addition to the two women of color who serve as governors, the women serving in statewide elective office include three Latinas (the lieutenant governor of Illinois, the secretary of state of New Mexico, and the secretary of state of Rhode Island); one African American (the state treasurer of Connecticut); one Native American (the superintendent of public instruction of Montana); one Asian Pacific Islander (the state controller of California); and one multi-racial individual (the attorney general of California).

Women may be slightly better represented among top appointed officials in state government than among statewide elected officials although it is not possible to know for certain since the most recent data available are from 2007. According to nationwide data collected by the Center on Women in Government and Civil Society at SUNY-Albany, in 2007 women constituted 32.2 percent of department heads with major policymaking responsibilities (including heads of departments, agencies, offices, boards, commissions and authorities) who were appointed by governors. This represented a substantial increase over 1997 when women constituted just 23.2 percent of department heads.

Women were even better represented in 2007 among top appointed advisors in governors' offices, with women holding 41.9 percent of these positions—a slightly higher proportion than the 39.5 percent of these positions they held in 1997. Women of color are still a rarity among appointed officials, with women of color constituting just 6.3 percent of all department heads and top advisors in governors' offices in 2007.

Justices on Courts of Last Resort

The first woman to win election to a state court of last resort was Florence E. Allen, who was elected to the Ohio Supreme Court in 1922 and re-elected in 1928. Nevertheless, it was not until 1960 that a second woman, Lorna Lockwood of Arizona, was elected to a state supreme court. Lockwood's colleagues on the Arizona Supreme Court selected her in 1965 to be chief justice, making her the first woman to preside over a state court of last resort.[8] She was followed by Susie Sharp of North Carolina who in 1974 became the first woman to be elected by popular vote to be chief justice of a state court of last resort.[9]

In 2003 Petra Jimenez Maes of New Mexico, who currently serves as an associate justice, became the first Latina chief justice of a state supreme court. Similarly, in 2005 Leah Ward Sears of Georgia became the first African American woman to preside over a state court of last resort.[10]

According to the National Center for State Courts, 125, or 36.3 percent, of the 344 sitting justices on state courts of last resort in early 2015 were women.[11] Of the 53 chief justices of these courts, 20, or 37.7 percent, are women. Women comprise a majority of justices on courts of last resort in nine states—Arkansas, California, Maryland, Massachusetts, New York, Ohio, Tennessee, Washington and Wisconsin. Women constitute at least 40 percent of the justices (but less than a majority) on an additional 21 courts of last resort.[12]

Legislators

Even before 1920 when women won the right to vote across the country, a few women had been elected to legislatures in states that had granted the franchise to women. By 1971 the proportion of women serving in state legislatures across the country had grown to 4.5 percent, and over the years this proportion has increased more than fivefold. As Figure B illustrates, the proportion of women legislators grew steadily throughout the 1970s and 1980s. However, the rate of growth slowed in the 1990s, and similar to the pattern for statewide elected officials, the numbers and proportions of women legislators nationwide have leveled off since the late 1990s. Following the 2014 elections, the number of women legislators actually decreased slightly, and the proportion of women legislators has increased less than 2 percentage points since 1999 (Figure B).

In early 2015 women held 436, or 22.1 percent, of all state senate seats. Women also held 1,350,

Figure B: Proportion of Women Among State Legislators

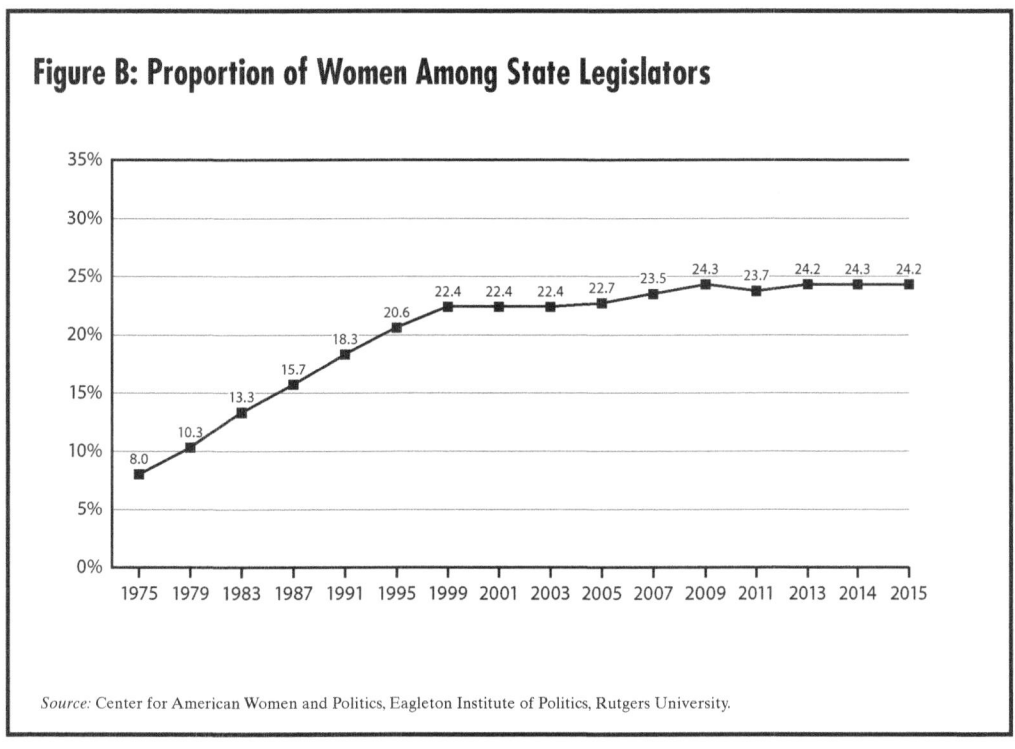

Source: Center for American Women and Politics, Eagleton Institute of Politics, Rutgers University.

or 24.9 percent, of all state house seats across the country. The 1,786 women who served in state legislatures in early 2015 were slightly fewer than the record number of 1,809 who served in 2010.

Great variation exists across the states in the proportion of legislators who are women. (See Table B.) Colorado ranks first among the states with 42.0 percent women among its legislators, followed by Vermont (41.1 percent), Arizona (35.6 percent), Minnesota (33.3 percent), and Washington (32.7 percent). With the exception of Minnesota and Illinois, all of the states ranked in the top 10 in the proportion of women in their legislatures are located in the West or Northeast. However, despite this geographic concentration, no easy explanation exists for why these states have risen to the top, and scholars who have statistically examined the variation among the states in the representation of women in their legislatures have found no simple patterns.[13]

At the other extreme, Louisiana with only 12.5 percent ranks last among the 50 states in the representation of women among its legislators. Accompanying Louisiana in the bottom five states are Oklahoma (12.8 percent), Wyoming (13.3 percent), South Carolina (13.5 percent), and Alabama (14.3 percent). Eight of the 10 states with the lowest proportions of women are southern or border states. Only one southern state, Florida, and one border state, Missouri, are slightly above the national average; each has 24.4 percent women. As these rankings make clear, the South as a region lags behind the rest of the country in the representation of women within its legislatures.

Nationwide, Republicans outnumber Democrats among all state legislators.[14] However, a very different pattern is evident among women legislators where Democrats outnumber Republicans. Among women state senators nationwide, 59.4 percent are Democrats; among women state representatives, 60.0 percent are Democrats.

About one-fifth of women state legislators, 21.7 percent, are women of color. Of the 100 senators and 287 representatives serving in legislatures in early 2015, all but 33 were Democrats.[15] African American women hold 66 seats in state senates and 184 seats in state houses across 40 states. Latinas are concentrated in 26 states; they hold 20 senate and 67 house seats. Asian American women count among their numbers 12 senators and 25 representatives in 12 states while Native American women hold two senate and 11 house seats in six states.

Table B: Women in State Legislatures 2015

State	Senate			House			Legislature (both houses)	
	Democrats	Republicans	% Women	Democrats	Republicans	% Women	% Women	State rank (a)
Alabama	3	0	11.4% (b)	11	5	15.2%	14.3%	46
Alaska.......................	1	4	25.0	2	10	30.0	28.3	14
Arizona......................	6	7	43.3	11	8	31.7	35.6	3
Arkansas...................	3	4	20.0	6	14	20.0	20.0	36
California	8	3	27.5	11	9	25.0	25.8	20
Colorado....................	8	4	34.2	19	11	46.2	42.0	1
Connecticut..............	8	1	25.0	25	19	29.1	28.3	14
Delaware	5	1	28.6	7	2	22.0	24.2	27
Florida	6	6	30.0	13	14	22.5	24.4	25
Georgia......................	8	1	16.1	28	17	25.0	22.9	29
Hawaii.......................	8	0	32.0	9	4	25.5	27.6	16
Idaho.........................	3	6	25.7	7	12	27.1	26.7	17
Illinois......................	11	4	25.4	32	8	33.9	31.1	9
Indiana......................	3	7	20.0	11	10	21.0	20.7	34
Iowa	6	1	14.0	21	6	27.6	22.7	30
Kansas.......................	4	9	32.5	11	17	22.4	24.8	24
Kentucky	2	2	10.5	11	8	19.0	16.7	43
Louisiana..................	3	1	10.3	9	5	13.3	12.5	50
Maine........................	5	3	22.9	30	16	30.5	29.0	12
Maryland	11	2	27.7	35	11	32.6	31.4	7
Massachusetts	12	0	30.0	29	9	23.8	25.0	21
Michigan...................	1	3	10.5	17	10	24.5	20.9	33
Minnesota.................	15	8	34.3	26	18	32.8	33.3	4
Mississippi	2	6	15.4	16	6	18.0	17.2	41
Missouri....................	5	1	17.6	19	23	25.8	24.4	25
Montana	12	6	36.0	21	8	29.0	31.3	8
Nebraska (c).............	···Nonpartisan···		20.4	·················Unicameral···················			20.4	35
Nevada......................	3	2	23.8	8	7	35.7	31.7	6
New Hampshire	4	4	33.3	69	45	28.5	28.8	13
New Jersey	8	3	27.5	15	10	31.3	30.0	11
New Mexico	3	3	14.3	13	10	32.9	25.9	19
New York..................	6	5	17.5	35	5	26.7	23.9	28
North Carolina........	7	5	24.0	14	12	21.3	22.4	31
North Dakota..........	4	4	17.0	11	8	20.2	19.1	38
Ohio	4	3	21.2	13	13	26.3	25.0	21
Oklahoma.................	3	3	12.5	3	10	12.9	12.8	49
Oregon......................	6	2	26.7	16	4	33.3	31.1	9
Pennsylvania	3	6	18.0	14	22	17.7	17.8	39
Rhode Island...........	9	1	26.3	17	3	26.7	26.5	18
South Carolina........	0	1	2.2	12	10	17.7	13.5	47
South Dakota..........	1	6	20.0	4	11	21.4	21.0	32
Tennessee	2	4	18.2	7	10	17.2	17.4	40
Texas........................	2	5	22.6	15	14	19.3	19.9	37
Utah.........................	3	3	20.1	7	3	13.3	15.4	44
Vermont....................	7	2	30.0	47	15	43.3 (d)	41.1	2
Virginia....................	7	1	20.0	12	4	16.0	17.1	42
Washington..............	10	8	36.7	18	12	30.6	32.7	5
West Virginia...........	0	1	2.9	6	13	19.0	14.9	45
Wisconsin	7	4	33.3	14	8	22.2	25.0	21
Wyoming	1	0	3.3	3	8	18.3	13.3	48

Source: Center for American Women and Politics, Eagleton Institute of Politics, Rutgers University. Figures are as of March 2015.
Key:
(a) States share the same rank if their proportions of women legislators are exactly equal or round off to be equal (AK, CT, FL, MO; IL, OR; MA, OH, WI).
(b) Includes one Independent.
(c) Nebraska has a unicameral legislature with nonpartisan elections.
(d) Includes three Independent Party members.

The Future

Although women have made substantial progress over time in increasing their presence in state government, the leveling off among state legislators and decline among statewide elective officials since the turn of the century are troubling developments. At a minimum, these developments provide evidence that increases over time are not inevitable.

The lack of growth in numbers has implications for women's representation not only among state

Table C: Women Statewide Elected Officials 2015

State	Governor	Lieutenant Governor	Attorney General	Secretary of State	Treasurer
Alabama	★	w	★	★	★
Alaska	★	★	★		
Arizona	★		★	w	★
Arkansas	★	★	w	★	★
California	★	★	w	★	★
Colorado	★	★	★	★	★
Connecticut	★	w	★	w	w
Delaware	★	★	★		★
Florida	★	★	w		★
Georgia	★	★	★	★	
Hawaii	★	★			
Idaho	★	★	★	★	★
Illinois	★	w	w	★	★
Indiana	★	w	★	w	w
Iowa	★	w	★	★	★
Kansas	★	★	★	★	★
Kentucky	★	w	★	w	★
Louisiana	★	★	★	★	★
Maine	★				
Maryland	★	★	★		
Massachusetts	★	w	w	★	w
Michigan	★	★	★	w	
Minnesota	★	w	w	★	
Mississippi	★	★	★	★	w
Missouri	★	★	★	★	★
Montana	★	w	★	w	
Nebraska	★	★	★	★	
Nevada	★	★	★	w	★
New Hampshire	w				
New Jersey	★	w			
New Mexico	w	★	★	w	★
New York	★	w	★		
North Carolina	★	★	★	w	w
North Dakota	★	★	★	★	w
Ohio	★	w	★	★	★
Oklahoma	w	★	★		★
Oregon	w		w	w	★
Pennsylvania	★	★	w		★
Rhode Island	w	★	★	w	★
South Carolina	w	★	★	★	★
South Dakota	★	★	★	w	★
Tennessee	★				
Texas	★	★	★		
Utah	★	★	★		★
Vermont	★	★	★	★	w
Virginia	★	★	★		
Washington	★	★	★	w	★
West Virginia	★		★	w	★
Wisconsin	★	w	★	★	★
Wyoming	★			★	★

Source: Data for elected officials are current as of February 2015 and have been provided by the Center for American Women and Politics, Eagleton Institute of Politics, Rutgers University.

Key:
★ — Denotes that this position is filled through a statewide election.
w — Denotes that this position is filled through a statewide election and is held by a woman.

legislators and nongubernatorial statewide office-holders, but also among governors and members of Congress. Probably the most striking positive development for women in state government in recent years has been the increase in women governors. Of the 36 women governors in the history of the United States, 22 have served all or part of their terms during the first few years of the 21st century. Of the six sitting governors, three held statewide elective office before running for governor—one as lieutenant governor, another as secretary of state, and a third as state treasurer.

In addition, four of the current women governors served in their state legislatures, where two were majority leaders and one was majority whip.

Similarly, many of the women who have run for Congress gained experience and visibility in state government before seeking federal office. Of the 84 women members of the U.S. House in the 113th Congress, 45 served in their state houses, 20 in their state senates, and three in statewide elective offices. Of the 20 female U.S. senators, seven served in their state houses, five in their state senates, and four in statewide elective offices.

Activists who are interested in increasing the number of women serving in office often refer to a political pipeline through which potential women candidates for higher office come forward from among the pool of women who have gained experience at lower levels of office. Clearly, the pipeline has worked well in recent years in the case of governors and members of Congress. But what if the pool of women candidates in statewide and state legislative offices continues to stagnate or decline? Then, the number of politically experienced women with the visibility and contacts necessary to run for governor or a seat in the U.S. House or Senate is unlikely to grow.

While several different factors may be responsible for the recent leveling off in the number of women in elective offices in the states, a lack of effective recruitment certainly is one of the most important. Statistics on the number of female candidates over time seem clearly to point to a problem with recruitment. For example, 2,528 women were general election candidates for the more than 6,000 seats up for election in state legislatures in 2014, which means more seats were uncontested by a woman than were contested. Moreover, there were 92 fewer female candidates in 2012 than in 2010 and only 70 more women than in 1992.[16] Clearly, then, a major factor contributing to the leveling off in the number of female officeholders is a lack of greater numbers of female candidates.

Research has found that women who run for office are less likely than their male counterparts to be self-starters. Women more often than men seek office only after receiving encouragement from others. In a 2008 nationwide study of state legislators, scholars at the Center for American Women and Politics found that only 26 percent of female state representatives, compared with 43 percent of their male counterparts, said it was entirely their own idea to run for their first elective office. In contrast, 53 percent of women state representatives, compared with 28 percent of men, said they had not thought seriously about running for office until someone else suggested it.[17]

Similarly, a study of major party candidates in state legislative races conducted a few years earlier found that only 11 percent of women, compared with 37 percent of men, were self-starters who said that it was entirely their own idea to run for the legislature; in contrast, 37 percent of women, compared with 18 percent of men, reported that they had not seriously thought about running until someone else suggested it.[18] Another recent study of people in the professions from which political candidates are most likely to emerge (i.e., law, business, politics, and education) found that notably fewer women (43 percent) than men (59 percent) had ever considered running for office.[19]

Findings such as these suggest the future for women in state government will depend, at least in part, upon the strength of efforts to recruit women for both elected and appointed positions. Legislative leaders, public officials, party leaders, and advocacy organizations can help by renewing their commitment and augmenting their efforts to identify and support potential women candidates, especially in winnable races with open seats or vulnerable incumbents. Recruitment efforts may well be key to determining whether the number of women officials continues to stagnate or again begins to move steadily upward as it did in earlier decades.

Notes

[1] All statistical information in this essay, unless otherwise noted, has been provided by the Center for American Women and Politics (CAWP), Eagleton Institute of Politics, Rutgers University. Additional information is available at www.cawp.rutgers.edu. This essay would not be possible without the tireless efforts of Gilda Morales who oversees the collection of data on women officeholders for CAWP. I also would like to thank Linda Phillips from CAWP and Deborah Wood Smith from the National Center for State Courts for their assistance with the data for this essay.

[2] Sila Calderon (Popular Democratic Party) served as governor of Puerto Rico from 2001 to 2004.

[3] Martin Gruberg, *Women in American Politics* (Oshkosh, WI: Academia Press, 1968), 189.

[4] Gruberg, 190.

[5] Women did serve as superintendents of public instruction in a few states earlier than this.

[6] These 78 women serving in statewide elective office include 42 Republicans, 35 Democrats, and 1 nonpartisan.

[7] These numbers do not include: officials in appointive state government positions; officials elected to executive posts by the legislature; officials elected as commissioners

or board members from districts rather than statewide; members of the judicial branch; or elected members of university Boards of Trustees or Boards of Education.

[8] Gruberg, 190, 192.

[9] "Susie Sharp (1906-1996)," North Carolina History Project. *http://www.northcarolinahistory.org/encyclopedia/40/entry*.

[10] Information provided by the National Center for State Courts.

[11] Unlike all the other statistics in this essay, these numbers from the National Center for State Courts include the District of Columbia as well as the 50 states.

[12] This includes the D.C. Court of Appeals, which is the court of last resort for the District of Columbia. Texas has two courts of last resort, one of which has more than 40% women and is counted here.

[13] See, for example, Barbara Norrander and Clyde Wilcox, "The Geography of Gender Power: Women in State Legislatures," in Sue Thomas and Clyde Wilcox, ed., *Women and Elective Office: Past, Present, and Future* (New York: Oxford University Press, 1998).

[14] According to Ballotpedia, as of February 2, 2015, 54.6 percent of state senators were Republicans and 41.8 percent were Democrats; 55.5 percent of state representatives were Republicans and 43.4 percent were Democrats. The remainder of the seats were vacant or filled by nonpartisans or independents. *http://ballotpedia.org/Partisan_composition_of_state_senates* and *http://ballotpedia.org/Partisan_composition_of_state_houses*.

[15] One is nonpartisan and 32 are Republicans.

[16] There were 2375 women candidates for state legislative seats in 1992; 2285 in 1994; 2277 in 1996; 2280 in 1998; 2228 in 2000; 2348 in 2002; 2220 in 2004; 2429 in 2006; 2337 in 2008; 2537 in 2010; and 2448 in 2012.

[17] Kira Sanbonmatsu, Susan J. Carroll, and Debbie Walsh, *Poised to Run: Women's Pathways to the State Legislatures* (New Brunswick, NJ: Center for American Women and Politics, 2009), 8. *http://www.cawp.rutgers.edu/research/reports/PoisedtoRun.pdf*.

[18] Gary Moncrief, Peverill Squire, and Malcolm Jewell, *Who Runs for the Legislature?* (New York: Prentice-Hall, 2001), Table 5.5, 102.

[19] Jennifer L. Lawless and Richard L. Fox, *It Still Takes a Candidate: Why Women Don't Run for Office*, Revised Edition (New York: Cambridge University Press 2010), 50.

About the Author

Susan J. Carroll is professor of Political Science and Senior Scholar at the Center for American Women and Politics of the Eagleton Institute of Politics at Rutgers University. Her most recent books are *More Women Can Run* (Oxford 2013, with Kira Sanbonmatsu) and *Gender and Elections* (Third Edition, Cambridge 2014, with Richard L. Fox).

Chapter Nine

SELECTED STATE POLICIES AND PROGRAMS

Proven Systems and Enhanced Approaches for New Threats

By Beverly Bell

It's not just cold air slamming against warm that creates disasters. Disasters come from a variety of threats: rising rivers and unprecedented snowfalls, cyberattacks and infectious diseases. There are also other kinds of risks, such as inadequate budgets and shifting political sands. Regardless of the cause, the consequences are predictable and can be tragic. Disasters hurt people and property. They tear lives apart. They can make political careers or bring them to a screeching halt. Disasters can change the course of history. While disasters can be difficult and present challenges to a neighborhood, community, state and a nation, their impact can be mitigated through strong and decisive action. Often, the only thing standing between the worst outcomes and manageable ones are citizens and public officials who refuse to be helpless pawns or victims, but instead prepare for the inevitable, conduct a thorough response and develop together a well-thought out recovery that acknowledges evolving threats without fear.

For those who work in disaster management, a year is often judged by two factors: the scope and destruction of any single disaster that occurred in that year and the total number of events that took place.

Using those parameters, 2014 was a quiet year in the United States. There were 51 presidential and emergency disaster declarations, the fewest since 2002. The country certainly had its share of disasters: tornadoes in the Southeast; the deadly landslide in Oso, Wash.; ice jams and flooding in Montana; dangerous lava flow in Hawaii and constant wildfires in the West. Still, the country breathed a collective sigh of relief because there wasn't anything like Hurricanes Sandy or Katrina.

Professionals call a so-called "down year" an opportunity. It's a chance to further test existing plans, to add another complexity to an exercise and to push the system beyond its breaking point without any real damages. It means taking a hypothetical event to the next level, and asking, "what if" so that a future disaster poses less harm than the last.

Ebola—A Deadly Disaster with Worldwide Consequences

According to the Centers for Disease Control and Prevention, the 2014 Ebola outbreak in several West African countries was the largest in the disease's history. An estimated 25,000 people were infected, resulting in more than 11,000 deaths. This includes four infections and one death in the U.S.

The crisis brought to light in this country the crucial relationship between state emergency management and health departments. These two critical agencies have been working more closely

together since the 2009 H1N1 influenza pandemic, resulting in improved information sharing and coordination that played a key role in the Ebola scare. In addition to this interface, some states also established task forces and planning groups that included state emergency management and homeland security. Other states created additional annexes for their emergency operational plans to address infectious disease scenarios.

It's important to note that many of these enhancements are possible because of federal grants. Sufficient funding in the grant programs allows more robust planning and exercises for an Ebola event.

Droughts, Rising Sea Levels and Weather Extremes

Drought remains one of the most insidious threats in the United States, compromising the potable water supply, reducing the ability to grow food and endangering millions of agricultural jobs. When it comes to drought, California is on the front lines, experiencing drought conditions for more than four years. For the first time, the state imposed mandatory water restrictions in 2015. Other states such Oklahoma, Oregon, Texas and Washington are starting to face similar issues.

So, how does drought affect emergency management? The growing number of wildfires—about 5,600[1] in California alone in 2014, up 20 percent from a five-year average—requires more firefighters, water, equipment and other resources. On a federal level, the resulting presidential disaster declarations demand additional funding at a time when many politicians are arguing for significant budget cuts. Another consideration is the Robert T. Stafford Disaster Relief and Emergency Relief Act (42 U.S.C. 5121 et seq.) itself. This is the legislation that guides the declaration process. It includes drought as a major disaster declaration eligible under the act. However, the Federal Emergency Management Agency doesn't have specific programs and policies in place to address drought emergencies.

Beyond drought, the changing climate is shaping other areas. FEMA is requiring states to include climate adaptation in their mitigation plans beginning in 2016. This could include rising sea levels or any condition that would influence long-term hazards and vulnerabilities. The goal is to assist states in reducing risk and increasing resiliency. For their part, state disaster management officials must deal with more intense and more frequent storms, even while state budgets have shrunk—perhaps permanently—leaving fewer resources to manage the threat and provide for people in need.

Emergency Management— A Shared Responsibility

Sixty-five years ago, Congress passed the Federal Civil Defense Act of 1950 and recognized that protecting citizens from hazards was a joint responsibility shared by the federal, state and local governments. Today, Congress continues that commitment by funding the Emergency Management Performance Grant. These grants are the only source of federal funding directed to state and local governments for planning, training, exercises and professional expertise for all-hazards emergency preparedness. It also requires a dollar-for-dollar match, which means every state and local jurisdiction must invest its own money in order to participate. Even as select state and local budgets have faced serious challenges and some within the federal government have proposed a higher federal cost share, state government has stood behind the match, believing that every level of government has a responsibility in building emergency management capacity nationwide.

Emergency Management Performance Grants and the capacity they afford, allow local jurisdictions and state government to coordinate most events rather than turning to federal support. Since 2011, state and local emergency management has provided an annual report to Congress, measuring deliverables of the program and demonstrating a return on investment. It quantifies the thousands of local and state warnings systems, operational, special needs and evacuation plans, training and educational classes, full-scale exercises, mutual aid agreements and outreach campaigns that are

possible in this country because of Emergency Management Performance Grant dollars.

Turnover in State Emergency Management

State emergency management has experienced a significant turnover in its ranks, with 19 new state directors appointed since March 2014. An additional 16 directors have been in their jobs three years or less. Only three people have been state director for 12 years or more. Much of the turnover is the result of 2014 gubernatorial elections, but some can be attributed to a normal maturation of the field. The question remains as to how emergency management can develop new talent, as well as retain its knowledge base, so that lessons learned can be applied to better prepare for and manage future disasters.

The Critical Role of Emergency Management

Regardless of whether a disaster is natural or manmade, state emergency management acts as the central coordination point for all resources and assistance provided during the event. When a disaster strikes, emergency management remains one of the most crucial functions of state government. It also has the overarching responsibility of saving lives, protecting property and helping people recover once a disaster has occurred. Typically, emergency management comes to the forefront once an event has taken place. In reality, much of the work comes before—in the form of disaster drills and exercises, plans and programs, public warning tests and preparedness education.

Emergency management includes four main parts, referred to as the Four Pillars:

- **Mitigation**—Activities that reduce or eliminate the degree of risk to human life and property;

- **Preparedness**—Activities that take place before a disaster to develop and maintain a capability to respond rapidly and effectively to emergencies and disasters;

- **Response**—Activities to assess and contain the immediate effects of disasters, provide life support to victims and deliver emergency services; and

- **Recovery**—Activities to restore damaged facilities and equipment, and support the economic and social revitalization of affected areas to their pre-emergency status.

On the state level, these four elements encompass many different aspects, from planning and implementation to training and exercises. A state

Table A: State Emergency Management: Agency Structure, Budget and Staffing

State or other jurisdiction	Position appointed	Appointed/ selected by	Organizational structure	Agency operating budget FY 2015 (excluding federal funds)	Full-time employee positions
Alabama	★	G	Governor's Office	$3,905,619	88
Alaska	★	G	Adjutant General/Military Affairs	$2,637,300	62 (a)
Arizona	★	ADJ	Adjutant General/Military Affairs	$2,239,733	50
Arkansas	★	G	Governor's Office	$5,274,373	100 (a)
California	★	G	Governor's Office	$139,376,686	910 (a)
Colorado	. . .	DHSEM	Public Safety	$971,183	113 (a)
Connecticut	★	PSS	Public Safety	$3,857,984	78 (a)
Delaware	★	G	Public Safety	$2,037,521	37
Florida	★	G	Governor's Office	$45,657,230	157 (a)
Georgia	★	G	Governor's Office	$2,780,105	121 (a)
Hawaii	★	ADJ	Adjutant General/Military Affairs	$2,400,000	75
Idaho	★	ADJ	Governor's Office	$1,854,100	41 (a)
Illinois	★	G	Combined Homeland Security/Emerg. Mgt.	$35,100,000	202 (a)
Indiana	★	G	Combined Homeland Security/Emerg. Mgt.	$25,967,796	263 (a)
Iowa	★	G	Combined Homeland Security/Emerg. Mgt.	$3,638,835	100 (a)
Kansas	★	G	Adjutant General/Military Affairs	$1,735,064	44
Kentucky	★	G	Adjutant General/Military Affairs	$4,600,000	81
Louisiana	★	G	Combined Homeland Security/Emerg. Mgt.	$3,116,681	53 (a)
Maine	★	G	Adjutant General/Military Affairs	$1,064,788	28 (a)
Maryland	★	G	Adjutant General/Military Affairs	$2,300,000	60
Massachusetts	★	G	Public Safety	$5,100,000	102
Michigan	★	G	State Police	$6,463,500	67 (a)
Minnesota	★	PSS	Public Safety	$9,565,630	83 (a)
Mississippi	★	G	Governor's Office	$4,874,868	160
Missouri	★	G	Public Safety	$3,078,435	92
Montana	. . .	ADJ	Adjutant General/Military Affairs	$1,300,000	24 (a)
Nebraska	★	ADJ	Adjutant General/Military Affairs	$1,271,627	37 (a)
Nevada	★	G	Public Safety	$341,800	33 (a)
New Hampshire	★	G	Public Safety	$5,872,877	42 (a)
New Jersey	★	G	State Police	$8,980,000	398
New Mexico	★	G	Combined Homeland Security/Emerg. Mgt.	$2,494,800	65 (a)
New York	★	HSD	Combined Homeland Security/Emerg. Mgt.	$10,672,000	392 (a)
North Carolina	★	G	Public Safety	$11,405,037	186 (a)
North Dakota	★	ADJ	Adjutant General/Military Affairs	$7,700,000	74 (a)
Ohio	★	PSS	Public Safety	$6,628,383	84
Oklahoma	★	G	Governor's Office	$700,000	30
Oregon	★	ADJ	Adjutant General/Military Affairs	$40,424,000	41 (a)
Pennsylvania	★	G	Governor's Office	$16,391,000	195
Rhode Island	★	G	Combined Homeland Security/Emerg. Mgt.	$2,166,720	32 (a)
South Carolina	★	ADJ	Adjutant General/Military Affairs	$2,887,701	58
South Dakota	★	PSS	Public Safety	$756,572	20
Tennessee	★	G	Adjutant General/Military Affairs	$3,384,400	111
Texas	★	PSS	Public Safety	$4,290,867	291
Utah	★	PSS	Public Safety	$1,396,500	60 (a)
Vermont	★	PSS	Public Safety	$2,225,000	28 (a)
Virginia	★	G	Public Safety and Homeland Security	$9,975,830	154 (a)
Washington	★	ADJ	Adjutant General/Military Affairs	$2,341,000	71 (a)
West Virginia	★	G	Public Safety	$3,343,821	53 (a)
Wisconsin	★	G	Adjutant General/Military Affairs	$3,031,018	60 (a)
Wyoming	★	G	Governor's Office	$2,503,909	25 (a)
District of Columbia	★	M	Combined Homeland Security/Emerg. Mgt.	$2,085,250	79 (a)
Guam	★	G	Combined Homeland Security/Emerg. Mgt.	$0	26 (a)
No. Mariana Islands	★	G	Governor's Office	$280,000	35 (a)
U.S. Virgin Islands	★	G	Combined Homeland Security/Emerg. Mgt.	$4,591,421	69 (a)

Source: The National Emergency Management Association, April 2015.
Key:
★ — Yes
. . . — No
G — Governor
ADJ — Adjutant General

M — Mayor
DHSEM — Director of the Division of Homeland Security and Emergency Management
HSD — Homeland Security Director
PSS — Public Safety Secretary/Commissioner/Director
(a) Includes homeland security and emergency management positions.

emergency manager will interact with all sectors of the population, including other state agencies, elected officials, local jurisdictions, all public safety personnel, the private sector, volunteer organizations and the general public.

State Emergency Management Organizational Structures, Budgets and Staff

States use a variety of structures when it comes to the emergency management function. A 2015 fiscal year survey[2] of 50 states, the District of Columbia and three U.S. territories found that 15 states have the emergency management office located within their department of public safety, an increase from 13 in the 2014 fiscal year. In 15 states, it's in the military department under the auspices of the adjutant general. This represents a decrease from 17 previously. Eleven states have it in the governor's office and in 10 states, it's located in a combined emergency management/homeland security agency. The remaining states use other organizational structures.

Regardless of how an agency's daily operations are organized, most governors make the final decision on who serves as the state emergency management director. The governor appoints the state emergency management director in 35 — or almost two-thirds — of the states.

Continuing a trend for the past few years, the majority of states — 36 — combine their emergency management and homeland security full-time equivalent positions. The total number of full-time equivalents for these states is about 3,964 and averages about 110 per state. For those states that have a stand-alone emergency management office, full-time equivalents total 1,976 or averaging about 110 per state. Agency operating budgets for the 2015 fiscal year range up to $139 million. Some states saw significant increases as the result of absorbing additional functions/departments into the state emergency management agency. As a result, the average state budget is approximately $9 million, while the median is about $3.2 million.

State Homeland Security Funding and Responsibilities

After several years of eroding budgets, the federal State Homeland Security Grant Program has remained steady for the 2015 fiscal year at $402 million, up slightly from $401 million in the previous year. The program is a central federal funding source that supports and sustains state and local government homeland security capabilities. As recently as the 2010 fiscal year, $842 million was allotted to states. The next year due to overall budget cuts, this amount fell to $527 million and the decline continued through fiscal year 2012, when the total was $294 million.

Fifteen states in 2014 relied solely on federal grants to fund their homeland security offices. This represents a decrease from the previous year, when 19 states depended on federal grants. Thirty-nine states receive 60 percent or more from federal money to fund their state homeland security office, down from 42 last year. On average, states rely on 75.7 percent federal funding, 20.4 percent state appropriations and 3.9 percent from other sources to pay for their homeland security function.

When it comes to the state homeland security offices, responsibilities and organizational structures vary from state to state. In some cases, state homeland security directors manage grants and budgets; in others, they have very limited roles. In 15 states, a combined emergency management/homeland security office oversees daily operations of the homeland security function. Thirteen states keep the homeland security function in their public safety department and nine states have it in the adjutant general/military affairs department. Nine states run it out of the governor's office. The rest of the states have other organizational structures for their homeland security function.

What's Next?

Growing Threat from Cyberattacks

Cyber vulnerabilities continue to threaten the nation and all sectors of the economy, government, education and even the White House. In an informal survey[3] of state emergency management and homeland security directors in 2014, cybersecurity was ranked as the top issue.

One of the most difficult aspects to address from an emergency management perspective is physical damage to infrastructure or to a community from a major cyberattack. How the response and recovery will be managed and the type of federal assistance available to states and jurisdictions are important questions that must be addressed if emergency management is to be an active and fully engaged partner.

Potential Changes for Disaster Assistance to States, Jurisdictions and Others

Two recent developments in the area of federal disaster assistance will have far-reaching implications on states, countless jurisdictions and tens of

Table B: Homeland Security Structures

	State homeland security advisor	Homeland security organizations	
State or other jurisdiction	Designated homeland security advisor	Day-to-day operations under	Full-time employee positions
Alabama	Homeland Security Director	Governor's Office	14
Alaska	Dual Title–Emerg. Mgt./Homeland Security Director	Adjutant General/Military Affairs	62 (a)
Arizona	Homeland Security Director	Adjutant General/Military Affairs	14
Arkansas	Dual Title–Emerg. Mgt./Homeland Security Director	Combined Emerg. Mgt./Homeland Security Office	100 (a)
California	Dual Title–Emerg. Mgt./Homeland Security Director	Governor's Office	910 (a)
Colorado	Dual Title–Emerg. Mgt./Homeland Security Director	Public Safety	113 (a)
Connecticut	Public Safety Secretary/Commissioner	Combined Emerg. Mgt./Homeland Security Office	78 (a)
Delaware	Homeland Security Director	Public Safety	1
Florida	Florida Dept. of Law Enforcement Commissioner	Florida Dept. of Law Enforcement	157 (a)
Georgia	Dual Title–Emerg. Mgt./Homeland Security Director	Governor's Office	121 (a)
Hawaii	Adjutant General	Adjutant General/Military Affairs	5
Idaho	Dual Title–Emerg. Mgt./Homeland Security Director	Combined Emerg. Mgt./Homeland Security Office	41 (a)
Illinois	Dual Title–Emerg. Mgt./Homeland Security Director	Combined Emerg. Mgt./Homeland Security Office	202 (a)
Indiana	Dual Title–Emerg. Mgt./Homeland Security Director	Combined Emerg. Mgt./Homeland Security Office	263 (a)
Iowa	Dual Title–Emerg. Mgt./Homeland Security Director	Combined Emerg. Mgt./Homeland Security Office	100 (a)
Kansas	Adjutant General	Adjutant General/Military Affairs	0
Kentucky	Homeland Security Director	Governor's Office	16
Louisiana	Dual Title–Emerg. Mgt./Homeland Security Director	Combined Emerg. Mgt./Homeland Security Office	53 (a)
Maine	Adjutant General	Combined Emerg. Mgt./Homeland Security Office	28 (a)
Maryland	Homeland Security Director	Governor's Office	2
Massachusetts	Dual Title–Emerg. Mgt./Homeland Security Director	Public Safety	9
Michigan	State Police Superintendent/Director/Commissioner	State Police	67 (a)
Minnesota	Dual Title–Emerg. Mgt./Homeland Security Director	Public Safety	83 (a)
Mississippi	Homeland Security Director	Public Safety	18
Missouri	Homeland Security Director	Homeland Security (stand-alone office)	11
Montana	Adjutant General	Adjutant General/Military Affairs	24 (a)
Nebraska	Lieutenant Governor	Combined Emerg. Mgt./Homeland Security Office	37 (a)
Nevada	Dual Title–Emerg. Mgt./Homeland Security Director	Public Safety	33 (a)
New Hampshire	Dual Title–Emerg. Mgt./Homeland Security Director	Public Safety	42 (a)
New Jersey	Homeland Security Director	Homeland Security (stand-alone office)	130
New Mexico	Dual Title–Emerg. Mgt./Homeland Security Director	Combined Emerg. Mgt./Homeland Security Office	65 (a)
New York	Homeland Security Director	Homeland Security (stand-alone office)	392 (a)
North Carolina	Public Safety Secretary/Commissioner	Public Safety	186 (a)
North Dakota	Homeland Security Director	Adjutant General/Military Affairs	74 (a)
Ohio	Homeland Security Director	Public Safety	23
Oklahoma	Homeland Security Director	Public Safety	20
Oregon	Adjutant General	Adjutant General/Military Affairs	41 (a)
Pennsylvania	State Police Superintendent/Director/Commissioner	Governor's Office	6
Rhode Island	State Police Superintendent/Director/Commissioner	Combined Emerg. Mgt./Homeland Security Office	32 (a)
South Carolina	State Police Superintendent/Director/Commissioner	State Police	19
South Dakota	Homeland Security Director	Public Safety	3
Tennessee	Assistant Commissioner, Department of Safety and Homeland Security	Dept. of Safety and Homeland Security	26
Texas	Homeland Security Director	Public Safety	50
Utah	Public Safety Secretary/Commissioner	Public Safety	60 (a)
Vermont	State Police Superintendent/Director/Commissioner	Combined Emerg. Mgt./Homeland Security Office	28 (a)
Virginia	Public Safety Secretary/Commissioner	Secretariat of Public Safety and Homeland Security	154 (a)
Washington	Adjutant General	Adjutant General/Military Affairs	71 (a)
West Virginia	Dual Title–Emerg. Mgt./Homeland Security Director	Combined Emerg. Mgt./Homeland Security Office	53 (a)
Wisconsin	Adjutant General	Adjutant General/Military Affairs	60 (a)
Wyoming	Dual Title–Emerg. Mgt./Homeland Security Director	Governor's Office	25 (a)
Dist. of Columbia	Dual Title–Emerg. Mgt./Homeland Security Director	Combined Emerg. Mgt./Homeland Security Office	79 (a)
Guam	Homeland Security Director	Governor's Office	26 (a)
No. Mariana Islands	Dual Title–Emerg. Mgt./Homeland Security Director	Governor's Office	35 (a)
U.S. Virgin Islands	Dual Title–Emerg. Mgt./Homeland Security Director	Combined Emerg. Mgt./Homeland Security Office	69 (a)

Source: The National Emergency Management Association, April 2015.
(a) Includes homeland security and emergency management positions.

millions of citizens. The first is an appeals court ruling in 2014 against FEMA.

FEMA had approved funding in 2004-06 for disaster repair work conducted by the Florida South Water Management District, but then reversed that decision, eventually demanding repayment of $21 million. Referred to as deobligation, the common practice has wreaked havoc on state, local and nonprofit budgets because they're expected to return sometimes millions of dollars—money they don't have. FEMA is now implementing numerous internal changes as a result of the ruling, but the full ramifications are unclear. It could mean the agency will take a more conservative approach in approving disaster assistance.

The second development involves FEMA's public assistance program, which is designed to help states, tribes, jurisdictions and certain private non-profit organizations after a presidentially declared disaster. It's a multi-billion dollar program that impacts the entire country. Because of persistent problems with the program, however, FEMA has initiated a redesign and has asked state emergency management to partner in the process. The new concept is expected to be piloted in 2015. If done effectively, the improved program could result in faster assistance to recipients, less bureaucracy, fewer deobligations and better coordination with other federal programs.

EMAC—Maturation of a Nationwide Capability

For more than 20 years, the Emergency Management Assistance Compact has served as the leading state-to-state mutual aid agreement, providing well-established mechanisms for states to help each other when a disaster occurs. Examples of this assistance across state lines include recent flooding events in New Mexico, Colorado and Alaska; severe winter storms in 2014 when 165 personnel were sent through EMAC to Connecticut and Massachusetts; and Hurricane Sandy in 2013, which resulted in more than 2,600 people on 142 missions helping in six states.

As the federal budget is further scrutinized and debated, more states will continue to use EMAC as a vehicle to leverage regional resources. For example, instead of each state investing in a search and rescue team, the compact gives states within a geographical area the option of sharing that capability. This also allows a broader leverage of federal grant dollars and individual state investments in providing a true nationwide, disaster management capability.

Notes

[1] http://cdfdata.fire.ca.gov/incidents/incidents_stats?year=2014.

[2] National Emergency Management Association, "NEMA FY 2015 Annual Survey of State Emergency Management Directors," March 2015.

[3] Conducted by National Emergency Management Association on behalf of the National Homeland Security Consortium, a group of 21 national associations representing first and second responders, government, business and key resources in the event of a disaster/threat.

About the Author

Beverly Bell is the policy and program manager for the National Emergency Management Association, an affiliate of The Council of State Governments. She assists in national policy coordination and grant implementation, while also conducting research and acting as an information clearinghouse for emergency management and homeland security issues.

Table 9.1
NUMBER AND TYPES OF PUBLIC ELEMENTARY AND SECONDARY SCHOOLS, BY STATE OR JURISDICTION: SCHOOL YEAR 2012–13

State or other jurisdiction	Total number of operating schools (a)	Type of school				Charter	Magnet (b)	Title I (c)	Title I schoolwide (c)
		Regular	Special education	Vocational education	Alternative education				
Reporting states (d).....	98,454	89,031	2,034	1,403	5,986	6,079	3,151	68,140	51,529
Alabama........................	1,637	1,402	44	72	119	†	32	906	884
Alaska...........................	509	436	3	3	67	27	17	367	347
Arizona.........................	2,267	1,955	22	225	65	542	19	1,794	1,318
Arkansas.......................	1,102	1,061	4	26	11	45	38	938	867
California	10,315	8,786	149	87	1,293	1,085	421	7,155	5,295
Colorado.......................	1,825	1,725	7	6	87	187	25	658	493
Connecticut..................	1,148	1,035	47	16	50	17	69	572	218
Delaware	224	191	21	6	6	22	3	183	175
Florida..........................	4,269	3,609	185	51	424	581	494	2,697	2,587
Georgia.........................	2,387	2,253	59	1	74	93	86	1,575	1,478
Hawaii...........................	286	284	1	0	1	32	†	228	210
Idaho.............................	719	629	11	10	69	47	19	570	517
Illinois..........................	4,266	3,978	140	0	148	58	108	3,330	1,734
Indiana..........................	1,925	1,860	29	27	9	72	32	1,497	1,194
Iowa	1,390	1,354	6	0	30	3	†	960	548
Kansas	1,351	1,338	10	1	2	16	33	1,057	858
Kentucky	1,568	1,301	6	126	135	†	42	1,116	1,069
Louisiana......................	1,407	1,218	28	9	152	104	77	1,181	1,139
Maine............................	617	587	3	27	0	2	1	529	398
Maryland.......................	1,449	1,327	39	26	57	52	92	385	337
Massachusetts	1,854	1,774	21	39	20	77	–	1,053	547
Michigan.......................	3,550	3,057	193	6	294	346	435	2,347	1,475
Minnesota.....................	2,403	1,626	279	11	487	176	82	867	322
Mississippi	1,063	908	4	90	61	0	17	721	710
Missouri........................	2,406	2,173	64	64	105	57	29	1,842	1,503
Montana	824	818	2	0	4	†	†	708	424
Nebraska	1,090	1,011	26	0	53	†	†	498	356
Nevada..........................	664	599	12	1	52	40	37	171	168
New Hampshire	481	481	0	0	0	22	†	419	137
New Jersey	2,598	2,360	59	62	117	86	–	1,640	478
New Mexico	877	829	8	1	39	94	2	782	752
New York	4,822	4,644	123	29	26	211	‡	4,429	1,927
North Carolina.............	2,557	2,444	25	7	81	108	106	2,120	2,004
North Dakota................	517	472	33	12	0	†	†	275	109
Ohio..............................	3,685	3,555	54	70	6	368	†	2,935	2,709
Oklahoma.....................	1,784	1,776	4	0	4	23	†	1,251	1,114
Oregon..........................	1,251	1,211	2	0	38	123	†	574	466
Pennsylvania	3,127	3,021	8	87	11	175	46	2,372	1,525
Rhode Island................	304	285	2	12	5	18	†	228	137
South Carolina.............	1,239	1,166	10	42	21	55	100	1,054	1,013
South Dakota...............	697	651	9	3	34	†	†	615	360
Tennessee	1,817	1,764	16	16	21	51	132	1,504	1,439
Texas.............................	8,731	7,710	22	0	999	628	242	6,970	6,707
Utah..............................	995	897	69	3	26	88	23	297	217
Vermont........................	318	302	0	15	1	†	2	241	189
Virginia........................	2,182	1,874	54	58	196	4	136	740	503
Washington...................	2,370	1,932	98	18	322	†	†	1,579	1,326
West Virginia...............	755	692	3	30	30	†	†	338	336
Wisconsin	2,238	2,125	10	5	98	238	4	1,519	639
Wyoming	364	337	3	0	24	4	†	173	96
Dist. of Columbia	230	208	7	3	12	102	34	180	175

See footnotes at end of table.

NUMBER AND TYPES OF PUBLIC ELEMENTARY AND SECONDARY SCHOOLS, BY STATE OR JURISDICTION: SCHOOL YEAR 2012–13—Continued

Source: U.S. Department of Education, National Center for Education Statistics, Common Core of Data (CCD), "Public Elementary/Secondary School Universe Survey," SY 2012–13 Provisional Version 1a. Table 3.

Note: Every school is assigned only one school type based on its instructional emphasis. Independent of school type, every school is assigned a separate charter status, magnet status, and Title 1 status. Numbers and types of schools may differ from those published by states. For the complete definitions, see Appendix B: Common Core of Data Glossary.

Key:

– — Not available.

† — Not applicable. Some states/jurisdictions do not have charter school authorization and some states/jurisdictions do not designate magnet schools.

‡ — Reporting standards were not met. Data missing for more than 20 percent of schools in the state or jurisdiction.

(a) Total number of operating schools excludes schools also reported by the Bureau of Indian Education (BIE). The number of operating schools shared with the BIE includes two in Arizona, one in Michigan, and eight in North Dakota.

(b) Massachusetts and New Jersey have magnet schools but were not able to provide data that indicate the magnet status of each school.

(c) A Title I eligible school is one in which the percentage of children from low-income families is at least 35 percent of children from low-income families served by the LEA as a whole. A schoolwide Title I eligible school has a percentage of low-income students that is at least 40 percent.

(d) A reporting state's total is shown if data for any item in the table were missing for some, but reported for at least 85 percent of all schools in the United States.

Table 9.2
NUMBER OF OPERATING PUBLIC SCHOOLS AND DISTRICTS, STATE ENROLLMENT, TEACHER AND PUPIL/TEACHER RATIO BY STATE: SCHOOL YEAR 2011–12

State or jurisdiction	Number of operational schools (a)	Number of operational districts	Membership (b)	Teachers (b)	Pupil/teacher ratio
United States (c)..........	98,328	17,992	49,521,669	3,103,263	16
Alabama	1,618	170	744,621	47,723	15.6
Alaska...........................	511	54	131,167	8,088	16.2
Arizona.........................	2,252	662	1,080,319	50,800	21.3
Arkansas.......................	1,108	289	483,114	33,983	14.2
California	10,170	1,187	6,287,834	268,689	23.4
Colorado	1,813	259	854,265	48,078	17.8
Connecticut	1,150	200	554,437	43,805	12.7
Delaware	221	44	128,946	8,587	15
Florida..........................	4,212	76	2,668,156	175,006	15.2
Georgia.........................	2,388	216	1,685,016	111,133	15.2
Hawaii...........................	287	1	182,706	11,458	15.9
Idaho............................	762	149	279,873	15,990	17.5
Illinois..........................	4,336	1,075	2,083,097	131,777	15.8
Indiana.........................	1,933	394	1,040,765	62,339	16.7
Iowa	1,411	361	495,870	34,658	14.3
Kansas	1,359	321	486,108	37,407	13
Kentucky	1,565	194	681,987	41,860	16.3
Louisiana......................	1,437	132	703,390	48,657	14.5
Maine............................	621	260	188,969	14,888	12.7
Maryland	1,451	25	854,086	57,589	14.8
Massachusetts	1,835	401	953,369	69,342	13.7
Michigan.......................	3,550	869	1,573,537	86,997	18.1
Minnesota.....................	2,392	555	839,738	52,832	15.9
Mississippi	1,069	163	490,619	32,007	15.3
Missouri........................	2,408	572	916,584	66,252	13.8
Montana	826	500	142,349	10,153	14
Nebraska.......................	1,090	288	301,296	22,182	13.6
Nevada..........................	649	18	439,634	21,132	20.8
New Hampshire	477	281	191,900	15,049	12.8
New Jersey	2,596	700	1,356,431	109,719	12.4
New Mexico	866	135	337,225	21,957	15.4
New York.......................	4,752	923	2,704,718	209,527	12.9
North Carolina	2,577	236	1,507,864	97,308	15.5
North Dakota	513	223	97,646	8,525	11.5
Ohio	3,714	1,079	1,740,030	107,972	16.1
Oklahoma.....................	1,774	575	666,120	41,349	16.1
Oregon..........................	1,261	221	568,208	26,791	21.2
Pennsylvania	3,181	784	1,771,395	124,646	14.2
Rhode Island	308	54	142,854	11,414	12.5
South Carolina	1,223	105	727,186	46,782	15.5
South Dakota................	704	171	128,016	9,247	13.8
Tennessee	1,802	140	999,693	66,382	15.1
Texas	8,697	1,262	5,000,470	324,282	15.4
Utah	1,020	126	598,832	25,970	23.1
Vermont.........................	320	369	89,908	8,364	10.7
Virginia.........................	2,170	221	1,257,883	90,832	13.8
Washington	2,365	316	1,045,453	53,119	19.7
West Virginia	759	57	282,870	20,247	14
Wisconsin	2,243	462	871,105	56,245	15.5
Wyoming	354	61	90,099	7,847	11.5
Dist. of Columbia	228	56	73,911	6,278	11.8
DoDEA	191	16	–	–	–
Bureau of Indian Education	173	195	–	–	–
American Samoa	28	1	–	–	–
Guam	40	1	31,243	2,291	13.6
No. Mariana Islands	29	1	11,011	496	22.2
Puerto Rico...................	1,464	1	452,740	33,079	13.7
U.S. Virgin Islands........	31	2	15,711	1,217	12.9

See footnotes at end of table.

NUMBER OF OPERATING PUBLIC SCHOOLS AND DISTRICTS, STATE ENROLLMENT, TEACHER AND PUPIL/TEACHER RATIO BY STATE: SCHOOL YEAR 2011–12—Continued

Source: U.S. Department of Education, National Center for Education Statistics, Common Core of Data (CCD), "Public Elementary/ Secondary School Universe Survey," SY 2011–12, Provisional Version 1a, "Local Education Agency Universe Survey," SY 2011–12, Provisional Version 1a, "State Nonfiscal Survey of Public Elementary/Secondary Education," SY 2011–12, Provisional Version 1a.

Note: Data for teachers are expressed in full-time equivalents (FTE). Counts of public school teachers and enrollment include prekindergarten through grade 12.

Key:

– – Not available.

(a) Total number of operating schools excludes schools also reported by the Bureau of Indian Education (BIE). The number of operating schools shared with the BIE include two in Arizona, one in Michigan, and eight in North Dakota.

(b) The membership and staff counts are from the State Nonfiscal Survey.

(c) U.S. totals include the 50 states and the District of Columbia.

Table 9.3
PUBLIC HIGH SCHOOL NUMBER OF GRADUATES, NUMBER OF HIGH SCHOOL DROPOUTS FOR GRADES 9–12, AND HIGH SCHOOL EVENT DROPOUT RATE FOR GRADES 9–12, BY GENDER AND STATE OR JURISDICTION: SCHOOL YEAR 2009–10

| | Number of graduates (a) | | High school dropouts (b) | | | |
| | | | Male | | Female | |
State or other jurisdiction	Male	Female	Number of dropouts	Dropout rate (c)	Number of dropouts	Dropout rate (c)
Reporting states (d)......................	1,514,185	1,556,052	280,648	3.8	206,424	2.9
Alabama.............................	20,844	22,271	2,185	2.0	1,606	1.5
Alaska.................................	4,010	4,235	1,554	7.4	1,262	6.3
Arizona...............................	29,608	31,109	13,429	8.3	11,061	7.2
Arkansas.............................	13,819	14,457	2,924	4.2	1,964	2.9
California	198,339	206,479	54,797	5.4	38,067	3.9
Colorado.............................	24,217	25,104	7,221	5.9	5,646	4.8
Connecticut	N.A.	N.A.	3,380	3.8	1,802	2.1
Delaware	3,885	4,248	871	4.5	647	3.4
Florida	74,094	78,468	10,404	2.7	7,325	1.9
Georgia...............................	43,664	47,897	10,741	4.5	7,025	3.0
Hawaii.................................	5,626	5,372	1,553	5.7	1,183	4.7
Idaho..................................	9,067	8,726	620	1.5	512	1.3
Illinois...............................	67,888	68,949	10,484	3.3	7,569	2.5
Indiana...............................	30,930	32,063	2,895	1.9	1,893	1.3
Iowa	17,080	17,382	2,784	3.7	2,065	2.9
Kansas	15,918	15,724	1,790	2.5	1,177	1.7
Kentucky	21,253	21,295	. . .	. . .	. . .	. . .
Louisiana............................	17,010	19,563	4,989	5.6	3,676	4.1
Maine	6,577	6,258	. . .	. . .	. . .	. . .
Maryland............................	29,049	30,029	4,385	3.2	2,695	2.1
Massachusetts	31,956	32,506	4,790	3.2	3,290	2.3
Michigan.............................	54,116	55,770	12,303	4.5	9,736	3.8
Minnesota...........................	29,846	29,821	2,573	1.8	1,740	1.3
Mississippi	11,735	13,586	. . .	. . .	. . .	. . .
Missouri..............................	31,915	32,079	5,535	3.9	4,010	2.9
Montana	5,041	5,037	1,094	4.8	807	3.8
Nebraska.............................	9,672	9,698	1,141	2.5	738	1.7
Nevada................................	9,976	10,699	2,995	5.0	2,305	3.8
New Hampshire	7,436	7,598	472	1.4	286	0.9
New Jersey	48,796	47,429	4,007	1.8	3,036	1.5
New Mexico	8,934	9,661	3,870	7.7	2,919	6.1
New York.............................	90,295	93,122	18,150	4.1	13,599	3.0
North Carolina....................	42,118	44,569	11,575	5.3	8,031	3.8
North Dakota......................	3,642	3,513	389	2.5	289	2.0
Ohio....................................	60,156	60,292	11,286	4.2	9,648	3.8
Oklahoma............................	19,255	19,248	2,375	2.6	1,908	2.2
Oregon................................	16,568	17,206	3,187	3.7	2,330	2.9
Pennsylvania.......................	65,393	65,200	6,919	2.4	5,119	1.8
Rhode Island.......................	4,883	5,025	1,303	5.5	863	3.8
South Carolina....................	18,424	21,230	3,727	3.5	2,513	2.4
South Dakota	4,081	4,076	540	2.8	459	2.5
Tennessee	30,780	31,628	4,527	3.1	3,052	2.2
Texas...................................	140,858	139,529	19,254	2.8	16,267	2.5
Utah....................................	15,505	15,870	2,345	2.9	1,740	2.3
Vermont..............................	3,306	3,232	397	2.9	284	2.2
Virginia...............................	39,341	40,899	4,563	2.4	3,235	1.8
Washington.........................	31,353	32,194	7,415	4.5	5,836	3.7
West Virginia.......................	8,861	8,790	1,870	4.4	1,424	3.6
Wisconsin............................	32,540	32,147	3,517	2.4	2,523	1.9
Wyoming	2,878	2,817	891	6.6	662	5.2
District of Columbia............	1,647	1,955	632	7.5 (e)	600	6.4 (e)
DoDDS: DoDs Overseas (f)........	N.A.	N.A.	N.A.	N.A.	N.A.	N.A.
DDESS: DoDs Domestic (f)........	N.A.	N.A.	N.A.	N.A.	N.A.	N.A.
Bureau of Indian Education	N.A.	N.A.	N.A.	N.A.	N.A.	N.A.
American Samoa	N.A.	N.A.	N.A.	N.A.	N.A.	N.A.
Guam	N.A.	N.A.	N.A.	N.A.	N.A.	N.A.
No. Mariana Islands	N.A.	N.A.	N.A.	N.A.	N.A.	N.A.
Puerto Rico..........................	N.A.	N.A.	N.A.	N.A.	N.A.	N.A.
U.S. Virgin Islands	397	543	256	10.4	131	4.8

See footnotes at end of table.

PUBLIC HIGH SCHOOL NUMBER OF GRADUATES, NUMBER OF HIGH SCHOOL DROPOUTS FOR GRADES 9–12, AND HIGH SCHOOL EVENT DROPOUT RATE FOR GRADES 9–12, BY GENDER AND STATE OR JURISDICTION: SCHOOL YEAR 2009–10—Continued

Sources: U.S. Department of Education, National Center for Education Statistics, Common Core of Data (CCD), "NCES Common Core of Data State Dropout and Completion Data File," School Year 2009–10, Version 1a; and "NCES Common Core of Data Local Education Agency Universe Survey Dropout and Completion Restricted-Use Data File," School Year 2009–10, Version 1a.

Key:

N.A. — Not available. State or jurisdiction did not report graduate counts or dropout counts by gender.

. . . — Reporting standards not met.

(a) Graduate counts were calculated using district-level data. Totals may differ from graduate counts on other tables due to different reporting levels. Graduation rates were not calculated due to missing data at the school district level.

(b) Ungraded dropouts are prorated by NCES into grades based on the graded dropout counts to calculate numerators for dropout rates. Ungraded student enrollments are prorated by NCES into grades based on graded enrollments to calculate denominators for dropout rates.

(c) The event dropout rate is defined as the count of dropouts from a given school year divided by the count of student enrollments within the same grade span at the beginning of the same school year.

(d) Reporting states totals include any of the 50 states and the District of Columbia that reported all data elements.

(e) Data were imputed based on prior year rates.

(f) DoDDS and DDESS are the Department of Defense Overseas Dependent Elementary and Secondary Schools and the Department of Defense Domestic Dependent Elementary and Secondary Schools, respectively.

Table 9.4
TOTAL REVENUES AND PERCENTAGE DISTRIBUTION, FOR PUBLIC ELEMENTARY AND SECONDARY SCHOOLS, BY SOURCE AND STATE OR JURISDICTION: FISCAL YEAR 2011

State or other jurisdiction	Revenues (in thousands of dollars)				Percentage distribution		
	Total	Local (a)	State	Federal	Local (a)	State	Federal
United States (b)	$604,293,209	$261,965,331	$266,786,402	$75,541,475	43.4	44.1	12.5
Alabama	7,386,471	2,307,983	3,827,907	1,250,581	31.2	51.8	16.9
Alaska	2,470,274	521,768	1,524,083	424,422	21.1	61.7	17.2
Arizona	9,764,472	4,200,211	3,924,369	1,639,892	43.0	40.2	16.8
Arkansas	5,273,728	1,711,386	2,703,033	859,309	32.5	51.3	16.3
California	67,864,062	20,203,727	38,411,425	9,248,710	29.8	56.6	13.6
Colorado	8,820,783	4,288,294	3,540,865	991,623	48.6	34.3	11.2
Connecticut	9,989,986	5,739,726	3,422,642	827,618	57.5	58.6	8.3
Delaware	1,748,658	516,279	1,024,557	207,823	29.5	34.4	11.9
Florida	26,358,355	12,492,913	9,069,113	4,796,329	47.4	41.7	18.2
Georgia	18,047,879	8,208,751	7,526,257	2,312,782	45.5	37.9	12.8
Hawaii (c)	2,470,432	63,280	2,059,791	347,361	2.6	83.4	14.1
Idaho	2,183,491	495,614	1,382,052	305,826	22.7	63.3	14.0
Illinois	28,895,633	16,691,051	9,304,471	2,900,110	57.8	32.2	10.0
Indiana	11,761,793	4,181,108	6,534,419	1,046,267	35.5	55.6	8.9
Iowa	5,906,171	2,742,097	2,550,546	613,528	46.4	43.2	10.4
Kansas	5,670,547	2,028,345	2,979,230	662,971	35.8	52.5	11.7
Kentucky	6,993,349	2,221,230	3,622,461	1,149,658	31.8	51.8	16.4
Louisiana	8,246,484	3,233,813	3,479,231	1,533,440	39.2	42.2	18.6
Maine	2,597,927	1,256,620	1,052,058	289,249	48.4	40.5	11.1
Maryland	13,437,322	6,672,768	5,508,344	1,256,210	49.7	41.0	9.3
Massachusetts	15,357,042	8,287,173	5,797,874	1,271,995	54.0	37.8	8.3
Michigan	19,466,487	6,042,795	10,717,934	2,705,858	31.0	55.1	13.9
Minnesota	10,938,581	3,635,648	6,397,541	905,392	33.2	58.5	8.3
Mississippi	4,483,191	1,405,267	2,071,471	1,006,453	31.3	46.2	22.4
Missouri	10,169,473	5,779,196	3,008,369	1,381,908	56.8	29.6	13.6
Montana	1,654,729	632,641	723,125	298,964	38.2	43.7	18.1
Nebraska	3,911,430	2,090,741	1,186,279	634,411	53.5	30.3	16.2
Nevada	4,212,793	2,360,780	1,388,359	463,653	56.0	33.0	11.0
New Hampshire	2,844,769	1,597,636	1,041,561	205,572	56.2	36.6	7.2
New Jersey	25,217,564	14,477,191	9,403,391	1,336,982	57.4	37.3	5.3
New Mexico	3,744,076	598,541	2,423,599	721,936	16.0	64.7	19.3
New York	57,538,128	29,072,179	23,097,859	5,368,090	50.5	40.1	9.3
North Carolina	13,228,999	3,401,425	7,688,360	2,139,214	25.7	58.1	16.2
North Dakota	1,258,921	442,351	629,843	186,727	35.1	50.0	14.8
Ohio	22,973,368	10,348,507	9,921,997	2,702,863	45.0	43.2	11.8
Oklahoma	5,874,001	2,125,560	2,754,252	994,189	36.2	46.9	16.9
Oregon	6,120,056	2,463,231	2,792,707	864,118	40.2	45.6	14.1
Pennsylvania	27,174,139	14,476,964	9,378,294	3,318,881	53.3	34.5	12.2
Rhode Island	2,278,564	1,198,154	830,217	250,194	52.6	36.4	11.0
South Carolina	7,873,340	3,373,102	3,414,705	1,085,533	42.8	43.4	13.8
South Dakota	1,307,520	661,188	380,410	265,922	50.6	29.1	20.3
Tennessee	8,915,680	3,608,119	3,995,291	1,312,271	40.5	44.8	14.7
Texas	50,874,695	22,476,413	20,430,187	7,968,095	44.2	40.2	15.7
Utah	4,597,983	1,679,229	2,340,850	577,903	36.5	50.9	12.6
Vermont	1,641,955	125,491	1,340,743	175,721	7.6	81.7	10.7
Virginia	14,444,511	7,668,024	5,349,193	1,427,295	53.1	37.0	9.9
Washington	11,801,402	3,677,484	6,757,950	1,365,968	31.2	57.3	11.6
West Virginia	3,499,055	1,033,700	1,951,616	513,739	29.5	55.8	14.7
Wisconsin	11,429,211	5,137,189	5,246,795	1,045,227	44.9	45.9	9.1
Wyoming	1,647,905	613,623	878,878	155,403	37.2	53.3	9.4
Dist. of Columbia (c)	1,925,824	1,698,626	0	227,198	88.2	0.0	11.8
American Samoa	82,921	225	10,689	72,007	0.3	12.9 (d)	86.8
Guam	333,235	190,469	0	142,766	57.2	0.0	42.8
No. Mariana Islands	87,377	0	29,758	57,619	0.0	34.1 (d)	65.9
Puerto Rico	3,911,167	43	2,328,968	1,382,157	0.0	62.8 (d)	37.2
U.S. Virgin Islands	243,250	198,392	0	44,858	81.6	0.0	18.4

Source: U.S. Department of Education, National Center for Education Statistics, Common Core of Data (CCD), "National Public Education Financial Survey (NPEFS)," fiscal year 2011, Preliminary Version 1a.

Note: Detail may not sum to totals because of rounding.

Key:

(a) Local revenues include intermediate revenues from education agencies with fundraising capabilities that operate between the state and local government levels.

(b) U.S. totals include the 50 states and the District of Columbia.

(c) Both the District of Columbia and Hawaii have only one school district each; therefore, neither is comparable to other states. Local revenues in Hawaii consist almost entirely of student fees and charges for services, such as food services, summer school, and student activities.

(d) Reported state revenue data are revenues received from the central government of the jurisdiction.

Table 9.5
TOTAL EXPENDITURES FOR PUBLIC ELEMENTARY AND SECONDARY EDUCATION: FISCAL YEAR 2011

| | | | Expenditures (in thousands of dollars) | | | | |
| | | | | Capital outlay | | | |
State or other jurisdiction	Total	Current for elementary/ secondary education (a)	Facilities acquisitions and construction	Land and existing structures	Equipment	Other programs (b)	Interest on debt
United States (c)	$604,214,912 (d)(e)	$527,166,106 (d)	$40,977,768 (d)	$3,415,999 (d)	$6,533,773 (d)(e)	$8,187,042 (d)(e)	$17,934,224
Alabama.......................	7,410,192	6,592,925	473,293	47,479	45,213	116,732	134,550
Alaska..........................	2,430,593	2,201,270	123,245	35,272	22,824	8,633	39,349
Arizona........................	9,889,232 (d)(e)	8,340,211	545,237	53,706	265,903	47,020 (e)	637,155
Arkansas......................	5,392,058	4,578,136	418,815	130,752	107,666	30,556	126,132
California	67,570,728	57,526,835	6,186,279	308,741	268,680	938,345	2,341,849
Colorado......................	8,743,142	7,409,462	582,201	104,968	148,097	58,479	439,936
Connecticut.................	9,944,121 (d)(e)	9,094,036	414,701 (d)	44,940 (d)	103,879 (d)	145,124 (e)	141,441
Delaware	1,855,007	1,613,304	175,069	1,956	12,741	28,277	23,660
Florida	27,433,536	23,870,090	1,949,441	117,526	150,097	570,458	775,923
Georgia........................	17,178,095	15,527,907	1,123,220	110,857	133,817	26,993	255,301
Hawaii (f)	2,342,924	2,141,561	70,923	0	14,553	17,627	98,261
Idaho...........................	2,107,272	1,881,746	116,378	13,425	30,281	4,151	61,292
Illinois.........................	27,621,033 (d)	24,554,467	1,434,733 (d)	163,487 (d)	495,276 (d)	151,196	821,873
Indiana.........................	11,037,564	9,687,949	430,547	210,123	231,192	139,215	338,537
Iowa.............................	5,859,335	4,855,871	722,810	17,179	131,168	30,310	101,997
Kansas	5,824,926	4,741,372	659,293	24,382	186,071	4,295	209,512
Kentucky	7,200,059	6,211,453	557,742	19,526	170,001	83,981	157,355
Louisiana.....................	8,502,295	7,522,098	719,957	42,952	49,848	45,343	122,086
Maine...........................	2,630,548	2,377,878	143,850	39	28,601	28,301	51,778
Maryland	13,251,725	12,035,719	944,925	795	76,362	28,220	165,704
Massachusetts	14,715,706	13,649,965	482,793	264,588	11,307	55,711	251,343
Michigan......................	19,444,952 (d)	16,786,444	1,106,005 (d)	113,027 (d)	215,801 (d)	332,187	891,488
Minnesota....................	10,816,918 (d)	8,944,867	806,694 (d)	85,820 (d)	159,690 (d)	417,151	402,695
Mississippi	4,268,801 (d)	3,887,981	119,992 (d)	21,995 (d)	139,049 (d)	28,526	71,258
Missouri.......................	10,072,167 (d)	8,691,887	650,207 (d)	26,945	177,181 (d)	198,591	326,725
Montana	1,653,315	1,518,818	72,650	9,095	25,459	11,231	16,062
Nebraska......................	3,739,179 (d)	3,298,536	201,619 (d)	20,654 (d)	134,369 (d)	2,629 (d)	81,372
Nevada.........................	4,244,029	3,676,997	237,773	25,194	34,187	25,308	244,570
New Hampshire	2,896,802 (d)	2,637,911	136,231 (d)	37,526 (d)	32,519 (d)	7,823	44,799
New Jersey	25,308,865	23,639,281	738,153	14,379	102,999	146,882	667,171
New Mexico	3,641,735	3,127,463	497,711	3,957	8,652	3,862	90
New York......................	57,350,534	51,509,285	2,064,981	82,587	366,207	2,165,740	1,161,734
North Carolina.............	13,277,669	12,322,555	694,146	51,936	132,511	67,080	9,442
North Dakota...............	1,198,926	1,049,772	68,039	12,015	43,351	8,143	17,605
Ohio.............................	23,500,247	19,988,921	2,108,997	56,804	369,551	436,310	539,664
Oklahoma.....................	5,618,816	5,036,031	365,991	66,604	75,491	13,899	60,800
Oregon.........................	6,201,702	5,430,888	421,403	7,063	32,871	25,737	283,739
Pennsylvania	27,393,554	23,485,203	1,923,223	40,186	308,409	569,951	1,066,582
Rhode Island................	2,316,164	2,149,366	22,992	2,687	22,196	69,475	49,449
South Carolina.............	7,919,837	6,461,884	719,941	203,997	61,543	65,127	407,345
South Dakota...............	1,347,213	1,126,503	132,638 (d)	14,872 (d)	42,718	2,947	27,535
Tennessee	9,294,028	8,377,599	416,662	52,663	172,016	84,493	190,595
Texas...........................	52,711,794	42,864,291	5,897,125	203,274	455,737	337,583	2,953,783
Utah.............................	4,642,830	3,704,133	431,406	188,329	81,697	103,832	133,434
Vermont.......................	1,515,638	1,424,507	33,613	249	30,082	13,106	14,079
Virginia........................	14,291,767 (d)	12,968,457	630,062 (d)	194,159 (d)	250,855	74,580	173,655
Washington..................	12,025,483	10,040,312	1,346,102	81,086	87,585	57,362	413,036
West Virginia...............	3,515,624	3,388,294	22,347	5,735	37,648	46,185	15,415
Wisconsin	11,359,841	10,333,016	328,363	35,206	175,530	265,689	222,038
Wyoming	1,643,359	1,398,444	167,709	18,914	47,788	8,844	1,660
Dist. of Columbia (f) ...	2,063,029	1,482,202	339,444 (d)	26,336	25,872 (d)	37,802	151,373
American Samoa	84,478	75,355	2,408	0	4,631	2,084	0
Guam...........................	342,273	266,952	0	68,973	3,223	0	3,124
No. Mariana Islands	2,405,388	84,657	0	0	1,145	2,319,587	0
Puerto Rico..................	3,664,247	3,519,547	0	0	62,172	82,528	0
U.S. Virgin Islands	215,278	212,112	0	0	94	3,071	0

See footnotes at end of table.

TOTAL EXPENDITURES FOR PUBLIC ELEMENTARY AND SECONDARY EDUCATION: FISCAL YEAR 2011
—Continued

Source: U.S. Department of Education, National Center for Education Statistics, Common Core of Data (CCD), "National Public Education Financial Survey (NPEFS)," fiscal year 2011, Version 1a.

Note: Detail may not sum to totals because of rounding.

Key:

(a) Current expenditures include instruction, instruction-related, support services and other elementary/secondary current expenditures, but exclude expenditures on capital outlay, other programs and interest on long-term debt.

(b) Other program expenditures include expenditures for community services, adult education, community colleges, private schools and other programs that are not part of public elementary and secondary education.

(c) U.S. totals include the 50 states and the District of Columbia.

(d) Value affected by redistribution of reported values to correct for missing data items and/or to distribute state direct support expenditures.

(e) Value contains imputation for missing data.

(f) Both the District of Columbia and Hawaii have only one school district each; therefore, neither is comparable to other states.

Table 9.6
CURRENT EXPENDITURES AND PERCENTAGE DISTRIBUTION FOR PUBLIC ELEMENTARY AND SECONDARY EDUCATION, BY FUNCTION AND STATE OR JURISDICTION: FISCAL YEAR 2011

State or other jurisdiction	Current expenditures (in thousands of dollars) (a)					Percentage distribution			
	Total	Instruction and instruction related (b)	Student support (c)	Administration (d)	Operations (e)	Instruction and instruction related (b)	Student support (c)	Admin. (d)	Ops. (e)
United States (f)	$527,166,106	$347,366,608	$29,345,585	$56,271,015	$94,182,897	65.9	5.6	10.7	17.9
Alabama......................	6,592,925	4,144,140	382,417	697,381	1,368,987	62.9	5.8	10.6	20.8
Alaska........................	2,201,270	1,372,728	180,052	246,601	401,888	62.4	8.2	11.2	18.3
Arizona......................	8,340,211	4,702,191	1,087,247	850,455	1,700,317	56.4	13.0	10.2	20.4
Arkansas.....................	4,578,136	3,007,670	233,099	469,976	864,392	65.7	5.1	10.3	18.9
California	57,526,835	38,179,602	3,004,958	6,830,236	9,512,039	66.4	5.2	11.9	16.5
Colorado.....................	7,409,462	4,671,285	361,218	1,173,925	1,203,034	63.0	4.9	15.8	16.2
Connecticut.................	9,094,036	6,050,126	555,702	901,670	1,586,538	66.5	6.1	9.9	17.4
Delaware	1,613,304	1,039,533	75,881	184,242	313,648	64.4	4.7	11.4	19.4
Florida.......................	23,870,090	16,107,806	1,066,264	2,198,973	4,497,048	67.5	4.5	9.2	18.8
Georgia......................	15,527,907	10,446,015	733,717	1,683,579	2,664,595	67.3	4.7	10.8	17.2
Hawaii (g)..................	2,141,561	1,314,131	201,020	192,772	433,638	61.4	9.4	9.0	20.2
Idaho........................	1,881,746	1,223,368	106,724	192,395	359,259	65.0	5.7	10.2	19.1
Illinois.......................	24,554,467	15,749,772	1,658,199	3,036,509	4,109,987	64.1	6.8	12.4	16.7
Indiana......................	9,687,949	6,070,134	456,293	1,051,068	2,110,454	62.7	4.7	10.8	21.8
Iowa	4,855,871	3,225,620	273,995	545,403	810,852	66.4	5.6	11.2	16.7
Kansas	4,741,372	3,075,990	275,382	539,000	851,001	64.9	5.8	11.4	17.9
Kentucky	6,211,453	3,979,356	279,805	627,356	1,324,937	64.1	4.5	10.1	21.3
Louisiana....................	7,522,098	4,790,410	369,620	827,621	1,534,447	63.7	4.9	11.0	20.4
Maine........................	2,377,878	1,566,401	155,421	232,588	423,468	65.9	6.5	9.8	17.8
Maryland	12,035,719	8,093,141	528,145	1,269,829	2,144,604	67.2	4.4	10.6	17.8
Massachusetts	13,649,965	9,479,401	953,027	1,055,474	2,162,063	69.4	7.0	7.7	15.8
Michigan....................	16,786,444	10,562,665	1,269,121	2,097,332	2,857,326	62.9	7.6	12.5	17.0
Minnesota...................	8,944,867	6,265,914	236,405	890,258	1,552,290	70.1	2.6	10.0	17.4
Mississippi..................	3,887,981	2,445,680	187,586	427,218	827,497	62.9	4.8	11.0	21.3
Missouri.....................	8,691,887	5,597,160	406,335	979,365	1,709,026	64.4	4.7	11.3	19.7
Montana	1,518,818	966,744	93,752	160,842	297,380	63.7	6.2	10.6	19.6
Nebraska	3,298,536	2,286,554	119,384	295,048	597,550	69.3	3.6	8.9	18.1
Nevada	3,676,997	2,384,767	187,908	442,503	661,819	64.9	5.1	12.0	18.0
New Hampshire	2,637,911	1,793,766	190,003	254,013	400,128	68.0	7.2	9.6	15.2
New Jersey	23,639,281	14,941,621	2,290,750	2,120,190	4,286,720	63.2	9.7	9.0	18.1
New Mexico	3,127,463	1,881,291	325,026	352,625	568,521	60.2	10.4	11.3	18.2
New York....................	51,509,285	37,322,510	1,708,221	4,199,169	8,279,385	72.5	3.3	8.2	16.1
North Carolina............	12,132,255	8,153,672	581,125	1,338,505	2,249,233	66.2	4.7	10.9	18.3
North Dakota..............	1,049,772	643,105	47,023	127,321	232,323	61.3	4.5	12.1	22.1
Ohio	19,988,921	12,708,443	1,268,590	2,620,729	3,391,159	63.6	6.3	13.1	17.0
Oklahoma...................	5,036,031	3,067,566	341,623	586,138	1,040,704	60.9	6.8	11.6	20.7
Oregon......................	5,430,888	3,384,393	387,583	763,461	895,451	62.3	7.1	14.1	16.5
Pennsylvania	23,485,203	15,249,185	1,215,179	2,615,308	4,405,531	64.9	5.2	11.1	18.8
Rhode Island...............	2,149,366	1,402,932	25,954	208,416	312,423	65.3	10.5	9.7	14.5
South Carolina............	6,461,884	4,085,004	474,538	662,745	1,239,598	63.2	7.3	10.3	19.2
South Dakota..............	1,126,503	713,125	62,504	131,201	219,673	63.3	5.5	11.6	19.5
Tennessee	8,377,599	5,837,140	342,363	871,928	1,416,115	69.7	4.1	9.3	16.9
Texas	42,864,270	27,943,247	2,081,440	4,619,275	8,220,330	65.2	4.9	10.8	19.2
Utah	3,704,133	2,529,923	143,615	362,564	668,031	68.3	3.9	9.8	18.0
Vermont.....................	1,424,507	939,789	111,637	160,568	212,514	66.0	7.8	11.3	14.9
Virginia......................	12,968,457	8,723,528	627,158	1,154,651	2,463,120	67.3	4.8	8.9	19.0
Washington.................	10,040,312	6,469,910	671,779	1,137,457	1,761,167	64.4	6.7	11.3	17.5
West Virginia..............	3,388,294	2,163,558	153,000	305,212	766,523	63.9	4.5	9.0	22.6
Wisconsin	1,033,016	6,826,970	490,843	1,309,372	1,705,830	66.1	4.8	12.7	16.5
Wyoming	1,398,444	918,209	81,181	156,360	242,694	65.7	5.8	11.2	17.4
Dist. of Columbia (g)...	1,482,202	869,415	86,134	204,013	322,640	58.7	5.8	13.8	21.8
American Samoa	75,355	40,753	535	8,602	25,464	54.1	0.7	11.4	33.8
Guam........................	266,952	154,611	27,736	29,736	54,869	57.9	10.4	11.1	20.6
No. Mariana Islands	84,657	40,862	11,416	13,244	19,134	48.3	13.5	15.6	22.6
Puerto Rico................	3,519,547	1,749,311	235,775	780,294	754,168	49.7	6.7	22.2	21.4
U.S. Virgin Islands.......	212,112	113,983	15,828	40,764	41,537	53.7	7.5	19.2	19.6

See footnotes at end of table.

CURRENT EXPENDITURES AND PERCENTAGE DISTRIBUTION FOR PUBLIC ELEMENTARY AND SECONDARY EDUCATION, BY FUNCTION AND STATE OR JURISDICTION: FISCAL YEAR 2011 — Continued

Source: U.S. Department of Education, National Center for Education Statistics, Common Core of Data (CCD), "National Public Education Financial Survey (NPEFS)," fiscal year 2011, Version 1a.

Note: Detail may not sum to totals because of rounding.

Key:

(a) Current expenditures include instruction, instruction-related, support services and other elementary/secondary current expenditures, but exclude expenditures on capital outlay, other programs and interest on long-term debt.

(b) Instruction and instruction-related expenditures include current expenditures for classroom instruction (including teachers and teaching assistants), libraries, in-service teacher training, curriculum development, student assessment and instruction technology.

(c) Student support services include attendance and social work, guidance, health, psychological services, speech pathology, audiology and other student support services.

(d) Administration expenditures include general administration, school administration and other support services.

(e) Operations expenditures include operations and maintenance, student transportation, food services and enterprise operations.

(f) U.S. totals include the 50 states and the District of Columbia.

(g) Both the District of Columbia and Hawaii have only one school district each; therefore, neither is comparable to other states.

Table 9.7
CURRENT INSTRUCTION AND INSTRUCTION-RELATED EXPENDITURES FOR PUBLIC ELEMENTARY AND SECONDARY EDUCATION, BY OBJECT AND STATE OR JURISDICTION: FISCAL YEAR 2011

Current instruction and instruction-related expenditures (in thousands of dollars)(a)

State or other jurisdiction	Total	Salaries	Employee benefits	Purchased services	Tuition to out-of-state and private schools	Instructional supplies	Other
United States (b)	$322,492,844 (c)	$212,849,042 (c)	$75,211,035 (c)	$14,692.931 (c)	$4,988,203 (c)	$13,280,584 (c)	$1,471,049 (c)
Alabama.....................	3,846,419	2,500,993	983,940	112,088	2,632	235,134	11,632
Alaska........................	1,218,685	666,919	413,655	61,055	365	67,196	9,495
Arizona......................	4,506,883 (c)	3,256,513 (c)	770,957 (c)	225.929 (c)	2,074	99,765 (c)	151,646 (c)
Arkansas....................	2,615,474 (c)	1,798,852 (c)	492,291 (c)	98.070 (c)	11,630	196,051 (c)	18,580 (c)
California	34,679,610 (c)	22,874,871 (c)	7,843,569 (c)	1,741,303 (c)	754,422	1,461,634 (c)	3,810 (c)
Colorado.....................	4,250,693	3,018,418	743,335	112.520	42,267	271,478	62,675
Connecticut	5,768,873 (c)	3,601,405 (c)	1,448,012 (c)	199.225 (c)	396,499	115,141 (c)	8,590 (c)
Delaware	1,018,491	643,671	281,665	24,378	5,547	54,010	9,220
Florida	14,690,696 (c)	8,826,445 (c)	2,860,946 (c)	2,196,960 (c)	960	582,507 (c)	98,479 (c)
Georgia......................	9,668,819 (c)	6,661,760 (c)	2,226,686 (c)	224,261 (c)	9,026	505,759 (c)	41,328 (c)
Hawaii (d)	1,242,693	801,451	263,734	68,519	6,494	64,916	9,770
Idaho..........................	1,148,131 (c)	829,549 (c)	265,057 (c)	40,803 (c)	1,292	39,309 (c)	219 (c)
Illinois.......................	14,690,696 (c)	9,447,166 (c)	3,839,639 (c)	678,624 (c)	161,448	397,632 (c)	166,186 (c)
Indiana......................	5,702,356 (c)	3,668,624	1,771,180 (c)	93,399	5,149	159,286	4,718
Iowa	2,994,346	2,111,774	670,350	82,724	2,602	99,366	4,120
Kansas	2,873,575	2,075,510	543,674	90.862	3,270	138,936	21,323
Kentucky	3,641,680	2,580,067	866,875	67,417	3,817	116,696	6,809
Louisiana...................	4,380,197 (c)	2,869,599 (c)	1,146,439 (c)	102,961 (c)	1,405	250,343 (c)	9,451 (c)
Maine.........................	1,442,329 (c)	914,977	387,202 (c)	31,789	66,125	37,564	4,672
Maryland...................	7,424,153 (c)	4,708,564	2,025,230 (c)	227,255	248,452	206,217	8,434
Massachusetts	8,867,542 (c)	5,644,823	2,247,917 (c)	57,083	642,126	261,104	14,435
Michigan....................	9,672,947	5,711,512	2,916,048	732,872	181	293,849	18,485
Minnesota..................	5,888,594 (c)	4,026,985 (c)	1,258,416 (c)	337,946 (c)	55,945	188,447 (c)	20,855 (c)
Mississippi	2,247,757 (c)	1,569,391 (c)	475,160 (c)	62,080 (c)	5,116	126,656 (c)	9,353 (c)
Missouri.....................	5,208,082 (c)	3,632,510	1,030,137	171,191 (c)	9,598	343,008	21,638 (c)
Montana	909,036	601,939	177,068	60,063	970	65,466	3,530
Nebraska	21,853,779	1,425,176	482,026	134,001	9,404	114,881	19,891
Nevada.......................	2,190,166	1,439,113	536,624	56,334	1,315	155,303	1,476
New Hampshire	1,712,141	1,045,326	440,816	44,965	135,465	42,637	2,933
New Jersey	14,209,004	9,006,686	3,647,162	470,068	580,169	377,576	125,344
New Mexico	1,793,031	1,227,588	387,735	71,269	0	106,129	310
New York...................	35,992,426 (c)	22,145,426 (c)	10,225,654 (c)	2,139,734 (c)	762,254	715,000 (c)	4,358 (c)
North Carolina..........	7,702,399	5,450,501	1,566,742	347,061	0	418,096	0
North Dakota............	607,522	426,980	131,943	17,890	692	27,023	2,995
Ohio...........................	11,372,653	7,419,242	2,578,234	578,882	234,400	412,847	149,048
Oklahoma..................	2,862,054	2,017,034	613,229	47,986	470	174,222	9,112
Oregon.......................	3,165,170	1,927,067	920,550	120,586	20,290	158,327	18,351
Pennsylvania	14,382,313	9,318,410	3,381,178	810,393	268,900	569,513	33,918
Rhode Island.............	1,324,326 (c)	861,668 (c)	347,020 (c)	10,339 (c)	79,309	25,252 (c)	738 (c)
South Carolina..........	3,688,634	2,569,308	796,285	128,228	2,521	171,226	21,066
South Dakota............	666,180	449,743	130,050	32,994	7,313	44,733	1,346
Tennessee	5,325,040	3,467,350	1,132,546	110,668	0	599,449	15,027
Texas.........................	25,719,093	19,881,449	3,074,615	865,178	58,715	1,602,088	237,090
Utah...........................	2,382,888	1,503,172	632,253	73,759	628	165,709	7,366
Vermont.....................	876,070	566,647	173,695	47,370	63,350	22,856	2,151
Virginia.....................	7,861,182	573,464	1,732,130	191,019	4,325	353,681	6,563
Washington................	6,067,366 (c)	4,120,582	1,294,236	349,878	15,825 (c)	249,485	37,359
West Virginia............	2,029,616 (c)	1,116,785 (c)	747,810 (c)	38,357 (c)	3,718	122,536 (c)	411 (c)
Wisconsin	6,322,480 (c)	3,855,317 (c)	1,997,077 (c)	103,837 (c)	137,966	211,031 (c)	17,252 (c)
Wyoming	826,891	539,711	212,491	27,788	1,110	44,554	1,237
Dist. of Columbia (d)...	754,454	451,341	79,700	52,967	135,240	18,961	16,256
American Samoa	32,770	20,734	3,593	1,599	0	2,670	4,174
Guam	149,292	102,505	40,305	5,134	0	1,348	0
No. Mariana Islands...	36,014 (c)	27,206 (c)	6,469 (c)	563 (c)	0	75 (c)	1,702 (c)
Puerto Rico...............	1,460,167 (c)	1,029,741 (c)	238,718 (c)	165,297	0	24,310	2,101
U.S. Virgin Islands	108,061	75,314	28,392	1,784	0	2,571	0

See footnotes at end of table.

CURRENT INSTRUCTION AND INSTRUCTION-RELATED EXPENDITURES FOR PUBLIC ELEMENTARY AND SECONDARY EDUCATION, BY OBJECT AND STATE OR JURISDICTION: FISCAL YEAR 2011 — Continued

Source: U.S. Department of Education, National Center for Education Statistics, Common Core of Data (CCD), "National Public Education Financial Survey (NPEFS)," fiscal year 2011, Version 1a.

Note: Detail may not sum to totals due to rounding.

Key:

(a) Current instruction expenditures include expenditures for activities related to the interaction between teachers and students, including salaries and benefits for teachers and teacher aides, textbooks, supplies and purchased services. These expenditures also include expenditures relating to extracurricular and curricular activities.

(b) U.S. totals include the 50 states and the District of Columbia.

(c) Value affected by redistribution of reported values to correct for missing data items, and/or to distribute state direct support expenditures.

(d) Both the District of Columbia and Hawaii have only one school district each; therefore, neither is comparable to other states.

Aligning Postsecondary Education with Regional Workforce Needs: A Tale of Two States

By Stephen Barkanic

The United States faces a pressing national security and competitiveness challenge rooted in a shortage of a diverse, highly skilled workforce, particularly in vital cross-disciplinary fields such as data science and analytics, cybersecurity, and information technology. To address this challenge, the Business-Higher Education Forum launched the National Higher Education and Workforce Initiative, employing a model of strategic business engagement with postsecondary education to meet the highest priority workforce needs. Through the initiative, the education forum plans, launches and assesses projects, partnerships and scaling strategies that are designed to enable business and higher education to move from transactional engagement in low-touch, piecemeal activities to strategic, long-term partnerships that align postsecondary education with workforce needs. Two of these projects—in Maryland and Ohio— offer models of such partnerships.

The Misalignment of Postsecondary Education with Emerging Workforce Demands

The number of job openings in the United States has grown to nearly 5 million, with many going unfilled for long periods of time because approximately half of employers now claim they cannot find employees with the competencies, skills and degrees they need. A 2012 study by the McKinsey Global Institute reported that by 2020, employers worldwide could face a shortage of 85 million high- and medium-skilled workers.

The President's Council on Jobs and Competitiveness noted that only 1.5 percent of 25- to 34-year-olds in the workplace in 2011 had earned a higher education degree in a science-related field, putting the United States in the bottom third of all 34 countries belonging to the Organization for Economic Cooperation and Development. The McKinsey Global Institute report also noted that by 2020, the supply of college graduates is projected to be 1.5 million less than the demand. The cumulative effect of these deficiencies impedes U.S. economic competitiveness and security, as well as equity and civic engagement.

Increasingly, innovation and competitiveness require new types of employees with either expert or enabled competencies in emerging, transdisciplinary fields. An example of such a competency is

data science, where The McKinsey Global Institute predicts a nationwide shortage of 140,000 to 190,000 data science workers with deep analytical skills, and a deficit of 1.5 million managers capable of using big data analytics for actionable insights in their decision-making. Whether driven by the demands of an increasingly competitive global workplace or the realities of a rapidly changing and evolving innovation economy, corporations also have come to place a high value on deeper learning.

Deeper learning, which has been championed by the William and Flora Hewlett Foundation through grants to the Business-Higher Education Forum— otherwise known as BHEF—and other partners, nurtures and enhances the skill sets required by many 21st century professions. These skills include competence in oral and written communication, and the ability to think critically and analytically, analyze and solve complex problems, apply knowledge to real-world settings, innovate, work in a team and make ethical decisions.

The P-16, preschool through higher education curriculum is not sufficiently aligned with workforce needs to provide students with the knowledge and skills needed to compete successfully in the workplace. Similarly, employers have failed to adequately articulate their expectations for the workforce. To bridge this gap, educators and business leaders increasingly are required to build deeper partnerships that enable the adaptation of curricula and applied learning experiences to build core competencies and promote deeper learning.

The BHEF National Higher Education and Workforce Initiative

The Business-Higher Education Forum, the nation's oldest organization of senior business executives and presidents of higher education institutions, brings together its members and other partners in flexible, mutually beneficial partnerships to address gaps in content knowledge and workforce skills at the undergraduate level. Through the collaboration of its business and academic members, BHEF has launched the National Higher Education and Workforce Initiative, which includes regional projects focused on business-higher education partnerships in selected states, as well as a national effort to disseminate information from the projects and scale effective practices. The initiative deploys a model of strategic business engagement in higher education to address the highest priority workforce development needs.

Recognizing the important role that business and academia can play in addressing workforce challenges together and the need to act based on evidence, over the past five years BHEF has engaged in intensive research, system dynamics modeling and project management. As a result, it has developed a robust process for initiating business-higher education partnerships that respond to local or regional workforce needs. Business and academic partners can use tools to assess their needs and available resources, and to identify interventions that can be deployed to attract and retain undergraduates in key emerging fields. Currently, regional projects are underway in data science and analytics, cybersecurity, water and energy sciences, materials sciences, engineering and other fields.

Based on its experience in designing, planning and implementing these projects, BHEF is compiling a set of tools and materials that enables business and higher education to move from transactional approaches to interaction—that is, limited to low-touch, piecemeal activities such as on-campus recruiting or support of research related to business products and services—to strategic and long-term partnerships to align human capital with workforce needs.

Building an Evidence Base with Research Tools

The Business-Higher Education Forum's process of building its evidence base for solutions involves several steps, the first of which is a comprehensive review of the research literature on science, technology, engineering and math—otherwise known as STEM—undergraduate education. The second is the development of a system dynamics model, which, in its initial version, produced powerful insights and informed BHEF's model of strategic business engagement. Modeling provides decision-makers with the information needed to understand their funding options and opportunities at scale. It can suggest potentially more productive avenues for investments in STEM undergraduate education and identify pathways to collaboration that leverage resources and efforts.

Modeling can play a critical role in informing policymakers about the most relevant and potentially effective actions to take in wedding workforce needs with academic programs. The Business-Higher Education Forum's original U.S. STEM Education Model® is a system dynamics model developed by systems engineers at Raytheon in collaboration with BHEF staff and donated to BHEF in 2009. It simulates the impact of various policies and programs on the number of graduates in the STEM disciplines who go on to pursue STEM careers. This first-of-its-kind model illustrates for policymakers, educators and researchers the complex structure of the U.S. STEM undergraduate education system and enables users to test different interventions that could help strengthen student outcomes in STEM. This initial model provided the first step in understanding the impact of individual discrete interventions, such as increasing teacher' salary or placing undergraduates into cohort living/learning programs, on the production of STEM-capable graduates.

Because of its interest in maximizing the impact of its investment in undergraduate STEM education, the U.S. Navy awarded the Business-Higher Education Forum a grant to develop a next-generation U.S. STEM Undergraduate Model™. Applying system dynamics, this model shows how implementation of high-impact strategies to retain students in STEM programs can have the strongest impact on the Navy's ability to satisfy its future workforce needs. This model has broader implications and can be used beyond the Navy environment. It retains components of the original model, but it deepens the ability to simulate interventions that can improve outcomes for students pursuing STEM degrees.

Research used in developing the U.S. STEM Undergraduate Model showed that implementing multiple interventions simultaneously (e.g., student learning communities and early undergraduate research experiences) can have a significant impact on the retention and academic success of undergraduates, particularly women and underrepresented minorities in the first two years of college. BHEF's model demonstrates similar outcomes with combined, integrated intervention strategies.

Even in the face of the intensifying demand for highly skilled workers, the production of graduates in fields fueling the innovation economy is stagnating. In recent years, the absolute number of degrees awarded in STEM fields increased modestly, but has decrease or remained flat in key fields. In computer science, for example, bachelor's degrees have declined, especially for women and underrepresented minorities. Understanding why students migrate away from STEM fields is a critical piece of evidence when designing an intervention.

The Consortium for Undergraduate STEM Success is a collaboration of postsecondary institutions interested in addressing issues relating to undergraduate degree completion in STEM fields, with particular focus on underrepresented students. It combines student academic data with survey responses from those same students to inform participating institutions about patterns of their students' migration into and out of STEM fields. The ability to track data over time allows academic departments, colleges and universities to make adjustments and monitor for improvement and make informed decisions regarding programmatic offerings, formulating funding requests and seeking partners. The consortium is a partner with the Business-Higher Education Forum on a multi-year grant from the National Science Foundation that studies the impact of industry-driven interventions on increasing the persistence of students transferring from two- to four-year STEM programs.

By focusing on key, high-demand sectors of the economy, a project has the potential to demonstrate new ways to strengthen the workforce and increase U.S. global competitiveness and national security. Project sites must have deep expertise in addressing the pipeline, significant workforce deficits in the sectors and disciplines to be addressed, and be particularly interested in adopting high-impact interventions that will improve transfer student retention from two- to four-year institu-

tions and baccalaureate degree completion for these students.

Each BHEF project addresses a unique workforce need in regions around the country. Examples include:

- Cybersecurity in the Maryland/Washington, D.C., region (University of Maryland, College Park and Northrop Grumman Corporation);
- Data science in Cleveland and Columbus, Ohio, (Case Western Reserve University and The Ohio State University with multiple corporate partners);
- Water science in Wisconsin (University of Wisconsin System with The Water Council); and
- Sustainability in the greater New York City area (City University of New York with IBM).

These partnerships not only leverage local resources toward undergraduate STEM education, but also bring in new corporate and government players who recognize the value of early engagement with students to building their future workforce. Thus, a critical step in establishing regional higher education and workforce development initiatives is assessing local or regional workforce needs. This activity creates the common framework for all parties in planning the project by documenting needs and identifying shared goals.

Often, regions conduct their own analyses of current and projected workforce needs that provide a framework for building regional partnerships. In Maryland, for example, a series of studies and reports by the governor's office, the University System of Maryland, and other agencies and foundations pointing to a sharp demand for workers specializing and enabled in cybersecurity was instrumental in planning and implementing projects, and, ultimately, a network in cyber for the region. In regions where such analyses are not available, BHEF has partnered with Burning Glass, a Boston-based company that conducts studies of regional and national job markets, in helping to understand skill demands of regions targeted for BHEF projects.

Business-Higher Education Forum Strategic Engagement Model

Using these tools and strategies, BHEF's members—Fortune 500 CEOs and college and university presidents—are implementing a new model of strategic business engagement with higher education that aligns five levers, or strategies, to move from transactional relationships to strategic partnerships

Figure A: BHEF's Strategic Engagement Model

BHEF's model of strategic business engagement with higher education aligns five levers, or strategies, to move from transactional relationships to strategic partnerships between the two sectors. When fully implemented, the model enables business and higher education to effectively build sustainable, high-impact regional projects to increase student interest and persistence toward degree completion and to align undergraduate education with emerging workforce needs.

Engage and deploy corporate and academic leadership. Specifically, C-suite executives and academic administrators provide grass-top engagement to (1) shape internal and external messaging to raise community awareness of 21st century workforce requirements and the academic response to those requirements; (2) build a critical mass of peers focused on the undergraduate education in support of workforce development goals; and (3) guide corporate and academic policy development to ensure that both sectors align with shared strategic education and workforce development goals.

Focus corporate philanthropy. When undertaken in concert with college or university strategic planning and regional workforce assessment, philanthropy can serve as a vital catalyst for positive, lasting and high-impact change in higher education and workforce alignment.

Identify and tap core competencies and expertise. Expertise is represented on the corporate side by managers, engineers and other subject matter experts and on the academic side by faculty members, researchers, postgraduate fellows and graduate students. These individuals bring intellectual resources, field experience, skills and competencies to bear on strengthening the education-to-workforce pipeline through efforts such as co-development of new courses focused on active learning, student research opportunities, and other learning experiences.

Facilitate and encourage employee and staff engagement. Partnerships can organize the hundreds or thousands of employees within an organization to support strategic education goals. This human capital can be mobilized to act both inside and outside the corporation or higher education institution, providing grassroots support and advocacy in the planning and implementation of educational reform.

Fund research. Research conducted in college and university laboratories can serve as platforms for early research experiences for freshmen and sophomores, which has been shown to increase student persistence. Corporate laboratories and research centers can provide unique real-world learning opportunities for undergraduates and can expand the capacity of higher education institutions to offer such experiences to students.

Source: Stephen Barkanic © April 2015.

between the two sectors. When fully implemented, the model enables business and higher education to effectively build sustainable, high-impact regional projects to increase student interest and persistence toward degree completion and to align undergraduate education with emerging workforce needs.

Positioning these strategies requires (1) commitment to sustained engagement to improve education outcomes; (2) collaboration to develop a shared understanding of academia's and business' interconnected problems, based on research and data that link college readiness and success to workforce requirements; (3) development of a shared vision for systemic solutions; (4) collaboration with each other and with other strategic partners to implement solutions; (5) advocacy for public policies needed to achieve goals; and (6) raising of public awareness about the urgency of these issues at the regional, state, and national levels.

BHEF catalyzes change by equipping its members with the information and tools they need to understand the challenges inherent in aligning education outcomes and workforce needs and by providing a strategic framework for addressing them. BHEF's goal is to develop regional demonstration projects that lead to national adoption. Lessons learned from BHEF's activities to date have significantly advanced knowledge in the area of four-year STEM undergraduate education. As the initiative evolves, validated evidence-based models will be available for others to adapt and adopt.

Cybersecurity in Maryland

Maryland has been an early and vigorous adopter of the type of program envisioned all along for the National Higher Education and Workforce Initiative, HEWI. At the time of the initiative's launch, Maryland already had identified cybersecurity as a strategic focus for education and economic development, given the presence in the region of such federal agencies as the National Security Agency, National Institute of Standards and Technology, and Department of Homeland Security, and major defense and high-tech companies.

Working with its membership, BHEF partnered with the USM to build a system-wide response to the state's (and nation's) cybersecurity workforce challenges. BHEF's leadership role in sparking innovation resulted in the creation of premier undergraduate programs in cybersecurity at two USM institutions and their adaptation at two additional institutions. Together, all partners have created vibrant and relevant educational programs to meet the needs of the cybersecurity industry, which provides proof of principle for HEWI, the workforce initiative.

With a three-year implementation grant from the Alfred P. Sloan Foundation to BHEF, USM, the university system, conducted a student migration analysis and focus groups with students and campus career services professionals. The initial undergraduate cyber project launched in the USM was the landmark Advanced Cybersecurity Experience for Students program, the nation's first honors undergraduate program in cybersecurity. Supported by a major grant from the Northrop Grumman Foundation and subsequent support from Parsons, the program educates future leaders in cybersecurity through rigorous, hands-on learning experiences, an intensive interdisciplinary curriculum, collaborative projects and professional insight from corporate leaders.

The advanced cybersecurity curriculum consists of two linked academic programs over the course of four years: (1) a freshman-sophomore living-learning program in a new honors dormitory leading to an Honors College Citation in Cybersecurity and (2) an upper-level course of study in cybersecurity. Students in this program take general cybersecurity courses as well as courses on cybersecurity forensics, reverse engineering, secure coding, criminology, and law and public policy, among other topics. Seniors complete a yearlong capstone project that addresses a foundational challenge in cybersecurity. Students graduating from the program receive a designation of completion on their academic transcripts. The first cohort of advanced cybersecurity students started their studies in fall 2013—less than two years after the program was first conceptualized—and in its first two years has approximately doubled its enrollments over projected demand.

As a second major achievement in its cyber-related work in Maryland, the Business-Higher Education Forum supported a partnership between the University of Maryland Baltimore County and Northrop Grumman that resulted in the launch of the UMBC Cyber Scholars program. The program has a strong focus on increasing diversity in the cyber workforce, and draws on significant insights gained through the university's nationally renowned Meyerhoff Scholars program—which is widely considered to be at the forefront of efforts to increase diversity among future leaders in STEM fields—and UMBC's Center for Women and Information Technology.

Like the ACES program, the Cyber Scholars program charts new ground in the delivery of effective undergraduate education in cybersecurity. Scholars receive financial awards with special opportunities for advanced research, directed internships, and other forms of academic and social support. They are matched with a faculty research mentor as well as an industry mentor. The program fosters a cybersecurity-focused community through common on-campus living-learning housing, events and activities. Each week, scholars engage in a cyber practicum that includes talks from field practitioners. Scholars also have the opportunity to visit government agencies and industry laboratories that engage in cybersecurity. Cyber Scholars take a combination of management-oriented and technically focused courses. All scholars are required to take an introductory seminar in their freshman year and at least one cybersecurity course in their junior year.

Industry involvement plays a vital role in the success, impact and sustainability of these programs. Companies and government agencies help shape curricula, work regularly onsite with program planning, and provide guest lecturers, program advisors, adjunct faculty, paid internships and mentors for students throughout their four-year experience. To scale effective cyber programs, the University System of Maryland-BHEF Undergraduate Cybersecurity Network was launched in 2013 with Sloan Foundation support. Comprising more than 30 representatives from academia, business, government and stakeholder organizations, the network supports an overarching system-wide goal of significantly increasing the number and diversity of graduates in cybersecurity fields.

The network supports projects aimed to strengthen business-government-higher education partnerships; focus on key policy challenges, such as accelerating student security clearances; sharing curricula and other resources; and developing a clearinghouse on effective cyber education practice and tools. With Sloan support, the network is seeding projects at key network institutions including Bowie State University, Towson University, UMBC, and UMD. These projects are enabling the institutions to expand partnerships with industry and government, and increase the size, diversity and capability of the region's cyber workforce. The work of the Maryland network feeds into BHEF's National Undergraduate Cybersecurity Network

Data Science in Ohio

The field of data science and analytics is experiencing explosive growth in both the specialist and enabled professions. Reports indicate that big data is growing at a rate of about 40 percent a year and has the potential to add some $300 billion of value to the nation's health care sector alone. Virtually all sectors, both public and private, are experiencing sharp demand for data science-trained employees.

Despite this growth, there are relatively few opportunities for undergraduates to learn about and become skilled in data analytics. A study by the Business-Higher Education Forum and supported by the Sloan Foundation revealed that most data science programs are available only at the graduate level and typically are offered through STEM departments that often lack the diversity needed in the workforce. Increasingly, employers and students

are calling for more courses, concentrations, minors and majors in data science, but significant challenges remain for academic institutions to develop undergraduate pathways in this rapidly evolving area. BHEF is aggressively moving forward to build partnerships between postsecondary institutions and employers across sectors whose goals are to launch undergraduate programs in data science.

Due in part to its high concentration of data-driven companies and regional efforts to catalyze innovation and workforce development around a rich diversity of leading higher education institutions, Ohio was a natural choice for BHEF to build partnerships focused on data science and analytics. In Cleveland, home to Case Western Reserve University—a major private research institution with a strong tradition in undergraduate education—and numerous companies acutely concerned about their data-skilled workforce, BHEF facilitated a process by which a range of partners came together to determine the workforce skills needed in data science and develop undergraduate tracks in the field. Case Western Reserve announced the launch of a new undergraduate major and minor in data science in 2014, designed to prepare a new generation of data science experts who will improve performance in health, production and manufacturing and energy.

Case Western Reserve's new undergraduate bachelor's of science degree in data science focuses on real-world applications. It consists of a core curriculum focusing on each of the specific domain areas of health, energy, and manufacturing and production. It includes such dimensions as mathematical modeling of data sources; examining raw data using analytics that focus on inference through the transformation of data to actionable information that improves decision-making; and visual analytics and user experiences. The program also features an experiential learning component through partnerships with industry that provide co-op assignments and internships to students.

To help bring the application of data science to a variety of fields, Case Western has developed an applied data science undergraduate minor that can be paired with any undergraduate major at the institution. Students can choose from eight subdomains within engineering and physical sciences, health, and business, all of which include a core curriculum that includes five three-credit courses. Among the tools and applications covered by the minor are data management, distributed computing, statistical analytics and informatics.

In Columbus, civic leaders, business executives and others launched the Columbus Collaboratory, an advanced technology company that brings together a range of noncompeting companies and other stakeholders to focus on regional workforce and economic development issues, and drive solutions in the areas of big data, analytics and cybersecurity. Attracting IBM's Client Center for Advanced Analytics to Central Ohio in 2013 was an early achievement of the group. The center brings new analytics and technology talent to the area and encourages existing talent to remain in Central Ohio.

To develop the kind of talent pool needed to help enable the region to continue this progress, the Ohio Board of Regents approved a new interdisciplinary undergraduate major in data analytics at The Ohio State University in 2014. Drawing upon the Business-Higher Education Forum's strategic engagement model, the university engaged deeply with regional business partners to identify the core elements for both the curricular and co-curricular dimensions of the program.

Opened to students in fall 2014, the major is made up of three basic parts: core courses, a specialization and a capstone—or internship—experience through business partnerships. The College of Arts and Sciences and the College of Engineering are partnering to deliver the core courses in computer sciences, mathematics and statistics. Students learn principles of data representation and management, computer programming and statistical modeling and analysis.

The core curriculum focuses on principles that are fundamental to all areas of data analytics and consists of courses taken by all majors. In these courses, students investigate the computational, mathematical and statistical foundations of data analytics, and develop such deeper learning skills as critical thinking and effective communication. Each student in the major chooses an area of specialization to learn how data analytics is applied in a particular field. Coursework in some specializations can be tailored based on a student's interests. The areas of specialization available in the major include biomedical informatics; business analytics; and computational analysis.

The program seeks to develop in students both highly technical skillsets and the ability to function in solutions-oriented teams. All students participate in a capstone or an integrative experiential component as part of their chosen specialization.

National Scaling and Networks

As part of its efforts to scale insights from its regional projects, the Business-Higher Education Forum is launching national networks of effective practice that bring together the kinds of network partners instrumental in building the regional work to focus on a more macro level. The National Undergraduate Cybersecurity Network has been underway since 2012 and has met on an annual basis.

BHEF's vision for this dimension of its work is to sustain a national network of experts from higher education, business and government who can serve as the intellectual hub of undergraduate cybersecurity and promote cooperation around cybersecurity education among the academic, business and government sectors. The group has been growing steadily. BHEF plans to launch its national data science network in Columbus in the fall of 2015, bringing together participants in data science projects under development in Florida, North Carolina, New York, Ohio and elsewhere.

BHEF also works with national partners to expand the reach of the National Higher Education and Workforce Initiative and launch joint initiatives of mutual benefit to a range of organizations representing both industry and higher education. In higher education, the Business-Higher Education Forum partners with the American Council on Education, Association of Public and Land-grant Universities, and Association of American Universities. On the corporate side, national partners include the Aerospace Industries Association and the Business Roundtable.

About the Author

Stephen Barkanic, senior vice president and chief program officer, joined the Business-Higher Education Forum in 2011. Barkanic provides overall leadership for the National Higher Education and Workforce Initiative, aimed at bridging industry and higher education to increase the persistence and diversity of students who go on to earn degrees or credentials in key emerging fields, and align undergraduate education with workforce needs. He also provides leadership in BHEF's work in Deeper Learning, or 21st century workforce skills and competencies that focuses on the business need for such skills as critical thinking, creative problem solving, and teamwork in the workforce of the future, and advocating for the importance of those skills on a national level.

Prior to joining BHEF, Barkanic was senior program officer at the Bill & Melinda Gates Foundation, where his work encompassed an array of policy and programmatic areas focused on improving student readiness and success in college.

Credit for Prior Learning: Transfer Models across the Nation

By Mary Beth Lakin

Credit for Prior Learning is gaining traction as one strategy for advancing postsecondary degree attainment. While much progress has been made in institutions across the U.S., challenges remain in the widespread acceptance and application of prior learning to provide transfer pathways. State and regional collaborations offer promising models.

Transferring academic credit across higher education institutions within and throughout state systems has a history of challenges and successes, beginning with the transfer of associate degrees articulated to four-year degree programs. The higher education system has made great strides in advancing academic mobility and the currency of academic credits through a variety of models. Such models have been built upon common course numbering, agreed upon core courses for general education, streamlined program reviews among institutions and implementing automated degree audits. Subsequently these efforts have expanded two plus two articulations within and across institutions and state systems, and produced dual-enrollment and reverse transfer agreements.

The higher education community is focused on the challenges of access, affordability and attainment. Most recently, higher education systems in Colorado, Ohio and Florida have found greater transfer rates, completion and tuition savings with transfer and articulation agreements in place.[1] A 2014 study of community college transfers reported that students who get the majority of their credits to transfer are 2.5 times more likely to earn a bachelor's degree than those who transferred less than 50 percent of their courses.[2]

Into the mix of state and national discussions on credit transfer, student mobility and completion rates has come a more robust discussion about credit for prior learning. That is in line with a recent Lumina Foundation/Gallup Poll survey on higher education (February 5, 2013) that found the general public is more aware of options for assessing prior learning from the workplace or military service, thinks that such recognition is warranted and would be more likely to return to college to complete a credential with those options in place.[3]

Meanwhile, recent research (CAEL, 2010; College Board, 2013) offers evidence of prior learning assessment boosting enrollment, persistence and attainment. That research has shown that adult students who earn credit for prior learning have better academic outcomes compared to their peers who do not earn credit for prior learning.[4] These findings held for ethnicity, gender, age and socioeconomic status.[5]

In spite of these trends, multiple challenges remain before credit for prior learning gains widespread acceptance. Those challenges are similar to issues that have been associated with articulation of two-year associate degrees to bachelor's programs, which primarily concern the quality and fit of programs external to the home institution. Principles and rubrics for evaluating extra-institutional learning have been provided for more than four decades through the American Council on Education's (ACE) programs evaluating workplace and military training; the Council for Adult and Experiential Learning for individualized assessment, in particular portfolio development and evaluation; and the College Board, in the production of national standardized subject examinations. A lack of awareness about these principles of practice has resulted in misperceptions about and mistrust in prior learning evaluation processes. Unfortunately, concerns about the quality of the evaluation process increase when "bad actors" exploit students and "sell" credit for experience in order to profit from that lack of knowledge.

What is Credit for Prior Learning?

The American Council on Education, also known as ACE, uses the term credit for prior learning and defines it "as academic credit granted for demonstrated college-level equivalencies gained through learning experiences outside of the college classroom".[6] Credit for prior learning encompasses several well-established methods for reviewing and evaluating extra-institutional learning, including third-party validation of formal training—for example, the ACE evaluation of military and workplace training—national or departmental exams and individualized assessment. Institutions use a broad range of terms and options—prior learning assessment, testing out, experiential learning and alternative credit, to name a few. With multiple terms and options in play, therein lies the confusion among stakeholders.

Credit for prior learning has been in place in U.S. higher education at least since World War I, as returning veterans looked for opportunities to earn high school and college credentials. The American Council on Education was organized as part of those early efforts, and the General Education Development (GED) tests, College Level Examination Program (CLEP), and other methods for verifying college-level equivalencies were developed. After World War II, ACE's Military Evaluation Programs, in collaboration with the U.S. Department of Defense and the service branches, began providing evaluations and academic credit recommendations through a faculty-driven review process.

By the mid-1970s, some institutions were offering individualized assessments, specifically the portfolio, and applied the Council for Adult and Experiential Learning standards. At the same time, a growing number of colleges began to standardize the acceptance of CLEP exams to meet general education requirements, while ACE broadened its third party validation process with the addition of military occupation reviews and the launching of ACE's College Credit Recommendation Service (CREDIT®). ACE CREDIT provides the same faculty-driven review process in the civilian workplace for formal training courses, certifications, and examinations offered through Fortune 500 companies, professional associations, labor unions, government agencies and online education vendors.

More recently Veterans Programs at ACE has created a network of institutions that share tools, training and resources in order to better serve student veteran populations. With the recent national focus on increasing attainment rates, ACE's College and University Partnerships is supporting the efforts of two- and four-year institutions, state higher education systems and multi-state organizations to implement effective credit for prior learning practices and related services. It disseminates institutional models for building infrastructure, engaging faculty, integrating programs, creating information-sharing pipelines and advising students.

The American Council on Education, as the major coordinating body for U.S. higher education, supports institutions in their efforts to identify and implement best practices in credit for prior learning that align to their mission, address issues of quality and support their student populations. Through this national lens, we are seeing trends on a number of fronts: 1) a move toward more comprehensive, integrated policies and practices in credit for prior learning; 2) an increase in collaborative efforts across states and beyond state borders; 3) a push toward articulation agreements within systems to decrease transfer barriers; 4) a focus on additional resources, including funding, to sustain and expand implementation; 5) a need for data that tracks the impact of credit for prior learning options on enrollment, persistence, and completion rates.

What do we know about trends in credit for prior learning?

A move toward more comprehensive policies through state initiatives recognizes the diversity of student groups and the different sources of learning they bring, in particular from military and workforce training. Institutions and higher education systems determine whether to transfer and award credit from other sources and create various models to reflect their mission, culture and infrastructure. Collaborative efforts at the state and regional levels have begun to produce examples of credit for prior learning implementation that engage campus stakeholders, address standards for quality degree programs, and meet the needs of their students and communities.

Pennsylvania's College Credit Fast Track, funded by a U.S. Department of Labor grant and developed through a collaboration of 14 community colleges, was launched in February 2015. It is one recent example of a state's implementation of comprehensive policies and practices, from third-party validation and national examinations to individualized assessment. These options are on ready display, actively promoting application of appropriate credit for prior learning. Potential and current students can easily access and understand what their CPL options are, how to get started and where to go if they need assistance.

The number of state higher education systems creating more transparent, comprehensive and integrated CPL practices—whether through a foundation grant, a board of regents' initiative, state legislation or a combination—is quickly growing. Tennessee, through its Begin Again Tennessee college completion initiative, provides a website which maintains CPL practices and points of contact through profiles of colleges and universities across the state.

Colorado's community college system has created a manual that explains standards. "We are taking incremental steps in expanding policy and practice that is built on history, rather than tearing down foundation," said Bitsy Cohn, the system's director of credit for prior learning during an American Council on Education webinar on credit for prior learning [7]).

The University of Wisconsin system applied a Lumina Foundation grant to expand CPL policy and practice and is exploring recognizing two-year institutions' practice as part of the system wide transfer agreements.

In these and other examples across the U.S., faculty have been engaged early and often in policy and practice implementation, with working groups of administrative, academic and student services professionals bringing their perspectives to the process. Stakeholders have provided their input on the policy review process, the roles in which they play and the ways in which information could best be shared. Consideration of strategies for shifting culture and building resources is critical to practice implementation, and subsequently, an increase in articulation and transfer of credit for prior learning. [8]

Many of those efforts began with community interest in supporting student veterans and helping them transition into the civilian workforce. As implementation takes root, more stakeholders are beginning to understand the quality of training that transitioning veterans have received—and the college-level learning that has accompanied much of that training. What helps in making that shift occur is the engagement of campus constituencies, primarily, but not exclusively faculty, in ongoing, experientially-based activity, such as participating in prior learning assessment activities, to better understand CPL evaluation processes. [9]

An increase in collaborative efforts across states and beyond state borders is fostering a wider dissemination of credit for prior learning implementation.

The University System of Georgia's Adult Learning Consortium has grown to 15 institutions, including three regional universities, five state universities and seven state colleges. The presidents signed a memorandum of understanding outlining working principles for providing adult-focused programs and services. The University System of Georgia's Regents Academic Committee on Adult

Learning promotes both statewide and leadership engagement in prior learning policy making and implementation while ALC offers continuous training and information sharing to practitioners in the field. This grassroots effort, funded by a state college completion grant, has garnered statewide and national attention with its developmental approach to implementing credit for prior learning practice. With this approach, the institutions are able to build on informal practices that are already in place. Go Back Move Ahead, initiated by the governor, provides opportunities to expand credit for prior learning options across Georgia institutions.

The New Jersey Prior Learning Assessment Network was initiated by Thomas Edison State College, a longstanding leader in programs geared to adult learners. It is another example of a voluntary group of higher education institutions organized to share effective CPL policy and practice. NJ PLAN also aids member institutions in building capacity to implement credit for prior learning options and related services, with a focus on creating statewide practices to expand and streamline articulation agreements. College Credit for Heroes, launched in 2011 by the Texas Workforce Commission through a five-year grant, began with seven institutions and has grown to 20. Central Texas College, a consortium member, created a manual to help institutions identify potential transfer credit for military training with consistent and appropriate guidelines.

On a regional level, the Multi-State Collaborative on Military Credit provides its 13 members, primarily Midwestern states, with opportunities to share information and best practices in the articulation of academic credit for military training and occupations. It also has addressed credit for prior learning transfer and satisfactory academic progress, outlining issues, potential solutions and recommendations. College Credit for Heroes and the Multi-State Collaborative provide noteworthy models for identifying, disseminating and advocating for effective credit for prior learning practice implementation and articulation beyond student veteran populations. Their strategies and resources could be adapted to serve other student populations with workforce training and industry certifications that may provide college-level competencies.

At a national level, the Western Interstate Commission for Higher Education facilitates effective CPL practices through its Adult College Completion Network. Funded by Lumina Foundation, ACCN encourages institutions, agencies, organizations and other stakeholders to share information about their work. Many of these projects, including 19 initiatives recently funded by Lumina, encompass credit for prior learning programs and services.

With this increased collaboration comes more easily available information for institutions, students and policymakers. What is truly exciting about this trend is that it addresses a major stumbling block for returning students and other stakeholders. A 2012 survey by the American Council on Education found that although most institutions apply at least one form of credit for prior learning, there remains a great deal of confusion about CPL.[10] On many campuses, a lack of awareness about credit for prior learning results in low demand by students, and subsequently, institutions perceive there is little or no need for credit for prior learning options for their students.

Findings in the 2015 American Council on Education brief on credit for prior learning suggest that "if institutions comprehensively and clearly define and manage credit for prior learning options and services, then staff, faculty, and administrators will be better prepared to effectively guide students throughout their academic careers on CPL options and benefits." Northern Virginia Community College is one institution that has addressed the lack of information sharing among campus groups through its creation of CPL guidebooks for students and advisors. The college's outreach begins before admissions and continues with orientation and throughout enrollment with CPL specialists.

A push toward articulation agreements within systems to decrease transfer barriers has grown with the development of comprehensive policies and greater collaboration. Much of the current articulation work has focused on the examination of military training and college-level equivalencies at the institutional, system and consortium levels. Many standout examples have existed for decades, including those at SUNY Empire State, Thomas Edison State College, Excelsior College and University Maryland University College, as well as higher education systems such as the Minnesota State Colleges and Universities System and Ivy Tech Community College, Indiana's statewide community college system.

New models continue to develop. The Ohio Values Veterans Initiative has set the stage for implementation of articulated military training.

Recent state legislation passed in 2014 requires the chancellor of the Ohio Board of Regents to develop standards and procedures for state institutions in the awarding of academic credit for military training. A process is now in place to articulate ACE credit recommendations to degree program requirements. The development of this process has engaged all of the institutional stakeholders: senior leadership in academic and student services areas, faculty, advisors, registrars, admissions staff and transfer coordinators. Teams of faculty experts representing two- and four-year public institutions are working together to identify potential course equivalencies to be included in transfer articulation databases and degree audit systems. These efforts build on several years of cross-institutional collaboration to study and develop a range of credit for prior learning practices, from national standardized subject examinations to individualized portfolio assessment. Coupled with the activities of the working groups have been early and ongoing information sharing and professional development opportunities through statewide and regional workshops.

Another challenge institutions face with credit for prior learning articulation is transcription. As with CPL policy in U.S. institutions, there is a wide range of transcription practices across institutions. The recent survey (January 2015) from the American Association of Collegiate Registrars and Admissions Officers underscores the variability in practice and highlights related issues, including Satisfactory Academic Progress, residency requirements and definitions, and financial aid restrictions. [11]

A focus on additional resources to expand and sustain implementation through private foundations, federal grants and state college completion initiatives, has opened up opportunities for building and disseminating CPL practices, and in turn, expanding articulation. The U.S. departments of Education and Labor continue to fund initiatives to advance CPL implementation. The Experimental Sites Initiative provides grantees with opportunities to develop solutions for the knotty issues surrounding competency-based education, financial aid and transferability. In the second round of the First in the World initiative, institutions can focus on creating completion pathways, with credit for prior learning as a major component where student outcomes can be measured. The new American Apprenticeship Initiative, funded by the U.S. Department of Labor, encourages community colleges to expand pathways to education and employment, join the Registered Apprenticeship College Consortium and articulate apprenticeship training to postsecondary credentials. State college completion initiatives also have provided funding, resources and training to support the building of the necessary infrastructure, from faculty engagement and policy creation to student services and data collection.

More data that tracks and analyzes the impact of credit for prior learning options on enrollment, persistence and completion rates will build CPL sustainability. Institutions have national research findings to make the case for credit for prior learning implementation, but much more specific data is required to demonstrate the impact of CPL options. While adult-focused institutions have created systems to track this information for some time, generally colleges and universities have had neither the infrastructure nor the incentive to collect and share CPL data.

The U.S. Department of Labor's Trade Adjustment Assistance Community College and Career Training grants support community colleges and other eligible organizations in expanding education and career training programs. These initiatives have focused on building credit for prior learning practices within and across states. That has been a massive effort, and now there is the opportunity to shine a light on the results of those efforts. The Colorado Community College System, for example has developed the structure for collecting baseline data. It is also carrying out audits of credit for prior learning usage and course enrollments, while working on standardization of credit for prior learning transcripting and transfer.[12]

More higher education state systems, from Tennessee to Washington state, are developing metrics to understand credit for prior learning usage, student performance and college completion rates. Sharing student outcomes and institutional benefits regularly and at multiple levels advances internal and external support.

What is next?

A variety of credit for prior learning models have emerged that represents the diversity of institutions and the students they serve. Stakeholders—higher education institutions and systems, state and regional consortia, policymakers and accrediting bodies—must continue to work closely together to identify effective CPL practice and remove barriers to implementation and collaboration (ACE, 2015). Continued cross-sector discus-

sions to review policy, receive stakeholder input and collaborate in the creation of quality standards would do much to advance credit for prior learning articulation practices. The result is shared benefits for students, institutions and their communities.

Notes

[1] Bautsch, Brenda. January, 2013. *State Policies to Improve Student Transfer.* National Conference of State Legislatures.

[2] Monaghan, David B. and Attewell, Paul. March 19, 2014. *The Community College Route to the Bachelor's Degree.* Education Evaluation and Policy Analysis.

[3] Lumina Foundation and Gallup. February 5, 2013. *America's Call for Higher Education Redesign.* Lumina Foundation.

[4] Hayward, Milan S. and Williams, Mitchell R. Adult Learner Graduation Rates at Four U.S. Community Colleges by Prior Learning Assessment Status and Method. *Community College Journal of Research and Practice,* 39(May 23, 2014): 44-54.

[5] Klein-Collins, Rebecca. 2011. *Underserved Students Who Earn Credit Through Prior Learning Assessment (PLA) Have Higher Degree Completion Rates and Shorter Time-to-Degree.* Council for Adult and Experiential Learning.

[6] Lakin, Mary Beth; Nellum, Christopher, Crandall, Jennifer; and Seymour, Deborah. *Credit for Prior Learning Charting Institutional Practice for Sustainability.* February, 2015. Washington, DC: American Council on Education.

[7] American Council on Education. April 7, 2015. *Internal Marketing: Building Credit for Prior Learning Engagement and Commitment across the Institution.* Washington, DC: ACE 2015 Credit for Prior Learning Webinar Series.

[8] ACE, February 2015.

[9] ACE, February 2015.

[10] Ryu, Mikung. 2013. *Credit for Prior Learning: From the Student, Campus, and Industry Perspectives.* Washington, DC: American Council on Education.

[11] American Association of Collegiate Registrars and Admissions Officers. 2014. *Credit for Prior Learning Practices: Results of the AACRAO December 2014 60 Second Survey.* American Association of Collegiate Registrars and Admissions Officers.

[12] American Council on Education. April 7, 2015. *Internal Marketing: Building Credit for Prior Learning Engagement and Commitment across the Institution.* Washington, DC: ACE 2015 Credit for Prior Learning Webinar Series.

References

American Council on Education. April 7, 2015. *Internal Marketing: Building Credit for Prior Learning Engagement and Commitment across the Institution.* Washington, DC: ACE 2015 Credit for Prior Learning Webinar Series.

American Association of Collegiate Registrars and Admissions Officers. 2014. *Credit for Prior Learning Practices: Results of the AACRAO December 2014 60 Second*

Survey. American Association of Collegiate Registrars and Admissions Officers.

Bautsch, Brenda. January, 2013. *State Policies to Improve Student Transfer*. National Conference of State Legislatures.

Berry, Carol L. 2013. *A Comparison of CLEP and Non-CLP Students with Respect to Postsecondary Outcomes*. The College Board.

Hayward, Milan S. and Williams, Mitchell R. Adult Learner Graduation Rates at Four U.S. Community Colleges by Prior Learning Assessment Status and Method. *Community College Journal of Research and Practice*, 39(May 23, 2014): 44-54.

Klein-Collins, Rebecca. 2010. *Fueling the Race to Postsecondary Success: A 48-Institution Study of Prior Learning Assessment and Adult Student Outcomes*. Council for Adult and Experiential Learning.

Klein-Collins, Rebecca. 2011. *Underserved Students Who Earn Credit Through Prior Learning Assessment (PLA) Have Higher Degree Completion Rates and Shorter Time-to-Degree*. Council for Adult and Experiential Learning.

Lakin, Mary Beth; Nellum, Christopher, Crandall, Jennifer; and Seymour, Deborah. *Credit for Prior Learning Charting Institutional Practice for Sustainability*. February, 2015. Washington, DC: American Council on Education.

Monaghan, David B. and Attewell, Paul. March 19, 2014. *The Community College Route to the Bachelor's Degree*. Education Evaluation and Policy Analysis.

Ryu, Mikung. 2013. *Credit for Prior Learning: From the Student, Campus, and Industry Perspectives*. Washington, DC: American Council on Education.

Sherman, Amy, Klein-Collins, Rebecca and Palmer, Iris. 2012. *State Policy Approaches to Support Prior Learning Assessment*. Council for Adult and Experiential Learning and HCM Strategists

About the Author

Mary Beth Lakin is the Director of College and University Partnerships (CUP) in the Center for Education Attainment and Innovation at the American Council on Education (ACE). CUP capitalizes on statewide, regional, and national initiatives to raise awareness, acceptance and application of credit for prior learning and boost postsecondary credential completion rates, assisting higher education institutions and systems in developing integrated programs and services that support and validate a diverse range of learning experiences. With 10 years at the American Council on Education, Lakin has concentrated on expanding educational pathways for adult learners, including military service members and veterans. Lakin has close to three decades of experience as a faculty member, academic advisor, and program administrator. In her previous position at Old Dominion University in Norfolk, Virginia, she developed and directed the University's Experiential Learning program and an interdisciplinary degree program geared to adult learners offered in a blended format. Her published articles, presentations, and research center on credit for prior learning policies and practices, adult learning, and trends in postsecondary education.

Table 9.8
AVERAGE UNDERGRADUATE TUITION AND FEES AND ROOM AND BOARD RATES IN INSTITUTIONS OF HIGHER EDUCATION, BY CONTROL OF INSTITUTION AND STATE: 2011–2012 AND 2012–2013 (In current dollars)

State or other jurisdiction	Public 4-year 2011–2012 Total	Tuition and required fees (in-state)	2012–2013 Total	Tuition and required fees (in-state)	Room	Board	Out-of-state tuition and required fees 2012–13	Private 4-year 2011–2012 Total	Tuition and required fees	2012–2013 Total	Tuition and required fees	Room	Board	Public 2-year In-state 2011–12	In-state 2012–13	Out-of-state 2012–13
United States	$16,805	$7,703	$17,474	$8,070	$5,241	$4,163	$21,847	$33,674	$23,460	$35,074	$24,525	$5,837	$4,712	$2,652	$2,792	$6,767
Alabama	15,550	7,528	16,546	8,073	4,695	3,777	20,380	21,037	13,041	22,486	13,983	4,378	4,124	3,864	4,048	7,736
Alaska	14,541	5,956	15,415	6,317	5,265	3,833	18,790	28,270	19,211	30,418	21,496	4,123	4,799	3,883	3,972	4,150
Arizona	19,274	9,030	19,064	9,694	5,948	3,421	21,201	20,391	11,865	20,394	11,650	4,979	3,765	1,802	1,842	7,870
Arkansas	13,100	6,377	13,936	6,604	4,113	3,219	15,669	23,939	16,888	25,267	18,004	3,690	3,573	2,435	2,633	4,605
California	20,670	8,830	21,029	8,892	6,474	5,663	30,765	39,177	27,379	40,599	28,345	6,990	5,264	977	1,225	6,267
Colorado	17,161	7,177	18,052	7,656	5,153	5,243	25,470	29,860	19,093	30,907	19,967	6,078	4,861	3,484	3,004	8,882
Connecticut	19,842	9,087	20,655	9,517	5,999	5,139	26,688	46,642	34,208	48,262	35,336	7,229	5,697	3,490	3,596	10,512
Delaware	20,926	10,470	21,940	10,929	6,595	4,416	26,228	23,521	13,182	23,701	12,943	5,135	5,623	3,086	3,242	7,562
Florida	13,622	4,042	14,170	4,377	5,813	3,980	17,050	29,598	19,925	30,123	20,155	5,522	4,446	2,485	2,486	6,889
Georgia	14,828	6,029	15,331	6,325	5,397	3,608	22,393	30,737	20,447	33,177	22,456	5,915	4,807	2,645	2,652	7,554
Hawaii	16,397	7,450	16,987	7,731	4,720	4,536	23,614	24,719	13,408	25,808	14,287	4,969	6,552	2,388	2,484	7,166
Idaho	12,347	5,673	13,476	5,980	3,368	4,128	17,736	13,916	7,118	11,544	6,752	2,356	2,436	2,672	2,915	7,276
Illinois	21,178	11,290	22,222	11,882	5,671	4,668	26,873	35,645	25,091	37,097	26,299	6,274	4,524	3,086	3,192	9,034
Indiana	17,034	7,937	17,758	8,269	4,956	4,533	26,538	34,380	25,259	36,368	26,794	4,901	4,672	3,354	3,455	7,302
Iowa	15,663	7,563	16,358	7,832	4,149	4,376	23,019	22,563	15,819	22,258	15,426	3,017	3,815	3,998	4,099	5,190
Kansas	13,432	6,660	13,901	6,970	3,426	3,505	17,646	27,425	20,023	28,525	20,852	3,635	4,039	2,601	2,621	4,023
Kentucky	15,921	7,942	16,581	8,416	4,150	4,015	19,040	26,450	18,658	28,654	20,639	4,056	3,959	3,268	3,391	11,789
Louisiana	12,596	5,205	14,245	5,817	4,991	3,437	17,405	36,998	27,163	39,088	28,691	5,783	4,614	2,584	2,837	5,781
Maine	18,631	9,294	18,676	9,295	4,450	4,930	24,397	41,456	30,765	42,745	31,558	5,635	5,552	3,409	3,409	6,053
Maryland	17,420	7,801	18,094	8,051	5,680	4,362	20,199	43,406	30,989	44,819	32,580	6,896	5,342	3,356	3,500	8,355
Massachusetts	20,328	10,094	21,094	10,632	6,378	4,084	24,399	48,159	35,586	49,871	36,795	7,457	5,619	4,006	4,186	9,516
Michigan	19,240	10,533	19,865	11,027	4,523	4,315	31,047	25,038	17,043	26,381	18,135	4,076	4,170	2,595	2,736	5,651
Minnesota	17,354	9,908	17,998	10,291	4,175	3,533	16,313	33,864	25,191	35,409	26,499	4,708	4,201	5,195	5,362	6,197
Mississippi	12,831	5,678	13,583	6,147	4,200	3,236	15,055	20,594	14,506	20,881	14,592	3,201	3,089	2,212	2,276	4,284
Missouri	15,665	7,609	16,236	7,815	4,804	3,617	18,885	26,788	18,186	27,615	19,020	4,717	3,878	2,600	2,716	5,384
Montana	13,074	5,995	13,572	6,267	3,463	3,843	20,164	25,590	18,468	27,320	19,737	3,547	4,037	3,120	3,151	8,351
Nebraska	14,577	6,749	15,291	7,023	4,371	3,897	16,702	25,956	18,485	27,212	19,478	4,006	3,727	2,470	2,594	3,415
Nevada	15,141	4,624	15,944	4,953	5,288	5,703	19,156	28,861	15,797	37,710	16,108	7,622	13,980	2,513	2,700	9,345
New Hampshire	23,314	13,339	24,705	14,435	6,098	4,172	24,945	41,411	29,805	42,310	30,202	7,118	4,990	7,194	7,218	15,697
New Jersey	23,151	11,580	23,773	11,955	7,590	4,229	24,447	41,201	29,700	42,831	31,195	6,779	4,857	3,682	3,782	6,591
New Mexico	12,877	5,275	13,225	5,483	4,134	3,608	14,327	24,128	15,417	25,144	16,256	4,727	4,161	1,372	1,399	4,558
New York	17,559	6,183	18,397	6,556	7,446	4,394	15,751	43,605	31,225	45,338	32,438	7,731	5,169	4,143	4,331	7,827
North Carolina	13,692	5,708	14,514	6,223	4,673	3,618	19,733	34,781	25,271	36,194	26,336	5,217	4,640	2,138	2,212	8,171
North Dakota	12,846	6,437	13,210	6,572	2,897	3,741	16,170	16,641	11,582	17,743	12,318	2,422	3,002	3,994	4,048	8,216
Ohio	18,737	8,860	19,453	9,301	5,607	4,545	21,683	34,832	25,568	35,367	25,756	4,884	4,728	3,349	3,480	7,421

See footnotes at end of table.

AVERAGE UNDERGRADUATE TUITION AND FEES AND ROOM AND BOARD RATES IN INSTITUTIONS OF HIGHER EDUCATION, BY CONTROL OF INSTITUTION AND STATE: 2011–2012 AND 2012–2013 (In current dollars)

State or other jurisdiction	Public 4-year							Private 4-year						Public 2-year, tuition and required fees		
	2011-2012		2012-2013				Out-of-state tuition and required fees 2012-13	2011-2012		2012-2013				In-state 2011-12	In-state 2012-13	Out-of-state 2012-13
	Total	Tuition and required fees (in-state)	Total	Tuition and required fees (in-state)	Room	Board		Total	Tuition and required fees	Total	Tuition and required fees	Room	Board			
Oklahoma	12,662	5,573	13,005	5,882	3,933	3,190	16,543	28,113	19,692	29,230	20,572	4,353	4,305	2,732	2,904	7,101
Oregon	17,601	7,978	18,526	8,294	5,684	4,549	25,067	38,411	28,555	40,655	30,195	5,411	5,049	3,561	3,752	7,689
Pennsylvania	20,978	11,817	21,637	12,184	5,604	3,850	22,891	42,432	31,402	44,407	32,949	6,286	5,173	3,936	4,133	11,009
Rhode Island	20,649	9,936	21,582	10,817	6,715	4,050	26,762	44,511	32,685	46,114	33,940	6,680	5,494	3,676	3,950	10,582
South Carolina	18,073	10,366	18,655	10,691	...	4,841	26,042	27,927	20,038	29,165	20,990	4,092	4,084	3,710	3,820	7,910
South Dakota	13,327	6,948	13,858	7,413	2,983	3,462	9,654	25,121	18,035	25,796	18,843	3,260	3,693	4,802	5,066	5,261
Tennessee	14,612	7,005	15,416	7,472	4,337	3,607	22,412	29,941	21,215	31,135	22,046	5,067	4,023	3,380	3,526	13,682
Texas	15,364	7,124	15,940	7,402	4,556	3,983	20,044	33,308	24,051	34,861	25,174	5,363	4,323	1,750	1,815	5,075
Utah	11,297	5,166	12,076	5,375	2,938	3,763	16,631	15,224	7,677	15,330	7,758	3,844	3,728	3,021	3,170	10,012
Vermont	22,504	13,084	23,290	13,524	6,160	3,607	32,650	43,752	33,174	46,255	35,130	5,983	5,142	5,236	5,452	10,804
Virginia	17,963	9,366	18,843	9,866	5,033	3,944	27,079	29,050	20,641	30,483	21,524	4,468	4,491	3,749	3,910	8,592
Washington	17,690	7,789	18,925	8,856	5,319	4,750	26,314	38,443	28,572	40,293	30,133	5,409	4,752	3,713	3,957	6,983
West Virginia	13,476	5,261	14,126	5,599	4,508	4,018	16,582	18,124	10,229	19,120	10,721	3,997	4,402	3,011	3,135	7,798
Wisconsin	14,718	7,864	15,446	8,339	4,166	2,940	20,146	32,830	24,303	34,199	25,500	4,689	4,010	3,874	4,073	6,824
Wyoming	12,022	3,501	12,479	3,642	3,901	4,936	10,962	...	14,177	†	13,562	†	†	2,305	2,420	5,998
Dist. of Columbia	...	7,000	...	7,244	...	...	14,540	47,365	33,774	48,440	35,524	8,557	4,358	...	...	...

Key: ... – Not applicable.

Source: U.S. Department of Education, National Center for Education Statistics, Integrated Postsecondary Education Data System (IPEDS), Fall 2011 and Fall 2012, Institutional Characteristics component; and Spring 2012 and Spring 2013 (This table was prepared December 2013.)

Note: Data are for the entire academic year and are average charges. In-state tuition and fees were weighted by the number of full-time-equivalent undergraduates, but were not adjusted to reflect student residency. Out-of-state tuition and fees were weighted by the number of first-time freshmen attending the institution in fall 2012 from out of state. Room and board are based on full-time students.

Table 9.9
DEGREE GRANTING INSTITUTIONS AND BRANCHES, BY TYPE AND CONTROL OF INSTITUTION, 2009–2010

State or other jurisdiction	Total	All public institutions	Public 4-year institutions							Public 2-year
			Total	Research, very high (a)	Research, high (b)	Doctoral (c)	Master's (d)	Baccalaureate (e)	Special focus (f)	
United States	4,706	1,649	682	73	73	28	270	191	47	967
Alabama........................	76	39	14	2	3	0	8	1	0	25
Alaska..........................	9	5	3	0	1	0	2	0	0	2
Arizona........................	87	24	4	2	1	0	0	0	1	20
Arkansas......................	51	33	11	1	0	1	6	2	1	22
California	460	150	35	8	1	0	21	3	2	115
Colorado......................	91	27	13	2	2	1	3	5	0	14
Connecticut..................	47	21	9	1	0	0	4	4	0	12
Delaware	12	5	2	1	0	0	1	0	0	3
Florida.........................	240	43	34	4	2	2	5	20	1	9
Georgia........................	139	66	27	3	0	1	11	11	1	39
Hawaii..........................	21	10	4	1	0	0	0	3	0	6
Idaho...........................	18	7	4	0	2	0	1	1	0	3
Illinois.........................	182	60	12	2	2	1	7	0	0	48
Indiana........................	107	29	15	2	2	1	6	4	0	14
Iowa	67	19	3	2	0	0	1	0	0	16
Kansas	67	33	8	1	2	0	4	0	1	25
Kentucky......................	79	24	8	2	0	0	5	1	0	16
Louisiana.....................	73	35	17	1	3	0	9	1	3	18
Maine...........................	32	15	8	0	1	0	1	6	0	7
Maryland	62	29	13	1	1	2	7	1	1	16
Massachusetts	124	30	14	1	2	0	7	2	2	16
Michigan......................	111	46	15	3	2	2	7	1	0	31
Minnesota....................	116	42	12	1	0	0	8	3	0	30
Mississippi	42	24	9	1	3	0	4	0	1	15
Missouri.......................	137	31	13	1	3	0	6	3	0	18
Montana	22	17	6	1	1	0	1	3	0	11
Nebraska......................	42	15	7	1	0	1	3	1	1	8
Nevada.........................	26	7	6	0	2	0	0	4	0	1
New Hampshire	29	12	5	0	1	0	2	2	0	7
New Jersey....................	68	33	14	1	2	0	10	0	1	19
New Mexico	44	28	9	1	1	0	4	1	2	19
New York......................	303	78	43	4	1	1	21	12	4	35
North Carolina..............	148	75	16	2	1	3	7	2	1	59
North Dakota................	21	14	9	1	1	0	1	4	2	5
Ohio.............................	222	60	36	2	8	0	1	24	1	24
Oklahoma.....................	63	29	17	1	1	0	8	5	2	12
Oregon.........................	62	26	9	2	1	0	3	2	1	17
Pennsylvania	265	61	44	2	1	1	17	21	2	17
Rhode Island................	13	3	2	0	1	0	1	0	0	1
South Carolina.............	77	33	13	1	1	1	5	4	1	20
South Dakota................	25	12	7	0	2	0	2	1	2	5
Tennessee	111	22	9	1	1	3	47	0	0	13
Texas...........................	260	108	45	3	6	7	16	5	8	63
Utah............................	42	11	6	1	1	0	2	2	0	5
Vermont.......................	24	6	5	0	1	0	1	3	0	1
Virginia........................	131	40	16	3	3	0	7	2	1	24
Washington...................	88	43	16	2	0	0	6	6	2	27
West Virginia................	46	23	13	0	1	0	3	8	1	10
Wisconsin.....................	88	31	14	1	1	0	10	2	0	17
Wyoming	11	8	1	0	1	0	0	0	0	7
Dist. of Columbia	20	2	2	0	0	0	1	0	1	0
U.S. Service Academies....	5	5	5	0	0	0	0	5	0	0
American Samoa	1	1	0	0	0	0	0	0	0	1
Federated States of Micronesia...............	1	1	0	0	0	0	0	0	0	1
Guam...........................	3	2	1	0	0	0	1	0	0	1
Marshall Islands.............	1	1	0	0	0	0	0	0	0	1
No. Mariana Islands..........	1	1	1	0	0	0	0	1	0	0
Palau...........................	1	1	0	0	0	0	0	0	0	1
Puerto Rico...................	85	18	14	0	1	1	0	9	3	4
U.S. Virgin Islands	1	1	1	0	0	0	0	1	0	0

See footnotes at end of table.

DEGREE GRANTING INSTITUTIONS AND BRANCHES, BY TYPE AND CONTROL OF INSTITUTION, 2009–2010 — Continued

State or other jurisdiction	All not-for-profit institutions	Not-for-profit 4-year institutions							Not-for-profit 2-year	For-profit institutions		
		Total	Rsrch., very high (a)	Rsrch., high (b)	Doctoral (c)	Master's (d)	Bacc. (e)	Special focus (f)		Total	4-year	2-year
United States	1,653	1,553	34	25	48	364	517	565	100	1,404	733	671
Alabama...........................	2	19	0	0	0	2	12	5	1	17	11	6
Alaska..............................	11	2	0	0	0	1	0	1	0	2	1	1
Arizona............................	13	11	0	0	0	2	3	6	0	52	35	17
Arkansas..........................	144	12	0	0	0	1	9	2	1	5	4	1
California	146	138	3	1	10	25	24	75	6	166	82	84
Colorado..........................	19	12	0	1	0	3	3	5	1	51	29	22
Connecticut	5	18	1	0	0	9	5	3	1	7	5	2
Delaware..........................	63	4	0	0	1	0	1	2	1	2	2	0
Florida.............................	35	60	1	1	3	12	22	21	3	134	58	76
Georgia............................	35	33	1	0	1	4	19	8	2	38	22	16
Hawaii..............................	7	7	0	0	0	2	2	3	0	4	3	1
Idaho................................	4	4	0	0	0	1	2	1	0	7	6	1
Illinois.............................	84	80	2	2	4	17	18	37	4	38	24	14
Indiana.............................	40	39	1	0	0	9	19	10	1	38	25	13
Iowa.................................	34	33	0	0	0	6	18	9	1	14	12	2
Kansas	24	22	0	0	0	6	12	4	2	10	5	5
Kentucky	27	27	0	0	1	6	13	7	0	28	19	9
Louisiana.........................	13	10	1	0	0	2	4	3	3	25	8	17
Maine...............................	15	13	0	0	0	3	6	4	2	2	1	1
Maryland	21	21	1	0	0	6	6	8	0	12	7	5
Massachusetts	83	80	5	3	1	15	24	32	3	11	6	5
Michigan..........................	50	49	0	0	1	11	23	0	1	15	12	3
Minnesota........................	36	35	0	0	3	6	12	14	1	38	32	6
Mississippi	9	9	0	0	0	3	4	2	0	9	3	6
Missouri...........................	57	54	1	1	1	11	12	28	3	49	26	23
Montana	5	4	0	0	0	0	3	1	1	0	0	0
Nebraska..........................	18	16	0	0	0	5	7	4	2	9	5	4
Nevada.............................	3	3	0	0	0	1	0	2	0	16	9	7
New Hampshire	15	13	1	0	0	5	5	2	2	2	2	0
New Jersey	26	26	1	1	1	10	2	11	0	9	5	4
New Mexico	3	3	0	0	0	1	2	0	0	13	10	3
New York..........................	179	163	6	5	7	40	27	78	16	46	19	27
North Carolina.................	49	48	1	1	0	7	27	12	1	24	16	8
North Dakota...................	6	6	0	0	0	1	1	4	0	1	1	0
Ohio.................................	75	66	1	1	2	20	19	23	9	87	24	63
Oklahoma........................	14	14	0	0	1	4	6	3	0	20	11	9
Oregon.............................	24	24	0	0	0	5	8	11	0	12	6	6
Pennsylvania	118	105	2	3	2	30	35	33	13	86	12	74
Rhode Island	10	10	1	0	0	5	1	3	0	0	0	0
South Carolina.................	24	22	0	0	0	5	14	3	2	20	13	7
South Dakota...................	8	7	0	0	0	0	5	2	1	5	5	0
Tennessee	49	45	1	0	2	11	15	16	4	40	23	17
Texas................................	63	54	1	2	2	17	15	17	9	89	37	52
Utah.................................	4	3	0	1	0	2	0	0	1	27	31	6
Vermont............................	17	16	0	0	0	4	10	2	1	1	1	0
Virginia............................	37	37	0	0	1	7	20	9	0	54	30	24
Washington......................	24	23	0	0	0	10	5	8	1	21	12	9
West Virginia....................	9	9	0	0	0	1	7	1	0	14	3	11
Wisconsin.........................	30	30	0	0	3	8	10	9	0	27	24	3
Wyoming	0	0	0	0	0	0	0	0	0	3	2	1
Dist. of Columbia	14	14	2	2	1	2	0	7	1	4	4	0
U.S. Service Academies...	n/a	n/a	n/a	n/a	n/a	n/a	n/a	n/a	n/a	n/a	n/a	n/a
American Samoa	0	0	0	0	0	0	0	0	0	0	0	0
Federated States of Micronesia................	0	0	0	0	0	0	0	0	0	0	0	0
Guam................................	1	1	0	0	0	0	0	1	0	0	0	0
Marshall Islands..............	0	0	0	0	0	0	0	0	0	0	0	0
No. Mariana Islands	0	0	0	0	0	0	0	0	0	0	0	0
Palau................................	0	0	0	0	0	0	0	0	0	0	0	0
Puerto Rico......................	48	44	0	0	3	12	18	11	4	19	8	11
U.S. Virgin Islands..........	0	0	0	0	0	0	0	0	0	0	0	0

See footnotes at end of table.

DEGREE GRANTING INSTITUTIONS AND BRANCHES, BY TYPE AND CONTROL OF INSTITUTION, 2009–2010 — Continued

Source: U.S. Department of Education, National Center for Education Statistics, Integrated Postsecondary Education Data System (IPEDS), Fall 2011. This table was prepared November 2012.

Note: Branch campuses are counted as separate institutions. Relative levels of research activity for research universities were determined by an analysis of research and development expenditures, science and engineering research staffing, and doctoral degrees conferred, by field. Further information on the research index ranking may be obtained from *http:// www.carnegiefoundation.org/classifications/index.asp?key=798#related*. Degree-granting institutions grant associate's or higher degrees and participate in Title IV federal financial aid programs.

Key:

n/a — Not applicable

(a) Research universities with a very high level of research activity.

(b) Research universities with a high level of research activity.

(c) Institutions that award at least 20 doctor's degrees per year, but did not have a high level of research activity.

(d) Institutions that award at least 50 master's degrees per year.

(e) Institutions that primarily emphasize undergraduate education.

(f) Four-year institutions that award degrees primarily in single fields of study, such as medicine, business, fine arts, theology, and engineering. Includes some institutions that have 4-year programs, but have not reported sufficient data to identify program category. Also, includes institutions classified as 4-year under the IPEDS system, which had been classified as 2-year in the Carnegie Classification system because they primarily award an associate's degree.

Table 9.10
AVERAGE SALARY OF FULL-TIME FACULTY ON 9-MONTH CONTRACTS: 2012–13

State or other jurisdiction	Total	All public institutions	Public 4-year Total	Public Doctoral (a)	Public Master's (b)	Public Other	Public 2-year	All not-for-profit	NFP 4-year Total	NFP Doctoral (a)	NFP Master's (b)	NFP Other	Not-for-profit 2-year	For-profit institutions
United States	$77,301	$73,909	$78,111	$84,316	$68,037	$60,575	$62,781	$85,448	$85,546	$99,877	$68,956	$67,640	$48,205	$45,727
Alabama	67,167	69,104	73,882	79,486	60,981	68,071	54,997	57,154	57,154	64,988	50,274	49,795	†	†
Alaska	76,295	77,374	77,440	81,152	75,075	†	69,050	54,063	54,063	†	54,063	54,063	†	†
Arizona	78,045	78,555	83,691	84,163	†	50,271	69,360	58,993	58,993	†	43,373	71,773	†	70,486
Arkansas	56,415	56,453	61,203	65,460	51,020	58,651	44,170	56,164	56,189	62,710	56,828	51,126	†	†
California	91,862	88,786	94,223	106,300	77,447	73,485	82,505	103,249	103,249	112,503	81,982	89,258	†	48,168
Colorado	72,613	71,234	76,705	83,645	59,353	63,659	47,339	82,152	82,152	83,972	82,306	62,503	†	31,893
Connecticut	94,524	85,944	91,336	101,798	81,403	†	69,383	103,640	103,640	112,537	89,205	81,456	†	61,939
Delaware	96,781	97,822	101,666	105,928	73,297	†	78,075	86,505	86,505	121,734	64,385	†	†	†
Florida	71,836	70,180	71,288	80,114	67,057	58,337	52,915	76,805	76,805	89,041	69,086	57,407	†	72,031
Georgia	69,625	67,874	69,973	77,358	58,527	53,359	45,489	74,959	74,973	91,874	64,862	60,681	†	†
Hawaii	78,967	79,346	85,115	86,873	67,937	69,041	66,139	72,539	72,539	†	67,883	83,502	†	†
Idaho	60,762	61,345	64,550	65,087	†	49,551	49,198	54,047	54,047	†	51,898	56,036	†	†
Illinois	81,749	76,090	79,669	83,428	66,138	†	69,859	90,298	90,298	105,930	64,910	62,048	†	39,951
Indiana	73,823	72,943	78,211	84,771	61,204	55,424	43,112	75,596	75,596	89,405	60,768	64,293	†	†
Iowa	71,614	77,617	86,911	90,905	70,469	†	54,966	62,330	62,330	68,849	55,444	62,916	†	56,041
Kansas	63,575	65,981	72,519	77,127	57,633	66,216	51,239	49,604	49,604	63,381	53,265	43,272	43,524	†
Kentucky	62,386	63,618	68,834	73,634	59,209	47,701	49,789	57,133	57,133	†	51,348	59,274	†	†
Louisiana	62,980	59,473	64,755	70,339	55,305	60,201	42,394	78,817	78,817	84,878	57,692	52,714	†	30,111
Maine	70,349	67,520	71,956	77,728	64,840	†	52,527	75,740	75,983	65,544	55,481	86,013	51,930	†
Maryland	76,229	73,484	77,145	86,128	73,804	†	66,417	86,284	86,284	101,660	65,462	74,397	†	†
Massachusetts	100,114	81,216	86,871	96,622	74,620	54,242	61,033	107,868	107,933	119,662	86,333	83,342	72,631	65,606
Michigan	81,811	84,387	85,904	88,478	68,281	59,928	77,403	65,402	65,402	79,232	61,156	63,493	†	†
Minnesota	71,861	71,506	78,936	95,717	52,356	†	59,761	73,034	73,034	76,028	65,302	75,049	†	49,740
Mississippi	58,709	58,853	63,476	65,740	59,628	57,484	51,099	57,340	57,340	66,696	58,912	42,475	†	†
Missouri	69,804	65,773	68,967	75,673	57,195	†	54,254	76,960	76,960	94,224	59,050	51,496	†	60,512
Montana	57,610	58,933	60,914	63,473	63,103	48,418	44,931	49,055	50,316	†	48,175	51,829	35,678	†
Nebraska	67,957	69,580	74,449	78,662	†	†	54,534	63,118	63,274	79,727	54,802	54,105	49,900	†
Nevada	78,888	79,091	80,526	89,020	†	63,724	63,164	62,703	62,703	†	62,703	†	†	†
New Hampshire	85,155	85,155	87,988	96,420	75,569	85,285	52,046	91,566	91,566	119,949	67,416	68,462	†	†
New Jersey	97,292	95,003	103,633	109,927	96,231	†	73,174	102,715	102,715	120,032	77,305	71,835	†	†
New Mexico	63,004	63,004	68,980	74,822	57,939	45,767	48,950	96,962	96,983	108,390	76,817	81,071	77,426	36,394
New York	89,275	76,415	80,644	98,701	70,054	64,098	68,333	81,882	82,121	101,958	56,745	58,840	40,111	87,040
North Carolina	71,164	67,222	78,149	83,585	68,189	68,477	48,827	49,086	49,086	52,188	†	46,726	†	†
North Dakota	63,228	65,675	67,413	73,864	57,536	52,125	52,128	69,350	69,393	†	62,087	68,987	52,909	15,127
Ohio	72,472	75,080	79,083	81,753	54,796	61,699	60,120	69,393	76,853	76,853	62,087	68,987	52,909	15,127
Oklahoma	64,747	64,345	67,698	73,084	60,036	49,493	48,293	66,603	66,603	72,657	56,611	39,580	†	†
Oregon	70,049	69,117	71,093	75,250	55,828	61,552	65,731	73,043	73,043	75,961	63,461	77,315	†	†
Pennsylvania	83,291	79,867	82,817	90,157	78,810	67,254	63,141	86,906	87,336	98,896	70,300	79,438	44,380	53,903
Rhode Island	89,435	72,374	75,990	80,797	67,731	†	61,249	101,310	101,310	123,303	86,115	†	†	†
South Carolina	63,668	65,590	74,226	86,607	65,284	54,533	48,092	57,640	57,777	†	59,777	54,774	49,852	52,308

See footnotes at end of table.

AVERAGE SALARY OF FULL-TIME FACULTY ON 9-MONTH CONTRACTS: 2012–13—Continued

State or other jurisdiction	Total	Public institutions						Not-for-profit institutions						For-profit institutions
		All public institutions Total	4-year Total	4-year Doctoral (a)	4-year Master's (b)	4-year Other	Public 2-year	All not-for-profit	Total	4-year Doctoral (a)	4-year Master's (b)	4-year Other	Not-for-profit 2-year	
South Dakota	59,058	60,422	63,240	63,966	64,365	45,440	45,751	52,963	52,963	†	52,736	53,076	†	†
Tennessee	68,335	64,605	70,088	72,142	61,226	†	46,719	75,854	75,854	96,669	55,252	54,249	†	†
Texas	72,450	70,521	77,644	83,178	63,561	56,632	55,647	81,470	81,551	93,833	65,434	56,048	34,305	‡
Utah	68,886	68,303	70,317	79,913	61,961	55,038	49,735	77,000	78,366	90,785	71,995	†	55,787	‡
Vermont	74,293	75,470	75,470	83,693	59,207	56,990	†	73,213	73,213	†	76,805	52,451	†	†
Virginia	70,365	75,299	80,399	87,402	66,980	67,732	58,644	59,719	59,719	60,066	57,810	59,863	†	35,498
Washington	69,240	68,108	73,585	81,826	67,714	55,280	56,170	73,338	73,364	78,875	61,247	70,157	‡	†
West Virginia	61,063	62,746	65,177	72,478	58,059	53,404	48,150	49,801	49,801	53,751	47,342	48,450	†	27,446
Wisconsin	70,431	72,250	71,073	80,487	58,689	90,577	75,483	64,284	64,284	72,291	59,833	57,743	†	55,687
Wyoming	69,566	69,566	78,955	78,955	†	†	58,606	†	†	†	†	‡	†	†
Dist. of Columbia	99,140	82,067	82,067	129,471	77,810	†	†	100,647	100,647	101,396	69,000	†	†	33,150
U.S. Service Academies	102,568	102,568	102,568	†	†	102,568	†	†	†	†	†	†	†	†
American Samoa	29,767	29,767	29,767	†	†	29,767	†	†	†	†	†	†	†	†
Federated States of Micronesia	24,674	24,674	†	†	†	†	24,674	†	†	†	†	†	†	†
Guam	62,641	62,641	66,229	†	66,229	†	53,606	†	†	†	†	†	†	†
Marshall Islands	58,174	58,174	†	†	†	†	58,174	†	†	†	†	†	†	†
No. Marianas Islands	43,216	43,216	43,216	†	†	43,216	†	†	†	†	†	†	†	†
Palau	†	†	†	†	†	†	†	†	†	†	†	†	†	†
Puerto Rico	59,357	65,265	65,265	49,191	71,629	56,733	†	26,788	26,788	31,402	29,979	17,028	†	14,815
U.S. Virgin Islands	62,810	62,810	62,810	†	62,810	†	†	†	†	†	†	‡	†	†

Source: U.S. Department of Education, National Center for Education Statistics, Integrated Postsecondary Education Data System (IPEDS), Spring 2013, Human Resources component, Salaries section. (This table was prepared March 2014.)

Note: Degree-granting institutions grant associate's or higher degrees and participate in Title IV federal financial aid programs. Data include imputations for nonrespondent institutions.

Key:
† – Not applicable.
‡ – Reporting standards not met (too few cases).
(a) Institutions that awarded 20 or more doctor's degrees during the previous academic year.
(b) Institutions that awarded 20 or more master's degrees, but fewer than 20 doctor's degrees, during the previous academic year.

Closing Skill Gaps

By Bryan Wilson

State policymakers hear frequently from employers that they cannot find skilled workers for open positions. Many of these positions are middle-skill jobs that require some form of postsecondary training, but not a bachelor's degree. This article discusses state strategies to close skill gaps and meet employer skill needs.

State policymakers hear frequently from employers that they cannot find skilled workers for open positions. Many of these are middle-skill jobs that require postsecondary training, but not a bachelor's degree. Even when the nation was slowly recovering from the Great Recession, employers expressed frustration.[1] As unemployment rates continue to fall, shortages of skilled workers will become more pronounced, especially with baby boomers retiring in increasing numbers.

Each state has multiple programs that help individuals prepare for middle-skill jobs. Most of these programs operate outside the traditional K-12-to-university pipeline. These programs include:

- Workforce Investment Act (WIA) Title I Program for Adults[2]
- WIA Title I Program for Dislocated Workers
- WIA Title I Program for Youth
- Employment Service
- Trade Adjustment Assistance Act
- Adult Basic Education
- Vocational Rehabilitation
- Temporary Assistance for Needy Families (TANF) Employment and Training
- Supplemental Nutrition Assistance Program (SNAP) Employment and Training
- Secondary Career and Technical Education
- Community and Technical College Workforce Education and Training (Postsecondary Career and Technical Education)
- Apprenticeship
- Corrections Employment and Training
- Customized Training for Employers

In addition, there is a vast sector of private, for-profit training institutions that are licensed by states and receive extensive public support indirectly in the form of student financial aid.

Too often these programs operate in silos rather than as part of a broad workforce development system, even though they serve many of the same individuals. When the programs do not work together, they are less effective in closing skill gaps.

Some states have coordinated middle-skill programs around common strategies. Key strategies are sector partnerships, career pathways, job-driven investments, and cross-agency data and measurement. These strategies align programs with employer skill needs and are incorporated in the newly enacted Workforce Innovation and Opportunity Act (WIOA) — the main federal law providing a workforce development framework for states.

Sector Partnerships

Sector partnerships are a proven strategy for closing skill gaps and meeting the needs of both workers and employers.[3] Sector partnerships bring together multiple employers within an industry to collaborate with colleges, schools, labor, workforce agencies, community organizations and other community stakeholders to align training with the skills needed for that industry to grow and compete. The partnerships identify skill gaps that are negatively affecting sector employers in the region, develop plans to close those gaps and implement the plans.

There are 21 states that have some form of state policy supporting local sector partnerships.[4] Of these, 15 provide financial assistance to local partnerships. States typically rely on either state general funds, an offset through the Unemployment Insurance system, or Workforce Investment Act/Workforce Innovation and Opportunity Act funds. State funding for local sector partnerships varies from a few hundred thousand dollars to $5 million per year.

Typically, an intermediary organization — such as a local workforce board, a nonprofit community-based organization or a community college — convenes the local partnership. Yet critically, employers lead the partnership so that it meets their skill needs. Common partnership activities include developing or modifying job training, establishing a K-12 to postsecondary pipeline, informing career pathways, identifying skill standards, and identifying or creating industry-based certifications.

Career Pathways

Career pathways align and integrate education, job training, counseling and support services to create seamless pathways to postsecondary credentials and employment.[5] Pathways may begin in secondary school with career and technical education. For low-skilled adults, career pathways may begin later in life. A complete career pathway system enables individuals to enter at any skill level, to stop when they need to and to re-enter without having to repeat what they already have learned.

Pathways involve a wide range of agencies and other entities. Potential partners include community colleges, state and local workforce boards, community-based organizations, support service agencies and providers, employers and labor. A state career pathway system should specify the different roles and responsibilities of each partner.

An estimated 36 million U.S. adults have low basic literacy and numeracy skills.[6] For these individuals, pathways may begin with adult basic education programs. In recent years, states have learned how to make these programs more effective by building bridge programs that prepare low-skilled adults to enter and succeed in postsecondary education, integrating adult education with occupational skills training in the same classroom and providing an occupational context for education.

Support services, such as transportation and child care, are critical for reducing barriers preventing low-income adults from persisting in career pathways. Counseling and career guidance connect individuals to needed services and draw a roadmap to a career. States increasingly are using professional navigators to work closely with participants—connecting them with the right support services and providing guidance on transitions from one program to the next.

Career pathway participants often need access to financial aid for postsecondary education. Traditional financial aid, however, is less accessible to students who are working, attending school less than half-time, or enrolled in non-credit occupational courses. Some states have responded to this challenge by providing financial aid for non-traditional students.

To help pay for pathway services, states can turn to the Supplemental Nutrition and Assistance Program (SNAP), formerly known as food stamps.[7] SNAP includes an Employment and Training program that pays for services for recipients. SNAP allocates some employment and training funds by formula and also offers 50-50 funds that can reimburse 50 percent of the costs of supportive services. There is no cap on 50-50 funds.

Job-Driven Investment

As U.S. Secretary of Labor Thomas Perez likes to say, we shouldn't just "train and pray" that there will be jobs at the end of training. We should invest in forms of training that are connected directly to jobs and training should be guided by the type and number of jobs that are available in the labor market.[8] Examples of training directly connected to jobs include incumbent worker training, on-the-job training, internships and apprenticeship.

Apprenticeship is the principle training strategy in many nations, but rare in the U.S. outside of construction. Some states are trying to change this. South Carolina offers a $1,000 tax credit to employers per apprentice and aggressively markets apprenticeship through its technical colleges. Virtually every state offers customized training for employers, often including training for incumbent workers. States may use WIOA funds, in addition to their own, to offer incumbent worker training and on-the-job training. Work-based learning opportunities like internships are a newly required element of the WIOA youth program.

Job-driven investment also means there should be a good match between the types of jobs that people are trained for and the types of jobs available. Middle-skill jobs account for the largest share of the labor market in each of the 50 states, yet most states don't have enough workers trained with mid-level skills. States also tend to invest far less in middle-skill training than other levels of higher education.[9]

All too frequently, there are mismatches between the fields students are being trained in and the occupations that are available. For example, there may be too few students preparing for careers in health care, manufacturing, information technology or certain fields of engineering. As discussed in the next section, states can take advantage of data tools to identify such mismatches and increase capacity where supply falls short of demand.

Cross-Agency Data and Measurement

While state policymakers generally have information on individual programs preparing people for middle-skill jobs, the often lack information on the workforce development system as a whole. They typically do not have information on:

- The total number of newly skilled workers programs supply;
- The employment and earnings outcomes of program participants across the system;
- How well the programs work together; and
- How well training matches employer demand.

States can use cross-agency data and measurement to better align workforce and education programs with each other and with employer skill needs. Three tools in particular can offer high-level information useful to state policymakers.

- *Dashboards* use a small number of common metrics to report education and employment outcomes across workforce development programs. Key metrics indicate completion rates, employment and earnings, and answer policymaker questions such as: *Do participants complete skills training? Do they get jobs? How much do they earn?* [10]
- *Pathway evaluators* show different patterns of participation across programs and the associated credential and labor market outcomes. They answer questions policymakers have about: *What pathways achieve the best employment and earnings outcomes for which groups of people?* [11]
- *Supply and demand reports* compare the number of newly trained workers with employer demand as measured by the number of job openings. Comparisons are broken down by level of education and occupational field. Supply and demand reports answer policymaker questions such as: *What fields need additional capacity in order to match employer demand?* [12]

A comprehensive cross-agency data and measurement system also includes postsecondary scorecards used to inform students' decisions. Scorecards use common metrics to show the performance of individual programs of study at local institutions—how many students graduate, how many get jobs and what the jobs pay. Scorecards can include other information, such as student costs and demographics, and links to information on career guidance and financial aid. Scorecards help students make market-based decisions, moving dollars from lesser- to better-performing programs.

WIOA

Many states already have implemented these strategies to better align middle-skill programs to meet employer skill needs. Congress built on state experiences and incorporated these strategies into Workforce Innovation and Opportunity Act. Under WIOA, effective July 1, 2015, states that have not already moved in these directions must soon make progress. [13]

Under WIOA, states must:

- Develop strategies for meeting the needs of employers, workers and jobseekers through sector partnerships;
- Develop strategies to use career pathways to provide low-income adults and youth with education, training and support services;
- Report state and local program performance using common metrics; and
- Expand training directly connected to jobs for out-of-school youth.

As we look to the future, there is great opportunity to move state workforce development systems forward using proven strategies to close skill gaps.

Notes

[1] For example, see, "Out of Inventory: Skill Shortage Threatens Growth for U.S. Manufacturing," Accenture, 2014.

[2] WIA will be replaced by the Workforce Innovation and Opportunity Act (WIOA) on July 1, 2015.

[3] "Connecting People to Work: Workforce Intermediaries and Sector Strategies," Edited by Maureen Conway and Robert P. Giloth, The Aspen Institute, 2014.

[4] Based on a National Skills Coalition scan of states.

[5] For more information on career pathways, see the web site of the Career Pathways Initiative, at: *https://learn-work.workforce3one.org/page/home*.

[6] "Survey of Adult Skills," Programme for the International Assessment of Adult Competencies, the Organization for Economic Co-operation and Development, 2013.

[7] "Training Policy in Brief: SNAP Employment and Training Program," National Skills Coalition, 2014.

[8] See, "Job-Driven Training and American Opportunity," The White House, July 2014.

[9] "Middle-School Job Fact Sheets," National Skills Coalition, 2015.

[10] "Are People Getting Credentials that Lead to Jobs: Using Dashboards for State Workforce Planning;" Heath Prince, Christopher T. King, Bryan Wilson, and Brooke DeRenzis; National Skills Coalition; February 2015.

[11] "Who is Being Served Well: Using Pathway Evaluators for State Workforce Planning;" Christopher T. King, Heath Prince, Bryan Wilson, and Brooke DeRenzis; National Skills Coalition; February 2015.

[12] "How Many More Skilled Workers Do We Need: Using Supply and Demand Reports for State Workforce Planning," Bryan Wilson, National Skills Coalition, June 2014.

[13] "Realizing Innovation and Opportunity: A Playbook for Creating Effective State Plans," Bryan Wilson and Brooke DeRenzis, National Skills Coalition, November 2014.

About the Author

As state policy director for the National Skills Coalition, **Bryan Wilson** leads the organization's efforts to assist state-based coalitions and policymakers in the development of specific policy proposals, including providing in-depth analyses of model state policies and proposals. He also provides assistance with policy implementation and measuring the impact of policy changes.

Signs Point to Affordable Care Act's Impact on Increasing Health Insurance Coverage

By Debra Miller

Two sources of contemporaneous data available from reputable national research institutions provide evidence that the Affordable Care Act has realized its principal goal of increasing the rate of health insurance coverage in the United States. The rates of uninsured Americans between late 2013 and early 2015 have dropped from 18 percent to 11.9 percent, according to Gallup, and from 17.4 to 10.1 percent, according to the Urban Institute. Further, the Gallup data which also provide state-by-state statistics show that the states with the greatest uptake in health insurance were more likely to have increased Medicaid eligibility and to operate state-based health insurance exchanges.

Large on-going survey efforts by both Gallup and the Urban Institute conclude that significantly fewer American adults remain without health insurance since the implementation of two key components of the Affordable Care Act in 2014: health insurance exchanges—and the availability of tax subsidies to offset premium costs—and Medicaid expansion.

Uninsured Rate Falls Nationally

The Gallup-Healthways Well-Being Index has tracked the percentage of Americans, ages 18 to 65, without health insurance since early 2008. According to Gallup's latest data for the first quarter of 2015, the rate of uninsured people has dropped to 11.9

percent from 18 percent in the last quarter of 2013, before the implementation of the ACA's major insurance coverage provisions.[1] (See Figure A.)

The Urban Institute's Health Reform Monitoring Survey data, in a national sample, indicate that 10.1 percent of adults remained uninsured in the first quarter of 2015, down from 17.4 percent in the last quarter of 2013.[2] (See Figure A.)

The end of the first quarter of 2015 coincided with the close of the 2014–15 open enrollment period for purchasing insurance and qualifying for tax subsidies through the ACA health exchanges, as well as the imposition of tax penalties for those who do not have health insurance. The 2014–15 open enrollment period was the second under the ACA.

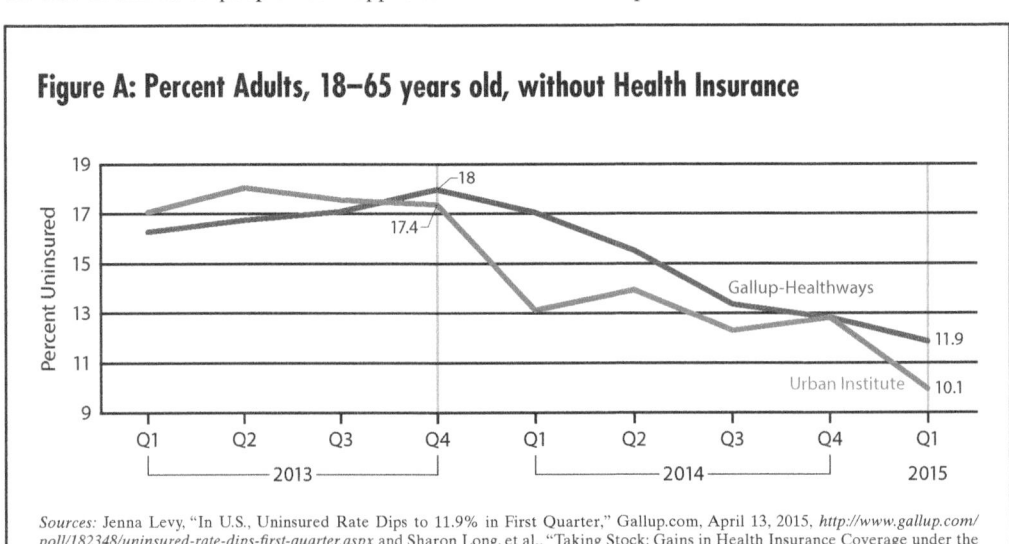

Figure A: Percent Adults, 18–65 years old, without Health Insurance

Sources: Jenna Levy, "In U.S., Uninsured Rate Dips to 11.9% in First Quarter," Gallup.com, April 13, 2015, *http://www.gallup.com/poll/182348/uninsured-rate-dips-first-quarter.aspx* and Sharon Long, et al., "Taking Stock: Gains in Health Insurance Coverage under the ACA as of March 2015," Urban Institute Health Policy Center, April 16, 2015, *http://hrms.urban.org/briefs/Gains-in-Health-Insurance-Coverage-under-the-ACA-as-of-March-2015.html.*

Table A: Uninsured Rates Drop, 2013 to 2014, in 49 States; Biggest Drops in States with Medicaid Expansion

State	Percent uninsured 2013	Percent uninsured 2014	Change in uninsured (% points)	Medicaid expansion in 2014	State-based exchange or partnership in 2014
Alabama	17.7	14.5	-3.2	No	No
Alaska	18.9	16.1	-2.8	No	No
Arizona	20.4	17.5	-2.9	Yes	No
Arkansas	22.5	11.4	-11.1	Yes	No
California	21.6	15.3	-6.3	Yes	Yes
Colorado	17	11.2	-5.8	Yes	Yes
Connecticut	12.3	6	-6.3	Yes	Yes
Delaware	10.5	9.6	-0.9	Yes	No
Florida	22.1	18.3	-3.8	No	No
Georgia	21.4	19.1	-2.3	No	No
Hawaii	7.1	6	-1.1	Yes	Yes
Idaho	19.9	15.2	-4.7	No	Yes
Illinois	15.5	11	-4.5	Yes	No
Indiana	15.3	13.6	-1.7	No (a)	No
Iowa	9.7	8.3	-1.4	Yes	No
Kansas	12.5	14.4	1.9	No	No
Kentucky	20.4	9.8	-10.6	Yes	Yes
Louisiana	21.7	17.2	-4.5	No	No
Maine	16.1	11.6	-4.5	No	No
Maryland	12.9	7.8	-5.1	Yes	Yes
Massachusetts	4.9	4.6	-0.3	Yes	Yes
Michigan	12.5	10.8	-1.7	Yes	No
Minnesota	9.5	7.4	-2.1	Yes	Yes
Mississippi	22.4	18.7	-3.7	No	No
Missouri	15.2	13.4	-1.8	No	No
Montana	20.7	15.8	-4.9	No	No
Nebraska	14.5	12.8	-1.7	No	No
Nevada	20	15.7	-4.3	Yes	Yes (d)
New Hampshire	13.8	12.8		Yes	No
New Jersey	14.9	11.7	-3.2	Yes	No
New Mexico	20.2	15.3	-4.9	Yes	Yes (d)
New York	12.6	10.1	-2.5	Yes	Yes
North Carolina	20.4	16.1	-4.3	No	No
North Dakota	15	14.1	-0.9	Yes	No
Ohio	13.9	10.5	-3.4	Yes	No
Oklahoma	21.4	18.5	-2.9	No	No
Oregon	19.4	11.7	-7.7	Yes	Yes (d)
Pennsylvania	11	10.3	-0.7	No (b)	No
Rhode Island	13.3	9.4	-3.9	Yes	Yes
South Carolina	18.7	15.4	-3.3	No	No
South Dakota	14	12.7	-1.3	No	No
Tennessee	16.8	15.1	-1.7	No	No
Texas	27	24.4	-2.6	No	No
Utah	15.6	13.3	-2.3	No	No
Vermont	8.9	7.4	-1.5	Yes	Yes
Virginia	13.3	13	-0.3	No	No
Washington	16.8	10.1	-6.7	Yes	Yes
West Virginia	17.6	10.9	-6.7	Yes	No
Wisconsin	11.7	8.4	-3.3	No (c)	No
Wyoming	16.6	12.4	-4.2	Yes	No

Sources: Gallup-Healthways Well-Being Index, *http://www.gallup. com/poll/181664/arkansas-kentucky-improvement-uninsured-rates.* aspx and on-going CSG research on state implementation of the Affordable Care Act.

Key:
(a) Indiana 1115 waiver started 2/1/2015.
(b) Pennsylvania 1115 waiver started 1/1/2015.
(c) Wisconsin did not technically expand under the ACA provisions but already was providing coverage to adults up to the poverty level.
(d) Nevada, New Mexico, and Oregon have state-based exchanges, using federal platform.

Figure B: States with Greatest Decrease in Rates of Uninsured, 2013–14

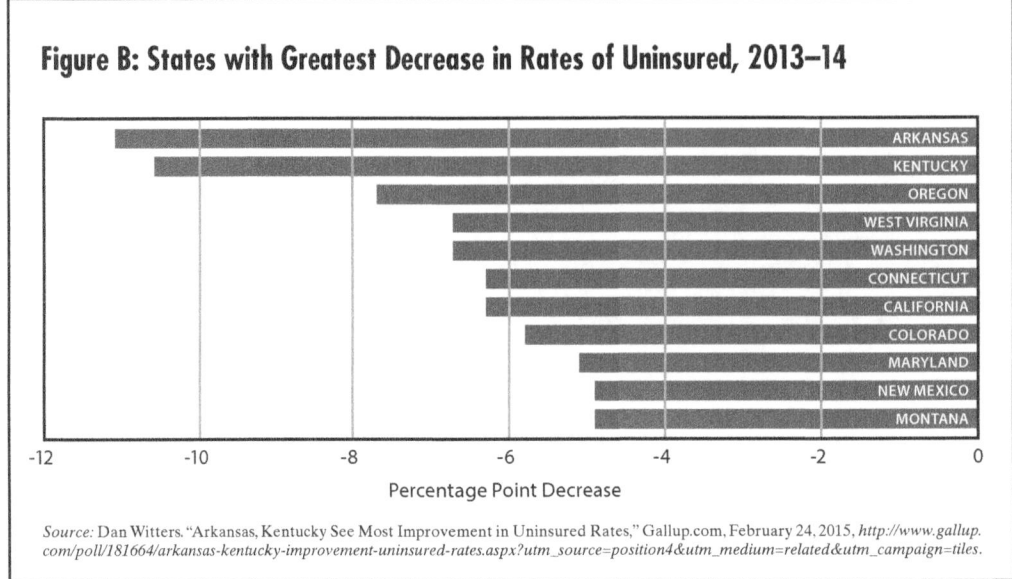

Source: Dan Witters. "Arkansas, Kentucky See Most Improvement in Uninsured Rates," Gallup.com, February 24, 2015, *http://www.gallup.com/poll/181664/arkansas-kentucky-improvement-uninsured-rates.aspx?utm_source=position4&utm_medium=related&utm_campaign=tiles.*

Uninsured Rate Falls in 2014 for all States Except Kansas

Between 2013 and 2014, according to the Gallup-Healthways data, uninsured rates fell in all states except Kansas.[3] (See Table A.)

The states with the 10 biggest drops in rates of the uninsured, with exception of Montana, made the state decision to expand Medicaid. These states range from Arkansas—with an 11.1 percentage point drop —to Montana and New Mexico, tied with 4.9 percentage point decreases. And all states, except Kansas, had some drop in their rate of uninsured residents.

In its methodology notes, Gallup reported the sampling error—the survey was conducted by landline and cellular telephone—is plus or minus one to two percentage points except for the states with the smallest populations, such as Alaska, North Dakota, Vermont and Wyoming, where the sampling error is close to plus or minus 4 percentage points. The vast majority of states' change in insurance coverage did not fall within the sampling error.[4]

Did the Affordable Care Act Make a Difference?

Of the states with the biggest drop in rates of the uninsured between 2013 and 2014 (see Figure B), only Montana did not chose to expand Medicaid eligibility. The June 2010 decision of the U.S. Supreme Court made Medicaid expansion a state option, not a state mandate.

During 2014, 25 states and the District of Columbia expanded income eligibility for Medicaid under the Affordable Care Act option. Wisconsin already had in place eligibility to the federal poverty level under a previously approved waiver. Pennsylvania's Medicaid expansion began on Jan. 1, 2015, and Indiana's expansion began on Feb. 1, 2015.

In the remaining 22 states, some low-income adults without children remain in the coverage gap between Medicaid and eligibility for tax subsidies to offset the premium prices of policies purchased through the health exchanges. This coverage gap in the states that have so far decided against expanding Medicaid eligibility has been estimated by the Kaiser family Foundation to impact about 4 million Americans.[5] Kaiser determined 43 percent of adults in the coverage gap are full-time workers, 36 percent are between 35 and 54 years old, 82 percent are in excellent, very good or good health; and 43 percent are white.[6]

Only three of the states with the top performance in terms of increasing health insurance coverage did not create state-based health exchanges. While the performance of the state-based exchanges and the federal exchange differed, all individuals who purchased insurance through the exchanges were assessed for eligibility for tax subsidies to increase the affordability of premiums. CSG estimated, based on U.S. Department of Health and Human Services data, that the total annual value of tax subsidies in 2015 will be approximately $34 billion.[7]

The decision of states to create their own state-based exchanges, or by default to depend upon the federally operated exchange, healthcare.gov, may have repercussions on health insurance coverage rates if the Supreme Court finds in favor of the plaintiffs in the *King v. Burwell* case. A decision is expected by the end of June 2015. CSG calculated the annual value of the subsidies at risk tops $24 billion and benefits 7.7 million individuals in the 34 states where the Supreme Court could declare subsidies unlawful.[8]

Notes

[1] Jenna Levy, "In U.S., Uninsured Rate Dips to 11.9% in First Quarter," Gallup.com, April 13, 2015, *http://www.gallup.com/poll/182348/uninsured-rate-dips-first-quarter.aspx*.

[2] Sharon Long, et al., "Taking Stock: Gains in Health Insurance Coverage under the ACA as of March 2015," Urban Institute Health Policy Center, April 16, 2015, *http://hrms.urban.org/briefs/Gains-in-Health-Insurance-Coverage-under-the-ACA-as-of-March-2015.html*.

[3] Dan Witters. "Arkansas, Kentucky See Most Improvement in Uninsured Rates," Gallup.com, Feb. 24, 2015, *http://www.gallup.com/poll/181664/arkansas-kentucky-improvement-uninsured-rates.aspx?utm_source=position4&utm_medium=related&utm_campaign=tiles*.

[4] Ibid.

[5] Rachael Garfield, et al., "The Coverage Gap: Uninsured Poor Adults in States that Do Not Expand Medicaid — An Update," Kaiser Family Foundation, April 17, 2015, *http://kff.org/health-reform/issue-brief/the-coverage-gap-uninsured-poor-adults-in-states-that-do-not-expand-medicaid-an-update/*.

[6] Ibid.

[7] Debra Miller, "Insurance Subsidies at Risk in Supreme Court's *King v. Burwell* Case," The Council of State Governments, March 30, 2015, *http://knowledgecenter.csg.org/kc/content/insurance-subsidies-risk-supreme-courts-king-v-burwell-case*.

[8] Ibid.

About the Author

Debra Miller is director of health policy in The Council of State Governments' national headquarters office in Lexington, Ky. She has over thirty years of experience analyzing states' health programs for low- and middle-income children and adults. Her work has appeared in the 2010, 2012 and 2014 volumes of *The Book of the States*.

Table 9.11
HEALTH INSURANCE COVERAGE STATUS BY STATE FOR ALL PEOPLE: 2013
(In thousands)

State or other jurisdiction	Total	Covered and not covered by health insurance during the year			
		Covered	Percent	Not covered	Percent
United States	311,158	265,977	85.5	45,181	14.5
Alabama	4,755	4,110	86.4	645	13.6
Alaska..	712	580	81.5	132	18.5
Arizona...	6,521	5,403	82.9	1,118	17.1
Arkansas.......................................	2,907	2,442	84.0	465	16.0
California......................................	37,832	31,331	82.8	6,500	17.2
Colorado.......................................	5,173	4,444	85.9	729	14.1
Connecticut...................................	3,541	3,209	90.6	333	9.4
Delaware	912	828	90.9	83	9.1
Florida..	19,245	15,392	80.0	3,853	20.0
Georgia...	9,801	7,955	81.2	1,846	18.8
Hawaii	1,345	1,254	93.3	91	6.7
Idaho..	1,592	1,335	83.8	257	16.2
Illinois..	12,705	11,086	87.3	1,618	12.7
Indiana...	6,472	5,569	86.0	903	14.0
Iowa...	3,045	2,798	91.9	248	8.1
Kansas	2,837	2,489	87.7	348	12.3
Kentucky.......................................	4,312	3,696	85.7	616	14.3
Louisiana	4,523	3,772	83.4	751	16.6
Maine...	1,314	1,167	88.8	147	11.2
Maryland.......................................	5,834	5,241	89.8	593	10.2
Massachusetts	6,614	6,367	96.3	247	3.7
Michigan.......................................	9,784	8,713	89.0	1,072	11.0
Minnesota.....................................	5,363	4,923	91.8	440	8.2
Mississippi....................................	2,925	2,425	82.9	500	17.1
Missouri..	5,931	5,158	87.0	773	13.0
Montana	999	835	83.5	165	16.5
Nebraska.......................................	1,841	1,632	88.7	209	11.3
Nevada..	2,757	2,187	79.3	570	20.7
New Hampshire	1,309	1,168	89.3	140	10.7
New Jersey	8,792	7,631	86.8	1,160	13.2
New Mexico	2,052	1,669	81.4	382	18.6
New York.......................................	19,400	17,331	89.3	2,070	10.7
North Carolina...............................	9,645	8,136	84.4	1,509	15.6
North Dakota	708	635	89.6	73	10.4
Ohio...	11,398	10,141	89.0	1,258	11.0
Oklahoma......................................	3,770	3,104	82.3	666	17.7
Oregon..	3,893	3,322	85.3	571	14.7
Pennsylvania	12,569	11,347	90.3	1,222	9.7
Rhode Island	1,036	916	88.4	120	11.6
South Carolina...............................	4,678	3,939	84.2	739	15.8
South Dakota	827	734	88.7	93	11.3
Tennessee	6,395	5,508	86.1	887	13.9
Texas..	25,977	20,228	77.9	5,748	22.1
Utah...	2,874	2,472	86.0	402	14.0
Vermont..	621	576	92.8	45	7.2
Virginia...	8,054	7,064	87.7	991	12.3
Washington....................................	6,864	5,904	86.0	960	14.0
West Virginia.................................	1,825	1,570	86.0	255	14.0
Wisconsin	5,669	5,151	90.9	518	9.1
Wyoming	573	496	86.6	77	13.4
Dist. of Columbia	636	594	93.3	42	6.7

Source: U.S. Census Bureau, 2013 American Community Survey. (Numbers in thousands)
URL: *https://www.census.gov/hhes/www/hlthins/data/incpovhlth/2013/acs-tables.html*

Table 9.12
NUMBER AND PERCENT OF CHILDREN UNDER 19 YEARS OF AGE, AT OR BELOW
200 PERCENT OF POVERTY, BY HEALTH INSURANCE COVERAGE AND STATE: 2013
(In thousands)

State or other jurisdiction	Total children under 19 years, all income levels	At or below 200 percent of poverty		Health insurance coverage			
		Number	Percent	With		Without	
				Number	Percent	Number	Percent
United States	76,194	33,917	44.5	30,394	39.9	3,523	4.6
Alabama	1,162	591	50.9	554	47.7	38	3.2
Alaska.................................	197	64	32.3	56	28.5	7	3.8
Arizona...............................	1,673	862	51.5	720	43.1	141	8.4
Arkansas.............................	732	403	55.1	376	51.4	27	3.7
California	9,518	4,507	47.3	4,018	42.2	488	5.1
Colorado.............................	1,289	489	38.0	428	33.2	62	4.8
Connecticut........................	817	249	30.5	235	28.8	14	1.7
Delaware	211	83	39.5	78	36.9	5	2.6
Florida................................	4,179	2,067	49.5	1,758	42.1	309	7.4
Georgia...............................	2,594	1,305	50.3	1,126	43.4	179	6.9
Hawaii	315	104	33.0	98	31	6	2.0
Idaho..................................	443	217	49.1	194	43.9	23	5.2
Illinois................................	3,128	1,291	41.3	1,212	38.7	79	2.5
Indiana................................	1,634	746	45.7	656	40.1	91	5.5
Iowa	747	280	37.5	263	35.2	17	2.3
Kansas	748	308	41.2	278	37.1	30	4.0
Kentucky	1,047	498	47.6	459	43.8	39	3.7
Louisiana	1,154	578	50.1	536	46.4	42	3.6
Maine..................................	267	112	41.8	104	39.1	7	2.7
Maryland	1,394	435	31.2	405	29.1	30	2.2
Massachusetts	1,444	447	30.9	437	30.3	10	0.7
Michigan.............................	2,322	1053	45.4	990	42.6	63	2.7
Minnesota...........................	1,322	438	33.2	396	29.9	43	3.2
Mississippi..........................	767	443	57.7	398	52	44	5.8
Missouri..............................	1,434	647	45.1	580	40.5	66	4.6
Montana	232	103	44.2	90	39	12	5.3
Nebraska.............................	479	198	41.3	179	37.5	18	3.8
Nevada................................	687	339	49.3	267	38.9	71	10.4
New Hampshire	279	79	28.4	74	26.5	5	1.9
New Jersey	2,106	690	32.7	620	29.4	70	3.3
New Mexico	533	291	54.7	261	49	30	5.7
New York	4,383	1,863	42.5	1,760	40.2	103	2.3
North Carolina....................	2,364	1,164	49.2	1,059	44.8	105	4.4
North Dakota	165	51	30.8	45	27.2	6	3.6
Ohio...................................	2,729	1,196	43.8	1,102	40.4	94	3.4
Oklahoma............................	980	494	50.4	434	44.2	60	6.1
Oregon................................	885	406	45.9	375	42.4	31	3.5
Pennsylvania	2,804	1,118	39.9	1,026	36.6	92	3.3
Rhode Island	219	88	40.1	81	36.9	7	3.2
South Carolina....................	1,118	576	51.6	523	46.8	53	4.7
South Dakota	211	87	41.0	78	37.1	8	3.9
Tennessee	1,544	777	50.3	715	46.3	62	4.0
Texas..................................	7,310	3,619	49.5	3,014	41.2	604	8.3
Utah...................................	929	363	39.1	304	32.7	59	6.4
Vermont..............................	128	47	36.6	45	35.3	2	1.4
Virginia..............................	1,930	670	34.7	611	31.7	59	3.0
Washington.........................	1,644	657	40.0	604	36.8	53	3.2
West Virginia......................	392	191	48.7	179	45.7	12	3.0
Wisconsin	1,349	533	39.5	493	36.5	41	3.0
Wyoming	143	46	32.2	43	30.0	3	2.2
Dist. of Columbia	114	54	47.5	53	46.4	1	1.2

Source: U.S. Census Bureau, 2013 American Community Survey.
URL: http://www.census.gov/hhes/www/hlthins/data/incpovhlth/2013/acs-tables.html.

Data in this table represent children under 19 in the poverty universe. Percentages are based on the total children under 19. For more information on poverty and the poverty universe see: *http://www.census.gov/hhes/www/poverty/methods/definitions.html.*

Transportation Innovations Present Policy Challenges Now and For the Future

By Sean Slone

They are known as ride-sharing or ride-hailing companies and in some circles as transportation network companies or TNCs. Uber, Lyft and other similar companies provide an update on the traditional taxi service, complete with a smartphone interface that has made them popular among the tech-savvy, millennial generation. State governments have found themselves playing catch-up in recent years, trying to authorize and regulate an upstart industry their laws never envisioned. But as policymakers navigate the particulars of basic operational questions like how to protect riders from unsafe or unsavory drivers, these services present a myriad of other policy questions for both the short and long terms.

When the taxi-like, smartphone app-enabled services Uber and Lyft began operating in Virginia in the spring of 2014, state officials had a problem.

"This technology forced us in Virginia to look at our ordinances, which clearly did not contemplate this type (of service)," recalled Delegate Thomas Davis Rust, who chairs the Transportation Committee in the Virginia House. "The Division of Motor Vehicles actually issued … a cease and desist order, which of course (the companies) objected to. Then the Division of Motor Vehicles, the attorney general, the governor's office worked something out and issued them a temporary license to operate with the understanding that we would do legislation that would … bring them in to our regulatory scheme, which basically had to be pretty much totally rewritten."[1]

The resulting legislation, House Bill 1662, which Rust sponsored and Gov. Terry McAuliffe signed in February 2015, includes background checks for drivers, a zero-tolerance policy regarding the use of drugs and alcohol, a 21-and-older age requirement and a $1 million insurance liability coverage requirement.

"When the rules that govern our taxi industry were first written many years ago, no one had any idea that companies like Uber and Lyft would come along," McAuliffe said upon signing the bill. "So we had to find a way to ensure Virginia's consumers were protected and that these new and innovative businesses could operate legally in the commonwealth."[2]

Rust's bill, which he says is among the statutes now being looked at closely by other states seeking to regulate Uber and Lyft, was the result of extensive negotiations among all the interests—the

Division of Motor Vehicles, the transportation network companies themselves, the taxi companies with which they compete, the insurance industry and the legislature.

"If you were to have told me six months ago that we would be able to bring everyone together, I would have thought it would have been … extremely difficult, because when there are cease and desist orders and lawsuits on both sides, you don't think you're going to get the parties together," Rust said.

While policymakers like Rust wrestle with the particulars of how to regulate—but not overregulate—companies like Uber and Lyft, analysts say the services are at the leading edge of a variety of innovations, trends and paradigm shifts that could dramatically reshape transportation and prompt even more policy and planning headaches for those trying to envision the future. Among them: the sharing economy that has helped popularize the services, the shifting preferences of the millennial generation, the potential impact for transportation funding, and the consumer choice and heightened expectations triggered by smartphones and smartphone apps.

Balancing Act for Policymakers

As they seek to deal with the myriad of short- and long-term issues presented by services like Uber and Lyft, policymakers must walk a tightrope between competing interests representing past and future.

"From the public policy perspective, it's always a balancing act between your critical job to make sure the public is protected and safe while also not putting in place onerous regulations that are going to stifle innovation and keep new products and services from coming on the market," said Paul Feenstra, senior vice president for government and external affairs at the Intelligent Transportation Society of America (ITS America), a Washington, D.C.-based organization that argues for the advancement of research, development and deployment of intelligent transportation system technologies to improve the nation's transportation system.[3]

Analysts say it's important for policymakers not to regulate out the efficiencies the services are able to provide to the point where they become indistinguishable from everything else in the marketplace.

"The more you legislate entrepreneurialism, you stifle innovation and so (policymakers) should consider a balance that lasts longer than one year in a law," said Darran Anderson, chief strategy and innovation officer at the Texas Department of Transportation. "If you want to make a lasting law, think about how well it might translate in the future. (That's) what I always try to tell (legislators). ... If you really feel that you must write legislation, ... you might just have a few rules or statutes in the first thing you establish and see where it goes from there. And then if you find that (other) things need to be addressed, then you have that opportunity. You didn't create an unnecessary restriction early on."[4]

Feenstra said fortunately cooperation and collaboration of the kind Rust experienced with Virginia's Uber bill has become commonplace when policymakers find themselves at the intersection of transportation and technology.

"We have automakers that now have Silicon Valley tech centers and we've got Silicon Valley companies that are now in Detroit and elsewhere," Feenstra said. "You've got partnerships that are developing and have developed between the GMs, Fords, Toyotas and the Googles and Apples and Intels and Qualcomms. The automakers know how to make automobiles. They know how to work with the state regulators and they have a lot of experience in developing vehicles that can operate safely on the road. You've got technology companies that know how to secure data transmission and know how to implement effective communication systems and provide the public with high tech consumer applications. And so having these two industries working closely together and in close collaboration with regulators so that everybody is on the same page moving forward I think is important."

The Sharing Economy

Uber and Lyft are two of the most successful companies considered a part of the "sharing economy," an evolving socio-economic trend involving the sharing of underutilized human and physical resources and consumer empowerment through technological innovation.

"The sharing economy is leveraging new technology and an apparently exceedingly pent up latent demand for convenience and quality that the public is looking for," said Joseph Coughlin, founder and director of the AgeLab at the Massachusetts Institute of Technology and an expert on demographic change and technology trends. "As long as you've got the connectivity and the convenience factor of a smartphone at your disposal to be able to get a ride when you want, how you want it, to go where you want, that is going to have profound implications over the priority and the value we place on having a car that sits unused in a driveway or on a street side."[5]

But Coughlin and others say one downside to the sharing economy is its potential to displace some of the transportation options that have become mainstays of the existing system.

"We see taxi companies fighting Uber and Lyft in metropolitan area after metropolitan area because their pre-existing way of providing the service is quite expensive and less effective, quite frankly, than these new generation services coming in," said Thomas Kern, interim president and CEO of the aforementioned ITS America. "Over time, what's going to happen is those more traditional services will have to change or they'll go out of business."[6]

Frank Shafroth, director of the Center for State and Local Leadership at George Mason University, wrote in a March 2015 article for *Governing* magazine that the explosion of services like Uber is "the beginning of an economic upheaval every bit as significant as the industrial revolution." The impact to the taxi industry and ultimately to state and local governments are but one reason.

"Uber and Lyft continue to undercut the licensed, regulated and revenue-producing taxi industry," Shafroth wrote. "State and local officials confront not just equity issues, but also declines in traditional taxi-related revenues — and a singular switch from a highly regulated industry of licensing and insurance requirements."[7]

Transportation Preferences of Millennials

Another aspect of the policy challenge presented by Uber and Lyft is the popularity of such services among millennials—those Americans born roughly between 1980 and 2000—who have expressed transportation preferences much different from previous generations.

"Younger people are less interested in owning cars," said Glen Hiemstra, founder and CEO of the website Futurist.com. "Some of that is financial for sure, but much is a shift in values. A car is less needed to achieve freedom, less needed to connect with friends, and more of us live in metro areas with transportation alternatives, alternatives are more sustainable, etc. Implications are that there will be a declining percentage of car ownership per population, and a desire for alternatives to be enabled and enhanced. Eventually, private car ownership will decline precipitously and shared ownership, single-use options and so on will dominate."[8]

But the differences of millennials may extend not just to their preferred mode of transport but to other aspects of their lives as well, said MIT's Coughlin.

"They're also putting off having kids," he said. "Well, if they're getting married later, having children later or not having children at all—which is a big issue—then maybe they will stay more urbanized and look for more urban transportation-like solutions, whether it's traditional public transportation or Uber or car-sharing, biking and the like."

Impact on Transportation Funding

If the future holds fewer cars on the roads, more Americans living in the city and driving shorter distances, it's likely to have a significant impact on what has been the major source of transportation funding for much of the past century at both the state and federal levels: the per gallon gas tax. Revenues from such taxes already have been in decline due to increasing fuel efficiency and other factors.

While a mileage-based user fee has long been touted by transportation researchers as a potential replacement for the gas tax, it would have little benefit in a future that involves less car ownership and more on-demand services like Uber and Lyft. Some say a revenue mechanism that would incorporate a larger base of Americans might be a better bet.

"The fact of the matter is that transportation … is a national benefit," said Coughlin. "Even if you don't drive, even if you don't even ride your bike, you are getting something delivered to your supermarket or to your doorstep using that infrastructure."

Coughlin said what's needed is a general use of infrastructure tax that incorporates not only the transportation infrastructure, but also the communications infrastructure because we already are seeing a convergence of the two.

"If people have lightened up on their VMT (vehicle miles traveled) to use their 3G, then maybe we need to start thinking (that) it's the nation's communications infrastructure that we need to finance and ensure is the best in the world to remain competitive and connected."

Smartphones Apps Enabling Mobility, Choice

That convergence is manifesting itself these days in the use of smartphones and smartphone apps to drive transportation systems and empower travelers.

"Mobile company Ericsson has just predicted that by 2020 there will be 50 billion connected devices in the U.S.," said ITS America's Feenstra. "That's just a phenomenal amount and that reflects the fact that … we're already seeing a ton of new consumer applications based on the smartphone."

Feenstra points to RideScout, an app that gives users real-time information about all transportation options available to them at a given time.

"Smartphones are key to enabling transportation choice, whether (it's) an Uber app, a one-bus-away app, … quick mapping of alternate routes and times, or simply substituting for travel," said Hiemstra. "This is all just getting started."

But the proliferation of these tools already is having a profound effect on the users of the transportation system and policymakers will soon need to take notice, many believe.

"I think the biggest thing that they have done is frankly, they have changed the consumer's expectation," said Coughlin. "I think what transportation is now up against is it is no longer going to be acceptable that the system has got a pothole here or that the train's not on time. …

"And Uber is only one little indicator. Of course it can pick me up exactly where I am and I'll know it's going to be here within three minutes with precision. So what the app has done is it has taught the consumer to expect more from an enterprise that is still built upon the legacies of the past decades. And we're all working hard both in research and practice, but it's really going to have to take a rethinking of the transportation enterprise to be more responsive to a consumer who is empowered by a smartphone."

Notes

[1] Telephone Interview with Del. Thomas Davis Rust. February 2015.

[2] Jacob Geiger. "McAuliffe signs bill setting rules for Uber, Lyft." *Richmond Times-Dispatch*. Feb. 17, 2015. Accessed from: *http://www.richmond.com/business/local/article_ecc1b973-d99d-57c0-9241-209da466ec42.html*

[3] Telephone interview with Paul Feenstra, March 3, 2015.

[4] Telephone interview with Darran Anderson, March 11, 2015

[5] Telephone interview with Joseph Coughlin, March 16, 2015.

[6] Telephone interview with Thomas Kern, March 3, 2015.

[7] Frank Shafroth. "The Unforeseen Fiscal Challenges of Uber-Like Services." *Governing*. March 2015. Accessed from: *http://www.governing.com/columns/public-money/gov-uber-unforeseen-fiscal-challenges.html*

[8] E-mail interview with Glen Hiemstra, March 13, 2015.

About the Author

Sean Slone is the director of transportation and infrastructure policy at The Council of State Governments. He staffs CSG's Transportation Public Policy Committee and writes about transportation policy for CSG publications, such as *Capitol Ideas* magazine, the Capitol Comments blog and Capitol Research policy materials. He is the author of two CSG national reports: *Transportation and Infrastructure Finance* (2009) and *Shovel-Ready or Not? State Stimulus Successes on the Road to Recovery* (2010). He has written an article for The Book of the States each year since 2010.

HIGHWAYS

Table 9.13
REVENUES USED BY STATES FOR HIGHWAYS: 2013 (In thousands of dollars)

State or other jurisdiction	Beginning balance total (a)	Highway-user revenues (b) Motor-fuel taxes	Motor-vehicle and motor-carrier taxes	Road and crossing tolls	Total	Appropriations from general funds (c)	Other state imposts	Miscellaneous	Bond proceeds Original issues	Refunding issues	Payments from other governments — Federal funds Federal Hwy. Admin.	Other agencies	From local government	Total receipts
United States	80,994,251	28,319,653	20,980,798	11,038,000	60,338,451	7,324,978	9,101,728	12,274,907	20,406,588	6,404,536	38,678,907	2,206,343	3,379,773	160,116,208
Alabama	272,402	591,378	162,256	…	753,634	168,682	43,601	6,940	401,293	…	832,948	68,475	1,487	2,277,060
Alaska	…	30,546	38,008	48,610	117,164	408,005	235	6,262	…	…	436,610	15,359	…	983,635
Arizona	1,292,300	589,588	299,893	…	889,481	50	679,458	31,272	302,723	541,610	810,740	36,165	3,015	3,294,514
Arkansas	527,088	377,526	148,054	…	525,580	54,895	46,049	245,888	230,752	…	552,413	43,661	14,568	1,713,806
California	24,537,267	4,335,676	2,516,751	850,619	7,703,046	1,900,564	640,150	736,644	1,922,654	191,931	3,368,589	154,714	1,059,412	17,677,704
Colorado	1,319,808	448,694	790,528	49,800	1,289,022	5,500	…	16,090	…	…	698,348	19,849	…	2,028,809
Connecticut	1,420,589	131,653	63,837	169	195,659	89,817	79,000	81,486	755,085	…	497,443	14,890	3,221	1,716,601
Delaware	1,945,002	62,614	82,467	562,160	707,241	125,985	…	193,732	…	…	192,216	3,414	4,714	1,227,302
Florida	2,993,915	1,177,523	1,093,385	1,328,132	3,599,040	…	288,202	1,410,113	(196,154)	2,027,118	1,718,924	330,029	254,923	9,432,195
Georgia	2,131,957	239,022	48,577	20,765	308,364	165,337	567,444	136,329	…	60,814	1,189,727	76,440	33,360	2,537,815
Hawaii	256,224	79,083	154,672	…	233,755	…	…	4,554	…	…	197,200	3,738	…	439,247
Idaho (e)	181,829	204,727	163,906	…	368,633	…	…	33,832	53,933	…	306,312	12,803	4,874	780,387
Illinois (e)	2,210,110	751,591	901,157	1,009,484	2,662,232	730,245	404	443,791	990,025	…	1,447,565	24,311	1,909	6,300,482
Indiana	37,996	613,682	206,933	195,781	1,016,396	103,675	18,647	543,735	2,070	…	1,088,338	8,893	38,578	2,820,331
Iowa	320,100	420,657	838,589	…	1,259,246	53,557	25,757	8,139	…	…	389,337	78,035	…	1,814,071
Kansas	662,500	338,500	46,621	94,224	479,345	…	407,270	75,029	29,658	20,732	341,616	10,283	35,140	1,399,073
Kentucky	395,987	747,873	596,526	…	1,344,399	5,637	…	171,318	…	…	672,509	7,006	…	2,200,869
Louisiana	2,428,636	583,022	172,529	16,248	771,799	257,964	54,051	147,566	238,731	479,819	823,802	33,354	2,145	2,809,231
Maine (e)	152,455	236,801	82,641	133,701	453,143	…	…	16,496	22,125	…	176,029	4,718	…	672,511
Maryland	1,339,838	244,361	370,487	479,882	1,094,730	90,679	101,576	152,508	326,096	…	551,627	9,503	128,845	2,455,564
Massachusetts (d)	650,734	335,747	114,082	310,232	760,061	407,635	617,205	290,765	684,681	…	522,773	7,772	…	3,290,892
Michigan	937,583	788,285	794,748	49,637	1,632,670	275,732	84,876	151,187	857	10,130	905,011	21,088	21,550	3,103,101
Minnesota	1,510,962	719,784	572,966	…	1,292,750	…	488,852	52,735	265,700	…	562,367	20,676	181,635	2,864,715
Mississippi	134,593	360,999	157,112	…	518,111	…	45,783	5,714	222,500	…	551,071	16,581	108,054	1,467,814
Missouri	1,246,757	617,910	267,383	…	885,293	2,994	336,925	19,422	…	…	905,287	46,676	49,980	2,246,577
Montana	51,888	106,404	108,043	…	214,447	297	7,049	47,063	…	…	407,553	31,634	1,938	709,981
Nebraska	132,333	294,015	81,564	…	375,579	48,746	210,422	16,800	…	…	345,209	9,122	497,230	1,503,108
Nevada (d)	216,894	264,692	208,590	620	473,902	…	839	47,967	21,453	138,030	344,750	8,965	30,087	1,065,993
New Hampshire (d)	1,975,375	129,663	148,658	116,425	394,746	…	…	79,166	226,193	16,543	139,218	86,010	1,024	942,900
New Jersey	2,146,462	372,272	852,450	1,741,567	2,966,289	…	…	344,175	4,192,490	…	605,967	23,712	3,849	8,136,482
New Mexico	466,768	165,434	208,764	…	374,198	16,127	25,783	47,863	1,324	261,769	420,585	20,928	…	1,168,577
New York (e)	194,530	472,014	524,791	1,212,399	2,209,204	672,531	1,563,511	1,830,556	944,479	680,610	1,802,197	27,277	23,013	9,753,378
North Carolina	2,042,775	1,795,980	594,835	2,061	2,392,876	…	561,920	73,544	…	47,887	1,168,029	61,181	21,083	4,326,520
North Dakota	331,960	193,948	114,779	…	308,727	192,760	…	9,879	…	…	333,370	7,229	20,728	872,693
Ohio	1,587,959	1,656,582	791,671	273,967	2,722,220	9,006	…	178,207	1,487,538	…	1,602,614	18,301	83,878	6,101,764
Oklahoma	802,341	89,349	82,352	238,204	409,905	…	621,358	234,405	…	…	529,162	16,214	33,771	1,844,814
Oregon	2,904,715	415,725	427,212	…	842,937	50,628	13,754	115,224	(67)	67	386,672	70,572	…	1,479,787
Pennsylvania	3,790,068	1,293,451	461,868	1,216,335	2,971,654	762,387	36,068	602,153	1,393,859	69,525	1,560,498	48,941	14,860	7,459,945
Rhode Island	81,894	55,740	28,784	18,806	103,330	30,990	…	21,233	29,500	…	268,248	5,185	…	458,486
South Carolina	369,637	535,615	191,781	14,935	742,331	57	2,546	7,655	…	…	617,583	8,459	32,033	1,410,664

See footnotes at end of table.

REVENUES USED BY STATES FOR HIGHWAYS: 2013 (In thousands of dollars) —Continued

State or other jurisdiction	Beginning balance total (a)	Highway-user revenues (b)				Appropriations from general funds (c)	Other state imposts	Miscellaneous	Bond proceeds		Payments from other governments			Total receipts
											Federal funds		From local government	
		Motor-fuel taxes	Motor-vehicle and motor-carrier taxes	Road and crossing tolls	Total				Original issues	Refunding issues	Federal Hwy. Admin.	Other agencies		
South Dakota	31,497	118,548	99,268	-	217,816	-	76,055	34,997	-	-	318,465	6,594	7,606	661,533
Tennessee	1,290,652	646,546	266,339	35	912,920	-	67,334	27,147	-	-	919,802	33,651	50,932	2,011,786
Texas	6,947,504	1,410,889	2,709,439	676,392	4,796,720	39,845	42,526	1,738,122	4,017,818	1,152,931	2,615,319	285,886	323,930	15,013,097
Utah	849,641	245,322	124,771	645	370,738	57,701	443,683	70,657	10,983	-	383,165	71,068	34,386	1,431,398
Vermont	7,277	75,167	128,105	-	203,272	29,611	-	17,866	-	-	197,143	61,855	2,543	523,273
Virginia	3,099,975	646,590	721,896	59,718	1,428,204	212,145	715,319	135,909	144,599	-	1,345,075	21,840	73,160	4,076,250
Washington	1,758,688	1,077,502	585,403	232,928	1,895,833	-	27,275	1,511,964	1,182,074	555,475	937,576	35,934	41,320	6,187,451
West Virginia........	140,951	399,037	271,670	83,519	754,226	20,414	3,315	37,034	-	-	463,471	19,172	541	1,298,173
Wisconsin	771,938	788,412	517,774	-	1,306,186	257,953	71,312	26,847	330,564	149,545	722,623	119,611	134,451	3,119,092
Wyoming	38,424	41,931	39,042	-	80,973	76,827	73,452	32,775	-	-	284,224	34,052	-	582,303
Dist. of Columbia ...	50,136	14,719	59,295	-	74,014	-	16,654	15	103,265	51,341	234,210	3,515	-	483,014

Source: U.S. Department of Transportation, Federal Highway Administration, *Highway Statistics,* 2012. (Dec. 2013).

Note: Detail may not add to totals due to rounding. This table was compiled from reports of state authorities.

Key:
(a) Any differences between beginning balances and the closing balances on last year's table are the result of accounting adjustments, inclusion of funds not previously reported, etc.
(b) Amounts shown represent only those highway user revenues that were expended on state or local roads.
(c) Amounts shown represent gross general fund appropriations for highways reduced by the amount of highway-user revenues placed in the State General Fund.
(d) Amounts shown represent data reported for 2010.
(e) Amounts shown represent data reported for 2011.

Table 9.14
STATE DISBURSEMENTS FOR HIGHWAYS: 2013 (In thousands of dollars)

State or other jurisdiction	Capital outlay State administered highways (a)	Capital outlay Local roads and streets	Capital outlay Total	Maintenance and service total State administered highways (a)	Maintenance and service total Local roads and streets	Maintenance and service total Total	Administration, research and planning	Highway law enforcement and safety
United States	68,864,703	5,547,563	74,412,266	21,222,139	798,723	22,020,862	8,470,808	9,413,902
Alabama	977,342	103,184	1,080,526	178,867	–	178,867	196,655	233,353
Alaska	592,321	–	592,321	226,048	–	226,048	80,587	47,529
Arizona	846,523	104,448	950,971	156,963	–	156,963	216,192	195,495
Arkansas	1,211,878	–	1,211,878	190,915	68,958	259,873	138,018	95,532
California	3,150,281	123,493	3,273,774	1,191,119	207,028	1,398,147	882,589	1,789,723
Colorado	889,930	58,979	948,909	464,304	–	464,304	141,016	143,321
Connecticut	794,825	–	794,825	118,301	–	118,301	339,728	17,511
Delaware	402,879	–	402,879	519,531	–	519,531	76,820	86,036
Florida	4,631,136	127,439	4,758,575	941,457	–	941,457	274,358	387,570
Georgia	1,174,364	200,882	1,375,246	277,918	–	277,918	290,520	230,324
Hawaii	207,202	–	207,202	64,472	–	64,472	79,177	9,677
Idaho	368,602	59,637	428,239	102,982	–	102,982	29,055	43,414
Illinois	3,375,680	88,749	3,464,429	694,609	12,106	706,715	302,416	107,937
Indiana	1,531,068	–	1,531,068	698,302	67,187	765,489	96,708	20,790
Iowa	735,152	–	735,152	194,358	–	194,358	117,764	121,934
Kansas	595,123	82,987	678,110	154,483	–	154,483	68,634	88,489
Kentucky	1,385,414	319,426	1,704,840	405,879	70,315	476,194	35,723	100,454
Louisiana	1,053,504	50,642	1,104,146	129,433	4,867	134,300	97,353	97,183
Maine (c)	380,032	18,435	398,467	211,599	–	211,599	20,954	25,724
Maryland	1,207,048	80,021	1,287,069	348,676	–	348,676	98,153	171,104
Massachusetts (b)	1,064,039	281,767	1,345,806	286,495	–	286,495	274,098	203,205
Michigan	1,081,219	990,603	2,071,822	290,501	–	290,501	98,277	266,590
Minnesota	978,918	–	978,918	507,597	–	507,597	184,983	130,999
Mississippi	935,623	112,174	1,047,797	81,173	–	81,173	73,537	32,861
Missouri	965,791	128,614	1,094,405	454,056	–	454,056	68,603	247,085
Montana	435,946	–	435,946	126,100	–	126,100	48,267	53,235
Nebraska	483,938	292,284	776,222	154,378	124,963	279,341	98,251	72,684
Nevada	499,589	–	499,589	114,828	–	114,828	130,317	98,195
New Hampshire (b)	319,550	12,837	332,387	80,126	–	80,126	95,025	91,799
New Jersey	2,811,302	–	2,811,302	780,218	–	780,218	150,104	388,616
New Mexico	409,549	–	409,549	39,489	–	39,489	315,661	21,363
New York (c)	2,869,968	513,867	3,383,835	1,514,762	–	1,514,762	381,201	402,611
North Carolina	2,641,080	–	2,641,080	810,317	–	810,317	285,668	375,877
North Dakota	791,560	16,174	807,734	42,103	–	42,103	23,715	29,168
Ohio	2,182,487	297,260	2,479,747	442,067	–	442,067	176,888	315,090
Oklahoma	1,107,209	105,228	1,212,437	198,569	–	198,569	82,261	102,513
Oregon	522,508	117,180	639,688	241,283	13,062	254,345	136,644	65,070
Pennsylvania	2,961,634	225,423	3,187,057	1,438,550	–	1,438,550	514,749	628,457
Rhode Island	246,706	25,073	271,779	97,955	1,454	99,409	45,196	26,506
South Carolina	861,775	–	861,775	310,814	53,564	364,378	101,980	127,199
South Dakota	477,740	54,451	532,191	60,659	–	60,659	45,690	37,154
Tennessee	1,367,091	35,418	1,402,509	293,688	–	293,688	171,538	30,201
Texas	8,721,805	304,045	9,025,850	1,999,832	–	1,999,832	302,763	819,539
Utah	495,620	–	495,620	534,759	–	534,759	87,299	71,733
Vermont	152,264	89,762	242,026	122,745	1,943	124,688	58,613	61,771
Virginia	1,585,919	–	1,585,919	1,623,047	–	1,623,047	314,374	212,389
Washington	3,836,147	50,763	3,886,910	666,517	167,651	834,168	209,037	322,063
West Virginia	734,790	–	734,790	295,956	–	295,956	113,313	43,853
Wisconsin	1,440,359	139,157	1,579,516	215,348	–	215,348	210,382	79,891
Wyoming	372,273	–	372,273	93,430	–	93,430	55,476	43,085
Dist. of Columbia	–	337,161	337,161	34,561	5,625	40,186	34,478	–

See footnotes at end of table.

STATE DISBURSEMENTS FOR HIGHWAYS: 2013 (In thousands of dollars) — Continued

State or other jurisdiction	Interest	Bond retirement Current revenues or sinking funds	Refunding bonds	Grants-in-aid to local governments	Total disbursements	Balances end-of-year Reserves for current highway work	Reserves for debt service	Total
United States	7,911,418	9,262,531	6,404,536	14,283,020	152,179,343	88,350,643	580,473	88,931,116
Alabama	78,554	14,540	–	205,844	1,988,339	561,123	–	561,123
Alaska...........................	9,918	22,120	–	12,111	990,634	(6,999	–	(6,999
Arizona........................	214,907	155,400	541,610	693,074	3,124,612	1,462,202	–	1,462,202
Arkansas......................	11,640	66,210	–	–	1,783,151	457,743	–	457,743
California	435,995	128,776	191,931	4,236,102	12,337,037	29,877,934	–	29,877,934
Colorado......................	44,063	187,620	–	651,003	2,580,236	768,381	–	768,381
Connecticut	165,432	513,580	–	32,515	1,981,892	1,155,298	–	1,155,298
Delaware	108,478	174,281	–	–	1,368,025	1,740,265	64,014	1,804,279
Florida.........................	443,154	328,523	2,027,118	386,201	9,546,956	2,874,681	4,473	2,879,154
Georgia........................	145,428	295,270	60,814	3,157	2,678,677	1,991,095	–	1,991,095
Hawaii..........................	20,245	30,813	–	51,278	462,864	232,607	–	232,607
Idaho............................	28,656	24,050	–	134,994	791,390	170,826	–	170,826
Illinois.........................	339,135	294,237	–	496,319	5,711,188	2,799,404	–	2,799,404
Indiana.........................	188,891	48,172	–	173,615	2,824,733	33,594	–	33,594
Iowa	–	–	–	667,837	1,837,045	295,151	1,975	297,126
Kansas	83,898	180,658	20,732	144,486	1,419,490	626,755	15,328	642,083
Kentucky	135,497	82,790	–	1,556	2,537,054	59,802	–	59,802
Louisiana.....................	134,130	30,573	479,819	1,633	2,079,137	3,158,730	–	3,158,730
Maine (c).....................	35,192	13,415	–	77	705,428	119,538	–	119,538
Maryland	195,559	221,776	–	160,598	2,482,935	1,312,467	–	1,312,467
Massachusetts (b)	349,534	295,437	–	168,447	2,923,022	1,018,604	–	1,018,604
Michigan......................	118,592	129,523	10,130	36,338	3,021,773	1,018,911	–	1,018,911
Minnesota....................	54,202	71,174	–	912,056	2,839,929	1,535,748	–	1,535,748
Mississippi	38,524	41,216	–	98,856	1,413,964	167,785	20,658	188,443
Missouri.......................	135,810	153,525	–	254,212	2,407,696	1,085,638	–	1,085,638
Montana	4,955	10,630	–	43,531	722,664	39,205	–	39,205
Nebraska......................	–	–	–	281,125	1,507,623	127,269	549	127,818
Nevada.........................	26,490	53,300	138,030	3,172	1,063,921	184,112	34,854	218,966
New Hampshire (b)	103,541	42,904	16,543	30,263	792,588	2,125,687	–	2,125,687
New Jersey	940,015	2,258,738	–	163,174	7,492,167	2,790,777	–	2,790,777
New Mexico	79,765	112,711	261,769	56,008	1,296,315	339,030	–	339,030
New York (c)................	851,044	928,994	680,610	372,545	8,515,602	1,432,306	–	1,432,306
North Carolina............	105,708	94,356	47,887	144,432	4,505,325	1,863,970	–	1,863,970
North Dakota..............	1,593	3,725	–	114,330	1,022,368	182,285	–	182,285
Ohio	61,410	256,960	–	1,102,979	4,835,141	2,854,582	–	2,854,582
Oklahoma....................	119,784	101,270	–	915	1,817,749	791,217	38,189	829,406
Oregon.........................	98,500	65,040	67	3,823	1,263,177	3,121,325	–	3,121,325
Pennsylvania	455,626	530,286	69,525	309,998	7,134,248	4,062,541	53,224	4,115,765
Rhode Island...............	37,323	31,052	–	–	511,265	29,115	–	29,115
South Carolina............	17,475	48,200	–	1,610	1,522,617	257,684	–	257,684
South Dakota..............	–	–	–	1,539	677,233	15,797	–	15,797
Tennessee	–	–	–	289,438	2,187,374	1,115,064	–	1,115,064
Texas...........................	1,014,366	264,183	1,152,931	444,404	15,023,868	6,624,645	312,088	6,936,733
Utah.............................	114,584	240,295	–	64,128	1,608,418	672,621	–	672,621
Vermont.......................	1,609	2,904	–	26,860	518,471	12,079	–	12,079
Virginia........................	143,919	220,660	–	386,726	4,487,034	2,654,070	35,121	2,689,191
Washington..................	37,805	168,626	555,475	476,778	6,490,862	1,455,277	–	1,455,277
West Virginia...............	19,962	56,566	–	10,978	1,275,418	163,706	–	163,706
Wisconsin	160,510	247,568	149,545	428,081	3,070,841	820,189	–	820,189
Wyoming	–	–	–	3,874	568,138	52,589	–	52,589
Dist. of Columbia	–	19,884	–	–	431,709	46,218	–	46,218

Source: U.S. Department of Transportation, Federal Highway Administration, *Highway Statistics, 2013*, (December 2014).

Note: Detail may not add to totals due to rounding. This table was compiled from reports of state authorities.

Key:
(a) Includes expenditures for local roads and streets under State control. Most local roads are under State control in Delaware, North Carolina, Virginia, and West Virginia.
(b) Amounts shown represent data reported for 2010.
(c) Amounts shown represent data reported for 2011.

Table 9.15
PUBLIC ROAD LENGTH MILES BY OWNERSHIP: 2013

State or other jurisdiction	Rural mileage						Urban mileage					
	State highway agency	County	Town, township & municipal (a)	Other jurisdictions (b)	Federal agency (c)	Total rural roads	State highway agency	County	Town, township & municipal (a)	Other jurisdictions (b)	Federal agency (c)	Total urban roads
Total	128,807	316	58	1,704	150	131,034	72,745	4,971	16,569	2,184	131	96,600
United States total	128,746	316	58	1,704	150	130,973	72,397	4,971	16,568	2,184	131	96,251
Alabama	2,760	9	—	—	—	2,769	1,384	17	106	—	—	1,508
Alaska	2,027	1	1	—	—	2,028	185	19	0	—	—	204
Arizona	2,096	19	5	—	15	2,135	805	123	1,035	—	1	1,964
Arkansas	2,502	1	—	—	—	2,503	1,164	5	79	—	—	1,248
California	4,413	96	20	—	—	4,529	4,103	729	4,650	2	—	9,484
Colorado	3,313	4	4	—	—	3,320	1,111	68	409	—	—	1,587
Connecticut	208	—	1	—	—	209	1,184	—	49	—	—	1,233
Delaware	170	—	—	—	—	170	253	—	1	—	—	253
Florida	3,632	40	2	—	—	3,672	4,517	319	203	—	—	5,039
Georgia	3,653	4	2	—	—	3,660	3,003	208	147	—	4	3,362
Hawaii	66	—	—	4	—	70	340	29	—	8	—	377
Idaho	2,239	2	—	21	—	2,263	309	8	71	124	1	512
Illinois	3,583	12	1	58	—	3,653	3,497	305	203	229	—	4,235
Indiana	2,367	10	1	—	—	2,378	1,839	175	420	—	—	2,433
Iowa	3,999	—	—	—	—	3,999	1,026	9	84	—	—	1,118
Kansas	3,527	—	—	177	—	3,704	611	65	408	61	3	1,149
Kentucky	2,480	—	—	—	—	2,480	785	3	23	—	—	811
Louisiana	1,589	—	—	12	—	1,601	1,460	41	136	14	—	1,651
Maine	1,008	—	—	85	—	1,093	210	—	—	26	—	235
Maryland	493	—	—	12	—	505	1,432	66	211	104	32	1,844
Massachusetts	181	—	4	—	—	184	1,719	755	999	64	1	2,783
Michigan	3,044	6	1	—	—	3,051	2,183	438	—	—	—	3,377
Minnesota	4,042	15	—	—	—	4,058	1,161	84	41	—	—	1,285
Mississippi	2,327	18	2	—	—	2,347	1,007	19	202	—	3	1,231
Missouri	3,801	1	3	—	—	3,805	1,724	11	344	1	—	2,080
Montana	3,867	—	—	—	—	3,867	311	—	3	—	—	315
Nebraska	3,185	—	—	—	—	3,185	372	18	150	—	—	540
Nevada	2,005	—	—	—	—	2,005	386	81	25	37	—	530
New Hampshire	517	—	1	12	—	530	244	—	77	80	—	401
New Jersey	191	9	—	38	—	238	1,690	583	87	371	—	2,732
New Mexico	2,560	—	—	—	—	2,561	521	—	229	—	—	750
New York	2,175	6	—	296	—	2,478	2,911	312	1,036	361	—	4,622
North Carolina	2,847	—	—	—	20	2,866	2,927	—	39	—	16	2,982
North Dakota	3,444	3	—	—	—	3,447	201	—	45	—	—	246
Ohio	2,310	7	—	151	—	2,468	3,581	65	404	91	—	4,140
Oklahoma	2,423	—	—	484	—	2,907	1,026	26	358	114	—	1,524
Oregon	3,330	21	1	1	—	3,352	734	47	224	3	—	1,008
Pennsylvania	2,782	—	2	277	—	3,060	3,633	19	217	272	—	4,141
Rhode Island	90	—	—	—	—	90	433	—	39	5	—	477
South Carolina	2,229	—	—	—	—	2,229	1,370	—	4	—	—	1,374

See footnotes at end of table.

PUBLIC ROAD LENGTH MILES BY OWNERSHIP: 2013—Continued

State or other jurisdiction	Rural mileage						Urban mileage					
	State highway agency	County	Town, township & municipal (a)	Other jurisdictions (b)	Federal agency (c)	Total rural roads	State highway agency	County	Town, township & municipal (a)	Other jurisdictions (b)	Federal agency (c)	Total urban roads
South Dakota	7,527	1	1	—	42	7,571	240	—	26	—	—	265
Tennessee	2,608	—	—	—	—	2,608	1,980	7	145	—	—	2,132
Texas	10,066	5	—	—	—	10,071	6,534	179	1,505	158	—	8,376
Utah	1,846	—	—	—	11	1,857	905	4	19	—	—	928
Vermont	596	—	7	—	—	603	101	—	43	—	—	144
Virginia	2,512	—	1	24	—	2,537	1,208	31	502	15	58	1,814
Washington	2,345	3	—	—	—	2,348	1,232	170	802	8	—	2,213
West Virginia	1,388	—	—	51	—	1,439	503	—	5	35	—	542
Wisconsin	3,645	23	1	—	—	3,669	1,912	368	316	—	—	2,595
Wyoming	2,740	—	—	—	62	2,802	316	2	12	—	—	331
Dist. of Columbia	—	—	—	—	—	—	113	—	—	—	14	126
Puerto Rico (d)	61	—	—	—	—	61	348	—	1	—	—	349

Source: U.S. Department of Transportation, Federal Highway Administration, *Highway Statistics, 2013.*

Key:
— Not applicable or unavailable
(a) Prior to 1999, municipal was included with other jurisdictions.
(b) Includes state park, state toll, other state agency, other local agency and other roadways not identified by ownership.
(c) Roadways in federal parks, forests, and reservations that are not part of the state and local highway systems.
(d) 2009 data.

Table 9.16
APPORTIONMENT OF FEDERAL FUNDS ADMINISTERED BY THE FEDERAL HIGHWAY ADMINISTRATION
FEDERAL-AID HIGHWAY PROGRAM APPORTIONMENTS UNDER THE MOVING AHEAD FOR PROGRESS IN
THE 21st CENTURY ACT (MAP-21) FOR FISCAL YEAR 2014 (a)(b) (In thousands of dollars)

State or other jurisdiction	National highway system	Surface transportation program	Highway safety improvement program	Railway- highway crossings program	Congestion mitigation and air quality improvement program	Metropolitan planning program	Appalachian apportioned total
United States total..	149,899	68,949	15,372	1,100	10,411	1,532	247,263
Alabama...................	457,293	210,341	45,720	4,532	11,397	2,980	732,263
Alaska......................	289,366	133,099	30,698	1,100	27,493	2,198	483,955
Arizona....................	413,210	190,064	42,731	2,676	51,829	5,671	706,182
Arkansas..................	309,421	142,324	30,242	3,761	12,302	1,665	499,714
California	1,930,325	887,889	196,843	15,280	463,638	48,493	3,542,468
Colorado..................	298,581	137,338	29,642	3,169	42,256	5,126	516,113
Connecticut.............	277,794	127,777	29,221	1,306	44,200	4,473	484,771
Delaware	95,480	43,918	9,392	1,100	11,651	1,727	163,268
Florida	1,143,438	525,946	117,189	8,464	13,585	20,068	1,828,689
Georgia....................	745,815	343,052	74,083	7,875	67,884	7,530	1,246,239
Hawaii......................	96,315	44,302	9,484	1,100	10,349	1,695	163,244
Idaho.......................	166,697	76,675	16,542	1,777	12,802	1,569	276,061
Illinois.....................	793,513	364,991	76,854	10,345	109,991	16,538	1,372,231
Indiana....................	552,613	254,185	53,355	7,372	47,071	5,073	919,669
Iowa........................	293,745	135,114	27,055	5,225	11,285	1,922	474,345
Kansas	225,079	103,529	18,847	5,887	9,507	1,888	364,737
Kentucky	398,221	183,169	40,108	3,653	13,686	2,455	641,292
Louisiana.................	421,573	193,910	42,305	4,021	11,436	4,167	677,413
Maine......................	105,801	48,665	10,401	1,226	10,287	1,785	178,166
Maryland	331,012	152,255	34,084	2,291	53,645	6,721	580,007
Massachusetts	327,494	150,637	33,563	2,425	63,361	8,712	586,192
Michigan..................	593,834	273,145	57,856	7,400	73,936	10,037	1,016,208
Minnesota................	377,579	173,675	35,537	5,955	32,196	4,432	629,373
Mississippi	289,164	133,007	28,398	3,378	11,208	1,648	466,804
Missouri...................	563,830	259,344	56,451	5,509	23,549	5,038	913,720
Montana...................	241,673	111,162	24,714	1,844	14,873	1,742	396,007
Nebraska	170,138	78,258	15,133	3,563	10,278	1,606	278,977
Nevada.....................	200,497	92,222	20,933	1,100	32,539	3,182	350,473
New Hampshire	94,020	43,246	9,232	1,100	10,339	1,532	159,470
New Jersey	539,935	248,353	55,705	3,628	103,995	12,066	963,683
New Mexico	217,521	100,053	22,289	1,614	11,402	1,560	354,440
New York.................	899,994	413,969	92,734	6,167	183,021	24,204	1,620,088
North Carolina........	605,016	278,288	60,040	6,445	51,204	5,638	1,006,630
North Dakota..........	144,907	66,653	12,299	3,625	10,510	1,627	239,622
Ohio........................	756,020	347,746	74,490	8,589	95,666	11,228	1,293,739
Oklahoma................	380,848	175,178	36,668	5,183	11,744	2,506	612,128
Oregon....................	292,722	134,643	29,279	2,889	19,382	3,508	482,423
Pennsylvania	934,243	429,722	96,084	6,580	104,402	12,572	1,583,603
Rhode Island...........	126,675	58,266	12,820	1,100	10,421	1,800	211,082
South Carolina........	401,416	184,639	39,889	4,222	13,087	3,053	646,307
South Dakota..........	164,488	75,659	15,754	2,322	12,255	1,713	272,191
Tennessee	492,999	226,764	49,464	4,712	37,007	4,659	815,605
Texas.......................	2,002,345	921,016	202,537	17,501	164,476	23,722	3,331,597
Utah........................	203,267	93,496	20,769	1,568	12,908	3,141	335,149
Vermont...................	115,947	53,332	11,641	1,100	11,835	2,032	195,887
Virginia...................	586,030	269,556	59,937	4,462	54,867	7,328	982,180
Washington..............	388,755	178,815	38,657	4,063	36,917	7,097	654,305
West Virginia...........	258,519	118,911	26,423	1,985	14,309	1,650	421,798
Wisconsin	442,348	203,466	43,000	5,610	27,372	4,431	726,227
Wyoming	149,899	68,949	15,372	1,100	10,411	1,532	247,263
Dist. of Columbia ...	90,575	41,662	8,853	1,100	10,092	1,720	154,003

Source: U.S. Department of Transportation, Map 21 Funding Tables/ FHWA Notice N4510.774, January 2015.

Key:
(a) Apportioned Federal-aid highway program funds authorized for FY 2014 pursuant to the Moving Ahead for Progress in the 21st Century Act (MAP-21), Public Law (Pub. L.) 112-141.
(b) Shows the state-by-state, program-by-program apportionment amounts, before post-apportionment set-asides, and before penalties available for MAP-21 for FY 2014.

Criminal Records and Employment

By Liam Julian

Tens of millions of Americans have criminal records, and for even the most qualified among them, finding a job can be incredibly difficult. When these people remain unemployed, it's bad for them, certainly, but also bad for their communities. Thus, a number of states and localities have adopted so-called "Fair Hiring" practices, which seek to ensure job applicants with criminal records can show a potential employer their qualifications before being required to reveal their criminal histories.

Some 65 to 70 million Americans of working age have criminal records. Finding a job isn't easy for anyone, but it's especially difficult for them.

Sometimes formerly incarcerated individuals simply lack the knowledge and skills that would make them employable; other times, they are barred from filling certain jobs by federal or state laws. In many instances, employers are simply reluctant to hire people with criminal records and eliminate such applicants from consideration before even reviewing their qualifications.

Yet hiring people with criminal records is not only good for them, it's also good for their communities. According to a 2013 The Council of State Governments' Justice Center report, reintegrating individuals with criminal histories into the workforce can make neighborhoods and families safer and more stable. "If releasees and supervisees are working," the report's authors write, "their time is being spent in constructive ways and they are then less likely to engage in crime and disorder in their neighborhoods."

"The question for me," former Nebraska state Sen. Bill Avery told me, "was why go to the expense and effort of preparing prisoners for jobs on the outside when we have barriers that impede their ability to even be considered for employment.'Ban the Box' was an important effort to remove one of those barriers."

"Ban the Box" is a catchy phrase describing a national political movement—often called "Fair Hiring"—that seeks to ensure job applicants with criminal records can show a potential employer their qualifications before being required to reveal their criminal histories. "Box" refers to the job application checkbox that people with criminal records are asked to tick.

State Actions

Though there have been some federal actions supporting Fair Hiring practices, such as the U.S. Equal Employment Opportunity Commission's 2012 guidance on the issue, most Ban the Box action has happened at the state and local level.

Avery introduced Nebraska's Ban the Box legislation—Legislative Bill 932—in January 2014. The bill prohibits public sector employers from asking about a job applicant's criminal past until they establish whether the applicant meets minimum job requirements. The Business and Labor Committee unanimously passed the bill, which was then attached to a larger prison reform bill that passed 46-0 and was signed it into law in April 2014.

The first state to pass such a law was Hawaii, which removed questions about criminal history from job applications for both public and private positions in 1998. But the phrase "Ban the Box" didn't appear until the early 2000s, when the activist group All of Us or None used the term to describe its California-based campaign. The slogan caught on, and Ban the Box became recognized shorthand for the movement behind an array of state and local legislation, ordinances, and orders focused on removing questions about criminal history from job applications.

Thirteen states and the District of Columbia have passed Ban the Box legislation, according to Michelle Natividad Rodriguez of the National Employment Law Project, which supports Fair Hiring. Nearly 100 cities and counties effectively have done the same. Six states and the District of Columbia—as well as some 25 localities and cities, such as Montgomery County and Baltimore, Md.; Philadelphia and San Francisco—have applied Ban the Box requirements to private as well as public employers. In fact, some private businesses like Wal-Mart and Target have voluntarily removed questions about criminal history from their job applications nationwide.

The belief at the heart of all these Fair Hiring laws is much the same—that steady employment for people with criminal records is a fundamental part of those individuals' successful reintegration into society. And it's good for society at large. A

Table A: Ban the Box Legislation

State (year reform adopted)	Relevant statutes	Employers		Job-related screening*	Limits information	Other protections
		Private	*Public*			
California (2010, 2013)	Cal. Lab. Code § 432.9	. . .	Public (S, Co)	. . .	Arrests, Expunged, Time limit	. . .
Colorado (2012)	Colo. Rev. Stat. § 24-5-101	. . .	Public (S, L)	Whether there is "direct relationship" between conviction and job	Arrests, Expunged	. . .
Connecticut (2010)	Conn. Gen. Stat. § 46a-80	. . .	Public (S, L**)	Consider nature of crime and relationship to the job	Arrests, Expunged	N, C
Delaware (2014)	Del. Code tit. 19. § 711(g); Del. Code tit. 29, § 6909B	. . .	Public (S, Co)	Consider nature of offense and job	. . .	. . .
Hawaii (1998)	Haw. Rev. Stat. §§ 378-2, 378-2.5	Private	Public (S, Co)	Conviction bears "rational relationship" to position	Time limit	. . .
Illinois (2013, 2014)	820 Ill. Comp. Stat.§ 75; Executive Order 1 (2013)	Private	Public (S)	. . .	. . .	. . .
Maryland (2013)	Md. Code Ann., State Pers. & Pens. § 2-203	. . .	Public (S)	. . .	. . .	. . .
Massachusetts (2010)	Mass. Gen. Laws ch. 151B, § 4 (9 ½); ch. 6, §§ 171A, 172	Private	Public (S, L**, Co)	. . .	Time limit	N, C
Minnesota (2009, 2013)	Minn. Stat. § 364	Private	Public (S, L**, Co)	Determine if conviction "directly relates" to position	Arrests, Expunged	N
Nebraska (2014)	Neb. Rev. Stat. § 48-202	. . .	Public (S, Co)	. . .	. . .	. . .
New Jersey (2014)	AB 1999	Private	Public (S, Co)	. . .	Expunged	. . .
New Mexico (2010)	N.M. Stat. §§ 28-2-1 to 28-2-6	. . .	Public (S, L**, Co)	Conviction "directly relates" to employment	Arrests	N
Rhode Island (2013)	R.I. Gen. Laws §§ 28-5-6, 28-5-7	Private	Public (S, Co)	. . .	Arrests	. . .

Source: National Employment Law Project, Jan. 2015. *http://www.nelp.org/page/-/SCLP/Ban-the-Box-Fair-Chance-State-and-Local-Guide.pdf?nocdn=1]].*
Key:
* Some of these components existed prior to the legislation listed here.
**Removal of conviction inquiry from the licensing application is not required.

C* — Copy of record
Co — Counties and cities
L — Licensing
N — Notification of denial
S — State
Arrests — Arrests not leading to convictions.
Expunged — Expunged or similar.
Time Limit — Time Limit on record.

study by the Economy League of Greater Philadelphia found that the employment of people who formerly were incarcerated has a significant positive impact on tax revenues. In a 2010 report, the Center for Economic and Policy Research found unemployment rates among ex-offenders costs the national economy about $60 billion a year in lost productivity and lowered output of goods and services.

Addressing a Problem

Many policymakers are convinced that Fair Hiring is part of the solution to this problem.

Former California Assembly Member Roger Dickinson is among them. He authored his state's Ban the Box legislation, Assembly Bill 218, which Gov. Jerry Brown signed into law in October 2013 and took effect in July 2014.

"California's recidivism rate is one of the highest in the nation," Dickinson said. "And there is growing consensus that we must do all we can as government agencies to reduce reoffending in smart, coordinated and cost-effective ways."

Much like Nebraska's law, California's law prohibits government agencies from asking a job applicant about his or her criminal history until those agencies have evaluated the applicant's basic employment qualifications. It doesn't apply to jobs that require a background check, such as jobs in child care facilities, or to criminal justice-related positions.

The bill had many supporters, but it had its critics, too. The California State Association of Counties, for example, wrote that the bill took away "the discretion of local agencies to design an employment policy that works locally."

According to Dickinson, some disagreement with this legislation stemmed from misconceptions. Certain critics, he said, believed the law "would require those with conviction histories to be hired." Others believed it "would put vulnerable populations, like children, in harm's way."

But since Assembly Bill 218 became law and its provisions have been clarified, some critics have softened their positions.

In Georgia, Ban the Box recently became law. The state's Criminal Justice Reform Council in 2014 recommended Georgia remove questions about criminal history from state agency job application forms and "instead require that the applicant disclose any criminal history during a face-to-face interview." In late February, Gov. Nathan Deal signed an executive order requiring state agencies to offer qualified applicants the chance in a follow-up interview to "contest the content and relevance of a criminal record" and demonstrate their personal rehabilitation.

"Such policies," the order read, "will allow returning citizens an opportunity to explain their unique circumstances in person to a potential employer."

New Jersey has also passed statewide Fair Hiring legislation, which was signed into law by Gov. Chris Christie in August 2014. New Jersey had been considering versions of Fair Hiring legislation for several years. Prior iterations were "much more restrictive on employers," Jill Cohen, a Trenton-based employment litigator, told Law360 in late 2014.

The legislation Christie signed disallows public or private employers with 15 or more employees from asking about a job candidate's criminal history until after the first interview. It also prevents employers from considering expunged or pardoned convictions in their hiring decisions.

In 2013 and 2014 alone, nine states—California, Delaware, Georgia, Illinois, Maryland, Minnesota, Nebraska, New Jersey and New Mexico—passed statewide Fair Hiring laws.

Local Campaigns

Fair Hiring campaigns have been especially successful at the local level.

Boston was the first locality to adopt Fair Hiring when it implemented several policies in 2004 designed to prevent undue discrimination against people in city government jobs who had criminal records. Boston expanded those policies in July 2006, by removing all questions about criminal history from city job applications and requiring private vendors that work with the city to do the same.

Boston also eliminated background checks for most city positions. On the occasions when background checks still are required, they're usually not conducted on an applicant until after a conditional offer of employment has been made.

In Indianapolis, the city council passed an ordinance in January 2014 disallowing city and county agencies and all their contractors from asking job applicants about criminal history until after the first interview. Indianapolis Mayor Greg Ballard strongly supported Fair Hiring.

"Re-entry has been one of the mayor's top priorities," Marc Lotter, Ballard's communications director, told me. Each year, Lotter said, about 5,000 formerly incarcerated individuals come to Indianapolis, and "most of them want to turn their lives around. With Ban the Box, it eliminates the chance they'll be instantly disqualified, and it encourages employers to first identify the potential these applicants hold."

Eliminating instant disqualification of applicants was certainly on the minds of Atlanta's city council, which in October 2014 passed a Fair Hiring ordinance that declared "lack of employment" to be "a significant factor in recidivism rates," and noted that "barriers to employment for formerly incarcerated people are significant factors in the creation of a permanent underclass."

Atlanta's ordinance mandates an applicant for a job with the city can be asked about criminal history only once it's been determined the applicant is otherwise qualified for the position. And if the city declines to hire a candidate after conducting a background check, the applicant must be notified within 30 days and provided a copy of the check that highlights the disqualifying convictions.

Ban the Box has been extended not only to public sector employers and the vendors they work with, but also to all private employers in 25 local jurisdictions across the country. Philadelphia became the first to do so when Mayor Michael Nutter signed the Fair Criminal Record Screening Standards bill into law in April 2011. The law prohibits every employer in Philadelphia from inquiring about or considering arrests that aren't pending and for crimes for which the individual was never convicted. It also disallows employers, with rare exceptions, from asking about an applicant's criminal history until after the first job interview.

In several cases, Fair Hiring proponents have seen their legislative victories tempered by implementation challenges, including pushback from employers, some of whom are reportedly finding ways around new Ban the Box laws. It's clear that employers must be included in the process of developing Fair Hiring practices and there is a growing national momentum to do just that. Many meetings—some organized in part by the CSG Justice Center—have been held to bring together employers, lawmakers and corrections officials for collaborative conversations about the ways to implement Fair Hiring most effectively, to hear employers' valid questions and concerns, and to better understand the legal issues surrounding Fair Hiring policies.

"Ex-offenders face many hurdles when reintegrating into the workplace, including lack of skills and limited education," Nutter said at Philadelphia's Fair Hiring bill signing. "One of their greatest challenges is overcoming their criminal records. This legislation will make it easier for ex-offenders to be judged by their abilities as opposed to their past. Everyone deserves a second chance."

About the Author

Liam Julian is a writer and editor at The Council of State Governments Justice Center.

Table 9.17
TRENDS IN STATE PRISON POPULATION: 2000, 2012 and 2013

| State or other jurisdiction | Total state prison population | | | Percent change 2012–2013 |
	December 31, 2013	December 31, 2012	December 31, 2000	
United States (a)...............	1,516,879	1,511,497	1,334,174	0.4
Federal (b)........................	195,098	196,574	125,044	-0.8
State (a)..........................	1,321,781	1,314,923	1,209,130	0.5
Alabama...........................	31,354	31,437	26,034	-0.3
Alaska (c).........................	2,682	2,974	2,128	-9.8
Arizona............................	39,062	38,402	25,412	1.7
Arkansas (d)	17,159	14,615	11,851	–
California	135,981	134,211	160,412	1.3
Colorado..........................	20,371	20,462	16,833	-0.4
Connecticut (c)	12,162	11,961	13,155	1.7
Delaware (c)......................	4,112	4,129	3,937	-0.4
Florida	103,028	101,930	71,318	1.1
Georgia............................	53,478	53,990	44,141	-0.9
Hawaii (c).........................	3,618	3,819	3,553	-5.3
Idaho...............................	7,549	7,985	5,535	-5.5
Illinois (e)........................	48,653	49,348	45,281	–
Indiana (f)	29,905	28,822	19,811	–
Iowa	8,654	8,686	7,955	-0.4
Kansas	9,506	9,398	8,344	1.1
Kentucky	20,330	21,466	14,919	-5.3
Louisiana.........................	39,298	40,170	35,207	-2.2
Maine	1,972	1,932	1,635	2.1
Maryland	20,988	21,281	22,490	-1.4
Massachusetts	9,643	9,999	9,479	-3.6
Michigan..........................	43,704	43,594	47,178	0.3
Minnesota........................	10,289	9,938	6,238	3.5
Mississippi	20,742	21,426	19,239	-3.2
Missouri...........................	31,537	31,244	27,519	0.9
Montana	3,642	3,609	3,105	0.9
Nebraska	4,929	4,594	3,816	7.3
Nevada (e)(g)....................	12,915	12,761	10,063	–
New Hampshire	2,848	2,790	2,257	2.1
New Jersey	22,452	23,225	29,784	-3.3
New Mexico	6,687	6,574	4,666	1.7
New York..........................	53,428	54,073	70,199	-1.2
North Carolina..................	35,181	34,983	27,043	0.6
North Dakota....................	1,513	1,512	994	0.1
Ohio................................	51,729	50,876	45,833	1.7
Oklahoma (f)	25,496	24,830	23,181	–
Oregon............................	15,180	14,801	10,553	2.6
Pennsylvania....................	50,083	50,918	36,844	-1.6
Rhode Island(c)................	2,039	1,999	1,966	2
South Carolina..................	21,443	21,725	21,017	-1.3
South Dakota....................	3,641	3,644	2,613	-0.1
Tennessee	28,521	28,411	22,166	0.4
Texas...............................	160,295	157,900	158,008	1.5
Utah................................	7,071	6,960	5,541	1.6
Vermont (c).......................	1,575	1,516	1,313	3.9
Virginia (f)	36,982	37,044	29,643	–
Washington.......................	17,947	17,254	14,666	4
West Virginia....................	6,812	7,027	3,795	-3.1
Wisconsin	21,285	20,474	20,336	–
Wyoming	2,310	2,204	1,680	4.8
Dist. of Columbia	0	0	5,008	0

Source: Bureau of Justice Statistics, National Prisoner Statistics Program, 2012–2013. *Prisoners in 2013* NCJ 247282 – p13t04.csv.

Note: Jurisdiction refers to the legal authority of state or federal correctional officials over a prisoner, regardless of where the prisoner is held. Counts are based on prisoners with sentences of more than a year under the jurisdiction of state or federal correctional officials. As of December 31, 2001, sentenced felons from the District of Columbia were the responsibility of the Federal Bureau of Prisons.

Key:
– – Not calculated.
(a) Includes imputed counts for Nevada. See Methodology for imputation strategy.

(b) Includes inmates held in nonsecure privately operated community corrections facilities and juveniles held in contract facilities.

(c) Prisons and jails form one integrated system. Data include total jail and prison populations.

(d) Changes to Arkansas' parole system in 2013 contributed to higher counts of inmates under jurisdiction.

(e) State did not submit 2012 NPS data.

(f) Counts for 2013 are not comparable to earlier years due to a change in reporting methodology.

(g) State did not submit 2013 NPS data.

Table 9.18
NUMBER OF SENTENCED PRISONERS ADMITTED AND RELEASED FROM STATE AND FEDERAL JURISDICTION: 2012 and 2013

State or other jurisdiction	Admissions (a)					Releases (b)				
	2012 total	2013 total	Percent change 2012–13	2013 New court commitments (c)	2013 Parole violations (c)(d)	2012	2013	Percent change 2012–13	2012 Unconditional (c)(e)	2012 Conditional (c)(f)
United States	608,442	631,168	3.7	450,150	164,065	636,715	623,337	-2.1	173,824	399,388
Federal	55,938	53,664	-4.1	48,818	4,845	56,037	54,785	-2.2	53,793	461
State	552,504	577,504	4.5	401,332	159,220	580,678	568,552	-2.1	120,031	398,927
Alabama	11,203	11,265	0.6	9,191	1,105	11,253	11,488	2.1	3,840	7,498
Alaska (b)(f)(g)	3,906	3,906	—	/	/	3,774	3,774	—	/	/
Arizona	12,970	13,538	4.4	11,069	2,357	13,000	12,931	-0.5	2,108	10,106
Arkansas	5,782	8,987	55.4	2,725	3,964	6,298	6,541	3.9	327	6,158
California	34,294	38,295	11.7	31,895	6,400	47,454	36,353	-23.4	/	/
Colorado	9,409	10,137	7.7	5,379	4,741	10,919	10,220	-6.4	1,454	8,609
Connecticut (f)	5,659	5,492	-3	4,597	827	6,014	5,177	-13.9	2,910	2,237
Delaware (f)	3,017	3,142	4.1	2,798	321	4,012	4,251	6	261	3,918
Florida	32,265	33,613	4.2	32,373	105	33,661	32,855	-2.4	20,736	11,776
Georgia	15,743	19,478	23.7	17,594	1,878	14,021	18,226	30	6,158	11,954
Hawaii (f)	1,524	1,380	-9.4	758	622	1,631	1,615	-1	293	802
Idaho	4,568	3,719	-18.6	3,539	180	4,617	3,761	-18.5	509	3,242
Illinois	30,877	30,959	0.3	21,761	9,026	30,108	31,370	4.2	4,460	26,742
Indiana	18,694	19,161	2.5	10,290	8,577	18,555	17,959	-3.2	1,534	16,367
Iowa	4,877	5,159	5.8	3,826	1,325	5,221	5,202	-0.4	1,150	4,002
Kansas	5,060	5,220	3.2	3,719	1,435	4,795	5,133	7	1,454	3,651
Kentucky	15,399	15,834	2.8	9,733	5,855	16,215	16,871	4	1,237	15,593
Louisiana	17,325	16,770	-3.2	11,958	4,774	17,104	17,646	3.2	1,393	16,066
Maine	846	929	9.8	607	322	1,108	971	-12.4	587	380
Maryland	9,396	9,223	-1.8	5,579	3,640	10,347	9,504	-8.1	1,311	8,108
Massachusetts (i)	2,635	2,567	-2.6	2,290	236	2,871	2,855	-0.6	2,062	763
Michigan	13,888	14,417	3.8	7,845	3,417	13,199	14,307	8.4	898	11,168
Minnesota	7,412	7,687	3.7	4,901	2,786	7,730	7,808	1	926	6,862
Mississippi	8,559	8,105	-5.3	5,972	1,915	7,725	8,201	6.2	1,329	6,727
Missouri	18,216	18,983	4.2	10,243	8,737	17,957	18,790	4.6	1,621	17,041
Montana	2,020	2,382	17.9	1,826	556	2,089	2,347	12.4	297	2,037
Nebraska	2,761	2,922	5.8	2,255	586	2,688	2,583	-3.9	761	1,799
Nevada (h)	4,929	5,855	18.8	4,817	1,018	5,556	4,903	-11.8	1,867	3,009
New Hampshire	1,696	1,659	-2.2	861	798	1,555	1,633	5	75	1,549
New Jersey	9,976	9,802	-1.7	7,203	2,598	10,817	10,766	-0.5	6,234	4,293
New Mexico	3,580	3,567	-0.4	2,453	1,114	3,371	3,345	-0.8	926	2,403
New York	23,065	22,740	-1.4	13,441	9,206	24,224	23,382	-3.5	2,541	20,550
North Carolina	12,098	14,077	16.4	12,721	1,356	12,327	13,829	12.2	6,341	7,412
North Dakota	1,160	1,222	5.3	684	536	1,069	1,173	9.7	158	1,008
Ohio	21,529	21,998	2.2	19,086	2,899	21,628	21,235	-1.8	9,092	12,003

See footnotes at end of table.

NUMBER OF SENTENCED PRISONERS ADMITTED AND RELEASED FROM STATE AND FEDERAL JURISDICTION: 2012 and 2013—Continued

State or other jurisdiction	Admissions (a)					Releases (b)				
	2012 total	2013 total	Percent change 2012–13	2014 New court commitments (c)	2013 Parole violations (c)(d)	2012	2013	Percent change 2012–13	2012 Unconditional (c)(e)	2012 Conditional (c)(f)
Oklahoma	7,697	8,019	4.2	5,618	2,401	6,947	7,374	6.1	3,804	3,476
Oregon	5,376	5,532	2.9	3,823	1,499	5,023	5,048	0.5	24	4,828
Pennsylvania (f)	18,492	20,455	10.6	11,479	8,201	18,805	19,632	4.4	3,690	15,773
Rhode Island (f)	868	810	-6.7	659	151	967	885	-8.5	614	270
South Carolina	6,802	6,431	-5.5	5,162	1,259	7,309	6,716	-8.1	2,709	3,931
South Dakota	1,986	1,842	-7.3	1,059	781	1,959	1,820	-7.1	268	1,544
Tennessee	13,922	13,803	-0.9	8,274	5,521	15,955	16,348	2.5	5,034	11,233
Texas	75,378	76,488	1.5	49,825	24,188	82,130	74,093	-9.8	10,661	61,581
Utah (f)	3,142	3,094	-1.5	1,963	1,131	3,063	2,988	-2.4	1,034	1,929
Vermont (f)	1,912	1,858	-2.8	662	1,196	1,963	1,752	-10.7	272	1,474
Virginia	11,727	11,636	-0.8	11,531	105	11,568	11,880	2.7	1,024	10,741
Washington	18,232	21,426	17.5	8,106	13,315	18,181	20,861	14.7	2,353	18,458
West Virginia	3,525	3,573	1.4	1,729	1,393	3,293	3,780	14.8	1,134	2,104
Wisconsin	6,200	7,343	—	4,645	2,671	7,724	5,475	—	287	5,134
Wyoming	907	1,004	10.7	808	196	878	895	1.9	273	618

Source: Bureau of Justice Statistics, National Prisoner Statistics Program, 2011–2012.

Note: As of December 31, 2001, sentenced felons from the District of Columbia are the responsibility of the Federal Bureau of Prisons.

Key:

/ — Not reported.

(a) Counts based on prisoners with a sentence of more than 1 year. Counts exclude transfers, escapes, and those absent without leave (AWOL). Totals include deaths, releases to appeal or bond, and other releases.

(b) Alaska did not report type of admission or release. Total admissions and releases include Alaskan reported values, but state and national totals by type of admission and release do not.

(c) Includes all conditional release violators returned to prison for either violations of conditions of release or for new crimes.

(d) Includes releases to probation, supervised mandatory releases, and other unspecified conditional releases.

(e) Includes expirations of sentence, commutations, and other unconditional releases.

(f) Prisons and jails form one integrated system. Data include total jail and prison populations.

(g) State updated 2011 admission and release totals.

(h) State did not report 2012 NPS data. Total number of admissions and releases imputed, and types of admission and release based on 2011 distribution.

(i) Changes made in the legislature to reduce discretionary paroles in 2011 are reflected in a higher parole rate in 2012.

Table 9.19
PRISON FACILITY CAPACITY, CUSTODY POPULATION, AND PERCENT CAPACITY, DECEMBER 31, 2013

State	Type of capacity measure			Custody population	Custody population as a percent of:	
	Rated capacity	Operational capacity	Design capacity	Custody population	Lowest capacity (a)	Highest capacity (a)
Federal (b)...........................	130,907	...	...	174,242	133.1	133.1
Alabama (c)........................	...	26,145	13,318	26,271	197.3	100.5
Alaska (d)	/	/	/	5,054	/	/
Arizona.............................	36,681	42,025	36,681	34,626	94.4	82.4
Arkansas............................	14,424	14,479	13,885	14,295	103	98.7
California (c)......................	...	...	86,054	122,798	142.7	142.7
Colorado............................	...	14,121	13,183	16,286	123.5	115.3
Connecticut........................	/	/	/	16,594	/	/
Delaware (c).......................	5,775	5,210	4,161	6,798	163.4	117.7
Florida (e)	...	114,995	...	100,940	87.8	87.8
Georgia (e).........................	60,638	54,583	...	53,701	98.4	88.6
Hawaii................................	...	3,327	2,291	3,752	163.8	112.8
Idaho (c)(e)........................	...	6,924	7,010	7,219	104.3	103
Illinois (e).........................	32,075	32,075	28,192	48,653	172.6	151.7
Indiana..............................	...	30,917	...	28,495	92.2	92.2
Iowa (f)..............................	...	...	7,109	8,106	114	114
Kansas	9,180	9,233	9,164	9,515	103.8	103.1
Kentucky	12,157	13,062	13,857	12,141	99.9	87.6
Louisiana (e)......................	18,121	15,531	16,764	18,794	121	103.7
Maine.................................	2,339	2,033	2,339	2,073	102	88.6
Maryland	...	23,465	...	21,676	92.4	92.4
Massachusetts	...	...	8,029	10,622	132.3	132.3
Michigan (c)(g)..................	44,846	43,985	...	43,704	99.4	97.5
Minnesota..........................	...	9,099	...	9,391	103.2	103.2
Mississippi (e)	...	25,691	...	15,591	60.7	60.7
Missouri (c)........................	...	31,681	...	31,499	99.4	99.4
Montana.............................	1,679	...	...	1,666	99.2	99.2
Nebraska (c).......................	...	3,969	3,175	5,012	157.9	126.3
Nevada (h)..........................	/	/	/	/	/	/
New Hampshire (c)	...	2,848	2,190	2,848	130	100
New Jersey	19,461	20,959	22,902	19,528	100.3	85.3
New Mexico	6,485	7,428	7,428	3,783	58.3	50.9
New York............................	52,855	53,408	52,330	53,312	101.9	99.8
North Carolina....................	...	39,206	33,615	37,176	110.6	94.8
North Dakota (i).................	1,044	991	1,044	1,571	158.5	150.5
Ohio	38,579	...	...	46,224	119.8	119.8
Oklahoma (c)......................	18,607	18,607	18,607	18,313	98.4	98.4
Oregon (i)...........................	...	...	14,362	14,605	101.7	101.7
Pennsylvania (c)..................	47,780	47,780	47,780	49,735	104.1	104.1
Rhode Island......................	3,989	3,774	3,973	3,168	83.9	79.4
South Carolina....................	...	23,806	...	21,534	90.5	90.5
South Dakota (c)	...	3,633	...	3,596	99	99
Tennessee	22,264	21,528	...	15,655	72.7	70.3
Texas (c)	161,173	154,901	161,173	140,839	90.9	87.4
Utah.................................	...	7,191	7,431	5,382	74.8	72.4
Vermont.............................	1,681	1,681	1,322	1,579	119.4	93.9
Virginia (c)........................	31,658	...	...	28,431	89.8	89.8
Washington.........................	16,799	16,488	...	17,760	107.7	105.7
West Virginia......................	4,948	5,778	4,948	5,708	115.4	98.8
Wisconsin (c)......................	...	22,923	17,181	22,443	130.6	97.9
Wyoming	2,288	2,288	2,407	2,036	89	84.6

Source: Bureau of Justice Statistics, National Prisoner Statistics Program, 2013, Prisoners in 2013 NCJ 247282, p13at01.csv, August 2014.
Key:
... — Not available. Specific type of capacity is not measured by state.
/ — Not reported. State does not report any capacity data.
(a) Population counts are based on the number of inmates held in custody of facilities operated by the jurisdiction. Excludes inmates held in local jails, other states, or private facilities unless otherwise stated.
(b) Federal custody count reported for the calculation of capacity includes an additional 412 inmates compared to the yearend custody reported in National Prisoner Statistics (NPS).
(c) State defines capacity in a way that differs from BJS's definition.

(d) Alaska did not report 2013 capacity data to NPS, and new facility construction prevents BJS from using prior years' data.
(e) Private facilities included in capacity and custody counts.
(f) Both capacity and custody counts exclude inmates in community-based work release facilities.
(g) Capacity counts include institution and camp net operating capacities and the population of community programs on December 31 since these programs do not have a fixed capacity.
(h) Nevada did not report 2013 NPS data.
(i) State did not report 2013 capacity or custody data to NPS. Data are from 2012.

Table 9.20
ADULTS ON PROBATION: 2013

State or other jurisdiction	Probation population				Change during 2013		Number on probation per 100,000 adult residents, 12/31/2013(a)
	1/1/2013	2013		12/31/2013	Number	Percent	
		Entries	Exits				
U.S. total............................	3,945,795	2,034,375	2,033,860	3,910,647	-35,148	-0.9	1,605
Federal............................	21,698	9,800	10,822	20,676	-1,022	-4.7	8
State................................	3,924,097	2,024,575	2,023,038	3,889,971	-34,126	-0.9	1,596
Alabama............................	62,368	20,741	21,308	61,801	-567	-0.9	1,655
Alaska (b)	7,154	...	...	7,167	13	0.2	1,308
Arizona.............................	72,452	27,048	27,173	71,527	-925	-1.3	1,418
Arkansas...........................	29,946	8,547	9,600	29,289	-657	-2.2	1,298
California	294,993	170,803	166,655	294,057	-936	-0.3	1,003
Colorado (b)	77,793	53,991	53,011	78,843	1,050	1.3	1,942
Connecticut.......................	47,798	21,554	25,162	42,723	-5,075	-10.6	1,515
Delaware	15,641	13,049	12,651	16,039	398	2.5	2,209
Florida (b)	240,607	165,208	171,448	233,128	-7,479	-3.1	1,491
Georgia (c)	515,896	290,462	291,881	514,477	-1,419	-0.3	6,829
Hawaii...............................	22,211	4,957	5,592	21,576	-635	-2.9	1,958
Idaho.................................	30,978	9,435	9,038	31,375	397	1.3	2,634
Illinois...............................	124,507	60,179	60,824	123,862	-645	-0.5	1,253
Indiana..............................	123,250	83,459	83,036	123,673	423	0.3	2,471
Iowa	29,333	16,421	16,453	29,301	-32	-0.1	1,233
Kansas	17,021	21,255	21,830	16,446	-575	-3.4	756
Kentucky (b)	57,720	31,876	18,569	51,027	-6,693	-11.6	1,505
Louisiana...........................	42,753	14,836	15,543	42,046	-707	-1.7	1,192
Maine.................................	6,942	3,209	3,432	6,719	-223	-3.2	629
Maryland	41,123	34,766	32,982	40,716	-407	-1	884
Massachusetts	68,673	73,505	74,394	67,784	-889	-1.3	1,273
Michigan (b)......................	183,031	99,214	100,105	176,795	-6,236	-3.4	2,305
Minnesota..........................	105,923	46,948	51,109	101,762	-4,161	-3.9	2,446
Mississippi	30,768	9,574	8,667	31,675	907	2.9	1,402
Missouri.............................	55,700	25,618	30,290	51,028	-4,672	-8.4	1,094
Montana	8,295	3,793	3,766	8,472	177	2.1	1,066
Nebraska	13,077	10,447	9,979	13,545	468	3.6	960
Nevada...............................	11,321	5,448	4,667	12,102	781	6.9	565
New Hampshire	4,088	2,759	2,853	3,994	-94	-2.3	379
New Jersey	114,594	41,451	42,814	113,231	-1,363	-1.2	1,639
New Mexico (b)	16,925	6,294	5,956	16,696	-229	-1.4	1,057
New York...........................	110,204	32,320	36,115	106,409	-3,795	-3.4	688
North Carolina...................	96,070	56,843	57,623	94,442	-1,628	-1.7	1,242
North Dakota......................	4,791	3,173	3,066	4,898	107	2.2	860
Ohio (b).............................	257,058	127,348	134,424	250,630	-6,428	-2.5	2,802
Oklahoma...........................	...	...	...	...	...	...	...
Oregon...............................	36,990	14,272	13,371	37,891	901	2.4	1,228
Pennsylvania	162,225	94,442	84,697	171,970	9,745	6	1,705
Rhode Island (b)................	23,818	...	...	22,988	-830	-3.5	2,737
South Carolina...................	34,625	13,923	12,723	35,825	1,200	3.5	964
South Dakota.....................	6,744	2,698	2,490	6,952	208	3.1	1,084
Tennessee	64,129	25,790	27,586	64,216	87	0.1	1,278
Texas.................................	405,653	156,509	162,507	399,655	-5,998	-1.5	2,043
Utah..................................	11,379	5,646	5,822	11,203	-176	-1.5	554
Vermont.............................	5,955	3,539	3,703	5,791	-164	-2.8	1,148
Virginia..............................	53,607	28,831	29,262	54,020	413	0.8	841
Washington (b)	85,270	47,883	34,818	95,217	9,947	11.7	1,762
West Virginia (b)	8,465	...	1,294	8,465	0	0	574
Wisconsin	45,777	22,741	21,760	46,758	981	2.1	1,051
Wyoming	4,899	2,824	2,516	5,207	308	6.3	1,165
Dist. of Columbia	8,051	5,411	6,111	7,351	-700	-8.7	1,362

See footnotes at end of table.

ADULTS ON PROBATION: 2013—Continued

Source: Bureau of Justice Statistics, Annual Probation Survey, 2013. *Probation and Parole in the United States,* 2013 NCJ 248029, ppus13at02. csv, Jan. 2015.

Note: Counts based on most recent data and may differ from previously published statistics. Counts may not be actual, as reporting agencies may provide estimates on some or all detailed data. Due to nonresponse or incomplete data, the probation population for some jurisdictions on December 31, 2013, does not equal the population on January 1, 2013, plus entries, minus exits. Reporting methods for some probation agencies changed over time, and probation coverage was expanded in 1998 and 1999.

Key:
…Not known.
(a) Computed using the estimated U.S. adult resident population in each jurisdiction on January 1, 2014.
(b) Data for entries and exits were estimated for nonreporting agencies.
(c) Includes private agency cases and may overstate the number of persons under supervision.

Table 9.21
ADULTS ON PAROLE: 2013

State or other jurisdiction	Parole population				Change during 2013		Number on parole per 100,000 adult residents, 12/31/13 (a)
	1/1/13	2013 Entries	Exits	12/31/13	Number	Percent	
U.S. total...........................	839,551	430,018	411,305	853,215	13,664	1.6	350
Federal.............................	108,679	49,212	46,665	111,226	2,547	2.3	46
State	730,872	380,806	364,640	741,989	11,117	1.5	304
Alabama	8,616	2,428	2,062	8,982	366	4.2	241
Alaska................................	2,000	1,103	800	2,303	303	15.2	420
Arizona.............................	7,460	11,929	11,753	7,636	176	2.4	151
Arkansas...........................	23,227	9,238	10,660	21,709	-1,518	-6.5	962
California (b)(c)	95,120	24,559	21,396	87,532	-7,588	-8	298
Colorado...........................	11,458	8,716	9,328	10,846	-612	-5.3	267
Connecticut......................	2,793	2,367	2,520	2,640	-153	-5.5	94
Delaware	601	579	523	657	56	9.3	90
Florida	4,538	6,252	6,107	4,683	145	3.2	30
Georgia.............................	24,673	14,565	12,627	26,611	1,938	7.9	353
Hawaii...............................	1,659	802	680	1,738	79	4.8	158
Idaho.................................	3,848	1,897	2,674	3,851	3	0.1	323
Illinois..............................	27,456	28,236	26,106	29,586	2,130	7.8	299
Indiana..............................	10,153	9,574	9,387	10,340	187	1.8	207
Iowa	5,151	3,675	3,231	5,595	444	8.6	235
Kansas	5,126	3,600	4,661	4,065	-1,061	-20.7	187
Kentucky	14,416	10,267	9,761	14,922	506	3.5	440
Louisiana..........................	27,092	16,058	14,406	28,744	1,652	6.1	815
Maine	21	1	1	21	/	:	2
Maryland	5,648	3,403	3,239	5,623	-25	-0.4	122
Massachusetts	2,130	2,785	2,749	2,166	36	1.7	41
Michigan...........................	19,113	10,539	11,213	18,439	-674	-3.5	240
Minnesota.........................	6,006	5,918	5,927	5,997	-9	-0.1	144
Mississippi........................	6,804	3,106	3,009	6,901	97	1.4	305
Missouri............................	20,679	13,863	15,141	19,401	-1,278	-6.2	416
Montana	943	608	530	1,021	78	8.3	128
Nebraska	1,383	1,764	1,901	1,246	-137	-9.9	88
Nevada..............................	5,379	4,085	3,942	5,522	143	2.7	258
New Hampshire	2,167	1,496	1,407	2,256	89	4.1	214
New Jersey	14,987	6,266	6,335	14,918	-69	-0.5	216
New Mexico	2,468	1,038	762	2,010	-458	-18.6	127
New York..........................	46,222	21,570	22,753	45,039	-1,183	-2.6	291
North Carolina..................	4,359	7,723	4,800	7,171	2,812	64.5	94
North Dakota....................	427	1,051	917	561	134	31.4	99
Ohio..................................	14,653	8,450	6,306	16,797	2,144	14.6	188
Oklahoma..........................	2,310	908	664	2,554	244	10.6	87
Oregon..............................	22,755	8,930	8,439	23,246	491	2.2	753
Pennsylvania.....................	92,315	57,654	46,167	103,802	11,487	12	1,029
Rhode Island.....................	481	408	430	459	-22	-4.6	55
South Carolina..................	6,000	2,105	2,549	5,556	-444	-7.4	150
South Dakota.....................	2,761	1,570	1,716	2,595	-166	-6	405
Tennessee	12,981	5,229	4,761	13,657	676	5.2	272
Texas.................................	112,288	35,076	36,062	111,302	-986	-0.9	569
Utah..................................	2,986	1,929	1,632	3,283	297	9.9	162
Vermont............................	1,037	568	510	1,095	58	5.6	217
Virginia.............................	1,891	534	568	1,800	-91	-4.8	28
Washington.......................	15,091	5,870	11,017	15,908	817	5.4	294
West Virginia.....................	2,052	1,917	1,416	2,553	501	24.4	173
Wisconsin	20,491	6,592	6,832	20,251	-240	-1.2	455
Wyoming...........................	729	538	491	776	47	6.4	174
Dist. of Columbia	5,928	1,467	1,772	5,623	-305	-5.1	1,042

See footnotes at end of table.

ADULTS ON PAROLE: 2013— Continued

Source: Bureau of Justice Statistics, Annual Parole Survey, 2013. *Probation and Parole in the United States*, 2013 NCJ 248029, ppus13at04. csv. Oct. 2014.

Note: Counts based on most recent data and may differ from previously published statistics. See Methodology. Counts may not be actual, as reporting agencies may provide estimates on some or all detailed data. Due to nonresponse or incomplete data, the parole population for some jurisdictions on December 31, 2013, does not equal the population on January 1, 2013, plus entries, minus exits.

Key:

: — Not calculated.

/ — Not reported.

(a) Computed using the estimated U.S. adult resident population in each jurisdiction on January 1, 2014.

(b) Data for entries and exits were estimated when data were incomplete.

(c) Includes post-release community supervision and mandatory supervision parolees: 38,781 on January 1, 2013; and 24,559 entries, 21,393 exits, and 41,947 on December 31, 2013.

Table 9.22
CAPITAL PUNISHMENT

State or other jurisdiction	Capital offenses by state	Prisoners under sentence of death	Method of execution
Alabama	Intentional murder with 18 aggravating factors (Ala. Stat. Ann. 13A-5-40(a)(1)-(18)).	198	Electrocution or lethal injection
Alaska............................	...	...	...
Arizona........................	First-degree murder, including pre-meditated murder and felony murder, accompanied by at least 1 of 14 aggravating factors (A.R.S. § 13-703(F)).	124	Lethal gas or lethal injection (a)
Arkansas......................	Capital murder (Ark. Code Ann. 5-10-101) with a finding of at least 1 of 10 aggravating circumstances; treason.	34	Lethal injection or electrocution (b)
California	First-degree murder with special circumstances; sabotage; train wrecking causing death; treason; perjury causing execution of an innocent person; fatal assault by a prisoner serving a life sentence.	743	Lethal injection
Colorado.......................	First-degree murder with at least 1 of 17 aggravating factors; first-degree kidnapping resulting in death; treason.	3	Lethal injection
Connecticut..................	... (c)	12	Lethal injection (c)
Delaware	First-degree murder (11 Del. C. § 636) with at least 1 statutory aggravating circumstance (11 Del. C. § 4209).	17	Lethal injection (d) or hanging
Florida (e)	First-degree murder; felony murder; capital drug trafficking; capital sexual battery.	403	Electrocution or lethal injection
Georgia.........................	Murder with aggravating circumstances; kidnapping with bodily injury or ransom when the victim dies; aircraft hijacking; treason.	87	Lethal injection
Hawaii............................	...	...	...
Idaho............................	First-degree murder with aggravating factors; first-degree kidnapping; perjury resulting in death.	11	Lethal injection
Illinois...........................	... (f)	0	...
Indiana..........................	Murder with 16 aggravating circumstances (IC 35-50-2-9).	14	Lethal injection or electrocution
Iowa	...	...	...
Kansas	Capital murder with 8 aggravating circumstances (KSA 21-3439, KSA 21-4625, KSA 21-4636).	10	Lethal injection
Kentucky	Capital murder with presence of at least one statutory aggravating circumstance; capital kidnapping (KRS 532.025).	35	Electrocution or lethal injection (g)
Louisiana (e)	First-degree murder; treason (La. R.S. 14:30 and 14:113).	85	Lethal injection
Maine.............................	...	...	...
Maryland	... (h)	4	Lethal injection or lethal gas (h)
Massachusetts	...	...	...
Michigan........................	...	...	...
Minnesota......................	...	...	...
Mississippi	Capital murder (Miss Code Ann. § 97-3-19(2)); aircraft piracy (Miss Code Ann. § 97-25-55(1)).	48	Lethal injection
Missouri........................	First-degree murder (565.020 RSMO 2000).	35	Lethal injection or lethal gas
Montana (e)	Capital murder with 1 of 9 aggravating circumstances (Mont. Code Ann. § 46-18-303); aggravated kidnapping; felony murder; capital sexual intercourse without consent (Mont. Code Ann. § 45-5-503).	2	Lethal injection
Nebraska	First-degree murder with a finding of at least 1 statutorily-defined aggravating circumstance.	11	Lethal injection
Nevada..........................	First-degree murder with at least 1 of 15 aggravating circumstances (NRS 200.030, 200.033, 200.035).	77	Lethal injection
New Hampshire	Murder committed in the course of rape, kidnapping, home invasion, drug crimes; killing of a police officer, judge, or prosecutor; murder for hire; murder by an inmate while serving a sentence of life without parole (RSA 630:1, RSA 630:5).	1	Lethal injection or hanging (i)
New Jersey	... (j)	...	...
New Mexico	... (k)	2	Lethal injection (k)
New York (l)	First-degree murder with 1 of 13 aggravating factors (NY Penal Law § 125.27).	0	Lethal injection

See footnotes at end of table.

CAPITAL PUNISHMENT — Continued

State or other jurisdiction	Capital offenses by state	Prisoners under sentence of death	Method of execution
North Carolina.............	First-degree murder with the finding of at least 1 of 11 statutory aggravating circumstances. (NCGS § 14-17).	158	Lethal injection
North Dakota...............	...	...	...
Ohio.............................	Aggravated murder with at least 1 of 10 aggravating circumstances (O.R.C. secs. 2903.01, 2929.02, and 2929.04).	145	Lethal injection
Oklahoma (e)...............	First-degree murder in conjunction with a finding of at least 1 of 8 statutorily-defined aggravating circumstances.	49	Electrocution, lethal injection or firing squad (m)
Oregon (n)	Aggravated murder (ORS 163.095-150).	36	Lethal injection
Pennsylvania	First-degree murder with 18 aggravating circumstances.	188	Lethal injection
Rhode Island................	...	...	...
South Carolina (e).......	Murder with 1 of 12 aggravating circumstances (§ 16-3-20(C)(a)).	45	Electrocution or lethal injection
South Dakota...............	First-degree murder with 1 of 10 aggravating circumstances.	3	Lethal injection
Tennessee	First-degree murder (Tenn. Code Ann. § 39-13-202) with 1 of 16 aggravating circumstances (Tenn. Code Ann. § 39-13-204).	73	Lethal injection or electrocution (o)
Texas (e).......................	Criminal homicide with 1 of 9 aggravating circumstances (TX Penal Code § 19.03).	276	Lethal injection
Utah..............................	Aggravated murder (76-5-202, Utah Code Annotated).	9	Lethal injection or firing squad (p)
Vermont........................	...	...	...
Virginia.........................	First-degree murder with 1 of 15 aggravating circumstances (VA Code § 18.2-31).	8	Electrocution or lethal injection
Washington...................	Aggravated first-degree murder.	9	Lethal injection or hanging
West Virginia................	...	...	...
Wisconsin	...	...	...
Wyoming	First-degree murder; murder during the commission of sexual assault, sexual abuse of a minor, arson, robbery, burglary, escape, resisting arrest, kidnapping, or abuse of a minor under 16 (W.S.A. § 6-2-101 (a)).	1	Lethal injection or lethal gas (q)
Dist. of Columbia	...	...	...
American Samoa	First-degree murder (ASC § 46.3513). (p)	0	Hanging (r)
Guam	...	...	...
No. Mariana Islands	...	...	...
Puerto Rico..................	...	...	...
U.S. Virgin Islands	...	...	...

Sources: The Council of State Governments' survey, May 2015; NAACP Legal Defense Fund, Death Row U.S.A. Winter 2015 (As of January 1, 2015); U.S. Department of Justice, Office of Justice programs, Bureau of Justice Statistics, Capital Punishment, 2013 — Statistical Tables, December 2013.

The United States Supreme Court ruling in *Roper v. Simmons,* 543 U.S. 551 (2005) declared unconstitutional the imposition of the death penalty on persons under the age of 18.

The United States Supreme Court ruling in *Atkins v. Virginia,* 536 U.S. 304 (2002) declared unconstitutional the imposition of the death penalty on mentally handicapped persons.

The method of execution of Federal prisoners is lethal injection, pursuant to 28 CFR, Part 26. For offenses under the Violent Crime Control and Law Enforcement Act of 1994, the execution method is that of the State in which the conviction took place (18 U.S.C. 3596).

Key:

... — No capital punishment statute.

(a) Arizona authorizes lethal injection for persons sentenced after November 15, 1992; inmates sentenced before that date may select lethal injection or gas.

(b) Arkansas authorizes lethal injection for those whose offense occurred on or after July 4, 1983; inmates whose offense occurred before that date may select lethal injection or electrocution.

(c) On April 25, 2012, Connecticut Governor Dannel Malloy signed into law a bill (SB 280) repealing the state's death penalty. The law replaces the death penalty with a sentence of life without parole for future cases, and does not apply to those already sentenced to death.

The Connecticut Supreme Court is currently considering whether the 11 inmates who remain on death row can still be executed.

(d) Delaware authorizes hanging if lethal injection is held to be unconstitutional by a court of competent jurisdiction.

(e) The United States Supreme Court struck a portion of the Louisiana capital statute on June 25, 2008 (*Kennedy v. Louisiana,* U.S. 128 S.Ct. 2641). The statute (La. Rev. Stat. Ann. § 14:42(D)(2)) allowing execution as a punishment for the rape of a minor when no murder had been committed had been ruled constitutionally permissible by the Louisiana Supreme Court. The U.S. Supreme Court found that since no national consensus existed for application of the death penalty in cases of rape where no murder had been committed, such laws constitute cruel and unusual punishment under the Eighth and Fourteenth Amendments. The ruling affects laws passed in Florida, Oklahoma, South Carolina, Texas, and Montana.

(f) Governor Pat Quinn signed a bill (SB 3539) on March 9, 2011, that abolishes the death penalty effective July 1, 2011. He commuted all death sentences to life without parole.

(g) Kentucky authorizes lethal injection for persons sentenced on or after March 31, 1998; inmates sentenced before that date may select lethal injection or electrocution.

(h) On May 2, 2013, Governor Martin O'Malley signed into law a bill (SB 276) that abolishes the death penalty for future crimes. Maryland currently has five people on death row, but they will not be affected by the legislation, although the governor has the option of commuting those sentences to life in prison.

CAPITAL PUNISHMENT — Continued

(i) New Hampshire authorizes hanging only if lethal injection cannot be given.

(j) New Jersey repealed its death penalty statute in 2007.

(k) Governor Bill Richardson signed a bill in March of 2009 abolishing the death penalty. The law is not retroactive and leaves two inmates on death row.

(l) The New York Court of Appeals has held that a portion of New York's death penalty sentencing statute (CPL 400.27) was unconstitutional (*People v. Taylor*, 9 N.Y.3d 129 (2007)). As a result, no defendants can be sentenced to death until the legislature corrects the errors in this statute. Efforts to restore the statute have been voted down.

(m) Oklahoma authorizes electrocution if lethal injection is held to be unconstitutional, and firing squad if both lethal injection and electrocution are held to be unconstitutional.

(n) In November 2011, Governor John Kitzhaber placed a moratorium on all executions in Oregon.

(o) Tennessee authorizes lethal injection for those whose capital offense occurred after December 31, 1998; those who committed the offense before that date may select electrocution by written waiver.

(p) Authorizes firing squad if lethal injection is held unconstitutional. Inmates who selected execution by firing squad prior to May 3, 2004, may still be entitled to execution by that method.

(q) Wyoming authorizes lethal gas if lethal injection is ever held to be unconstitutional.

(r) The last execution was in the 1920s.

Global Trade and Investment

By Justin Fisk and Jennifer Burnett

There was a time when trade policy largely was handed down from Washington. Today, states have more opportunities at their disposal to drive trade policy, making it very important for state leaders to understand those policies—particularly how free trade agreements affect their state—as they craft their job growth strategies.

More than 80 percent of global purchasing power and 95 percent of the world's population resides outside the United States; that's a lot of customers for U.S. businesses. More than 1 in 5 American jobs—38.1 million—depend on international trade. In addition, foreign-owned companies employ 5.3 million Americans.

Looking to the global marketplace for economic development and paying attention to export and import trends is no longer an option for state policymakers—it is a necessity.

A 2010 study by the International Trade Administration found that jobs in exporting industries actually pay better, with exports contributing an additional 18 percent to workers' earnings on average in the U.S. manufacturing sector. That earnings premium is even higher for blue-collar workers, who get a 20 percent boost over white-collar workers.

There was a time when trade policy largely was handed down from Washington. Today, states have more opportunities at their disposal to drive trade policy, making it very important for state leaders to understand those policies—particularly how free trade agreements affect their state—as they craft their job growth strategies.

According to a 2015 survey by the State International Development Organizations, or SIDO, only 5 percent of state trade offices do not have a role in trade policy. Most state trade offices play some role in policy, whether it is advising the governor or state legislature on trade policy, serving as a state point of contact for the U.S. Trade Representative's Office or responding to press inquiries.

Free Trade Agreements

The federal government does play the predominate role in negotiating trade agreements. Although these can be contentious, free trade agreements are, at their essence, an agreement between two or more countries to abide by certain rules that affect trade and offer protections for investors and intellectual property rights. They are designed to reduce barriers to trade, protect U.S. competitive interests abroad and enhance the rule of law among partner countries.

The U.S. is currently negotiating the Trans-Pacific Partnership agreement—or the TPP—which covers nearly 40 percent of global GDP. This agreement covers 12 countries along the Pacific Rim. In 2013, U.S. businesses exported nearly $700 billion in goods—or nearly 44 percent of total U.S. exports—to TPP countries.

The U.S. Department of Agriculture released a report in April of 2015 showing how a finalized trade agreement would benefit all 50 states. Food and agricultural exports in the U.S. reached $150 billion in 2014, supporting more than 1 million jobs. The report details the market potential for American-grown agricultural products, such as apples and wheat.

In addition to TPP, the U.S. government began ambitious negotiations with the European Union in 2013 to establish a Transatlantic Trade and Investment Partnership—or TTIP. This partnership would bring together two of the world's leading economies and estimates suggest the increase in bilateral trade could see a net employment gain of nearly 750,000 jobs for the U.S.

A report produced by the Atlantic Council, Bertelsmann Foundation and the British Embassy in Washington, D.C., "TTIP and the Fifty States: Jobs and Growth from Coast to Coast," suggests each state will see employment gains. States that currently have the highest unemployment rates should show better-than-average job growth. According to the report, states set to benefit the most by a transatlantic trade agreement in terms of employment are those that rank highest in population—California, Texas, New York and Florida. Some states—such as Georgia, North Carolina and Pennsylvania—will outperform the average in relation to population.

Federal and State Collaboration

Through the TPP and TTIP agreements, U.S. trade negotiators seek to eliminate tariffs and reduce many of the nontariff barriers that prevent American small businesses from exporting. In fact, only 1 percent of small businesses in America export. According to the National Small Business Association, one of the largest challenges of exporting is a lack of understanding about the export process. While small businesses benefit from free trade agreements, navigating the exporting process can be a major obstacle as well.

As the federal government focuses on concluding large free trade agreements on the international front, state trade offices are well positioned to help small businesses navigate the export process here at home. According to the 2015 SIDO survey, state trade offices predominately work with small businesses.

State trade offices vary in capability and resources, but many of them assist American business by facilitating foreign trade missions and local events, providing counseling and training, as well as offering a number of technical services to identify suppliers and produce pricing analyses. The Vice President of the Maine International Trade Center Wade Merritt once stated, "Although state programs are structured differently and our budgets range from zero to millions—our mission remains the same—boosting small business exports with the highest return on investment."

State Trade and Export Promotion Program

State trade office budgets have yet to reach pre-recession funding levels. To help offset budget reductions, Congress developed the State Trade and Export Promotion grant program, commonly referred to as the STEP program. Through STEP, the Small Business Administration provides matching grants to help state trade and export agencies support small businesses wishing to enter and succeed in the global market.

According to the SIDO survey, more than 80 percent of state trade directors find STEP to be "very important" or "extremely important" to the success of their export promotion efforts. In fact, eight states report that the STEP program provides more than half of their total budget for export promotion activities.

The STEP program has provided tangible benefits to U.S. small businesses too, supporting $575 million in actual and projected export sales in 2012.

"Through STEP awards, the [Small Business Administration] can work together with states to help more small businesses become exporters and expand their export sales," said Maria Contreras-Sweet, administrator of the Small Business Administration, in an April 2015 press release. "In the process, these small businesses will create jobs and strengthen the economies in their communities, across their state and the nation."

About the Authors

Justin Fisk is the Policy Associate for Federal and International Affairs at the Council of State Governments (CSG) and State International Development Organizations (SIDO).

Jennifer Burnett is the Program Manager for Fiscal and Economic Development Policy at The Council of State Governments headquarters in Lexington, KY.

Chapter Ten

STATE PAGES

Table 10.1
OFFICIAL NAMES OF STATES AND JURISDICTIONS, CAPITALS, ZIP CODES AND CENTRAL SWITCHBOARDS

State or other jurisdiction	Name of state capitol (a)	Capital	Zip code	Area code	Central switchboard (b)
Alabama, State of	State House	Montgomery	36130	334	242-7100
Alaska, State of	State Capitol	Juneau	99801	907	465-2111
Arizona, State of	State Capitol	Phoenix	85007	602	542-4331
Arkansas, State of	State Capitol	Little Rock	72201	501	682-2345
California, State of	State Capitol	Sacramento	95814	916	445-2841
Colorado, State of	State Capitol	Denver	80203	303	866-2471
Connecticut, State of	State Capitol	Hartford	06106	860	566-4840
Delaware, State of	Legislative Hall	Dover	19903	302	744-4101
Florida, State of	The Capitol	Tallahassee	32399	850	717-9337
Georgia, State of	State Capitol	Atlanta	30334	404	656-1776
Hawaii, State of	State Capitol	Honolulu	96813	808	586-2211
Idaho, State of	State Capitol	Boise	83720	208	334-2100
Illinois, State of	State House	Springfield	62706	217	782-0244
Indiana, State of	Statehouse	Indianapolis	46204	317	232-4567
Iowa, State of	State Capitol	Des Moines	50319	515	281-5211
Kansas, State of	The Capitol	Topeka	66612	785	296-3232
Kentucky, Commonwealth of	State Capitol	Frankfort	40601	502	564-2611
Louisiana, State of	State Capitol	Baton Rouge	70804	225	342-7015
Maine, State of	State House	Augusta	04333	207	287-3531
Maryland, State of	State House	Annapolis	21401	410	974-3901
Massachusetts, Commonwealth of	State House	Boston	02133	617	725-4005
Michigan, State of	State Capitol	Lansing	48909	517	373-3400
Minnesota, State of	State Capitol	St. Paul	55155	651	201-3400
Mississippi, State of	State Capitol	Jackson	39215	601	359-3150
Missouri, State of	State Capitol	Jefferson City	65101	573	751-0290
Montana, State of	State Capitol	Helena	59620	406	444-3111
Nebraska, State of	State Capitol	Lincoln	68509	402	471-2244
Nevada, State of	State Capitol	Carson City	89701	775	684-5670
New Hampshire, State of	State House	Concord	03301	603	271-2121
New Jersey, State of	State House	Trenton	08625	609	292-6000
New Mexico, State of	State Capitol	Santa Fe	87501	505	476-2200
New York, State of	State Capitol	Albany	12224	518	474-8390
North Carolina, State of	State Capitol	Raleigh	27601	919	733-5811
North Dakota, State of	State Capitol	Bismarck	58505	701	328-2200
Ohio, State of	Statehouse	Columbus	43215	614	466-3555
Oklahoma, State of	State Capitol	Oklahoma City	73105	405	521-2342
Oregon, State of	State Capitol	Salem	97301	503	378-4582
Pennsylvania, Commonwealth of	The Capitol	Harrisburg	17120	717	787-2500
Rhode Island and Providence					
Plantations, State of	State House	Providence	02903	401	222-2080
South Carolina, State of	State House	Columbia	29201	803	734-2100
South Dakota, State of	State Capitol	Pierre	57501	605	773-3212
Tennessee, State of	State Capitol	Nashville	37243	615	741-2001
Texas, State of	State Capitol	Austin	78711	512	463-2000
Utah, State of	State Capitol	Salt Lake City	84114	801	538-1000
Vermont, State of	State House	Montpelier	05609	802	828-3333
Virginia, Commonwealth of	State Capitol	Richmond	23219	804	786-2211
Washington, State of	Legislative Building	Olympia	98504	360	902-4111
West Virginia, State of	State Capitol	Charleston	25305	304	558-2000
Wisconsin, State of	State Capitol	Madison	53702	608	266-1212
Wyoming, State of	State Capitol	Cheyenne	82002	307	777-7434
District of Columbia................................	John A. Wilson Building	. . .	20004	202	727-6300
American Samoa, Territory of	Maota Fono Complex	Pago Pago	96799	684	633-4116
Guam, Territory of	Congress Building	Hagatna	96910	671	472-8931
No. Mariana Islands, Commonwealth of	Capital Hill	Saipan	96950	670	664-2280
Puerto Rico, Commonwealth of	The Capitol	San Juan	00902	787	721-7000
U.S. Virgin Islands, Territory of	Legislature Building	Charlotte Amalie,	00802	340	774-0001

Key:
(a) In some instances the name is not official.
(b) Numbers generally come from an executive branch office, such as the office of the governor.

Table 10.2
HISTORICAL DATA ON THE STATES

State or other jurisdiction	Source of state lands	Date organized as territory	Date admitted to Union	Chronological order of admission to Union
Alabama	Mississippi Territory, 1798 (a)	March 3, 1817	Dec. 14, 1819	22
Alaska	Purchased from Russia, 1867	Aug. 24, 1912	Jan. 3, 1959	49
Arizona	Ceded by Mexico, 1848 (b)	Feb. 24, 1863	Feb. 14, 1912	48
Arkansas	Louisiana Purchase, 1803	March 2, 1819	June 15, 1836	25
California	Ceded by Mexico, 1848	(c)	Sept. 9, 1850	31
Colorado	Louisiana Purchase, 1803 (d)	Feb. 28, 1861	Aug. 1, 1876	38
Connecticut	Fundamental Orders, Jan. 14, 1638; Royal charter, April 23, 1662	(e)	Jan. 9, 1788 (f)	5
Delaware	Swedish charter, 1638; English charter, 1638	(e)	Dec. 7, 1787 (f)	1
Florida	Ceded by Spain, 1819	March 30, 1822	March 3, 1845	27
Georgia	Charter, 1732, from George II to Trustees for Establishing the Colony of Georgia	(e)	Jan. 2, 1788 (f)	4
Hawaii	Annexed, 1898	June 14, 1900	Aug. 21, 1959	50
Idaho	Treaty with Britain, 1846	March 4, 1863	July 3, 1890	43
Illinois	Northwest Territory, 1787	Feb. 3, 1809	Dec. 3, 1818	21
Indiana	Northwest Territory, 1787	May 7, 1800	Dec. 11, 1816	19
Iowa	Louisiana Purchase, 1803	June 12, 1838	Dec. 28, 1846	29
Kansas	Louisiana Purchase, 1803 (d)	May 30, 1854	Jan. 29, 1861	34
Kentucky	Part of Virginia until admitted as state	(c)	June 1, 1792	15
Louisiana	Louisiana Purchase, 1803 (g)	March 26, 1804	April 30, 1812	18
Maine	Part of Massachusetts until admitted as state	(c)	March 15, 1820	23
Maryland	Charter, 1632, from Charles I to Calvert	(e)	April 28, 1788 (f)	7
Massachusetts	Charter to Massachusetts Bay Company, 1629	(e)	Feb. 6, 1788 (f)	6
Michigan	Northwest Territory, 1787	Jan. 11, 1805	Jan. 26, 1837	26
Minnesota	Northwest Territory, 1787 (h)	March 3, 1849	May 11, 1858	32
Mississippi	Mississippi Territory (i)	April 7, 1798	Dec. 10, 1817	20
Missouri	Louisiana Purchase, 1803	June 4, 1812	Aug. 10, 1821	24
Montana	Louisiana Purchase, 1803 (j)	May 26, 1864	Nov. 8, 1889	41
Nebraska	Louisiana Purchase, 1803	May 30, 1854	March 1, 1867	37
Nevada	Ceded by Mexico, 1848	March 2, 1861	Oct. 31, 1864	36
New Hampshire	Grants from Council for New England, 1622 and 1629; made Royal province, 1679	(e)	June 21, 1788 (f)	9
New Jersey	Dutch settlement, 1618; English charter, 1664	(e)	Dec. 18, 1787 (f)	3
New Mexico	Ceded by Mexico, 1848 (b)	Sept. 9, 1850	Jan. 6, 1912	47
New York	Dutch settlement, 1623; English control, 1664	(e)	July 26, 1788 (f)	11
North Carolina	Charter, 1663, from Charles II	(e)	Nov. 21, 1789 (f)	12
North Dakota	Louisiana Purchase, 1803 (k)	March 2, 1861	Nov. 2, 1889	39
Ohio	Northwest Territory, 1787	May 7, 1800	March 1, 1803	17
Oklahoma	Louisiana Purchase, 1803	May 2, 1890	Nov. 16, 1907	46
Oregon	Settlement and treaty with Britain, 1846	Aug. 14, 1848	Feb. 14, 1859	33
Pennsylvania	Grant from Charles II to William Penn, 1681	(e)	Dec. 12, 1787 (f)	2
Rhode Island	Charter, 1663, from Charles II	(e)	May 29, 1790 (f)	13
South Carolina	Charter, 1663, from Charles II	(e)	May 23, 1788 (f)	8
South Dakota	Louisiana Purchase, 1803	March 2, 1861	Nov. 2, 1889	40
Tennessee	Part of North Carolina until land ceded to U.S. in 1789	June 8, 1790 (l)	June 1, 1796	16
Texas	Republic of Texas, 1845	(c)	Dec. 29, 1845	28
Utah	Ceded by Mexico, 1848	Sept. 9, 1850	Jan. 4, 1896	45
Vermont	From lands of New Hampshire and New York	(c)	March 4, 1791	14
Virginia	Charter, 1609, from James I to London Company	(e)	June 25, 1788 (f)	10
Washington	Oregon Territory, 1848	March 2, 1853	Nov. 11, 1889	42
West Virginia	Part of Virginia until admitted as state	(c)	June 20, 1863	35
Wisconsin	Northwest Territory, 1787	April 20, 1836	May 29, 1848	30
Wyoming	Louisiana Purchase, 1803 (d)(j)	July 25, 1868	July 10, 1890	44
Dist. of Columbia	Maryland (m)	....	...	...
American Samoa	Became a territory, 1900			
Guam	Ceded by Spain, 1898	Aug. 1, 1950	...	...
No. Mariana Islands	...	March 24, 1976		...
Puerto Rico	Ceded by Spain, 1898	...	July 25, 1952 (n)	...
U.S. Virgin Islands	Purchased from Denmark, March 31, 1917			

See footnotes at end of table.

HISTORICAL DATA ON THE STATES — Continued

Key:

(a) By the Treaty of Paris, 1783, England gave up claim to the 13 original Colonies, and to all land within an area extending along the present Canadian to the Lake of the Woods, down the Mississippi River to the 31st parallel, east to the Chattahoochee, down that river to the mouth of the Flint, border east to the source of the St. Mary's down that river to the ocean. The major part of Alabama was acquired by the Treaty of Paris, and the lower portion from Spain in 1813.

(b) Portion of land obtained by Gadsden Purchase, 1853.

(c) No territorial status before admission to Union.

(d) Portion of land ceded by Mexico, 1848.

(e) One of the original 13 Colonies.

(f) Date of ratification of U.S. Constitution.

(g) West Feliciana District (Baton Rouge) acquired from Spain, 1810; added to Louisiana, 1812.

(h) Portion of land obtained by Louisiana Purchase, 1803.

(i) See footnote (a). The lower portion of Mississippi also was acquired from Spain in 1813.

(j) Portion of land obtained from Oregon Territory, 1848.

(k) The northern portion of the Red River Valley was acquired by treaty with Great Britain in 1818.

(l) Date Southwest Territory (identical boundary as Tennessee's) was created.

(m) Area was originally 100 square miles, taken from Virginia and Maryland. Virginia's portion south of the Potomac was given back to that state in 1846. Site chosen in 1790, city incorporated 1802.

(n) On this date, Puerto Rico became a self-governing commonwealth by compact approved by the U.S. Congress and the voters of Puerto Rico as provided in U.S. Public Law 600 of 1950.

Table 10.3
STATE STATISTICS

State or other jurisdiction	Land area — In square miles (2010)	Land area — Rank in nation	Population (a) — Size	Population (a) — Rank in nation	Percentage change 2013 to 2014	Density per square mile	Rank in nation	Number of Representatives in Congress	Capital	Population (j)	Rank in state	Largest city	Population (j)
Alabama	50,645	28	4,849,377	23	1.4	95.8	27	7	Montgomery	205,293	2	Birmingham	212,038
Alaska	570,641	1	736,732	48	3.7	1.3	50	1	Juneau	32,556	2	Anchorage (d)	298,610
Arizona	113,594	6	6,731,484	15	5.3	59.3	33	9	Phoenix	1,488,750	1	Phoenix	1,488,750
Arkansas	52,035	27	2,966,369	32	1.7	57.0	34	4	Little Rock	196,537	1	Little Rock	196,537
California	155,779	3	38,802,500	1	4.2	249.1	11	53	Sacramento	475,516	6	Los Angeles	3,857,799
Colorado	103,642	8	5,355,866	22	6.5	51.7	37	7	Denver	634,265 (k)	1	Denver	634,265
Connecticut	4,842	48	3,596,677	29	0.6	742.8	4	5	Hartford	124,893	4	Bridgeport	146,425
Delaware	1,949	49	935,614	45	4.2	480.2	6	1	Dover	37,089	2	Wilmington	71,292
Florida	53,625	26	19,893,297	3	5.8	371.0	8	27	Tallahassee	186,971	7	Jacksonville	836,507
Georgia	57,513	21	10,097,343	8	4.2	175.6	18	14	Atlanta	443,775	1	Atlanta	443,775
Hawaii	6,423	47	1,419,561	40	4.4	221.0	13	2	Honolulu	345,610	1	Honolulu	345,610
Idaho	82,643	11	1,634,464	39	4.3	19.8	44	2	Boise	212,303	1	Boise	212,303
Illinois	55,519	24	12,880,580	5	0.4	232.0	12	18	Springfield	117,126	6	Chicago	2,714,856
Indiana	35,826	38	6,596,855	16	1.7	184.1	16	9	Indianapolis	834,852	1	Indianapolis	834,852
Iowa	55,857	23	3,107,126	30	2.0	55.6	36	4	Des Moines	206,688	1	Des Moines	206,688
Kansas	81,759	13	2,904,021	34	1.8	35.5	40	4	Topeka	127,939	5	Wichita	385,577
Kentucky	39,486	37	4,413,457	26	1.7	111.8	22	6	Frankfort	25,583	13	Louisville (e)	605,110
Louisiana	43,204	33	4,649,676	25	2.6	107.6	23	6	Baton Rouge	230,058	2	New Orleans	369,250
Maine	30,843	39	1,330,089	41	0.1	43.1	38	2	Augusta	18,946	7	Portland	66,214
Maryland	9,707	42	5,976,407	19	3.5	615.7	5	8	Annapolis	38,629	7	Baltimore	621,342
Massachusetts	7,800	45	6,745,408	14	3.0	864.8	3	9	Boston	636,479	1	Boston	636,479
Michigan	56,539	22	9,909,877	10	0.3	175.3	17	14	Lansing	113,996	6	Detroit	701,475
Minnesota	79,627	14	5,457,173	21	2.9	68.5	30	8	St. Paul	290,770	2	Minneapolis	392,880
Mississippi	46,923	31	2,994,079	31	0.9	63.8	32	4	Jackson	175,437	1	Jackson	175,437
Missouri	68,742	18	6,063,589	18	1.2	88.2	28	8	Jefferson City	43,183	15	Kansas City	464,310
Montana	145,546	4	1,023,579	44	3.5	7.0	48	1	Helena	29,134	6	Billings	106,954
Nebraska	76,824	15	1,881,503	37	3.0	24.5	43	3	Lincoln	265,404	2	Omaha	421,570
Nevada	109,781	7	2,839,099	35	5.1	25.9	42	4	Carson City	54,838	6	Las Vegas	596,424
New Hampshire	8,953	44	1,326,813	42	0.8	148.2	21	2	Concord	42,630	3	Manchester	110,209
New Jersey	7,354	46	8,938,175	11	1.7	1,215.4	1	12	Trenton	84,477	6	Newark	277,727
New Mexico	121,298	5	2,085,572	36	1.3	17.2	45	3	Santa Fe	69,204	4	Albuquerque	555,417
New York	47,126	30	19,746,227	4	1.9	419.0	7	27	Albany	97,904	6	New York City	8,336,697
North Carolina	48,618	29	9,943,964	9	4.3	204.5	15	13	Raleigh	423,179	2	Charlotte	775,202
North Dakota	69,001	17	739,482	47	9.9	10.7	47	1	Bismarck	64,751	2	Fargo	109,779
Ohio	40,861	35	11,594,163	7	0.5	283.7	10	16	Columbus	809,798	1	Columbus	809,798
Oklahoma	68,595	19	3,878,051	28	3.4	56.5	35	5	Oklahoma City	599,199	1	Oklahoma City	599,199
Oregon	95,988	10	3,970,239	27	3.6	41.4	39	5	Salem	157,429	3	Portland	603,106
Pennsylvania	44,743	32	12,787,209	6	0.7	285.8	9	18	Harrisburg	49,279	9	Philadelphia (f)	1,547,607
Rhode Island	1,034	50	1,055,173	43	0.2	1,020.7	2	2	Providence	178,432	1	Providence	178,432
South Carolina	30,061	40	4,832,482	24	4.5	160.8	19	7	Columbia	131,686	1	Columbia	131,686

See footnotes at end of table.

STATE STATISTICS—Continued

State or other jurisdiction	Land area In square miles (2010)	Rank in nation	Population (a) Size	Rank in nation	Percentage change 2013 to 2014	Density per square mile	Rank in nation	Number of Representatives in Congress	Capital	Population (j)	Rank in state	Largest city	Population (j)
South Dakota	75,811	16	853,175	46	4.8	11.3	46	1	Pierre	13,914	8	Sioux Falls	159,908
Tennessee	41,235	34	6,549,352	17	3.2	158.8	20	9	Nashville (g)	624,496	2	Memphis	655,155
Texas	261,232	2	26,956,958	2	7.2	103.2	26	36	Austin	842,592	4	Houston	2,160,821
Utah	82,170	12	2,942,902	33	6.5	35.8	41	4	Salt Lake City	189,314	1	Salt Lake City	189,314
Vermont	9,217	43	626,562	49	0.1	68.0	31	1	Montpelier	7,787	6	Burlington	42,282
Virginia	39,490	36	8,326,289	12	4.1	210.8	14	11	Richmond	210,309	4	Virginia Beach	447,021
Washington	66,456	20	7,061,530	13	5.0	106.3	25	10	Olympia	47,698	24	Seattle	634,535
West Virginia	24,038	41	1,850,326	38	-0.1	77.0	29	3	Charleston	51,018	1	Charleston	51,018
Wisconsin	54,158	25	5,757,564	20	1.2	106.3	24	8	Madison	240,323	2	Milwaukee	598,916
Wyoming	97,093	9	584,153	50	3.6	6.0	49	1	Cheyenne	61,537	1	Cheyenne	61,537
Dist. of Columbia	61	...	658,893	...	9.5	10,801.5	...	1 (h)	...	...	...	...	...
American Samoa (b)	77	...	55,519	...	-3.1 (c)	721.0	...	1 (h)	Pago Pago	3,656 (b)	3	Tafuna	9,756 (j)
Guam (b)	210	...	159,358	...	2.9 (c)	758.8	...	1 (h)	Hagåtña (d)	1,051 (b)	13	Dededo (d)	44,943
No. Mariana Islands (b)	179	...	53,833	...	-22.2 (c)	300.7	...	1 (h)	Saipan (d)	48,220 (b)	1	Saipan (d)	48,220 (b)
Puerto Rico	3,424	...	3,548,397	...	-4.8	1,036.3	...	1 (i)	San Juan	389,714	1	San Juan	389,714
U.S. Virgin Islands (b)	134	...	106,405	...	-2.0 (c)	794.1	...	1 (h)	Charlotte Amalie, St. Thomas	18,481 (b)	1	Charlotte Amalie, St. Thomas	18,481 (b)

Source: U.S. Census Bureau, information available as of May 2015.
Key:
... — Not applicable
(a) July 1, 2014 Census Bureau estimates.
(b) 2010 Census Bureau counts.
(c) Population change calculations are from 2000–2010.
(d) Municipality.
(e) This city is part of a consolidated city-county government and is coextensive with Jefferson County.
(f) Philadelphia County and Philadelphia city are coextensive.
(g) This city is part of a consolidated city-county government and is coextensive with Davidson County.
(h) Represented by one non-voting House Delegate.
(i) Represented by one non-voting House Resident Commissioner.
(j) 2012 Census Bureau counts.
(k) 2012 Census Bureau counts.

Table 10.4
PERSONAL INCOME, POPULATION AND PER CAPITA PERSONAL INCOME, BY STATE, 2013–2014

State or other jurisdiction	Personal income (millions of dollars)				Population (thousands of persons) (a)	Per capita personal income (dollars)		
	2013	2014ᵖ	Percent change 2013–14	Rank of percent change 2013–14	2014ᵖ	2014ᵖ	Rank in U.S. 2014ᵖ	Percent of U.S. average 2014ᵖ
United States	$14,151,427	$14,708,582	3.9	—	318,857	$46,129	—	100
Alabama	176,341	181,816	3.1	37	4,849	37,493	47	81
Alaska	36,867	38,974	5.7	1	737	52,901	9	115
Arizona	245,070	255,089	4.1	18	6,731	37,895	41	82
Arkansas	108,603	111,984	3.1	36	2,966	37,751	43	82
California	1,856,614	1,944,369	4.7	8	38,803	50,109	10	109
Colorado	247,069	260,993	5.6	3	5,356	48,730	14	106
Connecticut	218,132	224,674	3.0	39	3,597	62,467	1	135
Delaware	41,487	42,984	3.6	29	936	45,942	22	100
Florida	811,377	848,357	4.6	11	19,893	42,645	28	92
Georgia	378,156	394,773	4.4	14	10,097	39,097	40	85
Hawaii	63,468	65,861	3.8	26	1,420	46,396	20	101
Idaho	58,272	61,347	5.3	6	1,634	37,533	46	81
Illinois	605,201	619,808	2.4	46	12,881	48,120	16	104
Indiana	253,779	260,133	2.5	45	6,597	39,433	39	85
Iowa	138,337	140,177	1.3	49	3,107	45,115	25	98
Kansas	128,541	132,267	2.9	42	2,904	45,546	23	99
Kentucky	159,172	166,182	4.4	13	4,413	37,654	44	82
Louisiana	190,590	196,621	3.2	35	4,650	42,287	30	92
Maine	54,359	55,958	2.9	40	1,330	42,071	31	91
Maryland	319,125	329,560	3.3	33	5,976	55,143	5	120
Massachusetts	383,152	399,204	4.2	17	6,745	59,182	2	128
Michigan	386,471	401,901	4.0	22	9,910	40,556	36	88
Minnesota	257,466	265,824	3.2	34	5,457	48,711	15	106
Mississippi	101,442	102,795	1.3	48	2,994	34,333	50	74
Missouri	245,771	252,325	2.7	43	6,064	41,613	33	90
Montana	39,963	41,558	4.0	21	1,024	40,601	35	88
Nebraska	88,114	88,569	0.5	50	1,882	47,073	19	102
Nevada	109,471	113,783	3.9	23	2,839	40,077	37	87
New Hampshire	67,513	70,519	4.5	12	1,327	53,149	8	115
New Jersey	492,897	507,749	3.0	38	8,938	56,807	3	123
New Mexico	74,996	78,428	4.6	9	2,086	37,605	45	82
New York	1,070,236	1,110,345	3.7	27	19,746	56,231	4	122
North Carolina	380,954	394,234	3.5	30	9,944	39,646	38	86
North Dakota	38,472	40,635	5.6	4	739	54,951	6	119
Ohio	474,973	493,578	3.9	24	11,594	42,571	29	92
Oklahoma	161,188	167,292	3.8	25	3,878	43,138	27	94
Oregon	156,605	165,484	5.7	2	3,970	41,681	32	90
Pennsylvania	590,171	610,295	3.4	31	12,787	47,727	17	103
Rhode Island	49,410	51,532	4.3	16	1,055	48,838	13	106
South Carolina	171,088	178,485	4.3	15	4,832	36,934	48	80

See footnotes at end of table.

PERSONAL INCOME, POPULATION AND PER CAPITA PERSONAL INCOME, BY STATE, 2013–2014—Continued

State or other jurisdiction	Personal income (millions of dollars)				Population (thousands of persons) (a)	Per capita personal income (dollars)		
	2013	2014[p]	Percent change 2013–14	Rank of percent change 2013–14		2014[p]	Rank in U.S. 2014[p]	Percent of U.S. average 2014[p]
South Dakota	38,897	39,541	1.7	47	853	46,345	21	100
Tennessee	256,969	266,260	3.6	28	6,549	40,654	34	88
Texas	1,160,079	1,224,548	5.6	5	26,957	45,426	24	98
Utah	106,289	111,141	4.6	10	2,943	37,766	42	82
Vermont	28,501	29,655	4.0	19	627	47,330	18	103
Virginia	403,425	413,898	2.6	44	8,326	49,710	11	108
Washington	332,655	350,130	5.3	7	7,062	49,583	12	107
West Virginia	65,889	67,804	2.9	41	1,850	36,644	49	79
Wisconsin	248,335	256,699	3.4	32	5,758	44,585	26	97
Wyoming	30,779	32,018	4.0	20	584	54,810	7	119
Dist. of Columbia	48,697	50,426	3.6	—	659	76,532	—	166

Sources: U.S. Bureau of Economic Analysis and Bureau of the Census.

Key:

p – preliminary

(a) Census Bureau midyear population estimate. Estimates for 2014 use state population estimates released in December 2014.

ALABAMA

Nickname..The Heart of Dixie
Motto..*Aldemus Jura Nostra Defendere*
(We Dare Defend Our Rights)
Flower .... Camellia
Bird... Yellowhammer
Tree... Southern (Longleaf) Pine
Song..*Alabama*
Entered the Union....................................December 14, 1819
Capital..Montgomery

STATISTICS

Land Area (square miles)...50,645
Rank in Nation...28
Population..4,849,377
Rank in Nation...23
Density per square mile 95.8
Capital City..Montgomery
Population...205,293
Rank in State...2
Largest City...Birmingham
Population...212,038
Number of Representatives in Congress 7
Number of 2012 Electoral Votes.....................................9
Number of County Governments....................................67
Number of Municipal Governments..............................461
Number of School Districts...132
Number of Special Districts 548

LEGISLATIVE BRANCH

Legislative Body .... Legislature

President of the Senate ....Lt. Gov. Kay Ivey
President Pro Tem of the Senate............................Del Marsh
Secretary of the Senate ....D. Patrick Harris

Speaker of the House...................................Mike Hubbard
Speaker Pro Tem of the House ....Victor Gaston
Clerk of the House ....Jeff Woodard

2015 Regular Session........................March 3 – June 4, 2015
Number of Senatorial Districts................................35
Number of Representative Districts 105

EXECUTIVE BRANCH

Governor .... Robert J. Bentley
Lieutenant Governor ....Kay Ivey
Secretary of State ....John Merrill
Attorney General ....Luther Strange
Treasurer.. Young Boozer
Auditor...Ronald L. Jones
State Comptroller ....Thomas L. White (Comptroller)

Governor's Present Term............................. 1/2011 – 1/2019
Number of Elected Officials in the Executive Branch.........................7
Number of Members in the Cabinet 23

JUDICIAL BRANCH

Highest Court..Supreme Court
Supreme Court Chief Justice.......................Roy S. Moore
Number of Supreme Court Judges 9
Number of Intermediate Appellate Court Judges...........10
Number of U.S. Court Districts.......................................3
U.S. Circuit Court..11th Circuit

ALASKA

Nickname...The Last Frontier
Motto..*North to the Future*
Flower ....Forget-Me-Not
Bird..Willow Ptarmigan
Tree...Sitka Spruce
Song...*Alaska's Flag*
Entered the Union.....................................January 3, 1959
Capital..Juneau

STATISTICS

Land Area (square miles)..........................570,641
Rank in Nation...1
Population..736,732
Rank in Nation...48
Density per square mile 1.3
Capital City..Juneau
Population...32,556
Rank in State...2
Largest City... Anchorage
Population...298,610
Number of Representatives in Congress 1
Number of 2012 Electoral Votes.....................................3
Number of Geographic Counties.................................16
(Number of Geographic Boroughs)
Number of County Governments..................................14
Number of Consolidated Governments..........................5
Number of Municipal Governments..............................148
Number of Special Districts 15

LEGISLATIVE BRANCH

Legislative Body .... Legislature

President of the Senate ....Kevin Meyer
Secretary of the Senate ....Liz Clark

Speaker of the House..................................... Mike Chenault
Clerk of the House ....Suzanne Lowell (Chief)

2015 Regular Session........................Jan. 20 – April 28, 2015
Number of Senatorial Districts................................20
Number of Representative Districts 40

EXECUTIVE BRANCH

Governor ....Bill Walker
Lieutenant Governor ....Byron Mallott
Attorney General ....Craig Richards
Treasurer.. Pamela Leary
Auditor...Kris Curtis
State Comptroller ....Scot Arehart (Director, Division of Finance)

Governor's Present Term............................. 12/2014 – 12/2018
Number of Elected Officials in the Executive Branch.........................2
Number of Members in the Cabinet 19

JUDICIAL BRANCH

Highest Court..Supreme Court
Supreme Court Chief Justice.......................Dana Fabe
Number of Supreme Court Judges 5
Number of Intermediate Appellate Court Judges...........3
Number of U.S. Court Districts.......................................1
U.S. Circuit Court..9th Circuit

ARIZONA

Nickname	The Grand Canyon State
Motto	*Ditat Deus* (God Enriches)
Flower	Blossom of the Saguaro Cactus
Bird	Cactus Wren
Tree	Palo Verde
Song	*Arizona March Song* and *Arizona*
Entered the Union	February 14, 1912
Capital	Phoenix

STATISTICS

Land Area (square miles)	113,594
Rank in Nation	6
Population	6,731,484
Rank in Nation	15
Density per square mile	59.3
Capital City	Phoenix
Population	1,488,750
Rank in State	1
Largest City	Phoenix
Population	1,488,750
Number of Representatives in Congress	9
Number of 2012 Electoral Votes	11
Number of County Governments	15
Number of Municipal Governments	91
Number of School Districts	242
Number of Special Districts	326

LEGISLATIVE BRANCH

Legislative Body	Legislature
President of the Senate	Andy Biggs
President Pro Tem of the Senate	Sylvia Tenney Allen
Secretary of the Senate	Charmion Billington
Speaker of the House	David Gowan
Speaker Pro Tem of the House	Bob Robson
Clerk of the House	Jim Drake (Chief)
2015 Regular Session	Jan. 12 – April 3, 2015
Number of Senatorial Districts	30
Number of Representative Districts	30

EXECUTIVE BRANCH

Governor	Doug Ducey
Secretary of State	Michele Reagan
Attorney General	Mark Brnovich
Treasurer	Jeff DeWitt
Auditor	Debra K. Davenport
State Comptroller	D. Clark Partridge (Comptroller)
Governor's Present Term	1/2015 – 1/2019
Number of Elected Officials in the Executive Branch	11
Number of Members in the Cabinet	36

JUDICIAL BRANCH

Highest Court	Supreme Court
Supreme Court Chief Justice	W. Scott Bales
Number of Supreme Court Judges	5
Number of Intermediate Appellate Court Judges	22
Number of U.S. Court Districts	1
U.S. Circuit Court	9th Circuit

ARKANSAS

Nickname	The Natural State
Motto	*Regnat Populus* (The People Rule)
Flower	Apple Blossom
Bird	Mockingbird
Tree	Pine
Song	*Arkansas*
Entered the Union	June 15, 1836
Capital	Little Rock

STATISTICS

Land Area (square miles)	52,035
Rank in Nation	27
Population	2,966,369
Rank in Nation	32
Density per square mile	57.0
Capital City	Little Rock
Population	196,537
Rank in State	1
Largest City	Little Rock
Population	196,537
Number of Representatives in Congress	4
Number of 2012 Electoral Votes	6
Number of County Governments	75
Number of Municipal Governments	502
Number of School Districts	239
Number of Special Districts	740

LEGISLATIVE BRANCH

Legislative Body	General Assembly
President of the Senate	Lt. Gov. Tim Griffin
President Pro Tem of the Senate	Jonathan Dismang
Secretary of the Senate	Ann Cornwell
Speaker of the House	Jeremy Gillam
Speaker Pro Tem of the House	Jon Eubanks
Clerk of the House	Sherri Stacks (Chief)
2015 Regular Session	Jan. 12 – April 22, 2015
Number of Senatorial Districts	35
Number of Representative Districts	100

EXECUTIVE BRANCH

Governor	Asa Hutchinson
Lieutenant Governor	Tim Griffin
Secretary of State	Mark Martin
Attorney General	Leslie Rutledge
Treasurer	Dennis Milligan
Auditor	Roger A. Norman
State Comptroller	Larry Walther
(Director, Department of Finance & Administration)	
Governor's Present Term	1/2015 – 1/2019
Number of Elected Officials in the Executive Branch	7
Number of Members in the Cabinet	47

JUDICIAL BRANCH

Highest Court	Supreme Court
Supreme Court Chief Justice	Jim Hannah
Number of Supreme Court Judges	7
Number of Intermediate Appellate Court Judges	12
Number of U.S. Court Districts	2
U.S. Circuit Court	8th Circuit

CALIFORNIA

Nickname	The Golden State
Motto	*Eureka* (I Have Found It)
Flower	California Poppy
Bird	California Valley Quail
Tree	California Redwood
Song	*I Love You, California*
Entered the Union	September 9, 1850
Capital	Sacramento

STATISTICS

Land Area (square miles)	155,779
Rank in Nation	3
Population	38,802,500
Rank in Nation	1
Density per square mile	249.1
Capital City	Sacramento
Population	475,516
Rank in State	6
Largest City	Los Angeles
Population	3,857,799
Number of Representatives in Congress	53
Number of 2012 Electoral Votes	55
Number of Geographic Counties	58
Number of County Governments	57
Number of Consolidated Governments	1
Number of Municipal Governments	482
Number of School Districts	1,025
Number of Special Districts	2,861

LEGISLATIVE BRANCH

Legislative Body	Legislature
President of the Senate	Lt. Gov. Gavin Newsom
President Pro Tem of the Senate	Kevin De Leon
Secretary of the Senate	David Alvarez
Speaker of the House	Toni Atkins
	(Speaker of the Assembly)
Speaker Pro Tem of the House	Kevin Mullin
	(Speaker Pro Tem of the Assembly)
Clerk of the House	E. Dotson Wilson (Chief)
2015 Regular Session	Dec. 1, 2014 – Sept. 11, 2015
Number of Senatorial Districts	40
Number of Representative Districts	80

EXECUTIVE BRANCH

Governor	Edmund G. Brown Jr.
Lieutenant Governor	Gavin Newsom
Secretary of State	Alex Padilla
Attorney General	Kamala Harris
Treasurer	John Chiang
Auditor	Elaine M. Howle
State Comptroller	Betty Yee (Controller)
Governor's Present Term	1/2011 – 1/2019
Number of Elected Officials in the Executive Branch	9
Number of Members in the Cabinet	11

JUDICIAL BRANCH

Highest Court	Supreme Court
Supreme Court Chief Justice	Tani Cantil-Sakauye
Number of Supreme Court Judges	7
Number of Intermediate Appellate Court Judges	96
Number of U.S. Court Districts	4
U.S. Circuit Court	9th Circuit

COLORADO

Nickname	The Centennial State
Motto	*Nil Sine Numine* (Nothing Without Providence)
Flower	Rocky Mountain Columbine
Bird	Lark Bunting
Tree	Blue Spruce
Song	*Where the Columbines Grow*
Entered the Union	August 1, 1876
Capital	Denver

STATISTICS

Land Area (square miles)	103,642
Rank in Nation	8
Population	5,355,866
Rank in Nation	22
Density per square mile	51.7
Capital City	Denver
Population	634,265
Rank in State	1
Largest City	Denver
Population	634,265
Number of Representatives in Congress	7
Number of 2012 Electoral Votes	9
Number of Geographic Counties	64
Number of County Governments	62
Number of Consolidated Governments	2
Number of Municipal Governments	271
Number of School Districts	180
Number of Special Districts	2,392

LEGISLATIVE BRANCH

Legislative Body	General Assembly
President of the Senate	Bill Cadman
President Pro Tem of the Senate	Ellen Roberts
Secretary of the Senate	Cindi Markwell
Speaker of the House	Dickey Lee Hullinghorst
Speaker Pro Tem of the House	Dan Pabon
Clerk of the House	Marilyn Eddins (Chief)
2015 Regular Session	Jan. 7 – May 6, 2015
Number of Senatorial Districts	35
Number of Representative Districts	65

EXECUTIVE BRANCH

Governor	John Hickenlooper
Lieutenant Governor	Joe Garcia
Secretary of State	Wayne Williams
Attorney General	Cynthia Coffman
Treasurer	Walker Stapleton
Auditor	Dianne E. Ray
State Comptroller	Bob Jaros (Controller)
Governor's Present Term	1/2011 – 1/2019
Number of Elected Officials in the Executive Branch	5
Number of Members in the Cabinet	21

JUDICIAL BRANCH

Highest Court	Supreme Court
Supreme Court Chief Justice	Nancy E. Rice
Number of Supreme Court Judges	7
Number of Intermediate Appellate Court Judges	22
Number of U.S. Court Districts	1
U.S. Circuit Court	10th Circuit

CONNECTICUT

Nickname	The Constitution State
Motto	*Qui Transtulit Sustinet*
	(He Who Transplanted Still Sustains)
Flower	Mountain Laurel
Bird	American Robin
Tree	White Oak
Song	*Yankee Doodle*
Entered the Union	January 9, 1788
Capital	Hartford

STATISTICS

Land Area (square miles)	4,842
Rank in Nation	48
Population	3,596,677
Rank in Nation	29
Density per square mile	742.8
Capital City	Hartford
Population	124,893
Rank in State	4
Largest City	Bridgeport
Population	146,425
Number of Representatives in Congress	5
Number of 2012 Electoral Votes	7
Number of Geographic Counties	8
Number of Municipal Governments	30
Number of School Districts	17
Number of Special Districts	447

LEGISLATIVE BRANCH

Legislative Body	General Assembly
President of the Senate	Lt. Gov. Nancy Wyman
President Pro Tem of the Senate	Martin Looney
Secretary of the Senate	Garey E. Coleman
	(Clerk of the Senate)
Speaker of the House	Brendan Sharkey
Speaker Pro Tem of the House	Bob Godfrey,
	Patricia Billie Miller, Bruce Morris,
	Linda Orange, Kevin Ryan,
	Peggy Sayers
	(Deputy Speakers of the House)
Clerk of the House	Martin Dunleavy
2015 Regular Session	Jan. 7 – June 3, 2015
Number of Senatorial Districts	36
Number of Representative Districts	151

EXECUTIVE BRANCH

Governor	Dan Malloy
Lieutenant Governor	Nancy Wyman
Secretary of State	Denise W. Merrill
Attorney General	George C. Jepsen
Treasurer	Denise L. Nappier
Auditor	John C. Geragosian and Robert M. Ward
State Comptroller	Kevin P. Lembo (Comptroller)
Governor's Present Term	1/2011 – 1/2019
Number of Elected Officials in the Executive Branch	6
Number of Members in the Cabinet	14

JUDICIAL BRANCH

Highest Court	Supreme Court
Supreme Court Chief Justice	Chase T. Rogers
Number of Supreme Court Judges	7
Number of Intermediate Appellate Court Judges	9
Number of U.S. Court Districts	1
U.S. Circuit Court	2nd Circuit

DELAWARE

Nickname	The First State
Motto	*Liberty and Independence*
Flower	Goldenrod
Bird	Blue Hen Chicken
Tree	American Holly
Song	*Our Delaware*
Entered the Union	December 7, 1787
Capital	Dover

STATISTICS

Land Area (square miles)	1,949
Rank in Nation	49
Population	935,614
Rank in Nation	45
Density per square mile	480.2
Capital City	Dover
Population	37,089
Rank in State	2
Largest City	Wilmington
Population	71,292
Number of Representatives in Congress	1
Number of 2012 Electoral Votes	3
Number of County Governments	3
Number of Municipal Governments	57
Number of School Districts	19
Number of Special Districts	260

LEGISLATIVE BRANCH

Legislative Body	General Assembly
President of the Senate	Vacant
President Pro Tem of the Senate	Patricia Blevins
Secretary of the Senate	Bernard J. Brady
Speaker of the House	Peter Schwartzkopf
Speaker Pro Tem of the House	Helene Keeley
Clerk of the House	Richard Puffer
2015 Regular Session	Jan. 13 – June 30, 2015
Number of Senatorial Districts	21
Number of Representative Districts	41

EXECUTIVE BRANCH

Governor	Jack Markell
Lieutenant Governor	Vacant
Secretary of State	Jeffrey Bullock
Attorney General	Matthew Denn
Treasurer	Ken Simpler
Auditor	R. Thomas Wagner
State Comptroller	Kristopher Knight
Governor's Present Term	1/2009 – 1/2017
Number of Elected Officials in the Executive Branch	6
Number of Members in the Cabinet	19

JUDICIAL BRANCH

Highest Court	Supreme Court
Supreme Court Chief Justice	Leo Strine Jr.
Number of Supreme Court Judges	5
Number of U.S. Court Districts	1
U.S. Circuit Court	3rd Circuit

FLORIDA

Nickname	The Sunshine State
Motto	*In God We Trust*
Flower	Orange Blossom
Bird	Mockingbird
Tree	Sabal Palmetto Palm
Song	*The Swannee River* (Old Folks at Home)
Entered the Union	March 3, 1845
Capital	Tallahassee

STATISTICS

Land Area (square miles)	53,625
Rank in Nation	26
Population	19,893,297
Rank in Nation	3
Density per square mile	371.0
Capital City	Tallahassee
Population	186,971
Rank in State	7
Largest City	Jacksonville
Population	836,507
Number of Representatives in Congress	27
Number of 2012 Electoral Votes	29
Number of Geographic Counties	67
Number of County Governments	66
Number of Consolidated Governments	1
Number of Municipal Governments	410
Number of School Districts	95
Number of Special Districts	1,079

LEGISLATIVE BRANCH

Legislative Body	Legislature
President of the Senate	Andy Gardiner
President Pro Tem of the Senate	Garrett Richter
Secretary of the Senate	Debbie Brown
Speaker of the House	Steve Crisafulli
Speaker Pro Tem of the House	Matt Hudson
Clerk of the House	Bob Ward
2015 Regular Session	March 3 – May 1, 2015
Number of Senatorial Districts	40
Number of Representative Districts	120

EXECUTIVE BRANCH

Governor	Rick Scott
Lieutenant Governor	Carlos Lopez-Cantera
Secretary of State	Ken Detzner
Attorney General	Pam Bondi
Treasurer	Jeffrey H. Atwater (Chief Financial Officer)
Auditor	David Martin
Governor's Present Term	1/2011 – 1/2019
Number of Elected Officials in the Executive Branch	5
Number of Members in the Cabinet	4

JUDICIAL BRANCH

Highest Court	Supreme Court
Supreme Court Chief Justice	Jorge Labarga
Number of Supreme Court Judges	7
Number of Intermediate Appellate Court Judges	61
Number of U.S. Court Districts	3
U.S. Circuit Court	11th Circuit

GEORGIA

Nickname	The Empire State of the South
Motto	*Wisdom, Justice and Moderation*
Flower	Cherokee Rose
Bird	Brown Thrasher
Tree	Live Oak
Song	*Georgia on My Mind*
Entered the Union	January 2, 1788
Capital	Atlanta

STATISTICS

Land Area (square miles)	57,513
Rank in Nation	21
Population	10,097,343
Rank in Nation	8
Density per square mile	175.6
Capital City	Atlanta
Population	443,775
Rank in State	1
Largest City	Atlanta
Population	443,775
Number of Representatives in Congress	14
Number of 2012 Electoral Votes	16
Number of Geographic Counties	159
Number of County Governments	153
Number of Consolidated Governments	6
Number of Municipal Governments	535
Number of School Districts	180
Number of Special Districts	510

LEGISLATIVE BRANCH

Legislative Body	General Assembly
President of the Senate	Lt. Gov. Casey Cagle
President Pro Tem of the Senate	David Shafer
Secretary of the Senate	David A. Cook
Speaker of the House	David Ralston
Speaker Pro Tem of the House	Jan Jones
Clerk of the House	Bill Reilly
2015 Regular Session	Jan. 12 – April 2, 2015
Number of Senatorial Districts	56
Number of Representative Districts	180

EXECUTIVE BRANCH

Governor	Nathan Deal
Lieutenant Governor	Casey Cagle
Secretary of State	Brian Kemp
Attorney General	Sam Olens
Treasurer	Steve McCoy
Auditor	Greg Griffin
Comptroller	Alan Skelton
Governor's Present Term	1/2011 – 1/2019
Number of Elected Officials in the Executive Branch	8

JUDICIAL BRANCH

Highest Court	Supreme Court
Supreme Court Chief Justice	Hugh Thompson
Number of Supreme Court Judges	7
Number of Intermediate Appellate Court Judges	12
Number of U.S. Court Districts	3
U.S. Circuit Court	11th Circuit

HAWAII

Nickname.. The Aloha State
Motto... *Ua Mau Ke Ea O Ka Aina I Ka Pono*
(The Life of the Land Is Perpetuated in Righteousness)
Flower .... Native Yellow Hibiscus
Bird.. Hawaiian Goose (Nene)
Tree.. Kukue Tree (Candlenut)
Song...*Hawaii Ponoi*
Entered the Union.. August 21, 1959
Capital..Honolulu

STATISTICS

Land Area (square miles)..6,423
Rank in Nation..47
Population...1,419,561
Rank in Nation..40
Density per square mile 221.0
Capital City...Honolulu
Population...345,610
Rank in State..1
Largest City...Honolulu
Population...345,610
Number of Representatives in Congress 2
Number of 2012 Electoral Votes..4
Number of Geographic Counties...4
Number of County Governments..3
Number of Consolidated Governments...............................1
Number of Municipal Governments 1
Number of Special Districts 17

LEGISLATIVE BRANCH

Legislative Body .... Legislature

President of the Senate .... Donna Mercado Kim
President Pro Tem of the Senate.................... Will Espero
(Vice President of the Senate)
Secretary of the Senate .... Carol Taniguchi
(Chief Clerk of the Senate)

Speaker of the House.......................................Joseph Souki
Speaker Pro Tem of the House .... John Mizuno
(Vice Speaker of the House)
Clerk of the House ....Brian Takashita (Chief)

2015 Regular Session.............................Jan. 21 – May 7, 2015
Number of Senatorial Districts...25
Number of Representative Districts 51

EXECUTIVE BRANCH

Governor .... David Ige
Lieutenant Governor .... Shan Tsutsui
Attorney General .... Doug Chin
Treasurer..............................Wesley Machida (State Budget Director)
Auditor...Jan Yamane
State Comptroller .... Douglas Murdock (Comptroller)

Governor's Present Term........................... 12/2014 – 12/2018
Number of Elected Officials in the Executive Branch.........................2
Number of Members in the Cabinet 22

JUDICIAL BRANCH

Highest Court..Supreme Court
Supreme Court Chief Justice............................. Mark E. Recktenwald
Number of Supreme Court Judges 5
Number of Intermediate Appellate Court Judges..............................6
Number of U.S. Court Districts...1
U.S. Circuit Court..9th Circuit

IDAHO

Nickname... The Gem State
Motto..*Esto Perpetua* (Let It Be Perpetual)
Flower .... Syringa
Bird..Mountain Bluebird
Tree..Western White Pine
Song...*Here We Have Idaho*
Entered the Union...July 3, 1890
Capital..Boise

STATISTICS

Land Area (square miles)..82,643
Rank in Nation..11
Population...1,634,464
Rank in Nation..39
Density per square mile 19.8
Capital City...Boise
Population...212,303
Rank in State..1
Largest City...Boise
Population...212,303
Number of Representatives in Congress 2
Number of 2012 Electoral Votes..4
Number of County Governments..44
Number of Municipal Governments 200
Number of School Districts 118
Number of Special Districts 806

LEGISLATIVE BRANCH

Legislative Body .... Legislature

President of the Senate ....Lt. Gov. Brad Little
President Pro Tem of the Senate............................Brent Hill
Secretary of the Senate ....Jennifer Novak

Speaker of the House.. Scott Bedke
Clerk of the House ....Bonnie Alexander (Chief)

2015 Regular Session.........................Jan. 12 – April 11, 2015
Number of Senatorial Districts...35
Number of Representative Districts 35

EXECUTIVE BRANCH

Governor ....C.L. "Butch" Otter
Lieutenant Governor .... Brad Little
Secretary of State...............................Lawrence Denney
Attorney General ....Lawrence Wasden
Treasurer .... Ron Crane
State Comptroller ....Brandon D. Woolf (Controller)

Governor's Present Term............................... 1/2007 – 1/2019
Number of Elected Officials in the Executive Branch.........................7
Number of Members in the Cabinet 39

JUDICIAL BRANCH

Highest Court..Supreme Court
Supreme Court Chief Justice.............................. Roger S. Burdick
Number of Supreme Court Judges 5
Number of Intermediate Appellate Court Judges..............................4
Number of U.S. Court Districts...11
U.S. Circuit Court..9th Circuit

ILLINOIS

Nickname... The Prairie State
Motto... *State Sovereignty-National Union*
Flower .... Native Violet
Bird.. Cardinal
Tree.. White Oak
Song.. *Illinois*
Entered the Union..December 3, 1818
Capital..Springfield

STATISTICS

Land Area (square miles)..55,519
Rank in Nation...24
Population...12,880,580
Rank in Nation...5
Density per square mile 232.0
Capital City...Springfield
Population...117,126
Rank in State...6
Largest City .... Chicago
Population..2,714,856
Number of Representatives in Congress 18
Number of 2012 Electoral Votes....................................20
Number of County Governments..................................102
Number of Municipal Governments 1,298
Number of School Districts 905
Number of Special Districts 3,227

LEGISLATIVE BRANCH

Legislative Body .... General Assembly

President of the Senate .... John J. Cullerton
President Pro Tem of the Senate........................ Don Harmon
Secretary of the Senate ....Tim Anderson

Speaker of the House............................. Michael J. Madigan
Clerk of the House .... Timothy Mapes

2015 Regular Session...........................Jan. 14 – May 14, 2015
Number of Senatorial Districts 59
Number of Representative Districts 118

EXECUTIVE BRANCH

Governor ....Bruce Rauner
Lieutenant Governor ....Evelyn Sanguinetti
Secretary of State...Jesse White
Attorney General .... Lisa Madigan
Treasurer.. Mike Frerichs
Auditor...William G. Holland
State Comptroller ....Leslie Munger (Comptroller)

Governor's Present Term... 1/2015 – 1/2019
Number of Elected Officials in the Executive Branch...........................6
Number of Members in the Cabinet 18

JUDICIAL BRANCH

Highest Court...Supreme Court
Supreme Court Chief Justice......................... Rita B. Garman
Number of Supreme Court Judges................................7
Number of Intermediate Appellate Court Judges.............................54
Number of U.S. Court Districts.......................................3
U.S. Circuit Court.. 7th Circuit

INDIANA

Nickname...The Hoosier State
Motto.. *Crossroads of America*
Flower ....Peony
Bird.. Cardinal
Tree... Tulip Poplar
Song.. *On the Banks of the Wabash, Far Away*
Entered the Union..December 11, 1816
Capital..Indianapolis

STATISTICS

Land Area (square miles)..35,826
Rank in Nation...38
Population...6,596,855
Rank in Nation...16
Density per square mile 183.1
Capital City...Indianapolis
Population...834,852
Rank in State...1
Largest City ....Indianapolis
Population..834,852
Number of Representatives in Congress 9
Number of 2012 Electoral Votes....................................11
Number of Geographic Counties...................................92
Number of County Governments...................................91
Number of Consolidated Governments...........................1
Number of Municipal Governments 569
Number of School Districts 291
Number of Special Districts 752

LEGISLATIVE BRANCH

Legislative Body .... General Assembly

President of the Senate .... Lt. Gov. Sue Ellspermann
President Pro Tem of the Senate....................... David C. Long
Secretary of the Senate ....Jennifer Mertz

Speaker of the House................................... Brian C. Bosma
Speaker Pro Tem of the House ....William C. Friend
Clerk of the House .... M. Carolyn Spotts

2015 Regular Session...........................Jan. 6 – April 29, 2015
Number of Senatorial Districts 50
Number of Representative Districts 100

EXECUTIVE BRANCH

Governor ....Mike Pence
Lieutenant Governor ....Sue Ellspermann
Secretary of State...Connie Lawson
Attorney General ....Greg Zoeller
Treasurer...Kelly Mitchell
Auditor.. Paul D. Joyce

Governor's Present Term................................... 1/2013 – 1/2017
Number of Elected Officials in the Executive Branch...........................7
Number of Members in the Cabinet 16

JUDICIAL BRANCH

Highest Court...Supreme Court
Supreme Court Chief Justice............................ Loretta Rush
Number of Supreme Court Judges................................5
Number of Intermediate Appellate Court Judges.............................15
Number of U.S. Court Districts.......................................2
U.S. Circuit Court.. 7th Circuit

IOWA

Nickname...The Hawkeye State
Motto.......... *Our Liberties We Prize and Our Rights We Will Maintain*
Flower ....Wild Rose
Bird...Eastern Goldfinch
Tree...Oak
Song...*The Song of Iowa*
Entered the Union.................................December 28, 1846
Capital..Des Moines

STATISTICS

Land Area (square miles)................................55,857
Rank in Nation..23
Population..3,107,126
Rank in Nation..30
Density per square mile 55.6
Capital City...Des Moines
Population..206,688
Rank in State...1
Largest City..Des Moines
Population..206,688
Number of Representatives in Congress 4
Number of 2012 Electoral Votes...................................6
Number of County Governments..................................99
Number of Municipal Governments...........................947
Number of School Districts.......................................366
Number of Special Districts 535

LEGISLATIVE BRANCH

Legislative Body .... General Assembly

President of the Senate .... Pam Jochum
President Pro Tem of the Senate......................................Steve Sodders
Secretary of the Senate ....Michael E. Marshall

Speaker of the House.. Kraig Paulsen
Speaker Pro Tem of the House ....Matt Windschitl
Clerk of the House ....Carmine Boal (Chief)

2015 Regular Session..............................Jan. 12 – June 5, 2015
Number of Senatorial Districts.....................................50
Number of Representative Districts 100

EXECUTIVE BRANCH

Governor .... Terry Branstad
Lieutenant Governor ....Kim Reynolds
Secretary of State..Paul Pate
Attorney General ....Thomas Miller
Treasurer... Michael Fitzgerald
Auditor...Mary Mosiman
State Comptroller......................................Calvin McKelvogue
(Chief Operating Officer)

Governor's Present Term.............................. 1/2011 – 1/2019
Number of Elected Officials in the Executive Branch.........................7
Number of Members in the Cabinet 30

JUDICIAL BRANCH

Highest Court..Supreme Court
Supreme Court Chief Justice.........................Mark S. Cady
Number of Supreme Court Judges 7
Number of Intermediate Appellate Court Judges................................9
Number of U.S. Court Districts.......................................2
U.S. Circuit Court... 8th Circuit

KANSAS

Nickname... The Sunflower State
Motto...*Ad Astra per Aspera*
(To the Stars through Difficulties)
Flower .... Wild Native Sunflower
Bird... Western Meadowlark
Tree...Cottonwood
Song...*Home on the Range*
Entered the Union............................. January 29, 1861
Capital..Topeka

STATISTICS

Land Area (square miles)................................81,759
Rank in Nation..13
Population..2,904,021
Rank in Nation..33
Density per square mile 35.5
Capital City...Topeka
Population..127,939
Rank in State...5
Largest City ....Wichita
Population..385,577
Number of Representatives in Congress 4
Number of 2012 Electoral Votes...................................6
Number of Geographic Counties.................................105
Number of County Governments.................................103
Number of Consolidated Governments..........................2
Number of Municipal Governments...........................626
Number of School Districts.......................................306
Number of Special Districts 1,523

LEGISLATIVE BRANCH

Legislative Body ....Legislature

President of the Senate ....Susan Wagle
President Pro Tem of the Senate................................Jeff King
(Vice President of the Senate)
Secretary of the Senate ....Corey Carnahan

Speaker of the House.. Ray Merrick
Speaker Pro Tem of the House .... Peggy Mast
Clerk of the House ....Susan W. Kannarr (Chief)

2015 Regular Session..............................Jan. 12 – June 12, 2015
Number of Senatorial Districts...40
Number of Representative Districts 125

EXECUTIVE BRANCH

Governor .... Sam Brownback
Lieutenant Governor ....Jeff Colyer
Secretary of State...Kris Kobach
Attorney General .... Derek Schmidt
Treasurer..Ron Estes
Auditor.. Scott Frank
State Comptroller ....DeAnn Hill
(Director, Office of Management, Analysis & Standards)

Governor's Present Term.............................. 1/2011 – 1/2019
Number of Elected Officials in the Executive Branch.........................6
Number of Members in the Cabinet 14

JUDICIAL BRANCH

Highest Court..Supreme Court
Supreme Court Chief Justice.........................Lawton R. Nuss
Number of Supreme Court Judges 7
Number of Intermediate Appellate Court Judges..............................14
Number of U.S. Court Districts.......................................1
U.S. Circuit Court... 10th Circuit

KENTUCKY

Nickname..The Bluegrass State
Motto..*United We Stand, Divided We Fall*
Flower..Goldenrod
Bird..Cardinal
Tree...Tulip Poplar
Song...*My Old Kentucky Home*
Entered the Union...June 1, 1792
Capital...Frankfort

STATISTICS

Land Area (square miles)..39,486
Rank in Nation..37
Population..4,413,457
Rank in Nation..26
Density per square mile..111.8
Capital City...Frankfort
Population..25,583
Rank in State..13
Largest City...Louisville
Population..605,110
Number of Representatives in Congress.................................6
Number of 2012 Electoral Votes...8
Number of Geographic Counties...120
Number of County Governments..118
Number of Consolidated Governments..................................2
Number of Municipal Governments....................................418
Number of School Districts...174
Number of Special Districts..628

LEGISLATIVE BRANCH

Legislative Body..General Assembly

President of the Senate....................................Robert Stivers
President Pro Tem of the Senate........................David Givens
Secretary of the Senate.....................................Donna Holiday
(Chief Clerk of the Senate)

Speaker of the House...Gregory Stumbo
Speaker Pro Tem of the House.........................Jody Richards
Clerk of the House..Jean Burgin (Chief)

2015 Regular Session.........................Jan. 6 – March 25, 2015
Number of Senatorial Districts...38
Number of Representative Districts....................................100

EXECUTIVE BRANCH

Governor..Steve Beshear
Lieutenant Governor..Crit Luallen
Secretary of State..........................Alison Lundergan Grimes
Attorney General..Jack Conway
Treasurer...Todd Hollenbach
Auditor...Adam Edelen
State Comptroller...................................Edgar C. Ross (Controller)

Governor's Present Term............................ 12/2007 – 12/2015
Number of Elected Officials in the Executive Branch.........................7
Number of Members in the Cabinet....................................10

JUDICIAL BRANCH

Highest Court...Supreme Court
Supreme Court Chief Justice............................John D. Minton
Number of Supreme Court Judges...7
Number of Intermediate Appellate Court Judges.............................14
Number of U.S. Court Districts..2
U.S. Circuit Court...6th Circuit

LOUISIANA

Nickname...The Pelican State
Motto..*Union, Justice and Confidence*
Flower..Magnolia
Bird...Eastern Brown Pelican
Tree..Bald Cypress
Song.............................*Give Me Louisiana* and *You Are My Sunshine*
Entered the Union.. April 30, 1812
Capital.. Baton Rouge

STATISTICS

Land Area (square miles)..43,204
Rank in Nation..33
Population..4,649,676
Rank in Nation..25
Density per square mile..107.6
Capital City... Baton Rouge
Population..230,058
Rank in State..2
Largest City...New Orleans
Population..369,250
Number of Representatives in Congress.................................6
Number of 2012 Electoral Votes...8
Number of Geographic Counties...64
(Number of Geographic Parishes)
Number of Consolidated Governments..................................1
Number of Municipal Governments....................................304
Number of School Districts...69
Number of Special Districts..96

LEGISLATIVE BRANCH

Legislative Body..Legislature

President of the Senate...John Alario
President Pro Tem of the Senate..................Sharon Weston Broome
Secretary of the Senate......................................Glenn Koepp

Speaker of the House...Chuck Kleckley
Speaker Pro Tem of the House..........................Walt Leger III
Clerk of the House...Alfred W. Speer

2015 Regular Session......................... April 13 – June 11, 2015
Number of Senatorial Districts...39
Number of Representative Districts....................................105

EXECUTIVE BRANCH

Governor..Bobby Jindal
Lieutenant Governor..Jay Dardenne
Secretary of State...Tom Schedler
Attorney General...James D. Caldwell
Treasurer..John Neely Kennedy

Governor's Present Term.............................. 1/2008 – 1/2016
Number of Elected Officials in the Executive Branch.........................7
Number of Members in the Cabinet....................................16

JUDICIAL BRANCH

Highest Court...Supreme Court
Supreme Court Chief Justice....................Bernette J. Johnson
Number of Supreme Court Judges...7
Number of Intermediate Appellate Court Judges.............................53
Number of U.S. Court Districts..3
U.S. Circuit Court...5th Circuit

MAINE

Nickname..The Pine Tree State
Motto..*Dirigo* (I Direct or I Lead)
Flower ....White Pine Cone and Tassel
Bird...Chickadee
Tree...White Pine
Song...*State of Maine Song*
Entered the Union...March 15, 1820
Capital...Augusta

STATISTICS

Land Area (square miles)..30,843
Rank in Nation...39
Population...1,330,089
Rank in Nation...41
Density per square mile 43.1
Capital City...Augusta
Population..18,946
Rank in State..7
Largest City...Portland
Population..66,214
Number of Representatives in Congress 2
Number of 2012 Electoral Votes.......................................4
Number of County Governments...................................16
Number of Municipal Governments.............................22
Number of School Districts...99
Number of Special Districts 237

LEGISLATIVE BRANCH

Legislative Body ....Legislature

President of the Senate ....Michael Thibodeau
Secretary of the Senate ....Heather J.R. Priest

Speaker of the House...Mark Eves
Clerk of the House ....Robert B. Hunt

2015 Regular Session................................Dec. 3, 2014 – June 17, 2015
Number of Senatorial Districts 35
Number of Representative Districts 151

EXECUTIVE BRANCH

Governor ....Paul LePage
Secretary of State..Matthew Dunlap
Attorney General ....Janet Mills
Treasurer..Teresa M. Hayes
Auditor...Pola Buckley
State Comptroller ....Douglas Cotnoir (Controller)

Governor's Present Term..............................1//2011 – 1/2019
Number of Elected Officials in the Executive Branch..........................1
Number of Members in the Cabinet 16

JUDICIAL BRANCH

Highest Court.....................................Supreme Judicial Court
Supreme Court Chief Justice................. Leigh Ingalls Saufley
Number of Supreme Court Judges 7
Number of U.S. Court Districts...................................1
U.S. Circuit Court...1st Circuit

MARYLAND

Nickname..The Old Line State and Free State
Motto...*Fatti Maschii, Parole Femine*
(Manly Deeds, Womanly Words)
Flower ....Black-eyed Susan
Bird...Baltimore Oriole
Tree...White Oak
Song ....*Maryland, My Maryland*
Entered the Union...April 28, 1788
Capital...Annapolis

STATISTICS

Land Area (square miles)..9,707
Rank in Nation...42
Population...5,976,407
Rank in Nation...19
Density per square mile 615.7
Capital City..Annapolis
Population..38,629
Rank in State..7
Largest City ....Baltimore
Population..621,342
Number of Representatives in Congress 8
Number of 2012 Electoral Votes....................................10
Number of Geographic Counties.................................24
Number of County Governments.................................23
Number of County Equivalents......................................1*
Number of Municipal Governments 157
Number of Special Districts 167

*The city of Baltimore is an Independent City and considered a
county equivalent.

LEGISLATIVE BRANCH

Legislative Body .... General Assembly

President of the Senate ....Thomas V. Mike Miller Jr.
President Pro Tem of the Senate......................Nathaniel J. McFadden
Secretary of the Senate ....William B.C. Addison Jr.

Speaker of the House..Michael Erin Busch
Speaker Pro Tem of the House .... Adrienne A. Jones
Clerk of the House .... Sylvia Siegert (Chief)

2015 Regular Session..Jan. 14 – April 13, 2015
Number of Senatorial Districts 47
Number of Representative Districts 47

EXECUTIVE BRANCH

Governor ....Larry Hogan
Lieutenant Governor .... Boyd Rutherford
Secretary of State...John Wobensmith
Attorney General ....Brian Frosh
Treasurer...Nancy K. Kopp
Auditor...Thomas J. Branickel
State Comptroller ....Peter Franchot (Comptroller)

Governor's Present Term.............................. 1/2015 – 1/2019
Number of Elected Officials in the Executive Branch..........................4
Number of Members in the Cabinet 25

JUDICIAL BRANCH

Highest Court...Court of Appeals
Supreme Court Chief Justice..................Mary Ellen Barbara
Number of Supreme Court Judges 7
Number of Intermediate Appellate Court Judges.............................12
Number of U.S. Court Districts...................................1
U.S. Circuit Court...4th Circuit

MASSACHUSETTS

Nickname...The Bay State
Motto..........................*Ense Petit Placidam Sub Libertate Quietem*
(By the Sword We Seek Peace, but Peace Only under Liberty)
Flower ....Mayflower (Epigaea repens)
Bird...Chickadee
Tree...American Elm
Song...*All Hail to Massachusetts*
Entered the Union...February 6, 1788
Capital..Boston

STATISTICS
Land Area (square miles)..7,800
Rank in Nation..45
Population..6,745,408
Rank in Nation..14
Density per square mile 864.8
Capital City...Boston
Population...636,479
Rank in State...1
Largest City...Boston
Population...636,479
Number of Representatives in Congress 9
Number of 2012 Electoral Votes..11
Number of Geographic Counties.......................................14*
Number of County Governments...5
Number of Consolidated Governments..................................2
Number of Municipal Governments 53
Number of School Districts 84
Number of Special Districts 417

*Seven counties have been abolished and are only geographic in
nature.

LEGISLATIVE BRANCH
Legislative Body ....General Court

President of the Senate ....Stanley C. Rosenberg
President Pro Tem of the Senate...........................Marc Pacheco
Secretary of the Senate ....William F. Welch
(Clerk of the Senate)

Speaker of the House...............................Robert A. DeLeo
Speaker Pro Tem of the House ....Patricia A. Haddad
Clerk of the House...................................Steven T. James

2015 Regular Session........................Jan. 7 – Nov. 18, 2015 (projected)
Number of Senatorial Districts 40
Number of Representative Districts 160

EXECUTIVE BRANCH
Governor ....Charlie Baker
Lieutenant Governor ....Karyn Polito
Secretary of State.......................................William F. Galvin
(Secretary of the Commonwealth)
Attorney General ....Maura Healey
Treasurer...Deb Goldberg
(Treasurer & Receiver General)
Auditor ....Suzanne Bump
State Comptroller ....Thomas Shack III (Comptroller)

Governor's Present Term.............................. 1/2015 – 1/2019
Number of Elected Officials in the Executive Branch.........................6
Number of Members in the Cabinet 10

JUDICIAL BRANCH
Highest Court....................................Supreme Judicial Court
Supreme Court Chief Justice..........................Ralph D. Gants
Number of Supreme Court Judges 7
Number of Intermediate Appellate Court Judges..............................28
Number of U.S. Court Districts...11
U.S. Circuit Court...1st Circuit

MICHIGAN

Nickname... The Wolverine State
Motto..........................*Si Quaeris Peninsulam Amoenam Circumspice*
(If You Seek a Pleasant Peninsula, Look About You)
Flower ....Apple Blossom
Bird...Robin
Tree... White Pine
Song..*Michigan, My Michigan*
Entered the Union.. January 26, 1837
Capital...Lansing

STATISTICS
Land Area (square miles)...56,539
Rank in Nation..22
Population..9,909,877
Rank in Nation..9
Density per square mile 175.3
Capital City...Lansing
Population...113,996
Rank in State...6
Largest City...Detroit
Population...701,475
Number of Representatives in Congress 14
Number of 2012 Electoral Votes..16
Number of County Governments...83
Number of Municipal Governments 533
Number of School Districts 576
Number of Special Districts 443

LEGISLATIVE BRANCH
Legislative Body ....Legislature

President of the Senate ....Lt. Gov. Brian Calley
President Pro Tem of the Senate............................Tonya Schuitmaker
Secretary of the Senate ....Carol Morey Viventi

Speaker of the House..Kevin Cotter
Speaker Pro Tem of the House ....Tom Leonard
Clerk of the House...Gary Randall

2015 Regular Session...................... Jan. 14 – Dec. 31, 2015
Number of Senatorial Districts 38
Number of Representative Districts 110

EXECUTIVE BRANCH
Governor ....Rick Snyder
Lieutenant Governor ....Brian Calley
Secretary of State.. Ruth Johnson
Attorney General .... Bill Schuette
Treasurer...Kevin Clinton
Auditor ....Doug Ringler
State Comptroller ....Michael J. Moody
(Director, Office of Financial Management)

Governor's Present Term............................... 1/2011 – 1/2019
Number of Elected Officials in the Executive Branch.........................5
Number of Members in the Cabinet 22

JUDICIAL BRANCH
Highest Court...Supreme Court
Supreme Court Chief Justice................................... Robert P. Young Jr.
Number of Supreme Court Judges 7
Number of Intermediate Appellate Court Judges.............................28
Number of U.S. Court Districts...2
U.S. Circuit Court..6th Circuit

MINNESOTA

Nickname..The North Star State
Motto......................................*L'Etoile du Nord* (The North Star)
Flower ....Pink and White Lady-Slipper
Bird...Common Loon
Tree...Red Pine
Song...*Hail! Minnesota*
Entered the Union...May 11, 1858
Capital...St. Paul

STATISTICS

Land Area (square miles)...79,627
Rank in Nation...14
Population...5,457,173
Rank in Nation...21
Density per square mile 68.5
Capital City..St. Paul
Population...290,770
Rank in State..2
Largest City ....Minneapolis
Population...392,880
Number of Representatives in Congress 8
Number of 2012 Electoral Votes...10
Number of County Governments...87
Number of Municipal Governments.................................853
Number of School Districts 338
Number of Special Districts 610

LEGISLATIVE BRANCH

Legislative Body ....Legislature

President of the Senate ....Sandra Pappas
President Pro Tem of the Senate..............................Ann Rest
Secretary of the Senate ....JoAnne Zoff

Speaker of the House.....................................Kurt Daudt
Speaker Pro Tem of the House ....Tim O'Driscoll
Clerk of the House ....Al Mathiowetz (Chief)

2015 Regular Session....................Jan. 6 – May 18, 2015
Number of Senatorial Districts 67
Number of Representative Districts 67

EXECUTIVE BRANCH

Governor ....Mark Dayton
Lieutenant Governor ....Tina Smith
Secretary of State..Steve Simon
Attorney General ....Lori Swanson
Treasurer...............................Myron Frans (Commissioner of Finance)
Auditor...Rebecca Otto

Governor's Present Term................................ 1/2011 – 1/2019
Number of Elected Officials in the Executive Branch.........................5
Number of Members in the Cabinet 25

JUDICIAL BRANCH

Highest Court...Supreme Court
Supreme Court Chief Justice..............Lorie Skjerven Gildea
Number of Supreme Court Judges 7
Number of Intermediate Appellate Court Judges...............19
Number of U.S. Court Districts...1
U.S. Circuit Court...8th Circuit

MISSISSIPPI

Nickname..The Magnolia State
Motto...*Virtute et Armis* (By Valor and Arms)
Flower ....Magnolia
Bird...Mockingbird
Tree...Magnolia
Song...*Go, Mississippi*
Entered the Union.......................................December 10, 1817
Capital...Jackson

STATISTICS

Land Area (square miles)...46,923
Rank in Nation...31
Population...2,994,079
Rank in Nation...31
Density per square mile 63.8
Capital City..Jackson
Population...175,437
Rank in State..1
Largest City ....Jackson
Population...175,437
Number of Representatives in Congress 4
Number of 2012 Electoral Votes...6
Number of County Governments...82
Number of Municipal Governments.................................298
Number of School Districts 164
Number of Special Districts 439

LEGISLATIVE BRANCH

Legislative Body ....Legislature

President of the Senate ....Lt. Gov. Tate Reeves
President Pro Tem of the Senate...................Giles K. Ward
Secretary of the Senate ....Liz Welch

Speaker of the House.....................................Philip Gunn
Speaker Pro Tem of the House ....Greg Snowden
Clerk of the House ....Andrew Ketchings

2015 Regular Session....................Jan. 6 – April 2, 2015
Number of Senatorial Districts 52
Number of Representative Districts 122

EXECUTIVE BRANCH

Governor ....Phil Bryant
Lieutenant Governor ....Tate Reeves
Secretary of State..Delbert Hosemann Jr.
Attorney General ....Jim Hood
Treasurer...Lynn Fitch
Auditor...Stacey Pickering
State Comptroller ....Diane Langham (Fiscal Management Director,
Department of Finance & Administration)

Governor's Present Term................................ 1/2012 – 1/2016
Number of Elected Officials in the Executive Branch.........................8

JUDICIAL BRANCH

Highest Court...Supreme Court
Supreme Court Chief Justice..............William L. Waller Jr.
Number of Supreme Court Judges 9
Number of Intermediate Appellate Court Judges...............10
Number of U.S. Court Districts...2
U.S. Circuit Court...5th Circuit

MISSOURI

Nickname	The Show Me State
Motto	*Salus Populi Suprema Lex Esto*
	(The Welfare of the People Shall Be the Supreme Law)
Flower	White Hawthorn Blossom
Bird	Bluebird
Tree	Flowering Dogwood
Song	*Missouri Waltz*
Entered the Union	August 10, 1821
Capital	Jefferson City

STATISTICS

Land Area (square miles)	68,742
Rank in Nation	18
Population	6,063,589
Rank in Nation	18
Density per square mile	88.2
Capital City	Jefferson City
Population	43,183
Rank in State	15
Largest City	Kansas City
Population	464,310
Number of Representatives in Congress	8
Number of 2012 Electoral Votes	10
Number of Geographic Counties	115
Number of County Governments	114
Number of County Equivalents	1*
Number of Municipal Governments	954
Number of School Districts	534
Number of Special Districts	1,854

*The city of St. Louis is an Independent City and considered a county equivalent.

LEGISLATIVE BRANCH

Legislative Body	General Assembly
President of the Senate	Lt. Gov. Peter Kinder
President Pro Tem of the Senate	Tom Dempsey
Secretary of the Senate	Terry L. Spieler
Speaker of the House	Todd Richardson
Speaker Pro Tem of the House	Denny Hoskins
Clerk of the House	D. Adam Crumbliss
2015 Regular Session	Jan. 7 – May 27, 2015
Number of Senatorial Districts	34
Number of Representative Districts	163

EXECUTIVE BRANCH

Governor	Jay Nixon
Lieutenant Governor	Peter Kinder
Secretary of State	Jason Kander
Attorney General	Chris Koster
Treasurer	Clint Zweifel
Auditor	Nicole Galloway
State Comptroller	Stacy Neal
	(Director, Division of Accounting)
Governor's Present Term	1/2009 – 1/2017
Number of Elected Officials in the Executive Branch	6
Number of Members in the Cabinet	17

JUDICIAL BRANCH

Highest Court	Supreme Court
Supreme Court Chief Justice	Mary R. Russell
Number of Supreme Court Judges	7
Number of Intermediate Appellate Court Judges	32
Number of U.S. Court Districts	2
U.S. Circuit Court	8th Circuit

MONTANA

Nickname	The Treasure State
Motto	*Oro y Plata* (Gold and Silver)
Flower	Bitterroot
Bird	Western Meadowlark
Tree	Ponderosa Pine
Song	*Montana*
Entered the Union	November 8, 1889
Capital	Helena

STATISTICS

Land Area (square miles)	145,546
Rank in Nation	4
Population	1,023,579
Rank in Nation	44
Density per square mile	7.0
Capital City	Helena
Population	29,134
Rank in State	6
Largest City	Billings
Population	106,954
Number of Representatives in Congress	1
Number of 2012 Electoral Votes	3
Number of Geographic Counties	56
Number of County Governments	54
Number of Consolidated Governments	2
Number of Municipal Governments	129
Number of School Districts	319
Number of Special Districts	763

LEGISLATIVE BRANCH

Legislative Body	Legislature
President of the Senate	Debby Barrett
President Pro Tem of the Senate	Eric Moore
Secretary of the Senate	Marilyn Miller
Speaker of the House	Austin Knudsen
Speaker Pro Tem of the House	Lee Randall
Clerk of the House	Lindsey Grovom (Chief)
2015 Regular Session	Jan. 5 – April 28, 2015
Number of Senatorial Districts	50
Number of Representative Districts	100

EXECUTIVE BRANCH

Governor	Steve Bullock
Lieutenant Governor	Angela McLean
Secretary of State	Linda McCulloch
Attorney General	Tim Fox
Treasurer	Mike Kadas
	(Director, Department of Administration)
Auditor	Tori Hunthausen
State Comptroller	Cody Pearce
	(Administrator, State Accounting)
Governor's Present Term	1/2013 – 1/2017
Number of Elected Officials in the Executive Branch	6
Number of Members in the Cabinet	19

JUDICIAL BRANCH

Highest Court	Supreme Court
Supreme Court Chief Justice	Mike McGrath
Number of Supreme Court Judges	7
Number of U.S. Court Districts	1
U.S. Circuit Court	9th Circuit

NEBRASKA

Nickname	The Cornhusker State
Motto	*Equality Before the Law*
Flower	Goldenrod
Bird	Western Meadowlark
Tree	Western Cottonwood
Song	*Beautiful Nebraska*
Entered the Union	March 1, 1867
Capital	Lincoln

STATISTICS

Land Area (square miles)	76,824
Rank in Nation	15
Population	1,881,503
Rank in Nation	37
Density per square mile	24.5
Capital City	Lincoln
Population	265,404
Rank in State	2
Largest City	Omaha
Population	421,570
Number of Representatives in Congress	3
Number of 2012 Electoral Votes	5
Number of County Governments	93
Number of Municipal Governments	530
Number of School Districts	272
Number of Special Districts	1,269

LEGISLATIVE BRANCH

Legislative Body	Unicameral Legislature
President of the Senate	Galen Hadley
	(Speaker of the Legislature)
President Pro Tem of the Senate	Bob Krist
	(Chairperson of the Executive Board)
2015 Regular Session	Jan. 7 – May 29, 2015
Number of Senatorial Districts	49

EXECUTIVE BRANCH

Governor	Pete Ricketts
Lieutenant Governor	Mike Foley
Secretary of State	John Gale
Attorney General	Doug Peterson
Treasurer	Don B. Stenberg
Auditor	Charlie Janssen
State Comptroller	Wes Mohling
	(State Accounting Administrator)
Governor's Present Term	1/2015 – 1/2019
Number of Elected Officials in the Executive Branch	6
Number of Members in the Cabinet	30

JUDICIAL BRANCH

Highest Court	Supreme Court
Supreme Court Chief Justice	Michael G. Heavican
Number of Supreme Court Judges	7
Number of Intermediate Appellate Court Judges	6
Number of U.S. Court Districts	1
U.S. Circuit Court	8th Circuit

NEVADA

Nickname	The Silver State
Motto	*All for Our Country*
Flower	Sagebrush
Bird	Mountain Bluebird
Tree	Bristlecone Pine and Single-leaf Piñon
Song	*Home Means Nevada*
Entered the Union	October 31, 1864
Capital	Carson City

STATISTICS

Land Area (square miles)	109,781
Rank in Nation	7
Population	2,839,099
Rank in Nation	35
Density per square mile	25.9
Capital City	Carson City
Population	54,838
Rank in State	6
Largest City	Las Vegas
Population	596,424
Number of Representatives in Congress	4
Number of 2012 Electoral Votes	6
Number of Geographic Counties	17
Number of County Governments	16
Number of County Equivalents	1*
Number of Municipal Governments	19
Number of School Districts	17
Number of Special Districts	139

* Carson City is an Independent City and considered a county equivalent.

LEGISLATIVE BRANCH

Legislative Body	Legislature
President of the Senate	Lt. Gov. Mark Hutchison
President Pro Tem of the Senate	Joseph P. Hardy
Secretary of the Senate	David A. Byerman
Speaker of the House	John Hambrick
	(Speaker of the Assembly)
Speaker Pro Tem of the House	John Ellison
	(Speaker Pro Tem of the Assembly)
Clerk of the House	Susan Furlong
	(Chief Clerk of the Assembly)
2015 Regular Session	Feb. 2 – June 1, 2015
Number of Senatorial Districts	21
Number of Representative Districts	42

EXECUTIVE BRANCH

Governor	Brian Sandoval
Lieutenant Governor	Mark Hutchison
Secretary of State	Barbara Cegavske
Attorney General	Adam Laxalt
Treasurer	Dan Schwartz
Auditor	Paul V. Townsend
State Comptroller	Ron Knecht (Controller)
Governor's Present Term	1/2011 – 1/2019
Number of Elected Officials in the Executive Branch	6
Number of Members in the Cabinet	21

JUDICIAL BRANCH

Highest Court	Supreme Court
Supreme Court Chief Justice	James Hardesty
Number of Supreme Court Judges	7
Number of U.S. Court Districts	1
U.S. Circuit Court	9th Circuit

NEW HAMPSHIRE

Nickname	The Granite State
Motto	*Live Free or Die*
Flower	Purple Lilac
Bird	Purple Finch
Tree	White Birch
Song	*Old New Hampshire*
Entered the Union	June 21, 1788
Capital	Concord

STATISTICS

Land Area (square miles)	8,953
Rank in Nation	44
Population	1,326,813
Rank in Nation	42
Density per square mile	148.2
Capital City	Concord
Population	42,630
Rank in State	3
Largest City	Manchester
Population	110,209
Number of Representatives in Congress	2
Number of 2012 Electoral Votes	4
Number of County Governments	10
Number of Municipal Governments	13
Number of School Districts	166
Number of Special Districts	131

LEGISLATIVE BRANCH

Legislative Body	General Court
President of the Senate	Chuck Morse
President Pro Tem of the Senate	Sharon Carson
Secretary of the Senate	Tammy L. Wright
	(Clerk of the Senate)
Speaker of the House	Shawn N. Jasper
Speaker Pro Tem of the House	Naida Kaen
	(Deputy Speaker of the House)
Clerk of the House	Karen O. Wadsworth
2015 Regular Session	Jan. 7 – July 1, 2015
Number of Senatorial Districts	24
Number of Representative Districts	204
Number of Senatorial Districts	24
Number of Representative Districts	204

EXECUTIVE BRANCH

Governor	Maggie Hassan
Secretary of State	William M. Gardner
Attorney General	Joseph A. Foster
Treasurer	William Dwyer
Auditor	Jeffrey A. Pattison
State Comptroller	Gerard Murphy (Comptroller)
Governor's Present Term	1/2013 – 1/2017
Number of Elected Officials in the Executive Branch	1

JUDICIAL BRANCH

Highest Court	Supreme Court
Supreme Court Chief Justice	Linda Stewart Dalianis
Number of Supreme Court Judges	5
Number of U.S. Court Districts	1
U.S. Circuit Court	1st Circuit

NEW JERSEY

Nickname	The Garden State
Motto	*Liberty and Prosperity*
Flower	Violet
Bird	Eastern Goldfinch
Tree	Red Oak
Song	*I'm From New Jersey*
Entered the Union	December 18, 1787
Capital	Trenton

STATISTICS

Land Area (square miles)	7,354
Rank in Nation	46
Population	8,938,175
Rank in Nation	11
Density per square mile	1,215.4
Capital City	Trenton
Population	84,477
Rank in State	6
Largest City	Newark
Population	277,727
Number of Representatives in Congress	12
Number of 2012 Electoral Votes	14
Number of County Governments	21
Number of Municipal Governments	324
Number of School Districts	523
Number of Special Districts	234

LEGISLATIVE BRANCH

Legislative Body	Legislature
President of the Senate	Stephen Sweeney
President Pro Tem of the Senate	Nia H. Gill
Secretary of the Senate	Jennifer A. McQuaid
Speaker of the House	Vincent Prieto
	(Speaker of the Assembly)
Speaker Pro Tem of the House	Jerry Green
	(Speaker Pro Tem of the Assembly)
Clerk of the House	Dana M. Burley
	(Clerk of the General Assembly)
2015 Regular Session	Jan. 13, 2015 – Jan. 1, 2016 (projected)
Number of Senatorial Districts	40
Number of Representative Districts	40

EXECUTIVE BRANCH

Governor	Chris Christie
Lieutenant Governor	Kim Guadagno
Attorney General	John Jay Hoffman
Treasurer	Andrew P. Sidamon-Eristoff
Auditor	Stephen Eells
State Comptroller	Charlene M. Holzbaur
Governor's Present Term	1/2010 – 1/2018
Number of Elected Officials in the Executive Branch	2
Number of Members in the Cabinet	23

JUDICIAL BRANCH

Highest Court	Supreme Court
Supreme Court Chief Justice	Stuart Rabner
Number of Supreme Court Judges	7
Number of Intermediate Appellate Court Judges	33
Number of U.S. Court Districts	1
U.S. Circuit Court	3rd Circuit

NEW MEXICO

Nickname	The Land of Enchantment
Motto	*Crescit Eundo* (It Grows As It Goes)
Flower	Yucca (Our Lord's Candles)
Bird	Roadrunner aka Greater Roadrunner
Tree	Piñon
Song	*Asi es Nuevo Mexico* and *O, Fair New Mexico*
Entered the Union	January 6, 1912
Capital	Santa Fe

STATISTICS

Land Area (square miles)	121,298
Rank in Nation	5
Population	2,085,572
Rank in Nation	36
Density per square mile	17.2
Capital City	Santa Fe
Population	69,204
Rank in State	4
Largest City	Albuquerque
Population	555,417
Number of Representatives in Congress	3
Number of 2012 Electoral Votes	5
Number of County Governments	33
Number of Municipal Governments	103
Number of School Districts	96
Number of Special Districts	631

LEGISLATIVE BRANCH

Legislative Body	Legislature

President of the Senate	Lt. Gov. John A. Sanchez
President Pro Tem of the Senate	Mary Kay Papen
Secretary of the Senate	Lenore Naranjo (Chief Clerk of the Senate)

Speaker of the House	Don Tripp
Clerk of the House	Denise Greenlaw Ramonas (Chief)

2015 Regular Session	Jan. 20 – March 21, 2015
Number of Senatorial Districts	42
Number of Representative Districts	70

EXECUTIVE BRANCH

Governor	Susana Martinez
Lieutenant Governor	John A. Sanchez
Secretary of State	Dianna J. Duran
Attorney General	Hector Balderas
Treasurer	Tim Eichenberg
Auditor	Tim Keller
State Comptroller	Ronald Spilman (Controller)

Governor's Present Term	1/2011 – 1/2019
Number of Elected Officials in the Executive Branch	7
Number of Members in the Cabinet	29

JUDICIAL BRANCH

Highest Court	Supreme Court
Supreme Court Chief Justice	Barbara J. Vigil
Number of Supreme Court Judges	5
Number of Intermediate Appellate Court Judges	10
Number of U.S. Court Districts	1
U.S. Circuit Court	10th Circuit

NEW YORK

Nickname	The Empire State
Motto	*Excelsior* (Ever Upward)
Flower	Rose
Bird	Bluebird
Tree	Sugar Maple
Song	*I Love New York*
Entered the Union	July 26, 1788
Capital	Albany

STATISTICS

Land Area (square miles)	47,126
Rank in Nation	30
Population	19,746,227
Rank in Nation	4
Density per square mile	419.0
Capital City	Albany
Population	97,904
Rank in State	6
Largest City	New York City
Population	8,336,697
Number of Representatives in Congress	27
Number of 2012 Electoral Votes	29
Number of Geographic Counties	62*
Number of County Governments	57
Number of Municipal Governments	614
Number of School Districts	679
Number of Special Districts	1,174

*New York City is coextensive with the five boroughs (counties).

LEGISLATIVE BRANCH

Legislative Body	Legislature

President of the Senate	Lt. Gov. Kathy Hochul
President Pro Tem of the Senate	Dean G. Skelos (Temporary President & Majority Leader)
Secretary of the Senate	Frank Patience

Speaker of the House	Carl Heastie (Speaker of the Assembly)
Speaker Pro Tem of the House	Jeffrion Aubry (Speaker Pro Tempore of the Assembly)
Clerk of the House	Laurene R. Kretzler

2015 Regular Session	Jan. 7 – Dec. 31, 2015 (projected)
Number of Senatorial Districts	63
Number of Representative Districts	150

EXECUTIVE BRANCH

Governor	Andrew M. Cuomo
Lieutenant Governor	Kathy Hochul
Secretary of State	Cesar Perales
Attorney General	Eric T. Schneiderman
Treasurer	Eric Mostert
State Comptroller	Thomas P. DiNapoli

Governor's Present Term	1/2011 – 1/2019
Number of Elected Officials in the Executive Branch	4
Number of Members in the Cabinet	75

JUDICIAL BRANCH

Highest Court	Court of Appeals
Supreme Court Chief Justice	Sheila Abdus-Salaam
Number of Supreme Court Judges	7
Number of Intermediate Appellate Court Judges	66
Number of U.S. Court Districts	4
U.S. Circuit Court	2nd Circuit

NORTH CAROLINA

Nickname.............................. The Tar Heel State and Old North State
Motto........................ *Esse Quam Videri* (To Be Rather Than to Seem)
Flower .... Dogwood
Bird.. Cardinal
Tree...Long Leaf Pine
Song... *The Old North State*
Entered the Union... November 21, 1789
Capital...Raleigh

STATISTICS

Land Area (square miles)...48,618
Rank in Nation...29
Population...9,943,964
Rank in Nation...9
Density per square mile 204.5
Capital City...Raleigh
Population...423,179
Rank in State...2
Largest City..Charlotte
Population...775,202
Number of Representatives in Congress 13
Number of 2012 Electoral Votes...15
Number of County Governments...100
Number of Municipal Governments 533
Number of Special Districts 320

LEGISLATIVE BRANCH

Legislative Body .... General Assembly

President of the Senate .... Lt. Gov. Dan Forest
President Pro Tem of the Senate...Phil Berger
Secretary of the Senate ....Sarah Lang
(Principal Clerk of the Senate)

Speaker of the House..Tim Moore
Speaker Pro Tem of the House ....Paul Stam
Clerk of the House ....Denise Weeks
(Principal Clerk of the House)

2015 Regular Session....................Jan. 14 – early July 2015 (projected)
Number of Senatorial Districts 50
Number of Representative Districts 120

EXECUTIVE BRANCH

Governor ....Pat McCrory
Lieutenant Governor ....Dan Forest
Secretary of State..Elaine Marshall
Attorney General ....Roy Cooper
Treasurer..Janet Cowell
Auditor...Beth Wood
State Comptroller ....Linda Combs (Controller)

Governor's Present Term.. 1/2013 – 1/2017
Number of Elected Officials in the Executive Branch.......................10
Number of Members in the Cabinet 9

JUDICIAL BRANCH

Highest Court...Supreme Court
Supreme Court Chief Justice.............................. Mark D. Martin
Number of Supreme Court Judges 7
Number of Intermediate Appellate Court Judges............................15
Number of U.S. Court Districts..3
U.S. Circuit Court...4th Circuit

NORTH DAKOTA

Nickname...Peace Garden State
Motto...*Liberty and Union, Now and Forever,*
One and Inseparable
Flower ....Wild Prairie Rose
Bird...Western Meadowlark
Tree..American Elm
Song...*North Dakota Hymn*
Entered the Union.. November 2, 1889
Capital...Bismarck

STATISTICS

Land Area (square miles)...69,001
Rank in Nation...17
Population...739,482
Rank in Nation...47
Density per square mile 10.7
Capital City... Bismarck
Population...564,751
Rank in State...2
Largest City...Fargo
Population...109,779
Number of Representatives in Congress 1
Number of 2012 Electoral Votes...3
Number of County Governments...53
Number of Municipal Governments 357
Number of School Districts 183
Number of Special Districts 779

LEGISLATIVE BRANCH

Legislative Body ....Legislative Assembly

President of the Senate .... Lt. Gov. Drew Wrigley
President Pro Tem of the Senate... Dick Dever
Secretary of the Senate ....William Horton

Speaker of the House... Wesley Belter
Clerk of the House .... Buell Reich

2015 Regular Session..Jan. 6 – April 29, 2015
Number of Senatorial Districts 47
Number of Representative Districts 47

EXECUTIVE BRANCH

Governor .... Jack Dalrymple
Lieutenant Governor .... Drew Wrigley
Secretary of State..Alvin Jaeger
Attorney General ....Wayne Stenehjem
Treasurer..Kelly Schmidt
Auditor...Robert R. Peterson
State Comptroller ....Pam Sharp
(Director, Office of Management & Budget)

Governor's Present Term.. 12/2010 – 12/2016
Number of Elected Officials in the Executive Branch.......................12
Number of Members in the Cabinet 18

JUDICIAL BRANCH

Highest Court...Supreme Court
Supreme Court Chief Justice............................ Gerald W. VandeWalle
Number of Supreme Court Judges 5
Number of Intermediate Appellate Court Judges...............................3
Number of U.S. Court Districts..1
U.S. Circuit Court...8th Circuit

OHIO

Nickname	The Buckeye State
Motto	*With God, All Things Are Possible*
Flower	Scarlet Carnation
Bird	Cardinal
Tree	Buckeye
Song	*Beautiful Ohio*
Entered the Union	March 1, 1803
Capital	Columbus

STATISTICS

Land Area (square miles)	40,861
Rank in Nation	35
Population	11,594,163
Rank in Nation	7
Density per square mile	283.7
Capital City	Columbus
Population	809,798
Rank in State	1
Largest City	Columbus
Population	809,798
Number of Representatives in Congress	16
Number of 2012 Electoral Votes	18
Number of County Governments	88
Number of Municipal Governments	937
Number of School Districts	668
Number of Special Districts	841

LEGISLATIVE BRANCH

Legislative Body	General Assembly

President of the Senate	Keith Faber
President Pro Tem of the Senate	Chris Widener
Secretary of the Senate	Vincent Keeran
	(Clerk of the Senate)

Speaker of the House	Cliff Rosenberger
Speaker Pro Tem of the House	Ron Amstutz
Clerk of the House	Bradley Young
	(Legislative Clerk of the House)

2015 Regular Session	Jan. 5 – Dec. 31, 2015
Number of Senatorial Districts	33
Number of Representative Districts	99

EXECUTIVE BRANCH

Governor	John Kasich
Lieutenant Governor	Mary Taylor
Secretary of State	Jon Husted
Attorney General	Mike DeWine
Treasurer	Josh Mandel
Auditor	David A. Yost
State Comptroller	Timothy Keen
	(Director, Office of Budget & Management)

Governor's Present Term	1/2011 – 1/2019
Number of Elected Officials in the Executive Branch	6
Number of Members in the Cabinet	24

JUDICIAL BRANCH

Highest Court	Supreme Court
Supreme Court Chief Justice	Maureen O'Connor
Number of Supreme Court Judges	7
Number of Intermediate Appellate Court Judges	69
Number of U.S. Court Districts	2
U.S. Circuit Court	6th Circuit

OKLAHOMA

Nickname	The Sooner State
Motto	*Labor Omnia Vincit* (Labor Conquers All Things)
Flower	Mistletoe
Bird	Scissor-tailed Flycatcher
Tree	Redbud
Song	*Oklahoma*
Entered the Union	November 16, 1907
Capital	Oklahoma City

STATISTICS

Land Area (square miles)	68,595
Rank in Nation	19
Population	3,878,051
Rank in Nation	28
Density per square mile	56.5
Capital City	Oklahoma City
Population	599,199
Rank in State	1
Largest City	Oklahoma City
Population	599,199
Number of Representatives in Congress	5
Number of 2012 Electoral Votes	7
Number of County Governments	77
Number of Municipal Governments	590
Number of School Districts	550
Number of Special Districts	635

LEGISLATIVE BRANCH

Legislative Body	Legislature

President of the Senate	Lt. Gov. Todd Lamb
President Pro Tem of the Senate	Brian Bingman
Secretary of the Senate	Paul Ziriax

Speaker of the House	Jeffrey Hickman
Speaker Pro Tem of the House	Lee Denney
Clerk of the House	Jan Harrison (Chief)

2015 Regular Session	Feb. 2 – May 22, 2015
Number of Senatorial Districts	48
Number of Representative Districts	101

EXECUTIVE BRANCH

Governor	Mary Fallin
Lieutenant Governor	Todd Lamb
Secretary of State	Chris Benge
Attorney General	Scott Pruitt
Treasurer	Ken Miller
Auditor	Gary Jones
State Comptroller	Lynne Bajema (Comptroller)

Governor's Present Term	1/2011 – 1/2019
Number of Elected Officials in the Executive Branch	8
Number of Members in the Cabinet	16

JUDICIAL BRANCH

Highest Court	Supreme Court
Supreme Court Chief Justice	John Reif
Number of Supreme Court Judges	9
Number of Intermediate Appellate Court Judges	12
Number of U.S. Court Districts	3
U.S. Circuit Court	10th Circuit

OREGON

Nickname	The Beaver State
Motto	*She Flies with Her Own Wings*
Flower	Oregon Grape
Bird	Western Meadowlark
Tree	Douglas Fir
Song	*Oregon, My Oregon*
Entered the Union	February 14, 1859
Capital	Salem

STATISTICS

Land Area (square miles)	95,988
Rank in Nation	10
Population	3,970,239
Rank in Nation	27
Density per square mile	41.4
Capital City	Salem
Population	157,429
Rank in State	3
Largest City	Portland
Population	603,106
Number of Representatives in Congress	5
Number of 2012 Electoral Votes	7
Number of County Governments	36
Number of Municipal Governments	241
Number of School Districts	230
Number of Special Districts	1,035

LEGISLATIVE BRANCH

Legislative Body	Legislative Assembly
President of the Senate	Peter Courtney
President Pro Tem of the Senate	Ginny Burdick
Secretary of the Senate	Lori Brocker
Speaker of the House	Tina Kotek
Speaker Pro Tem of the House	Tobias Read
Clerk of the House	Tim Sekerak (Chief)
2015 Regular Session	Feb. 2 – July 11, 2015 (projected)
Number of Senatorial Districts	30
Number of Representative Districts	60

EXECUTIVE BRANCH

Governor	Kate Brown
Secretary of State	Jeanne Atkins
Attorney General	Ellen Rosenblum
Treasurer	Ted Wheeler
Auditor	Gary Blackmer
State Comptroller	Robert Hamilton
	(Manager, Statewide Accounting, Chief Financial Office)
Governor's Present Term	2/2015 – 1/2019
Number of Elected Officials in the Executive Branch	6

JUDICIAL BRANCH

Highest Court	Supreme Court
Supreme Court Chief Justice	Thomas A. Balmer
Number of Supreme Court Judges	7
Number of Intermediate Appellate Court Judges	13
Number of U.S. Court Districts	1
U.S. Circuit Court	9th Circuit

PENNSYLVANIA

Nickname	The Keystone State
Motto	*Virtue, Liberty and Independence*
Flower	Mountain Laurel (Kalmia latifolia)
Bird	Ruffed Grouse
Tree	Hemlock
Song	*Pennsylvania*
Entered the Union	December 12, 1787
Capital	Harrisburg

STATISTICS

Land Area (square miles)	44,743
Rank in Nation	32
Population	12,787,209
Rank in Nation	6
Density per square mile	285.8
Capital City	Harrisburg
Population	49,279
Rank in State	9
Largest City	Philadelphia
Population	1,547,607
Number of Representatives in Congress	18
Number of 2012 Electoral Votes	20
Number of Geographic Counties	67
Number of County Governments	66
Number of Consolidated Governments	1
Number of Municipal Governments	1,015
Number of School Districts	514
Number of Special Districts	1,756

LEGISLATIVE BRANCH

Legislative Body	General Assembly
President of the Senate	Lt. Gov. Mike Stack
President Pro Tem of the Senate	Joseph B. Scarnati
Secretary of the Senate	Megan Totino Consedine
	(Secretary-Parliamentarian of the Senate)
Speaker of the House	Mike Turzai
Clerk of the House	Anthony Frank Barbush (Chief)
2015 Regular Session	Jan. 6 – Dec. 31, 2015 (projected)
Number of Senatorial Districts	50
Number of Representative Districts	203

EXECUTIVE BRANCH

Governor	Tom Wolf
Lieutenant Governor	Mike Stack
Secretary of State	Pedro Cortes
Attorney General	Kathleen Kane
Treasurer	Chris Craig
Auditor	Eugene DePasquale
State Comptroller	Anna Marie Kiehl
	(Chief Accounting Officer)
Governor's Present Term	1/2015 – 1/2019
Number of Elected Officials in the Executive Branch	5
Number of Members in the Cabinet	28

JUDICIAL BRANCH

Highest Court	Supreme Court
Supreme Court Chief Justice	Thomas G. Saylor
Number of Supreme Court Judges	7
Number of Intermediate Appellate Court Judges	32
Number of U.S. Court Districts	3
U.S. Circuit Court	3rd Circuit

RHODE ISLAND

Nickname	Little Rhody and Ocean State
Motto	*Hope*
Flower	Violet
Bird	Rhode Island Red
Tree	Red Maple
Song	*Rhode Island*
Entered the Union	May 29, 1790
Capital	Providence

STATISTICS

Land Area (square miles)	1,034
Rank in Nation	50
Population	1,055,173
Rank in Nation	43
Density per square mile	1,020.7
Capital City	Providence
Population	178,432
Rank in State	1
Largest City	Providence
Population	178,432
Number of Representatives in Congress	2
Number of 2012 Electoral Votes	4
Number of Geographic Counties	5
Number of Municipal Governments	8
Number of School Districts	4
Number of Special Districts	90

LEGISLATIVE BRANCH

Legislative Body	General Assembly
President of the Senate	M. Teresa Paiva-Weed
President Pro Tem of the Senate	William Walaska
Secretary of the Senate	Joseph Brady
Speaker of the House	Nicholas A. Mattiello
Clerk of the House	Frank McCabe
2015 Regular Session	Jan. 6 – June 25, 2015
Number of Senatorial Districts	38
Number of Representative Districts	75

EXECUTIVE BRANCH

Governor	Gina Raimondo
Lieutenant Governor	Dan McKee
Secretary of State	Nellie Gorbea
Attorney General	Peter F. Kilmartin
Treasurer	Seth Magaziner
Auditor	Dennis Hoyle
State Comptroller	Marc Leonetti (Controller)
Governor's Present Term	1/2015 – 1/2019
Number of Elected Officials in the Executive Branch	5
Number of Members in the Cabinet	24

JUDICIAL BRANCH

Highest Court	Supreme Court
Supreme Court Chief Justice	Paul A. Suttell
Number of Supreme Court Judges	5
Number of U.S. Court Districts	1
U.S. Circuit Court	1st Circuit

SOUTH CAROLINA

Nickname	The Palmetto State
Motto	*Animis Opibusque Parati* (Prepared in Mind and Resources) and *Dum Spiro Spero* (While I breathe, I Hope)
Flower	Yellow Jessamine
Bird	Carolina Wren
Tree	Palmetto
Song	*Carolina* and *South Carolina on My Mind*
Entered the Union	May 23, 1788
Capital	Columbia

STATISTICS

Land Area (square miles)	30,061
Rank in Nation	40
Population	4,832,482
Rank in Nation	24
Density per square mile	160.8
Capital City	Columbia
Population	131,686
Rank in State	1
Largest City	Columbia
Population	131,686
Number of Representatives in Congress	7
Number of 2012 Electoral Votes	9
Number of County Governments	46
Number of Municipal Governments	270
Number of School Districts	83
Number of Special Districts	279

LEGISLATIVE BRANCH

Legislative Body	General Assembly
President of the Senate	Lt. Gov. Henry McMaster
President Pro Tem of the Senate	Hugh K. Leatherman
Secretary of the Senate	Jeffrey Gossett (Clerk of the Senate)
Speaker of the House	James H. Lucas
Speaker Pro Tem of the House	Thomas E. Pope
Clerk of the House	Charles F. Reid
2015 Regular Session	Jan. 13 – June 4, 2015
Number of Senatorial Districts	46
Number of Representative Districts	124

EXECUTIVE BRANCH

Governor	Nikki Haley
Lieutenant Governor	Henry McMaster
Secretary of State	Mark Hammond
Attorney General	Alan Wilson
Treasurer	Curtis Loftis
Auditor	Richard H. Gilbert Jr.
State Comptroller	Richard Eckstrom (Comptroller General)
Governor's Present Term	1/2011 – 1/2019
Number of Elected Officials in the Executive Branch	9
Number of Members in the Cabinet	15

JUDICIAL BRANCH

Highest Court	Supreme Court
Supreme Court Chief Justice	Jean Hoefer Toal
Number of Supreme Court Judges	5
Number of Intermediate Appellate Court Judges	9
Number of U.S. Court Districts	1
U.S. Circuit Court	4th Circuit

SOUTH DAKOTA

Nickname..The Mt. Rushmore State
Motto...*Under God the People Rule*
Flower ....American Pasque
Bird..Ring-necked Pheasant
Tree..Black Hills Spruce
Song...*Hail, South Dakota*
Entered the Union.......................................November 2, 1889
Capital...Pierre

STATISTICS

Land Area (square miles)..75,811
Rank in Nation..16
Population..853,175
Rank in Nation..46
Density per square mile 11.3
Capital City...Pierre
Population..13,914
Rank in State..8
Largest City..Sioux Falls
Population..159,908
Number of Representatives in Congress 1
Number of 2012 Electoral Votes....................................3
Number of County Governments..................................66
Number of Municipal Governments............................311
Number of School Districts..152
Number of Special Districts 547

LEGISLATIVE BRANCH

Legislative Body ....Legislature

President of the Senate ....Lt. Gov. Matthew Michels
President Pro Tem of the Senate....................Gary Cammack
Secretary of the Senate ....Jeanette Schipper

Speaker of the House.....................................Dean Wink
Speaker Pro Tem of the House ....G. Mark Mickelson
Clerk of the House ....Arlene Kvislen (Chief)

2015 Regular Session........................Jan. 13 – March 30, 2015
Number of Senatorial Districts 35
Number of Representative Districts 35

EXECUTIVE BRANCH

Governor ....Dennis Daugaard
Lieutenant Governor ....Matthew Michels
Secretary of State...Shantel Krebs
Attorney General ....Martin Jackley
Treasurer..Richard Sattgast
Auditor...Martin L. Guindon

Governor's Present Term.............................. 1/2011 – 1/2019
Number of Elected Officials in the Executive Branch........................8
Number of Members in the Cabinet 19

JUDICIAL BRANCH

Highest Court...Supreme Court
Supreme Court Chief Justice..................David E. Gilbertson
Number of Supreme Court Judges 5
Number of U.S. Court Districts....................................1
U.S. Circuit Court..8th Circuit

TENNESSEE

Nickname..The Volunteer State
Motto...*Agriculture and Commerce*
Flower ....Iris
Bird..Mockingbird
Tree..Tulip Poplar
Song...*When It's Iris Time in Tennessee*;
The Tennessee Waltz; *My Homeland, Tennessee*;
My Tennessee; and *Rocky Top*
Entered the Union.......................................June 1, 1796
Capital...Nashville

STATISTICS

Land Area (square miles)..41,235
Rank in Nation..34
Population..6,549,352
Rank in Nation..17
Density per square mile 158.8
Capital City...Nashville
Population..624,496
Rank in State..2
Largest City..Memphis
Population..655,155
Number of Representatives in Congress 9
Number of 2012 Electoral Votes....................................11
Number of Geographic Counties..................................95
Number of County Governments..................................92
Number of Consolidated Governments..........................3
Number of Municipal Governments............................345
Number of School Districts..14
Number of Special Districts 465

LEGISLATIVE BRANCH

Legislative Body ....General Assembly

President of the Senate ....Lt. Gov. Ron Ramsey
President Pro Tem of the Senate.........................Bo Watson
(Speaker Pro Tem)
Secretary of the Senate ....Russell Humphrey
(Chief Clerk of the Senate)

Speaker of the House.....................................Beth Harwell
Speaker Pro Tem of the House ....Curtis Johnson
Clerk of the House ....Joe McCord (Chief)

2015 Regular Session........................Jan. 13 – April 22, 2015
Number of Senatorial Districts 33
Number of Representative Districts 99

EXECUTIVE BRANCH

Governor ....Bill Haslam
Lieutenant Governor ....Ron Ramsey
Secretary of State...Tre Hargett
Attorney General ....Herbert Slatery
Treasurer..David H. Lillard Jr.
State Comptroller ....Justin P. Wilson

Governor's Present Term.............................. 1/2011 – 1/2019
Number of Elected Officials in the Executive Branch........................1
Number of Members in the Cabinet 29

JUDICIAL BRANCH

Highest Court...Supreme Court
Supreme Court Chief Justice...........................Sharon G. Lee
Number of Supreme Court Judges 5
Number of Intermediate Appellate Court Judges............24
Number of U.S. Court Districts....................................3
U.S. Circuit Court..6th Circuit

TEXAS

Nickname..The Lone Star State
Motto.. *Friendship*
Flower .... Bluebonnet (Buffalo Clover, Wolf Flower)
Bird...Mockingbird
Tree..Pecan
Song...*Texas, Our Texas*
Entered the Union................................December 29, 1845
Capital..Austin

STATISTICS

Land Area (square miles)..................................261,232
Rank in Nation...2
Population..26,956,958
Rank in Nation...2
Density per square mile 103.2
Capital City..Austin
Population..842,592
Rank in State..4
Largest City...Houston
Population...2,160,821
Number of Representatives in Congress 36
Number of 2012 Electoral Votes...........................38
Number of County Governments.......................254
Number of Municipal Governments 1,214
Number of School Districts 1,079
Number of Special Districts 2,600

LEGISLATIVE BRANCH

Legislative Body ....Legislature

President of the Senate ....Lt. Gov. Dan Patrick
President Pro Tem of the Senate.....................Juan Hinojosa
Secretary of the Senate ....Patsy Spaw

Speaker of the House..Joe Straus
Speaker Pro Tem of the House ....Dennis Bonnen
Clerk of the House ....Robert Haney (Chief)

2015 Regular Session..........................Jan. 13 – June 1, 2015
Number of Senatorial Districts 31
Number of Representative Districts 150

EXECUTIVE BRANCH

Governor .... Greg Abbott
Lieutenant Governor ....Dan Patrick
Secretary of State...Nandita Berry
Attorney General...Ken Paxton
Auditor...John Keel
State Comptroller ....Glenn Hegar
(Comptroller of Public Accounts)

Governor's Present Term.............................. 1/2015 – 1/2019
Number of Elected Officials in the Executive Branch.........6

JUDICIAL BRANCH

Highest Court..Supreme Court
Supreme Court Chief Justice......................Nathan L. Hecht
Number of Supreme Court Judges 9
Number of Intermediate Appellate Court Judges.............80
Number of U.S. Court Districts................................4
U.S. Circuit Court...5th Circuit

UTAH

Nickname..The Beehive State
Motto.. *Industry*
Flower ....Sego Lily
Bird...California Seagull
Tree... Blue Spruce
Song...*Utah, We Love Thee*
Entered the Union................................January 4, 1896
Capital..Salt Lake City

STATISTICS

Land Area (square miles)....................................82,170
Rank in Nation...12
Population..2,942,902
Rank in Nation...33
Density per square mile 35.8
Capital City..Salt Lake City
Population..189,314
Rank in State..1
Largest City..Salt Lake City
Population..189,314
Number of Representatives in Congress 4
Number of 2012 Electoral Votes.............................6
Number of County Governments.........................29
Number of Municipal Governments 245
Number of School Districts 41
Number of Special Districts 307

LEGISLATIVE BRANCH

Legislative Body ....Legislature

President of the Senate .... Wayne Niederhauser
Secretary of the Senate ....Leslie McLean

Speaker of the House.......................... Gregory H. Hughes
Clerk of the House ....Sandy Tenney (Chief)

2015 Regular Session.....................Jan. 26 – March 12, 2015
Number of Senatorial Districts 29
Number of Representative Districts 75

EXECUTIVE BRANCH

Governor ....Gary R. Herbert
Lieutenant Governor ....Spencer Cox
Attorney General ....Sean Reyes
Treasurer..Richard Ellis
Auditor..John Dougall
State Comptroller ....John Reidhead
(Director, Division of Finance)

Governor's Present Term.............................. 8/2009 – 1/2017
Number of Elected Officials in the Executive Branch.........5
Number of Members in the Cabinet 24

JUDICIAL BRANCH

Highest Court..Supreme Court
Supreme Court Chief Justice................. Matthew B. Durrant
Number of Supreme Court Judges 5
Number of Intermediate Appellate Court Judges...............7
Number of U.S. Court Districts................................1
U.S. Circuit Court.................................. 10th Circuit

VERMONT

Nickname..The Green Mountain State
Motto.. *Freedom and Unity*
Flower .... Red Clover
Bird...Hermit Thrush
Tree .... Sugar Maple
Song... *Hail, Vermont!*
Entered the Union...March 4, 1791
Capital...Montpelier

STATISTICS

Land Area (square miles)...9,217
Rank in Nation..43
Population...626,562
Rank in Nation..49
Density per square mile 68.0
Capital City...Montpelier
Population...7,787
Rank in State..6
Largest City..Burlington
Population...42,282
Number of Representatives in Congress 1
Number of 2012 Electoral Votes...3
Number of County Governments.......................................14
Number of Municipal Governments 43
Number of School Districts 291
Number of Special Districts 153

LEGISLATIVE BRANCH

Legislative Body .... General Assembly

President of the Senate ....Lt. Gov. Phil Scott
President Pro Tem of the Senate...................John F. Campbell
Secretary of the Senate ....John H. Bloomer Jr.

Speaker of the House...Shap Smith
Clerk of the House .... Donald G. Milne

2015 Regular Session......................Jan. 7 – May 16, 2015
Number of Senatorial Districts 13
Number of Representative Districts 104

EXECUTIVE BRANCH

Governor ....Peter E. Shumlin
Lieutenant Governor ....Phil Scott
Secretary of State...Jim Condos
Attorney General ....William H. Sorrell
Treasurer..Elizabeth Pearce
Auditor... Douglas Hoffer
Comptroller..James Reardon
(Commissioner, Dept. of Finance and Management)

Governor's Present Term............................ 1/2011 – 1/2017
Number of Elected Officials in the Executive Branch.........................6
Number of Members in the Cabinet 12

JUDICIAL BRANCH

Highest Court...Supreme Court
Supreme Court Chief Justice......................... Paul L. Reiber
Number of Supreme Court Judges 5
Number of U.S. Court Districts..1
U.S. Circuit Court..2nd Circuit

VIRGINIA

Nickname.. The Old Dominion
Motto........................... *Sic Semper Tyrannis* (Thus Always to Tyrants)
Flower .... Dogwood
Bird.. Cardinal
Tree .... Dogwood
Song....................................*Carry Me Back to Old Virginia*
Entered the Union..June 25, 1788
Capital... Richmond

STATISTICS

Land Area (square miles)..39,490
Rank in Nation..36
Population...8,326,289
Rank in Nation..12
Density per square mile 210.8
Capital City...Richmond
Population..210,309
Rank in State..4
Largest City...Virginia Beach
Population...447,021
Number of Representatives in Congress 11
Number of 2012 Electoral Votes.......................................13
Number of Geographic Counties..95*
Number of Municipal Governments 229
Number of School Districts 1
Number of Special Districts 193

*In addition to the 95 counties, Virginia has 39 Independent Cities, considered county equivalents. Five cities in the Hampton Roads area were formed of entire counties and function at the county level of government. They are listed with the Independent Cities but counted as consolidated governments in Virginia.

LEGISLATIVE BRANCH

Legislative Body .... General Assembly

President of the Senate ....Lt. Gov. Ralph Northam
President Pro Tem of the Senate...........................Walter Stosch
Secretary of the Senate ....Susan Clarke Schaar
(Clerk of the Senate)

Speaker of the House.................................... William J. Howell
Clerk of the House ....G. Paul Nardo

2015 Regular Session.....................Jan. 14 – Feb. 27, 2015
Number of Senatorial Districts 40
Number of Representative Districts 100

EXECUTIVE BRANCH

Governor ....Terry McAuliffe
Lieutenant Governor .... Ralph Northam
Secretary of State.. Levar Stoney
(Secretary of the Commonwealth)
Attorney General .... Mark Herring
Treasurer...Manju Ganeriwala
Auditor..Martha Mavredes
State Comptroller .... David Von Moll (Comptroller)

Governor's Present Term............................... 1/2014 – 1/2018
Number of Elected Officials in the Executive Branch.........................3
Number of Members in the Cabinet 15

JUDICIAL BRANCH

Highest Court...Supreme Court
Supreme Court Chief Justice.................... Donald W. Lemons
Number of Supreme Court Judges 7
Number of Intermediate Appellate Court Judges............................11
Number of U.S. Court Districts..2
U.S. Circuit Court..4th Circuit

WASHINGTON

Nickname..The Evergreen State
Motto........................ *Alki* (Chinook Indian word meaning By and By)
Flower ....Coast Rhododendron
Bird..Willow Goldfinch
Tree..Western Hemlock
Song.................................. *Washington, My Home*
Entered the Union....................................November 11, 1889
Capital..Olympia

STATISTICS

Land Area (square miles)..............................66,456
Rank in Nation..20
Population..7,061,530
Rank in Nation..13
Density per square mile 106.3
Capital City..Olympia
Population..47,698
Rank in State...24
Largest City..Seattle
Population..634,535
Number of Representatives in Congress 10
Number of 2012 Electoral Votes 12
Number of County Governments..........................39
Number of Municipal Governments........................281
Number of School Districts 295
Number of Special Districts 1,285

LEGISLATIVE BRANCH

Legislative Body ....Legislature

President of the Senate ....Lt. Gov. Brad Owen
President Pro Tem of the Senate..........................Pam Roach
Secretary of the Senate ....Hunter G. Goodman

Speaker of the House....................................Frank Chopp
Speaker Pro Tem of the House ....Jim Moeller
Clerk of the House ....Barbara Baker (Chief)

2015 Regular Session.....................Jan. 12 – April 24, 2015
Number of Senatorial Districts 49
Number of Representative Districts 49

EXECUTIVE BRANCH

Governor ....Jay Inslee
Lieutenant Governor ....Brad Owen
Secretary of State ....Kim Wyman
Attorney General ....Bob Ferguson
Treasurer..James McIntire
Auditor..Jan Jutte
State Comptroller ....David Schumacher
                (Director, Office of Financial Management)

Governor's Present Term.....................1/2013 – 1/2017
Number of Elected Officials in the Executive Branch........9
Number of Members in the Cabinet 25

JUDICIAL BRANCH

Highest Court..Supreme Court
Supreme Court Chief Justice............................Barbara A. Madsen
Number of Supreme Court Judges 9
Number of Intermediate Appellate Court Judges...........22
Number of U.S. Court Districts.........................2
U.S. Circuit Court.....................................9th Circuit

WEST VIRGINIA

Nickname..The Mountain State
Motto.. *Montani Semper Liberi*
                (Mountaineers Are Always Free)
Flower ....Rhododendron
Bird..Cardinal
Tree..Sugar Maple
Song........................... *West Virginia, My Home Sweet Home*;
                The West Virginia Hills and
                This is My West Virginia
Entered the Union....................................June 20, 1863
Capital..Charleston

STATISTICS

Land Area (square miles)..............................24,038
Rank in Nation..41
Population..1,850,326
Rank in Nation..38
Density per square mile 77.0
Capital City..Charleston
Population..51,018
Rank in State...1
Largest City..Charleston
Population..51,018
Number of Representatives in Congress 3
Number of 2012 Electoral Votes 5
Number of County Governments..........................55
Number of Municipal Governments........................232
Number of School Districts 55
Number of Special Districts 317

LEGISLATIVE BRANCH

Legislative Body ....Legislature

President of the Senate ....Lt. Gov. Bill Cole
President Pro Tem of the Senate..........................Donna J. Boley
Secretary of the Senate ....Clark Barnes
                (Clerk of the Senate)

Speaker of the House....................................Timothy R. Miley
Speaker Pro Tem of the House ....Randy Swartzmiller
Clerk of the House ....Gregory M. Gray
                (Clerk of the House of Delegates)

2015 Regular Session.....................Jan. 14 – March 14, 2015
Number of Senatorial Districts 17
Number of Representative Districts 58

EXECUTIVE BRANCH

Governor ....Earl Ray Tomblin
Lieutenant Governor ....Bill Cole
Secretary of State ....Natalie Tennant
Attorney General ....Patrick Morrisey
Treasurer..John D. Perdue
Auditor..Glen B. Ganier III

Governor's Present Term.....................11/2010 – 1/2017
Number of Elected Officials in the Executive Branch........6
Number of Members in the Cabinet 10

JUDICIAL BRANCH

Highest Court..Supreme Court of Appeals
Supreme Court Chief Justice............................Margaret L. Workman
Number of Supreme Court Judges 5
Number of U.S. Court Districts.........................2
U.S. Circuit Court.....................................4th Circuit

WISCONSIN

Nickname.. The Badger State
Motto..*Forward*
Flower..Wood Violet
Bird..Robin
Tree... Sugar Maple
Song..*On, Wisconsin!*
Entered the Union...May 29, 1848
Capital..Madison

STATISTICS

Land Area (square miles)..54,158
Rank in Nation...25
Population..5,757,564
Rank in Nation...20
Density per square mile 106.3
Capital City..Madison
Population..240,323
Rank in State...2
Largest City .... Milwaukee
Population..598,916
Number of Representatives in Congress 8
Number of 2012 Electoral Votes...10
Number of County Governments...72
Number of Municipal Governments 596
Number of School Districts 440
Number of Special Districts 765

LEGISLATIVE BRANCH

Legislative Body ....Legislature

President of the Senate ....Mary Lazich
President Pro Tem of the Senate................................Richard Gudex
Secretary of the Senate ....Jeffery Renk
(Senate Chief Clerk)

Speaker of the House..Robin Vos
(Speaker of the Assembly)
Speaker Pro Tem of the House ....Tyler August
(Speaker Pro Tem of the Assembly)
Clerk of the House ....Patrick Fuller (Chief)

2015 Regular Session........................Jan. 5 – Dec. 31, 2015 (projected)
Number of Senatorial Districts 33
Number of Representative Districts 99

EXECUTIVE BRANCH

Governor ....Scott K. Walker
Lieutenant Governor ....Rebecca Kleefisch
Secretary of State................................Douglas LaFollette
Attorney General ....Brad Schimel
Treasurer..Matt Adamczyk
Auditor...Joe Chrisman
State Comptroller ....Steve Censky (Controller)

Governor's Present Term...............................1/2011 – 1/2019
Number of Elected Officials in the Executive Branch.........................6
Number of Members in the Cabinet 16

JUDICIAL BRANCH

Highest Court..Supreme Court
Supreme Court Chief Justice............................ Shirley S. Abrahamson
Number of Supreme Court Judges..7
Number of Intermediate Appellate Court Judges.............................16
Number of U.S. Court Districts..2
U.S. Circuit Court...7th Circuit

WYOMING

Nickname............................The Equality State and The Cowboy State
Motto..*Equal Rights*
Flower .... Indian Paintbrush
Bird... Western Meadowlark
Tree...Cottonwood
Song..*Wyoming*
Entered the Union...July 10, 1890
Capital..Cheyenne

STATISTICS

Land Area (square miles)...97,093
Rank in Nation...9
Population..584,153
Rank in Nation...50
Density per square mile 6.0
Capital City..Cheyenne
Population..61,537
Rank in State...1
Largest City .... Cheyenne
Population..61,537
Number of Representatives in Congress 1
Number of 2012 Electoral Votes...3
Number of County Governments...23
Number of Municipal Governments 99
Number of School Districts 55
Number of Special Districts 628

LEGISLATIVE BRANCH

Legislative Body ....Legislature

President of the Senate ....Tony Ross
President Pro Tem of the Senate........................Drew Perkins
(Vice President of the Senate)

Speaker of the House.....................................Kermit C. Brown
Speaker Pro Tem of the House ....Tim Stubson
Clerk of the House .... Patricia Benskin (Chief)

2015 Regular Session.........................Jan. 13 – March 5, 2015
Number of Senatorial Districts 30
Number of Representative Districts 60

EXECUTIVE BRANCH

Governor ....Matthew Mead
Secretary of State.. Ed Murray
Attorney General .... Peter Michael
Treasurer.. Mark Gordon
Auditor.. Cynthia Cloud

Governor's Present Term...............................1/2011 – 1/2019
Number of Elected Officials in the Executive Branch........................5
Number of Members in the Cabinet 20

JUDICIAL BRANCH

Highest Court..Supreme Court
Supreme Court Chief Justice............................E. James Burke
Number of Supreme Court Judges..5
Number of U.S. Court Districts..1
U.S. Circuit Court...10th Circuit

District of Columbia

Motto.......................................*Justitia Omnibus* (Justice to All)
Flower ....American Beauty Rose
Bird...Wood Thrush
Tree...Scarlet Oak
Song...*Washington*
Became U.S. Capital ....December 1, 1800

STATISTICS

Land Area (square miles)..61
Population..658,893
Density per square mile 10,801.5
Delegate to Congress* 1
Number of 2012 Electoral Votes...3
Number of Municipal Governments 1
Number of Special Districts 1

*Committee voting privileges only.

LEGISLATIVE BRANCH

Legislative Body .... Council of the District of Columbia

Chair... Phil Mendelson
Chair Pro Tem .... Kenyan McDuffie
Secretary to the Council .... Nyasha Smith
2015 Regular Session.............................. Jan. 2 – Dec. 31, 2015

EXECUTIVE BRANCH

Mayor...Muriel Bowser
Secretary of the District of Columbia .... Lauren C. Vaughn
Attorney General ....Karl Racine
Chief Financial Officer.. Jeffrey Barnette
Auditor... Yolanda Branche
State Comptroller..Anthony Pompa
(Deputy Chief Financial Officer)

Mayor's Present Term .... 1/2015 – 1/2019
Number of Elected Officials in the Executive Branch.......................10

JUDICIAL BRANCH

Highest Court.......................................D.C. Court of Appeals
Court of Appeals Chief Justice ....Eric Washington
Number of Court of Appeals Judges.......................................9
Number of U.S. Court Districts..1

American Samoa

Motto.......................*Samoa-Maumua le Atua* (In Samoa, God Is First)
Flower .... Paogo (Ula-fala)
Plant ....Ava
Song..*Amerika Samoa*
Became a Territory of the United States 1900
Capital... Pago Pago

STATISTICS

Land Area (square miles)..77
Population..55,519
Density per square mile 721.0
Capital City... Pago Pago
Population..3,656
Rank in Territory 3rd
Largest City ....Tafuna
Population..9,756
Delegate to Congress* 1
Number of School Districts 1

*Committee voting privileges only.

LEGISLATIVE BRANCH

Legislative Body ....Legislature

President of the Senate ....Gaoteote P.T. Gaoteote
Secretary of the Senate ....Leo'o V. Ma'o

Speaker of the House.............................. Savali Talavou Ale
Speaker Pro Tem of the House ....Fetu Fetui Jr.
Chief Clerk of the House.. Fialupe Lutu

2015 Regular Session........................... Jan. 12 – Dec. 31, 2015
Number of Senatorial Districts 12
Number of Representative Districts 17

EXECUTIVE BRANCH

Governor .... Lolo Matalasi Moliga
Lieutenant Governor .... Lemanu Peleti Mauga
Attorney General ....Talauega Eleasalo V. Ale
Treasurer ....Falema'o M. Pili
Auditor... Liua Fatuesi

Governor's Present Term........................... 1/2013 – 1/2017
Number of Members in the Cabinet 16

JUDICIAL BRANCH

Highest Court...High Court
High Court Chief Justice... F. Michael Kruse
Number of High Court Judges...6

Guam

Northern Mariana Islands

Nickname.. Hub of the Pacific
Flower .... Puti Tai Nobio (Bougainvillea)
Bird... Guam Rail
Tree.. Ifit (Intsiabijuga)
Song..*Stand Ye Guamanians*
Stone... Latte
Animal ....Iguana
Ceded to the United States by Spain ....December 10, 1898
Became a Territory .... August 1, 1950
Request to become a Commonwealth Plebiscite........ November 1987
Capital..Hagatna

Flower ....Plumeria
Bird... Marianas Fruit Dove
Tree...Flame Tree
Song..*Gi Talo Gi Halom Tasi*
Administered by the United States
a trusteeship for the United Nations ....July 18, 1947
Voters approved a proposed constitution.............June 1975
U.S. president signed covenant agreeing to
commonwealth status for the islands .... March 24, 1976
Became a self-governing Commonwealth .... January 9, 1978
Capital..Saipan

STATISTICS

Land Area (square miles)..210
Population...159,358
Density per square mile 758.8
Capital...Hagatna
Population..1,051
Rank in Territory 13th
Largest City ....Dededo
Population...44,943
Delegate to Congress* 1
Number of School Districts 1

STATISTICS

Land Area (square miles)..179
Population..53,883
Density per square mile 300.7
Capital City...Saipan
Population..48,220
Largest City ....Saipan
Delegate to Congress* 1
Number of School Districts 1

*Committee voting privileges only.

*Committee voting privileges only.

LEGISLATIVE BRANCH

Legislative Body ....Legislature

Speaker .... Judith T. Won Pat
Vice Speaker ....Benjamin J.F. Cruz
Clerk of the Legislature ....Rennae V. Meno

2015 Regular Session.......................... Jan. 12 – Dec. 31, 2015
Number of Senatorial Districts 15

LEGISLATIVE BRANCH

Legislative Body ....Legislature

President of the Senate ....Victor B. Hocog
Vice President of the Senate .... Francisco Borja
Clerk of the Senate..................................... Doris Bermudes

Speaker of the House...................................Joseph P. Deleon Guerrero
Vice Speaker of the House .... Rafael Demapan
Clerk of the House ....Linda B. Muna

2014 Regular Session.......................... Jan. 12 – Dec. 31, 2015
Number of Senatorial Districts 9
Number of Representative Districts 18

EXECUTIVE BRANCH

Governor ....Edward J.B. Calvo
Lieutenant Governor .... Ray Tenorio
Attorney General ....Elizabeth Barrett-Anderson
Treasurer...Rose T. Fejeran
Auditor... Doris Flores Brooks
Comptroller..Benita A. Manglona
(Director, Dept. of Administration)

Governor's Present Term............................... 1/2011 – 1/2019
Number of Elected Officials in the Executive Branch........................10
Number of Members in the Cabinet 55

EXECUTIVE BRANCH

Governor ....Eloy S. Inos
Lieutenant Governor ....Ralph Torres
Attorney General .... Edward Manibusan
Treasurer.. Antoinette S. Calvo
Auditor...Michael Pai
Comptroller...Connie S. Agulto
(Secretary, Dept. of Finance)

Governor's Present Term............................... 2/2013 – 1/2019
Number of Elected Officials in the Executive Branch........................10
Number of Members in the Cabinet 17

JUDICIAL BRANCH

Highest Court...Supreme Court
Supreme Court Chief Justice.................................... Robert J. Torres Jr.
Number of Supreme Court Judges 3

JUDICIAL BRANCH

Highest Court.....................................Commonwealth Supreme Court
Commonwealth Supreme Court
Chief Justice ....Alexandro C. Castro
Number of Commonwealth Supreme Court Judges 3

Puerto Rico

Nickname...Island of Enchantment
Motto..............................*Joannes Est Nomen Ejus* (John is His Name)
Flower ....Puerto Rican Hibiscus
Bird...Puerto Rican Spindalis
Tree.. Ceiba Pentandra
Song.. *La Borinqueña*
Became a Territory of the United States ....December 10, 1898
Became a self-governing Commonwealth ....July 25, 1952
Capital..San Juan

STATISTICS

Land Area (square miles)...3,424
Population..3,548,397
Density per square mile 1,036.3
Capital City...San Juan
Population..389,714
Largest City...San Juan
Resident Commissioner in Congress*...1
Number of School Districts 1

*Committee voting privileges only.

LEGISLATIVE BRANCH

Legislative Body ....Legislative Assembly

President of the Senate ....Eduardo Bhatia
Vice President of the Senate ....Jose L. Dalmau Santiago
Secretary of the Senate .... Tania Barbarossa

Speaker of the House.. Jaime R. Perello
Speaker Pro Tem................................. Roberto Rivero Ruiz de Porras
Clerk of the House ....Brunilda Ortiz-Rodriguez

2015 Regular Session..Jan. 12 – May 12, 2015

EXECUTIVE BRANCH

Governor ....Alejandro García Padilla
Secretary of State...David Bernier
Attorney General .... Cesar Miranda Rodriguez
Treasurer...Juan Zaragoza
Comptroller.. Yesmin M. Valdivieso-Galib

Governor's Present Term... 1/2013 – 1/2017
Number of Elected Officials in the Executive Branch........................10
Number of Members in the Cabinet 10

JUDICIAL BRANCH

Highest Court..Supreme Court
Supreme Court Chief Justice....................................... Liana Fiol-Matta
Number of Supreme Court Judges 7

U.S. Virgin Islands

Nickname..The American Paradise
Motto... *United in Pride and Hope*
Flower .... Trumpetbush
Bird... Yellow Breast or Banana Quit
Song.. *Virgin Islands March*
Purchased from Denmark .... March 31, 1917
Capital..Charlotte Amalie, St. Thomas

STATISTICS

Land Area (square miles)*..134
Population..106,405
Density per square mile 794.1
Capital City...Charlotte Amalie, St. Thomas
Population..18,481
Largest City ....Charlotte Amalie, St. Thomas
Delegate to Congress** 1
Number of School Districts 1

*The U.S. Virgin Islands is comprised of three large islands (St. Croix, St. John, and St. Thomas) and 50 smaller islands and cays.
**Committee voting privileges only.

LEGISLATIVE BRANCH

Legislative Body ....Legislature

President..Neville A. James
Vice President ....Janette Millin Young

2015 Regular Session.. Jan. 12 – Dec. 31, 2015

EXECUTIVE BRANCH

Governor .... Kenneth Mapp
Lieutenant Governor ....Osbert Potter
Attorney General ....James S. Carroll III
Commissioner of Finance .... Valdamier Collens

Governor's Present Term....................................... 1/2015 – 1/2019
Number of Elected Officials in the Executive Branch........................10
Number of Members in the Cabinet 21

JUDICIAL BRANCH

Highest Court...Supreme Court
Supreme Court Chief Justice... Rhys S. Hodge
Number of Supreme Court Judges 3
U.S. Circuit Court..3rd

Index

—G—

—S—

—T—

—U—